IRISH POLITICAL PRI
1848–1922

Modern Irish nationalism took form in the years 1848–1922. Campaigns ranged from the ballot box and civil disobedience and conspiracy to terrorism, insurrection and guerrilla war. While the punishment of offenders presented successive governments with seemingly intractable problems, imprisoned revolutionaries discovered and exploited numerous opportunities to continue and intensify their struggles.

This is the most comprehensive and detailed study yet offered of the political use of imprisonment in these years. Drawing extensively on archives and special collections in Ireland, England, the United States of America and Australia, many hitherto unused, Seán McConville shows how punishment came to shape the nationalist consciousness. Accounts of offenders' prison experiences and official reactions are given context by matching chapters, each describing the political and organisational components of successive phases in the nationalist and republican struggle. Government's response was conditioned by legal and constitutional factors as well as attitudes and opinions in Britain, Ireland, the United States of America and Australia. Considering these, as well as British and Irish party politics, McConville tells the full story of the part played by political imprisonment in the development of Anglo-Irish relations and the birth of the modern Irish state.

Seán McConville is Professor of Criminal Justice and Professorial Research Fellow in the Department of Law, Queen Mary, University of London. He has published widely on imprisonment and related political and legal issues, including work on Britain, Europe and the United States of America.

Books previously published by the author

A History of English Prison Administration
Volume I: 1750–1877

English Local Prisons, 1860–1900
Next Only to Death

FOR SALLY JAMES

IRISH POLITICAL PRISONERS, 1848–1922

Theatres of War

Seán McConville

Routledge
Taylor & Francis Group

LONDON AND NEW YORK

First published 2003
by Routledge
2 Park Square, Milton Park, Abingdon, Oxon, OX14 4RN

This edition published 2005
by Routledge
Simultaneously published in the USA and Canada
by Routledge
270 Madison Ave, New York NY 10016

Routledge is an imprint of the Taylor & Francis Group

Transferred to Digital Printing 2005

© 2003 Seán McConville

Typeset in 10/12pt Goudy by Graphicraft Limited, Hong Kong

British *Library Cataloguing in Publication Data*
A catalogue record for this book is available
from the British Library

Library of Congress Cataloging in Publication Data
McConville, Seán.
Irish political prisoners, 1848–1922 : theatres of war / Seán
McConville.
p. cm.
Includes bibliographical references and index.
ISBN 0-415-21991-4 (alk. paper)
1. Political prisoners—Ireland—History. 2. Political prisoners—
England—History. 3. Political violence—Ireland—History.
4. Government, Resistance to—Ireland—History. 5. Punishment—
England—History. 6. Irish question. 1. Title.

HV9650.3 .M33 2002
364.1'31'0941509034—dc21
2002073379

ISBN 0-415-37866-4

Printed and bound by Antony Rowe Ltd, Eastbourne

CONTENTS

ACKNOWLEDGEMENTS

The completion of a volume such as this, drawing heavily on archives and widely dispersed special collections, is inevitably costly. Several foundations and organisations provided essential support. A generous grant from the Leverhulme Trust met the bulk of the research expenses, including the employment of a research officer and certain other help. The Harry Frank Guggenheim Foundation (which has a special interest in the study of violence, aggression and dominance) has encouraged my work in many ways over the years. The Nuffield Foundation and the British Academy gave travel awards at critical stages, when access to overseas archives and collections was essential. The Home Office also made a grant which greatly assisted in the assembly of data: I should like to thank Ms Julie Vennard for smoothing the way, and for her sympathetic interest.

For the most part I have worked alone, but for two years I had the great fortune of having the assistance of Mrs Janette Martin, as research officer. Her interest in the project and her patience and conscientiousness were of the highest order. Together we came to know the many characters who decorate this history, and our numerous discussions of their virtues, vices and foibles were informative and stimulating. Mrs Martin was persuaded to return for several short spells of archive and library work. I am most grateful for her commitment and professionalism.

Despite the advent of word processors and sophisticated software I have needed a great deal of secretarial support, not least in balancing teaching and administrative duties and making time for research and writing. It gives me particular pleasure to acknowledge the ever willing, intelligent and loyal assistance of Mrs Linda Cox, my secretary at Queen Mary. The work of seeing the volume through its final drafts was cheerfully undertaken by Ms Susan Hemp, who completed the task with brio and much skill.

A number of colleagues have placed me in their debt. Professor Norval Morris of the University of Chicago Law School continued to show a generous interest in the work, and helped me immensely by comment and suggestion and by support in various funding applications. My friendship with Professor Roger Hood of All Souls, Oxford now extends for more than thirty years, and his encouragement at all times has been highly valued. The late Sir Leon Radznowicz discussed this work with me from the outset, and even in his final illness read and commented upon draft chapters. We had challenging, instructive and amusing conversations on political offenders, and on research and writing in general. With others I miss his advice and wit.

I have been fortunate to find a berth at Queen Mary, University of London. Professors Hazel Genn and (then Principal) Graham Zellick gracefully drew me into the College on my return from the United States. I consider myself lucky indeed to be among such friendly and supportive colleagues in the Department of Law and in the wider College. Professor Peter Hennessy, the distinguished modern historian, has been a particularly welcoming and supportive colleague in the Department of History. The heavy and time-consuming task of refining, rewriting and polishing the final drafts was immeasurably assisted by a year's sabbatical leave of absence from the College, for which I am most grateful.

As higher education has expanded in Britain and elsewhere, resources have dismally failed to grow apace. This is felt in many ways, including pressure on the libraries, archives and special collections. The goodwill and professionalism of librarians and archivists are of the greatest importance to researchers, and I am happy to acknowledge the numerous instances and forms of assistance I have received from the libraries and archives I list in the bibliography. Work on the Home Office papers was substantial and extended over several years. This task and various problems in location were greatly eased by the cooperation and assistance of the Departmental Records' Office. In particular, I wish to thank Mr John Lloyd for his knowledgeable and speedy responses to my queries, which must at times have seemed endless.

At a late stage in the publication process, Dr Garret FitzGerald, former Taoiseach and a distinguished author and academic, read and commented upon Chapters 9 to 15. This generous gift of his time, a very keen eye and his intimate knowledge of the period, its personalities and events, steered me safely away from several inaccuracies and errors.

All archives and publications on which I have drawn have been fully and properly identified in the text; few have been cited at length. I am grateful to all the owners and trustees of copyright for the use I have been allowed to make of this material.

Seán McConville
Department of Law
Queen Mary, University of London

ABBREVIATIONS

AOT	Archives Office of Tasmania	NLI	National Library of Ireland
BM	British Museum (now British Library)	NS	New Series
		NYPL	New York Public Library
CAB	Cabinet	OD	Outward Despatches
CO	Colonial Office	OS	Old Series
COIR	Chief Officer of the Irish Republic	P.Com	Prison Commission
		PP	Parliamentary Papers
CSO	Chief Secretary's Office	PRO	Public Record Office (London)
CUA	Catholic University of America		
		Q	Question
DNB	Dictionary of National Biography	RA	Royal Archives (Windsor)
		RAMC	Royal Army Medical Corps
DORA	Defence of the Realm Act	RCP	Report of the Commissioners of Prisons and the Directors of Convict Prisons
DORR	Defence of the Realm Regulations		
FBP	Fenian Brotherhood Papers	RIC	Royal Irish Constabulary
FO	Foreign Office	ROIA	Restoration of Order (Ireland) Act, 1920
GO	Governor's Office		
HMSO	Her (His) Majesty's Stationery Office	RP	Registered Papers
		SCRO	Somerset Co. Record Office
HO	Home Office	SROWA	State Records Office of Western Australia
ID	Inward Despatches		
IRB	Irish Republican Brotherhood	TCD	Trinity College, Dublin
		TP	Tasmanian Papers
LB	Letter Book	UCD	University College Dublin
LOO	Law Officers' Opinion	USNA	United States National Archives
MCIHP	Maloney Collection of Irish Historical Papers		
		VDL	Van Diemen's Land
MLS	Mitchell Library, Sydney	WO	War Office
NAI	National Archives of Ireland		
NIPRO	Northern Ireland Public Record Office		

Note: In the citation of newspapers and certain journals the letter following the page number indicates the column.

INTRODUCTION

This book is about Irish political violence – promoted, plotted and carried out – and the imprisonment in England of successive generations of rebels. The story starts in 1848 with a great deal of noise and fury and the slightest kind of insurrection. It ends with the years of intense guerrilla war, terrorism and counter-terror, which were the hard birth of the Irish Free State. Young Ireland is the starting point since this was the first uprising to follow Catholic Emancipation (1829) and the Reform Act of 1832. These transformed politics at Westminster and in Ireland, in turn conditioning the response to rebellion. The establishment of the modern Irish state and the consequent amnesties and releases make 1922 an obvious finishing date.

The narrative extends to Australia, since three batches of Irish political offenders were despatched there: the Young Irelanders and some of their follow-ers in 1849 to 1850, and the sixty-two Fenians who in September 1867 sailed on the *Hougoumont*, the last convict ship. Transportation, with its supporting prisons and penal stations in Australia, was conducted under the authority of imperial government, with policy determined by the Colonial and Home Offices in London. The account on occasion also includes happenings in Irish prisons, since these led to the removal of inmates to England. These instances apart, I do not consider imprisonment in Ireland. The substantial local element in the administration of Irish prisons, and the general political climate of the country, obliged and allowed them to operate in ways which differed quite considerably from their English counterparts. Political imprisonment in Ireland deserves its own volume.

This study deals in detail with political imprisonment over some three-quarters of a century and is very much a tale of two cities, Dublin and London. Here the word-spinning revolutionary, the insurrectionist, rebel, guerrilla and terrorist; there the politician, official, administrator and journalist. The only way to enter such different worlds, and to understand them in relation to each other, is to sift through those private words, letters and documents intended always to be kept within the camp. Officials are rather better at preserving their records than revolutionists, but a surprisingly large number of the latter's documents, letters and memoirs have survived: the ordinary man or woman touched by history clings to recollections. If history is about imaginative sympathy as much as detached analysis – and surely it must be – the handling and interpretation of such documents, with all their uncertainties and imperfections of haste and incomplete knowledge, is as near as we come to time travel. The newspapers and journals of the day, while more deliberate and polished, share many of the characteristics of private documents and are indispensable to this re-creation of time and place.

This volume is part of a wider enterprise. For some years I have been researching and writing a history of penal ideas, policies and administration. This has focused principally on imprisonment in England since 1750. Many different elements have come together in these studies – a variety of philosophical, economic and political approaches as well as changing administrative patterns and standards. The books have included the many crises, scandals and institutional contingencies which shaped short-term policy. Pages and chapters have been peopled with thinkers, reformers, politicians and administrators, together with a rich variety of prisoners.

Into this broader picture there has from time to time intruded a man or woman of a very different cast. This is the person whose crime comes not from viciousness, malice or dishonest gain, but from political conviction, an irreconcilable difference with some aspect of state or religious policy, or the demands of an ethic out of kilter with the times.

In any analysis there comes a point at which the frequency of exceptions becomes an embarrassment. By the time I reached the early twentieth century my narrative had encountered a wide range of conscionable offenders. These included activists of various phases of the labour and trade-union movements, communists and anarchists; religious offenders of the mid-century 'bells and smells' controversies of the Church of England and Salvationists whose zealous marching and outdoor preaching led them into public-order offences; parents who would not send their children to school, or have them vaccinated; unruly litigants; unauthorised imperialists; a campaigner against paedophile vice; direct-action female suffragists; those who opposed or refused conscription and campaigners for equity in local taxation. Like a thread through all this there ran several generations of Irish nationalists and republicans. Numbers apart (and all these offenders never amounted to more than a tiny percentage of those who annually passed through the courts and prisons), this was too great an accumulation of protests and disobedience to treat as an aside to the story of punishment. And mere numbers were misleading. By the nature of their crimes these men and women often had a disproportionate impact on national life. The manner of their punishment, the continuation of protest in custody, and the official and political response they provoked, extended their campaigns and heightened their notoriety and influence.

For these reasons I could not avoid the task of putting together a book dealing with the imprisonment of the conscionable offender. Reading and searching began, and within two years a considerable volume of material lay in its boxes and files. The difficulty came (as it always does in this work) when I began to sort, organise, plan and write. Most of the campaigns, episodes and persons mentioned above could be dealt with in fairly self-contained chapters. After a great deal of drafting and frustrating rewriting I was forced to conclude that the Irish simply would not fit in. They were not a part of the British political, cultural and religious story in the way of other conscionable offenders, and attempts so to treat them were precisely part of the conflict and their rage. Early plans and preliminary drafts had assumed perhaps two Irish chapters. In this space I had thought that it would be possible to deal with offences, lives in custody, and officials' and politicians' responses. Ruefully and reluctantly I had to conclude that the nature and complexity of this story demanded a separate book.

The concept of the political offender

Part of my interest in the conscionable offender is the common-law unwillingness to distinguish between political and ordinary crime. This is a controversy which has dogged English jurisprudence for centuries without resolution, though periodically subject to fierce debate. The classic defence of a refusal to differentiate was that in a free society, where political expression and organisation was not stifled (the Chartists would have said that it was), where the rule of law and a separation of powers guaranteed a judiciary free of politics (another point of some dispute) and where the jury guarded against executive intervention and tyranny (absent jury-packing), there was no reason to engage in unconstitutional politics and certainly no justification for political trials and *custodia honesta*.

Nor was this a solely English reaction. Speaking to a meeting of the American Bar Association about the campaign to pardon Eugene Debs, the many-times-imprisoned union activist, socialist and pacifist, United States Attorney General Daugherty argued that in America there were no excuses to step outside the rules of conventional political contest. Unlike the old-world countries, in America 'The sovereign will of the people can express itself and . . . the ballot box is available'.[1] Writing a few years later, Sir Edward Troup, Permanent-Under-Secretary at the Home Office, argued against special treatment for political offenders, even in the limited form allowed by English law.[2] In those days the indulgence was rarely granted (he was writing in the early 1920s) because some of the suffragettes to whom it had been given had used their entitlements 'to conduct political propaganda from the prison'.[3]

---

1 'Respect for Law', *American Bar Association Journal*, 7 (1921), 505 (see also 508–9).
2 Sections 40 and 41 of the Prison Act, 1877 (40 & 41 Vict., c.21) extended the courts' power to order the privileges of the first-class misdemeanant to persons imprisoned for sedition and seditious libel, and those committed for contempt of court. A first-class misdemeanant was subject to little more than civil detention.
3 Sir Edward Troup, *The Home Office*, London and New York, G. P. Putnam's Sons, 1925, p. 119. He enlarged on the point (while adding little): 'When persons not really of the criminal class

3

Indeed, it was the willingness of the political offender to grasp imprisonment as an opportunity to further his or her cause which had led some continental jurisdictions to restrict or withdraw privileges given in the latter part of the nineteenth century because of feelings of guilt or liberal angst about state repression.[4] This unease, particularly after the events of 1848, had allowed the courts when sentencing to recognise the honourable motivations of political foes. Otto Kirchheimer suggested that clemency was discontinued for practical reasons: 'What had begun as a means to enforce public order while making desirable moral differentiations turned against this order itself.' Political offenders used their privileges to exert 'massive pressures against the state apparatus'. And quite apart from the will of the offender and followers, the chivalrous state was surely in a confused position: 'It is difficult to prosecute a heretic while explicitly recognising the purity of motivation which triggered his action.'[5] The state's weakness and the rebel's opportunities in this moral contest were recognised by Eoin MacNeill (former Commander-in-Chief of the Irish Volunteers). Around 1920 he summarised four years of his organisation's experience of the criminal process and penal system in an epigram:

> Imprisoned, we are their jailers,
> On trial, their judges,
> Persecuted, their punishers,
> Dead, their conquerers.[6]

These lines were written in the concluding terrible phase of the Anglo-Irish war, and before its outcome was discernible. They are facile in their contrived symmetry, and have an element of bravado in the face of possible failure. But they hit home. Bringing the conscionable offender into the criminal process the state seeks to head off threats to public order and its own security. By spurning the mechanism of democratic debate, persuasion and the ballot box, the offender has confessed the weakness of his case and wilfully and unnecessarily threatened the legal order. Whatever the offence that brings him before the court, his guilt is aggravated by this general attack on the state. So the argument goes, as sentence is imposed and punishment begins. But as the events which are variously

---

force their way into prison for the purposes of political propaganda, suffragettes, conscientious objectors, or recalcitrant town councillors – and set themselves to defy the prison rules, questions arise which require very delicate handling from the Home Secretary who is bound to maintain the necessary safeguards of prison discipline' (p. 125).

4 Barton Ingraham offers an instructive survey and analysis in his *Political Crime in Europe: A Comparative Study of France, Germany and England*, Berkeley, University of California Press, 1979.

5 Otto Kirchheimer, *Political Justice: The Use of Legal Procedures for Political Ends*, Princeton, NJ, Princeton University Press, 1961, p. 241.

6 National Library of Ireland (NLI): Kathleen McKenna Napoli Papers: Ms. 22, 744. Annotated in the hand of Arthur Griffith: 'This is an epigram by MacNeill. It is worth publication.'

examined in this book will show, the constitutional argument was from first to last rejected by the Irish political prisoners, who denied the legitimacy of British rule in Ireland. Nor was this simply a matter of courtroom speeches. Within the prison walls many found means to continue to challenge state authority, drawing into their battles wider circles of supporters and sympathisers. The prison became a stage on which the rebel could play out his drama.

The captive insurgent was aware that he was not totally at the mercy of the state. Laws, rules and regulations, institutional procedures and the channels of accountability that led to Parliament, ensured that caprice and excess were restrained. Eoin MacNeill's claim 'we are their jailers' would privately have been accepted by many prison and Home Office officials. Where functionaries had to tread with care, the embarrassment and ire of superiors and ministers a constant anxiety, the prisoner could misbehave with relative impunity. The political prisoner could thus turn the prison inside out.

Violence as virtue

A few words on terminology. The term 'conscionable offender' includes, but is not restricted to, the prisoner of conscience, the non-violent opponent of governments whose cause is promoted by Amnesty International and other organisations. Neither should the term exclusively be the preserve of purely political crimes such as sedition and treason. I use it for all those offenders with political or other conscionable motivation, whose crimes range from the non-violent to the extremely violent, from unlawful words, uttered or published, to armed insurrection, the terror of indiscriminate arson and bombing, and the special brutality of individual killing. Many of the deeds done in the name of political ideals must fill any decent person with horror and revulsion. But passion makes its own rules and is governed by its own ethics – a reason why the ancients saw it as an affliction.

Most of the research and all of the writing has been carried out in times when political nationalism and ethnic exclusiveness have been in a particularly efflorescent phase. The long drawn-out aftermath of colonialism in the Congo, Burundi and Rwanda; the resurrection of vile and lethal nationalisms in the Balkans; the tangled and seething hatreds of what was Soviet Central Asia; East Timor under the torch and gun; the wholesale slaughter of civilians in Algeria; bombs and machine guns in San Sebastian, Jerusalem and Bethlehem – all came through the news-waves as I wrote this book: here are the forces which nationalism can unleash, the beast behind the door. The September 2001 attacks on New York and Washington revealed a new dimension of cold and pitiless hatred. Every sentence that follows was formed in months and years during which there was only rarely interrupted news of violence and hatred both within and coming out of Northern Ireland. At times it seemed that the awful years of 1920 and 1921 in which I was immersed had by some curse been endlessly revisited upon the land. I have no desire therefore to conceal the sombre mood in which I explored my subject. I recognise that only some aspects of nationalism and related ideologies spawn violence. It is also true that nationalist ideas and movements can and do connect the individual with the transcendent, carry people's lives beyond the present, inspire sacrifice and confer dignity and self-respect; cultural diversity, which springs from national and ethnic roots, immeasurably enhances our lives. I hope I have dealt fairly and evenly with the several faces of nationalism, but I remain deeply concerned about the dark side of this powerful and seemingly strengthening current in our lives.

It seems fair to put this on the table, if only to save the reader the trouble of unpicking my biases. At the risk of infuriating a wholly different set of readers, I must add that my approach does not include a justification of imperialism or a defence of British rule in Ireland. Both, while they had their virtues, were fraught with too many injustices to make an ethical case for their survival, and politically were unwilling or incapable of adapting to new ways of thinking and living. Whatever dispute there may be about the manner of its birth, the modern Irish state has enriched and improved the lives of its people and achieved a respected place in the community of nations.

Coming as it did in the midst of the Great War, the 1916 eruption of Irish republicanism was a tocsin of the modern age – the arrangements and way of life which would follow the fall of centuries-old empires, customs and patterns of obligation, and see the redrawing of many a map and ultimately a complete loss of political innocence. The Irish story, full of interest in itself, is of considerable significance for these wider developments. And there is perhaps no better way to understand Irish republicanism than its doctrine of suffering: sacrifices past, present and future have in the past two centuries repeatedly demonstrated their power to move to action. Conferring a mandate of history, they challenge the earthbound and venial qualities of the ballot box and the law. In the course of the conflict between Irish nationalism and British ascendancy the prison and the gallows have exerted a tidal force, pulling together Irish constitutional politics and extra-parliamentary agitation, moral and physical force. Sacrifice and suffering conspicuously endured, when accompanied by a devotion to religion, and eventually allowed the always-cautious and conservative Roman Catholic Church to throw its weight into the balance on the republican side.

The rational and the romantic

This book is an exploration of the limits of democracy and the criminal process. Irish rebels would shrug aside the notion that their acts were a test of either law or democratic government: whose law and whose democracy was precisely the matter at issue. But for those who worked within the status quo, Irish political violence posed perplexing problems. Some went to the deepest meaning of the British state, its restraint, balances and Christian values: departures from these were constantly tempting, and to the extent that politicians and officials yielded in 1920 and 1921, they accelerated the collapse of British authority and power in Ireland.[7] The daily contest of forces and the hundreds of consequent decisions revealed the limitations and weaknesses of constitutional administration. Violent and unlawful acts were dealt with under law and offenders were duly passed to the penal system. With ordinary crimes this process usually works, if only to contain, but the passage of the political offender through the prison gate was simply so much more fuel for the engine that one wished to destroy or at least shut down. Punish and be damned; hesitate and be damned; pardon and be damned.

Great material and political interests were at issue in Ireland, but this was also a conflict between the rational and romantic worlds. The philosophical outlines of these two have been discussed in a variety of contexts. Romanticism is hard to define, and its elements may even be found in the writings of antiquity. One influential approach traces it to a German reaction to Enlightenment ideas.[8] Romanticism thus challenges the assertion that reason alone is the key to man's fate; it favours the particular and individual to the universal, variety to uniformity, the crooked to the straight. It emphasises the virtues of nature (and the supernatural) rather than civilisation and artifice, and in social arrangements the organic and symbolic over the mechanical, legal and functional. The approach is sympathetic to elitist politics and is suspicious or antagonistic towards democracy. It favours the great man and the towering leader.

The first group to appear in this narrative is a textbook example of political romanticism. Young Ireland's leader was an aristocrat of a long defunct order, fretting constantly about his chivalric honour, gleaning the past for identity and values. Another of the inner group had idealised notions of an agrarian civilisation, based on a self-sufficient peasantry. Several used the language and forms of an earlier generation of revolutionaries, but rejected the Enlightenment thought on which their politics was based. Fenianism, the organisation which followed on Young Ireland's heels, also had a strong romantic element. The name referred back to a band of Celtic warriors, and the objective was national regeneration through sacrifice and victory on the field of battle. The Easter rising of 1916 was cut almost entirely from this cloth. All was epitomised in the immolative romanticism of its leader, Patrick Pearse, whose final declaration, summing up the insurrectionists' achievement in four days of battle, with defeat and death looming, insisted that 'Ireland's honour has already been redeemed'.[9]

---

7 Contemplating the European experience some decades later, Otto Kirchheimer noted that when organisations succeeded in fusing the ideological and material interests of large groups, a government which does not wish to take the totalitarian path of total repression 'may face major problems of political mass control' (*op. cit.*, p. 9). He particularly notes Irish nationalism as an example of this conundrum.
8 Isaiah Berlin, *The Roots of Romanticism*, London, Chatto & Windus, 1999.
9 'The Provisional Government to the Citizens of Dublin', *The* Irish Times, *1916 Rebellion Handbook* (facsimile, ed. Declan Kiberd), Dublin, The Mourne River Press, 1998, p. xiii.

Two of the groups dealt with in these pages did not subscribe to notions of romantic honour, either in their objectives or in their tactics. The dynamitards of the 1880s followed a purely terrorist agenda, using explosions and arson to create the conditions which would force the British government to withdraw from Ireland. The IRA which regrouped after the 1916 rising initially thought in terms of another Fenian-style general rising, but by trial and error found in guerrilla tactics and assassinations the means to harass, exhaust and then paralyse British administration. Honour gave way to effectiveness.

The criminal process and penal system which these men and a handful of women entered was of course based on legal and bureaucratic principles. It had been designed to assess harm, allocate blame and to punish according to deserts. Moral opprobrium attached to all offenders, and acknowledgement of guilt, the authority of the state and the justice of punishment were demanded as expiation. Prisons were intended to be retributive and deterrent and, as a means of achieving both these ends, were run on lines of strict uniformity: everyone was to be treated in exactly the same manner by a staff which itself was minutely regulated and supervised. The human element was to be removed as far as possible, punishment to be delivered as though by a machine. Only one group was spared this penal experience. It was decided that as gentlemen under punishment the Young Ireland leaders would be given wide privileges. This grace did not extend to later groups, only a minority of whom were gentlemen according to the criteria of the times, and the times themselves were changed.

Imprisonment is a contest for moral domination. The sociology of the prison traces patterns of resistance and compensation among ordinary criminals, who reject the institution's attempt to define and control. Defiance was a prime virtue for political offenders during the seventy-five or so years of this narrative. On the one side there is a determination to use the well-tried tools – silence, isolation, convict uniform, hard and crushing labour, penal food, minimum stimulation, personal contamination and association with criminals: a regime crafted and thoughtfully modified over the years to compel submission, and to bewilder, belittle and demoralise. The political prisoner has his or her own tools – essentially a succession of refusals to cooperate, to accept the state's definitions and rules. He or she may refuse to wear a uniform, or destroy it, refuse to associate with criminals, to be silent, to do demeaning work, to 'sir' authority, or to stand, remove a cap or to show any deference whatsoever. These acts bring punishment, but that itself is resisted, perhaps through hunger-striking or cell-smashing. Eventually there is established the spiral of disobedience, punishment and further disobedience, and as the stakes rise the news seeps under the gate and heightens the strength of feeling among supporters and the wider circle of sympathisers.[10]

---

10 And beyond even that. When the political offender leaves prison, his or her account will acquire an audience, its size determined by fame, notoriety or literary skill. Even those who have

This was the state of affairs in 1920 and 1921. The war in Ireland was being waged ever more widely and ruthlessly and neither side permitted neutrality. Decency was in hibernation. The contest for hearts and minds was as fiercely and carefully fought as the war of guns, bombs, searches and ambushes. Government had by now conceded political status and a liberal regime to most of the Irish political prisoners, though there were constant disputes as to what constituted political and what were the entitlements of the status. Such prisoners had no intention of reaching agreements but sought simply to sap officials' energy and cast government in a poor light in the eyes of the Irish people throughout the world, their sympathisers and (particularly in America) those who competed for the Irish vote.

An ordinary offender enters the criminal process shamed, isolated and vulnerable. The political offender, should his or her group of supporters and sympathisers be large and confident enough, embraces and transcends captivity. To know that one is cherished and respected revivifies the prisoner and directs a confrontational energy on the many irksome restrictions of institutional life. The balance of advantage shifts, with the prisoner becoming ever more assertive and the retreating administrator and his staff demoralised. The only route to failure for an Irish political prisoner was to be seen as a traitor or backslider. Martyrdom – either in suffering or in death – consecrated the movement and magnified the individual.

There follows another step. The passage of time and the prisoner's suffering overshadow and largely obliterate the original offence. A shift in the popular mood turns the offender into a hero or (remarkably so in the case of the dynamitards) a victim. In these circumstances punishment produces perverse outcomes: deterrence becomes encouragement and retribution transfiguration. Honour resides in the offenders' intention, and cannot be removed by the legal process and punishment. Dishonour is cast upon the state and its agents, no matter that all the rules were followed and safeguards enforced.

Resonances

As noted above, conflict has continued in Ireland throughout the years of this research and writing. Burrowing daily into the archives and literature, an ever-stronger realisation grew that many of the events and nearly all the personages with whom I was dealing were part of the familiar discourse of modern paramilitaries and their political associates. Concepts, phrases and words current in

---

no sympathy with the rebel cause may recognise the intelligence of the offender and the value of his or her prison testimony. 'It is something', wrote Professor Gilbert Murray in 1919, 'to have an intelligent man or woman who has been through the experience of prison and can tell us what it is like.' (Preface to Stephen Hobhouse, *An English Prisoner from Within*, London, George Allen & Unwin, 1919, p. 7.) Murray was referring to the suffragettes, conscientious objectors, and Sinn Féiners who had recently been imprisoned.

the 1990s had been used seventy years previously, and indeed seventy years before that. The battle for control of the prison continued unabated, and was being fought minutely and tenaciously, point by point and hold by hold, by both sides, and all by means of long-tested tactics. As in the 1860s, 1890s and after 1916, the prison was projected into the foreground. It continued to link constitutional nationalism and republicanism, to be an icon of suffering and a motivator for the faithful.[11] A large part of modern Irish republicanism is the assertion of claims of legitimacy based on historical continuity. The history of Irish political imprisonment is central to the education of republican activists and their self-assumed obligation to keep faith with the past. To many the remembrance of the penal servitude of the Fenians, the release, insane, of the dynamitard Dr Thomas Gallagher, the death of Thomas Ashe and the hunger-strike of Terence MacSwiney are wholly familiar events, cornerstones of their own political edifice.

Perhaps more surprising is the poor official memory of the three-quarters of a century of political imprisonment chronicled here. No one who had researched the files from those years, and who entertained the most slender belief that lessons could be learned from history, could have imagined that the August 1971 arrests and internment without trial in Northern Ireland would do more than provide the opportunity to consolidate republicanism, or that its camps and prisons could avoid becoming further and higher education campuses for the study of republican culture and beliefs, a selection process for leaders and paramilitary staff academies. It may well be, of course, that officials studied the files but did not find them relevant, or found their politicians deaf to the lessons. Irish history, it seems, is stuffed with endlessly reprised passages and themes.

The human element

Introductions have a tendency to be overly abstract, and this one is perhaps no exception. The author, impatient to send his book out into the world, empties his head of distillations of the themes that have so long preoccupied him. The characters and the complicated and intriguing events that are the stuff of the story are boiled down into a bland preamble. This volume is indeed a history of politics, penology and administration, written to the standards of scholarship, and within its conventions. But it is also an account of the lives, deeds and emotions of people who were swept up into extraordinary events.

Minimalism in its many forms has been a powerful influence in the past fifty years and longer. Narrative history has lost ground to historiography and works

11 Kieran McEvoy provides a scholarly and gripping account of these events in his *Paramilitary Imprisonment in Northern Ireland: Resistance, Management and Release*, Oxford, Oxford University Press, 2001. A comparison of the modern with earlier periods shows many striking parallels.

more of theory than substance. It has sometimes seemed that the apocryphal admonition to Mozart of Emperor Joseph II ('Too many notes') has been taken unduly to heart. This is not to claim more than a share of the virtues for my own approach. In history's house there are many mansions, and rooms for all types and styles of scholar and writer. But the human element should never be forgotten as the final reference – men and women as actors, acted upon or merely bewildered. This book is full of stories, episodes, characters, sayings, heroes, villains, fools, sages, tragedies and even some comedy. There can be no apology for presenting such a cast, such a serpentine scenario and so many facts.

1

THE YOUNG IRELANDERS

Personages and politics

No Irishman in 1845, at home or abroad, was held in greater esteem than Daniel O'Connell. Prophet and chieftain to the poorer classes, educated Roman Catholics and liberal Protestants admired his statesmanship, vision and political skills. In his sixty-ninth year he had received a sentence of one year's imprisonment, the fruit of his revived campaign for repeal of the Act of Union and the incitement and threat of his monster meetings. His confinement in Richmond Prison must count among the most luxurious and least oppressive in the history of imprisonment. His conviction was overturned three months into the sentence, yet in the eyes of his compatriots he had added martyrdom to his other heroic attributes. His achievements, personality and capacity had given him a unique position in national life and had made the civilised world familiar with his country's problems. But at the zenith of his fame and renown, a great change in spirit came upon him. His accelerating decline, physical and mental, contributed to the splintering of constitutional nationalism and thus to the Young Ireland insurrection of 1848.

Adulation and a long tenure in office engender proprietorial feelings; successes and failures and hard-won experience make for impatience and the intolerance of opposition. Add to these the protective dogmatism of old age, the fears and uncertainties of declining health, and an unhappy tendency to surround oneself with sycophants, and the result was reflexive and unthinking reaction.[1] And at

---

1 This phase of O'Connell's life is described by Sir Charles Gavan Duffy, perhaps the most moderate of his Young Ireland opponents. Duffy's account is certainly partisan, but this is tempered by the retrospect of some forty years, the historical certainty of O'Connell's achievements, and Duffy's own assimilation into the ranks of respectable eminence. It was one of O'Connell's fatal weaknesses, Duffy wrote, 'to surround himself by men whose chief characteristic was abject submission; men capable of wilfully misleading him for their private ends, more than one of whom would have scuttled the ship to carry off an armful of plunder' (Sir Charles Gavan Duffy, *Four Years of Irish History, 1845–1849*, London, Cassell, Galpin & Co, 1883, p. 115). A nationalist of a later generation struck an even harsher note: 'The policy of O'Connell had brought

precisely the time that O'Connell's imperiousness and political inertia became most evident, he was challenged by a talented, educated and energetic group from within nationalist ranks.[2] Where the skills of his earlier days would have conciliated, assimilated or neutralised, O'Connell now bowed to the advice of his son John[3] and sought their suppression or exclusion.

Of the several men of talent who came to oppose O'Connell, two in particular embodied distinctive impulses and forces which would shape Irish nationalism thereafter – William Smith O'Brien and John Mitchel. The former was a most unlikely candidate for nationalist leadership, whether of moral or physical force. Born in 1803 into an old Irish landowning family which had been Anglican for several generations, O'Brien was ever conscious of the descent which his family traced back to the last High King of Ireland, Brian Boru.[4] For hundreds of years O'Briens had been the principal family in Co. Clare, and for seven generations had provided parliamentary representatives either for the county or for the county town, Ennis. They had served at Westminster and also in the Irish Parliament in Dublin, where they had opposed the Act of Union.

great reforms. But his personal influence had been almost entirely evil. His violent nature, his invective, his unscrupulousness, are the chief cause of our social and political divisions. . . . In his very genius itself, there was the demoralisation, the appeal – as of a tumbler at a fair – to the commonest ear, a grin through a horse-collar. We have copied all that, but have not copied his simplicity, his deep affectionate heart' (William Butler Yeats, *Tribute to Thomas Davis*, Cork, Cork University Press, 1947, p. 15). There are several analytical studies of O'Connell. Still impressive in its scholarship and clarity of expression, Denis Gwynn's *Young Ireland and 1848* (Cork, Cork University Press, 1949, chs 1–12) provides an account both incisive and sympathetic to O'Connell's declining years and his relationship with the various factions of Young Ireland; it also brings together a number of useful original documents. Oliver MacDonagh, with the perspective of 140 years and the advantages of modern scholarship, covers much the same ground, but providing the contrast with O'Connell's prime years (*The Emancipist*, London, Weidenfeld & Nicolson, 1989: see esp. chs 10–12).

2 Quite apart from political differences, the gap in age between O'Connell and his radical critics contributed to the inability of the two sides to work together, as a writer sympathetic to both sides pointed out: 'Of course the name *Young Ireland* was not a misnomer for men who, as compared with O'Connell, then approaching 70, were nearly all in their 20s. In 1842 when the *Nation* was founded Smith O'Brien was 39, but Davis was only 28, Dillon and Duffy 26, Martin 30, Mitchel 27, McManus 31, O'Doherty and Meagher 19 each, and D'Arcy McGee 17' (Cardinal Tomás O'Fiaich, 'The North and Young Ireland', *Tipperary Historical Journal*, 1998, p. 20).

3 (1810–58). Third son of Daniel. Read law and was called to the Bar, but never practised. Elected for Youghal at twenty-two, and thereafter acted as his father's chief assistant. Became the leading force in the Repeal Association. His animosity towards the Young Irelanders contributed to their departure from the Association in July 1846. Sided with Tories in 1851, and afterwards became ever more conservative in his politics. William Dillon, Mitchel's biographer, wrote of him: 'he had none of his father's greatness, and most of his father's faults' (*Life of John Mitchel*, London, Kegan Paul, Trench & Co, 1888, Vol. 1, p. 116).

4 Richard Davis, Young Ireland's principal scholar, provides an excellent biographical account of O'Brien in his essay, 'The Reluctant Rebel: William Smith O'Brien', *Tipperary Historical Journal*, 1998, pp. 46–55.

Educated at Harrow and Trinity College, Cambridge,[5] and Lincoln's Inn, the highly Anglicised William Smith O'Brien on his father's nomination became MP for the pocket borough of Ennis in 1828. Given the weak and fluid nature of party politics at the time, it is not altogether easy to attach a party label to the man: Whig on some issues, Tory on others, in the parliamentary line-up he was Tory. He supported Catholic Emancipation, having joined the Catholic Association before his election as an MP. His patriotism was Irish as well as British. Unlike some of the Young Irelanders he was no republican, and expressed a strong attachment to the Crown – even in the political crisis of his life supporting the British constitution, save only that there should be a Dublin as well as a Westminster parliament. But these disputes lay ahead when in 1835 he was elected as member for Co. Limerick, with politics which were liberal and patriotic in tendency, but still evolving. In that election he was endorsed by O'Connell and the Roman Catholic clergy; thereafter he sat as an independent Liberal, in broad support of the Whig administration.

O'Connell's final agitation for repeal acquired such momentum by 1843 that the British government took steps to counter it. O'Brien objected to some of these measures, particularly the dismissal as justices of various prominent men who had attended repeal meetings. Although not yet a repealer, O'Brien achieved national notice when he subsequently resigned his own commission; several other protesting landowners followed his lead.

In the summer of 1843 O'Brien commenced a tour of several continental countries, returning home with the conviction that there was 'more misery in one county in Ireland than throughout all the populous cities and districts which I had visited'.[6] A consciousness of the continuing misgovernment of his country, and the same sense of fairness which had led him to resign as a magistrate, moved him further into the repeal camp in October 1843. O'Connell's fortunes and cause were at a particularly low ebb following his cancellation of the Clontarf monster meeting in the face of a government prohibition. It was at this moment that O'Brien publicly applied for Repeal Association membership. This support from a well-known Protestant landowner, a defector from Unionism, whose family claimed such a special place in Irish history, was a coup and an act of support which O'Connell never forgot. O'Brien's application arrived in time to be read aloud at the first public meeting to be held in the Repeal Association's

---

5 Of Cambridge he was later to insist 'I learnt there much that was evil and little that was good'. His son Edward was sent to Trinity College, Dublin, because he was thought to be less likely to form bad associations there. (National Library of Ireland: O'Brien Papers, Ms. 8653/28: William to Lucy Smith O'Brien, 28 June 1852.) Richard and Marianna Davis provide a brief account of O'Brien's rakish young adulthood in their selection of his papers (*The Rebel in His Family: Selected Papers of William Smith O'Brien*, Cork, Cork University Press, 1998).

6 The lines are taken from O'Brien's letter of application for membership of the Repeal Association, 20 October 1843: *Nation*, 28 October 1843, 35d–36a.

new headquarters, Conciliation Hall. The reading was accompanied by repeated cheering and noisy appreciation.[7]

Just as O'Connell welcomed this unexpected bounty, the Young Irelanders, when O'Brien moved to their side, saw his support as a substantial strengthening of their cause. At that point one of the Young Irelanders wrote to him, arguing that 'our chance of effecting anything important depends on your continuing our recognised Leader'. O'Brien, Duffy observed, was 'providentially gifted with qualities and attributes for the time and place'. He was blunt in what he meant by this: 'The Protestants and the landed gentry must be won, and you, a man of property and family, and a Protestant, can and will, win them. What chance of their listening to young men, most of whom are Catholics and all of them spring directly from the trading class.'[8] O'Brien had determined to retire from parliamentary politics, and absented himself from Ireland for the 1847 elections. On his return he discovered that through the efforts of Young Irelanders and the Roman Catholic clergy of the diocese of Limerick he had been elected for that constituency.[9] It was a measure of Young Ireland that so much depended on this complicated man, whose sensibilities and refinement of political beliefs periodically caught him in a paralysing vice. This was a leader with dangerously deceptive properties.

John Mitchel came to national notice several years later than O'Brien, but in times and with such a voice and antecedents that he was marked for gaol almost from the start. His instincts and energies contrasted with O'Connell's Catholic nationalism and O'Brien's Whiggish nationalism. O'Connell's character and galvanic energy had turned him inexorably to populism and demagoguery, the arts of which he practised with historic genius. O'Brien would have been equally at home in an English shire, where they would have recognised his cool, distant and aristocratic liberalism. Mitchel was of a far more radical hue, of Ulster nonconformist stock (and of the least conformist strain of that highly individualistic breed). He was a type for whom political orientation was never difficult, since he lived in a state of permanent opposition: his compass always pointed away from the establishment.[10] In all his writings it is difficult to find the Ulster nonconformist's condemnation of the Roman Catholic Church; it is equally

---

7 The letter, O'Connell delightedly proclaimed, 'was not a document – it was a fact in history – an event of the utmost importance' (ibid., 36a).

8 NLI: O'Brien Papers: Ms. 434/1303, Duffy to O'Brien, 26 December 1846.

9 Ibid., Ms. 449: personal memorandum.

10 Duffy saw Mitchel's wide popularity in Ireland as a measure of British misgovernment. He was a barometer of the 'profound depth of bitterness which generations of injustice and scorn have created in Ireland'. In his time, he had advocated nothing reasonable or practical and hurt England no more 'than the prick of a pin'. Yet Mitchel continued to be loved by multitudes of Irishmen because it was certain that 'he execrated England'. He was not a guide who could be followed – 'in the main he pointed to no road which led anywhere, but he was a constant trumpet of resistance to England, and this was enough' (Duffy 1883, p. 585).

difficult to find any mention of England or things English that is not accompanied by a sneer or imprecation. Hatred of England drove him as much, if not more, than love of his own country.[11]

John Mitchel was born into the manse in 1815. His maternal grandfather had been a United Irishman.[12] His father – a Presbyterian minister educated at the University of Glasgow – had embraced Unitarianism, incurring much condemnation from the Ulster Synod. Dissent and defiance were Mitchel's family traditions, and faith in individual conscience and action was in his blood; there was much of the anarchist, though none of the democrat about him. He was educated at Trinity College, Dublin (but was not a resident student) and became a solicitor in Banbridge, Co. Down. From an early age, and despite mutual love and regard, he brought much unhappiness upon his parents, commencing with a scandalous elopement when he was twenty-one and the girl, Jane Verner, only seventeen. Apprehended in Chester by Captain James Verner, Mitchel was committed briefly to prison. Despite Captain Verner's efforts to keep the couple apart, and the strong disapproval of his own parents, Mitchel succeeded in carrying her off again, this time marrying by special licence. In best romantic fashion (and Mitchel was highly romantic in his makeup) the marriage succeeded, despite politics always coming first: to all appearances it was a happy union.

Mitchel's character made cooperation and any form of collective discipline difficult; his career was punctuated by breaches with colleagues. In his writings and actions there is a manifest and continuing rejection of any authority.[13] The individual was the measure of things, and if that individual had the ability to push the levers of history, it was his right and duty so to do.[14] Resentment and distaste extended to radical and revolutionary organisation – open individual action was preferred to the hierarchies, discipline and claustrophobia of conspiracy, not only on grounds of effectiveness, but also aesthetics – and aesthetics and temperamental incompatibility preceded and drove the functional arguments. The observations of a close relative (probably his brother William) throw light on this side of his character. While tolerant of human frailties, Mitchel was

---

11 Yeats assessed Mitchel's political influence to have been 'almost wholly mischievous'. He played upon international suspicions, and 'exalted the hate of England above the love of Ireland' (Yeats, *op. cit.*, p. 18).

12 This society, founded in Belfast in October 1791, sought parliamentary reform. It brought together men of various political tendencies, liberal to revolutionary, and those of Anglican, nonconformist and Roman Catholic backgrounds. Suppressed in 1794, it reformed as a secret, oath-bound revolutionary body. It was effectively destroyed in the wake of the 1798 rising, in which some of its members were prominent.

13 Although – or because – he was a clergyman's son, Mitchel, not a religious bigot, had what one historian noted as 'a natural dislike for clergy of all denominations' (Gwynn 1949, p. 53). One might add 'and of all callings'.

14 Well schooled in Greek, Mitchel referred to Archimedes, and to America as the 'very standing-ground' where a lever might be planted 'that shall move the world' (*New York Daily Times*, 20 December 1853, 1d).

moved to 'inappeasable wrath' by the pretensions of authority, 'whether it clothed itself in ermine or other official trappings, or walked at noon-day as cant, poisoning the general air'. He could bear criticism, the account continued, 'but if there were any attempt to overbear, his manner changed instantly, and he became stern, almost fierce. At such times his speech was a cutting instrument, and one of the keenest.'[15]

Exaggerated individualism fuels impulsiveness in judgement and haste in action; it can also make it impossible to work with others as equals. These aspects of Mitchel's character were recognised by admirers and sceptics alike. An account of the man published by a sympathetic nationalist journal described him as being 'at once gentle and impetuous, enthusiastic and sagacious; his impulses were irresistible'.[16] A sometime comrade, later bitter opponent, Charles Gavan Duffy – the man who brought Mitchel from his Banbridge obscurity to work on the *Nation* – summed him up with a degree of kindness reserved for the dead. In his Young Ireland days, and throughout his career, Mitchel, Duffy insisted, lacked 'the gift ordinarily called judgement'.[17] John Martin, Mitchel's devoted friend and follower, came to lose confidence in him because of his views on negro slavery and his tendency to antagonise rather than unite.[18] Years before, in a mood of intense and despondent introspection during his confinement on board a convict hulk at Bermuda, Mitchel's judgement had been equally harsh:

> I wish no darker memories crowded upon me . . . but my whole life lies mirrored before me; and it is not bright nor fair to see. I would that I could find in it one single good action (besides the action for which I was convicted as a felon). I wish the mild shade of my father were a less reproachful aspect – and I wish he had less reason.[19]

Towards revolution

Young men of principle and mettle with their blood up were affronted by what they took to be O'Connell's arrogant bullying. Whether of the ilk of O'Brien or of Mitchel, a large part of their political chemistry was the rejection of unjust authority. On his side, O'Connell saw these young radicals as a threat to

15 William Dillon, *Life of John Mitchel*, 1888, vol. 2, pp. 309–10.
16 *Irishman*, 10 June 1848, 1c.
17 *Op. cit.* (1883), p. 12. Mitchel had died in 1875.
18 'I lost the confident hopes I had rested on him. I saw that his power for uniting and organising the Irish patriots was gone, and the haughty violence he was displaying and the wrongheadedness that I attributed to some of his acts made me despair of his ever regaining his power.' Yet, Martin added, 'Nobody else appeared to possess the qualities for a leader in our cause so eminently as Mitchel' (Diary of John Martin, Northern Ireland Public Record Office (NIPRO), D. 560/5; *Paris Journal*, July 1858, f. 134).
19 John Mitchel, *Jail Journal; or Five Years in British Prisons*, London, R & T Washbourne, n.d.

constitutional nationalism and the safety of the electoral machine and arrangements he had constructed.[20] Underlying differences on the relationship between
Irish nationalism and Roman Catholicism grew more acute as O'Connell became
careless, in public and private, of the distinction. The remembrance of the hierarchy's past support led O'Connell to take a sectarian line in educational policy;
the Repeal Association appeared to some to be becoming a priests' organisation,
neglecting or dismissing the sensibilities and concerns of Protestant nationalists.[21]
To this mixture of discontents was added a sharp disagreement on the tactics to
be pursued towards the expected new government: O'Connell favoured a type of
alliance with the Whigs; the other Young Irelanders would have nothing to do
with it, and saw in Ireland no significant distinction between Tory and Whig.

All societies have to cope with the demands of young men in a hurry. The
activities of the Young Irelanders might have been absorbed in the usual fashion
had it not been for the great economic and social challenges then facing the
country and its government. The tides of popular discontent and nationalism
gained strength and surged. Those who had placed themselves at the forefront
were propelled forward and, almost without thinking about it, found themselves
in what they imagined to be a revolutionary position.

The Irish Confederation was the body formed in January 1847 by the Young
Irelanders who had broken with O'Connell's Repeal Association six months
before.[22] Radical though some of the Confederation's members were, most were

20 The intemperance and hauteur with which all opposition was received by the leaders of the
    Repeal Association was epitomised in the infamous reception of a petition got up by working
    men (and supported by 1500 signatures) who wished to see healed the breach between the
    Association and the seceded Young Irelanders. The petition was duly presented at Conciliation
    Hall on 24 October 1846. On the orders of John O'Connell this petition was thrown in the
    gutter, widening the gulf of bitterness between Old and Young Irelanders (see Michael Doheny,
    The Felon's Track, Dublin, M. H. Gill & Son, 1914, p. 113). Yet wherever intra-party despotism
    and indulgence of his son's arrogance led him, O'Connell's liberal credentials were, on the
    broader political stage, as sound or sounder than some of his Young Ireland opponents – notably
    Mitchel (scarcely a democrat and later a notable supporter of negro slavery) and O'Brien, who
    had reservations about household suffrage and the secret ballot (*see* MacDonagh, *op. cit.*, p. 267).
21 O'Connell's form of Roman Catholicism was narrow and rigid. One biographer notes that he
    regarded non-Catholics as being irremediably spiritually disadvantaged because they did not
    have access to the true sacraments, which only the Church could dispense. While admitting
    that no one can see into another's soul, the writer continues, it appears that from outward signs
    O'Connell was 'an ultra-conscientious, fearful, straitened type of Catholic, almost morbidly
    observant.... He may even have been a victim – to a small degree – of a form of religious
    neurosis' (ibid., pp. 211–12).
22 The breach between O'Connell's Repeal Association and the Young Irelanders took place on 29
    July 1846. They objected to O'Connell's backstairs dealings with the incoming Whig govern-
    ment, and to the suppression of dissent within the Repeal Association. Subsidiary disagreements
    were the refusal to oppose a Whig candidate in a parliamentary election, and accepting and
    distributing Whig patronage. The first public meeting of the Confederation was held at the
    Rotunda, Dublin. William Smith O'Brien, who had helped in the formation of the organisation,
    was on the platform and spoke at length.

not republicans, and the organisation's objectives did not exceed what would later be called Home Rule. Proclaiming a right to Irish self-government, the Confederation repudiated physical force as a means to achieve its ends, and was content to maintain the constitutional link with Britain.[23] Like most associations, however, it was a coalition. A group of radicals wished to press for land reform and republicanism. From this group emerged the would-be insurrectionists.

Political and religious sects, repelled by the world, are gripped by an amoebic impulse for division. The body which emerges from a split, especially one originating in disputes over hypotheticals, principles and words, will frequently go on dividing. Mitchel, despairing of change through what he saw as a hopelessly restricted Irish franchise, and indignant at the introduction of another Coercion Act, began to urge on the Confederation a policy of preparation for agrarian revolution. Few of the other leaders found this acceptable since it violated their commitment to peaceful change, and would isolate them from support in the country. Although Mitchel had the support of his friend John Martin and of the young journalist Thomas Devin Reilly, and of some of the Confederation's Dublin Clubs, he had little if any following from the population at large. In these circumstances, Mitchel's tactic was to publish letters and articles which he hoped would provoke the government, thus exposing the oppressive nature of the regime and garnering popular support. O'Brien and the other leaders were concerned about the effect this would have on the Confederation, both legally and politically.[24]

---

23 For a contemporary's account see Michael Doheny's *The Felon's Track*, *op. cit.* Sir Charles Gavan Duffy's *Young Ireland: A Fragment of Irish History 1840–1850* (London, Cassell, Petter, Galpin & Co, 1880) is essential reading, giving a comprehensive and detailed account from the perspective of a moderate at the centre of the movement. It should be read together with his *Four Years of Irish History 1845–1849* (1883). Although generous in his judgements and apparently scrupulous in narrative, both volumes were written half a lifetime after the events with which they dealt, by one who had played a leading and partisan role in intra-party affairs. Richard Davis, in *The Young Ireland Movement*, (Dublin, Gill & Macmillan, 1987) provides a modern account of the personalities and events of the 1848 uprising; his *William Smith O'Brien: Ireland – 1848 – Tasmania* (Dublin, Geography Publications, 1989) is an excellent short account of O'Brien's family, his trial and transportation to Van Diemen's Land. Denis Gwynn's *Young Ireland and 1848* (1949) remains an essential text, despite some trivial and irritating errors. Sir Llewellyn Woodward provides a wider context for Irish grievances and British responses in *The Age of Reform 1850–1870*, Oxford, Oxford University Press, 1962 (2nd edn), pp. 328–64.

24 On 8 January 1848, breaking with Duffy and on Duffy's invitation, Mitchel addressed a long letter to the *Nation* setting out his militant policy of agrarian resistance and preparation for rebellion. He used words which were particularly likely to provoke government action: 'I desired that *The Nation* and the Confederation should rather employ themselves in promulgating sound instruction upon military affairs – upon the natural lines of defence which make the island so strong – upon the construction and defence of field-works, and especially upon the use of proper arms – not with a view to any immediate insurrection, but in order that the stupid "legal and constitutional" shouting, voting and "agitating" that have made our country an abomination to the whole earth, should be changed into a deliberate study of the theory and practice of guerrilla warfare; and that the true and only method of regenerating Ireland might in course of time recommend itself to a nation so long abused, and deluded by "legal" doctrines' (*Nation*, 8 January 1848, 28b).

Mitchel's views appeared to O'Brien to be 'very dangerous in their character – both in regard to the interests of the Repeal Cause and in regard to the general well-being of Society'.[25] On 31 January 1848, a public debate opened which was to last for three days, and concluded with the defeat of Mitchel's propositions by 317 votes to 188. The final resolution insisted, *inter alia*, 'That to hold out to the Irish people the hope that, in this present broken and divided condition, they can liberate their country by an appeal to arms, and consequently to divert them from constitutional action would be, in our opinion, a fatal misdirection of the public mind.'[26]

The following week Mitchel and his supporters, Martin and Reilly, resigned from the Confederation.[27] Mitchel at this time had a reckless desperation about him, and although he was little known outside Dublin,[28] he had a following among the rank and file of the Confederation clubs in the city, and was accomplished in inflammatory and seditious prose. It was only a matter of time before Dublin Castle reached out and took him.

Two other events made up the insurrectionary mix: the potato famine which had commenced with the crop failure in September 1845, and recurred ever more disastrously in succeeding years, each of which government failed properly to address; and the French Revolution of February 1848. Of the former not much need be said – the horror and suffering of the event are well known, and have reverberated down the generations. The tardiness and inadequacy of the government's response (and that of a large section of landlords) was obvious at the time, and infused the nationalist cause with great bitterness, which has continued to poison Anglo-Irish relations into modern times.[29] The only

25 NLI: O'Brien Papers: Ms. 449; personal memorandum. O'Brien emphasised that his criticisms of Mitchel were of a political rather than a personal nature: 'I believed him to be an enthusiastic lover of Ireland, a warm friend, an excellent husband, father and brother – amiable in all the relations of life. Fairminded and truthful, though wayward and capricious.'

26 Doheny, *op. cit.*, p. 124. Later there may have been some ironic satisfaction for Mitchel in the fact that all the leaders of the subsequent insurrection – O'Brien, Dillon, Meagher, O'Gorman and Doheny himself – spoke against him in the debates.

27 For an account of the debate and surrounding events, see Charles Gavan Duffy 1883, pp. 503–23. A brief account is also given by Mitchel's biographer, William Dillon (vol. 1, pp. 176–83). Mitchel's version of the debate (which was conducted in a courteous and fair manner by both sides) is given in *The Crusade of the Period and Last Conquest of Ireland (Perhaps)*, New York, Lynch, Cole & Meehan, 1873, pp. 257–60.

28 Meagher, then a candidate in a by-election in Waterford, wrote to Duffy at this time that 'the people of Munster know as little of Mitchel as of Mahomet' (Duffy 1883, p. 494).

29 Cecil Woodham-Smith's *The Great Hunger: Ireland 1845–9* (London, Hamish Hamilton, 1962) remains the best introduction to the famine. Recent studies have amplified and to some extent modified earlier understandings. See, for example, Chris Morash and Richard Hayes (eds), *Fearful Realities: New Perspectives on the Famine*, Dublin, Irish Academic Press, 1996; Christine Kinealy, *This Great Calamity: The Irish Famine 1845–52*, Dublin, Gill & Macmillan, 1994. Colm Tóibín's *The Irish Famine* (London, Profile Books, 1999) is an incisive contribution to the historiography and politics of the famine and injects some necessary passion into the subject.

organisation which had the standing and resources to lead the people through the political trials of the famine was the Repeal Association, but this, as we have seen, was riven and moribund. As one of the leading writers on the famine observed, during the fearful winter of 1846 to 1847, 'the all-absorbing issue in the Repeal Association was not the failure of the potato but the crushing of Young Ireland'.[30] In fairness, it must also be noted that, apart from its demands for Home Rule, Young Ireland had also failed to address the famine.

Looking back to the winter of 1847 to 1848, Charles Gavan Duffy described the ruination of agriculture, trade and rural society, and the mass emigration that seemed to be emptying the country: 'There were not many of us who would not have given his life cheerfully to arrest this ruin, if only he could see a possible way; but there was no way visible.'[31] By the autumn of 1847 Mitchel, the most extreme of the leaders, wanted revolution and saw it as a spontaneous force, ready to explode.[32] Complete independence, a republic and immediate action were the planks of his platform.[33] Unable to carry his Confederation comrades with him, he split from them and used his newspaper, the *United Irishman*, openly to call and organise for revolution.[34] Mitchel's inflammatory language

30 Woodham-Smith, *op. cit.*, p. 330.

31 Mitchel 1883, p. 532.

32 Mitchel opposed clandestine organisation, on grounds of both principle and good practice. Influenced by Carlyle (with whom he had several meetings, and whose *French Revolution* he greatly revered) he believed that revolutions had to be spontaneous popular upheavals. With good cause, he also believed that a secret organisation would from the start be penetrated by government agents, and thus literally be worse than useless. (William Dillon, *op. cit.*, vol. 1, pp. 195–6). Any insurrection, Mitchel believed, could only hope to succeed were England engaged elsewhere. (This became a Fenian dogma: see below.)

33 Ten years later Mitchel, asked about the possibility of resuming his long-stilled relationship with O'Brien in the nationalist cause, insisted 'I am no republican doctrinaire, and would accept an Irish monarchy or Irish anything'. He differed with O'Brien, he insisted, not on theories of government 'but as to possibilities of action'. He was convinced that the mass of the Irish people could not be roused for anything less than social revolution – 'destruction of landlordism, and denial of all tenure and title derived from English sovereigns' (letter to a friend (unnamed), 20 June 1858, *cit.* Dillon, *op. cit.*, vol. 2, p. 130).

34 The first issue appeared on 12 February 1848, the last on 27 May 1848 (John Mitchel's final contribution was to the issue of 20 May – a letter to Ulster Protestants, written from Dublin's Newgate). The newspaper's motto was taken from Wolfe Tone, the revolutionary of United Irishmen of fifty years before: 'Our Independence must be had at all hazards. If the men of property will not support us, they must fall; we can support ourselves by the aid of that numerous and respectable class of the community, the men of no property.' Such was the interest and demand that a price of two shillings could be got for a copy of the *United Irishman* on its first day. A run of 5000 had been ordered, but Mitchel claimed he could have sold 15,000, given the volatility of the times. It is worth noting the rapidity with which Mitchel had moved away from the Repeal Association's constitutional methods, of which he had written not many months before: 'This is a legally organised and constitutional society seeking to attain its object, as all the world knows, by peaceable means and none other. Constitutional agitation is the very basis of it; and nobody who contemplates any other mode of bringing about the independence of the country has a right to come here, or consider himself a fit member of our Association' (Doheny, *op. cit.*, p. 105).

alarmed most of his erstwhile comrades as much as the government. Urging William Smith O'Brien to use his influence to counter Mitchel, Duffy wrote that an outbreak was certain, but unless O'Brien provided against it, it would be

> a mere democratic [i.e. popular] one, which the English Government will extinguish in blood . . . if things are left to take the course they are tending towards, we will see the life of the country trampled out under the feet of English soldiers, suppressing a peasant insurrection; or you and I will meet on a Jacobin scaffold, ordered for executions as enemies of some new Marat or Robespierre.[35]

Disunity and despair were swept aside by the French Revolution of February 1848, and the wave of insurrections which followed across the Continent.[36] The moment seemed right for a reunited nationalist movement to treat once more with the British government, and, if that failed, the moral ground had been cleared for direct action. Those who had only weeks before opposed direct action now embraced it: 'From that time forward until the final catastrophe, all the confederate leaders were for a policy which may fairly be described as a policy of physical force.'[37] Even O'Brien responded to the apparent promise of the French Revolution. Recalling its impact, he wrote that 'Its opening scenes were characterised by alternations of moral grandeur and of moral beauty. . . . A passionate enthusiasm for liberty was preserved from excess by a universal love of order. . . . All Europe felt the electric sensation. Wherever oppression had been sustained by Power – there the shock produced a convulsion.'[38] His impulse was to bind up the divisions within the Confederation and between Young and Old Ireland. But conciliation and revolution pulled in opposite directions, and the latter won O'Brien.

On 20 March 1848, at a public meeting at Dublin's North Wall, organised by the Confederation and attended by some 10,000 to 15,000 people, O'Brien moved an inflammatory message of congratulations to the French people ('As slaves we address freemen . . .'). He called for the unity of Repeal and Confederation, and for the formation of a national guard. This, he improbably claimed, could be done 'in a manner perfectly constitutional' – but privately he must

---

35 Duffy 1883, p. 543n.

36 Mitchel remembered the effect that the February revolution had on the militants of the Confederation – the news 'burst in upon us . . . for between the French people and the Irish there has always been all electric telegraph, whose signals never failed' (1873, p. 262).

37 See William Dillon, *Life of John Mitchel, op. cit.*, vol. 1, p. 213. Mitchel began to attend Confederation meetings again, moving a resolution that the clubs should arm themselves. The resolution was passed with acclamation. He recalled 'Nobody would be listened to there, who proposed any other mode of redress for Irish grievances than the sword' (1873, p. 262).

38 NLI: O'Brien Papers: Ms. 449; personal memorandum. The implied reference to the excesses of the first French Revolution is significant.

have realised that it could not.[39] Five days before, at a Confederation meeting, he had recalled his previous opposition to guerrilla war, 'but the state of affairs was totally different now'. Every lover of his country should come forward to be enrolled in the National Guard.[40] It was not pure Mitchelism, but it was getting close, and made nationalist unity impossible.

Mitchel himself had been brought to near rapture by the French Revolution. The astonishing reception of his *United Irishman* provided him with popular confirmation and validation.[41] This added to the pressures on the less extreme members of Young Ireland. Caught up in factional hopes and rhetoric, imagining that government reaction would unite the country behind their cause, the various activists inevitably deluded themselves that fervour and self-sacrifice could bring their hopes and desires to fruition. Strong language and bellicose threats too often repeated invite ridicule; words and poses may pass into action through little more than the embarrassment and self-regard of revolutionists. The overthrow of firmly established authority is a rare event, and to have any chance of success, those who undertake it require conspiratorial experience, military skill, boldness, true ruthlessness, luck and some popular support; they also need a failure of tactics and nerve on the other side. The Young Ireland insurrectionists, mainly intellectuals and amateur politicians, went forward with little more than the poetry of hopelessness. As Mitchel would recall, 'A kind of sacred wrath took possession of a few Irishmen at this period. They could endure the horrible scene no longer, and resolved to cross the path of the British war of conquest, though it should crush them to atoms.'[42]

Later in the century Irish nationalists – particularly the Davitt–Parnell Land League – would devise a range of measures of civil disobedience and direct action which would show that between the pressures and implied threats of the mustering of great numbers of supporters (O'Connell's method) and the act of armed rebellion (Young Ireland), there existed a field which gave scope for action and initiative. Rent strikes, local campaigns of protest and boycotting all

---

39 *Freeman's Journal*, 21 March 1848, 2d.

40 Ibid., 16 March 1848, 3d. Twenty years later Mitchel's recollections were of a more violent speech: see *The History of Ireland from the Treaty of Limerick to the Present Time: Being a Continuation of the History of the Abbé Macgeoghegan* (Glasgow, Cameron & Ferguson, 1869, vol. 2, p. 229). It was probably this speech on 15 March 1848, which O'Brien himself described as being 'of a more warlike tendency than any which I had previously spoken and it was made the ground of a prosecution against me for sedition. The Government exhibited no little skill in directing against me a large amount of prejudice by coupling [my case] with Mr Meagher who had also spoken in language of a very violent character' (NLI: O'Brien Papers: Ms. 449; personal memorandum).

41 Doheny insisted that the Dubliner who did not read that first issue 'might indeed be pronounced a bigot or a fool'. So great was the sale, Doheny recalled, that the press was kept busy for three days and nights and a police guard was necessary. Mitchel claimed that the paper was in substantial circulation among the soldiers, the English and Scots, who shared Chartist ideas, as well as the Irish soldiers who had nationalist sympathies.

42 John Mitchel, 1869, vol. 2, p. 224.

stayed within the criminal law. Cattle driving and the destruction of crops and livestock, long-established forms of rural protest, broke the law, but in ways that were difficult to bring home to individuals, never mind a parent organisation. In an atmosphere of mounting disorder and illegality, intimidation easily and spontaneously passed from riot, arson and assault to murder, again without any links of legal culpability to the Land League organisers. Well short of overt armed rebellion, the pressures on government forced far-reaching policy changes. John Mitchel and his Confederation colleagues conceived of some of the measures later used by the Land League, but they lacked the organisational means to achieve them – and none of their leaders in their own time achieved the immense popular veneration of Parnell or Davitt.[43]

While the Land League's political achievements stopped well short of independence, they wrought economic and social changes in the Irish countryside that were far more extensive than those contemplated by some of the Young Ireland leaders. It was left to even later generations to devise means of civil protest which could achieve independence from colonial rule. Gandhi and his Congress showed how a centuries-old and highly efficient system of government could be brought down. The shades of Mitchel, O'Brien and the other Young Irelanders might protest that the first steps to Indian and other colonial independence were taken in Ireland. But in 1848 the tactics of nationalist campaigning remained marooned on the narrow spit between monster meetings and armed insurrection.[44]

With a minimal repertoire of civil protest, it was but a short step from the pressure of assembled multitudes to other direct action menaces. Threats of force (including studied speculations on the suitability of Ireland for guerrilla warfare) at a time when Britain faced hostility from France and the internal threat of Chartism seemed to many (and not only the timid) to be a way in which social and political objectives might be extracted without an actual recourse to violence; the more extreme elements persuaded themselves that armed insurrection was a

43 James Fintan Lalor (1807–49) in 1846 and 1847 set out ideas for land reform and for direct action by the tenantry which attracted the attention and support of the more militant Young Irelanders. Among the proposals which he called 'Moral Insurrection' was a notion of a national rent-strike. Although the majority of the activists, conscious of the influence of O'Connell and the priests, thought Lalor's idea of a moral insurrection impracticable, these notions were the basis of the Davitt–Parnell Land League, and Lalor's influence extended to the generation of the 1916 uprising and beyond. See his *Collected Writings*, Dublin and London, Maunsel & Company, 1918. For a biographical note see n. 89, below.

44 This point was enlarged upon by Mary Robinson, President of Ireland, in a tribute to Daniel O'Connell on the 150th anniversary of his death (15 May 1997): 'A weapon of political action of the magnitude of that developed by O'Connell does not spring into effective operation overnight. It requires organisation, education, discipline, control and flexibility. . . . No political philosopher and with no pretensions to be one, O'Connell became, however, the great pioneer of political empowerment of deprived peoples' ('Tribute to Daniel O'Connell', Reform Club, London, 15 May 1997).

practical programme. Language and posturing became wilder by the day. Having allowed a good airing of these seditious utterances and publications (Home Secretary Sir George Grey was later to characterise Mitchel's *United Irishman* as 'the ravings of a disordered imagination'),[45] government concluded that the cause of the Confederation had been sufficiently discredited among the clergy and respectable classes. The leaders were cornered by their own rhetoric, leaving government to claim that it had exercised forbearance to the utmost extent, and so the time was ripe for prophylactic action.[46] As the megaphone of revolution, John Mitchel was the first in line for attention.

Mitchel's prosecution

The legal background to Mitchel's prosecution was a change in the law of treason and sedition. The former, depending on a statute of Edward III, was characterised by the legal scholar Sir James Fitzjames Stephen as 'a crude, clumsy performance, which has raised as many questions as it can have settled, and which has been successful only when it was not required to be put in force'.[47] In the Irish context, the main difficulty was that this law dealt with deeds rather than threats or conspiracies. The archaic penalty for treason,[48] moreover, was in itself an obstacle to its implementation – especially (as was notoriously the case

45 3 *Hansard* XCVIII, col. 22; 7 April 1851. O'Brien held scarcely less critical views of Mitchel's effusions. They had, he recorded, 'alienated from the cause of Repeal and from the Confederation an incalculable number of persons belonging to the higher and wealthier classes of society'. The revolutionary opinions of Mitchel and Reilly were expressed in language which 'while it is often very powerful was frequently revolting to men of fastidious tastes [and] had excited no little alarm and disgust amongst those who have something to lose. Many interpreted the doctrines of the United Irishman as stimulants to plunder. They now began to regard the agitation for Repeal as synonymous with the Confiscation of Property' (NLI: O'Brien Papers: Ms. 449; personal memorandum).

46 O'Brien, in retrospect, was convinced that government had let Mitchel have his head for several weeks when they could have acted, and had ample evidence to bring a charge of treason against him, in order to confound in the public mind his own more moderate approach and Mitchel's revolutionary doctrine (O'Brien Papers, ibid.). This may have been true, although, as noted, after the February revolution O'Brien had himself begun to support and to advocate armed action. The difference, perhaps, was that he wanted a revolution such as he had seen in France – a transfer of political power while leaving the social, economic and legal pillars of society intact; Mitchel had a more apocalyptic vision.

47 Sir James Fitzjames Stephen, *A History of the Criminal Law of England*, London, Macmillan, 1883, vol. 2, p. 283. The statute was the Treason Act, 1351: 25 Ed. III, c.2.

48 Until discontinued by s.31 of the 1870 Forfeiture Act (33 & 34 Vict., c.23) this remained, at least notionally, hanging, beheading and quartering, and the display of the remains at the will of the government. The evisceration while still alive ('drawing') of earlier years was no longer required. The last aggravated death sentence in England for high treason was carried out on Brandreth, Turner and Ludlam on 7 November 1817. The Prince Regent remitted that part of the sentence relating to quartering (see Sir Leon Radzinowicz, *Adventures in Criminology*, London and New York, Routledge, 1999, pp. 278–9).

in Ireland) where juries were apt to bend to public sentiment; and indeed, were the aggravated death penalty executed, an inflammatory effect was as likely as fearful submission. The offence of sedition was a misdemeanour (rather than a felony), subject to relatively mild penalties, allowed for bail, did not include forfeiture of property, and prosecution was not unwelcome as fuel for political careers: the law was in need of strengthening.

The Treason Felony Bill

The English political mood was febrile, and while there were grounds for the widespread fear of disorder, there were fewer for the exaggerated statements about revolution. The third and most heralded of the Charters was about to be presented to Parliament by tens of thousands of radical working men from all over the country. Following the events in France, it seemed briefly that the provisional government might be willing to assume the role of European revolutionary headquarters. Authority was threatened in Austria, Germany and Italy; Europe seemed poised to return to an instability more than thirty years in the past. People deemed to be extremists had been in Paris to solicit assistance for Irish insurrection. The Irish peasantry was in a state of sullen desperation as a result of one of the most destructive famines in modern European history. Even the most sanguine politician recognised the imponderabilities of the moment. In Ireland, the government's policy was the familiar mixture of conciliation and coercion. There was little of the former, and the latter was twofold – a consolidation and extension of coercive powers in Ireland, and the creation of a new offence of treason felony. The new law was ostensibly intended to dampen extremist political agitation throughout the United Kingdom, but was especially intended for the suppression of Irish militants, and used against them throughout the rest of the nineteenth and well into the twentieth century. The Treason Felony Bill provided a penalty of transportation for between seven years and life, or imprisonment for up to two years.[49]

This legislation was carried forward in a setting which emphasised all the dire possibilities. The second reading debate was preceded by an extended and anxious exchange on the impending presentation of the Chartists' third petition. (The debate was on Friday, 7 April 1848; the demonstration was to take place on Monday, 10 April.) There were reports in radical circles and newspapers that as many as 300,000 or even 500,000 demonstrators would present the petition: widespread civil disorder was in prospect, and the more nervous politicians feared revolution.[50] In the Commons, members drew attention to the connection

---

49 This would be enacted as the 1848 Treason Felony Act (11 & 12 Vict., c.12).
50 The right to petition Parliament was enshrined in the Bill of Rights, but common law limited to ten the number who could bring the petition to Parliament. Exceptions had been made to this rule, which was intended to prevent the disruption or intimidation of Parliament.

between the Chartists and the extreme party in Ireland. Despite the loyal prot-estations of Feargus O'Connor, the Chartist leader,[51] the majority of MPs were apparently convinced that the Irish and the Chartists were colluding or even conspiring jointly to promote their causes by disorderly and extra-legal activities.[52]

The Treason Felony debate was to be followed by a second reading debate on the Landlord and Tenant (Ireland) Bill, a measure which was promoted as a step towards the reorganisation and reform of Irish land tenure. Several Irish members who spoke insisted that the effect of the new measure would be a diminution of tenant rights. William Smith O'Brien claimed that the Bill had been drawn 'with great dexterity in such a manner as to excite universal condemnation. It gave equal dissatisfaction to both Landlords and Tenants.'[53] Certainly it proved almost wholly ineffective in dealing with Ireland's land tenure problems.

What was needed, Home Secretary Sir George Grey told the Commons, was a law to deal with offences which in seriousness fell between sedition and treason. The Bill would deal with those who would contrive ('compass') various treason-able acts, short of offences against the person of the Sovereign, and who promoted such intentions by 'open and advised speaking'. The offence of treasonable incitement would become a felony, instead of the misdemeanour of sedition.

The Bill was overwhelmingly supported; opposition was confined to a handful of mainly radical and Irish members. Among these, however, there were several who, while deploring Confederation activities, argued that the Bill would aggra-vate Irish affairs. The precipitator of the split between the Repeal Association and the Confederation, John O'Connell, declared the Young Irelanders to be to Repeal what the United Irishmen of 1798 were to the progress of Irish liberty ('for it was notorious that the acts of the United Irishmen were the cause of the Union'), but he opposed the Bill, not from the slightest sympathy whatever towards those likely to be affected but because it would inflame and irritate Irish opinion.[54]

Feargus O'Connor affirmed his own radical principles, but insisted that they had not been and would not be furthered illegally. Should the Bill go forward, public expressions of opinion would give way to the foundation of secret clubs

---

51 (1796–1855). Educated at Trinity College, Dublin, and Gray's Inn. Elected MP for Co. Cork in 1832, but subsequently unseated. Founded the radical newspaper the *Northern Star* in 1837. Imprisoned 1840–1. Leading figure in Chartism for many years; MP for Nottingham 1847–52. Advocated an alliance between the Irish peasantry and the English working class. An early quarrel with Daniel O'Connell was never made up.

52 3 *Hansard*, XCVIII, cols 6–20; 7 April 1848, but see also cols 26–7 for references to Feargus O'Connor's attitude to Ireland. At the time of William Smith O'Brien's trial in September 1848, his family feared that the government might attempt to implicate him in Chartist offences (Robert to Ellen O'Brien, 24 September, 1848: Trinity College, Dublin (TCD): O'Brien Papers: Ms. 10610/21). O'Brien denied any such connection, and none was proved against him.

53 NLI: O'Brien Papers: Ms. 449; personal memorandum.

54 3 *Hansard*, XCVIII, cols 34–7 *passim*; 7 April 1848.

and associations.[55] Another radical, George Thompson,[56] warned that the Bill would make it a felony to talk politics. Government should watch out, 'lest, by passing this Bill, they ennobled felony; let them beware lest they converted that which ought to be a badge of degradation into a badge of honour and renown.'[57] Other radicals including Joseph Hume[58] and George Muntz[59] opposed the Bill in more measured terms, Hume asking that the phrase 'or by open and advised speaking' be struck out. Were it left in, 'there would be nothing but secret meetings, private associations, and a hateful system of espionage.' Muntz could not consent to any Bill which made it possible to charge anyone with a felony on the evidence of a single person; he was persuaded that juries and judges took 'vast liberties' with facts where politics were concerned.[60]

Several speakers, who sympathised with neither the Irish nor the Chartists, also opposed the Bill. Sharman Crawford objected to a Bill which made a man liable for spoken words.[61] Sir William Clay characterised the measure as a gagging Bill which would have counterproductive effects, making men's minds 'rankle and fester, and induce them to do what otherwise they would never have thought of doing'. Indeed, had the law been in effect during the agitation of 1831 and 1832 many reformers (some in Parliament) would have been transported: this was a dangerous check on freedom of speech.[62]

Much had ensued between the first Friday and Monday second reading sessions. William Smith O'Brien had returned from his mission to revolutionary France, en route to Ireland, where he was to surrender to his Queen's Bench bail on a charge of sedition. He was accompanied by Thomas Francis Meagher and a provocative new Irish flag – a tricolour which was a gift of the French revolutionaries. The great Chartist demonstration had fizzled out, and whatever bluff of menace that lay behind it had been called. Despite this reassertion of order, and the vigorously (but nearly always reasonably) expressed views of those members who opposed what they saw as a dangerous intrusion of law into politics, Sir George Grey pressed on with the Bill and carried the second reading by 453 to 36.

---

55 Ibid., cols 83–5; 10 April 1848.
56 (1804–78). Free-trader and radical reformer; East India proprietor; opposed to all endowments for ecclesiastical purposes.
57 3 *Hansard*, XCVIII, cols 85–6; 10 April 1848.
58 (1777–1855). Held various medical and other offices in India; returned home as East India proprietor. Justice of the Peace in several petty-sessional divisions. Variously Member for Weymouth, Montrose, Middlesex and Kilkenny. A radical reformer.
59 (1774–1857). Merchant and inventor of German descent. In 1837 convicted in connection with a Church Rate meeting riot, but the conviction quashed on appeal. A reformer who also opposed any further grant of political power to the Roman Catholics.
60 3 *Hansard*, XCVIII, col. 112; 10 April 1848.
61 Ibid., col. 351; 14 April 1848. William Sharman Crawford, MP for Rochdale, was an Ulster Liberal.
62 Ibid., cols 351–3. Sir William Clay (1791–1869) was a merchant who had been Secretary to the Board of Control, 1839–41. A reforming Liberal, Member for Tower Hamlets, 1832–57.

Grey's inflexibility was not driven by political panic. Irish developments were disturbing, but he must have known that much of what was happening was merely talk; only forces of gossamer were ranged against the government. What probably strengthened his determination, and cemented support from all but the more extreme or eccentric of Liberals, Radicals and Irish Members, was O'Brien's own defiant speech to the Commons. His apparent attempt to secure material support from France had been wrecked by Lamartine's prudence.[63] All of this had been well trailed in the English press,[64] as had the increasingly bellicose statements of the Irish Confederation, *The Nation* and Mitchel's *United Irishman*.[65]

O'Brien had been warned not to appear in the Commons, which was bitter and hostile. Even so, his long service and many friends might have allowed him to argue for conciliation. Knowing that his cause had faint chance of success, O'Brien instead defied and threatened, and seemingly did all he could to strengthen government's case against him. This was not simply a matter of misjudgement: a romantic craving for defiant failure apparently drove him on. The Bill, he observed, was an attempt to meet Ireland's claims with coercion rather than conciliation. He emphasised his Chartist support ('from five millions of whom there has been a petition presented this evening'). Lord John Russell had called him a traitor, but O'Brien repudiated the charge, warning, 'if he plays towards this government the part of Guizot or Metternich . . . I tell him, it is not I, but he and his colleagues, that are traitors to the country, the Queen and the constitution'.[66]

The speech, delivered to a noisy and seething Commons, was courageous and certainly defiant, but politically pointless.[67] It could not overawe or intimidate government, nor could it rally moderate opinion to his side. Had O'Brien been

---

63 Revolutionary delegations from many European states made their way to Paris for an audience with the provisional government. O'Brien's memorandum of the events of 1848 emphatically denied having sought armed assistance. '[I]n the conversations which I had with Mr La Martine (sic) . . . and others I carefully abstained from soliciting armed succour from France.' He did own to having asked 'to be placed in friendly communication with the Irish officers in foreign service' adding 'But . . . we had no immediate intention of calling upon our fellow countrymen to appeal to arms'. This could be read to mean that while no formal request was made for men or *matériel* such assistance, unofficially given, would have been welcome (NLI: O'Brien Papers: Ms. 449; personal memorandum).

64 See, for example, the *Daily News*, 3 April 1848, 2e; 5 April 1848, 3b–c; *The Times*, 4 April, 4d–e ('The Irish traitors only prove by all this the perfect freedom they enjoy under our laws').

65 *The Times*, 10 April 1848, 2b–c.

66 3 *Hansard*, XCVIII, cols. 74–80; 10 April 1848.

67 That is, on the pragmatic plane. It immensely elevated his position within the narrow church of extreme nationalism. John Mitchel, ambivalent in his feelings towards O'Brien, and, from time to time his opponent, afterwards wrote: '[T]hose to whom the name and fame of that good Irishman are dear, will always remember with pride that his last utterance in the London Parliament was one of haughty defiance, in the name of his oppressed and plundered country' (Mitchel 1869, p. 231).

directed by the government to convict himself of all their charges he would have made such a speech, word for word: it demonstrated the need for a Treason Felony Bill because it was a prime example of 'open and advised speech' with seditious intent. O'Brien had isolated himself from moderate opinion in England, and by the language which he used and the posture he adopted committed himself and his friends to revolt and failure.

In a bombastic editorial as intemperate in language as that for which it condemned O'Brien and his associates, *The Times* surely scored a point when it observed that as he stood to oppose the second reading of the Treason Felony Bill, he must have had 'some terrible misgivings of what the next few weeks will produce to himself and his associates in treason'. Events must now reach their crisis: 'with the provisions of this measure hanging over their heads the Irish traitors must act or desist.' Were treason to go out of fashion there would be no remembrance of past folly, but public security seemed to require the committal to Bedlam of O'Brien and one or two others: 'Seclusion and cooling diet is the regimen that charity would fain suggest in their cases.'[68]

Mitchel's arrest and trial

Back in Dublin, Mitchel had continued his course as revolution's John the Baptist, publishing violent and abusive tirades against the government in the *United Irishman*.[69] He was, of course, well practised in incendiary writing, having as far back as November 1845 caused a great deal of trouble between Duffy's *Nation* and O'Connell by a leading article on how, should the railways be used for the movement of troops on missions against a rebellious population, they might be disabled, by lifting track, filling cuttings, breaking embankments, and then ambushing the detrained soldiers. Duffy had published the piece as a response to a rather gloating article in the *Standard*, a pro-government newspaper, but even though he approved of Mitchel's riposte, he thought he had gone into 'somewhat needless detail'.[70] That episode had done much to establish Mitchel's name as an extreme nationalist. The article had tweaked O'Connell's tail and caused much annoyance to the general body of respectable Repealers, and, of course, their Unionist opponents. In the two years since, Mitchel had much enlarged his stockpile of provocation.

In an article directed to the 'small farmers of Ireland' he pointed out that the landlords and their families numbered no more than 8000; the small tenant-

---

68 *The Times*, 12 April 1848, 5a–b.

69 The journal's masthead was in itself provocation, being a reference and act of homage to the revolutionary secret society, the rebellions of 1798, and the various supportive activities of the French.

70 Duffy tells the story in his *Four Years of Irish History*, pp. 116–18. See the *Nation*, 22 November 1845, 88c. What came to be called 'The Railway Article' is also quoted extensively by Dillon in his *Life of John Mitchel*, vol. 1, pp. 93–4.

farmers amounted to more than a million. There was no help for the small farmers in laws or government: 'The state of the case . . . appears to be exactly this – you are surplus, or else the "gentry" are surplus – the million or the eight thousand – and it seems plain that you or they must die.'[71] This statement came close to direct incitement, but probably left some room for legal doubt. A few weeks later Mitchel directed an open letter to the Lord Lieutenant, the Earl of Clarendon, 'Her Majesty's Detective-General, High Commissioner of Spies, and general suborner in Ireland'. This could leave no legal doubt of his intent. The only question was the seriousness of the threat. As noted above, Mitchel believed that revolution was a spontaneous explosion that none could stop: it was a force of nature, or it was nothing. On this basis he taunted government with the idea of men openly preparing 'to overthrow a powerful government, *by force*, and giving a programme of their plans beforehand'. It must seem absurd to the Lord Lieutenant, but that was what was under way: 'The Irish People, or a competent number of them, will simply continue so to arm, and so to organize . . . fearlessly, zealously, with passionate ardour . . . for the blessed hour that organization may find itself ranked in battle array, and when these arms may wreak the wrongs of Ireland in the dearest hearts-blood of her enemies.'[72] This was far across the line that separated intemperate political discourse from sedition.

Mitchel also published his own inflammatory speeches in the *United Irishman*. This device gave some protection from the law of sedition (which was more tolerant of seditious speech than seditious writing) while at the same time placing on the publisher no more than the responsibility for reporting a speech. The disadvantage of this proceeding was to provide a record for the authorities, and in the second reading debate on the Treason Felony Bill, Sir George Grey, the Home Secretary, had quoted one of Mitchel's speeches *in extenso*: it was compelling evidence against him.

Addressing a meeting of the Irish Confederation on 27 March 1848, Mitchel (having by then been charged and bailed for sedition) boasted: 'I did write seditious articles, and I will write seditious articles. I will incite the people to discontent and disaffection. . . . On the day this Confederation was formed, I . . . declared myself a disaffected subject, and promised to devote myself continually to excite disaffection in others. I think I have kept that promise; and come what may, I will continue to do so.' He would take issue with the government in the lawcourts, 'boldly and desperately' and if unsuccessful there, 'we shall throw them on a broader field. It must be done'. He referred to the continuing

---

71 *United Irishman*, vol. 1, no. 3; 4 March 1848, 56a–c. This was a message to those who had suffered or were threatened by the 'consolidations' of holdings which had followed the famine's course. A few years thence it would have been a futile message, since the lot of those who survived famine, eviction and consolidation was sufficiently improved to transform them into a cautious and politically conservative force.

72 Ibid., vol. 1, no. 9; 8 April 1848, 136b. See also col. a, where in an item headed 'Answer to Correspondents', Mitchel gives specific advice on arming and on material suitable for a street barricade.

revolutionary upsurge in Europe: 'The news this morning announces that Vienna is in the hands of the people. Stand by us, citizens, and it shall be done.'[73]

But a sedition conviction was not enough for the government, Mitchel claimed (with some justification), and the Treason Felony Act had been brought in with the immediate intention of crushing the *United Irishman* and kindred organs. Had a sedition charge succeeded, there would have been no forfeiture of property (since sedition was only a misdemeanour), and in consequence, new editors could have taken over: '[C]ompetent men would not be wanting to give a voice to treason, even though editor after editor should be chained up.'[74] That was not to happen, however. Mitchel was arrested on 21 March 1848 (together with William Smith O'Brien and Thomas Francis Meagher)[75] and charged with sedition. His two comrades were acquitted, and on the eve of his trial the sedition charges against Mitchel were dropped.[76] On the same day, however, further charges – the first ever brought – were laid against Mitchel under the newly passed Treason Felon Act.[77] It appears that the jury was well packed (though of Mitchel's eager guilt there could be little doubt) to the indignation of a wide

---

73 All these quotations given by Grey in the second reading debate: 3 *Hansard*, XCVII, cols 23–4; 7 April 1848. The same issue of the *United Irishman* carried a speech by Thomas Devin Reilly, Mitchel's co-worker, calling for the formation of a National Guard, and envisaging barricades and blood in Dublin and fighting throughout Ireland. The people should arm and 'show the tyrant out of Ireland by the light of the burning gaols'. He also referred to European revolution: 'Democracy had crossed the Alps and entered Austria. Last week he was in Paris, and there was smashed the strongest dynasty in the world. He would presently come to Ireland. 300,000 Englishmen, Chartists, would assemble in London next week, and then they would have London in their hands' (*Hansard,* ibid., cols 25–6). See also Reilly's article 'The French Fashion', which appeared in the *United Irishman*. (Emigrating to the United States of America following the collapse of the Young Ireland insurrection, Reilly worked as a journalist until his death in March 1854.)

74 John Mitchel, *Jail Journal*, p. 18.

75 Meagher (1823–67), educated at Clongowes Wood and Stonyhurst Colleges. Intended for a career at the Irish Bar. One of his two brothers entered papal military service; the other was a barrister. His father, a prosperous Waterford merchant, represented his city in the Commons for ten years, 1847–57. A founder-member of the Irish Confederation. Made numerous speeches in favour of physical as distinct from moral force. After one such oration satirised by W. M. Thackeray as 'Meagher of the Sword' – a title he bore with some pride. As an orator considered by Charles Gavan Duffy to have had 'astonishing power', an 'intense but limited' range of abilities (1883, pp. 8–9). See Robert G. Athearn, *Thomas Francis Meagher: An Irish Revolutionary in America*, Boulder, Colorado University Press, 1949. In 1852 Meagher was described as being 'very corpulent' and of 'a dark, swarthy appearance'. At the same time it was noted that he was 'in excellent health' (*New York Times*, 29 May 1852, 2d).

76 Mitchel (1873, pp. 273–4) contended that the charges were dropped because he was able to block the government's jury-packing plans. O'Brien and Meagher were each acquitted because of a solitary hold-out juror. Isaac Butt's defence of O'Brien and Meagher marked his formal and public switch from Unionism to Repeal (Gwynn 1949, pp. 186–7).

77 It had received the Royal Assent on 22 April 1848 as an Act for the Better Security of the Crown and Government of the United Kingdom: 11 & 12 Vict., c.12 (generally known as the Treason Felony Act, 1848).

section of moderate Catholic opinion.[78] The trial was held on 26 May 1848, and Mitchel was found guilty. The following day, amidst noisy courtroom demonstrations, he was given the heavy sentence of fourteen years' transportation, and his property was forfeited to the Crown.[79] To avert possible rescue attempts he was removed from Dublin within a few hours under heavy police and military guard.[80] The warship *Shearwater* took him down the coast to Spike Island convict depot and from there on 1 June Mitchel embarked to Bermuda, on board the *Scourge*, arriving on 20 June 1848.[81]

The open conspiracy

If we are to accept his retrospective account, this had been a knowing sacrifice by Mitchel. By provoking a prosecution under specially wrought legislation, and trial before an egregiously packed jury, he claimed to have exposed the hollowness

---

78 '[I]t is not that I deny the matter charged to me, but that I deny having been tried at all. The false pretence was the trial' (Mitchel 1873, p. 285). The *Daily News* lamented the packed jury, its reporter stating that he shared his readers' 'sense of shame at beholding such a proceeding as this takes place in the name of our sovereign Lady, the Queen' (29 May 1848, 2b–c). Twenty-seven years later John Martin, by then an MP for Meath, in a speech to the Commons detailed the packing of Mitchel's jury, which, he claimed, had resulted in a trial which was a 'solemn farce of justice'. See 3 *Hansard*, CCXXII, cols 964–72; 26 February 1875. This speech was published as a pamphlet, and was reprinted in P. A. Sillard's *The Life and Letters of John Martin*, Dublin, James Duffy & Co, 1901), pp. 272–83. In a speech to the Confederation, O'Brien, who at this point completely rejected Mitchel's views, also condemned the jury-packing (NLI: O'Brien Papers: Ms. 449; personal memorandum).

79 See 3 *Hansard*, CCXXII, cols 493–539; 18 February 1875; cols 964–83; 26 February 1875; *The Times*, 25 May 1848, 8c; 27 May, 8a; 29 May, 5f; the *Irishman*, 1 July 1848, 14b–c; *Return to the Honourable The House of Commons, dated 16 February 1875 for Copy of 'Certificate by the Clerk for the County of Dublin of the Conviction and of the Judgement in the Case of the Queen Against John Mitchel, etc. etc.'* (hereafter *Certificate of the Conviction and Judgement of John Mitchel*), PP, 1875 [50], LXII, 155, 1. (This return was moved in consequence of Mitchel's attempt to resist his disqualification from the Tipperary seat which he had won in a by-election on 16 February 1875. Two days later Disraeli had moved the writ for another election on the grounds that Mitchel, being a convicted felon who had (by his escape from Van Diemen's Land) not purged his offence, was not qualified to sit in the House.) The forfeiture of his property had left Mitchel's wife and children in a difficult position, but a public subscription raised some £1800 for their use. In passing sentence Baron Lefroy intimated that had Mitchel's case not been the first under the new Act, he would have felt obliged to pass a life sentence (Doheny, *op. cit.*, p. 136).

80 See the reports in the *Nation*, 3 June 1848, p. 358d; *Freeman's Journal*, 29 May 1848, 4c; *Cork Examiner*, 28 May 1848, 2a–g, 3a–f.

81 *The Times* (5 June 1848, 6e–f) quoted a Cork report on Mitchel's departure: 'Even in the summary way in which this noble man has been dealt with he has his triumph. Government dared not wait to transmit him with the freight of scoundrels to whose level their baseness thought to sink him.' The report referred to Bermuda as 'one of the strongest fortresses in the Queen's dominion, another St Helena'. Gavan Duffy abandoned legal caution in his lament (*Nation*, 3 June 1848, 360c) for Mitchel's easy removal: 'He is borne through an Irish City, carried on Irish Seas, degraded within Irish confines, and no blow is struck for his deliverance.'

of constitutional protections, and the futility of O'Connell's type of moral force campaign.[82] But his immediate revolutionary expectations were unrealised. The Confederation had established clubs which, after a fashion, had been arming and drilling, and Mitchel had hoped that this force would come to his rescue.[83] The other leaders took a different view. A sober assessment led them to believe that any attempt at rescue 'would eventuate in a street row which would entail not only defeat but disgrace'.[84] They countenanced action only after harvest, when the peasantry would march on full bellies. That had previously been Mitchel's view: 'We hoped, and the Government feared that no armed collision would be made necessary until September, when the harvest would be all cut, and when the commissariat of the people's war, the cause of the war, and the prize of the war, would be all bound up in a sheaf together. But the foe we had to deal with was no weak fool.' Club leaders, fearing a futile bloodbath, had visited Mitchel at Newgate, the day before his trial, and had asked him to issue a letter to the Clubs, counselling against a rescue. This, Mitchel recalled, 'I refused utterly; and perhaps too bitterly'.[85]

Mitchel's prosecution did nothing to reconcile the Repeal Association and the Confederation, but it did unify and animate the latter.[86] Many who had not agreed with Mitchel's provocative tactics had been in court to show their general

---

82 Mitchel n.d., pp. 24–6.
83 'The Clubs of Dublin, as I was credibly informed, were vehemently excited; and the great majority of them were of opinion, that if an insurrection were to be made at all, it should be tried then and there – that is, in Dublin streets, and on the day of my removal' (ibid., p. 20). He repeated this view in a later book, insisting that the rescue should have been attempted while he awaited his trial in Dublin's Newgate. 'This was the right counsel. I thought so then; and, after many years, I deliberately think so still' (1873, p. 285). Other accounts confirm that he had a considerable following in the Dublin clubs.
84 Doheny, op. cit., p. 130. Dillon distinguishes between club members and their leaders in this matter. The leaders thought an attempted rescue would lead to a slaughter, but among ordinary members in Dublin there was a fierce determination that Mitchel should not be removed: 'It needed the utmost efforts of the leaders to restrain their followers' (op. cit., p. 247; see also Gwynn, op. cit., pp. 190–3). O'Brien considered that there was insufficient support for a mass uprising, and that even had there been, 'the resources of the country would not at that time allow the Irish people to sustain a conflict with the Power of England' (NLI: O'Brien Papers: Ms. 449; personal memorandum).
85 Mitchel 1873, pp. 268 and 290.
86 There had been another split. Following the February revolution Mitchel had resumed an uneasy membership of the Confederation, while reserving his own programme and continuing to publish the United Irishman. The reconciliation did not last long, however, and there was another parting following the 'Battle of Limerick' on 29 April 1848. On this occasion anti-Mitchel protests by O'Connellites, incensed at an attack on O'Connell's memory which Mitchel had recently made in the United Irishman, resulted in O'Brien being stoned and injured by an angry mob. O'Brien, aware of the feeling against Mitchel, had previously asked him not to attend the soirée on which the attack was made. After the attack fulsome apologies were made to O'Brien by local Repealers, but his dignity had been so injured that he threatened to resign from the Confederation. In the event, Mitchel and Thomas Devin Reilly resigned and O'Brien

sympathy and support. Mitchel's fate transformed the situation: his sacrifice changed everything, including (in public at least) his relationship with his previously estranged colleagues.[87] With Mitchel sentenced and removed, Doheny recalled, 'everything wore a sterner aspect, as if, whether they willed it or no, an imperious obligation required fulfilment at their hands'. Even between those who had favoured a rescue attempt and those who had not, unity asserted itself and preparations for insurrection began; Mitchel had managed to light the fuse.

They conspired, but were no conspirators. Mitchel's disastrous tactic of open preparation was revived. Within a month two newspapers took the baton from the United Irishman. Mitchel's friend, John Martin,[88] published the Irish Felon, assisted by James Fintan Lalor,[89] while Richard D'Alton Williams[90] and Kevin

then agreed to go on. See Gwynn (op. cit., pp. 174–80) for an account of this incident. It is also discussed at length by O'Brien in his personal memorandum (NLI: O'Brien Papers: Ms. 449). After an interval of many years the humiliation and rejection remained painful to him.

87 Once Mitchel had been taken, O'Brien recorded, it was impossible for him to be repudiated, even though O'Brien totally disagreed with his ideas, which he regarded as dangerous and divisive. Had he made a public statement of these differences 'it would have been said with some degree of justice that I was anxious to save myself by presenting him as a victim to the Government. Such a course seemed to me to be so ungenerous that I could not adopt it' (NLI: O'Brien Papers: Ms. 449; personal memorandum).

88 (1812–75). Farming and factory-owning Presbyterian family. Educated at Trinity College, Dublin. An inheritance in 1835 gave him financial independence and he travelled in America and Europe. A friend of Mitchel from schooldays at Dr Henderson's in Newry. In his fifty-seventh year (November 1868) he married Mitchel's youngest sister Henrietta, to whom he had long been romantically attached. Described by Charles Gavan Duffy as a 'simple, modest, upright gentleman'. Another Young Irelander, P. J. Smyth admired Martin's excellent qualities but noted that he had some peculiarities, including 'a spirit of contradiction – a desire to do the thing which his friends advise him not to do' (NLI: O'Brien Papers: Ms. 445/2846). Curiously, Martin's own sister, Mary Simpson, considered Mitchel's 1853 escape from Van Diemen's Land to be 'inconsistent with honour' and after 1854 was estranged from him (NIPRO: John Martin Papers: Paris Journal, D.560/5). Martin in his later years distanced himself from violent republicanism, being a founder-member of the Home Government Association. In January 1871 he was elected MP for Meath, in the Home Rule interest. He died only nine days after John Mitchel, whose election as a more extreme nationalist he had generally supported. P. A. Sillard provides a helpful if occasionally inaccurate and generally uncritical life of Martin in his The Life and Letters of John Martin. Fragments of his papers – a diary of his voyage as a convict to Van Diemen's Land, and a journal of some weeks in Paris in the summer of 1858, are held in the Northern Ireland Public Record Office (D/560–5).

89 (1807–49). Son of Patrick Lalor, a landowning MP. Contributed to the Nation and the Felon in 1847–8. After years of ill-health he died in 1849, attempting to organise another rising. His synthesis of nationalism and land reform had a long-lasting influence on the course of Irish nationalism. Charles Gavan Duffy wrote of him: 'Of all the men who have preached revolutionary politics in Ireland, this isolated thinker, who had hitherto had no experience either as a writer or an actor in public affairs, was the most original and intense' (1882, p. 465); see also Gwynn, op. cit., ch. 13.

90 (1822–62). Natural son of Count D'Alton, a landowner, studied medicine and obtained his diploma in 1849. Three years after his acquittal he emigrated to the United States of America, where he had a career as an academic and doctor, before an early death from consumption.

Izod O'Doherty[91] (both students in Dublin) published the *Irish Tribune*. With Mitchel's fate before them, these men can have had no doubts as to their own, but they were gathered up in the logic, morality and momentum of their politics, and in ties of friendship. These journals served government as well as had the *United Irishman* – providing a chronicle of the rebels' intentions, names of the leading figures and, through the distribution system, an indication of supporters and their organisation. Their offices were convenient collection points when the moment came.

With some consciousness of these dangers, the Confederation council reorganised, and an inner committee (which excluded O'Brien) began to plan for an autumn rising. Military training of a sort continued; aid was solicited from American sympathisers, and there were attempts to create a diversion using Irish immigrants in Britain.[92] Lacking any degree of ruthlessness, the leaders deluded themselves as to the violence and loss of life a serious insurrection would involve. Their various memoirs indicate that they collusively willed themselves not to think about this aspect of things, although they more easily contemplated self-sacrifice. Without experience, with only a rudimentary organisation to support them and working to a hopeless timetable, the uprising had not the slightest chance of success. In so far as it had a strategy, it could be summarised in the phrase of a later and far more ruthless and successful revolutionary – 'A single spark can start a prairie fire.' Looking back to the great rebellion of 1798, but drawing only some of its lessons,[93] they believed that they could unleash a seething peasantry by getting among them in arms, offering little more than the standard of national liberation. The insurrectionists were chivalric, eschewing guerrilla tactics, and remote from terrorism. To be seen to act with honour was for most of the leaders essential, not simply a matter of style or personal preference – national representation was as much the point of the rebellion as any hope of success. The corruption and futility of Irish politics, and the consequent demoralisation of the people, could be addressed in no

---

91 (1823–95). Son of a Dublin solicitor. Joined the Young Irelanders while still a medical student at Dublin's Catholic University. Upon release from transportation he qualified as a doctor and returned to Australia, where he remained for twenty-three years. He was a member of the Queensland legislature, and on returning to Dublin in 1885 became MP for North Meath. He again returned to Australia, where he died.

92 Davis 1987, pp. 158–9; Duffy 1883, ch. 3.

93 For an account of the 1798 rebellion, and the rebels' organisational and military failures, see Thomas Pakenham, *The Year of Liberty: The History of the Great Irish Rebellion of 1798*, London, Hodder & Stoughton, 1969. Partisan and blindly one-sided though it is, John Mitchel's account of 1798 has much intrinsic interest, throwing light on his social, political, religious and military ideas, and his implacable hostility to English power in Ireland: *The History of Ireland from the Siege of Limerick to the Present Time*, Glasgow, Cameron & Ferguson, 1869, vol. 1, pp. 255–304; vol. 2, pp. 13–39.

other way. In particular, there could not be another episode of bombastic and cowardly leadership.[94]

From the moment of conception the insurrection was penetrated by informers; police and military preparations intensified, and there was lavish spending on informants. On 2 March 1848, the Commander-in-Chief, the Duke of Wellington, informed Lieutenant-General Sir Edward Blakeney that the Irish revolutionary leaders had made enquiries in Paris about the construction of street barricades, 'which have been used there, and have been considered so formidable'. Pointing out certain differences between the buildings and streets in Paris and Dublin, Wellington observed that 'on the other hand there is in Dublin as in London no want of construction of a Barricade'.[95] Three months later Wellington wrote again, about the military situation in Ireland and England in the face of insurgent threats, though he was not disposed to take the Chartists as seriously as the Confederation.[96]

Dublin Castle was in a state of alert from the early spring of 1848, on 11 March issuing a 'Secret and Confidential' police circular to county inspectors, calling for greater preparedness against possible attacks, and giving detailed instructions for the deployment of troops and the protection of communications. These operations would test the fidelity and discipline of the Royal Irish Constabulary, but officers and men were assured that those who showed zeal and valour 'in the suppression of tumult, and in the vindication of law and order'

94 O'Brien's explanation for his actions emphasised this. Faced with detention without trial or with fleeing abroad, he chose to stay at liberty and do what he could: 'So much had been said by the party with which I was associated and by myself, about the necessity of preparation for conflict, that we should have been exposed to ridicule and reproach if we had fled at the moment when all the contingencies which we had contemplated as justifying the use of force were realised' (NLI: O'Brien Papers: Ms. 449; personal memorandum). Duffy took a similar line: 'No struggle for liberty has greatly prospered which has not had willing martyrs. And now, once again, there was about to be seen the spectacle, for ever grand and touching to the human soul, of men who in the midst of corruption and cowardice offered up their lives for the truth. . . . A ministerial journal afterwards admitted, as a fact fit to be noted by men of honour, and to be recorded by other men of honour, that there was not one conspicuous Confederate who had encouraged the people to resistance, but staked his own head on the issue' (Duffy 1883, pp. 642–3).

95 Wellington to Blakeney, 2 March 1848: NLI: Larcom Papers: 7698 (unfoliated). Wellington sent Blakeney a detailed plan for the defence of Dublin Castle, and other key points. He had drawn this up on the basis of his memory of the street layout in Dublin, though 'It is forty years since I was in Dublin'.

96 Wellington to Field Marshal the Marquess of Anglesey (former Lord Lieutenant), 17 June 1848: NLI: Larcom Papers: 7698 (unfoliated). Wellington again noted that both the Irish and English insurrectionists had paid attention to the tactics of street fighting in France. In this memorandum he overestimated by far the strength of the Young Irelanders. Other memoranda on military issues followed on 20 July and 15 August 1848. The main danger, to Wellington, was not of the success of the Irish insurrectionists (which he considered unlikely) but rather, as a reaction and countermeasure, the establishment of a National Guard, separate from the Army. Even in his eightieth year Wellington was ever watchful of French institutions and the Bonapartist spirit.

would be amply rewarded with promotion, 'or other substantial proofs of His Excellency's approbation'.[97]

The foolhardy publishers who had stepped into Mitchel's shoes were conveniently gathered in. Warrants were issued in early July 1848, and the proprietors of the two journals were sent for trial on treason felony charges. Kevin Izod O'Doherty was at first lucky, and his jury refused to convict; John Martin was convicted and given ten years' transportation. A second jury refused to convict O'Doherty, but a third trial returned a guilty verdict, and he was also transported for ten years. The other publisher of the *Irish Tribune*, Richard D'Alton Williams, was acquitted after a lengthy trial. Charles Gavan Duffy, publisher of the *Nation*, was also arrested, but his trial was postponed, and after five attempts the government resigned itself to his acquittal.

While these trials were proceeding the other leaders attempted to regroup. There was a short-lived reconciliation with the Repeal Association, in the form of a league into which the Confederation dissolved itself: it swiftly became clear that there was no basis for such a union. The Confederation clubs which (in Doheny's words) 'continued a precarious and unintelligible existence' came together and (French revolutionary style) elected a directory.[98] This seems to have been little more than a gasconade: it apparently never met, and its members left town separately in hopeless confusion.[99]

A proclamation was issued on 19 July, requiring all persons in certain districts to surrender their arms on penalty of imprisonment: the cities of Dublin, Cork, Drogheda and Waterford were included. More sweeping measures were to follow. On 22 July, Parliament assented to a suspension of habeas corpus[100] and, faced with arrest and detention without trial, the principals haphazardly set about rousing the peasantry – pursued by the authorities. This is not the place to describe the confused and hopeless preparations, inspections and meanderings that ensued.[101] With no strategy, supplies or military experience, relying on a crushed, resourceless and traumatised peasantry, and opposed by a substantial section of the clergy,[102] the leaders' position was utterly hopeless. O'Brien had the standing – at least in the minds of his colleagues – to get something serious

---

97 NLI: Larcom Papers: 7698 (unfoliated).
98 Its members were John Blake Dillon, Thomas D'Arcy McGee, Thomas Francis Meagher, Richard O'Gorman and Thomas Devin Reilly.
99 See Duffy's account of events: 1883, ch. 4.
100 3 *Hansard* C, cols 696–756; 22 July 1848. This Act (11 & 12 Vict., c.35) allowed the Lord Lieutenant to detain suspects without trial until 1 March 1849, constituting what today would be called internment. For a list of those detained see Duffy 1883, pp. 756–7.
101 There are various accounts of these events. See Doheny, *op. cit.*, pp. 153–90; Duffy 1883, p. 641–99; Gwynn, *op. cit.*, pp. 212–14, 227–70.
102 Apart from its inherent conservatism and understandable pastoral concerns, the Irish clergy had been greatly alarmed by the communistic insurrections in France, and by Italian republicans' moves against the temporal power of the papacy.

under way, and the initial enthusiasm of excited crowds of peasants fuelled his hopes.[103] But having reluctantly accepted leadership of the insurrectionary force he had no stomach for bloodshed, and had even forbade the seizure of private property.[104]

Reflecting on O'Brien's character a decade after these events John Martin (who was not given to gratuitously critical observations) identified those attributes which disqualified O'Brien from revolutionary leadership. He had indeed excellent qualities – 'firmness, honour, clear judgement, love for Ireland, public spirit, and very respectable powers as a writer and speaker'. But these had to be set alongside his limitations. He was, Martin thought, lacking in the 'élan, fierce activity or indefatigable persistence in effort' necessary in leadership. O'Brien was inclined to leave it to others to form their opinions without his intervention and 'rather

103 On the second anniversary of his capture O'Brien looked back on the events which had propelled him into high treason: 'Upon what trifling circumstances does the fate of man depend. If T. F. Meagher had not overslept himself and lost his place on the coach in which he intended to proceed to Dublin with a view to embark for America he would never have been a convict in Van Diemen's Land.. . . . If he had gone to America it is probable that my fate would also have been very different from what it has since been. He would not have gone to the County of Wexford to announce to me the intention of the Government to cause me to be arrested under the Suspension of Habeas Corpus Act. We should not have formed our united resolution to offer resistance to that Act. I should probably have gone home to Cahermoyle and have allowed *myself* to be taken prisoner unless the population had risen spontaneously to defend me.' In that event no charge of high treason could have succeeded since 'I had not compromised myself but on the contrary had upon . . . several occasions been mainly instrumental in preventing a rising of the people' (NLI: O'Brien Papers; Ms. 449, 'Journal of a Residence in Maria Island Van Diemen's Land Written by William S. O'Brien for his Wife' [hereinafter 'Maria Island Journal'], Part 2, ff. 17–18 (6 August 1850)).

104 Proposals were put to O'Brien to confiscate the property of landlords, and to issue promissory notes drawn on the provisional government: 'O'Brien, who was ready to die,' Duffy recorded, 'would not consent, and this decision starved the insurrection' (1883, p. 668). With skirmishing under way, and police advancing on their position, O'Brien forbade the felling of trees across roads unless the estate owners granted permission. Few were inclined to give it (Duffy, ibid., p. 661, citing a letter from Charles Kickham). John Blake Dillon protested to O'Brien that it was 'an act of futility to engage in such a movement, and utterly impossible to prolong it for any time, without resorting to the usual expedient of making the property of the country support those who were battling for the interests and independence of their country' (cit. Revd Philip Fitzgerald, *A Narrative of the Proceedings of the Confederates in '48 from the Suspension of the Habeas Corpus Act to their Final Dispersion at Ballingary*, Dublin, James Duffy, 1868, p. 24). Patrick O'Donohoe, who played a minor part in the events, reflected on O'Brien's respect for property: 'It was truly ridiculous to hear the leader of a revolution which to be successful should have sanctioned all the wild and savage passions of the hordes of oppressed wretches who followed its standard, inculcating those virtues which are practised in the best ordered communities. . . . It was a pitiable sight to behold a man possessed of so many great qualities so deficient in the one most necessary to achieve the great task he designed' (NLI: O'Donohoe Papers: Ms. 770, f. 27 ob., f. 28: Patrick O'Donohoe, 'Incidents Connected with Political Disturbances in Ireland in 1848: Origin, Progress and Failure of the Movement' (28 August 1848)).

wait for their invitation before he will act for them'. To lead Irish revolutionaries, it was necessary, while accepting the freedom of opinion of others, to exert every effort to infuse them with nationalist opinion – 'to inspire them with the hopes, the pity, the shame, the love, all the feelings which may bind them together and organise to conquer our independence'. A leader needed 'a divine impulse which keeps him ever at the work of the leader . . . though he need not be at all deficient in the modesty & gentlemanly feeling which make O'Brien keep back and behave with too much reserve.'[105]

Martin's observations were accurate as far as they went, but they overlooked another significant strand in O'Brien's character – a melancholia which at times of stress fed his indecision, and which is fully in keeping with Charles Kickham's observation that when during the insurrection he met O'Brien in Tipperary he seemed to be 'like a man in a dream'.[106] Faced with the failure of the uprising, O'Brien's resilience collapsed completely, a condition concealed only by his withdrawn nature and a tight control over his emotions in public.[107]

O'Brien's qualities – his appeal and charisma, his patrician's easy command of leadership, and his muddle, inappropriate scruples and paralysis – were magnified and exaggerated during these days. After a great deal of fretful wandering, O'Brien, Dillon, Meagher and various followers encountered a police column on 29 July. Awaiting reinforcements, the police – some forty in number – barricaded themselves in Widow McCormack's house at Boulah, near Ballingarry, Co. Tipperary.[108] The well-armed police held Mrs McCormack's children in the besieged house, and even a man more ruthless than O'Brien might have hesitated to burn or storm the property. Despite a foolhardy display of bravery on his part, the encounter therefore ended in débâcle, with the rebels' demoralised and

---

105 NIPRO: John Martin Papers: *Paris Journal*, D. 560/5, f. 134 (entry late July 1858).

106 Duffy 1883, p. 660. Kickham was later to become a prominent Fenian.

107 His journals are seamed through with this melancholic spirit, and reveal a private world with few sources of joy. The following is not atypical (written on board the ship carrying him to Van Diemen's Land). He laments not having been executed at Clonmel and wishes that his existence had been ended 'by some circumstance not occasioned by myself. Life has never had much charm for me. Whatever personal interest I have felt in it apart from my public functions has been derived from domestic enjoyment and from the hope of seeing my children possess happiness greater than that which had fallen to the lot of their father' (NLI: O'Brien Papers: *Transportation Journal*, Ms. 3828; 9 July 1849).

108 This was then a remote district more than twelve miles from the nearest market town. John O'Mahony, who gave a better account of himself than many 'out' in 1848, and who later founded Fenianism in America, considered Ballingarry an utterly inappropriate place for an armed insurrectionary encounter. O'Brien, he wrote, 'could not have commenced in a much worse place. Strangers up to that to the action and resolves of the party, they could not well understand what it was about, nor I believe, did anyone else. Not one in the hundred of those thousands assembled had ever seen O'Brien's face before, or that of any one of the companions then with him' (NLI: Father Michael O'Hickey Papers: Ms. 868, Box 58, f. 7, 'Personal Narrative of my Connection with the Attempted Rising of 1848 by John O'Mahony').

diminishing forces in retreat.[109] A week later O'Brien was arrested at Thurles railway station, en route to his home. The remaining leaders were taken the following week. Some spasms of rebellion continued, but on a very different basis to O'Brien's unwieldy and vulnerable progresses.[110] By harvest time it was all over. The leaders had been arrested or had fled the country.[111] That portion of the peasantry which had been affected was subdued, and the cause of insurrectionary nationalism was, for that generation, completely lost. Mitchel's comment a quarter of a century later was bitter but accurate:

109 The *Liverpool Mercury*, which followed the subsequent trial closely, probably typified the reaction of the British press. The evidence, the *Mercury* observed, showed 'a set of men [who] aspire to the dignity of patriot rebels and insurgent leaders, but without the most ordinary judgement to discriminate or the most common prudence to exercise caution. . . . Treason is plotted with the recklessness of insanity; and after a vast display of frothy wisdom and vaporous heroism, everything is done which ignorance, improvidence and poltroony could suggest to bring defeat, disaster, and contempt upon the whole affair' (6 October 1848, 640b). *Punch* poured scorn on the battle in Widow McCormack's cabbage-patch. Even the sympathetic *Hobarton Guardian*, which did much to assist O'Brien in his place of penal exile, poked fun: 'The courage of Mr Smith O'Brien in slinking under the fire of the police . . . among the cabbages in Widow McCormick's garden, may be questioned, but it is to be remembered that the hero if he crept out of the way of the bullets, betrayed no fear of the slugs' (6 January 1849, 4c). For a less hostile account see Revd P. Fitzgerald, PP, *Personal Recollections of the Insurrection at Ballingarry*, Dublin, John F. Fowler, 1861. Fitzgerald assisted in avoiding a bloody outcome to the incident. This pamphlet provoked a reply from the RIC sub-inspector who had charge of the besieged party: Thomas Trant, *Reply to Father Fitzgerald's Pamphlet Entitled His 'Personal Recollections of the Insurrection at Ballingarry in July, 1848.' With Remarks on Irish Constabulary, and Hints to All Officials*, Dublin, McGlashan & Gill, 1862. (Both pamphlets are rare, but may be found in NLI: Larcom Papers, Ms. 7698.) There was a bitter and well-ventilated disputation between the two men in the immediate aftermath of the action (*Freeman's Journal*, 15 November 1848, 3c–d) and Trant complained that the incident and its consequences blighted his career. Doheny, who was desperately roaming the country at the time, also provides an account of O'Brien's rout (*op. cit.*, pp. 180–3).

110 John O'Mahony together with two Dublin men, John Savage (a student) and Phil Grey (a mechanic), attacked police barracks on the Tipperary–Kilkenny border. John O'Leary, 'out' in 1848 (and also to become an active and influential Fenian), described these attacks as 'a sort of final flash in the pan' (John O'Leary, *Recollections of Fenians and Fenianism*, London, Downey & Co, 1896, Vol. 1, p. 15; see also the facsimile reprint: Shannon, Irish University Press, 1969, edited by Marcus Bourke).

111 Among those who escaped to the United States of America were John Blake Dillon, Michael Dohery, Thomas D'Arcy McGee, Richard O'Gorman, Thomas Devin Reilly and Patrick James Smyth. From the British point of view this self-exile had certain advantages, not least of which was to take these men out of circulation without the glory and uncertainties of trials. Michael Doheny, James Stephens and John O'Mahony escaped to France, whence the latter two would eventually return to build the Irish Republican Brotherhood; Doheny and O'Mahony were the co-founders of the Fenian Society in the United States of America. Altogether 118 persons were detained under the Lord Lieutenant's warrant up to 14 December 1848. The majority of these were freed on bail; the remainder put on trial (see *Return of All Persons Committed to or Detained in Prison in Ireland by Warrants of the Lord Lieutenant or Chief Secretary for High Treason or Treasonable Practices, or Suspicion Thereof*, PP, 1849 [13], XLIX, 381, 1. This return lists all the detainees by name and place of detention).

In fact there had been no insurrection. The people in those two or three counties did not believe that O'Brien meant to fight; and nothing would now persuade them but some desperate enterprise. . . . The English ought to be grateful to O'Brien, that his extreme punctilio about not striking the first blow, and his tender regard for human life, suffered the passion of the people to cool, and enabled the enemy to draw their toils around him.[112]

The treason trials

Two sets of trials were put in hand, in September and October 1848. Those who had acted, and against whom there was sufficient evidence, were indicted for treason; those who had merely exhorted and supported faced the lesser but still very serious charges of treason felony. Of the latter John Martin and Kevin Izod O'Doherty were, as has been seen, sentenced to transportation for ten years. Richard D'Alton Williams was acquitted, while James Fintan Lalor – in poor health – was released after a few months' imprisonment. William Smith O'Brien, Terence Bellew MacManus,[113] Thomas Francis Meagher and Patrick O'Donohoe[114] were tried for high treason before the Irish Lord Chief Justice and others sitting in Special Commission at Clonmel, Co. Tipperary. The case was prosecuted by the Irish Attorney General. The men's guilt was obvious, but the government had been careful to ensure that the jury should not suffer the inconvenience of dissident members. Verdicts were duly brought in after trials lasting several days, the jury by a majority recommending mercy 'for various reasons'.[115] On

---

112 Mitchel 1873, p. 304. In this assessment Mitchel is not wholly faithful to his own politics, and fails to acknowledge what he indubitably knew and had then believed: the point of the insurrection was not only or necessarily to succeed, as much as to offer sacrifice and make a gesture.

113 (1823–60). Born in Ireland, but commenced work as a shipping agent in Liverpool. On his return in 1843, joined the Young Irelanders. Took part in O'Brien's Ballingarry fracas and was arrested in Cork, on board a ship bound for the United States of America. Transported, he escaped Van Diemen's Land and settled in San Francisco, where he died in poverty. His body was returned to Ireland and given a large political funeral by the Irish Republican Brotherhood (Fenians) providing impetus to that movement, and bestowing credibility upon it (see p. 116, n. 18 below).

114 (1815–54). Born into a middle-class Roman Catholic family in Clonegal, Co. Carlow. Married with a daughter, a law clerk and conveyancer at the time of his arrest. A founding member of the executive council of the Irish Confederation, though subsequently inactive. A relatively minor figure among the Young Irelanders (see Richard Davis, 'Patrick O'Donohoe: Outcast of the Exiles', in Bob Reece (ed.), *Exiles from Erin: Convict Lives in Ireland and Australia*, London, Macmillan, 1991; Garry Owens, 'Patrick O'Donohoe's Narrative of the 1848 Rising', *Tipperary Historical Journal*, 1998, pp. 32–3).

115 A verbatim account, including Grand Jury proceedings, is provided in one volume: John George Hodges, *Report of the Trial of William Smith O'Brien for High Treason at the Special Commission for the Co. Tipperary. Held at Clonmel, September and October, 1848: With the Judgement of the Court of Queen's Bench, Ireland, and of the House of Lords, on the Writs of Error*, Dublin, Alexander Thom, 1849. See also *The Times*, 6 October 1848, 4c; 24 October, 4b; R. V. Smith O'Brien, 7 *State Trials*, NS 1; TCD: O'Brien Papers: Ms. 10610/30. Robert O'Brien (himself a

23 October the Lord Chief Justice sentenced all to death in the traditional form for this offence. They would be drawn on a hurdle to the place of execution to be hanged by the neck until they were dead.[116] After death their heads would be struck off and their bodies quartered, to be disposed of as Her Majesty might direct.[117] O'Brien's application for a writ of error was authorised by the Irish Attorney General and heard before the Queen's Bench in Dublin and then by the Lords. This addressed sixteen points concerning jurisdiction, procedure, the disallowance of jurors and defective evidence.[118] The objections were overruled and the judgement of the Special Commission as to the conviction and sentence were upheld.[119]

Government's problem was to find means to avoid execution of this atavistic penalty. The uprising had failed, but it would be extremely unwise to make martyrs of these inept revolutionaries; it was indeed unlikely that English politics would support it. The death sentences were commuted to transportation for life.[120] There was some doubt whether persons found guilty of treason could be transported, and O'Brien instructed his counsel, Sir Colman O'Loghlen,[121] to obtain a writ of habeas corpus if the authorities attempted to carry out the transportation order: 'I emphatically repeat that I do not consent to be transported and if as I am assured is the case the law does not authorise the government to transport me, I claim the protection of the Law.'[122] The prisoners also petitioned

Protestant) pointed out that in the whole jury panel for the county there were only nineteen Roman Catholics, although Roman Catholics comprised 95 per cent of the county's population.

116 There is a telling comment in the O'Brien Papers. Robert O'Brien (William's brother) described the men in the dock at the indictment: 'William looked Pale and Gentlemanlike, Mr McManus Farmer like & the 3 others are peasants. Sad indeed to see them in the Dock & my heart shook within me' (Robert O'Brien to his wife Ellen, 24 September 1848: TCD: O'Brien Papers: Ms. 10610/17).

117 *The Times*, 25 October 1848, 4f–5a and b; 'Conviction of the Irish Rebel Leaders', *Fraser's Magazine*, 38 (November 1848), pp. 592–4. As convicted felons the men's property was forfeit to the Crown. To avoid this, O'Brien on his mother's advice had in April 1848 transferred his property to his trustees for the benefit of his wife and children (Richard Davis, 'The Reluctant Rebel', *op. cit.*, p. 54). As late as 25 September 1848, Robert O'Brien seemed to think that his brother's property might still be forfeit. Conviction would involve attainder which could be removed only by an Act of Parliament: 'This is certainly the strongest reason that can be urged for not giving up without a struggle' (Robert to Ellen O'Brien, 23 September 1848: TCD: O'Brien Papers: Ms. 106010/18).

118 Hodges, *op. cit.*, pp. 923–5.

119 Judgment at Queen's Bench was given on 16 January 1849, and by the Lords on 11 May 1849 (Hodges, *op. cit.*, pp. 926–84); 3 *Hansard*, CVI, cols 159–60; 14 June 1849; PP, 1849 [290], XLIX, 443.

120 On the day the death sentences were passed O'Brien's lawyers were told by both the Solicitor and Attorney General that the government would not carry them out (TCD: O'Brien Papers: Ms. 10610/32).

121 (1819–99). Second baronet, son of the Master of the Rolls. Became MP for Clare; Irish Privy Councillor and Judge Advocate General.

122 O'Brien to O'Loghlen, 5 June 1849: NLI: O'Brien Papers: Ms. 443/2550.

the Commons,[123] contending that there was no legal authority or precedent without his consent to transport from the United Kingdom any person convicted of treason and sentenced to death. It was O'Brien's hope that he could avoid transportation, since even a long sentence of imprisonment served in the United Kingdom would leave him close ('encircled') by his family and friends.[124] The Commons refused to hear the petition, but the Home Secretary, Sir George Grey, announced that in order to clear up any doubts, a short Bill would be introduced.[125] There was some concern that the proposed legislation was retroactive, and therefore wrong in principle, but Grey prevailed and the measure passed into law.[126] With all doubts removed, the treason prisoners[127] were on 9 July 1849 transferred from Richmond prison to the warship *Swift*, for transportation to Van Diemen's Land.[128] Virtually all of the Young Ireland leadership had been removed from the country, either as fugitives or as transported convicts.[129]

123 O'Brien to Speaker of Commons, 6 June 1849: NLI: O'Brien Papers: Ms. 443/2551; to Under-Secretary of State for Ireland, 7 June 1849, Ms. 443/2553. The petition is at Ms. 443/2559.

124 NLI: 'Maria Island Journal', *op. cit.*, Part 2, f. 17 (3 August 1850).

125 3 *Hansard*, CVI, cols 158–62; 14 June 1849; 'Maria Island Journal', *op. cit.*, Part 2, f. 17 (3 August 1850): 'I did not imagine that the British Government would condescend to such an *ex post facto* law for the purpose of sending me out of the United Kingdom.'

126 The prisoners greeted this news with dismay. They may have prepared themselves for death, but equally likely, realising the political impossibility of executing the death sentences, they hoped for pardons – perhaps following some further and none-too-arduous confinement in Dublin's Richmond Prison (3 *Hansard*, CVI, cols 389–449; 18 June 1849; cols 823–30; 25 June 1849; PP, 1849 [394], XLIX, 463). The statute was the Transportation for Treason (Ireland) Act, 1849 (12 & 13 Vict., c.27).

127 Kevin Izod O'Doherty and John Martin had been convicted under the Treason Felony Act, and since there was no doubt about the legality of their transportation they had been removed from Richmond on 15 June, and dispatched some three weeks before the four treason prisoners.

128 During the months of legal action an attempted rescue had been got up, but was discovered by the authorities. Among those involved in the plot was John O'Leary – then barely twenty years old – who would later become a leading Fenian. Thus (and there were several other examples) was the militant nationalist tradition passed on (see Duffy 1883, 719n.).

129 Charles Gavan Duffy had been charged with treason on the basis of a letter of his addressed to and found in O'Brien's luggage. The case was not conclusive and Duffy was ably defended by Isaac Butt (later to become leader of the Irish Party in the Commons). (On Butt at this time see David Thornley, *Isaac Butt and Home Rule*, London, MacGibbon & Kee, 1964, pp. 18–19.) Public scrutiny hampered jury packing, and after five trials and nine months in prison Duffy regained his freedom. Six years later, ironically, he emigrated to Australia convinced that Ireland was but a 'corpse on the dissection table'. The independent Irish Parliamentary Party which he had put together had been thwarted by place-seekers and the actions of the Roman Catholic hierarchy. Having decided to go to Australia he directed a number of questions to O'Brien about the country's conditions and prospects. For an account of his disillusionment and intentions see his letter to O'Brien (who by then had served a term in Van Diemen's Land), 2 December 1854 (NLI: O'Brien Papers: Ms. 445/2877). It should also be noted, as an indication of the obstinacy on both sides, that a full year after the treason trials had been concluded two men – John O'Donnell and Richard Shea – remained in prison for having failed to give evidence at the trial of O'Brien (*Nation*, 20 October 1849, 121a).

2

GENTLEMEN CONVICTS

Prison conditions

The Young Irelanders' prison treatment was undoubtedly influenced by the fact that the local politicians and personages of Dublin Corporation who supervised the administration of Dublin's Newgate and Richmond prisons were either sympathetic or felt they had to take account of nationalist sentiment. They had, moreover, a strong set of precedents to follow. Daniel O'Connell's imprisonment with several companions at Richmond Penitentiary from 30 May to 6 September 1844 had, by laxness and indulgence, been reduced to a farce. His entry into the prison was accompanied by a procession of thousands of supporters. He had been given the use of the governor's house, in which he and his fellow prisoners had suites of rooms. Married prisoners' wives resided with them; in O'Connell's case, two daughters and a daughter-in-law acted as hostesses. So many were the visitors that O'Connell had to limit times of admission to the prison. There were political soirées every evening, and the Repeal Association issued weekly bulletins (to be read throughout the country) on the health and condition of the prisoners. When the House of Lords overturned their conviction O'Connell and the others went home for the night, returning the following day in order to leave the prison at the head of a grand procession, and in a triumphal carriage of fantastic construction. The prison had been graced by O'Connell and his fellow offenders and allowed to play a part in a repeal pageant. The same municipal authorities responsible for Richmond Prison had accompanied the processions to and fro, clad in their civic robes and wearing the insignia of office.[1]

---

1 *Freeman's Journal* (which appeared in mourning columns), 31 May 1844, devoted almost all editorial and news space to the state trial, and the removal of O'Connell and his colleagues to Richmond Prison. There was a ceremonial procession (with carriages) through Dublin, and the men were greeted at the entrance to Richmond by the Lord Mayor and the governor. On 6 and 7 September the procession was repeated, again consuming columns of the *Freeman's Journal* (7 September 1844, 2b–f; 9 September, 2c–d, 3a–f, 4a–d). See also Oliver MacDonagh, *The Emancipist: Daniel O'Connell, 1830–47*, London, Weidenfeld & Nicolson, 1989, pp. 247–52.

The Young Irelanders were not of O'Connell's status, and their misdeeds had gone far beyond his monster demonstrations. Yet O'Brien's standing as a man and politician could not be overlooked. Relations between Old and Young Ireland had decayed in the last few years of O'Connell's life, and even more thereafter, but few could forget that while he had been in prison, O'Connell had handed to O'Brien the formal leadership of the repeal movement. The Dublin prison authorities would not provide for O'Brien on the scale of O'Connell, but they would, for several sets of reasons, seek by generosity and deference to put themselves beyond reproach.

This sentimental and opportunistic largesse was bestowed even before O'Brien's committal. John Mitchel had distanced himself from all but the most extreme boundaries of nationalism, but even he was indulged. He did not leave a record of his fortnight in Dublin's Newgate (which was controlled by Dublin Corporation), but in an account otherwise bitter against authority, he does not mention any particular hardship. Duffy recorded that there was 'liberality and consideration' during his pre-trial detention. The men wore their own clothes; food was sent in from a hotel, and a prison servant waited at table. Visitors were freely admitted, and there was no restriction on correspondence. So generous were the conditions that Duffy suggested that the authorities were using the traffic with the prisoners to collect information on friends and sympathisers.[2]

As the verdicts came in and sentences of death and long periods of transportation were handed down, Duffy, O'Doherty and Williams determined on escape, with the intention of fleeing to America. Outside help was secured, a small boat hired, and a night fixed for the attempt. They hoped that an escape would have a positive political effect, perhaps enabling them to continue the struggle. Above all they were young men who, in Duffy's words, 'felt the pulse of action beating too strong within us to subside willingly into perpetual bondage'. They may have been the victims of a ploy, since their plot was betrayed by an ostensibly friendly guard, and the three men were removed from their comfortable

---

2 Sir Charles Gavan Duffy, *Four Years of Irish History 1845–1849*, London, Cassell, Petter, Galpin & Co, 1883, pp. 626–7. After an escape attempt Duffy was forbidden to correspond or receive letters without the permission of the governor, and the Lord Lieutenant was enraged when he succeeded in smuggling out a letter which was published in the *Freeman's Journal* (ibid., p. 707). Nor were the various privileges much curtailed after conviction. John Martin, convicted but with his appeal pending, read and exercised a great deal and sent and received correspondence unhindered; he was also allowed to receive food from the outside. On 5 November 1848, he made the following entry in his journal: 'Had quite a "party" for tea. Elizabeth and Todd, Mary and Simpson. Todd came to town yesterday. Lill brought various presents of eatables and drinkables – a fine large cake from Mrs Todd, eggs and fowl from Mrs Boyd on Longhorne, butter from Lill herself, wine from Todd, jam and honey from Mrs Todd and herself. I shall become quite a glutton' (Northern Ireland Public Record Office (NIPRO): Diary of John Martin: D560/1, 5 November 1848, f. 4). Two days later he observed, 'It is remarkable how many extra visitors have been admitted to me during the last fortnight' (ibid., f. 6).

quarters to a secure cell.[3] These new quarters had no access to a separate yard, and it was therefore necessary for them to exercise with the criminals. The latter, Duffy records,

> [E]xhibited a fine trait of natural politeness or national feeling . . . by which I was touched at the time, and have never forgotten. Whenever I arrived they huddled into one corner and left me the greater part of the yard for undisturbed exercise during my brief stay . . . it seems to me a club or a drawing-room could scarcely have surpassed this courtesy.[4]

The escape attempt was an expensive venture. The part of the prison to which they were subsequently removed, Duffy recorded, was one of 'filth, foul air, darkness and horror': the abode, in other words, of the common criminal. There were cells where 'light was as effectively excluded as from the grave'. Claiming that the prison had been built on an ancient monastic burial ground, Duffy insisted that it reeked of 'odours of unknown origin', and was infested with insects. After several months in such conditions, suffering also from the strain of his repeated and inconclusive trials, Duffy's health began to fail, and his doctor unavailingly petitioned for his patient's removal to more healthy surroundings.[5] It was not until his fourth trial and hung jury that Duffy was removed from Newgate to Richmond Bridewell. He continued in close confinement and was not allowed to associate with O'Brien, Meagher and the others, who were now convicted prisoners awaiting the outcome of their legal challenge. From his silence on the matter, and from our knowledge of the favourable conditions enjoyed by the other political prisoners, we may safely infer that Duffy was restored again to the status of state prisoner.[6]

Like Newgate, Richmond Bridewell came under the jurisdiction of Dublin Corporation. One modern writer suggests that public opinion in Dublin was the reason why the Young Irelanders were treated leniently while they awaited the outcome of their various legal moves.[7] This was probably true, though what

---

3 Duffy 1883, pp. 722–3. The cell to which they were removed had been the one, according to tradition, where the United Irishman Lord Edward Fitzgerald had died half a century previously – a felicitous and patriotic coincidence.

4 Ibid., p. 723.

5 Ibid., p. 728.

6 The Irish government, through an intermediary, suggested that if Duffy were to show public signs of repentance it would be possible to grant an amnesty to all the Young Irelanders. All the prisoners were allowed to consult together for an evening and the answer was sent that Duffy would not make any concession, and so he embarked on his fifth trial. The incident is important as an indication of the government's desire to have done with the affair, and also the great care not to be seen ill-treating the prisoners (ibid., pp. 749–50).

7 Blanche M. Touhill, *William Smith O'Brien and His Irish Revolutionary Companions in Penal Exile*, Columbia, University of Missouri Press, 1981, p. 14.

passed for public opinion was segmented and in any event somewhat confused. It must also be remembered that the indulgences granted to O'Brien and the others were no more than had been extended to middle-class persons recently convicted of political offences in England.[8]

On 18 November 1848, Martin and O'Doherty learned that their application for a writ of error had been refused.[9] On the same day O'Brien and the other prisoners were brought up from Clonmel and delivered to Richmond Bridewell. Conditions were now greatly improved for the Clonmel prisoners.[10] They were allocated adjacent rooms and allowed freely to associate with each other; visits, letters and newspapers were virtually unrestricted.[11] In a curious acknowledgement either of his social pre-eminence or of his leadership in the affair, O'Brien received special treatment. His servant attended him, the chief officer's wife cooked his meals, using food provided by his family, and he was given rooms in Governor Marques' house, with access to two gardens.[12] O'Doherty

---

8 These cases are reviewed by Sir Leon Radzinowicz and Roger Hood in 'The Status of Political Prisoners of England; the Struggle for Recognition', *Virginia Law Review*, 65, 8 (1979), pp. 1423–33. For a list of prisoners convicted of political offences in England in 1839–40, and of their treatment, see *A Return for Each Gaol and House of Correction in the United Kingdom, Stating (1) The Name and Designation of Every Person Confined for Charges for Printing and Publishing Seditious and Blasphemous Libel, or for Uttering Seditious Words, or for Attending any Seditious Meetings, or for Conspiring to Cause Such Meetings to be Held, or for Any Offence of a Political Nature . . . (2) Exceptions to this Treatment . . . (4) Comparative Treatment of Persons Confined for Misdemeanour*, PP, 1840 [600], XXXVIII, 691.

9 As late as 3 June 1849 (some three weeks before embarkation) Martin doubted that he and O'Doherty would be transported with the others. Mitchell Library Sydney (MLS); John to David Martin: A M 87, f. 2. Martin was stoical about the decision of the judges, who ruled against him on all points: 'Sorry to have spent so much money for nothing. Though originally the only object contemplated by my friends in applying for the writ was to keep me from being sent out of the country' (NIPRO: Diary of John Martin: D561/, 18 November 1848, ff. 8–9).

10 Martin noted of their arrival: 'O'Brien looks but poorly – thin sallow & rather low spirited, or as if he were struggling to keep up his spirits. McManus and O'Donohoe complain of suffering from the damp and uncomfortableness of their cell in Clonmel and say they were obliged to drink plenty of whisky punch in contending against the rheumatic tendencies of their condition' (ibid., f. 10).

11 In a letter to Duffy, who was in the midst of his series of trials, and thus separated from the men who had been convicted, John Martin confessed to an uneasy conscience about the sociable time he and his comrades enjoyed: 'For the last ten or twelve days . . . we are permitted sufficient intercourse with each other. Any of us may visit our lodging of any other of us, from breakfast-time till 9 at night. And when some three or four of us are met, and engaged in friendly chat and interchange of thoughts, about subjects so dear to you, I can't help recollecting with vexation that you are so solitary' (P. A. Sillard, *The Life and Letters of John Martin*, Dublin, James Duffy & Co, 1901, pp. 138–9). Correspondence was not censored at Richmond, O'Brien would later point out to the convict authorities in Van Diemen's Land. (National Library of Ireland (NLI): O'Brien Papers: Ms. 443/2375.)

12 O'Brien to Archdeacon Marriot, 16 November 1849: NLI: O'Brien Papers: Ms. 443/2575. This letter was written to contrast his generous treatment in Richmond, 'under the eye of Lord Clarendon', with the close confinement imposed on him in Van Diemen's Land.

was given the daytime use of the parlour of Matthews, the chief turnkey. Duffy (freed after his fifth trial) found him on a visit, 'labouring at the eternal task of his correspondence'.[13]

On the warship *Swift* transporting him to Van Diemen's Land, O'Brien reflected on his eight months at Richmond: 'I could scarcely call my imprisonment an infliction and were it not for the prospect of the dismal separation which has at length commenced I might have been perfectly content with my lot.' Apart from the suffering which he had inflicted on his family he 'could scarcely wish (for a season at least) to be placed in more happy circumstances than those which surrounded me in Richmond Prison'. He had been isolated from the outside, surrounded by his family, visited by his friends and received letters of sympathy 'and not infrequently of admiration' from all over the world. During his imprisonment he had 'commanded to an unlimited extent literary resources calculated to gratify intellectual tastes'. All in all, he was to look back on Richmond as 'a period during which I have lived more for myself and experienced more of the personal enjoyments of life than I have known for many years'.[14]

The other prisoners fared almost equally well. John Dillon's wife Adelaide visited Richmond and reported to him that Meagher had his cell 'settled with all his beautiful pictures – books & carpeted & made as comfortable as possible'.[15] MacManus was allowed a box of tools, and made knick-knacks. All the younger prisoners, Duffy reported, 'were in excellent, sometimes exuberant, spirits'.[16] When, after several months' confinement, the men appeared in court to hear the judgment in their appeals, they were reported by the *Irishman* to be in good health, showing 'the same firmness and composure that characterised their manner and bearing from the beginning of the proceedings against them'.[17]

The voyage to Australia

Mitchel

A decision had also been taken to continue favourable treatment during the prisoners' shipment to Van Diemen's Land and during their time there. In the case of Mitchel, imprisoned two months before the others and shipped more than a year ahead of them, the decision may have been a last-minute one: uncertainty mixed with caution and a desire not to inflame opinion or incite

13 Duffy 1883, p. 758.
14 NLI: O'Brien Papers: *Transportation Journal*, Ms. 3923, 15 July 1849.
15 Trinity College Dublin (TCD), Dillon Papers: Ms. 6455/90: Adelaide to John Dillon, 5 January 1849. 'He *looked much* better too – quite himself – not at all stupefied as before – dear glorious little fellow.'
16 Duffy 1883, p. 758.
17 *Irishman*, 20 January 1849, 34a.

sympathy for the prisoner. In his *Jail Journal* Mitchel recorded that shortly after sentence had been passed he was instructed to put on convict clothes, but no sooner had he done so than there came the countermanding order – 'Let him be removed in his own clothes.'[18] Mitchel was obliged to wear chains, but was then so hurried on board ship that these were affixed to one leg only, and he had to carry the loose links in his hands. The chain was removed as soon as he boarded the *Shearwater* (he was never to be fettered again), and he was given a restorative sherry and water.[19] During his run down the coast to Spike Island, Mitchel had what he described as a 'good berth', and took his breakfast with the ship's officers. On Spike Island (a convict depot) he was given a large cell opening on to its own courtyard. He was obliged again to don convict uniform, but only for two days.[20] Orders then arrived from Dublin Castle directing Grace, the Spike Island governor, that Mitchel was not to be treated as an ordinary convict, but should have his own clothes and be left unchained; he was also allowed to write to his wife on condition that no reference was made to politics.[21] The captain of the warship *Scourge* which would take him to Bermuda had been instructed before leaving Portsmouth that Mitchel was to be treated 'as a person of education and a gentleman'. This injunction procured him a 'very handsome' cabin, furnished with couches, chairs and a table. Subject only to the restriction of a

18 John Mitchel, *Jail Journal or Five Years in British Prisons*, London, R. & T. Washbourne, n.d., p. 221 (original edn New York, 1854).

19 The myth of 'Mitchel, bound in chains' was nevertheless firmly established, as his fellow Young Irelander Gavan Duffy (himself soon to go on trial) put it in a leader for the *Nation*: 'The first "felon" is borne away by England, manacled with her irons and guarded with her soldiers.' The article was headed 'Departure of the Prisoner in Irons for Spike Island' (Saturday, 3 June 1848, 360c). Years later, in his first public speech in America (indeed, his first speech since his imprisonment in Dublin) Mitchel charged the British government with seeking to degrade Irish patriots 'to the rank and to the society of cut-throats and rick-burners', and of 'bolting me in irons and carrying me to Bermuda' (*Daily Alta California*, 26 October 1853, 2d).

20 A *Times* report, based on a government briefing ('undoubted authority') claimed that Mitchel, 'so far from having any ground of complaint on the score of severity, has expressed his gratitude for the consideration with which his case has been met'. Mitchel in his memoirs recalled that at Spike Island he was obliged to wear convict uniform for two days, but the government-inspired report insisted that he was not put into convict clothes; it also insisted (what was true) that his hair had not been cut nor was he obliged to associate with 'any of the other criminals undergoing their sentences at the same prison' (*The Times*, 3 June 1848, 6e). *Lloyds Weekly* reported (4 June 1848, 2c and 2d) that Captain Atkins, the Inspector of Penitentiaries (a post superior to that of the governor), had directed that Mitchel should be given a separate room and 'should not be interfered with' on the day of his arrival, but that on the morrow 'he would be obliged to wear the convict dress, and be treated in all respects as an ordinary convict'.

21 Here also there is a conflict between Mitchel's recollection and the report given to *The Times*. According to the latter, permission to write to his wife and to receive letters from her was given conditional only on Mitchel's word not to write about political matters. Mitchel recalled being told he could write a letter home, but that it had to be submitted to the governor (*The Times*, 3 June 1848, 6e; Mitchel, *op. cit.*, p. 28).

marine escort when he went on deck, Mitchel was allowed to come and go as he pleased, and took his meals with the captain.[22]

The regime continued at Bermuda, where Mitchel was given special accommodation on board the hulk *Dromedary*, moored off Ireland Island. Having suffered severe asthma on the voyage, Mitchel had been certified as unwell by the surgeon of the *Scourge*, and despite his protestations, was left for only a few days in his new quarters before being removed to the hospital ship *Tenedos*.[23] Protesting that he was not an invalid, Mitchel nevertheless admitted that his new quarters were pleasant. The accommodation was excellent, and the ship was moored about a quarter of a mile offshore 'in a most beautiful bay, or basin, formed by well-wooded island, and far out of sight of the prison hulks and the batteries'.[24] A scare that Irish-Americans might attempt a rescue caused his removal back to the *Dromedary*, where he continued to enjoy superior quarters, food and conditions. He could, within reasonable limits, come and go around the ship and the adjacent quay. Even at the height of the rescue scare, when guns were being mounted on nearby vessels, he was, according to his own account, given his letters from home unopened – merely being asked to promise that should they contain anything on public affairs he would give them up. Despite this easy regime an account of some ill-treatment was got up and published in Hobart (his eventual destination) long before Mitchel arrived there.[25]

The shrieks of ordinary convicts being flogged were clearly audible to Mitchel in his cabin. Some floggings were inflicted merely for provocative language, causing him to reflect on the insolent manner in which the hulk officers issued their orders to the convicts. As to his own position, 'Your gentlemanly

22 Ibid., pp. 31–2. Far from grateful at this treatment, Mitchel took it as confirmation of government's confusion or deviousness: 'A person of education and a gentleman! And if such a person has indeed committed a felony, is he not just all the more felonious? . . . how does his education entitle him to indulgence over other felons?' (ibid., p. 31).

23 Bermuda was at that time an unhealthy place for convicts, many of whom arrived in poor condition. Dispatches from the governor to Sir George Grey, Home Secretary, reported a 'considerable' mortality rate, especially among the Irish prisoners, 'attributable entirely to their low state of health from previous wretchedness and destitution'. The medical superintendent reported the deaths of forty-four Irish prisoners between 24 January and 1 November 1848. (PRO HO 45/50916, 2 December 1848). John Martin, Mitchel's devoted friend, nevertheless wished to join him there; writing on 20 November 1848 that Mitchel had expressed a wish that Martin could join him in Bermuda, and commenting 'I wish I may' (Diary of John Martin, *op. cit.*, D.560/1, f. 11).

24 *Jail Journal*, p. 57.

25 *Hobarton Guardian*, 6 January 1849, 4c. Although Mitchel gave an unadorned and, as far as one can see, accurate account of his treatment in his *Jail Journal*, verisimilitude did not always serve his ends and other accounts he gave of his confinement were more propagandist. In a letter to Thomas Devin Reilly, intended for publication, and justifying his escape from Van Diemen's Land, he gave a very different description of his time at Bermuda from that of the *Journal*. He was, he wrote, 'kept ten months in a solitary cell of a hulk . . . and with much more rigour and less liberty than any of the real convicts at that place' (*New York Daily Times*, 24 November 1853, 3a).

convict . . . must have deference and accommodations, and attendance and literary leisure; – but in the hulk, as elsewhere, there is the hard word and the hard blow, and unremitting, ill-requited toil, and fetters for the limbs, and a scourge for the back of the poor.' Yet the great ease and privileges of his position slipped his mind when the latest newspapers arrived from England, for although they circulated freely among the officers and staff, he was denied them: 'Here is a violent provocation to me.'[26]

A possible Irish-American rescue meant that Mitchel was confined under the guns of the battery and warships.[27] At the same time his asthma, and other respiratory troubles, apparently aggravated by confinement and the humid climate of Bermuda, were a cause for concern. Security and health could be reconciled only by his removal to another place remote from the Americas. Eight months after his arrival, Mitchel was told that he was to go to the Cape, where he would be granted conditional liberty. Two and a half months were fretted away on board *The Neptune* before this trip commenced. The voyage, which had been expected to last for two months, actually took five, being so unfavourable that it was necessary to revictual in Brazil; such was the delay that *The Neptune* was presumed lost.[28] On this voyage Mitchel was given an indeterminate status which meant he could mix neither with convicts nor crew, causing him to complain that he was in virtual solitary confinement. He described his cabin as 'a close, unclean, and unhealthy cavity under the poop deck.'[29]

The prospect of conditional liberty had lifted Mitchel's hopes, but he was severely disappointed when he arrived at the Cape on 19 September 1849 to discover that he had missed by a week O'Brien and the others on board the *Swift*. The proposal to establish a penal settlement at the Cape had provoked the colonists into such furious agitation that convict landings were impossible, and the ship's officers were boycotted on shore; even getting supplies was very difficult.[30] Both in Cape Town and in the prosperous hinterland, opposition was

---

26 *Jail Journal*, pp. 66–7. Elsewhere Mitchel refers to the officers as generous and courteous, 'gentlemen worthy of an honester service' (*New York Daily Times*, 24 November 1853, 3a).

27 The state of tension was described by a former steward at Bermuda (*Hobarton Guardian*, 6 January 1849, 4c). According to this account (taken from the *New York Herald*) all Irish civil staff at the Bermuda convict establishment were dismissed at the time of the rescue scare. Mitchel records that one of his guards, an Irishman, was dismissed 'because he had spoken some words favourably of me before another, who straight reported it' (*Jail Journal*, p. 67).

28 John to David Martin, 16 November 1849: MLS; A M 87, f. 1). See also *Hobart Town Courier*, 31 October 1849, 2d; *Hobart Town Advertiser*, 30 October 1849, 2b.

29 *New York Daily Times*, 24 November 1853, 3a.

30 The *South African Commercial Advertiser* carried an incandescent editorial. The attempt to convert an old-established free colony into a penal settlement was 'injurious, despotic and tyrannical in itself [and] beyond the Constitutional prerogatives and recognized powers of the Crown of Great Britain' (22 September 1849, 2a; see also cols b–e). This was the flavour of opposition in the months during which the policy was being contested. See *Convictism: Report of the Proceedings of a Public Meeting Held in the Court House at Grahams Town on Wednesday,*

well organised, powerfully backed and implacable.[31] Since Mitchel could not be landed, London had to be consulted and new arrangements made, and for five months the ship lay at anchor in Simon's Bay.[32] The final leg of Mitchel's penal wanderings did not therefore begin until 19 February 1850, and it was not until 6 April 1850 that the *Neptune* arrived off Van Diemen's Land – completing in just thirteen days under a year what must have been the most costly voyage in the history of transportation. In consideration for the hardships they had suffered, the ordinary convicts on board were given immediate conditional pardons.[33]

4 *July, 1849 on the Subject of the Order in Council Constituting the Cape of Good Hope a Penal Settlement*, Graham's Town, Godlonton & White, 1849. See also *The Reception of Convicts at the Cape of Good Hope*, PP, 1850 [1139], XXXVIII, 223, 1. The colonists had been outraged that any convict should be sent thither, 'as dangerous to the security of life and property in this settlement'. Arrival of the Young Irelanders caused further offence – 'desperate men, who instigated the lower orders of their countrymen to acts of unparalleled wickedness' (ibid., 'Resolutions passed at a Public Meeting of the Inhabitants of Graham's Town, held in the Court House, 7 December 1848'). The success of the Cape colonists in blocking London's plans (news of which arrived with Mitchel) was widely reported and discussed in the Australian colonies. (See the *Sydney Morning Herald*, 18 April 1850, 2b; the *Argus* (Melbourne), 22 April 1850, 4a–e; 24 April 1850, 4b–c; 26 April 1850, 4a–b). For the reactions in Britain (which were not great) see William Shakespeare Childe-Pemberton, *Life of Lord Norton (Right Hon. Sir Charles Adderley, K. C. M. G., MP) 1814–1905: Statesman & Philanthropist*, London, John Murray, 1909, ch. XIII.

31 A meeting of the principal landowners and wine-growers of Stellenbosch declared their support for the Cape Town anti-convict movement which, they stated, had 'our fullest confidence. . . . It is our firm resolution to support them in carrying out the Pledge, until the *Neptune* shall have quitted our shores.' Nothing short of the departure of the vessel would quiet the inhabitants 'and prevent the total alienation of the affections of the colonists from the mother country' (Residents of Stellenbosch, *Letter to the Governor*, Stellenbosch, 1849 (National Library of South Africa)).

32 In a later account Mitchel insisted that his ship's predicament at Simon's Bay had been anticipated before his dispatch from Bermuda: 'The British Ministers, indeed, knew that I should most probably never land at the Cape, where, accordingly, I never did land' (*New York Daily Times*, 24 November 1853, 3a). Mitchel was wrong in this assertion. For accounts of the Cape controversy in the wider context of convict and colonial policy see A. G. L. Shaw, *Convicts and the Colonies*, London, Faber & Faber, 1966, pp. 327–30; Alan Frederick Hattersley, *The Convict Crisis and the Growth of Unity*, Pietermaritzburg, University of Natal Press, 1965, chs 3–10.

33 Except for some thirty men who had misconducted themselves on the voyage (*Sydney Morning Herald*, 18 April 1850, 2b; *The Irish Exile*, 13 April 1850, 3a). Mitchel was in a poor state of health when he arrived, and was reported by Meagher as looking 'wretchedly ill, apparently excessively worn and haggard, and bore in his features the most piteous evidence of long ailing, and severe exhaustion'. Meagher added that Mitchel's constitution did not seem to be affected, and that he was soon restored to health by 'this pure and beautiful climate' (NLI: Meagher to O'Brien, 11 May 1850, O'Brien Papers: Ms. 444/2690). The colonists knew well the extent of the dispute between Earl Grey and the Cape, and, in an increasingly strong mood against the status of Van Diemen's Land as a penal colony denounced the vessel's arrival as ministerial 'cowardice and meanness' (*Hobart Town Courier*, 6 April 1850, 2c; 10 April 1850, 2c). Mitchel's confederate, Patrick O'Donohoe, now had his own newspaper, and reported the arrival of 'Our beloved friend, the bold, the chivalrous, the self-sacrificing John Mitchel' (*Irish Exile*, 6 April 1850, 4a).

Although no special instructions had been received from the Colonial Office regarding Mitchel, Lieutenant-Governor William Denison decided to treat him the same as his companions, who had already arrived.[34] Accordingly, on giving his parole not to escape, he was offered a ticket of leave, allowing him to live in any police district he chose. He was obliged to report monthly to the district magistrate, but otherwise was at liberty.[35] Acceptance of a ticket of leave meant a promise not to escape from the colony. Parole might at any time be resigned, in which event his fate would be the same as if he refused to accept it – close confinement in a penal depot. Brooding on the matter three and a half years later, Mitchel saw the grant of parole as a cunning ploy to make him and his companions their own gaolers: 'If we had been dealt with here as any of the classes of real convicts are – if we had got the ordinary ticket-of-leave without parole, or had been hired out to settlers as "pass-holders", we would all instantly have left the island.'[36]

John Martin and Kevin O'Doherty

The party which had next followed Mitchel into exile was a small one, consisting of the seditious editors John Martin and Kevin O'Doherty. They embarked on the convict ship *Mountstewart Elphinstone* on 28 June 1849. There had been hopes that O'Brien and the others would also join the ship, but their departure was delayed further. Martin and O'Doherty were given a large cabin, and were consulted as to its arrangements. Originally intended for five occupants, the two decided to keep two extra beds to sit on, and to allow them to spread out their possessions; the fifth bed was removed and replaced by a second washstand. Enough space remained for Martin to have his own dressing room. All in all, these were comfortable quarters – certainly more commodious than most private passengers could afford for a voyage to Australia, and grander than any officer's, short of the captain. Martin wrote approvingly that they were 'very snug and comfortably accommodated'. The cabin was well ventilated, but there were smells from the adjacent infirmary and from a hole by the cabin door, against which the

---

34 Mitchel had been ten months at Bermuda, and almost a year in transit thither to Van Diemen's Land, so the two other parties – Martin and O'Doherty, and O'Brien and his companions – although dispatched thirteen months after Mitchel, and having also experienced unfavourable winds, had arrived in the penal colony some five months before him.

35 Archives Office of Tasmania (AOT): Governor's Office, Inward Despatches (GO, ID), GO1/76 f. 107–8. His freedom included the privilege of publishing his writings, and he embarked upon the serial publication of a life of the sixteenth-century Irish chieftain Hugh O'Neill in the *Hobarton Guardian* (first published in Ireland in the autumn of 1845). This allowed a strong subtext of Irish nationalist thinking, albeit in Mitchel's rather idiosyncratic mode.

36 The grant of parole, he maintained, was contrived 'not out of courtesy, God knows, to us, but as a security to them – the only security they could have that we would stay one week in the Island'. As to why he had submitted to this duplicitous device, Mitchel insisted the alternative was 'a lingering death in a dungeon' (*New York Daily Times*, 24 November 1853, 3a).

chloride of lime with which the men had provided themselves proved ineffectual. Martin also doubted whether this solution would guard against vermin,
especially those they might expect to encounter in the tropics – 'thousands of
them of all abominable varieties'.[37]

Martin and O'Doherty lived well. The steward appointed to serve them,
Martin recorded, was 'attentive and desirous to please us in our meals'. Breakfast
was at 8 a.m., dinner at 1 p.m. and tea at 6 p.m. Meat was served twice a day,
and they both had healthy appetites. O'Doherty was not at all bashful about
asking for any extra comfort or luxury that the two required, obtaining brandy
and wine from the Captain, together with lemonade. Martin was so taken with
O'Doherty's boldness that he told him that 'I must worship him as a divinity of
face'. O'Doherty also contrived to get himself a bath, prompting Martin to
confide to his diary, 'I really must pluck up courage and get a bath too, at least
occasionally'.[38]

Relations with the officers and crew were easy and security precautions
minimal. Four days out, permission was given for the two to be on deck for an
extra hour each evening until 10 p.m., and all other restrictions were removed.
The Captain, mates, crew and officers of the military guard were all pleasant:
'Nobody offers us the slightest incivility in any word or look; but everybody
seems respectful and obliging.' The ship's doctor was rather more formal in his
manner, but, Martin recorded, never meddled once they were well out to sea
'beyond a very brief & civil salute and inquiry after my health or the like'. The
other convicts could be seen going about their routines, but Martin and
O'Doherty had no contact with them.[39]

The men were being forcibly transported, but this is hardly discernible in
Martin's record of the voyage, which has all the qualities of a pleasure cruise.
Days were spent reading, conversing and observing sea life and enjoying a
pleasant climate; evenings were passed in an equally jolly manner. On 8 July
1849, the two celebrated the first anniversary of their arrest, enjoying with their
dinner some of the sherry which the Captain sent them each Sunday: 'Success
to felony! With our whole heart!' On another evening they stayed on deck
until past 10 p.m., 'walking upon the poop and conversing with the mate and
smoking and enjoying the delightful sea breeze of this latitude'.[40] A week later
another pleasant evening was noted, consisting of a luxurious dinner, accompanied by wine and brandy ('we take a couple of glasses each every day, besides
our ale'). In guilty rationalisation, Martin observed that at sea the water was so

37 These details and Martin's account of his voyage are taken from the manuscript diary of John
Martin (hereinafter Martin Diary): NIPRO: D560/2.
38 Ibid., f. 25. This was 10 July 1849, and three days later Martin was still debating with himself
whether to have a bath (ibid., f. 31).
39 Ibid., f. 26. There were repeated appreciative entries about the civility of all on board, e.g. 19
July (f. 40); 5 August (f. 57); 10 August (f. 60); 25 August (f. 67).
40 Ibid., ff. 23 and 18.

bad that 'people are strongly tempted to drink wine or the like in hot weather'. The dinner itself had consisted of a roast duck, 'very tender & quite another thing from the tough dry lean fowls we have hitherto got. Also a plum pudding . . . I shall become quite a bon vivant.'[41]

The dinner table was not the only source of pleasure, and evenings on deck were delightful.

> Ever since we reached [the] latitude of the Azores the air is a continual feast, that is when any wind is stirring. The night air in these latitudes is delightful at sea. Every night O'D and I lie upon the benches or sides of the poop feasting on the cool soft balmy night breeze. Sometimes I fall asleep for a few minutes.[42]

Balmy nights and epicurean feasts took their toll, however, and both men felt that their health was suffering from overindulgence. Four weeks out Martin confessed:

> My drinking and smoking don't suit my constitution well, particularly as I have no exercise for my arms: for I don't make use of the ropes for exercise they are so hard & harsh upon my soft hands. But I must force myself to exercise my arms and shoulders. As to *drinking* etc. I now take daily 2 glasses of port sherry or Marsalla (all excellent as supplied us by the Captain) besides an occasional 'nip' ($^1/_3$ or $^1/_4$ of a glass) of brandy and my share of our bottle of porter. I must quit smoking for a few days.[43]

Three weeks later both men were feeling rather indisposed and not sleeping too well. Martin confessed that 'probably we both drink & smoke too much, having so little exercise'.[44]

The Captain and the two men would have expected that the luxuries enjoyed during the voyage would be paid for on arrival, but neither man had adequate funds. On 1 October they were told that the ship was nearing land, and began to pack their things. They discussed the gratuities they should pay their steward and other members of the crew and their now large mess-bill, and discovered that they had only £10 between them. Martin decided to ask the Captain for a loan of £12 or £14, to be drawn on the security of their relatives in Ireland. Not surprisingly the Captain, already substantially out of pocket, did not reply to

---

41 Ibid., f. 33. Almost a month out, Martin recorded that he was in the habit of taking two or three glasses of wine each day 'besides my ale or porter, or sometimes a little brandy. O'D says I am decidedly fatter than when I left Dublin – that is less thin. I think so myself' (ibid., f. 46).
42 Ibid., f. 47.
43 Ibid., ff. 48–9; 26 July 1849.
44 Ibid., f. 63; 14 August 1849.

this application. The men then applied to the colonial authorities, and the Deputy Commissary, General Ramsay, told them to make a formal application. Mere indigency put on the garb of honour. A note was submitted asking the government to meet their expenses on board ship, together with the cost of getting them to their places of exile and associated expenses. Martin and O'Doherty insisted that this was not an application, for they could not submit such to the British government. Any sum expended by the government would be repaid as soon as the two received money from home or began earning it. The letter was signed 'with a due sense of the courtesy we have received from Mr Ramsay and yourself, your obedient servant John Martin convict for treason and felony.'[45]

The men had made land at Sydney harbour – which place greatly impressed Martin, who compared it favourably with Cove.[46] Arrangements had to be made for their transhipment to Hobart Town. It was first intended that they should go on board the brig *Palmyra*, where they would be confined until departure. This order was countermanded and they were allowed to stay where they were until the *Palymra* was ready to depart. The authorities apparently received information from the Captain of the *Mountstewart Elphinstone* and respectable passengers that Martin and O'Doherty were gentlemen, and had behaved as such throughout the voyage. It was then decided that the accommodation on the *Palymra* was not good enough, and instead to send them on the brig *Emma*.[47] This vessel, Martin was pleased to hear, belonged to a Mr McNamara, a wealthy Irish merchant. His pleasure was increased when the *Emma* entered harbour, and they saw upon her stern 'a conspicuous gilt Irish harp, surrounded by a wreath of shamrocks'. Martin and O'Doherty were told that the Commissariat was making arrangements for their comfortable passage to Hobart Town, and that they would travel in the ladies' cabin with the government paying to have them mess with the ship's officers.[48] Martin asked for an account of the expenses but was told that no charge would be made and no payment accepted. (Although Martin noted that he wished to pay, there is no record in his papers of payment for this journey or for the messing charges for the long voyage out from Ireland.) These arrangements were discussed at a meeting between Martin and O'Doherty, General Ramsay, Deputy Commissary, and Captain McClean, Inspector of Convicts. The tone of the meeting, Martin recorded, was 'even more [courteous]

---

45 NIPRO: Martin Papers; D.560/3: letter dated 12 October 1849.
46 'But the sun & sky of this climate are wanting at Cove except in some favoured June or September days. And alas the huts of wretchedness are always there, or if not always seen are always in my mind [and consciousness]' (Diary, f. 93; 3 October 1849).
47 There may also have been some pressure from the Irish community in Sydney, which convened a meeting to petition government on the men's behalf, requesting an easing of their conditions (*Argus* (Melbourne), 17 October 1849, 2d).
48 The *Hobart Town Advertiser* described their accommodation as the 'State cabin' – indicating that it was sometimes put at the disposal of the Lieutenant-Governor (30 October 1849, 2b).

than the first if possible'.[49] Writing to his brother, Martin confessed surprise at 'the respectful manner of the government officials, and the general respect that has been exhibited by the English and Scotch colonists'.[50]

One matter threatened to disturb these amicable relations – the formal registration of Martin and O'Doherty as convicts. The two men had been told (by whom it is not recorded) that they would be made to parade on deck before the Inspector of Convicts and his assistant, 'stripped up to the knees & bare headed and open mouthed and with shirt sleeves rolled up to our shoulders and our collars open to exhibit our necks and breasts to the public gaze'. Martin and O'Doherty resolved to refuse any personal examination beyond how they appeared in their everyday clothes. They told the Inspector that should any indignity be offered them they would refuse to consent to be examined, and would protest in writing to the Governor. Martin also mentioned Sir George Gray's undertaking to Sir Lucius O'Brien that no indignity would be offered to his brother on the passage or afterwards. This statement equally applied to the other state prisoners. The Inspector explained that he intended to treat them in all respects with civility and courtesy and would not ask them to submit to a public inspection or stripping: 'he rather impetrated our consent to an interview in our cabin with [the Assistant Inspector] for the purpose of taking our height, colour of eyes and hair and complexion. To this we had no great objection.'[51] The inspection was duly carried out, and the two men were registered as convicts. Shortly thereafter they were embarked for Hobart Town.

O'Brien and his companions

O'Brien, MacManus, Meagher and O'Donohoe left Dublin on 9 July 1849, eleven days after Martin and O'Doherty. Some weeks before, Lucy, O'Brien's wife, had written to Sir Thomas Rodington at Dublin Castle, asking about the conditions under which the men would be transported. He was quick to assure her:

> any extra bedding & other articles for their convenience & including the baggage *within reasonable limits* will not be objected to, and the prisoners will be permitted to take money out with them. The accommodation provided is more ample than is usual in the ships ordinarily supplied on this service but it will not admit of each prisoner having a separate apartment.[52]

---

49 Ibid., ff. 103–4; 16 October 1849.
50 John to David Martin, 16 November 1849: Mitchell Library, Sydney (MLS); A M 87, f. 1. He also reported that the Irish in Sydney regarded them both as patriots and martyrs – very pleasant, no doubt.
51 Martin Diary, ff. 98–9; 16 October 1849.
52 Lucy O'Brien to Sir Thomas Rodington, 19 June 1849; NLI: O'Brien Papers: Ms. 443/2554. Lucy had also been worried about the men's diet on the voyage and Rodington assured her that the

O'Brien and the others were removed under armed escort from Richmond in a closed prison van, O'Brien reflecting on his eleven months in confinement, 'nearly eight of which had been spent in monotonous though not disagreeable residence in Richmond Prison'.[53] The men were first taken by boat to the warship *Dragon*, whose Commander, Captain Hall, introduced himself 'and exhibited much kindness and courtesy in his conversation'.

At Kingstown the men had been transferred to the warship *Swift*, which was to carry them to Van Diemen's Land. Before departure their craft was surrounded by many small boats carrying friends and relatives, as well as sightseers.[54] To prevent any demonstrations, the prisoners were not allowed on deck until their vessel had cleared Kingstown harbour. Instructions on this matter appear to have come from London.[55] The ship's appearance disappointed O'Brien, who thought that 'being greatly in want of paint she looked more like a collier than a man of war'. But there was no complaint about accommodation: 'In fact the best cabin in the ship was placed at our disposal as a sitting room and the sleeping berths adjoining it are airy and comfortable.' Despite Sir Thomas Rodington's letter to Lucy O'Brien, the men *were* given separate cabins. A sketch made by O'Brien shows the men in small cabins grouped around the captain's cabin, while their mess adjoined the officers' mess. All the berths were fitted with venetian blinds and were, O'Brien recorded, 'immediately under the deck, well lighted and ventilated'. Even on board ship O'Brien appears to have received more favourable treatment than his companions, and he was allocated, in addition, to his cabin, 'a sort of little dressing room'.[56]

The regime was slightly stricter than Martin's and O'Doherty's on the *Mountsteward Elphinstone* – but theirs was a convict ship used to the carriage of prisoners, whereas the *Swift* was a man of war, whose captain was new to this work and doubtless anxious about the sensitivity of the task. No conversation was allowed between the prisoners and the officers or men. Access to the deck was fairly liberally given between 8 a.m. and 8 p.m., but not for more than two of them at a time, and they could not go forward further than the mainmast. Smoking 'for the sake of health' was allowed on deck, but not below, between 12 noon and 1 p.m. and between 5 and 6 p.m. Nor did they fare so well in the matter of food, being allowed rations calculated as two-thirds of those given to

rations would include both fresh and salt meat 'as long as the supply of the former remains'. He was unable to supply further information. O'Brien undid his wife's good intentions by sending back the bedding and other materials which – once he was under way – he realised would have increased his comfort and that of his companions (NLI: O'Brien Papers: *Transportation Journal*, Ms. 3923, 18 July 1849. Unless otherwise indicated O'Brien's account of his voyage is taken from this source).

53 *Transportation Journal*, 9 July 1849.
54 *Freeman's Journal*, 10 July 1849, 2a–b, 3e–f.
55 Fears of further demonstrations meant that action was taken to avoid a river steamer which had put out from Cork to intercept the *Swift*, with the intention of handing over money and supplies for some of the prisoners (*Hobarton Guardian*, 1 December 1849, 4a).
56 NLI: O'Brien Papers: Ms. 443/2564; sketch and notes by O'Brien.

working men – no succulent ducks were provided by the cook or wine and brandy by the Captain. Upon O'Brien's complaining that the rations were inadequate, the ship's surgeon directed that the men should receive full rations. A day out, after a breakfast of biscuit and tea without milk, O'Brien lamented, 'Did I sigh for the couple of eggs daily administered by the care of Mr Marques in Richmond Prison on first trying a Prisoner's fare at sea.'

As the voyage progressed, the quality of the rations declined, and O'Brien and the others were obliged to eat what remained in the meat cask, a common experience on a long trip. One such meal O'Brien described as about a pound and a half of 'hard dry red carrion' which he thought had been in the cask for many years and had thereby lost 'every particle of its nutritious qualities'. Had it not been for additional food which had been sent to the prisoners by the ship's officers, 'I should have been nearly starved by this time'.[57] There were other adjustments to be made, though the regime could be scarcely described as draconian. On his second day at sea O'Brien momentously noted in his journal: 'Today I made my bed for the first time in my life and am resolved except when prostrated by sea-sickness to continue the practice throughout the voyage.'[58] He was less philosophical about the 9 p.m. lights-out rule. He had counted upon the late evenings for quiet reading and writing: the rule was 'a great privation'.[59]

Instructions had been sent that the prisoners were not to be allowed to send back personal mail by passing homebound ships. They were naturally anxious to assure their families and friends as to their safety and welfare, and this prohibition – clumsily intended to prevent political communications – seemed harsh. On the first occasion, when the Swift came alongside a homebound ship, O'Brien rushed below to scribble a note to his wife, only to find the ship gone when he returned on deck. He was told then by Captain Aldham of the orders prohibiting the sending of correspondence.[60] A fortnight later the Swift encountered another British warship, and O'Brien took his letter unsealed to Captain Aldham,

---

57 *Transportation Journal*, 12–17 August 1849. The food had been good during the first weeks of the voyage, O'Brien recording that 'we have had as yet little reason to complain of our fare. We have had fresh meat very often for which I believe we are indebted to the officers. The only beef is tough, dry and scanty, but the pork, biscuits, preserved meat and tea provided for the ship's company and supplied to us has been on the whole as good as we could have expected' (ibid., 22 July 1849).

58 There followed a little homily to himself (and there would be a number of these): 'Self-reliance is a principle which I have laboured to instil into others. Let me now practice it myself . . . I will now at length endeavour to wean myself from my former habits and learn also never to ask another to do for me what I can do for myself' (ibid., 10 July 1849).

59 And then the lesson: 'On board a ship or in a prison it is much better for a prisoner at once to accommodate his habits to the circumstances in which he is placed rather than to fret himself by discontent or resistance.'

60 O'Brien's apostrophising was on this occasion more justified than usual: 'Savage orders! Could the man who framed those orders know what it is to feel that there is one to whom even the most trivial information respecting his fate would under such circumstances as ours be interesting.' The Captain, perhaps not too happy with his orders, had sent a message back to the men's friends in Ireland saying that they were well (ibid., 26 July 1849).

to be transmitted home via the Admiralty: 'My spleen rises more than I can describe when I find myself thus compelled to submit my correspondence to officials for inspection.'[61]

Apart from the irksomeness inseparable from their penal state, the men seem to have enjoyed the exotic and strange sights, sounds and smells of the voyage. One month out the Captain allowed the prisoners an extra hour on deck each evening, which O'Brien found by far the most agreeable of the day. There were walks on deck, beautiful sunsets and sea creatures to observe, and the ship passed some islands so striking that O'Brien lamented not having taken his sister's gift of a sketchbook with him. On crossing the equator, the whole ship's company, including the prisoners, had a day of fun and pageant, as was the custom. The sensation of isolation on the ocean and removal from all that was familiar could be both depressing and uplifting and this was reflected in O'Brien's various journal entries, which ranged from melancholic self-pity to an apprecia-tion of novelty and strangeness which transcended the circumstances of captiv-ity. In good weather, with a following breeze, he recorded his satisfaction: 'I have seldom enjoyed an hour more than the one spent yesterday by myself in the poop of the vessel. A warm breeze fanned my cheek which was protected from the excessive heat of the sun by the shade of a sail.'[62]

Transportation as a convict – even with the status of state prisoners – inevitably had its bitter and melancholic periods. Yet within these limitations the men recognised that they had been well treated. Thomas Meagher described the ship's commander, Captain Aldham, as a 'most courteous, gentle, amiable, good man' neither officious nor inquisitive, who granted what favours he could.[63] O'Brien, reflecting the confusion of feelings which permeated his journal, claimed that from the moment of his embarkation on the *Swift* he was treated with 'unbecoming severity', but confounded this assertion by admitting that Captain Aldham had behaved towards his charges 'as a gentleman and a naval officer'. This was confirmed in writing at the end of the voyage when the prisoners presented Aldham with a letter thanking him for the 'tact and gentlemanlike feeling with which he carried out his orders'.[64]

---

61 Ibid., 10 August 1849. He went on to express indignation and contempt over what he saw as ungenerous treatment.

62 Ibid., 20 July 1849. He was glad to have escaped for a season from the newspapers and the demands of everyday life, and rejoiced above all 'to have no more the cry of starving multitudes and the whining murmurs of discontented but spiritless slaves. For a brief moment I could almost fancy myself happy.'

63 Arthur Griffith (ed.), *Meagher of the Sword*, Dublin, M. H. Gill & Son, 1916, p. 238.

64 *Freeman's Journal*, 22 June 1850, 2c. Aldham thanked the prisoners for their 'flattering senti-ments, far beyond my deserts' (NLI: O'Brien Papers: Ms. 443/2565). John Martin reported to his brother David: 'The four traitors had quite a pleasant voyage on the Swift. The officers [and] men were all very civil to them & several of them (but of course that is a secret) very familiar & jovial. All the traitors enjoyed right good health at sea' (John to David Martin, 16 November 1849; MLS: A M 87, f. 5).

O'Brien may have been tempted in his public comments to hint at severity, but writing privately to his brother Lucius, he stated that he and the others had disembarked in Van Diemen's Land 'with feelings of the kindliest nature towards Captain Aldham as well as towards the officers and crew of the vessel'.[65] And in a journal which he wrote for his wife (and posted back to her in instalments) O'Brien observed that 'upon the whole my recollections of the *Swift* are far from being as painful as might be expected . . . we had been totally exempt from annoyances on the part of those to whose custody we had been entrusted, so that we parted with feelings of goodwill and esteem'. Indeed, on leaving the ship, he had feelings 'such as those with which we quit a domicile which we may never see again'.[66]

In Van Diemen's Land

The colony to which the men were consigned was far from being the hellhole of moral pestilence which in Britain and Ireland it was imagined – and certainly portrayed – to be. After transportation to New South Wales ceased in 1841 Van Diemen's Land was for some years the only Australian convict penal colony; Western Australia had only months before been so designated.[67] At the time of the state prisoners' arrival, therefore, a very high proportion of the island's population – probably more than half of the adults – were convicts with unexpired sentences, and of the remainder a substantial proportion had either been convicts or were of convict stock.[68] Despite the fearsome demographics, and past economic and administrative difficulties, by 1850 the island seems to have been a tranquil and generally law-abiding place, albeit with an apparent crime rate twice that of England. William Denison, sometime lieutenant-governor, recalled that despite its 'very formidable-looking census' and a tendency on the part of visitors to have 'a sort of morbid dread' of every person they met, and to keep loaded pistols in their pockets, 'life and property were as secure, I may indeed say with truth more secure, than in England: there were no shutters on the windows, no locks to the doors . . . a little after nine o'clock there was not a

---

65 William Smith O'Brien to Sir Lucius O'Brien, 6 December 1849; NLI: O'Brien Papers: Ms. 443/2567.

66 *Maria Island Journal*, Part I, f. 1; NLI: O'Brien Papers: Ms. 449. The *Swift* arrived at Hobart on 27 October 1849 (*Hobart Town Courier*, 31 October 1849, 2d). The arrival of O'Brien and his associates was widely reported in the Australian colonies (see *Argus* (Melbourne), 29 October 1849, 2a).

67 On 1 May 1849, by Order in Council. The first consignment of convicts arrived at Freemantle on 1 June 1850 (James Edward Thomas and Alex Stewart, *Imprisonment in Western Australia*, Nedlands, University of Western Australia Press, 1978, pp. 20–1).

68 In 1847 the population of Van Diemen's Land was around 66,000 of whom 29,000 were convicts. Of the remaining 37,000, several thousand were children and young people (Sir William Denison, *Varieties of Vice-Regal Life*, London, Longmans, Green & Co, 1870, vol. 1, p. 15. See also A. G. L. Shaw, *op. cit.*, p. 343).

sound to be heard, although [Hobart Town] was a seaport'. The various Young Irelanders would discover how tranquil and safe the island actually was, but as they looked on Hobart Town for the first time, they must have shared the 'morbid dread' which Denison found in his visitors.[69]

By the time the first of the exiles arrived the policy on their treatment, only partly formed when Mitchel embarked on his penal wanderings, was well settled. The Colonial Secretary, Earl Grey,[70] instructed Sir William Thomas Denison,[71] Governor of Van Diemen's Land, on the line to be taken. The men had been found guilty of 'the most grave offences against good order and the peace of the country', and they were to be punished. At the same time the punishment was to be appropriate for those 'who belonged to a superior class in society'. It was 'scarcely practicable' and unfair to place them on the same footing as their fellow convicts. The essence of their punishment was banishment and the loss of 'fortune and station'. These were a heavier affliction than for persons from humbler ranks: 'On the whole therefore the practice appears to have been to place such persons in situations of less physical hardship than the generality of convicts although with the liability of being thrown back among the ordinary offenders in case of any misbehaviour or attempt either to escape or create disorder.'[72]

69 Despite his endless imprecations ('Every sight and sound that strikes eye or ear on this mail road, reminds me that I am in a small misshapen, transported, bastard England') Mitchel had to concede that although living in a lonely and unsecured cottage, with two or more prisoner-servants about the place, 'my family have felt as secure, and slept as peacefully, as ever they did in Banbridge' (*Jail Journal*, pp. 238 and 256).

70 (1802–94). Statesman, elder son of second Earl Grey; Colonial Secretary in Lord John Russell's administration, 1846–52. Although, according to the *Dictionary of National Biography* (*DNB*) he was 'somewhat unsympathetic and on all occasions didactic and dogmatic', he was wise enough not to force his favourite projects on unwilling colonists. One of these was the attempted establishment of a convict colony at the Cape in 1849, which the *DNB* notes 'was much resented', and would doubtless have been actively resisted if enforced.

71 (1804–71). Royal Engineer variously employed in Canada, Bermuda and England, having charge for a time of the works at Woolwich dockyard. Appointed as a reforming governor of Van Diemen's Land in 1846 and took up his post in 1847. He saw the colony into its first legislature, and through the labour crisis resulting from the Californian gold rush of 1849. In 1854 appointed Governor of New South Wales. Opposed to the ticket-of-leave system, he believed that punishments should be fully and strictly enforced. Refers to his time in Van Diemen's Land in his memoirs *Varieties of Vice-Regal Life* (vol. 1, pp. 17–279).

72 Earl Grey to Sir William Denison, 5 June 1849, PRO CO/408/32/3874; Governor, Cape of Good Hope to Lieutenant-Governor, Van Diemen's Land, 18 February 1850; MLS: Tasmanian Papers, 102. The precedents (although not directly quoted) went back fifty years, to the rebels of the 1798–1803 uprisings. Whereas the rank and file were treated as ordinary convicts, gentlemen among their leaders were conditionally freed on arrival, or shortly thereafter: class displaced culpability (see A. G. L. Shaw, *Convicts and the Colonies, op. cit.*, pp. 166–71; Patrick O'Farrell, *The Irish in Australia*, Kensington (NSW), New South Wales University Press, 1987, p. 31; see also George Rudé, *Protest and Punishment: The Story of Social and Political Protesters Transported to Australia 1788–1868*, Oxford, Clarendon Press, 1978; Robert Hughes, *The Fatal Shore*, London, Collins Harvill, 1987). Bob Reece's *The Origins of Convict Transportation to New South Wales* (Basingstoke, Palgrave, 2001) is an excellent overview of Irish transportation.

Provided that they had behaved well during the voyage, and gave their parole, they were to be offered tickets of leave. They were each to live in different districts, at a distance from Hobart Town.[73] Other conditions could be decided by Denison. Offences against discipline were to be punished according to the nature of the offence; it was even possible that they could be reduced to the level of common convicts.[74] This lenity was determined largely by the need to calm Irish popular sentiment and to placate the constitutional politicians. The Commons intercession of Smith O'Brien's elder brother Sir Lucius O'Brien was accordingly well received, and his plea may have been behind the statement of Home Secretary Sir George Grey that 'no indignity should be offered on the passage or afterwards'.[75]

For Denison, only nine months in the post, expected to address many pressing colonial problems and a man quite as ambitious as the next, the arrival of the Irish political prisoners was an unwelcome complication. He would, his wife recorded, 'have been full as well pleased if they had been sent anywhere but here, and placed under anybody else's jurisdiction than his'. Matters would have been simplified greatly had he been able to treat them as ordinary convicts.[76] The orders from London were vague to some extent, but what was *very* clear was that they were not to be treated as ordinary criminal convicts. They were, in consequence, 'neither . . . convicts nor . . . free men'.[77] Denison's wife objected

73 Mitchel was made an exception to the separate residence requirement. Dr Gibson, the surgeon of *Neptune* on which Mitchel arrived, certified that because of his state of health he was 'incapable, not merely of maintaining himself, but of performing those ordinary offices which are essential to his existence'. In consequence Mitchel was allowed to live in Bothwell with his friend John Martin (Denison to Grey, 2 May 1850; AOT GO Outward Despatches (OD), GO 33/70, ff. 483–6); see also *Return to the Honourable The House of Commons, dated 16 February, 1875 for Copy of 'Certificate of the Conviction and of the Judgement in the Case of the Queen Against John Mitchel'* [hereinafter *Certificate of the Conviction and Judgement of John Mitchel*], PP, 1875 [50], LXII, 155, 1, 2). Mitchel had no difficulty in requesting this privilege, later explaining to O'Brien: 'I had no scruple at all about asking for this further "indulgence", any more than I w[oul]d hesitate – if I were in an actual Bastille, & knew that a friend was confined in the same, to ask the governor to let me be transferred to *Martin's Corridor*' (Mitchel to O'Brien, dated June 1850, NLI: O'Brien Papers: Ms. 444/2696). The *Irish Exile* described the concession as 'an act of undoubted clemency on the part of Sir William Denison' (13 April 1853, 2d).
74 *Certificate of the Conviction and Judgement of John Mitchel*.
75 John Martin Diary, 16 October 1849; NIPRO; D/560/3, f. 98. See also 3 *Hansard*, CXI, col. 1233; 14 June 1850. Sir George Grey then insisted that 'The government, wishing to act with as much indulgence in this case as was consistent with their public duty, had departed from the usual practice pursued towards ordinary convicts'. This may have been true of the practice towards *ordinary* convicts, but Grey's letter to Denison of 5 June 1849 implied that there was already established a quite different practice for convicts of superior social status (PRO CO/408/9874).
76 And, at least in his early years, Denison favoured individualisation in punishment, and the encouragement of reformation (Denison, *op. cit.*, vol. 1, p. 40). After some years in the colony, however, he became a firm believer in uniformity in retribution and deterrence, which he saw as the primary objectives of punishment (ibid., vol. 1, pp. 281–3 and ch. 8, *passim.*).
77 Ibid., vol. 1, pp. 130–2.

strongly to the inconvenience to which her husband and his colleagues would be subjected by these anomalous exiles; she was also scornful of the thinking behind their treatment. It was true that transportation would fall more heavily on gentlemen than on the lower classes, but so it ought: the education and social position of the gentleman made his crime less excusable; O'Brien, Meagher and the others had used their superiority to lead their ignorant and uneducated countrymen into crimes. But the directions of the Colonial Secretary were as clear in spirit as in language, and, provided the men behaved well, they were not to be degraded to convict status.[78]

Behind the frequently sarcastic and bitter comments of William Denison and his wife lay a good deal of social insecurity and tension, and a realisation that much could go wrong, and there would be little recognition if things simply proceeded as normal – whatever normal meant in the custody of these prisoners. O'Brien was the first (and would be the only) MP to be transported, and his social and political connections had not been sundered by a crime of infamy or moral turpitude. His arrival in this last and least regarded of places of settlement in the Empire was bound to have a local effect and perhaps he would become a focus for popular discontent – free as well as convict. In an imperial society based on precedence he was an acute embarrassment to the Lieutenant-Governor and his lady, and during his years in the colony they took care never to meet him. Next in seniority in the ranks of the political convicts – and the only other man who had a serious potential for trouble-making – was John Mitchel. His was not a social or conventional political danger, but he was possessed of one of the most vitriolic pens then writing in English, loathed the British Empire and all its works, and conducted himself with deliberation. He was open to no inducements and would not easily place himself at the mercy of petty authority. And remote though the colony was, the standing of all the convicts in the eyes of their countrymen across a swathe of opinion and countries of Irish exile was only too clear.

Denison had his foot on the first significant rung of the imperial ladder of dignity and promotion, and well understood the rules for advancement – avoid political troubles, and constantly balance on that point between using one's initiative, making few demands and referring appropriate matters upwards to the Colonial Office. The last was a fundamental problem for all civil servants and required sensitivity, judgement and luck for its resolution. Too frequent and detailed a correspondence meant that one would be seen as lacking in judgement

---

78 This was well received by the colonists, who generally were sympathetic to the men's plight. On arrival they were advised by the *Hobart Town Courier* (31 October 1849, 2b) to 'yield with submission to an inevitable lot'. *Britannia and Trades Advocate*, which maintained a hostile stance, and which thought they were being treated too leniently, compared their lot with that of the Chartists, especially John Frost, who had been well behaved in the colony for some years. Why could he not have the same privileges as the Irish? (*Britannia and Trades Advocate*, 1 November 1849, 2d–e).

and confidence; failure to communicate on what became a key issue indicated lack of judgement and recklessness. Denison correctly calculated that Earl Grey, the Colonial Secretary, would want far more than the usual level of information on these men, but with a time lapse of seven or eight months in the exchange of correspondence with London there could be no shedding of responsibility upwards.

And they were far from being cowed or submissive. Although all but one of the exiles accepted a ticket of leave, they regularly broke its conditions.[79] Despite prohibitions, they contrived regular reunions.[80] Living conditions in the colony were favourable – political rather than penal exile. Before disembarkation the Assistant Registrar took details of their appearance and family circumstances, but, as with Martin and O'Doherty, these interviews were in private, and were conducted with a considerable degree of deference.[81] More sinister was the presence in the colony of two former members of the Confederation, who while in comradeship with O'Brien, Mitchel and the others supposedly had been acting as spies. Mark O'Callaghan and J. D. Balfe (who had been a member of the Confederation Council) were, according to Charles Gavan Duffy's later account, used to watch the exiles in Van Diemen's Land. Balfe, indeed, was allegedly rewarded for his former services by being appointed Deputy Assistant Comptroller of Convicts and a Justice of the Peace with, as Mitchel noted, 'a handsome salary, and a large grant of land'.[82]

Meagher and Mitchel have left a detailed record of their living conditions. The former was assigned to Ross, a small village some seven miles from Campbelltown, his district's principal town. There, looked after by a general servant, he initially had the use of a four-roomed cottage, with a small garden and vegetable plot. The district's settlers included several Irish families who, with

79 Mitchel drew a distinction between his parole, which he was honour-bound to uphold, and the governor's regulations: 'If I disregard them I know the penalty, and run the risk. If I observe them, it is simply to avoid that risk and penalty' (*Irish Exile*, 15 March 1851, 6d).

80 They were each assigned to a separate police district, and it was a condition of their parole not to leave it without a pass. This condition was regularly evaded, seemingly with the connivance of the local authorities. Following the punishment of MacManus, O'Donohoe and O'Doherty for one such illegal gathering, it was argued in the House of Commons that the restriction was not authorised by law. Chisholm Anstey claimed that the Transported Convicts Amendment Act, 1843 (6 & 7 Vict., c.26) rendered earlier convict regulations obsolete. Following the passage of this statute the only obligation on those who were granted a ticket of leave, Anstey insisted, was not to attempt to leave the colony (3 *Hansard*, CXVII, cols 634–8, 12 June 1851). The government's position was that Denison was entitled to set parole conditions, and generally to enforce order and discipline in the colony (ibid., cols 638–40).

81 Griffith, *op. cit.*, pp. 245–6.

82 Mitchel, *Jail Journal*, p. 239. Although Duffy accepted Mitchel's charge that Balfe had been an informer, a more militant nationalist with an even greater reason to detest informers described Mitchel's accusation as 'groundless', and reproached him for having made it. Michael Davitt, *Life and Progress in Australasia*, London, Methuen, 1898, p. 335.

other inhabitants, were happy to welcome him (and subsequently help him).[83] At a later point he moved to a hotel in Ross, and later still began to build his own cottage at Lake Sorell. After sixteen months in the colony Meagher married Catherine Bennett, the daughter of a local farmer, and the couple went to live on Lake Sorell. Even the stern Mitchel began to reflect on domesticity, confessing to his journal that he was 'dreaming how blessed a privilege it is to have a *home*'.[84]

Mitchel's life was equally pleasant – at first an easy bachelor existence near Bothwell with his house-mate Martin, a routine of roaming and exploring the country, spiced with regular illegal but apparently not very risky meetings with his companions. His wife wished to join him and to bring their children. As late as April 1850, Mitchel wrote home dissuading her, but three months later relented: 'I do so pine for something resembling a home. . . . Pray God, I have done right.'[85] To O'Brien Mitchel explained that before arriving in Van Diemen's Land he was insistent that his family should not join him, no matter how long his confinement. He could not think of 'exposing a woman & five children to the felonious atmosphere which I suppose penetrated into the most retired valleys & afflicted the most secluded families'. But in all of this, he admitted, 'I was, if not quite wrong, at least very exaggerative.' His family needed him, and 'I have got rid of so much of my abhorrence of V. D. Land & find some of the people here (Scotch generally) so amiable, so friendly & so anxious to see Mrs Mitchel amongst them . . . that I have actually written to her . . . to come out, & make herself a prisoner here with me.'[86]

With a lifelong love of wild nature and country walking, Mitchel was at once attracted and repelled by his exotic surroundings. The mountains, glens, lakes and streams, and the hours and days he and Martin spent exploring them in boats and on good horses clearly gave him the greatest of pleasure. The native

---

83 T. F. Meagher, 'Personal Recollections', *Irish News*, 17 January 1857, 229c (this was Meagher's New York *Irish News*). Meagher at the time informed O'Brien that he was in 'pretty good spirits' and that he passed his time pleasantly enough 'with my books, my pen and my horse' (Meagher to O'Brien, 11 May 1850; NLI: O'Brien Papers: Ms. 444/2690). Denison disapproved of the men being allowed entry into decent colonial society and, Mitchel alleged, even complained in his dispatches about those colonists who received them (*New York Daily Times*, 24 November 1853, 3a).

84 *Jail Journal*, p. 222. Privately, Mitchel regarded Catherine Meagher, who came from convict stock, to be an unfit bride for his companion.

85 Ibid., pp. 224–5. A letter to Father Kenyon revealed that Mitchel was expecting his wife's arrival 'evidently in delight, poor fellow' (Adelaide to John Dillon, 30 June 1851: TCD: Dillon Papers: MS. 6455–7/146).

86 Mitchel to O'Brien, dated June 1850; NLI: O'Brien Papers: Ms. 444/2696. A factor in Mitchel's change of mind may have been bouts of disagreement between him and John Martin. The latter recorded one such on 22 September 1850 (*after* Mitchel had decided to send for his family, it is true) resulting in a broken sofa and chair. Mitchel, it would seem, was also prone to episodes of demonstrative silence (John Martin Diary, D.560/4; f. 2).

flowers were 'abundant'; many were 'splendid' and one was 'superb'. The whole of the bush was 'adorned with a wonderful variety of plants . . . bearing purple, crimson, scarlet, white, or rose-coloured bells'. The settlers' sweet-briar hedges were 'more uniformly and all over radiant, both summer and winter . . . than I ever saw hedges before'.[87] In the early months of 1851 a letter to his friend, Father Keynon, showed him to be in the highest spirits. Had he remained in Ireland he would by now have been dead, but he was in such health as he had never previously enjoyed.[88] In yet another mood Mitchel found the countryside almost repulsive. Other than the river, nothing sounded or looked like home: 'The birds have a foreign tongue: the very trees whispering to the wind, whisper in accents unknown to me. . . . Yes, all sights and sounds of nature are alien and outlandish.'[89]

But whatever the intermittent consolations of the countryside, ennui, exile, isolation, inactivity and helplessness gnawed at the exiles; their very existence was permeated with self-reproach. They had been involved in the passion and tumult of agitational politics and had cast for their lives in revolutionary times. The contrast between captivity and freedom is the torment of the prisoner, and even on the lakes, heaths and mountains of Van Diemen's Land, with all the freedom of their parole and with the comforts that their private resources could buy for them, their captive condition was corrosive. They resided in a limbo where they could gather news of the real world but, like ghosts and spirits, were unable to affect it. Just two months after his arrival, Meagher, gripped by this realisation and in a deep depression, wrote pitifully to O'Brien:

> So far as we can see, our lives are purposeless for ever – devoid of all high and ennobling pursuits, and cast within a community with which we can have little or no sympathy. . . . Ah! I would prefer, a thousand times, to be back in the old dark cell at the top of Clonmel Gaol [where they stood trial] than remain here, with a 'ticket-of-leave', – sur ma parole d'honneur, for another three weeks. Separation from those whose tastes, sympathies and ideas in great measure harmonize with your own is, in truth, as severe a punishment as could be imposed.[90]

To Mitchel, when he became conscious of it, contentment or any stilling of the agitation of the captive, any transitory contentment or enjoyment betokened

---

87 *Jail Journal*, pp. 228–9: Meagher found the hedges, gardens and cottages of the settlers 'Charming in the extreme' (Griffith, *op. cit.*, p. 241).
88 Reported by Adelaide to John Dillon, 30 June 1851 (TCD: Dillon Papers: Ms. 6455–7/146).
89 *Jail Journal*, p. 226.
90 NLI: O'Brien Papers: Ms. 443, 2591a; Meagher to O'Brien, 16 December 1849. A curious feature of this expression of near despair is that with O'Brien in confinement on Maria Island, Meagher knew that the letter was likely to be read by the Comptroller of Convicts. That being so, what message did he wish to send to Denison?

the more sinister aspect of the island. It was the land of the Lotophagi, those who lived on the soporific lotus, which caused forgetfulness and indolence.[91]

Settling in

But whether it was the effect of the lotus leaf or simply the human need for comfort and routine, the men adapted as best they could, bringing funds from home to rent land and homes. As noted, Meagher had married a local girl;[92] Mitchel sent for his family and settled on a 200-acre livestock farm.[93] Kevin O'Doherty, it is true, pined for a romance broken by his exile; he was allowed to live in Hobart Town, where, having produced his qualifications and passed the local examinations, he practised medicine and was reported to be 'universally respected'.[94] MacManus was said to be the most comfortably off of the group, drawing money quarterly from his Liverpool firm, and spending time farming, hunting and socialising.[95] Patrick O'Donohoe's lack of private means made it

91 'We also, John Knox [Martin] and I, have eaten narcotic lotus here; and if it has not removed, it has surely softened the sting, even of our *nostalgia*' (*Jail Journal*, p. 251). (It will be remembered that some of Odysseus' men who ate the lotus had to be forced back to their ships.) Martin had anticipated this state, writing in his journal aboard ship that although he had been reading about Van Diemen's Land and considering what his life there might be, he was 'wonderfully apathetic. If I can only find an easy & not annoying employment by which I can earn food clothes & lodging, that's all I want' (Diary, *op. cit.*, 21 July 1849; f. 42).

92 A report by William P. Dowling to the *Galway Vindicator* referred to Meagher who 'still resides in his solitary domicil at Lake Sorrell, save that the solitude is now somewhat disturbed by the presence of his amiable and beautiful bride' (reprinted in the *New York Daily Times*, 11 June 1852, 1c).

93 Mitchel's wife Jane and their five children had arrived in June 1851. Mitchel (who ever after would live an itinerant life, and inflict many moves of home on his family) regretted bringing them to Van Diemen's Land. In April 1853, he wrote about his intended escape. It was impossible to contemplate his family staying in Van Diemen's Land for the nine remaining years of his sentence: 'Long since, I have seen that it was unjust and selfish to permit them to come hither at all. . . . Think . . . of a child of mine being christened, married, buried here, – here in these kingdoms of Dis, and under the poisonous shadow of the British flag!' (*New York Daily Times*, 25 November 1853, 3b).

94 O'Doherty to O'Brien, 27 May 1850; NLI: O'Brien Papers: Ms. 444/2691. See also the *New York Daily Times*, 11 June 1852, 1c (letter of William P. Dowling). Mitchel the married man (and whose much desired reunion with his own family was then but a week or so away) could write with some complacency that Kevin O'Doherty was brooding on 'a dark-eyed lady', then in Ireland, 'with hair like blackest midnight; and in the tangle of those silken tresses she has bound my poor friend's soul: round the solid hemisphere it has held him, and he drags a lengthening chain' (*Jail Journal*, p. 231). The 'dark-eyed lady' was Mary Eva Kelly (1826–1910), who under the *nom de plume* 'Eva' wrote patriotic verse for the *Nation*. Hers was the first letter to reach O'Doherty in his exile. She waited for him, and they married on his return to Ireland in 1855. For a brief personal account of the pair see Mark F. Ryan, *Fenian Memories*, Dublin, M. H. Gill & Son, 1945, pp. 172–3.

95 J. Ryan Sheehy (Hobart Town) to J. Sheridan Moore, 3 December 1851(?); MLS: A M/38/15, ff. 3–4.

necessary for him to live in Hobart so that he could earn his living, ostensibly in a lawyer's office.[96] There, to Mitchel's 'utter amazement', he was allowed to establish a newspaper called the *Irish Exile and Freedom's Advocate*, whose politics and preoccupations were much as the masthead suggested.[97] The newspaper carried political and religious articles and fiction, as well as the usual ration of local news, and was reasonably successful in attracting advertising. It says much about the confidence of the authorities that such an enterprise was allowed.[98] Rebel rhetoric might generate a little pro-forma civic heat in Van Diemen's Land, but revolution and disorder were as remote as the island itself.

The strains of political and cultural isolation were never likely to be eased – certainly for most of the men – by the diversions of exotic surroundings, or pioneering, local politics or uxorious domesticity. The arrival of Mitchel's family, Meagher's marriage, O'Donohoe's venture into journalism and the various efforts to adapt that the others made, failed to overcome the tormenting sense of isolation and the bitter passing of time. They were in no way masters of their fate, never mind the destiny of their country. Their manhood was diminished and daily insulted by their reduction to domesticated provincials in the last territory of the Empire. Escape attempts were inevitable, subject only to the demands of honour and of practicality.

---

96 *Hobart Town Advertiser*, 2 November 1849, 2f; *Hobarton Guardian*, 3 November 1849, 2f.

97 Even in Van Diemen's Land convict status and the enmity of government were poor recommendations for employment in a law office. Unable to get work O'Donohoe had persuaded various Hobart sympathisers to fund the newspaper. Mitchel and the other exiles distanced themselves from it, on the grounds that it was published with the indulgence of the authorities. (For a discussion of the authorities' vacillating attitude towards O'Donohoe's *Irish Exile* see Richard Davis, 'Exiles from Erin', *op. cit.*, pp. 254–7.)

98 The more conservative newspapers in Van Diemen's Land and New South Wales were critical of the decision to allow O'Donohoe to publish (see the *Irish Exile*, 23 February 1850, 3a–c; 16 March 1850, 3d). Denison in a letter to Earl Grey appears to have had second thoughts, perhaps in the light of such complaints. He had not expected the newspaper to appear, 'and even now I question very much whether it will be able to drag on its existence for any lengthened period'. Through the Comptroller General of Convicts, Dr Hampton, O'Donohoe had been informed that he could not publish 'any comment whatever upon the acts of measures of the government'. If he did so he would be dealt with as a convict. This had brought an abject letter of submission (Denison to Grey, 29 January 1850 (with enclosures); AOT: GO, OD, GO 33/69, ff. 417–29). With his dispatch Denison enclosed a copy of the *Irish Exile*. Grey's response was blunt. '[I]f these prisoners should abuse the indulgence which has been shewn to them by an endeavour to create misconduct, and disturb society, they should . . . be immediately deprived of their ticket-of-leave, and remanded to the condition of ordinary convicts' (Grey to Denison, 29 April 1850; ibid., GO, ID, 1/77, ff. 223–5). Government was less sensitive about O'Donohoe giving offence to private individuals, and when one Thomas Reading complained that he had been named by the *Irish Exile* as a person who had given evidence against O'Brien in 1848, he was advised to seek the usual civil remedy (MLS: Tasmanian Papers, 103; Thomas Reading to (Hobart) Colonial Secretary, 27 November 1850).

Honourable escapes

Terence Bellew MacManus fled on 21 February 1851. He had challenged Governor Denison's order committing him to penal labour at the Cascades penal station (a punishment for an illegal meeting with O'Doherty and O'Donohoe),[99] obtaining his release on a writ of habeas corpus. Since Denison had suspended his ticket of leave MacManus considered it possible to escape without formally withdrawing his parole.[100] He arrived in San Francisco on 5 June 1851, where, in what was to become a pattern, he received an effusive welcome from members of the Irish community.[101] On 3 January 1852, he sent letters and business cards from his safe haven to his various friends in Van Diemen's Land, and to Governor Denison and the Comptroller-General of Convicts.[102] Thomas Meagher resigned his parole by sending a note to the local magistrate giving twenty-four hours' notice of his intention. He claimed that, protected by friends, he had presented himself to the officers who came to arrest him. He also reached America, arriving in New York on 26 May 1852, to many demonstrations of welcome and regard. This account he gave of withdrawing his parole was said to be untrue, and it followed that his escape had been dishonourable.[103] Disturbed

---

99 *Irish Exile* (15 March 1851, 6a–b) gave an account of MacManus' escape, arguing that he was driven to it. MacManus' description of his time under punishment, and other interesting information, is given in Brendan O'Cathaoir's 'Terence Bellew McManus: Fenian Precursor', *Irish Sword*, 16 (63), 1985, pp. 105–9. In the colony – among sympathisers at least – MacManus' stock was high, and his escape was considered honourable – 'pure and untainted' (J. Ryan Sheehy (Hobart Town) to J. Sheridan Moore, 3 December (?)1851; MLS: A M 38/5, f. 3).

100 The pro-government *Hobart Town Advertiser* claimed that MacManus' legal victory was due to a technical error in the legal proceedings; it also defended Denison's treatment of the prisoners (25 February 1851, 2d; 4 March, 2d; 7 March, 2b–c).

101 See report of British Consulate to Australian Governor General, 19 June 1851; MLS: Tasmanian Papers (TP), 101 [FM4/8512]. There were several celebratory demonstrations and a week after his arrival the honour of a public dinner and ball. The event was chaired by Charles Brenham, Mayor of San Francisco, and guests included Senator William Gwin and various judges, local politicians and army officers. A silver pitcher was presented to the captain of the ship in which MacManus had made his escape (see the *Daily Alta California*, 6 June 1851, 2c; 7 June 1851, 2c; 8 June 1851, 2c; 13 June 1851, 2c; 14 June 1851, 2c; 4 August 1851, 2a). The arrival of MacManus and later escapers were significant episodes in the early history of California (which had entered the Union as a state only nine months before MacManus' arrival). For accounts of the Irish in California, and reaction to MacManus, see Jay Monaghan, *Australians and the Gold Rush: California and Downunder*, Berkeley, University of California Press, 1966, pp. 205–22, *passim.*; Patrick J. Downling, *California: The Irish Dream*, San Francisco, Golden Gate Publishers, 1988, pp. 199–201; R. A. Burchell, *The San Francisco Irish: 1848–1880*, Manchester, Manchester University Press, 1979, pp. 6–7; Dr Quigley, *The Irish Race in California and the Pacific Coast*, San Francisco, A. Roman & Co, 1878, pp. 322–6.

102 *New York Daily Times*, 11 June 1852, 1c. Deninson may have sent one of these letters with a dispatch to Earl Grey (Denison to Grey, 10 October 1851; AOT: GO, OD, GO 33/74, f. 497).

103 Mitchel and John Martin investigated Meagher's story, and disbelieved his claim that he had given the constables a chance to arrest him. They therefore wrote and asked him to return to Van Diemen's Land (O'Doherty to O'Brien, 1852; O'Brien Papers: NLI: MS. 444/2799).

71

by reports which had been copied from the European and Australasian papers, Meagher set out his version of events in a letter to the *New York Daily Times*. The essence of the story was that on 3 January 1852, he had written a letter to the police magistrate of the District of Campbelltown, stating his intention to withdraw his parole at his residence at noon on the following day, 4 January. Meagher lived thirty miles from the District Police Office and did not expect a quick response, but shortly after 7 p.m. on the day of the letter his friends told him that a police patrol was approaching, intending to arrest him. He left his house and hid in the bush. When the police arrived, Meagher claimed that he presented himself on horseback at the front of his house, challenged them to arrest him, and fled, accompanied by his friends.[104] He made his way to the west, where after a short delay he was taken up by their ship which he had arranged to collect him.[105]

So concerned was he, even at liberty, that anyone should think that he had behaved dishonourably that he offered good bourgeois references in support of his story to the leading newspaper of the colony: 'The men who vouched with their signatures for the truth of the statement then made, and now repeated, are men of considerable property and highly creditable position in the Colony, and no one there would be rash enough to speak a single word derogatory to their honour.'[106]

O'Doherty would have none of this: 'I, for my part, lament nothing now in his escape except the letters which Mitchel and Martin wrote him, which I fear will either draw him back here or embitter his life much.' To the colonial authorities Meagher's escape was merely proof of his rapscallion nature. Lady Denison conceded that he had gone through the form in writing to the authorities, 'But he took care to be off before this intimation could reach them, or at any rate, before they could possibly take any steps in consequence.' She thought he had broken his word as completely as if he had never given notice at all, since he had clearly taken advantage of the liberty he had enjoyed under his ticket of leave to prepare his escape, and to flee before steps could be taken against him. The Irish rebels' idea of honour was a strange one and perhaps the home government would now recognise that 'they made altogether a mistake in treating them like honourable men, as prisoners of war, rather than as convicted felons'. Had Meagher been recaptured, her husband had determined to send him to the convict barracks, where he would be put to penal labour – a 'bottom sawyer' under a very good 'top one' (*op. cit.*, vol. 1, pp. 181–2).

104 Denison gave a different account to Earl Grey: Meagher was gone when the police arrived; there was no mention of his presenting himself (Denison to Grey, 27 April 1851; AOT: GO, OD, GO 33/76, ff. 245–8).

105 Denison was convinced that the ship was the *Elizabeth Thompson*, captained by Betts, who had assisted in MacManus' escape (for which he had received a silver cup and large reward in San Francisco): Denison to Earl Grey, 31 January 1852; AOT: GO, OD, GO 33/75, ff. 332–5.

106 *New York Daily Times*, 7 June 1852, 2c. O'Brien reported to his wife that Meagher with 'the assistance of faithful and energetic friends . . . has been enabled I trust to place himself beyond the reach of the petty persecutors who rule this Colony'. A great and bright career would be open to him in America, but had he remained in Van Diemen's Land 'nothing would have prevented him from degenerating into something very unlike the being which nature formed him to be!' O'Brien had seen Catherine Meagher who appeared to be 'very cheerful and hopeful about him – but cannot expect to see him for more than a year – or to hear of him in less than six months' (William to Lucy, 18 January 1852; NLI: O'Brien Papers: Ms. 8653/28).

All of this must have seemed arcane and bizarre to the City of Tammany. Meagher was safe under the stars and stripes. Many Irish-Americans loathed the government which had condemned him. The notion that there could be rules for escape would have been hard to grasp, and even harder to take seriously: in the real world the punctilio of honourable escape counted for nothing at all.[107] Meagher gave lectures to packed halls on his Van Diemen's Land experience, obtaining £300 for his first New York appearance, with the expectation of a further few thousand in the following year.[108]

On 2 December 1850 MacManus, O'Doherty and O'Donohoe visited O'Brien at New Norfolk to celebrate his release. Subsequently O'Donohoe was arrested for being drunk and disorderly, and together with O'Doherty and MacManus was, in January 1851, on Governor Denison's orders, committed to a penal station (on the Tasman Peninsula) for breaking the conditions of parole.[109] This was described by the *Hobarton Guardian* as 'petty tyranny'.[110] The three men were subject to the usual regime of penal labour. O'Doherty was put to splitting shingles and MacManus to loading timber. Because of the injuries sustained during his drunken escapade, O'Donohoe was at first too weak to work, but on his recovery he too was put to logging.[111] Released after three months, O'Donohoe lost his ticket of leave six months later, possibly for an escape attempt. Although his detention on this occasion did not last long, O'Donohoe was in trouble again in January 1852 when he drunkenly renounced his parole. On recovering

---

107 For a description of Meagher's reception in New York, which included addresses, military parades and a presentation (he declined a public dinner), see the *New York Daily Times*, 29 May 1852, 2d; 11 June 1852, 1b–c; *New York Tribune*, 29 May 1852, 7a; 7 June 1852, 11a).

108 Dillon to O'Brien, 12 December 1852; NLI: O'Brien Papers: Ms. 445/2842. Dillon reported that Meagher had 'borne his honour, with modesty, dignity and distinction'.

109 The police magistrate had reprimanded the men. Denison evidently considered this too light a punishment, and ordered their incarceration. AOT: GO, OD, GO 33/75, ff. 736–9. There was a great deal of local indignation at this official mean-mindedness. The *Hobarton Guardian* asked why the state prisoners were denied a freedom of movement available to other ticket of leave convicts (25 December 1850, 3a). Their punishment was imposed at Denison's direction, overturning the police magistrate's decision simply to reprimand the men. This was regarded as excessively harsh, since a reprimand was the usual penalty (ibid., 28 December 1850, 2c). This denunciation was followed by several local newspapers – the *Cornwall Chronicle*, *Colonial Times* and *Launceston Examiner* (ibid., 1 January 1851, 3a–d). Denison had taken care to report the matter immediately to the Colonial Secretary, however, who on 29 May signified his approval (AOT: GO, ID, GO 1/81, ff. 403–4).

110 21 December 1850, 2d.

111 O'Donohoe had got into a brawl with John Moore, editor of the *Hobarton Guardian*. Both men had been placed in the New Norfolk lock-up and fined the next day. It was this that attracted Denison's ire. The *Hobarton Guardian*, ironically, was a champion of the men's cause (ibid., 4 January 1851, 2b–e). The *Irish Exile* (edited by Patrick McSorley during O'Donohoe's incarceration) insisted that while at Port Arthur O'Donohoe had been placed under the supervision of the thrice-convicted Booth, the overseer of the scavengers. O'Donohoe 'is now plunged neck-deep in the disgusting cess-pool called Port Arthur – working in a gang with the refuse of the penal colony' (8 February 1851, 7a).

sobriety he reinstated it, but was sentenced to a fortnight in Launceston Gaol for his drunkenness. In the course of that confinement it was claimed that he was put on the tread-wheel – a degrading and humiliating punishment reserved for petty offenders.[112] O'Donohoe took his repeated sentences of imprisonment as evidence of Denison's breach of the implicit compact between the authorities and the exiles, and accordingly felt free to escape, even though he was at large on a ticket of leave.[113] With the assistance of friends he was able to make his way to the Australian mainland and thence, via Tahiti, to San Francisco, arriving on 22 June 1853.[114]

In 1848 the Irish Directory in New York had raised substantial funds to support the Young Ireland rising. Before the funds could be disbursed, news came of its suppression. Despite subsequent appeals to spend the money on cultural and religious projects in America, the fund was preserved. This reserve was now applied to the deliverance of the remaining exiles in Van Diemen's Land. Priority was given to O'Brien, whose liberation would have been a considerable coup, but there were funds enough to take more than one person. Patrick James Smyth,[115]

112 *Hobart Town Courier* (14 January 1852, 3c), citing *Cornwall Chronicle* (10 January 1852, 19c). O'Donohoe's lack of sobriety and occasional wild episodes led to rumours that his companions were ashamed of him. On at least two occasions he published denials of this including support- ive letters from Mitchel, Martin and O'Meagher (*Irish Exile*, 4 May 1850, 2a–d). His wider reputation was blasted, however. A resident of Hobart Town, very sympathetic to the political convicts, in December 1851 wrote that 'O'Donohue [*sic*] has disgraced himself, his country and fellow exiles, he's in fact – a b[lackguar]d the name given him by them, and by every other respectable person in the island' (J. Ryan Sheehy to J. Sheridan Moore, 3 December 1851 (?); MLS: A M 38/5, f. 4). See also Roger Therry (New South Wales lawyer and judge) to J. A. Donaldson, 10 July 1856, defending the political character of the Young Ireland prisoners – by that time pardoned or escaped: 'O'Brien was more of a fool than a felon. . . . Yet he was a gentleman . . . Michell [*sic*] was a truculent madman, & Donohue [*sic*] a most disreputable fellow but still their offence was a political one' (MLS: 17/3, ff. 1–4, *passim.*).

113 It seems that it was Mitchel who developed this doctrine. P. J. Smyth explained it to O'Brien: 'an arrest by any authorised officer of the Government, no matter in what quarter of the Island it may be made, discharges the parole' (Smyth to O'Brien, 5 August 1853; NLI: O'Brien Papers: Ms. 445/2846).

114 While still in Van Diemen's Land, O'Donohoe had written an account of his persecution by Denison and his administration. This was to have been published in the colony, 'but in consequence of the gold discovery printers cannot be procured at any price – they are all gone to the diggings' (*New York Daily Times*, 11 June 1852, 1c). O'Brien considered that O'Donohoe *had* escaped in violation of his parole but thought that the circumstances had mitigated the offence: 'Though I could not have counselled or assisted him to escape under the circumstances, yet I am not sorry that he is gone. He has been most infamously treated by the local gov[ernmen]t and if ever the doctrine that an extorted promise is not binding is applicable, it is applicable in his case' (William to Lucy O'Brien, 12 January 1853: NLI: O'Brien Papers: Ms. 8653/29).

115 (1826–85). In America had worked as a journalist. Returned to Ireland in 1856, where he was called to the Bar, but did not take up legal practice. Elected MP for Westmeath in 1871 as a member of Butt's Home Rule Party, and from 1880 until 1882 sat for Tipperary. Opponent of Parnell and Land League. Accepted a government appointment in late 1884 amidst much nationalist criticism, but held the post for only a few weeks before his death.

one of the leaders who had escaped in 1848 to America, was sent by the Directory to Van Diemen's Land to conduct the affair. He arrived early in January 1853. O'Brien considered the possibility of an honourable escape to be so high that he warned his wife that the attempt might come within the year.[116] After further consideration, however, he decided to continue to wait for the pardon which would allow him to return to Ireland.

In the light of O'Brien's decision not to escape, Smyth arranged for Mitchel to make the attempt.[117] As always for the Young Irelanders the etiquette was elaborate and strictly observed, so that the authorities could not afterwards charge dishonour; Mitchel's was to be another chivalrous escape. He would have been content to take any arrest by any officials as a discharge of his parole, and such an arrest could have been contrived in circumstances favourable to an escape. Prompted by O'Donohoe's escape, O'Brien and O'Doherty had enunciated a different doctrine – only a personal surrender in the district police office would suffice. Possibly concerned that his companions might criticise him for dishonourable behaviour (as he and Martin had judged Meagher), Mitchel felt obliged to abide by their interpretation of the requirements of parole.[118] In consequence, on 9 June 1853, accompanied by Smyth, he delivered to the Bothwell District Assistant Police Magistrate a note withdrawing his parole (which he called his 'comparative liberty'). With a certain amount of menace he then made his exit, and, according to his account, faced only with feeble attempts to stop them, he and Smyth rode off.[119] The Assistant Police Magistrate

---

116 12 January 1853; NLI: O'Brien Papers: Ms. 8653/29. 'I think I ought to inform you that unless some change for the better takes place during the present year it is my firm intention to resign my ticket of leave and to take the chance of an escape.' He would accept from the authorities any enlargement of the conditions of his parole, 'but nothing short of an absolute and unconditional amnesty will be considered by me as a boon'.

117 Martin was also offered the chance of escape, but declined it, a decision which P. J. Smyth thought he had subsequently regretted (Smyth to O'Brien, 5 August 1853; NLI: O'Brien Papers: Ms. 445/2846).

118 The issue was discussed by Smyth in a letter to O'Brien, after Mitchel's escape (5 August 1853; NLI: O'Brien Papers: Ms. 445/2846).

119 Mitchel, *Jail Journal*, pp. 275–7. According to Duffy, Mitchel had arranged that bribes should be paid so that he would not be stopped by the convict constables as he rode off. How Duffy came by the information is not clear, but it is consistent with the circumstances (Duffy to O'Brien, 2 December 1854; NLI: Ms. 445/2877). In a letter to Reilly, dated 26 April 1853, Mitchel set out the justification for his intended escape – essentially the packed jury at his trial and the ill-treatment he received after conviction. He also indicated the means by which he intended to escape, including the withdrawal of his parole (see the *New York Daily Times*, 20 November 1853, 3a–b, for the full text). In a letter to a mutual friend John Martin gave more detail of Mitchel's escape (P. A. Sillard, *The Life and Letters of John Martin*, pp. 152–6). It is interesting that Martin wrote and posted this account while he was still in Van Diemen's Land. He evidently had enough confidence in the government's honour to believe that the letter would not be intercepted, just as O'Brien had had, when he warned his wife that he might escape during 1853.

told a different tale. Mitchel entered his office and, handing over a letter addressed to the Lieutenant-Governor, 'instantly quitted before I could peruse the note, and mounting a horse, which he had waiting at the gate, galloped furiously off'. Mitchel's note withdrew his parole and concluded 'I shall forthwith present myself before the police magistrate of Bothwell at his police office, show him this letter, and offer myself to be taken into custody'. The Assistant Police Magistrate described the last part of Mitchel's letter as 'a deliberate lie'.[120] Then and thereafter Mitchel had no doubt that he had acted in an honourable way, nor had that *doyen* of honourable prisoners, O'Brien.[121] The escape was well planned, but ran into some difficulties. After several weeks concealed by sympathisers (including some time in the costume of a Roman Catholic priest) he obtained passage, first to Sydney, and from there onward to San Francisco, which he reached with his family (who had joined him en route) on 9 October 1853.[122]

120 *Certificate of the Conviction and Judgement of John Mitchel*, p. 3. Mitchel's escape was well received by some sections of colonial society. On 11 June the *Hobarton Guardian* was enthusiastic: 'We have much pleasure in announcing the escape of another of the Political Victims of '48.' It would be better to pardon them all, the newspaper observed (2f).

121 William Dillon, *op. cit.*, p. 14. Charles Gavan Duffy, who had become a bitter enemy of Mitchel after Mitchel's attack on his character, told O'Brien that 'nothing in my life surprised me so much as your justifying the course he took'. Duffy disputed Mitchel's reasoning; were he excused the obligations of his parole by the oppressiveness of his gaolers, then why was it necessary to stage the farce of offering himself for arrest? While it would not, in Duffy's view, have been honourable or admirable to run off without notice, then at least that would have been more consistent with Mitchel's rationale of oppressiveness (Duffy to O'Brien, 2 December 1854; NLI: O'Brien Papers: Ms. 445/2877). Duffy and Mitchel were now enemies and therefore the former's criticism might be discounted. More telling was John Martin's retrospective view of the matter: 'There was also the distressing subject of his escape from V. D. Land which was condemned as inconsistent with honour by some honest and friendly persons, in particular by the Simpsons. I lost the confident hopes I had rested on him' (Diary, *op. cit.*, *Paris Journal*, f. 133). But Michael Davitt, who visited Tasmania more than forty years later, and who was fairly critical of Mitchel, was able to meet and interview several of those who assisted in the escape. He acquitted Mitchel of any dishonour in the matter. One of Mitchel's felonious helpers had later become a justice of the peace and an MP (Michael Davitt, *Life and Progress in Australasia*, p. 317).

122 He described his adventures in a letter to George Barker (who had sheltered him) written in Hobart Town in July 1853, before he made his final departure. The letter was signed 'John Mitchel, alias Johnston, alias Baker, alias Macnamara, alias Blake, alias Wright' (Mitchel to Barker, ?13 July 1853; MLS: A M 141/2). See also the detailed account by one of his helpers, Daniel Burke. From attached correspondence this appears to have been written many years after the events (MLS: A M 141/1). An account of Mitchel's escape was also given by P. J. Smyth in a letter to O'Brien, sent from Sydney after he had seen Mitchel and his family safely of their way (Smyth to O'Brien, 5 August 1853; NLI: O'Brien Papers: Ms. 445/2846). Mitchel's success in eluding capture, according to Smyth, was due to the government's failure to mount a sufficiently vigorous search, and the strong sympathy of the colonists: 'There is not, I believe, a respectable colonist in the Island to whose house Mitchel might not have gone at any hour of the day or night with the certainty of finding a refuge, and of being provided with horses, guides, and if need were, money for his escape.' Such was the strong feeling in their favour, Smyth insisted, that none of the remaining prisoners need remain in captivity any longer than they chose.

Although urged by the Irish community to remain in California, Mitchel pressed on to New York, which he and his family reached on 29 November 1853. At both cities he was met with many demonstrations of honour and acclaim.[123]

As might be expected, local politicians and community leaders, in conveying congratulations and good wishes to Mitchel and his family, also sought a measure of reflected glory and glamour. The reception of the escaped Young Irelanders established a pattern which would repeat itself several times in the following twenty years, culminating in a fracas which bordered on kidnapping when the amnestied Fenians reached the United States of America in 1871. But the faults were not all on one side, and Mitchel, vehement in his public persona, used the attention which was heaped upon him to vilify the British.[124] This was probably fair enough: he was an Irish revolutionary and entitled to castigate his enemies. What was less acceptable in a man who claimed always to act in accordance with a code of honour was his misrepresentation of the treatment he had received since conviction, and the conditions of his exile.

Two weeks after Mitchel's arrival in San Francisco a public dinner was held in his honour, attended by between 400 and 700 people.[125] The Governor of California presided, assisted by the Mayor of San Francisco, and a number of other prominent state, city, military and religious figures: it was a ceremony prepared and carried through without stinting. The numbers, the conviviality, the romance of the escaped exile and the fervour of patriotism, Irish and American, brought great emotional heat to the evening. This was not an occasion for lame and rather lacklustre fact; only fable and rhetoric met the mood. Mitchel, whose romantic impulses had pitched him into prison, was equal to the challenge.

After five weary years of living death, 'immured in dungeons by land and sea or eating the bitter bread of penal exile in the depths of the forests of a convict colony', he was, he said, one who had to open his eyes slowly, bedazzled by 'this Republican festival'. His thoughts went to his still-imprisoned comrades and his broken country. He was scornful of the attempts to ameliorate conditions in Ireland, and promised that the deaths and forced emigration of the famine years would not be forgotten or forgiven. He had been freer in a Bermudan hulk than

123 *Daily Alta California*, 13 October 1853, 1f, 2a and 2b; 14 October, 2b; 15 October, 2a; *New York Tribune*, 30 November 1853, 4,e–f; *New York Daily Times*, 30 November 1853, 1b.

124 In his insistence, both in San Francisco and New York, that the welcome and public honours he received amounted to an insult to England, Mitchel went further than many of his hosts thought appropriate – business was business, and Britain remained a major trading partner. His speech in New York shows signs of pique at the criticism of this aspect of his remarks (*New York Daily Times*, 20 December 1853, 1c–d).

125 *Nevada Journal*, 4 November 1853, 1a. The *Daily Alta California* (15 October 1853, 3a) gave a lower figure – 400 – for attendance.

the 'unhappy Irishman who saunters and simpers in the Dublin Crystal Palace'. Even though a false and malign peace and order now reigned there, he looked forward to the next European convulsion when 'thrones and principalities will totter and rush down into chaos before the stormy wrath and execrations of God and men'. Justifiably, he charged the British with having brought in special legislation to net him, and of having packed his jury – but went on to denounce them for 'bolting me in irons and carrying me to Bermuda and . . . to the Cape of Good Hope, and to Van Diemen's Land and [for] deliberately endeavouring for two whole years to procure my death underhand in secret dungeons'. Yet 'In the worst and blackest of my many dungeons my enemies never extorted from me one word of submission.' He had always worn his fetters 'lightly as wreaths of roses'. Rage, scorn, vengeance and a belief in God's justice had kept him alive when his enemies had sought to kill him by 'long and rigorous confinement in an unwholesome den'. He was grateful that his enemies had refused to liberate him and that he had been freed by the daring and energy of his brave confederate (Patrick James Smyth) who sat at the table.[126]

This was a wished-for martyrdom, a catalogue of imagined sufferings. His stay at Bermuda had been terminated because government feared for his health, and wished, if not for altruistic then for political reasons, to protect it. And he could hardly blame the British Empire for the ill winds which prolonged his voyage to the Cape, or for the rebelliousness of the settlers which prevented him from landing here. That left his treatment in Van Diemen's Land, and this, by his own *Jail Journal* (at that time still to be published), was painful mainly for its ennui and suspended animation. His career as a convict was limited indeed: he may have *wished* it more, or in the spotlight of that moving 'Republican festival' have believed it more – but it is hard to construct martyrdom from the actual history of his exile.

A revolutionary of a later generation, one who undoubtedly sat in dungeons and ate the bitter food of captivity, passed his judgement on Mitchel's experience. Between the punishment of the rank-and-file pikeman of 1798 and the Young Irelanders there was no comparison: '[W]e see the men of [1848] "sitting placid under a honeysuckle tree, basking in the balmy air", as John Mitchel writes of himself at Bothwell but must to Marcus Clarke's book [*The Term of His Natural Life*] to learn what tortures and indignities had to be endured by the men [of 1798]'. As for himself, 'With recollections of Millbank and Dartmoor in my mind, during my stay in Tasmania, I could not help being a little envious of my immediate and more fortunate political forbears of the Irish movement.'[127]

---

126 Ibid., 26 October 1853, 2c–d. Many other speeches were made, and the dinner did not finish until past 1 a.m.
127 Michael Davitt 1898, p. 333.

Honourable captivity

Since his arrival in Van Diemen's Land William Smith O'Brien had acted with scrupulous regard for his honour.[128] He alone had refused a ticket of leave.[129] In an effort to make him agree to accept parole, he claimed, he was told that Maria Island was 'a sort of hell upon Earth' where he would be subject to 'whatever torments and provocations, the malignant injustice of man could suggest'.[130] O'Brien's sense of his leadership determined him to resist and set an example. The British and Irish press had cast him in the role of leader of the insurrectionists, as had the other Young Irelanders. He was the oldest among them, a generation ahead, and well into middle age when most of them were in young manhood. One of a relatively small group of liberal Protestant landowners who had vented Irish social and political grievances, O'Brien was an established public figure. His twenty years in Parliament had gained him a respectful if not always sympathetic hearing there. Even among revolutionaries – and certainly in the public mind – his status as a landowner, MP and former magistrate added considerably to his standing: at the very least it was concluded that he had something to lose. That the imprisoned O'Connell had chosen him as his deputy, in charge of the Repeal Association, had been a clear certification of his national status. None other among the insurrectionists came close in Irish (or British) esteem. Conscious of his personal, social and political standing, and claiming a place in his country's history, O'Brien decided not to treat with the enemy.[131] He would not, by giving his parole, become his own gaoler; he saw his duty to preserve every chance of honourable escape; he may also have calculated that this was a way of maintaining the pressures for a pardon. Captain Aldham of the *Swift* told

---

128 To his enemies, O'Brien was devoured by vanity. When the emergency legislation to remove doubts about the commutation of his death sentence came before the Lords, Lord Brougham spoke of 'perverted love of distinction . . . that absurd and preposterous personal vanity' (3 *Hansard*, CVI, cols 161–2; 14 June 1849). Duffy insisted that he was 'proud, not vain', though he conceded that he was 'a little too anxious, perhaps' that his conduct should be always seen to correspond with his long descent: 'But he never sought to derive from his rank anything but its obligations, and his standard of a gentleman's duty was more strictly enforced against himself than against any one else' (1883, p. 199). Denis Gwynn closely reviewed O'Brien's convict diary (comprising the letters O'Brien wrote from exile to his wife) and found it courageous and patriotic in sentiment, 'combined with great personal dignity, a genuine humility and deeply religious sense, and a remarkable keen and highly cultured intelligence'. It is fair to note, however, that Gwynn's evaluation of O'Brien may have been affected, to some extent at least, by the fact that he was his subject's great-grandson (Preface, pp. ii and iii).

129 MacManus at first determined to stand with O'Brien in withholding his parole, and to accept the consequent close confinement on Maria Island, but changed his mind at the last moment and accepted a ticket of leave (Denison, *op. cit.*, Vol. 1, p. 134).

130 *Maria Island Journal*, f. 2.

131 John Martin speculated that O'Brien must have considered the giving of parole to be an acknowledgement of the justice of the proceedings against him, and of his own criminality, 'But certainly [?] I don't understand the matter in that way' (John to David Martin, 16 November 1849; MLS: A M 87, f. 4).

Governor Denison that O'Brien wished to be made a martyr: '[H]e would really like to be treated with severity, that he might have something to a sensation, and excite commiseration with . . .'.[132]

Since he would not give his parole O'Brien was not permitted to land at Hobart Town, but was kept on board ship until arrangements were made for his transfer to the probation station on Maria Island, some ten miles off the coast of Van Diemen's Land.[133] This was an exclusively penal settlement, populated only by convicts and prison staff and their families. No civilians were allowed access to the island without government permission. He was told that he should expect to remain there for as long as his parole was withheld.[134] Even so, he continued to enjoy special treatment. He wore his own clothes and was not subject to the penal regime. Accommodated in a cottage and garden in the officers' quarters he was allowed an officer's fuel and light allowance, a hospital ration of food, a servant to wait on him, and as many books as he wanted.[135] For a few initial days he was allowed to associate with the senior staff and their families, a number of whom, including the Superintendent, were Irish. All treated him with courtesy and friendliness.[136] He was given 'every indulgence that was consistent with my safe custody.'[137] But Denison soon concluded that a policy of laissez-faire would not lead O'Brien to accept a ticket of leave with its implied submission and acceptance of obligations. Dr John Stephen Hampton, Comptroller-General of Convicts, arrived with more stringent instructions.[138]

132 Denison, *op. cit.*, Vol. 1, p. 134. This report was probably true, but must be treated with some caution since it was recorded by Denison's wife who, largely for reasons of domestic convenience, was hostile towards the Young Irelanders. To her record of Aldham's remarks she added the caustic observation that Maria Island would probably disgust O'Brien since she would have 'no martyrdom, no grievance and *nobody to hear of it* if he had one!' (ibid.).

133 The term 'probation station' may mislead the modern reader. 'Probation' referred to the preliminary stage of convict progress, and was a form of imprisonment. Good behaviour earned promotion to the higher and freer stages, culminating in the ticket of leave.

134 NLI: O'Brien Papers: Ms. 443/257: Assistant Comptroller of Convicts to William Smith O'Brien, 29 October 1849. He had initially been threatened with assignment to a convict labour gang and the convict uniform, according to the *Hobarton Guardian* (24 November 1849, 2c). Denison had immediately informed the Colonial Office of his decision on O'Brien. This had brought back a letter of approval from Earl Grey (Grey to Denison, 29 April 1850; AOT: GO, ID, GO 1/77, ff. 221–2).

135 Mitchel to Dillon, 9 November 1850: *cit.* William Dillon, *op. cit.*, vol. I, p. 318.

136 *Hobarton Guardian*, 26 October 1850, 3c; ibid., 20 November 1850, 4a. See also PRO CO 280/249/2759; *Maria Island Journal*, ff. 4–5 (31 October to 6 November 1849).

137 William Smith O'Brien to Sir Lucius O'Brien, 6 December 1849; NLI: O'Brien Papers: Ms. 443/2567.

138 (?1810–69). Would play a major part in convict and colonial affairs during his career. An Edinburgh medical education was followed by six years as a naval surgeon, including convict ship postings. Comptroller-General of Convicts, Van Diemen's Land 1846–55. After a dispute with the Legislative Council and allegations of corrupt practices Hampton went on half pay to Canada. Governor of Western Australia, 1862–8, where he again became closely and controversially involved in convict administration.

A regime of what O'Brien called 'petty persecution' now began. He was not to be received by the officers who, other than in the course of their duties, were also forbidden to speak to him. His freedom of movement at the probation station was restricted to 200 yards of the convict buildings; all incoming and outgoing mail was to be inspected and he was forbidden to write 'in disrespectful terms' about the conditions of his confinement.[139] He was not allowed access to his private funds until he should accept a ticket of leave. This meant that he could not make any purchases of additional food.[140] A week later conditions were further tightened, effectively consigning O'Brien to his cottage and its potato garden – to separate and silent imprisonment. He was locked in his bedroom from sunset until the morning muster of the convicts. The Super-intendent of Convicts, Samuel Lapham, visited him four times a day, and the fastenings of his bedroom were inspected three times each night. In order that the keys to O'Brien's quarters should not fall into other hands, Lapham person-ally locked his door at night and unlocked it in the morning. The rules strictly forbade any person 'male or female, child or fullgrown, convict or free' to speak to him[141] – a level of custody imposed on no other convict except for those under punishment for an offence.[142] Writing to his MP brother Lucius (in a letter which he knew would be seen by the convict authorities – including Governor Denison himself), O'Brien stated that death would have been better than such a fate, with some bravado he insisted that he was in 'excellent health', and that 'this contemptible system of paltry persecution far from depressing my spirits has a tendency to evoke whatever fortitude belongs to my nature'. In fact his health was failing, and it was this and the fear of the political consequences of any

---

139 O'Brien was denied a copy of the convict regulations, or a statement in writing of the special conditions to which he was subject. Instead these were communicated to him verbally (NLI: O'Brien Papers: Ms. 443/2576; see also *Maria Island Journal*, f. 7 (7 November 1849)). Lady Denison could not resist gloating over O'Brien's difficulties – wholly self-imposed in her view. In early December 1849 when he was some four weeks into his Maria Island confinement he wrote to O'Meagher. His letter, according to Lady Denison, contained 'verses of his own composing, setting forth how he had been oppressed, ill-used, *murdered*, and I do not know what besides, by the "tyrant Denison."' The letter was opened and returned to him 'with an intimation that he could not be allowed to disseminate ebullitions of that sort' (Denison, *op. cit.*, vol. I, p. 135).

140 He was, however, allowed to buy some necessary clothing (Denison to Earl Grey, 18 March 1850; AOT: GO, OD, GO 33/69, ff. 1024–6).

141 Copy of letter from Superintendent Samuel Lapham to Comptroller-General Dr Hampton, 16 November 1849; ibid., GO 33/69, f. 196–200 (copy sent to Earl Grey); *Maria Island Journal*, f. 9 (13 November 1849); *Colonial Times*, 29 October 1850, 2e–f (reprinting O'Brien's letter to Isaac Butt).

142 PRO CO 280/249/2759. In an account published in the *Freeman's Journal* (22 June 1850, 22c) O'Brien reported that he had been kept without human contact for several weeks, and observed that the policy seemed to be to isolate him from 'every human being who can feel the smallest interest in my fate'.

drastic deterioration which forced the authorities to ease his conditions.[143] Food (which had been strictly restricted to the convict allowance) was improved, as was his freedom of movement and exercise. Staff and their families were again allowed to talk to him.[144]

Although he wanted O'Brien to accept a ticket of leave, Denison was strongly opposed to the home government's lenient policy, and in dispatches to Earl Grey he expressed doubts about treating the men as state prisoners. Several other convicts, he pointed out, had been of high social standing, and had committed politically motivated offences, yet had been denied special treatment. And the Irish prisoners' privileges, in Denison's view, had unfortunate local effects, causing them to be admitted into respectable society and even official circles.[145] On 12 January 1850, Denison wrote to Grey about O'Brien's 'morbid state of mind'. He could at any time relieve himself from the restraints under which he lived, but would not do so: 'The simple fact is that [he] is anxious not merely to be a martyr but to be recognised and honoured as such; his vanity, the great and prominent feature of his character, induced him to refuse the indulgence offered to him.' O'Brien hoped to be at the centre of attention of 'an admiring and wondering multitude', but on Maria Island he was neither known nor cared for. He was 'bitterly disappointed' but his obstinacy would not allow him to own that he was mistaken.[146]

But it was Denison who was mistaken in imagining that O'Brien would be forgotten. Colonial sympathisers condemned what they saw as an attempt to coerce and bully him: the fact that he had been offered and had refused favourable conditions was dismissed as irrelevant. A fiery editorial in the Irish-owned *Hobarton Guardian* denounced O'Brien's treatment as an attempt to kill him 'by a species of torture'.[147] O'Donohoe's *Irish Exile* received many letters about O'Brien, but could not publish them because of the editor's convict status.[148] O'Brien was

143 William Smith O'Brien to Sir Lucius O'Brien, 6 December 1849; NLI: O'Brien Papers: Ms. 443/2567.

144 See letter from O'Meagher to Denison, 17 January 1850; NLI: O'Brien Papers: Ms. 443/2632. The Comptroller-General, Dr John Hampton, who had immediate responsibility for O'Brien, and for executing the general orders of the governor, was a zealous gaoler, forbidding O'Brien any purchases to supplement his convict diet (*Freeman's Journal*, 22 June 1850, 22c).

145 Denison to Earl Grey, 6 December 1849 and 11 December 1849, PRO CO 280/249/2757 and 2759. Denison and other local officials were not persuaded by O'Brien's argument that the government intended him to have a liberal regime, as was demonstrated by the treatment he had received while at Richmond. He was then, they pointed out, awaiting the result of his action on a writ of error. To this O'Brien replied that his companions had been sentenced to transportation but were allowed while waiting at Richmond to enjoy all the privileges which he had himself enjoyed.

146 Denison to Grey, 12 January 1850; AOT: GO, OD, GO 33/69, ff. 312–17; see also Denison to Grey, 13 December 1849, PRO CO 280/249/96 and 24 December 1849, PRO CO 280/249/269.

147 *Hobarton Guardian*, 24 November 1849, 2c–d. See also the comment on 22 December 1849: 'Cruelties have been perpetrated repugnant to humanity, and disgraceful to the British Character' (ibid., 2f).

148 9 February 1850, 3a.

an energetic correspondent, and conceived of the idea of sending letters via the Secretary of State to his family and friends, thus ensuring that any decision on interception would be made in England.[149] By this means and others news filtered back to England and Ireland, provoking heated press and political debate. This largely followed the contours of the various political and national allegiances, but worryingly for government there were signs that, across a spectrum of Irish opinion, sympathy was growing for O'Brien, whose treatment was represented as a form of gratuitous oppression.[150] In the Commons, Sir Lucius O'Brien repeatedly drew attention to the matter without much obvious effect. He always emphasised that he disagreed with his brother's politics and methods, and that he had urged him to accept the ticket of leave. At the same time, he argued that should his brother die or lose his reason, the cause of constitutional government in Ireland would suffer.[151] In reply, the Home Secretary Sir George Grey, while sympathising with such fraternal feelings, insisted that if government was open to any charge it was of granting O'Brien too many indulgences.[152] There were other attempts to bring parliamentary pressures to bear, even to obtain a pardon, but in these O'Brien's friends were as unsuccessful as his brother had been.[153] Given the general treatment of other convicts in Van Diemen's Land – political as well as criminal – many took the view that, having refused a ticket of leave, he should sleep in the bed he had made.[154]

---

149 Denison forwarded the letters to Earl Grey with a covering commentary on O'Brien's various claims. This met with the approval of the home government, Grey writing that when O'Brien's letters were sent on to the various members of Parliament Denison's comments went with them (Grey to Denison, 20 April 1850; AOT: GO, ID, GO 1/77, ff. 231–3; see also OD, GO 33/69, ff. 434, 912–13, 1024–6).

150 O'Brien's letter to Isaac Butt sent on 31 January 1850 was reprinted in the *Dublin Evening Mail* on 8 July 1850. This caused a great deal of indignation, including an all-party meeting in Limerick which protested at the treatment of their former MP (*Freeman's Journal*, 22 June 1850, 2b–d). See also *Colonial Times*, 29 October 1850, 2e–f: the letter filtered back to the colony).

151 3 *Hansard*, CXI, cols 1231–3; 14 June 1850. This line would be followed by many constitutional politicians in later years in respect of other groups of prisoners.

152 Ibid., col. 1234.

153 Ibid., CXII, cols 151–3; 21 June 1850; 786–95; 1 July 1850. Early in 1850 O'Brien took advice as to the legality of his confinement on Maria Island, and received conflicting opinions from local lawyers (NLI: O'Brien Papers: Ms. 443/2647 and 2648). Such was the discretionary power of the Secretary of State and of the governor that it was unlikely that any legal remedy could be obtained by O'Brien (ibid., 2656; Denison to Grey, 11 April 1850; AOT: GO, OD, GO 33/70, ff. 389–93).

154 R. F. Shaw, sometime assistant superintendent of the Maria Island settlement (and whose former residence had been assigned to O'Brien) contended that having refused a ticket of leave O'Brien was 'enjoying mildness of treatment quite unprecedented'. Over years of duty in the convict service Shaw had seen all classes and grades of convicts – 'the high-born embezzler, the educated Chartist, the political offender of every class and degree of respectability'. All had been equally treated, subjected to the same discipline and work ('drawing bricks in hand-carts with rope harness, or stone breaking, etc.'). Apart from O'Brien, no distinction had been made between these offenders and 'the common felon or murderer who never enjoyed refinement'.

Concern over O'Brien's health led sympathisers in Van Diemen's Land, backed by pledges of financial support from the Irish Directory in New York, to contrive his escape. The authorities had been warned of the plot by the captain of the cutter *Victoria* on which the escape was to be made, and had taken the necessary steps to foil it.[155] On the surgeon's advice, O'Brien had been released from close custody and for several months had been allowed to ramble the island, accompanied only by his guard. In the days before the escape attempt an armed constable kept secret watch on O'Brien and the guard he had bribed. On the afternoon of 12 August 1850, as the rescue party was about to land, the constable arrested O'Brien, his corrupt guard and the three rescuers. The three boatmen ('cowardly wretches', according to O'Brien) immediately surrendered. Since he refused to walk back to the convict station (about a mile distant), O'Brien's would-be liberators were made to carry him, allowing Denison later, and with much truth and mirth, to observe: 'Was not this a most absurd termination?'[156] There may have been chagrin and embarrassment on O'Brien's part at this failure, but there was no sense of dishonour, since his attempt had been made from conditions in which his parole had been explicitly withheld. Denison's reaction was remarkably mild, contrary to O'Brien's expectations. A decision had already been made to wind up the Maria Island station, and quarters had been prepared for O'Brien at Port Arthur, whence he was immediately transferred.[157] An even

O'Brien's exceptional treatment gave his sympathisers little ground for complaints of cruelty (*The Times*, 21 June 1850, 6f).

155 Mitchel considered Ellis, the captain of the rescue schooner had been the traitor, and that the colonial authorities had rewarded him for his treachery (*Jail Journal*, p. 242). This was also the view of O'Donohoe, who described Ellis as a 'swindling coward' (*Irish Exile*, 7 September 1850, 6d). Shortly after his arrival in the United States of America, MacManus and others kidnapped Ellis from his ship in San Francisco harbour. Taking him into the countryside, they conducted a trial and acquitted him for lack of evidence. Had he been convicted, they supposedly would have hanged him (Brendan O'Cathaoir, 'Terence Bellew McManus: Fenian Precursor', *Irish Sword*, 16 (63), 1985, 107). Despite dark theories that O'Brien had been the victim of a carefully and cynically engineered plot, Denison's account to Grey is straightforward. Suspicions had been aroused because of the character of Ellis, master of the cutter, a watch had been kept and the attempt successfully foiled. Funds for the escape had come from Hobart Town, though Denison did not know from whom. (Denison to Grey, 30 September 1850; AOT: GO, OD, GO 33/71, ff. 1348–57).

156 Denison, *op. cit.*, vol. 1, pp. 144–5. In his account of the incident O'Brien claimed that by refusing to walk he hoped to provoke the constable to shoot him – but it is possible that chagrin and despair prompted the sit-down. O'Brien later gave an account of the matter to Mitchel, when the two men had their first clandestine meeting, after O'Brien accepted his ticket of leave (*Jail Journal*, pp. 242–3). He also gave a detailed account of it in his *Maria Island Journal* (Part 2, ff. 19–24; 14 August 1850). Denison's and O'Brien's accounts are in complete agreement. The trial of William Ellis and John Hunt (mate) was reported in full in the local newspapers (see, for example, *Irish Exile*, 7 September 1850, 8a–d). A fine of £100 was paid immediately. The *Launceston Examiner* had no doubt that O'Brien had been entrapped and that he had not acted dishonourably, but urged him to accept parole (17 August 1850, 523d).

157 He arrived at Port Arthur on 22 August 1850 (AOT: CON 37/5, p. 1612).

closer watch was now kept including an armed military guard. However, although the conditions under which the ordinary convicts laboured and lived were sometimes crushingly arduous, O'Brien was assigned quarters he considered superior to those he had occupied at Maria Island, and he was told, in effect, that he would not be punished for his escape attempt even though an ordinary convict would have been severely flogged.[158] Denison warned him that another attempt would result in his being treated as a common convict, and placed in a work gang.[159]

Behind the scenes there was another sordid set of circumstances, which may have precipitated O'Brien's escape attempt, and which had drastic consequences for Superintendent Lapham and his family.[160] Three men – one a recently freed convict, the other two serving convicts promoted respectively to the office of constable and coxswain – claimed that on 18 July 1850, through a telescope at a distance of 400 yards, they had seen O'Brien embracing Lapham's younger daughter Susan.[161] One of them, Convict Constable Hamerton, claimed that he

158 As John Mitchel had good reason to know, the practice at Bermuda had been to flog re-captured convicts from hulk to hulk – twenty lashes on each ship. Mitchel certainly did not think this punishment too severe, and noted this in his journal with the comment 'But when even felons are getting mangled, I had rather, as a matter of personal taste, be out of hearing' (*Jail Journal*, p. 102). O'Brien's cottage (which for some years was a youth hostel) may still be seen in Port Arthur. Richard Davis, with much atmospheric material in his *William Smith O'Brien: Ireland – 1848 – Tasmania* (Dublin, Geography Publications, 1989) provides photographs.

159 *Maria Island Journal* Part 3, ff. 23–4 (24 August 1850). See also Denison, *op. cit.*, vol. 1, p. 145. Denison surmised that the escape attempt had been in O'Brien's mind from the beginning, and this was why he had not given his parole, '[W]hich I believe his sense of honour would not allow him to break; but this scheme, like all others in which he has meddled, has been a failure'. The Colonial Office was delighted that O'Brien had been foiled. Denison had reported that this was due 'entirely to the intelligence, resolution and fidelity of the convict Constable Flowers Hamerton'. Lord Grey granted Hamerton an immediate free pardon and a gratuity of £50, but expressed alarm that O'Brien had been allowed to walk about so freely (AOT: GO, ID, GO 1/80, ff. 131–3).

160 This incident, and the connected papers, remained hidden until uncovered by Thomas Keneally in research for his highly accomplished *The Great Shame* (London, Chatto & Windus, 1998). I have examined the relevant papers, but come to a rather different interpretation of the incident.

161 The three were Daniel Griffiths, Thomas Hamerton and William Rogerson. Griffiths was a 26-year-old, transported for seven years for theft, with a criminal record in England, and offences of idleness, lying, misbehaviour, criminal damage and theft in the colony. For these offences he had served many spells of hard labour, solitary confinement, and had been whipped. His sentence having expired, however, he had been freed on 8 May 1850 (AOT: CON 33/34; CON 14/23). Thomas Hamerton had been transported for fifteen years for arson. At the time of this incident he was twenty-nine, and had been a convict constable for just over two years. His record in the colony was of minor infractions only (ibid., CON 33/83; CON 17/1, p. 264). William Rogerson, a Bermondsey clerk, was serving a life sentence for stealing a postal package containing a considerable amount of jewellery and money. A married man with three children (his family was in England) he had a very good disciplinary record; he had been a convict constable for some years. In October 1853 Rogerson was granted a conditional pardon but subsequently committed suicide (ibid., CON 33/8; CON 14/5).

had seen an act of indecency; Susan Lapham was around thirteen years of age.[162] Various other allegations were also made of the two kissing and being together after dark, although until this point there had been no suspicion of any kind of impropriety. Hamerton, according to his account, was urged by Mrs Lapham (to whom he reported what he had seen) to keep the information to himself, since it would bring disgrace on the family and would blight her husband's career. Dr Thomas Christie Smart, the Maria Island surgeon and Visiting Justice,[163] was suspicious of Hamerton's visit to the Lapham household and extracted the story from the convict by way of a formal statement. This was put to O'Brien, who utterly denied any impropriety, but admitted that loneliness had led him to act with a lack of prudence by being unaccompanied in Susan Lapham's company. There followed an angry exchange of words between Dr Smart and O'Brien.[164]

The matter rested for almost two months, but eventually came to the attention of Dr John Hampton, who on 6 September asked for further details. The tone of Hampton's letter indicated that he thought Smart remiss in not previously having informed him of the incident.[165] Sworn statements were then taken by Dr Smart from the other two convicts who claimed to have witnessed the incident – all three saying that they had seen it through a telescope at a distance of nearly a quarter of a mile. Smart made his report to Hampton, enclosing the various statements and claiming that Mrs Lapham had admitted that O'Brien had taken liberties with her daughter, and that she had been anxious to keep the matter from her husband.[166] At his first interview with Mrs

162 Tasmanian records show Susan's christening to have been registered in 1837 which would make her around and not less than thirteen in 1850 (no date of birth is given). It is no extenuation of O'Brien's conduct – even as discussed here – that she married three and a half years later, in February 1854, and that at age fifteen her sister had married a 31-year-old clergyman. Girls at this time married young, and necessarily therefore men some years older than themselves. Social contact between the two groups would not have been exceptional, subject to the chaperonage requirements of the day. The lonely man and imaginative girl were undoubtedly drawn to each other on the isolated penal station. In later life Susan, who had gone to New Zealand with her husband, published a number of essays on colonial life. She died in 1880 (AOT: Marriage/Birth Registrations; 67/248).

163 (1816–96). Educated Edinburgh; Licentiate, Royal College of Surgeons. Appointed Assistant Surgeon, Fingal Convict Station, 1842. Became justice of the peace 1849. Private practice from 1856, thereafter prominent in medical and public life.

164 Smart had the watch over O'Brien intensified. When O'Brien complained Smart refused to speak to him: 'I told him I considered his conduct most disgraceful and that I should bring it under the notice of the Government' (Smart to Hampton, 12 September 1850; MLS: TP: 102 (unfoliated)).

165 Hampton to Smart, 6 September 1850; ibid.

166 There was much agitated discussion between Mrs Lapham, William Rogerson and Dr Smart. The latter reported to Hampton that Mrs Lapham had been 'in great distress at what had come to her knowledge and begged me in the most earnest manner to take no steps to make known what had transpired as it would prove the ruin of her family and the death of Mr Lapham'. Smart made no promise (Smart to Hampton, 12 September 1850; ibid.).

Lapham, Smart had not given an undertaking of secrecy, but following further entreaties he had promised that 'nothing short of absolute necessity should induce me to take further steps'. This was his plea in mitigation of not having made a report.[167] Apart from agreeing that a closer watch be kept on O'Brien, who had already been removed to Port Arthur, neither Governor Denison nor Dr Hampton used the information against O'Brien. Given Denison's intense irritation with O'Brien this is at first sight surprising. But since O'Brien had already been moved, Lapham dismissed and Maria Island station wound up, it is hard to see what, short of criminal proceedings, could be done.

The whole episode could, however, be played in two ways. The Laphams never broke their friendship with O'Brien, for whom they had the highest regard, and it is inconceivable that they could therefore have believed that he had sexually abused their young daughter.[168] In October 1851, Lapham described O'Brien as 'One of the most highly honorable estimable and kind hearted men ever breathed'.[169] O'Brien's offence was to be so much alone with the girl that it created a scandal and, in the intense atmosphere of a convict settlement, surrounded by those who would lie easily to blackmail or secure official favour, this allowed false allegations of sexual intimacy. Beyond all doubt, had the affair become public it would have destroyed Susan Lapham's reputation and marriage prospects. O'Brien, the older, worldly man, who placed claims to personal honour at the front of everything, had paid scant regard to the honour of a daughter of the family which had shown him much kindness.[170] The Laphams had equally neglected their duty. Far short of sexual impropriety, Susan Lapham and her family did suffer and would have suffered more had the matter become public.

Denison and Hampton also had to be careful. A number of adverse readings of the incident were possible, ranging from their neglect of duty in failing to

---

167 Ibid.

168 In an unfavourable review of Thomas Keneally's 'novelised' account of Irish transportation and life in Australia and the United States of America (*The Great Shame: A Story of the Irish in the Old World and the New*, London, Chatto & Windus, 1998) Fintan O'Toole castigates Keneally for glossing over incidents unworthy of the Irish tale, O'Brien's alleged molestation of Susan Lapham among them. O'Toole's general criticism has weight, but a careful examination of these papers allows us only to say that three convicts made allegations; that the family did not appear to believe them, but was distressed that they *could* be put; and that the authorities made no further reference to the matter (see Fintan O'Toole, 'O'Schindler', *The New Republic*, 11 October 1999, pp. 48–52).

169 See n. 192 below.

170 Asserting his innocence to Smart, O'Brien acknowledged his error in being alone with her: 'I would rather lose my life than do an injury to one for whom I entertain a most sincere affection and esteem. I now deeply regret that I allowed her to be seen alone with me under circumstances which appear to have excited censorious observation but this want of prudery on her part arose from a kindly desire to mitigate the loneliness of my solitude combined with the innocent confidence of a guileless nature' (O'Brien to Smart, 28 July 1850; MLS TP 102).

ensure proper supervision for their most important prisoner, to creating a plot against O'Brien on the back of statements from convicts of blasted and infamous character. Both also had to consider the position of the official class in the colony. It existed as a caste, and damage of such a scandalous kind to the family of one of their number was damage to all.

How the matter was kept from public knowledge in the colony is unclear. Even the most confidential clerk would have been tempted to indiscretion by such sensational material. The papers are fragmentary, consisting only of Dr Smart's report and one or two items of correspondence with the Comptroller-General. The incident did not make its way into the detailed reports on the political convicts which Denison so dutifully sent to Grey. Two readings of that are possible – that Denison did not trust his clerks and copyists, and no report was sent, or (equally likely) that Grey was informed by a private and confidential communication from Denison himself, bypassing the usual clerical processes. In the latter case it is possible that Grey replied confidentially, and told Denison to bury the matter.

In fairness to O'Brien it must be noted that there had never been such an incident alleged against him before, nor was there afterwards. There had been sexual misbehaviour and an illegitimate child while he was at Cambridge, but this was the not uncommon lechery and wildness of a rich and unrestrained young man of his time. It is also telling that on eventually giving his parole and being released from Port Arthur, O'Brien was allowed to take up a position as tutor to the sons of Dr Henry Brock in a remote quarter of the island. Denison and Hampton would never have permitted this employment within a family had they believed that a further scandal might result.

With the whirlwind of scarcely averted scandal, attempted escape and ignominious capture behind him, O'Brien, now at Port Arthur, reassessed his position. Although he did not at first see it, the failed escape attempt cleared the way for an acceptance of a ticket of leave without compromise to his principles or scruples.[171] The physical conditions under which he was living were decent but he was almost entirely cut off from social intercourse. His days were spent reading and writing, and working in the gardens attached to his quarters.[172] Because of the attempted escape, and the supposed indulgence (including close

---

171 At a later point Patrick O'Donohoe wrote to him, insisting that 'there is not a shadow of inconsistency in your accepting [parole] . . . you refused them in the first instance from too delicate a sense of duty and attachment to a cause which was lost, and could not be retrieved by your further martyrdom; and having made a last and final effort to release yourself, without terms of any kind, and failing in it – surely you must see, as everybody else sees and feels, that a continuous suffering would not be consistent with the duty you owe yourself, your family, and your friends at home and abroad' (O'Donohoe to O'Brien, 7 October 1850, NLI: O'Brien Papers: Ms. 444/2742).

172 At some point he had been deprived of books, which brought protests in the local press (*Colonial Times*, 1 November, 2f–3a).

contact with his family) extended to O'Brien, Lapham had been dismissed.[173] With this example before them officials had reason to restrict their dealings with O'Brien.[174] Denison and Hampton showed no sign of relenting, and rejected O'Brien's conditions for accepting a ticket of leave.[175] O'Brien also enquired whether he would be allowed to live in Hobart Town were he to accept parole, and on being refused determined to continue in close custody at Port Arthur. There were continuing pleas to O'Brien from his family and sympathisers at home to accept parole. They had concluded that until O'Brien had at least taken his ticket of leave, government would be reluctant to consider a greater measure of clemency.

The combination of pressures was such that towards the end of October 1850, O'Brien sought a face-saving way out of the impasse, and enquired of Mitchel and Martin how expensive it would be to live in conditional freedom at the standards of a single gentleman.[176] An acceptable occasion arose when,

173 Lapham appealed to his Colonial Office contacts for assistance, writing on 30 October 1851 that his sole offence was not to have carried out to the fullest extent 'the (inhuman) instructions of the Comptroller General in reference to the treatment of the Irish State Prisoners!! And I have thus incurred the vindictive animosity of Doctor Hampton because I would not become the willing instrument of slow torture to my suffering Countryman who whatever may be his political principles is one of the most highly honorable estimable and kind hearted men ever breathed. Were it in his power . . . at any cost or sacrifice neither myself or family would have suffered loss or privation' (AOT: GO, ID, GO 1/80).

174 Captain Samuel Lapham (1805–76) arrived in Van Diemen's Land in 1832. He was the second son of Joseph Lapham of Skerries, near Athy, Co. Kildare. Although he came with sufficient capital to develop a farm, he was too late for a land grant. With good references from home he was appointed police magistrate and held various other government appointments, before becoming Superintendent of Convicts on Maria Island. He had a large family and when dismissed by Denison was left without means of support. Lapham, his wife and O'Brien himself wrote to Lucius O'Brien, who raised the matter in the Commons, apparently to no effect (3 *Hansard*, CXVII, cols 640–1; 12 June 1851). See *Maria Island Journal*, Part 3, f. 25 (8 September 1850). In 1852 Lapham went to Victoria, where he re-entered government service. On being pensioned in 1855, he returned to Van Diemen's Land (Tasmania) (*Hobart Mercury*, 7 June 1876, 2d).

175 Bidding from a weak hand, O'Brien tried to make his acceptance of the ticket of leave conditional on Lapham being pardoned by Denison. The ploy was doomed, of course, and as soon as the offer was made Denison was able to record that 'he is beginning to nibble at the bait, [and] I dare say I shall soon get rid of him' (*op. cit.*, Vol. I, p. 145). Lapham's appeal, and appeals on his behalf, were finally turned down in April 1852 (AOT: GO, ID, GO 1/84 ff. 100–27). Following this decisive rejection Lapham went to Victoria.

176 To this Mitchel replied, extolling the inexpensiveness of the comfortable lodgings that he and Martin had obtained. He could not resist a preachy social commentary, however: 'You ask how one may live "*as a gentleman*" on this £80 per ana. The notion of gentlemanhood has always seemed rather vague to me. And it has grown more confused since I came to this place, but I find that I can live as I please, take as much as I like of the best society of the place, ride a good horse, & occasionally (in conjunction with O'Meagher, Martin, etc.) see some little company on the lakes – and all for £80' (Mitchel to O'Brien, 6 November 1850; NLI: O'Brien Papers: Ms. 444/2762). It did not occur to Mitchel, it would seem, that O'Brien could be short of money, but at least for a time he was, and found it necessary to borrow money from a local

on 29 October 1850, a well-attended Hobart Town public meeting unanimously adopted an address requesting O'Brien to accept a ticket of leave on the same basis as his companions.[177] This address was subsequently signed by more than 900 residents, the list headed by five magistrates, and the rest persons of substance and respectability. Considering the sparse population of the island, such a collection of signatures in so short a time was a remarkable demonstration of local feeling. At the same time Mitchel, Martin and O'Donohoe urged O'Brien to yield to the request that had been made.[178] Accepting the address, on 9 November O'Brien agreed to give his parole, and on 18 November 1850 entered into conditional liberty.[179] He took up a position as tutor to the children of an Irish physician, Dr Henry Brock, in a remote district of the island. In Denison's view O'Brien was 'tired out at last' and had taken the address as an excuse for changing his mind on the ticket of leave.[180] Whether politically tired or not, O'Brien stuck to teaching for only ten months, returning in December 1851 to New Norfolk, where he lived in an hotel, socialising with colonists in the area.[181]

doctor. The expense of bringing his family from England and maintaining them in the colony may have been beyond him (O'Brien to McCarthy, 24 and 25 May 1852; NLI: O'Brien Papers: Ms. 444/2816–17). O'Brien attempted to earn some money by entering into a trading venture, but this went wrong and he evidently made a loss (see ibid.: Ms. 445/2821 et seq.).

177 Hobarton Guardian, 16 November 1850, 2f.

178 See letters to O'Brien from Mitchel, 6 November 1850 (NLI: O'Brien Papers: Ms. 444/2762); O'Donohoe, 5 November 1850 (ibid., 2761); 8 November 1850 (ibid., 2764); Martin, 7 November 1850 (ibid., 2763). Both Mitchel and Martin urged O'Brien to accept the conditional liberty of parole in order to refute false rumours being circulated by Denison's staff.

179 Launceston Examiner, 20 November 1850, 748d, 749a; Hobarton Guardian, 13 November 1850, 3f. There was a large and cohesive Irish community in Van Diemen's Land, many members of which held influential positions and (as the Hobarton Guardian repeatedly indicates) were antagonistic towards the colonial authorities (for some discussion of this see Merrilyn Graham and David Bamford, 'Chartists and Young Irelanders: Towards a Reassessment of Political Prisoners in Van Diemen's Land', Tasmanian Historical Research Association Papers and Proceedings, 32, June 1985, pp. 68–74). One consequence of O'Brien's acceptance of a ticket of leave was the punishment of three of his companions (MacManus, O'Donohoe and O'Doherty) for the offence of leaving their assigned police districts personally to congratulate him. This was an offence but hardly a serious one, and in the circumstances Denison could have ordered the convict authorities to turn a blind eye. Instead he revoked the tickets of leave of the three men, and placed them under punishment in the Port Arthur convict establishment. As noted above, MacManus took the revocation of his ticket of leave as the de facto withdrawal of his parole, and escaped on 21 February 1851. Chisholm Anstey berated Sir William Denison for his lack of generosity in the matter (apparently unaware of MacManus's escape) (3 Hansard, CXVII, cols 636–7; 12 June 1851).

180 Denison, op. cit., vol. I, p. 146. Scornfully (and inaccurately) he described those who had sent O'Brien the letter as 'a deputation of Irish convicts'. Mitchel had been in correspondence with O'Brien before the Hobart public meeting, and on 9 November 1850 wrote to Dillon that O'Brien was beginning to entertain the idea of accepting a ticket of leave (Mitchel to John Dillon, 9 November 1850; cit. William Dillon, op. cit., p. 317).

181 To his wife O'Brien confided that 'My effort to escape from Maria Island was my last effort to procure for myself a new career. Since that time I have felt that I have now nothing more to

Time dragged, however, and the government did not seem disposed to act in his case. In early 1853 O'Brien had rashly sent a statement about his continuing exile to *The Times* indicating, *inter alia*, that he intended to surrender his parole – doubtless with the hope of forcing the hand of government.[182] O'Brien was informed (on doubtful authority, as it turned out) that the letter had destroyed all hope of amnesty. The situation distressed O'Brien's friends – both his fellow revolutionaries and his politically influential friends in Dublin and London.

Fresh from organising the escape of Mitchel, Patrick Smyth, then in Sydney, wrote to O'Brien asking him to consider his own escape and to do nothing about surrendering his parole. He was particularly worried that O'Brien might persuade Martin and O'Doherty to follow his lead in the matter. Their cases were very different from O'Brien's (they had been sentenced to ten years trans-portation, O'Brien to life) and it was probable that both would be freed before the expiration of their time. Rather, O'Brien should remain as he was, on a ticket of leave, until he should determine to escape. When that time came, Smyth concluded, 'I beg that you will inform us in America of it. Assistance will then be sent to you. There must be no more failures. For my own part I would esteem it a proud privilege to be permitted to return here for the purpose of aiding in your liberation.'[183]

Neither man knew it, of course, but at almost exactly the same time Sir David Norrey, one of O'Brien's great friends and supporters from the respectable side of his life, was writing to inform him of a favourable interview with Palmerston, and hinting in fairly blunt terms that provided there were no more letters to *The Times*, and O'Brien did nothing else imprudent, he had reasonable hopes of a not-too-distant release.[184] In the event, O'Brien's path to freedom, as he saw it, lay not in escape and perpetual exile, but in persuading the British government to release him. His lack of reality in the matter lay in his imagining that pressure could probably be brought to bear by surrendering his parole and returning to custody. Smyth, the revolutionary, was much more of a realist than the man who had spent twenty years in the House of Commons. O'Brien's voluntary return to a convict depot would be misunderstood, he wrote: 'People would say it was Quixotic – that it was dictated by a morbid craving after martyrdom. The consequence would be that it would deprive you of that sympathy which is now your strongest sup-port, and the guaranty of your ultimate liberation.' In any case, his health had suffered before, and the chances were that a return to close confinement would oblige O'Brien again to accept a ticket of leave, 'on the same terms as before'.[185]

---

do than quietly and patiently to abide my fate – merely paddling along upon the surface of Life's stream with just enough exertion to prevent myself from sinking' (William to Lucy O'Brien, 18 January 1852: NLI: O'Brien Papers: Ms. 8653/28).

182 It appeared in *The Times* on 25 March 1853 (5c).

183 P. J. Smyth to O'Brien, 5 August 1853: NLI: O'Brien Papers: Ms. 445/2846.

184 See n. 192 below.

185 Smyth to O'Brien, 5 August 1853, *op. cit.*

Caught between vistas of perpetual exile in the United States of America and a return to the 'petty persecution' of close confinement in a convict depot, O'Brien chose to do nothing – which in his circumstances was by far the best course.

The amnesty campaign

Apart from his unfortunate letter to *The Times*, O'Brien's position with the British government had improved over the years, his standing rising as his companions gave notice and effected what they claimed to be honourable escapes but which the authorities considered to be breaches of their pledges. Despite his own attempt which, had it succeeded, would have meant permanent exile, O'Brien at heart wished to return unconditionally to Ireland, his family and his property.[186] Adherence to his parole gave government an opportunity to acknowledge and reward his honourable conduct without the appearance of weakness. Many clemency petitions were lodged with the Home Office; the signatories included many responsible and influential people.[187] Constitutional nationalists found favour with their constituents by taking a stand for a man led astray by an excess of patriotism and the horrors of the famine. Advised privately by members of the government, O'Brien's brother Henry helped to organise a petition for his pardon, aided by Sir Colman O'Loghlen and other supporters and friends. Signatures were harder to obtain than O'Brien's brother had expected, and he told his brother that many more would have supported him had there been any expression of regret on his part.[188] This, of course, O'Brien could not do; government would have to read his disposition rather than expect declarations from him.

---

186 He told Mitchel and Smyth that his earlier failure to escape from Maria Island had affected his decision. Mitchel had stronger motives to go to America than had he, 'and you will be more at home there'. He also thought that the British government might at some time set him free without an act of submission on his part: '[I]n that case I return to Ireland: if I break away against their will, Ireland is barred against me for ever' (*Jail Journal*, p. 269). From the beginning O'Brien had refused to countenance his family coming to join him, despite his wife's plea on her own behalf and their children's. O'Brien wrote his first emphatic refusal in the form of a dialogue: 'Lucy and William: A Dialogue' (Richmond Prison, 4 July 1849; TCD: William Smith O'Brien Papers: Ms. 10611/2). As soon as he arrived on Maria Island he repeated his wish. Writing to his brother Lucius, he insisted that his wife should not think of coming to join him: 'I *implore* her not to think of bringing our family to this colony. If I could communicate freely with her I could state many many reasons which might prevent her from taking this step' (William Smith O'Brien to Sir Lucius O'Brien, 6 December 1849; NLI: O'Brien Papers: Ms. 443/2567).

187 See, for example, the April 1852 petition from the Mayor, Aldermen and citizens of Montreal on behalf of 'The Irish political exiles of 1848' (PRO HO 12/81). There had also been certain discreet approaches by the United States government (see letter of 27 December 1851: Daniel Webster (Sydney) to John Appleton (State Department, Washington, DC), MLS: DOC 821).

188 'You certainly owe it to your friends and family to make every exertion consistent with honour and truth to obtain your release, for believe me many are suffering and will suffer with you as long as you remain in exile from your home and family' (Henry to William Smith O'Brien, 26 May 1852; NLI: O'Brien Papers: Ms. 444/2818).

Despite O'Brien's unwillingness to express regret, by 1854 conditions favoured mercy. The last convict ship had departed for Hobart in November 1852. On 29 December the following year the order-in-council, designating Van Diemen's Land a penal colony, was withdrawn.[189] O'Brien's presence on the island was growing more anomalous, and it was undesirable that he should continue to attract the sympathetic regard of disaffected colonists. There had been vast social, demographic, economic and political changes in Ireland, and it was unlikely that O'Brien would again become a danger, even if he could find it within himself to resume agitation. It was widely recognised that he was no revolutionary, but a reformer whose impatience had led him to use force – and that of a very limited kind. His actions during the insurrection had not been revolutionary. He had made his gesture and was reconciled to its failure. Remaining substantially in support of law and order in Ireland, he would carry the authority of the Irish patriot when he urged his moderating views on others. That irreconcilable revolutionary John Mitchel recognised all this well, and spelt it out to O'Brien in a private letter, written when both were in Van Diemen's Land:

> You admit there is Law in Ireland, & that you were virtually & sub-stantially tried by that Law. I deny that there is any law at all and that if there be, I was not tried at all. Therefore I regard myself as a Captain in the hands of pirates. You are content to accept the defeat of the insurrectionary attempt, as a pronouncement of the country for British dominion, & you would now, if permitted settle quietly in Ireland and disturb English dominion no more. But the breath of my nostrils is rebellion against that accursed Empire. I shall die either a rebel or the citizen of a free Irish State. And wherever the British flag throws its poisonous shadow I may find a prison or a grave, but a home *never*. Then there are institutions, social & political in Ireland which you would not overthrow or declare war upon, even if that were proved needful in order to wrest the island from Britain. But I would claim our country of the English, at the price of leaving the surviving inhabitants as bare of all social & political order and garniture as were the men of Deucalion when they ceased to be stones.[190]

In Van Diemen's Land, O'Brien was a reproach to British authority; in Ireland he would demonstrate the administration's security and magnanimity: he could be a force for reconciliation rather than division. Finally, the political, diplom-atic, financial and even military potential of the famine-swollen Irish-American

---

189 *Correspondence on the Subject of Convict Discipline and Transportation*, PP, 1852–3 [1601], LXXXII, 1, 105; A. G. L. Shaw, *op. cit.*, p. 351.

190 Mitchel to O'Brien, 6 October 1852; NLI: O'Brien Papers: Ms. 444/2813.

population was announcing itself to the world.[191] An untamed, unreconciled and venerated O'Brien at large in the United States of America was considerably more dangerous than a domesticated O'Brien in Ireland: the extravagant receptions given to Mitchel, Meagher and the others had shown what an appetite existed for Irish rebel heroes. And so long as he enjoyed a ticket of leave, the chances of O'Brien organising a successful escape were high, even allowing for the self-imposed handicaps and etiquette of honourable escape.

Behind the scenes, representations were being made at the highest level. On 7 August 1853, Sir David Norrey wrote to O'Brien reporting a conversation which he had had with Palmerston:

> He spoke kindly of you – still nothing favourable has resulted from our conversation. He states that he has had much conversation with Sir Geo. Grey [the Home Secretary] about you & that they both are of the opinion that it is *not expedient at present* to recommend to the Queen that a free pardon should be granted to you, yet that neither desired 'to shut the door of hope against you'.

The Prime Minister had not yet felt it his duty to speak to the Queen on the subject, but even if he favoured O'Brien's return he would be obliged to consult Her Majesty's private wishes on such a subject before he could move officially on it: 'It is a question of free pardon for high treason & . . . her views must be ascertained on so serious a point.' Palmerston had additionally said that O'Brien's case could not be considered on its own and that it had bearing on other cases – 'cases which they were not prepared to pardon at present'. Agreeing with Norrey that O'Brien would do well to remain quiet for some time, Palmerston added: 'His own conduct will have much effect on our decisions.' Summarising the result of this interview, Norrey felt justified in offering O'Brien hope that his case was moving foward.[192]

191 John Bright had warned of this danger as early as August 1848, just a month after the collapse of the Young Ireland rebellion. The Irish, driven out by poverty and famine, would settle in their millions in America. Their feelings about Britain would not dissipate. In the event of a crisis between Britain and the United States of America 'it is certain . . . the Irish in that country will throw their whole weight into the scale against this country' (3 *Hansard*, CI, cols 533–9; 25 August 1848). This reservoir of anti-British feeling would remain at flood level, regularly replenished throughout the nineteenth century. Twenty years after Bright's warning J. S. Mill spoke in similar terms, in the wake of the Fenian insurrection: the number of Irish in the United States of America was constantly increasing, Mill pointed out, as was therefore their power in American politics, and, he asked, '[I]s there any probability that the American-Irish will come to hate this country less than they do at the present moment?' (ibid., CXLI, col. 32; 12 March 1868).

192 He added, 'You have at least the satisfaction that you have many sincere friends & that they have placed you in a far better position than you stood in at the beginning of the Session. Lord P. admitted this' (Sir David Norrey to William Smith O'Brien, 7 August 1853; NLI: O'Brien Papers: Ms. 445/2847).

Six months later Palmerston was ready to act. On the opening of the new parliamentary session the Irish member Francis Beamish[193] asked an agreed Parliamentary Question. Whereas some of his companions had broken their parole, Home Secretary Palmerston declared, 'Mr Smith O'Brien himself, whatever might have been his faults and guilt, has acted like a gentleman, and has not taken advantage of opportunities for escape of which, if he had been a less honourable man, he might have availed himself.' In consequence, government would advise exercise of the Crown Prerogative so that O'Brien might be placed in the same position 'in which those other persons have placed themselves by a violation of the pledges which they had given.'[194]

Fairness required similar lenience for John Martin and Kevin O'Doherty, who, according to the rules and language of Palmerston, had also behaved as gentlemen. They had also helped their case immeasurably by living quietly and uncontroversially in the colony, O'Doherty following his calling as a doctor and Martin (after Mitchel's escape) employed as a private tutor.[195] When Isaac Butt presented their case for pardon, he was pushing at an open door. A fortnight after the announcement about O'Brien, Palmerston confirmed that his two companions, as well as the Chartist prisoners Frost, Jones and Williams, would be granted conditional pardons.[196]

It was not until 27 June, 1854, that O'Brien received his pardon. He and his companions immediately began to make their departure arrangements.[197] There were festive leave-takings and deputations in New Norfolk, Hobart Town, Geelong and Melbourne.[198] The three made various appearances in Victoria, with O'Brien always outshining his two companions. There were several great celebrations by the Irish community. Meetings were also held in Sydney, and a

---

193 (1802–68). Liberal MP for Cork 1837–41, 1851–9.

194 3 *Hansard*, CXXX, cols 1112–13; 22 February 1854. O'Brien so established himself in the British political consciousness that twelve years later, when he was safely dead, he was compared favourably with the Fenians, especially in the matter on which O'Brien himself had placed such value: 'As it happens, with the exception of poor Mr Smith O'Brien, we have not had a rebel for many years who was a man of honour' (*The Times*, 27 November 1866, 8c).

195 Martin to O'Brien, 5 September 1853 and 29 November 1853; NLI: O'Brien Papers: Ms. 445/ 2848 and 2852. On 5 September Martin asked O'Brien (who had his own financial concerns) for a loan of £12. This lack of funds was probably the reason for Martin taking up his job as a tutor – a position in which he was comfortable enough, but in which he had little privacy.

196 3 *Hansard*, CXXX1, cols 448–9; 7 March 1854. The condition was expatriation. The pardons were signed on 13 March 1854, and despatched to Van Diemen's Land on 1 April, arriving there on 26 June. AOT: GD, ID, GO 1/92/1 and GO 1/92/6–10.

197 William to Lucy Smith O'Brien, 28 June 1854; NLI: O'Brien Papers: Ms. 8653/30. Characteristically O'Brien had determined not to apply for his certificate of conditional pardon lest such action on his part should be considered as a confession that he considered himself a criminal 'in regard of the transactions of 1848'.

198 See *Hobart Town Daily Courier*, 5 July 1854, 2c–d; 10 July, 2c–d; 11 July, 2c–d. Opinion about them remained divided, the *Courier* continuing to deplore their offence, while praising O'Brien's personal manner and 'simple and gentle manners'.

125-ounce 22-carat gold cup was commissioned and manufactured in Melbourne and sent to O'Brien in Europe.[199] With these delays it was not until 26 July 1854 that O'Brien and Martin left Australia. O'Doherty and Patrick Smyth (who had returned with new funds and instructions to rescue the exiles) wished to investigate the possibilities of the newly opened gold-fields. Martin arrived in Paris at the end of October 1854, and by 24 November O'Brien, having taken a month en route to visit his wife's brother in Madras, and a further three weeks to make a tour of Spain, was in Brussels.[200] Full pardons had to await a propitious political occasion, a further gathering of parliamentary support and sufficient assurances as to O'Brien's political course in Ireland.[201] Doubts were sufficiently overcome and an appropriate occasion for clemency was provided by the end of the Crimean War. On 9 May 1856, in response to a question from Thomas Duncombe, Palmerston announced that full pardons would be given to all sentenced political offenders 'with the exception of those unhappy men who had broken all the ties of honour and fled from their place of banishment'.[202] With all conditions removed, the three remaining Irish exiles (together with the Chartists Frost, Williams and Jones) returned to the United Kingdom.[203] Illuminations

199 The cup was 19 inches high, decorated with Irish symbols and cost more than £800. For the meetings and presentations see *Argus* (Melbourne) 12 June 1854, 5f; 15 June, 5f; 10 July, 5b–c; 15 July, 5g; 24 July, 4d–e, 5a–c; 26 July, 5a; 25 August, 4g. See also *Illustrated Sydney News*, 22 July 1854, 171a and 171c; 29 July 181b–c (portrait) and 5 August 1854, 186a. The dispatch of the testimonial gold cup is described in the *Argus*, 28 December 1854, 5f.

200 O'Brien's excursions delayed his return to Europe by almost two months – strange decisions for someone who had been separated from his family for five years (William to Lucy Smith O'Brien, 21 August 1854 (at Galle, Ceylon); NLI: O'Brien Papers: Ms. 8653/30). It may have been these delays, or the usual difficulties of re-establishing an easy and intimate family relationship after a prolonged separation that led to Lucy's postponement of her departure for Brussels once O'Brien arrived there, and a decision on his part not to meet her in Antwerp (ibid., 16 November 1854 (from Spain) and 21 November 1854 (Paris)). Having himself presumably spent freely on his journey and excursions O'Brien cautioned his wife about their living expenses and forbade her to bring a governess with her to Brussels. All of this was conveyed in worried, slightly irritated and certainly businesslike letters (ibid.,William to Lucy Smith O'Brien, 29 November 1854).

201 Duffy, now promoting an Independent Irish Party in the Commons, and doubtless conscious of his obligations to his former comrades in rebellion, was energetic in obtaining all-party support for a full pardon and permission to return to Ireland (Duffy to O'Brien, 2 April 1855; NLI: O'Brien Papers: Ms. 445/2855–66, *passim*. These letters are filed out of sequence).

202 3 *Hansard*, CXLII, cols. 264; 9 May 1856. Duncombe, a radical, was MP for Finsbury, 1834–61.

203 PRO HO 12/81. Full free pardons were granted under the Great Seal, though several months elapsed before they were issued, causing O'Brien to protest to Lord Palmerston (NLI: O'Brien Papers: Ms. 445/2936; 8 December 1856). O'Brien had spent much of the period between his being granted a conditional pardon and the announcement of a full one travelling in Italy and Greece in the company of his eldest son Edward (see NLI: O'Brien Papers: Ms. 8653/32). In 1859 Edward accompanied his father on an extended tour of the United States of America,

and popular celebrations in Clare and Limerick marked O'Brien's return to Ireland on 8 July 1856. He declined various invitations to return to public life, and as the years went by acquired a broad-based respect within Ireland, and some indirect influence in public affairs.[204]

The followers

There remained another group of Young Ireland exiles – followers rather than leaders – of whom we know tantalisingly little. Before departing the island on receiving his conditional pardon in 1854, John Martin drew attention to the plight of eight Irish political offenders who had not received their pardons.[205] These men comprised a group of seven sentenced for their part in the attack on a police barracks at Cappoquin, Co. Waterford, on 16 September 1849 – more than a year after O'Brien and the other leaders had been taken into custody. The barracks was not taken, but one policeman was killed, as was one of the insurgents.[206] The attack was part of a small-scale conspiracy organised by James Fintan Lalor with a handful of the lower-ranking Confederation members who remained at liberty, and who had been able to assemble a small quantity of primitive arms. The leader of the Cappoquin attack was Joseph Brenan, who had been a contributor to the *United Irishman* and to the *Irish Felon*, and was for a time editor of the *Irishman*. Brenan himself escaped to the United States of America, but several of his followers were taken and, in September 1849, sentenced at Waterford for their part in the attack, arriving

and the following year to Spain. Having attained a degree of fame and affection among his countrymen, but not wishing to return to politics, O'Brien evidently found it difficult to settle to a domestic existence. He avoided travel to England, responding to one invitation that it was his 'earnest desire never again to set foot on the shores of England' (NLI: O'Brien Papers: Ms. 445/2916; letter, 19 July 1856).

204 His pardon had been unconditional, so there was no formal barrier to his return to public life and politics. He was unable to accommodate himself to renewed membership of the House of Commons, or to develop the energy to seek a new departure in Irish politics (see, for example, his letter to the Liberal Club of Tipperary declining an invitation to accept their parliamentary nomination; NLI: O'Brien Papers: Ms. 445/2917; 18 July 1856).

205 *Hobart Mercury*, 15 July 1854: cit., *Irish American* (New York), 25 November 1854.

206 For accounts of the Cappoquin attack of varying degrees of accuracy and partisanship, see *Freeman's Journal*, 20 September 1849, 2b–c; 21 September, 2b–c; 24 September, 4d; 27 September, 1e–f; 28 September, 4c. The attack on the barracks was strongly condemned by prominent members of the Roman Catholic clergy, who (not very originally) denounced the rebels as 'Wolves in sheep's clothing' (ibid., 28 September 1849, 4c). Small-scale unrest continued for some days, and a soldier on night guard duty was attacked by pikemen. There was also a raid on a 'big house' for firearms (ibid., 10 October 1849, 4f). Strong forces of military and police were swiftly moved into the area. Order was restored, but not before a large mass of local people attempted to prevent the removal of the captives to prison. Some sixty armed police had to await the arrival of priests before the crowd let the party pass (*Nation*, 29 September 1849, 68c).

in Hobart on 13 December 1850.[207] William P. Dowling, who had played an active part in the Chartist movement, had been convicted of arson attempts in London in August 1848, and when arrested had Confederation documents in his possession. For his offence (treason felony), Dowling was sentenced to transportation for life on 30 September 1848.[208] His comrades in the enterprise, also transported for life, were William Gaffney, William Lacey, George Mullins and Joseph Ritchie.[209]

True to the government's stated policy on Irish rebels, class determined the treatment of the men. William Dowling was an art student, and on arrival in Van Diemen's Land was granted a ticket of leave. This allowed him to settle in Hobart, where he entered into business as a portrait-painter, achieving some success. He married his fiancée, who had followed him from Ireland. Changes in the convict regulations made him eligible for a conditional pardon after only six years in the colony. In October 1854, Denison recommended him to the Colonial Office.[210] A conditional pardon was granted in August 1855. He received a full pardon in 1857, but chose to remain in Van Diemen's Land, where he died twenty years later.[211]

Of the seven Cappoquin convicts, three were given fourteen-year terms for participation in the attack; the remaining four had received seven-year sentences

207 Duffy wrote of the attack '[I]t failed so hopelessly that scarcely a memory of it remains' (1883, p. 766). See Richard Davis, 'Unpublicised Young Ireland Prisoners in Van Diemen's Land', *Tasmanian Historical Research Association Papers and Proceedings*, 38 (3 and 4), December 1991, p. 133. Edmund Sheafy was transported for attacking a police barracks on 12 September 1848. Thomas Donovan, John Walsh and Thomas Wall appear to have been transported in connection with the Cappoquin attack, but little is known about them. Their convict records in Hobart show them to have been working men – a printer, two farm labourers and a top sawyer (AOT: CON 33/104; 33/100). The Cappoquin incident was mentioned in the memoirs of one of the leaders of the conspiracy, John O'Leary (later a Fenian), *Recollections of Fenians and Fenianism*, London, Downey & Co. (rpt. Shannon, Irish University Press, 1969), 1896, vol. 1, pp. 29–43. He noted that this and Lalor's abortive assembly of men in Tipperary had produced the same results that O'Brien's had achieved the previous year: 'The mountain in labour was not so big, and the mouse that came forth was not appreciably smaller, but still there was no gainsaying the fact that the product was only a mouse, and in so far ridiculous' (ibid., vol. 1, p. 41). See also *Freeman's Journal*, 20 September 1849, 2b.
208 *The Times*, 2 October 1848, 6f–7a. Although convicted earlier, Dowling was sentenced with his co-defendants on 30 September 1848.
209 This list was requested by O'Brien from the convict authorities in Van Diemen's Land. William Lacey died on 11 February 1854 (NLI: O'Brien Papers: Ms. 445/2854; letter of 7 July 1854).
210 Denison to Grey, 4 October 1854; AOT: GO, OD, GO 33/81, ff. 426–7.
211 The *New York Daily Times* (11 June 1852, 1c) carried a letter from Dowling (reprinted from the *Galway Vindicator*) giving an account of the various Young Irelanders and Chartists then in Van Diemen's Land. Earlier that year Dowling was in correspondence with O'Brien, reporting a severe paralytic seizure. Even at this point he appeared to have a substantial interest in local political developments, presaging his decision to remain in the colony (Dowling to O'Brien, 21 October 1852; NLI: O'Brien Papers: Ms. 444/2814).

for soliciting the attack. All bar one (who was a sawyer) were labourers, and on arrival in Van Diemen's Land were put to work in the normal convict fashion, progressing from the probationary labour gang after a year and a half to the status of paid pass-holders for a similar time. There followed a full ticket of leave and, after a further year, conditional pardons. In all, these men served relatively short sentences, after which they lived uneventful private lives: all seem to have settled in Australia.[212]

To modern eyes it appears anomalous that the leaders of an insurrectionary movement should be given penal conditions superior to their followers; even at the time there were voices of dissension. Following Lady Denison, it could plausibly be argued that the gentlemen leaders had committed the greater crime. To this, Grey or Palmerston would have replied that both were being treated in proportion to their offence, and this required acknowledgement of their prior stations in life. Those who were gentlemen were quite properly permitted to continue living as such, seeking employment or drawing on their private resources. Those who had been labourers scarcely suffered more from being obliged to pass through the convict system.

The political expediency of this answer was clear – as was the distinction being drawn between political and 'ordinary' crime. In the latter case – theft, forgery or fraud – there was not the slightest suggestion of adjusting the convict regime to take account of the offender's previous way of life. For the Confederation rank and file truly equal treatment would have meant tickets of leave on their arrival, allowing them to make their way as free labourers as best they could; passing them through the convict system meant that their political status was ignored. O'Brien was stung by the accusation in a critical local newspaper that his humble followers were in the labour gangs while the leaders were enjoying privileged conditions. The accusation was unfounded in the strict sense that none of O'Brien's 1848 followers had been transported (Dowling's offence had occurred a month after O'Brien's arrest; Cappoquin a year later), but O'Brien saw the moral force of the argument. Had any followers been transported it was unworthy on the part of the government to treat them more severely than the leaders. For his part, O'Brien insisted, 'I can truly say that I have no desire to receive from the British Government, any indulgences which are not shared by the humblest of those who followed me in the unsuccessful effort which I made to secure my country from ruin'.[213] A sceptic might have found this disavowal unconvincing and convenient.

---

212 Richard Davis, 'Unpublicised Young Ireland Prisoners in Van Diemen's Land' (*op. cit.*) sets out and discusses such information as is available about these men's lives as convicts and thereafter. See also 'Our Dead Comrades', *Celtic Magazine*, XI (February 1884), pp. 91–7, which stated, without giving direct evidence, that *ten* working-class Young Ireland followers remained in custody after the leaders had been pardoned.

213 *Op cit.*, pp. 131–2.

Hons and rebels

The 'terms of engagement' followed by most of the Young Irelanders, and espe-
cially upheld by O'Brien, both in insurrection and then exile in Van Diemen's
Land, mark them out as pre-revolutionary conspirators. By refusing to countenance bloodshed or attacks on personal property, O'Brien completely doomed
the 1848 Rebellion, which was already a most improbable military venture. *The
Times*, in common with the rest of the English press, had poured ridicule on
O'Brien's indecisive and aimless anabasis, presumably to deride the notion of
Irish military prowess (though whether they would have been better pleased had
the rebels acted with effective ruthlessness is questionable). Permeated with the
superiority and condescension with which Ireland and the Irish were then viewed,
The Times leader which supported the decision to allow O'Brien to Ireland
referred to Ballingarry as 'a paltry riot in a cabbage garden', and to the denoue-
ment as a burst bubble, after which 'the foolish persons who had amused themselves with playing at treason found themselves within the grasp of the constables,
and in due course lodged in gaol'.[214] *Punch* heaped on contempt. Why not allow
O'Brien to return to Ireland? 'We think his presence there would be of enduring
good; he would be like a bankrupt linen draper; a living memento of an alarming failure; an old musket barrel without a lock; a firework case, with the
combustibles quenched in a gutter.'[215]

In the conduct of the rebels and the reaction of the government, there was
a harking back to the age of chivalry, when wars were fought according to
rules which protected non-combatants, and required clemency and honourable
treatment for the vanquished. The rebels were uncomfortable with methods of
secrecy and conspiracy. Mitchel taunted the British administration with the
openness of the rebellion – 'The idea of men preparing in broad day-light to
overthrow a powerful government *by force*, and giving them a programme of
their plans beforehand, seemed to you wholly absurd'.[216] O'Brien took a similar
line against conspiracy, and on his return to Ireland disavowed the Irish Republican Brotherhood, which sought to present itself as a successor to the Irish
Confederation. Writing in the constitutional nationalist organ of his friend
Duffy, O'Brien urged his countrymen not to join the Brotherhood because it
was a secret organisation. In part his objection was tactical – conspiracy and
secrecy strengthened the government's hand since such organisations immediately attracted spies, and became instruments for provocation and intelligence
gatherings. 'Either through indiscretion or through treachery,' he cautioned
the *Nation's* readers, 'the *secrets* of such associations become known almost

---

214 *The Times*, 13 March 1856, 8d.
215 *Punch*, 22 March 1856, p. 113.
216 *United Irishman*, 8 April 1848, 136b. Looking back on his actions years after their failure
   Mitchel was unrepentant – 'Sedition, treason, were openly preached and enforced; and the
   United Irishman was established specifically as an Organ of Revolution' (*Jail Journal*, p. 17).

immediately to the government, and furnish a pretext for invasions upon public liberty.'[217]

One's fellow criminals?

Over the past century and a half a recurrent theme in the memoirs of Irish political offenders and their sympathisers and supporters has been the indignity of being forced to associate with criminals – especially those drawn from the slums and rookeries of England's large cities, guilty of morally repulsive crimes. This indignation certainly stirred the Young Irelanders. They gloried in their country's predominantly agricultural economy and rural society, and its religious peasantry. They identified the great cities and conurbations of Britain with the abhorrent national characteristics of their opponents, and with moral corruption on a scale unknown in Ireland. Crimes of simple dishonesty, it is true, could be viewed with a certain detachment, even sympathy. Offences of moral turpitude and vice, and the obscene language and immoral behaviour of urban criminals in captivity, evoked special horror – the more so, understandably, when political offenders might be expected to live with such offenders. In civil society, manners, etiquette and a range of customs and social arrangements existed to regulate contact between the classes. The control and regulation of servants showed that these anxieties were most keenly felt where contacts were close and familiar.

John Mitchel was ambivalent in his attitude towards convicts. He had a modicum of sympathy with them as underdogs, but little sense of comradeship. He had no doubt that they were a class, a people apart, their very physiognomy showing that they were 'burglars and swindlers from the womb'.[218] In penal philosophy Mitchel was as conventional as his nationalism was extreme; his views would not have been out of place in the more conservative English drawing-rooms. Transportation violated the principles of less eligibility. If the convicts' conditions were superior to those of the poor, 'what can be more natural than that famished honesty should be tempted to put itself in the way of being sent to so plentiful a country?' With its material inducements and lack of penal effect transportation encouraged and entrapped rather than deterred: 'It is not uncommon to find families who have been hulked for three or four generations.' The cost of the whole exercise appalled him. The number of convicts was increasing 'in much comfort, with everything handsome about them, at the cost of the hardworking and ill-fed, and even harder working and worse-fed people of England, Scotland, and Ireland. That there is a limit to all this, one may easily see.[219]

---

217 *Nation*, 30 October 1858, 137b; the *Nation* itself took a strong line against secret societies.
218 *Jail Journal*, p. 77. Here he echoes the writing of his sometime idol, Carlyle (See 'Model Prisons', in *Latter Day Pamphlets*, *The Works of Thomas Carlyle* (ed. H. D. Traill), London, Chapman & Hall, 1896–1901, vol. 10, pp. 50 *et. seq.*).
219 *Jail Journal*, p. 125.

What then was to be done with convicts? 'Why hang them, *hang* them.' This was a penal philosophy of the unreconstructed eighteenth-century Whig.[220] Mitchel denounced the liberal jurists who had done so much to reform the sanguinary code, and looked back to a happier, bloodier time:

> In criminal jurisprudence, as well as in many another thing, the nine-teenth century is sadly retrogressive; and your Beccarias, and Howards, and Romillys are genuine apostles of barbarism – ultimately of canni-balism. 'Reformation of the offenders' is not the reasonable object of criminal punishment, nor any part of the reasonable object, and though it were so, your gaol and hulk system would be the surest way to defeat that object and make the casual offender an irreclaimable scourge of mankind. Jails ought to be places of discomfort; the 'sanitary condition' of miscreants ought not be better cared for than the honest, industrious people – and for 'ventilation', I would ventilate the rascals in front of the county gaol at the end of a rope.[221]

These views were almost certainly more reactionary than those of the ministers and senior officials of the day. Having served their sentences and secured their tickets of leave and conditional pardons through good conduct, former convicts were regarded by the authorities as being restored to civic life, including eligibil-ity for public office. Their punishment completed, they regained something of a presumptive good character (at least in Australia). But Mitchel would have none of this. Convicts were irremediably tainted stock, as were their children – presumably unto the seventh generation. Many of the former convicts who had acquired farms grew 'rather decent', he acknowledged, but he hastened to add: 'it would be too strong to say honest.' Such improvement as there was came from 'the mere contact with their mother earth here'. These farmers were friendly to one another, and to travellers, 'and otherwise comport themselves partly like human beings'. But this was mere surface appearance for 'human they are not. Their training has made them subterhuman, preterhuman; and the system of British "reformatory discipline" has gone as near to making them perfect fiends, as human wit can go. . . . What a blessing to these creatures, and to mankind, both in the northern hemisphere and the southern, if they had been hanged.'[222]

220 A type found in England and the Southern States of America. Mitchel would eventually become a staunch and prominent supporter of the Confederacy (and serve time in a Federal fortress, alongside the Confederate President Andrew Davis) but his views on slavery were already discernible. En route to the Cape he saw slaves when the *Neptune* touched the Brazil-ian coast. Here he found the slaves 'fat and merry, obviously not overworked nor underfed, and it is a pleasure to see the lazy rogues lolling in their boats, sucking a piece of green sugar-cane, and grinning and jabbering together' (ibid., p. 150).

221 Ibid., pp. 125–6.

222 Ibid., p. 224. Later he reflected on the ex-convict day labourers whom he employed on his farm in Van Diemen's Land: '[I]nstead of rejoicing in *their* improved conditions, and behaviour, I

To a lady in Ireland Mitchel wrote of the 'high attractions' of farming in Van Diemen's Land despite 'the drawback of the hideous people one must employ and see about one'.[223] As for those former convicts who had advanced themselves to become minor functionaries in the administration, these were, in the main, 'the very offal of mankind'.[224] Indeed, Mitchel confessed to a deep-seated dread of the penal colonies: '[I] have all my life determined a violent horror of Australia and Van Diemen's Land. To live among utter savages in Dahomey or Namaqualand, might be tolerable – but these Colonies are peopled for [the] most part by far more detestable Savages, Savages decivilized.'[225]

Given this fountain of disgust, Mitchel was oddly willing to turn the natural secrecy and solidarity of convict society to his own advantage. During his escape from Van Diemen's Land he wanted to communicate covertly with his wife, and sent a note which, had it been turned in to the authorities, would doubtless have brought the informant a reward or some advantage, and may have led to his own capture. But Mitchel did not hesitate: 'This man is an Englishman and has been an old prisoner; yet I know he would not sell that note to the enemy for a thousand pounds.'[226] It would seem that the tainted stock of Van Diemen's Land thought better and did better by Mitchel than he ever did by them. Even in death he loathed convicts and withheld all pity. He said of a convict cemetery he had seen, 'I have a respect for my own body, and wish that it may mingle with earth, if not in consecrated ground, at least not in an unblessed company.'[227]

---

gaze on them with horror, as unclean and inhuman monsters, due long ago to the gallows – tree and oblivion; and then the very sunlight in this most radiant land takes a livid hue to my eyes! the waving, whispering woods put on a brown horror . . .' (ibid., p. 256). All this horror rode easily with his admission, in the same paragraph, that in his remote and unsecured farmhouse in a land peopled largely by ex-convicts his family felt as secure and slept as peacefully as they ever did at his home in Ireland (Mitchel to Miss Thompson, 4 October 1852; cit. William Dillon, op. cit., vol. 1, p. 338).

223 Michael Davitt, who of all the Irish political offenders was probably the most sympathetic to ordinary prisoners, had, as a nationalist, long cherished Mitchel's Jail Journal. On a visit to Tasmania more than forty years after the Young Irelanders had escaped or been released, he reread it. He praised Mitchel's condemnation and defiance of British rule, but looking at the book 'from the broad humanitarian standpoint' he was taken aback: 'I discovered its appalling narrowness of spirit and lamentable want of fairness towards friends as well as foes.' He particularly deplored Mitchel's attitude towards his fellow prisoners: 'The injustice and harshness of his sentiments as expressed in his book towards the unfortunates who had sinned against the rights of that property which he had himself so eloquently denounced – after reading all this in the land in which Hobart, Port Arthur, and Macquarie Harbour prisons had existed, I almost regretted having opened the Jail Journal again' (1898, p. 335).

224 New York Daily Times, 24 November 1853, 3a.

225 Mitchel to O'Brien, dated June 1850; NLI: O'Brien Papers: Ms. 444/2696.

226 Jail Journal, p. 280.

227 Ibid., p. 58. In a letter to Reilly on the eve of his escape, he again expressed horror that his remains or those of his family should mix with those of the convicts: 'Imagine how our bones would rest in one of those devil's acres they name churchyards' (New York Daily Times, 24 November 1853, 3b).

Mitchel's views may have been the most extreme among the Young Irelanders, and one must make some allowance for exaggeration in pursuit of literary effect. But among the rebels anti-convict sentiment ran deep and strong. When William Smith O'Brien was transported (in some considerable comfort), John Dillon's wife, Adelaide, wrote indignantly that he shared the ship 'with 250 common English convicts'.[228] And when Thomas Meagher married in Van Diemen's Land, Mitchel wrote to Father Keynon that all the exiles were displeased. According to Adelaide Dillon, Mitchel regarded the bride, Catherine Bennett as 'an amiable girl enough herself' (Adelaide adding 'I hate *amiable* girls') but commented that 'she is the daughter of a common *English* convict, and all her relations, etc. etc. are convicts too, and that altogether they [the exiles] seem to think it is an unfortunate match altogether [*sic*].'[229]

Patrick O'Donohoe for a time poisoned relations between his comrades and the population of Hobart Town by remarks he made in a letter to his wife in Ireland, which she rather foolishly made public. It first appeared in Duffy's *Nation* on 27 April, 1850, and thence found its way into the *Hobarton Guardian* (which had done so much to support the Young Irelanders), where it provoked understandable complaints about O'Donohoe's lack of gratitude. The observation which particularly offended may have had some truth in it (which made it the more wounding): 'I suppose the earth could not produce so vicious a population as inhabits this town; vice of all kinds, in its most hideous and exaggerated form, openly practised by all classes and sexes.'[230]

228 *Cit.* Brendan O'Cathaoir, *John Blake Dillon, Young Irelander*, Dublin, Irish Academic Press, 1990, p. 119. One gets the sense that to Adelaide *English* convicts were worse shipmates than Irish convicts would have been.

229 Passing this news in a letter to her husband (he in New York, she in Grace Field, Ireland), Adelaide Dillon emphasised that it was confidential. She entirely endorsed Mitchel's condemnation: 'Is it not *too* bad, of course she is not *one bit* fit or worthy of him and now I think will be *ruined*, a noble really good wife would be his happiness & salvation, but now – it makes me melancholy to think of it' (Adelaide to John Blake Dillon, 30 June 1851; TCD: Dillon Papers: Ms. 6455-7/146). Catherine was in fact of Irish extraction, her father having been transported in 1818 for holding up a mail coach at Trim, Co. Meath. At the time of her marriage her father farmed 100 acres at New Norfolk. Catherine Meagher's first child, born in Van Diemen's land, died. She herself died in 1854 giving birth to a second child at her father-in-law's house in Waterford.

230 *Nation*, 27 April 1850, 552d. This letter appeared in the *Hobarton Guardian* on 17 August 1850 (3d–e), and produced a clamour of protest – not least from the prosperous townsmen who had financed O'Donohoe's controversial newspaper the *Irish Exile*. The *Hobarton Guardian* denounced O'Donohoe in an outraged editorial (21 August 1850, 3a and e–f). Wisely, O'Donohoe made a full and immediate apology, giving details of all the financial and moral assistance he had received from numerous local people. The letter had been written hurriedly and he never supposed it would be published. It had, moreover, been misinterpreted. It was, he argued, intended to mean that there were vicious individuals in all classes, 'and could not have been meant to embrace every member of the community' (ibid., cols e–f). The *Irish Exile* also reprinted the letter, with O'Donohoe's apologetic comments (24 August 1850, 5b–d, 6a–c).

Despite this distinctly unfortunate beginning (for which he was obliged publicly and abjectly to apologise) O'Donohoe used his journal, the *Irish Exile*, to argue against the bigotry with which free settlers regarded convicts, 'emancipatists' (those who had served their sentences) and the poorest class of immigrant. Although he used various defences of these lower orders, the essence of O'Donohoe's approach was that all men were sinners, and only God's intervention could elevate them from their base condition.[231] In contrast to Mitchel's violent penal opinions, he considered flogging and like forms of punishment as 'the bitterest satire on the wisdom of Omnipotence, and likely only to prove counter-productive'.[232]

Australia itself was seen as a cesspool of the British Empire, and consignment there under any conditions was regarded with the same anger and repulsion that imprisonment would have provoked. Despite their relative freedom of movement, the Young Irelanders felt the odium of criminal associations forced upon them by the remoteness of the place, the convict ancestry of so many of its free inhabitants, and the convict or ex-convict status of so many more. Writing home, John Martin expressed some of this sense of contamination: '[W]e are branded convicts here at the uttermost end of the earth in this loathsome den of depravity of the whole Empire, by the relentless Enemy, and alas as yet triumphant Enemy, of our country.'[233]

It is remarkable that these men, one and all, had put themselves in the path of the law's severest penalties for the sake of the poorest of the Irish peasantry, yet (with the exception of the hapless O'Donohoe) showed little or no interest in the common Irish among whom they lived in Van Diemen's Land. Few are the words of understanding about the social conditions in which they had committed their crimes, or the lives which they led as convicts, freedmen or immigrants. Mitchel would freely have resorted to the gallows or lash for English convicts, but said little of the Irish criminals among whom he lived: had they lost their nationality through crime, and entered into the new one of 'detestable Savages, Savages *decivilized*'?[234]

As for how their fellow-convicts viewed them, the evidence, while unclear, is that they were venerated for their part in the national struggle: O'Brien had become a talisman. The Irish names in the lists of tradesmen and the respectable asking O'Brien to give up his parole, or bidding him farewell on his departure

---

O'Donohoe had disclosed in his original letter the regular Monday meetings between Martin, O'Meagher and O'Doherty, which can hardly have pleased them.

231 Richard Davis provides a succinct outline of O'Donohoe's social and religious thought in 'Patrick O'Donohoe: Outcast of the Exiles', in Bob Reece (ed.), *Exiles from Erin: Convict Lives in Ireland and Australia*, London, Macmillan, 1991, pp. 246–83.

232 *Irish Exile*, 17 August 1850, 2c.

233 Cit. Patrick O'Farrell, *The Irish in Australia*, Kensington (NSW), New South Wales University Press, 1993 (rev. edn), p. 49.

234 Mitchel to O'Brien, dated June 1850; NLI: O'Brien Papers: Ms. 444/2696.

from the island, or commenting on the treatment of the Irish political convicts in letters to the colony's many newspapers, all indicate a deep fund of sympathy and admiration. But whatever the escapades of O'Donohoe, Irish convicts, ticket-of-leave men or recent convict stock were not in their circle of acquaintances. O'Brien kept himself within the most respectable social circles and comported himself with great care, as did Mitchel. Between them and the man in the street, convict-connected or free immigrant, a great gulf loomed. Writing in May 1851 to a former servant who had emigrated to New South Wales, William Dalton, a Tipperary farmer, indicated the extent of the divide when he face-tiously enquired: 'You do not Say a word about your friend Smith O'Brine did you Call to See him.'[235] As likely indeed for the common Irish as a call on Lieutenant-Governor Sir William Denison.

The cause of militant nationalism required a sacrifice for its sanctification. The rigged trials of the Young Irelanders provided some grounds for seeing them as martyrs – except that they were obviously and determinedly guilty, and the partiality of all juries in Ireland was likely to be determined by their religion. The commutation of their sentences and gentlemanly transportation to Van Diemen's Land hardly constituted martyrdom, any more than their conditional liberty in the colony. Except when they breached the rules by drunkenness or a too-obvious defiance of their parole conditions (as had O'Donohoe, O'Doherty and MacManus in January 1851), the Young Irelanders had no more contact with the convict population of Van Diemen's Land than had the free settlers. Oppression and suffering had to be found to a greater degree than mere civil banishment afforded: the nobility of the cause deserved no less. The solution for Mitchel and several of his comrades was to rail against the indignity and insult offered to them by being placed on the same island as convicts and those of convict stock. Irish revolutionists of succeeding generations would be given the opportunity to form a much closer acquaintance with their criminal companions.

---

235 William Dalton to Ned Hogan, 15 May 1851: David Fitzpatrick, *Oceans of Consolation: Personal Accounts of Irish Migration to Australia*, Ithaca and London, Cornell University Press, 1994, p. 287. (This scholarly work provides an outstanding insight into the Irish emigrant experience in Australia and its perception and effects in Ireland.)

3

THE FENIANS

A dream of revolution

'A dangerous feeling of aversion . . .'

No substantial social or political reform followed the events of 1848. Famine passed, death and emigration depopulated an agrarian economy which had been unable to sustain such numbers. With the removal of tiny and unsustainable tenancies landlords consolidated – either taking land into their own cultivation or letting larger holdings. A measure of well-being – albeit still very low on that scale – began to grow among those who had variously survived the terrible years. It became easy (and certainly convenient) to imagine that the old order could continue, improved, and strengthened even, by the experiences and results of famine, eviction and the Young Irelanders' paltry and ultimately absurd challenge to authority.[1]

But the grievances of Irish Roman Catholics had not been addressed and continued to fester. Where the experience of 1848 had bolstered the complacency of those who wished to be complacent, it fanned the hatred of those who had long been disaffected. Almost twenty years after the Young Irelanders had been suppressed, Lord Strathnairn, then Commander-in-Chief of British forces in Ireland, passed a remarkable document to his superior, the Duke of Cambridge, for submission to the Cabinet. This was a frank appraisal of the root causes of Fenianism, and could, in many ways, have reflected the reasoning of many constitutional nationalists, if not the Fenian leadership itself.

---

1 This view was well expressed in an article in the loyalist *Dublin University Magazine*, at a time when Fenianism appeared to have been forestalled: 'Celtism has found a home in Australia and in America, but its own excesses have expelled it from Ireland, and the great rural population are prepared for the new era of industry and peaceful progress. . . . After the Young Ireland failure of 1848 there was a rapid development of practical effort, and a substantial advance in prosperity; and now that probably the last of the series of plots generated by long years of false agitation has become matter of history, it may be expected that every reasonable man and lover of his country will prefer the practical progress possible within his own lifetime to the fostering of delusions which can only provide perils for his children' (Anon., 'The Fenian Conspiracy in America and in Ireland', *Dublin University Magazine*, 68 (April 1866), p. 480).

There was widespread disaffection with British rule in Ireland, Strathnairn informed the Cabinet. It existed not only among the lower social classes but also in a large portion of the middle classes. Shopkeepers, artisans, second-rate civil engineers, some of the young clergy, as well as small farmers and farmers' younger sons, were in sympathy with the Fenians. As for the rest of the middle class and the Roman Catholic clergy, their opposition to Fenianism was based more on its threat to their basic interests rather than Fenianism's hostility to British rule. In short, with the exception of the Catholic aristocracy and almost all the gentry, there existed in Ireland among a large portion of the population 'A dangerous feeling of aversion to British rule, which can be called nothing but disloyalty'.[2] And those who did not sympathise with Fenianism stood disapprovingly aloof from the government, which had the effect of increasing ill-will and disaffection in the lower classes.

The disaffection and lack of loyalty had several causes. Centuries before, the Roman Catholic hierarchy had lost its lands and revenues and still bitterly resented the deprivation. The laity was obliged to support its own church and that of the alien, Protestant Church. There remained bitter memories of conquest, dispossession and severe penal laws directed against Roman Catholics, and these engendered 'irreconcilable social animosities' between the two religious groups. It would be a dangerous illusion, Strathnairn warned, to imagine that these feelings of disloyalty and division were of a passing nature, 'temporary and evanescent'; they were ingrained – imbibed and retained from earliest youth.

The social composition of the country and the associated agrarian problems contributed to the dangerous condition of things. Absentee landlordism was a significant but not conclusive factor in disaffection, as was the poor state of agriculture and the small size of holdings. Then there were combined the Irish lack of talent for agriculture and the effects of free trade. Without capital, or talent, pasturage was preferred to cultivation. With large families struggling on smallholdings, this 'indigent class of small farmers who in England would be labourers' found themselves insolvent and evicted. These experiences, in their turn, led to 'Irish vindictiveness, assassination, agrarian outrage and intimidation'. The effect of *these* was further economic and social dissolution. Ireland, even in times of peace, was 'a source of grave anxiety', a place where conflict and threat discouraged investment and reduced property to half its value.

In its existing state Ireland was also a strategic threat to Britain's security. Irish-American sentiments were inflamed, and had their political effect in the United States of America. Ireland's south and west coast offered safe anchorage for a large number of ships, for whom, should war develop with France or America, Irish fisherman would be pilots. One-third of the privates and non-commissioned officers of the British army were Irish Roman Catholics, and,

---

2 National Library of Ireland (NLI): Larcom Papers: Ms. 1188(5); Strathnairn memo to the Cabinet, June 1867; the quotations and summaries which follow are taken from this source.

both on grounds of continued supply of such numbers of men and their loyalty in time of war, the Irish political situation was dangerous.

When it came to remedial policies, Strathnairn was as much at sea as the politicians themselves. Religious reconciliation was at the top of his list, because of the influence of the Roman Catholic Church, the injustice with which it had been treated, and its unremitting indignation and hostility to British rule. There should be agricultural reform, but how this was to be achieved Strathnairn could not say. Peace would encourage investment in manufacture, which in turn would spread the prosperity that encouraged loyalty. Emigration – not least because it increased the ranks of discontented Irish-Americans – was no solution. Casting around, Strathnairn even found favour in allotments for labourers which, having served so well in England, might 'with advantage' be introduced to Ireland.

Conciliation and pacification should be carried as far as possible, but there should simultaneously be vigour in countering conspiracy, incitement and rebellion. The laws and punishments for subverting soldiers needed tightening, as did those against the publication of sedition and the activities of secret societies. There should even be some switch from civil to military law, and those who sought to tamper with soldiers should be brought before courts martial. But as to the repeated and continued suspension of habeas corpus, and similar coercive measures, Strathnairn was sceptical. These were but 'a cumbrous and temporary palliative . . . not a permanent remedy'. Such were the thoughts of the leading military man in Ireland in the midst of the Fenian emergency. Pacification and conciliation would be the basis of British policy in the years to come, but the problems that Strathnairn outlined – the seemingly unalterable religious, political and social conflict – had become the bedrock on which a new Irish revolutionary organisation would be built.

In a society which had been so decisively deprived of native sources of authority, loyalty to those which remained was fierce. The Roman Catholic Church provided moral authority and secular services and organisation. Through its membership of the wider Roman Catholic community, its members could claim a place in the world which was neither mediated nor controlled by the British Empire. It was a strict church which subordinated laity in the clergy and shared its authority with none. Its Jansenist approach to moral teaching gave it great power over the personal lives of adherents, but to a people who longed for authority to which they could yield without scruple or reservation, this was a welcome yoke. And although there had been various conflicts between nationalist leaders and the Roman Catholic clergy, and no considerations of nationality could weigh more heavily than the claims of a universal Church, there was in the minds of the people an almost total identification between religious affiliation and nationality. The Protestant nationalist was an anomaly, and lionised when he appeared.

The business of the Roman Catholic Church was, quite understandably, the Roman Catholic Church. The cure of souls necessarily blurred some of the boundaries between the secular and the sacred, and involved the Church in social and political matters. Despite strict rules of hierarchy and an iron discipline, individual clergy sometimes stepped further across the boundary and into the affairs of the world than the hierarchy deemed prudent.[3] When this was done in support of national aspirations it usually evoked a warm response from the faithful. However, despite its dissatisfaction with the existence of the established Anglican Church, the Roman Catholic hierarchy recognised its obligation to support the established order, and to protect the faithful from political extremism and revolution. In part this arose from its own moral teachings, and in part from the calculations of an institution which was very much of the world, and with many political and material interests. Revolutionary developments in Europe, especially France and Italy, had taught the Church how closely linked were the privileges and prerogatives of the secular and sacred establishment, and how vulnerable both could be. Strathnairn had castigated the Roman Catholic Church in Ireland (and its Protestant counterpart) for unsettling bigotry, but in truth it was a conservative and stabilising force in Irish society, dedicated to achieving its institutional objectives through the cultivation of the established political order, and therefore utterly opposed to subversion and insurrection.

There is a level of individual and collective psychological and spiritual need which churches and political movements may meet. This is a desire to be part of a wider entity, to be more conscious of oneself as an individual, even while participating in the greater body – because, indeed, one is part of that transcendent entity. This is a ground where church and party may compete and conflict, and were particularly likely to do so where each made claims in the other's territory. Romantic Ireland, with its other-worldliness; its authority derived from history and various utopias; its invitation to sacrifice and its pantheon of martyrs; its ability to transcend the meanness of individual life, to resolve doubts and dissolve frustrations; its offer of emotional and spiritual experience far beyond the ordinary – in all of this, nationalism met the religious as much as the political and civic needs of its devotee. The austere self-discipline which looked to joy and fulfilment after death was bound to be challenged by the offer of reward – moral and material – in the here and now.

Irish revolutionary nationalism was strengthened rather than weakened by the events of 1848. The cause had been validated by bravery, adventurous display and, above all, by sacrifice. It would have been better, more potent, had the sacrifice been one of blood rather than imprisonment and exile, but these

---

3 In September 1866, John Mitchel, then in Paris, had visited the Irish College, in company with his friend Father John Keynon. When the seminarians and staff heard of the visit they lined the corridors and cheered Mitchel, who, deeply touched, reflected that in a year or two these young men would be curates in towns and country parishes throughout Ireland: 'What is his Eminence Cardinal Cullen going to do about it? How will he ever make the young priests, educated in this Irish College, good faithful West Britons?' (William Dillon, *Life of John Mitchel*, London, Kegan, Paul, Trench & Co, 1888, vol. 2, p. 247).

were mysterious and awful enough, and could be enlarged upon in the mind. And on the other side, oppression, cruelty and wickedness had been displayed. Going forward, there would be an attempt to avoid the organisational errors of Young Ireland, but organisation, in the end, was less important than spirit. The conspiracy would be more refined, better prepared, but the outcome was intended to be the same – an army of Ireland, under its colours and uniformed commanders, taking the field against its enemies, upholding the honour of the nation and summoning all its children to the decisive struggle. As against a campaign of murder, terror, sabotage and intimidation, this national flourish looked an unlikely victor in a contest with British administration – but the romantic idealism from which revolutionary morality was fashioned allowed no other course.

Paths from Young Ireland

Constitutional politics

All political movements are coalitions of various tendencies, some closely allied, others fleeting in their cooperation, and potentially antagonistic: the formation, splitting and re-formation of alliances is the circulatory system of politics. Young Ireland was no exception to this process, and before, during and after the 1848 uprising the division of the Irish Confederation into several factions was obvious, as were the shifts in alliances. Following the suppression of the movement and the punishment of its leaders, those various formations reacted in different ways – withdrawal from political activity; assimilation into conventional politics and the repudiation of earlier beliefs; new departures in constitutional nationalism; and, for some, a renewal of revolutionary activity. From the last two groups emerged traditions which would dominate Irish political life until our own times.

At least in the short term, constitutional nationalism was strengthened. Acquitted after his multiple trials, Charles Gavan Duffy was one of the few Young Ireland leaders remaining in the country. Even while a member of the Irish Confederation, he had floated a plan for the creation of an independent and aggressively national Irish Parliamentary Party. Anticipating tactics which Parnell would deploy so devastatingly a generation later, Duffy wished Irish members to obstruct Westminster business until an Irish parliament was granted. Should the campaign fail, the MPs would return to Ireland and sit as a national council, to pave the way for an Irish parliament.

Despite early and favourable signs, the times were not right for Duffy's scheme. Forty-eight candidates supporting his programme were returned in the general election of July 1852. This was not an Irish majority, since the total number of MPs in the representation of Ireland at that time was 105. But this small party held the balance of power in the Commons and, by voting with the Liberals, was able, in December 1852, to turn out Lord Derby's first administration. This was the high point of their campaign. Within a short time the Irish party broke up as a result of internal dissent, acceptance of patronage, conflicts with the

Roman Catholic clergy and problems with the landlord-dominated electoral system.[4]

Defections from the Irish party's ranks, and acceptance of office by men who had previously denounced place-seeking, did much to discredit the movement, and the constitutional approach to nationalism. This hiatus was an opportunity for the British government to take action to relieve Irish grievances and to divert politics away from confrontation. Other affairs of empire took up ministerial time and energy.[5] Nor was it simply a matter of full agendas. Political thought in the principal English political parties had a long way to go before confronting the scale of the change that would be necessary to conciliate the Catholic Irish and draw them into willing citizenship. With few obvious gains available, constitutional nationalism languished.

Even John Martin, Mitchel's closest friend, a more committed revolutionary than Duffy, despaired of the political climate of the mid-1850s. Reading of various nationalist developments in Europe, and considering the achievements of the Italians and Hungarians, he reflected on the 'fine spirit' of these peoples, which he contrasted with the 'slavishness' of the Irish.[6] He was greatly disappointed by the popular reaction in Ireland to the Crimean War, and the support that was being given to the British forces – 'I saw that great progress had actually been made towards the denationalisation of Ireland' – and there were more far-reaching changes. Many who were nationalists had emigrated, as had many who 'from their youth, spirit and social position' would most likely have become nationalists. Such had been the impact of the famine, Martin believed, that the mass of the people were 'delighted to get the coarsest food' and, remembering what they had passed through, 'felt such a state of things prosperity'. The famine, though generally felt to be the fault of the English rule had yet to be charged against England 'as a crime to be punished, or as a wrong to be avenged'. But worst of all was the pro-British sentiment – 'war-spirit' – of Irish public opinion regarding the conflict between the British and the French and Russian governments: 'When I reflected a little I admitted that this spirit, however absurd, was not to be wondered at.'[7]

Martin's pessimism and political misery were heightened by the state of the Irish leadership. Mitchel had lost much support and had provoked a reaction among his political friends and supporters to his pro-slavery views. His 'haughty violence' and wrongheadedness convinced Martin that he had lost his capacity for uniting and organising Irish nationalism (though few among his other

4 Theodore William Moody, *Davitt and Irish Revolution 1846–82*, Oxford, Oxford University Press, 1981, p. 39; R. F. Foster, *Modern Ireland 1600–1972*, Harmondsworth, Penguin, 1989, pp. 383–4.
5 Sir Llewellyn Woodward, *The Age of Reform 1815–70*, Oxford, Oxford University Press, 1962, p. 350.
6 Northern Ireland Public Record Office (NIPRO): John Martin Papers: *Paris Journal*, D.560/5, f. 119.
7 Ibid., ff. 133–4.

contemporaries would ever have thought that he had possessed these qualities). O'Brien, despite his many excellent qualities, had shown that he lacked the capacity for revolutionary leadership, and now had no interest in it. Martin had hoped that he could himself have contributed to the nationalist cause, even if from Europe and America, but given the divisions among the Irish nationalist leadership, 'this abominable quarrel between Mitchel and Duffy', their incapacity and the state of Irish public opinion, he had been reduced to a prolonged period of political depression. Reflecting on what had been and what might be, ten years after the Young Ireland insurrection, Martin could see no way forward. In this he probably reflected the despair of a substantial section of what had been advanced nationalist opinion.[8]

Fenianism

Yet the embers still glowed. The events of 1848 showed that physical force nationalism was much more effective as an idea than an organisation. Its continuing appeal was shown by the persistence of fragments of the revolutionary movement. Young Ireland's failure had lain, as a later and more experienced revolutionary observed, in the fact that the movement was 'virtually all leaders, with practically no organized followers'.[9] This had been the basis of the débâcle – leaders half-heartedly wandering around in search of followers. The lack of organisation and practical results meant that government could be content to deride and dismiss the episode, to prosecute and punish a handful of leaders, and pay little attention to the local clubs and associations. The well-disseminated knowledge that government had lists of members who could easily be gathered in was a useful device to ensure the good behaviour of all but the small core of hardened activists. Many clubs nevertheless remained in being, or at least capable of resuscitation, after the 1848 leaders had been transported, or had lapsed into internecine polemics, indifference or despair. What remained was not material of outstanding promise, but was sufficient for local contacts to be made between men who held strongly nationalist views, some of whom had been willing to arm and train for insurrection: these groups would provide a basis for Fenianism. Pitiful though it was as an insurrectionary body, on the plane of romantic politics the Irish Confederation had achieved far greater success than was evident at the time. Fenianism was an attempt to harness the powerful poetic, symbolic and emotional elements in the Irish political consciousness which Young Ireland had reanimated, and to direct that force into an effective revolutionary organisation. Although few of its founders would live to see it, many of the goals of Fenianism would be achieved. It became the most

---

8 These various reflections are set out in his *Paris Journal*, written between May and late July 1858 (NIPRO, D. 560/5, ff. 131 *et. seq.*).
9 Michael Davitt, *Life and Progress in Australasia*, London, Methuen, 1898, p. 333.

enduring and successful revolutionary secret society in Europe. Fenians of a later generation would establish an independent Irish state, and the ideology of Fenianism – some would say its direct organisational descendants – remains a significant force in modern Irish politics.[10]

The revolutionary, unknown and without resources, daily confronted by the immensity of the power of the state, dreams of transformations. He can continue this existence only if he can nourish and maintain those cravings in the face of his own powerlessness and unimportance. As the various revolutionary movements of the past 200 years have shown, theoretical and organisational work can sustain the activist and keep alive the revolutionary vocation. But theories must offer the comfort and encouragement of fulfilled predictions and favourable omens from time to time, and there must be evidence of advance, at least organisationally. For the Young Irelanders the French Revolution of February 1848, and other upsets of the European order, provided the bridge between contemplation and action. The key doctrine, which had been articulated in 1846 (but which went back to the United Irishmen and beyond) was that British military power must be engaged in a major struggle elsewhere for revolution to have a chance of success in Ireland. The Young Irelanders waited anxiously for a Britain at war, and had persuaded themselves that the events in Europe were the beginning of a wholesale *risorgimento*.

For those who in the 1850s had revolutionary dreams, there were portents and omens more encouraging than the false spring of 1848. The Crimean War tested British military power and found its weaknesses, and showed for the first time since Waterloo and the Congress of Vienna that the country's resources could be committed to a war with a major European power. Britain emerged from the Crimea having succeeded (with its allies) in blocking Russian expansion to the West, but for all that, somewhat humbled, with her enemies emboldened. (The Irish revolutionaries did not grasp the wave of military and civil reform that had been spurred by criticisms of the war effort.)

Even more encouraging for the Irish revolutionary was the Sepoy Mutiny of 1857 to 1858: an overstretched empire dependent upon colonial levies to maintain its army, popular dissatisfaction with the political, cultural and religious

---

10 John Devoy (1842–1928) bridged the generations and was the outstanding example of a lifetime in Fenianism. Joining the movement in his teens he then enlisted in the French Foreign Legion to gain military experience. On returning to Ireland he was directed by James Stephens to recruit in the British Army. Following the arrests in the autumn of 1865 he became chief organiser of the Fenians. Arrested himself in February 1866, he was sentenced to fifteen years' penal servitude; with the other leaders he was granted conditional freedom five years later. For several decades he worked as a professional revolutionary in the United States of America, raising funds and operating at arm's length in Ireland and Britain. He played a significant part in the organisation of the Easter rising of 1916, and lived long enough to take the salute of the army of the Irish Free State in 1924. (For an interesting, but wholly partisan account of this key figure in the history of revolutionary Irish nationalism, see Stephen Rynne, *John Devoy*, Kildare, The John Devoy Memorial Committee, 1964.)

domination of the conqueror, and a soldiers' revolution which spread with uncontrollable rapidity. The parallels were tantalising. The Roman Catholic Irish comprised one-third of the ranks of the British army.[11] If Irish soldiers could be neutralised or even turned, chances for revolution in Ireland were immeasurably strengthened. At the very least, was it to be imagined that Irish Catholics could be relied upon to prosecute a repressive war against their countrymen? Perhaps it would be possible to fashion a secret organisation in the British Army which would, as had the sepoys, strike when instructed by their leaders.

Two men saw the revolutionary potential of the times in the debris of the Irish Confederation: both had been 'out' in 1848. They were prepared to face up to the immensity of the task of overthrowing British authority in Ireland, and to live the conspirator's life. Although their organisation would not carry the day, it established an extraordinarily durable ideology and organisational form: these men and their comrades crossed the all-important bridge from thought to action. They infused their ideas with the energy that led to desperate action and communicated them convincingly to large numbers of followers. Their few triumphs were glorified, their sufferings and their martyrs gave them historical stature among their countrymen; over several generations they were formidable opponents.

The two who achieved this process were James Stephens[12] and John O'Mahony.[13] Following the 1848 defeat both escaped to France, to which revolutionaries again looked for inspiration. Together with many other exiles, Stephens and O'Mahony lived in the milieu of the numerous Paris-based secret societies.[14] In 1853 Stephens returned to Ireland, where, in company with another

---

11 NLI: Larcom Papers: Ms. 11188(5): Strathnairn memo to the Cabinet, June 1867, p. 4.

12 (1825–1901). Railway engineer. Wounded in Young Ireland's Ballingarry skirmish. Chief of the Irish Republican Brotherhood, which he founded in Dublin on 17 March 1858. Went to America in 1858 and 1864 to raise funds and founded a successful paper, the *Irish People*. Dismissed from the Fenian leadership in late 1866. In exile until 1891, when he was permitted to return to Dublin. In a Commons speech in 1866, James Whiteside, Conservative MP for Dublin University, and a former Irish Attorney General, outlined much of what was then known about Stephens. The serving Irish Attorney General, James Lawson, added further comment (3 *Hansard*, CLXXXII, cols 740–74; 22 March 1866). A more sympathetic account of the man and his achievements is given by Desmond Ryan in *The Fenian Chief: A Biography of James Stephens*, Dublin, Gill & Son, 1967.

13 (1816–77). Gentleman farmer and scholar. After several years in France following the 1848 failure, went to the United States of America where in 1858, in association with James Stephens and Michael Doheny, he founded the Fenian Brotherhood, initially as a support body for the Irish Republican Brotherhood.

14 Little is known of the details of Stephens' life in Paris. What can be gleaned has been set out in Desmond Ryan's *The Fenian Chief* (*op. cit.*, ch. 5). The form of organisation he chose for his revolutionary society shows the influence of Blanqui's Society of the Seasons. Stephens claimed to have fought on the Republican side in the 1851 *coup d'état* of Louis Napoleon (E. L. R. Green, 'The Fenians', *History Today*, 8 (1958), pp. 700–1). Frank Jellinck (*The Paris Commune of 1871*, London, Victor Gollancz, 1937, pp. 19–60) describes the background and aftermath to the February revolution and the regrouping on the 1848-ers, all of which would have engrossed

Young Irelander Thomas Clarke Luby,[15] he travelled the country to take a measure of conditions and popular feeling. He established contact with the remnants of the Confederation Clubs and other surviving militants such as O'Donovan Rossa had gathered in his Skibbereen-based Phoenix Society. After protracted discussions and reorganisation, the way was cleared for a new organisation, and on St Patrick's Day, 1858, the Irish Revolutionary Brotherhood (later called the Irish Republican Brotherhood (IRB)), familiarly the Fenians, was inaugurated.[16] Shortly afterwards Stephens made his way to the United States of America, where he visited prominent Irish-Americans and the remnants of the Young Ireland leadership.[17] The movement nevertheless dawdled, but achieved a certain credibility and was given a considerable infusion of new strength in 1861 after its inspired organisation of a public funeral for the Young Irelander Terence Bellew MacManus, whose body had been brought back from the United States of America for that purpose.[18]

Stephens and O'Mahony, who came to Paris with their revolutionary credentials already established. Auguste Blanqui, who embodied the notion of vanguard revolutionary – acting on behalf of a people as yet unenlightened – had been a pupil of one of the most extreme of the Jacobins. His life was one entirely of conspiracy, and his activities lasted for almost half a century. He became known (as would Stephens) as the 'Old One' or the 'Old Man'. See Samuel Bernstein, *Auguste Blanqui and the Art of Insurrection*, London, Lawrence & Wishart, 1971, chs 5, 8 and 9; Leon O'Broin, *Fenian Fever: An Anglo-American Dilemma*, London, Chatto & Windus, 1971, pp. 1–2; One Who Knows, 'Fenianism: A Narrative', *The Contemporary Review* 19 (December 1871 to May 1872), pp. 302–3.

15 (1821–1901). Son of a Church of Ireland clergyman; educated at Trinity College, Dublin. Briefly imprisoned after the 1848 rising. Formulated the oath taken by members of the Irish Republican Brotherhood. Arrested and imprisoned for Fenian activities in 1865. Released under the 1871 Amnesty, but forbidden to return to Ireland until the expiration of his sentence; settled in the United States of America, where he died.

16 At the time of its foundation the organisation was given no name, and for several years thereafter was apparently known only as 'the organisation'. The Fenians, strictly speaking, were the revolutionists organised by O'Mahony in the United States of America. The name (which was adopted in 1863) was taken from the legendary band of warriors, the Fianna. Usage applied the term to the IRB, and it eventually became generic (and even now is used as a term of sectarian abuse in Ireland). For the sake of convenience I shall use the term interchangeably with IRB, to denote the revolutionists both in Ireland and overseas, making more specific distinctions only when required.

17 Stephens visited Mitchel in Knoxville in November 1858. He stayed two days, Mitchel remembered, 'telling me romantic tales of his armed, sworn, organized forces in Ireland. All he wanted was that I should publicly call on my fellow-countrymen in America for money, and more money, and no end of money to be remitted to him for revolutionary purposes' (William Dillon, *op. cit.*, Vol. 2, p. 120).

18 The passage of the body across the United States of America, from San Francisco to New York, further stimulated the flourishing American movement Manchester (R. A. Burchell, *The San Francisco Irish: 1848–1880*, Manchester University Press, 1979, p. 100. See also *Daily Alta California*, 24 July 1861, 3a; 20 August, 1a; 21 August, 1a). 'One Who Knows' (and who *did* know, since he was Sir Robert Anderson, a principal in the anti-Fenian moves of government) contended that from the time of the MacManus funeral 'fenianism rapidly gained ground in

As a revolutionary body, the IRB seemed more fitted for the task than the Irish Confederation had been. It was a hybrid military hierarchy and secret society, and though not democratic it did attempt to provide elements of accountability and collective decision-making. Security and discipline were organised on continental lines. Initiates were bound by oath, and members were organised in circles. A 'centre' (known as A) was chosen, corresponding to the rank of colonel; he appointed nine captains (known as B) each of whom selected nine sergeants (C), and each sergeant appointed nine men (D). (Overall, and choosing the 'centres', was the Head Centre, James Stephens.) The resultant unit was a 'circle' of 820 men (though in practice it varied in size). In theory, the lower ranks did not know the identities of those in other units, and thus were limited in the damage they could do, should they turn traitor.

Fenianism's *raison d'être* was violent struggle against British rule; parliamentary and other constitutional action were anathematised. Such a stark doctrine of force left little room for illusions about enemy strength, thus emphasising the need for patience and restraint until British military capacity should be stretched elsewhere by imperial responsibilities. From history, both ancient and modern, the Fenian leaders drew the lesson that an empire so dependent upon levies of the conquered was vulnerable. After some initial hesitation it was decided to swear to the organisation as many Irish soldiers as possible. Irish emigrants in Britain, although removed from the critical battlefield, could provide useful recruits and material support, and might stage diversions and sabotage at the critical time, and so were brought into the conspiracy. The Irish in the United States of America were to provide money, arms and trained men, all channelled through the Fenian Brotherhood. In contrast to the Young Irelanders, the Fenians recruited from the clerical, commercial and working classes, making the members

Ireland'. 'Fenianism: A Narrative', *The Contemporary Review*, 19 (December 1871 to May 1872), p. 305. See Joseph Denieffe's memoir (*A Personal Narrative of the Irish Revolutionary Brotherhood*, New York, The Gael Publishing Co, 1906, ch. 9 and appendices V and VI) for an account of the use of the MacManus funeral by the Fenian leadership. An anonymous contribution to the *Dublin University Magazine* gave the loyalist view of the funeral and its aftermath: 'The Fenian Conspiracy in Ireland and America', *Dublin University Magazine*, 68 (April 1866), pp. 465–7. For a biographical note on MacManus, see above (p. 42, n. 113). Relations between several of the surviving leaders of Young Ireland and the Fenians were at best mixed. Mitchel repudiated its conspiratorial methods (though not physical force in the national struggle); Martin took to the constitutional path; and O'Brien repeatedly condemned Fenianism. Some merely drifted away from nationalist (and probably all) politics. One such was Thomas Meagher to whom the *Irish Republic* gave a mixed obituary: 'Many of us have borne him grudge, because of his latter day indifference to Irish matters; some have spoken uncharitably of his failings . . . but in memory of his youthful patriotism . . . let the venomed tongue be hushed' (27 July 1867, 9a). MacManus, in contrast to all of these, had not tarnished his credentials of militant nationalism. Death at a relatively young age and in obscure poverty had caught him safely in amber: Fenianism would suffer no embarrassment by celebrating his life and using his death (see Brendan O'Cathaoir, 'Terence Bellew McManus: Fenian Precursor', *Irish Sword*, 16, 63 (1985), pp. 105–9).

an integral part of the organisation, rather than casting them as elemental forces to be set in motion when banners were unfurled by an élite leadership.[19]

Informers, spies and revolutionaries exist everywhere and at all times in symbiosis – but especially so in Ireland. Each conspiracy had an accompanying flock of informers; for some, loyalties, identities and even objectives were in a near-constant state of flux. Secrecy, the oath and the compartmentalisation of the 'circle' were intended to provide some form of protection against penetration. Fatally for their enterprise, Stephens, O'Mahony and their comrades did not fully embrace the conspiratorial method. This was due partly to their military strategy, which envisaged conventional rather than guerrilla or terrorist action.[20] It was intended to wage a lightning campaign, to overthrow the occupation garrison and draw strength from the swift establishment of a revolutionary government; international recognition would follow, and reconquest would be impossible. The plan required a demonstration of nationhood – an army, a flag, uniforms and large bodies of men in the field in conventional military formation. Secrecy, always difficult with large numbers, was made utterly impossible by the necessity to recruit, assemble, train, equip and fund on such a scale. Whatever else Stephens had learned in Paris, he had failed to heed Blanqui's crucial distinction between a mass and a conspiratorial organisation. Reflecting this, and in another echo of 1848, Stephens set up his own newspaper in Dublin, the *Irish People*. This served to stimulate support, but also became an invaluable

---

19 For an interesting insight into the social class composition of the IRB see John Newsinger, *Fenianism in Mid-Victorian Britain*, London, Pluto Press, 1994, pp. 29–30. Analysing the occupations of the 1100 men interned under the suspension of habeas corpus powers between 1866 and 1868, Newsinger points out that no less than 47.8 per cent were artisans or skilled workers, 6.4 per cent town labourers, 5.3 per cent farm labourers, 9.1 per cent clerks or schoolteachers, and 3.6 per cent shop assistants. This socially flat pyramid had certain consequences. The impecuniousness of even the leaders is indicated by a letter from O'Donovan Rossa to his wife, while still on remand, awaiting his trial. He advised her to go immediately to America, and to use his gold watch and chain, worth £7 or £8, to help meet the cost. The watch, he told her, had been bought in a pawn shop, to which she should seek to resell it (Rossa to Mary O'Donovan Rossa, 25 September 1865: Catholic University of America; Fenian Brotherhood Papers, Box 2, item 23). Of the Fenians, Michael Davitt was one of the most incisive and politically sophisticated. Looking back several decades to compare Young Ireland and the Fenians, he noted of the former that 'they were virtually all leaders, with practically no organized followers'. The Fenians had 'organization, numbers, and a menacing power, but no leaders in the later attack upon Castle rule in Ireland' (*Life and Progress in Australasia*, London, Methuen, 1898, p. 333).

20 In later phases Fenianism – or at least strands of it (like many revolutionary movements it had strong centrifugal tendencies) – did adopt terrorist tactics, in particular the dynamite campaign of the 1880s. Terrorism, in the sense of a deliberate or reckless harm to civilian life and property, and the calculated use of atrocities to alarm the population and undermine authority, was not acceptable to Fenianism as conceived by Stephens, O'Mahony and other founders. When some groups in the Fenian tradition – such as Clan na Gael, the Triangle and the Invincibles – did engage in terrorism and committed atrocities, they were denounced by authoritative Fenians. Such tactics violated Irish revolutionary honour, as defined by the Fenians. In this important sense, Fenianism was a pre-terrorist organisation.

intelligence conduit for the authorities, by its content, and by surveillance of those involved in its production and distribution.[21] Only the most restricted of conspiracies can hope to resist penetration by counter-conspirators using the culture of secrecy to advantage.[22] The Young Irelanders were not entirely naive about this matter, and gave it as one of their reasons for preferring open to secret organisation.[23]

21 The temptation to publicise the movement was all the greater since there appeared to be a considerable popular appetite for revolutionary journalism. In his June 1867 memo to Cabinet, Lord Strathnairn lamented the influence of the Fenian press: 'The lower orders read nothing but these treasonable effusions. They pore over them in their leisure hours, and the more extravagant they are in their descriptions of Ireland's wrongs and misfortunes, and the more they point to a violent and illegal remedy, the more they are engrossed with them. Few are too poor to buy these penny papers, which are passed from hand to hand' (NLI: Larcom Papers, Ms. 11188(5)). Such popular responses would, understandably, have been encouraging to the Fenian leaders, and provided an important stimulus for the movement. Unfortunately, they also stimulated the police. The G Division of the Dublin Metropolitan Police reported on the newspaper from its inception, although the first report (23 December 1863) showed that the police at that time did not know that Stephens had established a conspiratorial organisation in Ireland – commenting that 'the existence of such a society in this country would be illegal and its proceedings not tolerated' (National Archives of Ireland (NAI), Chief Secretary's Office (CSO), Registered Papers (RP): 1863/11941). The authorities were soon disabused on this point.

22 In the Irish context, the classic example of this ability to turn a conspiracy 'inside out' was, of course, the Englishman Henri Le Caron (1841–94; real name Thomas Billis Beach), who for twenty-five years spied on Irish revolutionaries in the United States of America. To increase his espionage effectiveness Le Caron established his own branch of Clan na Gael (a Fenian organisation) in Illinois. As founder of the branch he received communications from headquarters and travelled widely on Clan business. He recalled that, by cautiously advancing himself, and 'by taking advantage of the varied openings given me, I was enabled to extend my usefulness as a Special Service agent to a very appreciable extent' (Twenty-five Years in the Secret Service, London, William Heinemann, 1893, p. 128). For a more concise and accessible account of Le Caron, see Charles Currant, 'The Spy Behind the Speaker's Chair', History Today, 18 (1968), pp. 745–54. The continuing vulnerability of secret organisations to penetration by spies or informers using the conventions and facilities of secrecy is demonstrated in the account of a recent Irish Republican informer, Sean O'Callaghan, The Informer, London, Bantam Press, 1998.

23 John Mitchel was ambivalent but not wholly unsympathetic towards the Fenians. They were very helpful in securing his release when in 1865 he was incarcerated by the victorious Union in Fortress Monroe (alongside Jefferson Davis) because of his services to the Confederate cause; he subsequently acted as the Fenians' financial agent in Paris. But, as his biographer notes, save for that brief period, Mitchel never believed that the Fenians could be successful: 'Secret organization and secret conspiracy were the essence of Fenianism, and these very things he had always regarded as sure to do more harm than good in Irish politics' (William Dillon, op. cit., vol. 2, p. 228). Mitchel's friend John Martin took a different course in politics after his pardon and return to Ireland, and was a co-founder of the (wholly legal and constitutional) National League. He described Fenianism as a 'delusion' which he expected to be gone by the end of 1865. When the Fenian leaders were arrested in September of that year he wrote that he would be relieved of heavy anxiety 'if I felt confident that the arrests will prevent any attempt at rising' (P. A. Sillard, The Life and Letters of John Martin, Dublin, James Duffy & Co, 1901, pp. 178–9). See also his letter to the Nation (1 December 1866, 233a–b) warning against the planned insurrection.

The conspirators further put themselves in the hands of the government by failing to separate covert from overt personnel, since the staff of the *Irish People* largely overlapped with the central committee of the IRB. Identities and affiliations were thus announced to the world, and it was an easy matter for the police to watch premises and people, and to insert a spy into the staff.[24] Incriminating documents, arms and ammunition were, against all common sense, kept in the *Irish People* office, where they awaited a raid at a time to be chosen by the police.[25] In the meantime, the newspaper's steady flow of sedition provided abundant evidence for action when desired. The constant blending of covert and overt action undoubtedly influenced the psychology of the Fenian leaders, perhaps blinding them to the nature of what they were attempting, and the inevitable response of the authorities.

Revolutions

The first phase

Irish politics, as John Bright had anticipated in 1848, and J. S. Mill would reiterate in 1868, would forever be changed by the flood of Irish emigrants to the United States of America.[26] Here the Irish diaspora would find resonances, affinities and opportunities which no other country offered. A state constantly

24 Their principal spy was Pierce Nagle. The police also kept close observation on all comings and goings. Thus, on 11 September 1865, the Dublin Metropolitan Police reported that O'Leary, Luby, O'Mahony, O'Donovan Rossa and fourteen other recognised leading Fenians had met at the *Irish People* offices. The report commented that such an assembly had not been seen before. The inference that an outbreak was at hand would have been impossible for a prudent official or policeman to avoid (NAI: Fenian Papers; Fenian Police Reports, 1857–83, carton 3, no. 237, Daniel Ryan, Superintendent of G Division to Under-Secretary Thomas Larcom, 11 September 1865). But although the authorities knew that an insurrection was being planned, they did not have a grasp of detail until they seized papers when the *Irish People* offices were raided (Anon., 'The Fenian Conspiracy in America and in Ireland', *Dublin University Magazine*, 68 (April 1866), p. 475).

25 The offices were raided on the night of Friday, 15 September 1865, following numerous reports of an impending insurrection. Thirty-five were arrested, and Cork city and county 'proclaimed' under the Peace Preservation Act, 1856: 19 & 20 Vict., c.36. (See *Freeman's Journal*, 18 September 1865, 2g–3a, 3h). The papers which were seized were kept more or less intact (except for those abstracted for use in the prosecution of the Fenian leaders) but remained in the disorganised state in which the police had removed them. The State Paper Office (now absorbed into the National Archives of Ireland) received the papers in 1933. An account of the papers is given in Breandán MacGiolla Choille's pioneering essay, 'Fenian Documents in the State Paper Office', *Irish Historical Studies*, 16 (1968–9), pp. 258–85.

26 The famine had greatly increased the pace of Irish emigration, driving particularly large numbers across the Atlantic. By 1850 New York had 133,000 Irish residents – more than half the population of Dublin. In the United States of America at large there were 1.6 million persons of Irish birth by 1860 (E. R. R. Green, 'The Fenians Abroad', in T. Desmond Williams (ed.), *Secret Societies in Ireland*, Dublin, Gill & Macmillan, 1973, p. 79).

and visibly growing in power, established in revolutionary conflict with the hated British; religious freedom and equality as high constitutional doctrine (though not always social or political realities); and above all, an authority to which the displaced Irish could give wholehearted loyalty without feeling disloyal to their own national origins. All of this was reinforced by the constantly improving fortunes and status of the Irish in civic life, the professions and commerce. At home treated as rural aboriginals, irremediably backward through some defect of race, the Irish responded to the opportunities of their new home with a fervent and demonstrative American patriotism. That they were divided by the American Civil War did not detract from this communion with the new nation; Irish valour and prowess on both sides of the conflict raised their standing in the new, post-bellum state. The martial strain in Irish culture was confirmed by the string of honours won by generals and colonels and other officers and ranks of Irish birth or blood. Irish-Americanism entered a powerful and florid phase.

Nor in America did the emigrant Irish and their descendants cease to dwell on their national grievances. Success, intermarriage and the passage of time wholly absorbed many in their new country, and the images lost their colour and fury. But even for these an instinctive and easily aroused Anglophobia remained, while for others cultural traditions, activities and organisations kept alive strong national attachments. Lord Cornwallis, in the 1790s, when Irish emigration to America was but a comparative trickle, foretold the consequences: 'They will embark with a spade, and return with a musket.'[27]

The American Civil War, with all the unsettling bellicose and triumphalist emotions it unleashed, had the same seismic effects on Irish politics. Leading Fenians hoped that the Anglo-American tensions of those years would erupt into a full-scale conflict. Besides Union resentment over British relations with the Confederacy, there was potential trouble in the border disputes between Canada and the United States of America.[28] A confident, remade and still martially inclined America might apply the Monroe Doctrine offensively, rather than defensively. Indeed, the Fenians hoped that the anti-imperial sentiment which had run through the Americas for some generations could be wedded to a desire to expand the Republic by incorporating British North America. The Irish presence in America's great cities was already large and influential. Electoral leverage grew by the day, honed political skills, and yielded national opportunity as well as local advantage. Attendances of Fenian demonstrations and social events (some called picnics) were large, and emotions unleashed in

---

27 NLI: Larcom Papers: Ms. 11188(5); Strathnairn memo to Cabinet (*op. cit.*, p. 6).

28 Twenty years before John Mitchel had optimistically pondered these possibilities in a boundary dispute between Britain and Oregon. Here, perhaps, was a revolutionary alliance, for 'distant and desolate as are those tracts beyond the Rocky Mountains, even there may arise the opportunity for demanding and regaining our place among the Nations' (*Nation*, 6 December 1845, 120b–c).

the sympathetic ethos of the American Republic were intensified by the flags, uniform, music and military formation and order of the marchers; in years in which pageantry flourished, Irish-Americans were in the first rank of showmanship. All of this was interpreted by the Fenian leaders as a mass willingness to act and to support action; another interpretation (which they ignored) was that these were substitutes for action – symbolic rather than actual venting of nationalist sentiment; and, at an even more prosaic level, these could be seen as the cultural and recreational activities of a confident but still nostalgic immigrant community.[29] Even so, the enemy (who took all this into account) was worried.

Intelligence reports from the United States of America and almost all parts of Ireland grew steadily more alarming throughout the summer of 1865.[30] Significant numbers of Americans were already in Ireland, and new drafts were in preparation or on their way.[31] There was widespread drilling, and rumours of the stockpiling of arms.[32] Certain evidence existed of subornation in the army: soldiers were being prepared to mutiny, to throw their weight behind the rebels in the event of an insurrection; others were instructed to obstruct or kill their loyal comrades.[33] Fenian influences and membership grew in other public services such as the railways, post office and telegraphs, and even the police. And all the time the Fenian leadership was promising a rising in 1865.

Attempts were made to develop an alliance with the extreme wing of English radicalism, then confronting authority in the campaign for further electoral reform.[34] Contacts were made with continental socialists, and the revolutionary

29 R. A. Burchell (op. cit., p. 101) notes that the Fenian movement for a time provided a focus for Irish activity throughout the United States of America: 'The balls and picnics gave a chance for outings, meetings and gossip on the grander scale.' A picnic in May 1868 was attended by 8000 to 10,000 people, who travelled in a train half a mile long, pulled by three or four engines.

30 NAI: Fenian Papers: Reports on Fenianism, No. 252: A files (Reports from Police and Consular Officials in the United States, No. 23).

31 The dispatch of these men was a mixed blessing for the Irish section. O'Mahony had provided them with between £50 and £100 each, with the promise of a reasonable salary when they reported for service in Dublin. Stephens' resources, however, were so meagre that on arrival the men were paid only very small sums (Anon., 'The Fenian Brotherhood', Blackwoods Magazine, 190, 1151 (September 1911), p. 388).

32 The police were aware of the location of some of the arms dumps, and deemed it advantageous to keep them under observation, rather than raid them. See, for example, the report from Superintendent Daniel Ryan, G Division, Dublin Metropolitan Police, to Commissioners of Police, 5 March 1867, noting the movement of arms from a Dublin dump, and naming several of the principal persons involved (NAI: CSO, RP, 1867/3820).

33 The government had reports of Fenian recruiting in the army in England and Scotland, as well as Ireland. In one case (Private Simpson) a Fenian soldier was allegedly intent on putting poison in his comrades' food, and, with others, shooting them should the alarm to turn out be given (NLI: Larcom Papers: Ms. 11188(5); Strathnairn memo to Cabinet, op. cit., p. 10).

34 The background to these contacts is set out in John Newsinger's instructive 'Old Chartists, Fenians and New Socialists', Eire-Ireland, 17, 2 (summer 1982), pp. 19–45.

soldier Gustave Paul Cluseret[35] was offered and accepted command of the embryonic Fenian army. The condition upon which Cluseret accepted this post was that no fewer than 10,000 men would be available. This prerequisite would never be met, nor was Cluseret's demand for 5000 men, and so he returned to France. For the short period of his involvement with Fenianism, however, Cluseret and some other experienced officers who served with him dangerously strengthened Fenianism's military capacity.

Government struck, and, on the night of 15 September 1865, widespread police raids netted hundreds of incriminating documents, most of the principal conspirators, and a good number of the rank and file. They also seized a substantial portion of the available funds, which, unbelievably, had simply been placed on deposit in the account of Thomas Luby, the IRB paymaster. Stephens eluded the police and remained at large until 11 November, when he too was arrested at Sandymount, Dublin, together with Charles Kickham, Hugh Brophy and Edward Duffy. There was considerable satisfaction in the Irish administration with this decapitation.[36]

Special Commissions in Dublin, Cork and Limerick tried the principal offenders, making deadly use of the Fenian papers which had been seized at the *Irish People* offices.[37] Fortunes were reversed and government confidence shattered when, only thirteen days after his arrest, James Stephens was spirited out of Richmond Bridewell in a brilliant coup that revitalised the revolutionists and led the Lord Lieutenant to confess: 'I was in a fool's paradise about the safety of prisoners . . . I feel like a general who has let his camp be surprised in the night

---

35 (1823–1900). Had been an officer in the French Army. He received French and (it was said) English decorations for his service in the Crimea. Forced to resign his commission because of his strong republicanism, he campaigned with Garibaldi in Sicily in 1859–60. He fought in the Union Army, rising to the rank of brigadier-general. He was introduced to Stephens by Colonel Thomas Kelly. Later, and after other incendiary involvements, Cluseret's career as a revolutionary and soldier of fortune culminated in his military command of the Paris Commune. He gives an account of the events of 1867 from the fairly close perspective of five years in his article 'My Connection with Fenianism', *Frazers Magazine*, VI, 31 (NS) (July 1872), pp. 31–46. From this there emanates a distinct, if affectionate, bemusement with the Irish and their affairs.

36 *Freeman's Journal*, 13 November 1865, 3g. (There was irony in the juxtaposition of this report with one from the United States of America: John Mitchel had been released from custody by order of the President.) The *Irish Times* saw the arrest as a 'death blow to Fenianism in Ireland'. Stephens had been 'the very soul of the Confederacy' (14 November 1865, 2i). The blow was all the more telling because Stephens had concentrated so many functions in his own hands (see Anon., 'The Fenian Brotherhood', *op. cit.*, pp. 384–5). On Stephens' arrest, detention and escape see Desmond Ryan, *The Fenian Chief, op. cit.*, ch. 19.

37 A loyalist writer who appears to have been in some way involved in the prosecutions was emphatic on the importance of the *Irish People* raid and seizures. Had government acted before it did, it ran the risk of securing evidence for no more than treason-felony charges, and these may not have convinced juries. But by laying its hands on virtually the entire correspondence of the Fenians, 'the innermost secrets, thoughts and workings, of all its members, were unmasked' (Anon., 'The Fenian Conspiracy in America and in Ireland', *op. cit.*, p. 477).

and lost half his army.'[38] The Special Commissions proceeded, lasting through the autumn. The newspapers were filled with them, and Ireland was agog. O'Donovan Rossa made a speech of some eight hours, a large portion of which was directed to taunting the judge, William Nicholas Keogh[39] (who had at one point supported constitutional nationalism); not surprisingly, he received a particularly heavy sentence. As they were sentenced, the men were immediately removed under heavy guard.[40]

Events were to show that these arrests, convictions and sentences had dealt the Fenians a critical blow, but this was far from obvious at the time. The movement still possessed considerable resources, widespread support, a potent mystique and great momentum. This was shown by the atmosphere of intimidation which persisted in the aftermath of the trials. The judges and juries which had tried the Fenians had to be placed under military guard. No person, soldier

---

38 Wodehouse to Clarendon, 27 November 1865; Bodleian Library, Oxford, Ms Clarendon Dep., c.99. For the escape see *Freeman's Journal*, 25 November 1865, 8a–c; 27 November, 4e–g. The loyalist *Irish Times* described the report of the escape as falling 'like a thunderbolt upon the city' (25 November, 3b). A bitter opponent of Fenianism, writing just four months after Stephens' escape, confirmed Wodehouse's assessment: great had been the triumph when Stephens was arrested, and proportionately greater were the feelings when he escaped. It was a feat worthy of some admiration, the writer confessed: '[T]he Fenians in the position of leaders must have been much more than vulgar conspirators, and must have been truer to each other than Irish patriots usually have, otherwise Stephens could never have got out of prison, and having escaped could not have baffled the police aided by a reward of £2000, and finally made his way out of the country. A plot whose principal machinators displayed so much ability and constancy was certainly not contemptible' (Anon., 'The Fenian Conspiracy in America and in Ireland', *op. cit.*, p. 478).

39 (1817–78). Had been the Tory MP for Athlone – the only Irish Roman Catholic of that party in the Commons. He was one of the founders of the Catholic Defence Association, and became a member of the Irish Party, which Duffy and others hoped would further constitutional nationalism. He became one of the defectors and saboteurs of that party when he accepted appointments as Irish Solicitor General. Subsequently became Attorney General and Judge. Regarded by the nationalists as a turncoat, Rossa reviled him in court. Keogh's resolute performance on the Special Commission gave him a particular standing with the Irish government, which two years later was somewhat panicked when Keogh indicated that he was unable to sit on another Special Commission to deal with Fenians. Abercorn, the Lord Lieutenant, writing to Mayo, the Chief Secretary, described Keogh's absence from the Commission as 'very serious', adding that Keogh's son-in-law had been sent to persuade him to change his mind. The trials had been adjourned, but should Keogh persist in his decision not to take part, the next judge in line would be O'Brien – 'and his being the Judge is looked upon as being somewhat unfortunate for the ends of justice' (NIPRO: Abercorn Papers: D.623/A/301/21: Abercorn to Mayo, 28 October 1867). It is doubtful if there would have been such crude executive interference with the judiciary in England, but in Ireland justice and the machinery of politics were intertwined.

40 There survives in the Fenian Brotherhood Papers a letter from O'Donovan Rossa to his wife Mary, written in the cells beneath the court, where he awaited verdict and sentence. As he wrote, troops arrived to escort those convicted to Mountjoy Convict Prison. In this extremity, Rossa wrote that his position had brought him 'as much suffering as man can endure bravely' (Rossa to Mary O'Donovan Rossa, 1 December 1865; Catholic University of America: Fenian Brotherhood Papers: Box 2, item 23).

or civilian, who had given evidence was safe out of barracks or without armed protection. A soldier who had given information against his comrades had all six chambers of a revolver emptied into him on one of the Dublin quays, and a further attempt was made to kill him later, as he was recovering from his wounds. Various other murders were attempted, and the military authorities had to transfer abroad various soldiers who were under threat. Fear of retaliation extended to the magistrates who were reluctant to pass severe or even appropriate sentences. In one case the magistrate sent to goal for two weeks persons convicted of incitement to mutiny, and directed that they should not be put to hard labour.

The hundreds of Irish-American officers and men so rapidly demobilised after the American Civil War were sinew and muscle for Fenian plans.[41] Hardened and fresh from the traumas, losses and conquests of war, these included a small but determined group who were battle-ready, constituting a potentially dangerous cadre around which larger forces could be organised. The story of Fenian failure to realise this potential is familiar. The American supporters on whom Stephens had relied for _matériel_ failed to deliver what they had promised.[42] For reasons of character or calculation Stephens dithered, and the moment – a desperate and far from certain moment it was – passed.[43] By the spring of 1866 prospects

41 In April 1865, at the conclusion of the American Civil War, the Union had armies of more than one million men. Such was the speed of demobilisation that a year later the army was only 80,000 strong (James M. McPherson, _Battle Cry of Freedom: The Civil War Era_, New York, Oxford University Press, 1988, p. 853). In such a torrent of men passing from military into civilian life there would be many not yet ready for the disciplines of peace; among these some could be found to take up the Fenian cause. Some 150,000 Irishmen had served in the Union Army, and it was from these that most recruits came for action in Ireland. A smaller number would also come from the shattered armies of the Confederacy.

42 Whether Stephens lacked the courage to go forward it is hard to say. He was one of very few who had already taken armed revolutionary action – in 1848, and maybe also (in France) in 1851. What is certain is that both sides of the organisation – Irish and American – misled each other about their capacities and strength: O'Mahony promising more money and supplies than he could deliver, and Stephens exaggerating the enrolment and state of preparedness in Ireland (see Anon., 'The Fenian Brotherhood', _op. cit._, pp. 382–3). Several armouries had been set up in Dublin, mainly, it would seem, for the manufacture of pikes and bullets. Money was more easily smuggled from America than weapons, and so it made sense to have weapons made in Ireland. This severely limited the type of item that could be made, since gunsmithing was a skilled trade and required special tools and materials. The intention appears to have been to use the pikes in the initial phases of the uprising, and the bullets when weapons had been seized from barracks or from confederates in the army. There was a great shortfall in arms. In February 1867, there were said to be ready for muster 15,000 men in Dublin and 18,000 in Cork, but only 4500 weapons were available (One Who Knows, 'Fenianism: A Narrative', _op. cit._, p. 628).

43 Looking back on the arrests after an interval of some twenty months, Lord Strathnairn, the Commander-in-Chief of British forces in Ireland, was able to see them as a critical turning point. Had Stephens and his comrades not been gathered in and left to proceed with their plans before Fenianism had been neutralised in the army, 'something disagreeable might and would probably have occurred' (NLI: Larcom Papers: Ms. 11188(5): Strathnairn to Cabinet, June 1867, p. 4).

withered further, when the conspiracy in the British Army was suppressed.[44] Stephens had been blamed for the postponements which had nullified any advantage of surprise. On 15 December 1866 he was removed as leader, never again to exercise revolutionary command.[45]

Irish-American leadership

With Stephens and the other Irish leaders gone – to prison or to exile – a new energy flowed into Fenianism from the Irish-American element. Stephens' close friend and adviser, Thomas J. Kelly,[46] now assumed command, and consignments of arms and contingents of men again made their way into Ireland. A steamer which had been purchased for a raid on Canada was sold, and the Fenian treasury replenished.[47] Plans were made for a multi-pronged uprising, and an amount of training took place. All of this was fairly comprehensively penetrated by spies and betrayed by informers. As the months passed, the authorities, scared in 1865, made their own preparations, and took care to have all necessary forces appropriately deployed.[48] The revolutionists also gave notice of their intentions. In some consultation with English radicals and republicans a proclamation of the Irish Republic was issued in London on 10 February

---

44 Altogether some 150 courts martial were held. Several sentences of death were passed, but all were commuted. A number of other men were flogged in front of their regiments (John Newsinger, *Fenianism in Mid-Victorian Britain*, op. cit., p. 45). The newspapers carried numerous accounts of these courts martial. See, for example, *The Times*, 9 January 1867, 7c; 17 January 1867, 10a.

45 See Desmond Ryan, *The Fenian Chief: A Biography of James Stephens*, op. cit., ch. 22. Stephens spent twenty-five years in impoverished exile before being allowed to return to end his days in Ireland. His papers include a pitiful collection of some forty letters from Paris to his wife in Ireland – many delayed homecomings and much worry about tiny sums of money (NLI: James Stephens Papers: Ms. 10, 491 (1)).

46 (1833–1908). Born in Loughrea, Co. Galway. Emigrated to the United States of America, where he served as a subaltern in the Signal Corps of the Union's Army of the Potomac. Wounded and invalided out, Kelly was active in the Fenian movement from the earliest days of its establishment in the United States of America. Appointed colonel by Stephens, with whom he enjoyed a close friendship.

47 During the period 1864–7 funds were also raised by the issue of 6 per cent bonds, whose redemption was contingent on the establishment of the Irish Republic. At a later phase in the Irish struggle the first Dáil (which had reaffirmed the Irish Republic) accepted responsibility for these bonds (Piaras Béaslaí, *Michael Collins and the Making of a New Ireland*, London, George C. Harrap, 1926, vol. 1, pp. 327–8).

48 Lord Naas, the Irish Chief Secretary, wished to let the conspiracy develop before acting. In particular he wanted to wait until the leaders were in the country, and then make a number of simultaneous raids and arrests, gathering up papers, arms, uniforms and the like. Were the authorities to move too soon, they might miss arresting the leaders. He cast doubt on the policy followed the year before – 'shutting up poor and insignificant men'. It was preferable, he argued, to cage the leaders – 'and the smaller fry will disappear' (NIPRO: Abercorn Papers: D623/A/304/2; Naas to Abercorn, 15 November 1866).

1867.[49] There was certainly no panic, and although some in the administration anticipated a serious challenge, the Irish Chief Secretary Lord Naas,[50] daily in receipt of copious intelligence, had no doubt that the army could easily deal with any Fenian effort. In mid-November 1866, he assured Lord Abercorn, the Lord Lieutenant, that the army would not have to fight a campaign or even a pitched battle: 'All we can expect and the worse we should be prepared for can be the assembling of an undisciplined mob of half armed desperados who might plunder . . . houses and attack isolated Police Barracks.' Small bodies of between 200 and 400 troops, ready to move rapidly, would be the most suitable response.[51] This forecast was highly accurate. In support of the main rising there were several provincial raids, notably in the republican districts of Kerry, Cork, Clare, Limerick and Tipperary.[52] The much heralded and once postponed general insurrection, centred on Dublin, took place on 5–6 March 1867.[53]

As Naas had anticipated, it was an utterly irresolute and fragmentary action, hardly more than the 1848 débâcle: an unrealistic mobilisation and deployment of bodies of men and their inglorious dispersal through a combination of vastly superior resources, good intelligence and discipline on the one side, and lack of leadership, confusion, general maladroitness and minimal supplies on the other.[54]

---

49 The text of the proclamation displays the influence of English radicalism, appealing as it did to English workers: 'Republicans of the entire world, our cause is your cause; our enemy is your enemy; let your hearts be with us. As for you, workmen of England, it is not only your hearts we wish, but your arms. Remember the starvation and degradation brought to your firesides by the oppression of labour' (One Who Knows, 'Fenianism: A Narrative', *op. cit.*, p. 633).

50 (1822–72). Richard Southwell Bourke; later sixth Earl Mayo. Irish Chief Secretary 1852, 1858 and 1866. Conservative politician who sought to combine conciliation and coercion in Ireland. Governor General of India 1869–72.

51 NIPRO: Abercorn Papers: D 623/A/304/2; Naas to Abercorn, 15 November 1866.

52 *Freeman's Journal*, 7 March 1867, 3h, 4b–c; 8 March, 3f–h. For an account of the Tipperary rising – a very small thing in military terms – see William Rutherford, '67 *Retrospection: A Concise History of the Fenian Rising at Ballyhurst Fort, Tipperary*, Dublin, O'Loughlin, Shields & Boland, 1903. See also William McGrath, 'The Fenian Rising in Cork', *Irish Sword*, 8, 33 (1968), pp. 322–5; Peter Nolan, 'Fariola Massey and the Fenian Rising', *Journal of the Cork Historical and Archeological Society*, 75, 221 (January to June 1970), pp. 1–11.

53 *Freeman's Journal*, 7 March 1867, 3b–g, 4a–d. The archives show that the Irish government had almost comprehensive advance knowledge of the rising and its preparation (see NAI: CSO, RP, 1867/3813–35, *passim.*). These and other documents are comprehensively reviewed by Shin-Ichi Takagami in his Ph.D. dissertation 'The Dublin Fenians, 1858–79' (Trinity College, Dublin, 1990) and his essay 'The Fenian Rising in Dublin, March 1867', *Irish Historical Studies*, 29, 115 (May 1995), pp. 340–62.

54 Takagami (*op. cit.*) provides the most carefully researched account of the rising in and around Dublin, and shows that some contemporary accounts and reminiscences have to be treated with caution. It is certain, however, that Cluseret and his Chief of Staff Fariola had intended there to be an initial period of small-scale military and civil engagements, with guerrilla bands acquiring experience and confidence before embarking on general engagements. This plan was set aside by Godfrey Massey, who had been appointed by Thomas Kelly to lead the Fenians through the

The leadership was conspicuously absent from the scene of action. Cluseret had agreed that he would not take the field until a provisional government had been proclaimed in Ireland. He remained in England, ironically enough, inspecting English military depots, as part of a perfectly bona-fide mission for the Governor of New York State. Inexplicably, Kelly, the chief executive of the organisation, stayed in London.[55] The suspension of habeas corpus, and the detention of several hundred men under the Lord Lieutenant's warrant, had the effect of neutralising many of the Irish-American soldiers, deterring others from coming, and driving out all but the most resolute of those still at liberty.[56] For all its weaknesses, British administration in Ireland was not going to be toppled without a high level of counter-organisation and serious fighting, and of these there was little sign.[57] Lord Strathnairn, the Irish Commander-in-Chief, warned the Cabinet that the rising – 'partial and weak though it was' – had not collapsed through lack of disaffection, and that only fear had prevented it from assuming larger proportions.[58]

early campaign (Peter Nolan, 'Fariola, Massey and the Fenian Rising', op. cit., pp. 5–7). Thirty years later the nationalist William O'Brien, who had been a child in the 1860s, described the event as a 'fizzle': 'A couple of dozen American officers, ashamed of going home without something to show for rather liberal promises in newspaper interviews, invited some thousands of young men to rise up one fine night (or rather one very foul night), without arms enough all told to fight a single company of soldiers, and without the slightest idea where they were to get their breakfast the next morning. They passed the night in taking or failing to take a few isolated police-barracks. A fortnight of pitiless sleet and snow came down, and saved the troops the trouble of dispersing the insurgents.' O'Brien argued that 1867 was but a sputtering out of 'a movement whose pride and strength had really been crushed more than eighteen months before'. But, he argued, in 1865 Fenianism *had* formidable military capacity ('Was Fenianism Ever Formidable?', *Contemporary Review*, 81 (January to June 1891), pp. 680–1). He was referring, of course, to the September 1865 round-up.

55 One Who Knows, 'Fenianism: A Narrative', op. cit., p. 628. It is possible that Kelly wished to avoid detention under the Lord Lieutenant's warrant, but if this were so, it demonstrated a low level of revolutionary confidence and competence.

56 Lord Naas had hoped to let the Suspension of Habeas Corpus Act (29 & 30 Vict., c.119) lapse in the spring of 1867 (NIPRO: Abercorn Papers: D623/A304). The March rising and continued tension ensured that it remained in force for a further two years, lapsing in March 1869. In May 1867 there were 211 prisoners detained under the Lord Lieutenant's warrant. By the following year only ninety-six remained in custody, despite eighty-one arrests during that time. Some 1050 arrests were made during the currency of the Act (One Who Knows, 'Fenianism: A Narrative', op. cit., p. 642, n.). The prospect of detention on the Lord Lieutenant's warrant also had the consequence (not fully anticipated by the authorities) of sending a number of activists to Scotland and England, where they reinforced the local Fenian organisations.

57 By the mid-1860s an extensive railway and telegraph network had been established in Ireland, and troops could be rapidly deployed throughout the country. This capacity was augmented by the establishment of several flying columns. Rebels would therefore have had to confront regular troops, including artillery and cavalry, and it is hard to imagine that they would have been successful.

58 NLI: Larcom Papers: Ms. 11188(5), p. 3.

There were occasional flashes of brilliant derring-do, but these served only to light a landscape grown dismal for the revolutionists. It had been the intention of one group of Fenian leaders that the Irish rising should be powered by a shipment of arms stolen from England. A plan was made by the Irish-American Captain John McCafferty and the journalist John Flood.[59] This idea and its organisation showed the bravura of some of the Irish-American officers. They had discovered (probably through an IRB man in the British army) that some 30,000 stands of arms were held at Chester Castle, guarded by only one company of soldiers. Chester was on a favourable line of communication with Dublin. The plan was to assemble there a large force of men from the various towns of the north of England in which the IRB had been organising. Aided by Fenians among the guard, the Castle would be captured and, using a commandeered train and the Holyhead steamer, men and *matériel* would be dispatched to Ireland. Resonances would have been great, and the lifting of hopes enormous. The whole scheme was one of audacity, recalling a similar but never realised plan of 1848,[60] and the infiltration guerrilla tactics of the American Civil War.[61] Speed, secrecy, and above all luck, were prerequisites if the scheme were to come off: none was achieved. On the evening before the attack (Monday, 11 February 1867), the authorities had received accurate intelligence, and immediately alerted the garrison, as well as drafting in troops by express trains.[62] Seeing that their plans were known, and countermeasures had been adopted, the leaders decided

59 Dr Mark F. Ryan, *Fenian Memories*, Dublin, M. H. Gill & Son, 1945, pp. 16–17.
60 Thomas D'Arcy McGee had been dispatched to Scotland by the Young Ireland insurrectionists with the intention of landing men and arms in the north-west of Ireland. The scheme miscarried and McGee returned to Ireland. (See 'Thomas D'Arcy McGee's Narrative of 1848', in Michael Doheny, *The Felon's Track*, Dublin, M. H. Gill & Son, 1914, pp. 289–97.)
61 John McCafferty, organiser of the Chester raid, according to some accounts, had, as a Confederate officer taken part in guerrilla raiding behind Union lines, as an officer with Morgan's Raiders, a cavalry unit which severely damaged Union rail communications in the western states. Research, however, has cast some doubt on these claims, and has suggested that McCafferty followed a more mundane occupation prior to his enlistment in the Fenian cause. Truth here may be relatively unimportant, since the power of a legend to shape reality has been demonstrated on many occasions. (See Patrick Quinliven and Paul Rose, *The Fenians in England 1865–1872: A Sense of Insecurity*, London, John Calder, 1982, pp. 26–8.)
62 John Joseph Corydon, an American officer, was the informant, via Head Constable McHale, a Royal Irish Constabulary (RIC) man stationed at Liverpool. Corydon first gave a warning and then confirmed the intelligence, enabling preventive measures to be taken (Sir Robert Anderson Papers: Public Record Office (PRO) HO 144/1537/Pt. 1(b)). Corydon's reports at this time were invaluable in disclosing all the major Fenian moves in Ireland and England. The advance notice given by Corydon allowed extensive countermeasures to be taken, by sea as well as on land. Arrests were made of groups of men arriving in Dublin on the Liverpool ferry; arms and ammunition were hurriedly discarded. Quite apart from Corydon's betrayal, however, the Fenian plan was advertised locally by groups of purposeful and burly young Irishmen travelling to Chester in large groups (*The Times*, 12 February 1867, 9b; *Freeman's Journal*, 13 February 1867, 3c–d).

to call off the raid, and, discarding weapons as they went, more than 1000 IRB men rapidly dispersed.[63] Some immediate arrests were made.

But whatever maladroitness the Fenians had shown in military matters, there were signs of stamina in the organisation, which should have caused the authorities some concern. With news of the defeat of the rising still fresh, the O'Mahony faction of Fenianism got up an expedition in the brigantine *Jackmel*, a vessel of 115 tons. Some forty men embarked with what was said to be several thousand rifles, including some up-to-date breech loaders, three small field pieces and ammunition for the whole. After an adventurous voyage lasting some six weeks, the *Jackmel* arrived off the Sligo coast. Amidst some muddle and cruising to and fro along Ireland's western coast, thirty-one men disembarked, and the *Jackmel* returned to New York without landing a single weapon. All the disembarked revolutionists were arrested.[64] In this instance also the Fenians showed themselves to be capable of bold and brave ventures, but far from the mastery of the detail necessary to carry them through.[65]

Both the Chester raid and the rising itself had given government a scare, although neither in England nor Ireland had the rebels constituted a serious threat to regular troops, or (with the possible exception of Chester) even the constabulary. Such at least is the judgement of hindsight, secure in the knowledge that the fortunes and uncertainties of war had failed to tip the expected balance. By the middle of 1867 all resistance seemed to be over, and a further set of leaders and a few of the rank and file were brought to trial before special commissions.[66] Pressure from the United States of America and the Roman Catholic hierarchy reinforced official and political caution, and no death sentences were carried out.[67]

---

63 *The Times* reported that from 4 p.m. on the day of the aborted raid until late the following evening, 'about 2000 Irish roughs passed through the New Ferry tollbar on their way from Chester to Birkenhead. They came in gangs of 30 or 40, and seemed to be much jaded and dispirited' (15 February 1867, 9f).

64 For technical reasons, and the difficulty of finding a jury sympathetic to the government in that part of Ireland, only two of the thirty-one landed from the *Jackmel* were convicted (of treason felony) and even these convictions were found to be unsafe and the men discharged (One Who Knows, 'Fenianism: A Narrative', *op. cit.*, p. 636).

65 For an account of this expedition, which he describes as 'the most romantic episode connected with the Fenian conspiracy', see ibid., pp. 634–6.

66 Between 8 April and 19 June 169 prisoners were put on trial before the Special Commissioners in Dublin, Cork and Limerick. The great majority (110) pleaded guilty; fifty-two were convicted after jury trial and seven were acquitted. Eight persons found guilty of high treason were sentenced to death, their sentences being commuted. Twenty-five received lengthy sentences of penal servitude, and the remainder were variously imprisoned (ibid., p. 633).

67 The British Ambassador in Washington, Sir Frederick Bruce, on 28 May 1867, reported back to London on a meeting which he had with the US Secretary of State William Seward. In the name of the President, Seward had said that any executions would increase sympathy for Fenianism in America. It was important not to stimulate a fresh Fenian raid on Canada, but in the event of such a raid the US government 'would be more inclined to act if popular feeling was not

Aftershocks

Then there was an apparent lull. Between March and September 1867, the public heard little of Fenianism, and some at least in government became more optimistic.[68] Their rising had failed, their leaders were in prison or abroad and there was little outward sign of their continued activities. The authorities had some idea of the continuing conspiracy, but even they failed to grasp the formidable spirit which the organisation retained. Before the Fenian campaign had completely fizzled out, however, there would be hangings. The man who had taken command from Stephens was an Irish-American, Colonel Thomas J. Kelly. For a time Kelly made his headquarters in Manchester, where he was eventually arrested, ironically on a holding charge of vagrancy. Although the police were initially unaware of the importance of their captives, he and the companion with whom he had been taken (another American officer, Captain Timothy Deasy) were swiftly identified, and as they were being moved from court to the county gaol, following a remand hearing, on 18 September 1867 (a week after their arrest) a rescue was mounted by their comrades. A raiding party of about thirty ambushed the Black Maria and easily dispersed its unarmed police guard. In opening the van, Sergeant Charles Brett, the key-holding policeman, was shot and killed. The two Fenian leaders were released and got away. There was intense police activity, including a number of armed raids.[69] Eventually twenty-eight men were put on trial for their part in the affair, of whom twelve were convicted, five capitally.

The scale and audacity of the attack stunned a public which had been thoroughly alarmed by Fenian activities; even in respectable circles there was a lynching mood. Rather than wait until the next Manchester Assizes, *The Times*

excited by executions' (Sir Robert Anderson Papers, PRO HO 144/1537/Pt/ 1(a)). See Peader MacSuibhne, *Paul Cullen and His Contemporaries* (Naas, Leinster Leader, 1961, vol. 1, pp. 397–406) for an account of the anti-Fenianism of much of the Roman Catholic hierarchy of the time. Intervention to prevent severe punishment of Fenians was prompted by Cullen's belief that severity would increase popular support for the revolutionists.

68 Gathorne Hardy (then President of the Poor Law Board, but in May 1867 to become Home Secretary) noted in his diary on St Patrick's Day, 1866, that he hoped the day would not bring any trouble in Ireland – 'nor do I think it will for Fenianism seems pretty well checked there and Stephens it is said has gone away' (Nancy E. Johnson (ed.), *The Diary of Gathorne Hardy, Later Lord Cranbrook, 1866–1892; Political Selections*, Oxford, Clarendon Press, 1981, p. 6).

69 It was, *The Times* pronounced, 'an incident unprecedented in this country within recent times . . . we thought it was a recognised thing among us that none but downright thieves and murderers would resist law by open violence. But we have now to face, it seems, the most audacious practices of American rowdyism, even if this be all' (19 September 1867, 6b–c; report 7c). See also University of Durham: Sir Charles Grey Papers: Ms. II, 12; General Grey to Sir James Fergusson, 13 October 1867. Reports arrest of Liverpool Head Centre and three others: 'He was clearly identified as having taken part in the rescue of prisoners from the police van at Manchester . . . resistance was made and . . . the arrest was only completed easily by the fact of the police officers being armed with revolvers drawn.'

urged trial before a Special Commission, observing that 'One execution in October may save the necessity of many executions in December.' Unlawful terrorism 'must be repelled by lawful terrorism'. The accused should have all their legal rights, but 'Let speedy justice be done in this instance, and we shall probably hear no more of Fenianism in England; let it be encouraged by the hope of impunity for the next two months, and it may cost us dear to quell it.'[70]

A Special Commission was promptly agreed, amidst some liberal doubts, as represented by the Pall Mall Gazette, which feared that the Commission would 'make more haste than good speed'.[71] This side of the political spectrum may also have been dismayed by the controversial decision of the Manchester magistrates that during their committal proceedings the prisoners should be shackled hand and foot. Defending this decision, the conservative Saturday Review pointed out that 'English prisoners are tried before our Courts without gyres and fetters, because it is not usual for their sympathizers and confederates out of Court to combine for their rescue and the assassination of their warders'. After the attack on the prison van, 'it would have been idiotic for the Manchester magistrates to act on such an assumption'. The Review went on to warn that 'the feeling against Irishmen is unfortunately gaining strength every day'.[72]

In such an atmosphere, moderate loyalist opinion welcomed the acquittal of several of the lesser accused as well as the convictions of those who were seen as principals. The fact that there had been acquittals was taken by the Ulster liberal Northern Whig as evidence of the impartiality of the Commission, and of the merciful drawing by the jury of a distinction between leaders and followers.[73] But the atmosphere of crisis and vengeance remained.

Of the five men found guilty of the murder of Sergeant Brett, one (Thomas McGuire) was pardoned on grounds of wrongful conviction and another had his sentence commuted to life imprisonment.[74] The remaining three – William

---

70 The Times, 8 October 1867, 6d. In his Diary (op. cit., p. 49) Home Secretary Gathorne Hardy was equally indignant: 'England will never endure that such an event should go unpunished.'

71 Pall Mall Gazette, 9 October 1867, 1a.

72 Saturday Review, 12 October 1867, pp. 460–1. It is impossible now to assess the state of public opinion then prevailing, but it is clear that the Manchester rescue and the killing of Sergeant Brett evoked mixed reactions in radical circles. Certainly the response was not reflexively anti-Irish. Writing to his sister just over a week after the rescue of Kelly and Deasy, John Murgatroyd (a member of a Manchester Methodist family) described the rescue and observed that 'These Irish agitators are called Fenians. Ireland has before and since the union of that country with England been badly and sometimes wickedly treated by the English so that these Fenians are not altogether wrong in frightening us in return' (Manchester Central Library: Murgatroyd Papers: M476/16/1/6; letter of 27 September 1867).

73 Northern Whig, 9 November 1867, 3b.

74 Having attended the trial and closely observed all the defendants, John Greenwood, the Treasury Solicitor, advised Home Secretary Gathorne Hardy on the pardons. Excluding McGuire, Greenwood considered the men who had been sentenced to death to be 'a bad lot – very'. He considered Allen (who fired the fatal shot) to be 'wrongheaded, vain, discontentedly active

O'Meara Allen, Michael Larkin and Michael O'Brien (tried and convicted as Gould) – were publicly executed on Saturday 23 November 1867.[75] Between 8000 and 10,000 assembled to witness the executions amidst great military and police security. Some 500 constables were on duty, supported by 2000 special constables. The army was also deployed, and the 500 soldiers included cavalry, infantry and (astonishingly) two batteries of artillery. Commercial enterprises also took precautions lest there should be rioting and looting.[76]

Because of their bravery in court and on the gallows, their public and devout reception of the ministry for the dying from the Roman Catholic Church, the cause in which they were engaged, popular misunderstanding of the common-law doctrine of joint enterprise, and the view that the killing of the constable was an accident, the men's execution aroused great feeling among the Irish at home and abroad.[77] It is hard to overstate the impact of the executions on Irish

minded, a mischevious person – a dangerous tool to be worked by others'. Larkin (with Gould) played the most conspicuous part in the attack. Greenwood was especially scathing about Gould (O'Brien) – 'the worst man of all'. He had been prosecuted on arms offences the previous year and acquitted, and Greenwood considered him to be a determined and deliberate offender. It was his performance in court which particularly incensed Greenwood, however: 'the most odious in manner and in the exhibition which he made of himself throughout the trial, and in his speech'. Greenwood went on to observe that if four were to be selected from the rest (for execution) they should be Allen, Gould, Shore and Larkin. If only three, Larkin ('a poorer creature than the others') or Shore might be excluded from the list (Greenwood to Gathorne Hardy, 6 November 1867; Cranbrook Papers, BM Add. Ms. 62,537, ff. 16–17). For a note on this section of the papers, which had been lost to scholars for several decades, see Robert A. H. Smith, 'The Cranbrook Papers: Stray Letters from a Politician's Archive', British Library Journal, 12 (1986), pp. 172–5. In the end Cabinet decided to reprieve Shore (Gathorne-Hardy, Diary, op. cit., pp. 54–5).

75 One of the hangings (Larkin) was bungled, though its extent did not become public knowledge at the time (see my English Local Prisons 1860–1900, London, Routledge, 1995, p. 414, n. 94; The Times, 25 November 1867, 9e).

76 See Alfred Gathorne-Hardy (ed.) Gathorne Hardy, First Earl of Cranbrook: A Memoir, with Extracts from his Diary and Correspondence, London, Longmans & Co, 1910, Vol. 1, pp. 231–2; The Times, 23 November 1867, 9f.

77 Writing four years after the executions, an American commentator (who may have witnessed them) noted that the scene reminded Americans of the martyrdom of John Brown in Virginia. Of the condemned he observed that their 'noblest act in life was the manner in which they met their death' (Anon., 'An American Opinion of Fenianism', Dublin University Magazine, 68 (November 1871), p. 493). Mock funerals were held throughout Ireland to express sympathy with the executed Fenians. Some of these processions attracted very large crowds, including some 20,000 to 30,000 in Dublin. A similar demonstration in Cork was described as 'one of the most remarkable and significant exhibitions of popular feeling ever witnessed not alone in this city but throughout Ireland' (Cork Examiner, 23 December 1867, 2g). An RIC head constable assigned to surveillance work in the Manchester area reported that 'The speeches of Allen and the others, from the dock, have had a most pernicious effect on the Fenian mind' (8 November 1867). A month later he reported further: 'Notwithstanding the apparent quietness of the Fenians here, they were never more determined in wickedness than now. A great change has taken place since the executions here, in persons whom I hitherto considered to be loyal. I do not think that 1000 of the 150,000 Irish Roman Catholics in this district are loyal. The Fenians

republicanism and nationalism more generally. The incompetence and shameful failure of the March rising were washed away by this blood sacrifice. The 'Manchester Martyrs' galvanised national sentiment. The executions became iconic in their depiction, a saga in the telling, an anthem in the singing: a touchstone of political authenticity.[78] All this was quickly discernible. The public policy lessons were not hard to learn, and strengthened the hand of the conciliators in the British and Irish administrations.[79] From the opposite end of the political spectrum, Engels noted that the Manchester executions had reinforced the revolutionists: 'The only thing the Fenians still lacked were martyrs.

will be better aided in money than they have ever been before' (Sir Robert Anderson Papers: PRO HO 144/1537/Pt 1 (b)). The anti-Stephens Fenian newspaper, the *Irish Republic* (then published in Chicago) described the Manchester rescue in which Sergeant Brett had been killed in the most disingenuous terms. Had ordinary prisoners been released 'nobody would have cared', but since they were Fenians, 'the affray is magnified into a political disturbance' (19 October 1867, 6a). A very different tone was taken when the death sentences were announced and carried out (9 November 1867, 3a; 28 December, 3a–c). The tyrant had 'strangled before the gaze of a besotted and abandoned multitude of the scum of English cut-throatism Allen, O'Brien and Larkin' (for a note on the *Irish Republic*, which is a useful source in these and later years, see William O'Brien and Desmond Ryan (eds), *Devoy's Post Bag*, Dublin, C. J. Fallon, 1953, vol. 2, p. 177).

78 Eleven years later Charles Stewart Parnell, then a parliamentary newcomer, electrified the Commons and attracted the attention of militant nationalists (including the Fenians) by insisting that the shooting of Sergeant Brett had not been murder: 'I wish to say as publicly and directly as I can that I do not believe and never shall believe, that any murder was committed at Manchester' (3 *Hansard*, CCXXX, col. 808; 30 June 1876). Such was the potency of the Manchester executions that this assertion that Brett's killing had been an accident, not murder and the corollary that the executions had been unjust, was the first step towards Parnell's eventual displacement of Butt as leader of the Irish Party. See Francis Stewart Leland Lyons, *Charles Stewart Parnell*, London, Fontana, 1977, pp. 54–5. Robert Kee (*The Laurel and the Ivy: The Story of Charles Stewart Parnell and Irish Nationalism*, Harmondsworth, Penguin, 1994, pp. 114–16) points out that Parnell's remarks attracted no public attention at the time. There is sound evidence, however, that Fenian interest in Parnell commenced at this point.

79 RIC Head Constable Meagher reported from Liverpool on 27 September 1867 that since the Manchester rescue and the executions, 'the Fenians had fallen in the estimation of many of the old Chartists, who had till then sympathised with them'. This, however, was somewhat contradicted by another police report just eleven days later – this time from the Dublin Metropolitan Police: 'In every part of England, but especially in the north, there was great activity among the Fenians, and many of the Chartists were said to be supporting them' (Sir Robert Anderson Papers: PRO HO 144/1537/Pt.(b)). Two days before the executions the Reform League (the principal working-class radical organisation of the times) held a meeting at Clerkenwell Green, attended, it was claimed, by 20,000 to 25,000 working men. The meeting asked for mercy for Allen, Larkin and O'Brien. Gathorne Hardy, the Home Secretary, refused to receive a deputation of Reform League officers which wished to present the memorial. The officers then attempted to present the memorial to the Queen at Windsor, but this was refused on the grounds that it should go to the Home Secretary, 'by whom alone, as the responsible adviser of the Queen, it can be submitted to Her Majesty' (*The Times*, 23 November 1867, 9e). Yet radical and working-class opinion was split by Fenianism, and there were several working-class anti-Fenian demonstrations. In Manchester these were combined with anti-Papist protests, and there were attacks on Roman Catholic churches (ibid., 9f).

They have been provided with these.'[80] Marx took a similar line: 'Fenianism has entered a new phase. It has been baptised in blood by the English government. The political executions at Manchester remind us of the fate of John Brown at Harpers Ferry. They open a new period in the struggle between Ireland and England.'[81] In Ireland, although the Roman Catholic hierarchy remained firm in its condemnation of Fenianism, it was clear that many of the clergy were more in tune with the sympathetic outpourings of their parishioners.[82]

Government's intention to match firmness with fairness and conciliation was certainly tested in what would prove to be the last major incident of the first Fenian campaign – and like the Manchester incident this was another rescue attempt, and also involved an American officer. The anger within militant nationalism at the Manchester executions spurred insurrectionary activity. Arms were still in short supply, and the Fenians intensified procurement efforts. The authorities had good intelligence and kept a special watch on arms dealers; there were also rewards to informers to help identify the leading figures in arms procurement. On 27 November 1867, as a result of these efforts, Ricard O'Sullivan Burke,[83] the leader of one of the two factions of Fenians in England,[84] was

---

80 Karl Marx and Friedrich Engels, *Ireland and the Irish Question*, Moscow, Progress Publishers, 1971, p. 145. The Manchester executions were also the subject of an article by another revolutionary, Louis Blanc, who was then the London correspondent of the Paris *Temps*. Castigating the authorities for the display of force surrounding the executions, and praising the men as martyrs, Blanc concluded, somewhat bemused, 'But what a country is that where it is permitted to wear mourning in public for Irishmen in rebellion against England, and where each man may freely cry, "Cursed for ever be those who make use of the scaffold"' (*The Times*, 29 November 1867, 8a).

81 Notes for (an undelivered) speech, 19 November 1867, Karl Marx and Frederick Engels, *Collected Works*, London, Lawrence & Wishart, 1985, Vol. 21, p. 189.

82 The loyalist *Dublin Evening Mail* protested that the Catholic bishops had made insufficient efforts to stop the requiem masses which were being said for Allen, Larkin and O'Brien. One bishop (Dr Gillooly) had appeared to suggest that the Clerkenwell explosion might have been some form of punishment on the English for supporting Mazzini's attack on papal power (2 January 1868, 2c).

83 (1838–1922). Born Kinneigh, Co. Galway, son of a tenant farmer. Family evicted, and he eventually enlisted in the South Cork Militia. Deserting, he went to sea for several years, visiting many countries and serving for a time in the Chilean Army. He joined the Union Army, fought throughout the Civil War, and was demobilised as a Captain in the Engineers, breveted a Colonel. An adventurous and resourceful man, Burke had established his own arms firm in Birmingham (which traded as E. C. Winslow & Co) and thus obtained large quantities of arms and ammunition. Burke planned and carried out the Manchester rescue of Kelly and Deasy. Convicted of treason felony and sentenced on 6 April 1868 to fifteen years' penal servitude, Burke apparently became mentally unbalanced while in prison (see below, p. 185).

84 The history of Fenianism is littered with splits and schisms. The first of these occurred in the United States of America when the Fenian Brotherhood, at its Philadelphia Convention, split into the William Roberts and John O'Mahony factions. The former group then decided to organise a raid in Canada. Not to be outdone, O'Mahony also organised a raid. Both of these actions ended in routs, humiliation and demoralisation, and consumed resources which had been assembled for an Irish rising. Stephens then asserted his control over the entire Fenian movement in the United States of America, but it continued to be riddled with dissent, factions and defections.

arrested in Bloomsbury. The following day he was, with Casey, the companion with whom he had been arrested, remanded for trial and sent to the Clerkenwell House of Detention.

Another rescue attempt was decided. The plan was to breach the prison perimeter wall while Burke was in the adjacent exercise yard. The neighbourhood had a large Irish population and a tradition of working-class radicalism, and it would no doubt have been easy for Burke to vanish into the many narrow streets and courts, his way eased by sympathisers and supporters. A first attempt to blow the wall foundered on 12 December 1867, when the explosives failed to detonate. A try was to be made for the following day. Once again, however, an informer intervened and Burke was removed to a more secure part of the prison.[85] Unaware of these precautions, the conspirators pressed ahead, and the prison wall was blown apart by a massive explosion. A barrel of gunpowder was fired with a short-fuse squib; no warning was given.[86] No prisoners escaped, but there was grave loss of life and damage to property. Twelve died, 120 were injured, and a great swathe of domestic and commercial buildings was destroyed or damaged. It was a national tragedy, and an atrocity against a whole community – one of the poorest and most helpless in the capital.[87] Ironically, the atrocity had been committed 100 yards or so from Clerkenwell Green, where only weeks before thousands had gathered in protest both before and after the Manchester executions.

85 The authorities had reliable advance information of the explosion, but the Commissioner of the Metropolitan Police, Sir Richard Mayne, failed to take adequate protective steps. Following the explosion, he tendered his resignation to the Home Secretary, but the offer was refused (Gathorne-Hardy, *Diary*, *op. cit.*, p. 57; Sir Basil Thomson, *The Story of Scotland Yard*, London, Grayson & Grayson, 1935, pp. 158–9). Quinliven and Rose (*op. cit.*, chs 6–9) provide an authoritative account of the Clerkenwell explosion, the trials arising therefrom and the aftermath.

86 So immense was the explosion that opinion was divided as to whether gunpowder or the much stronger (and newly employed) nitroglycerine had been used. Some experts thought that various fragments collected in the aftermath of the explosion smelled of nitroglycerine (*Daily Telegraph*, 16 December 1867, 2c).

87 See *The Times*, 14 December 1867, 6d; 16 December, 9d–f; 18 December, 5c–f; 21 December, 5c–d; Mark F. Ryan, *op. cit.*, pp. 125–7. For a discussion of the aftermath see Norman McLord, 'The Fenians and Public Opinion in Great Britain', in Maurice Harmon (ed.), *Fenians and Fenianism*, Dublin, Sceptre Books, 1968. John Newsinger, *Fenianism in Mid-Victorian Britain*, *op. cit.*, provides an interesting account of English radical and working-class attitudes following the Clerkenwell outrage (see esp. ch. 4). Such was the strength of the public reaction that Edward Keneally, the barrister who had been retained to defend Burke and Casey, withdrew from the men's defence, claiming that he had no option since Burke and Casey had not given him assurances that they were not privy to the plot (*Daily Telegraph*, 16 December 1867, 2d–e). Keneally later achieved fame – and professional ruin – through the Tichborne trial (see Arabella Keneally, *Memoirs of Edward Vaughan Keneally, LLD*, London, John Long, 1908). Although he had not withdrawn from the case, Digby Seymour, who had, as ably as possible, defended Allen, Shore and O'Brien, following the Manchester rescue, opened his address to the jury with a personal disclaimer: it was a case 'from which he would gladly have been dissociated' (*The Times*, 2 November 1867, 7c).

Whatever was happening in English radical circles since the escape of Stephens in November 1865, general anti-Fenian sentiment had mounted in England, fed further by the Manchester rescue, discoveries of arms, and rumours of an Irish-American invasion led by Stephens. It was also believed that some of the Irish-Americans who had been conditionally released from internment the previous year had broken their word and had returned to Ireland. Fenian activities constantly stoked the fires of anxiety and anger. At the end of September a man was shot in Holborn for publicly denouncing Fenianism. The *Pall Mall Gazette* warned that though open rebellion had been defeated, terrorism still hoped to drive the government to despair.[88] Threats against the Irish in England – oblique and direct – found space in several of the other national newspapers. There was some reaction from the Irish community, to the extent that an Irish loyalist warned that should the Irish be attacked there would be a united response.[89]

The Times had long insisted that leniency had fed Fenianism. Conspiracy, 'happily abhorrent to Saxon and Norman natures', was getting a new start in Ireland. But let the conspirators beware: 'a rebel in this country is not the romantic personage we imagine in Continental politics; he is a mere robber and ruffian'.[90] Government would certainly defeat another uprising, but (referring to the excesses which followed the suppression of the Sepoy Mutiny) might not be able to restrain the soldiery, 'half-maddened by the sight and report of recent atrocities'. The Fenian leaders might reflect that 'A rebellion is always possible to stop in time, but not its suppression. That cannot be stopped, and most certainly will not.' Warning should be taken from the bloody counter-atrocities of earlier centuries: 'The Englishman and the Irishman, the Saxon and the Celt of this day, are substantially the same as they were in 1641 and 1798, and it entirely depends, as we believe, on Ireland whether there is to be a repetition of those dreadful scenes.' But the Irish appeared to be unheeding and 'the pestilence seem[ed] to be spreading over the country'.[91]

Competing national sentiments, fear, threats, ancient prejudices and anger were twined together in a tinder-dry undergrowth when the Clerkenwell explosion occurred. The monstrous size of the bomb, and the callous disregard of the consequences, challenged British national sentiment as much as it outraged

88 1 October 1867, 1a and b.

89 Ibid., 10 October 1867, 9b. There was at least one killing of a supposed Fenian: see 'Hanging of a Professed Fenian by Lynch Law at Barnsley', *The Times*, 25 September 1867, 12b.

90 *The Times*, 27 November 1866, 8c. The editorial continued: 'As it happens, with the exception of poor Mr Smith O'Brien, we have not had a rebel for many years who was a man of honour. So, should there be another Irish rebellion, there will be no false sympathy, nor even respect, for those who take part in it.'

91 Ibid., 29 November 1866, 12b. For a constitutional nationalist remonstrance against such inflammatory rhetoric, see *Dublin Evening Post*, 29 November 1866, 2e–g: 'the indestructibleness of the Irish race, as of its rights and aspirations, has only received additional confirmation from defeat'.

humane feeling. The then Liberal *Daily Telegraph* described the episode as 'diabolical', and insisted that 'the whole heart and brain of the realm are now animated with the full sense of an enormous and cowardly outrage, of indignation against the criminals and their secret abbetors, and of sympathy for the innocent victims'.[92] The Fenian movement, or at least sections of it, whether from reasons of tactical embarrassment or genuine regret also condemned the explosion.[93] Karl Marx, always ambivalent about Irish revolutionary nationalism, believed that Clerkenwell had caused great damage to the development of English revolutionary politics.[94]

Three persons were arrested and charged with murder. One, a spy who had been involved in the plot under police instructions, was subsequently discharged. Further arrests were made, and eventually, on 20 April 1868, six persons went on trial for murder; the cases against Ann Justice (who had been visiting Casey, Burke's companion) and another were subsequently withdrawn. The remaining charges went to the jury and produced three acquittals and one conviction. The convicted man, Michael Barrett, was sentenced to death – the last person to be hanged publicly in England.

The Clerkenwell explosion further discredited the Kelly faction and encouraged the Roberts section of American Fenianism in its bid for leadership of a reunited movement. Meetings had been held in Paris between Roberts and IRB delegates from Britain and Ireland, and on 4 July 1867 a compact had been signed whereby the Roberts faction would provide material support for an uprising in Ireland, which would be coordinated with an attack upon Canada from the American side. Attempts to bring together the factions of American Fenianism under the leadership of John Mitchel failed, Mitchel (who did not think highly of Fenianism) refusing the proffered position. Various changes were made in the Fenian leadership however, and pledges of substantial funding were given by the various circles in the United States of America.

Fenianism had been ever stronger on rhetoric than action, and the poetry of names – Congress, Senate, President – and flags, uniforms and demonstrations absorbed much of the rebellious and patriotic energy of its Irish-American

---

92 *Daily Telegraph*, 16 December 1867, 2a. The explosives (an estimated quarter of a ton of gunpowder) were pushed against the prison wall in a handcart – a forerunner of the car bombs of more recent times.

93 The perfervid (and anti-O'Mahony) *Irish Republic* reported the extensive damage and loss of life caused by the explosion, commenting that it had caused 'great indignation at the reckless disregard of life and property.... Thousands of persons were attempting to get near the scene of the outrage' (18 January 1868, 3a–c).

94 He considered the Clerkenwell explosion to be 'a very stupid thing'. The London working class, hitherto sympathetic to Ireland, would in reaction support the government: 'One cannot expect the London proletarians to allow themselves to be blown up in honour of the Fenian emissaries' (Karl Marx and Friedrich Engels, *Ireland and the Irish Question*, Moscow, Progress Publishers, 1971, p. 149).

adherents. Declaration and promise followed one another, yet months passed with no action. The Fenian Convention of the Senate or Roberts faction which met in Philadelphia in November 1868 learned that less than one-third of the money which had been pledged had been paid, and even that had seeped away. Of $100,000 collected only $23,000 remained. Factionalism continued, and by 15 March 1870 this amount had shrunk to $70. In Ireland and Britain the American infighting stimulated what one of the government's chief anti-Fenian officers described as 'an air of activity which was in large measure fictitious'.[95] Arms, however, were being procured and distributed to the circles of both factions.

Lodged firmly in the politics of romance, Fenianism needed a gesture to find its way forward. Arms were brought to the Canadian border and General O'Neil launched an attack on 25 May 1870. Early reports were of 'Thousands of Fenian soldiers, well armed and equipped . . . swarming over the Canadian frontier at various points'.[96] The reality was very different. Once again there had been ample forewarning, both by Fenian posturing and through the activities of agents. O'Neil had expected some 2000 men to meet him for the invasion, but in the event only 200 turned up. The action, which had been a leap in the dark, predicated upon an influx of support from the United States of America once territory had been conquered and held, collapsed completely when faced with determined and overwhelming Canadian forces. O'Neil fell back with his men, and was arrested as soon as he crossed into the United States of America. By 11 June 1870 the *Nation*, which had at first reported the invasion as a serious and powerful threat to Canada, was writing of 'The Fenian Fiasco'.[97] The American courts handed down various sentences of imprisonment upon O'Neil and his principal lieutenants, but these were curtailed by political action shortly before the US elections.

To Robert Anderson, that astute observer of Fenianism, it seemed just months after these events that 'the game of American Fenianism seems well nigh played out'. He had some doubts, however, recalling the observation of Lord Kimberley, the former Lord Lieutenant, that as long as the American organisation of Fenianism lasted, the danger would continue.[98]

95 One Who Knows, 'Fenianism: A Narrative', *op. cit.*, p. 642.
96 *Nation*, 28 May 1870, 649b.
97 Ibid., 11 June 1870, 681a; see also 675a–d. For a contemporary overview of these events see *The Times*, 13 June 1870, 12a–b.
98 One Who Knows, 'Fenianism: A Narrative', *op. cit.*, p. 644.

4

THE FENIANS IN PRISON

Prisons, politics and policy

Fenianism brought politics again into British prisons. As always, Irish policy was a constantly shifting search for the balance between coercion and conciliation, demonstrating strength while seeking to engage the populace in the lawful political structure. By the 1860s, Irish Catholics' political, social and economic confidence had advanced considerably. Nationalism had tactical allies in the Commons, and while it had not yet achieved the parliamentary potency and ruthlessness of Parnellism, it was no mean force. Towards Fenianism the increasingly prosperous and settled urban and rural classes in Ireland had a range of attitudes, only some of which they were comfortable in acknowledging. In Britain, the United States of America and Australia, sizeable Irish immigrant communities grew more cohesive and assertive, and advanced themselves socially and economically. At Westminster the flux of its Whig, liberal and radical elements sometimes made the Liberal Party seem an odd beast even while it moved to the dominance of Gladstonism that would prevail for the rest of the century. British Conservatism was a weakening element on the Irish political scene, its place filled uncertainly by Southern Unionism's inchoate doctrines, as it adjusted – thirty years on – to Catholic Emancipation and the rapidly broadening franchise.

This new influx of political prisoners could enjoy no rerun of 1848 to 1849. Their numbers were so much greater, their insurrectionary enterprise of a different order, and the political structure was much changed in the intervening years. For their part, the Fenian prisoners did not grasp the opportunity to continue their fight within the walls. There would be some combat, but this was at the individual level (notably O'Donovan Rossa). An attempt was made to gather outside support around the issue of prison conditions, and eventually there would be a campaign for amnesty. Prison had yet to be viewed by the militant as a theatre of revolutionary war, in which a surprising amount of initiative could be seized and damage done to government. In the imprisoned Fenians we begin to discern new patterns and methods of political struggle in which captivity became an opportunity as well as an incapacity.

The principles by which the Fenians would be dealt with in prison were published at the outset. The political nature of the offences was recognised, but government was not willing to repeat the Young Irelanders' 'gentleman convict' arrangement. While undergoing their sentences, whether imprisonment or penal servitude,[1] the Fenians would be treated in the same way as non-political offenders.[2] They and their supporters protested: Fenians were not 'common criminals' and should not be treated as such; they also complained that their prison treatment was *worse* than that inflicted on ordinary offenders.

Government would not concede the first of these points, even though this drew down on them repeated and particularly heated charges of hypocrisy. In the winter of 1850/1 Gladstone had visited the Neapolitan prisons of Vicaria and Nisida, and attended the political trial of the liberal minister of the Neapolitan government of 1848, Baron Carlo Poerio. Poerio and his companions were held in conditions which one Gladstone biographer described as being such that 'On the day of Gladstone's visit a veritable *Fidelio* scene was enacted.'[3] Gladstone angrily denounced the requirement that these men should be forced into the uniform of common criminals. Horrified and angered by this and other conditions, he hurried back to England to launch a protest campaign. He condemned the governance of Naples in some of the strongest public language he would ever use: the regime was 'one of the most purely satanic agencies upon earth'; Bourbon rule 'the negation of God erected into a system of government'.[4] Naples brought Gladstone to the attention of the continental liberals, and was a decisive juncture in his own political evolution; to taunt him with Naples was to question his integrity.[5] And at much the same time that political status was being withheld from Fenian offenders, powerful voices were raised in England against the treatment of his political offenders by Louis Phillippe.

1 For an explanation of the distinction between penal servitude and imprisonment see my essay 'The Victorian Prison', in Norval Morris and David J. Rothman (eds), *The Oxford History of the Prison*, New York, Oxford University Press, 1995, esp. pp. 131–9.

2 Both the Irish and British administrations turned their faces against political treatment. O'Donovan Rossa petitioned against his treatment in Portland, and the Home Office asked Dublin Castle for comment. On 26 November 1866, the Lord Lieutenant responded that he had 'no wish that the Fenian Convicts should be treated in any way differently from ordinary Convicts under like sentences' (National Archives of Ireland (NAI), CSO LB 266, f. 383).

3 Roy Jenkins, *Gladstone*, London, Macmillan, 1995, p. 122.

4 See H. G. C. Matthew, *Gladstone 1809–1874*, Oxford, Clarendon Press, 1991, pp. 80–1; E. J. Feuchtwanger, *Gladstone*, London, Allen Lane, 1975, pp. 72–3. Gladstone had powerfully set out his case against the government in Naples in two public letters to Lord Aberdeen, which went into multiple editions and aroused national and international indignation (*Two Letters to the Earl of Aberdeen on the State Prosecutions of the Neapolitan Government*, London, John Murray, 1851).

5 Gladstone argued that his letters to Aberdeen had been a condemnation of the illegality and corrupt tyranny of the Neapolitan government, and that there was not the slightest comparison between that odious system and the rule of law on which British government was based.

Policy was shaped by several considerations. First, the precedent of 1848 was hardly applicable to the Fenians. There had been some violence in 1848, but minimal loss of life and little damage to property. The stance of the Young Ireland leaders had been more political than military, and they had acted in the extremities of the famine. The Fenians, by contrast, in times of peace and growing prosperity attacked life and destroyed property in order to destroy British government in Ireland. Young Ireland had conducted its campaign almost entirely in the open; the IRB was a clever and determined conspiracy, reaching into the army and public administration. Finally, the Young Irelanders could perhaps be treated leniently because they appeared to be laughably ineffective – a few shots in a cabbage patch. The Fenians required tough handling because they were a danger and source of much public apprehension at home and in the empire.[6] Michael Davitt, analysing the rebellions of a century, argued that the Fenians and the 1798 men were treated much more severely than those of 1848 because what Mitchel had described as 'a rueful and pitiful rebellion' had appeared to the English to have, in Davitt's words, 'the inherent harmlessness of a mere newspaper and rhetorical warfare'.[7]

As already noted, the IRB drew its members from the lower-middle and working classes.[8] One of the reasons government had found it expedient to deal indulgently with the Young Irelanders was that most of the leadership was middle class, even (as with William Smith O'Brien) aristocratic. Although there were some criticisms at the way in which government treated them, the designation 'gentleman', and the frequently repeated determination of O'Brien and his colleagues to act honourably, allowed government to proceed as though these were prisoners of war of the officer class, to whom appropriate respect could be properly accorded.[9]

The treatment of the Young Irelanders was also affected by the lobbying of relatives and friends. And since O'Brien, the most powerfully connected, was also its leader, any indulgence extended to him – necessarily the most blameworthy – carried over to his followers. The Fenians, by contrast, were unconnected, and were, moreover, the object of the hostility of the Roman Catholic

---

6 While urging stern treatment, *The Times* considered the danger over with the close of the Special Commission and the imposition of severe sentences: 'We now have reason to feel that, though Fenianism may be troublesome for a time, it never can be in any way formidable' (3 February 1866, 9a). The words struck a defiant chord in the rebel psyche, and were remembered.

7 Michael Davitt, *Life and Progress in Australasia*, London, Methuen, 1898, p. 333.

8 See p. 118, n. 19 above: see also John O'Leary, *Recollections of Fenians and Fenianism*, London, Downfy & Co, 1896, Vol. 2, pp. 237–9.

9 *The Times* was clear on this: 'Smith O'Brien's movement was to some extent a gentlemanly rebellion, whereas Fenianism has been too strong for the taste of any but the lowest' (3 February 1866, 8f). The power of the term 'gentleman', and the moral entitlements of the rank, had been reflected in Gladstone's indignant depiction of the plight of such mingled with common criminals in the prisons of Naples (See *Two Letters*, *op. cit.*, pp. 15–16, 30–2).

hierarchy.[10] They were also so numerous that there could be no question of secreting them in some cranny of the penal system. If special treatment were conceded government would be setting up a distinct class of offender, venturing into unknown territory.

On the larger stage there were other considerations. Relations with the United States of America remained uneasy, having reached a particularly low ebb over the *Alabama* affair. With two other British-built warships being prepared for the Confederate Navy, in September 1863 the Union had been on the point of breaking off diplomatic relations: much resentment remained.[11] The Irish vote had assumed a strategic importance in the United States of America, and it could be won with anti-British rhetoric and action.[12] It appeared to many that, driven by these pressures, the United States of America might welcome an excuse to seize British North America. Such a war would have answered Fenian prayers, draining British strength while clearing the way for American support for a Fenian insurrection.[13] Diplomacy was hard at work, and war-weariness counterbalanced bellicosity. In this context, resolute but restrained action in

10 Archbishop Paul Cullen had many times denounced the Young Irelanders and Fenianism. Of the latter he wrote, in a pastoral letter of 10 October 1865, 'As to what is called Fenianism . . . it [is] a compound of folly and wickedness wearing the mask of patriotism to make dupes of the unwary . . . the work of a few fanatics or knaves, wicked enough to jeopardise others in order to promote their own sordid views' (Peadar MacSuibhne, *Paul Cullen and His Contemporaries: With Their Letters from 1820–1902*, Naas, Leinster Leader, 1961, Vol. 1, pp. 397–8). Sixteen months later Bishop David Moriarty of Kerry preached a sermon in which he proclaimed, *inter alia*, that 'when we look down in to the fathomless depth of this infamy of the heads of the Fenian conspiracy, we must acknowledge that eternity is not long enough, nor hell hot enough to punish such miscreants'. He referred to the Fenian leaders as 'criminals' and 'execrable swindlers' and dramatically called down 'God's heaviest curse, His withering, blasting, blighting curse on them' (*Irish Times*, 19 February 1867, 3f). E. R. Norman provides a scholarly and penetrating account of the attitude of the Roman Catholic Church towards Fenianism in his study, *The Catholic Church and Ireland in the Age of Rebellion: 1859–1873*, London, Longmans, 1965, ch. 3.

11 In an 1867 secret report to Cabinet, Lord Strathnairn, the Commander-in-Chief in Ireland, referred to the American problem: 'In the event of hostilities with us, America (and with no country are our relations so delicate) enjoys the special advantage that a million of her most military and stirring subjects are Irish Roman Catholics, bitterly opposed to British rule in Ireland and Canada, and ready to make any . . . sacrifice to overthrow it' (PRO HO/45/9303/11188(5), p. 4).

12 The Irish vote, if Henri Le Caron is to be believed, had by 1868 achieved such a weight in the United States of America that President Andrew Johnson was prepared to go to the brink of illegality to placate and aid the Fenians (Major Henri Le Caron, *Twenty-five Years in the Secret Service*, London, William Heinemann, 1893, p. 59).

13 In his recollections, John O'Leary discussed the dismal relations between Britain and the United States of America from which he and his comrades had drawn much encouragement: 'Had the *Alabama* difficulty but then come to the front, what might not these Irish millions [in the United States of America] have done to arouse or exasperate popular feeling? and there were the hundreds of thousands of hands, with hearts behind them, ever ready and willing instruments for use against England' (*op. cit.*, vol. 2, p. 241).

Ireland signalled British intentions internationally. The Prime Minister, Lord Derby, responded to the Fenians' abortive rising of March 1867 by insisting that revolution needed to be smothered immediately, rather than be tackled piecemeal. To accomplish this he wanted the leaders, particularly the Irish-Americans, tried before Special Commissions: 'It would be quite necessary to make a prompt and severe example of them; and much as he shrank from capital punishment, it would have, in this instance, to be resorted to without scruple and was indeed real mercy.'[14] But this would not be a rerun of the counter-terrorism of 1798: Special Commissions were not martial law, and in its speed and severity punishment would be civil, deliberate and discriminating, not martial, impetuous and general.[15] While the incendiary and adventurous in America would be warned off, conservative and even liberal opinion in that country should not be alienated.

As the Fenians began their sentences policy towards them was still evolving. Decisions were divided between two departments of government: the Irish administration and the Home Office. Relations between the two were not always easy, and there were the normal bureaucratic suspicions and cautions: neither wished to be responsible for a wrong decision, particularly one with unwanted political repercussions. With some energetic passing of the parcel it became clear that any radical departures from defensive administration needed political underwriting. In a series of exchanges between the Home Office and Dublin Castle over Rossa, Denis Mulcahy, John O'Leary and Charles O'Connell, the directors of convict prisons sought precise directions on matters such as extra letters and special visits. The invariable reply was that these should be granted so far as they were consistent with convict discipline, in the opinion of the directors.[16] Caution went so far on one occasion that Thomas Larcom blankly replied to a petition from Rossa, forwarded by the Home Office with a 'no comment'.[17] All this was intensely frustrating for the Home Office, which regarded the Fenians as an Irish problem unfairly wished upon it.

Administration

Penal policy and management are often determined by crises and scandals, and the defining moment for the Fenians was the escape of James Stephens, the IRB

---

14 Leon O'Broin, *Fenian Fever: An Anglo-American Dilemma*, London, Chatto & Windus, 1971, p. 154.

15 For an account of military justice in suppressing the 1798 rebellion, and of the lessons learned, see Thomas Packenham, *The Year of Liberty*, London, Panther Books, 1972, esp. pp. 59–87.

16 See National Archives of Ireland (NAI), Chief Secretary's Office (CSO), Letter Book (LB), 266/383 (26 November 1866); ibid., 405 (17 December 1866); ibid., 94 (16 January 1866); ibid., 299 (20 August 1866); ibid., 311 (10 September 1866); ibid., 376 (16 November 1866); ibid., 405 (17 December 1866); ibid., 411 (22 December 1866).

17 'I am to state that the Convicts' petition does not appear to call for any remark on the part of His Ex[cellency]' (ibid., 383; Larcom to Walpole, 26 November 1866).

Head Centre. Arrested on 11 November 1865, Stephens vanished from Richmond Bridewell in the small hours of 24 November, creating a national sensation – elation among followers and sympathisers, confusion and embarrassment in the Irish government, anger among loyalists.[18] The Fenian cause was electrified and its morale boosted to unexpected levels.[19]

Three lessons were drawn from the fact that Stephens' escape was an 'inside job': safe custody could probably not be provided in Ireland; portions of the civil as well as the military administration were tainted with Fenianism; and any further escapes would damage not only British administration in Ireland, but perhaps the basis of government itself.[20] An anonymous analyst, whose views carried sufficient weight for his communications to be preserved in the Chief Secretary's papers, gave an alarming estimate of the extent of Fenian infiltration. There were 15,000 sworn men in the army and militia; 100 in the Royal Irish Constabulary and 1200 sympathisers; another eighty in the Dublin Metropolitan Police, and 250 sympathisers.[21]

18 See above, p. 123. The escape was organised by Stephens' substitute in command of the IRB, Colonel Thomas Kelly, assisted by Captain Timothy Deasy (who would themselves be arrested and rescued in Manchester ten months later). Crucial inside assistance was given by Jim Breslin, the prison infirmary superintendent, and Dan Byrne, the night-watchman (see Robert J. Bateman, 'Captain Timothy Deasy, Fenian', *Irish Sword*, 8 (1967–8), pp. 130–7).

19 The *Nation* had been in a high satirical mood over the Stephens escape: 'The Special Commission on Monday next will look rather farcical now. Their "most timely capture" has been but a moment's triumph for the government. This "most untoward escape" constitutes a far more lasting humiliation' (25 November 1865, 216d); see also National Library of Ireland (NLI): Larcom Papers: Ms. 7687; Sir Thomas Larcom (1801–79) was, from 1853 to 1868, Under-Secretary in the Irish administration. His archive on the Fenian emergency is invaluable.

20 The subornation of the Irish in the British Army and Irish Civil Service was extensive, and might have proved decisive had revolutionary upheaval proceeded. For a concise account of Fenian recruitment of soldiers, police, gaolers and others see Leon O'Broin, *Fenian Fever: An Anglo-American Dilemma*, op. cit., 1971, chs 1–3. Looking back some thirty years, William O'Brien gave a colourful account of military and civil subversion, partly from personal experience, in his *Contemporary Review* article, 'Was Fenianism Ever Formidable?' (vol. 71 (January to June 1897), pp. 680–93). For the inquiry into Stephens' escape (which includes references to 'the unsatisfactory character of the prison staff') see NAI, CSO RP 1866/9904 (2449). Byrne, the prison's night-watchman, was found (rather foolishly) to have fifty copies of the Fenian oath in his possession (Larcom Papers: Ms. 7687 (unfoliated) (26 June 1866)).

21 Ibid., 'The Story of the Fenian Brotherhood', f. 24. This document may have been compiled by Larcom himself, or on his instructions, and is derived from several sources. In addition to the subversion of the military and police, it was estimated that the Fenians had at their disposal 34,000 half-drilled men throughout the country, together with the support of 9000 Ribbonmen and members of other secret societies. The document emphasises that Stephens had to act soon or not at all, and set out the other circumstances which were favourable to the Fenians – the stance of the Americans, the British defeats and weaknesses in the Crimea, the military commitments to the Ionian Isles, the Sepoy Mutiny and so forth. In addition, Stephens' escape had been a great boost for his organisation. See also 'Strathnairn Report, 1867', op. cit., pp. 9–10.

Action was swift and apparently decisive. Irish military units were rotated out of the country. Fenian recruiters in the army were rounded up, together with a small number of sworn rank-and-file soldiers of whom an example would be made. Extra pay and allowances had been given to many police officers during the Fenian emergency, and to those civilians whose work was particularly sensitive and important, such as telegraph clerks and railway workers. (These emoluments were known as 'Fenian Pay' or 'Fenian Gratuities'.) There were moves to put this largess on a permanent basis, reinforcing the loyalty of the various functionaries; resident magistrates and grand juries (the backbone of loyalist administration and sentiment in the countryside) were especially vociferous in urging financial liberality.[22] The oath of allegiance was administered to prison warders.[23]

The internees

The safe custody of the Fenians remained a major cause for concern. One category was relatively easily dealt with: those – mainly Irish-Americans – who had been interned on the Lord Lieutenant's warrant during the suspension of habeas corpus. By August 1866 there were 320 political detainees at Mountjoy and other Irish prisons; a total of 756 had up until then been imprisoned.[24] These were civil detainees, many of whom were able to obtain some protection from the United States' Consul in Dublin, although a distinction was drawn between native-born and naturalised American citizens.[25]

Being unconvicted, prison precedent indicated that the internees should have superior conditions: fairly free association, recreation and exercise, and a generous and varied diet.[26] As the emergency continued, however, these congregations of large numbers of fit, militarily trained and increasingly frustrated young men posed obvious problems for prison security and control; there was in addition an

22 NAI, CSO LB 266/383, ff. 97–8, 107–8, 141, 159 and 250. See also the long letter from Chief Secretary Lord Naas to the Treasury, urging rewards for members of the Irish constabulary (ibid., ff. 123–8, March 1867).
23 NLI: Larcom Papers: Ms. 7687 (unfoliated).
24 3 Hansard, CLXXXIV, col. 1912; 2 August 1866: statement by Lord Naas, Irish Chief Secretary.
25 The American-born were in a stronger position than naturalised citizens, and appeared to be protected from arrest under the suspension of habeas corpus. Thus in April 1866, one John Sullivan was released on proof being presented that he was an American-born citizen (ibid., f. 188; NAI, CSO RP 1866/8757). There was some suspicion of the bona fides of the US Consular Service at a later point. In July 1869 Dublin Castle passed to the Home Office a report that James Haggerty, US Consul in Glasgow, would assist the passage to Ireland of arms bought in England (NAI, CSO LB 268/397).
26 Speaking as Chancellor of the Exchequer in Russell's second administration, Gladstone confirmed that the government 'held firmly by the principle that unconvicted prisoners who were arrested under the Habeas Corpus Suspension Act were to be treated in the same manner as all other untried prisoners' (3 Hansard, CLXXXII, col. 446; 16 March 1866).

element of malign neglect, an implicit desire that they should experience the incidental deterrence and retribution that an earlier generation described as *squalor carceris*. There were questions in the Commons about the conditions under which the men were being held,[27] and it was important that security considerations should be balanced by a politically defensible custodial regime.[28] The product of rules made on 18 February and 8 March 1866 was a hybrid: neither the minimal custody and control of the debtor or first-class misdemeanant, nor yet the total separation, restrictions and elements of discomfort and degradation reserved for convicted criminals. Importantly – if only on the symbolic level – detainees could not be compelled to wear prison uniform, and if they had funds, they might send out for food.

Supposedly to hinder plotting, if not entirely to prevent it, the internees were forbidden to converse with each other. This was a major hardship, a feature of the punitive regime for convicted criminals, but not imposed on those awaiting trial on criminal charges.[29] Some prisons had no separate cells, and so it was impossible to enforce the injunction everywhere.[30] To avoid possible damage to mental or physical health, it was agreed that detainees might exercise in pairs (each pair at a distance from the next), provided the partnerships were approved. So great was the concern to strike a balance between security and the scandal which would erupt should the detainees' health be damaged that Lord Kimberley, the Lord Lieutenant, took a direct hand in the final draft of the revised rules.[31] As the weeks and months passed, however, it became clear that the regime was overly demanding of physical and mental health.

Apart from silence and a degree of separation, the detainees were forbidden to have any paper or writing materials other than those issued for the purpose of writing a letter;[32] these had to be surrendered when the letter was completed.

---

27 3 *Hansard*, CLXXXII, cols 440–7; 16 March 1866; CLXXXIII, cols 445–63; 4 May 1866; CLXXXIV, cols 494–9; 15 June 1866.

28 The Mountjoy authorities screened the detainees' letters for intelligence, copying and filing important items. Some of the extracts seem to have been intended for political use, particularly to refute charges of ill-treatment. A letter from 'Head Centre Morris' to his brother on 10 April 1866 includes the following felicities: 'I like it here very much. . . . Our cells are very comfortable. . . . The beds are very comfortable. . . . Since the fine weather came it's a delightful place to live in.' A less effusive letter was sent by D. L. Burke to his wife on 14 April 1866. He reported seeing a friend or acquaintance, but not being allowed to speak to him – 'However it is a consolation to see him looking so remarkably well. I never saw a man improved so much as he has during his confinement' (NLI: Larcom Papers: Ms. 7590).

29 'Colonel Feather' (apparently a released detainee) wrote that the criminal prisoners (i.e. remands) were allowed at Mountjoy to talk and play as they pleased, 'within our view' ('Specimens of British Liberty in Ireland: Mountjoy Government Prison', *Irish Republic*, 18 May 1867, 11b).

30 At Mountjoy Prison the silence rules could be enforced, while at Limerick they were not (NAI, CSO RP, 1866/13009).

31 Ibid., Kimberley's memorandum of 7 July 1866.

32 It was alleged in the Commons that the Inspector of Prisons (who in Ireland had executive authority) had in the first weeks of internment issued an instruction that detainees were not to

Newspapers were prohibited, though friends could send in books (which could not be 'improper'). The prison library comprised largely moral and religious tracts chosen by the Anglican chaplain. Incoming and outgoing mail was read, and visits (which were allowed once a week) were conducted through bars and in the presence of a warder. The regime for criminal prisoners was run on progressive lines: good behaviour and the passage of time could win progressive ameliorations. After eight months a convicted criminal was brought into association with his fellows. Some of the detainees, by contrast, served much longer than that without their separation being eased (save for walking exercise in pairs).[33] Even before he was formally advanced from the separate stage of his sentence, the convicted prisoner could expect some casual contact with his fellows at school or in the infirmary. Detainees, by contrast, were not allowed to attend school and, as far as possible, were treated in their cells when sick.

Conditions varied between the prisons. At Waterford, where by March 1866 a dozen or more persons were interned, the regime was overseen by the local Board of Superintendence, advised by a stipendiary magistrate. Because the government had directed that the men should exercise alone, the governor, having two yards at his disposal, and the non-political prisoners also to exercise, could not provide the detainees with their full entitlement to exercise.[34] There was also a prohibition on visits from friends, family and even legal advisers. As a security precaution, cells were lit by gaslights all night. The Irish Attorney General denied that the Waterford detainees were subject 'to any severe restrictions' but did not specifically refute the allegations. John Francis Maguire, MP for Cork (and proprietor of the *Cork Examiner*) alleged severity of treatment in Cork prison – 'greater vigour than ordinary untried prisoners'. Only two hours' exercise a day were allowed; visits from relatives were restricted to two per week, and communications with legal advisers were conducted in the presence of a warder. Gladstone, promising an inquiry into any credible complaints,

---

have visitors or paper on which to communicate with their friends and relatives, despite a ruling to the contrary from higher authority (3 *Hansard*, CLXXXIII, cols 445–52; 4 May 1866). It is certainly true that great care was taken to guard against uncensored post in either direction. Prisoners' friends were allowed to send in food, with the safeguard that 'all such food and utensils must be most carefully searched, and the utensils examined when going out to see there is no writing on them' (NAI, CSO RP 1866/13009: letter of 18 February 1866).

33 By January 1867, fifty-three detainees had undergone more than eight months' separate confinement, and one had endured some sixteen months, according to Dr McDonnell, the Mountjoy medical officer. This report was suppressed. In February 1867, Dr McDonnell reported on the mental and physical state of the detainees, drawing attention to the injury being caused by the strict regime. These observations were not passed on to the Irish government by the Directors of Convict Prisons. At this point McDonnell leaked his reports to nationalist MPs and the matter was raised in the Commons by J. A. Blake (3 *Hansard*, CLXXXVI, cols 1933–4; 3 May 1867).

34 The details which follow are taken from speeches in the Commons by J. A. Blake (Waterford), J. F. Maguire (Cork City) and J. Bagwell (Clonmel) – all moderate nationalists (3 *Hansard*, CLXXXII, cols 440–7; 16 March 1866).

insisted that at Waterford and Cork, as elsewhere, the detainees would be treated as untried prisoners.[35]

Native-born and naturalised American citizens enjoyed one considerable advantage as detainees: the interest and protection of the United States' Consulate in Dublin.[36] This kept the authorities on their toes, and frequent contacts with the Consul allowed the prisoners to vent their grievances.[37] In view of the unsettled international situation, the Irish government was anxious to persuade the Consul that his citizens were being properly treated, and in this it appears to have succeeded.[38] The Consul was given the same access to American internees as legal advisers, and allowed to conduct interviews in the prisoners' cells, in sight but out of hearing of a warder.[39] The American detainees had additionally a steady flow of visits from relatives and friends, to whom they could report their grievances.[40]

Although the internees would claim that they had been subjected to especially harsh or unsavoury conditions as an act of political malice and oppression, the

35 A fortnight after these Commons exchanges the *Irishman* (quoting the *Waterford Gazette*) insisted that the claims of ill-treatment at Waterford were well founded. It compared the Fenians with the Irish Confederates: 'The prisoners of 1848 had a large day-room, where they met and spent the day in pleasant intercourse; they had books and papers to read; they had pens and ink to write with; they were treated like human beings, not like "caged hyenas"' (*Irishman*, 31 March 1866, 636c).

36 Behind the Consulate there were open pressures from Congress and the President. See, for example, 39 *Congress: H. Exdoc.* 139 (39–40), 1267; 40 *Congress: H. Misdoc.* 46 (40–1), 1312; 157 (40–2), 1339. These documents variously deal with the arrest, trial and conviction of American citizens in Great Britain and Ireland on suspicion of or for offences connected with Fenianism. None of these messages to the British government dictated US policy on the issue, which was cautious and conciliatory. But the rhetoric was a form of pressure. For some informative observations on the Irish in American politics at this time see the introductory chapter to Alan J. Ward's *Ireland and Anglo-American Relations 1899–1921*, London, LSE/Weidenfeld & Nicolson, 1969, pp. 1–6.

37 Any able-bodied male with an American accent or clothing was at risk of arrest during the emergency and it seems likely that some of the detainees were innocent of any association with Fenianism (see, for example, the case of John Sullivan, who claimed to have come to Ireland on family business, but who was nevertheless held from August 1865 until April 1866, when he was permitted to leave the country (NAI, CSO RP 1866/8757).

38 On 22 March 1866, the Consul stated that he was satisfied with the treatment of the Mountjoy detainees (NAI, CSO RP 1866/6278). West (the US Consul) had been privately instructed on the approach of the US government by Secretary of State Seward on 10 March 1866: 'Americans, whether native or naturalized, owe submission to the same laws in Great Britain as British subjects while residing there and enjoying the protection of that Government. We applied the converse of this principle to British subjects who were sojourning or traveling in the United States during the late rebellions' (cit. *New York Times*, 4 April 1882, 4c).

39 NAI, CSO RP 1866/10808. The detainees' ordinary visitors had their meetings in a wire-partitioned room in the presence of a warder.

40 A sad little story concerning these visitors found its way into the official papers: 'The mother of a man named Byrne wished to see him but finding she was very poorly dressed he declined the visit, stating she was a washerwoman, although I know she supported his two children while he was in America' (NAI, CSO RP 1866/10, 808).

normal conditions of imprisonment ensured a punitive experience, even on civil detainees. One of the Americans described the physical conditions in Mountjoy as being 'arranged with the most demonical ingenuity, with a view to intensify the tortures of imprisonment'. Overlooking the fact that it was a defect in the majority of Irish and English prisons, he complained that 'the soil-pan in each cell is so fixed that it is not more than 14 or 16 inches away from the prisoner's nose while in bed'.[41] He insisted that the internees were poisoned by the Mountjoy bread: 'I did not eat it, for, on tasting it, it created a nausea, and I could use no food for several days after . . . it did kill some, and sent at least one [Thomas Burke of Clonmel] to the lunatic asylum.' To those more familiar with the prison bread of the times, however, such gut-wrenching reactions were not unusual: this was bad bread, but within the normal range of prison baking.

Used to eating well, the Americans and Irish-Americans found prison fare monotonous and inadequate, but here again they were not being singled out. The Irish prison diets had been revised during the famine years to discourage the starving peasantry from taking refuge in gaols and prisons, and had not been revised since. Comparing the two countries, the *Pall Mall Gazette* noted that '[T]he prison diet of an English criminal exceeds enormously that of the Irishman. Against the Irishman's 98 oz. of bread and 56 oz. of meal a week the Englishman gets 148 oz. of bread.' Listing other differences the article concluded that the allowance 'is positive starvation to prisoners of a higher grade accustomed to a liberal diet'.[42] It certainly would have been so to the free-feeding American and Irish-American detainees, not many of whom had the funds to exercise their entitlement to purchase food from the outside.

As the months of their detention passed, with no release in sight (the suspension of habeas corpus was further extended in February 1866),[43] the detainees

---

41 'Colonel Feather', 'Specimens of British Liberty in Ireland. Mountjoy Government Prison', *Irish Republic*, 18 May 1867, 11b. The water-valved lavatory pan had not at that time been developed. Effluvia permeated prisons. 'Colonel Feather's' views were not shared by all inmates. The authorities preserved two letters in which prisoners praised the facilities. One described the cells as 'very comfortable . . . well lighted and ventilated' with gaslight until 9 p.m. each evening. This prisoner was also impressed by the fittings: 'We have water pipes in the cell, closet, washstand tables, stool, shelves, everything that is requisite.' There was also praise for the priest, who visited every day, 'giving and exchanging books, and hearing confessions'. At about the same time another prisoner wrote of a companion whose health had improved greatly during his confinement: 'In fact ye can hardly credit how well and stout [he] is.' The fact that these are the only two extracts from prisoners' letters in the Larcom Papers casts doubt on their representativeness, and calls into question the reason they were preserved, but it is entirely understandable that among the detainees there were various reactions to their conditions (NLI: Larcom Papers: Ms. 7590 (April 1866)).

42 *Pall Mall Gazette*, 14 May 1867, 1a–b.

43 Suspension of Habeas Corpus (Ireland) Act, 1866; 29 & 30 Vict., c.1 (Royal Assent, 17 February 1866). This was continued in 1867 by 30 & 31 Vict., c.1: Habeas Corpus (Ireland) Continuance Act. The measure was renewed in 1868 (31 & 32 Vict., c.7) and was allowed to lapse the following year.

grew ever more depressed and restive. At Mountjoy they were locked in their cells for all but two hours out of the twenty-four. Already in virtual solitary confinement, little more could be done to punish them. As unconvicted men they could not be flogged, and for misbehaviour were subject only to dietary punishment, the removal of articles of warmth and comfort from their cells or (most severely) removal to an unheated punishment cell. Those to be punished had first to be examined and certified as fit by the prison medical officer. By refusing in a number of cases to certify fitness and expressing general concern about the use of dietary and related punishments, and by raising the matter in his section of the annual report of the prison, the medical officer, Dr Robert McDonnell, provoked an embarrassing public row.[44] Despite the discomfiture of his colleagues, McDonnell returned to the matter in his next report, noting that apart from specific illnesses, 'the health of a good many of these prisoners has deteriorated from their prolonged confinement'. This, and the necessity of treating sick detainees in their cells rather than in hospital wards, had increased the demands on staff.[45] In a section of his report which was suppressed by the authorities (but which inevitably found its way into the public domain) McDonnell listed a number of cases of insanity, insisting that there was a clear connection between insanity, prolonged confinement and severe discipline. He also warned of the political consequences should any of the detainees be driven to suicide.[46]

---

44 *Twelfth Annual Report of the Directors of Convict Prisons in Ireland*, PP, 1866 [3745], XXXVIII, 465, 20–2. McDonnell (1828–89) was educated at Trinity College, Dublin, and had been a surgeon in the Crimea. He was a Fellow of the Royal College of Surgeons in Ireland. His later career was distinguished in professional, academic and administrative posts (see Cliona McDonald Buckley, 'Robert McDonnell (1828–1889)', *Journal of the Irish College of Physicians and Surgeons*, 3 (1973), pp. 66–9). He took a liberal view of his duties as a medical officer, using his powers to ease the lot of individuals. One inmate, for example, reported that McDonnell had ordered him tobacco and chew once a week (NLI: Larcom Papers: Ms. 7590).

45 *Thirteenth Annual Report of the Directors of Convict Prisons in Ireland*, PP, 1867 [3805], XXXVI, 273, 21.

46 'An Ulsterman' (pseudonym George Sigerson), *Modern Ireland: Its Vital Questions, Secret Societies and Government*, London, Longmans, Green, Reader & Dyer, 1868, pp. 375–6. Dr McDonnell had probably caused particular offence by describing the punishment of the convict John Murphy (actually Pagan O'Leary, one of the Fenian leaders). Murphy/O'Leary refused to choose one of the designated religions – Anglican, Presbyterian or Roman Catholic – and it was ordered by Patrick Joseph Murray, the Director of Convict Prisons responsible for Mountjoy, that Murphy/O'Leary should be confined to a punishment cell on a bread-and-water diet until he opted for one of the officially approved religions. McDonnell admitted him to the hospital, but on determining that he was not insane he was returned to his punishment cell and diet. O'Leary had insisted that he would rather die than conform to one of the approved religions, even though he was not an atheist. The Director was sufficiently embarrassed to insert an explanatory footnote, pointing out O'Leary's notoriety as a leading Fenian. It was this Director, Patrick Joseph Murray, who initiated the process leading to McDonnell's dismissal (*Thirteenth Annual Report, op. cit.*, p. 20).

Given the general unease at the prolonged detention of unconvicted men, McDonnell's report was bound to have consequences. Lord Naas, the Chief Secretary, immediately ordered an inquiry, as a result of which several relaxations were made, doubling the amount of exercise and allowing the men to smoke while they walked in pairs. To emphasise the change in treatment, Naas spoke to McDonnell himself, later reporting to the Commons that conditions had improved, and quoting a confirmatory letter from McDonnell.[47] These changes had been forced, and shortly afterwards McDonnell paid the penalty by being removed from his Mountjoy post, supposedly because he lived two miles away from the prison, and his private practice made him unsuitable to be medical officer in such a large prison.[48] This was naked retaliation, and was widely seen in Ireland as injustice to a humane official bound by his medical and ethical obligations; it also suggested that the authorities had something to hide.[49]

The 1866 to 1867 internments hardened the views of constitutional nationalists. Although they may have been justified on immediate police and military grounds, politically they were unhelpful, making martyrs of rank-and-file Fenians and building a bridge of sympathy between the two wings of the nationalist movement. A few years later, Isaac Butt, then leader of the Amnesty Association, set out the constitutional objections. Unlike those remanded in prison on criminal charges against whom, at the minimum, a prima facie case had to be made out, internees were held without evidence of wrongdoing being brought before a court; they were held by administrative fiat. Persons facing criminal charges, he pointed out, were entitled to apply for bail, and to some extent they had the power of bringing about their trial. The internee could not obtain bail, could not demand a trial and faced imprisonment of unknown duration – he was at a distinct disadvantage when compared to the criminally accused.[50]

This legal and political argument, when added to the harsh conditions of confinement, created an impression of unfair, arbitrary and oppressive use of power – the more so as fears and memories of the emergency faded. On the

---

47 3 Hansard, CLXXXVI, cols 1933–4; 3 May 1867. The diet had also been improved and additional blankets issued; books were available from the prison library, and from the detainees' friends.

48 Return of Correspondence Relative to the Change in the Medical Management of the Mountjoy Convict Prison, whereby Dr McDonnell was Deprived of Office of Medical Superintendent without Compensation, PP, 1867–8 [502], LVII, 519, 1–32.

49 For a discussion of Dr McDonnell's removal see Beverly A. Smith, 'Irish Prison Doctors: Men in the Middle, 1865–90', Medical History, 26 (1982), pp. 373–7. The viewpoint of a constitutional nationalist of the times is given in George Sigerson's Political Prisoners at Home and Abroad, London, Kegan Paul, Trench, Trübner & Co, 1890, pp. 63–8. McDonnell established a high standing among the Irish nationalists of various degrees of militancy. See, for example, the exchanges between John Francis Maguire, MP, and the Earl of Mayo (formerly Lord Naas) when an extension of the suspension of habeas corpus was again being considered on 18 February 1868 (3 Hansard, CXC, cols 932–3).

50 Isaac Butt, Ireland's Appeal for Amnesty, Glasgow and London, Cameron & Ferguson, 1870, p. 70. Butt had been defence counsel for the leading Fenians in 1865–6.

government side, by contrast, as the weeks and months passed, a view may have grown that it was no bad thing to give the Americans and Irish-Americans such a prophylactic taste of imprisonment; and certainly they should be kept out of circulation while the emergency continued. The internees, for their part, were gripped by the uncertainty of their situation. New legislation and extensions of the suspension of habeas corpus might indefinitely prolong their incarceration. But with the collapse of the uprising in March 1867, the emergency – at least as far as it involved Irish-American soldiers – appeared to be over and it was possible to release the bulk of the detainees; nearly all were liberated on condition that they left the country.

The civilian convicts

Severe and implacable punishment was reserved from the outset for those who were accused of being at the centre of this very dangerous conspiracy, and who were to stand their trial. Unlike those detained on the Lord Lieutenant's warrant, these men were criminal remands. Their regime was not that fondly imagined by the executive detainees, however, and was far from that which O'Brien, Mitchel and the other Confederation leaders had experienced while they awaited trial. In a letter from Kilmainham (where the Dublin remands were held) Colonel William Halpin described conditions.[51] The diet, which was disgusting and inadequate, included gruel which, he wrote, 'looks more like a fly-stew or a spider fricassee'. The men rose at 6 a.m. and (it being winter) went to bed at 5 p.m. Twenty-two of the twenty-four detainees were locked in separate cells; strict silence was enforced at all times.[52]

A long series of state trials commenced on 27 November 1865 and lasted until 2 February 1866. These, together with the arrests made as a result of the uprising and other actions in March 1867, yielded a total of 105 convicted prisoners.[53] The sentences were severe.[54] Convicted by the Dublin Special Commission on

---

51 William G. Halpin was born in Co. Meath, emigrated to America, and commanded a Kentucky regiment in the Civil War. He was a member of the Fenian Military Council, and commanded the Dublin district in the March 1867 rising, having given up a $10,000 per annum post as City Engineer and County Surveyor in Cincinnati to return to Ireland. Sentenced to fifteen years' penal servitude by the Dublin Special Commission. At a later stage (1871) made a lone stand and refused to accept amnesty (and release) under conditional pardon. He relented when he was left the sole Fenian leader still imprisoned.

52 Kilmainham was 'a wonderful place to recuperate over-taxed digestive organs' and more likely to cure gout than a mountain of pills. Halpin also complained of the swarms of fleas (Irish Republic, 16 November 1867, 3a–b).

53 This figure is roughly correct but must be treated with some caution. There is in the official papers, unfortunately, no systematic tabulation of Fenian convictions.

54 O'Donovan Rossa (who was sentenced to life) in an eight-hour speech did his best to provoke Judge William Keogh, a former nationalist and placeman whom the Fenians despised. This (at least marginally) may have affected the other sentences then passed.

1 December 1865, Thomas Clarke Luby was sentenced to twenty years' penal servitude. Within half an hour of sentence, he was removed under military escort to Mountjoy Convict Prison, where he was stripped, dressed in prison uniform and locked in his cell.[55] An extra guard of fifty soldiers had been placed on Mountjoy 'where the strictest military discipline will be preserved'.[56] The same procedure followed as the other sentences came in.

The Lord Lieutenant, Lord Kimberley, determined that security was best served by getting the convicts over to England. This would minimise the chances of a repetition of the Stephens affair, and dampen political excitement.[57] This option raised certain legal problems, as Home Secretary Sir George Grey pointed out; and it would not do to transfer the men to England only to find that their custody was illegal. It was decided to seek a Law Officers' Opinion which, when tendered, did not suit Kimberley. The Fenians, the Law Officers determined, could be transferred to an English convict prison only by order of the Home Secretary, since the Lord Lieutenant's authority was restricted to transfers within the Irish prisons, or to places 'beyond the seas' (that is, outside the United Kingdom – in effect convict depots at Bermuda, Gibraltar and Western Australia). They recommended the latter as being 'much more effectual as a public example than their removal to England and we strongly recommend a direct removal by ship from Dublin'.[58]

Despite this advice, Kimberley insisted that the prisoners be transferred to Pentonville, to commence their first (separate) stage of convict discipline. This was necessary because 'in Ireland they cannot be in such safe custody as over the water, and their presence here keeps up excitement'. Kimberley's will prevailed, and warrants for the transfers were accordingly prepared for joint signature.[59] On Saturday, 23 December 1865, six convicts were transferred to Pentonville; another batch followed a few days later, and a group of ten in mid-January 1866.[60]

---

55 See the letter from Rossa to his wife, 1 December 1865, written in a court cell as sentencing and removal were going on (Catholic University of America (CUA): Fenian Brotherhood Papers (FBP): Box 2, item 23).

56 *Freeman's Journal*, 2 December 1865, 4g.

57 Political interest in the Stephens affair was intense, and government faced criticism from all quarters (see 3 *Hansard*, CLXXXII, cols 740–74; 22 March 1866).

58 NLI: Larcom Papers: Ms. 7687 (unfoliated). Transportation may initially have been rejected because of the escapes from Van Diemen's Land of the Young Irelanders.

59 Ibid. By the Penal Servitude Act, 1853 (16 & 17 Vict., c.99) various terms of penal servitude were substituted for transportation, and by the 1857 Penal Servitude Act (20 & 21 Vict., c.3) transportation was notionally abolished. (It was renamed removal, and became an executive act rather than a judicial sentence.) Sections 6 and 8 of the 1853 Act allowed convicts to be confined in any part of the United Kingdom. The law officers therefore thought it prudent to have both the Home Secretary's signature *and* the Lord Lieutenant's on each warrant (see also PRO HO 45/9329/19461/2).

60 The *Irish Times* hailed the transfer to England 'where no sympathiser outside the walls can even talk of an effort to release them' (27 December 1865, 2f). When the third group was transferred

Before, during and after transfer there was strict security. But of Mountjoy's efficiency, even under direct government supervision, and with the extra safe-guard of a military guard, Kimberley was only lukewarm: 'We can I apprehend count on keeping the prisoners securely in Mountjoy, at all counts for the present.'[61]

A brisk processing routine was established. Sentence was followed by immediate removal to Mountjoy, where the convicts were stripped and searched. Facial hair was removed, and the men received the distinctive 'convict crop' – a cut which left only stubble on the scalp and face. All were dressed in convict uniform and put in separate cells. At night, all clothing was passed out of the cell, and the prisoners were inspected at quarter-hour intervals: this was a positive iden-tification, which meant that the warder had to examine the prisoner so closely that the man was woken up.[62] Some prisoners were placed under direct military guard in addition to the usual supervision by prison staff.[63] As well as the usual locks, padlocks were fitted to cell doors, and these were kept fastened at all times, the keys being held by principal warders.[64]

Much the same security precautions were followed in England, where at Pentonville the prisoners were greeted with a full body search, including a lantern-assisted examination of the rectum and private parts. Strip-searches were thereafter conducted each week during the prisoners' time at Pentonville. Describing these procedures, the author of *Things Not Generally Known* objected not only to the stripping and probing, but also to the warders' accompanying scoffing and sneering. Men of education and feeling were being treated 'with

the nationalist *Irishman* was subdued, emphasising the security precautions that had been taken and noting that the men had been handcuffed: 'There was no excitement, as no previous notice had been given of the departure' (20 January 1866, 469b).

61 NLI: Larcom Papers: Ms. 7687 (unfoliated). This feeling of insecurity persisted, and may have been behind the January 1867 proposal of Lord Naas (shortly to become the Earl of Mayo) to remove from Irish local prisons to the (government-controlled) convict prisons all those serv-ing sentences of three months and over. The proposal was vigorously resisted by the convict authorities, who argued that it could inflict 'very serious injury on the character of the Irish Convict System' (NLI: Larcom Papers: Ms. 9591).

62 'The Convict of Clonmel', *Things Not Generally Known Concerning England's Treatment of Fenian Prisoners* [hereinafter *Things Not Generally Known*], Dublin, The *Irishman*, 1869. (This was prob-ably written by Richard Pigott, who was in close touch with the families of the imprisoned men. It was published in his newspapers the *Irishman* and (later) *The Flag of Ireland*; it also appeared in pamphlet form. The ostensible reason for publication was a response to the 1867 whitewash-ing report by Knox and Pollock: *Report of the Commissioners on Treatment of the Treason-Felony Convicts in the English Convict Prisons* [hereinafter *1867 Commission*], PP, 1867 [3880], XXXV, 673.)

63 Jeremiah O'Donovan Rossa, *My Years in English Jails*, Tralee, Anvil Books, 1967 (rev. edn), p. 57. This deployment of soldiers inside the prison as well as on the perimeter was because of Kimberley's distrust of the Irish staff.

64 NAI, CSO RP 1866/16, 399.

less decency than they would a wretch convicted of [the most atrocious acts of bestiality]'.[65]

In addition to putting out their clothing each night the Irish prisoners also had to put out all cell furniture and utensils, except for beds. This rule was so enforced, they complained, that they could stand naked for up to a quarter of an hour on the cold asphalt floor before warders came to collect clothing and other items.[66] 'Pat-down' searches were conducted on leaving the cells for exercise, and again on return. At Portland, in the depth of the severe winter of 1866 to 1867, the prisoners, having come in cold from their labour, were frequently made to strip naked outside their cells; they then stepped inside where they stood while item by item their clothing was examined and passed in to them.[67] Exercise, during their first two months at Pentonville, was taken in pens, iso-sceles triangular in shape, some twenty-five feet on the longer sides, and fifteen feet across the base. Subsequently the men were allowed to exercise in a ring, but always with ordinary prisoners interspersed among them, to prevent con-tact or communication. As a cell task there was tutoring in tailoring, but the threads were cut short for reasons of security.[68]

The connivance of staff in Stephens' escape caused the Home Office to take extra precautions even in England. The fear was probably less that there was an IRB man or cell among the English warders (though even that was possible, since some were of Irish origin)[69] than that there would be bribery – the Fenians supposedly having a considerable treasury. It was directed, therefore, that during the separate stage at Pentonville Prison, the prisoners' meals would be taken to their cells by two prison officers. As a further precaution, meal-flaps on the cell doors were sealed, so that staff could speak to inmates only when the door was

---

65 *Things Not Generally Known*, p. 8. Despite the body searches O'Donovan Rossa managed to secrete small pieces of slate, which he used, during exercise, to pass messages to his companions. For some curious reason the Pentonville schoolmaster, having asked Rossa to read a passage, assessed him as a Class 3 reader (equivalent to a nine- or ten-year-old). Rossa had been a newspaper editor, and his letters show him to have a high standard of literacy. It may have been an act of mercy, to give Rossa a more congenial cell occupation. There is some confirmation of this, since Rossa records – in an exceptional comment on prison officials – that the Pentonville school-master treated the men considerately (Rossa 1967, pp. 70, 84–6).

66 *Things Not Generally Known*, pp. 8–9. There were penalties for letting down the bed before the bell rang, and prisoners were not allowed to get into bed before their clothing was collected. Equally, not to have the clothing instantly ready for collection incurred a rebuke.

67 Letter of Thomas Duggan, *Nation*, 17 October 1868, 184d.

68 Ibid., p. 9; NAI, CSO RP 1866/13, 684; Rossa 1967, p. 72.

69 In July 1866 a magistrate wrote to Under-Secretary Sir Thomas Larcom from Cork reporting that the son of a man in the district was a warder at Dartmoor. This son had been in the Papal Brigade and was a friend of some of the Cork Fenian convicts: 'Therefore I deem it prudent to write to you that the authorities at Dartmoor may make enquiries on the subject – perhaps prevent a secret escape plan' (NLI: Larcom Papers: 7690 (Fenian Supplement, 1866)).

opened, which required the presence of at least two warders: there could be no casual communication.[70]

There were other restrictions. Since there were no facilities for Roman Catholic services at the time, the men received cell visits from the prison chaplain. Ellen O'Leary noted that for the first eight weeks of their confinement at Pentonville there was no Roman Catholic chaplain.[71] When eventually appointed, this functionary was of little comfort. He attempted to persuade Rossa[72] to renounce his Fenian oath, and refused to give him information about his wife and children, his fellow-prisoners or anything happening in the outside world; he apparently told the prisoners that he believed them to be excommunicated.[73]

70 Rossa jeered that 'Those great English people would not even trust their English jailers with us without making them act as spies upon each other' (1967, p. 80).
71 The *Irishman*, 7 July 1866, 28a.
72 Jeremiah O'Donovan Rossa (1831–1915) was prominent in Fenianism for more than fifty years. Born Rosscarbery, Co. Cork. In 1856 founded the Phoenix Society – a body intermediate to the Young Irelanders and the IRB. Became an IRB organiser in 1858; sentenced to penal servitude for life in 1865. Conditional pardon and expatriation in 1871 took him to New York, where he lived for the rest of his life. Took an independent hand in promoting dynamitardism in the 1880s. Alcoholism and erratic behaviour caused breaches with his former comrades, though he continued to be widely regarded by extreme nationalists because of his imprisonment, defiant attitude and uncompromising anti-British writings and speeches. The IRB arranged for the return of his body and for a public funeral of great significance in August 1915.
73 Ibid., pp. 74–9; *Irishman*, 7 July 1866, 28a; 4 August, 93a; *Cork Examiner*, 6 January 1866, 2f. Then and later the Roman Catholic chaplains were scrupulous in their duty to the prison. A few days after the arrival of the Fenians in Pentonville, Captain Edmund Du Cane, one of the directors of convict prisons, wrote to Larcom at Dublin Castle: 'I think it proper to tell you that the Roman Catholic priest visited the Irish prisoners in Pentonville yesterday and that Luby and another of them asked him almost the first thing whether there had been a rising in Ireland yet – as it seems to show they expect a rising to occur at any moment – and they do not consider their own arrest to have materially damaged the plans of the rebels' (NLI: Larcom Papers: Ms. 7690). The priest, the Revd Vincent Zanetti, refused to assist O'Donovan Rossa's wife while she was in New York, and Rossa was under punishment, and therefore, in strict conformity with the rules, denied correspondence. Mary O'Donovan Rossa wrote asking his assistance on 16 January 1868. Zanetti handed the letter to the governor, who wrote, informing Mrs O'Donovan Rossa that through continued misconduct her husband had forfeited the privilege of writing a letter, adding 'He is in his usual state of health' (21 February 1868: CUA: FBP, Box 2, item 23). Years later, just ten months before his release under amnesty, Rossa's wife asked the chaplain to pass a message to him, and received the following brusque reply: 'I am in receipt of your letter but I regret to say that I cannot comply with your request as it is strictly forbidden for officers to become a medium of communication between prisoners and their friends. I cannot regret that I missed seeing you on your visits and that you failed to see me for to have had to refuse to listen to you (as I should have been obliged to do) would have been hurtful to you and have been painful to me' (NLI: O'Donovan Rossa Papers: Ms. 10,974 (iii) (unfoliated), 16 February 1870). The Roman Catholic chaplain at Pentonville, the Revd Vincent Zanetti, was referred to as 'the jailor priest Zennetti [sic]' (*Things Not Generally Known*, p. 8).

The rules provided that on arrival at a convict prison a prisoner was allowed to write one letter to family or friends.[74] At Mountjoy at least some Fenians had been denied this privilege, and were refused it again in England 'until further instructions came'. This angered Rossa, who argued that although it had been decided that the Fenians would be treated as strictly as other convicts, 'the ordinary rules were set aside and special instructions received to treat us worse than the thieves and murderers of England'.[75] On appealing to the directors against the denial of a reception letter, Rossa was told that he could write neither to his wife, nor to the Liberal MP James Stansfield.[76] He was, however, allowed to write to the Home Secretary. A request from Michael O'Regan to write to the American Ambassador in London was granted on condition that he restricted it to his property in the United States of America, since the Lord Lieutenant (or, rather, Thomas Larcom) took the view that 'it is very questionable whether matters concerning convict discipline or treatment ought to be made the subject of correspondence with a foreign government'.[77] John O'Leary was later refused a visit from his wife, and Devoy was given a similar answer to a request for a visit from his children. The Fenians' special treatment was underscored by the consultations which took place between Dublin Castle and the Home Office on these issues.[78] It should be noted, of course, that correspondence and visits were regulated by the progressive stage system and could be suspended as part of a prison punishment – but there was no question of punishment regarding these reception letters.[79] This was simply an exercise of executive discretion in suspending the rules.

74 See *Rules and Regulations for the Government of Convict Prisons*, London, George E. Eyre & William Spottiswoode, 1858, Rule 14. The same privilege was enjoyed in the Irish convict prisons (see *Rules to be Observed in Mountjoy Male Prison*, Dublin, Alexander Thom, 1867, Rule 21; it appears that this rule was in effect the previous year).

75 Rossa 1967, p. 68.

76 There is a mystery here. On the arrival of the first batch of Fenians, Mark Gambier, one of the directors of convict prisons, had written to Horatio Waddington, the Permanent-Under-Secretary at the Home Office, enquiring if the men were to have the usual privilege of writing and receiving a reception letter. Sir George Grey, the Home Secretary, insisted that the prisoners should be treated like other convicts, but directed that the Irish government's views should be sought. Dublin Castle replied on 16 January, stating that the Lord Lieutenant had no objection to the convicts having their reception letters, on the usual conditions. It is hard to know, therefore, where the difficulty lay, since there was no reason why Rossa and the others should not have had their letters (PRO HO 45/9329/19461/6 and /10; NAI, CSO LB 266/94). Stansfield was MP for Halifax and on the Radical wing of the Liberal Party. In later years he was a Home Ruler. It is not known why Rossa wished to write to him.

77 NAI, CSO LB 266/311.

78 NAI, CSO LB 267, f. 85 (24 April 1867); f. 177 (5 August 1867).

79 On a number of subsequent occasions Rossa's correspondence and visiting privileges were withdrawn while he was under punishment. See, for example, letter from the governor of Millbank to Mrs O'Donovan Rossa, 31 December 1867: CUA: FBP, Box 2, item 23.

Nine months was the usual stay in the separate stage ('probationary') prison, but this was shortened for the Fenians, who were moved after three or four months.[80] The next stage was a public works prison, where the men would labour in association. The Home Secretary directed that five who were in failing health, and therefore unfit for convict labour, were to go to Woking Convict Prison (which was reserved for invalids).[81] There remained twenty-four about whom Colonel Edmund Henderson, then Chairman of the Directorate of Convict Prisons, wrote to Horatio Waddington, Home Office Permanent-Under-Secretary. In his opinion, it was not desirable to send the men to Portsmouth Convict Prison, 'where there are already over 500 Roman Catholic Convicts, mostly Irish, or to Dartmoor where there are nearly 200 many of them, owing to physical ailments, liable to be very troublesome'. Portland was believed to be the most suitable and secure prison to which they could be sent.[82]

If Rossa's recollection is to be trusted, he was transferred to Portland prison on 14 May 1866.[83] Here high security continued, and the men were lodged in the basement (which Rossa claimed had not been used previously for accommodation). These were small night-cells, the partition walls of which were of corrugated iron. They had stone floors and so were very cold; they were also prone to flood when it rained.[84] Natural light was so poor in some cells that reading was impossible, except in winter when candles were issued. Permission to write a reception letter to their families was again denied, and the governor refused without special orders to put the men to temporary work, as was customary with newly arrived prisoners.[85] Since Portland had not previously been a prison to which Roman Catholics were sent, it was necessary to erect a temporary chapel and to get Treasury approval for the employment of a visiting priest.[86] Pending this appointment, permission was given for one of the Fenians to read morning and evening prayers each Sunday. The men chose Denis Mulcahy,

---

80 *Commission of Inquiry into the Treatment of Treason-Felony Convicts*, PP, 1871 [C.310], XXXII, 1 (hereinafter *Devon Commission*); *Minutes of Evidence*, q. 83, p. 4; q. 188, p. 7.

81 An article in the *Irish Republic* claimed that within twelve months of conviction seven or eight men (including Charles Kickham, who at the age of thirteen had been maimed in an accident) had been certified as invalids and sent to Woking ('A Statement of Facts with Regard to the Treatment of State Prisoners', 18 May 1867, 7c: hereinafter 'A Statement of Facts').

82 PRO HO 45/9328/19461/Pt.1/23, Henderson to Waddington, 18 April 1866. Portland, situated on an easily guarded peninsula, also had security advantages. Over the years care would be taken to restrict as far as possible the mixing of Irish criminal and political prisoners.

83 This is also the date Ellen O'Leary gives in a prisoner's letter (possibly her husband) which she cited in her own letter in the *Irishman*, 4 August 1866, 93a–b. But Henderson reported the transfers to the Home Office on 18 April 1866 (PRO HO 45/9329/19461/23).

84 The cells were said to be so damp that the men invariably went to bed in their damp shirts ('A Statement of Facts'). See also Rossa 1967, p. 98; *Things Not Generally Known*, p. 10.

85 Rossa 1967, p. 100. A labour assignment – temporary or permanent – meant time out of cell, and the opportunity to mix with other prisoners.

86 PRO HO 45/9329/19461/23 and 30.

who managed to select Bible passages which, Rossa recorded, 'harmonized best with our positions'.[87]

When the Fenian prisoners were eventually assigned to quarry labour, William Fagan, one of the directors of convict prisons,[88] ordered that they should be put to work in a spot 'where their safe custody or the officers' honesty will not be tampered with'. The chosen place was no more than 300 yards from the prison, where both the Fenians and their guards would be clearly visible to the senior officers.[89] Each prisoner worked at his own station, about three yards away from his nearest companions. They could speak, but only about their work, and the conversation had to be loud enough to be heard by the supervising guard. The use of Gaelic was forbidden, the official view being that it counted as 'slang'.[90]

The men were now allowed visits, but these were subject to special arrangements. A visiting cage was constructed, consisting of a row of three barred compartments. The prisoner sat in one of the outer cages, his visitor in the other; sandwiched in the middle was a warder. Contact was thus restricted to conversations conducted over a distance of four feet through two sets of closely set bars and past the invigilating warder. The reason for the extra security and supervision was that the Irish government believed that the Fenians' wives and female relatives had taken a hand in the Fenian organisation.[91] According to Things Not Generally Known the ordinary prisoners considered it their unlucky day that the Fenians had been sent to English prisons: discipline had been made

87 'It was pleasing to me to hear him read from the Holy Book denunciations of tyrants and oppressors, perjurers and liars, and sympathy for their victims . . . and blessings for all who suffered persecution for justice sake. It was the most treasonable preaching ever I heard, and we had it for Sunday after Sunday for eight weeks till the priest came' (Rossa 1967, p. 101).

88 William Fagan, who came from a well-known Cork family, had served with Henderson at the convict establishment in Western Australia. Rossa had a particular dislike for Fagan, and noted of him in his memoirs: 'Mr Wm. J. Fagan (one of the Catholic Fagan family of Cork) is a Director of prisons in England. He gets charge of the prisons that the Irish Fenian prisoners occupy. In transferring some of us from Pentonville prison in London to Portland prison in the Southern point of England, he writes this way to Governor Clifton: "The Irish prisoners are to be worked in a separate party at labour equal to their ability, and are to be kept and exercised by themselves on all occasions; and they are to be worked by protestant officers who are English, and in whom you have full confidence. You must therefore locate them on the works in a secure position, where their safe custody, or the officers' honesty, will not be tampered with."' It would have been significant to Rossa and others that Fagan's letter was sent on St Patrick's Day, 1866. Rossa's comment was characteristic: 'You see that England would not trust an Irish protestant – even an Irish Orangeman with having any charge of us' (NLI: O'Donovan Rossa Papers: Ms. 10,974 (iv), unfoliated).

89 Rossa 1967, p. 102.

90 Ibid., pp. 104 and 109.

91 John O'Leary's sister applied for a private visit in November 1866. This request was passed by the Home Office to Dublin Castle, and refused because 'there is reason to know that Fenian affairs are managed very much by female Emissaries' (Larcom to Waddington, 16 November 1866; NAI CSO LB, 266/376).

twice as severe, talking prohibited and their friends were shut up in a cage when they visited. Somewhat fancifully, the criminal prisoners also contended that, but for the Irish political prisoners, the Home Secretary would have improved their food and clothing.[92]

The convict authorities and the Home Office had in the first year apparently not reached a final position on details of the Fenians' treatment. As noted, they had refused (at least for a time) the letter-writing privileges extended to ordinary convicts, but in November 1866 the directors issued an order (quickly countermanded) that, provided they committed no disciplinary offences, the Fenian prisoners would be permitted an allowance of letters more generous than that of the ordinary convicts.[93] In response to events in the outside world – the Chester Raid, the March 1867 rising, the Manchester rescue, the Clerkenwell explosion, and (two years later) Rossa's sensational (invalidated) election as an MP for Tipperary – security arrangements were tightened.[94]

Penal servitude was intended to be a severe and oppressive punishment and, even without the additional hardships which the Fenians claimed were inflicted on them alone, taxed body and spirit to the limit. The sentence was divided into what were called 'progressive stages', advancement through which required a combination of elapsed time and earned marks.[95] During the first stage, normally nine months in duration, the convict was in separate confinement. This meant that as many as twenty-three hours a day were spent in his cell, where he both ate and worked. At exercise he could see but was forbidden to communicate with other prisoners. Following this ordeal, he moved on to a public works prison where, supposedly to the extent that his health permitted, he was put to heavy labour such as quarrying, stone-dressing and stone-breaking.[96] During this stage, the well-behaved advanced through several classes, each of which carried with it slight improvements in diet and privileges. Although apparently marginal to the outside observer, so arduous was the basic discipline that these

92 *Things Not Generally Known*, p. 20.
93 Ibid. This pamphlet attributes the change to the pending insurrection in Ireland, though the author was uncertain whether the authorities' intention was to placate Irish opinion, or to use the extra letters as an intelligence net. Either explanation is possible, but simple confusion is more likely, given that the privilege was withdrawn at the end of January 1867, that is, *before* the expected insurrection.
94 Rossa 1967, pp. 152–3, 174 and 214. Rossa's victory in a by-election was an explicit and unmistakable declaration of sympathy for the Fenian prisoners. Election material described him as being 'of Portland Prison, or Pentonville, England'. In the *Irishman* his supporters exhorted 'Remember the record of his unparalleled sufferings – remember his thirty-five days torture with hands manacled behind his back' (*Irishman*, 13 November 1869, 323c).
95 For a more detailed description of the progressive stage system in the convict prisons, see my *History of English Prison Administration*, London, Routledge & Kegan Paul, 1981, pp. 400–4.
96 This labour sapped the energy of men who were on a restricted diet, and severely tested their powers of endurance (see letter of Thomas Duggan describing his labour at Portland in the winter of 1866–7, *Nation*, 17 October 1868, 184d).

small ameliorations were valued greatly by the convicts, and their loss through demotion ('degradation') was a weighty sanction.

Each stage of the sentence was severe and trying, especially to persons such as the Fenians, who had never previously experienced imprisonment. Their resilience was severely tested when they arrived from Ireland, fatigued by the long journey, humiliated by the procedures of imprisonment, their sentences before them and, perhaps above all, with their hopes of rebellion dimming or in tatters. Depression, even despair, must have accompanied them as each was rushed to a separate cell where isolation ate at morale and sapped endurance. Monotony in sight, sound and taste, lack of any mental stimulation and near-complete seclusion constituted a burdensome and progressively grinding punishment. There were the usual cell tasks such as cleaning and laying out equipment in the military style and, should the inspecting principal warder find anything out of order, the whole lot was pulled from the shelf on to the floor and had to be done again.[97] For ordinary prisoners this was humiliating, but for those who detested British authority it was an almost intolerable goad.

Even in sleep the prisoner was subject to penal discipline. There was a finely calculated inadequacy in the bedding, and such a hardness in the bed that in winter sleep was nearly impossible. The prisoner, going to sleep cold, woke shivering and shaking in the small hours. Years later, Rossa recalled that 'in the way of metaphysical discomfort, I do not know that I ever experienced anything worse than those early mornings in Pentonville'.[98] The bed itself was a virtual instrument of torture, consisting of a board covered by a mattress, 'About half as much thick, not quite so hard as the board'. The pillow was made of layers of boards nailed to the bed-board. To sleep at all the prisoner had to employ a special technique, described by Rossa as an automatic rolling from side to side every fifteen minutes or so, without waking.[99]

During waking hours cold was also a problem, since the Pentonville cells received little benefit from the system of heating.[100] In addition, prisoners were

---

97 In a letter to the *Irishman* Ellen O'Leary contended that hard work and insufficient food were minor problems compared with the 'moral torture they undergo. . . . To be liable to be ordered about twenty times a day by some of the lowest in creation . . . takes all their stoicism quietly to endure' (7 July 1866, 28a).

98 Rossa 1967, p. 65.

99 Ibid., p. 67. He could not completely shake off the habit after release. His daughter reported that towards the end of his life Rossa suffered from recurrent prison nightmares. She also referred to his spinal injury, which he claimed had resulted from a beating inflicted on him in prison. This injury may have been exacerbated by the years of convict bedding (Margaret O'Donovan Rossa, *My Father and Mother Were Irish*, New York, The Dervin-Adair Company, 1939).

100 Pentonville's flue and ventilator system of heating was a fanciful design by the prison's chief architect, the Surveyor General Major Joshua Jebb. Even when well maintained and worked correctly it was of doubtful reliability. Numerous complaints from prisoners of many different sorts over the years indicate that it was imperfectly operated and at times next to useless (see

denied their flannel underwear which they had worn when at liberty and whose loss they felt keenly.[101] Their work provided no relief since cell tasks were sedentary. In combination with a restricted diet and the natural depression of imprisonment, the constant feeling of being cold must have been extremely oppressive; it is no wonder that Rossa remembered it as 'most cruel'.[102] On transfer from Pentonville to Portland, Rossa was found to have lost eight pounds in weight during his months in separate confinement.[103]

Besides the pervasive cold, there was also the smell of sewer-gas, which issued from the poorly valved water-closets with which the cells were then equipped.[104] These gases were supposed to be drawn off by the hot-air system, but in practice this did not happen. Some relief was given while the prisoners were at exercise, since for a time they were out of doors and because cell doors were then left open, thus permitting general ventilation. There were complaints from the Fenians about the stench (which all prisoners had to endure) and of their unoccupied cells not being left open to air (a security precaution applied only to them).[105]

Jebb's *Modern Prisons: Their Construction and Ventilation*, London, Privately Printed, 1844). For the reactions of an experienced prisoner to prison heating, see my *English Local Prisons 1860–1900: Next Only To Death*, London, Routledge, 1995, p. 716.

101 Homes and workplaces were nowhere as well heated in the nineteenth century as they are now. Warm clothing, including flannel underwear, was worn indoors. In the matter of underwear, there was no extra severity towards the Fenians. By a standing order of 4 March 1865, no convict could be issued with flannels of any kind except upon medical recommendation (*Standing Orders (Convict Prisons)*, London, George E. Eyre and William Spottiswoode, 1865, p. 127). Rossa had evidently felt the cold of the cells keenly since the beginning of his imprisonment. While on remand at Richmond Prison he asked his wife to send in his flannels, even though summer had just ended (Rossa to Mary O'Donovan Rossa, Monday, 25 September 1865: CUA: FBP, Box 2, item 23). John O'Leary suffered similarly (see letter from his sister, Ellen O'Leary, *Irishman*, 7 July 1866, 28a).

102 Rossa 1967, p. 63. In 1904, almost forty years after his incarceration at Millbank, Rossa annotated an envelope which had contained a letter from John Lynch, a former Fenian 'Centre' from Cork City: 'Died in an English prison in 1866. In Millbank prison London he whispered to me, Rossa: the cold is killing me' (New York Public Library (NYPL): Maloney Collection of Irish Historical Papers (MCIHP); Correspondence of Jeremiah O'Donovan Rossa, 1HP61, Box 4). John Casey ('The Galtee Boy') on his way to Western Australia on board the *Hougoumont*, passed through the iceberg zone of the South Atlantic and remembered 'many bitter days spent in Portland with hands benumbed and feet almost frozen with cold' (John Sarsfield Casey, *Journal of a Voyage from Portland to Fremantle on Board the Convict Ship Hougoumont*, ed. Martin Kevin Cusack, p. 28 (on deposit in the British Library).

103 Rossa 1967, p. 96. This was in addition to the twenty pounds which he claimed to have lost during his preliminary imprisonment in Dublin.

104 See my *English Local Prisons 1860–1900*, pp. 283–4, 716.

105 *Things Not Generally Known*, p. 8: 'each cell was a water closet, and . . . we had the full benefit of the stench that rose from it twenty-three out of the twenty-four hours.' The author also complains that while the Fenians were at Pentonville 'a current of fresh air or hot air did not pass through our closet-dungeons. The political prisoners alone were treated with this exceptional severity, the necessity for which I could never see' (Ibid., p. 9).

There were other hardships. Clothing, for example, was in common, and both outer- and underwear were issued only on the basis of approximate size. This meant that the prisoners returned their clothing at certain times and received back items, many no doubt laundered imperfectly, which had been worn by others. *Things Not Generally Known* referred to the Fenians being compelled 'to wear the shirts and flannels of the vilest criminals, many of whom suffer from the most loathsome and infectious diseases, syphilis, etc.'. There were, he wrote, 'few things more disgustingly horrible than to be obliged to put on a shirt or a flannel worn by one of those leprous outcasts of society'.[106] But perhaps one of the more disgusting things was to have to bathe in water in which other convicts had also bathed. The Fenians objected to being bathed en masse and to being paraded naked on such occasions, and also when they were taken for inspection in the surgery.

When the prisoners passed from the separate-stage prisons (Pentonville and Millbank) to the public works prison (as noted above, most went to Portland), there were other sanitary hardships and humiliations. The public works prisons had much smaller cells – apparently half-sized – since the convicts were expected to be out of them for a full day's work.[107] They were not equipped with water-closets, and besides being half-sized were less well lit and more poorly ventilated than Pentonville or Millbank cells. Sanitary needs were met by a chamber-pot. Even on Sunday, when they were locked in their cells, the convicts were reprimanded if they used these pots. And because these vessels had to be burnished to silver-brightness, and kept thus always, some prisoners used their dinner-tins for defecation should they have bowel trouble. Those same tins might then be used by another prisoner as a dinner-tin. Equally disgusting, the tin and zinc vessels with which the cells were provided (water containers, chamber-pot, wash-basin, knife, plate and drinking pot) were all wiped and burnished with the same rags: requests for a separate set of rags were refused.[108] The sense of contamination, of pollution, of continuing and ineluctable filth would have been a most debilitating torment to men of normal sensibilities.

It is a humiliating device frequently employed oppressively to assert control over prisoners' bowel and bladder movements by obliging them to seek permission to visit the lavatory, and by restricting the time spent there. Whether these restrictions arose from bureaucratic expedience, the requirements of a tightly timetabled regime, or simply from calculated petty tyranny, or a combination of these factors, the Fenians were not spared their quota of mortification. *Things Not Generally Known* claims that even when suffering from dysentery prisoners were forbidden use of the lavatory, or were rationed in its use. Some Fenians

---

106 Ibid.
107 Examples of cells of this size may be seen at Fremantle Prison, Western Australia (now a museum).
108 *Things Not Generally Known*, pp. 10–11.

were assigned to the laundry, where they washed the clothing and sheets of their fellows, including the infirmary inmates. As can be imagined, this was disgusting and taxing work, since some clothing and sheets were filthy and stinking.[109] Some also drew lavatory duty – cleaning the common water-closets in the prisons, and digging out the dry toilets on the public works.[110]

A substantial amount of public works labour was in the open air, where labour parties permitted contact with comrades, as well as exercise and fresh air. But it was arduous work and, because no regard was paid to the weather, could be gruelling both in the heat of the summer and cold of the winter. The day was long. Prisoners rose at 5 a.m., marched to the works at 6.50 a.m. and returned at 5.45 p.m.; permission to put down their beds was not given until 7.45 p.m. When working in inclement weather – cold, wet or hot – no protective clothing was issued, nor, except in the most extreme of conditions, were convicts allowed to shelter. In consequence, there were occasions when men took their wet clothing to the cold cells with them at night.[111] These conditions were the common lot of convicts, and despite their harshness some Fenians, including Rossa, preferred them to the indoor tasks of laundry and closet-scouring.[112] At least one Portland prisoner looked back fondly on his Pentonville days, complaining that the privilege of being transferred after only four and a half months meant only that the Fenians were subject to five more Portland months: 'the labour [at Pentonville] was comparatively light, and you had meal hours, and an hour after work for mental recreation'. Four days a week there was an hour's exercise, and two hours of exercise on three days. At Portland, by contrast, from 5 a.m. until 8 p.m. 'you can scarcely call ten minutes your own'.[113]

The Fenian soldiers

It was not until several months after the civilian trials that the Fenian soldiers (although arrested in February 1866) were brought before courts martial. A number of sentences were especially severe – initially death, but this was commuted to life penal servitude; others received this sentence in the first instance; twenty-, ten- and five-year sentences were also imposed. Soldiers were viewed as double traitors – to their oaths of loyalty as well as to their duty as subjects. Because of their training, physique and particular comradeship, they were also

---

109 It was improbably claimed that the temperature in the wash-room was 140 degrees Fahrenheit. More plausibly, it was reported that men became sick from washing the infirmary linen and that Charles Underwood O'Connell 'fainted with loathing' ('A Statement of Facts').

110 *Things Not Generally Known*, pp. 11, 13, 16, 20.

111 Ibid., pp. 16–18.

112 Letter of Mrs Mary O'Donovan Rossa to the *Irishman*, reporting a visit to her husband, whom she said was suffering from eye trouble through working in the Portland quarries (11 August 1866, 104a).

113 Ellen O'Leary, quoting a prisoner's letter (*Irishman*, 4 August 1866, 93a–b).

taken to be a greater threat to security than the civilians. Their prosecutor, Colonel W. Fielding, was said to have 'peculiar aptitude and thorough knowledge of the matter of the Fenian Conspiracy'. In a letter to Lord Strathnairn, he counselled their swift removal from Ireland:

> 1st . . . I have good reason to believe that the Military Fenian Convicts hold communication with their friends in this City. 2nd . . . they entertain a firm conviction that they will be liberated from their prison by their friends (the Fenians). I have moreover good grounds for my belief that Fenian Movement is still vigorously in progress in this Country and that the leniency shown to Col. Sergt. McCarthy has had bad effects among the soldiers both loyal and disloyal. The loyal say that a soldier who had struck his officer on parade would have got as much and that they will be murdered. The disloyal say that the Government did not dare to carry out the sentence of death against a Fenian for fear that [the] whole country should rise.[114]

It was agreed that on arrival in England the men would be formally discharged from the army, and that they would thereafter be treated as ordinary civilian convicts.[115] The course of their confinement generally followed that of the other Fenian convicts with two exceptions: they were not exempted from flogging and failed to benefit from the 1869 to 1871 amnesties.

In the early years of the IRB, as John O'Leary recalled, James Stephens had directed that there should be no attempt to recruit among the Irish soldiers in the British Army.[116] When in 1863 recruitment did begin (under the direction of John Devoy), it was very successful, O'Leary claiming that there was no limit to those willing to be sworn, 'save the natural ones of time and opportunity'.[117] The plotting, apparently from the beginning, was well known to the authorities. Irish regiments thought to be infected with the Fenian virus were moved overseas, and at home certain men were arrested and severely punished. Their crimes, it was felt, had brought shame on their regiments and the Irish in the British Army; their very existence was corrosive of that trust which was the focus of all military training and beliefs.[118] Officer sentiment, powerfully represented by

---

114 PRO HO 45/9329/19461/31.
115 Ibid., /34, /36, /38–40.
116 O'Leary, op. cit., Vol. II, p. 229.
117 Ibid., p. 230.
118 A few men had enlisted in anticipation of an uprising, to obtain military training. One such was James Clancy (1846–1911), who joined the Royal Engineers, deserting when the 1867 rising was imminent. He assisted in the reorganisation of the IRB in England after 1867. Recognised by a detective as a deserter, Clancy shot the man, but was nevertheless arrested and sentenced to penal servitude for life. There was no mention of Fenianism in the charge, and it took determined efforts by Isaac Butt to secure Clancy's release after ten years (see William

HRH, the Duke of Cambridge, Commander-in-Chief, was so outraged that the men were excluded from the amnesties of 1869 and 1871, and served large portions of their sentences. This was a manifest injustice, since the leaders of the conspiracy, under whose orders the soldiers had acted, were among the first to be released. The last three Fenian soldiers were not released until January 1878.[119]

In the normal course, soldiers or sailors sentenced to penal servitude, even for purely military or naval offences, were sent to civilian convict prisons. The Fenian soldiers were first subjected to a ceremony of military degradation, being taken to the parade ground where in front of the regiment they were stripped of uniform, dressed in convict clothes and removed to prison. As with the civilian Fenians, there was a short period of detention in Mountjoy Prison, Dublin, and then shipment to England. For this, the prisoners were chained together and marched in their convict uniforms through the streets, under heavy escort.[120]

In the separate-system prison, special precautions were taken to keep the Fenian soldiers incommunicado. In chapel they knelt apart from the other prisoners, with a warder stationed nearby. Even in their cells they were denied freedom of movement, being ordered either to sit on the covered bucket which served for a stool, or to stand stationary. This was a constant punishment, and immobility was undoubtedly a hardship in cold weather in the poorly heated cells.[121]

Close custody continued in the public works' prison, where soldiers were strip-searched four times a day. At Chatham they were given end cells, which had no direct access to the cell-block wall, and therefore were more secure; these cells were next to the lavatories and also had no direct ventilation, so conditions can be imagined. The prison authorities, however, doubtless felt justified in all this when John Boyle O'Reilly and two others attempted to escape from Chatham. They were recaptured and punished (but not flogged).

O'Brien and Desmond Ryan (eds), *Devoy's Postbag, op. cit.*, Vol. 1, p. 365). Thomas Hassett was another who joined to acquire military training for revolutionary purposes. He deserted in January 1866 with his weapon, and was arrested the following month and sentenced to penal servitude for life. For an escape attempt in Australia he spent two years in chains. He was one of the *Catalpa* escapers (see Z. W. Pease, *The Catalpa Expedition*, New Bedford, Mass., George S. Anthony, 1897, p. 67).

119 *The Times*, 5 January 1878, 9f; 7 January, 7a. The three were Colour-Sergeant Charles McCarthy, Thomas Chambers and John Patrick O'Brien.
120 A. G. Evans, *Fanatic Heart: A Life of John Boyle O'Reilly 1844–1890*, Nedlands, University of Western Australia Press, 1997; see also Mrs John Boyle Roche (ed.), *Life of John Boyle O'Reilly*, by James Jeffrey Roche, *Together with his Complete Poems and Speeches*, New York, The Mershen Company, 1891, p. 47. For a more systematic account of O'Reilly's later years see Francis G. McManamin, 'The American Years of John Boyle O'Reilly: 1870–1890', Ph.D. dissertation, The Catholic University of America, 1959. There is some discussion of the Fenian soldiers in William Rutherford, '67. *Retrospection*, Dublin, O'Loughlin, Shields & Boland, 1903, pp. 6–8.
121 Roche, *op. cit.*, pp. 51–5.

At Portsmouth, to which O'Reilly was transferred, he again attempted to escape, was again recaptured and punished. Security precautions at Dartmoor consisted of location in a cell block which was so constructed that the cells had no access to an outside wall. The cells were very small, and through poor construction were poorly ventilated and dimly lit, and provided little protection against extreme temperatures.[122] At Dartmoor, the Fenian soldiers were put to heavy labour, but since they were fit young men at the time of their committal this was to be expected. O'Reilly made a final escape attempt, but was recaptured after two days and punished by a bread-and-water diet and confinement to a punishment cell. (It is notable that though some of the civilian Fenians plotted escape, none, as far as we know, actually tried it.)

Given the security precautions exercised over the Fenian prisoners in general, the particular detestation of military traitors and O'Reilly's escape attempts, it is curious that the decision was taken to transport so many of the soldiers to Western Australia in October 1867. The Young Irelanders had shown that once convicts were given a degree of liberty in Australia (as they almost invariably were) it was impossible to prevent their escape. In Australia, O'Reilly remained true to form, and escaped little more than a year after his arrival.

Punishments

Such harsh conditions could be maintained and such arduous labour extracted only by the threat and use of punishment. This ranged from the comparatively mild loss of marks to the extreme severity of a flogging. The Fenians had one enormous advantage: with the exception of the soldiers they were exempted from corporal punishment. To those who were bold and hardy enough to endure the intermediate punishments, this immunity meant that they could show considerable defiance of authority.[123] The decision that they should not be flogged was not made known to them, but as they tested the limits of authority it became

---

122 This type of cell, widely used in the United States of America, where it was known as the Auburn cell, was not usual in England. The cells were stacked, back to back, within the cell house, so that none had access to an outside wall, nor, of course, to direct light or ventilation. Besides the extra security which this provided, such cells were much cheaper to construct. At Dartmoor (which had a mixture of types of cell house) the Auburn-type cells were constructed of corrugated iron, with stone floors. Because cells were intended mainly for sleeping, they measured only 7' × 4' × 7' in height. This is not much larger than the cells which the Vietnamese Communist administration in the 1970s used for punishment and which were much dreaded by the prisoners (see Doan Van Toai and David Chanoff, *The Vietnamese Gulag*, New York, Simon & Schuster, 1986, p. 242). John Boyle O'Reilly gives a detailed account of his initial four months at Millbank in his semi-autobiographical novel, *Moondyne: A Story from the Underworld*, London, G. Routledge & Sons, 1889, ch. 7.

123 Rossa, by his own admission, misbehaved continuously at Portland. The 1867 Commission, which explicitly charged him with inciting the other treason-felony prisoners, and being a perpetual source of discontent, noted that instead of being fully punished at Portland Rossa

clear that this ultimate sanction had been deemed politically unacceptable.[124] It would have been a blast of oxygen for the flames of sympathy and indignation had reports reached Ireland or America that, in addition to their heavy terms of penal servitude among common criminals, Fenians were also being flogged. Government was conscious of this propaganda contest, and was careful to insist that there was no ill-treatment – going so far, it would seem, to plant or encourage ostensibly independent letters in the Irish press, attesting to the decency of prison conditions.[125] Dublin Castle received warnings even from magistrates, with one (John Cunningham of Londonderry) insisting that flogging would cause more sympathy with the Fenians than would be consistent with law and order: 'I myself would feel for O'Donovan Rossa – tho' I believe without egoism I successfully resisted his making any *inroad* in the North.'[126] A paragraph about alleged floggings was carried in the *Cork Examiner*.[127] J. S. Whitty (one of the

had been transferred to Millbank Prison: 'Had he been an ordinary convict, he would have been subjected to corporal punishment for his constant and open defiance of the prison authorities and prison rules' (*1867 Commission, op. cit.*, p. 4). The Commission regretted that Rossa's energies of mind and body had been so misapplied that 'the end of it all was the convict's cell and a duel between himself and the authorities. . . . The convict Rossa is a dangerous man, and must remain the object of unceasing anxiety and vigilance to the authorities. The senior warder at Millbank, a man of no mean experience in convict life, said that in the whole course of his career he never met with the equal of this unfortunate man. . . . He must mend his ways or abide his fate' (ibid., p. 23).

124 Even when Rossa threw the contents of his chamber-pot over the governor of Chatham prison – an offence which officials justifiably characterised as 'foul and insubordinate' and 'unprovoked and disgusting' – it was decided that flogging could not be inflicted 'without special authority'. This meant political authority, and the then head of the convict service, Colonel Edmund Henderson, was unwilling to raise the possibility with ministers, writing to Captain Du Cane, the Director who oversaw Chatham, 'I am unwilling to resort to corporal punishment in the case of this man, whose conduct savours of imbecility, except in the last resource' (*Devon Commission*, PP 1871 [C.319], XXXII, Appendix H, p. 60).

125 In this propaganda war it is difficult to distinguish one side from the other. A supposedly anonymous letter to the *Irishman* could have been a ham-fisted ploy of the authorities – or could have been intended by Fenian sympathisers to seem as though it were. The letter, dated 29 July 1866, purported to convey assurances from an influential and extremely reliable source that the Fenians were not suffering unusual hardships: 'They are treated just like the rest, and have a Catholic Chaplain to visit them – the allegations of cruelty, etc. are quite unfounded, their relatives need not be alarmed, a doctor examines them and does not allow overwork.' This rather bland statement was hardly likely to reassure, but was a useful peg for a concerned editorial in the *Irishman* (4 August 1866, 93a).

126 NLI: Larcom Papers: 7690 (Fenian Supplement, 1866). Lord Kimberley, the Lord Lieutenant, evidently did not like the tone of Cunningham's letter, and directed that it should have neither acknowledgement nor reply.

127 6 January 1866, 2f. The *Examiner* indicated that it did not know whether the story of flogging was true, but insisted there should be 'no additional degradations . . . of these unhappy men'. The men were not felons 'except in a mere legal sense; they are not robbers, ravishers and murderers – they are political prisoners, the victims of heated imaginations and illdirected patriotism – and not men branded with moral infamy'.

directors of Irish convict prisons) forwarded this to Henderson, and was assured that 'Truth in Cork lies at the bottom of the sea I should think – the whole story is a pure fabrication and does great credit to the imagination of the writer'.[128] As late as 1870 warning questions were being asked in the Commons, particularly regarding Rossa.[129]

Forgoing the lash, the authorities had sanctions with more limited deterrent value. From the perspective of twenty years or life penal servitude, the loss of marks[130] which might mean an extra month or year of imprisonment was almost meaningless. After one such infliction Rossa asked the governor who had sentenced him, 'Do you really mean to tell me that you are going to keep me a year and a half in prison without burying me after I'm dead?'[131] The reply is not recorded. Loss of food and confinement to a punishment cell or a dark cell were severe punishments, but they were limited by the prisoner's powers of physical endurance. Death under such circumstances would have the same political repercussions as death, disfigurement or permanent ill-health through flogging. This is not to say that the intermediate punishments were wholly negligible. Forfeiture of marks delayed promotion or caused degradation in class, and this had immediate consequences for both diet and privileges. Several of the political prisoners were physically unable to perform their tasks, and although the rule clearly stated that prisoners must be certified fit for labour, they were punished as if they had been deliberately idle at their work.[132] As a result of being judged guilty of not having fulfilled their tasks, O'Leary, Luby, Kickham and Cain were denied promotion in class, and, in consequence, for three years

128 Henderson insisted that the convicts were very well behaved, and indeed had no opportunity to be otherwise under their strict discipline. 'They appear to be much depressed at being here; but are quite satisfied they are fairly treated' (NLI: Larcom Papers: Ms. 7690). There was a tone of condescension in Henderson's letter which appears to have irritated Larcom, to whom it was passed, and he scored through the reference to truth at Cork lying at the bottom of the sea.

129 3 *Hansard*, CXCIX, col. 533; 18 February 1870. The aristocratic Liberal Home Ruler, Captain Charles William White, raised the matter. Home Secretary Henry Austin Bruce (later Lord Abordare) gave a categorical assurance that there had been no flogging.

130 Marks were awarded for good conduct over and above the marks which accrued for good behaviour. By ensuring maximum marks a convict could reduce his sentence by a quarter or more. For a life sentence prisoner, however, this inducement was slight, even theoretical. Marks were not awarded during the probationary (separate) stage, or if a man should be obliged to re-enter the probationary stage (as Rossa had). Misconduct could be punished by the withdrawal of marks (Standing Order No. 146: 'Regulations – Mark System', 22 July 1864, *Standing Orders (Convict Prisons)*, London, George E. Eyre and William Spottiswoode, 1865).

131 Rossa 1967, pp. 106–7.

132 The author of *Things Not Generally Known* mentions O'Leary, Luby and Kickham as being among the prisoners put to work beyond their capacity, and punished when they failed to fulfil their tasks (*op. cit.*, p. 18). O'Donovan Rossa, who was repeatedly punished, was in the different category of those who could but would not work.

received only bread and water for their evening meal, not having qualified for the tea allowance of the second class.[133]

Besides the political limitations on their punishment, the Fenians enjoyed psychological defences not generally available to ordinary prisoners, who had only their own resources on which to draw, and, having committed criminal offences may have felt isolated, ashamed and vulnerable. Very different the reaction of someone fortified by the correctness of his cause, and the moral reinforcement of his suffering. Dr Robert Lyons,[134] one of the Commissioners appointed in 1870 to enquire into the treatment of the treason-felony convicts, described their psychology:

> As the consciousness of guilt breaks the spirit of the ordinary convict committed for a crime which involves moral turpitude, and all the more readily if he have been, as sometimes happens, a man of education or position, he recognises at once and submits to the dictates of prison discipline. But the political prisoner, purely such, is, on the contrary, led to a higher and even exaggerated sense of his position by confinement in association with ordinary criminals. He considers that his sufferings ennoble his acts, and he rebels against prison rule.[135]

Rossa claimed that he entered prison resolved to be passive and patient. He was, he insisted, 'determined to obey in everything, as I conceived that the dignity of the cause of liberty required that men should suffer calmly and strongly for it.' These good intentions were soon discarded. The problem was that the more docile he was, 'the more my masters showed a disposition to trample upon me, the more they felt disposed to give us that annoyance which had no other object but to torment us'.[136] Given the character of the man, the effect of prison punishment was inevitably counterproductive. Recalling the first of his numerous bread-and-water punishments, Rossa, his dignity and self-respect outraged, found that his whole nature

> [A]rose in arms, and I felt that even against prison government I could be a rebel too. It was measuring me by the same rule as that by which they measured their thieves and pick-pockets; and though we were wearing the same jackets, I had inside of mine some kind of Irish pride which made me wish to have the authorities learn they were mistaken in supposing that the application of this rule to Irish revolutionists was

---

133 At one point Kickham was said to be in such a low state from the diet that his comrades smuggled mugs of tea to him (ibid., p. 22).
134 For a biographical note see p. 197, n. 244.
135 *Devon Commission, op. cit.*, Report, p. 32.
136 1967, p. 56.

to have the same effect upon them as the garrotters and Sodomites of England.[137]

In his war against authority Rossa endured a fearsome amount of punishment. The authorities' determination to break him ratcheted up his defiance. Sometimes the punishments were justified by his behaviour, Rossa admitted, but on other occasions he claimed that they were unjustified.[138] From bread and water, punishments increased to a prolonged special diet and deprivation of all books. The authorities' difficulty was that, in common with all other convicts, Rossa, even when not under punishment, lived at such a basic level that little could be taken away from him; physical and mental endurance could be severely tested, but not ultimately broken. Defiance and determination made for a dangerous, possibly fatal outcome. By the end of his time at Portland Rossa was refusing all work, and nearly all orders. It may have been that he believed his survival was at stake, since by then he was 'very much emaciated and reduced in strength'. Working out of doors in cold weather he keenly felt every blast of wind: '[w]hatever little flesh was on my hands seemed to be rotting off them.'[139]

Having exhausted Portland's punishments, the directors of convict prisons classified Rossa as refractory, and returned him to second probation – another dose of separate confinement – this time at Millbank.[140] Defiance and punishment continued. Between June 1867 and February 1868 Rossa was the least well-behaved prisoner at Millbank (and possibly in the fifty-year history of that prison), committing a total of nineteen offences. These included shouting out 'I am a Fenian', singing Fenian songs, making a great deal of noise in his cell destroying his spoon and porridge bowl, and saying 'I must do something to amuse myself, by Jesus I will'.[141] The authorities continued to respond to and punish each episode, even after a letter which Rossa managed to have smuggled out of the prison led to an official inquiry into his treatment. A wholly biased

---

137 Ibid., pp. 107–8.
138 His own restless nature seemingly led him to court punishment to relieve the monotony of cellular confinement at Pentonville. He described it thus: 'The history of one day ... contains the history of nearly every day of prison life, the same cheerless food, the same solitary confinement, the same dreary monotony, except that if you grew discontented with any of these things you could have a change for the worse in dark cells, bread and water, handcuffs, or anything that way you desire to choose as a variety. And I got into such a state of mind that, to get a change, even from bad to worse, was a kind of relief to me' (ibid., p. 73).
139 Ibid., pp. 142–3 and 134.
140 While at Millbank on second probation Rossa was treated as being under punishment, and for all or most of his time there he was denied the privilege of receiving or sending correspondence. Since his wife was then in New York this lack of communication must have been a great worry to them both (see letters of 31 December 1867 and 21 February 1868, governor of Millbank to Mary O'Donovan Rossa: CUA: FBP, Box 2, item 23).
141 PRO HO 45/9329/19461/104. This report was compiled by the Director responsible for Millbank (and punishing Rossa), Captain Mark Gambier.

inquiry exonerated the authorities, and the battle of wills continued.[142] Refusing all work and orders, Rossa barricaded himself in his cell. The punishment for this was four months in a darkened cell on a special penal diet, the first twelve days of which were to be bread and water. During this severe punishment Rossa was ordered, but refused to pick oakum.[143] Because of his unwillingness to conform, Rossa went for long periods under punishment and restrictions in privileges. During almost five years in prison, his wife was able to record, he had been able to send her only five letters, and she had been granted only five visits.[144]

It was in the midst of these punishments that the first sign came of a softening in the line of the authorities. It was decided to send a batch of convicts to Western Australia and Rossa was asked if he would volunteer to join them. He refused, and was told that he would be sent anyhow.[145] Shortly thereafter this order was rescinded – Rossa thought because of the events surrounding the Manchester rescue.[146] Defiance and punishment continued unceasingly, and in February 1868, having spent a year at Millbank, Rossa was removed to Chatham – his second public-works prison. On being taken to the stone-breaking yard, he threw his hammer over the prison wall, telling the astonished warders that he had no need for it since he would not work. Punishment followed, culminating in Rossa throwing the contents of his chamber-pot over the governor.[147] This provoked the authorities to the self-defeating severity which they had thitherto resisted. Rossa was placed in irons, with his hands manacled behind his back except when eating and sleeping.[148] This regime continued for thirty-five days

---

142 *1867 Commission, op. cit.*, p. 24. 'The convict authorities . . . must do their duty to all alike. The only true cause of complaint the treason-felony convicts have against them is that they can't get out.'

143 Rossa 1967, p. 172.

144 *Freeman's Journal*, 6 July 1870, 4a: Letter of Mary O'Donovan Rossa to the Earl of Devon. The visits had all taken place in the presence of at least two prison officials, who had constantly interrupted their conversation to prevent any discussion of politics or prison treatment.

145 This is Rossa's recollection. The official records tell a somewhat different story. Rossa, it was noted, on being asked if he would agree to go to Western Australia replied that he wished 'to place himself at the disposal of the government but without consulting his wife or friends, cannot express his wishes in a more definite form' (PRO HO 45/9329/19461/64).

146 Rossa 1967, p. 173. He preferred to be in England: 'I felt a kind of pleasure in seeing them treat us brutally in England, and I could not enjoy this feeling under similar treatment, in the Antipodes' (ibid., p. 174).

147 Rossa claimed in his memoirs that he had thrown only clean water from his slop bucket, but the authorities were probably correct in their claim.

148 The *Irishman* (then owned by Richard Piggot, who was closely involved with Rossa's family) carried a long account of Rossa's ill-treatment, and asserted that he had never for a moment in the thirty-five days been released from the manacles, and that his hands had remained behind his back. Piggot claimed that Rossa had told him this when he interviewed him in prison. Bad though Rossa's treatment was, this story was not true, and Rossa made no such claim in his own prison memoirs. Piggot was, of course, subsequently found (in relation to the forged Parnell letters) to be an egregious cheat and liar (*Irishman*, 5 June 1869, 776a and b; *The Times*, 14 June 1869, 6b).

on the orders of Captain Edmund Du Cane, confirmed by Colonel E. Y. W. Henderson, Chairman of the Directorate.[149]

On the official side there appears to have been a change of heart about this time, and this was matched by Rossa. It may have been that Du Cane and his colleagues realised that through the prolonged manacling they had gone too far, venturing beyond political protection. There may also have been a recognition that Rossa was not going to be compliant, that he had a daring and obdurate spirit, and the spiral of defiance and punishment could end in disaster. In September 1868, Du Cane and Rossa had a conversation, the details of which, tantalisingly, have not survived. What is certain is that the exchanges of defiance and punishment ceased, and, indeed, from that point on Rossa was never punished in prison.[150] It may have been that part of the agreement was the granting of special privileges regarding letters and books, easy work – to be performed as a group – and perhaps other concessions. From a letter of July 1870, it would seem that Rossa was able to receive, through one of the directors (probably Du Cane), extra correspondence including books, poems and photographs.[151]

149 Rossa 1967, pp. 197–200. Rossa claimed that he was handcuffed for thirty-five days. The Commission of Inquiry found on a 'preponderance of testimony' that he had been manacled for thirty-three days. This was sophistry, since the shorter term was based on the fact that he was released from the handcuffs for two and a quarter hours before being manacled again for a further two days for another offence. In the eyes of the Commissioners, this gap was enough to constitute the second manacling as a new period (see *Devon Commission, op. cit.*, pp. 14–16 and 15n.). Many would have thought the difference was not worth haggling over: it was an outrageous and illegal punishment. Colonel Henderson was an experienced manager of convicts, having served for thirteen years in Western Australia as Comptroller General. Du Cane had for six years been Henderson's subordinate in the convict administration, and it was on Henderson's recommendation that he was appointed to the English service in 1863.

150 On 17 February 1870, Home Secretary Henry Bruce confirmed that Rossa had never been flogged, 'nor do I believe that he ever received the slightest punishment beyond his ordinary imprisonment since September 1868' (3 *Hansard*, CXCLX, col. 533). In their summary of opinions, the Devon Commission referred to those of the Fenian prisoners who 'brooding over the supposed injustice of their sentence, displayed a spirit of insubordination' which it was the duty of the authorities to repress. Notwithstanding this obligation on the authorities to uphold discipline, the Commission, without naming him, drew attention to Rossa's case as 'one notable instance of an opportune remission of punishment accompanied by a few kindly words of remonstrance was followed by a marked improvement in conduct, which coercive measures had altogether failed to produce' (*Manchester Guardian*, 4 January 1871, 5e).

151 Rossa to Mary O'Donovan Rossa, 9 July 1870: CUA: FBP, Box 2, item 23. When Mary O'Donovan Rossa had in December 1867 attempted to send books to her husband (possibly as a Christmas gift) she was informed that the regulations prohibited all convicts from receiving books (Governor, Millbank Prison, to Mary O'Donovan Rossa, 31 December 1867: CUA: FBP, Box 2, item 23). But by February 1869, Rossa was able to obtain permission to write a special letter to his wife which, against all the regulations, he wrote in tiny script, cramming three lines into each ruled line on the paper – even writing on the fold of the envelope. By this time, it would seem, the regulations on such matters were regularly being set aside. The letter is marked 'Director's Order' (Rossa to Mary O'Donovan Rossa, 18 February 1870: ibid.).

Ordinary convicts were emphatically forbidden to receive such material, and their limited reading matter had to come from the prison library.

The illegal punishment of Rossa marked the extremity of the severity towards the Fenian prisoners. Gladstone's first administration came into office in December 1868, and a new spirit was immediately apparent. At this time – three years after he had been imprisoned – Rossa was told that he would be put to work with the other Fenian prisoners, as he had demanded.[152] One of their number, William Halpin, refused to work, even in the Fenian work party, and after a first petty punishment was left alone.[153] The work party also indulged in other minor acts of defiance, such as refusing to doff their caps to the prison doctor.[154]

Ill-treatment

The gist of the Fenians' complaints was that they were treated as ordinary convicts. This was a refrain repeated from first to last, in every possible form and variation. They bitterly resented being mixed with common criminals[155] and

152 He had argued that by being obliged to work with the criminal prisoners, no distinction was being made between criminal and political offenders: 'They classed us as they classed their criminals, and, as many of these often said to me, they treated us worse. They would make us feel degradation, putting us into association with them' (Rossa 1967, pp. 132–3). The easing of regime was general. Towards the end of 1868 or early 1869, *Things Not Generally Known* reported, the hospital treatment of the Fenians improved, and the doctors dealt with them in a more civil way. The writer commented, 'To what this change is to be attributed we know not' (p. 20). This was a coy reference to Gladstone's incoming administration.

153 'Every morning his needle and thread were handed to him. He graciously received them from the hands of the warder, and as graciously laid them down on the stool. Then he occupied his time and amused us by telling stories all day long. His bad and idle example had an influence on myself, and I suggested that we would invent something else to kill time.' The prisoners accordingly made a draught-board and played games throughout the day (Rossa 1967, p. 212).

154 Convict prisons were permeated by the military culture of most of the governors and directors. There was an insistence that convicts should show respect to the superior officers of the prison by standing to attention and uncovering their heads or saluting (*Things Not Generally Known*, pp. 15 and 20). O'Donovan Rossa and James O'Connor had each previously been sentenced to three days on bread and water in the dark cells for refusing to salute the prison doctor.

155 In evidence to the Commission of 1867 Charles Kickham (who was a devout and pious Roman Catholic) was asked if he had anything to complain of except mixing with criminals. Before going on to outline his other complaints he replied, 'I consider being mixed with criminals the greatest punishment in the power of man to inflict. Why should I complain of their conduct or conversation? It is not their fault that I am among them, but the loathing with which association with them has inspired me will cling to me while I live' (*Things Not Generally Known*, p. 21). Enjoying the comparatively liberal convict regime of Australia, at least one of the Fenians transported in 1867 expressed a preference for Pentonville and Portland. The position of the political offender was worse in Fremantle than in the English convict prisons since they were obliged 'to associate with two or three hundred robbers, forgers, and not a few murderers' (John Sarsfield Casey, *Journal, of a Voyage from Portland to Fremantle on Board the Convict Ship 'Houguoumont'. Cap Cozens Commander Oct. 12th 1867*, ed. Martin Kevin Cusack, Bryn Mawr, PA, Dorrace & Co, 1988, Appendix B).

regarded it as an insult and provocation, for example, that Ricard O'Sullivan Burke was transferred from Millbank to Woking prison chained to 'a vile and hideous-looking criminal, who he had been credibly informed, had been convicted of having [committed bestiality]'.[156] They protested at being called 'fellows' and at being accused of lying.[157] They generally and frequently complained that they were being treated as the sodomites were, and that they were being bullied and spoken to rudely.[158] Indeed, echoing Mitchel, they objected to burial in prison, where their remains might mingle 'with that of England's vilest criminals in the felon's bone-yard'.[159] But this was no more than a reiteration of the view that they should not have been treated as ordinary convicts. All convicts were bullied, spoken to harshly, restricted, repressed, subjected to petty tyranny and sometimes capricious punishments, and were denied justice: the Fenians were hardly being singled out.

It would seem, however, that in the early days of their imprisonment, a determined and conscious effort was made to cow the Fenians collectively, and to break those among them who were especially contumacious and rebellious. From the officials' point of view – especially at institutional level – the need for early and decisive repression was clear. Here was a body of men which had tried to overthrow government itself. Some were former soldiers; all had some kind of military involvement: none was cowed or ashamed. They had acted in concert before, and with resourcefulness and audacity had rescued their leader. If a similar incident were to be prevented, and if the men were to be denied the possibility of concerted action, then they had to be harassed and repressed above the ordinary. A disturbance, mutiny or riot, or another successful escape, was simply unthinkable.[160] And all of this must be seen in the context of

---

156 *Things Not Generally Known*, p. 8. The complaint that they were being treated on a par with sex criminals was frequently repeated. Ellen O'Leary insisted that the government had itself behaved abominably by mixing the political offenders with such outcasts: 'That political prisoners some of whom are even of high intellect, refinement and education, should be placed on a level with the most degraded and basest of mankind – men stained with the worst crimes – is a thing which will reflect eternal disgrace on the British government' (*Irishman*, 4 August 1866, 93a–b).

157 *Things Not Generally Known*, pp. 15, 19, 20 and 26.

158 The Fenians and their supporters found the proximity of sexual offenders (perhaps even the knowledge of their existence) intolerable. Thus D. D. Mulcahy 'was bullied as though he had been guilty of some of the bestial crimes so common in English prisons that no two criminals – no, nor even two political prisoners – are permitted to be together in a room for a second of time, lest they should commit one of those abominable crimes on each other' (ibid., p. 7).

159 Ibid.

160 In his memoirs Rossa admitted that his wife had attempted to organise his escape, borrowing £100 to bribe the guards. It is hard to say how serious this episode had been (and curious that his wife, rather than the IRB had taken the lead), but it was foiled by the frequent cell moves and other security precautions (Jeremiah O'Donovan Rossa, *My Years in English Jails*, New York, American News Co, 1874, pp. 164–5).

continuing Fenian activity in Ireland, England and America, great public and political anxiety, and the possibility of another insurrection.

Stripping and body-searching are essential to prison security. These procedures may be conducted in reasonable privacy and with some consideration, or they may be made intentionally degrading. The latter course was chosen with the Fenians. The prisoners were, on reception at both their separate stage prisons (Pentonville and Millbank) and public works prison (Portland) stripped naked and dealt with as a group. They were also made to stand in their underwear while waiting to see the doctor, and had to discard their clothing entirely before passing into his surgery.[161] Ricard O'Sullivan Burke, on his reception into Mountjoy, was stripped naked in the presence (it was claimed) of a dozen warders. Body searches – with all their opportunities for humiliation – were conducted with great frequency. Every time a prisoner left his Pentonville cell he was searched, and although not stripped, his clothing was undone and a close examination made; there were also surprise body and cell searches.[162] Such frequent searching must produce a sense of insecurity, vulnerability and disorientation. In his evidence to the 1869 Commission, Charles Kickham disclosed how close he had come to breakdown. Having described how he was variously harassed in his cell, he continued, 'About once a week I was stripped and made to stand naked in the middle of my cell, with my arms extended and my mouth open. This torture was carried SO FAR on one occasion that in spite of the scorn I felt for my torturers, I was obliged to burst into tears.'[163]

Prisoners may also be subdued and disoriented by constant and unpredictable verbal harassment and abuse. At Portland, for example, failure to burnish tin and zincware to the warders' satisfaction provoked such vituperation, delivered in the presence of the criminal prisoners. This campaign continued for several months.[164] Security was reason and excuse for entering the cell at all hours, and searching it and the person. Disturbed sleep and the insecurity of random searching greatly increased stress. *Things Not Generally Known* considered this regime 'well calculated to drive men mad'.[165] There is no evidence in the papers and archives to support the claim of calculation at official level, but the effects of such ad-hoc intimidation and bullying would have been immediately visible

---

161 *Things Not Generally Known*, p. 9.

162 Ibid., pp. 9 and 13.

163 Ibid., p. 21. Kickham's personal sensibility is described (albeit by admirers) in Matthew Russell's 1887 Introduction to Kickham's novel: 'There was much of what is best in woman and in child in his nature; and it was impossible . . . to know him well without feeling that he was trustful, and kindly, and sympathetic as a woman' (*Knocknagow: or The Homes of Tipperary*, Dublin, Gill & Macmillan, 1978, p. x).

164 *Things Not Generally Known*, pp. 10 and 11.

165 Ibid., p. 11.

(and welcome) to the warders and their supervisors.[166] There is also some indication that the Fenians were punished on a quota basis, whether or not they had committed an offence. The Portland Governor, Captain George Clifton, was alleged on two occasions to have ordered warders to bring four or five of the Fenians before him the following day for a disciplinary hearing.[167]

In Rossa's case it is unclear how much of the harsh treatment arose from an official intent to subdue him because he was a leading Fenian, and how far it was a response to his constant and provocative misbehaviour.[168] Some of his fellow prisoners disagreed with his confrontational conduct, considering it undignified and unworthy of an Irish rebel.[169] Rossa himself made few complaints, apparently believing such to be beneath his dignity and a form, even, of 'treating with the enemy'.[170] His memoirs list only acts of officiousness and callousness, such as the denial of permission to send or receive letters – even on important family matters.[171]

166 Examples of subjugation through harassment are legion in the historical and contemporary record of imprisonment and interrogation. Isolation, denial or interruption of sleep, humiliation, guards shouting and screaming, sparse diet, excessively hot or cold cells – all these stopped short of physical torture, but constituted a psychological battering which reduced the victim to a state of compliance and terror. The long-term effects of such treatment can be profound, as we know from medical and psychological studies of post-traumatic stress disorder. For the Soviet Union see, for example, Robert Conquest, *The Great Terror: A Reassessment*, London, Pimlico, 1992, pp. 121–7; China: J. P. Bao Ruo-Wang and R. Chelminski, *Prisoner of Mao*, Harmondsworth, Penguin, 1976, pp. 29–43, 129–35; Vietnam: Doan Van Toai and David Chanoff, *The Vietnamese Gulag*, New York, Simon & Schuster, 1986, pp. 17–24, 41–63, 242–3; South Africa: Albie Sachs, *The Jail Diary of Albie Sachs*, London, Harvill Press, 1966 – a particularly gruelling account of prolonged solitary confinement. The bibliography of such works runs into thousands and perhaps tens of thousands of volumes, all with common experiences, patterns of oppressive behaviour and outcomes – both heroic and dismal.

167 *Things Not Generally Known*, pp. 15 and 16. It is difficult to assess this claim, since the author fails to say how he came by the information. 'A Statement of Facts' mentions that on 14 September 1866 several men were punished for speaking, Luby and O'Leary receiving sentences of bread and water and dark cells.

168 An article apparently written in the autumn of 1866 mentions that at Portland 'O'Donovan Rossa was almost in constant punishment' ('A Statement of Facts').

169 Even *Things Not Generally Known* hints at this. See also John O'Leary, *Recollections of Fenians and Fenianism*, London, Downy & Co, 1896, vol. 1, p. 90n. O'Leary's correspondence in *Devoy's Post Bag* (ed. William O'Brien and Desmond Ryan, Dublin, C. J. Fallon, 1948–53), and elsewhere, lacks the sharp edge of criticism and execration often found in revolutionists' exchanges. Indeed, he had a widespread reputation for amiability: this increases the credibility of his criticism of Rossa.

170 In a smuggled letter to the French paper *La Marseillaise* Rossa asserted: 'I make no complaint of the penalties which my masters require me to endure – my fate is to suffer.' Despite such stoicism, however, he did go on to complain (the letter was published in translation in *The Times*, 10 March 1870, 5e).

171 For example, when notified of his son's birth, Rossa was not allowed to hold his wife's letter: it was at first summarised and then, at his request, read to him. He was then refused permission to write to her on the grounds that six months must elapse between letters. But this was not exceptional treatment – any convict would have been given the same disinterested benefit of the rules.

His wife wrote to tell him that she was taking their child to the United States of America, but this information was withheld. When she came for her final visit, Rossa had had no warning of the purpose of the meeting, yet the encounter was limited to only twenty minutes.[172] It is difficult to characterise such actions as other than official sadism, but whatever the intention, the only outcome was to increase Rossa's bitterness and determination. At the same time it must be remembered that this was the way ordinary convicts were treated, and had questions been raised about it, the Home Secretary would have emphasised the need to act within the rules.[173] And however bitterly he complained about the callousness of the authorities, Rossa had the benefit of at least one important indulgence, that of being allowed to hold his baby, born after his imprisonment. This was a privilege not extended to ordinary convicts.[174]

The ill-treatment of Rossa which went beyond the bounds of legality, as well as decency, was the order that as a punishment his hands should be manacled behind him. Released only to sleep (when eating he was front-handcuffed), Rossa was kept in this state for thirty-five days.[175] The prison authorities attempted to persuade the commission of enquiry that the handcuffs were a measure of restraint (which was legal) rather than a punishment (which was not), but the commissioners showed their impatience with such evasion: handcuffs, they contended, 'should never be employed in any case as a measure of punishment, and upon a review of all the circumstances, we fail to discover any

---

172 Ibid., pp. 164–5. An equally inhumane incident was recalled by one of the soldier-convicts, John Boyle O'Reilly. When many of the Fenians were transported in October 1867, a young girl rushed out of the crowd on the wharf, watching the chained men embark. The girl, O'Reilly related, 'threw herself on the breast of a man in our chain, poor Thomas Dunne. She was his sister. She had come from Dublin to see him before he sailed away. They would not let her see him in prison, so she had come there to see him in his chains. Oh! May God keep me from ever seeing another scene like that which we all stood still to gaze at; even the merciless officials for a moment hesitated to interfere' (cit. Francis G. McManamin, 'The American Years of John Boyle O'Reilly: 1870–1890', Ph.D. dissertation, The Catholic University of America, 1959, p. 20).

173 In so far as it was consulted (mainly in the early years of Rossa's confinement) the Irish government consistently replied that Rossa and the others should be dealt with according to the convict rules (see NAI, CSO LB 266/94, 311, 383, 405).

174 Rossa's wife Mary had written to the Home Secretary asking for a privileged visit, and the request was granted on 1 August 1866 (see her account of the visit in the Irishman, 11 August 1866, 104a). This was her first visit. Rossa was allowed to take his child on his lap, and the visit was extended from twenty to thirty minutes (My Years in English Jails, op. cit., pp. 116–17).

175 Devon Commission, op. cit., paras 82–93, pp. 15–16. There was some suggestion that, for a time at least, Rossa had to eat his meals from a dish on the floor, while his hands were manacled behind him (ibid., letter of 19 August 1869: James Farquherson, deputy governor of Chatham to Captain Stopford, one of the directors of convict prisons, reporting on a conversation between Rossa and McCarthy Downing, MP, and John Blake, MP, on 30 July 1869). This allegation, however, was not raised by Rossa in his interview with the Devon Commission.

sufficient justification for their employment for so long a period as a measure of restraint'.[176]

John Boyle O'Reilly's daughter and biographer was convinced that the British government had decided to treat the Fenian prisoners harshly. She referred not to the denial of political status but simply compared the Fenians' lot to that of ordinary criminal prisoners.[177] It was helpful in the political struggle to portray the British as unrelentingly severe, and to pump up popular indignation by describing the indignities forced upon those who were struggling for Ireland's freedom: perception, not truth, was the issue. In one of the street-ballads in praise of John Mitchel, the Young Ireland leader, the listener was asked to 'Remember John Mitchel, a convict bound in chains';[178] yet, as we have seen, Mitchel was fettered lightly only once – when he was taken from prison to the ship which was to remove him to Dublin: thereafter he was never chained and was a privileged civil detainee. But the image of a chained felon was more powerful by far than the fairly banal reality, and this was as true for the Fenians as it had been for the Young Irelanders.

Indeed, the idea that the Fenians were being starved, overworked, thrust into association with sodomists and syphillitics, driven mad and denied medical treatment was powerful, politically rousing material: moderate nationalists and fair-minded loyalists *should* have been roused to indignation. There was some truth in these statements about prison conditions, but the anger of sympathisers rested largely on the basic assumption that Irish political offenders should not be treated as common criminals. If the treatment of the civilian Fenians (at least up until the amnesties) were looked at from a different perspective – how severely they were being treated as ordinary convicts – then the conclusions drawn would not be so dramatic. Immunity from flogging; a shortened period of separate confinement; de facto exemption of many from hard labour; the setting up of a separate regime of work (or non-work) for some; a degree of liberality regarding letters and visits, and, most importantly, amnesty after serving only a portion of their sentence – all these concessions and indulgences placed the Irish political prisoners (though not every one of them) in a position of considerable privilege over the common criminals.

---

176 Ibid., para. 93, p. 16. Dr Robert Lyons, one of the Commissioners, added an even more forthright note. In his opinion, 'by keeping Rossa in handcuffs both the Governor and the visiting Director exceeded the power and authority entrusted to them' (ibid., pp. 30 and 31). There was at this time some uncertainty about the punitive use of restraints. It was not until 1893 that the practice was prohibited by rule, but the Home Office view was that manacling as a punishment was illegal since it constituted an unauthorised aggravation of imprisonment (see PRO HO 45/9695/A49757/15).

177 Fenians were 'systematically subjected to harsher treatment than the hardened criminals with whom they were associated; and this was done as a fixed policy of the government, to make treason odious' (ed. Mrs John Boyle Roche, *op. cit.*, p. 62).

178 See Colm O'Lochlainn (ed.), *More Irish Street Ballads*, Dublin, The Three Candles, 1968 (2nd edn).

There was ill-treatment, especially in medical provision, and this was catalogued by the sympathetic 1871 Commission. But the Fenians were not being treated *worse* than ordinary convicts, simply the same. Convicts lied to escape work, and the case-hardened and sceptical prison officials exerted pressure to keep to an absolute minimum time off work through sickness or even for medical examination;[179] medical officers – even the more benign – were caught in the middle. The result was that some sick convicts – ironically including the least devious – were worked to a breakdown or even to death. But this was a hazard for all convicts. The first wave of Fenians gradually extracted special and privileged treatment. Government did not want explicitly to concede political status, but it did so in fact.[180] Political instinct and bureaucratic caution meant that greater care would be taken to ensure that Fenians avoided mishap than would have been the case with an ordinary prisoner who did not have voluble and influential outside supporters.

There were occasions when the Fenians were ill-treated, or did not receive their rights, or were handled maladroitly, but it is difficult to disagree with Du Cane that, for the most part, these were 'mere ordinary incidents of prison life'.[181] The Devon Commission expressed its concern about Ricard O'Sullivan Burke, whom it considered to be manifestly mentally ill. But on his release Burke lent support to the medical officer who had been most sceptical about his claims: he had, he said, been feigning insanity in order to obtain early release. He embarked on a successful lecture-tour of the United States of America, and subsequently obtained employment as an engineer.[182]

The Devon Commission upheld some of the Fenian complaints, particularly on medical issues, labour assignment and the treatment of O'Donovan Rossa. It was an enquiry which Rossa himself pronounced to have been conducted 'in a completely honest and unbiased manner'.[183] Yet after its 'patient and minute

---

179 Prisoners who sought medical attention were often, for example, required to see the medical officer during their lunch-hour. This was, and was intended to be, a deterrent against seeking medical treatment. The practice was condemned by the 1878 Penal Servitude Commission (*Report of the Commissioners Appointed to Inquire into the Working of the Penal Servitude Acts*, PP, 1878–9 [C.2368], XXXVIII, 1, xviii).

180 And so carefully that no explicit instructions were given to staff. In his close examination before the 1871 Commission Edmund Du Cane, then Chairman of the directors of convict prisons, agreed that various privileges had been conceded. He was asked how staff had come to know that the treason-felony prisoners were to be allowed to work 'rather easily, without any extreme exertion' and not to be reported. His reply was uncharacteristically imprecise: the staff 'must have been told it, or given to understand it, or something of that kind; probably they were told it'. This was an uncharacteristically clumsy evasion from a man who throughout his career as a prison administrator enforced the rules, regulations and standing orders to the letter, and who insisted upon accountability (*Devon Commission, op. cit.*, Minutes of Evidence, qq. 44–5, p. 2).

181 Ibid., q. 76, p. 3. He seemed unaware of the implications of his statement.

182 See below, p. 185, n. 200; p. 249, n. 135.

183 *Devon Commission, op. cit.*, p. 10.

investigation' the Commission found no ground for the belief that the treason-felony prisoners had 'as a class' been subjected to any exceptionally severe treatment or had 'suffered any hardships beyond those incidental to the condition of a prisoner sentenced to penal servitude'. On the evidence of officials, supported at times by prisoners, it appeared to the Commission that various relaxations had been granted. And since they had protested from the outset that they should not be classed as common criminals, every privilege granted to the Fenians 'has but confirmed their belief in the justice of this demand'.[184]

And so the debate completed the circle. The Fenians demanded political status, but the politicians and officials did not want them to have it: as prisoners, revolutionists were not to be allowed to establish the legitimacy of a cause which they had failed to carry in the field. But while there was little room for overt compromise, some de-facto acknowledgement emerged that these men were not just another criminal group – offenders whose malice, immorality or pursuit of self-interest had led them to crime. Special security requirements and the pressures of sympathisers and supporters inevitably meant distinctive treatment. This apparently conceded the Fenian prisoners' case that they were a morally distinct and superior class, and raised the question why they did not receive the rest of their privileges. The Devon Commission attempted to recast the Fenians' argument in pragmatic terms, without endorsing their political assumptions. The issue, as the Commission saw it, was the treatment of prisoners convicted of a crime 'so exceptional in its nature that it has been thought right to modify prison discipline in their case to a certain extent'. Might it not be better, the Commissioners wondered, to separate them completely from other convicts? There were difficulties, even dangers, in granting exceptional treatment to any few individuals in the midst of a large prison population. That being so, 'we are led to the conclusion that the difficulties attendant upon the location and treatment of political prisoners, may perhaps be most readily and effectually overcome by setting apart from time to time a detached portion of some convict prison for prisoners of this class, and we recommend this subject to the consideration of Her Majesty's Government'.[185] But with all but a handful of the Fenians by this time in Australia or released under conditional pardons, politicians and officials saw no need to address the issue further. In this they miscalculated.

Medical treatment

Despite their relative youth, a number of the Fenian prisoners were in uncertain or poor health on reception into custody – as would be expected from men of

184 *Op. cit.*, report, paras 204–7, p. 27.
185 Ibid., para. 209, pp. 27–8.

their walks of life at the time.[186] As has been noted, within the first year seven or eight men had been removed to Woking, the prison for invalid convicts. Several of their complaints of ill-treatment concerned medical treatment – given or withheld – or assignments to labour which were beyond their capacities, even though they had been certified fit. At any time death in custody raises questions about the adequacy of medical care and creates suspicions of harsh discipline or other ill-treatment. These concerns were bound to be acute in the case of the Fenians and, for various reasons, would be vociferously expressed by their sympathisers as well as constitutional nationalists and English radicals and liberals.[187] The case of William Pherson Thompson brought to a head a series of complaints about the medical treatment.

Thompson had been sentenced to life penal servitude for his part in the Manchester rescue and arrived at Portland prison on 15 April 1869. He was admitted to the infirmary on 26 March 1870, where he died two months later. At the inquest, evidence was given by the principal warder in charge of the infirmary, as well as William Roupell, the disgraced former radical MP for Lambeth. Roupell, who by connections and diligence (it was said) had worked himself into an easy berth in the prison,[188] gave evidence as one of the orderlies who had nursed Thompson. Roupell's account, and his character and vested interest in giving it, may have inflamed rather than soothed suspicions.[189] While

---

186 See above, p. 118, n. 19, for the occupational background of the Fenians. Nor was ill-health confined to the rank and file. Charles Kickham, disabled in a childhood accident, appears generally to have been in poor health. 'A Statement of Facts' reported that in the autumn of 1866 Kickham had ulcers all over his body, but was nevertheless successively sent to the Portland laundry and then to the quarry. Both of these assignments were terminated by removal to the infirmary, as his health broke down completely. He was eventually admitted to Woking Invalid Prison.

187 The more extreme organs of Irish nationalism were convinced that the Fenians were systematically being tortured. The *Irishman*, drawing attention to Rossa's thirty-five days in handcuffs, had called for the punishment of his torturers, insisting that worse than torture had occurred: 'We are convinced that MURDER has been done in the government prisons, by the horrible system they countenanced. We are convinced that morally, and, it may be legally, the deaths of a score of prisoners – young, healthy, able-bodied men – were in several instances nothing else than Murder – Murder the result of a system abominable in the extreme' (5 June 1869, 776a).

188 In September 1862 Roupell was convicted of forgery and sentenced to penal servitude. An account of the indulgences he supposedly procured for himself is given by a fellow convict, 'Ticket-of-Leave Man' in his book *Convict Life or Revelations Concerning Convicts and Convict Prisons* (London, Wyman & Sons, 1879). The author claimed that Roupell took his share of the food and drink prescribed for the sick, that he had access to newspapers and unlimited correspondence, and had a small flower garden in the infirmary grounds. 'He made a great display of his piety . . . was "hail-fellow-well-met" with governors, doctors and chaplains. To the schoolmasters and principal warders he assumed a patronising air. Altogether he had quite a jolly time of it' (p. 94). Roupell served some seven years, and was released in 1869.

189 Four years previously Ellen O'Leary had dismissed Roupell's defence of the regime: 'If model convicts, such as the distinguished swindler and ex-MP Roupell, enjoy such luxuries as puddings and porter at Portland, the Fenian prisoners certainly do not' (*Irishman*, 4 August 1866, 93b).

in the infirmary, Roupell reported, Thompson had 'every reasonable indulgence', including oranges, jellies, eggs, wine, brandy, lean chops, bone chicken, boiled mutton and sherry. His requests 'were granted immediately', and there was no limit to the supply of sherry. Thompson had spoken several times to Roupell about the acts of kindness of the governor and medical officer. There was no doubt that Thompson had been suffering from consumption on admission into the prison, and that little could be done to save him. Equally, sherry as well as spirits and a number of 'delicate' foods were frequently given to consumptives – even in prison. But Roupell's evidence as to the extravagance of Thompson's treatment bordered on the fantastic; no other account by any prisoner of the time bears it out. That the authorities brought such a man forward indicates their immense sensitivity about any Fenian death, as well as their political naivety. It is doubtful whether Roupell's evidence was needed, since the case appeared to be clear-cut. A verdict of death from consumption was duly recorded.[190]

Certainly in the case of Charles Underwood O'Connell,[191] the Devon Commission exposed concerns about prison medical officers. One doctor stated that O'Connell had a 'slight aortic disease'; another denied this but claimed that he had heart palpitations. In giving his evidence to them, the Commission reported, O'Connell exhibited 'a condition of excessive and unceasing nervous tremor, visibly affecting his whole person'. Chatham's medical officer, Dr John Burns,[192] considered that O'Connell's frequent weight changes were produced by malingering, but admitted that he had not tested this belief.[193] The Commission deprecated the fact that O'Connell had on several occasions been placed in close confinement and on a bread-and-water diet. Since it was reasonable to assume that on these occasions he had been suffering from aortic disease, the Commission commented on his unfitness for such punishment.[194] This was a

190 *The Times*, 2 July 1870, 5e.
191 A clerk from Frankfurt, King's Co. (now Offaly), on 14 December 1865, sentenced to ten years' penal servitude for treason felony by the Cork Special Commission.
192 John James Douglas Burns, MD, member of the Royal College of Physicians. Joined the convict service in 1849, retired 1874. Allegations of callousness and hostility towards the Irish political prisoners were made against him during the inquiry into the death of Charles McCarthy (see *Inquiry as to the Alleged Ill-treatment of the Convict Charles McCarthy in Chatham Convict Prison*, PP, 1878 [C.1978], LXIII, 769, 13 and 18). It should be noted that Burns' zealousness against malingering would lead to an inquiry into allegations of his scandalous ill-treatment of Daniel Reddin. Although his medical colleagues in the convict service stood by him, and the allegations were dismissed, Burns resigned shortly thereafter at the age of only 58 (*Copy of All Affidavits Used in the Court of Queen's Bench, Either in Obtaining or Showing Cause Against a Conditional Order for a Criminal Information Made in Last Hilary Term, on the Application of Daniel Reddin Against Dr Burns, the Medical Officer of Chatham Convict Prison*, PP, 1873 [366], LIV, 287, 1–24).
193 Devon Commission, report, paras 104–6, p. 17.
194 Ibid., para. 107, p. 17. The Commission urged immediate action in O'Connell's case: 'his health and condition are such as to make his ultimate location and treatment a question which demands the special attention of the authorities'.

more or less direct criticism of Dr Burns, who, by the regulations, was required to certify each prisoner's fitness to undergo punishment.

The Commission was similarly unimpressed by the medical care of Patrick Lennon.[195] On reception into Millbank it was noted that Lennon had a 'debility with phthisical tendency'. He was not further examined when he was transferred to the taxing climate of Dartmoor, where his weight dropped by nineteen pounds.[196] The Commission considered that this loss (suggestive of serious illness) required a closer examination of his chest; the Commission also recommended his removal from Dartmoor before the onset of winter.[197]

But the case which caused the Devon Commission most concern was that of Ricard O'Sullivan Burke.[198] 'We have,' the Commission reported, 'with very great care and anxiety inquired into the case of Rickard [sic] Burke.' On reception into Millbank, Burke did not display any symptoms of mental illness, but while at Chatham he underwent a change. Dr Burns thought this was another case of malingering. Despite these reservations, Burke was transferred to Woking Invalid Prison where his weight loss continued, and he made statements about being poisoned. The Woking medical officer, Dr John Campbell, concluded that Burke was insane, which opinion was shared by Dr Meyer of Broadmoor.[199] Others who had contact with Burke, including the warder who had special charge of him, the deputy governor of Woking prison, and the Revd John O'Leary, the Woking visiting priest, also considered Burke to be of unsound mind. The Commission interviewed Burke three times and was so concerned by what it found that, while still in session, it made special recommendations to the governor of Woking prison. In its final report the Commission stated that Burke was not of sound mind and that his case demanded 'the immediate consideration of the authorities as to his future location and treatment'.[200]

---

195 Born 1843 in Dublin, a cork-cutter by trade. Sentenced by the Dublin Special Commission, on 10 February 1868 to fifteen years' penal servitude.

196 Despite its harsh climate (or perhaps because its high elevation and 'bracing' weather were thought to be healthy) Dartmoor was considered to be an invalid prison (see evidence of Captain Edmund Du Cane to Devon Commission: op. cit., Minutes of Evidence, q. 9, p. 1).

197 Devon Commission, op. cit., para. 116, p. 18.

198 See p. 181 above.

199 This diagnosis was the more impressive since Campbell set himself up as a great scourge of malingerers: see p. 187 below.

200 Devon Commission, op. cit., para. 155, p. 22. As noted, it appears that Dr Burns' obsession with malingerers was, ironically, fully justified in the case of Burke, who was released in 1872, and went to the United States of America, where he undertook a lecture-tour and subsequently obtained employment as an engineer. There, he claimed that he *had* shammed insanity to obtain release. This decision, he said, had been taken after he concluded that Dr Campbell had attempted to poison him. He produced the evidence of an analytical chemist and the testimony of the Roman Catholic chaplain in support of his claim (see William O'Brien and Desmond Ryan (eds), Devoy's Postbag, op. cit., Vol. 1, pp. 35–6; Mark Francis Ryan, Fenian Memories, Dublin, M. H. Gill & Son, 1945, p. 127). Burke may have been convinced that he was being poisoned – though why he should have been singled out for medical assassination is

Weight loss seemed to be widespread among the imprisoned Fenians, and allowing that in some instances this could be attributed to the depressing effects of imprisonment, other cases of weight loss betokened illness. Malingering so obsessed some medical officers that it would be difficult to contend that the Fenians were being singled out when their symptoms were dismissed or ignored.[201] Denis Mulcahy[202] was received into Pentonville on 10 February 1866 and was eventually transferred to Portland. There he was certified fit for hard labour and put on stone-dressing. After two episodes of what was called 'blood-spitting', he was diagnosed as suffering from haemoptysis – a condition that is usually due to haemorrhaging of the lungs. Despite fits of coughing, and further visits to the medical officer, he was kept at his dusty, arduous and completely unsuitable work. Having reviewed his record, the Devon Commission disagreed with the prison authorities that Mulcahy was then fit to be kept at hard labour, 'or that due care and caution were exercised in his regard'.[203] On transfer to Dartmoor in the particularly harsh winter of 1867 Mulcahy was nevertheless again certified for hard labour, and was put to work on the moor, trenching and clearing land and carrying slabs of stone on his back.[204] After three weeks there was renewed lung haemorrhaging and Mulcahy was admitted to the prison hospital. Only then was it decided to transfer him to Woking invalid prison. The Dartmoor medical officer claimed that he had mislaid Mulcahy's medical notes for the period before his transfer.[205]

Brian Dillon[206] was described by the Devon Commission as 'a weak and deformed man, of middle age, and delicate appearance'. In a voluminous statement to the Commission, Dillon made several complaints of ill-treatment, in

unclear – and thus have become temporarily insane, even while thinking that he was shamming. It is unlikely that the truth will ever be known.

201 On medical officers and malingering see my *History of English Prison Administration*, p. 398.

202 Denis Downing Mulcahy, born Tipperary 1840, medical student. On 20 January 1866 sentenced in Dublin to ten years' penal servitude for treason felony.

203 Devon Commission, *op. cit.*, para. 161, p. 23.

204 *Things Not Generally Known* claimed that the 'atrocious punishment' of Mulcahy at Dartmoor included having to associate with criminals, and to clean the privy after them. Mulcahy also had to draw stones in a cart 'to which he was yoked by a collar fastened round his neck; to carry rough granite slabs (for the purpose of draining) on his *bare back* a distance of 400 or 500 yards across a mountain' (p. 13). Elsewhere it appears that 'on his back' meant on his shoulder, which would not have been an unusual way for an unaided to man to carry a slab or boulder. This does not invalidate the point being made.

205 Devon Commission, *op. cit.*, report, paras 158–65, pp. 23 and 24. Mulcahy refused to give evidence to the 1871 Commission, which, because it had insufficient information, could not investigate a number of other complaints of ill-health and poor treatment. It was also alleged that Mulcahy had been punished for giving evidence to the 1867 inquiry into the condition of the treason-felony prisoners – which may have been his reason for failing to cooperate with the 1871 Commission.

206 Born Cork 1830, law clerk. On 14 December 1865, sentenced by Cork Special Commission to ten years' penal servitude for treason felony.

particular that he was given work unsuitable for his physique and state of health. At Pentonville he was put to sewing from 6 a.m. until 7.45 p.m. This statement was not controverted, the Commission merely observing that during that time he was allowed meals.[207] Transferred to Woking invalid prison after only three months, he was put, in the winter of 1867, to clean a heap of frozen bricks. At his own request he was moved to the carpenter's shop, where he remained until taken into hospital the following year. When discharged, and still very weak, he was put to brick-cutting in a wooden shed in very cold weather. The bricks which he was cutting were soaked in water. In intense summer heat, and while suffering from dysentery (he claimed), Dillon was obliged to hoist bricks by rope and pulley. 'We feel bound to say', the Commission commented,

> [T]hat some of the work on which Dillon appears to have been from time to time employed was of a nature hardly suitable to his delicate and deformed frame. His weight is 7 stone $4^{1}/_{2}$ lbs, his height is 4 feet 10 inches, and the delicacy of his constitution is clearly shown by his personal appearance, and by his frequent admissions to hospital, especially during the last two years. Dillon's condition, at the time of our visits, in consequence of an accidental fall, appeared to be such as to render him incapable of any manual labour. He is hardly able to walk without assistance.[208]

Those who sympathised with the political prisoners were vociferous in drawing attention to these cases of ill-health, poor medical treatment and inappropriate labour assignments. The convict medical service did not need to victimise the Fenians in order to show itself callous and inefficient. There was a general mission against malingering, particularly where symptoms were not cut and dried. Medical officers reflexively believed that the convict was a malingerer, and would await developments which proved otherwise. John Campbell, who in the 1870s was medical officer at Woking (and who showed sympathy in the case of Ricard Burke) used both galvanism (electric shocks) and the cold douche as treatments, not least because they tested the genuineness of aspiring patients.[209] Nor were the fears of malingering groundless. Labour at the public works prisons was so severe that some convicts self-mutilated to avoid it. At Chatham, Dr John Burns reported that forty-one of the injuries which he saw in the course of

---

207 Devon Commission, *op. cit.*, report, para. 174, p. 24.
208 Ibid., paras 174–7, pp. 24–5. The list of work to which Dillon was put in itself draws attention to the curious nature of the regime for persons who were, after all, sent to Woking because of admitted ill-health.
209 'Patients suffering from the real disease gladly submit to this or any other remedy likely to benefit them, but malingerers show a great repugnance' (John Campbell, *Thirty Years' Experience of a Medical Officer in the English Convict Service*, London, T. Nelson & Sons, 1884, p. 67).

a year had been self-inflicted with the intention of avoiding labour.[210] So the Irish political prisoners, although they might be thought to be more devious than the common run, were probably not singled out for harsh or indifferent medical treatment: that was what one got in the convict prisons.

The case of Daniel Reddin[211] shows how far prison doctors could go in their attempts to detect malingering. On completing his sentence on 25 October 1872, Reddin and his supporters launched a campaign of protest against his treatment by Dr Burns at Chatham. He was substantially paralysed in his legs, alleged the paralysis had developed while in prison and that while ill he had been severely and grotesquely ill-treated by Burns and staff acting under his direction.[212] The Freeman's Journal, which publicised Reddin's charges, described them as astounding and appalling, and some 'too horrible for print'.[213] Reddin's case provoked widespread comment and condemnation, and sufficient support was forthcoming for an application to the High Court to direct that Dr Burns and Dr Wilson (assistant surgeon at Millbank) should show cause why criminal information should not be issued against them for assaults committed on Reddin.[214]

After some incidents of unsympathetic treatment by Burns, in October 1870 Reddin claimed to have a paralytic attack in his lower limbs. A warder removed him to the infirmary, but Burns turned him out, saying that he was fit for work. Persisting in his claim to be unwell, Reddin was confined to a cell and placed on a diet of bread and water. At some point Dr Burns transferred Reddin to the infirmary, but directed that he should go to the parade ground for exercise. Reddin stated that he was unable to walk, and Burns directed two prisoners to drag him, replacing them when they tired with two warders. Burns then proceeded to test Reddin for malingering. These tests included pricking with needles and burning with a hot iron, with Reddin spending time alternately in the infirmary and then the solitary cell.

Burns was a self-appointed witchfinder-general for malingerers – quite apart from any animus he may have had against the Fenians. The ultimate device he employed against malingering was an electric shock machine. This may have been developed by another prison medical officer, Dr John Campbell, but was also used by Burns on Reddin. Pricking, burning and shocking all failed to expose Reddin's supposed malingering, and on 10 March 1871 he was transferred from Chatham to Millbank, where, he alleged, an even more determined campaign was waged against him.

---

210 Report of the Directors of Convict Prisons 1871, PP, 1872 [C.649], XXXI, 385, 269. Burns' definition of 'self-inflicted' must, of course, be treated with caution.

211 Reddin had been sentenced to five years' penal servitude for his part in the rescue of Kelly and Deasy at Manchester.

212 Freeman's Journal, 13 November 1872, 5f–g; Flag Ireland, 16 November 1872, 3c–d; 23 November, 4b–c.

213 Ibid., 3 December 1872, 2d.

214 The rule was granted on 30 January 1873 (Freeman's Journal, 31 January 1873, 3a–b). The substantive case was heard on 29 May 1873.

Placed in the reception cell at Millbank, Reddin was immediately visited by the principal medical officer, Dr Robert Mundy Gover[215] and his assistant, Dr Wilson, together with three warders. Reddin's feet were pricked with needles for, as he deposed, 'about the space of an hour, as far as I would judge'. When this failed to produce the desired effect, Reddin claimed, he was dragged by his feet out of bed and some distance along the floor into the surgery. He was then clamped into a specially fitted chair and electric shocks were applied 'to different parts of my body as well as to my private parts; the application to my private parts caused me intense pain'.[216] The following day he was again dragged to the surgery, and when he screamed as the galvanic battery was applied to his genitals a towel was placed over his face. Reddin also complained of being thrown around, held under water until he became unconscious and being beaten violently in the stomach. The latter 'caused me to vomit in the corridor, which enraged Dr Wilson, and he ordered the warders to wipe the discharge up with my face, which they accordingly did'. In August Reddin was removed from the ward of the infirmary to a solitary cell, where until 8 September he was kept without a bed. He complained about his treatment to the Visiting Director, Captain Fagan, who ordered his removal to more comfortable quarters, where he remained until his release.[217]

This was an appalling tale of torture. On Reddin's side there was a deposition from William O'Leary, a surgeon at St Vincent's Hospital, which attested that Reddin was debilitated and unable to walk, his left leg being completely paralysed and his right one almost as badly so. His left arm was paralysed and rigid and he was suffering from an impairment of speech. O'Leary testified that Reddin's condition was 'evidence of his having been the subject of a paralysis of the limbs . . . for a considerable time, certainly more than one year'. A fellow prisoner deposed that he had seen Reddin unable to walk, and being dragged to chapel and around the parade ground, and being carried between his cell and the infirmary on another prisoner's back. The assistant surgeon at Chatham stated that Reddin had been in good health, but in January 1871 he had formed the opinion that there was an incomplete paralysis of Reddin's lower limbs.

The defence was that Reddin had not been treated cruelly, and that the pricking, application of a hot iron and use of electric shocks were simply tests

---

215 (?–1897). A prominent figure in the convict service by this time. Member of the Royal College of Surgeons of England, 1856; Licentiate of the Society of Apothecaries; member of the Royal College of Physicians. Joined the convict service in 1857 (Portsmouth). Posted to Millbank 1860, becoming head of its medical department in 1865. In 1878 he was appointed to the newly nationalised local prisons as medical inspector. Adviser to Du Cane (Chairman of Directorate of Convict Prisons and the Prison Commission) on diet, lunacy and the mentally subnormal.

216 *Freeman's Journal*, 30 May 1873, 6c.

217 Ibid. The remainder of the account of the hearing is taken from the same source. The affidavits are set out in full in a return moved by Isaac Butt (see *Copy of all Affidavits Used in the Court of Queen's Bench, etc., op. cit.*, pp. 1–24).

for paralysis. A needle had not been used to prick Reddin, but a quill pen had been passed over the sole of his foot. When it came to the electric shock treatment at Millbank, Dr Wilson was in a difficulty. He admitted that the treatment had continued for three days. If he further admitted that Reddin had shown pain and screamed, then the continuation of the tests could only be taken as torture and punishment. If, on the other hand, Reddin had not appeared to be in pain, then clearly he must be suffering from paralysis. Wilson deposed that when Reddin was placed in the armchair and given electric shocks he showed no symptoms of pain; he did not explain why the tests had continued for three days. For the rest, affidavits were produced by Dr Gover supporting Dr Wilson in his denial of cruelties and claiming, somewhat improbably, that 'During his stay at Millbank Reddin was treated with the greatest indulgence and kindness'. The Millbank governor and several warders gave similar depositions. Dr Burns of Chatham Convict Prison and various prison officials took a similar line, Burns insisting that the tests were all per-formed with Reddin's permission in order to ascertain whether or not he was paralysed.

Reddin's application was refused by the court. If the acts had taken place as Reddin had alleged, then the rule should have been granted, but his claims were contradicted by the medical and other evidence of the other side. 'Without any motive it was suggested that these gentleman had been guilty of the greatest cruelty, and they denied the charges, to which there did not appear to be any corroboration.' Reddin, Mr Justice Blackburn was convinced, had been treated as a patient, and not punished. With the agreement of his two fellow judges the rule was discharged with costs.

At this distance it is impossible fully to judge the relative weight of Reddin's application, and its refutation by the prison officials. Given the strong fear of malingering in the convict prisons, and the determination of officials, medical and administrative alike, that it should not succeed, and Dr Campbell's admis-sion in his memoirs that he used both electric shocks and cold baths on sus-pected malingerers, it is more than likely that Reddin was grossly ill-treated to the point of torture. In this situation a stack of affidavits from prison officials counted for little: there was a culture of secrecy and solidarity against prisoners and the outside world, and they all, moreover, had a lot to lose. Whether Reddin had been ill-treated *as a Fenian* is very difficult to say. His political status was probably irrelevant: this was simply another convict trying to swing the lead. The Attorney General, for the defendants, had argued that it was improbable that prison officers would have acted as Reddin alleged, knowing that he had 'many sympathisers outside who would take up any complaint which might be made'. This was (and is) a well-known and last-chance defence ploy – 'Would my client have been so stupid as to do something for which he might so easily be caught?' The answer, all too often, is 'Yes'. It is perhaps significant that the directors of convict prisons would subsequently reserve for themselves approval for painful tests for malingering.[218] In the pressure cooker of prison life zeal could turn into excess, and excess into scandal, all too easily.

In Ireland, of course, the case and its outcome played very differently. The moderate nationalist *Freeman's Journal* expressed its reservations about Gover's claim that Reddin had been treated with the greatest indulgence and kindness. It also noted that this was not the only case of its kind. Virtually all recently released political offenders had complained of ill-treatment. Whatever else came out of the Reddin case, it should act as a warning 'to those holding so terrible a power over poor creatures undergoing sentence that, should they abuse that power, they do so at the risk, at least, of a public exposure, even though they may have little cause to dread a more substantial punishment'.[219] The case confirmed the views of the more extreme nationalists about the cruelty and unfairness of the British administration. Reddin's case also found a response in the broad ranks of nationalist sympathisers and even those hardly committed at all: the Fenian prisoners were martyrs rather than perpetrators. The effect of Reddin's story, and all other accounts of ill-treatment in prison, was to stimulate the nationalist movement and the Amnesty Association.[220]

Reddin's case showed the cruelty and self-protective secrecy of the convict system. But it, and a recital of the medical ill-treatment of a handful of the treason-felony prisoners, could give the wrong impression of the Fenian prisoners as a whole. The majority (many of whom had been soldiers in the British or American army) were young men in good health, and had no need of the attentions of the medical officers. Referring to the Portland treason-felony convicts, the 1867 Commission (which, admittedly, took a dim view of their complaints) noted their generally healthy condition:

> As a rule, with scarcely an exception, they were wiry, robust, bronzed looking men. Not one of them had been subject to any serious illness; not one had been attacked during the prolonged cold winter of 1866–67 with any acute or inflammatory action of the organs of respiration

218 Rule 84, *Rules and Regulations for the Government of Convict Prisons*, London, HMSO, 1886.
219 *Freeman's Journal*, 30 May 1873, 2a–b.
220 Death in prison had a particularly powerful effect and, in the absence of what could be seen as independent investigation and accountability, reinforced all other complaints about brutality and cruelty. Under the caption 'Done to Death', the *Nation* reported the death of William Pherson Thompson as follows: '[T]he dampness of his cell brought on a painful affliction which was desperately aggravated by the brutal cruelty of the warders . . . even when his limbs would no longer bear up his body, he was dragged from his cell to continue such toil as would try the strength of the most robust.' Thompson's dying wish, the report continued, was to be buried in Ireland. The Amnesty Association had arranged for his body to be brought back from England, and he was buried at Ballycastle, Co. Antrim (*Nation*, 2 July 1870, 729a; 23 July, 775c). Such general charges of cruelty and ill-treatment were impossible to refute without a public inquiry – and very likely not even then.

or other effects of exposure to cold or damp. In fact their ailments were simply slight, and such as any ordinary labourer would have suffered from in such a severe winter, such as chilblains and chapped hands.[221]

The Devon Commission gave several critical accounts of the medical treatment and labour assignments of the Fenian prisoners who were sickly, and adopted conclusions and recommendations which were scarcely veiled condemnations of the general state of medical services and the severity of the English convict system. Yet the Commission could find no support for the belief that the treason-felony prisoners, *as a class*, had been subjected to exceptionally severe treatment, or that they had suffered any hardships 'beyond those incidental to the condition of a prisoner sentenced to penal servitude'.[222] Rossa considered that the Devon Commission had conducted a good-faith inquiry and he certainly did not accuse it of a whitewash.[223] This being so, and given that the Fenians were likely to be the most confident complainers,[224] and were certainly among the most articulate of prisoners and could count on the strongest outside assistance in ventilating their complaints, we may conclude that many such medical, dietary, disciplinary and industrial hardships befell 'ordinary' convicts, and all were treated as no more than 'incidental to the condition of a prisoner sentenced to penal servitude'.

Special treatment

Ostensibly the Fenian prisoners were supposed to receive no exceptional treatment, yet in certain important ways this rule was not followed. The official line was that there was no such thing as a political prisoner in England. Captain

221 1867 Commission, *op. cit.*, p. 14. This was a somewhat misleading statement, as the case of Mulcahy clearly shows: the phrase 'with scarcely an exception' is a telling qualifier.

222 Devon Commission, *op. cit.*, report, para. 204, p. 27.

223 'To their lasting credit be it stated that these gentlemen – with the possible exception of Dr Greenhow – conducted their examination in a completely honest and unbiased manner' (*My Years in English Jails* (1967), p. 219). Dr Greenhow had issued a minority report, disputing some of the Fenian claims. (Greenhow (1814–88) studied medicine in Scotland and France and graduated MD at Aberdeen in 1853. Settling in London, he played an increasingly important part in public health policy and administration. Served on several Royal Commissions; delivered Croonian lectures at the Royal College of Physicians in 1875.)

224 T. Folliott Powell, the Chatham governor, wrote to William Fagan, on 28 May 1869. Referring to Rossa's outrageous behaviour in some detail he continued: 'The feeling of one and all of these prisoners appears to be to give as much trouble as possible to every individual with whom they in any way come in contact, to do as little work as they can help, to oppose the orders given them so far as they dare, or consider prudent, and to imagine that they are ill-treated because the ordinary rules of the prison are not entirely dispensed with in their cases and they are not allowed a different diet to other prisoners; and I regret to add, that in stating their supposed grievances an adherence to facts appears to be one of the last things considered requisite' (Devon Commission, *op. cit.*, Appendix G, p. 59).

Mark Gambier,[225] the director responsible for Pentonville, explained this notion to Rossa. 'England,' he said, 'has no political prisoners now-a-days; you are here no more than any other prisoner, and you are treated like every other prisoner.'[226] The Portland governor told Rossa that the government was treating the Fenians too kindly and 'Twenty years ago you'd have been hanged.'[227]

Although the official line was maintained, in several ways the first wave of Fenians were treated as an exceptional group – and looked at purely administratively that is what they were. No other cause since the Chartists had produced so many prisoners at once; no other offenders possessed, as a group, so many moral and intellectual resources; and no other prisoners had on them so continuously the constant and anxious scrutiny of tens or hundreds of thousands of sympathisers and the electorally stimulated attention of a powerful foreign government. The doctrine of 'no political prisoners here' was the official line, but neither officials nor politicians believed or acted as though it were true.[228] The security precautions attested to this. It is true that there may have been individual non-political offenders for whom it was thought necessary to subject frequent strip-searches and body-cavity examinations, and whose cell lights were kept on all night or who might be confined in a special sleeping cell. But it was unknown for such precautions to be applied to a whole group of prisoners, irrespective of prior prison behaviour.[229]

---

225 Gambier was at first deputy governor at Millbank Prison, and then (in 1850) the first governor of the reopened Dartmoor, moving from there to Portsmouth and then (as governor) back to Millbank. He was promoted to a directorship in 1858 and retired in 1872.

226 Rossa 1967, p. 157. Rossa left an amusing pen-portrait of Gambier, his old adversary: 'He was a tall, smooth-tongued old gentleman of about seventy, with very white hair, a glass eye, and a large red jolly-looking nose which I could never look at without thinking of the good old times of Irish whiskey punch and jolly company. He could order you fifty lashes on the bare back and twenty-eight days on bread and water, in the most pathetic tones of regret that your bad behaviour and the necessity of maintaining discipline called for it; and you'd think his glass eye, as well as his unglazed one, was swimming in tears over your misery' (ibid., p. 71).

227 Ibid., p. 115.

228 This was the case from the outset. Prior to the arrival of the first of the treason-felony prisoners on 23 December 1865, Captain Gambier went to Pentonville to direct the arrangements for the Fenians' reception. He told the 1867 Commission that their cells had been equipped with new mattresses and pillows and clean bedding; new uniforms were provided. Although the boat-train was late the governor, deputy governor, medical officer and steward all remained in the prison to supervise the prisoners' arrival (1867 Commission, op. cit., pp. 5 and 6). Just four years later, however, the Devon Commission was told a different tale, when Du Cane insisted that no special instructions had been given at Pentonville or Millbank regarding the Fenian prisoners (Devon Commission, op. cit., Minutes of Evidence, qq. 21–2, pp. 1–2). This was untrue, as the official correspondence of the times shows.

229 None of the twenty-six treason-felony prisoners who remained in English prisons at the time the Devon Commission was making its enquiries had a prior criminal or prison record (Devon Commission, op. cit., Appendix A, pp. 42–5). The Commission's report was submitted on 20 September 1870, although not published until 1871. By then the civilian Fenians had been given their conditional freedom, and had left the country for exile in the United States of America.

Like the Young Irelanders before them, the Fenians looked with disdain upon their fellow prisoners; attempts to make them mingle were but another British attempt to degrade them and their cause. As with John Mitchel, there was a certain amount of hypocrisy in the Fenians' stance, since they benefited from the solidarity and support of fellow convicts, even while affecting complete moral superiority towards them. In one of his many bouts of punishment, Rossa received bread, meat and tobacco (the last being particularly valuable contraband) from his fellow convicts – yet he found it degrading to work alongside these men who had befriended him, and who had taken risks on his behalf.[230] On another occasion he obtained food and writing materials, and noted 'I was supplied by these unfortunate convicts'.[231]

With some sympathy for the situation of the political prisoners, the Devon Commission nevertheless noted that, by the time of their inspections, they were a class apart. For the most part they were now assigned to comparatively light indoor work, and were therefore spared exposure to the elements to a greater extent than their fellows. Worn down by the difficulties of pretending that these were ordinary prisoners, and yet conscious all the time that they were not, and that any mishap could have dire consequences; and subject as well to unceasing provocation from Rossa, the authorities had, over a five-year period, retreated from even their nominal determination to treat the Fenians as ordinary convicts. By 1870 they were generally not incarcerated with criminal prisoners. They were given a superior cell and diet, and the regulations on letters were relaxed. When they worked, they did less than other prisoners, and some merely went out to a place of labour where, under a special warder, they remained idle.[232] This was political status – niggardly, extracted piecemeal, and with some suffering – but political status none the less.[233] There were advantages for politicians and administrators in this vagueness and equivocation.

The inquiries

Within a space of three years there were two inquiries into complaints about the treatment of the Fenians, and a comparison of the two sets of conclusions

230 Rossa 1967, pp. 132–3.
231 Ibid., p. 158. It was not all moral superiority and disdain, of course. Familiarity can breed compassion. He observed of the criminal prisoners that 'Nearly half these men were of Irish parents, and their crimes were traceable to poverty and whiskey – two things which the Irish people could well afford to get rid of and which are a curse to any people they afflict'.
232 Devon Commission, op. cit., para. 73, p. 14 and para. 206, p. 27.
233 This did not apply to soldier Fenians who had therefore been sentenced for military offences and (as was usual) sent to the civil prisons to serve out their sentences. In 1867 there were seventeen such who, the Commission of that year was informed, were serving out their sentences 'precisely in the same way as other convicts, and are treated precisely as ordinary convicts are' (op. cit., p. 3).

shows the distance that English opinion – that is of the political and official classes – had travelled in the intervening years. The first inquiry was authorised by the Conservative Home Secretary Gathorne Hardy, and was conducted by Alexander Knox and George Pollock – men who could hardly have been expected to take an impartial view.[234] No transcript of their inquiry survives, but Rossa smuggled a letter to the Paris *La Marseillaise* in which he denounced both Knox and Pollock for refusing to listen or take note of his complaints on the curious grounds that neither had anything to do with the discipline of the prison. 'What a mockery it was,' he insisted, 'to send two government officials to ascertain the truth concerning English prisons!'[235] The two certainly showed a general unwillingness to consider Fenian complaints. They achieved an admirable level of philosophical detachment, and some literary elegance in their refutation of the Fenian complaints:

> A convict's bread is bitter food at the best. Place him under the best sanitary conditions, treat him with what humanity you will, the privation of liberty, the enforced seclusion, and equally compulsory labour; the terrible monotony of life; the stern order, and the instant obedience, constitute a very terrible punishment. We know that these men have a better diet, sleep in better beds, are more cared for in sickness, have lighter labour than the bulk of the labouring classes in the three kingdoms, and that the stories of their ill-treatment are simple falsehood; but the meanest and poorest labourer in the empire would scarcely change places with them. Penal servitude, we repeat it, is a terrible punishment; it is intended to be so, and so it is. The convict authorities however, must do their duty to all alike. The only true cause of complaint the treason-felony convicts have against them is that they can't get out.[236]

Three years later the volume of complaint, both inside and outside the prisons, had become so great that another inquiry was necessary. There had been a

---

234 Knox was a barrister and stipendiary magistrate. George David Pollock (?–1897) came from a military and legal family. His father was Major-General Sir Frederick Pollock, who won great fame in the retreat from Afghanistan; his uncle Sir Charles Edward Pollock was one of the most eminent judges of the times. George Pollock trained in medicine and, at the time of the 1867 Commission was a surgeon at St George's Hospital, London. He was brought up, his obituarist noted, 'in traditions of honourable exertion and a strict sense of duty'. His politics were 'of the strictest sect of Conservatism' (*British Medical Journal*, 20 February 1897, pp. 496–7).

235 *The Times* reprinted the letter on 10 March 1870, 5e. Thomas Duggan, another of the Fenian prisoners, commented that 'if the governor of the prison and his chief warders were the exclusive members of that commission they could not have given a more favourable report, as far as the prison authorities were concerned' (*Nation*, 17 October 1868, 184d).

236 1867 Commission, *op. cit.*, p. 24.

change of government, and Gladstone was in the midst of the first of his attempts to conciliate and pacify Ireland.[237] Philip Callan, the MP for Dundalk,[238] moved in the Commons for a select committee on the treatment of the Fenian prisoners. This was initially refused by Gladstone, but another application, more narrowly contrived, by George Moore, the Member for Co. Mayo, was accepted.[239] (Given Gladstone's attempt to balance palliation with firmness, it was no coincidence that the concession was announced immediately before Fortescue, the Irish Secretary, rose to introduce yet another coercion measure – the Peace Preservation (Ireland) Bill.) The inquiry was intended to be a fairly narrow fact-finding exercise, to last no more than fifteen days.[240] The lesson of the earlier exercise had been learned, however, and to provide credibility the new committee was chaired by the venerable and widely respected Earl of Devon.[241] Other members

237 For the famous description of Gladstone's supposed response to the impending mandate from Queen Victoria to form his first administration see H. C. G. Matthew, Gladstone 1809–1874, Oxford, Oxford University Press, 1986, p. 147: 'My mission is to pacify Ireland.'

238 (1837–?). Educated Clongowes Wood College, Inner Temple, 1864; Irish Bar, 1865; an Irish nationalist.

239 The establishment of the inquiry was agreed by Gladstone, having first refused one on the grounds that the 1867 Commission had refuted the allegations of ill-treatment that were being made (3 Hansard, CIC, cols 1140–1; 3 March 1870). Only a fortnight later, however, he conceded that there was sufficient support in the House to justify an inquiry 'of a perfectly impartial character, conducted by impartial persons' (ibid., CC, col. 79; 17 March 1870). Gladstone emphasised that the form of the inquiry was a matter solely for the government. A Royal Commission, with the implicit admission that an issue of national importance was involved, and with an uncertain political momentum, was clearly not acceptable, nor, for similar reasons, was a Commons Select Committee. A high-powered departmental committee was the answer. (See my English Local Prisons (op. cit., pp. 585–7) for a discussion of the scope of various types of committees of inquiry.) The Devon Committee was at the time generally referred to as the Devon Commission, and I have followed this nomenclature. Henry Bruce, the Home Secretary, gave details on 8 April 1870, stating that the committee 'would be constituted with utmost care, and its members would be so selected that the public would repose full confidence in them. Two Irish gentlemen and two from England would be appointed members of that Commission, which would be presided over by a gentleman of high position' (3 Hansard, CC, col. 1582). Such was the Liberal government's desire to demonstrate impartiality that Bruce invited Dr Robert McDonnell, the controversial former medical officer at Mountjoy Prison, to serve on the Commission, 'both on account of his professional eminence and of the independence of character of which he had given conspicuous proof'. McDonnell declined the invitation, believing that the remit of the inquiry prejudged the question of whether the Fenians should be treated as political prisoners – as he believed they should (ibid., CCIII, col. 954; 26 July 1870).

240 PRO HO 45/9330/19461A/8.

241 William Reginald Courtney, eleventh Earl of Devon (1807–88), educated Westminster and Christ Church, Oxford; First in Classics, Fellow of All Souls. Called to Bar (Lincoln's Inn) 1832; Secretary, Poor Law Board, 1850–9, Chancellor of Duchy of Lancaster in Derby's third administration, 1866–7; President of Poor Law Board, 1867–8. Inherited heavily mortgaged estates in Devon and Ireland. He was, according to the DNB, 'for many years the most influential man in his country and was generally known as "the good earl".'

were less eminent, but were persons of standing and some independence of mind. George Brodrick was a leader writer for *The Times* and had been a Liberal parliamentary candidate.[242] Stephen De Vere came from an Irish landowning family, and had converted to Roman Catholicism in 1848; he had earned a reputation for philanthropy in the service of his countrymen.[243] Reflecting the government's belief that the inquiry would be largely a technical fact-finding exercise, there were also two eminent physicians. Dr Robert Lyons was a Cork-born doctor who had rendered medical service in the Crimean War, and who had experience of public and institutional health issues.[244] His colleague, Dr Edward Greenhow was a Scottish doctor who had settled in London in 1853, also with a background in public health.[245] A barrister, William Ollivant, was appointed as Secretary, and took a rather narrow view of his role.[246]

The difference between the Devon Commission and the 1867 inquiry was at once made apparent. Shortly after its appointment Isaac Butt requested that he be allowed to act on behalf of the Fenian prisoners. He wished, *inter alia*, to be able to question witnesses and to suggest witnesses and topics for inquiry, as well as to examine released prisoners. This, Butt maintained, would do much to convince Irish opinion of the Commission's independence and impartiality, and its dissimilarity to the 1867 Knox and Pollock investigation. Although refusing Butt's submission, Lord Devon made a concession of some importance, which greatly irritated the Home Office. At reasonable times and for reasonable periods friends of prisoners would be allowed to visit in order to assist in their preparation of statements to the inquiry.[247] 'Reasonable' was interpreted generously, so that

---

242 Hon. George Charles Brodrick (1831–1903), educated at Eton, Balliol and the University of London. Distinguished university career: barrister, 1859–60, when he joined *The Times*. Thrice unsuccessful Liberal candidate; elected Warden of Merton College, Oxford, 1881. In later years anti-Gladstone on the Home Rule issue – a stance which may have coloured his memories of the Devon Commission.

243 Stephen Edward De Vere (1812–1904), educated Trinity College, Dublin; called to Irish Bar in 1836; Liberal MP for Limerick, 1854–9. Succeeded to baronetcy in 1880.

244 Dr Robert Spencer Dyer Lyons (1826–86), educated Trinity College, Dublin; Licentiate Royal College of Surgeons of Ireland; served in Crimea and visited Lisbon to investigate yellow fever; staff of St George's Hospital, Dublin; Professor of Medicine at the new Roman Catholic medical school. In later years (1880–5) Liberal MP for Dublin.

245 Dr Edward Headlam Greenhow (1814–88), educated Edinburgh, Montpellier and Aberdeen; served on several Royal Commissions; reported to Privy Council on epidemics and other matters of public health.

246 William Spencer Ollivant (1834–76). Eldest son of Bishop of Llandaff. Educated Corpus Christi, Oxford; called to Bar in 1860. Appointed assistant boundary commissioner under the Reform Act in 1867. Revising barrister for Chester parliamentary lists. See also HO 45/9330/19461A for Ollivant's secretarial correspondence concerning the Commission.

247 PRO HO 45/9330/19461A/18, 9 June 1870. A few days before this concession was granted, the *Freeman's Journal* had insisted that an inquiry without proper representation for the prisoners would in Ireland be considered to be 'a sham – a mockery, a delusion, and a snare' (6 June 1870, 3c).

prisoners could have in their cells the friend or family member designated as an assistant every day, and throughout the day, until the inquiry and pending its completion. The prisoners were also permitted to carry on an extensive correspondence on issues connected with the inquiry.[248] Butt at once communicated this concession to the Irish newspapers, ensuring that it could not be withdrawn without much political upset and the discrediting of the committee.[249]

Several of the prisoners were apparently unwilling to take part in what, not unnaturally, they suspected would be a rerun of the 1867 whitewashing exercise. The generosity of Devon's gesture won them over, and ensured their participation. Such was the suspicion of the Fenians and their supporters, however, that Rossa and his wife Mary exchanged some testy – even bitter – correspondence on the matter.[250] Mary also had a heated correspondence with Lord Devon, contending, with some justification, that the Home Office and the prison authorities had, either by design or carelessness, nullified the concession of allowing her to assist her husband in the preparation of his evidence.[251]

---

248 Rossa to Mary O'Donovan Rossa, 9 July 1870: CUA: FBP, Box 2, item 23. Rossa also received advice from wider circles of friends, who channelled their views through spokesmen (Richard Pigott to Rossa, n.d. (? mid-1870): ibid., Box 2, item 22).

249 See *Freeman's Journal*, 29 June 1870, 2i. Sir Adolphus Liddell, Permanent-Under-Secretary at the Home Office, minuted his dissatisfaction: 'It is very much to be regretted that Lord Devon did not consult Mr Bruce [Home Secretary] before the communication ... was made to Mr Butt which has I understand been published in the Irish newspapers, and may lead to some difficulty and embarrassment' (ibid., 1/19). Devon's concession had to be honoured, but it was required that the names of prisoners' friends who wished to assist in the preparation of statements had to be submitted in advance for the Home Secretary's approval.

250 Having received assurances, Rossa was willing to give evidence, and asked that Mary should be admitted to Chatham to help him prepare his submission to the Commission. Fearing that the government would take a propaganda advantage from the concession, she reproved him, writing (words he quoted back to her) that 'Even while I could understand another man putting aside all considerations but the satisfaction of meeting his wife, I cannot understand it in you who have since I first knew you held public interest far in advance of mine or your own gratification, to take advantage of this permission to assist you in preparing your statement for the Commission of Inquiry.' Rossa thought it hard his wife should take this line since her unwillingness to visit under the circumstances meant that he could not in future 'with any face' apply for a public or private visit, since the governor or director might respond, 'How do you know that your wife wants to visit you?' (Rossa to Mary O'Donovan Rossa, 9 July 1870: CUA: FBP, Box 2, item 23).

251 Mary O'Donovan Rossa had travelled from Co. Cork to London in anticipation of being allowed to help her husband. She sent a request to Ollivant, the Commission Secretary; he forwarded the letter to the Home Secretary. Having waited for five days without a reply, Mary left London for Cork, only to be summoned by a telegram which was forwarded from her London lodgings. The telegram was dated Saturday, 2 July, and requested her to be at Chatham on 4 July to assist her husband. At this distance one can scarcely be conclusive but it is more likely that muddle rather than malice lay behind these events. Mrs O'Donovan Rossa saw it as the latter – a plot by the authorities to claim that they had offered the facilities, while ensuring that she could not take advantage of them (see the exchange of correspondence in the *Freeman's Journal*, 6 July 1870, 4a–b).

Lord Devon indicated in other ways that he wished to give the prisoners every opportunity to make full representation. Evidence would be taken in private rooms, and no prison officials would be present; an undertaking was given that there would be no retaliation for any statement made to the committee. Prisoners could make written submissions, as could any friend or person acting on their behalf; those who had already been released could also submit evidence. Finally, it was promised that both report and evidence would be published.[252] It is hard to see what further assurances could have been given that this was to be a serious and full inquiry, and as unbiased as these events ever can be.

The Home Office was not pleased. Instead of the fairly narrow technical inquiry which was planned, Lord Devon had taken a course, an official subsequently observed, which was 'altogether unanticipated'.[253] There was a fear that the various concessions would lead to collusion and the fabrication or exaggeration of complaints. When four of the prisoners petitioned to be allowed to consult their comrades in preparing their statements, Henry Bruce, the Home Secretary, refused their request: 'Most decidedly not in my opinion. The ordinary trial of the truth in any criminal investigation is that the witnesses should be examined separately and not hear what the others state. To allow these men to meet and concoct a story wh[ich] all should stick to w[oul]d be to [avoid] this test.'[254]

In retrospect at least one of the committee members believed that the prisoners had managed to concert their responses. Despite agreeing to serve, George Brodrick (writing thirty years later and by then an anti-Home Ruler) claimed that he had thought that Gladstone's agreement to an independent inquiry was 'an act of weakness', and that the Home Office itself could easily have investigated the allegations. He objected to prisoners being given three days' notice that the Commission would be coming to take evidence. During this intervening period paper and pen was to be provided so that statements might be prepared. To prevent collusion the prisoners were supposed to be separated. But this precaution was frustrated when there was a Sunday in one of the days of notice, '[F]or my Roman Catholic colleagues, supported by Lord Devon, would not hear of Catholic prisoners being kept away from mass in the chapel, where the facilities are great for the secret telegraphy which is an occult science of jails. The result was a highly suspicious family likeness between the papers handed to us in prisons where such communication had been possible.'[255] This

---

252 *The Times*, 28 June 1870, 9f.

253 'Instead of being as had been expected almost a purely medical examination lasting for about a fortnight, it developed into a general inquiry occupying more than 3 months' (PRO HO 45/9330/19461A/62).

254 Ibid., /20.

255 Hon. George Charles Brodrick, *Memories and Impressions 1831–1900*, London, James Nisbet & Co, 1900, pp. 166–7. Brodrick later recorded that he thought committees of inquiry were generally carried on 'with an enormous waste of time and energy'. His own experience had been 'specially unfavourable'. As to why he had accepted membership of the Devon Committee, 'I was advised that, as there was to be a Commission, I might be of some public use by serving on it'.

interpretation does not find support in Rossa's correspondence with his wife, where, rather than welcoming the opportunity to have a platform to blacken the prison authorities, and mindful of his bitter experience with Knox and Pollock, he debates with her the wisdom of submitting *any* evidence. He had come to the decision to do so somewhat uneasily, and because he 'would not leave it in the gentlemen's power to say that my refusal to give evidence was proof that these statements could not be substantiated'.[256]

Whatever reservations individual members and officials may have had about the prisoners collaborating, the Devon Commission expressed a number of concerns about the treatment of the Fenian prisoners. All of these, it is true, probably boiled down to little more than the fact that the Irish prisoners were being treated with the same callousness as ordinary convicts. Rossa surely had a point when he wrote to his wife that whatever political use the government envisaged in the Commission, the history of his prison life would counterbalance it.[257] There *may* have been some collusion between the men in the production of their statements, but no evidence of this appears in the official records. Certainly the Devon Commission did not find that the charges of ill-treatment were, in Brodrick's words, 'most extravagant and mendacious', and it is difficult to imagine how Brodrick could have signed the report had he believed this to be the case. Rather, the several observations of the committee on which I have drawn show that there was dismay at the harshness of the regime, condemnation of Rossa's illegal punishment, and (straying well beyond the Commission's terms of reference) a general feeling that political offenders such as the Fenians might better be segregated completely:

> It is the question whether prisoners convicted of a crime so exceptional in its nature that it has been thought right to modify prison discipline in their case to a certain extent, might not with advantage be more completely separated from the general body of convicts. We are led to the conclusion that the difficulties attendant upon the location and treatment of political offenders, may perhaps be most readily and effectually overcome by setting apart from time to time a detached portion of some convict prison for prisoners of this class, and we recommend this subject to the consideration of Her Majesty's Government.[258]

The *Spectator* supported this approach, and condemned the refusal to treat the Fenians as political prisoners. In Ireland this view was that in dishonouring these men, Irishmen at large were dishonoured. 'These men are nobler than many of us, for they acted on the impulses which we had either too much

---

256 Rossa to Mary O'Donovan Rossa, 9 July 1870: CUA: FBP, Box 2, item 23.
257 Ibid.
258 *Op. cit.*, pp. 27–8.

prudence or too little courage to act upon. And in casting insults on them you render us implacable.'[259] But with the release of the Fenian leaders, which coincided with the publication of the Commission's report, the problem of political prisoners seems to have gone away. The *Manchester Guardian* probably voiced the general mood, hoping that 'it may be long before the problem comes again to have more than a theoretical interest for the English people'.[260] This sentiment was widely shared, and a sense of the issue being shelved was encouraged by the coincidence of the publication of the Devon Commission report and the announcement of a conditional amnesty for the civilian Fenians. Few could have foreseen that Irish political offenders would continue to be found in English prisons, more or less continuously, into the twenty-first century.

Transportation

Penal options had narrowed in the twenty years since the Young Irelanders were transported. Even for 'ordinary' offenders transportation meant conditional liberty at an early point. In 1848 transportation was the usual penalty for felony; by 1865 the position was reversed. Transportation was being phased out (indeed formally it had been abolished as a sentence of the court)[261] and only a tiny minority of offenders were removed to Western Australia, which alone of the Australian colonies accepted their labour and, eventually, their settlement. Banishment to the further ends of the earth was a retribution in itself – wrenching the miscreant from home, family and friends, with little expectation of return: for some generations quarter sessions and assizes had echoed with the shrieks and sobs of those who would never meet again. And far from the scene of their crimes, the penal objectives of deterrence, containment and denunciation were not greatly undermined by dealing liberally with offenders.

Two objectives clashed in the disposal of the Fenians: the desire to punish the most grievous offenders, and the policy of removing at least some of the long-sentence prisoners from English convict prisons. Following Irish representations – especially from the Roman Catholic hierarchy – consideration was given to sending the Fenians to Western Australia. Authority for this was provided by the 1857 Penal Servitude Act.[262] Unusually, some of the convicts were asked whether they were willing to be transported. It is unclear how much

---

259 *Spectator*, 19 March 1870, 369a.

260 *Manchester Guardian*, 5 January 1871, 5a. See also *Freeman's Journal*, 4 January 1871, 2i; 5 January, 3g. The *Spectator* was indignant at the abuses the Commission had uncovered. In the case of Rossa 'punishment was carried to the extent of torture – torture of a novel kind certainly, but quite as brutal as the boot, and protracted with a vindictive pertinacity' (14 January 1871, 35a).

261 See my *History of English Prison Administration*, ch. 12.

262 20 & 21 Vict., c.3. This Act substantially replaced transportation by penal servitude, while retaining (s.3) executive power to remove any convict 'to any place or places beyond the Seas'.

the decision to offer transportation was the result of the prisoners' initiative. On 31 August 1867 William Fagan passed a list of five Fenian prisoners to the Home Office. These men had 'expressed a desire to be sent to Western Australia in the next convict ship and as a similar request on the part of prisoner Michael Moore has been granted I recommend the cases of these prisoners for favourable consideration'. Fagan's letter was minuted by George Everest, the Criminal Clerk: 'It would be a convenient mode of disposing of the whole of the Irish Treason Felony Convicts, who are likely to be a source of trouble as long as they remain in this Country.' The Home Secretary, Gathorne Hardy, assented to the proposal.[263]

Convict prison conditions were harsh and the men's sentences were long. In Australia, by contrast, there would be a speedy easing of confinement, and even the time spent in the labour gangs while working for a ticket of leave would be made easier by the relaxation of custody and living in the open air. Besides these inducements, the men may also have been mindful of the Young Irelanders' escapes. Against these advantages there was the hardship of removal far from family and friends, but since they were by regulations and practicalities restricted – at best – to one or two short visits each year, this consideration may not have weighed too heavily.

Throughout September 1867, the Home Office recruited for the transportation party, which, it had been decided, would be the last one to be sent.[264] It would be a mixed shipment, and ordinary criminals would accompany the Fenians. The men were marshalled at Portland Convict Prison, and by late September, amidst great security, all was made ready.[265] On Saturday, 12 September 1867, the *Hougoumont*, chartered by the government, left Portland. Because of a feared rescue attempt while the *Hougoumont* was travelling down the coast, it was escorted by the steam warship *Earnest* as far as 'the Chops of the Channel'.[266]

Better to travel . . .

On board the *Hougoumont* the sixty-two Fenians were divided into two parties. Forty-five civilians were accommodated in quarters on the main lower deck astern. The seventeen soldier Fenians were quartered with the criminal prisoners in the midship section of the lower deck, although days were spent with their

---

263 PRO HO 45/9329/19461/64. The following week four more prisoners volunteered to be transported (ibid., 65).
264 *The Times*, 17 October 1867, 9a.
265 Ibid., 26 September 1867, 7e. No women were transported.
266 Ibid., 15 October 1867, 7f. This report, like the previous one, was juxtaposed with a continuing appeal for funds for the family of Sergeant Brett, killed during the Manchester rescue, and accounts of the trial of those accused of his murder. The removal of the Fenians to the far end of the world was not likely to be opposed by those who read such reports.

civilian comrades.[267] In the eyes of captain and crew the Fenians were in a very different category from the 218 criminal prisoners on board; relations between the crew and the political prisoners were amiable.[268] The awful isolation of the separate cell was gone, conversation and association were unlimited, and the penal diet was replaced by ship's rations, prepared by each of the messes to which the men were assigned. The main meal included salt beef, soup, potatoes and plum duff. A glass of wine was served daily, and tobacco and fruit were issued occasionally. The quantity was somewhat less than healthy young men would have liked, but this was a very long way indeed from Dartmoor, Portland and Millbank fare. Concerts were staged every second night or so, a ship's journal was produced (and ran to seven issues before completion of the voyage), and there was regular and extended access to the top deck for exercise and relaxation in the air.[269] There were frequent religious services, at which the men's devotion to their church was made clear. The voyage through the Tropics was as entrancing for the Fenians as it had been for the Young Irelanders. There was some consciousness of the historic nature of their circumstances, a sense that extended to the captain and crew who requested souvenir copies of 'The Wild Goose' – a few spares of which were produced.[270] On arrival the captain characterised the men's behaviour on the voyage as 'exemplary'.

Western Australia was one of the Empire's most remote places of settlement, but the doings of the Fenians had reached even there – Stephens' escape, the

---

267 There are several accounts of the voyage of the *Hougoumont*, which draw on original sources, including the diary kept by Denis Cashman from 15 October 1867 to 8 January 1868; the diary of John Sarsfield Casey, 7 October 1867 to 9 January 1868 and a journal produced by the Fenian prisoners 'The Wild Goose: A Collection of Ocean Waifs'. These documents are available in the Battye Library, Perth, The Mitchell Library, Sydney, and the National Library of Ireland. Casey's diary has been privately printed and is additionally available in the British Library (John Sarsfield Casey, 'Journal of a Voyage from Portland to Fremantle on Board the Convict Ship Hougoumont Cap Cozens Commander October 12th, 1867', ed. Martin Kevin Cusak). Some of this material did not become available to scholars until the late 1960s, and therefore a rather misleading account of the voyage was disseminated, based on John Boyle O'Reilly's *Moondyne: A Story from the Underworld* (London, G. Routledge & Sons, 1889). This novel (which is known to be semi-autobiographical) contains passages suggesting that the Fenian convicts were transported under conditions of maximum security and a great deal of cruelty, which was certainly not the case.

268 Keith Amos (*The Fenians in Australia*, Kensington (NSW), New South Wales University Press, 1988, ch. 5) provides a thoroughly researched account of the voyage.

269 'The Wild Goose' was produced in very fine calligraphy, and consisted of verse and prose with, as would be expected, a heavy emphasis on Irish patriotic verse and themes of exile. There was a great deal of humour, and the mast-head was an indication that the editors could poke fun at themselves – the Wild Geese being the venerated exiles from Ireland following the Williamite victories of the late seventeenth century.

270 Through good fortune a complete set of 'The Wild Goose', the property of John Flood (a Dublin man sentenced to fifteen years), was preserved and passed down in his family. In 1968 his great-granddaughter presented it to Sydney's Mitchell Library.

raid on Chester, the rising, the Manchester rescue and the Clerkenwell atrocity. The raids on Canada and rumours of Fenian privateers created an immediate sense of vulnerability, while the Protestant–Catholic, Irish–English divides in the colony itself made for fear and prejudice-driven hostility on both sides. Despite their exemplary conduct on board the *Hougoumont* the Fenians were viewed with the greatest apprehension by some colonists.[271] All of this was wrapped in resentment that the imperial government had violated the spirit if not the letter of a pledge to end transportation.[272] The news of the Fenians' arrival had not long preceded them, which imported an urgency into the protests of colonists who fretted that if the Fenians were capable of such outrages even in England, what might they and their sympathisers not do in this remote part of the world?[273] Pressure on the colonial government was considerable.

By coincidence Dr John Hampton, who had been Comptroller General of convicts in Van Diemen's Land at the time of the Young Irelanders' transportation, was now Governor of Western Australia, and was the man on whom the duty of reassuring the colonists fell.[274] Hampton was aided in this task by one of the most powerful men in the colony – the banker, publisher and editor Francis Lochee.[275] Privately Lochee reported on the widespread fears of the Fenians.[276] Hampton requested a naval and military show of strength. While he considered the alarm in the colony to be greatly exaggerated, he was not a little on edge himself, writing to the Commodore of the Australian squadron that as 'Fremantle

271 See comment in *South Australian Weekly Chronicle*, 25 January 1868, reprinted by the Perth *Inquirer and Commercial News*, 12 February 1868, 3e: 'The insurgent Fenians . . . the most atrocious characters yet exported from British prisons.'

272 Government had promised to end transportation by 26 November 1867. By interpreting this as the date on which the vessel should be dispatched, there was a feeling that government had engaged in sharp practice. On the other hand, the Perth *Inquirer* refuted claims that a specially depraved and desperate cargo of humanity had been sent to the colony. The *Hougoumont* had carried 'the most orderly body of men ever transported to the colony'. Conditions on board had been appreciably better than those of free immigration vessels (*Inquirer and Commercial News*, 15 January 1868, 3e; see also 22 January 1868, 2f).

273 *Perth Gazette*, 27 December 1867, 2e. See also the *Gazette's* sensational reports on Fenian activity in England (18 December 1867, 2d–e; 14 February 1868, 3e). On 20 December 1867 (3c–d) the paper reported that 'preparations for a regular revolt have been going on in open day'. The generally confused state of mind then prevailing in the colony was shown by the *Gazette's* report that the *Hougoumont's* voyage had been a quiet one and the Fenian convicts had been 'especially well behaved and amenable to the regulations of the ship' (17 January 1868, 2d).

274 For Hampton see p. 80, n. 138, above.

275 (1811–93). Born London of Huguenot stock. Settled in Fremantle in 1838 and almost immediately entered into the public affairs of the colony. Began publication of *Inquirer* in 1840, and manager of Western Australian Bank the following year. Did much to encourage immigration to the colony.

276 State Records Office of Western Australia (SROWA): Francis Lochee to John Hampton, 31 December 1867: Acc. B6/1187/10.

might without any difficulty be destroyed by a Fenian pirate with only one heavy gun, I think it would be a good policy to grant the town and harbour the protection of a ship-of-war until a decision is received from Her Majesty's Government'.[277] Although tightly stretched, Lambert dispatched the gunboat *Brisk*, which arrived at Fremantle some six weeks after Hampton's request had been sent.[278] The War Office also responded (somewhat tardily in the event that the emergency had been a real one) by sending two companies of the 14th Regiment from Tasmania.[279] It was emphasised that both the naval and military show of force was a mood-calming exercise, and the deployments were purely temporary.

The upsets and fears came to nothing, and at the end of February 1868, Hampton, thanking Lambert for sending the *Brisk*, had somewhat sheepishly to confess that the alarm and excitement had decreased on it becoming known that the Fenians' behaviour on the voyage had been very good. Fears had been further lessened 'by their quiet demeanour after disembarkation and by the opportune arrival of the *Brisk*'. Despite this favourable state, however, Hampton wanted the *Brisk* to remain on station, since its expected departure might cause a revival of fears.[280] It was clear that whatever difficulties the Fenians might present (and there were to be some) an outbreak of public disorder was not among them. Sentiment remained volatile, however, and was aggravated and reanimated by the attempted assassination of Prince Albert, Duke of Edinburgh, in Sydney on 12 March 1868. The would-be assassin, Henry O'Farrell, was of Irish Catholic stock and claimed, until an eve of execution confession, to be acting on behalf of a Fenian organisation; in fact, he was a mentally unstable isolate. The event, as may be easily imagined, sent shock-waves through all the Australian colonies, generating feelings of shame and anger and anti-Irish and anti-Catholic bigotry. Western Australia re-entered its Fenian fever.[281]

Throughout the months that followed there were further requests for a show of force in the isolated colony. The two companies of the 14th Regiment arrived, but stayed for only two months. On 11 August 1868, Colonel Brice, commanding the troops, informed Hampton that he did not consider it necessary to retain his men in Western Australia: 'Good order prevails throughout the length and breadth of the Colony, and were it otherwise I should have full confidence in the power and the loyal spirit of the enrolled pensioners force.'[282] A month later members of the Western Australia Council and magistrates

---

277 Ibid.: J. S. Hampton to Commodore Lambert, 23 December 1867; Acc. 392/1232/3.

278 Ibid., Acc. 136/1187/11; Lambert to Hampton, 17 January 1868; *Inquirer*, 5 February 1868, 4e.

279 Ibid., Acc. 136/1187/11, Major-General Chute to Hampton, 26 February 1868.

280 Ibid., Acc. 392/1232/3; Hampton to Lambert, 29 February 1868.

281 The attempted assassination, and its effect on Australian public opinion is thoroughly examined by Keith Amos (*op. cit.*, ch. 3). A Loyal Address was adopted at a Perth public meeting on 24 April 1868, assuring Queen Victoria that the attempt did not reflect the sentiment of Western Australia which was assuredly loyal to the Crown (SROWA: Acc. 136/1187/11).

282 Ibid., Acc. 136/1187/11; Brice to Hampton, 11 August 1868.

submitted a memorial to Hampton (possibly with his connivance), deploring the withdrawal of the 14th Regiment's men and the decision not to replace them. There were in the colony 'many sympathisers with Fenianism' who might be in contact with Fenians in England, Ireland and America. The memorialists referred to the Fenian preparations then reportedly being made to wage war on Canada and their fear that a force could be sent to Western Australia to release the Fenian prisoners. As the Home government had 'placed the safety of this Colony in peril they are bound to protect it from foreign invasion'. They asked Hampton to request further protection or the removal of the Fenians.[283] Hampton was more than happy to comply with this request. The answer, sent on 19 January 1869, was blunt. The War Office saw no reason in the present state of Western Australia 'or in the circumstance of some of the Convicts now there having been convicted of treasonable offences for thinking it necessary to maintain a detachment of Troops of the Line in the Colony'.[284] With this final and definite refusal the colonists were left to get on with their Fenians.

In Western Australia

Convict life in the colony was very different from that privileged existence enjoyed by the Young Irelanders, to whom ennui and exile were the greatest hardships. Apart from a closer attention to their security, there was no attempt to provide a separate regime. Even their custody was, for the most part not a major issue. Although it had been decided in 1853, when transportation to Van Diemen's Land ceased, that only those serving sentences of fourteen years or more would thenceforward be transported,[285] the *Hougoumont* Fenians were in the great majority short-sentence men, twenty-four serving sentences of five years, eleven serving seven years and ten serving ten years.[286] It is true that in 1857 another Penal Servitude Act (20 & 21 Vict., c.3) restored executive discretion over the shorter-sentenced men, but at the time the Home Secretary, Sir George Grey, had informed all judges and recorders how government intended to exercise its discretion. As far as possible, seven-year men would not be transported, and selection would take place when about half the sentence

283 Ibid., Acc. 136/1187/11; Memorial, 10 September 1868.
284 Ibid., Acc. 392/1232/3; Edward H. Lawrence, on behalf of the Duke of Buckingham and Chandos to Hampton, 19 January 1869.
285 Penal Servitude Act, 1853: 16 & 17 Vict., c.99.
286 Compiled from nominal roll and sentences published in the *Inquirer*, 15 January 1862, 2f. In addition two were serving fifteen years, two twenty years and eleven life. Of the last, three had originally been sentenced to be hanged, drawn and quartered (Patrick Doran, Dublin; Thomas Bowler, Ballymacody; David Joyce, Ballymacody), respited, and commuted to life. The total of sixty in the *Inquirer* does not agree with other sources which give the figure of sixty-two. Keith Amos (*op. cit.*, pp. 87–9 and 289–90) gives this last figure, and also differs slightly in the distribution of sentences. At some point, evidently, there had been clerical errors.

had been served.[287] The short-term Fenian prisoners had therefore been treated exceptionally. The relatively short sentences of so many, moreover, when combined with time already served in England, meant that several could look forward to early release on tickets of leave.

The men were allowed to work their way through the normal stages of convict discipline, each of which entailed an easing of custody and increase in privileges. They were not segregated from the ordinary convicts. Six or seven worked on a party in and around Fremantle Convict Prison; others were assigned to labour gangs throughout the colony. They were under discipline, but provided they did not break the rules their custody was not arduous; and though the work was hard, it was out of doors, and relations with their guards seem to have been amiable enough. Above all, the awful oppressiveness of English convict life was behind them. One of them, writing to his family, stated that despite all the hardships of climate and labour in Western Australia, life was preferable to that at Portland.[288]

Many, if not most of the Fenian convicts entered easily enough into colonial life and settled in the colony. They were generally well-behaved men, decent in character, and advanced rapidly through the disciplinary stages, at least one gaining his conditional liberty by August 1868 – a mere seven months after arrival. Besides those released on the expiration of their sentences, others were freed as an act of clemency under the amnesty of May 1869.[289] In July 1869, an advertisement appeared in the *Inquirer* on behalf of the Irish State Prisoners' Fund informing those who had been released that a fund had been raised to enable them to return to their homes, or to go elsewhere, and that an agent was on his way to the colony to assist them.[290] On 11 September 1869, twenty-five men left Perth in triumphant procession, en route for Albany, King George's Sound, the only port from which former convict passengers could then depart.[291] Of those freed, ten made their way back to Ireland and fifteen went to the United States of America. Nine chose to remain in Western Australia.[292] In December

---

287 Circular, Sir George Grey, 27 June 1857, to all judges, recorders, etc.: see Appendix I.E., *Royal Commission on Transportation and Penal Servitude*, PP, 1863 [3190], XXI, 1, 129.

288 Letter of Thomas Duggan, *Nation*, 17 October 1868, 184d and 185a. Duggan had one complaint. He had left his encampment in the bush in search of mushrooms. Arrested and taken before a magistrate, he was sent back to his work party: 'Such is the liberty a convict has in Western Australia' he grumbled. Indeed.

289 See below, pp. 226–32.

290 *Inquirer*, 21 July 1869, 1c.

291 On the way to Sydney their ship berthed in Adelaide. The Fenians were prevented from landing, but Adelaide's Irish gave them a warm reception in the form of a four-day party on board their steamer, the *Rangatira* (see *Inquirer*, 2 November 1870, 8b–d; Amos (*op. cit.*, ch. 8) gives an account of the departure of the amnestied men).

292 The discontented mushroom-gatherer, Thomas Duggan (ten years) was one of these, as was Hugh Brophy (ten years), Joseph Noonan or Nunan (ten years), James O'Reilly (five years) and others. Two men were not granted amnesty at this time, but on release one went to another of the Australian colonies, while the other married locally and stayed. See the reminiscences of Thomas Duggan in *Clare's Weekly*, 14 May 1898, 10b.

1870 there were further pardons extended to all those still in Western Australia who were not soldier-convicts. These pardons reached the colony in March 1871, and eight men were released. Only one of this group chose to stay in the colony.

As shall be seen, the Duke of Cambridge, the Commander-in-Chief, allegedly objected to amnesty for the solider-convicts.[293] A number of these were serving short sentences, and were released as a matter of course. Several had long sentences, however, and with little hope of mercy determined on escape. The first of these was John Boyle O'Reilly, serving twenty years, who, as we have seen, had already made at least two escape attempts in England. Aided by a sympathetic Irish Catholic priest Father Patrick McCabe, and driven by the prospect of the long confinement stretching ahead of him (and perhaps an unhappy love affair with a warder's daughter), O'Reilly made an escape attempt on 17 February 1869, but was unable to board the whaler *Vigilant* as arranged. A second attempt was successful, and O'Reilly boarded the whaler *Gazelle*. In July 1869 he transferred to the American barque *Sapphire*, bound for Liverpool. At Liverpool he signed as third mate on another American ship *Bombay*, reaching Philadelphia on 23 November 1869 after an odyssey of some nine months.[294]

There was a great deal of shutting the stable door, always slowed by the imperial bureaucracy. Thus on 30 March 1870, Frederick Weld,[295] who had replaced Hampton as Governor of Western Australia at the end of 1868, had to solicit permission from Home Secretary Henry Bruce to employ two additional water police constables. It had come to his knowledge, he wrote, that Fenian sympathisers had sent money to the colony to assist escapers, and Fenian agents were at work.[296] Two months later Weld was supplying details of the treatment of the remaining Fenian prisoners, which had become a matter of some concern.[297] In October 1870 he was fretting that Fenian sympathisers and agents were at work, and that prison staff (including Father Patrick McCabe, who had, unknown to Weld, assisted O'Reilly's escape) could not be wholly relied upon.[298]

---

293 See pp. 303–5, below.

294 Keith Amos (*op. cit.*, ch. 7) provides a detailed account of O'Reilly's escape. It is also described (though in a more guarded way) in Mrs John Boyle O'Roche (ed.), *Life of John Boyle O'Reilly*, London, T. Fisher Unwin, 1891. A. G. Evans provides more detail in his *Fanatic Heart: A Life of John Boyle O'Reilly 1844–1890*, Nedlands, University of Western Australia Press, 1997 (see esp. chs 16–21). Thomas Keneally (*The Great Shame*, London, Vintage, 1999, pp. 500–12) makes an engaging story of this incident, as with much of the other material he handles so deftly. Michael Davitt (*Life and Progress in Australasia*, *op. cit.*, 455–63) also deals with O'Reilly's escape.

295 (1823–91). Born in Dorset into one of England's leading Roman Catholic families. Followed usual career of colonial administrator in Australia and South-East Asia. Had a special attachment to Western Australia.

296 SROWA: Weld to Bruce, 30 March 1870; Acc. 390/1174/47.

297 The Fenian prisoners had themselves acknowledged that they had received 'fair, honourable and even kind treatment'. He regretted that on their release some of the men had not acknowledged this (ibid., Acc. 390/1174/47; Weld to Bruce, 20 May 1870).

298 Ibid., Acc. 390/1170/42; Weld to Home Office, 13 October 1870.

Catalpa

Weld's anxieties were well founded, but he was a lucky administrator and had the good fortune to be long removed from the scene when disaster struck on 17 April 1876. The unhappy incumbent at that time was William Robinson.[299] Among those Fenian leaders given conditional pardon by Gladstone in January 1871 was John Devoy.[300] The condition was that the pardoned convicts should expatriate themselves for the duration of their sentences. In practical terms this meant exile to the United States of America. Devoy, perhaps the most determined, level-headed and methodical of the Fenian leaders, quickly found his feet in America, and determined to carry on his fight against British rule in Ireland from that haven. This was not an easy thing to do, and there was much vaporous invective and sabre-rattling among the Irish groups with revolutionary aspirations. Devoy's success in rescuing six of his comrades from Western Australia was a great triumph, permanently secured his place in the revolutionary leadership and reanimated Fenianism. As will be seen in the next chapter, it also indirectly initiated a campaign of terrorism in England – not foreseen by Devoy, and without his support.

By the mid-1870s releases on the expiration of sentence and the Gladstone pardons had reduced Fenian prisoners to eight, seven of whom were soldiers under life sentences to whom it had been made clear that clemency could not be expected.[301] Even the short-sentence soldiers had not received pardons. The men had been treated differently from their civilian comrades on the *Hougoumont*, and on arrival were dispersed throughout the colony, whereas the civilians were allowed to work together. Convinced that they would never receive pardons, those remaining in captivity wrote increasingly pressing letters to comrades in the United States of America. After some time Devoy (who had been the Fenian's chief organiser in the British Army) succeeded in persuading his branch of Fenianism, Clan na Gael, to finance an escape.[302] Since the men to be rescued were in Fremantle Prison there was talk of an armed attack to rescue them, but eventually a more subtle plan was developed. It was decided to buy and equip a whaler, to sail her under an experienced captain and crew, and to effect the escapes surreptitiously. The 202-ton barque *Catalpa* was purchased, refitted, equipped and crewed. The ship would engage in whaling and aim to be

---

299 (1834–97). Born in Co. Westmeath, Ireland. Colonial career, including Montserratt, Dominica, the Falkland Islands and Prince Edward Island. Governor Western Australia 1874–7. In 1880 reappointed Governor of Western Australia, then South Australia, Victoria and (for the third time) Western Australia in 1890.

300 See below (pp. 246–50).

301 Thomas Delaney was a soldier (5th Dragoon Guards). Serving ten years, he had already been released on licence. He was in Fremantle Prison for repeated bouts of drunkenness while on ticket of leave, serving a local sentence of twelve months' hard labour.

302 A selection of Devoy's correspondence on the project (and it must have been considerable) is to be found in the Devoy Papers (NLI: Ms. 18,135 (i) and (ii)).

profitable in order to assist with finances. The crew was a regular one and information about the mission was closely guarded. One Fenian only was put on board (another joined later). In the meantime agents were dispatched to Western Australia, where they went about their seemingly normal lives of work and recreation while they prepared the rescue.[303]

The American Fenians had been a major target of British intelligence efforts for some time, and the British government was not unaware that an attempt might be made to spirit the Fremantle convicts away. The Colonial Secretary, Lord Carnarvon, had send confidential instructions to the Governor of Western Australia, now William H. Robinson. These were acknowledged on 13 April 1876. There were, he reported, only ten Fenian convicts left. Two were on tickets of leave in outlying districts, and under watch. The eight in Fremantle Prison would be carefully supervised: 'I think I may assure your Lordship that any scheme of the nature referred to which may possibly be set on foot, will end in total failure.'[304] Only six days later Robinson was woefully impaled on his own confidence: 'it is my painful duty to report . . . that six of the convicts in question have escaped from the Imperial Prison at Fremantle, and gone to sea, as we believe, in a boat belonging to the American Whaling Barque "Catalpa".'[305] This was an international embarrassment, and Robinson immediately set up a committee of inquiry, including three reasonably independent members. The committee described what had happened and placed the blame on the prison authorities rather than on Robinson.[306] When the findings of the committee reached London, Sir Edmund Du Cane, Chairman of the Directorate of Con-vict Prisons recommended a number of disciplinary measures. The Comptroller General, Fauntleroy, was pensioned out of the service. The dismissal of Superin-tendent Doonan was confirmed. A warder who had allowed two men to leave his party was dismissed; a principal warder was reduced in rank, and two other warders were to be interviewed and further considered for dismissal. Two

---

303 A collection of letters dealing with the rescue and its preparation is to be found in William O'Brien and Desmond Ryan (eds), *Devoy's Postbag, op. cit.*, vol. 1, pp. 174–7 and 219–23. Michael Davitt, in Australia some twenty years after the event, collected some interesting information (*Life and Progress in Australasia, op. cit.*, pp. 464–70). Amos (*op. cit.*, chs 9 and 10) draws a number of sources into an accomplished narrative.

304 SROWA: Acc. 390/1174/47; Robinson to Carnarvon, 13 April 1876.

305 Ibid., Acc. 390/1174/47; Robinson to Carnarvon, 19 April 1876. Robinson went on to describe the steps he had taken on receipt of Carnarvon's dispatch. With due deference he attempted to throw some of the responsibility for the failure on Carnarvon's insistence that total secrecy be observed, which meant that no untoward and obvious steps could be taken. It had been intended to disperse the men so that they could not easily communicate, but Robinson's instructions had not been implemented by Fauntleroy, the Comptroller General.

306 The Acting Colonial Secretary (Imperial Government's other eyes and ears and counter-check in the colony), A. O'Grady Lefroy, chaired the committee. The other members were the Assistant Commissary General A. R. Thompson and J. G. Slade, Visiting Magistrate at Fremantle Prison (see SROWA: Acc. 392/1232/4 and 390/1168/37).

warders (including one who had been dismissed) were found to be blameless. Various steps were taken to improve procedures and to tighten security. It was a moderate amount of blood-letting for such a crushing embarrassment.

The escape had been carried of in a manner which, if anything, increased the discomfiture of government. On Easter Monday (17 April 1876) six convicts assembled, having by various ruses left their assigned places. The telegraph wires between Perth and Fremantle had been cut to delay attempts at recapture. The convicts made their way to Rockingham Beach, some twenty miles distant from Fremantle, where they embarked on a *Catalpa* boat. An alarm was given fairly quickly and the escape ran into trouble when the rowing-boat initially failed to make contact with the *Catalpa*. The *Georgette*, a government-commandeered steamship had been sent out to the *Catalpa* by this time, but had been refused permission to board. The escapees managed to get on to the *Catalpa* only the following day, pursued by a police-cutter. The *Georgette* returned to the pursuit, refuelled and with a party of armed constables and pensioner soldiers. On Wednesday, 19 April the *Catalpa* came in sight, but in international waters. A shot was fired across her bows. The two boats being within hailing distance, *Catalpa's* captain was asked to surrender the convicts. The Fenians had armed themselves, but were outgunned by the *Georgette*. A fight however proved unnecessary since the *Catalpa* was flying the stars and stripes, and being in international waters claimed its protection. The *Georgette* had been instructed to board by force only within the three-mile limit, and so the *Catalpa* had to be allowed to proceed.[307] The *Catalpa's* defiance, the drama of the chase and, above all, the protection of the American flag, all burnished the story for Fenian and Irish-American legend. In a colony so far-flung and isolated, the *Catalpa* affair remained a topic of public interest for many years.[308]

The six who escaped were all Fenian soldiers serving life sentences.[309] There were seven in Fremantle Prison, but one had been left behind because of his

307 The escape was a sensation in the colony, whose local newspapers reported it extensively. See *Herald*, 22 April 1876, 2g–h. The *Inquirer*, nine days after the escape, gave the fullest report, based on interviews with many of those who had taken part in the pursuit (26 April 1876, 3c–d). The *Western Australia Times* (28 April 1876, 2f, 3a) commented that the plan had been skilfully laid 'and succeeded quite as well as the absconders and their abettors could possibly have expected. Not a blow was struck, and not a shot fired; but a lesson had been learnt which the authorities will no doubt profit by hereafter.' The *Herald* criticised the Home government for not giving better protection to the colony.

308 Warder Booler, in charge of a party from which two of the Fenians had escaped was a year later dismissed by order of the Home government. This, after his twenty-nine years' service, was considered by the *Herald* to be an 'excessively severe punishment' (12 May 1871, 3h). When a play about *Catalpa* was put on in Boston, it was noted by the *Western Australia Times* (22 June 1877, 2b).

309 Thomas Darragh had been in the 2nd Queen's Regiment; Martin Hogan and James Wilson (McNally) in the 5th Dragoon Guards; Michael Harrington and Robert Cranston, 61st Foot and Thomas Hassett in the 24th Life Guards (*Inquirer*, 15 January 1868, 2f; *Western Australia Police Gazette*, 11 (10 May 1876), pp. 43–4. The latter includes detailed physical descriptions).

treachery some years before.[310] While the men were on the high seas Disraeli turned down an amnesty petition for the convict soldiers signed by 138 MPs.[311] This inflexibility increased justification for the escape, when it became known. (A break in the submarine telegraphic cable just off Australia meant that news of the event did not reach London until 5 June 1876.)[312] Reactions were predictable. *The Times* complained of American attitudes towards the escapers.[313] The Irish newspapers reacted to the news according to their political complexion. There were nationalist demonstrations of triumph in Dublin, Cork and elsewhere. Irish newspapers in America were jubilant, and even the Anglophile *New York Times* reflected on Disraeli's earlier refusal to give the men amnesty. On board the ship there had been something of a quarrel between the various parties. The prisoners insisted on making landfall in America, rather than continuing with the whaling trip which had been intended to recoup a substantial amount of the expenses. The *Catalpa* accordingly moored in New York in the small hours of 18 August 1876. The men were feted at meetings in all the major Irish communities: a great Fenian victory was celebrated.[314]

This last event was of great importance. Internal divisions, public squabbling, accusations of embezzled and misspent money and, above all, two farcical attacks on Canada, had laid Fenianism low in the eyes of the Irish community. By this one stroke this ignominy had been wiped out. John Devoy and other Fenian leaders took due credit for the exploit, and ever afterwards were in an impregnable position of authority because of it.[315] But the *Catalpa*, if it taught lessons

---

310 Amos, *op. cit.*, pp. 230–1.

311 3 *Hansard*, CCXXIX, cols 1040–3; 22 May 1876. Parnell and Butt both intervened in the subsequent heated exchanges.

312 *The Times*, 6 June 1876, 5e. A fuller account of the escape was given on 26 June (9a).

313 Ibid., 21 August 1876, 3d and 5c. There was increased security for the remaining Fenian convicts in England – the unpardoned soldiers, and some arrested after Glastone's amnesty. Michael Davitt, then at Dartmoor, was moved from an outdoor to an indoor working party; similar precautions were taken with the others (Theodore William Moody, *Davitt and Irish Revolution 1846–82*, Oxford, Oxford University Press, 1981, p. 152; *Inquiry as to the Alleged Ill-treatment of the Convict Charles McCarthy in Chatham Convict Prison*, PP, 1878 [C. 1978], LXIII, 769, 4).

314 The arrival of the escapers was overshadowed by the intense coverage of the election campaign then in progress, but it did have interest outside the Irish community (*New York Times*, 21 August 1876, 5e).

315 There was intense interest in the details of the escape, and Clan na Gael fed carefully screened stories to the press. These stories made their way into the Irish and English press and in due course were reprinted in Australia. The *Herald* was evidently sensitive to the political ambiguities in running such Fenianism triumphalism, and prefaced its five-column story with the pander's disclaimer: 'There can be no doubt . . . that the American Government is heartily ashamed of the violation of international honour committed under cover of its flag' (18 November 1876, 3g–h, 4a–d). The *Inquirer* dealt with the American stories more briefly (8 November 1876, 3c). Nor did this interest falter in the colony. Some ten years after the *Catalpa* rescue, Michael Harrington, one of the six escapees, died in New York. The *Inquirer* ran a story on him, the *Catalpa* and the whereabouts of his five companions (25 August 1886, Supplement, 1h).

about the fruits of secrecy, careful planning and financial control, also taught a false lesson which, within a few years would take sections of Fenianism into terrorism. If a relatively small investment in a well-thought-out scheme could produce such good results, what more might not be possible with well-financed and carefully placed attacks on the mercantilism which was the heartbeat of the British Empire – her shipping and great commercial centres?

5

AMNESTY
Gladstone takes a chance

Amnesty and Irish politics

Romantic causes require sacrifices if they are to materialise and prosper. Loss of life and the spilling of blood are critical: they actualise what may otherwise be dismissed as rhetoric and wind; and for the insecure and rootless among the followers they confer seriousness and self-regard. Martyrs and mythology make any movement stronger, but are essential where the primary appeal is to sentiment and symbol rather than self-interest. The difficulty for government is obvious. Law and order must be upheld and thus rebellion's plotters and doers must be suppressed. Yet by any killing and punishment the rebellious movement is strengthened rather than weakened.

Such extreme attachments and desires acquire a spiritual character, a communion from which the zealous may not be deterred. Suppress and encourage the fanatical and make more fanatics; fail to act, and the web of loyalty to the state is torn and the confidence and support of the law-abiding are eroded. In a society as fractured by race, religion and property as Ireland was, pragmatic government found it extremely difficult to counter rebellion and subversion.

The imprisonment of the Fenians created a current of opinion in Ireland which daily grew more threatening. To the extremists, the prisoners were living sacrifices, whose indignities and sufferings added to their nobility and confirmed the wickedness of the British oppressor. To the rank and file, whose participation had been overlooked as an act of clemency, the sufferings of the leaders dignified their own momentary participation in history, and bound them anew to Fenian ideas and organisation. To onlookers, sympathetic or initially indifferent, the prisoners were an opportunity for safe – even humanitarian – defiance, and became the basis for mass campaigns in Ireland, the United States of America and Australia. Even those who had disapproved of Fenianism were not excluded: 'Look,' they could say, 'where their foolishness has taken them. But perhaps it was an excess of love rather than wickedness, and now in calmer times they should have mercy.' A noble and forgiving posture – and at so little cost.[1]

For the constitutional nationalists participation in amnesty campaigns held several advantages. They would not be outflanked by extremists and could, by virtue of their offices and public position, exert some control over the direction and tone of the movement. Gladstone himself had argued that Fenianism was a product of English misgovernment – something which constitutional nationalists had pointed out. The rhetoric of mercy in the nationalist cause bolstered their own position, allowing them safely to appropriate the fervour and drama of extremism. Fenianism could be portrayed as a matter of foolish rather than wicked means, directed to the noble ends which both streams of nationalism sought.

Trial and imprisonment fulfilled government's duty to suppress rebellion. Thereafter and rapidly, advantages turned into liabilities. The plight of the imprisoned scarcely acted as a deterrent, but rather as a device to tap and distil sympathy and to enlist recruits for extremism. Severe treatment enhanced the martyrdom of the offenders, and yet the ordinary regime of penal servitude was severe. Attempts to extinguish the political character of the offences and to emphasise criminal guilt simply backfired. Associating the men in prison with the ordinary criminal was easily portrayed as an outrage. Here, sympathisers and supporters said, was gratuitous insult and indignity. Rumours of brutal treatment, impossible to counter, ceaselessly hatched and buzzed around ever more fantastically; some proved to be true and thus all were validated. Complaints from wives and families of bureaucratic obstruction and callousness went forth ringing of truth. Whereas it would have been acceptable for the contaminated dependants of morally guilty criminals to have been treated thus (and would such have complained, and if so who would have listened?), the respectable wives, sisters and mothers who made the trip to England and who fretted about the condition of their men were not to be denied sympathy.[2] Some of *them* were as committed to the cause as the prisoners, adept in their publicity, able to use helplessness and apparent innocence, and willing to act as messengers and couriers.

Campaigns for improved prison conditions and for amnesty, with central roles for the prisoners' families, were effective vehicles for gathering funds

---

1 Several of these sentiments were brought together in an address presented by the Amnesty Association when the first group of Fenian leaders were released. '[T]he years of your imprisonment have placed you in your true light before your fellow-men . . . Irishmen of all creeds and classes have learned to appreciate your fidelity and devotion to the cause you have at heart. Those who were opposed to you are, perhaps, the most ready to do homage to your sincerity and fidelity. . . . The whole Irish race protested against the continuance of your imprisonment as a wrong' (*Freeman's Journal*, 10 January 1871, 4f).

2 Sending £200 to Mrs Luby, Treasurer of the appeal fund for the prisoners' families, the Fenian Brotherhood in the United States of America hoped that 'the men who pine in British dungeons can feel in their misery that their wives and children will not suffer the pangs of hunger' (*Irish Republic*, 19 October 1867).

and sympathy, pointing all the while to the pitiful state to which decent women and children were reduced by punishment which in its prolongation became cruel. Haughty and indifferent government became the offence, and the act of rebellion was eclipsed. Meanwhile the gathering of sentiment, funds and supporters increased the organisational strength, appeal and versatility of nationalism.

International relations – especially those with the United States of America – were affected by the plight of the prisoners and by amnesty campaigns.[3] Little effort and much gain made it irresistible for aspiring and established politicians to milk the strength and cohesiveness of the Irish-American vote by denouncing the cruelty and oppressiveness of the continued imprisonment of misguided but good-hearted men.[4] And in a country which only ninety years before had fought for its independence such politics did not need to be cynical. Congressional debates and inquiries put pressure on the president, and letters of concern and appeal were duly dispatched. In these, and the answers to them, there was always room for offence – intended or not, taken or not. At such a level words could be dangerous; one grievance could attract another, and soon there would be a nest of them. An appeal could become improper interference or even a threat; rejection, if not perfectly phrased (and even then) could be construed as disdain and insult. Diplomacy strained that in times of ease and peace these exchanges should not fray relations, and in other times should not throw oil on the embers and flames.

In prison, therefore, the Fenians promoted their cause far more effectively than at liberty. Entering their long terms of penal servitude, an embarrassment to the constitutional nationalists, anathema to the greater part of the Roman

---

3 The pamphlet *Things Not Generally Known* had a considerable effect on American opinion. An 1879 San Francisco petition to the US Senate on the treatment of Fenian prisoners made use of the pamphlet. The petition then appeared in the Senate proceedings, and was also printed in the *Washington Daily Globe* (12 July 1870). The British Consul confirmed the enormous effect of the pamphlet on America opinion (Public Record Office (PRO) HO 45/9330/1946/A). There were also various petitions on behalf of individual prisoners. See, for example, the petition on behalf of William J. Nagle from the St Patrick's Society of Brooklyn, 1 January 1868. United States National Archives (USNA), Washington, DC, 40th Congress, Committee on Foreign Affairs, HR 40A-H6.1 (folder 2). There were numerous petitions on behalf of naturalised citizens detained in Ireland (ibid., folders 2 and 3).

4 Even when Fenian activities were much closer at hand the politicians put votes before consequences. Thus the comments of a New York newspaper on the Fenian fair or picnic at Buffalo, which was seen as a possible cover for a raid on Canada in November 1867: 'Republicans and Democrats are equally anxious to secure the Irish vote. Republicans and Democrats, therefore, though they may not openly encourage the Fenians, will not go out of their way to discourage them.' The newspaper (probably the *New York Herald*) condemned the Fenians for disregarding US laws and bringing disgrace on the country: President Johnson should intervene (Enclosure, Lord March to Duke of Buckingham and Chandos (Colonial Secretary), 30 May 1868: Buckingham Papers, British Museum (BM) (now British Library) Add. Mss. 41,860, ff. 68–70).

Catholic hierarchy, and thinly supported in the country, few could have seen the changes in public sentiment and the developments in high politics which would effect their liberation and redefine their actions.[5] And yet there is a strong current in Irish history which should have alerted even contemporary observers to these possibilities. Public opinion in Ireland had been apathetic, even hostile to the Fenian rising, yet there was sensitivity about the rebels' punishment. Demands for clemency became a touchstone in Irish political life: 'For years to come "amnesty" was to be a means of keeping the cause of irreconcilable republicanism vivid in the minds of the people.'[6]

The disestablishment election of 1868, which Gladstone fought on the basis of justice for Ireland, produced an unprecedented closeness and mutual confidence in the alliance between Irish and English liberalism, and effusive praise for Gladstone as Ireland's saviour. The stoutly anti-Fenian Roman Catholic Bishop of Kerry, Dr David Moriarty,[7] in a letter congratulating Gladstone on his election victory, assured him that 'Since the days of O'Connell the public mind has not been so deeply stirred, nor has the people's faith been so trustingly given as it is now to you'.[8] The veteran Repealer Sir John Gray,[9] speaking in the second debate on the 1869 Irish Church Bill,[10] insisted that Gladstone was

5 There was an early (and largely unnoticed) indication that government might be prepared to look sympathetically at the Fenians' sentences. John Stuart Mill asked whether 'the very heavy sentences' passed on John Warren and Augustine Costello, the only two members of the crew of the *Jackmel* not to be released, might be remitted or mitigated. The Irish Chief Secretary, the Earl of Mayo, described the offences of the two prisoners and concluded that 'He was afraid the time *was hardly yet come* when it would be possible to enter into anything like a general consideration of the sentences passed upon the Fenian prisoners with a view either to a commutation or a remission of their sentences, and, therefore, he did not see any exception in the case of these two prisoners.' (3 *Hansard*, CXCIII, cols 1282–3; 16 July 1868: my emphasis). Five members of the *Jackmel* crew (William Nagle, Patrick Nugent, Andrew Leonard, Daniel Lee and Frederick Fitzgibbon) were indicted for treason felony but having been a year in custody were released from Mountjoy Prison on 5 and 6 May 1868, without being brought to trial. They gave undertakings to leave Ireland and not to return. Nagle promised to leave within five days and in the meantime not to communicate 'with any persons who I understand to be connected with the Fenian conspiracy, neither will I attend any public meeting or in any way place myself before the Public whilst I remain in Ireland'. The five left Ireland without fuss or notice (PRO FO 115/473).

6 Francis Stewart Leland Lyons, *Ireland Since the Famine*, London, Fontana, 1985, p. 137.

7 (1814–77). Educated in Ireland and France. In 1867 delivered an abusive sermon against the Fenians which was controversial at the time, and has since dogged his historical reputation. At one time suspected of Young Ireland sympathies, in later years he became a Unionist and anti-Home Ruler.

8 Moriarty to Gladstone, 28 November 1868, W. E. Gladstone Papers. BM Add. Mss. 44416, f. 273. In this long letter Moriarty went on to discuss Cabinet appointments.

9 (1816–75). Stood trial with Daniel O'Connell and others in 1843–4; editor, then proprietor of *Freeman's Journal*. MP for Kilkenny City.

10 Established Church (Ireland) Bill. Received Royal Assent as 32 & 33 Vict., c.42: Irish Church Act, 1869.

The leading Statesman of the day – the man whom the world would recognize hereafter as the great Statesman who gave peace and prosperity to Ireland, and strength and liberty to the Empire by the just and wise Irish policy he was originating – a policy that would identify his name with the first great effort during three centuries of English rule, to extend religious justice to the Irish people.[11]

But separatist (or advanced, as it was sometimes called) sentiment had not been extinguished, either by the Fenian débâcle or by the Liberal consensus; indeed the latter may well have served to revivify and stimulate a certain critical nationalism. Since a practical programme of separation had little scope in the 1868 election, amnesty for the Fenian prisoners became the vehicle to carry forward this apparently instinctive and ineradicable strain of Irish politics. The nationalist politician and poet Stephen Gwynn, an infant at the time of the Fenian campaign, was expressing the sentiment then already powerfully established when he described Ireland as a land 'Where to fail is more than to triumph/And victory less than defeat'.[12]

The amnesty campaign

In the summer of 1866 the wives and sympathisers of the Fenian leaders launched an appeal for the relief of the prisoners' dependants.[13] Thereafter began a campaign of resolutions and petitions praying for the release of the Fenians. Town councils and city corporations submitted clemency pleas, and throughout the autumn of 1868 candidates at the impending general election were canvassed and asked to declare themselves on amnesty.[14] An amnesty committee was

11 3 *Hansard*, CXCIV, cols 1834–5; 19 March 1869.
12 'A Song of Defeat'(1903), *Collected Poems*, London, Brickwood & Sons, 1923.
13 Mary O'Donovan Rossa was Secretary and Letitia Luby Treasurer. Their appeal was for support for the families of the rank and file. Under the heading, 'The State Prisoners: An Appeal to the Women of Ireland' they described the plight of the families: 'Every post brings us fresh applications from all parts of the Country. Our hearts are wrung with grief at the distressing accounts that daily reach us; but alas! We can give little help for our funds are almost exhausted, and money comes in very slowly' (*The Irishman*, 18 August 1866, 113a). The same issue reported the founding of an aid society in Australia: 'The movement was initiated a few weeks ago in aid of the wives and children of those Irishmen who have brought themselves within the power of the English authorities ruling in Ireland is progressing very satisfactorily' (ibid., 117a).
14 See David Thornley's scholarly *Isaac Butt and Home Rule* (London, MacGibbon & Kee, 1964, ch. I) for an account of the 1868 election and the several currents then moving through Irish politics. See also PRO HO 45/9329/19461 for a selection of the many petitions addressed to the Queen. One, dated 2 January 1869, is typical: 'The political prisoners have already suffered sufficient to vindicate the power of British Law . . . it would be most consonant with your Majesty's Royal Dignity and Honour, and more conducive to the peace of the Empire, to release the prisoners, than to permit them to remain longer in a captivity, the character and severity of which is opposed to the intelligence of the age, and the practice of all civilised countries in

established, counting among its leaders Sir John Gray. In the election itself amnesty became an important issue in several constituencies, although there was not sufficient time to rouse popular sentiment to the pitch it would achieve the following year.[15]

Gladstone's pledges, the first of which was redeemed with the disestablishment of the Anglican Church in Ireland, both satisfied Irish opinion and raised further expectations. Land tenure and educational reform were in the offing, and Gladstone's conciliatory inclinations were thought to extend to clemency for the Fenians.[16] The Roman Catholic hierarchy, anxious to receive the prize of denominational education from the Liberal government, and unremittingly suspicious of any movement associated with Fenianism, refused to endorse the amnesty campaign.

There was much disappointment when, in the midst of petitions, memorials, resolutions and collections for dependants, Gladstone announced a partial amnesty. Only forty-nine of eighty-one remaining Fenian prisoners were to be released, and of these the only leader was the frail and crippled Charles Kickham.[17] That decision, it has been argued, was critical to Irish politics: 'From that moment on a disappointed public opinion read with growing anger the reports which appeared continually in the popular press of prison harshness to the captives, of their shattered physical, and in some cases mental, health.'[18] With feelings rising, the amnesty movement split over tactics. One faction urged vigorous action such as monster meetings and strong proclamations to exert maximum pressure on Gladstone and his government; the moderates considered such a course to be self-defeating, likely to impede amnesty. The activists established a new Amnesty Association (as distinct from the Amnesty

relation to Political Offences.' In the aftermath of the Civil War the Americans had not thus harshly punished their defeated opponents. The petition concluded with the prayer that the Queen should exercise her prerogative of mercy 'during this Holy Christmas season, by restoring to their sorrowing relatives the political prisoners' (ibid., /79). By November 1868 nineteen of the largest Irish corporations and councils had adopted amnesty resolutions (*Nation*, 14 November 1868, 199c).

15 Thornley, *op. cit.*, pp. 54–6.
16 Typical of these raised expectations of amnesty was a meeting of Cork Town Council held on 6 November 1868. One of the speakers referred to the change of government, then imminent, and trusted that Gladstone would 'terminate the sufferings of those men. It was possible that Mr Disraeli who was rather eccentric, might do it; but they could not depend upon him, while they might with some confidence expect a Liberal Ministry to accede to the wishes of the country' (*Nation*, 14 November 1868, 199a).
17 Fifteen men were released in England, thirty-four in Australia (*Return of the Names and Sentences of the Fenian Convicts Now Proposed to be Released, Stating What Portion of Their Sentences is Unexpired, and Distinguishing Between Those Confined in Australia and Those in Great Britain and Ireland*, PP, 1868–9 [72], LI, 531). The sentences of those released ranged from life to five years' penal servitude.
18 Thornley, *op. cit.*, p. 66.

Committee) at a public meeting in Dublin on 28 June 1869. Newly out of debtor's prison, Isaac Butt was elected President,[19] and a number of leaders of Irish nationalist opinion, constitutionalists as well as revolutionists, followed him on to the committee. Demonstrations were immediately organised by the Association throughout the country, culminating in a meeting at Cabra (a Dublin suburb) on Sunday, 10 October 1869. This was attended, it was claimed, by 200,000 people.[20] Between 1 August and 31 August 1869, Butt claimed that a total of more than one million people had attended forty-three meetings organised by the Association. A national petition to the Queen carried 250,000 signatures.[21]

The shift in public opinion was demonstrated in the Tipperary by-election of November 1869. This arose from the death of the sitting MP, Charles Moore, a Liberal. Tipperary had a reputation for militancy on the national issue, and Isaac Butt was invited to contest the seat. He declined, on the grounds that he would be more effective working outside what he described as an alien Parliament. A replacement was found, a distinguished Roman Catholic barrister, Denis Caulfield Heron. Unanimously supported by the moderate nationalists, Heron was not acceptable to the militants because of his professional association with government.[22] It was in these circumstances that the convict Jeremiah O'Donovan Rossa was nominated, at a packed and boisterous meeting which bore every sign of prior preparation by Fenian organisers.[23] The contest that ensued tested the reforming and moderate nationalists against the more militant party which comprised Fenian sympathisers of various degrees, as well as those of strong, if unfocused, nationalist sentiment. In the event, there was a low poll, and, amidst allegations of intimidation, Rossa was elected.[24]

---

19 *Freeman's Journal*, 29 June 1869, 4c–e. Having been detained in Kilmainham Prison for some eighteen months, Butt made an agreement with his creditors (who were to receive his fees as they came in) and was released. See Terence de Vere White, *The Road of Excess*, Dublin, Browne and Nolan, 1946, p. 233.

20 *Freeman's Journal*, 11 October 1869, 3f–i, 4a–e.

21 Isaac Butt, *Ireland's Appeal for Amnesty*, London and Glasgow, Cameron & Ferguson, 1870, pp. 81–3.

22 The *Irishman* reminded electors of O'Connell's advice that they should not choose lawyers as their representatives because they would become legal officials and not be independent. 'As Castle counsel, Solicitor General, Attorney General, Mr Heron would have to pack juries, exclude Catholics, patronise informers, and persecute patriots. Save him from such a destiny of degradation, Men of Tipperary' (13 November 1869, 324c).

23 See the detailed account of the nomination meeting in the *Nation*, 27 November 1869, 227a–d.

24 The *Nation* was clear that Rossa's election was the result of the climate of fear in the constituency. Out of a registered electorate of 10,000 only 2500 turned out, and Rossa was elected with about 1200 votes. Those priests who had supported Heron had to have a police guard 'to protect them from a thrashing at the hands of enraged Christians of their own flocks' (23 December 1869, p. 558a and b). The Ballot Act of 1872 (35 & 36 Vict., c.33) was a response to allegations of intimidation, largely in Ireland. Certainly, by providing for secret voting (s.2) it reduced the opportunities for unfair pressure, from whatever source.

By-elections are apt to produce fluke results, easily overturned in general elections and signifying little. Despite the atmosphere of heavy intimidation in which it was conducted, the Tipperary by-election was widely recognised to fall into a different category. The *Nation*, A. M. Sullivan's organ of advanced (but constitutional) nationalist opinion, described it as 'unquestionably the most remarkable event of the kind which has taken place in Ireland since the memorable contest for Clare in 1829'.[25] Sir John Gray's pro-Liberal *Freeman's Journal*, swallowing its disappointment, agreed that something quite out of the ordinary had occurred. The result was 'one of the most remarkable and suggestive events of this the most critical period of our history'.[26] Indeed, this result foreshadowed the alliance between the 'direct action men' and the constitutional politicians which ten years later would lead to the formation of the Davitt–Parnell Land League. Dublin Castle was in no doubt that it had been disgraced by the result.[27]

As a convicted felon, Rossa was disqualified from taking his seat. The only difference electoral victory made to his prison life appears to have been a tightening of security. But the Tipperary by-election confirmed to Gladstone and the Irish constitutional politicians the importance of the amnesty issue. Undertaking reform in religion, land tenure and education, Gladstone sought to remove the loam from which sprang insurrection, conspiracy and unconstitutional politics. The Amnesty Association, the flood of memorials and petitions from the respectable and established classes of Ireland, and the Tipperary by-election all indicated that to his initial list of reforms he had to add the palliation of amnesty for Fenians.

Gladstone and amnesty

In his monumental study of Gladstone and Ireland, J. L. Hammond suggests why, in the middle years of his career, Gladstone appeared to neglect Ireland. It was not the disregard of ignorance but of necessity. Apart from his first Cabinet appointment (Secretary for War and the Colonies) in 1845, Gladstone's ministerial career was spent as Chancellor of the Exchequer; he was even, for a period of four months (1874) and then for more than two and a half years (1880 to 1882) both Prime Minister and Chancellor of the Exchequer. If it is for his

---

25 The *Nation*, 27 November 1869, 233a. The historic Clare by-election of 1829 confirmed Daniel O'Connell in the seat which he had won the previous year, but from which, refusing to subscribe to the Oath of Supremacy, he had been debarred at the King's insistence.

26 *Freeman's Journal*, 26 November 1869, 2d.

27 Fortescue to Gladstone, 25 November 1869, W. E. Gladstone Papers: BM. Add. Mss. 44122, f. 21. ('We are watching now for the telegrams from Tipperary, to see whether we are to undergo the disgrace of having O'Donovan Rossa elected. If he is not, he will be very near it. Heron has pandered to the mob as far as he dared, wearing a green sash on the hustings etc., and has failed in making himself popular.')

efforts to resolve the Irish problem that Gladstone is frequently remembered, to his contemporaries he achieved his pre-eminence through an overhaul of the nation's finances. This task, Hammond argues, precluded all others.[28] In his diary for December 1868 Gladstone thus referred to the insatiable demands of politics: 'Swimming for his life, a man does not see much of the country through which the river winds, and I probably know little of these years through which I busily work and live.'[29]

Immurement in office was not the only reason for Gladstone's silence on Ireland. His own mind was moving to the understanding and radical balance which would shape the politics of the latter part of his life, and tie so much of his ambition and reputation to the Irish conundrum. Ireland was certainly long embedded in his conscience. Had he followed Mary Tudor he could have said no more: 'When I am dead and opened, you shall find "Calais" lying in my heart.' For Gladstone it was Ireland. In 1845, at the age of 36, he had visited the French statesman and historian François Guizot on ministerial business. More or less in passing, Guizot had spoken about Ireland, saying that Britain would gain the sympathies of Europe in giving Ireland justice. Nearly thirty years later Gladstone reminded Guizot of the exchange, which he 'ever after saved and pondered. It helped me on towards what has been since done.'[30] To his wife he had written at the time,

> Ireland, Ireland! That cloud in the west, that coming storm, the minister of God's retribution upon cruel and inveterate and but half-atoned injustice, Ireland forces upon us these great social and great religious questions – God grant that we may have courage to look them in the face and to work through them.[31]

Gladstone's first reaction to the telegram of 1 December 1868, intimating the Royal Summons to government, is well known, if perhaps too convenient to be entirely sound in its provenance: 'My mission is to pacify Ireland.'[32] This determination and confidence had been solidifying into a definite shape for most of the preceding year. In a speech at Southport on 19 December 1867 (delivered,

---

28 *Gladstone and the Irish Nation*, London, Longmans, Green, 1938, p. 70.

29 John Morley, *The Life of William Ewart Gladstone*, London, Macmillan, 1903 (3 vols), Vol. 2, p. 256. He further recorded, 'I feel like a man with a burden under which he must fall and be crushed if he looks to the right or left or fails from any cause to concentrate mind and muscle upon his progress step by step.'

30 Gladstone to Guizot, Morley, *op. cit.*, Vol. 2, 240.

31 Gladstone to Catherine Gladstone, 2 October 1845, *cit.* Roy Jenkins, *Gladstone*, London, Macmillan, 1995, p. 276.

32 Supposedly recorded by Evelyn Ashley (Palmerston's former private secretary) who was with Gladstone at Hawarden when the telegram arrived. To complete the historic appositeness of the moment, Gladstone was at the time felling a tree (see Morley, *op. cit.*, Vol. 2, p. 252; E. J. Feuchtwanger, *Gladstone*, London, Allen Lane, 1975, p. 146).

it must be remembered, only six days after the Clerkenwell atrocity) Gladstone urged an analytical rather than an emotional response to Fenianism. He urged calmness, so that the processes of justice should not be disturbed, either in the jury-box or on the bench. And while he denounced the Fenian invasion of Canada ('inexcusable and abominably wicked'), he insisted that Irish grievances had to be addressed so that 'instead of hearing in every corner of Europe the most painful commentaries upon the policy of England towards Ireland we may be able to look our fellow Europeans of every nation in the face'.[33]

It was sometimes alleged against Gladstone that he had legitimised the Fenians by making it possible even for constitutional nationalists to concede that the Fenians had brought Irish grievances to centre stage.[34] In one sense that accusation is true: the activities of the Fenians convinced Gladstone of the urgent need to isolate the revolutionists. He wished to draw the Fenians apart from the people of Ireland, to isolate them politically. Time and again during the years 1868 to 1872 he emphasised the importance of Fenianism in questions of Irish policy.

In contemplating the insight, moral stature and craggy independence of mind which so elevated and commended Gladstone to his contemporaries and to history, it is inadvisable to forget that he was also a pre-eminent politician. His friend, disciple and biographer Morley considered him to be an opportunist.[35] Hammond read this as meaning that '[I]f you want to carry a reform you had better choose the moment when you are most likely to address yourself to public opinion with success'.[36] In politicians of the highest range of skill and vision, this sense of timing cannot be confused with a Robespierrian slavishness to popular sentiment. It was surely Gladstone's genius that in so many issues he penetrated the immediate and conventional to the paradoxical necessity: Ireland, it is true, ultimately proved to be his flaw, but so it has proved to every British politician since. In 1868 he told Lord Granville (then Secretary of State

33 *The Times*, 20 December 1867, 6a–c. On 2 December 1868, accepting the Queen's commission to form a government, Gladstone had a long conversation with General Grey, the Queen's personal secretary. He disclosed that he had made up his mind about the disestablishment of the Church of Ireland 'when reading, in the railroad, the account of the rescue of the Fenian prisoners at Manchester'. Gladstone emphasised that the decision had not been taken for party political reasons, believing, indeed, that 'it would have the effect of weakening his personal position, and he had been *astonished* by the way in which it had been taken up' (memorandum by General Grey, 4 December 1868, in George Earle Buckle (ed.), *The Letters of Queen Victoria*, London, John Murray, 1926, Vol. 1, p. 562).

34 Gladstone saw Fenianism as a symptom of misgovernment. This assessment was distorted by the Fenians' supporters and sympathisers. Writing to the Fenian leaders amnestied in January 1871, the Amnesty Association produced the following travesty: '[T]he Prime Minister of England has repeatedly and distinctly avowed that it is to the boldness of your conduct that Ireland owes the passing of those remedial measures to which English statesmen point as concessions to the Irish people' (*Freeman's Journal*, 10 January 1871, 4f).

35 Morley, *op. cit.*, Vol. 2, p. 241.

36 J. L. Hammond, *op. cit.*, p. 78.

for the Colonies) that for years past he had been 'watching the sky with a strong sense of the obligation to act with the first streak of dawn'.[37] The Fenian campaign of 1865 to 1867 was the dark interval which preceded that dawn.

There was abundant truth in the proposition that if the Fenians were a symptom of the misgovernment of Ireland, there was room for mercy in their punishment. Indeed, the darker Gladstone painted Ireland's grievances, the paler grew the Fenians' sins. Certainly in 1867 and 1868, amidst all the democratic promise of the new Reform Act, and talk of a conciliated and peaceful Ireland, expectations were growing that church, land and educational reform would be topped with clemency towards the Fenians. Only eighteen months before Gladstone formed his first administration, John Bright, who would be President of the Board of Trade in that government, presented the famous 'Positivist' petition to the Commons, praying, *inter alia*, for restraint of the soldiery, fair treatment of the Fenians before trial, and sentences 'as lenient as is consistent with the preservation of order'. In their imprisonment, it was urged, the Fenians should be spared punishment 'of a degrading nature' as inappropriate to men 'whose cause and whose offence are alike free from dishonour, however misguided they may be as to the special end they have in view, or as to the means they have adopted to attain that end'.[38]

From first to last, Gladstone's Irish policy was one of condemnation of Fenianism and all forms of extremism, combined with a programme of reform. Taking Fenianism as a symptom of bad government, it followed, or so Gladstone hoped, that good government would erode its influence, and, finally, wash it away. Speaking a month after the Manchester executions, he denounced Fenianism as 'a foul disease afflicting society'. He derided the defence of accidental death which had been offered by the Manchester defendants and refused to criticise the government in any way for its denial of petitions for mercy. The Clerkenwell explosion and the Canadian invasion fell into a similar category of crimes. In its calm and equable administration of the law in the face of such crimes, government deserved the strong and unflinching faith of the people. The lenient treatment of political offenders was 'a great advance in modern civilisation', as the civil war in America had shown, but he altogether denied that the recent crimes in England and Canada were entitled to 'partial immunity and leniency'. All of this, as might be expected, won the applause of his audience. But Gladstone was equally emphatic that indignation about Fenianism should not obscure Ireland's problems. The Fenian outrages might 'in the designs of providence'

---

37 Morley, *op. cit.*, Vol. 2, p. 240.

38 3 *Hansard*, CLXXXVI, col. 1931; 3 May 1867. The petition, which was angrily greeted by some Conservative members, also asked that during their sentences the Fenians and other political offenders should not be confined 'in common with prisoners suffering for offences against the ordinary criminal laws of their country'. It was known as the Positivist Petition because of the prominent Positivists, such as Congreve, Beesly and Harrison, who were among its signatories.

be intended 'to incite the nation to a greater searching of its own heart and conscience' regarding the condition of Ireland. There had to be long and patient reforms – he particularly mentioned education and land – in order to remedy the condition of Ireland and to capture 'those sympathies in Ireland which were now floating between law and lawlessness'.[39]

Two years later, having won government, his argument was bolder, less veiled. Penal and ascendancy laws had gradually been removed for a century or more, but he observed that agrarian disturbances had continued in Ireland, and indeed had grown. After Catholic Emancipation there were campaigns for the abolition of the tithe, and reduction of the county cess and rents: 'Still we went on without touching the laws that immediately affect the condition of the agricultural masses, except to aggravate the mischief at its sorest point by the Landed Estates Act, & the sale of the Tenant's improvements over his head.' Political reform, in other words, had failed to address the central issue, which was the land question. There was a paradox at the heart of Irish affairs. While political agitation had become more hostile and extreme, agrarian violence had become less savage – 'personal torture & wanton cruelties are not heard of'. The extreme and violent impulse seemed to have become political: 'Now therefore comes the last & extremist development of the political disease in the shape of the monster we term Fenianism – which represents the "irreconcilables" of France . . . Fenianism aims at giving to resistance the noble form of public war.'[40] The logic of this was clear. A constructive and pacific political and social agenda could proceed only if Fenianism were headed off.

Gladstone's allies and followers took a similar line of condemnation and reform. Only nine months before Gladstone took power, John Stuart Mill, the radical but influential voice of political economy, attacking Disraeli's Irish policy (a 'beggarly account of empty boxes'), urged generosity and imagination. As for the Fenians, their rebellion had been contemptible and there was no chance of conciliating them. The situation was more serious than at any time since 1798 because of several millions of Irish in America, whose political influence was constantly increasing and who hated Britain. Action on a much grander scale than had previously been contemplated was essential – the land tenure reform which Mill set out in some detail. It was a compelling speech because of the way in which it marshalled the facts that underlay the 'dangerous state of Ireland' and popular feelings of 'general discontent and wide disaffection'.[41] With the backing of such as Mill, and with the wind of triumphant reform behind him, Gladstone was as much the prisoner as the beneficiary of Irish hopes. Was it entirely reassuring that Dr Nicholas Conaty (Roman Catholic

---

39 Speech at Southport, Thursday, 19 December 1867: *Nation*, 28 December 1867, 293a–c, *passim*.
40 Gladstone to Fortescue, 26 November 1869, W. E. Gladstone Papers: BM Add Mss. 44122, ff. 23–4.
41 3 *Hansard*, CXC, cols 1516–32, *passim*.; 12 March 1868.

Bishop of Kilmore) should be moved to eulogy?: 'You have gained the esteem and won the confidence of every honest and well-disposed Irishman; for we are thoroughly convinced that since the Norman Invasion no statesman whether English or Irish ever entertained so sincere a desire or so honest a determination to do us justice.'[42]

These were the expectant circumstances in which Gladstone embarked on amnesty. It would, perforce, be carried out in two stages, the first being the release of the rank and file, and twenty-one months later (not anticipated at the outset) that of the leaders. The Fenian soldiers were excluded, together with several civilians who were not deemed eligible either because of the late date of their offences, or because their crimes were not thought to be exclusively political.

The first amnesty

Rumours of releases circulated through the autumn of 1868.[43] In early February 1869, Cabinet agreed to the release of some of the offenders, but the announcement of the first amnesty did not come until 21 February 1869 in response to an agreed question by The O'Connor Don.[44] The Chief Secretary for Ireland, Chichester Fortescue,[45] was emphatic that there would be no general amnesty.[46] Following the advice of Thomas O'Hagan (the Irish Lord Chancellor),[47] Spencer

---

42 Conaty to Gladstone, 3 August 1869, W. E. Gladstone Papers: BM Add. Mss. 44421, f. 230.

43 See, for example, the *Evening Star* (London), 10 October 1868, 5d, reporting that six Fenians were to be released from Dartmoor.

44 In early January 1870, The O'Connor Don had written confidentially to Fortescue about the prisoners, warning of a formidable campaign for their release (Fortescue to Gladstone, 7 January 1869, W. E. Gladstone Papers: BM Add. Mss. 44121, f. 92). Of the Cabinet only Lowe (the Lord Chancellor) opposed any amnesty at all.

45 Fortescue (1823–98) was born in Co. Louth, for which he became Liberal MP. Irish Chief Secretary during much of the Fenian period (1865–6 and 1868–70). Assisted Gladstone with measure to disestablish the Church of Ireland and 1870 land legislation. Granted peerage in 1874 on losing his seat. Influential voices had been raised in favour of a general amnesty.

46 W. Monsell, Liberal MP for Co. Limerick, and Under-Secretary of State for the Colonies, had urged the release of all the Fenian offenders who were not convicted of acts of personal violence, suggesting that it be linked to the repeal of the Party Processions Act, 1850 (13 & 14 Vict., c.2), which mainly affected the Orange Order. Monsell wished some of the amnestied to be expatriated for a number of years, 'but no act of repentance should be required of them – such a requirement would lead to lying and hypocrisy and would probably exclude from amnesty the most honest and best men. Simultaneously with these acts of grace, there should be the greatest determination shown by the government in dealing with agrarian outrage' (Monsell to Granville (Foreign Secretary), 7 January 1869; Somerset County Record Office (SCRO): Carlingford Papers: CP3/74). Granville had asked Monsell's opinion on the question of amnesty.

47 (1812–85) Roman Catholic. Advocated local government for Ireland. Solicitor General for Ireland, 1861; Attorney General, 1862; Irish Privy Council, 1862; Judge of Common Pleas; Lord Chancellor of Ireland, 1868 and 1880–8; Peer, 1870; Vice Chancellor, Royal University of Ireland, 1880; Knight of St Patrick, 1881.

(Lord Lieutenant)[48] and Fortescue, and in accordance with the Cabinet's uneasy acceptance of Gladstone's lead, distinctions were to be drawn between the prisoners in order to identify those who might with safety be released.[49] These were 'young men, hot-headed men, who were led in an excited moment into criminal acts . . . men, some of whom might be described as the dupes and tools of others'. As far as government could judge these would not be capable of leading any future insurrection.[50] The soldier Fenians were in a very different position, and would be denied amnesty. There were eighty-one Fenian prisoners under sentence of penal servitude – forty-two in Australia and thirty-nine in England – and of these it was proposed to release forty-nine unconditionally.[51] Of the men to be freed thirty-four were in Australia and fifteen at home. Thirty-two men would therefore remain in custody.

Those denied their freedom, Fortescue insisted, were 'deeply responsible' for the Fenian conspiracy, 'men whom the Government and the Lord Lieutenant felt it would not be consistent with their duty to discharge, or whose freedom would be compatible with the public safety'. There was no opposition comment, excepting a query from the former Home Secretary, Gathorne Hardy, as to whether those in Australia would have their passages paid home. A decision on this had not been reached, and Fortescue promised an answer the following day.[52]

Without advance notice, a first batch of eight men was released from Portland Convict Prison on 4 March 1869. Collected from their work party at 10 a.m. and returned to the prison, the men exchanged their convict uniforms for civilian clothing. Each was given £2 and a discharge notice and, at about 4 p.m., all

48 (1835–1910) The fifth Earl and was appointed to the Lord Lieutenancy by Gladstone in 1869. A strong supporter of Gladstone's Irish policies then and later, he helped to draft the first Home Rule Bill (1886).

49 The distinctions between the various categories had been proposed by Spencer and Fortescue. In drafting his announcement of the releases, Bruce (Home Secretary) advised Fortescue to be as clear as possible since it was certain that those for whom the weakest cases for amnesty could be made would be the basis of political attacks (Bruce to Fortescue, 2 February 1869; SCRO: Carlingford Papers: CP3/77). Bruce thought that conditional pardons would be useless and should not be required, short of expatriation on tickets of leave.

50 The only leader to be released was Charles Kickham whose case, Home Secretary Bruce observed, 'stands upon special and suff[icien]t grounds'. These were his illness and infirmity (Bruce to Fortescue, 2 February 1869; SCRO: Carlingford Papers: CP3/77).

51 These figures for Western Australia do not seem accurate, since although there had already been some releases of short-sentence men, this had not amounted to twenty by February 1869. It may be that Fortescue was discounting in Australia those who had been given tickets of leave, and thus were no longer prisoners, nor yet free.

52 3 Hansard CXCIV, cols 159–161, 22 February 1869; Flag of Ireland, 27 February 1869, 3c. On the question of passages home, Chichester Fortescue equivocated. The general policy was not to pay, unless conviction had been erroneous, but he gave no undertaking as to whether this general rule would be followed (3 Hansard, CXCIV, col. 209; 23 February 1869). The government clearly wished to avoid creating another difficulty by leaving any of the pardoned men stranded in Western Australia for want of passage money. In the event, abundant funds for repatriation (or travel to the United States of America) were raised by sympathisers in Australia.

were released.[53] Three others – Charles Kickham, C. M. O'Keeffe and William Moore Stack – were released from Woking Invalid Prison. No conditions were attached to the releases and, with one exception, all the men immediately made their way to Ireland. There was speculation that a general amnesty was imminent.[54]

Intense excitement greeted the releases, and this doubtless fuelled what would be counterproductive demonstrations and wild remarks: there was no indication of Fenian orchestration of these events. Enthusiasm was greatest in Cork. Although only three rank-and-file men returned there,[55] the rumour went around that three Fenian leaders – Captain Mackey, Colonel O'Brien and Colonel Burke – were on their way.[56] The news had been received late in the day, but a demonstration was immediately organised and a large crowd paraded the streets, accompanied by a band, and made its way down to the landing stage. The three

---

53 *Dublin Evening Post*, 9 March 1869, 4c; *Flag of Ireland*, 13 March 1869, 5a. The eight were: Coghlan, Barry and Sullivan; James F. X. O'Brien (sentenced to death for treason in 1867); Edward Butler and Terence Byrne convicted of participation in the rising outside Dublin; Michael O'Regan of Cork and John Haltigan, foreman printer of the *Irish People*. The *Manchester Guardian* reported that all complained of their treatment at Portland, 'which they assert to be of the most rigorous character permitted by prison discipline' (8 March 1869, 3e).

54 See, for example, *Irish Times*, 8 March 1869, 3g.

55 The three were John Coghlan, who had been shot by one of his own side in the attack on Ballyknockane police barracks, and sentenced to five years' penal servitude; Patrick Barry, who in 1865 had received ten years for seducing a soldier from his allegiance; and William O'Sullivan, who in 1867 had been sentenced to five years' penal servitude for participation in the rising (*Manchester Guardian*, 8 March 1869, 3e).

56 Captain Mackey (as his name is spelled in the official records; it was given as Mackay in the Irish newspapers) was in fact William Francis Lomasney (1841–84) who had been sentenced to twelve years' penal servitude for his part in the 1867 Fenian rising, and the attack on Ballyknockane barracks, Co. Cork. Born in Cork, he went to the United States of America at an early age, at that time assuming the name Mackey. He became a printer, and subsequently enlisted in the Union Army, where he attained the rank of corporal. He returned to Ireland in 1865 to take part in the Fenian rising, but was arrested on suspicion and shortly afterwards released for want of evidence. This brush with captivity notwithstanding, he became active in Fenian circles in England, where he was an associate of Deasey, Kelly and Michael O'Brien (who was executed for his part in the Manchester rescue). In the course of his arrest in February 1868 (on suspicion of the robbery of a gunsmith in Cork) he shot a policeman and was tried for murder but acquitted. He was then convicted of treason felony and sentenced to twelve years' penal servitude. Released in 1871, he settled in Detroit, where he ran a Roman Catholic bookshop. Described by Thomas Burke, the Irish Under-Secretary, as 'a man of intelligence' and a 'determined conspirator . . . more of the character of a Filibuster than a Patriot' (Burke to Fortescue, 25 September 1869, W. E. Gladstone Papers: BM Add. Mss. 44121, ff. 172–3). He continued as an active and daring Fenian, and returned to England to wage a dynamite campaign. In December 1884 he blew himself up while attempting to place a bomb under London Bridge. Colonel O'Brien was James Frances Xavier O'Brien (1828–1905) who had been sentenced to death for leading the attack on Ballyknockane barracks. His sentence was commuted to life penal servitude, and after release in 1869 (he had gone to Waterford rather than Cork) O'Brien took little part in Fenian activities, and became MP for Mayo (1885–95) and then Cork (1895–1905). Colonel Burke was Ricard O'Sullivan Burke (1838–1922): see p. 185 above.

leaders did not appear, but cheers were given anyway for the released prisoners. Another rumour had it that Mackey would arrive from Dublin by train, and large crowds, accompanied by four bands, made their way to Mrs Mackey's house and then dispersed peacefully.[57]

On the following evening the Cork demonstrations continued, reinforced by crowds of Saturday shoppers. Bonfires were lit, and bands paraded playing Irish airs; there were lighted tar-barrels and constant cheering. At 2 a.m. the crowds converged on the railway station, to welcome the Mayor, Daniel O'Sullivan (who was one of the founders of the amnesty movement), and in the vain hope of seeing 'Captain Mackay'. The enthusiasm scarcely waned, and on the Sunday morning rumours of Mackey's imminent arrival again brought crowds to the railway station and landing stage. Numbers were said by the *Flag of Ireland* to have far exceeded anything seen in the city since the day of the Manchester Martyrs' Procession.[58]

These may have been the largest demonstrations, but similar events took place in other cities, townlands and villages, particularly where there was a connection with the released prisoners: Kilmallock, Co. Cork, mounted a massive celebration for William O'Sullivan. Cheering crowds stood beside the railway line and gathered at intermediate railway stations. On alighting, O'Sullivan was escorted by several hundred people through decorated streets to his father's house. That evening, bonfires and tar-barrels were lighted and there were continuing processions.[59]

The Roman Catholic Church was divided in its response to the releases and the outbursts of popular enthusiasm – as it was on the national question generally.[60] Dr George Butler, Bishop of Limerick, willingly gave permission for a collection to be made on St Patrick's day at churches throughout his diocese in aid of the political prisoners and their families, expressing his sympathy 'for the sufferers' to a deputation which had waited on him for the purpose of soliciting permission.[61] Collections were also allowed by Bishop Keane in the diocese of Cloyne.[62] These concessions were strongly disapproved of by Cardinal Cullen, who, to the disgust of the nationalists and delight of the English newspapers, prohibited similar collections at churches under his control. The *Flag of Ireland*

---

57 *Dublin Evening Post*, 9 March 1869, 4c–d; *Flag of Ireland*, 13 March 1869, 5a–c. Thomas Burke, the Irish Under-Secretary, agreed that Mackey's release would be popular with the lower classes in Cork ('I am sure they would hail his return with delight') but thought that the respectable and loyal citizens had not 'the slightest sympathy with this mischievous and obscure conspirator' (Burke to Fortescue, 25 September 1869, W. E. Gladstone Papers: BM Add. Mss. 44121, f. 173).

58 *Flag of Ireland*, 13 March 1869, 5b.

59 Ibid., 5c.

60 For a discussion of the different factions within the Roman Catholic hierarchy see E. R. Norman, *The Catholic Church and Ireland in the Age of Rebellion: 1859–1873*, London, Longmans, Green, 1965, ch. 3 and *passim*.

61 *Dublin Evening Post*, 9 March 1869, 4d.

62 *The Times*, 18 March 1869, 7d.

sarcastically congratulated Cullen for his uncompromising support of the govern-ment, 'at the expense of those martyrs by whose sacrifice his Eminence hopes to secure the equality of his Church with all others'.[63] The *Pall Mall Gazette* pointed to the Cardinal's repeated condemnation of Fenianism and noted that his denunciation of the collections would encourage the middle and prosperous lower classes to 'defy the communists and be supported by their clergy'.[64]

On the basis of a parliamentary briefing, the *Irish Times* reported a halt to further releases, because of the recurrence of agrarian crime as well as the 'violent language' of some of the amnestied. Chichester Fortescue had asked the MPs John Maguire and McCarthy Downing[65] not to press him in the Commons, but to leave the issue of further clemency in the hands of the government 'on the understanding that they were not indisposed to consider it favourably in all cases where guarantees or assurances could be given of the convicts and refugees resolve not to renew their attempt against the public peace'. Active consideration had previously been given to the cases of three convicts who had not been part of the first group of releases, 'But the fiat has gone forth that further liberation cannot be sanctioned, and Ministers refuse listening [sic] to all representations on the subject.'[66]

But this was a halt rather than a cessation. Two and a half months earlier the Lord Lieutenant, Lord Spencer, had taken important soundings in Ireland, possibly at Gladstone's behest. He had asked Thomas O'Hagan, Ireland's Lord Chancellor, for his comments on amnesty. Starting from the fact that Fenianism was still smouldering in Ireland, and that it had great vigour in America, O'Hagan argued that under favourable circumstances it could be revived and developed, though he had never looked upon the organisation as 'substantially formidable' except in the event of a struggle with America, but it was an evil and retrograde influence in Ireland.

Popular representatives would press the government for an absolute and universal amnesty, but O'Hagan did not see how this could be granted, 'regard being had to the comparatively brief period which has elapsed since the outbreak and subsequent convictions, the open continuance of the movement in America and the want of any expressions of repentance or relinquishment on the part of its favourers here'. Something might be done, however. Distinctions might be made between various categories of the Fenian prisoners. The state of health of some might allow their release. Another group might be given clemency in view of the 'probable settlement of International relations on the subject of

---

63 *Flag of Ireland*, 20 March 1869, 4a.
64 *Pall Mall Gazette*, 23 March 1869, 11b, 12a. The paper added that 'still greater numbers, who joined the Fenian movement from sheer terror, will be reassured by the attitude of the Roman Catholic priesthood'.
65 McCarthy Downing (1814–79) was a Liberal Home Ruler. MP for Co. Cork December 1869 until his death in 1879. For Maguire see p. 234, n. 79 below.
66 *Irish Times*, 22 March 1869, 3h; *Manchester Guardian*, 22 March 1869, 2f.

naturalized citizens'. And for those who were not to be released it might be possible to mitigate their punishments by treating them as political prisoners: past usages and current continental practice would justify such a step. Concluding, O'Hagan urged serious consideration of this policy or some modified form of it, which might include expatriation 'or abandonment of treasonable practices or any other conditions'.[67] This statement from the Irish Lord Chancellor carried great weight with Gladstone and the Cabinet – the more so since it offered a politically prudent way forward. The first releases, of Fenian rank and file, the sick, and some Americans had followed within just eight weeks. The conditions of Rossa and the other leaders also improved around this time.

But, as noted above, government's hopes that graduated releases might avoid political excitement and nationalist triumphalism were dashed. The enthusiasm of the demonstrations surprised and alarmed loyalist opinion in Ireland, provoked criticism in England, and laid government open to the charge of political miscalculation. It is indicative of its degree of embarrassment that on the occasion when the inflammatory remarks of one of the men (Augustine Costello) were raised in the Commons, Gladstone was also asked about the claim of the Mayor of Cork, that he (Gladstone) was on their side, and would release the rest of the Fenian prisoners. Gladstone, who at that very time was attempting to convince his colleagues to agree to the release of the Fenian leaders, was able to reply, 'I have only to say that Her Majesty's government have formed no intention to release any more of the Fenian prisoners.'[68] Typically Gladstonian, this sounded much more decisive and final than was actually the case.

The behaviour of the amnestied and their supporters cut off further releases. In the words of the *Pall Mall Gazette*, a consistent critic of the amnesty, 'The Fenians shouted before they were fairly out of the wood, and now they have the satisfaction of knowing that they turned the locks securely on many of their friends.'[69] Yet it is easy to imagine the explosive emotions of men who had

---

67 O'Hagan to Spencer, 9 January 1869; NLI: O'Hagan Papers: Ms. 17, 873 (unfoliated). An imperfect copy of this letter survives as well as the original, indicating that Spencer may have sent a copy to Gladstone.

68 3 *Hansard*, CXCIV, col. 1999; 23 March 1869. At the time, Gladstone made the statement that he was in arms'-length contact with O'Donovan Rossa, via the nationalist MP McCarthy Downing, on the question of conditional amnesty.

69 30 March 1869, 4a. On release, the *Gazette* observed, 'the prisoners pass from the position of the Church under persecution to the Church triumphant. They are received everywhere with sympathetic acclamations. They glory in their crimes. They avow their determination to repeat them on the first favourable opportunity' (ibid., 25 March 1869, 1a). Fortescue resisted attempts to halt the releases then under way in Western Australia (3 *Hansard* CXCV, cols 856–7; 8 April 1869). Two years later, when the Fenian leaders were released, *The Times*, generally welcoming the step, cautioned against public receptions and demonstrations such as occurred during the first batch of amnesties: 'The friends of the captives have reason to remember with bitter regret the reckless language then used by conceited demagogues who cared only for self-display. The base ingratitude which they evinced towards the Government was calculated to check its generous impulses' (*The Times*, 20 December 1870, 7b).

been locked away for several years. Whatever caution they may have had (and these were inexperienced and rash young men of the rank and file) could easily be swept aside. Augustine Costello, freed from a twelve-year sentence, told a welcoming meeting at Ballinasloe that 'he would, as long as he had breath, conspire and plot against the English government'.[70] Asked about these remarks, Chichester Fortescue could only agree that Costello and his companion Warren (released from a fifteen-year sentence) had 'grossly and disgracefully abused the clemency of the Crown'. He added that as far as he knew, these were the only two who had so acted.[71]

On the nationalist side *some* lessons were learned. The embarrassment which the various demonstrations had caused the government (and Gladstone in particular) greatly moderated the welcome given to those amnestied in Australia, and who reached Ireland almost a year after those released from England. A large crowd assembled on the quay to greet ten men who arrived on 18 February 1870. There was none of the raucousness of the previous year and the crowd confined itself to cheering. That evening the men attended a performance at the Theatre *Royal*, and there were further demonstrations of welcome. The pit and gallery audiences stood, singing 'God Save Ireland' (a song eulogising the Manchester Martyrs), and the performance was suspended 'for a considerable time'.[72] This showed enthusiasm, but was much less provocative than the marches, bonfires, torchlight processions and incendiary speeches which had greeted the men's comrades. Subsequently there were some attempts at public demonstrations, but these lacked the support of the previous spring, and were dealt with easily by the police.[73]

The second amnesty

Despite the public embarrassment, Gladstone, behind the scenes, was already pressing for the far more difficult release of the Fenian leaders. The first mention of his campaign was probably on 27 January 1869; on 2 February, he brought the

---

70 Together with John Warren, Costello was arrested following the abortive voyage of the *Jackmel*, a Fenian arms supply ship which arrived on the west coast of Ireland after the Fenian rising had been defeated. Costello (who had not been transferred to an English prison, pending his appeal) had earlier rejected conditional amnesty (*Nation*, 27 February 1869, 441a).

71 3 *Hansard*, CXCIV, cols 1997–8; 23 March 1869. Rather confusingly, Fortescue compared the first release of the Fenians to the amnesty of the Chartists. In the latter case there had been free pardons, but after 'very careful consideration' it had been decided to discharge the Fenians without conditions, 'our deliberate opinion being that we were not discharging any person on whom it would be worth while to make the attempt to impose those conditions'.

72 *The Times*, 19 February 1870, 5e. At Cork the Mayor issued a proclamation forbidding processions with tar-barrels and bands to greet the released men (*Freeman's Journal*, 19 February 1870, 2h).

73 3 *Hansard*, CXCLX, cols 687–89; 22 February 1870. There were complaints, however, about Isaac Butt's speech at a welcoming banquet. The government chose not to make much of this, seemingly putting it down to the fervour of the occasion.

matter to Cabinet. A general feeling that further amnesty was premature was bolstered by indications that the Fenian conspiracy spluttered on in Ireland.[74]

In arguments with Spencer, Gladstone fully deployed a range of casuistical skills. It was not only a matter of choosing a quiet interlude to release the Fenians; their release emphasised the strength of government and would drive a wedge between Fenianism and the Irish people. The Irish law officers, Gladstone complained, seemed to think that the Fenian prisoners should be held until Fenianism itself had been suppressed. This, however, was 'a wrong conception of the question'. Rather, 'what we have to do is to defy Fenianism, to rely on public sentiment, and to provide (as we have been doing) the practical measures that place the public sentiment on our side, an operation which I think is retarded by any semblance of severity to those whose offence we admit among ourselves to have been an ultimate result of our misgovernment of the country'. Local (i.e. loyalist) opinion in Ireland had 'habitually & traditionally' exercised too much influence and had 'greatly compromised the character of the Empire'.[75]

Once embarked, for all his 'opportunism' Gladstone was single-minded, obstinate and tenacious. There was the difficulty of the reaction to the release of the first batch of low-ranking prisoners. The Queen read the Pall Mall Gazette's account of triumphant return, and its editorial condemnation of government's policy of clemency.[76] Alarmed by the prospect of disorder, and danger to the Prince of Wales, who was shortly to visit Ireland, she immediately wrote to Gladstone, who passed the letter to Spencer – 'obviously the proper person to give an opinion with authority' – who would consult with his law officers, the Under-Secretary and the Chief of Constabulary. As for himself,

> I cannot be surprised at the Queen's anxiety, we must not of course raise any phantoms, but nothing that rational & well informed persons would deem a risk ought to be run. I am rather sanguine in the matter but in Ireland they are better judges. I have not seen the article in the Pall Mall Gazette to which you refer, nor should I attach much authority

74 Thus on 22 March 1869, Colonel Hugh Annesley, MP for Co. Cavan, raised in the Commons the arrest in his county of one Smith, who had in his possession printed Fenian documents dated 1869. (This was strongly suggestive of the Fenian organisation continuing to function at a worrying level.) Was it the government's intention, Annesley enquired, to recommend the liberation of any more Fenian convicts? Confirming the facts of the arrest, Chichester Fortescue stated the government's ostensible position that no further advice would be offered to the Crown on the matter of Fenian releases (3 Hansard, CXCIV, col. 1904).

75 Gladstone to Spencer, 29 September 1870, W. E. Gladstone Papers: BM Add. Mss. 44539, f. 38.

76 Government policy, the Gazette contended, was taken in Ireland to be 'a distinct admission on the part of the Government of two things, each of which ought to have been denied in the most emphatic and strenuous manner. It admits, in the first place, that there is no moral guilt in insurrection . . . and in the next place, that the Government are afraid of the Fenians' (25 March 1869, 1a): see also Pall Mall Gazette for 27 March 1869, 3b).

to the opinion of that journal, & I own I do not infer that the purpose of the release of the prisoners has failed on account of improper or seditious language among them since their release. For our purpose & duty is to endeavour to draw a line between the Fenians and the people of Ireland, and to make the people of Ireland indisposed to cross it. But as to the general connexion of those who are Fenians already I do not expect much – when they have once committed themselves, their self love & pride become enlisted and the mere sense that their chances of proselytism are diminishing (if so it were) might increase their wrath.[77]

Spencer was an uncertain ally, at best, and in forwarding the Queen's expressions of concern, Gladstone sought to reassure and fortify. While the Queen's uneasiness was not to be wondered at, Gladstone wrote, he could hardly suppose that the Prince of Wales would be in any personal danger, though Spencer and his staff would be better judges of that. The *Pall Mall Gazette* may be right, but little weight was to be given to its authority. Gladstone could not agree that there was any proof of failure in conciliation. The object was to stop the manufacture of Fenians 'which has so flourished of late years'. It was even possible that success in this purpose 'might exasperate the Fenians that are & might make them more outrageous'.[78]

On 4 August 1869, Gladstone wrote to Chichester Fortescue, enclosing a letter from the Cork MP and newspaper owner, John Francis Maguire, who had proposed the release of the remaining Fenians.[79] He had not, Gladstone assured Fortescue, committed himself, 'but I thought it quite worth while that he should put his point in his own way'.[80] Fortescue responded that further releases were 'not open to consideration for the present'; The Irish Attorney General agreed.[81] Several weeks later Fortescue again confirmed that he could see no possibility of

77 Gladstone to General C. Grey, the Queen's Private Secretary, 28 March 1869, W. E. Gladstone Papers: BM Add. Mss. 44536, f. 134.

78 Gladstone to Spencer, 28 March 1869, W. E. Gladstone Papers: BM Add. Mss. 44536, f. 135. Gladstone knew that Fenianism could never be conciliated, as the pronouncements of the various factions into which it had by then split made abundantly clear. An address from the American faction led by John Savage was typical. It set aside as largely inconsequential the disestablishment of the Anglican Church in Ireland. Only Irish autonomy would suffice. As for amnesty, Gladstone should know 'that when released the political prisoners will not be regarded as pardoned felons, but as unjustly punished patriots', Catholic University of America (CUA): Fenian Brotherhood Papers: Box 4, item 12: Address of the Chief Executive and Council of the Fenian Brotherhood, 10 November 1869).

79 John Francis Maguire (1815–72), journalist, novelist, barrister, politician and newspaper owner. Founded the still-extant *Cork Examiner*; MP for Dungarvan, 1852–65, and for Cork, 1865–72. Four times Mayor of Cork.

80 SCRO: Carlingford Mss. CP1/58.

81 Fortescue to Irish Attorney General, 6 August 1869, W. E. Gladstone Papers: BM Add. Mss. 44121, f. 151. (Gladstone minuted this letter on 7 August 1869, noting, no doubt, the phrase 'for the present'.)

releasing the prisoners – 'or any of them' – at that time. 'Our conduct, if we did it would be regarded with indignation by all England & Scotland by all the upper classes here [in Ireland] and by a great many quiet law loving people who w[oul]d not venture to express their feelings.' Government had publicly asserted that it was holding only the dangerous Fenian leaders, and 'We have no sign of regret from them, nor promise of future peace.' The amnesty agitation being got up by Fenians and their sympathisers was being used by some politicians and joined unwillingly by some respectable people who had not the courage to refrain. There was some genuine feeling in the movement, but it was 'mistaken and mischievous'. It 'glorifies these men as heroes, denies the moral right of the Gov[ernmen]t to carry out the sentence of the law upon them, and in many cases demands their release in the name of justice instead of praying for it in the name of mercy.'[82]

That a section of respectable opinion had swung behind the amnesty campaign there could be no doubt. On Sunday, 10 October 1869, Isaac Butt's Amnesty Association organised a large demonstration at Cabra, on the outskirts of Dublin. This, Fortescue wrote to Gladstone, was not as large as the newspapers had reported (some 200,000) but it was, nevertheless, 'a most remarkable popular demonstration, very numerous, very orderly, very respectable in its composition'. On the platform, however, Fortescue observed, 'there was nobody of any social or political standing, and the speeches were such as to make compliance impossible, if it had been possible before.'[83]

As the petitions from solid constitutional nationalists and liberals continued to come in, Gladstone, Cabinet opposition notwithstanding, grew more convinced that some step had to be taken. In September 1869, Algernon Greville-Nugent, MP for Westmeath, forwarded a petition from citizens of Longford.[84] In response, Gladstone indicated that the amnesty question was 'assuming such an aspect' that it would have to go to Cabinet. Continuing agrarian crime 'is practically though not logically a bar so far as it goes in the way of leniency'. Gladstone had tried to obtain promises of future good conduct from those prisoners, 'but with a very limited measure of success'. He also privately informed Greville-Nugent that the soldier Fenians appeared to raise a 'special difficulty'.[85]

---

82 Fortescue to Gladstone, 25 September 1869, W. E. Gladstone Papers: BM Add. Mss. 44121, ff. 163–77, *passim*.

83 Fortescue to Gladstone, 12 October 1869, W. E. Gladstone Papers: BM Add. Mss. 44121, ff. 191–2, *passim*. Following this event Fortescue pondered the advisability of prohibiting large open-air demonstrations. There were also demonstrations in England by Fenian supporters and Radical sympathisers, but these, in the aftermath of Clerkenwell, were relatively small and ineffectual (see Bruce to Fortescue, 26 October 1869; SCRO: Carlingford Papers: CP3/95; *Freeman's Journal*, 11 October 1869, 3f–i, 4a–e).

84 See W. E. Gladstone Papers (BM Add. Mss. 44537, f. 70) for Gladstone's acknowledgement of the petition. Greville-Nugent (1841–1910) was Liberal MP for Westmeath, 1865–74. Groom-in-waiting to the Queen, December 1868 to April 1872.

85 W. E. Gladstone Papers: BM Add. Mss. 44537, f. 70; accompanying private letter.

There were growing signs that the amnesty campaign was drawing support from ever-widening circles, and was inflaming even moderate (and certainly constitutional) nationalist opinion. George Henry Moore, MP for Co. Mayo for more than ten years, addressed a Castlebar amnesty meeting on 12 September 1869. He referred to England as a country whose sceptre had been the sword, diadem the black cap and throne the gallows – 'that great pharisee of nations'. Every country in Europe wished to resist its oppression: 'England is steeped deep in the blood of India; red handed from the massacre of the women of Jamaica, she exists with the blood of 20 generations of dead Irishmen standing between her and God on high, and, with the bones of Irishmen still suffering in her dungeons, she calls upon us to applaud the proud policy of her government.'[86] Only a call for revolution was necessary to transform this oration into Fenianism. Despite the pressures on constitutional nationalism, Gladstone's public stance was apparently unyielding. Following an amnesty meeting at Limerick, Isaac Butt wrote asking Gladstone to show the same sense of justice that he had shown to prisoners in other lands. The reference was, of course, to Naples, and with acerbity Gladstone denied the parallels: 'In due course of justice, as fixed by the law of the land, the Fenian prisoners received a free and open trial, under a lawful government; and they were found guilty by juries of their fellow countrymen.' At Naples there had not been such due process, judicial sentencing or constitutional government. 'The acquaintance, Sir, which you possess with Italian history and affairs in addition to your many other distinctions, renders me glad to have the opportunity of addressing to you this reference to the facts.'[87]

To Henry O'Shea, who had written on behalf of the Amnesty Association, Gladstone was more conciliatory. The sentences had been justly imposed, the Fenian conspiracy was not extinct either in the United Kingdom or America, the prisoners had not abandoned their designs, and some Irish journals continued to be seditious. It was his desire to carry leniency 'to the furthest point which the supreme consideration of the public safety permits', and this had been shown by the release of the Fenian rank and file. The wider process of reform would continue in Ireland, but government could not now release the Fenian leaders: 'Were public mischief to arise in consequence of an ill-judged act of indulgence, wishes expressed even by large numbers of the people, would not avail to excuse the advisers of the Crown or to relieve them in any degree of their responsibility.' This 'painful question' should be left in the hands of

---

86 *The Times*, 17 September 1869, 10a. George Henry Moore (1811–70), MP for Co. Mayo, 1847–57 and 1868–70, educated at Oscott College, Birmingham, and Christ's College, Cambridge; an exemplary landlord; a founder of the soon-defunct Independent Irish Party. A substantial – even major – figure in Irish politics. For an interesting and informative short sketch of Moore and his associates see Terence De Vere White, *The Road of Excess*, op. cit., pp. 234–6.

87 Gladstone to Butt, 23 October 1869, W. E. Gladstone Papers: National Library of Ireland (NLI): Ms. 15, 738. This letter appeared in *The Times* (23 October 1869, 5d) and other newspapers.

government 'who have to decide if with the fullest knowledge and under the heaviest responsibility'.[88]

Even at ministerial level the Irish government remained unconvinced that amnesty was a timely or appropriate step, and in mid-October 1869 Fortescue drafted a letter to Isaac Butt which was generally agreed by the principal officers of the Irish government. Seeking to corral him he forwarded this for Gladstone's approval and signature.[89] The manoeuvre was clumsily executed, and Gladstone prepared his own version.[90] On its drafting, Gladstone commented, 'As you would not be satisfied without a rap at the Fenians I inserted a passage of that kind: but I feel afraid to mention "the constitution" as I suppose that the word has but a cold and hollow sound in the ears of the Irish people.' Gladstone had put in a passage of Bright's 'heartily adopting the refusal'.[91] Amended, the letter appeared in *The Times* the following week.[92] Henry Bruce, the Home Secretary, was against releasing the Fenian leaders, and Gladstone also gave him reassurances. At the same time Gladstone did not, privately at least, rule out the possibility of a further concession to Irish nationalism, provided that the government was not seen to be acting under duress. Writing to Archbishop Manning in the spring of 1870 he explained government's need to steer a middle course between the forces promoting and resisting change in Ireland. He was going as far as practical politics would allow.[93]

Chichester Fortescue felt overwhelmed by these pressures and his responsibility for law and order. A further amnesty was out of the question – indeed increased coercive powers seemed essential. Towards the end of November 1869, he urged Gladstone to give no encouragement to petitions, no matter how loyal and well intentioned the petitioners. He could not conceive of granting any such petition:

> The fact is that Fenianism has not been anything like as active or dangerous as it is now since the rising of March '67 – and every week proves this activity to be increasing. If we were to believe some of our best informants we should think an actual outbreak to be not far off, but things have not come to that yet. There is however great excitement,

88 *Freeman's Journal*, 22 October 1869, 2g.
89 Fortescue to Gladstone, 12 October 1869, W. E. Gladstone Papers: BM Add. Mss. 44121, ff. 190–1.
90 Dated 16 October 1869, W. E. Gladstone Papers: BM Add. Mss. 44422, ff. 216–19.
91 Gladstone to Fortescue, 16 October 1869, SCRO: Carlingford Mss. CP1/64.
92 *The Times*, 23 October 1869, 5d.
93 'But an undoubted terrorism prevails & if our remedy is refused by those in whose interest it is offered . . . & if through its refusal terrorism continues, on the one hand we shall be at the end of our tether as regards concession to justice, on the other we shall remain under one absolute obligation with regard to the maintenance of peace & order. These are grave subjects of reflection.' In thanking Manning for the support which his policy had received from the Irish bishops, Gladstone hoped that their 'discernment patriotism and influence' would continue to be exercised. (Gladstone to Manning, 1 March 1870, W. E. Gladstone Papers: BM Add. Mss. 44538, f. 86).

uneasiness & expectation of disturbance in some parts of the country. I hardly see the possibility of continuing to govern the country much longer without increased powers.[94]

Fortescue's senior officials were equally alarmed. Larcom's successor, Thomas Burke, wrote to Larcom about Fenianism, asserting that the country was in a worse state than it had been in the 1840s, 1850s or even during the more recent upheavals. The first amnesty had had a malign influence: 'Fenianism has been wonderfully stimulated by the release of the prisoners last Spring, the popular notion that the Irish Church Act was a concession made on its behalf, and lastly the Tipperary Election.' Ribbonism had also been revived by tenant-right agitation and the promised Land Bill. Added to these evils, 'a certain class of protestants' had a deep hatred of Gladstone's government: 'The result is that Sedition has become, one might almost say, the religion of the people.'[95] Burke worried that Fenianism had become much more secret and effective in its organisation than in 1867, making it hard for the Castle to learn its plans. Butt was the legal adviser to the Fenians (that is, the amnesty movement): 'I do not mean to say he is a Fenian, but he is all the more useful to them on that account.'[96]

Despite any exaggeration which might flow from Burke's distaste for Gladstone and his Irish policy, the picture he painted was not wholly inaccurate. Reports from police and resident magistrates were alarming. Cases which were serious enough to be reported to the Castle included murder, attempted murder, arson, cattle-maiming, sheep-killing, assaults, threats, ribbonmen activities, damage to property and to churches, Protestant meetings, illegal oath-taking and attacks on police. MPs were threatened and trains fired on, and Rossa's election in Tipperary was greeted by celebratory meetings in many of the principal towns.[97] Government's anxiety was reflected in the number of rewards offered, and the authorisation of gratuities to police. A rough count of these reports, as recorded

94 These views were shared by Spencer, Fortescue added. He also mentioned Judge Fitzgerald's opinion ('one of the coolest and most sagacious men on the Bench') that complete or partial suspension of habeas corpus would be necessary (Fortescue to Gladstone, 25 November 1869, W. E. Gladstone Papers: BM Add. Mss. 44122, ff. 19–20).

95 Burke to Larcom, 19 December 1869; NLI: Larcom Papers: Ms. 7694.

96 Ibid. Butt's motive was his 'overweening vanity' and a desire as far as possible 'to lower every one else to a level from which he can never again hope to rise'. Lord Spencer, the Lord Lieutenant, seemed a sensible man, interested in all developments, 'and if his mind were not warped by evil influences brought to bear on him' would form sound judgement about the state of the country. 'Evil influences' referred to Gladstone: Thomas Burke was, of course, thoroughly anti-Gladstone. This remarkable letter concluded with an unmet plea to Larcom: 'Now I have but one favour to ask of you – that you will burn this when you have read it.' Larcom's instinct as a collector of Fenian memorabilia was stronger than his obligation as a gentleman, or his bureaucratic caution.

97 National Archives of Ireland (NAI) Chief Secretary's Office (CSO): Registered Papers (RP): 1869, 136, *passim*.

in the registers, shows that in 1868 they numbered approximately 1500, compared to about 2300 in 1869 and 1870, and some 1900 in 1871. Thereafter, it is true, there was a gradual decline, but it was slight, and by 1875 the level of reporting was still the same as in 1868 – about 1500 cases.[98] Reviewing these reports one can see how cynically civil servants may have received the claims of Gladstone and some of his ministers in 1869 to 1870 that amnesty was possible because Ireland was progressively ever more peaceful.

The deteriorating situation in Ireland led Gladstone to conclusions diametrically opposed to Fortescue and his colleagues. Convinced that the cycle of disturbance, sedition, violence and state repression had to be broken, or it would continue indefinitely, he became more convinced of the rightness and urgency of his strategy, and the need for deft manoeuvre, even in the midst of what seemed to be a worsening crisis of security. John Bright was one of the strongest Cabinet advocates of further clemency, and in October 1869 Gladstone informed him that the time had come to answer the Irish petitions. Cabinet consent was required, yet the opinion of their colleagues was 'without exception against the release'. Amnesty's strongest point was that 'it would soften the popular feeling and facilitate the passing of a moderate Land Bill'. But Gladstone could not resist the Irish government – liberally minded and upright men – whose objections were strong and who, moreover, were 'answerable for the peace of the country & the working of the law'.[99] The time was therefore not ripe for Cabinet consideration. To this Bright replied that the agitation in Ireland had made release more difficult – but also 'more necessary at no distant period'. The response to the Irish petitions 'should be soothing but firm'. It was a matter of timing: 'to release the prisoners immediately after the meetings and *menaces* in Ireland would be to prostrate the Government at the feet of the movement.'[100] Gladstone was taken with Bright's approach, and communicated it to the Prince of Wales and the Queen: 'I like so much the mode of expression that I must try to crib some of it for my reply now on the anvil.'[101]

Agrarian violence continued, and Fortescue repeatedly pressed for a strong legislative response such as the suspension of habeas corpus. To Gladstone this was simply another turn in the spiral from which he sought escape. He temporised by suggesting (improbably) that Irish opinion should be gathered behind the government *before* enacting emergency legislation. Unjust land laws had to be changed in order to give the agricultural population proper conditions of life,

98 Ibid.: 1868: 133; 1870: 139; 1871: 142; 1872: 145; 1873: 148; 1874: 151; 1875: 154. For Chichester Fortescue's summer of agrarian outrages see his first reading introduction to the Peace Preservation (Ireland) Bill on 17 March 1870: 3 *Hansard*, CC, cols 81–106.

99 Gladstone to Bright, 13 October 1869, W. E. Gladstone Papers: BM Add. Mss. 43385, f. 46.

100 Bright to Gladstone, 15 October 1869, W. E. Gladstone Papers: BM Add. Mss. 44112, ff. 95–7.

101 Gladstone to Bright, 16 October 1869, ibid.: BM Add. Mss. 43385, f. 49. A piece of manipulative flattery from a man who never needed to borrow words from another?

and, once that had been done, there might be support for the suspension of habeas corpus – 'if it shall then prove to be our deplorable & disgraceful necessity which God forbid, or for anything else.'[102] Reading this exchange, one is tempted to conclude that Gladstone's reaction was simply a *show* of unwillingness. He knew that a strengthening in the coercive response to lawlessness was desirable and inevitable, but while clearing the way for the necessary legislation he wished to draw Fortescue into agreement – even if it were only tacit – with his own Irish strategy. This was not far from horse-trading.

In Dublin, Fortescue and his colleagues fretted away, daily police and intelligence reports confirming their worries. There was general agreement between them, Fortescue wrote to Gladstone:

> Fenianism embodies the issue of national independence, and of national vengeance upon England, which has sprung up hotly in many Irish minds under the influences of freedom and education, following a dreadful & humiliating period of serfdom, submission & ignorance – and it is certainly the highest form of 'disturbance' that has yet arisen in R[oman] Catholic Ireland, excluding the Protestant revolutionists, Wolfe Tone, Emmet, etc.

That the Fenians dreaded a successful Land Bill was proved by their disruption of land law reform meetings. But all that having been said, the immediate duty of the Irish government was to keep down Fenianism and Ribbonism and avert insurrection and murder under a constitution 'framed for Yorkshire & the Lothians'. He hoped it would not be necessary to ask for exceptional powers and would only do so out of dire necessity.[103]

The Land Bill proceeded, and the dialogue between Gladstone and Fortescue scarcely altered – strategic ambitions on the one side and domestic urgency on the other. In the midst of a long and complex letter about the Land Bill, Fortescue again ventilated his worries: 'I don't like the state of the country at all. The recent murderous outrages have been very bad, & the system of terrorism & sense of alarm in some districts are more intense than ever.' He promised for the Cabinet (though Gladstone may have wished otherwise) a printed statistical report on the previous year's crime, together with 'very instructive' accounts from the Crown Solicitors of the disturbed counties.[104]

---

102 Gladstone to Fortescue, 26 November 1869, ibid.: BM Add. Mss. 44122, f. 23.

103 Fortescue to Gladstone, 30 November 1869: BM Add. Mss. 44122, ff. 30–2. The Law Officers were examining the back copies of the *Irishman* and the *People of Ireland* to see if treason-felony prosecutions might be brought. Both editors, 'we have great reason to believe', were 'leading and trusted members of the Fenian Society'. No steps would be taken, however, without the assent of Gladstone or the Cabinet (ibid., ff. 33–4).

104 Fortescue to Gladstone, 7 January 1870: BM Add. Mss. 44122, ff. 124–5. It is interesting that Fortescue's pessimism was shared from the dispassionate distance of the Washington *Nation*

Reversion to traditional repressive legislation would unhinge Gladstone's hoped-for Irish policy. Before the Cabinet could agree on the suspension of habeas corpus, he told Fortescue, the whole case for it would have to be set out, and it should be realised that there would be a considerable political backwash: 'I can hardly overstate the gravity of the case: the first effect of it would be – I feel satisfied – Bright's resignation, and you may readily judge of the aspect that would bear in Ireland.'[105] And while the forces of law and order called for action, demands for clemency for the Fenian leaders continued. Travelling back from the United States of America to seek a personal interview with Gladstone, Rossa's wife had submitted another plea for his release, stating that on her recent visit to him at Chatham she had obtained his agreement to permanent expatriation as a condition of liberty.[106] Mary O'Donovan Rossa had pleaded her husband's case well, but whatever his inclinations, Gladstone was at pains not to alarm Fortescue, whom he assured that there could be no movement on Rossa's case: 'It is too plain I fear that circumstances do not allow us to comply with his wife's prayer.'[107]

By the spring of 1870, Gladstone's balance between firmness and palliation had begun to assume legislative form and practical effect. The Irish Church would be disestablished as from 1 January 1871; land tenure laws would be reformed, and steps taken to strengthen law and order. The rank-and-file Fenians – dupes and tools – had been released, and the prospect was held out of an amnesty for the leaders. On St Patrick's Day 1870, Gladstone had signalled his intentions to the Commons, and to the Irish nationalist leadership there and in Ireland.

which described Gladstone's Irish problems as having entered 'a new and extraordinary phase . . . a sea of trouble, of which no man can see the end'. All of Gladstone's concessions had the appearance of coming in response to intimidation: 'There is probably not an Irish Catholic who does not ascribe the change of policy to pure, unadulterated fear.' Fenianism and agrarian violence supported each other: 'The tenants "help along the cause" . . . by killing landlords, robbing houses of arms, and serving notices of an early death on persons interfering with actual possessors of arms. They no longer, as a priest remarked the other day . . . take the trouble to form organisations for the commission of outrages; each individual, when he finds himself in the vein for it, without communicating his purpose to anybody "takes his revolver and tumbles his landlord" without more ado. Nobody sees him, or, if anybody does, he knows better than to swear against him, and juries know better than to convict him' (*Nation*, 234 (23 December 1869), 557b, 558a). The piece could have been written by Fortescue himself.

105 Gladstone to Fortescue, 2 March 1870: SCRO: Carlingford Papers: CP1/104.

106 See W. E. Gladstone Papers: BM Add. Mss. 44306, ff. 247–9; Mary O'Donovan Rossa to Gladstone, 15 February 1870: 'Sir, You have denied me the favour of a personal interview and I felt deeply disappointed at that denial.' She pointed out that she had travelled 3000 miles in midwinter 'for the sole purpose of pleading a cause which you will not hear'. Rossa would prefer to go to America if released, but would accept exile elsewhere should that be required 'and I am willing to share it'. It was a thoughtful, dignified and moving plea for her husband. Gladstone immediately began to make inquiries (ibid., ff. 250–68, *passim.*).

107 Gladstone to Fortescue, 2 March 1870, *op. cit.* He also asked Fortescue for further information on 'marked or palpable signs . . . of Fenian action in Ireland at this moment, which justify our regarding it as an obstacle to our efforts'.

Government was engaged in an extensive programme of legislative reform, but was being compelled to interrupt this with a measure (the Peace Preservation (Ireland) Bill) which was necessary to secure life and property in Ireland. Only when a better state of affairs prevailed in Ireland – and that would come in part from the mixture of repressive and reformatory legislation – would it be possible to extend the programme of amnesty which had begun the previous year. Until Ireland was in a peaceable state it would be 'cruel to encourage the friends of these prisoners to cherish any hopes whatever with regard to their release'.[108] Coercion and firm language helped to rebalance the scales, which had begun to swing against Gladstone because of the many reservations in his own party, Tory opposition, and reckless and inappropriate Irish responses to the first wave of releases. Retrimmed, Gladstone resumed his course.

The Irish government had to listen to the concerns and daily complaints of landowners, magistrates and the loyalist community generally; it was also acutely aware of where blame would fall should the fabric of order rupture. The differences of emphasis, and even of approach between the Irish ministers and Gladstone therefore persisted. Unconditional amnesty could not be carried in these circumstances, and so Gladstone struck out in a new direction. On 3 September 1870, he addressed Spencer on amnesty. 'Has not the time now arrived', he wrote, 'when we may again consider the question of releasing the batch of Fenian prisoners whom we still hold in durance?' Having deliberated with the Foreign Secretary (Granville) and with Fortescue, Gladstone now proposed a significantly modified scheme which would avoid the embarrassing scenes and excesses of the earlier releases. Timing was important, and it would be 'a great advantage' to release the men 'when the agitation for their release seems absolutely dead'. Although the campaign might thereafter revive 'I suppose that banished from this country as a condition of release, they would be very little able to do mischief'. Fenianism, moreover, 'had its root in bad laws' and there was therefore 'something of pain & scandal in prolonging the memory of this outbreak after we launched our main remedies, unless it be absolutely required by the necessities of public order, of which you will be the proper judge'.[109]

Exercising what amounted to his veto, Spencer replied immediately that the time had not yet arrived to release the remaining Fenians.[110] His letter

108 3 *Hansard*, CC, cols 80–1; 17 March 1870.
109 Gladstone to Spencer, 3 September 1870, W. E. Gladstone Papers: BM Add. Mss. 44539, f. 22, *ob*. The notion of exile following release had variously been discussed throughout 1870. In January, the Irish bishops, in Rome for the First Vatican Council, favoured amnesty as a means of stopping the 'wild and seditious meetings' then going on in Ireland. They argued that the Fenians ('wild beasts') could subsequently be deported (Bodleian Library, Oxford, Clarendon Papers: c.487, f. 120: Odo Russell to Clarendon, 24 January 1870). The precise origin of the idea of expatriation is, however, unclear. (Odo Russell was the British agent to the Vatican; Lord Clarendon was Foreign Secretary.)
110 Spencer to Gladstone, 5 September 1870, W. E. Gladstone Papers: BM Add. Mss. 44306, f. 312.

crossed with one from Gladstone informing him that the American government was being pressed by Congress to endeavour to obtain the release of William Halpin.[111] The applications thus being made 'cannot long be withheld'. Gladstone raised the matter because 'the moment of calm [is] so plainly the proper one for considering this subject'.[112] Spencer and several of his officials (including the Irish Attorney General and Thomas Burke, the Under-Secretary) remained unconvinced, and sent a full statement of their views to Gladstone. He well understood Gladstone's desire to be rid of the political prisoners, Spencer wrote, since their continued detention kept up an angry feeling between the two countries 'and affords an argument by which Fenians can enlist the sympathies of other Irishmen who are not revolutionary in their views'. He acknowledged the importance of granting any amnesty in tranquil times, and also accepted that Fenianism, at least in part, had its origins in laws, some of which had recently been altered by Parliament and 'it would be agreeable & proper to release those who are now in prison; if necessities of public order admitted it'.[113] The last, however, was the hook on which Spencer continued to hang his objections.

Fenianism, Spencer argued, was by no means dead: 'its organisation is still complete & is supported by large numbers of the population'. In seizures of arms and papers and in continued fund-raising there was evidence of the persistence of the Fenian organisation, which awaited 'any occasion of English difficulty' to make a move. To grant an amnesty would indicate that government thought Fenianism all but finished, and this would encourage the active plotters to proceed. There was also the matter of agrarian violence in the coming autumn and winter. Even if Fenianism were quite unconnected to agrarian crime it would have an unfortunate effect if amnesty were to be accompanied by agrarian troubles; and amnesty might, indeed, be taken as a relaxation of law. At this time migrant farm workers were returning from England to the West of Ireland, and were said to be 'steeped in Fenianism': no doubt these were the men who contributed to the disturbances of the previous winter, and if Fenians were to take a hand in agitation things could be even worse. An amnesty should not be considered until January 1871, when it would be possible to see how these various forces had developed. Should there be a quiet winter, Spencer assured Gladstone, 'I should be the first to recommend the release which with all submission I fear would not be judicious now'.[114]

---

111 On Halpin see above, p. 153, n. 51; below, pp. 249–50.

112 Gladstone to Spencer, 5 September 1870, W. E. Gladstone Papers: BM Add. Mss. 44539, f. 25. A copy was sent to Fortescue.

113 Spencer to Gladstone, 13 September 1870: SCRO: Carlingford Papers: CP2/15, f. 1.

114 Ibid., ff. 2–3. Spencer mentioned the possible adverse effects of the Franco-Prussian War as yet another reason for caution. He also wondered what effect an amnesty would have on the work of the Devon Commission: would it not 'bring its work to a sudden conclusion, and prove that it was never necessary'. This last, he conceded, 'may be of small moment'.

This was a comprehensive, if somewhat eclectic and contrived statement of the arguments against amnesty and Fortescue added his voice to that of his colleagues. 'Grave as the responsibility will be of releasing the remaining, and the leading, Fenians,' he wrote, 'I hope we shall find our way to it before long – but I see great difficulties in coming to that decision at this moment.' Fenianism was still alive, and if it should revive after the release of the leaders, it was desirable that Parliament should be sitting. The existing measures dealt far more effectively with agrarian than political crime ('with wh[ich] nothing copes more effectually but the suspension of the Habeas Corpus'). The releases should be no earlier than January 1871; in other words, so that if need be the amnestied leaders and whatever new ones came forward might be reimprisoned by executive action.[115]

Once again French and Irish affairs were seen to intersect. The Second Empire had been overthrown, and the forces which would establish the Commune were already mobilising. Perhaps another wave of incendiary republicanism was about to break across Europe. Would it not be better to await the outcome of these momentous developments, Fortescue wondered, before going forward with amnesty for the Fenian leaders? 'There w[oul]d be an appearance of weakness and untimeliness in letting out our Irish republicans at a moment when a French republic has started, which may possibly degenerate into something Red and revolutionary. I think we shall be in a better position to decide the question say two months hence.'[116]

All of this vexed Gladstone, but caused him little pause. He took Spencer's letter to Granville, his new Foreign Secretary, who pronounced himself unconvinced by the case that the Irish government had made.[117] Fortified, Gladstone then replied to Spencer. Release 'belongs to a policy of confidence, their continual confinement to a policy of mistrust & apprehension.' While government could not put down Fenianism, it should surely aim to estrange it from the Irish people, and especially the rising generation. This was the context in which amnesty ought to be considered. 'We know,' Gladstone insisted, 'from unexceptionable evidence' that the sufferings of the Fenians 'by which I mean simply their continued imprisonment' tended to gain them the sympathy of 'multitudes of men who are not Fenians'. As to their influence when removed to the United States of America, Gladstone discounted it. But even were they to reinforce the American Fenians, 'there would be more than a countervailing advantage in liberating the American government from its difficulties, strengthening our case for urging on them a course of systematic repression of hostile manifestations & emboldening them to face the clamours that have made them at times slack in their duty'. Should the Fenians refuse release because of the condition

---

115 Fortescue to Gladstone, 9 September 1870: BM Add. Mss. 44122, ff. 161–2.
116 Ibid., ff. 162–3.
117 Granville, formerly Colonial Secretary, had been promoted to the Foreign Office in June 1870, on the death of Clarendon.

of expatriation, 'then we stand clear'. As had Fortescue, Spencer also raised the possibility of the Fenians removing themselves to France, whose new Republic was viewed with considerable suspicion by liberal as well as conservative Europe. Gladstone's response verged on the derisive: 'As to the Republic in France, is it meant that these men are to be prisoners as long as it exists?' Answering his own question, he said only until that Republic was proved harmless, and that looked like a mere matter of weeks. 'The difficulty is more likely to be, to prevent the French Republic from becoming ridiculous.'[118]

As Lord Lieutenant, Spencer did not sit in the Cabinet; Fortescue, as Irish Chief Secretary, did, and Gladstone (perhaps anxious to avoid a memorandum to the Cabinet) encouraged Spencer to state his views through Fortescue. This he did in almost exactly the same terms as he had to Gladstone in his long letter of 13 September. He added one point which would become significant. The Fenian organisation was intact and arms were actively being imported. Prosecutions were impending (this almost certainly referred to Michael Davitt and his associates) and it would surely be inconsistent 'to let out one batch of prisoners & prosecute others for recently committed acts of the same character as those for which the released men were punished'.[119]

On 30 September 1870 Gladstone took his amnesty proposals to the Cabinet, where he failed to secure the support of his colleagues.[120] The door was not completely shut, since it was decided to accept the advice of the Irish government and to postpone action until there had been a chance to digest the experience of the short days. Gladstone's minute on this decision also makes it clear that the Fenian soldiers would not be included in any eventual amnesty.[121]

This emphatic defeat was no greater an inconvenience than an adjustment in Gladstone's timetable – and it may even be that he had anticipated that the plea for a few months' delay would triumph, and was happy enough to trade that against the unequivocal commitment of Fortescue and Spencer that amnesty could proceed should serious agrarian trouble be avoided during the usual season. In any case, events on the ground were always open to interpretation, and Gladstone was not to be prevented from reading the runes as he wished. It was also likely that, having overruled its leader on one occasion, the Cabinet would

---

118 Gladstone to Spencer, 14 September 1870, W. E. Gladstone Papers: BM Add. Mss. 44539, f. 28. Napoleon III had been captured at the rout of Sedan on 1 September 1870, and the Second Empire had fallen. France again wore a revolutionary aspect, but Gladstone's estimation of its weakness was correct.

119 Spencer to Fortescue, 28 September 1870; SCRO: Carlingford Papers: CP2/16. He concluded, 'I shall be most anxious to hear the result of the Cabinet.'

120 Fortescue immediately passed the good news to Spencer, whose joy was tempered by fear of Gladstone's reaction: 'I was greatly pleased to receive your letter about the Cabinet, I am hoping to see Mr G. this afternoon but rather tremble at his reception. I hear that no one backed him up' (Spencer to Fortescue, 2 October 1870; SCRO: Carlingford Papers: CP2/17).

121 H. C. G. Matthew (ed.), *The Gladstone Diaries*, Oxford, Clarendon Press, 1995, Vol. 7, p. 372. The proposal considered by the Cabinet excluded 'those not merely political offenders'.

be unlikely to do so a second time, except for the most compelling of reasons –
and the continued seething and low-level violence of the Irish peasantry was
hardly such a cause.

In those seasons of short days matters developed in such a way (or so were
represented by Gladstone) that just over two months after his Cabinet defeat
Gladstone was able to dispatch to Dublin a letter which prepared the way for
a public announcement of the amnesty.[122] There was a last-minute hitch while
the clause of the conditional licence requiring expatriation was checked by the
English law officers. Fortescue complained to Gladstone of delays in getting a
response, although he was emphatic that the legality of the licence had to be
assured and exile enforceable – 'unassailable by Butt & Co., who w[oul]d pounce
upon a flaw or a doubt in a moment, and we sh[ould] never hear the end of it.'[123]
A few days later, the English law officers advised conditional pardon rather than
release on licence, and, despite the consequent misgivings of the Irish law officers,
on 15 December 1870, a letter was sent over Gladstone's signature to Sir William
Carroll, former Lord Mayor of Dublin, who had headed the amnesty petition.[124]
Carroll was an obvious person to whom the news should be communicated, since
the debate on the resolution of Dublin Corporation in favour of amnesty had made
clear the Corporation's total antipathy to the course the Fenians had taken.[125]

---

122 To the very last Fortescue remained doubtful about the releases. Events in Europe seemed to
be developing towards war, with Britain being dragged in. Release under such circumstances,
Fortescue argued, 'w[oul]d be set down to fear by all evil disposed persons and partizans here
[in Ireland]' (Fortescue to Gladstone, 27 November 1870, W. E. Gladstone Papers: BM Add.
Mss. 44122, f. 172).

123 Fortescue to Gladstone, 11 December 1870, ibid., f. 181. The problem the Irish law officers saw
was that a conditional pardon might not give the power of re-arrest were the condition
violated. Fortescue tried to postpone the release yet further to allow more checking, but was
pre-empted by Gladstone privately informing McCarthy Downing, the nationalist MP, who
immediately telegraphed the news to Dublin (Fortescue to Gladstone, 18 December 1870,
ibid., ff. 195–8; Gladstone to Fortescue, 23 December 1870, ibid., ff. 205–6; Fortescue to
Gladstone, 24 December 1870, ibid., ff. 207–10).

124 Gladstone to Fortescue, 9 December 1870, ibid., ff. 179–80; the Nation, 24 December 1870,
295c. The letter was drafted by Fortescue in consultation with Spencer. Fortescue was keen
that it should come from Gladstone ('As the memorials have been generally addressed to you
and last year's refusal was signed by you') rather than himself – there was no desire to partake
in this particular piece of glory (Fortescue to Gladstone, 1 December 1870, W. E. Gladstone
Papers: BM Add. Ms. 44122, ff. 175–6). The draft, with two amendments, was approved by
Cabinet on 9 December, with instructions that it be issued immediately. Fortescue had, with
the amnesty, reached the end of his tether in Ireland. The work was gruelling and had imposed
a great strain on his relationship with Gladstone. He was offered removal to the Board of Trade
– a sideways move rather than a promotion – and was urged by his friend W. K. Grenfel to
accept: 'The education question will crucify you between the thieves of bigotry and Enlightenment, the pandering to Fenianism & popery which Gladstone seems to be doing will be held
rightly or wrongly to be caused by you and your Irish constituency' (Grenfel to Fortescue
(marked 'Secret'), 20 December 1870: SCRO: Carlingford Papers: CP3/115).

125 Freeman's Journal, 24 November 1870, 3b, 4a–c.

The central points of the announcement were that the prisoners had been justly convicted, for had they succeeded in their conspiracy they 'would have filled Ireland with misery and bloodshed'. Ireland was secure and at peace, however ('a most marked improvement upon that which prevailed a year ago') and amnesty was therefore possible. The step was perfectly compatible with public safety, and would 'tend to strengthen the cause of peace and loyalty in Ireland'. Those amnestied would be required to quit the United Kingdom, and not return for various specified terms.[126] The latter was a condition over which the prisoners themselves had at first baulked, and which Rossa described as 'our banishment from prison'.[127]

Negotiations had been going on with the prisoners since the spring of 1869, partly through Mary O'Donovan Rossa, and also through McCarthy Downing. The issue of exile was an extremely sensitive one among the prisoners, and no one wished to assume the lead lest it was taken as a break in solidarity and a weakening. Rossa, in March 1869, gave McCarthy Downing a letter accepting expatriation as a condition of amnesty, but asked him to keep it confidential until it became clear that this proposal was going to be acceptable to government. He wished to avoid the humiliation of agreeing to conditions which the government might reject; he also did not wish it to appear that he had asked Downing to intercede on his behalf. His wife gave a hint to some supporters in America that conditional release might be in the offing, and they indicated their opposition to the idea. This long-distance patriotism infuriated Rossa, who fumed to his wife, 'By jove they *are* spunky . . . I have met hundreds of men who would die for Ireland and have often lamented my own deficiency in this respect. I could never work myself up to more than a revolution to risk life, and then ever permeated with a strong hope and desire of living.'[128] But while he was willing to agree to expatriation, he would not himself approach the government, nor was he content that his wife should do so. She had written to Gladstone (without Rossa's permission) and his view was that if Gladstone agreed to amnesty and expatriation that was acceptable, but, should Gladstone not agree, she should take the

---

126 *The Times*, 19 December 1870, 9f. The decision had been taken not to discriminate between the various treason (and treason-felony) cases – the military men and those convicted in Manchester were not to be included, in any event. There was some consideration as to whether any of the released men ought, on grounds of health, to be allowed to remain in the country (Fortescue to Gladstone, 11 December 1870: BM Add. Mss. 44122, f. 177).

127 William O'Brien and Desmond Ryan (eds), *Devoy's Post Bag 1871–1928*, Dublin, C. J. Fallon, 1948, Vol. 1, p. 1.

128 Rossa to Mary O'Donovan Rossa, 18 February 1870 (CUA: Fenian Brotherhood Papers (FBP): Box 2, item 23). He continued, 'I am weak, and whatever I may think of leaving Ireland *before* conviction, once I find myself in England with 9549 on my arm, I find myself also holding the opinion that I do nothing dishonorable or demoralising by getting rid of this badge if my masters allow me the choice of doing so by leaving the country. Doing such a thing [would not] be deemed improper in the Frenchman, the Italian, the Pole or any other nationality in chains. But, as the poet asks "where is the nation can rival old Erin" etc. etc.'

matter no further. He advised her to beware of 'that sickness of heart . . . which is caused by deferred hope. . . . Do not Mollis waste your energies in this fashion by feeding at the feet of the British lion, on hopes which may be vain.'[129]

Several months later Rossa maintained this caution. In the last weeks of detention the prisoners were not as responsive to the conditional amnesty as government wished. None wished to take the initiative, which delayed their release. Rossa had accepted the terms put before him, and William Fagan, the Convict Director, asked him to advise the others to do likewise. He refused, saying that he would take responsibility for himself, but to do so for the others would cause his motives to be suspected. He was unwilling even that a copy of his reply to the terms of amnesty should be sent to John O'Leary (then at Portland) since it seemed that an unfair construction might be placed upon this also.[130]

This unease, and their delay in agreeing to the conditions, showed that the Fenian leaders did not trust Gladstone, nor did they see their amnesty as any kind of victory.[131] Gladstone's announcement brought mixed feelings. Some agreed with John Mitchel, the still-active link with Young Ireland, that the release was a 'sham amnesty'. To the last they were concerned lest it should be represented that they had treated with the British government, and had thus compromised their cause. '[I]t being clearly understood,' wrote Thomas Clarke Luby from prison, 'that I gave no promise or pledge as to my future conduct.'[132]

---

129 Ibid. ('I am decidedly averse to your proceeding further.')

130 Rossa to Mary O'Donovan Rossa, 28 December 1870(?), CUA: Fenian Brotherhood Papers: Box 2, item 23.

131 The terms of exile related to their original sentences, and ranged from twenty years each for O'Donovan Rossa and John McClure to five years for John Devoy and four years for Charles O'Connell (see *The Times*, 9 January 1871, 10c; 16 January 1871, 10d; see also *Pall Mall Gazette*, 9 January 1871, 6b). The three-week delay between notifying the prisoners of their amnesty and actually releasing them was due to a query about the enforceability of the condition of exile and – once that had been settled – the drafting of the letters of pardon. Both show the lack of preparation. The Irish law officers, who oversaw the drafting of the letters, did not complete their work until 29 December. The documents were then sent to England for signature, and so the 9 January departure was probably the first passage that could be arranged thereafter (NAI, CSO, LB, 270/77: 29 December 1870). For the text of the conditional pardons, a list of the released prisoners in Australia and Great Britain, and the terms of expatriation, see *Return of the Conditional Pardons Granted to Persons Convicted of Treason-Felony and Other Offences of a Political Character Since and Including the Year 1865*, PP, 1881 [208], LXXVI, 381.

132 *Freeman's Journal*, 14 January 1871, 2i. See also his bitter letter of 31 December 1870 (*Flag of Ireland*, 421a). The prisoners had been presented with a release document which could be taken as an attempt to get an undertaking as to future conduct, or to allow the government to say that such had been given. The document (which the prisoners were asked to sign) stated that the pardon was accepted 'unconditionally and without reserve'. Luby refused to sign, explaining that he could not bind himself as to future conduct. This was relayed to the Home Office, which accepted that in signing no such undertaking would be implied. The Visiting Director, Captain Stopford, and the governor and deputy governor of Portland Prison, confirmed

Some with shorter sentences bitterly complained that, having served half of their time (and they could have expected a normal remission of between a quarter and one-third), they were, in effect, being resentenced.[133] But whatever their declarations, by accepting conditional release and leaving the country, the Fenians had been gathered in.[134] Apart from Ricard O'Sullivan Burke, who was not released because of his supposed state of mind, and his inability to understand the conditions of his release,[135] two men refused amnesty. William Halpin at

this understanding to Luby, who (with five other Portland prisoners) then signed the documents. To make sure that his position was not misrepresented, Luby wrote to his wife explaining what had happened; she passed the letter to the press. John O'Leary also communicated with the press: 'I have the happiness to learn after five years of the most exquisite mental and physical suffering that it is (or rather may be) the intention of Mr Gladstone to exile me for the remaining term of my sentence' (the *Irishman*, 7 January 1871, 444a.).

133 See the letters of Denis Mulcahy (ten years, served five and a half) and William Roantree (ten years, served about half), both addressed to their families and carried in the *Flag of Ireland*, 31 December 1870, 5a.

134 A last-minute attempt was made to waive the expatriation condition for at least some of the released men. Dr Robert Lyons (who had sat on the Devon Commission) asked Fortescue if some discrimination might be possible between the various cases. He singled out Bryan Dillon, who by reason of infirmity could not support himself abroad; D. D. Mulcahy, who was the sole support of an aged and decrepit father; Ricard Burke, whose friends could not support him abroad; and Patrick John Ryan, on grounds of ill-health and inability to support himself. Lyons warned that as exiles the men would have more political appeal than at home in Ireland. Neither Dublin Castle nor the Home Office was impressed by this argument and plea for the men (Lyons to H. A. Bruce, 19 December 1870: W. E. Gladstone Papers, BM Add. Mss. 44 122, f. 213). Writing about the matter to Gladstone, Fortescue hoped that changing conditions might allow the return to Ireland of at least some of the men before too long, but for now the discrimination advocated by Dr Lyons was not possible (Fortescue to Gladstone, 27 December 1870, ibid., ff. 211–12).

135 See *The Times*, 6 January 1871, 3e. The Home Office stated that 'The mode of dealing with the case is under the consideration of the Government, and is not yet decided.' Burke's ill-health might have entitled him to more lenient treatment, but for his record in the Fenian leadership. In March 1870 there had been an exchange of letters between McCarthy Downing and Henry Bruce, the Home Secretary. Bruce did not deny that Burke's ill-health and insanity were such that 'in ordinary cases I might be justified in recommending him to the mercy of the Crown'. But he was 'a conspirator of a desperate character' whose plans for Clerkenwell, had they been carried through, would have resulted in even more loss of life than had actually occurred. Even in his present condition, therefore, he was 'an improper recipient of pardon' (*Freeman's Journal*, 17 March 1870, 4c). Burke had planned and supervised the Manchester rescue, but had not been charged with any offence in that connection. He was, however, subsequently convicted for his part in the purchase of arms, and received a sentence of fifteen years' penal servitude. The Clerkenwell explosion, of course, was an attempt to rescue him. Shamming or actually becoming insane while in prison, Burke moved first to Woking Invalid Prison, and then to Broadmoor (the asylum for criminal lunatics) (3 *Hansard*, CC, cols 79–80; 17 March 1870). He was deemed to be ineligible for release because he could not understand the conditions attaching to the amnesty (*The Times*, 6 January 1871, 3e). He was released in July 1871, and travelled to Cork. Since he was not expected, there was no demonstration (*The Times*, 11 July 1871, 5b). *Devoy's Postbag* is in error in giving 1872 as the date of his release (*op. cit.*, Vol. 1, pp. 35–6).

first rejected conditional release, but soon gave way.[136] The other refuser, Brian Dillon, was a Cork Fenian sentenced to ten years for treason felony. He refused a conditional pardon, claiming that he was too ill to cross the Atlantic. In February 1871, he was released under very liberal terms, but his health, never strong, was completely broken, and he died the following year.[137] Altogether twenty-four men were released from English prisons, with another nine from Australian convict depots.[138]

The removal of the Fenian leaders from the United Kingdom was for Gladstone less a matter of security than domestic politics. That they could make mischief in the United States of America (their inevitable destination) he had conceded, but he thought that this disadvantage would be offset by an improvement in Anglo-American relations, and a consequently firmer line against Fenian activities in that country.[139] The political reaction to a series of triumphant progresses and receptions in Ireland would, however, have been intolerable, and could well have affected his own position, given the considerable ambivalence towards the amnesty in government, Parliament and the press. The reception given to the released rank-and-file Fenians in 1869 made it imperative now to eject the prisoners so smartly that their sympathisers and supporters would be unable to organise demonstrations. This ploy was successful, and when the first five men embarked (as the *Freeman's Journal* reported) beyond a few people who had been informed of the event by telegraph, no one was present to give them

---

136 Halpin had been the subject of special interest from the US government, which had instructed its conciliatory ambassador, Reverdy Johnson, to use his good offices to seek clemency. The ambassador duly approached the Foreign Office, which passed the request to Dublin Castle. On 8 March 1869, Chichester Fortescue indicated that there could be no clemency. A direct approach was made to Lord Spencer two months later with the same result. The Irish authorities, indeed, asked for further enquiries to be made about Halpin, whom they suspected had been prosecuted in Ohio in 1856, on the instigation of the British Consul, on a charge of conspiring to organise a piratical and revolutionary expedition to Ireland (NAI, CSO LB 268/359: 21 May 1869; PRO FO 115/487).

137 See *Spectator*, 11 February 1871, p. 151. Dillon was allowed to return to Ireland on licence, the conditions of which required him to report to the authorities once a year. The Devon Commission (PP, 1871 [C.319], XXXII, 1) described Dillon as 'a very weak and deformed man, of middle age, and delicate appearance', and set out in some detail his complaints, including assignment to inappropriate work and poor medical treatment (pp. 24–7). See also *Devoy's Postbag*, op. cit., Vol. 1, pp. 34–5. (These authors are, however, in error in giving Dillon's release date as 1870.)

138 *Return of the Fenian Convicts Recently Released, Showing in Each Case the Offence; the Date of Conviction; the Sentence; the Term of Sentence Unexpired; the Cost of Passage Money Provided; and the Total Expenses Incurred in Connection with the Release*, PP, 1871 [144], LVIII, 461. There is an inexplicable discrepancy in numbers. In February 1869, when the first batch of releases was announced, the figures indicated that there remained (excluding the soldiers and the Manchester rescue prisoners) thirty-two remaining prisoners. Somehow one man must have been missed from the earlier counting.

139 Gladstone to Spencer, 14 September 1870, W. E. Gladstone Papers: BM Add. Mss. 44539, f. 28.

a send-off.[140] The *Cuba*, the vessel of exile, went from Liverpool to Queenstown (Cork), where it touched briefly, and where Mary O'Donovan Rossa joined her husband. The Home Office had suggested that here also steps might be taken to prevent the men from landing and to guard against demonstrations, and this was done.[141] When a second batch of nine men was removed the following week it was arranged that they would arrive in Liverpool at 3.30 a.m., and be transferred immediately to their waiting steamer, the *Russia*. Only two relatives of Peter Mohan were on hand when the men embarked.[142] The unobtrusive departure of the Fenians was further aided by the fact that Parliament was then in recess. This was a Gladstonian slight of hand which did not pass unnoticed by some who considered the amnesty to be a 'very serious mistake'.[143]

The releases and deportation were handled in a decent and humane way, with the exception of providing insufficient opportunities for departure meetings with family and friends, which was part of the larger plan to curtail demonstrations and publicity. At the same time, care was obviously taken to avoid giving sympathisers grounds for criticism: the men were treated with respect and consideration. Rossa initially had some grumbles about his discharge clothes, and

---

140 Though the newspaper's correspondent added that had their presence in Liverpool been known 'there would have been a demonstration' (9 January 1871, 4c). No contact was allowed between the prisoners and the few who had turned up to see them off 'beyond a mere formal recognition and the waving of handkerchiefs'. Rossa and his companions were escorted by Captain Arthur Griffiths, the deputy governor of Chatham, and a complement of warders. They had been held overnight at Liverpool police headquarters, and the following morning were transferred by tender to the *Cuba*, which was already slowly under way (*The Times*, 7 January 1871, 7b; 9 January 1871, 10c).

141 NAI, CSO LB 270/84: Spencer to Home Office, 7 January 1871. As a measure of protection against an illegal return by the released men their photographs were circulated to the Irish constabulary (ibid., /97 and 101). The Amnesty Association had wished a delegation to go abroad the *Cuba* formally to present an address, but this was regarded as a demonstration and was refused. The Association's long and militantly nationalist address was handed over by the authorities, as were several other such documents from various parts of the country (*Freeman's Journal*, 10 January 1871, 4f). Some personal contact was permitted. Relatives visited, and a deputation from Cork was allowed on board to present clothing and £10 to each man. A few hours later Isaac Butt, President of the Amnesty Association, John Nolan, its secretary and Richard Pigott, were also allowed to present £10 each to the men. Although demonstrations directly involving the men were not permitted, as the *Cuba* sailed bonfires were lighted along the shore, bands played and cheers were given: an American barque in harbour dipped her colours (ibid., 9 January 1871, 4c). See also *Pall Mall Gazette*, 9 January 1871, 6b.

142 *The Times*, 16 January 1871, 10d.

143 Earl Grey in the Lords, 9 March 1871; 3 *Hansard*, CCIV, col. 1604. There was an unexpected protest from J. G. Moylan, the Canadian government's immigration agent in Dublin. By forcing the Fenian leaders to go to the United States of America, Canada was being exposed to 'dangers far more formidable and probable than the Premier is disposed to encounter at home, notwithstanding all the moral and physical force at his command'. To this Gladstone replied dismissively that government should not be expected to allow these men 'to remain in the midst of the community whom they had sought and probably would seek again, to disturb' (*Manchester Guardian*, 29 December 1870, 3d).

wrote somewhat humorously from Chatham Prison about this to the Amnesty Association, which in turn passed the note to the press.[144] The suit in which Rossa was convicted was held at the prison with the rest of his belongings, but after some five years was hardly in a fit state to wear. William Fagan offered money for the purchase of a new outfit, to which Rossa (who would later be very critical of Fagan in his memoirs) replied: 'whatever was laid before me in this matter I would receive reasonably'.[145]

At Cork, Rossa expressed no dissatisfaction with the amnesty terms and said that he considered the prisoners had been fairly treated. The *Freeman* noted that as the men were nominally travelling as second cabin passengers they were 'admitted to all the privileges of first-class, and have received an excellent outfit and £5 from Government'.[146] Accounts published the following month showed that the men's passages had cost between seventeen guineas and eighteen pounds, and other expenses (clothing and pocket money, in the main) were for most of the men between £34 and £43. A total of £328 was spent on passages and £755 on the men's expenses.[147]

The remaining prisoners

The dispatch of these two groups and a further ten men, less prominent as leaders, almost concluded the business of the Fenian amnesty, but there remained eighteen prisoners who for reasons of background or date of offence were denied pardons: eleven of these were in Western Australia (all soldiers) and seven (including three soldiers) in England.[148] Because of the attitude of the army, Gladstone could not

---

144 *Freeman's Journal*, 9 January 1871, 4c–d.
145 Rossa to Mary O'Donovan Rossa, 28 December 1870(?), CUA: Fenian Papers: Box 2, item 23; Rossa's wife had asked permission to send a tailor to measure him for a new outfit. The Chatham governor had been unable on his own authority to give this permission, and the issue had thus been referred to Fagan.
146 Ibid., 9 January 1871, 4c. The provision of first-class travel caused some critical comment, and the government denied that it had done so (3 *Hansard*, CCIV, cols 164–6; 13 February 1871). Some special arrangement had, however, been made which would allow the men first-class privileges without actually travelling at first-class rates. This point was confirmed the following month but did not prevent *The Times* from repeating the canard: 10 March 1871, 10a; 13 March 1871, 9e).
147 *Return of the Names of the Fenian Convicts Recently Released*, op. cit., PP, 1871 [144], LVIII, 461.
148 *Return of the Names of Any Persons Now Suffering Imprisonment on Account of Their Conviction, Either as Principals or Accessories, of the Murder of Serjeant Brett at Manchester, 1867; Of the Names of Any Persons Now Suffering Imprisonment under Convictions for Treason-Felony Under the Crown and Government Security Act of 1848; And, of the Names of Any Persons Suffering Imprisonment Under Sentences of Courts Martial in Ireland for Offences Against the Articles of War, Appearing to be Connected with their Complicity with the Fenian Conspiracy; Specifying in Each Case the Date and Nature of the Sentence, the Court before Which They Were Convicted, the Nature of the Charge, and the Mode in which the Sentence is Carried Out*, PP, 1874 [119], LIV, 493. The eleven men in Western Australia were sidelined with the comment that since their arrival in the Colony 'the Home Office is not in possession of any information respecting them'.

hope to amnesty the fourteen Fenian soldiers. Those imprisoned for their part in the Manchester rescue and the Clerkenwell explosion also seemed beyond amnesty because of the notoriety of their offences, and the fact that they had been committed in England.[149] Their infamy in one country brought them regard in the other, however, and this in turn put them in Gladstone's sights.

For the soldiers there was a distinct and curious silence – indeed a pronounced indifference – on the part of the amnesty groups, but there existed widespread sympathy in Ireland for those who had been sentenced for their part in the Manchester rescue. In addition to Allen, Larkin and O'Brien, who were hanged, eight men had been sentenced to penal servitude. For being accessories to murder, Edward Shore and Patrick Melody had been sentenced to death, commuted to life penal servitude. Six men had been found guilty of lesser offences, and sentenced to five years' penal servitude with concurrent terms of two years' imprisonment at hard labour.[150] These last offenders, having been sentenced on 26 October 1867, were (with the remission granted for good behaviour) in any event close to release through expiration of sentence, but Shore and Melody would have many years to serve before being considered for release on licence.

In Home Office records it is rare to find a prime minister interesting himself in the fate of an individual prisoner, and probably unique for that prisoner's case to be pressed by him on a reluctant Home Secretary, but such was Gladstone's action regarding Melody. Rebuffed at first, Gladstone again approached his new Home Secretary, Robert Lowe.[151] He was prepared to leave in prison Melody's two remaining companions, since they had used firearms, 'a great fact' which in Gladstone's opinion had brought them close to murder. Melody, however, was a different case: 'I cannot but feel doubtful whether in such a case as this, which has only a technical relation to murder, there is not room for the mercy of the Crown.' He asked Lowe if the matter should be referred to the trial judge, and apologised for pursuing the issue: 'If you think me pertinacious in this matter, it is perhaps because the people outside have from the first insisted on making it mine at every step.'[152]

---

149 Through *The Times* (which had made an erroneous report to the contrary on 10 March 1871 (10a)) government emphasised that no Clerkenwell or Manchester prisoner had been amnestied (13 March 1871, 9e).

150 *Return of the Names, the Dates of Conviction, and the Sentences of the Irish Convicts Still Remaining Under Punishment in English Gaols, or in the Penal Settlements, for Complicity in One or Other of the Offences Known as the Manchester Rescue and the Clerkenwell Outrage, Both Committed in the Latter Part of the Year 1867*, PP, 1871 [430], LVIII, 463.

151 (1811–92). Lowe had been Chancellor of the Exchequer, December 1868 to August 1873. Educated at Winchester and Oxford, he had lived in New South Wales for eight years where he practised law and took part in Sydney politics.

152 Gladstone to Lowe, 4 December 1873, W. E. Gladstone Papers: BM Add. Mss. 44543, f. 21. In the form of particularly fractured Gladstonian punning there was an attempt at contrived emollience in this letter: 'Though our correspondence, protracted as it is, about the Brett case cannot be said to be a sea without a shore, yet its Melody is certainly rather unmelodious.'

When Lowe continued to resist,[153] Gladstone, casting around for an ally, approached his Lord Chancellor, Lord Selborne. The question of releasing the remaining Fenian prisoners was more than a departmental one, he assured Selborne, and 'the whole pressure of the correspondence and demands for their release has been on me for a long time past'.[154] One group had been ruled out for consideration: 'There are 16 soldiers still confined, with respect to whom I am hardly able to form an opinion, the military authorities silence one.' Besides these, he continued, there were four other men 'in two pairs'.[155] Of the pair still in prison for the Manchester rescue, one had carried firearms, and it had been sworn that he had used them once. But Melody, the other man, had not carried firearms although he had assisted in the rescue:

> On *his* case Lowe & I differ. I suggested communication with the judge but he says this is unusual. It seems to me that if it had been a murder in an attempt to release an ordinary criminal Melody w[oul]d by this time after 5 or 5½ years of imprisonment have been released: & the political circumstan[ces], I think it is admitted, ought not to aggravate the punishment. I wish you w[oul]d kindly look into the matter.[156]

In the event, Selborne agreed with Gladstone rather than Lowe, and wrote accordingly.[157] Melody was released in early 1874.

The attitude of the Amnesty Association towards the remaining prisoners (seven in England, eleven in Australia) was curious. As soon as Isaac Butt had heard of the intended release of the Fenian leaders he wrote to the Association (of which he was president) calling for dignity and restraint in any celebrations and stating that the work of the Amnesty Association was now at an end. With the funds that remained the released prisoners should be helped, but the main work of the Association had been accomplished. Its accounts should be audited

---

153 See the long and detailed letters (ibid., 44302); 25 November 1873, ff. 153–6; 29 November ff. 157–64.

154 Among these pressures, of course, there were numerous official, semi-official and private representations from the United States of America. Sometimes the levels of representation were combined. Thus in July 1870, for example, a petition from some citizens of San Francisco regarding the treatment of Fenian prisoners was received by the US Senate, ordered to be printed in the Senate proceedings, and was carried in various US newspapers. The British Embassy in Washington duly forwarded a file on the matter to London (PRO HO 45/9330/19461A/25).

155 One of the pairs was Davitt and his accomplice Wilson, whom Gladstone himself had ruled out of consideration for pardon, since their offence had been committed after the main Fenian campaign. It is not clear where Gladstone got the figure of sixteen soldiers (see n. 148 above).

156 Gladstone to Selborne, 27 December 1873, W. E. Gladstone Papers: BM Add. Mss. 44296, f. 345.

157 Selborne to Gladstone, 30 December 1873, W. E. Gladstone Papers: BM Add. Mss. 44296, ff. 348–9. He did not dissent from Lowe's legal or moral judgement, but considered Melody's subordinate role in the affair opened the door to mercy.

and the organisation wound up.[158] Those attending the meeting seemed to agree with Butt, and there was no mention of the military or Manchester prisoners, or of Michael Davitt or John Wilson who had been sentenced to long terms of penal servitude in July 1870.[159]

The more moderate Amnesty Committee claimed the releases as a result of its own 'judicious proceedings', and expressed its thanks to McCarthy Downing 'for the wise discretion which he used in presenting our petition at the most fitting moment, and with merited success'. It was true, the Chairman observed, that the amnesty was not unconditional, as had been hoped, 'But beggars can't be choosers, and we have only to take what we get and be thankful, and, taking it on account, leave the rest to the healing hand of time to smoothen down the roughness and remove all blemish from the act of grace.' The Committee adopted a resolution hoping that the amnesty conditions could soon be relaxed to allow the men to return to Ireland.[160] Conspicuously again, there was no mention of the military prisoners, or of the remaining civil prisoners.

Attitudes towards amnesty

Queen Victoria

The formality of constitutional monarchy meant that the Queen's name validated all pardons and commutations. She had a right to be informed and consulted, and to give her advice, but otherwise was almost completely a cypher of government. In a matter of delicacy, such as the Fenian pardons, however, her determination could tip the scales. In greater constitutional affairs, such as the Lords' defiance of the Commons over the disestablishment of the Irish Church, Victoria had played an important, perhaps decisive role.[161] She was perpetually alert for any hint of lèse-majesté, and despite her constitutional position frequently put ministers to the inconvenience of wooing her to positions or decisions which she suspected or disliked: she was not to be presumed upon. There were several strands in Victoria's opinion of the Fenian amnesty. Together they acted as a further brake on Gladstone's policy, and towards one group (the Fenian soldiers) they constituted a veto.

---

158 Freeman's Journal, 19 December 1870, 4e; Dublin Evening Post, 19 December 1870, 3f. There appears to have been some difficulty with the accounts. A sum of £510 had been sent to Australia to aid the Fenian prisoners. It was not required and was returned directly to the Amnesty Association, rather than the trustees. Thereafter the money may have been dispensed somewhat irregularly by Butt, causing a public protest from the trustees of the rival Amnesty Committee (Freeman's Journal, 11 January 1871, 4b; Dublin Evening Post, 22 December 1870, 5d).

159 For a list of those remaining in custody for Fenian offences see the Return moved by Isaac Butt, 15 April 1874 (at PRO HO 144/6/19461, with minutes and correspondence).

160 Dublin Evening Post, 22 December 1870, 5d.

161 George Earle Buckle (ed.), The Letters of Queen Victoria, London, John Murray, 1926 (Second Series), Vol. 1, pp. 603–22.

Framing the Queen's attitude and responses to questions of Fenian policy was her general and abstract dislike of Ireland and the Irish. She was notoriously ignorant of Irish affairs, and travelled to the country only four times during her long reign. Her first visit (in 1849) was a great success, and engendered warm feelings towards Ireland and the Irish.[162] Three further visits – two during Albert's lifetime, and a final one in the last year of her life – produced similar effusions, but they seem to have been of a passing nature on both sides. Albert, normally a broadening influence on Victoria, found the Irish politically and culturally baffling. Religious perceptions were a further complication. Victoria was strongly attached to Presbyterianism, and to the Low Church within Anglicanism,[163] and if her objections to the Anglo-Catholic movement were strong, they were mild in comparison to the visceral and traditional rejection of papism and priesthood – and it was the Roman Catholic Church which so shaped and characterised Irish life. Gladstone, by contrast, although unshakeable in his adherence to the Anglican Church, was sensible of the influence of the papacy for good as well as ill, and saw the universality of the Church, Anglican and Roman, as a defining factor in European civilisation.

By the end of 1868, when the worst of the Fenian threats were over, Victoria was confirmed in her deep dislike and distrust of the Irish. Her Personal Secretary,

162 This first visit was in the aftermath of the famine, and she was much struck by the enthusiastic demonstrations of loyalty. Whatever the state of Irish political opinion in the preceding years there had been a willingness among nationalists – particularly O'Connell – to distinguish between monarch and government. Victoria wrote to her mother of the visit: 'The enthusiasm and loyalty of the Irish is most striking – and we never can forget, or feel otherwise than most warmly and kindly towards them' (Richard Mullen and James Munson, *Victoria: Portrait of a Queen*, London, BBC Books, 1987, p. 53).

163 Towards the end of 1866 protests reached the Queen from Scottish Presbyterians, who objected to Anglican proselytising in Scotland. Victoria wrote to the Dean of Windsor seeking advice: she would make a protest, but what form would be best? She pointed out the legal position, and her coronation oath to maintain the Presbyterian Church in Scotland. She also observed that the reformation had not been completed in England and (alluding to Anglo-Catholicism) 'had we applied the pruning knife more severely, we should never have been exposed to the dangers to which the Church of England is *now* exposed'. Victoria affirmed that she felt '*more strongly* than words *can* express, the duty which is imposed upon her and her family, to maintain the *true* and *real principles* and *spirit* of the *Protestant* religion; for her family was brought over and placed on the throne of these realms *solely* to maintain it; and the Queen will *not* stand the attempts made to destroy the simple and truly Protestant faith of the Church of Scotland, and to bring the Church of England as near the Church of Rome as they possibly can' (Victoria to Wellesley (Dean of Windsor), 23 November 1866, Buckle, *op. cit.*, Vol. 1, p. 377). See also (as one example among many) her strong denunciation of Anglo-Catholicism in a letter to Dean Stanley of 13 November 1873 (ibid., Vol. 2, pp. 290–1). Yet Victoria's Low Church sensibilities and Protestant preferences could be set aside in the face of her duty to guard against religious discord among her subjects. Deprecating any public act which could give needless offence to Roman Catholics, she queried in 1868 the proposed appointment of a clergyman of strongly Protestant views (Dr McNeile) to be Dean of Ripon. He had, she informed Disraeli, 'rendered himself conspicuous by his hostility to the Roman Catholic Church' (Sir Thomas Biddulph to Disraeli, 16 August 1868: Buckle, *op. cit.*, Vol. 1, p. 533).

General Charles Grey, discussed with her the possibility of a Royal visit to Ireland, which Gladstone had proposed. This provoked an eruption. She attached the general character of the Irish as being 'untruthful and impossible to be depended upon'. Grey maintained that they had been made so by a long course of mis-government and the lesson taught them by the Duke of Wellington, that agita-tion and the threat of rebellion were the only means of obtaining redress for their acknowledged grievances. The Highlander (beloved by the Queen) and the Irishman were very little different, Grey pointed out, only that one had been petted and the other insulted and oppressed: 'She would not have of this and said the *Danish* element prevailed in the Highlander.'[164] She was willing to agree in principle to an Irish visit, but would not fix a time.

Not having experience of the well-to-do and professional Irish – or indeed of any class outside the ascendancy – Victoria was also inclined to associate the Irish with poverty. Travelling through Wolverhampton, having unveiled a statue of Prince Albert, she passed 'wretched-looking slums'. The crowds were enthusiastic but all in tatters, 'and many very Irish-looking'.[165] When, to con-ciliate Irish opinion, Disraeli persuaded the Queen to allow the Prince of Wales to visit Ireland, she strongly resisted the proposal that he might later make a longer visit, and reside in the country for a while. If such an arrangement were made for Ireland, she protested, 'Wales, and the Colonies even, might get up pretensions for residence, which are out of the question'. And more specifically, 'For health and relaxation, no one would go to Ireland, and people only go who have their estates to attend to. But for health and relaxation thousands go to Scotland.'[166]

The Fenian campaigns in Ireland, England and Canada from 1865 to 1868 may, in historical retrospect, appear haphazard, ill-prepared and pitiful in the face of British power and resources. But that was not how these events were seen by contemporaries, and in those years a very definite 'Fenian panic' was established in the public consciousness.[167] A diligent reader of the newspapers, and constantly informed of developments by her ministers, Victoria partook of the panic, even while she chafed at the security restrictions which it imposed on her daily routine.

---

164 University of Durham: General Charles Grey Papers: memorandum, General Charles Grey, 29 December 1868, Ms. XIII/10.

165 Ibid., p. 380: Journal, 30 November 1866.

166 Victoria to General Grey, 7 March 1868 (Buckle, *op. cit.*, Vol. 1, p. 514). On his part, the Prince of Wales wanted a house in Ireland, and felt that one should be provided for him. See Alfred E. Gathorne-Hardy (ed.), *Gathorne Hardy First Earl of Cranbrook*, London, Longmans, Green & Co, 1910, Vol. 1, p. 258.

167 Alfred Gathorne-Hardy, the Home Secretary's son, writing in 1910, refers to the months of the Manchester Rescue and the Clerkenwell explosion thus: 'I am old enough to remember the panic which possessed all classes during the next six months' (Gathorne-Hardy, *op. cit.*, Vol. 1, p. 243).

From the beginning of the Fenian campaign Victoria favoured a hard line, and was difficult to persuade in the matter of commutation of death sentences. Spencer Walpole, who had ceased to be Home Secretary in May 1867 (but who remained in Derby's Cabinet as a minister without office) had to present a detailed defence of the government's position while staying at Balmoral. To General Grey he wrote that commuting the death sentences of 'The Fenian Traitors' was the correct decision. This was not what he would have said a month before, but 'the interval which has elapsed makes all the difference, not indeed as a matter of justice, but as a matter of policy'.[168] Grey conferred with the Queen, and on the same day wrote to the Home Secretary, Gathorne Hardy, to say that she had approved of the commutation for Burke:

> H.M. commanded me to say that she had had serious doubts on the subject, even when she agreed to comply with the recommendations of her government; but she has since had a full explanation of the case from Mr Walpole, and is satisfied that the gov[ernmen]t have taken the course which . . . was most expedient.[169]

Pressures from the United States of America for lenient treatment of the Fenian prisoners exasperated Victoria. President Andrew Johnson had telegraphed recommending pardons in appropriate cases, and the Queen took umbrage, despite the President's expressed desire not to exceed the proper limits of diplomacy. Walpole (still at Balmoral) wrote to Lord Stanley, the Foreign Secretary, informing him of the Queen's displeasure. She did not want it thought that she acquiesced in 'the interference of any foreign government between Herself and her rebellious subjects.'[170]

Throughout the summer and early autumn of 1867 the Fenian campaign distressed and angered Victoria as much as any of her subjects, as she freely informed her ministers. A letter to the Prime Minister, Lord Derby, is typical of the tone she took: 'These Fenian outrages are becoming very alarming, and the Queen thinks the Government must show much firmness and determination, as these people are really dreadful, and her good English subjects will become (and with right) thoroughly exasperated at last.'[171]

---

168 To have carried out the decisions would have encouraged anger and made it more difficult to coax Ireland back to the ordinary administration of law and justice. Walpole also pointed to the Lord Chief Justice's support of the decision, concluding 'May it answer! If it does not – there must be no trifling with such traitors in future' (Royal Archives (RA), 23/74: Walpole to Grey, 27 May 1867).

169 Ibid., 23/75: Grey to Hardy, 27 May 1867. The Queen regretted that the decision was not taken sooner, before the Lord Lieutenant had refused a petition for clemency.

170 Ibid., B23/76: Walpole to Stanley, 1 June 1867. Walpole thought the information was pertinent 'in case she should have to communicate again with this or any other American government upon such a subject'.

171 Ibid., A36/22: Victoria to Derby, 2 October 1867.

The Manchester rescue on 18 September was bad and alarming news in itself, only partly allayed by the immediate capture of twenty-nine of the rescuers. But beyond the shock at such an outrage in the streets of Manchester was deep concern at the threat posed by the two freed Fenian leaders (Thomas Kelly and Timothy Deasy). The Queen remained at Balmoral, unhappy with the resultant precautions. Intelligence was received of a kidnap plot.[172] The government, for reasons of safety, wished her to travel back to Windsor by day. Victoria consented to this, but only after much persuasion, since she found daytime train journeys (and the inevitable public attention) disagreeable. She was in the midst of her period of unpopular seclusion, and was quite happy to remain at Balmoral, but this caused other concerns.[173] The Prime Minister believed the Queen was as safe there as in any part of her dominions, but 'it is impossible to calculate on what may be done or attempted by men so witless and desperate as these have proved themselves to be'.[174] This uncertainty was immediately communicated to Victoria and cannot but have increased her own fears and detestation of Fenians, Fenianism, and the Irish classes from which they were drawn.

Threats continued, even after the Queen's safe arrival at Windsor. From Ireland, Lord Mayo, the Irish Chief Secretary, brought news of an assassination society formed by Kelly, the freed leader. The Duke of Cambridge warned of alliances with communistic forces abroad in a campaign of murder and arson. Victoria's anger was further fanned by a message from Lord Monck, the Canadian Governor General, that vessels had set out from New York with the intention of abducting her from Osborne.[175] Victoria protested that since every precaution

---

172 Robert Neill, Mayor of Manchester to Balmoral (copying letter of chief constable), 14 October 1867; University of Durham: General Sir Charles Grey Papers: Ms. II/12.

173 See the exchanges between Grey and Gathorne Hardy, 14–22 October 1867; University of Durham: General Sir Charles Grey Papers, Ms. II/12. On government's concern about her persistent seclusion, and the complication of the Fenian emergency, see Grey to Home Secretary Henry Bruce, 16 December 1868, ibid.

174 Ibid., 6/25: Derby to Grey, 15 October 1867. In fact the precautions against attack or abduction seem to have been rather slight. The Sheriff of Aberdeen reported that the Queen's train would pass through the wild and thinly inhabited country eight miles from Balmoral, where only one constable was stationed. 'This is perhaps the most vulnerable point in our police arrangements. A few determined men could come from Dundee to Grantown by the Highlands Railway and could reach Tomintoul in a few hours on foot. There, it is said, they would easily be harboured. I understand the population is about 600 and is chiefly Roman Catholic' (Andrew Jameson to Gathorne Hardy, 23 October 1867, Buckingham Papers: BM Add. Mss. 43742, ff. 13–14; see also Gathorne Hardy to General Charles Grey, 17 October 1867; University of Durham; General Charles Grey Papers: II/12).

175 At this time a vast amount of correspondence in cypher passed between Archibald, the British Consul in New York, and the Home and Colonial Offices (see Buckingham Papers: BM Add. Mss. 41860 and 43742). The Duke of Buckingham wished to publicise the impending threat, and to raise a general alarm. If a public announcement were made it would increase vigilance – something that mere rumour would not do (see letters of Buckingham to Disraeli and Gathorne Hardy, 21 December 1867; Buckingham Papers: BM Add. Mss. 41860, ff. 14–19).

had been taken in the grounds, and she never went out after dark, she would not be confined to the house, and General Grey reported to the Home Secretary, 'if I tried to prevent her going out, I should make her ill'.[176] (This conversation and Victoria's determination not to be made a prisoner in her own house have a particular significance since they took place the day after the Clerkenwell explosion.) A few days later Grey returned to the topic, this time by letter. So that he should not alarm her he refrained from giving her the full extent of the information to hand, but for her own safety he now warned her of the threat of assassination and entreated her not to return to Osborne: '[T]he most unsafe places for Your Majesty at this moment, are those where the population is most thin & scattered.' Against four or five determined men, as the Fenians had shown themselves to be, a few policemen would offer little protection, and, stating that he was probably going beyond his duty, Grey 'on his knees' beseeched Victoria to consider whether she would not be better off at Windsor.[177] The Duke of Cambridge ordered cavalry to be sent to the Isle of Wight as extra protection. He wished the Queen would stay safely at Windsor, but this could not be accomplished unless the Cabinet expressed its opinion on the matter.[178]

Clerkenwell outraged Victoria, and her feelings of sorrow and anger were intensified by its proximity to the sixth anniversary of the Prince Consort's death.[179] Writing to Home Secretary Gathorne Hardy, she referred to Albert's death ('the distressing thoughts which this sad anniversary always renews') and to Clerkenwell: 'Her heart bleeds to think of the misery thus wantonly inflicted on so many innocent victims by the atrocious wickedness.' She urged that more effectual steps be taken for the protection of the public, and hoped that 'neither those who planned nor those who perpetrated the outrage may escape the punishment they deserve'.[180] Her personal physician was directed to visit the surviving victims of the explosion, and sent her a vivid description

176 Grey to Hardy, 14 December 1867, Alfred E. Gathorne-Hardy, *op. cit.*, Vol. 1, p. 248. (Chapter 13 of this volume contains much correspondence on the various reported plots against Queen Victoria and her responses to the continuing warnings and alarms.)

177 Grey to Victoria, 19 December 1867, Buckingham Papers: BM Add. Mss. 43742, ff. 31–3. See also Grey to Gathorne Hardy, 19 December 1867; University of Durham: General Sir Charles Grey Papers: Ms. II/12.

178 Duke of Cambridge, 20 December 1867, Buckingham Papers: BM Add. Mss. 43742, ff. 34–5.

179 The explosion took place on 13 December 1867; Albert had died on 14 December 1861. The Queen had immediately been informed of the attack in a letter from the Home Office Permanent-Under-Secretary, Sir Adolphus Liddell, to General Sir Thomas Biddulph, Keeper of the Privy Purse. The letter was written at 6 p.m. (the explosion had been at 4 p.m.) and provided a detailed account of what had happened together with subsequent steps to increase security and to deploy police and the army. The immediacy and comprehensiveness of the letter shows what importance was attached to keeping the Queen informed (RA B24/39).

180 General Grey to Gathorne Hardy, 14 December 1867, Buckle, *op. cit.*, Vol. 1, p. 474. See also Nancy E. Johnson (ed.), *The Diary of Gathorne Hardy, later Lord Cranbrook, 1866–1892: Political Selections*, Oxford, Clarendon Press, 1981, pp. 57–60.

of the terrible injuries which had been inflicted on women, children and poor working men.[181]

The Queen took a close interest in the proceedings against those allegedly involved in the Clerkenwell explosion, and Gathorne Hardy wrote expressing his regrets at the failure of the case against many of them, while confirming that 'one of the chief culprits' had been convicted. Quite improperly, since no formal representation had yet been made to him for pardon, Hardy anticipated that attempts would be made to corroborate Barrett's alibi. It would be his duty to consider all that might be argued, 'but assuming the verdict to be just it does not appear to him that he would be justified in interfering with the due course of law. Threats begin again but they may be disregarded.'[182]

The Clerkenwell atrocity, the following threats, and the several letters and exhortations which Victoria received about her own safety, confirmed her support for the government's resolve to execute Fenians for their part in the Manchester rescue. Informed by the Home Secretary of the course which it was proposed to take with the four men convicted of the murder of Sergeant Brett – three were to be hanged and Edward Shore was to be reprieved – the Queen replied that the government had taken the proper course, 'and that which true humanity itself would dictate'. She hoped the execution of the three men would have the effect of deterring others 'from the perpetration of crimes which they have appeared to believe they might commit with impunity'.[183]

The Fenian campaign accentuated Victoria's timidity, and further fuelled her sweeping judgements and prejudices about the Irish. She was kept informed about Fenianism from its early stages, Palmerston in equal parts cautioning her about it and urging more royal visits to Ireland as an antidote.[184] Fraught relations between the United Kingdom and the United States of America caused Victoria to worry about the defence of Canada, and the possibilities for war – an

---

181 Dr William Jenner to Queen Victoria, 16 December 1867, Buckle, *op. cit.*, Vol. 1, pp. 475–6.

182 Hardy to Victoria, 2 May 1868: RA B24/80. Hardy criticised the Lord Chief Justice: 'The informers as usual were of low and discreditable character and the Chief Justice took a view of the want of corroboration which Mr Hardy hears does not meet with general acquiescence.'

183 Grey to Hardy, 20 November 1867, Buckle, *op. cit.*, Vol. 1, pp. 469–70. See also Derby to Queen Victoria, 5 November 1867, RA A36/29; Queen's Journal, 1 December and 20 December 1867; Grey to Victoria, 19 December 1867, Buckle, *op. cit.*, Vol. 1, pp. 476–8; Victoria to Grey, 19 December 1867, ibid., pp. 478–9; Victoria to Hardy, 19 December 1867, ibid., p. 479; Derby to Victoria, 19 December 1867, ibid., pp. 479–83; Victoria to Derby, 20 December 1867, ibid., p. 484. Grey himself (and as a conduit between Queen Victoria and her ministers his views were important) thought that the acquittal of a number of the lesser figures in the Manchester rescue showed that the prosecution had overplayed its hand: 'You will not easily get an English Juryman to admit the Law by which *every* man engaged in [a] lawless act, where death ensues, is made to answer for that death, tho' it is certain he neither inflicted it nor intended it, and I think after the Conviction of the actual Murderer, the rest should have been tried on some minor Charge' (General Grey to Stanley, 7 November 1867: RA B24/24).

184 Palmerston to Victoria, 17 February 1865, Buckle, *op. cit.*, Vol. 1, pp. 251–2.

opportunity greatly desired by the American Fenians.[185] At home there were Fenian plots against herself and her family, and security precautions to be endured, which were of such a stringent character that, following an increasingly vigorous exchange of correspondence, she complained to Lord Derby from Osborne (her favourite house, designed and built under Albert's supervision) that 'Such precautions are taken here that the Queen will be little better than a *State* prisoner. She may consent to this for a *short time*, but she *could* not for long.'[186] In a letter the same day to Gathorne Hardy, she resisted attempts to make her leave Osborne: 'Windsor the Queen does not consider nearly so safe, for there are a great many nasty people always about there.' She repeated that she was willing to submit to being a state prisoner (with its 'irksomeness of constant gêne and being constantly watched and surrounded') but wanted it clearly understood that she could not continue 'these great precautions' for very long.[187]

When the inadequacy of government's intelligence became apparent,[188] as in the case of Lord Monck's inaccurate warning about the embarkation of New York Fenians intent on abducting her from Osborne, Victoria's anger was mixed with relief. To Hardy (who managed to keep in her good graces) she wrote that Monck's warning had been '*absurd* and *mad*' and that Monck and the government should be 'utterly ashamed' at having believed the tale. The discrediting of the warning she regarded as '*a great satisfaction and a great triumph. She never* for one moment credited the absurd ideas of *danger* either *here* or at *Balmoral*, from the *utter impossibility* of the plans being carried out.'[189] Victoria contrasted her supposed calm with the panic of the government:

> The Queen has now reigned nearly 31 years, is 48 years old, has lived in troubled times . . . she has been shot at 3 times, once knocked on the head, threatening letters have over and over again been received, and yet *we never* changed our mode of living or going on! This the Queen hopes will be a lesson for the future, and that these *panics* (which have

185 See, for example, Palmerston's letter to Victoria, 13 March 1865, Buckle, *op. cit.*, Vol. 1, pp. 262–3; Derby to Victoria, 16 November 1866, Buckle, *op. cit.*, Vol. 1, p. 374.

186 Victoria to Derby, 20 December 1867, Buckle, *op. cit.*, Vol. 1, p. 484. See also the report to the Queen of her Private Secretary, General Grey, on his conversations with the Home Secretary concerning rumoured plots against her (Grey to Victoria, 19 December 1867, ibid., 476–8).

187 Victoria to Hardy, 20 December 1867, Gathorne-Hardy, *op. cit.*, Vol. 1, p. 249.

188 See Lord Monck to Buckingham and Buckingham to Gathorne Hardy, 7 and 9 January 1868, Buckingham Papers: BM Add. Mss. 43742, ff. 68–72.

189 In keeping with what could be a very personal way of conducting business Victoria exempted Hardy from her scolding: '*She* thinks *he* was never himself inclined to share in the extravagant alarm which took possession of everyone almost' (Gathorne-Hardy, *op. cit.*, Vol. 1, p. 251). This may have been a criticism of the Duke of Buckingham (Colonial Secretary), who seems to have involved himself in intelligence details he could not possibly resolve, instead of taking a wider and more measured view (see Buckingham to Monck, 28 December 1867: BM Add. Mss. 41860, ff. 62–3).

affected the Queen's health very *much* from the annoyance and worry which they entailed) will not be again recurred to *every 2 or 3 months*.[190]

Even though it had been Derby's Conservative administration she accused of mishandling her security, Victoria carried over to the new government her reluctance to take a positive role in Irish affairs. Embarked on his new policy, however, Gladstone was persistent in urging royal visits to Ireland, which Victoria stonewalled with vague promises of largely private visits. She repeated her doubts about the practicality of establishing a royal residence in Ireland, for herself or the Prince of Wales, but assured Gladstone that it was her 'anxious wish, when-ever circumstances permit . . . to take an opportunity of making herself acquainted with the fine scenery of Ireland, and with the character of its peasantry, by visits of a few weeks from time to time'. But this was conditional on her not being pressed to make 'public entrances into any large towns, or to hold receptions. If, in short, she can visit the country quietly, as she makes excursions in Scotland, without going near Edinburgh or Glasgow.'[191] Such inconspicuousness, of course, would largely have nullified the effect of an Irish visit, and would hardly have met the case that Gladstone pressed on her for visits of conciliation.

But only weeks after making this offer, Victoria was particularly (and under-standably) incensed by an incident arising out of the first wave of Fenian releases. On St Patrick's Day 1869, the Mayor of Cork (Daniel O'Sullivan), at a banquet in honour of two amnestied Fenians, Warren and Costello, referred to 'that noble Irishman' Henry O'Farrell, who had attempted to assassinate the young Prince Alfred, Duke of Edinburgh, near Sydney on 12 March 1868.[192] The

---

190 Gathorne-Hardy, *op. cit.*, Vol. 1, p. 251. The letter continued in similar fashion, with Victoria asking Hardy to relax the extensive security precautions which had been taken as a consequence of 'this *disgraceful* and ludicrous hoax'. Hardy – rather strangely – appears to have denied knowledge of the security measures, which disclaimer from the Home Secretary was hardly reassuring, causing Victoria to write saying how sorry and shocked she was at this lack of know-ledge, continuing, 'But really that Friday 20th December every one lost their heads and seemed to think the whole island teemed with danger, excepting herself, her children, the Ladies, and *one* or 2 other Men' (ibid., p. 252).

191 Grey to Gladstone, 8 January 1869, Buckle, *op. cit.*, Vol. 1, p. 576. The Queen and her advisers were also doubtless aware of the sectarian minefield that surrounded all acts of state. The previous year, for example, in discussing the proposed installation of the Prince of Wales into the Order of St Patrick, Lord Strathnairn, Commander-in-Chief of Ireland, pointed to the religious sniping between the Roman Catholic and Anglican churches which would surround what was intended to be a conciliatory occasion of pomp and royal splendour (Strathnairn to Abercorn, 13 March 1868, Rose Papers: BM Add. Mss. 42828, ff. 9–10).

192 O'Farrell (who was tried for attempted murder, convicted and executed) at first insisted that the attempt was part of a Fenian plot, and that he had been one of a team of ten men sent out to New South Wales to arrange the assassination. He produced no evidence to support his claims, however, and a second (and final) confession stated that he had acted alone, out of vanity. Some of the more extreme Protestant MPs believed the first version of O'Farrell's account, and made vague and foreboding accusations of the involvement of the Roman Catholic priesthood

remarks were cruel, reckless and exhibitionistic, and in any event could not but be provocative.[193] Considering that O'Sullivan was speaking about the attempted murder of her son (and was perhaps aware that the date was close to the first anniversary of the attack) it was entirely to be expected that Victoria would be angered and revolted.[194] She wrote immediately to Gladstone, who replied that the government viewed the speech as a matter of great gravity: 'Though the individual may be insignificant, he represents public authority, for local purposes, in the second city of Ireland.' The matter would be prosecuted 'with care and diligence'.[195] Legal proceedings against O'Sullivan looked as though they would be difficult and protracted, and so the government decided on a Bill to deprive him of office.[196] In the event, his colleague John Francis Maguire (MP for Cork City) and The O'Donoghue (MP for Tralee) persuaded O'Sullivan to resign, and a potentially inflammatory situation was avoided.[197] O'Sullivan's brutal remarks further confirmed Victoria's views on Ireland and the Irish. These were little modified by Gladstone's vacuous assurances that because public sentiment had failed to rally to the Mayor against the Crown and the law, authority 'cannot fail to derive an accession of moral weight and force from such an incident'.

Victoria's reluctant agreement to the first batch of releases, and her anger at the intemperate remarks and lavish celebrations that greeted them, made it

in the original plot, and what they saw as a subsequent cover-up, beneath which lurked a more extensive conspiracy (for an account of the assassination attempt see Keith Amos, *The Fenians in Australia 1865–1880*, Kensington (NSW), New South Wales University Press, 1988).

193 'When that noble Irishman O'Farrell fired at the Prince in Australia, he was imbued with as noble and patriotic feelings as Allen, Larkin, and O'Brien were.' He believed that O'Farrell 'would be highly thought of as any of the men who had sacrificed their lives for Ireland'. This pronouncement was greeted with 'great cheering and cries of "he was"' (*Nation*, 1 May 1869, 581c).

194 Sullivan had also praised Allen, Larkin and O'Brien (hanged for their part in the Manchester rescue) and Barrett (hanged for his part in the Clerkenwell outrage) as 'good Catholics and good patriots'. Referring to an attempted assassination of the Tsar by a Polish nationalist, Sullivan said that O'Farrell was 'as noble an Irishman as the Pole, and as true to his country, for each was impelled by the same sentiments to do what they did' (3 *Hansard*, CXCV, col. 1950; 30 April 1869; *Nation*, 1 May 1869, 581b–d).

195 Gladstone to Victoria, 1 May 1869, Buckle, *op. cit.*, Vol. 1, p. 595.

196 In September 1868, O'Sullivan introduced an amnesty resolution to Cork Council. The motion was unanimously agreed, and O'Sullivan had it copied and sent to other councils throughout the country, of which nineteen formally adopted it (*Nation*, 14 November 1868, 199c). Daniel O'Sullivan had been outspoken throughout the latter part of the Fenian emergency. When the Fenian leader Burke was under sentence of death (his reprieve was due largely to Cardinal Cullen) O'Sullivan wrote to the *Freeman's Journal* stating that the execution would 'in all probability' be followed by a blood-letting 'of many an Englishman across the Atlantic'. He threatened to resign as a justice of the peace (an office he held ex-officio as mayor) should the execution go ahead (27 May 1867, 8b).

197 Gladstone to Victoria, 11 May 1869, Buckle, *op. cit.*, Vol. 1, p. 599; 3 *Hansard*, CXCV, cols 357–8; 8 April 1869; see also cols 1948–54; 30 April 1869. Writing to Fortescue, Spencer expressed relief that O'Sullivan 'is to be brought to book. We shall have to transfer him to a lunatic asylum' (30 April(?) 1869; SCRO: Carlingford Papers: DD/SH325: CP2/5).

much more difficult to reconcile her to the amnesty of the leaders.[198] Given an equally reluctant Cabinet, this meant that Gladstone could not carry through the clean sweep for which he had hoped, thus weakening, in his view, the political impact of amnesty. As the second amnesty was being finalised in November 1870, the Queen's new Private Secretary, Colonel Ponsonby, by her direction wrote to Gladstone, who on 11 November had set out the case for release on condition of expatriation.[199] Referring to the Fenian leaders, Ponsonby stated, 'the Queen cannot avoid remarking that no expression of regret or sorrow has been pronounced by any of them, but that on the contrary they have maintained a defiant attitude and will probably regard their release as a triumph of their party'. She hoped that some guarantee for the men's good behaviour would be exacted, 'since the presence in America of these reckless men at the present moment might lead to disastrous consequences'.[200]

There was no prospect of Victoria agreeing to the release of the Fenian soldiers, and given her attachment to the army, both personal and constitutional, Gladstone did not pursue the matter. The Queen's inclinations were strongly reinforced by her staff and advisers. Colonel Ponsonby informed Victoria that while he supposed the release of the Fenian leaders to be advisable he could not help regretting it. Their crime was most serious and they had shown no sign of contrition; some, indeed, might refuse release on the terms that were to be offered. Yet despite all this 'if it will allay agitation the pardon should of course be granted'. As to the Fenian soldiers, Ponsonby considered their crime to be double that of the civilians, and so they should not be included in the amnesty.[201] The following day Victoria endorsed Ponsonby's views in a letter to Gladstone: 'Her Majesty understands that as it is intended to release only those whose crimes were purely political the soldiers convicted of Fenianism will not be included in the pardon.'[202]

---

198 Sir Thomas Biddulph (Private Secretary) to Gladstone, 20 September 1869. Victoria found the amnesty petition which Gladstone had sent her 'very properly and respectfully worded' but went on to worry about the activities of the Fenians in the United States of America. Until there was reason to suppose that the prisoners would have neither the desire nor the means of doing mischief, clemency 'could hardly fail to be a cause of danger, and to create alarm in the minds of all peaceable and well-disposed subjects of the Queen' (Buckle, op. cit., Vol. 1, p. 628).

199 Gladstone explained that Fenianism had been losing energy and support. During the 1869 Amnesty one or two among them had indulged in 'unseemly triumph', and to prevent any such occurrence release would be conditional on exile. He also argued that the Devon Commission had completed its report. This, while finding that the prison authorities were generally innocent of any abuse, had indicated that by treating the Fenians as ordinary criminals the law was over-severe. 'The publication of this report,' Gladstone asserted, 'would not be favourable to the reputation of this country, if at the time when it occurs these men are still detained' (Buckle, op. cit., Vol. 2, p. 82).

200 Ponsonby to Gladstone, 13 November 1870: RA A40/76.

201 Ponsonby to Victoria, 12 November 1870: RA A40/76.

202 Ponsonby to Gladstone, 13 November 1870: RA A40/77.

Despite her fear and detestation of Fenianism, and her unease and perplexity with Gladstone's policy of conciliation – especially the disestablishment of the Anglican Church in Ireland and the Fenian amnesties – Victoria submitted to the advice of government. In an age that was becoming more obviously democratic Gladstone's mandate to seek far-reaching change in Ireland could not be doubted. Regardless of her acquiescence and even (as when she intervened on Gladstone's side when the Disestablishment Bill was being obstructed) her duty of support, her scepticism was known to all in the Cabinet, and was another obstacle which Gladstone had to avoid as he manoeuvred forward with his Irish policy.

The Queen's disclaimers and objections behind the scenes were, in the end, probably of much less consequence than her refusal to use the grace and majesty of her position actively to conciliate, warm and woo Irish opinion. As noted, from the days of O'Connell, Irish nationalism – even William Smith O'Brien, the chief Young Irelander, and John O'Mahony, co-founder of Fenianism[203] – had distinguished between the Crown and the deeds of government. Royalty was a thing of romance and mystery appealing across parties and affiliations to the affections of the heart and to those emotions which resonated with the symbolic rather than the actual. A sympathetic and embracing monarchy might perhaps have filled some of the void which lay so dangerously close to the heart of Irish life, and where Fenianism had found a home. Not fully realising the great power of emotion in Irish public life, Gladstone failed to deploy the Crown in support of conciliation (and being personally so little at ease with the Queen he may not have been able to do so, even had he wished). For her part, Victoria failed to overcome what had become her general dislike of Ireland and the Irish, and therefore cut herself off from the personal relations which might in time have engendered in her for the Irish the same warm feelings that she felt for the Scots. Strangeness, disloyalty and menace were what she saw, and which the Fenian crisis set forever in her mind. Far from crossing the bridge which Gladstone's policies opened between the Irish and the English, Victoria was driven even further from engagement with this, the most troubled of her kingdoms. Unknowingly, she ceded the battleground of imagination, symbol and affection to the Fenians.

---

203 John O'Mahony had protested to the incendiary and at times scurrilous *Irish Republic* about the language it used referring to Queen Victoria. He did not believe it 'necessary to our purpose to assail female honor and soil our pages with indecent assaults on the reputation of such ladies as may be unfortunate enough, in these republican days, to have royal honors thrust upon them'. This infuriated the editors of the *Irish Republic*, who asked: 'Can it be possible that he is in the pay of the English government. . . . What next, O Warrior of the bloodless sword? 'Publicly this woman is HEAD AND REPRESENTATIVE OF THE SYSTEM WHICH ROBS AND MURDERS THE PEOPLE OF IRELAND. Privately she is . . . the mistress of a Scotch dragoon' (*Irish Republic*, 6 July 1867, 6b).

English political opinion

The crisis of the Fenian campaign had passed, and, as memories of insurrection, escapes and explosions faded, they began to slip down the ranks of English concerns. The question of amnesty continued to exercise Irish groups and organisations in England, together with some radical and liberal sympathisers. On the Conservative side there was generally acquiescence to Gladstone's policy, but some politicians strongly doubted its wisdom and said so in Parliament.

As has been noted, the Fenians were released in two main tranches – the spring of 1869 and the winter of 1870 to 1871. The first group, the government insisted, were '[P]artly young men, hot-headed men, who were led in an excited moment into criminal acts . . . men, some of whom might be described as the dupes and tools of others; men incapable, as far as could be ascertained, of doing mischief hereafter as leaders in any future insurrectionary attempts.'[204] This was an understandable reassurance to the public. But this announcement was also an argument for the continued retention of the leaders. Excluding the military convicts and the Manchester prisoners, there were eighty-one Fenians in penal servitude in February 1869. Forty-nine fell into the 'dupes and tools' category, and would be released. The remaining thirty-two, Chichester Fortescue told the Commons, 'included almost all the main founders, leaders and organizers of the Fenian movement; it included men who were deeply responsible for the attempted revolution of the last two or three years'. The Irish executive and the British government did not think it would be safe to discharge these men; indeed, if released they might again attempt to resume 'their unhappy and criminal, although desperate enterprise'.[205] This was an unwise and unnecessarily categorical choice of words, which would stick like burrs when it became necessary to justify amnesty for these same 'founders, leaders and organizers'.[206]

But even the release of hotheads, dupes and tools provoked concern and protest. The possibility that government might pay to repatriate those released in Australia was viewed with repugnance, and after some dithering it was put out that the prisoners would have to pay for their own return.[207] In response to the callous, inflammatory and offensive remarks of the Mayor of Cork, Sir George Jenkinson vented the feelings of a swathe of English opinion when he asked whether these and like words were not grounds for stopping the Australian

---

204 3 *Hansard*, CXCIV, col. 160; 22 February 1869.
205 Ibid. *The Times* blundered by including O'Donovan Rossa in its list of names of released prisoners (13 March 1869, 10a).
206 *The Times*, for example, reminded the government that it had initially denied release to the leaders as 'men concerned in the most heinous outrages known in our time' (10 March 1871, 10a).
207 3 *Hansard*, CXCIV, col. 161; 22 February 1869; CXCV, cols 356–7; 8 April 1869. The government refused to bind itself in respect of the expenses of future cases, but insisted that no public money would be spent on the repatriation of those released in Australia.

releases. Seditious language had been used by two or three men, the Irish Secretary agreed, but this had been 'very generally reprobated in Ireland', had only damaged the Fenian cause, and had not altered the government's policy on clemency.[208] There was more of the same when ten prisoners returned from Australia in mid-February 1870, and were greeted with what Jenkinson called 'uproarious demonstrations', including a night-time procession with blazing tar-barrels.[209]

However well they played in nationalist Ireland, the 1870 to 1871 releases took place against the background of much English unhappiness over Gladstone's disestablishment of the Church of Ireland, and his impending legislation on land tenure and educational reform. Memories of the rebellion were still sufficiently fresh to fuel doubts and recriminations over the release of Fenian leaders. These protests grew louder and more challenging, as agrarian violence in Ireland demonstrated that rebelliousness and social disorder continued.

Because Parliament had been in recess, the principal political attack on Gladstone's policy came some weeks after the Fenian leaders had reached America. Earl Grey,[210] who had been a reforming Colonial Secretary, and who had stood on the Whig side of the Liberal Party before joining the Conservatives, spoke in a Lords debate on 9 March 1871. The amnesty was an accomplished fact, he acknowledged, but 'a very serious mistake has been committed'. The Fenian leaders had received a double measure of clemency. They had not been prosecuted for treason, as they would have been in the past, or even now in almost all other countries. He thought that this first display of clemency was wise, but not so the decision to grant a second amnesty after such a comparatively short time. Those disposed to treason would draw the lesson: if they failed they would not be hanged, and though penal servitude for life might sound terrible, 'we know very well that after a time we shall be discharged; so that if we succeed there is a grand prize for us, and if we fail we run, after all, no great risk'.[211]

Lord Derby[212] believed that the Irish were a people with a virtually incurable wish for national independence, a nation 'where, as we have had abundant proof, law is not respected, where order is not desired, where human life is not held sacred, and where the general sympathy of the population go with the

208 3 *Hansard*, CXCV, col. 357; 8 April 1869. Jenkinson (1817–92), Conservative Member for North Wiltshire, 1868–80. Voted against disestablishment of the Church of Ireland.

209 Ibid., CXCLX, cols 688–9; 22 February 1870.

210 Henry George Grey, Viscount Howick, third Earl Grey (1802–94). See above, p. 63, n. 70.

211 This, and other quotations and summaries of this Lords debate taken from 3 *Hansard*, CCIV, cols 1604–64; 9 March 1871. Other speakers included the Duke of Somerset, Lord Cairns and Lord Derby.

212 Edward Henry Stanley (1826–93), fifteenth Earl of Derby. A distinguished ministerial career in successive governments, including Foreign Secretary in his father's third and Disraeli's first administrations. He would return to the Foreign Secretaryship in Disraeli's second administration (1874–8), join the Liberals in 1880, become Colonial Secretary under Gladstone in 1882–5, and become a Liberal Unionist in 1886.

assassin and not with the law'. As a preliminary, the Duke of Richmond[213] blasted Gladstone's Irish legislation with both barrels. The Church Bill was 'a most wanton destruction of the Irish branch of our Church' and the Land Bill was 'one of the most revolutionary measures ever passed by this or any other Parliament'. It was wrong to yield to the amnesty agitation. There was no distinction between political offenders and ordinary criminals:

> What description of crime do you call shooting the policeman at Manchester? Was that a political or an ordinary crime? No doubt it was murder, but it was in connection with the Fenian conspiracy. What was the crime of attempting to blow up Clerkenwell Prison, and involving in death, or injury, hundreds of persons who had no connection with Fenianism? Was that political or ordinary crime? What was the attempt to seize the arms stored at Chester Castle? What is the shooting of policemen in their barracks? Political and ordinary crime seem to be so mixed up that you cannot distinguish one from the other.

Liberal speeches were lukewarm. For the most part they adhered to arguments which Gladstone had contrived and made familiar. Lord Dufferin, for the government, stated the abhorrence of treason of all right-minded people. The 'utmost penalty of the law' should be inflicted on such offenders as long and as far as necessary to restore order and maintain tranquillity. But there *was* a difference between political and ordinary criminals – the 'moral guilt' was not the same. In conditions of tranquillity the fate of the remaining Fenian prisoners 'forced itself upon the attention of the Government' at the same time that a 'very intense feeling as to their future fate was expressed by the great mass of the Irish people'.[214]

Much the same line was taken by the Lord Chancellor, Lord Hatherley,[215] but with a great deal more confidence and verve. He drew a bold distinction between the Fenians and ordinary criminals:

> The crime of which these men were convicted was political. However mischievous, it was not of a sordid character – persons accused of political offences, bad as they may be, and great as the evils they may

---

213 President of the Council and Leader of the Lords in Disraeli's second administration. His father (fifth Duke) had resigned from Grey's government in 1834, over what he took to be a partial disendowment of the Church of Ireland.

214 *The Times*, in its leader the following day, derided the Devon Commission Report (to which Dufferin had referred). It was 'a document which we could hardly imagine any one treating seriously'. As to Lord Dufferin's arguments on the need for special treatment for political offenders: 'They will really amaze the public' (10 March 1871, 10a).

215 Formerly Sir W. Page Wood (1801–81). Liberal MP for Oxford, 1847–53. Appointed to various legal offices; Lord Chancellor, 1868.

produce, are generally by comparison men of education, of high moral sensibility, and of good feeling towards those with whom they were not brought into immediate political antagonism. Are these men to be placed in the condition of common felons, thieves and murderers? . . . It is, I hold, simply a play upon words to speak of political offences and thefts and murders being placed in the same condition. The universal instinct of modern civilized nations draws a line of distinction between the two classes of offenders.

It was neither wise nor just to punish political offenders of education and refine-ment, beyond the point necessary to vindicate the law. Punishment continued after that point 'is only calculated to turn the tide of sympathy in their favour, and ultimately to produce a state of feeling in the public mind ten times more mischievous in its effects than any amount of clemency the Government might show to such prisoners'. Gladstone could scarcely have put it better.

Press reaction

Outside Parliament, the conservative reaction to the 1869 releases was led by the *Pall Mall Gazette*, which at that time claimed to be the organ of independ-ent liberalism. The releases undermined government in Ireland, where they were seen as a victory for the Fenian cause. The amnestied gloried in their crimes and 'avow their determination to repeat them on the first favourable opportunity'. . . . The Fenians and their supporters would seize upon signs of softness, yet government, fearing rebellion, was pampering and flattering the rebels.[216] The Conservative *Saturday Review* was of similar mind. Cost and trouble would have been saved by keeping the men in prison: 'The English people have a right to be exempted from the annoyance and worry of constantly hunting down dirty and disaffected Hiberno-Americans.' The continued deten-tion of the leaders was welcome, and it was good to learn that gaolers were not soon to lose the personal acquaintance of Luby and O'Donovan Rossa 'who were at one time supposed to be among the objects of Mr Gladstone's unreason-able compassion'.[217]

And when Gladstone's 'unreasonable compassion' led to the release of the Fenian leaders, press comment also followed party lines. *The Spectator* (generally pro-Gladstone) was against it. The main purpose of punishing political offend-ers was not reform, but prevention – 'to deter the sufferer, whenever he again becomes free – to deter those who are disposed to imitate the sufferers, but who dread the risks'. Those who had benefited from the first amnesty heaped con-tempt and menace on the government. Demands were being made in tones so

216 *Pall Mall Gazette* (25 March, 1869, 1a–b); see also *The Times*, 7 April 1869, 4c.
217 *Saturday Review*, 27 March 1869, 1b.

threatening and insolent that the government could not possibly give way: 'It would be pure insanity to grant an amnesty demanded by these swaggering ranters.[218] Six months later *The Spectator* repeated these objections to amnesty, but at the same time strongly urged political status be granted to the prisoners.[219] Yet when the amnesty was announced, *The Spectator* accepted Gladstone's assurances that it would not to be taken for weakness. It was critical of the condition of expatriation, which it mistakenly thought would be in perpetuity. In a sly swipe at Gladstone's Neapolitan campaign it noted that it knew of no political amnesty which had been granted on condition of expatriation, 'except that of Poerio and his comrades, who, having been deported to the United States by the King of Naples, mutinied on the voyage, and carried their transport into Cork'. The choice for America for exile was 'so inconsiderate as to be almost appalling'. The leaders would arrive to popular adulation, the Irish vote would be at their disposal, and they would reinforce an almost collapsed Fenian organisation.[220]

The Times had always opposed amnesty as an encouragement to rebellion. A year after Stephens' spectacular escape from Richmond Bridewell, *The Times* speculated that he might be back in Ireland again where 'he reckons, if not on success, at least on impunity. He sees how easily rebels have been let off of late years, and thinks the game, if the worst comes to the worst, at least a safe one.' Objecting to the release of the Fenian leaders, it further condemned the decision to send them to the United States of America. The men's exile had been triumphal: their first-class passages across the Atlantic; fast craft setting out to meet them; a vote of the House of Representatives; their reception by President Grant. They had become, indeed, 'the lions of the hour'. It was difficult enough to mount a trial in Ireland, but where in future could reliable witnesses and juries be found, when the outcome would be 'a short imprisonment . . . followed by a triumphant liberation of the traitor and the honours of a cheap martyrdom'.[221]

The Conservative *Standard* was also strongly disapproving of what it saw as lenient treatment: 'A great many honest burglars and meritorious pickpockets have suffered and are suffering even more severely than the Fenians.' The release of the Fenian leaders was 'a weak and foolish use of the Queen's prerogative'.

---

218 *Spectator*, 18 September 1868, pp. 1088–9, *passim*.

219 *Spectator*, 19 March 1870, pp. 368–9. At this time the *Spectator* described itself as Whig, its articles written in a spirit of 'perfect independence'.

220 Ibid., 24 December 1870, pp. 1540–1. The *Spectator*'s fears were confirmed by the Congressional reception for Rossa and his companions – an action which it thought misrepresented the views of the American people (ibid., 4 February 1871, 127a). In practical terms it mattered little where the Fenians were first exiled since unless imprisoned they could subsequently make their way to America.

221 10 March 1871, 10a and b. *The Times* trusted that there would never be another Fenian rising, but should there be, 'the liberation of Rossa and his comrades cannot but become a source of weakness'.

Gladstone himself was clearly not convinced of the men's good intentions – why otherwise were they being sent out of the country: 'Either they are capable of mischief or they are not. If they are, they should be kept in prison: if they are not, then there can be no harm in letting them go where they please.' The real reason they were being released was that Gladstone could not afford to quarrel with the Irish Party.[222]

For the Liberal *Manchester Guardian* the first releases were enough: all had been liberated 'who have the smallest claim to mercy'. The imprisoned leaders were 'stained with crimes which would make it an unpardonable weakness to send them out again upon the world'. It was through no want of effort on their part that Ireland was not deluged with blood. They deserved no sympathy, and sympathetic meetings would be popularly interpreted as support, if not for Fenianism, then for 'that chronic agitation which has been the curse of Ireland'.[223]

In the end, however, the *Guardian* was willing to go along with Gladstone. It had found renewed cause for alarm in the remarks of Augustine Costello at Ballinasloe and in the Cork demonstrations, and argued that in future substantial guarantees for good conduct should be required.[224] The condition of expatriation attached to the leaders' release twenty-one months later assuaged these anxieties. Taken with Gladstone's programme of legislative reform, the leaders' exile convinced the newspaper that the unthinkable could be contemplated, and that what had been 'unpardonable weakness' was 'a pledge of generous intention designed to give additional effect to the conciliatory policy on which Parliament and the Government have entered'. Despite the speeches and writings of some of those released, the bulk of the Irish people, whatever their policy differences with the British government, 'accept the boon . . . in the spirit in which it is offered'.[225]

Other provincial newspapers took the same, somewhat uneasy line of support for Gladstone's policy. The *Leeds Mercury*, commenting on the Lords' attacks, argued that the Conservatives erred by failing to distinguish between the anti-British feeling 'so largely and deeply impregnating the mass of the Irish people, and the outrages and rebellions which occasionally burst out from this smouldering sentiment'. If that line were to be followed, the *Mercury* argued, 'the prisoners would never be released, but fresh batches would be perpetually added to their

222 20 December 1870, 4d–e, *passim*.
223 17 March 1869, 7f.
224 *Manchester Guardian*, 22 March 1869, 2f.
225 Ibid., 29 December 1870, 4d and e. Even the ghost of the now sanitised William Smith O'Brien was summoned to express support for Gladstone's policy. Had he lived to see disestablishment, and the Land Act, and Parliament's honest sympathy with Irish grievances, 'He would have perceived the needlessness, if not the hopelessness, of aiming at the objects which he had in view through the unspeakable horrors of insurrection and civil war'. (O'Brien was sufficiently restored to respectability for his statue to be erected in Dublin's Stephen's Green, where it was unveiled on 26 December 1870.)

numbers'.[226] It had no doubt that government had exercised 'a wise discretion'. The *Mercury* quibbled only with the expatriation condition which attached to the pardons, and hoped that the released Fenians would so conduct themselves in the United States of America that it would be possible to revoke the exile which 'so long as it continues, will be a source of irritation'.[227]

Amnesty and Irish opinion

Irish nationalists were united on the undesirability of the American exile. Richard Pigott's *Irishman* contrasted the response of the government to the Hyde Park Riot, which had preceded the 1867 Reform Bill, with the negative response to the amnesty campaign's 'orderly and peaceful manifestations'. What was being granted was exile, not amnesty. Had the Fenians' revolt been without cause there would have been no injustice in exiling them or continuing their imprisonment. But this and previous administrations had admitted that the wrongs done in Ireland were unbearable. The outcome was 'in the highest degree unfair'.[228]

A. M. Sullivan's *Nation* was hardly less dismissive. In response to the first amnesty, the newspaper observed that Russia and Britain apart, no country in Europe was holding political prisoners, despite all the upheavals of recent years. The leaders of the Confederacy were, almost to a man, pardoned by the Union at the end of the war, and even Turkey had been more magnanimous to its rebels than England. The partial amnesty was an example of English clemency and liberal magnanimity: 'Nations of the world, hear it! Men of Ireland, hold your breath and bide your time! Thirty-two of your fellow-countrymen are still the prisoners of your English master.'[229] The partial amnesty had been intended to conciliate, but what had been given would confuse, perplex and perhaps irritate the public mind: the government had made 'a miserable blunder'.[230]

Seeing the 1870 to 1871 releases also as a partial amnesty, the *Nation* reiterated those objections, though less vehemently. Expatriation had taken some of the 'grace and sweetness' out of the act of clemency, thus depriving it of 'those

---

226 *Leeds Mercury*, 22 March 1869, 2e and f.

227 Ibid., 20 December 1870, 5c. The editorial concluded with a look to the future. Was it too much to hope, it pondered, 'that we have really entered upon a better state of things; that it will be long before our gaols again become the homes of political prisoners'.

228 Especially as the Fenians had been 'flung amongst the lowest of scum of England's criminals . . . made to bear the brunt of the ill-will of turnkeys who loathed their country, and of scoundrels who detested their honour, honesty, and birth'. Completely carried away, the editorial proclaimed that 'The agony of their torture, material as well as moral, is unparalleled in the punishments of political offenders' (*Irishman*, 24 December 1870, 408b and c).

229 *Nation*, 27 February 1869, 441c–d.

230 Ibid., 440c. 'The country,' the editorial continued, 'expected of them a large, bold, and generous measure; they have replied with a half-hearted and disappointing one, an act of clemency so constrained and limited that, as Grattan said of another halting and incomplete concession, the "liberty withheld will poison the good communicated".'

qualities of courage and generous confidence which always touch the Irish heart'. Allowed unconditionally to return to Ireland, the men's sense of gratitude would have ensured their future peaceable behaviour. In America no such obligation was created, and there could be no expectation that they would abstain from Irish politics. There existed in America 'a powerful organization of armed Irishmen, pledged to the work of overthrowing British rule in Ireland', and therefore, the *Nation* suggested, 'the more kindly and trustful course in this matter would have been the wiser one'.[231]

Like other origins of the 'advanced' nationalist press, the *Flag of Ireland* did not moderate its hostility in response to either of the amnesties. 'Over the length and breadth of the land,' the newspaper insisted, 'whilst the prisoners released will be hailed with delight, the cry will resound, "This is no amnesty".'[232] The spirit of dissatisfaction with the partial amnesty was, if anything, stoked by the accounts given of the severity of their treatment by those who were first released. Both John Haltigan[233] and Michael O'Regan[234] described their imprisonment as 'most inhumanely severe' and 'horrible'. Charles Kickham, whose health was fragile before his imprisonment, was a living reproach to the policy of continued imprisonment for the other leaders. On his arrival in Dublin he became ill as a result, the *Flag of Ireland* hypothesised, of 'the change from the horrible prison fare to the diet of human beings'.[235]

One of the most inflammatory fruits of the 1869 amnesty was the endorsement of the pamphlet *Things Not Generally Known Concerning England's Treatment of Fenian Prisoners*, which was first published serially in March 1869 in Richard Pigott's *Irishman* as a repudiation of the 1867 inquiry by Pollock and Knox.[236] An inspired piece of political campaigning, this material was in preparation well before the first amnesty, and its publication coincided almost exactly with the releases. Charles Kickham, C. M. O'Keeffe and James O'Brien all validated its claims. Their endorsements were the more telling since they were careful to confine themselves only to matters of which they had personal knowledge. By serialising the material in his newspaper, and then publishing it as a pamphlet, Pigott ensured maximum publicity, in Ireland, England and the United States of America. Substantial portions of it were reprinted in the *Flag of Ireland*,[237] and it was referred to in other newspapers. What lent particular immediacy and impact

---

231 Ibid., 24 December 1870, 297c; see also 295c for the announcement of the Amnesty.
232 *Flag of Ireland*, 27 February 1869, 4d; see also 3c and d – 'The Sham Amnesty'.
233 The foreman printer of the *Irish People*, sentenced to seven years' penal servitude by the Special Commission in December 1865.
234 Seven years' penal servitude imposed by the Cork Special Commission in January 1866.
235 *Flag of Ireland*, 13 March 1869, 5a.
236 See p. 155, n. 62 above for an account of the provenance of this pamphlet. The Pollock and Knox Inquiry was published as *Report of the Commissioners on the Treatment of the Treason-Felony Convicts in the English Convict Prisons*, PP, 1867 [3880], XXXV, 673, 1.
237 See the issues of 6,13, 20, 27 March and 3 April 1869.

was the claim that its author ('a chivalrous young Irishman of superior education and spotless honour') was still imprisoned and thus enduring the conditions he described. The pamphlet had a significant effect on Irish opinion, and so worried Gladstone as to be a factor in the establishment of the Devon committee.

This impression of harshness of treatment and severity was reinforced in 1870 to 1871 with the release of the leaders. The *Flag of Ireland* was emphatic in its condemnation of the condition of expatriation,[238] and printed letters to their relatives from Luby and Power. Imploring his wife and children not to travel to Portland to see him before his deportation, Luby struck a note of pathos and helplessness that cannot have failed to evoke anger as well as sympathy in the ranks of nationalists. Power, who wrote from the invalid prison at Woking, confirmed that there was no question of the released men visiting friends and relatives in Ireland before their departure for America: they were to be treated as prisoners until they embarked, and any farewells would be restricted to the prison.[239]

The venerable *Dublin Evening Post*, Liberal and free trade, predictably came closest to understanding Gladstone's position, and lavishly praised his clemency. The amnesty of the Fenian leaders was 'an act of grace and healing with scarce a parallel, that we can call to mind, throughout the associated history of England and Ireland. . . . There has never existed heretofore a government whose assumed good will to adopt the policy of forgive and forget would have been in any sort of proportion to its means.' The editorial did not suppose that British opinion was fully convinced by the government's policy of amnesty and, while it would eventually see its correctness, in the meanwhile 'it is certain that the government has put a heavy strain upon English opinion by its resolution to discharge the prisoners'.[240] This was an appeal to forgo that boasting triumphalism which had cut across Gladstone's hopes for the 1869 amnesty. Tranquillity in the short term, conciliation in the long were in Irish no less than English interests.

238 'It has been intimated to the prisoners by the agents of the English government that their sentences have been changed to exile, and they have been directed to communicate with their friends with the means to defray the expenses of their banishment' (31 December 1870, 1d). The latter statement was completely untrue, of course.
239 *Flag of Ireland*, 31 December 1870, 7b and c.
240 *Dublin Evening Post*, 19 December 1870, 2d.

6

THE CONVICT MICHAEL DAVITT

Latecomers excluded

The case of Michael Davitt marked an important transition. After a determined fight on both sides, the Fenian prisoners had eventually been conceded political status. Davitt served the whole of his first period of penal servitude as an ordinary convict but, as an act of political clemency, was released some four years earlier than would ordinarily have been possible. For Davitt the experience was a protracted ordeal, as penal servitude was intended to be, and he later wrote about it in a partisan but dignified and scrupulous manner. If his and the official account do not always agree, such further enquiries as now are possible generally resolve discrepancies in Davitt's favour. Reading the extensive surviving official records, public accounts and private papers dealing with Davitt's imprisonments (there were three in all) he emerges as a person of integrity, one who for his own sake above all would not wilfully misrepresent his experiences. In the bibliography of prison writings this is a rare quality, and, being thus perceived by his contemporaries, it enhanced his moral and political stature, and gave weight to his utterances and writings on prison matters. He was no turbulent Rossa: his prison record shows only a handful of disciplinary reports, and those of the most trivial kind. This was a man who tried to survive in the convict system, keeping his mental and emotional balance, and limiting the damage which could undoubtedly arise from a long confinement.

The question of amnesty arose early in his imprisonment. Davitt had the misfortune to be a late Fenian – he certainly was no dynamitard – and thus was excluded from the 1869 to 1871 amnesty, even though his offence was no greater than most of those who were released, and was less serious than many. This is not to say that he was a trivial offender. Indeed, from 1868, when he succeeded Ricard O'Sullivan Burke as the chief IRB organiser and quartermaster in England, Davitt was a dangerous threat to public order and security. He was only 22 years old when he assumed these IRB positions, but he was intelligent, self-disciplined and well schooled in conspiratorial method.[1] He travelled about the country on various organisational tasks, but his principal work was the procurement of arms (mainly from legitimate gunsmiths) and organising their smuggling to Ireland. Years later he cheekily described himself to the Kimberley Commission as a 'commercial traveller in fire-arms'.[2] There was no way he could be represented as an immature dupe, or released with the senior Fenians – Devoy, Rossa, Luby, O'Leary et al. – even though their time in prison overlapped with his. He was convicted on 11 July 1870 and sentenced to fifteen years' penal servitude for treason felony, and was still serving the solitary confinement stage of his sentence in Millbank when the Fenian leaders and a number of their followers were released and expatriated. The practical politics of the Cabinet meant that Gladstone, even had he wished to do so, could not have treated Davitt and his English accomplice John Wilson as 'afterthoughts' and slipped them into the amnesty.[3] There could not be a rolling programme of offending, imprisonment and amnesty. Davitt's was as good a case as any to establish this point.

Yet the issue was a difficult one to state in terms of principle, and to detach from political necessity and expediency. With Davitt three years into his sentence,

---

1 See Theodore William Moody's definitive *Davitt and Irish Revolution* (Oxford, Oxford University Press, 1981, ch. 2) for an overview of this phase in Davitt's revolutionary career. Davitt's exceptional qualities were evident at an early age. Born in the famine years (1846) his family was evicted from its Co. Mayo smallholding and emigrated to Haslingden in Lancashire. Davitt commenced work in a cotton mill at the age of 10, and two years later lost his right arm in the machinery. The accident compelled him to work in a print shop, and the opportunities he thus gained, and his natural intelligence, curiosity and determination, meant that he was able to educate himself to a surprising degree. In an autobiographical fragment Davitt observed that in the three or four years after he lost his arm he obtained 'all the schooling it has been my good fortune to get outside of my own exertions in the task of mental improvement' (Trinity College Dublin (TCD): Davitt Papers: Ms. 9639, f. 358 *ob.*). By his fortieth year he had published his *Leaves from a Prison Diary* (London, Chapman and Hall, 1885, 2 vols), which displays first-rate intellectual abilities in an account of his imprisonment and an exposition of his various criminological, penal, political and economic views. Because his formative years were spent in a mill town Davitt, of all the Irish revolutionary leaders of his time, was most sympathetic to the English working class and to his fellow prisoners. An election to the Commons (for Co. Meath) during a second imprisonment (1881–2) was declared invalid. He was returned for North East Cork in 1893 and in 1895 for Mayo, South. In 1899 he resigned his seat and travelled to South Africa to further his sympathetic interest in the Afrikaner cause. He died on 30 May 1906.
2 *Royal Commission to Inquire into the Working of the Penal Servitude Acts* (hereinafter *Kimberley Commission*), PP, 1878–9 [C.2368], XXXVII, 1, q., 6532, p. 529.
3 The first amnesties, as has been seen, were carried by Gladstone almost alone, in the face of strong Cabinet doubts and opposition from the Irish government and the Queen. By the spring of 1873 Gladstone was unclear what justification there was for his administration remaining in office. His relationship with his Cabinet colleagues was troubled. On the basis of the defeat of his Irish University Bill he tried to slip away, but the Conservatives were unwilling to assume office, and he had to soldier on. The Fenian amnesties had been part of his wider Irish policy, which had since identified other priorities: Gladstone had neither reason nor means to deliver further amnesties (see Richard Shannon, *Gladstone: Heroic Minister 1865–1898*, London, Allen Lane, 1999, ch. 4).

Isaac Butt pleaded for his release. Gladstone, feeling for the firm footing of principle, floundered and threw up his smokescreen of fine-sounding words. When a convulsion had been put down by the law, he argued, it was a sound principle of modern administration to treat leniently those who through 'a contagion of strong feelings' had been led to join it. But there was no reason to deal leniently with those who 'without the apology of contagion' had sought to bring about bloodshed: 'I look upon it as an abuse and morbid symptom of the feeling of the day to bring such a class into the category of political prisoners.' Davitt's and Wilson's offences were committed 'quite apart from Fenian offences' during 1870. They were part of a secret organisation for distributing arms and laying the basis for future revolution.[4]

Gladstone's public and private assessments may have differed, and certainly his freedom of action in Davitt's case was hampered by a behind-the-scenes attempt to secure agreement from his colleagues for the release of Melody, one of the Manchester rescuers. There was strong resistance to this, and Gladstone could not afford to take on a second hard case. Later that year a new Home Secretary (Robert Lowe) informed Gladstone of his strong opposition to releasing Davitt: the Fenian conspiracy was continuing and Davitt was 'a very dangerous man and deep in all the counsels of the Fenians'.[5] This blocked Davitt's release and made it difficult to ameliorate his penal regime.

This line had been taken from the outset. At the end of April 1871, Davitt and Wilson had completed nine-and-a-half months' separate confinement and were eligible to be transferred to a public works prison. Colonel Edmund Du Cane, thinking of the just-departed Fenian leaders, sought political guidance. Were the pair to be kept apart from other prisoners, and to be treated different-ently?[6] Swiftly came the reply: They were to be treated as ordinary convicts.[7] Thus during his first imprisonment Davitt received none of the privileges which had eventually been conceded to the earlier Fenians.

The convict life

Of the post-amnesty Fenian prisoners Davitt's is the most reliable testimony. The details of his prison life are particularly well known because of his eventual

---

4 Repeating the point Gladstone went on: 'In ordinary convictions for political offences we can positively and confidentially [sic] say that once public excitement and hazard have passed away, it may be well to stretch a point on the side of mercy: but we are not able to do so in this case' (3 Hansard CCXVII, cols 997–8; 25 July 1873).
5 Robert Lowe to Gladstone, 25 November 1873; W. E. Gladstone Papers: BM Add. Mss. 44, 302, ff. 154–5. Lowe continued: 'The Fenian conspiracy still exists. It is not dead but sleepeth.' He referred to arms purchases in Liverpool and in Ireland.
6 Col. E. F. Du Cane to Henry Austin Bruce (Home Secretary), 28 April 1871: PRO HO 144/5/ 17869/2.
7 Ibid., Minutes.

importance in constitutional politics, his reputation of integrity and the consequent credence which attached to his several accounts of his own imprisonments.[8] He lacked the need for self-dramatisation of many political activists; even after the ordeal of penal servitude there was a remarkable absence of any self-blinding bitterness and, indeed, remarkable objectivity and even-handedness. His evidence to a Royal Commission on which he was cross-examined sustained his credibility.[9] Since he represented his treatment as *not* having been aggravated or mitigated because of his political status, what he said was deemed important by the 1878 Kimberley Commission: twenty years later, when an MP, he was able to speak in the Commons with authority on penal issues and to obtain great respect (if not always agreement) for his views.[10]

The psychological state of the prisoner at the commencement of his sentence is critical to his adaptation to imprisonment. Some of the Fenians were in a pitiful state, but most were able to cope. For all his youth, Davitt had considerable reserves of moral courage. Many had this at the beginning, but to sustain it through the months of solitary confinement and the years beyond was no common thing. The death of his father eighteen months into his sentence intensified the ordeal. Writing to his parents while awaiting his trial, Davitt thought the evidence against him was weak but stated that he was prepared for a conviction (and thus he sought to prepare them). He insisted that, in any event, he was not a common criminal: 'Remember, I am accused of no heinous or dishonest crime, which could cause you to blush for your son, or bring disgrace upon you.'[11] Three weeks later he affected still to hope for an acquittal,' but took another step to prepare his mother:

> Even should the worst happen, what is a few years more or less, when the mind is still the same. A contented mind, supported by health, can even in a prison enjoy the comforts of content which even liberty denies to frail humanity. . . . If I were satisfied that my mother would

8 He smuggled letters out of prison, some of which led to questions and debates in the House of Commons. In 1878 he gave evidence to the Kimberley Committee on penal servitude. Finally, he published a book on his imprisonment, *Leaves from a Prison Diary: or Lectures to a 'Solitary' Audience* (London, Chapman and Hall, 1885 (2 vols)).

9 This was the 1878–9 Kimberley Commission, *op. cit.* Davitt's evidence was given six months after his release (20 June 1878): pp. 515–45; qq. 6383–691.

10 Augustine Birrell (Irish Chief Secretary, 1907–16) inscribed a telling tribute to Davitt in a copy of his book *Leaves from a Prison Diary* which he owned (and which was sold when Birrell's library was broken up after his death): 'Michael Davitt died May 30, 1906. A most lovable man – his life comprised the whole tragedy of Ireland within its compass. I had many delightful conversations with him in the House of Commons and one or two pleasant walks in Battersea Park' (Archives Office of Tasmania, Irish Convicts File: Mimeographed article, T. J. Kiernan, Irish Minister in Australia).

11 TCD: Davitt Papers: Ms. 9321/5, f. 1 *ob.*; 18 June 1870. He hoped to be acquitted and to leave England to join them.

not give way to useless sorrow, or regrets, I would not care one pin for whatever term of imprisonment I might receive.[12]

His resolve held when he was convicted and sentenced to fifteen years' penal servitude. He still hopes to see his family again:

> They may keep me in their prisons . . . but they cannot deprive me of the companionship of my own conscience which tells me I am guilty of no crime, and the hope that God will strengthen and succour the guiltless and cause them to triumph in his own good time . . . I was never in better health in my life, and am quite reconciled to my fate.[13]

Security

Davitt's Home Office file shows that the extra restrictions imposed on him all related to security – a need to minimise his possibilities of escape, or ability to cause trouble.[14] Having reviewed Davitt's complaints and the official record, his sympathetic biographer, Theodore Moody, concluded that as far as the authorities – government, Home Office and convict service – were concerned 'There was no intention of treating him with exceptional severity. The official intention was to treat him according to the ordinary rules of the prison system, and broadly speaking that was how he was in fact treated.'[15]

The extra security to which Davitt was subject during his first imprisonment was fairly predictable. At Millbank, the receiving convict prison, a well-behaved man might after several months be given the greatly valued privilege of working outside his cell, but in Davitt's case the directors issued an order that he should not have this privilege.[16] On first arriving at Dartmoor, he was assigned to the punishment cells and protested to the governor that he was being kept awake at night by the shouting and screaming of the refractory prisoners. In addition to this, both Davitt and Thomas Chambers (one of the three remaining Fenian soldiers) were inspected hourly throughout the night, and this also broke their sleep, since to effect a proper identification the warders shone a lantern on them.[17] But the punishment cells were in the most secure part of the

---

12 Ibid., 11 July 1870; 9321/5, f. 2.
13 Ibid., 22 July 1870; 9321/7, f. 3. He *was* guilty, and in later life never pretended otherwise.
14 PRO HO 144/5/17869. See also his evidence to the Kimberley Commission, *op. cit.*, especially questions 6425–6; 6446; 6452–4; 6579: 6662–6680, pp. 518 *et seq.*
15 Theodore William Moody, *Davitt and Irish Revolution 1846–82*, *op. cit.*, p. 159. See pp. 156–9, *passim*.
16 *Kimberley Commission*, *op. cit.*, qq. 6425–6, p. 518.
17 The two other Fenian soldiers, Charles McCarthy and John Patrick O'Brien, were at Chatham Convict Prison.

prison, and Davitt was not dealt with in any other way as being under punishment. After a week or so he was assigned to one of the general population cells, but an inside one. Throughout his stay at Dartmoor he was frequently moved around cell houses, from one cell to another.[18] In August 1876 he was again assigned to the punishment cells, and remained there for some fifteen months until a few weeks before his release on ticket of leave. This cell allocation, however, was a prudent precaution in the wake of the *Catalpa* escape, news of which had taken some time to reach England.[19] Another abiding grievance was Davitt's choice of exercise companion. As a privilege the Dartmoor Governor, Major Hickey, allowed the men to choose a partner with whom to walk around the exercise yard on Sundays. Davitt naturally chose Thomas Chambers, and his request was turned down.[20]

Letters and visits were restricted to relatives and respectable friends, and Davitt also complained about this. He was allowed three letters from friends who were not relatives, but these friends had not been permitted to visit him, and he objected both to the ban and the fact that he had not been given the reason for it. This was a particular hardship as his family were all in the United States of America, and the strict reading of the rules meant that he received no visits at all. The authorities justified the decision on security grounds – the friends might be fellow-conspirators, or might carry messages on behalf of Davitt's Fenian associates. Davitt objected that he would not be so foolish as to deliver co-conspirators into the hands of the authorities.[21] In all of these matters (including labour assignments) security rather than malice was paramount for the directors and the governors, for whom the consequences of Davitt's escape (or even a half-way decent escape attempt) would have been disastrous. Davitt was a reasonable man, who attempted to be as fair as he could on prison matters, but he would have none of this.[22]

It was central to penal servitude that the regime should get as close to uniformity as was humanly possible. Staff discretion was curtailed to the greatest practical extent through an extensive code of rules and regulations. These were accompanied by a constant flow of detailed interpretive standing orders: all aspects of the prison day and the thousand-and-one minute details of institutional

---

18 Ibid., qq. 6448–55, p. 521; qq. 6679–80, p. 543.

19 Ibid., qq. 6676–8, p. 543. The *Catalpa* escape took place on 17 April 1876, but since the submarine telegraphic cable linking Australia and Britain broke on 24 April news of the escape had to be taken to England by ship. See above, p. 212.

20 This privilege was granted only during Major Hickey's governorship, and was discontinued after 1873, the men being obliged to walk with whomsoever the warders decreed (ibid., qq. 6597–8, p. 535; qq. 6674–5, p. 543).

21 Ibid., qq. 6662–70, pp. 541–2.

22 Asked why he considered himself to have been treated with exceptional harshness he responded: 'I was more strictly watched while I was in Dartmoor and Millbank than any other prisoner . . . while conforming to the prison rules in the very letter, I was deprived of the privileges to which such conformity to the rules entitles all the prisoners' (ibid., q. 6662, p. 541).

life were micro-managed. This apparatus of control was cross-checked and rein-forced by direct supervision and a strict hierarchy of control by numerous ledgers and books of record, by frequent letters of enquiry and visitations from an inspector (an in-house auditor and assistant director) and the director with particular responsibility for the prison. At the centre of the web of control, Edmund Du Cane energetically and unrelentingly enforced accountability and demanded an adherence to the rules as complete for staff of all grades as it was for convicts.[23] Provided he abided by the rules, any member of staff, from the governor to the newest assistant warder, was safe, whatever the outcome. Any exercise of discretion was hazardous, even were there a favourable outcome, and always at risk of being discovered. This knowledge in itself – and it was con-stantly emphasised – was enough to scour the machine of almost every vestige of human sympathy. Convicts were so many objects to be processed, constantly unpredictable risks to the official's career. In these circumstances a cold impersonality was the safest course for a reasonable man.

The bitter herbs of captivity

The convict diet was considerably more generous than that of the local prisons (or, as many contemporary commentators pointed out, the workhouses), but given the extreme demands of their heavy labour it was barely adequate for the convicts, especially those with larger frames. Precise calculations had been made so that quantity should be enough to sustain life, while flavour, smell and quality should deprive it of all enjoyment: diet was an instrument of the punishment – little more than the unvarying sustenance of brutes. In a pamph-let published after his first penal servitude, Davitt recalled that at Dartmoor it was quite common to find black beetles in soup, skilly (a porridge mixture) and other foods: the convicts removed the insects and ate the food. In a particularly graphic and horrible paragraph Davitt explained that men were also frequently reported and punished for eating candles, boot oil and other substances,

> and notwithstanding that a highly offensive smell is purposely given to prison candles to prevent their being eaten instead of burned, men are driven, by a system of half-starvation, into an animal-like voracity, and anything that a dog would eat is nowise repugnant to their taste. I have seen men eat old poultices buried in heaps of rubbish, and have seen bits of candles pulled out of the prison cesspool and eaten after the human soil was wiped off them.[24]

23 Sir Edmund F. Du Cane, *The Punishment and Prevention of Crime*, London, Macmillan, 1885, ch. 6, *passim*; Seán McConville, *A History of English Prison Administration 1750–1877*, London, Routledge & Kegan Paul, 1981, pp. 417–19.

24 Cited by Francis Sheehy Skeffington, *Michael Davitt: Revolutionary Agitator and Labour Leader*, London, MacGibbon & Kee, 1967, p. 49. The Kimberley Commission took evidence from

He also complained of putrid meat in the soup, of bad bread, and of vegetables that in the free world would have been animal feed. Dartmoor prisoners frequently did not even get the proper measure of this awful food. Cookhouse trustees stole that intended for their comrades, and although they were entitled to have their allowance weighed, few prisoners did so, since the extra trouble this caused to staff might have invited retaliation.[25]

Twenty years after his release from Dartmoor, Davitt spoke in a Commons debate on the 1898 Prisons Bill. Prison diet was so seared into his memory that, even after all those years, he conjured up the pangs of hunger. There was no bodily punishment more cruel, he told them, 'than that remorseless, gnawing, human feeling which tortures the mind in thinking of the sufferings of the body, and tending to make life an unbearable infliction under a denial of the element-ary cravings of nature'. And this was the full allowance of the ordinary diet. Of the punishment diet (of which he had several doses), he told the Commons, 'You would not punish a dog in that manner – you would shrink from inflicting any such inhuman penalty upon any animal in your possession.'[26]

Hygiene and health

Sanitary standards in the convict prisons (as in the local prisons and work-houses) were by the 1870s generally sufficient to prevent the deadly epidemics of earlier generations, but they did not go much beyond that. Apologists for these institutions insisted that they reflected the conditions in which the poor lived, and standards were a great deal higher than many if not most prisoners had procured for themselves when free. For respectable working men such as Davitt, however, there were many occasions when the sensibilities were revolted, and a powerful feeling of contamination took hold. During his period of Millbank solitary confinement (and Davitt did not speak ill of the prison – even its food) he did not recollect seeing any of the bedding being washed. Two blan-kets, one sheet and a rug were allowed to each man (sufficient in summer, but not in winter). When Davitt was moved from cell to cell (which was done frequently for security reasons) he was not allowed to take any of his bedding – even the sheet – with him. The result was that one had to sleep in bedding which another man had used and, Davitt told the Kimberley Commission,

---

Davitt and vigorously examined him on these points. Apart from admitting that he had seen only one man eat a poultice, Davitt insisted on the truth of all he had written. He had, however, to admit that some of his claims and accusations were based on hearsay (*Kimberley Commission*, qq. 6504–9; 6517–20, pp. 526–8).

25 Ibid., qq. 6494–6500, p. 525. At Millbank and Portsmouth, Davitt recalled, the food had been much better. At the former, he stated, 'the food in quality was what it was expected to be, and it was in quantity, I think, fair to the prisoners' (ibid., q. 6514, p. 527).

26 4 *Hansard*, LV, col. 1183; 28 March 1898. Prison diet was a 'scale of scientific starvation'.

'I have often found bedclothes soiled with human soil. . . . Sheets and blankets too'.[27]

Bathing arrangements were minimal at Millbank and Dartmoor, and conducted in a way that a man with any sense of personal cleanliness would have found disgusting and repulsive. At Dartmoor, where men were engaged in heavy and dirty labour, a full bath was usually given only once a fortnight, and feet washed once a week. Despite the official requirement that the water should be fresh for each man, Davitt recalled, 'prisoners are not often fortunate enough to get a clean bath for bathing all over'. Three wards might bathe in one night, and only the first get clean water. The prisoners who had charge of running the baths might not run fresh baths 'and so we would have to use water already used by one or two men'. The warders who supervised the baths were there for security purposes only, and the bathhouse prisoners might refuse to go to the trouble of filling and emptying thirty or forty baths. And when it came to the weekly feet-bathing the expectation was that the water would not be changed. Two or three wards would wash their feet in the same water, 'and that is according to order'.[28]

Ventilation and the circulation of air was a matter to which much official attention was paid. Sir Joshua Jebb, the first Surveyor General of Prisons (and first Chairman of the Convict Directorate), had devised a system of foul-air extraction operated by hot-air flues. However satisfactory on the engineer's drawing-board, in practice this was frequently unsatisfactory, and there were many complaints about its inadequacies.[29] When one considers that some of the cell blocks at Dartmoor did not even have Jebb's imperfect ventilation, and takes into account the men's heavy labour, infrequent baths and clothes changes, the air must indeed have been foul. It was indeed so bad, Davitt insisted, that in some of the top cells it was difficult to breathe. This situation was made worse by the materials from which these small sleeping cells were constructed – iron and slate – and from the fact that they were Auburn-type inner cells without direct access to the outer walls and windows of the cell house. The effluvium of unwashed men meant that in the summer, and especially in the mornings, the air was particularly foul.[30]

---

27 Ibid., qq. 6428–9, p. 519. He added that he thought that the rules had since been changed and that on moving cells men could take their blankets with them.

28 Ibid., qq. 6569–74, p. 532. When working in the prison laundry, Davitt said, he had been allowed the privilege of a weekly bath 'as the work was very laborious, and the men sweated very much' (q. 6569, p. 532). At Millbank the practice was also to bathe one's feet once a week, and to have a full bath once a fortnight. Here also the same water was made to serve several men: 'One bath often served half a dozen men, to my knowledge.' The Millbank ward of thirty men had access to six baths, 'and it was very seldom that the water would be renewed more than twice for the 30 men' (ibid., qq. 6434–5, pp. 519–20).

29 See my *English Local Prisons 1860–1900: Next Only to Death*, London, Routledge, 1995, pp. 282–4.

30 *Kimberley Commission*, qq. 6472–9, p. 523.

This situation, onerous and disgusting though it was, was far worse for those men (such as Davitt, for a time) who were located close to the dry-earth lavatories. These consisted of three tubs between eighty-four men. The excrement was used for manuring the fields, and as each man excreted he was supposed to throw dry earth over his faeces. This, Davitt insisted, was not sufficient to keep down the foul smell. The tubs, moreover, were not emptied from Saturday night until Monday morning, and his cell was only ten feet away from them. In addition to this stench, night slops were collected each morning from the cells (each man had a chamber-pot) and were emptied into a sink in the closet. This also produced a foul smell. Davitt complained of the poor ventilation and odours, but the governor refused to move him to another cell. When some type of rash broke out on his chest, however, the doctor authorised a shift.[31]

As might be imagined in such circumstances, there were continuing problems with infestation. Davitt had described finding 'black beetles' (presumably some form of cockroach) in his food. This arose, he believed, from the fact that these insects swarmed in the kitchen: 'I have heard some of the officers at Dartmoor remark that they throw boiling water over the floor at night time, but that does not destroy them.' Indeed, hygiene practices in the kitchen must have been another reason for a sense of contamination (and poor health). The food trays on which the men were fed were inadequately washed. Only three men were allocated to this duty, and a thousand trays had to be washed each day. The result, Davitt said, was that the trays were 'very dirty, and often filthy, as if they had not been at all washed from the previous day, and those dirty tins would give a taint to the food which was contained in them, when, perhaps it was not the fault of the food.'[32]

Davitt smuggled letters out of Dartmoor describing conditions in much the same terms (though not at such length or as comprehensively) as the evidence that he later gave to the Kimberley Commission.[33] Despite the certainty that he would be punished for this breach of the rules, he asked Irish MPs to use the information, which they did during the debate on the 1877 Prisons Bill. John O'Connor Power,[34] the former Fenian (and for six months an internee in Dublin), now MP, read out extracts from the letters. He had been put in stone-breaking, wrote Davitt, of which in warm weather he did not complain, but which in the

---

31 Ibid., qq. 6481–9, pp. 523–4.

32 Ibid., q. 6510, p. 526. In addition to black beetles Davitt also sometimes found horsehair in his food and 'pieces of old broom with which the bakehouse and cookhouse were swept out . . . and bits of stone occasionally. I have also found pieces of coal in the shins of beef soup' (ibid., q. 6521, p. 527).

33 The first of these appeared in the *Freeman's Journal*, 3 September 1872, 6d.

34 See pp. 307–8. In secret papers O'Connor Power was described as having been the associate of a Fenian group in England which at one point plotted to kidnap the Prince of Wales (Sir Robert Anderson to Sir William Harcourt, 5 November 1883; Sir Robert Anderson Papers: PRO HO 144/1537/Pt. 1(c)).

very coldest weather was a hardship. He described the sanitary conditions and also complained that his reasonable requests were refused. His cell was directly opposite and only ten to twelve feet away from the water-closet where the faecal matter from ten wards was kept in tubs before being used to manure the fields. He asked to be moved, but this was refused, even though there was a vacant cell available. His seven-by-four-foot cell was constructed of iron and slate, and during the long and severe Dartmoor winter he suffered from catarrh and incessantly spat phlegm. This, he insisted, must inevitably produce lung disease. In general terms he observed that 'the food was so abominable bad and filthy, that the wonder was how men could bear up against two of the greatest hardships of life – cold and hunger'. The system of administration was as bad as the regime which it enforced: 'there was not one prison official, from the Visiting Director to the lowest of the crowd, that would not lie to save themselves from blame or exposure.'[35]

Medical services

Davitt gave various instances of men whose serious condition was overlooked or misdiagnosed by the surgeons. One man had several times reported himself sick, but had never been admitted to the infirmary, as far as Davitt knew: 'One morning I observed him drop dead on the parade, and I believe it was from heart disease, or from bursting a blood-vessel or something of that sort.' Another man, also misdiagnosed, had died of lung disease and yet another when being operated on for a stricture. It was generally believed among the prisoners, Davitt recalled, that the latter had died 'owing to the unskilful manner in which he was treated'.[36] He also told the Kimberley Commission that Dartmoor men attending morning sick parade had to strip naked in the infirmary porch in preparation for the doctor's examination. The porch was covered, and had a door which opened directly on to the prison yard. Having stripped, the prisoners were searched and admitted to the infirmary where they waited (clothed again) for some two hours before seeing the doctor.[37] Those who applied in the morning (rather than the previous evening) had to forfeit almost three-quarters of their lunch-hour for the examination.[38] This evidence was not contradicted in official evidence to the Commission.

---

35 3 Hansard, CCXXXIV, col. 1312; 5 June 1877. Replying, Richard Assheton Cross, the Home Secretary, emphatically denied Davitt's statements, and observed 'that prisoners from a class of life like that of Davitt found the discipline, the restraint, and the food of a prison irksome and distasteful was likely enough; but it must be remembered that the man had been convicted of felony' (ibid., col. 1317).

36 Ibid., qq. 6606–7, p. 536.

37 Ibid., qq. 6617–24, pp. 537–8.

38 Ibid., qq. 6634–5, p. 538.

We have seen that convict service doctors were constantly – some obsessively – on guard against malingering,[39] and Davitt fell victim to this fixation at Portsmouth. Davitt believed he had been suffering from quinsy, tonsillitis or bronchitis. Having examined Davitt's throat and asked him to put out his tongue, the medical officer said that there was a little inflammation, but nothing serious. He then ordered that Davitt should be put on disciplinary report for 'falling out without sufficient reason'. Brought before the governor, Davitt was admonished: 'I was not punished, as the officer in charge of the ward testified that I had been unable to eat food for two days.'[40]

In a pamphlet on his prison experiences Davitt had claimed that a paralysed man had asked for water, but had been told by the deputy governor that he had water in his cell, and if he wanted it he could get up for it. Questioned by the Kimberley Commission, Davitt gave further details. The doctor had suspected the man of shamming, and in consequence once a year put him in the punishment cells where he was left for two or three weeks to test whether the paralysis was genuine. Since the man had been in prison he had not walked, Davitt insisted, nor done anything that would suggest dissembling. But the doctor was certain that he was faced with a determined malingerer: 'I have seen that man twice in the punishment cell, and I have heard them drag him along the floor from the governor's office.'[41]

Ill-treatment

Davitt contended that he was singled out for ill-treatment. As will be seen, apart from certain security restrictions, it is doubtful that this was the case. Far more shocking was the lack of consideration for his disability, the insistence that he did much the same work as a two-armed man. Uncompromising demands were made from the beginning. Of his remand at Clerkenwell House of Correction (and of Fenianism's infamous connection with that place) he had little to say, and we may assume that no lack of consideration was shown to him there.[42] As a sentenced prisoner at Millbank he was compelled to pick oakum and coir, as were all the prisoners, and while doing this was obliged to sit on his upturned slop-bucket in the centre of the cell (denying him back support) for ten hours a day. Oakum-picking normally required two hands, and Davitt was able to do it only by grasping the material between his knees and tearing at it with his free hand.[43] No daily quota of oakum was set for him, but he had to work throughout

---

39 See above, pp. 182–92.

40 Ibid., qq. 6636–40, pp. 538–9; *Freeman's Journal*, 3 September 1872, 6d.

41 *Kimberley Commission, op. cit.,* qq. 6688–90, pp. 544–5.

42 He was body-searched (including an intimate examination) at Clerkenwell and on reception into Millbank (*Kimberley Commission*, q. 6568, p. 532). This was standard procedure.

43 Ibid., q. 6398, p. 516. A warder suggested that he might compensate for his infirmity by tearing at the material with his teeth, but he refused to do this (ibid., q. 6412, p. 517).

the allotted ten hours. The strain on his back – especially given that he had to bend and twist – must have been considerable. He was not excused the washing and scrubbing of his cell, even though the wringing out of the wash-cloth meant that it took him three times as long to clean his cell as an able-bodied prisoner.[44] Each Dartmoor wing (seventy or so men) emptied their chamber-pots into a slop-tub. Since so many used the tub, it may be imagined that the weight of the vessel and its contents was considerable. Davitt was ordered to empty the tub and refused, saying that he could not lift it. He was brought before the governor on a disciplinary charge and sent to the punishment cells. The following day, however, the medical officer decided that the tub was indeed too heavy for a one-armed man, and Davitt was released.[45]

At Dartmoor Davitt was put to stone-breaking (which was considered to be light labour) but after a week or two, because his hand had blistered, was transferred to a cart party. Davitt's cart supplied the various parts of the prison with coal, and also hauled rubbish, human waste and stone. He wore a harness for this work, and eventually this caught on the remnant of his amputated arm, almost forcing the bone through the skin.[46] He was returned to stone-breaking for some six months, and then worked as a labourer on a new cell block which was being built. This required him first to mix mortar and then to take his part on a four-man crew which operated a crank for lifting stones. For this last task, he recalled, he had to make as much effort as a two-handed man since he would otherwise be putting the work on his crew-mates, and making their labour harder. With twenty to thirty other disabled and weakly men Davitt was employed for most of one summer in the breaking of putrid bones which were used for fertiliser on the prison farm. He objected to this labour because of the offensive smell of the bones, but despite an appeal to the governor and the doctor was refused a transfer.[47]

In the summer of 1872 Davitt was temporarily transferred to Portsmouth, which he preferred to Dartmoor. The journeys to and from Portsmouth were conducted with an indifference to his condition – even, he claimed, with malice towards him. He was one of a batch of thirty prisoners, each of whom was manacled one hand to another. Davitt requested that instead of being cuffed by his single hand a body-belt might be used, but this was refused, as were his pleas that he might be attached to the extreme end of the party. Instead he was

44 Ibid., q. 6408, p. 517.
45 Davitt to 'M', 1 August 1872. This illicit letter was published in the *Freeman's Journal*, 3 September 1872, 6d.
46 This incident occurred in October 1871. The doctor warned him to be careful and told him that there could be 'serious consequences' should there be another incident. Instead of removing him from the cart party, however, he said he would have a protective pad made up. The prison shoemaker was sent to measure, but said it was a job for the tailor, who was apparently reluctant to become involved (*Freeman's Journal*, 3 September 1872, 6d).
47 *Kimberley Commission*, qq. 6515–25, pp. 527–8.

handcuffed between what he claimed were 'two of the dirtiest men of the 29'. Davitt had seen one of these men eat a candle from the prison cesspool, and he had particularly offensive breath (he died not long after); the man on Davitt's other side was, he said, 'equally dirty'. Cuffed by his single hand for the entire journey from Dartmoor to Portsmouth Davitt's plight took a particularly disgusting turn when the candle-eater (hardly unexpectedly) had an attack of 'looseness of the bowels' and had to use the toilet on the train while Davitt remained shackled to him. The warder in charge (no doubt following the security standing orders to the letter) insisted that he could not detach Davitt from the chain.[48]

On the return journey from Portsmouth some weeks later, Davitt was scarcely more fortunate, being handcuffed to an equally undesirable companion – 'a notorious character, who had the name of being a madman, or, as is expressed in prison slang, a "balmy bloke"'. Davitt's companion ('He is a notorious gaol-bird, and is, in fact, literally a mad-man') succeeded in removing some of his clothes while the men waited at Exeter to change trains.[49] Reading Davitt's account of these two nightmarish journeys it is hard not to believe that someone was capitalising on his one-handedness in order to have some cruel fun: at the very least it was an indifferent and callous way in which to treat a disabled man.

But it should not be imagined that Davitt was being singled out from other amputees or otherwise disabled convicts. There was little allowance for these, apart from the most grossly crippled or physically or mentally ill. Since he had one perfectly good arm Davitt was expected to use it, and it was simply his misfortune if on occasion this resulted in having to work twice as hard in order to keep up with the able-bodied.[50] It was equally his misfortune if he had to pass a journey of several hours in an all but helpless state. From Davitt's evidence to the Kimberley Commission a minor but telling example of the authorities' unwillingness to make any allowance for the disabled stands out. As a well-behaved prisoner Davitt could in time have expected to have tea instead of gruel. This privilege was withheld, however, until, despite his crippled condition, he had performed the necessary quantum of hard labour.[51]

Labour

Quite apart from his special difficulties as a one-armed man, Davitt had to endure the demanding nature of Dartmoor labour, made harder by a harsh

---

48 Ibid., qq. 6646–9, pp. 539–40. Davitt, in a letter to a friend, complained that while he remained in this position the escorting officers were laughing (*Freeman's Journal*, 3 September 1872, 6d).

49 Ibid., q. 6650, p. 540.

50 His work at Portsmouth was the stacking of wet bricks. After a fortnight of this work he was put on a reduced diet. On complaining to the medical officer that what was light labour for a two-handed man was heavy labour for him, he was told, 'Oh yes, 'tis all the same' (*Freeman's Journal*, 3 September 1872, 6d).

51 *Kimberley Commission*, q. 6671, p. 542.

climate. Stone-breaking from morning to night was not considered hard labour at Dartmoor, and Davitt was put to it because of his handicap. It was not fatiguing, he said: '[M]y objection to it was being employed in winter in the open air.' Should it start to rain once the labour party had been marched out, warders were reluctant to allow them to shelter since, if they did so without what was considered good cause, the warder was likely to be fined.[52] During severe weather some shelter was allowed, but Davitt was required to break stones while snow was falling and while it lay on the ground: 'I had to remove the snow in the morning from the stones in order to find the stones to break, and I had to stand in the snow.' From 1872 prisoners were issued with small bags of the same material as their jackets to cover their hands in the very cold weather. Davitt saw this less as a humanitarian measure than a means of enforcing the labour regime: 'The men were laid up with chilblains and were incapable of work, and then an order was issued, I think, that they should be supplied with those bags or gloves.'[53] Clothing was adequate for the summer, but not for the winter. The authorities seem to have recognised this, however, and at the same time that they issued mittens, a jersey was added to the convicts' winter uniform.

In addition to the work being arduous and demanding, and the draining effects of the Dartmoor climate, Davitt complained that there was insufficient care for prisoners' safety. When the old iron and slate cells and Auburn-type cell house were being replaced with a new, convict-built block, four men perished: three on the building works and one man in quarrying stone. Supervision of the scaffolding and building works was inadequate, and it was from a lack of knowledge of scaffolding in particular that the three men lost their lives. The general belief of the convicts was that the subsequent inquests were biased, with the jury being composed of former prison warders who had gone into business supplying the prison or were otherwise associated with it. He was strongly pressed on this point by the Kimberley Commission, however, and had to agree that he had no direct knowledge of how the coroner's jury was constituted, but that in his statements to the Commission and in a letter which he had smuggled out, and which was read in the Commons, he was simply stating what he had been told 'and what was the general belief of the prisoners'.[54] On this, and on a number of other points, Davitt's evidence as to conditions was somewhat weakened by having to rely on hearsay, but he insisted that he found the accounts which he had been given wholly credible, and repeated them because he believed them.

52 Ibid., qq. 6527–31, pp. 528–9.
53 Ibid., qq. 6534–5, p. 529.
54 Ibid., qq. 6654–60, pp. 540–1; qq. 6681–2, p. 543.

Brutalisation

Disabled or able-bodied, the effect of this type of regime – and, despite the official denials, Davitt's complaints and assessments were substantially true and sound – was to degrade the convicts physically and mentally and to sustain a climate of brutality. Writing in his own (short-lived) newspaper in 1890, Davitt argued that the monotony and unchanging routine were in themselves debilitatory, and a man coming out of prison after a long sentence would be 'so brutalised and degraded by the everlasting sameness of prison life as sometimes to be incapable of joining in social intercourse'.[55]

The convicts were, of course, completely subordinate to the warders, and while many staff performed their difficult duties fairly and decently (and they were themselves subject to a ferocious disciplinary code and unremitting surveillance), there was more than ample scope for bullying and victimisation. Davitt related a story of words passing between a warder and a convict over a work matter. The convict had probably been right regarding the detail of the work, and a principal officer to whom the matter was taken was inclined to overlook it. The convict (who was dressed in yellow clothes and wore irons as an escaper) had unfortunately expressed himself in an insolent manner – 'an unpardonable sin in the eyes of prison officials'. The offending prisoner was removed to the punishment cells by two or three warders, who used their staves on him. He was taken before the governor, who had ordered three days' bread-and-water punishment. On returning to work the prisoner had borne a great grievance, and had confided to Davitt, his workmate, that he was going to batter the warder to death with a crowbar (one of the tools of the stone-dressing on which they were working). Davitt kept a close watch on the man and managed to foil the attempt without giving him away: the other convict never spoke to him again. This incident and its near tragic outcome demonstrated to Davitt the brutalising and counterproductive culture of the convict system.[56]

The ultimate brutality, perhaps, was the punishment of those who found their lives insupportable under such circumstances, and who attempted suicide. This, were it unsuccessful, Davitt sardonically observed, 'generally leads to an interview with the grim and muscular warder, whose particular function is "bashing" the unruly members of the establishment. This gentleman does his duty as a true-born Briton should, as a sore back for a month or two eloquently testifies.'

Davitt strongly objected to what he saw as the warders' brutal behaviour, and gave evidence to the Kimberley Commission about searching and rough handling, without claiming that this was in any way exceptional treatment. It was indeed his case that the instances he cited were all the worse for being part of the normal routine. Searching was inevitable in a prison, but Davitt found the practice of having prisoners strip in groups particularly objectionable. This was

55 Michael Davitt, 'The Tortures of Convict Life', *The Labour World*, 4 October 1890, 2b.
56 Ibid., 2c.

done at Millbank, when the men bathed and when, roughly each month, cells were searched.[57] On reception at Dartmoor and Portsmouth prisons, the entire group of thirty convicts who were being processed were stripped.[58] In the daily rub-down searches, where the warders' hands were run over a prisoner's clothing, Davitt claimed that certain officers would by touching the man's private parts attempt to provoke the men into insubordination, although he noted that such behaviour was not typical of 'the generality of officers'. He had himself been touched on the private parts during rub-down searches, but never during strip-search.[59] He was subject to an examination of his rectum at Clerkenwell House of Correction, and when received into the convict system at Millbank. Such searches were not conducted upon him again.[60] Davitt's view was that a man who is not capable of murdering a warder should be excused from searching, likewise those whose offence involved 'no moral obloquy'; this of course included political offenders. Generally he thought that some other method should be adopted 'less offensive to a man's honour and feelings' although (contradictorily) he agreed that 'some system of searching is necessary in order to keep up prison discipline'. He was not prepared to say what measures should be adopted, leaving that to those who were in charge of prisons.[61]

Davitt himself was never subject to staff violence – but he saw others who were. Prisoners suspected of having contraband, such as tobacco, would be rushed by the warders and seized by the throat to prevent any swallowing; he had 'scores of times' seen this 'choking'. At Millbank he saw only 'choking', but at Dartmoor warders often used their staves to knock prisoners down.[62] These incidents were usually in response to threatening language towards a warder. He had also seen a man 'in a very weak state of health' knocked down for what he took to be failure or inability to keep up with a work party. In Davitt's view (and it was an opinion certainly shared by contemporary prison reformers) warders recruited from the army and navy were more severe in their treatment of the convicts than those warders with a civilian background.[63]

Unlike almost all Irish political prisoners, Davitt was not inclined to look down on his fellow convicts or to revile them as 'scum' and 'dregs'. He did, however, unequivocally object to the foul language and behaviour of the convict prison. He had heard much such language, and indeed 'the general run of prisoners appeared to be men who delighted in that sort of conversation'. He

---

57 *Kimberley Commission*, qq. 6437–40, p. 520.
58 Ibid., q. 6545, p. 530.
59 Ibid., q. 6547, p. 530; qq. 6565–7, p. 532.
60 Ibid., q. 6568, p. 532.
61 Ibid., qq. 6548–51, p. 530.
62 Ibid., qq. 6441–3, p. 520.
63 Ibid., qq. 6579–84, pp. 533–4. Former soldiers and sailors 'like to show their authority more than warders drafted from the artizan class' (ibid., q. 65584, p. 534). On militarisation and its critics see my *History of English Prison Administration 1750–1877*, *op. cit.*, pp. 454–6.

had often heard foul language during religious services. Men pretended to be following the service but, taking advantage of the prayers which were said loudly, they carried on conversations with the prisoners around them, 'passing remarks on the ceremony, and using foul and filthy language'. There was also a great deal of boasting about criminal exploits, especially 'to men who have not had the honour of being convicted three or four times. An offender of that sort is looked up to in prison by the general run of convicts.' Davitt thought that these undesirable conversations should be suppressed. He did not believe that the privilege of Sunday association should be stopped altogether, however, since that would punish men who did not deserve to be punished. He wished convicts to be classified and properly separated according to class, with habitual offenders being separated from first-time convicts, 'and that old gaol birds should on no account be allowed to associate with young boys. Even in chapel I have noticed what I should be almost ashamed to mention, attempts made even in chapel.'[64] This last point was studiously ignored by the Kimberley Commission, which immediately passed on to the problems arising from prisoners illicitly acquiring pencils.

Communicating with the outside world

Davitt was well supported by the Fenians, who did what they could to keep his case alive and to give him personal support. In January 1872, John Francis Maguire, Member for Cork and proprietor of the *Cork Examiner*, disingenuously sought permission for John O'Connor Power to visit Davitt. Power had been Secretary to the Supreme Council of the IRB, and continued to be a member of that body – something that Maguire must have known, since it was known to the convict service. Colonel Edmund Du Cane pointed out that convicts were not allowed visits and communications with those suspected of 'being connected with them in crime' and consequently refused to authorise the visit.[65]

In November 1872, Richard Pigott's *Flag of Ireland* alleged that Davitt, Chambers and John O'Hara were being ill-treated at Dartmoor.[66] Davitt had smuggled out a letter describing prison conditions and Pigott claimed that this had provoked retaliation. Davitt, he claimed, had been put to the most severe and degrading labour available and had been yoked with nine others to a heavy cart which they had to pull in place of draught animals. In an echo of the brutalities

---

64 Kimberley Commission, qq. 6588–9, p. 534.
65 Du Cane to Adolphus Liddell, 3 January 1872: PRO HO 144/5/17869/4. Power was at this time an assistant teacher at St Jarlath's College, Tuam, where he had for a time studied for the priesthood. He became an MP the following year (Co. Mayo) and in 1877 was expelled from the IRB Supreme Council. He and Davitt had been friends from their childhood in Lancashire (see n. 34, above and pp. 307–8, below).
66 30 November, 1872, 5d–e.

visited on Rossa, Pigott insisted that for a trivial breach of the rules Davitt had his single arm heavily ironed and fastened to his leg all day long for several days. Other severities included the denial of privileges and excessive personal searching. Similar claims were made for O'Hara and Chambers.

The Dartmoor governor replied to each charge, and his letter was passed to the Home Secretary by Du Cane.[67] The reply shows how far the men's political status – or at least political sensitivity – was acknowledged by the authorities. Since Davitt's smuggled letter had appeared he had committed one further prison offence, for which he had been cautioned, 'although the offence is usually punished'. Chambers had also committed an offence for which he had been placed on bread and water for two days. O'Hara had not been reported for any offence. As for Davitt's labour being degrading, he had been assessed for light labour only, because of his having only one arm, and had been put to stone-breaking with other light-labour prisoners. It was true that he had been harnessed to a cart, but the governor maintained that he asked for this work since he preferred it to sitting still, breaking stones. There was a complete denial ('it is utterly false') of the story that Davitt had been put in solitary confinement for objecting to his employment and that he had had his sole arm shackled to his leg. In two-and-a-half years in prison he had only once been put on bread and water, and had been cautioned six times for offences which usually would have been more seriously dealt with. He had not been denied his privileges or correspondence and was not searched more than any other prisoner, nor had he made my complaint about this. Indeed, nearly all the requests he had made had been granted. There were similar rebuttals of the allegations regarding O'Hara and Chambers. The latter was generally insubordinate, yet in eighteen months had received only five days' dietary punishment.

A table was attached, listing all the men's offences and punishments. Davitt had variously been disobedient and had small items of contraband in his posses-sion – a piece of mirror on one occasion, paper on another and (twice) pieces of knife blades. The offences, many of which were connected with illicit writing, included an occasion when he had been caught writing in his cell and had eaten the paper when ordered to give it up. (For this he had been given a day's bread and water and lost twenty-four marks.)[68] He clearly had an aversion to having his beard and moustache clipped and had twice been cautioned for this. He had given bread to another prisoner, supposedly asked to see the doctor unnecessarily and left the ranks without permission, caused confusion, had been

67 Du Cane to Bruce, 16 January 1873: PRO HO 144/5/17869/6. The *Flag of Ireland* article appeared on 30 November 1872; its provenance is not clear.

68 Later in life, when he had acquired fame as one of the leading nationalist politicians, Davitt received letters from prisoners, asking for help with their cases. At least one of these was illegally written and smuggled out: 'written in a dark corner of my cell, with the possibility of getting twenty-one days, on bread and water for it' (TCD: Davitt Papers: Ms. 9458/3743/6 *ob.*: Michael Walshe, Mountjoy Prison, to Davitt, October 1892).

insolent and had a dirty cell. Since all of these offences, apart from illicit possession, were a matter of interpretation rather than fact (and the warder's word
would invariably rule), it would seem that Davitt was generally well behaved, but
occasionally and mildly failed to knuckle down as completely as was demanded.
His punishments were lenient, but the offences were trivial: certainly there is
no sign of victimisation. Chambers had a rather shorter catalogue of offences
and punishments – again with no evidence of undue severity.[69]

Davitt's letters from prison – legitimate and illicit – give some indication of
the toll of the years. The isolation meant that he had to assure his mother that
his health was holding up and that conditions were not too bad: 'An Irishman
is not so easily "kilt" as you seem to think, and it is only the upbraiding voice of
conscience adding remorse to merited punishment that would make prison the
inferno your imagination pictures it to be.'[70] In another letter he assured her that
the passage of time in prison was not as slow as inexperienced people imagined
it to be:

> *time* must be dreadfully slow when it forms the barriers between an
> unfortunate individual and his liberty; but I assure you it is not so to
> me as yet. Our correspondence I make a calendar, and four letters [his
> entitlement under the rules] knock down a twelvemonth. The past five
> years have been satisfactorily accounted for by some twenty of my
> precious epistles, and something like three dozen more will 'backward
> turn the iron screws of fate'.[71]

The official quarterly letters were not Davitt's only link with the outside world
(as his disciplinary record of illicitly obtaining the means of writing shows), and
there survive some letters which he had smuggled out, either by a prisoner who
was released, or a sympathetic (or avaricious) warder. In these the language is
less literary, since there was no prison censor to confront and confound with
erudition and polish. In February 1876, some five and a half years into his
sentence, he remains defiant, although there are signs of strain:

> They have done their worst so far as their treatment of me is con-
> cerned and continue to deny me even the privileges of the common
> herd I am compelled to associate with. But I am sustained by the
> consciousness of my imputed 'crime' being an honourable one and that
> no degradation can lower me in the esteem of my friends.[72]

---

69 Du Cane to Bruce, 16 January 1873, *op. cit.*: all details taken from this document.
70 TCD: Davitt Papers: Ms. 9321/11, f. 15; 2 June 1874.
71 Ibid., Ms. 9321/14, f. 18; 1 March 1875. It is hard to see how Davitt imagined his elderly mother
   might draw comfort from this grim arithmetic, but it was the best consolation he could manage
   in the circumstances.
72 Ibid., Ms. 9321/36; 7 February 1876.

Three months later, his correspondence privileges suspended as a punishment, he managed to send out another letter to reassure his family, who would have been worried had they not received the usual quarterly 'blue letter' (the colour of the official letter-form). They were not to be troubled by this suspension of his writing privileges (which would not be reinstated for a further quarter): 'Their cowardly, inhuman conduct can never break my spirit.'[73]

When he sent out (officially) the letter with which he marked the seventh year of his imprisonment, Davitt's stoicism seemed to have broken. For the prison censor the literary style was again elaborate and allusive rather than direct, but the underlying uncertainty and vulnerability could not be completely disguised: his seven years had been an apprenticeship in adversity 'in its most hideous form and under conditions that would reflect credit on Procrustean hospitality'. If contrast were to enhance experience, then no happy soul who reached Paradise after a 'purgatorial probation' would be more enraptured than he would be should he live 'to emerge from my Inferno to taste again the pleasures of being free – free to mingle in the world's commotion again'.[74] At the time of writing Davitt did not know and could take no encouragement from the fact that he had only ten months left before he would again experience 'the world's commotion'.

The amnesty campaign

Appeals to Gladstone

In the years of Davitt's incarceration he had not been forgotten, nor had the few other Fenian prisoners. After euphoria over the 1871 release of the Fenian leaders had passed and a more sober assessment had been made of the conditional amnesty, a new start was made on the amnesty campaign. And, as with the campaign to free the Fenian leaders, the constitutional nationalists were able to tap into the fervour of the more extreme faction, to validate their own nationalist credentials, and to have at their service an organisation which could help deliver the vote. For the Fenians and their supporters the titular leadership of Butt and other constitutional nationalists made the amnesty movement respectable, allowed the Roman Catholic hierarchy and clergy to endorse it, and attracted mass support. This was a marriage of convenience which would survive in various organisational forms for some five decades more, and which was mutually advantageous to the two wings of nationalism.[75]

---

73 Ibid., Ms. 9320/3, f. 9; 13 May 1876.

74 Ibid., Ms. 9321/21, f. 25; 28 February 1877.

75 These various facets of the amnesty campaign were demonstrated in a Dublin meeting of the Amnesty Association on 10 October 1871. The ostensible purpose was to celebrate Butt's return as MP for Limerick. Butt represented that election as a vote for amnesty (or, rather, the completion of amnesty). P. J. Smyth (who had assisted Mitchel's escape from Van Diemen's Land twenty years before) made the point that the amnesty campaign had given impetus to the

The argument in favour of the release of the remaining prisoners was that Ireland was in a wholly peaceful and stable condition, and that the men's continued detention was based on unjustified distinctions. Of the Fenian soldiers and the Manchester rescuers, Butt argued that it was

> a miserable quibble to assert that these men were not guilty of a political offence. Every one knew that their offence was political, and it was not changed by the mere form of the trial carried out. In the Manchester case, for murder instead of treason; in the military cases, for the violation of the Military Act, instead of treason.[76]

The campaign appealed to several different constituencies. Addressing the Queen's opposition to clemency for the military Fenians, there was got up a memorial of Irish ladies, addressed to Princess Louise, asking for her intervention. This was presented at several Dublin churches for signature, and was signed by Lady Wilde, Lady Corrigan, Mrs George Henry Moore and other leading figures.[77] Meetings were also held in England and were well attended by the Irish community and, it would seem, by numbers of English radicals and other sympathisers. In a message to one such meeting, held in Liverpool, Richard Pigott of the *Irishman* contended that the punishment of the military prisoners for breaking their oath of allegiance was disproportionate: they were less guilty than those who had seduced them (and who had been pardoned and expatriated). The remaining prisoners were 'in the lowest hell of Britain jails'. Butt, writing to the same meeting, referred to Gladstone's Neapolitan pamphlet and hoped that he would not tolerate 'worse cruelties towards Irishmen who had struck wildly, and perhaps unwisely, for freedom'.[78]

The venerable Young Irelander and gentleman convict John Martin, who had become MP for Meath in 1871, wholeheartedly supported the amnesty movement, arguing that the two previous amnesties had been achieved because of the demonstrated strength of Irish popular opinion. The continued detention of fifty Irish political prisoners[79] after the liberation of comrades convicted of the same type of offence, many of whom were more prominent and important conspirators, Martin attributed to 'the English idea of striking terror in Ireland, and keeping the Irish people always impressed with a sense of the absolute and irresistible power of England'. The capriciousness of this action probably seemed

Home Rule movement. With very different objectives both sides were able to appear very pleased with each other (*Freeman's Journal*, 11 October 1871, 4e).

76 Ibid., 4e. There was no mention of Davitt or Wilson in Butt's speech.

77 *Freeman's Journal*, 20 March 1871, 3c.

78 Ibid., 1 March 1871, 3g.

79 The government said that the figure was twenty: sixteen soldiers, two Manchester rescuers, Davitt and Wilson (see p. 302, n. 98). Martin's calculation included those in Western Australia, while the government's referred to the prisoners held in English prisons only.

to government a demonstration of English national power 'which in dealing with subject Ireland, is accountable neither to the Irish people nor to common sense'. Martin was by no means certain that action in 'the imperial Parliament' would hasten the release of the prisoners, but it did serve to remind the nations that the English press had the impudence to lecture to about morality, 'the mean and cruel conduct of England in this matter'.[80]

The *Freeman's Journal*, which backed the amnesty campaign throughout, contrasted the reception of the Fenian leaders in the United States of America with the government's 'timid' amnesty policy. The US House of Representatives had given a public welcome to the expatriated prisoners by a majority of 172 to 21, and there had been effusive demonstrations in New York. Hampered and narrowed, the amnesty had satisfied no one, *Freeman's* declared, and had 'only afforded opportunity for renewed agitation at home and anti-English manifestations abroad'. The amnesty campaign had, in effect, been relaunched, and the newspaper, an important voice of middle-class, constitutional nationalism, was behind it.[81]

The new campaign certainly attracted wide support, meeting in Dublin's Rotunda on 1 February 1871, with a crowded platform including solicitors, a doctor, a justice of the peace, a professor of Trinity College, Dublin, local politicians and, of course, the veteran Fenians P. J. Smyth and John ('Amnesty') Nolan. Perhaps more significant than the platform party, however, were the letters of support read to the meeting. These came from Dr John MacHale (an old Repealer) the Archbishop of Tuam, as well as the Bishops of Monaghan, Clogher and Down and Conor, and several senior members of the Roman Catholic clergy. The usual range of local notables and politicians completed an impressive list. Nationalist speeches roused the audience, which heard a preliminary report from the Investigation Committee established by the Amnesty Association to consider the treatment of the Irish political prisoners.[82]

The Association now devoted itself to branch activity throughout Ireland and among Irish communities in England and Scotland.[83] Local authorities controlled by nationalists, or sympathetic to them, issued a series of resolutions and memorials.[84] All of this was periodically punctuated by large – sometimes

---

80 *Freeman's Journal*, 14 August 1873, 3f.

81 Ibid., 2 February 1871, 2h.

82 Ibid., 4c.

83 See, for example, reports of meetings held at Clerkenwell, Poplar, Chelsea, Deptford and the London assembly rooms of the Irish Home Rule Confederation, all on the evening of Saturday, 28 March 1874 (*Freeman's Journal*, 30 March 1871, 3d). It would seem that the level of agitation and interest in amnesty among the Irish in Britain was considerable (ibid., 11 September 1871, 2e).

84 An early example of these is the September 1871 meeting of the Castlebar Board of [Poorlaw] Guardians begging in respectful and flattering terms for the release of the remaining prisoners. Copies of the resolution were to be sent to the Prime Minister, Lord Lieutenant and Chief Secretary (*Freeman's Journal*, 11 September 1871, 2e).

'monster' – gatherings aspiring to be in the style of O'Connell. On Sunday, 7 September 1873, the Amnesty Association marshalled some tens of thousands on to Danes' Field at Clontarf, with echoes of O'Connell's frustrated meeting on that spot thirty years before, of the Irish victory over the Danes in 1014, and a reprise of the Cabra amnesty meeting four years before. The *Freeman's Journal* claimed that between 100,000 and 150,000 people were present, and hailed the meeting, its peaceful conduct and dispersal; it was but a very small proportion of the millions who supported amnesty. It was not wise government to deny the people what they asked, and at this moment 'it is almost certain that no other cause, political or otherwise, could draw together so huge and so orderly a congregation as that proclaimed from the platform in the Danes' Field'.[85]

The march to Clontarf, well marshalled and entirely peaceful, filled the entire route from the city centre, a distance of some four miles, and took two hours and forty minutes to pass a given spot. Twelve marching bands accompanied the demonstrators, and the procession was made colourful with the banners of numerous trade unions and other associations. Many middle-class families came in their own or hired carriages, and members of the associations also travelled on foot and in a variety of horse-drawn conveyances. Almost as many women as men were present, *Freeman's* reported, their dresses enlivening the scene; all wore green ribbons, sashes, badges, rosettes or hat adornments. The event was as much a nationalist pageant as a demonstration: the boost to the twin causes of amnesty and nationalism was considerable.

Throughout the autumn of 1873 a campaign of outdoor meetings continued. On each Sunday from 28 September to 23 November there were large gatherings and demonstrations at various Irish towns, and in Blackheath, near Greenwich (then a major Irish community). The numbers reported at these meetings by the nationalist press were doubtless on the optimistic side, but in any event constituted an important statement of public interest, ranging from an estimated 10,000 at Blackheath to a supposed 300,000 at Glasnevin, Dublin.[86] Gladstone requested the Irish Chief Secretary, Lord Hartington, to review the cases of the remaining prisoners. The Home Office took the view that only Davitt and Wilson might be possible cases for amnesty, but Hartington reported against any amnesty or reduction in sentences.[87] In a heated pre-election atmosphere, and despite the fact that a decision against clemency would damage the Irish support for his party in Britain, Gladstone announced his decision, evoking a predictable reaction.[88]

85 *Freeman's Journal*, 8 September 1873, 5d. The account which follows is taken mainly from this source (5d–f, 6a–e).
86 *Irishman*, 25 October 1873, 262; 29 November 1873, pp. 342–3. *The Times*, 27 October 1873, 11b.
87 W. E. Gladstone Papers: BM Add. Mss. 44144, ff. 129–33 *ob.*, 7–18 October 1873.
88 *Irishman*, 27 December 1873, 409c.

During the election campaign Gladstone's Neapolitan philanthropy came back to haunt him, as did his promise, given before the Fenian leaders were released, to open the prison doors once conditions in Ireland should permit. It was also repeatedly argued that it was a mere niggle to try to distinguish between categories of political offenders. The release of the Fenian leaders also provided a kedge anchor with which to draw the campaign forward. From Monaghan, an amnesty meeting declared that Britain had granted asylum to French soldiers who had broken their oaths and fought against their government in the days of the Paris Commune. Men who had 'killed an archbishop who massacred hostages, who burned splendid buildings are in your eyes political offenders only. If they were Irishmen you would say they were guilty of murder, arson, burglary etc., etc. As they are French, they are merely revolutionists.' The Monaghan memorialists also pointed out that when Orsini and his comrades had made an attempt on the life of the Emperor Napoleon, Gladstone was part of the government which refused to surrender them because their offence was political. There were two prisoners for whom there could be no defence for their continued detention: Davitt and Wilson: 'They were tried as Fenians who supplied arms to the brotherhood. No attempt was made to impute any offence but Fenianism to them. By your own statement they should be released.'[89]

These themes continually resurfaced in general resolutions and in correspondence addressed to Gladstone, the formula being most completely set out in a letter from the Council of the Amnesty Association on 2 May 1872, which quoted *in extenso* Gladstone's Commons reply to George Henry Moore on 17 March 1870.[90] Endorsing the Amnesty Association's argument, *Freeman's* insisted that Gladstone's 1870 response to Moore had been a promise 'which, whether direct or implied, had certainly the force of an engagement'. Ireland was profoundly at peace, with life as secure as in the most Arcadian village in England. Even the Coercion Act had failed to secure a conviction. In these circumstances the newspaper hoped Gladstone would find 'sufficient and substantial grounds for a complete forgiveness'.[91] Butt suggested that Gladstone was himself in favour of redeeming his promise and completing the amnesty, but that he had been overruled by the Cabinet.[92]

There was some truth in this for, as we have seen, behind the scenes Gladstone had tussled with senior colleagues for the release of Melody, one of the Manchester rescuers.[93] Military prerogatives continued to be asserted over the Fenian soldiers, blocking their release. There could be no public wavering, however, and Gladstone continued to adhere to the formula he had first used when

89 *Freeman's Journal*, 12 September 1872, 3i.
90 Ibid., 7 May 1872, 4a–b; see 3 *Hansard*, CC, cols 78–81; 17 March 1870.
91 *Freeman's Journal*, 12 September 1872, 2i–3a.
92 Ibid., 12 June 1872, 2e.
93 See above, p. 253.

questioned about Davitt. An Irish organisation in his Greenwich constituency forwarded the resolution of a public meeting attended by 10,000 people, reminded him of the part played by the Irish vote in his election as MP, and called on him to honour the pledge he had given to George Moore three years before to release the Irish political prisoners when conditions in Ireland were propitious. The letter praised Gladstone's policy of conciliation in Ireland and respectfully urged clemency to help complete the process. Responding, Gladstone discharged his usual bank of verbal stage-fog. Of the twenty Irish prisoners, sixteen were soldiers. It could not be argued that a soldier who conspired against the Queen was in the same category as a similarly placed civilian. Without any commitment as to the outcome he confirmed that all these cases continued to be considered on their merits. All of this was wrapped in his doctrine of the mitigating heat and tumult of revolution:

> Mr Gladstone is unable to agree . . . that these prisoners are entitled to share in the same measure of indulgence as is properly accorded to those who are drawn by the passion of the moment into the tide of proceedings which partake, even though in a remote degree, of the nature of civil war.[94]

Conservative rebuffs

There would have been many Irish electors in the drenched Greenwich crowd which Gladstone addressed on 28 January 1874. Three days previously Parliament had been unexpectedly dissolved as Gladstone sought a new mandate in the face of Liberal Party indiscipline, the need to reanimate Liberalism, a wish to avoid a draining away of energy in by-election defeats, and a desire to secure a majority which would avoid dependence on the Irish nationalists.[95] The outcome was certainly decisive, but not as Gladstone had hoped: Disraeli was returned to office with a majority of more than fifty. The campaign for amnesty could no longer rely on Liberal needs and holding Gladstone to his promise: the Conservative victory, on a scale not seen for some forty years, was an immense setback.

The election was marked by two important developments. Under the leadership of Isaac Butt the Home Rule League entered the Commons with fifty-nine

---

94 M. J. Cunningham (Secretary, Greenwich Irish Election Committee) to W. E. Gladstone, 30 October 1873; reply 5 November 1873. *Freeman's Journal*, 8 November 1873, 5e. Gladstone's last reference was to the Union amnesty after the American Civil War – a frequently cited instance of victorious generosity. Eighteen months later the two sides still differed about the number of Irish political prisoners in custody. The Amnesty Association insisted there were fifty-four such prisoners, the government eighteen (3 *Hansard*, CCXXII, col. 1760; 12 March 1875).

95 Richard Shannon, *Gladstone: Heroic Minister 1865–1898, op. cit.*, pp. 135–8. In his sixty-fifth year Gladstone undertook a fitful and mutually irritating leadership of his party in opposition.

members. The size and relative cohesiveness of the new party would make it felt not only in Irish but also in English politics, and in the business of the House. The arrival of this new parliamentary force allowed the baton of the Amnesty Association to be passed on. There is a logic in public meetings, no matter how huge they might become: if the government remains obdurate the meetings must pass on to civil disobedience, with a good chance that they will pass out of the hands of the leadership; or they must be brought to a conclusion and the focus must return to the committee room, and to Parliament. Daniel O'Connell had learned that lesson thirty years before and had backed down, partly smothered by the collapse of his followers' expectations. The appetite for outdoor meetings declined as winter came on, and the advent of the new, or at least repackaged Irish Parliamentary Party allowed the points to be switched. The Amnesty Association remained in being, but from 1874 onwards seems mainly to have concentrated on relief for the prisoners' families.[96] After many years as its chief organiser, John Nolan retired and removed himself to the United States of America.[97]

Within a month of the new administration taking office an amnesty petition supported by seventy-seven MPs – mainly but not exclusively Irish – had been presented and rejected. The new Home Secretary, Richard Assheton Cross, made it clear that he would continue the policy of the previous government. He side-stepped the question of what constituted a distinctly political offence, listed those still serving sentences for their involvement in Fenian activities, and indicated that it was not the government's intention to grant an amnesty.[98] Great offence was taken at the tone of the announcement, which was greeted with Tory cheers. The *Freeman's Journal* drew the conclusion that 'in the English Parliament, as at present constituted, there is no tolerance of Irish sentiment and no desire to defer to the opinions or feelings of the Irish members'. And in the ranks of the Liberal opposition there was said to be a certain enjoyment at the amnesty setback: '"Serve them right" would appropriately convey their sentiment of sympathy if they gave expression to the feelings which they restrain from motives of political prudence.'[99] The best that could be done in

---

96 Moody, *op. cit.*, p. 177.
97 *Irishman*, 10 July 1875, 19.
98 3 *Hansard*, CCXVIII, col. 347; 27 March 1874. The prisoners were as follows, according to his reckoning: Shore and Condon, the two remaining Manchester rescuers, serving life sentences; Davitt and Wilson; eleven soldiers serving life sentences (three in England, eight in Australia); three soldiers in Australia serving shorter sentences – one fifteen years, two ten years. These, he said, were 'probably' on tickets of leave. In addition, he mentioned two prisoners serving sentences in Ireland – twenty and ten years' penal servitude respectively – for shooting at the police. This amounted to a total of twenty prisoners or ticket of leave men in England, Australia and Ireland.
99 *Freeman's Journal*, 30 March 1874, 3d. The Irish Party had flirted with Disraeli before the election: Liberals had reason to feel aggrieved.

the circumstances was to move for a return on the political prisoners, and this Butt proposed to do.[100]

At the head of the Amnesty Association, Isaac Butt was anxious not to revive ill-feeling between the Irish parliamentary group and the Conservatives. He quoted with approbation a 'very remarkable speech' of Disraeli's in which the Prime Minister had said that it was a mistake to suppose that old Tory principles were those of enmity to Ireland, and that 'history attested that when red Toryism was in the ascendant Ireland had hope'. Butt also regretted that a demonstration had been organised on Sunday, 15 March 1874 in Hyde Park, and emphasised that this was not under the auspices of the Amnesty Association.[101] He invited Disraeli to 'seize upon the imagination and the heart of the Irish nation by one bold and masterly act of generosity'; he should make up even if he could not repair the shortcomings of his predecessor.[102] To these and other overtures, however, Disraeli remained unheeding.[103]

By 1875, Disraeli's unwillingness to move on amnesty spawned a rumour: it began to be said that he wanted to act but could not. In his case it was not the Cabinet but the Commander-in-Chief, the Duke of Cambridge who was the obstacle. This allegation was first raised in the Commons by Mitchell Henry,[104] who stated that there was in Ireland a widespread belief that the government was not averse to releasing the soldier Fenians, but that the military authorities were unwilling to agree to an amnesty.[105] Henry gave an example of oath-breaking which had been rewarded: 'Had not Churchill broken his oath to his Sovereign James and gone over to the King whom hon. Gentleman opposite [Conservatives] delighted to honour; and did the pious and immortal William, Prince of Orange make him Duke of Marlborough as a reward for his perfidy?'[106] This gibe against William, the Orange Order[107] and the Conservative Party, had Lord Randolph Churchill on his feet to defend his ancestor: 'The so-called

---

100 3 Hansard, CCXVIII, cols 411–12; 30 March 1874.

101 For an account of this good-humoured meeting see the Daily Telegraph, 16 March 1874, 2a.

102 Freeman's Journal, 16 March 1874, 3e–f.

103 A few days later, for example, he refused to receive a deputation of English working men who wished to press for amnesty (ibid., 23 March 1874, 2f).

104 (1826–1910). Born near Manchester. Educated at University College, London. Consulting surgeon, 1848–62. Partner in trading firm. Liberal Home Ruler. MP Galway Co., 1871–85, then Hutchesontown division of Glasgow, 1885–6, when defeated while standing as Liberal Unionist.

105 3 Hansard, CCXXII, cols 1759–64; 12 March 1875. See also 3 Hansard CCXXVI, col. 686; 7 August 1875. Mitchell Henry, on the latter occasion, was joined by three English MPs as well as one Irish MP in his mercy plea.

106 3 Hansard, CCXXII, col. 1762; 12 March 1875.

107 The toast, originally the charter oath of a forerunner of the Orange Order (the Aldermen of Skinner's Ally), began: 'To the glorious, pious, and immortal memory of the great and good King William' (see Ruth Dudley Edwards, The Faithful Tribe, London, HarperCollins, 1999, pp. 172–3).

treachery of Churchill was one of the most disputed historical questions, whereas the treachery of these soldiers was not disputed.' The dukedom had been awarded by Queen Anne for Churchill's victory at Blenheim. Mitchell Henry ought to inform himself of 'the commonest facts of history before again aspersing the character of heroes whom the country revered.'[108] Despite Lord Randolph's ire, another Irish MP, Sir Patrick O'Brien, returned to the point. Mitchell Henry, he was sure, had not meant to detract from the honour and glory of an illustrious name, but had for the purposes of his arguments stated a fact: 'the Duke of Marlborough, having been in the service of James II, within 24 hours was in the camp of William III.'[109] It is difficult to see how this knockabout furthered the case in hand.

But whatever the government's intention (and Cross simply repeated Gladstone's 'apology of contagion' doctrine) the Irish party had indicated the strength of feeling over the matter within its ranks and in Ireland: it was clear that amnesty would not be removed from the agenda. And for all Churchill's fuming that the case of his ancestor and those of the Fenian soldiers were different in kind, it was obvious that the distinction lay in the fact that one oath-breaker had been successful and the others not. Removed from the sacramental plane, the consequences of breaching the oath of allegiance became a matter of luck and history, and the punishment of the Fenian wrongdoers a penalty for failure, rather than a deed of infamy so heinous as to place it beyond normal political calculation. There was a pragmatic judgement that the offenders must pay the penalty of their failure as those who ventured into unsuccessful treason and rebellion have ever had to do. And some – perhaps most – MPs still looked with particular horror on the act of mutiny and disaffection, but their country's history provided too many examples of successful treason for the Fenian soldiers to remain as objects of worked-up indignation, for whom mercy was inconceivable. And if the soldiers were released, the others could not be retained.

Discussing Henry's speech, the *Freeman's Journal* instanced other rumours which had been calculating – that when the deputation of MPs had first waited on the Prime Minister in 1874, he and the Cabinet had been in favour of amnesty, but they had reversed their decision because of the strong protest by the Duke of Cambridge: 'This was stated in a manner and on authority which certainly gave the statement the semblance of truth.' It had also been said that Disraeli favoured an amnesty but the Cabinet did not, and this was why in 1874 the amnesty deputation of MPs had been asked to await their answer in the House of Commons and from the Home Secretary rather than Disraeli himself. Another (and wholly unfounded) theory was that the Queen had expressed 'the strongest desire' for the prisoners' release.[110]

---

108 3 *Hansard*, CCXXII, col. 1764; 12 March 1875.
109 Ibid., col. 1765.
110 *Op. cit.*, 14 August 1875, 5d.

Since the matter of the veto of the Duke of Cambridge had been raised in the Commons, *Freeman's* felt free to discuss it. It was mischievous that the Duke's popularity as 'the soldier's friend' should be marred by the belief that he was blocking the releases, which were favoured by nine out of ten soldiers – 'Upon the minds of the Irish soldiers the effect [of this belief] would be peculiarly undesirable.' Enlistment had already become unpopular among Irishmen because of the denial of pardon to soldiers when far more guilty civilians had been freed. The newspaper hoped that the Duke would reconsider, but if he did not the government should make the decision without referring to him: 'This is a question for the Cabinet, not the Horse Guards.' The Cabinet ought to consider how far it was fair to the Queen to let it be known that her close relative had been able to interpose his veto between the Irish people and this act of mercy.[111]

Freeman's was unaware of the Queen's attitude towards Fenianism, the Fenian pardons, and – to her – the special and unforgivable wickedness of a soldier betraying his sworn allegiance. Gladstone, who had battled almost his entire Cabinet to secure the first and second wave of amnesties, had encountered stronger and more persistent opposition from the Queen.[112] The idea that Disraeli, who lacked entirely Gladstone's drive to transform Irish politics, would risk the ire of his 'faery Queen' by challenging her deeply ingrained attitudes towards Irish rebellion and mutinous soldiers was fantastic: in his seventy-second year Disraeli wanted no more than quiet in Ireland, and cosy tranquillity with his Queen.

The link between the Home Rule League and the cause of the political prisoners became clearer on 14 September 1875 at a public meeting in Dublin's Rotunda, which expressed itself in favour of both.[113] The event was said to be the most successful ever organised by the League. Meanwhile a private appeal was made by A. M. Sullivan for Davitt's release. His accomplice, John Wilson, would be freed on completion of his sentence (less remission) in January 1876. Could not Davitt be released at the same time? To ease the political difficulties Sullivan indicated that Davitt would be willing to follow the example of the Fenian leaders released in 1871, and to accept expatriation to the United States of America, where his elderly mother was living. There was a flaw in the appeal, however. How could it be right for Davitt to serve the same sentence as his far less culpable accomplice? In any event, as it was bound to do, the Home Office took account of the judge's remarks on the respective degrees of culpability of the two men, and the aggravating circumstances he found in Davitt's case.[114]

---

111 Ibid., 5e.
112 See above, pp. 264–6.
113 *Freeman's Journal*, 15 September 1875, 6f–g, 7a–g; *The Times*, 16 September 1875, 7f.
114 A. M. Sullivan to R. A. Cross, 27 November 1875 and 10 January 1876; Cross to Sullivan, 12 and 26 January 1876; TCD: Davitt Papers (02); PRO HO 45/9329/19461/91; PRO HO 144/5/1/17869/9, 10, 23. The aggravating circumstances came mainly from a lightly coded letter

But any circumstances, even conspiracy to murder, could have been set aside by political decision. This would have required a sense of direction and strength quite lacking in Disraeli's Irish policy. It had been widely expected that the Liberals would return to office, and Disraeli found himself Prime Minister without a programme. The 1874 Queen's Speech was a purely pro-forma fragment announcing some stale items of news and some domestic legislation already in the pipeline.[115] Richard Assheton Cross recalled the first Cabinet meeting, at which Disraeli enquired successively of each minister what his policy was to be.[116] The instinct of the Conservative Party was Unionist and pro-ascendancy in Ireland, but Gladstone's Irish legislation had created a new political landscape in which Conservatism had yet to find its way. It would be some time before the question of amnesty would be ready for serious consideration. In the last few days of the Liberal administration, and possibly in the heat of the hustings, Disraeli had referred to the most recent Coercion Act for Ireland. The country, he said, was 'governed by laws of coercion and stringent severity that do not exist in any other quarter of the globe'. He was careful then, however, to qualify this observation with the remark 'I am not saying the severity is not necessary; I refrain from entering on any question of that kind.' If the observations about severity and stringency were intended to suggest a more lenient approach (as they were) Irish MPs must have been disappointed. When Disraeli was confronted in the House with his earlier statements he declined to express any further opinion.[117]

written by Davitt to Arthur Forrester on 15 December 1869. The letter, which appeared to sanction the murder of a supposed informer in Fenian ranks, was seized when Forrester was arrested and was passed by the police to Robert Anderson, who advised the Home Office on Fenian matters. In the letter Davitt urged Forrester himself not to carry out the murder because of his importance to the Fenian organisation. He also advised that consent for the act be obtained from two Fenian leaders. Most damningly, the letter insisted on precautions to avoid any link being made between the murder and Davitt's arms procurement and smuggling enterprise: 'Whoever is employed [to do the murder]; *don't let him use the pen we are & have been selling.* Get another one for the purpose – a common one' (cit. Moody, *op. cit.*, p. 60). 'Pen' was Davitt's code for gun, and the letter subsequently became known as the 'Pen Letter'. Davitt denied that this was a murder instruction, insisting that the advice to get permission from Forrester's comrades before the killing was carried out was a means of averting the murder. The letter was produced at Davitt's trial, as a means of connecting him to the Fenian conspiracy. Forrester, was called in defence and told various lies under oath in an attempt to exculpate Davitt. In sentencing Davitt, however, the judge described Forrester's explanation of the letter as a story that no sensible man could believe; the letter itself he viewed with the utmost horror. This aggravating circumstance would later be cited by Home Secretary R. A. Cross as a reason for denying clemency (Moody, *op. cit.*, pp. 98–102; 3 *Hansard*, CCXXXI, col. 317; 1 August 1876). One of the Manchester convicts, William Thompson, had died of consumption in Portland Prison in June 1870 (*Daily Telegraph*, 2 July 1870, 2d).

115 3 *Hansard*, CCXVIII, cols 22–5; 19 March 1874.
116 Richard Assheton Cross, A *Political History*, London, privately printed, 1903, p. 25.
117 3 *Hansard*, CCXVIII, col 543; 14 April 1874.

The Home Rulers (as they had now come to be known) presented in the 1876 session a clemency motion which attracted the signatures of 136 MPs. By this time the eighteen Irish political prisoners had shrunk to fifteen, three having been freed on the expiration of their sentences. Another six had been liberated from Western Australia aboard the *Catalpa* (though at the time of the debate this was not yet known). Nine Irish political prisoners remained, therefore, comprising Davitt, the two remaining Manchester rescuers (Shore and Condon) and six Fenian soldiers.[118] The debate followed a familiar course, but with a number of English members joining in the plea for amnesty. The principal points of contention were whether the punishment of the two Manchester men had gone far enough, and, as before, the particular guilt of soldiers who broke their oaths. There was also a cameo debate between John Bright, who deplored the fact that three men had been hanged for the murder of Sergeant Brett at Manchester, and Gathorne Hardy, the Home Secretary who had advised on the exercise of the Prerogative in the case.[119] At the conclusion of these lengthy exchanges Cross reiterated the government's position: 'The late Government as well as the present Government had totally denied that there were any political prisoners now in prison.' The men's treatment was 'as lenient as that of any other convicts who were in confinement at the present time'. Had they been political prisoners they would have been freed: 'As the late Government decided, so the present Government had decided, that there was no reason why the prisoners should be set at liberty.'[120]

As a means of meeting its election promise to reduce the burden on ratepayers – especially in the counties – in 1876 Disraeli brought in a Bill to nationalise local prisons, which until that point had been run by the magistrates, and substantially financed by the rates. The measure ran out of time and had to be reintroduced in the 1877 session.[121] The debates on this legislation, and a parallel provision for Irish local prisons, provided further opportunities to press the amnesty case, notably in the speech of O'Connor Power in June 1877. This was a detailed catalogue of the alleged ill-treatment of the Irish political prisoners, referring to the cases of O'Donovan Rossa, Davitt, Colour-Sergeant Charles McCarthy and Corporal Thomas Chambers. As long as the political prisoners were to be kept, they should be treated 'as men, and not as brutes'. Should the

---

118 Ibid., CCXXXI, cols 287–8; 1 August 1876.

119 Ibid., cols 302–8. In private, Gladstone expressed concern that three men had been hanged for one murder.

120 Ibid., cols 315–18. On Davitt, Cross confessed that the case had at first caused him some worry, but on consulting the papers he had discovered that the reason the judge had imposed a sentence of fifteen years was that 'there was in the mind of Davitt a direct intention of private assassination which could not possibly be referred to the question of a political offence' (ibid., col. 317).

121 See my *History of English Prison Administration* (*op. cit.*, pp. 468–82) for a discussion of the passage of this legislation.

Commons assert that there was no difference between political and ordinary crimes it would be following a course not taken by any other country, and would be 'rolling back the tide of civilisation'.[122]

O'Connor Power was supported by Dr M. F. Ward, MP for Galway, who insisted that if a full and fair investigation were carried out it would be found that a system of cruelty was practised in English convict prisons.[123] Parnell was in a threatening mood. The treatment of the political prisoners deeply interested the Irish people:

> [I]t was a question that they would push on the attention of this House, and . . . they would make inconvenient to this House if necessary . . . no exertion of theirs would be left undone to ensure that the attention of the Home Secretary should be directed to the consideration of the treatment of the few political prisoners still in prison.[124]

Gladstone intervenes

By the summer of the following year, when O'Connor Power initiated another amnesty debate, there were only six political prisoners left in England: three Fenian soldiers, who had been in prison for eleven years, the two Manchester rescuers, and Michael Davitt.[125] O'Connor Power was followed by Major P. O'Gorman, MP for Waterford, who undertook a memorably tedious, rambling and bizarre review of English, French, Austrian, Hungarian, Roman, Spartan and American history to prove that regicides, rebels and assorted malefactors had attained power and been recognised as legitimate rulers. The whole confection was topped with a dollop of Portia and an appeal to Queen Victoria.[126] There followed a heated speech from Gathorne Hardy on the question of the Manchester rescue and subsequent hangings: he remained understandably sensitive about his advice on the exercise of the Prerogative. Significantly, however, he concluded by stating that while he would always oppose a grant of mercy to the prisoners, were that taken as a criticism of the actions of the government of the day, he was far from saying that he would not be a party to the remission of the prisoners' sentences 'when the proper time had arrived'.[127]

Of the several members, English and Irish, who spoke in the debate, Gladstone's intervention was probably the most significant. Apart from his obvious

---

122 3 *Hansard*, CCXXXIV, col. 1315; 5 June 1877.
123 Ibid., col. 1322.
124 Ibid., col. 1324. Parliament should investigate the treatment of these men so that there should be some alleviation of 'the terrible and cruel lot and fearful treatment that they had hitherto experienced'.
125 Ibid., CCXXXV, col. 1591; 20 July 1877.
126 Ibid., CCXXXV, cols 1591–8, *passim*.
127 Ibid., cols 1604–8.

pre-eminence, Gladstone had been in office when a decision had been taken on Davitt and Wilson, and when the other offenders had been under preliminary consideration. Now considering all six cases, he made it clear that the time had come for an amnesty. At Manchester, three lives had been taken as punishment for the murder of Sergeant Brett and 'The cases are very rare indeed when the taking of a single life is avenged by the law by the taking of three lives.' The view now taken of the two remaining Manchester prisoners would determine the decision to be made on the Fenian soldiers, and 'hardly any one would think it necessary to prolong the punishment of the soldiers, who have already suffered longer periods of imprisonment – one 11 and the other 10 years'. On Davitt's case Gladstone appeared to change his stance of 1873. This man 'as to whom some hopes have been held out of separate consideration' was, he agreed with Butt, in 'a class strictly political'. The Manchester men had served ten years, and Gladstone wondered whether this, representing as it did 'so large a fraction from the ordinary term of life' was not 'quite sufficient' a punishment for their crime. While deferring to the government, Gladstone hoped that 'either the time may now have arrived, or that the time will be very speedily considered to have arrived, when the cases of these men may be examined with a view to the exercise of the prerogative of mercy'.[128]

Cross was rather peeved at this change of tack, and contrasted Gladstone's actions when in government with the course he now appeared to be urging. It was clear, nevertheless, that there was to be movement in the matter, even as Cross checked the files and upheld the decisions in all the cases. Davitt was now under review, and the cases of the other men would be considered at the proper time, 'but the question must be left to the discretion of the Advisers of the Crown'.[129] But there was an inescapable logic in the matter. Just as Gladstone had argued that the course of action taken with the Manchester prisoners would govern the decision on the Fenian prisoners, it was all but unthinkable – especially after Gladstone's speech – that Davitt would be released and the other men retained: and Davitt's pardon would not be long in coming.

Release

What was not known to the Commons at the time was that Cross had already approved Davitt's early release. On 11 July 1877 he had minuted Davitt's file, indicating that he might be released two years after his accomplice, John Wilson, had been given his ticket of leave.[130] Since Wilson had been released in January 1876,[131]

---

128 Ibid., cols 1614–19, *passim*.
129 Ibid., cols 1622–3.
130 This decision Cross directed was 'Not to go into the office or be made public till the time arrives' (PRO HO 144/5/17869/19a).
131 PRO HO 45/9329/19461/91.

this meant that Davitt's release was contemplated within six months of the July 1877 debate. It was then decided to give Davitt his liberty just before the Christmas holiday, and he was freed on a ticket of leave on 19 December 1879. Early in January the Fenian soldiers McCarthy, Chambers and O'Brien were also released.[132] The grant of a ticket of leave avoided government having to deal with the vexed question of the political status of the prisoners. It also meant, however, that Davitt and the others could not be expatriated. Especially in the case of Davitt this would have far-reaching implications for the development of Irish nationalist politics. It was a significant sign of what was to come that when Davitt reached London on the evening of his release, he was met by Isaac Butt and other Irish MPs.

Another consequence of releasing Davitt and the three Fenian soldiers on tickets of leave was that they could not be prevented from returning to Ireland, where they were certain to be met with extravagant demonstrations.[133] Opportunity was taken to reflect the broad basis of the amnesty campaign, and when Davitt and his companions arrived at Kingstown harbour on the evening of 13 January, the reception committee consisted of constitutional politicians such as Parnell and John Dillon, and a number of Fenians and others interested in the Irish national cause. The triumphal procession in Dublin was lit by thousands of torches and accompanied by many bands; it took three hours to traverse the few miles from the railway station to the hotel. So dense had become the crowd in front of the hotel that two of the four had to be taken in through a window rather than the main door.[134] Various reception ceremonies took their toll on men tired from travelling, excited and exhausted from conversation and intense socialising, and only hours away from the oppressive seclusion and hardship of convict life. A day and a half after arriving in Dublin Charles McCarthy, at breakfast with his three comrades, Parnell, Dillon, T. D. Sullivan, Richard Pigott and others, suddenly collapsed and died. A Dublin coroner's jury inevitably found that he had died from heart disease, accelerated by prison ill-treatment. There was a pitiful and tragic quality in McCarthy's death. Public feeling surged, especially in the light of the evidence given at the inquest by Davitt, Chambers and O'Brien. On 20 January, a week after his arrival in Dublin, McCarthy was given a hero's burial at Glasnevin Cemetery, with a cortege that took hours to pass through the streets, and was said to be the largest since the burial of Daniel O'Connell.[135] Irish nationalists now *knew* that the convict system tortured Irish

132 *The Times*, 5 January 1878, 9f.
133 Sections of nationalist opinion, according to *The Times*, had not been especially grateful for the releases (7 January 1878, 7a).
134 *Freeman's Journal*, 14 January 1878, 7a–c; *Irishman*, 19 January 1878, 451a–d; 452a.
135 *Freeman's Journal*, 21 January 1878, 7f–h. It was estimated that half the population of Dublin was on the streets to watch or participate in the funeral, which was, according to *Freeman's*, 'conducted bravely as a soldier's; mightyly as a patriot's; and solemnly as a devoted Catholic's' (ibid., col. f). See also the *Irishman*, 26 January, 1878, 467a–d.

political prisoners. An inquiry, promptly agreed by the government, did nothing to dissipate this opinion.[136] The deliberate and cruel sins of government washed away the Fenians' passing culpability.

There remained in prison after the release of Davitt and the three Fenian soldiers a further eight men.[137] Revulsion at the death of McCarthy and the details of their convict life disclosed by Davitt, Chambers and O'Brien to the official inquiry and in well-reported speeches built up great feeling for the release of the remaining prisoners. The notion that daily cruelty was being inflicted on them, and that their health was being irreparably damaged, charged efforts for a final amnesty. The first of what was planned as a series of public meetings took place at St James's Hall, Piccadilly, on 9 March 1878, with an audience of some 2500 London Irish. Twelve MPs sat on the platform – ten Home Rulers and two English Liberals – together with Davitt, Chambers and O'Brien. The presence of William Tallack, the respectable and widely respected Secretary of the Howard Association, put a question-mark over the whole issue of convict discipline. The meeting was presided over by John O'Connor Power. Home Rule associations sent messages of support from their various district organisations, and several groups attended the meeting with banners and bands. Three resolutions were passed with acclaim – unconditional release of the remaining prisoners; condemnation of the treatment of the political prisoners and a demand that they should have first-class misdemeanant status; and the agreement of the meeting that the two substantive resolutions should be conveyed to the Home Secretary and the Irish Chief Secretary.[138] The high point was Davitt's speech, which greatly moved the audience and was rewarded with a standing ovation of several minutes' duration.[139]

Other meetings followed throughout the English and Scottish provincial towns with Irish populations. The boost to the Fenian cause and to Home Rule was

136 *Inquiry as to the Alleged Ill-treatment of the Convict Charles McCarthy in Chatham Convict Prison*, PP, 1878 [C.1978], LXIII, 769, 1.
137 These were Thomas Ahearn, James Clancy, Edward O'Meagher Condon, John Dillon, Robert Kelly, Patrick Melody, Edward O'Connor and Edward O'Kelly (*Freeman's Journal*, 11 March 1878, 7c; Moody, *op. cit.*, p. 197). O'Connor Power stated that the eight had been in prison for between eight and twelve years. The background of only some of the eight is known. James Clancy was active in the IRB reorganisation in England after the failure of the March 1867 rising. He shot a detective who attempted to arrest him and was sentenced to life at penal servitude for attempted murder: Fenianism did not feature in his indictment (see William O'Brien and Desmond Ryan (eds), *Devoy's Post Bag*, Dublin, C. J. Fallon, 1948, Vol. I, p. 365). Edward O'Meagher Condon was one of the Manchester rescuers. He was condemned to death but his sentence was commuted to life imprisonment. On release in 1878 he returned to the United States of America, of which he was a citizen, and became active in Clan na Gael. The other men on the list were not in Western Australia, so it is possible they were in Irish prisons.
138 *Freeman's Journal*, 11 March 1878, 7c–h.
139 Ibid., cols e–f. This speech was read, and the manuscript survives in the Davitt Papers. It was subsequently expanded into a pamphlet and this in turn became the core of Davitt's evidence to the Kimberley Commission.

as considerable as the marshalling of Irish opinion (and much of Liberal and radical English opinion) behind the cause of amnesty. The coming together at these meetings of Fenian organisers and constitutional politicians was a harbinger of a movement which would reshape Irish (and to an extent English) politics in the 1880s. Without the focus and cohesion provided by the amnesty campaign it is doubtful whether this fateful alliance could have been formed. The relatively speedy success of the campaign helped to underline what might be accomplished by nationalism's two wings if they joined hands. The final releases took place (while Parliament was in recess) between August and November 1878, so that by the end of that year no Irish political prisoners remained in custody.

The second imprisonment

The re-arrest decision

Davitt's exit from Dartmoor may have surprised the governor, who put it down to the effects of his good advice to Davitt: in fact a political decision had been taken upon which Davitt's prison record had minimal effect.[140] This was not a conditional pardon, such as the Fenian leaders had been granted, but early release on a ticket of leave, on the authority of the Home Secretary. Ironically, British policy in Ireland might have been better served had Davitt been freed as an act of clemency, with the condition of expatriation. Since his mother was in the United States of America, Davitt would almost have certainly accepted exile, and once in America his energies may well have been absorbed in Irish-American politics, thus preventing or delaying him from playing a key part in the formation of the Land League, and the establishment of an alliance between Fenianism and Parnellism.

Davitt's role in the Land League and his fiery speeches made a move against him inevitable. Because of his popularity, much anxious thought went into the question of his re-arrest. Technically, he had been in breach of the reporting requirements of his licence from the outset. A close watch was kept on his movements and various instances were noted where he and other men released on tickets of leave were travelling around Ireland without notifying the police.[141]

---

140 The governor's homily, as Davitt recalled it, went as follows: 'On several occasions I have spoken to you about how good conduct in prison is rewarded and I am very happy to say that the Secretary of State has taken your case into consideration, and I have now the pleasure of telling you that your good conduct has met with its reward. I have received a communication from the Secretary of State to the effect that you are to be discharged on a ticket of leave for the remaining portion of your sentence.' Davitt was thereupon given a new suit, £3 and put on a train for London (*Universe*, 20 December 1877, at TCD: Davitt Papers: Ms. 9354/604).

141 Inspector George Talbot of the Dublin Metropolitan Police (who had special political duties) reported on 26 January 1878 that Davitt was moving about the country without reporting himself, that he had asked hotel staff to keep his departure secret; and (entirely at odds with the latter) that he had been the guest of honour at a torchlight celebration in Castlebar (near

This was behaviour which would have caused any other convict to be arrested, but for political reasons it was decided not to bring the matter to a head. No action was taken because Davitt was not considered to be 'in the ordinary category of habitual criminal'.[142]

The intention of the reporting requirement for ticket of leave men was to enable the police to keep track of habitual or serious offenders and, through the reporting requirement, to impress on the offender the knowledge which the police possessed of his identity and movements. In Davitt's case there was no concern that he was travelling around secretly committing crimes. The worry was almost exactly the opposite: he was very public in what he was doing, inciting enthusiastic disaffection by his mere presence.

In the autumn of 1879, faced with the increasingly successful and threatening activities of Davitt and the Land League, Home Secretary Cross asked whether he could revoke Davitt's licence, while rather doubting that he could.[143] In response Godfrey Lushington, his Permanent-Under-Secretary, set out five grounds on which action might be taken. Davitt could be prosecuted for sedition on the basis of his speeches, but it might be difficult to get a conviction in Ireland. His licence could be revoked on the grounds that he had broken the law by making seditious speeches. The objection to this was that it was contrary to custom to revoke a licence without a conviction, and this consideration would weigh even more strongly where the violation of the law was the questionable matter of sedition. Third, he could be proceeded against for failing to report himself: but the Secretary of State had determined that he should not be required to report. It appeared that Davitt himself had not been informed of this, but something might have been said to Parnell or to O'Connor Power. In any event, he had been allowed to go for almost two years without the requirement being enforced, and without having given him a warning, it would be harsh now to take action. There was a residual power to revoke the licence at pleasure, but this would also be unduly severe, especially as these general powers had never been previously used. Lushington proposed that Davitt be warned. He had been convicted of treason felony and his sentence was still running. The Secretary of State should call attention to the language which he was reported to have used, and warn him that if he again used it a revocation would be recommended to the Queen.[144] This would not be unfair. It 'will effectually

to where he originated); *Freeman's Journal* (29 January 1878, 7e–f) carried a half-column report of the Castlebar processions, at which Davitt was careful not to comment on his prison treatment, 'as it might be prejudicial to his imprisoned countrymen' (PRO HO 144/5/17869/19).

142 PRO HO 144/5/17869/35; 7 February 1881.
143 Cross to Lushington, 11 November 1879: PRO HO 144/5/17869/22b.
144 The Queen was already quite familiar with Davitt's name and on the eve of his eventual arrest wrote to Gladstone: 'The Queen hopes it may be possible to shut up Davitt' (Victoria to Gladstone, 25 January 1881: RA D30/65). The words 'shut up' in this context meant 'lock up'.

stop him, as if the licence is revoked he will be liable to 7 years penal servitude. And the warning to him may have a salutary effect on others.'[145]

This caution, and moderation of tone by Davitt, meant that his re-arrest did not take place for another two years. On 3 February 1881, however, he was arrested discreetly and without difficulty in the centre of Dublin and immediately removed to England to resume his sentence.[146] The arrest caused consternation and indignation in nationalist circles, but when announced in the Commons there was 'a tempest of cheering' which provoked Parnell and the Irish party into an immediate campaign of obstruction. Gladstone told the Queen that the uproar in the House was 'the most extraordinary night known in Parliament certainly for fifty years and probably for a much longer time'.[147]

The arrest had been keenly awaited and was welcomed by the Queen, whose attitude towards Davitt and the Land War was at one with her attitude to Fenianism and all moves by the government to palliate rather than repress. In an exchange with Lord Hartington (then Secretary of State for India) Victoria implicitly criticised Gladstone by her extravagant praise of Hartington's speech and silence upon Gladstone's: 'The times are so dangerous – the tendency to destroy and level – so great – that it behoves every loyal statesman to hold strong and firm language [sic]. The Queen trusts that means will be found to prevent these dreadful Irish people from succeeding in their attempts to delay the passing of the important Measures of Coercion.'[148] As with the Fenians, these views were framed by rumours (wholly believable in the cirumstances of the times) about attempts at her assassination or kidnapping. Extra precautions

---

145 Lushington to Cross, 13 November 1879: PRO HO 144/5/17869/22b.
146 The Irish Permanent-Under-Secretary wrote to H. J. Jephson, Private Secretary to the Irish Chief Secretary, William Forster, on 21 January 1881, describing Davitt as 'the most dangerous conspirator of the lot'. The Cabinet discussed the case and determined to wait, although both Gladstone and Granville (Foreign Secretary) were in favour of immediate action. It was agreed, however, that should Davitt make another violent speech he would be arrested. This he did at Carlow on 30 January 1881, and a warrant was accordingly issued, with the injunction 'Take care . . . to expose him to no needless indignity in the arrest' (Burke to Jephson, 21 January 1881; Jephson to Burke, 31 January 1881; Jephson to Cowper, 31 January 1881: PRO HO 144/72/A19/3 and /1/10).
147 Gladstone to Victoria, 3–4 February 1881: RA D30/102. See Daily Telegraph (4 February 1881, 2c–f) for a description ('Extraordinary Scenes') of the announcement and reaction in the House, including the expulsion of five Irish Members. Years later Davitt would refer bitterly to the Liberals who had 'yelled themselves hoarse with triumphant delight when my recommittal to penal servitude was announced to the House of Commons by . . . Sir William Harcourt on the 3rd of February 1881' (Pall Mall Gazette, 4 March 1889, 2b).
148 Victoria to Hartington, 16 January 1881: RA D30/30. Hartington (later the eighth Duke of Devonshire and, during the uncertain interregnum following Gladstone's 1874 election defeat, and supposed retirement, Liberal leader) did not share Gladstone's views on Irish Home Rule.

were taken at Osborne and Windsor Castle.[149] So much was Ireland in Victoria's mind at this time (the Land Bill, which she fretted was too much in favour of the Irish, as well as another Coercion Bill, were passing through the Commons) that special arrangements were made to send her, without any ministerial instruction, all Fenian material passing through the Foreign and Home Offices.[150]

By this time Davitt was Victoria's special *bête noire*. Her remarks on Gladstone's initial failure to return Davitt to prison as Land League activities and associated rural unrest burgeoned had so irked the Prime Minister that he wrote stiffly, outlining Disraeli's lack of energy in dealing with Davitt and concluding: 'In this recital Mr Gladstone does not presume to form my judgement on the proceedings of the late administration, with the grounds of which he may not be perfectly acquainted: but only to state the facts for your Majesty's information.'[151] Victoria then took the unusual (and slightly improper) step of getting her Private Secretary to get information on Davitt from Cross, the former Home Secretary. In his reply, however, Cross was careful to avoid comment and confined himself wholly to the facts.[152] But the Queen's dissatisfaction with Gladstone's attitude towards the Irish militants and extremists was hardly softened by this demonstration of bipartisanship. Newspaper and other accounts of disturbances in Ireland and the declaration of a rent strike brought more royal complaints. One, which contrasted the official assurances the Queen had received about the state of Ireland with newspaper and other reports, concluded with a call for stronger action – more troops and legal action: 'let no effort be spared for putting an end to a state of affairs which is a <u>disgrace to any civilised Country</u>.'[153] The Queen's anger and anxiety at what she saw as growing public disorder was heightened greatly when on 1 March 1882 a shot was fired at her when she left Windsor railway station. Gladstone's immediate letter of shock and declaration of the Commons' joy and thankfulness at her escape understandably did little to dispel her anger and irritation and lack of confidence in his Irish policy.[154] The extent and strength of that feeling was shown by her strong objection to the decision to parole Parnell to attend the funeral of his nephew in Paris: her natural family feelings were submerged in her irritation and displeasure with what she saw as an over-lenient and mistaken policy.[155]

---

149 See the exchanges between Ponsonby, Victoria's Private Secretary, 1881: ibid., 157–64; D28/55 and 56.
150 Ibid., Granville to Victoria, 18 February 1881.
151 Ibid., /47, Gladstone to Victoria, 19 January 1881.
152 R. A. Cross to Ponsonby, 24 January 1882: RA D28/56.
153 Ibid., D28/89. The underlining was characteristic of Victoria's letter-writing.
154 Gladstone to Victoria, 2 (or 3) March 1882: RA D28/136–7.
155 See RA D32/13a, 15, 15a and 16: 13–18 April 1882.

A gentle regime

Davitt's importance in Irish politics was immeasurably greater than it had been on his first arrest eleven years before.[156] Sir William Harcourt determined that he should be given the most lenient treatment that could be contrived in a convict prison: no grounds were to be given for allegations of ill-treatment.[157] He and other freed prisoners had repeatedly and powerfully depicted the cruelties of the convict regime, and the notion that Davitt was being returned to them would have given a boost to extreme nationalism and perturbed the moderates. More than eight years later Sir William Harcourt, stung by a letter of Davitt's in the *Pall Mall Gazette*, outlined the steps he had taken to alleviate as far as possible the penal character of Davitt's second imprisonment. He revealed that immediately on his release Davitt had written to him: 'Learning since my release from Portland that I am indebted to you for whatever kind treatment I have received while incarcerated there, I beg you will accept this as an expression of my grateful acknowledgement of such kindness.[158]

Harcourt's direction that Davitt was not to be treated as an ordinary convict raised certain legal problems. Since the convict rules were enshrined in legislation, Harcourt claimed that he had exercised his discretion through the Prisons Act, which vested all control in the Home Secretary.[159] He summoned Sir Edmund Du Cane and told him to transmit his orders to Colonel George Clifton, Governor of Portland Prison. Davitt was not to have his hair cut (the convict crop) and was not to be transferred to the prison in convict uniform. He was required (supposedly as a precaution against escape) to wear the uniform, but

156 Though his relationship with the Fenians – or at least a section of them – had changed, Sir Robert Anderson warned Harcourt that the absence of Fenian-inspired disturbances and outrages on the occasion of Davitt's re-arrest could not be taken as a precedent indicative of the Fenian temper and capacity for such things – 'for there is no doubt that Davitt had "sold" the Fenians, in his relations with the Land League, & there was a certain under current of satisfaction at his punishment' (Anderson to Harcourt, 23 July 1881: PRO HO 144/1537/Pt. 1(c); marked 'Confidential').

157 He also took a supervisory role in Davitt's case, requiring that he was minutely and immediately kept informed of any material change of circumstances. On one occasion, when a request was made to visit Davitt and the correspondence dawdled through the offices of the convict service, Harcourt (whose outbursts of temper were well known) angrily minuted 'Send this to the Irish Office for opinion. *Why is this letter of May 3 ten days in coming to me?* There seems no reason for such a delay' (PRO HO 144/5/17869/56).

158 3 *Hansard*, CCCXXX, col. 1264; 8 March 1889. Harcourt became a hate-object with some Irish and Irish-American militants after Davitt's arrest. His press-cuttings contain a piece from Ford's *Irish World* pointing to his unpopularity and consequent fears that he or his family would be attacked with dynamite (Bodleian Library, Ms. Harcourt dep. 348, f. 14).

159 This was quite spurious reasoning, as he must have known. Davitt was being returned to a convict prison to serve out the unexpired portion of his sentence of penal servitude, the terms of which were set by the various Penal Servitude Acts, and not the Prison Act, 1865 (28 & 29 Vict., c.126) and the Prison Act, 1877 (40 & 41 Vict., c.21).

Harcourt ordered that various ladies, including the wife of A. M. Sullivan, MP, should be allowed to visit, to provide an independent verification that he was being properly treated. There was laughter in the House when visits from lady friends were mentioned. Harcourt explained that he wanted Davitt to be visited by friends, but did not want politics to be discussed – hence the female visitors. He also ordered that Davitt's friend and medical attendant Dr Kenny should visit and report back on his condition: this Kenny did on several occasions. Orders were given that Davitt was not to be associated with the other prisoners, 'that he should have no disagreeable labour, and that he should amuse himself as he pleased'. He was to have whatever books and writing materials he requested, and was also to be allowed to occupy himself in a garden. A request was made for Davitt to receive *Hansard* and Harcourt allowed this. ('The matter had not occurred to me, but I replied that no one cared to read *Hansard*, and that, so far as I was concerned, I should have thought it would have been an additional punishment to supply it.') The result of this regime was that Davitt had gained six pounds while at Portland and was said by a visitor to be 'in wonderful spirits, and wrote and read every day'.[160]

This second imprisonment was little more than civil detention, albeit rather more removed from the world at Portland than Davitt would have been at Dublin's Richmond Prison. Harcourt had reason to be irritated by Davitt's attack in the *Pall Mall Gazette* some years later ('I was a little surprised at the tone of that letter, but I do not complain of it. In these days one ought not to be surprised at anything'). Among other attacks on Liberal policy towards Ireland, which Davitt absurdly insisted was almost identical with Conservative policy, was a repudiation of Gladstone's assertion that while at Portland Davitt's treatment was 'in a point of decency and indulgence, everything that could reasonably be desired'. On the contrary, insisted Davitt, 'I was treated as a convict, and treated in every respect – save one – as a convict located in the infirmary of a convict prison.'[161]

The facts, as shown in the official papers and in Davitt's own account of his Portland imprisonment, do not support these assertions. Four days after Davitt was received at Portland, Du Cane wrote to Sir Godfrey Lushington, transmitting a report from the Portland Governor. Du Cane was evidently not entirely convinced by Harcourt's exposition of his authority as Home Secretary, and had resorted to a device which he frequently used when he wanted to circumvent the regulations and at the same time cover himself against any possible charges of

---

160 3 *Hansard*, CCCXXX, cols 1264–8; 8 March 1889. For the original question and response see 3 *Hansard*, CCLXVII, cols 1275–7; 20 March 1882.

161 'This was, of course, a more humane and considerate treatment than the old Dartmoor practice of making me wear a collar and yoking me to a cart to do the work of a beast of burthen; but it is not deserving of the self-complacent encomiums bestowed upon it by Mr Gladstone' (*Pall Mall Gazette*, 4 March 1889, 2b).

abuse of authority: he had involved the prison's medical officer in the transaction. This pliable functionary had examined Davitt and determined that he needed special treatment – location in the infirmary and a special liberal diet. To ensure that there should be no misunderstandings, Du Cane had directed that Davitt should not be moved out of the infirmary without reference to headquarters.[162]

The wisdom of this preferential treatment was immediately apparent when a week after his arrest 104 MPs, substantially Irish, but with a good representation of English and Scots, signed a petition asking that Davitt be treated as a first-class misdemeanant.[163] This status was the least restrictive form of imprisonment available.[164] It would have been legally impossible to treat Davitt as a first-class misdemeanant: the order had to be made by magistrates in the course of sentencing. This requirement was to be overridden by Harcourt on other occasions – in the face of objections and warnings by his officials[165] – but Davitt's was a case in which it would have been impossible to act: he had not been sentenced to imprisonment (which had to be served in a local prison) but was a convict returning to resume serving his sentence of penal servitude. So far as was possible, however, with the curious exception of being obliged to wear convict uniform, Davitt was dealt with in the manner of a first-class misdemeanant – the only instance in the history of English *convict* prisons.[166]

Understandably, Davitt's lenient treatment at Portland did nothing to reconcile him to his position, and on 24 February 1881 he addressed a long petition (the fruit of some days' work) to Harcourt. He had been arrested in a 'clandestine' manner, and had therefore been deprived of the opportunity of defending himself before a justice of the peace. He had not broken the conditions of his licence:

---

162 Du Cane to Lushington, 9 February 1881, PRO HO 144/5/17869/37a. George Clifton, the Portland Governor, reported that Davitt was located in a central cell in the infirmary where 'every consideration is shown him'. The 'Hospital Full Chop Diet' which Davitt received included roast mutton, tea, sugar, milk, butter and a bottle of ale, besides bread and the usual vegetables.

163 PRO HO 144/5/17869/44.

164 The status of first-class misdemeanant originated in the Prisons Act, 1840 (3 & 4 Vict., c.25) and exempted such prisoners from the severe discipline provided for criminal prisoners. First-class misdemeanants had many privileges. They could, for example, provide their own food, have beer and wine, wear their own clothes, furnish their own cell and employ another prisoner to clean it. They were completely separated from criminal prisoners. For a fuller account of this classification and its use see my *English Local Prisons 1860–1900*, *op. cit.*, pp. 369–77; see also PRO HO 45/9710/A51143 for the papers concerning several controversial cases involving this status.

165 Harcourt would intervene a few months after this in the case of Johann Most, the anarcho-communist imprisoned for seditious libel and incitement at the time of the assassination of Tsar Nicholas II. Significantly, Most was defended by A. M. Sullivan, KC, the MP for Meath.

166 The Young Irelanders had been convicts, but were not held in any English prison. The requirement that Davitt wear a convict uniform was probably a political blind allowing the Home Secretary, if questioned, to escape into vagueness on the regime: a convict in civilian clothes would have been difficult to explain.

he had a visible and reputable means of livelihood; his place of residence was known to the authorities; and he had not violated the conditions upon which he had been liberated. (The last, he argued, had been confirmed by the Irish Chief Secretary in the Commons only three days before the arrest.) In any event, although it had been called a ticket of leave, Davitt continued, his release from Dartmoor had in fact been an amnesty. He would not have been entitled to release on licence for another four years, and had been freed as a result of the agitation in England and Ireland for the release of the remaining 'Irish State Prisoners', of whom he was one. The public had accepted that he had been amnestied, and the authorities had acted as though he had. His evidence for the latter was the failure to revoke his licence when, in November 1879, he had been arrested on the charge of using seditious language at a meeting in Co. Sligo: any ordinary ticket of leave holder would then have been returned to prison.

Arrest and recommittal in these circumstances, Davitt concluded, was a violation of the spirit of English law. The assertion that the Crown could cancel a ticket of leave without giving a reason left the 'legally pardoned offender' (a self-description which the Home Office would not have accepted) 'at the mercy of an irresponsible authority'. The real reason he had been arrested was his political activity, an endeavour to curb the privileges and despotic actions of a dominant class in the state. That class had used its influence to have him returned to prison. Davitt had no hope that his petition would be successful, and its sole purpose was to put on record his 'most solemn protest' against an act of political vengeance which no sophistry could disguise – an act 'without a precedent or parallel in the actions of preceding Administrations towards individual opponents'.[167]

Bitter at the manner of his arrest, Davitt was nevertheless a cooperative prisoner who was pleasant to staff and caused no trouble. He was obviously as anxious to keep abreast of political developments as government was to keep him isolated. His Land League colleagues made various attempts to visit him, but even where these contacts were allowed, care was taken to monitor what passed. On the whole, however, a liberal approach was taken to visitors. I. M. Wall, who was known to the Dublin Metropolitan Police as a leading Land Leaguer, applied to make a visit: the Dublin police advised against it, but the Home Office allowed it on the grounds that although a political associate of Davitt, Wall was also a close personal friend.[168] An American, J. H. Smith, made a similar application, which was refused, although Smith's letter to Davitt was forwarded.[169] This process of vetting requests continued, and a number were declined without reasons being given. By September 1881, Davitt had received

---

167 PRO HO 144/5/17869/51.
168 Ibid., /54.
169 It is likely that Smith was a clandestine Fenian emissary (ibid. /55).

six visits over a period which, had he been an ordinary convict, he would have been entitled to only one.[170]

One visit which was very difficult to prevent, and yet which was largely political rather than personal, was that of Dr J. E. Kenny. Kenny had been active in the Land League, and it was probable that he wished to see Davitt on League business. At the same time, Kenny could legitimately claim that as Davitt's personal physician he had good reason to see him: it was also in government's interest that Kenny be assured about Davitt's health. As a precaution, however, Dr Robert Gover, Chief Medical Officer of the Convict Service and Medical Inspector of the local prisons, attended Dr Kenny's examination of Davitt. From the manner in which Kenny went about his business, the questions he asked of Davitt, and the way in which he seemed to encourage Davitt to exaggerate or manufacture his symptoms, Gover formed the impression that Kenny was 'not acting in a *bona fide* capacity as a physician'. The objective was to get Davitt out of prison, or, short of that to Kilmainham or if that were not possible to Woking. 'I have no doubt whatever, that he [Kenny] wishes to communicate something to Davitt, & that he is much disappointed in having been foiled in his purpose.'[171]

Davitt's health was of the greatest political interest and Dr Gover was directed to make a number of special reports to the Home Secretary. Because of some of the long-term consequences of Davitt's childhood loss of his arm, and evidence of some past lung damage, Gover at first recommended that he be removed from Portland during the winter of 1881 to 1882. Possibly in response to pressure from Du Cane, who may not have wished to have the trouble of resettling Davitt elsewhere, in July 1881, Gover urged that Davitt be left where he was. He gave several reasons for this about-turn. Davitt's health was improving and he appeared to be 'as cheerful and contented as a man can be in prison'. Both the building in which he was lodged and the garden in which he worked were south-facing; he had become comfortable in his surroundings and got on well with all the staff. All of these were considerations to set alongside questions concerning climate. Gover would examine him again once or twice during the winter, and he would be kept under close medical supervision; should there be any deterioration, he could immediately be moved. There was a coda. It was generally desirable to avoid treating any one prisoner differently from another,

---

170 The visitors were Mrs A. M. Sullivan (15 February); Dr J. E. Kenny (3 March); Mrs J. E. Kenny (2 June); Mrs A. M. Sullivan (2 June); Archbishop of Cashel (8 September); Bishop of Ross (8 September). (Ibid. /79). Among requests which were refused were Thomas Brennan, W. Sharman (of Plymouth), John Lowther (Land League), Francis Soutter, Alfred Webb and John Daly (Land League). The two lady visitors (Kenny and Sullivan) published an account of their visit (Bodleian Library: Ms. Harcourt dep. 348, Lewis Harcourt Diaries, Vol. 2).

171 Ibid., /64. 'Dr Kenny speaks of Davitt's ability & powers of management with the greatest respect and it is evident that his [Davitt's] presence is deemed of great importance.'

and therefore Davitt should be left at Portland.[172] No early decision was made on the matter, but after a further health report at the end of the summer the Home Office in early November agreed that Davitt should stay at Portland.

The writer's cell

Only ten days before making this report, Gover had pointed out that although Davitt had healthy employment and relaxation in his garden through the spring and summer, he needed something to occupy him during the winter. Davitt had himself asked for writing materials so that during the winter months he might work out his ideas in politics, economics and other subjects. Gover thought that the winter days and evenings would be very trying to Davitt were he only to have available 'the passive occupation of reading'. For reasons based on Davitt's past health record, his present condition, his active life prior to his second imprisonment and 'a certain eagerness and excitability' of temperament, Gover thought that writing materials should be supplied. As a safeguard against illicit correspondence, only a limited number of sheets of paper would be issued each time, and these would be handed back and counted at the end of each session. The completed manuscript would be retained by the governor, and handed back to Davitt on his release.[173]

Sir Edmund Du Cane did not welcome this proposal, which would create 'a very inconvenient precedent'. He acknowledged that Davitt, more than most of the men who had been convicted of similar offences, could be trusted not to abuse any privilege of this kind. If it were understood that in the case of abuse the privilege would be immediately removed, that anything objectionable would be destroyed, and that no prison subjects would be dealt with, 'the inconvenience would be limited to the difficulty of preventing other prisoners claiming the privilege on the same ground as Davitt'. Du Cane recommended that any decision on the matter be put off until the seasonal deterioration in the weather compelled Davitt to cease his garden work.[174] This was agreed, and when the matter came up for consideration Harcourt directed that writing materials be issued with the necessary precautions. So that no general precedent should appear to be created, Harcourt indicated that his decision was being taken 'Under the special circumstances of the case'.[175]

The outcome of Gover's recommendation and Harcourt's liberality was Davitt's two-volume *Leaves from a Prison Diary: Or Lectures to a 'Solitary' Audience*.[176]

---

172 Dr R. M. Gover to Sir Edmund Du Cane, 6 July 1881: PRO HO 144/17869/64.
173 Gover to Du Cane, 26 June 1881: PRO HO 144/5/17869/64.
174 Du Cane to Lushington, 7 July 1881: PRO HO 144/5/17869/65.
175 Ibid. /65. Considering how many privileges Davitt enjoyed it was curious that Harcourt should be so coy about this one.
176 *Op. cit.* The subtitle – '*Lectures to a 'Solitary' Audience* – refers to a young blackbird which came into Davitt's possession through, as he later recalled, 'the kindness of the governor'. The bird

Portions of the manuscript entitled 'Jottings in Solitary' survive in Davitt's papers at Trinity College, Dublin. This does not comprise the final and published version which, dealing with topics on which in prison he was forbidden to write, was a combination of Portland and post-Portland writings. The foolscap sheets (of the kind used in official correspondence) each bear the royal coat of arms (though this has been carefully erased from one). Davitt's script is well formed and educated, and throughout he uses Irish, Latin, German, Spanish, Italian and (most frequently) French phrases. Many of the jottings are abstracts from books or comments upon them, showing the wide range of material he obtained. In the fashion of the times there is a deal of maudlin, dolorous and sentimental verse, accompanied by many aphorisms and 'wise sayings'. There is much of the commonplace book about the script, but taken altogether it is a document of considerable interest, and a very great credit to a self-educated man.[177]

Release again

Davitt's second imprisonment was as little onerous as was possible in the penal system. Following the clampdown on the Land League in the autumn of 1881, culminating in the arrest of Parnell and some 800 of his followers under new coercion legislation, Irish policy had to find a new way forward. In the spring of 1882 Gladstone took the first steps in a new initiative, which he announced to the House on 2 May 1882. Parnell and others who had been interned in Kilmainham Prison were to be freed.[178] In these circumstances Davitt's release was also a certainty. William ('Buckshot') Foster, the Irish Chief Secretary, resigned. Gladstone appointed his nephew-in-law Lord Frederick Cavendish in his place, and on 4 May 1882, explained his policy in the House of Commons and heard Forster's bitter resignation statement.[179] Two days later, Cavendish, newly arrived to take up his post, was walking in Dublin's Phoenix Park with

---

became Davitt's cell companion ('Solitary Audience'), but when he thought it could survive he released it and without hesitation it flew away. Davitt drew a predictable political conclusion: 'The instinct of freedom was too powerful to be resisted though I had indulged in the fond hope that it would remain with me. But he taught me the lesson which never be unlearned by either country prisoner or bird, that nature will not be denied, and that liberty is more to be desired than fetters of gold' (TCD: Davitt Papers: Ms. 9641, f. 345).

177 There are striking similarities between the circumstances surrounding the production of this script and Oscar Wilde's *De Profundis* some fourteen years later. In each case a political decision was taken to ameliorate conditions. The authority of the politicians who took the decisions – Harcourt in Davitt's case, Asquith in Wilde's – was questionable, and to protect them (and themselves) the prison officials and civil servants deployed the versatile authority of the prison medical officers: pen, ink and paper straight from the penal pharmacopoeia (for Wilde's prison treatment see PRO PCOM 8/432–5/13629; see also Richard Ellman's *Oscar Wilde*, London, Hamish Hamilton, 1987, chs 19 and 20, and esp. pp. 474–84).

178 3 *Hansard*, CCLXXVIII, cols 1965–70; 2 May 1882.

179 Ibid., CCLXIX, cols 106–18; 4 May 1882; see also Shannon, *op. cit.*, pp. 294–8.

Thomas Burke, the Irish Under-Secretary. Within sight of Viceregal Lodge, the two were slashed to death by members of a Fenian splinter group, 'The Invincibles'. This atrocity coincided with Davitt's release from prison, and was ever afterwards remembered by him with especial pain as one of the blackest days in Irish history.[180]

It was an ill-omen that Davitt was freed from Portland on the day of the Phoenix Park murders. Care was taken to record his physical condition on release (this was generally done very cursorily). On the morning of 6 May 1882 he was examined by Dr G. Herbert Lilly, Portland's assistant surgeon. He was suffering from slight dyspepsia and heartburn, but his lung condition had greatly improved, as had his general health. During his time at the prison Davitt had put on twelve pounds.

Parnell, John Dillon, James O'Kelly, nationalist MPs and Land League associates travelled to Portland to escort Davitt back to London. The prisoner was brought to the governor's office, where he placed himself in their hands, remarking (in the governor's presence) 'that he intended to ignore *in toto* the conditions of his licence'. Davitt asked that the Roman Catholic priest be summoned to receive the thanks of his friends for the kindness shown to him. Parnell and the others asked to see Davitt's cell and the garden where he had worked. When shown these Dillon remarked that the cell (which was in the infirmary) was larger than the one he had occupied at Kilmainham.[181] At the prison gates Davitt asked to see Mrs Clifton, the governor's wife, to thank her personally for her attention to his friends on their various visits, and to introduce Parnell and the others. This was arranged, and before leaving Davitt told Colonel Clifton that 'he was perfectly satisfied with his treatment in Portland

---

180 On 6 May 1883, Davitt was again in prison – this time interned under the Lord Lieutenant's Warrant, arising from the continuing land campaign. He remembered how at 5 a.m. one year previously news which he and Parnell had initially discredited had been confirmed: Cavendish and Burke had been murdered. Henry George came into Davitt's bedroom with a telegram confirming the news. To Davitt this was 'horrible', 'a calamity', 'a catastrophe' and 'a thunderbolt upon our cause' (TCD: Davitt Papers: Ms. 9537/53). Sixteen years later Davitt returned to Portland, but this time as an MP on a visit of inspection. He visited his old cell ('How little this place seemed changed. It looked as if I had only left it yesterday'). His reflections were again drawn to the day of his 1882 release: 'Sixteen eventful years have passed since that tragic day. Reflect how on our journey we were so elated at the overthrow of the Buckshot regime [the nickname of W. E. Forster, given because of his use of the Coercion Acts] & so full of hope for the future! So little did we know what our feelings & hopes were to be inside of twenty-four hours!' (TCD: Davitt Papers: Ms. 9571, f. 32).

181 Davitt remembered it differently. Parnell 'on hearing me describe it as a "palace cell" [compared with the corrugated slate and iron cells at Dartmoor] he shuddered and said such a cell would drive him mad if he were shut up in it for a month' (TCD: Davitt Papers: Ms. 9571, ff. 31 *ob.*, 32). Parnell's reaction is interesting. Although he had been in prison and was consequently familiar with general conditions he had had no idea of the severity of the convict regime.

Prison'. He also thanked him and his staff for their consideration and courtesy. Despite these courtesies Clifton ensured that the usual procedures were followed: Davitt was again photographed for the Habitual Criminals' Register, and the photograph and various identity papers were forwarded to the Metropolitan Police.[182]

Davitt's release would under any circumstances have provoked conservative feeling: next to Parnell he was probably the best known of the Irish agitators, and his Fenian past had certainly not been forgotten. That his release coincided with the brutal murder of Cavendish and Burke outraged a wider section of opinion, and wounded Gladstone's Irish policy. On the evening of 5 May (the murders took place the following day), Sir William Harcourt, the Home Secretary, had to try to placate the Queen, who had protested by telegram that she had not been informed before the announcement of the impending releases was made to the Commons.[183] She objected in particular to the release of Davitt, and Harcourt made his explanation in a sixteen-page letter. The policy had been fully explained, he insisted, and among the 'political suspects' (as Parnell and the other internees were called) a distinction was made between those held for political agitation, and those detained for incitement to outrage and crime. The first category would be released, and the latter would continue in custody. No preferential distinction could be made between MPs and other detainees.

As for Davitt, Harcourt continued, a question had been put down in the Commons and a quick decision had been needed. Davitt was discussed at an afternoon Cabinet, which sat until proceedings began in the House. No grounds could be found for distinguishing between him and the others to be released: 'Mischevious as he had been as an agitator he has never been suspected of promoting outrage or encouraging intimidation.' Both before and during his imprisonment he had condemned violence, and of all the prisoners 'he is the one who is most likely with effect to use his influence to discourage and prevent the terrible crimes which have lately so shocked and alarmed loyal people in Ireland'. To have kept Davitt in prison would have undermined the whole policy of clemency; it would have been impossible for Parnell and his followers to help repress outrage and crime, and Davitt's detention would have been a continuing irritant in Irish politics. Finally, Harcourt pointed out, Davitt's release was not unconditional, but on a ticket of leave. He was therefore free on good behaviour and liable to be returned to custody for any

---

182 George Clifton to Du Cane, 6 May 1882: PRO HO 144/5/17869/93.

183 'Is it possible that Michael Davitt known as one of the worst of the treasonable agitators is also to be released? I cannot believe it! 3 suspects were spoken of [for release] but no one else' (cypher telegram, Victoria to Gladstone, 4 May 1882: RA D32/56. The Queen's characteristic underlinings and exclamations on this occasion did not make their way to Gladstone, but her anger was obvious).

misconduct.[184] None of this assuaged the Queen's anger or her particular dislike of Davitt, which was stoked by her personal private secretary, General Sir Henry Ponsonby.[185] In the Irish section of Victoria's demonology Davitt had found his place alongside Mitchel and Rossa.

184 Harcourt to Victoria, 5 May 1882: RA D32/59. There were several rather tart passages in the letter. In constitutional matters Harcourt's whig principles were at their strongest, and (as his private remarks recorded by his amanuensis son Lewis frequently show) he was sensitive to what he saw as the Queen's interference in the conduct of government. His irritation notwithstanding, he was obliged four days later to write at even greater length to the Queen (twenty-four pages), again apologising for not informing her in advance about Davitt's release, discussing the Burke and Cavendish murder and generally explaining the government's Irish policy (Harcourt to Victoria, 9 May 1882: RA D32/115).

185 See, for example, his letter to Victoria of 10 January 1881, condemning Davitt ('his speeches are worse than the others') and wondering why his ticket of leave was not cancelled (RA D30/13).

7

THE DYNAMITARDS

Nobel's marvel

From the vantage point of the third millennium the possibility of high explosives being detonated in large cities is no longer seen as marking the end of civilisation; it seems, rather, to be inseparable from the way we live now. The vigorous life of London, on which fell some 19,000 tons of high explosive, many hundreds of thousands of incendiaries and several thousand rockets between 1940 and 1945, is but one of many such instances.[1] The response of the United States of America to the September 2001 attacks on New York and Washington is another. But there was a time when the detonation of a few sticks of dynamite and the use of phosphorus-based 'Greek Fire' were viewed with utmost alarm by governments, and with the greatest glee by a new style of Irish revolutionist. Indeed, the invention of dynamite was thought by many to presage the end of civilisation.[2] When at a New York meeting in April 1885 O'Donovan Rossa called for the Prince of Wales to be killed during his visit to Ireland, and proclaimed that he would hurl 'the fires of hell at England' if he could get them within his grasp, he was cheered to the rafters[3] by an audience which needed to believe that dynamite and phosphorus could accomplish what Rossa promised: these were instruments so terrible in rebel hands that the British Empire would fall to its knees.

The advent of dynamite brought renewed life to the violent faction of Irish nationalism that by the end of the 1870s was in the doldrums. The material itself dated to 1867 when Alfred Nobel managed to stabilise the powerful and extremely dangerous explosive, nitroglycerine, in such a fashion that it could be manufactured commercially. By absorbing the nitroglycerine into an inert base such as sawdust or certain types of earth, a substance which previously was

---

1 See Tom Harrisson, *Living Through the Blitz*, London, Collins, 1976, pp. 331–2. Harrisson's Mass Observation archive gives a remarkable account of how ordinary people lived under such conditions.
2 But see Julius H. Sheelye, 'Dynamite as a Factor in Civilisation', *North American Review*, 320 (July 1883), pp. 1–7, where it is argued that it is not dynamite but man's use of it that is the source of danger.
3 *United Irishman*, 4 April 1885 1e; see also PRO HO 144/133/A34707/34.

difficult to transport and easy accidentally to detonate, became safe to use.[4] Nobel perfected his invention by combining it with a percussion cap, which simultaneously provided heat and a minor explosion, both of which were necessary for detonation. Yet dynamite could be burned in certain ways without risk, and was stable enough to resist shock – even an explosion within its vicinity. Such a powerful, safe and portable explosive had many uses, civil and military, and these were rapidly explored. By the early 1880s gunpowder, except for certain mining operations and as a propellant in guns, was displaced by dynamite and various other nitro-compounds.[5]

Dynamite could have been tailor-made for the terrorist. Being almost one hundred times more powerful than gunpowder, well-placed small quantities could accomplish vast destruction. Its stability enabled it to be carried and placed without risking premature explosion from a jolt or stray spark. With the use of the percussion cap, various timers could be devised which would allow the bomber to get safely away from the scene: no need for an uncertain and easily discovered fuse. Finally, although elaborate forms of nitro-compound explosive (such as guncotton) required a complicated form of manufacture, basic forms of the explosive could be made in a simple workshop rather than a factory or laboratory: backstreet access to the power of Titans.

The headlines were its testimonials. The most notorious was the nihilist assassination on 13 March 1881 of the liberal Tsar Alexander II: the civilised world was horrified by this regicide. Two nitroglycerine-based bombs were used, and the appalling injuries inflicted at the scene demonstrated beyond peradventure the destructive power of the explosives. This carnage and the subsequent panic delighted revolutionaries of many different hues in Europe and in the United States of America. The more the apparatus of the establishment – church, press and politicians – execrated the bombers and their acts, the more they commended them to the extreme of the extreme. In the wake of Alexander's assassination, the London *Globe* – one among a multitude of newspapers and journals to do so – condemned dynamiting in terms which to a questing terrorist would have been an attractive prospectus. The bombs 'almost inevitably destroy many others who are not only innocent of any special crime, but in no degree objects of hatred to the murderers themselves'. This was an appalling level of barbarity made worse by the ease with which the atrocities could be committed: 'the immunity enjoyed

---

4 A series of accidents in Britain, Europe and the United States of America on land and at sea led to the stringent controls of the 1869 Nitro-glycerine Act (32 & 33 Vict., c.113). The use of pure nitroglycerine was prohibited, but the Home Secretary was given powers to license compounds in which it was used.

5 Vivian Dering Majendie, 'Nitro-glycerine and Dynamite', *The Fortnightly Review*, 33 (January to June 1883), p. 643 (Majendie was a leading explosives' expert). See also the letter from 'A.W.G.' to *Science*, 8, 188 (10 September 1886), pp. 231–2. Commercial exploitation of the explosive proliferated after 1881 when Nobel's patent expired and a number of other manufacturers came on to the market.

by the conspirators in many cases seems thus far to show that the use of infernal machines is safer than the use of the pistol or the dagger'.[6]

Terrorism is the policy of indiscriminately, deliberately, recklessly and uncaringly destroying civilian life, property and security in the pursuit of military and political ends: randomness and ruthlessness are intended to sap confidence in the state, to create irresistible pressures on government to reach an accommodation with the terrorists. Since fear and panic are the true objects of terrorist action, the amount of property incidentally destroyed and number of innocent lives taken or blighted are of little consequence, despite token expressions of regret, and are certainly outweighed by the symbolic and threat value of the carnage and destruction. An individual terrorist assassination is a statement of the lives that might thereafter be taken; the 'accidental' by-products of the attack attest to the awful haphazardness of this form of warfare and to the fierce indomitable will of the terrorist. It is a product of this logic as well as practical difficulties that attacks are much less often directed at hard military targets than at soft ones. While to the law-abiding this is cowardly behaviour, to the bomber it is proof of the vulnerability of the supposedly mighty enemy. Government offices, public buildings and monuments, museums and art galleries, underground trains, restaurants and crowded thoroughfares all commend themselves to the terrorist not only because they may be attacked with ease, but also because the carnage is indiscriminate and the horror is universal.

Strands of Fenianism

From William Smith O'Brien's quixotic insistence upon honourable and open warfare to bombs on the London Underground is an enormous transformation in revolutionary morality and tactics. To understand the transition we must look again briefly at Fenianism's development in the aftermath of the defeat of the 1865 to 1867 insurgency. Terrorism, strictly defined, issued not from the Fenian organisation which survived in Ireland and Britain, but from the various strands of Irish revolutionary thought and organisation which were transplanted to and developed in the United States of America.

Nothing is more conducive to splits in political and revolutionary organisations than abject failure, and when that organisation has been set up on highly centralised and autocratic lines, splintering is inescapable. Stephens' escape on 24 November 1865 electrified the movement and gave it a myth, but, as General Strathnairn observed, having had a taste of imprisonment, Stephens was demoralised.[7] The moment to strike was immediately after his escape, with

6 The *Globe*, 13 March 1881, 1d.

7 In this Strathnairn and at least some of the Irish revolutionists agreed. Joseph Denieffe, one of the founding members of the Irish Republican Brotherhood, considered that Stephens had shown the white feather at the meeting he held with the Fenian Centres on the night of his release (*A Personal Narrative of the Irish Revolutionary Brotherhood*, Irish University Press, 1969, p. 129).

Ireland agog, Fenian invincibility established in the popular mind, and the British garrison wrong-footed. Looking back at that moment with the advantage of two years' hindsight, the British Commander-in-Chief in Ireland informed the Cabinet that 'something disagreeable might and would probably have occurred' had the Fenians pushed ahead with their plans.[8] But that would have required nerveless leadership and exceptional moral courage, and Stephens, for all his remarkable qualities, was not cut from that cloth: this was no Danton. Promises bravely given, expectations repeatedly fanned into flame and quenched, a series of postponements that punctured rhetoric and reputation and made the movement ridiculous – all these led to a rancorous division of the Fenian Brotherhood in the United States of America.

One of the principal factions, known as the Roberts or Senate wing, prepared for an attack on Canada. An assortment of arguments supported the venture, the chief of which was that an Irish uprising could not succeed unless Britain were engaged in a major war. By attacking Canada, and possibly provoking cross-border retaliation, such a draining conflict with the United States of America might be precipitated: relations between the two countries continued to be frosty and war a possibility while the *Alabama* claim remained outstanding. In any event, were the Fenians to secure and hold a port, they would have advanced their cause both militarily and politically.[9] This Senate scheme attracted such enthusiasm among the rank and file that it was taken up by the rival O'Mahony group, whose raid on the island of Campobello, New Brunswick, ended in utter fiasco in April 1866. The Senate Fenians launched their attack on 31 May 1866, crossing into Canada at a point near Buffalo, and pressing on to Ridgeway. After some fighting they retreated to the United States of America, where they were indulgently treated by the American government.

Stephens had fled to Paris shortly after his prison escape, and from there crossed the Atlantic determined on an attempt at unification of the American movement. Arriving in New York after the Campobello expedition, Stephens was immediately placed at the head of the O'Mahony faction, but failed to regain control of the Senate group. A revolutionist drawn to doctrine and posture rather than politics, his autocratic pretensions and scathing denunciations of the Campobello raid and Roberts' proposed move on Canada cast oil on the flames of factionalism.

8 General Lord Strathnairn, 'Annual Report to the Cabinet', June 1867; NLI: Mayo Papers: Ms. 11188 (5), f. 4. Strathnairn (Hugh Henry Rose, 1801–85) was born in Berlin and had a successful career soldiering throughout the British Empire. Commanded British forces in Ireland from 1 July 1865 to 30 June 1870. Sworn of the Irish Privy Council, 1865; created Baron Strathnairn and Sansi, 31 July 1866.

9 For an account of the split in the Fenian movement in the United States of America, see 'One Who Knows' (pseudonym Robert Anderson), 'Fenianism: A Narrative', *The Contemporary Review*, 19 (December 1871 to May 1872), pp. 301–16; see also Denieffe, *op. cit.*, p. 131, n. 1).

With the defeat of the Senate expedition another opportunity came. Since he had warned against these futile expeditions, Stephens' authority rose and was reinforced in a series of public meetings at which he gave messianic pledges to take the field in Ireland before the end of the year. At his last public appearance in New York on 28 October 1866, Stephens committed himself irrevocably. The cause of Irish independence would be decided within the next two months: 'I speak to you now for the last time before returning to Ireland. . . . My last words are, that we shall be fighting on Irish soil before the 1st of January, and I shall be there in the midst of my countrymen.'[10] Such a bid could not be reneged: Stephens staked and lost his reputation. Still pleading for more time and resources, he was deposed as military leader in December 1866, and was shortly thereafter eased out of the leadership altogether.

Stephens' replacement was Colonel Thomas J. Kelly, designated Chief Officer of the Irish Republic (abbreviated in Fenian documents to COIR), whose men were behind the events which galvanised Ireland and Britain throughout 1867, including, of course, his own famous rescue from the black maria at Manchester.[11] Kelly had already established his name as a man of action in Fenian eyes, having led the 1865 rescue of Stephens. But even under this leadership, as we have seen, the combination of astute policing aided by well-rewarded informers, and the overwhelming military strength and preparedness of Britain, proved to be unshakable.

The dynamite campaign

Fenianism, both in Ireland and in America, had thus been devastated organisationally and politically by the beginning of the 1870s, when rescue came from an unexpected quarter: Gladstone's release of the Fenian leaders, and their exile to the United States of America. Their reputation and moral stature was made unassailable by their years in prison, and there were hopes that they would heal Fenianism's wounds and divisions. This they attempted, by setting up the Irish Confederation, which was intended to allow the various revolutionary organisations to come together, while maintaining their own identities and

---

10 'One Who Knows', *op. cit.*
11 In February 1867, there was an attempt to unite the two principal Fenian factions under Mitchel's leadership, an honour he peremptorily declined. New divisions would have broken out around him, he wrote to Martin, and he would have been expected to implement the Fenians' 'ridiculous' constitution – 'to carry on the sham of a provisional government, and to commission "generals" for an imaginary army. All this, even if it were not illegal, is still ludicrous.' (William Dillon, *Life of John Mitchel*, London, Kegan Paul, Trench & Co, 1888, Vol. 2, p. 256). Mitchel's criticism of the Fenians was characteristically acid, and not at all softened by the fact that in October 1865 they had secured his release from federal internment at Fort Monroe. Subsequent to this he had been, for some six months, the Fenians' financial agent in Paris, resigning that post in June 1866 (ibid., Vol. 2, p. 244).

structures. But even the charisma of the Fenian exiles failed to overcome the feuding and personality conflicts which by then were endemic, and the Confederation collapsed.

While Fenianism had attempted to honour its various pledges of war and had failed dismally, a new Irish-American secret society, Clan na Gael, was formed on 20 June 1867. Rather than follow the autocratic model of the IRB, the Clan adopted a democratic structure on to which was grafted the usual apparatus of secrecy – restricted membership, compartmentalisation, hierarchy, a significant centralisation of funds, and a fanciful password, secret signs and symbols.[12] Although the details are unclear, the Clan also acknowledged the authority of the executive committee of the IRB, which was based in Ireland and Britain. Whereas Stephens was given to fire, fury and dramatic pledges, capable of inflaming but not realising patriotic fervour, the Clan worked diligently at local organisation. Above all, the Clan recognised the need to tap and meet the needs of the whole range of sympathisers, from postal subscribers to would-be soldiers. By providing opportunities for regular social contacts and an outlet for immigrants' anti-British feelings, and operating at both national and local levels, the Clan attracted a sizeable membership and accumulated a useful war-chest.[13]

The Clan secured its place in the leadership of militant Irish-Americans in 1876 when it organised the rescue of the six Fenian soldiers still serving their sentences at the penal depot in Western Australia. As noted, the operation was organised by John Devoy and executed by John J. Breslin in some style, and, despite its complexity and protracted preparation, was not betrayed to the British government.[14] The *Catalpa* success had far-reaching consequences. The movement was, by definition, adventurist, and the *Catalpa* satisfied a desperate need for success, buoyed up the extreme men, both in America and Ireland. But by confirming the possibilities of some audacious action against the British, this episode hopelessly exaggerated the potential of such actions in general. Why, the militants asked themselves, if a mission could be conducted against a target on the other side of the world, could not even more successful blows be landed closer to home? Could not they repeat the success of the Confederate raider *Alabama* against the Union and ruin the commerce of the British Empire? Could England's chief cities be damaged or destroyed and her shipping sunk?

---

12 The English spy Henry Le Caron (Thomas Billis Beach) was a member of the Clan from 1876, and by being active in its leadership betrayed many of its secrets (see his *Twenty-five Years in the Secret Service*, London, William Heinemann, 1892).

13 K. R. M. Short estimated a subscribing membership of 20,000 by 1884 (*The Dynamite War: Irish-American Bombers in Victorian Britain*, Dublin, Gill and Macmillan, 1979, p. 29).

14 See above, pp. 209–13. Breslin (?1836–88) was the hospital warder at Richmond Prison who procured the keys that allowed the escape of James Stephens in November 1865. Breslin (who was an associate of John Devoy, rather than Rossa) became active in Clan na Gael after his emigration to the United States of America. Besides the *Catalpa* rescue he also played a major part in the Fenian Ram submarine scheme.

Those ideas were being discussed by Rossa and his followers some time before dynamite ('scientific warfare') revealed itself in all its revolutionary glory, and before the *Catalpa* berthed in New York to such heartfelt acclaim. In December 1875, the *Irish World* published a letter from Rossa calling for funds for parties of skirmishers who would mount repeated small attacks on England while work continued for a general insurrection.[15] This idea might well have languished, or spluttered along ineffectually. The *Catalpa* success – in which Rossa had played no part – supercharged it. Patrick Ford (publisher and editor of the *Irish World*) was asked to allow his newspaper to be the conduit for donations. Ford was initially reluctant to become involved in the enterprise and returned early donations. After further negotiations he agreed to make the *Irish World's* columns available for fundraising. Rossa was to provide regular appeal copy, and two trustees suggested by Ford – James J. Clancy and Augustine Ford – were to handle and be accountable for the money. Ford imposed another condition: any donor requesting a refund within six months was to be refunded 'without asking any uncivil questions'.[16]

At first the fund languished. The public was told that action would be taken as soon as $5000 had been collected and that the general intention was to strike as the opportunity permitted and to 'make way for the efforts of the regular revolutionary organisations'. From an early point, however, Rossa entertained ambitions vastly wider than merely harassing the British government. He suggested that Liverpool shipping be burned, adding to this the principal cities in England – indeed he was 'in favor of anything'. Any loss of life would not be 'one-tenth that recorded in the least of the smallest battles between the South and the North'. At this point Ford accepted Rossa's reasoning, contending that a dozen arsonists could, on a propitious winter's night, lay London in ashes. Ford also believed that by attacking the City of London, Britain's economy and therefore her world political position could be destroyed. That accomplished, the dream went on, Ireland might become 'England's regenerator as well as her own emancipator, and over the blackened ruins the English Republic and the Irish Republic, forgetting and forgiving the past, would sign a treaty of perpetual peace'.

Before this consummation, however, certain practical matters needed attention. Primary among these was the collection of money, which at first did not go at all well – especially when James Stephens, John O'Leary and Thomas Clarke Luby denounced the Skirmishing Fund. These doldrums were left behind, however,

---

15 William O'Brien and Desmond Ryan (eds), *Devoy's Post Bag*, Dublin, C. J. Fallon, 1948, Vol. 1, pp. 141–2.
16 These details of the Skirmishing Fund are taken from what appears to be an authoritative background article in the *New York Herald* (20 April 1883: at PRO FO 5/1861/141 *et seq.*). Most of the article's information was culled from Patrick Ford's account of the origin and development of the Fund. The details which follow here are based on this source.

when the *Catalpa's* marvellous news reached America. Although this was a Clan na Gael affair, with no connection whatsoever to the Rossa fund, it epitomised what audacity and a relatively modest fund might do. Money poured in, and Rossa's $5000 target was soon reached and exceeded. No 'work' was commissioned by Rossa and his colleagues, but in February 1877 the fund paid some $2300 for the transportation of the body of John O'Mahony back to Ireland and for the expenses of a public funeral. Following this event, concern was expressed that the trusteeship of such a large fund (it had risen to $23,000 by March 1877) was so narrowly based. Ford, Clancy and Rossa resigned and were replaced as trustees by Thomas Clarke Luby, Thomas F. Bourke, Dr William Carroll, John J. Breslin, John Devoy and James Reynolds. Because of his personal debts Rossa was not made a trustee, but instead became fund secretary.[17]

The new trustees renamed the fund the 'National Fund' and largely abandoned Rossa's pledges of immediate, violent and destructive action. They promised in a more general way that donations would be used to further the Irish national struggle, and would be disbursed according to their discretion. Money continued to come in from the United States of America, Canada, Australia, and from Ireland and Britain. By 1880 some $90,000 had been accumulated, but none expended on the terrorist attacks which Rossa and his supporters originally had in mind. Instead, large sums were spent on the development of a submarine, designed by an immigrant Irish engineer, John Philip Holland. Various proto-types were unsuccessful, but a practical machine always seemed tantalisingly imminent, and between 1876 and the end of 1883, when Holland and the revolutionaries discontinued their association, a goodly portion of the National Fund went into the project. So alarmed was the British government that it requested the authorities to seize Holland's vessel should it attempt to leave US jurisdiction.[18] Although Holland's work is now recognised as having con-tributed to the development of the modern submarine, the enterprise was a

17 Rossa gave a full accounting for the $23,000 in the Fund, but shortly afterwards two of his cheques (one for $300 and another for $500) were refused payment. Rossa promised to make up the deficit and was allowed to remain as Secretary after the trustees guaranteed his pledge. The debt was eventually repaid by the Fund voting Rossa the sum of $1000 for his work as Secretary, and deducting $800 from this payment. Because of the amount of work involved the Trustees considered this a reasonable arrangement – though the whole episode was hardly to Rossa's credit.

18 The British government obtained details of Holland's submarine. The Home Secretary (Sir William Harcourt) told his son that the plans were 'very formidable'. The project appears to have failed because of faulty construction rather than defective design (Lewis Harcourt Diaries, Bodleian Library: Ms Harcourt dep. 348, 17 August 1881, f. 146). Two years later, however, the British government still remained apprehensive about the 'Fenian Ram' (as the submarine was known) and applied to the US Secretary of State 'for a watch to be kept on the movements of the Torpedo Boats reported to be at New Haven, New Jersey [sic.]'. The Ambassador reported that in response 'such steps have been taken as may prevent any violation of the neutrality law' (PRO FO 5/1862/282-3).

failure for the National Fund, and lent weight to Rossa's contention that Irish-American money could be put to more immediate and devastating use. On this and various other grounds Rossa eventually split from the National Fund and set up his own organisation, complete with newspaper, national convention and terrorist units.

Rossa's position at this time sheds interesting light on the micro-economics of terrorism. He had arrived in America without a profession and made his living, by inclination and necessity in proportions known only to himself, as a revolutionary organiser and publicist. Shortly after his expatriation he, with the other Fenian exiles, had received testimonial gifts amounting to several thousand dollars.[19] This money ran out, and Rossa had to earn, since he could not expect to live indefinitely on Irish-American hand-outs. With name and reputation as capital, he set himself up as a steamship and railroad ticket agent, operating from offices on Broadway. This must have been an uncertain and thin living, however, and there are besides indications that Rossa lent money to some of his fellow exiles, who through improvidence or ill-luck had found themselves in an even worse position than his. By mid-1878 Rossa's wife, Mary, was calling in those debts because of Rossa's own pressing financial difficulties.[20]

Rossa had urgent political and financial reasons for breaking with the Clan and setting up his own newspaper (inevitably the *United Irishman*). Politically, he freed himself to take his own line, and to publicise and execute it how he wished. Financially, he attracted more funds to himself and, since he was a one-man operation, the blurred line between personal and operational expenses could be resolved to his benefit – and he could without dishonour draw a regular emolument for himself.

Rossa's problems were greatly aggravated by his alcoholism. Writing to James Reynolds[21] on 6 February 1878, Devoy described Rossa as 'a drunken man bringing us into disgrace by raving in the papers'. It was not safe to go into revolutionary work with those who could not keep a secret. A month later he

---

19 From Patrick Ford's *Irish World* alone Rossa received $3859 (*Irish World and American Industrial Liberator*, 16 February 1884, 10c–e).
20 See the letter dated 26 July 1878 from John Devoy to Mary O'Donovan Rossa, enclosing $20 as an instalment of his debt to Rossa. Devoy strenuously denies that he and his friends are indifferent to Rossa, or that they have sought to ruin him. Such false stories, if continued, Devoy warns, 'may lead to exposures which will be much more unpleasant to Rossa than to us'. This can only refer to Rossa's defalcation (see n. 17 above). Despite alluding to this brewing scandal, Devoy promised Mary O'Donovan Rossa that he would 'make any sacrifice in my power to take him out of the condition he is now in' (Devoy to Mary O'Donovan Rossa, 26 July 1878: Catholic University of America, Fenian Brotherhood Papers (CUA, FBP): Box 2, item 24). This would be a hopeless task, however, as long as Rossa refused to shake off the men who were clinging to him. It was around this time that Rossa was obliged to resign his Skirmishing Fund secretaryship.
21 One of the *Catalpa* organisers, a leading member of the committee appointed by Clan na Gael in July 1874 to carry out the work.

wrote again: 'He is now so bad that I fear the only way to save him is to put him under restraint. He can't eat or sleep.'[22]

Such matters would not be discussed or held against Rossa by his erstwhile colleagues – or at least not in public – since scandal and splits damaged all, politically and organisationally, and reduced the overall flow of donations and subscriptions. Behind the scenes, however, there were sharp exchanges. The initial split over the use to which the Skirmishing Fund should be put produced a demand from Rossa that Thomas Luby and Thomas Bourke should resign as trustees because of statements condemning bombing and adventurism which they had made in the New York newspapers.[23] Rossa had long been a supporter and beneficiary of Patrick Ford's *Irish World* (his ticket-agency letterhead included an appeal for subscribers to the *World*), but when he ventured out on his own this association also turned sour. To succeed, Rossa needed the ringmaster's flair, and frequent announcements well larded with sensational and dramatic state-ments and promises.[24] These attracted a certain type of exhibitionistic follower, inevitably heightening the appetite for hyperbole. This accelerating unreality caused Patrick Ford, at this point a committed dynamitard, to decline Rossa's invitations to participate in his 1880 'Convention of the Irish Race' which was to be held in Philadelphia.[25] Among Rossa's associates, Ford observed, there were many for whom self-promotion and jealousy rather than duty were the motivating forces: 'Rossa, when you can raise up a body of men who are willing to do their duty in silence, and who are not seeking self-glorification, I will do all I can to strengthen their arms. Not a step will I move otherwise – as it would be labour in vain.'[26]

22 Devoy to Reynolds, 10 March 1878, NLI: Devoy Papers: Ms. 18, 351 (ii). Rossa had quarrelled with his wife and had not gone home; she wanted to return to Ireland. For his part Rossa was thinking of changing his name and going to Australia. Patrick Ford, publisher of the *Irish World*, could not afford to keep him on the payroll and Rossa would therefore soon be without a livelihood.

23 'I consider both of you condemn the policy on which the skirmishing money was contributed and I told Bourke that I think both of you ought in decency resign' (Rossa to Luby, 27 March 1878, CUA, FBP: Box 3, item 33).

24 Typical of these was a Rossa warning that after a certain date it would not be safe to travel in British vessels – a considerable amount of notice and worry for no cost or risk (see Bodleian Library: Lewis Harcourt Papers: Ms Harcourt 749/99 – no date, probably early 1882). The British government rose all too easily to Rossa's bait – his threats, bluffs and claims – and solemnly catalogued a selection of them for presentation to Parliament and the public (see *Correspondence Respecting the Publication in the United States of Incitements to Outrages in England*, PP, 1882 [C.3194], LXXX, 53, 1–3).

25 This was the week-long 'Dynamite Convention' at which Rossa hoped to receive widely drawn Irish-American support for his policies, particularly the use of dynamite in England (CUA, FBP: Box 3, item 30: 'Convention of the Irish Race, 1880'). Apart from Rossa, however, the organising committee of the Convention included no prominent Fenian or Irish-American leader.

26 Ford to Rossa, 17 March 1880: CUA, FBP: Box 3, item 33. ('I am in entire accord with any honest body of men who believe in harassing England in every way in their power.') On 8 July 1880, there was a serious breach between Rossa and Devoy (NLI: Devoy Papers: Ms. 18, 351 (ii)).

Cut off from the support and restraint of his former comrades, and their solid organisational resources, Rossa had no option but to continue as a type of revolutionary showman, a self-publicist perhaps more familiar in our own times than in his. This career could not have been sustained but for the mercurial and sensation-seeking element in his own character. As a headline-chaser, he became the most notorious of the exiled Fenian leaders, an object of execration in England, infuriation mixed with a type of pity to his former colleagues, and adulation to the less-educated and more demonstrative among Irish immigrants and the Irish-Americans.[27] To the establishment *New York Times*, Rossa's antics were those of a disreputable mountebank. In a leader excoriating a certain Mr Hartmann who for reasons of self-promotion claimed to be behind the assassination of Tsar Alexander II, the *New York Times* referred to Rossa 'and a number of other lazy patriots [who] are collecting a rich harvest of sixpences from Irish servant girls by pretending to be dynamite fiends'. The article went on to explain how the scheme worked: 'Whenever an explosion occurs anywhere on English soil or on board an English vessel, Mr O'Donovan Rossa and his pals instantly claim that it was their own dynamite that did the work. In the intervals between accidental explosions they hold secret meetings, at which they are making active preparations to blow the greater part of the British Empire into fragments.'[28] But the newspaper thought that only the credulous would believe that 'with whisky and cigars at their present price' Rossa and his colleagues would waste their accumulated money on dynamite. This was only slightly unfair as a parody of Rossa's self-advertising money-collecting schemes. It was for good reason that the various groups of Fenians in America always appointed trustees when funds were collected, and took care to publish accounts. Even so, complaints about misspent and misappropriated funds were perennial. Rossa thought he had bypassed all of this by being his own collecting and accounting officer, but the arrangement made it even more certain that he would become the target of criticism and suspicions.

27 Typical of Rossa's provocations was an advertisement in his *United Irishman*: '$10,000 REWARD FOR THE BODY OF THE PRINCE OF WALES. DEAD OF ALIVE.' The notice continued in a similar vein and was best ignored, but the Foreign Office decided to take it up with the US government, recalling the case of Johann Most, who had been prosecuted and punished in England and America for incitement and sedition (see *United Irishman*, 11 February 1885, 1b; PRO FO 5/1863: Foreign Office to State Department).

28 *New York Times*, 22 August 1881, 4e. The leader went on to demand capital punishment for pretending to be a dynamite fiend. The only defence would be to show that they had actually killed someone with dynamite, in which case they should be hanged anyway. The *Nation* (Washington) had also drawn attention to the benefits which Rossa derived from claiming responsibility for explosions, when he had boasted that he had been behind the destruction of the warship *Doterel* in the Magellan Straits: 'O'Donovan Rossa had certainly no more to do with the explosion . . . than with the Scio earthquake, and to appear to believe that he had is the greatest service that could be rendered him, next to lending him fifty dollars' (ibid., 23 June 1881, 435a).

The 'new departure'

Before the submarine project was abandoned, the Clan took a critical strategic decision. In June 1879, John Devoy and Michael Davitt, representing the revolutionary wing of Irish nationalism, and Charles Parnell its militant but constitutional wing, agreed on the so-called 'New Departure', which, on certain conditions, put the resources of Fenianism behind parliamentary politics, and committed the parliamentary party to the Land War.[29] Neither side represented anything more than a fraction of their respective groupings, but the alliance was soon to show its enormous potential and to recast Irish politics, marrying the romantic nationalism and dedicated revolutionary organisation of the IRB to pragmatic demands for land reform, thereby creating the conditions for successful mass agitation and organisation.

But while Clan na Gael was reaching out to militant constitutionalists, it had not abandoned armed struggle. In Ireland the ballot box was combined with civil disobedience and rural crime in a potent mix. The Clan also continued to fund arms smuggling into Ireland, and at the same time its Revolutionary Directory drew up a plan for a dynamite campaign in Britain, placing operations under the charge of the veteran revolutionist Captain William Mackey Lomasney.[30] Early in 1881 Lomasney set off on a four-month reconnaissance mission to England and Ireland. Fearing a backlash against the Irish community in England and military reprisals in Ireland, Lomasney recommended to the Clan leadership that the business of arming and organising supporters in Ireland and Britain should proceed much further before a major dynamite campaign was launched.[31] Changes were then made in the Clan's national organisation in anticipation of terrorist operations and the need for even greater secrecy. Training and other preparations continued for another eighteen months. In the spring of 1883 it was agreed to proceed, and Clan dynamiters began to make their way to England.[32]

29 The alliance with Parnell had been prepared by Devoy over the preceding several months and in November 1878 the Clan na Gael executive had approved the 'New Departure' and had authorised the necessary negotiations with Parnell and the IRB (see Theodore William Moody, *Davitt and Irish Revolution 1846–82*, Oxford, Clarendon Press, 1982, ch. 8). For an interesting (but inconclusive) examination of suggestions that Parnell was actually sworn to the IRB see Patrick Maume, 'Parnell and the I. R. B. Oath', *Irish Historical Studies*, 29, 115 (May 1995), pp. 363–70.
30 See above, p. 228, n. 56.
31 Short, *op. cit.*, pp. 57–8.
32 Rossa had made another attempt to obtain control of the Clan Skirmishing Fund, but this had been thwarted, prompting a break in the cooperative association between the two groups (Agent's Report, via British Consul General, Philadelphia: PRO FO 5/1861/229 *et seq.*, 5 May 1883).

The skirmishers

By the time the Clan's bombers arrived in England, however, several explosions had already taken place or had been attempted. These were the fruit of Rossa's own Skirmishing Fund and skeletal but surprisingly effective organisation. He had launched the *United Irishman* in June 1880, together with his own appeal for funds to carry the war to England and Ireland – the United Irish Reserve Fund. The formula was quite simple: if supporters would send him the money Rossa would undertake to find the men to set fires and place explosives in England.[33] The network of so-called auxiliary clubs – social and benevolent societies loosely attached to Clan na Gael – provided a pool from which suitable recruits could be drawn for the work.[34]

This was a complete departure from the basic doctrine of Fenianism – the people's army carrying the nation's will and honour against a beleaguered enemy – national renaissance as much in the form of victory as its substance. If such a logic were accepted, assassination, bombing and the other deeds of terrorism could give birth only to a creature of dishonour, endlessly devoured from within by the moral incapacity of its ministers and soldiers. Established by the authority of those who had fought against English oppression, and who had suffered for it, the classic Fenian doctrine was widely disseminated among the Irish-Americans and found consonance in certain of their religious beliefs and idealistic nationalism. Such a doctrine of honour and patient vigilance could lead to torpor, and certainly justify inaction. For money to flow, blood to rise and men to volunteer, Rossa and others believed, more urgent, brutal and pragmatic tactics were required – at least as interim measures. The strength (and convenience) of traditional Fenianism was the principal ideological obstacle that baulked Rossa and the Clan in the 1880s. By trial and error, and an accretion of arguments, the extremists developed the politics and ethics of the dynamitard movement.

Terror explosions were presented as an oppressed people's last recourse in a war with a mighty and ruthless opponent. The very nature of dynamite itself was heralded as a providence-given and easily manufactured equaliser in a struggle in which hitherto all the advantages had gone to the strong: David's sling against

33 A Rossa supporter in England was overheard to say that '£1 of dynamite was worth more than any resolution at a public meeting' (Bodleian Library: Lewis Harcourt Diaries: Ms Harcourt dep. 348; 10 April 1881, f. 39). At around the same time Sir Robert Anderson, Home Office adviser on Fenian matters, warned Sir William Harcourt that recent developments had re-established Rossa as a leading influence on American Fenianism: 'If the men who hitherto have exercised a definite control, give place to desperate men like Rossa, whose only thought is of wild & reckless revenge, we shall have trouble in the near future far greater than any we have known in the past' ('Secret', Anderson to Harcourt, 29 March 1881: PRO HO 144/1537/Pt. 1(c)).

34 See the *New York Times* report 'Fenian Work in New York' describing the connection between the auxiliary clubs (with names such as the Emerald Club and the Thomas Davis Club), Clan na Gael and Rossa; 20 April 1883,1a–d. This report was thoroughly researched, and was published in conjunction with reports of the appearance in Bow Street Magistrates' Court of Dr Gallagher and his dynamite team.

Goliath. Aware that indiscriminate slaughter might raise certain moral – but mainly political – problems, Rossa took steps to lay the foundations for a deontology and theology of explosives, and even found a priest willing to accompany him on this journey of moral speculation.

As a means of recruiting support and raising money, while at the same time giving a revolutionary benediction to the substance itself, Rossa began to run classes in dynamite-making. The United Irishman, under the heading 'Educate That You May Be Free', announced one such series. Classes were to be free to those whom the 'advanced nationalists' intended to send to England as 'Missioners' or 'Skirmishers'; other societies or individuals would pay a fee of $30 for the course. There was a whiff of the snake-oil salesman in the claimed results: 'Our professor says he can, in thirty days, instruct any man of average intelligence and make him able to manufacture dynamite in America, England, Ireland, Scotland, or any other part of the world.'[35] The 'professor' was Mezzeroff, whose public lectures (as distinct from tutorials) were paens of praise for dynamite: 'The Resources of Science Against the Resources of Civilization.' Mezzeroff would show dynamite to be 'the best way for oppressed peoples from all countries to get free from tyranny and oppression'.[36]

A pamphlet outlining the moral and political case for dynamite, followed by detailed instructions for its manufacture, for a delayed-action detonator and for making the phosphorus-based 'Greek Fire', was published a few years later, under the pseudonym 'Glencree', and may be supposed to contain the substance of Mezzeroff's lecture. (The Russian-sounding name was a convenient reference to the explosives expert's knowledge of Russian nihilists.) This was what today would be called a bomber's cookbook, in which the recipes and, even more importantly, the method of mixing, are described with the warning that 'care is needed'. Dynamite was presented as a 'wonderful compound' and it was asserted that 'there is more potency in the knowledge and use of a one-pound bomb than in a million speeches'.[37] Certainly the pamphlet gives sufficient information to manufacture powerful explosives and incendiary devices, but in this case a little knowledge may have been a truly dangerous thing, and one wonders how many deaths and injuries there were among those who experimented without the benefits of Mezzeroff's practical classes.[38]

---

35 United Irishman, 30 September 1882, 4e. By January 1883, according to a British agent, Rossa claimed to have trained sixty-three students to manufacture explosives and combustibles 'from most simple and inexpensive materials' (PRO FO 5/1860/35).

36 Ibid., 4c. The phrase 'the resources of civilisation' had been used by Gladstone in response to terrorist attacks.

37 'Glencree', Scientific Warfare or the Resources of Civilization, Private Circulation, 1888, p. 5.

38 At a meeting to pronounce the death penalty on the Prince of Wales, held on 3 April 1885 in Chickering Hall, New York, Mezzeroff, introduced as 'England's invisible enemy', dared the US Congress to make laws preventing Irishmen from using dynamite in England (PRO HO 144/133/A34707: extracts from United Irishman, f. 1). Congress certainly had an interest in the American-based apprentice phase of the bombers' trade.

Orthodox Fenianism's various leaders spoke out. John O'Leary condemned the outrages in the *Celtic Magazine*, stating that he had yet to learn of any well-known Fenian who had ever advocated that hated doctrine, and he had not the slightest moral doubt that his views were shared by Stephens, Luby 'and every other prominent Nationalist in Ireland or America'. Of Rossa he said that the time when he had any claim 'to represent any appreciable section of the Fenians is long past. I firmly believe that he has not the means to carry out his insane schemes, and I more than suspect that despite all his mouthings, he is far from being the desperado he would pass for.'[39] John Boyle O'Reilly, the first Fenian to escape from Western Australia, was also horrified by the outrages, and stated so repeatedly, going so far as to offer a reward through the *Boston Pilot* for the apprehension of the Phoenix Park murderers.[40] Some former Fenian activists including Edward O'Meagher Condon (condemned and reprieved for his part in the Manchester rescue) did insist that British policy in Ireland justified the dynamite campaign, but these views were repudiated by the bulk of the old-style Fenians.[41]

Recognising the need to justify his doctrine, Rossa enlisted the aid of an unnamed clergyman in a pamphlet published in preparation for the Philadelphia Dynamite Convention of 1880. The priest (if indeed he was one) argued that if attacked at home England was 'very destructible', going on to observe that 'her cities invite destruction. The loss of them would so cripple England as to leave her unable to take care of herself, and much more unable to overpower any other country.' As for the laws of war, 'Ireland is not a free nation, and therefore not subject to the laws which should regulate the conduct of a free nation in its belligerent relations to its antagonist'. Since that enemy was England, 'the situation demands such methods as are justifiable when a captive is endeavouring to rescue his property, his liberty and his life from his piratical captor.'[42]

This was the basic line: any measures were justified for the weak and oppressed to win Irish freedom from its cruel and implacable conqueror. The theme permeated public meetings, pamphlets and articles throughout the 1880s. Two more examples will suffice. P. J. Sheridan spoke at a meeting in Philadelphia on 27 September 1883 on the subject of 'Scientific Warfare' (which had become the accepted euphemism for bombing campaigns). A British agent was in the

---

39 CUA, FBP: Box 4, *Celtic Magazine*, 1 June 1882. By this article Rossa has pencilled 'Lady O'Leary'.
40 Ibid.: Box 4. This portion of the Fenian Brotherhood Papers includes many articles and reactions to the outrages from the Irish community. The majority were horrified by this form of warfare.
41 Condon, who served eleven years' penal servitude after his reprieve, emigrated to the United States of America, where personal and political influences secured him a post in the US Treasury. There was a sharp press reaction when in April 1883 he gave an interview to the *Washington National Republican* justifying dynamiting as a just means of retaliation against Britain's Irish policy (*Washington National Republican*, 7 April 1883, at PRO FO 5/1861/31). The *New York Tribune* called for his silence or resignation as a civil servant (22 April 1883, at PRO FO 5/1861/97).
42 'Le Sagart', 'The Coming Convention. Its Policy', *The Society of United Irishmen: Preamble and Constitution*, Philadelphia, United Irishmen, 1880, pp. 18 and 19.

audience and recorded his remarks. Sheridan said he was there to object to what was hypocritically called 'honorable warfare'. This concept entailed 'injustice, inhumanity and evil results'. It was unjust because it involved in a terrible war men who had no interest in the cause of the strife; inhuman because of the loss of life and suffering which it entailed. Its evil results would be the 'desolation and sorrow which it would bring to Ireland under any circumstances'. But there was an alternative to honourable warfare: 'Some will call it scientific warfare, others fiendish warfare, but it is at any rate a war for the emancipation of Ireland.' Instead of waging war on the innocent soldiers of the English army 'we should turn our attention to the legislators and cabinet ministers'. All of this and more was received with cheers and applause (according to the transcript) and the meeting adopted a resolution recognising as 'just and right the use of every weapon which nature and science has placed at our disposal', and insisting that 'it was no more sinful to use dynamite and nitroglycerine than for the English to use viler tools in any endeavor to crush the hope of freedom in Ireland'.[43]

Professor Mezzeroff was as well versed in the ethics of bomb warfare as in the manufacture of explosive substances, and set out his beliefs in a pamphlet promoted, apparently with equal vigour, by Rossa's fire-eating dynamitards as by the more restrained Clan and Land League organisation. The title of the publication seemed to make its contents redundant: *Dynamite Against Gladstone's Resources of Civilisation or The Best Way to Make Ireland Free and Independent.* Drawing examples from the Crimean War and American Civil War (and from those of the Israelites, Ancient Greeks, Romans, Egyptians, Assyrians, as well as the Swiss, Austrians, Scots, Germans and French), Mezzeroff argued that there was no Christian doctrine as to what constituted honourable warfare ('He [Jesus Christ] made no law and gave no directions how Christians should fight'). Nor was there customary law, since weapons and methods of warfare were constantly changing, 'and what is called dishonorable today is called honorable tomorrow'.[44] He poured scorn on those who maintained they practised only honourable warfare, and those who attempted to distinguish between war and murder ('wholesale or retail work?') and gave various examples of the killing of innocents in war. 'Secret devices,' he concluded, 'are as honorable weapons of war as pistols, guns or cannon; and as they have been used for the last hundred years by all the tyrants in Europe to enslave the people, it is perfectly just that Ireland should use them to achieve her liberty and independence.'[45]

The lectures and pamphlets of Mezzeroff and the other apostles of dynamite were concerned to still doubts, and to set out, in an easily mastered form, a convenient political and moral argument. Among a section of extreme nationalists

---

43 'Notes of a lecture delivered at Horticultural Hall Philadelphia by P. J. Sheridan on September 27 1883', PRO FO 5/1862, ff. 211–13.

44 Professor Mezzeroff, *Dynamite Against Gladstone's Resources of Civilisation or The Best Way to Make Ireland Free and Independent*, pp. 4–5 (at PRO FO 5/1861).

45 Ibid., pp. 22–3.

this succeeded so well that in January 1884 a contributor to the California *Bee* could write that 'Dynamite will speed the blessed day when peace shall dwell upon the earth, and good will shall reign among the nations. Condemn it not, for it bids fair to be the benefactor of mankind.'[46] In this, as in the reams of Rossa's contrived dynamitology, there is the familiar adolescent desire, *épater les bourgeoisie*.

The campaigns

Despite their operational and organisational disagreements, Rossa and the Clan took a common approach to recruitment: no bombers would be taken from Fenian or other revolutionary ranks in Ireland or Britain, since these must be supposed to have been compromised by government penetration. Alexander Sullivan of Chicago, who became the leader of the triumvirate (the so-called 'Triangle')[47] which in the 1880s directed Clan na Gael, explained how men were selected for dynamite missions. No volunteer was to be accepted, and before a man was chosen there would be a detailed and secret inquiry into his background. Men without families would be preferred, and new members would be avoided.[48] These were effective precautions against penetration by an agent on one of the missions, but they were not proof against betrayal by a high official of the organisation, nor against surveillance by Royal Irish Constabulary officers operating in the United States of America and Britain. The abiding and fatal disadvantage of using Irish-Americans was that once a dynamite campaign was under way, such men, because of their manner of dress, speech and their general demeanour, became conspicuous targets for units of the Irish and English police assigned to anti-Fenian duties; they also became objects of suspicion to members of the general public.

Rossa's skirmishers

On 14 January 1881 Rossa turned words into action with an explosives attack on Salford barracks. Four civilians were injured, including a boy of 7 who died two days later.[49] Steps were immediately taken to guard public buildings and possible military targets. There is, however, no defence against terrorism except effective intelligence, and at this point the authorities were without it. It was only mistiming, therefore, that foiled Rossa's next outrage – an attempt on 16 March

---

46 Cit. *Irish World*, 3 January 1884, 8d.

47 The other two were General Michael Kerwin and Colonel Michael Boland, both of New York.

48 The conversation with the English agent, Henry Le Caron, took place in late May 1883. See Le Caron, *op. cit.*, pp. 217–18.

49 The attack, carried out in dense fog, was on the Regent Road Barracks, then in occupation by the 8th Light Infantry. Debris from the powerful explosion was cast for some hundred yards around (*Salford Weekly News*, 15 January 1881, 2e). Within a few days Salford's Parnell Defence Committee had condemned the explosion as the work of agents provocateurs intent on discrediting constitutional nationalism. The committee also asserted its improbable disbelief in the existence of 'any so-called Fenianism' (ibid., 22 January 1881, 2e).

to blow up the City of London's Mansion House. A constable on his regular beat found the bomb with its fuse still burning (but very close to the device's twenty-five pounds of gunpowder) and extinguished it.[50] By this time the police thought that they knew the identity of the chief bomber (an activist in the Land League). A squad was dispatched to the man's lodgings, where, according to the Home Secretary's son, they were to ask for him under his real and assumed names, to show that both were known: 'They were then to search the place and generally terrify the man.'[51] The somewhat haphazard targeting of Rossa's skirmishers was revealed when the police located the cabbie who had driven the bombers to the Mansion House. According to his version of events, the men had at first wanted to go to the Horse Guards (War Office), 'but finding that they had not enough money they said that the Mansion House would do just as well'.[52]

Police intelligence was inadequate or misinformed, and Rossa's men continued to elude capture. The first team, supposed by the police to be Coleman, O'Donnell and Mooney, got safely out of the country – the first two to New York, and Mooney to France.[53] James McGrath,[54] who had been instructed by Rossa to mount attacks in the north of England, and who was probably responsible for the Salford explosion, moved to Liverpool, where he took up lodgings with another Rossa associate, James McKevitt.[55] On 16 May 1881, the two planted a bomb at the Liverpool police headquarters. Because the bomb was poorly manufactured, however, little damage was caused.[56] Despite the fumble, and having greatly increased the state of alertness of the local police, the pair immediately began to plan another attack, this time using dynamite instead of gunpowder. In the early hours of 10 June they carried a large and heavy bomb through the streets and placed it against the west door of Liverpool Town Hall. Again a patrolling constable (alerted by a passing cabbie) foiled the operation. Help was summoned, and the bomb was pulled away from the building and exploded in the street. The two bombers were pursued and, although armed, allowed

---

50 See *The Times*, 18 March 1881, 8b; 19 March, 10b; 21 March, 10d; 24 March, 12a; 25 March, 9b; 28 March, 10d.

51 Lewis Harcourt's Diaries, *op. cit.*, 17 March 1881, f. 10. Harcourt hoped that this intimidation would cause 'a stampede of the worst characters, which is all we can hope for' (ibid., f. 11).

52 Ibid., 24 March 1881, f. 19.

53 This report, from police agents in New York, was definite that these were the Mansion House bombers (ibid., 10 April 1881, f. 39).

54 Alias Robert William Barton. Born Glasgow 1854 of Irish parents; emigrated to New York, where he eventually came under the influence of O'Donovan Rossa.

55 See *The Times*, 11 June 1881, 9e.

56 *The Times*, 18 May 1881, 12c. 'It looks like an old piece of glass or waterpipe, about sixteen inches long and three inches in diameter, with two plugs at either end firmly embedded in the bore to the depth of two inches and a half.' This improvised bomb had been very crudely constructed, and the fact that the powder was packed rather loosely in it, and that the plug was first blown out, considerably minimised the effect of the explosion. 'Very little damage was done to the building beyond the breaking of several panes of glass at the top and sides of the floor and the singeing of the woodwork.'

themselves to be captured.[57] After a trial lasting only a day, both were found guilty. McGrath (aged 31) was sentenced to penal servitude for life and McKevitt (aged 30) to fifteen years.[58]

Despite these setbacks, Rossa put in a new set of men the following year. This campaign started with another attempt on the Mansion House on 12 May 1882. Again the bomb failed to explode, and succeeded only in putting the police on heightened alert. The device was so poorly made – a mixture of gunpowder and blasting powder, placed at the strongest part of the building – that the press conjectured that the operation had been no more than a trouble-causing hoax.[59] Certainly failing in the one objective, it succeeded in the other, and the spring of 1882 was passed in the larger British cities in some apprehension of further Fenian actions, relieved only in part on 17 June by the discovery of an IRB arms dump at Clerkenwell.[60] The caretaker of the cache, John Walsh (alias Sadgrove), was charged and found guilty on arms charges and received a sentence of seven years' penal servitude.[61] This blow against the IRB's regular gun-running activities

57 *The Times*, 11 June 1881 9e; see also *Liverpool Courier*, 11 June 1881, 4h and i; 5c and e–g. The *Courier* praised the police. 'The vile scheme was partially frustrated by an inquisitive cabman and the vigilance of the constables on duty. By one of the constables the bomb was thrown into the middle of the street, where it almost immediately exploded doing considerable damage to the surrounding buildings. The police had an exciting chase after the two conspirators, and one of the constables displayed a quick presence of mind and sterling courage. McKevitt and Barton were captured, and will be brought before Mr Raffles today' (ibid., 4h).

58 PRO HO 144/194/A46664C/99. For an account of remand and trial proceedings see the *Liverpool Courier*, 13 June 1881, 4g; 20 June, 4f; 3 August, 4g–h; 5f–i and 6a–c. Both men having been found guilty of attempting to blow up the town hall (the jury retired for only fifteen minutes), McGrath was then charged and found guilty of the attack on the police barracks, on the evidence of a joiner who had made the plugs for his bomb. While condemning the men's crimes the *Courier* noted that it had not been expected that the sentences would be so severe (ibid., 3 August, 4h).

59 *The Times*, 13 May 1882, 12d; *Globe*, 15 May 1882, 5c; 16 May, 2d. There was speculation that the bomb was meant to be discovered since there was attached to it 'an inscription derogatory to the Lord Mayor and the Irish landlords, who are supposed to be the main recipients of the Defence of Property Fund raised at the Mansion House early in his mayoralty' (*Globe*, 15 May 1882, 5c). The suspicion was that the bomb was connected with the equally inept bombing attempt on the Mansion House fourteen months before (see *Globe*, 17 March 1881, 5a; 18 March, 6d; 19 March, 5c).

60 *The Times*, 19 June 1882, 7d: 'About 400 stand of Snieder rifles and needle guns with bayonet, 25 large cases of six-chambered revolvers, some marked "Colt" and others "Hartford USA" together with many kegs of gunpowder and between 90,000 and 100,000 rounds of fully charged ammunition have been found in a large stable in Rydon Crescent, Clerkenwell.' See also *The Times*, 20 June, 10f; 21 June, 12c; 22 June, 5e; 23 June, 5f; 24 June, 7e; 26 June, 7d; 27 June, 5d.

61 PRO HO 144/84/A7323B; *The Times*, 3 August, 1882, 9c; 5 August, 10f; 7 August, 10a; 9 August, 10d; 10 August, 12c. This arms dump was not connected with the bombing campaign, but was part of the IRB's smuggling network. The procurement of arms was constant, so far as funds and opportunity allowed (Mark F. Ryan, *Fenian Memories*, Dublin, M. H. Gill and Son, 1945, p. 108). The IRB can hardly have been happy to lose such a cache, and may have reflected that the increased police vigilance and activity arose from the activities of the marauding Irish-Americans over which they had no control.

confirmed Lomasney's earlier denunciation of Rossa's activities (and the police vigilance they stimulated) as 'imbecile and farcical'.[62] Indeed, so concerned had Lomasney been that Rossa would provoke even more police activity against the Irish community and thus endanger the activities of Lomasney's own operation, that attempts had been made to find and scare off Rossa's bombers. For a time Rossa's freelance operation thus had the distinction of being the target both of the British authorities and the Clan.

But although Lomasney considered Rossa's campaign inept and bungling, it had heated a climate of fear and growing panic. The assassination of Tsar Nicholas II had shocked the world, and England especially, where extra precautions were immediately taken to protect the Queen.[63] In March 1882 there was an attempt on the Queen's own life (one of several during her reign) by the demented McClean. Most shocking of all, perhaps, was the murder of the Irish Chief Secretary, Lord Frederick Cavendish, and Thomas Burke, the Irish Under-Secretary, in the Phoenix Park, Dublin, by the Fenian breakaway group, the Invincibles. The extreme and calculated brutality of the deed – the men were slashed to death with surgical knives – and its audacity, challenged law and order throughout the kingdom. The Queen did not trust the government to protect her, and refused to set foot in London or to open Parliament. All of this delighted the dynamitards, and those who supported them. And the bombings went on, allowing the Irish-American journal *An Gaodhal* to proclaim that 'England is now in a panic and every European monarch feels like a hunted stag'.[64] The journal may have been surprised to learn that Victoria was of similar mind, complaining to her Home Secretary that 'she did not see why sovereigns should be less taken care of or more exposed to assassination than other people'.[65]

Since he had no organisation to speak of, Rossa made his decisions virtually alone. The advantage of this mode of operating was that if he could get both volunteers and money, he could put men to work willy-nilly; he was also fairly impervious to penetration attempts. The money came in through his *United*

---

62 He continued, 'The affair would seem more like a burlesque than anything else, but the trouble is, it is sure sooner or later, to involve our cause in trouble and disgrace if steps are not at once adopted to counteract these presumptuous fools' (William Mackey Lomasney to John Devoy, March 1881: O'Brien and Ryan, *op. cit.*, Vol. 2, p. 52).

63 See Bodleian Library: Lewis Harcourt Diaries: Ms Harcourt dep. 348; 14 March 1881. There were, of course, close family ties between the royal families of Europe. Queen Victoria's daughter-in-law, the Duchess of Edinburgh, was a daughter of Nicholas II, and there were many other links between the two families. Lewis Harcourt (son of the Home Secretary, Sir William Harcourt) wondered if the revival of torture might not be necessary to prevent assassinations since there seemed to be a ready supply of assassins who were willing to sacrifice their own lives (ibid., 15 March 1881).

64 The writer considered nitroglycerine 'a solvent of tyranny', and when rightly used 'a blessing to men', but fretted that 'unfortunately it is more liable to be used for criminal purposes' (*An Gaodhal*, 2, 8 (May 1883), p. 312).

65 Lewis Harcourt Diaries, *op. cit.*, 1 April 1881, f. 30.

Irishman appeals and willing men, it would seem, could always be found. On 20 January 1883, Rossa's ill-luck turned when his bombers made a successful attack on Glasgow Corporation's Tradeston gasworks, where they spectacularly ruptured one of the large gas storage tanks, causing extensive fire damage and some injuries. What made this operation the more formidable was two other explosions the same night – a failed attempt to destroy an aqueduct, and damage to railway property. This apparent capacity to cause simultaneous explosions was a success in itself, since it created the effect of the town being laid siege to by terrorists.[66] The police looked in the usual places and offered a substantial reward, but Rossa's men initially escaped. There was a flaw in the operation, however. Rossa had been forced to recruit Ribbonmen for the Glasgow operation and these could not be spirited out of the country, and the longer they remained the greater the chance they would come to the attention of the police – possibly for a reason quite unrelated to the bombing. And so it proved. They were denounced to the police for other matters, and the conspiracy unravelled. The full story was told at their trial, at which ten men were convicted for their various parts in the explosions. Five received sentences of life penal servitude, and the other five – considered to have been dupes – seven years' penal servitude apiece.[67]

The next operation, on 15 March 1883, also displayed Rossa's capacity for multiple explosions. On that evening two pillars of the Empire – *The Times* and the civil service – were attacked. At *The Times* the bomb failed to go off properly and merely blackened a window, but the attack on government offices was a demonstrative success. A bomb, comprising a sophisticated fuse detonator and ample dynamite, exploded with a bang that was heard forty-six miles away.[68] By great good chance there was no loss of life or injury, but very considerable damage was done to the buildings, part of a complex housing several departments, including the Home Office, Foreign Office, Colonial Office, India Office and – the principal casualty – the Local Government Board. Nearby structures, including

66 *The Times*, 22 January 1883, 6f; *Glasgow Weekly Citizen* (27 January 1883, 4e): 'Between Saturday night and Sunday morning three explosions occurred in Glasgow, within so short a time of each other as to suggest that they had been caused by the same agency. The first and most alarming was the explosion of a large gasometer at Tradeston Gasworks, which was heard with startling effect for miles around. Nine persons living in small dwellings close beside the holder were more or less seriously burned. The damage to the gasometer was not very great. Investigations are being made by the local and Home Office authorities with the view of discovering the cause of this and of the other two explosions. One of the latter blew up a disused shed at the Buchanan Street station of the Caledonian Railway, and the other took place at Possil Park. In the last case, as a party of men and women were passing, they discovered a tin box on the parapet of the canal bridge. While it was being handled the box exploded, and several persons were injured.'

67 The five who received life sentences were Terence McDermott aged 18; Thomas Devaney (41); Peter Callaghan (45); Henry McCann (48); James McCullagh (31); seven-year sentences were given to James Donnelly (33); James Kelly (48); Patrick McCabe (48); Patrick Drum (62); Denis Casey (37) (PRO HO 144/194/A46664C/99; HO 144/127/A33559/5; *The Times*, 24 November 1883, 7e).

68 The Revd W. D. Parish, Vicar of Selmeston, Sussex, claimed to have heard the explosion.

the 'A' division police station, were damaged by the flying debris.[69] There was popular outrage, well ventilated in the newspapers, and the authorities offered a £1000 reward for information. In New York Rossa was a jubilant sphinx. This was, by any reckoning, a telling blow, and it was only with difficulty that he restrained himself from claiming it to his credit.[70] Unbeknownst to Rossa, however, the Local Government Office bomb was to be the apogee of his pay-as-you-go bombing campaign. But without a doubt he had severely shaken the confidence of the British government in its ability to maintain law and order.[71]

Rossa's activities in the United Kingdom (he had agents in Cork, London and Glasgow) were brought to a halt in August 1883, when five of his bombers took their place in the dock. Four were convicted of treason felony and sentenced to life penal servitude; one man was acquitted.[72] These arrests and trials had aborted a Rossa scheme to manufacture bombs in Cork and to detonate them simultaneously in Counties Cork and Kerry, and in Liverpool, St Helens, London and, possibly, somewhere in Scotland. Deasy's arrest, as he stepped off the Cork steamer with some of the explosives in his possession, led to the other arrests, and, with the Glasgow bombers in prison awaiting their trials, left Rossa powerless to continue with his own campaign.[73]

---

69 PRO HO 144/144/A25908/11; *The Times*, 16 March 1883, 9c–d. Having described the explosion, *The Times* observed that these and other actions had caused political and popular sympathy to Ireland and her grievances to wane, being replaced by feelings 'of deep and profound disgust with Ireland and her people'. It warned of the growth of anti-Irish feelings that could get out of control. See also the long editorial in *The Times* on 17 March (11e–f). The US Legation immediately sent a message confirming its government's 'horror and detestation' at the 'dastardly crime' (PRO HO 144/144/A25908D).

70 Rossa was, for a time, at the centre of press attention, but had to take care lest he ran foul of US law, however unlikely that was. The *New York Herald* described his demeanour as mixed jubilation and portentousness. P. K. Horgan had telegraphed a caution to Rossa: 'Do not open your lips to mortal man or woman today on the subject of explosions in London.' The *Herald* reporter, in something of a send-up, described the upshot: '"I mean to follow that advice", said Rossa, toying with one of a couple of dynamite bombs rested on the table before him. However, I will say this: – "England is at war with Ireland and Ireland is justified in carrying the fight into the very heart of London"' (*New York Herald*, 17 March 1883, 5b; the *Herald* covered the explosion itself over three columns (3a–c)). See also the *New York Times*, 17 March 1883 (1c–d), to which Rossa revealed that he received congratulatory messages from various parts of the United States of America, 'and better than all, some money; not as much as we ought to have though; only about $100'.

71 Behind the scenes there was considerable concern about a warning sent from the British Ambassador in Washington, Sackville-West, that the dynamitards intended to blow up the Prince of Wales, Lord Derby and Herbert Gladstone in their homes (PRO FO 5/1860/5).

72 *The Times*, 8 August 1883, 5e. The four were Timothy Featherstone (aged 30); Patrick Flanagan (26), Henry Dalton (38) and Denis Deasy (PRO HO 144/194/A4664C/99).

73 PRO HO 144/115/A26302/2; see also PRO HO 144/194/A46664C/99. A useful review is provided by Anon. (? Robert Anderson or Howard Vincent), 'The Dynamite Party: A Word in Season for British Electors', London, The British Protestant, c.1886, p. 3 (British Library Pamphlet 8145 ss 17) (this article first appeared in *The Times*). In substantial part the Liverpool arrests were due to the work of a long-established and well-funded British agent, James McDermott, to whom

Clan na Gael strikes

While Rossa had been making the running, Clan na Gael had been preparing for a campaign supposedly of much greater destructiveness. Certainly the British authorities considered the organisation to be much more formidable than Rossa's inspired one-man terrorist directorate. It had, wrote a leading expert, 'resources, determination and the power of acting with extraordinary secrecy'.[74] The difference in capability was matched by a difference in ambitions, as may be grasped by comparing Rossa's arithmetic of terror with Lomasney's. According to Rossa $30,000 would have put sixty men into London to burn or dynamite – a neat $500 per head.[75] In January 1881 the Clan had given Lomasney $5500 to get his 'work' under way. Having studied the needs of the proposed campaign he wrote to Devoy two months later saying that twenty times that sum (i.e. $110,000) would be required 'to do the work completely'. He cautioned that 'If it is to be done at all it should be complete, for otherwise we would finally get the worst of it'.[76] A secret circular to Clan branches from the executive committee spelled out their war aims. The executive committee, members were informed,

> had no delicacy or sentimentality about how it would strike the enemy, or when or where. . . . They meant war, they meant that war to be unsparing and unceasing. They meant it to be effective. Their policy would be to make assaults in all directions, so that the suffering, bitterness and desolation which followed active measures should be felt in every place.[77]

The Clan failed to realise its destructive ambitions. Following Lomasney's reconnoitre, it dispatched Dr Thomas Gallagher[78] to England. In early November 1882, Gallagher made preliminary arrangements for a spring bombing campaign. Returning to the United States of America, he dispatched James Murphy (alias Alfred George Whitehead) to Birmingham to obtain premises in which explosives could be manufactured. At the same time, Gallagher entered into a secret operational

---

Rossa had foolishly given credentials as the representative of his *United Irishman* (see *New York Times*, 14 August 1883, 2d).

74 Anon., 'The Dynamite Party', *op. cit.*, p. 3.

75 PRO FO 97/472/1932A.

76 O'Brien and Ryan, *op. cit.*, Vol. 2, pp. 33 and 57. Lomasney feared that a half-hearted campaign would not bring the British to their knees, but would stir up revenge attacks against the Irish in England (ibid., p. 57).

77 Le Caron, *op. cit.*, p. 238.

78 (1851–1925). Born in Glasgow, and, when aged about 15, emigrated to the United States of America with his family. At first working in a foundry, Gallagher studied medicine, eventually setting up a practice in Greenpoint, Brooklyn. As an educated and professional man, Gallagher moved easily in circles which were closed to other Clan agents. He was said often to have been in the House of Commons, and, according to Henri Le Caron, had even been introduced to Gladstone (*op. cit.*, p. 218; some caution is necessary here, however, since Le Caron was almost as strongly opposed to Gladstone as he was to the Irish revolutionaries).

agreement with Rossa, which allowed him to draw on Rossa's experience and contacts, but which also meant that Gallagher was no longer fully under Clan control.[79]

By manufacturing explosives rather than smuggling them into the country, Gallagher avoided some dangers of detection.[80] But bulk purchases of the chemicals necessary to make nitroglycerine also carried a risk of exposure, especially when these transactions were conducted by persons who were obviously Irish-American. The inevitable occurred, and through exceptionally large purchases of materials, Gallagher's Birmingham bomb factory was discovered. The police held their hand and mounted surveillance. By this means, and because of the conspirators' inexperience and carelessness, on 5 April 1883, Gallagher's team of would-be bombers, and Gallagher himself, were netted together with 400lb of nitroglycerine and a large sum of money, much of it in dollars.[81] On being brought to trial for treason felony and various other charges, four of the six who had been arrested were convicted and sentenced to life penal servitude; the other two were acquitted.[82] The Lord Chief Justice presided over the trial, assisted by the Master of the Rolls and another senior judge. The prosecution was conducted by the Attorney General and Solicitor General. The setting, the line-up of the senior judiciary and the conduct of business emphasised the exceptional seriousness with which the dynamite campaign was viewed.[83]

---

79 Short, *op. cit.*, p. 126.

80 A point which was at once recognised by the press. The *Nation* (Washington) commented that 'Dynamite is so easily manufactured anywhere, and is so powerful an explosive in small quantities, that economy as well as prudence forbids its transportation for criminal purposes over long distances' (29 January 1885, 88a).

81 3 *Hansard*, CCLXXVII, col. 1506; 5 April 1883. The detailed Scotland Yard account of the case against Gallagher and his associates is at PRO HO 144/116/A26493/59. See also in that file (unfoliated) a summary of evidence to be given ('if necessary') by Head Constable Shea, dated 23 April 1883. A précis of the events is also at PRO HO 144/194/A46664C/99.

82 For detailed accounts of the trial see *The Times*, 12 June 1883, 3a–d; 13 June, 5a–c; 15 June, 3a–d; for an account of the reaction to the trials among those in the New York revolutionary circles (including Rossa) see *New York Herald*, 20 April 1883 (at PRO FO 5/1861/141). The *New York Times* hoped that the trial and sentences would be a lesson to the American-based organisers of the dynamitards ('certain well-known Irish blatherkites'): 'Sooner or later, justice, aided by the ever-present informer, and by circumstantial evidence, overtakes the dynamiter and his abettors' (15 June 1883, 4e). The *New York Tribune* agreed. The men had had a fair trial, as evidenced by the acquittal of Thomas Gallagher's brother Bernard and of William Ansburgh (15 June 1883, at PRO FO 5/1862/35). One of Gallagher's team W. J. Norman (alias William Joseph Lynch) turned Queen's Evidence, and helped to seal the case against his comrades. Besides Thomas Gallagher (aged 32) the convicted men were Alfred Whitehead (22), Henry Wilson (alias Thomas Joseph Clarke) (21) and John Curtin (33).

83 The trial's political character was well advertised, and proceedings were conducted with majesty and grandeur. No fewer than eleven ex-officio justices – aldermen, MPs and under-sheriffs – took the bench on the opening morning. The Lord Mayor went in state from the Mansion House, accompanied by the Mace-bearer and City Marshall. Many members of the Bar were in attendance, entrance to the Old Bailey being by ticket only. For security reasons the prisoners were lodged in Millbank rather than Newgate or Holloway, and were escorted to and fro by a strong force of mounted police (*The Times*, 12 June 1883, 3a).

Within a week of the Gallagher trial an emergency Explosive Substances Bill had been rushed through Parliament. This measure ('an indispensable, imperative, and unavoidable necessity') was intended to deal with the possession of explosives with intent to cause an explosion; possession of explosive substances under suspicious circumstances; and the causing of explosions. Penalties ranged from a minimum of two years' imprisonment to penal servitude for life.[84] Thenceforward the possession of explosives or the making of explosives could be vigorously dealt with, and the onus was placed on the suspect to provide a lawful reason for possession.

The true test of a terrorist is not whether he is prepared to contemplate the loss of civilian life (that is a prerequisite), but whether he seeks it in order to increase the effectiveness of his action: this is the difference between terrorism and a military action which accepts but does not seek civilian death and injury. The Clan was unambiguously terrorist in its next operations. On 30 October 1883, a bomb exploded on the Metropolitan Line of the London Underground close to Paddington Station. Carriages were wrecked and many passengers were injured, some seriously, by flying glass. It was thought that the bombers had dropped their device on the line (presumably allowing them to get away). Almost simultaneously several miles away, a bomb exploded between Charing Cross and Westminster Underground stations. Forty or fifty passengers were badly cut and bruised by flying glass and woodwork, and by concussion, but there was only limited damage to the railway.[85] Government was again faced with its own virtual impotence in the face of such attacks: the targets were too many and protective resources manifestly inadequate.[86]

The ease with which railways could be bombed was noted by the Clan's agents, and a few months later there were attacks on some of the mainline terminals, this time bombs being deposited as left luggage. In the early morning of 26 February

---

84 The Bill became law as the Explosive Substances Act, 1883 (46 Vict., c.3). The measure went through in a matter of hours, prompting protests from Tory Lords about an abuse of the parliamentary process, and the argument that because of its 'remarkable' character the Bill should have been designated as an emergency measure with the requirement that it should lapse after a number of years unless renewed (3 *Hansard*, CLXXVII, cols 1802–11; 9 April 1883; col. 1642; 6 April 1883).

85 *Globe*, 31 October 1883, 1b and 5a–b. See also Patrick Ford's tongue-in-cheek report under the heading 'The Authorities Alarmed, The Police Losing Heart, and Business Paralysed', the *Irish World*, 17 November 1883, 5c.

86 There was a very good idea of who was who in the organisation of the bombings. At the end of October 1883, Robert Anderson at the Home Office informed the Home Secretary that Mackey Lomasney was not connected with Rossa's men, but 'He is a leading member of the V. C. [United Brotherhood] organ[isation] & was one of the trio who sent over Gallagher and his set. He is a most prominent & dangerous Fenian.' Anderson also knew that John McCafferty (who had organised the raid on Chester Castle) had, in violation of his conditional pardon returned to England in the autumn of 1883. He was, Anderson observed, a 'daring man'. Police were given instructions to arrest him on sight ('Secret' to Home Secretary Sir William Harcourt, Anderson Papers: PRO HO 144/1537/Pt. 1(c)).

1884 there was a large explosion at London's Victoria Station; damage was extensive, but again, largely due to the time of the day, no lives were lost.[87] Other left-luggage offices were immediately searched, and unexploded bombs were found at Charing Cross, Paddington and Ludgate stations, their detonating mechanisms in each instance having failed to operate.[88] No arrests were made, even though the police obtained some clues from the makings of the bombs.

In the meantime, the Birmingham police had mounted intensive surveillance on an Irish-American named John Daly, who had probably been identified by an informant.[89] After several months of apparently blame-free activity, in April 1884 Daly was arrested at Birkenhead Station in possession of three well-made brass-cased bombs. When his dwelling was searched a bottle of nitroglycerine and some cartridges were found in the back garden. Subsequent experiments at Woolwich arsenal showed that the brass grenades were extremely effective weapons.[90] The intention had been to throw them from the Strangers' Gallery of the House of Commons, and to kill government and opposition front-benchers. Amidst quite extraordinary security precautions, Daly and two associates (James

---

87 PRO HO 144/133/A34707; see also PRO HO 144/194/A46664C/100. On 2 March the Home Secretary, Sir William Harcourt, directed that a reward of £1000 be offered for the detection and apprehension of the dynamiters. Pardons would be given to accomplices who informed (/9). The amount of the reward was later increased to £2000.

88 *Globe*, 26 February 1884, 1b; 4e, 5a–b; 27 February, 3c; 28 February, 5c; 29 February, 7b. The last gives an indication of the panic then abroad. Under the heading 'Another Infernal Machine Found at Paddington Station' it was reported that a brown leather portmanteau 'containing over 20 lbs of the most dangerous description of dynamite, the explosion of which would have blown the room – a very large one – into atoms and devastated the houses in the neighbourhood . . . the clock had ceased working, but . . . the slightest shake would have set it going again'. The bag when opened was 'found to contain 46 cakes of the Atlas Powder, some in a cash box and others packed around it. In this case, however, the label Atlas Powder had been torn off nearly all the packets. The arrangement of the clock and the pistol here was exactly as in the Charing Cross bag.' See also *Globe* (5 March 1884, 5c) in which rewards were posted. Ford's *Irish World* was delighted with the explosions: 8 March 1884, 5d; 22 March, 4a; 29 March, 1a–g.

89 Daly (1845–1916) had emigrated to the USA following the 1867 rising. On his return to Ireland some twelve years later, he became a member of the IRB Supreme Council and an organiser for the movement. He moved to England (where Dr Mark Ryan found him work as an asylum attendant) and provided direction and support for the dynamitards. The editors of *Devoy's Post Bag* suggest that Daly was betrayed by a fellow Fenian, 'Big Dan O'Neill', who had manoeuvred him into collecting the explosives from one of the crew of an American ship then in Liverpool. At that precise moment – the first time Daly had had the devices in his possession – the police pounced (O'Brien and Ryan, *op. cit.*, Vol. 2, pp. 242–3). At his trial Daly was identified as a Fenian by the informant Moran who had known him in 1871. Geoffrey Lushington (Permanent-Under-Secretary at the Home Office), reviewing the evidence some years later, cautioned that the use of agents and informers made it necessary to emphasise how strong the case against Daly had been, 'for if the doubts raised . . . against the good faith of Government agents are not quieted, an agitation is sure to spring up for re-opening other Fenian cases of the same date' (PRO HO 144/193 A46664B/24c: Lushington to Home Secretary Matthews, 1 August 1891).

90 PRO HO 144/133/A46664B/13; Jenkinson to Harcourt, 12 April 1884, Harcourt Papers, *op. cit.*, Lewis Harcourt's diary entries 11 and 27 April 1884).

Egan and William McDonnell) stood their trial for treason felony at Warwick Assizes on 30 July 1884, the prosecution again being conducted by the Attorney General. All three were found guilty, the jury retiring for only fifteen minutes. Daly was given penal servitude for life; James Egan, the man with whom he had lodged, and whom he had tried to exonerate, got twenty years. William McDonnell was bound over in the sum of £200 for an 1874 offence.[91] There remained for many years some doubt about James Egan's part in the affair – Daly insisted that Egan had not known about the bottle of nitroglycerine buried in his garden.[92]

Luck and informers had their limitations, however, and other Clan bombers remained at large. Three attacks were mounted on the night of 30 May 1884. The targets were the Junior Carlton Club, the home of Sir Watkin Wynn,[93] and the office of the Irish Special Branch at Scotland Yard.[94] A bomb in Trafalgar Square, placed against Nelson's Column, failed to detonate. Five people were injured and there was some damage to property. But the most serious political harm was at Scotland Yard. Offices were damaged, and a portion of the records dealing with Irish revolutionary conspiracy were destroyed.[95] Showing as it apparently did both a good knowledge of the layout of Scotland Yard, as well as audacity and advancing (though still imperfect) mastery of the technology of bombs and timers, the attack on the Special Branch was perhaps the most alarming yet mounted. Had all the cases of dynamite gone off, a major disaster would have occurred in the heart of Whitehall.[96]

91 *Globe*, 30 July 1884, 2c; 1 August, 5b; 2 August, 1b. The men were unrepresented, but Daly had defended himself with vigour and intelligence: he was uncowed by his predicament and was highly articulate. A full report of the trial is at PRO HO 144/193/A46664B. William McDonnell had some years before renounced his membership of the IRB and was consequently commended to the judge by the Attorney General.

92 Some years later a confidential review of the trial of Egan and Daly was conducted by the Home Office. The tentative view then taken was that Egan had been a member of the IRB and a friend of Daly's, but that the evidence that he knew of the dynamite in his garden was slender. But 'there is no possibility of doubt that Egan had belonged to the IRB and was guilty of treason felony' (PRO HO 144/193/A46664B/24a). In a letter of 13 December 1887, the Chief Constable of Birmingham informed the Home Secretary that the evidence against Egan was 'very slight indeed!' (ibid., /13). The *Freeman's Journal*, which condemned the men's actions, nevertheless praised Daly for seeking to exonerate Egan from guilt in the enterprise (2 August 1884, 4g).

93 (1820–1855). Conservative MP for Denbeighshire, Military and Yeomanry background. It is not clear why his home was a target.

94 The *Globe* and other newspapers reported these incidents in detail; see 31 May 1884, 5b–c.

95 One man was injured in the attack, but in the end the damage was not as bad as had first appeared. Total repair costs were less than £500 (PRO HO 144/137/A35842/10). The report on the explosion was doctored to avoid disclosing certain sensitive information about the Special Branch (ibid., /7).

96 *Globe*, 31 May 1884, 5b. The recovered dynamite was 'Atlas' brand, the same that had been used in Paddington, Charing Cross and elsewhere. It is possible that the placing of the bomb so that the Irish records were damaged was merely a matter of luck, but the coincidence seems too great.

There then followed a break of several months. Public buildings were well guarded, and there must have been some concern among the bombers that, as evidenced by the capture and conviction of Daly, spies had penetrated their ranks. The campaign was entering its final phase, which for the Clan would hold tragedy as well as success. At 5.45 p.m. on Saturday, 13 December 1884, amidst the bustle of the evening rush-hour, there was an explosion at the south-west end of London Bridge. There was little damage to the bridge, and its structure remained sound; windows a considerable distance away were broken.[97] The bombers were William Mackey Lomasney, his brother and John Fleming.[98] In attempting to fit a bomb to one of the bridge piers the men evidently detonated their device and blew themselves to smithereens.[99] So complete was their destruction, and of the boat which they had used to get to the pier, that it was some time before it was realised that the men had been killed rather than escaped. Their mutilated remains and the debris of the boat were carried away by a strong ebb tide and westerly wind. From that time on Lomasney was never heard of again, and Clan na Gael began to pay a pension to his widow.[100]

At the time of the London Bridge explosion yet another Clan team was about to cross the Atlantic. This comprised three or four men, equipped with a large amount of dynamite and the requisite detonators. Their first attack, on 2 January 1885, was another Underground explosion, just outside Gower Street Station.

97 PRO HO 144/145/A3008. The Common Council of the City of London offered a reward of £5000 for the apprehension of the perpetrators (ibid., /1a). *The Times* (15 December 1884, 10a–b) indicated considerable police uncertainty about how the bomb had been placed. Under the headline 'Alarming explosions at London Bridge – supposed Fenian outrage', the *Globe* gave its account of the incident: 'Shortly before six o'clock on Saturday evening an explosion, which was heard and some of its effects felt for many miles around, took place near one of the buttresses of London Bridge. Large numbers of persons were then passing over the structure, and the vehicular traffic was still large. Suddenly a deafening explosion occurred, and at the same moment a sheet of flame shot up from the southern side of the river . . . people who were walking on the bridge were thrown down, and some, it is said, received slight personal injuries. . . . The detonation was heard in the suburbs of Highbury, Leytonstone, and Epping Forest, Woolwich, Bromley (Kent), and at Tooting.' Some connections were conjectured: 'It should be mentioned that Saturday was the anniversary of the [1867] Clerkenwell explosion. At an Anarchist Meeting held in Paris yesterday the London Bridge outrage was applauded' (Monday, 15 December 1884, 6b–c).

98 See O'Brien and Ryan, *op. cit.*, Vol. 2, p. 8. Lomasney had, with his brother, apparently been running a bookshop in Harrow Road, using the alias Marshall. The landlord reported Marshall missing, and in February 1885 the police broke into the premises, where they found dynamite and electrical detonators ('The Dynamite Party', *op. cit.*, pp. 2 and 3 (British Library Pamphlet 8145 ss 17).

99 Scotland Yard had long expected an attack on London Bridge, and gratings had been fitted to the piers to deny access to their interiors (BL: Lewis Harcourt Diaries: Ms Harcourt, dep. 362, ff. 87–8, 20 December 1884).

100 'The Dynamite party' (*op. cit.*, pp. 2–3) confirmed that the police had at first thought that no lives had been lost, but the sequence of events soon became evident, and the payment of a pension by the Clan was conclusive.

Three weeks later, on 24 January there were coordinated attacks on the Tower of London and on the Palace of Westminster. The Tower bomb exploded prematurely and the man who placed it, James Cunningham, was arrested as he was leaving the precincts. Despite the presence of numerous visitors, including schoolchildren (it was a Saturday) no lives were lost, although four people were seriously injured.[101] At the Palace of Westminster there were to be two bombs, one serving as a diversion so that the Chamber of the House of Commons could be attacked. The plan worked well. There was extensive damage, and the two bombers (probably Luke Dillon and Harry Burton) escaped.[102] Amidst alarm and confusion in official circles there was sharp press criticism of the Criminal Investigation Department, and behind the scenes infighting and recrimination between the Criminal Investigation Department and the Special Branch.[103] In the United States of America there were renewed demands that the dynamitards should be prevented from using that country as a base, particularly for the collection of funds.[104] Rossa, despite requests from his associates and Clan na Gael, refused to moderate his language or tone down his political theatre. In April 1885, for example, he chaired a meeting at Chickering Hall, New York, at which the death sentence was passed on 'Albert Edward Guelph, commonly called, "The Prince of Wales"'.[105]

But whatever extravagances Rossa permitted himself in New York, being an Irish-American in London in any kind of doubtful circumstances was, at that time, rather unhealthy. One of the Clan team, Harry Burton, had the misfortune

101 *Globe*, Saturday, 3 January 1885, 5a: 'Dynamite outrage – explosion on underground . . . in the tunnel of the Metropolitan Railway between Gower Street and King's Cross stations about a quarter-past nine o'clock last night – a few slight injuries, no fatalities.' There was sensation, alarm and some fear in the reports on the Tower and Westminster explosions: 'This afternoon two explosions occurred within three minutes of each other, one in the House of Commons itself, and the other in Westminster Hall.' Two policemen were seriously injured – PCs Cole and Cox – together with a man and a woman. And on the Tower the *Globe* reported: 'It being a Saturday and a free day there were a large number of visitors in the building, some of whom were seriously injured, one having his leg smashed and another his ear cut off, while several others were more or less hurt' (*Globe*, 24 January 1885, 5c–d).

102 *The Times*, 5 January, 6d; 26 January, 10a–f, 11a–d and (editorial) 9a–b.

103 The conservative *Saturday Review* castigated the CID for its lack of results: 'When every allowance has been made, the fact of the failure of the force in the capital remains. . . . Our Criminal Investigation Department . . . is talkative, indolent and unintelligent' (31 January 1885, p. 132).

104 See *Nation* (Washington), 29 January 1885, 88a–c. 'We . . . wish to bring those who feel that the United States are disgraced by being made the scene in which the dynamiters hatch their plots, face to face with the real problem. . . . No dynamite is sent from this country; but money to buy dynamite and pay those who use it, is sent, and is collected for this purpose without the slightest concealment' (ibid., 88c).

105 It was at this event that Professor Mezzeroff was introduced as 'England's invisible enemy' and Rossa said he would hurl 'the fires of hell at England' if he could get them within his grasp. See 'Extracts from the *United Irishman* of April 4, 1885' (PRO HO 144/133/A34707). This issue of Rossa's journal also called for dynamite bombs to be dropped from Dublin roof-tops on to soldiers and police. There was advice to Irish soldiers in the British army to desert, or if that were not possible to kill their officers in battle.

unwittingly to take lodgings in the same house as a City of London constable. When Cunningham was arrested Burton was consequently identified as having been with him on an earlier date, and was arrested also. The two men stood trial on 11 May 1885. Cunningham was charged with the Tower explosion and also with the bombing of the Metropolitan Line on 2 January; Burton was accused of planting the bombs at Charing Cross and Paddington stations in February 1884.[106] Both were found guilty, and received life sentences of penal servitude.

By the spring of 1886 the dynamite campaign had been defeated. Three dynamitards had blown themselves up and twenty-five had been given penal servitude – sixteen for life, two for twenty years and the remainder for seven years apiece. One had died in prison (Denis Deasy) and another, serving seven years, had been released because he was dying. This depressing toll was well known to the extreme nationalists in Ireland and America, on whom the campaign depended for funds and support. The sobering realisation that dynamite could not defeat the resources of civilisation was unavoidable. And there were other factors. Clan splits and quarrels, the IRB's continuing disapproval of dynamite attacks, the success of Parnell's militant constitutional politics and Gladstone's conversion to Home Rule all help to explain why after the Tower and Westminster explosions, there was a significant pause in dynamite attacks.[107] But Queen Victoria's Jubilee, celebrated in 1887, was a magnet for the dynamiters – to whom British claims of peace, progress and prosperity were a provocation.

In June 1887, what would be the last team of bombers entered the country, jointly supported by Rossa and a wing of the now split Clan. One of the Clan leaders, long in the pay of the British government, had warned of the expedition, and Scotland Yard watched the men throughout. Two were arrested in London; another died before arrest; and the leader of the group escaped.[108] Michael Harkins and Thomas Callan were convicted of conspiring to cause explosions and were each sentenced to fifteen years' penal servitude.[109] An associated group of some eleven men who were preparing attacks in Liverpool and other cities was broken up and, with documents and weapons seized when their lodgings were raided, the men fled the country by various routes.[110] The realisation that their organisation was thoroughly compromised – perhaps at the highest levels – splits and scandals, and the striking advances in constitutional and land reform in Ireland, all contributed to the cessation of dynamite attacks. And from first to last, although its

---

106 *Globe*, 13 May 1885, 5c; 14 May, 5e; 15 May, 3c–d; 18 May, 5b–c.
107 Parnell was conspicuously silent on the matter of the bombings, doubtless because of his Land League allies Davitt and Devoy. This failure to speak out prompted some bitter comment from the English newspapers (see, for example, 'Friends of Dynamite', *Saturday Review*, 31 January 1885, p. 134).
108 The man who died at his lodgings used the alias Joseph Cohen (for the inquest see *The Times*, 27 October 1887, 12; see also 29 October, 7d).
109 *Pall Mall Gazette*, 27 October 1887, 8a, 10a; 28 October 1887, 7a and 9a.
110 *Pall Mall Gazette*, 29 October 1887, 8a.

individual members may have thought and acted otherwise, the IRB remained opposed to dynamite attacks.[111]

The American base

The dynamitards had had the enormous advantage of a secure American base, from which they could advocate the use of violence against British rule, solicit funds, organise, recruit and train. Without this haven the dynamite campaign would have been impossible. Unlike the raising of armies on American soil and the crossing of international frontiers (as in the Canadian raids), agitation and incitement to violence in a foreign country for political ends did not violate American neutrality laws, and political crime was specifically exempted from extradition under the Anglo-American treaty of 1842. Both governments recognised the domestic and international invulnerability of the bombers and their directors, but this did not hinder regular appeals from the British to the United States government for assistance in preventing the dispatch of bombing missions and curbs in incitement to murder prominent politicians, royalty and other public figures. The September 1872 settlement of the *Alabama* claim had permitted a rapid re-establishment of cordial relations, but federal government had very limited criminal justice powers and, for various political reasons, there was a lack of will to act at state and local level. In all the reports emanating from the United States of America at this time – official, journalistic and Irish-American – there is little evidence of police or judicial action against the dynamitards, or of exchanges of intelligence on their activities.

At the beginning of the 1880s, some British officials had hopes of US government action – presumably because of the reaction to the Canadian raids ten years before. The shooting of President James Garfield on 2 July 1881, his protracted suffering and his death on 19 September were thought to have changed attitudes towards political violence.[112] An official wrote to Lord Granville, the Foreign Secretary, in October 1881, insisting that if the Fenians were to attempt any 'nonsense' the US government would act 'where we can give substantial proofs of their villainous intentions and acts'. Indeed, 'they would be most pleased to have the chance of crushing them'.[113] This enthusiasm faded in the face of the limited powers of the US authorities, the British Ambassador Sackville-West

---

111 Though there was a period when the organisation, in order to ensure continued Clan na Gael subventions, acquiesced to the operations of the dynamitards. It has also been argued that the IRB and Fenian leaders might have refrained from a more vigorous and open condemnation of the dynamite campaign because of the feelings of their followers (see Louis N. Le Roux, *Tom Clarke and the Irish Freedom Movement*, Dublin, The Talbot Press, 1936, pp. 22–3).

112 See Bodleian Library: Lewis Harcourt Papers: Ms Harcourt 749/26 (undated, but probably July 1881).

113 Victor Drummond to Earl Granville, 24 October 1881: *cit.* American Historical Society, *Annual Report, 1941*, Washington, DC, 1942, p. 150.

writing to Granville in 1883 that 'There is nothing in the extradition treaty to warrant the surrender of a Dynamite conspirator, and that even if his machinations resulted in murder it would be a question as to whether it was murder as contemplated by the Treaty, and that the mere blowing up of public buildings in England would be unquestionably considered in the case of Irish complicity as a political offence.' The United States government condemned murder and outrage, but these were the grounds on which it refused to intervene in the dynamitard organisation, 'the objects of which it thus tacitly admits to be legitimate'.[114]

The English newspapers either did not know, or chose to ignore or minimise, the legal constraints which bound the Americans.[115] The British government was itself a notable adherent to the doctrine of political asylum and had controversially sheltered many who sought to overthrow what they saw as tyranny in their own countries, but this aspect of the matter was on the whole ignored.[116] There were repeated condemnations from the English press of American inactivity in the face of murder and outrage, and the authorities' apparent indifference to public endorsements and celebrations of atrocity and incitement to yet more crime. For the most part, the principal American newspapers followed a line very similar to their government's: they deplored terrorism, but were resigned to the fact that the dynamitards' legal immunity could not be overturned. Early in the bombing campaign Washington's *Nation* pointed to the legal limitations: the US government could not act, and while soliciting funds to commit outrages might be punishable under state laws: 'it is to the last degree improbable that any prosecution of the Fenian newspapers by the state could be carried through effectively'. Public feeling would be against imprisoning an editor who ran such material and it might be impossible to find a jury who would return a guilty verdict. In any event, there was the pragmatic objection: incendiary publications were a good source of intelligence.[117]

The *Nation* and other journals had over the years variously considered whether US neutrality laws (which prohibited the organisation or embarkation from American soil of a military expedition or enterprise) could be used against the dynamitards. The difficulty was with the term 'military', suggesting, as it did, an armed and organised body. 'Modern science,' the *Nation* observed, 'has furnished

---

114 Sackville-West to Earl Granville, 29 April 1883: PRO FO 5/1861/159-67.

115 The *Saturday Review* caustically praised the New York press for inching towards the realisation that the dynamite campaigns were being planned, funded, supplied and manned by Rossa and his colleagues. In the *Alabama* affair Britain had paid a large compensation, but had secured the agreement that a neutral state was obliged in a matter such as the dynamitards 'to raise its municipal law to the standard of its international obligations, and that it fails of due diligence in the discharge of these obligations if it neglects or refuses to do so' (24 January 1885, p. 102).

116 It was raised by William Dillon (John Mitchel's biographer) in his article 'Assassination and Dynamite': 'Men who had advocated and even attempted political murder were not only harboured, but their conduct was, to say the least, not very emphatically condemned by English public opinion' (*Fortnightly Review*, 35 (January to June 1884), p. 512).

117 *Nation*, 4 August 1881, 87c.

conspirators with means of attack equally hostile, but at the same time non-military.'[118] To attempt to amend the neturality laws, to take account of the new possibilities offered by dynamite, would have invited the same political failure as an attempted implementation of state laws against incitement to outrage.[119] The *New York Herald*, probably drawing on legal advice, explored the possibility of using the state's conspiracy laws to deal with the problem, since the conspiracy was formed and completed in the state.[120] Although some domestic and international precedents might have supported this line of reasoning, political will would have been necessary to test it, and, as with the other possible remedies, this was not present, and the *Herald's* speculations remained just that.

With their base secure, and almost certainly immune from any kind of state or federal policing action, Rossa and the Clan could continue their activities. An important section of the east coast press nevertheless kept up a steady barrage of condemnation. This intensified with each explosion. The *New York Tribune*, immediately following the bombing of the offices of the Local Government Board on 15 March 1883, wondered whether the British government was not over-reacting: it was not clear that it was the work of Irish extremists, and in any event it was 'a trivial incident'. At the same time the *Tribune* denounced 'the cowardly crew of so-called Fenians' who took responsibility for the bomb (a claim the newspaper doubted), seeing in it 'a chance to wring a few more dollars from the working men and servant girls who have long been their dupes'.[121]

The *New York Times*, which abominated Rossa (it appears to have known little about the Clan at this stage) argued that should it emerge that there was an extensive plot to destroy life and property in a friendly country, the US government should act, but when and in what form should be left to the government itself.[122] Reacting to the committal evidence given in the Bow Street proceedings against the Gallagher bombing team, the *Boston Daily Advertiser* took a very much sharper line. The evidence of the conspiracy was such as to attract international attention and cause immediate action. Americans did not care to have among them criminals and conspirators plotting against a friendly nation: 'Respect for good order at home, friendship for England, and abhorrence of crime – these are

---

118 Ibid., 88a. See also *New York Tribune*, 7 April 1883 (at PRO FO 5/1861/37) and 9 April 1883 (at PRO FO 5/1861/44) which makes much the same point.

119 The *Nation* (Washington) pointed out that the Democrats would control Congress until 1885, but that a move to change the extradition laws would bring derision from both sides of both houses. And should such a measure be brought forward, 'Nearly every Democratic member would greet it with a terrible speech containing an epitome of Irish history. . . . In fact, supplements to the *Congressional Record* would have to be issued to accommodate the statesmen who would be eager to put on record their burning hatred of British tyranny and their sympathy with the Irish race, to which it would probably appear that nine-tenths of them belonged by descent' (26 April 1883, 256b).

120 *New York Herald*, 21 April 1883 (at PRO FO 5/1861/94).

121 *New York Tribune*, 18 March 1883 (at PRO FO 5/1861/94).

122 *New York Times*, 10 April 1883, ibid.

the reasons why the Irish conspiracies in this country must cease immediately unless the conspirators wish to bring down upon themselves the terror of the law. And if the law against crime is not terrible now, let it be made so.' The Irish should not forget that the issue was not politics, freedom or ambition, but 'crime of the heinous kind, crime committed in this country, and crime committed by Irishmen who came here as guests, but have betrayed all that is honourable'.[123]

A bad press was made worse by the actions and demeanour of O'Donovan Rossa, who became an object of dislike, derision and some contempt in the mainstream press, and who took a perverse delight in his hate-figure status. When veteran Fenians went so far as to denounce him publicly, as did Luby and O'Leary, they were clearly concerned about the effect he was having on the reputation of Irish nationalism and the standing of the Irish community generally: every newspaper denunciation of Rossa as a fraud could not but affect the credibility of other nationalist organisations, whatever their degree of militancy. And Rossa courted publicity, presenting himself as an Othello 'Horribly stuffed with epithets of war'. There was something unwholesome about one who hurled words and men against the English from the safety of his Broadway office, an impression heightened by the whiff of whiskey and financial impropriety that inescapably clung about him.[124]

Rossa became – certainly in the 1880s – perhaps the most quoted, and reviled, of the Irish exile leaders. A few instances will serve to give the overall flavour of his portrayal in the respectable press at the height of the dynamite scare. Marking St Patrick's Day 1883, the *New York Times* stated: 'There is not a right-thinking man in this country who does not detest the principles and practices of O'Donovan Rossa and his fellow-Fenians. . . . Who is responsible for their existence, and why do they come over here to try our patience with this violence and make the name of Irish-American fairly hateful to us?'[125] And in response to what emerged in the prosecution of Gallagher and his associates, the *New York Herald* asserted that Irish-Americans saw Rossa's dynamite campaign as setting back the cause of self-rule and would be 'the first to adjust the noose and pull the rope, were it lawful to hang O'Donovan Rossa and his fellow cowards and blatherskites as the worst enemies Ireland has'. It also referred to 'Rossa and his gang of dupes, fools and rascals' and repeated that he was a 'blatherskite and despicable coward'.[126] Showing some impatience with English criticisms of American attitudes and apparent inaction, the *New York Tribune* asserted that 'if English newspapers could be made to comprehend with what

---

123 *Boston Daily Advertiser*, 21 April 1883, 4b–c; see also 1a–b.
124 See above, pp. 333–6.
125 *New York Times*, 17 March 1883, 4d. 'The American people know very well that for the most part these fellows are cowardly, lying braggarts, who go about bawling for war on England in order that they may have the chance to steal the money which simpletons contribute for that purpose. But there are some among them who are less noisy and far more dangerous.'
126 *New York Herald*, 20 April 1883 (at PRO FO 5/1861/137).

contempt and ridicule [Rossa's] proclamations and pretensions are regarded in this city, and throughout the United States, they would put a stop to the wretched drivel about American sympathy with Irish ruffianism and rascality'.[127]

All of this was sticks and stones, but it was bound to have a long-term effect – especially when the toll of prison sentences began to mount and Rossa's continuing immunity from legal consequences threw a question mark over his right to commit others to what was a wicked and counterproductive campaign. Luby, O'Leary, Stephens and the others were correct in their fears: the dynamite campaign diminished all physical-force Irish nationalists in America. Far in the past were the huge civic dinners and parades which had greeted the escaped Young Irelanders and the Fenian exiles of 1871: dynamite, and Rossa's capering, had expended a great deal of the moral capital of the extreme party and made its organisational task in America much more difficult, without affecting British policy in Ireland, or bringing closer by one inch the goal of an Irish Republic. And quite apart from British concerns and protests, the major European countries, many of which had their own political and labour extremists and violent nationalists to worry about, raised their concerns that the United States of America was becoming a base for dynamite terrorists. This placed the issue within a broader international context, and generalised and further reinforced the British case.[128] This is not to say that a residual Anglophobia ever left the American press. The history of the two countries, their political and commercial rivalries, and the skein of ambivalences which bound them, ensured that from time to time there would be support for attempts to twist the lion's tail. But in the end, dynamite terrorism was not easy for the wider Irish community to stomach, notwithstanding periodical mercy and amnesty campaigns for the perpetrators.[129]

---

127 *New York Tribune*, 18 March 1883 (at PRO FO 5/1860/278).

128 Following the Victoria Station explosion on 26 February 1884, and the discovery of several other undetonated bombs at railway stations, the German, Austrian, Spanish, French and other ambassadors in Italy convened under the chairmanship of the Italian Foreign Minister to demand that the USA legislate against dynamitards. They also proposed to impose travel restrictions against persons arriving from America (*The Times*, 6 March 1884, 1d).

129 The campaign to reprieve Patrick O'Donnell (a naturalised American citizen), who had murdered the Invincible informer James Carey on board the *Melrose Castle*, was one such episode. Despite the atrocious nature of the Phoenix Park murders and Carey's cold-blooded stalking and murder, a wider group of Irish-Americans than would ever have supported political extremism petitioned for O'Donnell's reprieve. The President complied with a House request to intercede with the British government on O'Donnell's behalf. The British government's subsequent refusal to stay the execution produced a strong but short-lived reaction among Irish-American politicians (see interview with Congressman Finnerty, *Washington Sunday Herald*, 18 December 1883 (at PRO FO 5/1862/380)). Both the *New York Times* (17 December 1883, 4b) and the *New York Tribune* opposed the US government's intervention on O'Donnell's behalf, the latter noting that O'Donnell deserved his fate and that 'the impertinent representations of the United States Government seem to have been received with much more civility' than would have been expected had such an intervention been made the other way (at PRO FO 5/1862/211–12).

8

THE DYNAMITARDS IN PRISON

Du Cane's kingdom

We have examined closely Michael Davitt's convict experiences, which are sufficiently close to those of the dynamitards to allow us to minimise repetitive description. The convict service under Sir Edmund Du Cane was almost entirely shielded from outside scrutiny, and he was adamant that any change in such a minutely meshed system would have deleterious consequences. Alteration also carried the implication that what had gone before was unsatisfactory, and this was a conclusion which Du Cane could not abide. From the moment he entered the home convict service as a director in 1863, and particularly when he assumed the chairmanship of the Directorate of Convict Prisons in 1869, Du Cane turned a face of stone to the outside world – which on many occasions included the Home Office, its ministers and senior officials. Davitt's shocking recollections of Dartmoor life and the recommendations of the Kimberley Commission therefore had little effect. All the key dimensions of convict life – the hours and type of work, food, cells, marks, stage privileges and remission of sentence – remained unchanged. Du Cane, moreover, now had an extensive experience of Irish political prisoners and a finely tuned appreciation of the shifting attitude of politicians towards them. The Fenians had benefited from Gladstone's monumental shift in Irish policy; Davitt had also been a beneficiary of political necessity – but only after seven years as an ordinary convict. Moving in London official and social circles, and with an intelligent interest in current affairs, Du Cane constantly watched the political barometer, and knew how it affected Irish political offenders. When the dynamitards began their sentences in the mid-1880s, there was formed the first Conservative government in thirteen years. Gladstone was out of office, and at the age of 76 it seemed inconceivable that he should again occupy it. These domestic party political considerations apart, there was little question that dynamitards were men with precious few friends on either side of the Irish Sea or the Atlantic. And without the restraint of policy, friends and influence, the full and crushing experience of convict life awaited them.

The Gallagher team and others

Gallagher's imprisonment commenced with an incident which further increased the authorities' security concerns – which were already high. Shortly after his arrest it was agreed that a Mr de Tracey Gould, an American lawyer, settled in London but not a member of the English Bar, should be allowed to visit Gallagher. This was a matter of favour, since only a lawyer admitted in the United Kingdom should have been allowed legal visits. Whatever Gould's intent, he entirely spoiled his chances when, at the completion of an interview with Gallagher, he offered money to the principal warder who had been on duty outside the visiting room. The tip – one sovereign – was half a week's wages, but the officer refused and reported it. The offer was a breach of regulations, and perhaps the first step in a more sinister campaign of subornation. The Home Office immediately barred Gould from further visits. Anxious that there should be no misrepresentation in America, and seeking to head off a complaint that Gallagher had made to his embassy, Adolphous Liddell, Permanent-Under-Secretary at the Home Office, wrote to his Foreign Office counterpart, asking that the circumstances be explained to the American Ambassador. Liddell emphasised that there was no objection to Gallagher employing any respectable solicitor of his choice in place of Gould.[1]

In the event, no legal advice could have saved Gallagher and his colleagues. The whole team returned to Millbank from court on 14 June 1883 as life-sentence convicts.[2] They would normally have served a further nine months at Millbank in solitary confinement. Whether because of the time they had spent on remand or for other reasons, Gallagher, Whitehead and Curtin, together with Thomas Clarke (alias Wilson), were transferred to Chatham – one of the public works prisons – towards the end of 1883. By the spring of 1884 all or most of the dynamitards under sentence had been assembled there, and were known as 'The Special Men'.[3]

---

1 In a letter to the Home Secretary Gould denied that he had offered a bribe, but said that he had merely enquired whether a gratuity was permissible, and on being told that it was not he did not persist. Principal Warder Benjamin Price, however, reported that Gould had actually slipped the sovereign into his hand in the process of a handshake. Gould's nationality and the substantial financial resources thought to be available to the dynamitards rang many alarm bells. The truth of the matter is now impossible to fathom (see PRO HO 144/116/A26493/25–31 and 32, and PRO FO 5/1861/280–2).

2 Gallagher insisted that he was entirely innocent, had never intended to break English law, and that exculpatory evidence had been suppressed. In somewhat abject tones he pleaded for a further hearing and for legal assistance (Gallagher petition, Millbank Prison, 26 June 1883: PRO HO 144/116/A26493/46).

3 Thomas J. Clarke, *Glimpses of an Irish Felon's Prison Life*, Dublin and London, Maunsell & Roberts, 1922, pp. 5–6 (this book was first published as a series of articles in the IRB's front journal *Irish Freedom*). See also Louis N. Le Roux, *Tom Clarke and the Irish Freedom Movement*, Dublin, The Talbot Press, 1936, pp. 36–53.

Although not under punishment, following the practice adopted with the Fenians, the men were assigned to the punishment cells in order to ensure greater separation from the general population and to provide closer custody. They had the usual clothing, diet, cell equipment and daily routine; they do not appear to have offended excessively, or to have been punished out of the ordinary.[4] Special precautions were, however, taken throughout their sentences – isolated cells and a high degree of surveillance. This last involved hourly cell checks, in the course of which warders opened the cell door inspection flap. When this inset steel trapdoor was shut smartly it made a noise, Thomas Clarke recalled, 'something like the report of a small cannon being fired close beside me'.[5] Since the noise was made hourly through the night the effect was to deny the prisoners a sound sleep. This, Clarke justifiably observed, had baneful effects on men whose nervous systems were already strained by imprisonment.[6] Such repeated

4 A hardship of the penal cells – even when fully equipped – was the absence of a hammock. In place of a stool these cells were equipped with a block of wood firmly anchored to the floor: the bed was a hard platform. These arrangements were intended to cope with violent and refractory prisoners. The items, being fixed, could not be easily removed, and certainly made the cells more uncomfortable than the ordinary accommodation. John Daly argued that he was being treated as 'an ordinary prisoner under punishment' because of these conditions (*Report of the Visitors of Her Majesty's Convict Prison at Chatham as to the Treatment of Certain Prisoners Convicted of Treason Felony* (hereinafter *Chatham Visitors' Report*), PP, 1890, XXXVII [C.6016], 629, Minutes of Evidence, qq. 243–50, p. 9, q. 1690, p. 52). Daly and the others also protested that their slates and pencils had been removed, a step the authorities said was to stop the practice of 'telegraphing' between cells. (The prisoners wrote the tapping code out on their slates.)

5 *Op. cit.*, pp. 7–8. Thomas (usually Tom) Joseph Clarke (1858–1916) was one of the more famous of the dynamitards, and eventually became a republican and nationalist martyr, being executed in May 1916 for his part in the Easter rising. His father was a Protestant, his mother a Catholic, and Clarke was baptised in his mother's faith. Clarke's father was a British Army sergeant who served in the Crimea, South Africa and in various home postings. Thomas was born on the Isle of Wight. His father was posted to Dungannon in 1865, whence at the age of 22 Thomas emigrated to the United States of America. He had already been sworn to the IRB (by John Daly) and in New York joined Gallagher's conspiracy. He returned to the USA and to Clan na Gael on his release from penal servitude in 1898. In 1907 he moved to Dublin and established a tobacconist's shop which became a meeting place for revolutionary nationalists. Elected to the IRB Supreme Council, he was the guiding spirit in developing the policy that culminated in the Easter rising (see Le Roux, *op. cit.*, pp. 1–96). A sanitised version of his early life was given by Edward Morton, MP for Devonport, in an 1898 Commons debate. This had him living in Ireland, where he was a pupil teacher – 'a boy of the highest possible character' – also engaged in temperance work. A drop in school numbers resulted in a loss of position and emigration to America at the age of 19 (4 *Hansard*, LIII, cols 449–50; 11 February 1898). In fact, before leaving Dungannon Clarke had been an active and successful IRB organiser.

6 These comments were confirmed by Henry Dalton in his evidence to the Chatham visitors, who said in March 1883 (six and a half years into his sentence) that he still woke up each time the trapdoor was banged shut ('a thundering noise, slamming to'). *Chatham Visitors' Report*, Minutes of Evidence, qq. 243–50, p. 9. As a result of the prisoners' complaints, the practice of banging closed the cell trapdoors stopped towards the end of 1886 (ibid., evidence of John Daly, qq. 1386–90, pp. 39–40; *Daily Chronicle* interview, 12 September 1896 3e).

interference with sleep was authorised at the highest levels of the convict service, but it is doubtful if the Home Office had exact knowledge of the regime and its draining effects – either at the official or the political level. The charge against them is indifference rather than vindictiveness.

But there can be no doubt that tight security was necessary. These were determined and ingenious men with resources in the outside world and comrades more than willing to aid their escape. Thomas Clarke was perhaps the most resolute and astute of all the prisoners, and his prison memoir shows that he was able to communicate more or less at will with his companions, that they had a cell telegraph and post office and, on one occasion, a properly printed and highly treasonable newspaper.[7] An even more serious threat to security was the channel which Clarke later established via a paid English collaborator at Woolwich dockyards. Through this contact, cleverly cultivated by Clarke, newspapers and cuttings were sent into the prison and letters were sent out. The Fenian leader, Dr Mark Ryan, and Clarke's former prison companion James Francis Egan, were at the other end of this channel and paid the dockyard worker.[8] So smoothly did this arrangement work that Clarke determined on an escape plan, and was on the verge of taking the first step when he was moved (as a matter of routine security) to another working party, and the contact was broken.[9]

To face a sentence of penal servitude for life, and to be told (as the men were, on admission) that there was 'no hope of release for life prisoners till they have completed twenty years, and then each case will be decided on its own merits' was a terrible test of moral courage.[10] Faced with such desolation even the strongest cordial of fanaticism and self-sacrifice ceased to warm. The closeness of their confinement, and the encouragement that the men's special security

7 Le Roux, *op. cit.*, pp. 40–3. Clarke was able to print the newspaper because of his assignment to the print shop (PRO HO 144/925/A46664/35).

8 Ryan (1844–1940) had been sworn to the IRB by Michael Davitt in 1865. He studied medicine in Galway and Dublin, and practised in England, where he became a member of the IRB Supreme Council. He was a founder of the Gaelic League. (See Mark F. Ryan, *Fenian Memories*, Dublin, M. H. Gill & Son, 1945.) Egan, who had been released on health grounds in 1893, was by this time healthy enough to take a hand in conspiracy once more. His claims of innocence of the possession of explosives – very likely true – did not amount to innocence of other revolutionary activities.

9 See Clarke (*op. cit.*, pp. 42–9) for an account of this episode. After his release John Daly, in a Philadelphia lecture, alleged that Assistant Warder Cooper had been bribed to bring in contraband, including tobacco, press cuttings and occasionally whisky. 'It wasn't any humanity on his part; it was purely avarice.' Ten shillings a week (around a quarter of his regular salary) was paid via a relative of Cooper's. Cooper (still in the convict service when the allegations were published) emphatically denied them and demanded an investigation. Wisely, the Home Office decided to probe no further (PRO HO 144/925/A46664/145).

10 Clarke, *op. cit.*, p. 3. An extra degree of pressure was applied by withholding the prison rules from at least some of the men. James Egan complained that they were not read to him until he had been in prison for some twelve months (*Chatham Visitors' Report*, Minutes of Evidence, qq. 2038–55, pp. 61–2).

status gave to some warders and more senior officials to be officious, assiduous and unrelenting in enforcing the discipline, further intensified the punishment. Under such severe pressures it was no wonder that several of the dynamitards would suffer breakdowns in their mental and physical health, and that some would die, apparently prematurely.

As ever, there were allegations of ill-treatment and replies that this was normal convict discipline. Tom Clarke insisted that Captain W. F. V. Harris, the Chatham Governor, had given his warders special licence to harass the Irish prisoners. The rules and regulations, Clarke observed, to some extent shielded prisoners from the 'foul play and the caprice of petty officers' but these were set aside for Harris' 'scientific system of perpetual and persistent harassing'. This consisted of the constant application of pressure 'always and at all times', of punishments, denial of sleep and other tortures. The system was applied to the Irish prisoners only and was at its most intense for the first six or seven years, and it was then that all of those who succumbed went mad. 'The horror of those nights and days will never leave my memory. One by one I saw my fellow-prisoners break down and go mad under the terrible strain – some slowly and by degrees, others suddenly and without warning.'[11]

From evidence given by James Egan and others to the Chatham Visitors' Inquiry, it would seem that the men were subject to a range of harassments, from provocative goading, to false and sadistic intimations that release was imminent, to disarranging a man's cell in his absence. Egan and Daly have to be treated with some scepticism because of their persistent complaining and tendency to magnify incidents – irritating and coarse, but none the less an inevitable part of male institutional life under discipline. Sifting their evidence there is nevertheless much of the cruel trick-playing and petty tyranny that rings true. Egan, for example, confined in his cell, overheard bogus conversations in the corridor between staff suggesting that he should be bathed because of his imminent release. On another occasion his cell was wrecked in his absence, and when he complained to Deputy Governor Captain Burgoyne he was warned that further complaints would get him into trouble. Egan also objected, understandably, to being issued with underwear that had not been washed. This had happened regularly, he claimed, and some of the items were 'soiled in a very bad manner . . . [and were] filthy'. These incidents in which dirty linen was substituted for clean, he seemed to agree, were not specially directed at the Irish prisoners, but were a scam by other prisoners taking advantage of neglectful officers. In any event, the system of exchanging laundry was altered.[12]

---

11 Clarke, *op. cit.*, p. 8. Yet in February 1890, neither Clarke nor any of the other prisoners made complaints when interviewed by a director, who visited for that purpose (PRO HO 144/925/ A46664/32–4).

12 *Chatham Visitors' Report*, Minutes of Evidence, qq. 2370–9, p. 73; q. 2387, p. 74; qq. 2458–65, p. 76; qq. 2511–14, p. 77; q. 2567, p. 79.

Even Egan conceded that some of the incidents of which he complained were fairly common in prison life, that senior staff rebuked assistant warders for inappropriate behaviour towards prisoners, and that latterly (especially after 1888) things improved.[13]

John Daly complained of being given (in November 1890) three very nearly fatal overdoses of belladonna, the circumstances of which were thoroughly investigated by the inquiry. This incident almost certainly arose from error rather than intent, though Daly had grounds for complaint about the lack of skill and care by Joshua Durbin, the infirmary's compounder.[14] He also made various complaints about what was callous and possibly cruel treatment while he was ill, vomiting and suffering from diarrhoea and back pain.[15] He told of one particularly disgusting occasion when, possibly through another ill-prescribed medicine, he soiled his clothing while at chapel, and was made to get into a cold bath where he was instructed to wash both himself and his clothes in the same water.[16] Daly also mentioned being issued with dirty rather than clean clothing – shirts or undershirts smelling so badly that they would 'make a sensitive person sick'. He had also been given blankets 'which were full of the filth of self-abuse from some prisoner that had used them before'. These blankets had eventually been exchanged but he was given others that were similarly stained.[17]

In the midst of all this sordid and disgusting detail of convict life it is hard to say how far Daly, Egan and the others were being singled out for abuse, since according to their own evidence other weaker prisoners were repeatedly assaulted and ill-treated by some of the warders. A simple-minded man was knocked down when he failed to keep step during the men's marching exercise, and as he fell he cried out for his mother. Devaney, one of the dynamitards, was beaten as he was pushed into a cell, but so were the other non-Irish prisoners. One old and heavily burdened man who accidentally bumped into an officer in a workshop was struck so heavily that he nearly fell over. An infirmary

---

13 The reason for the improvement, it might be supposed, was the renewed interest in the Irish prisoners by members of the Irish Parliamentary Party and the willingness of MPs to raise questions in the House about the men's prison treatment. Sir Edmund Du Cane was well aware of this Irish Parliamentary interest.

14 The compounder had made an error as to the strength of the medicine he dispensed. As punishment he was reduced in rank, though later reinstated and transferred (PRO HO 144/925/A46664/48–55). An internal inquiry was conducted, and on reviewing the facts the Permanent-Under-Secretary commented, 'I am afraid it was a very bad mistake indeed' (ibid., /30). Daly had nearly been killed, and he and his supporters thereafter used the error and near-tragedy to maximum political advantage.

15 *Chatham Visitors' Report*, qq. 833, p. 22, *et seq.* On the overdosing with belladonna see qq. 989–1062, pp. 27–30; qq. 1095–245. pp. 31–5.

16 Ibid., qq. 877–96, pp. 23–4.

17 Ibid., qq. 1613–14, p. 49; qq. 1620–2, p. 49.

prisoner, suspected of feigning insanity, was severely beaten, said Daly, in 'the most brutal manner I ever saw in my life'. Another elderly prisoner, blind in one eye, was beaten 'in a most awful manner' because he was slow getting back into bed after saying his prayers. He claimed that a mentally handicapped convict, 'an idiot . . . named Moore', was made by a warder to put his penis on a table where it was beaten with a club with such force that he subsequently could not urinate.[18] A number of other instances of gratuitous and sadistic brutality were mentioned by Daly – none except for Devaney involving Irish prisoners. While exposure to such cruelty was in itself a fearful and constantly intimidating experience (as it was doubtless intended to be) its unpredictability, frequency and apparent focus on the weaker prisoners confirmed that the dynamitards were not being singled out. Indeed, of Principal Warder Ruffell, Daly observed that since he had known him 'I have seen him display the truest and kindest humanity towards all prisoners in his dealings'. Perpetual harshness and eruptions of savagery were products of a primitive penal regime, and the perverse and sadistic impulses of a minority of officers, who when unsupervised felt free to act. Such was convict life.

All of this was framed by a deep concern which faces all who serve long terms of imprisonment: the passage of years, and the process of ageing.[19] The liberal regimes of modern prisons allow inmates, even those categorised as maximum security, to take steps to maintain their fitness, to obtain mental stimulation, and to improve themselves through educational and other courses. These can be effective means of reducing the fear of rotting away in prison. With a close-knit group, such as the dynamitards, linked to each other by nationality, religion, politics, prior friendships, fate and proximity, the mental and physical health of one became a deep concern to the others: one man going under was both a reason for compassion and a warning. '"[W]ho next" was the terrible question that haunted us day and night – and the ever-recurring thought that it might be myself added to the agony.'[20] Early in his imprisonment, Clarke had devised means to communicate with his comrades, both through a form of telegraph

18 Ibid., qq. 1551–68, pp. 45–6.
19 See Stan Cohen and Laurie Taylor's *Psychological Survival: The Experience of Long Term Imprisonment* (Harmondsworth, Penguin, 1972) for a thoughtful exploration of the demands of and responses to long-term imprisonment.
20 Clarke, *op. cit.*, p. 8. He recalled Whitehead's (Murphy's) onset of insanity: 'Can I ever forget the night that poor Whitehead realised that he was going mad. There in the stillness, between two of the hourly inspections, I heard the poor fellow fight against insanity, cursing England and English Brutality from the bottom of his heart, and beseeching God to strike him dead sooner than allow him to lose his reason. Such episodes are ineffaceable in the memory, they burn their impress into a man's soul' (ibid., pp. 8–9). At one point Clarke began to hear a buzzing in his ears and thought that this was the long-feared onset of insanity. He spent a night in mental agony, only to discover the next morning that the buzzing was caused by a new telegraph wire affixed outside his cell (ibid. pp. 72–3).

(tapping on cell walls) and by passing notes.[21] Since the men were concentrated in one part of the prison and in constant communication with each other, it was possible to notice changes, and Clarke claims that he saw both Gallagher and Whitehead become insane step by step – to 'get queer'. On release, both men were unquestionably insane, but Clarke maintained that they were then in no worse condition than they had been for the previous seven or eight years. If this was true, it was evidence of official cruelty or callous indifference.[22]

Short of flogging, the dynamitards were not exempted from prison punishments.[23] Thomas Clarke insisted (and it seems more than possible) that on occasion warders provoked offences in order to get the men punished. Having served several weeks of a sentence of forty days' cellular punishment – that is, close confinement in a stripped and unheated cell on a reduced diet – Clarke was allowed out to answer a call of nature. The cold of the cell and the sparse diet had reduced him to such a state of starvation that he had chewed his cleaning rags to allay his pains.[24] In the corridor Clarke saw several lumps of bread, accidentally, as it were, spilled on the floor. The warder, who had put Clarke on the charge which had earned him some of his punishment, was apparently looking the other way:

> I was absolutely starving and could have eaten it ravenously, but like a
> flash a revulsion of feeling came, and in my impotent rage and misery
> I uttered curses fierce and bitter against English villainy as ever Irishman
> uttered. . . . He stood pretending to look into the ward below, but his

---

21 In his evidence to the 1890 Chatham Visitors' inquiry John Daly (still a prisoner) was simply lying when he stated that telegraphing between cells was impossible and that he had never done it: 'I never telegraphed a word to a single prisoner. I declare it upon my word.' He had, however, twice been convicted of the offence, which Thomas Clarke described in detail. Daly had used his cell slate to write out a telegraphic code, and when this was found the slate was removed (*Chatham Visitors' Report*, qq. 1339–52, p. 38; Le Roux, *op. cit.*, pp. 41–3).

22 Clarke, *op. cit.*, p. 12; see also pp. 13–20.

23 The men seem to have been well behaved. A summary of their punishments, compiled in March 1889, shows that loss of marks and other minor punishments were imposed mainly for talking and communicating and idleness. Gallagher was punished for irreverence in chapel, 'foul language and worse'. He was also punished for assaulting Clarke, and for 'improper conduct in the separate cells' (PRO HO 144/195/A46664C/149). John Duff was punished for 'apparently trying to injure himself in the print shop' (PRO HO 144/925/A46664, 22–3). The dynamitards were fully aware that they could not be flogged, James Egan informing an American newspaper on his release, 'No, they don't touch the lash to political prisoners. That's one thing they cannot do to us' (*New York Press*, 4 October 1896, PRO HO 195/A46664C/294A). John Daly, who over-egged the pudding where possible, claimed to have lived 'in absolute terror' that by means of trickery officers would lead him to violence and thus to a flogging: 'that thing was on my mind to an awful extent that I would be by some means or other forced to commit myself, and that I would ultimately be flogged' (*Chatham Visitors' Report*, Minutes of Evidence, qq. 1570–1, p. 46). Had one of the dynamitards attacked an officer it is likely that he would have been flogged – but prisoners could be flogged for very much less serious offences, such as persistently refusing to work.

24 The modern phrase 'sparse diet' is misleading. This was a starvation diet, intended to produce unceasing pangs of hunger.

eye was on my every movement, and had I touched the bread he would have pounced upon me and taken it from me, and would have had me up before Pontius Pilate [the Governor] to be awarded still more punishment for 'stealing bread'.[25]

Having completed his 'terrible' forty days' punishment, Clarke recalled he was so weak and exhausted that he could not stand upright or walk without staggering.[26] Bearing in mind that in modern times dietary punishment (which in English prisons ended in the late 1960s) was restricted to three-day periods it is unlikely that he was exaggerating.

But although the Irish prisoners generally experienced no more than the normal brutality of the system, hostility towards them naturally intensified as the campaign of terror and Rossa's threats continued in the outside world.[27] There was great scope to victimise should an officer wish to do so. Work was obligatory, for example, but no provision was made for teaching the several trades of the prison. The prisoner was therefore placed in the position of having to complete a task in order to avoid punishment for idleness, while at the same time scarcely knowing how to do it. The only remedy was to look carefully at what was being done by the other prisoners (conversation was forbidden) and to do one's best. This situation, Clarke insisted, afforded 'countless opportunities' for trade-shop officers to victimise the Irish prisoners – though it is not clear from his account to what extent the vulnerability of *all* the novice prisoners was exploited by those of the trade officers with a penchant for bullying.[28]

Towards their fellow prisoners Clarke and his comrades displayed the same attitude of repulsion and raw contempt which (with the notable exception of Michael Davitt) had been a mark of the Irish political offenders from the time of the Young Irelanders. The ordinary convicts were 'dregs raked in from the gutters' and 'criminals, guilty of almost every crime in the calendar, ranging from

---

25 Clarke, *op. cit.*, pp. 33–4. John Daly made a complaint of a similar nature, arguing that there were fair and unfair methods of catching the prisoners talking: 'Every man when he gets the chance considers that he has a fair right to talk . . . I quite admit that I would if I got the chance.' He objected to warders concealing themselves to detect talking. 'It is the duty of the warders to suppress talking, but to encourage it by their pretended absence is, I submit, not fair' (*Chatham Visitors' Report*, Minutes of Evidence, qq. 1529–30, p. 44).

26 Ibid., p. 34.

27 '[I]t must be remembered that at the time of our conviction all England was panic-stricken. . . . There was blood on the moon and a skirmisher or Irish Fenian to be seen at every turn . . . the prison gates did not close out from us the spirit of vengeance that was holding sway throughout England. That spirit held inside the walls with far greater intensity than it did outside' (Clarke, *op. cit.*, pp. 51–2).

28 Ibid., pp. 51–4. Clarke records acts of kindness towards him by two warders, but these largely confirmed his nationalist perceptions. An Irish infirmary nurse would give extra bread whenever he had the chance, and would also whisper interesting items of news. An English warder would also sometimes pass on outside news. For years Clarke puzzled why this man had been so friendly. The mystery was solved when he discovered that the man had an Irish wife (ibid., pp. 85 and 87).

the multi-murderer down to the court martialled soldier'.[29] These men did not even have the one essential virtue of the prisoner: solidarity against the authorities. In breaking the rules Clarke was as watchful of his fellows as of the warders, since 'they would have been only too glad to give me away to curry favour'.[30] From the experience of Michael Davitt (and indeed the Young Irelanders) this is probably a misfounded belief: prisoners' solidarity against the authorities generally transcended any national prejudice, and (if events in the outside world were any guide) such informers as there were were hardly in a greater proportion among the ordinary criminals than among the dynamitards.

The men also complained of the language of some of the warders, and it is probable that as ex-soldiers and sailors in the main, their vocabulary was sometimes earthy, scatological and obscene – especially when they were unsupervised. James Egan told the Chatham Visitors' Inquiry of language so 'filthy and disgusting' that when he complained to the governor about it he could not bring himself to use the words. He did say that when he was bathing, the officer who was supervising called the cleaner to look at him, saying, 'Look here, come here, here is a bloody little arse'. He complained that another officer also frequently used filthy language, and had shouted into the cell, 'Go and scrape the cakes of shit off your arse'. Egan strongly objected to this language, observing, 'We may have been poor, but are never accustomed to such language as that.'[31]

If the degradation and depravity of his fellow convicts and some of the warders was apparent to Clarke, so also was his own national and natural superiority. Brutal punishments were unsparingly heaped upon him over the years, he insisted, 'but never for one moment did I forget I was an Irish political prisoner, and, in

29 Ibid., p. 62. Quite a different view was taken by the *Saturday Review* in the wake of the explosions at the Tower and House of Commons. In a previous generation the dynamitards would have been hanged, yet in the convict prisons they were now being treated with the same indulgence as the luckless clerk 'who in dread of ruin forged his employer's name, or a manslayer whose guilt accrued in a single moment of perhaps provoked passion'. Dynamitards had planned crimes which might, and, had they more boldly been carried out, must have inflicted death and injury to scores of innocent lives. The treatment of the dynamitards was 'a ridiculous and disastrous leniency' (31 January 1885, pp. 130–1).

30 By the time the dynamitards entered the convict prisons the 'Star' system had been introduced. This separated first offenders from those previously convicted in a rather futile attempt to prevent contamination. According to Clarke, he was at first refused entry into the 'Star' class, and an attempt was made to get from him the names of friends who would vouch to his not having been previously convicted. Clarke (who had been convicted under the name Henry Hammond Wilson and whose antecedents had been obscured by his shipwreck off New Foundland *en route* to England) refused to give names, considering the request to be an attempt at intelligence-gathering. He was eventually placed in the 'Star' class notwithstanding (Clarke, *op. cit.*, pp. 97–100; Le Roux, *op. cit.*, pp. 24–5).

31 *Chatham Visitors' Report*, Minutes of Evidence, qq. 2100–4, p. 63; q. 2117, p. 64. It is hard to know what to make of such complaints: were they sanctimonious or point-scoring tittle-tattle, or genuine shock at language which was used widely by rougher sections of the English working classes? If the latter, in what circles had the England-based dynamitards moved? Was there no such language used in Ireland and the United States of America?

spite of it all, never felt any degradation'. Treated as an ordinary criminal – forced to wear the uniform, to have a shaven head – Clarke took satisfaction in the thought that despite all their power the authorities could not force him to regard himself as one of the criminal class.[32] Despite this moral posturing, however, the dynamitards had not been wholly immune from the usual temptations of the world, and one of them had the secondary symptoms of syphilis.[33]

One's sense of personal worth and dignity was severely tested by the invasive routine of personal searching to which all the 'Special Men' were subject. Like Rossa and the other Fenians before them, Clarke and his comrades found this particularly provocative and indecent; it was 'inspired by a spirit of devilry and aimed at galling the finer feelings of a man's nature and was calculated to blur and deaden the moral sense'.[34] This remained Clarke's view, even while he recounted the various means by which he and his colleagues had concealed and passed on contraband. Unlike Rossa, Clarke apparently did not use the body cavity for concealment (he may have thought it indecent to disclose that he done so), but other prisoners were less fastidious. Had they not regularly carried out intimate body searches prison staff would have been open to charges of neglecting their duties: issues of safety as well as enforcement of penal discipline were involved. It is more than likely, however, that there were good grounds for objecting to the manner of the searches. The warders, according to Clarke, sometimes kept up 'a running fire of comments' which he implies were indecent, since they were 'in keeping with the nature of the work they were engaged in'. He also complained about the indecent and hurtful way some staff mauled him while conducting the much more frequent 'pat down' (i.e. fully clothed) searches.[35] Every day Clarke saw his fellows being patted down, since all had to submit to the procedure four times a day as they went to and came back from work. He did not claim that the searches to which he was subject were conducted any more roughly on the Irish politicals than on ordinary convicts; rather that the indignity offered to the Irish was greater because of their sensibilities.[36]

32 Clarke, *op. cit.*, p. 62.
33 This was John Daly, who said that he had contracted syphilis in 1878, with secondary symptoms, including ulcers, manifesting themselves in Chatham (*Chatham Visitors' Report*, Minutes of Evidence, qq. 966–71, pp. 26–7).
34 Clarke, *op. cit.*, p. 63. According to Daly, ordinary convicts were strip-searched six times a year, and the Irish prisoners twelve times (*Daily Chronicle*, 12 September 1896, 3e).
35 Ibid., p. 64; Le Roux, *op. cit.*, pp. 44–5.
36 Daly most strongly objected to the strip-searching – 'utterly demoralising . . . I call the search indecent and an outrage upon humanity' (*Daily Chronicle*, 12 September 1896, 3e). A point that emerged almost casually in the course of the Chatham visitors' inquiry was that toilet paper was rationed to fourteen sheets a week, but that regularly less than that was given out and sometimes as little as five small sheets for a week (see PRO HO 144/194/A46664C/1. Egan submitted a specimen sheet of the toilet paper, which is still attached to the file of the Visitors' Report). This rationing was both humiliating and disgusting and compelled the prisoners to beg for toilet paper. Once more there was no suggestion that the Irish were being singled our for special treatment (*Chatham Visitors' Report*, Minutes of Evidence, qq. 2110–11, p. 64).

Penal servitude demanded and enforced unremitting, unreserved and manifest submission, and this principle was especially emphasised during Edmund Du Cane's headship of the convict system. At this time convict prisons were largely staffed by former military and naval men, and an atmosphere of rigid discipline prevailed for both prisoners and warders. Complaints, unless delivered with the utmost tentativeness, humility and deference, were likely to be taken as insolence and confirmation that one was a malcontent or liar. Knowing this, the lodging of a complaint was at the very least a risk, and often must have been an act of defiance. Adverse or contrary results might follow. Clarke recounts one such sequence. He complained that his library book did not match his educational level; he received only 'girls' and boys' trashy story books'. Bumble-like, the governor's indignation on hearing this request was such that he ordered Clarke to be removed from the office. Clarke's next volume was a book of nursery rhymes, and subsequently a fiercely anti-Popery tract, stamped 'Protestants Only'. A letter protesting at this interference with his library privileges was suppressed.[37] In a duel with the authorities a prisoner had only the faintest chance of winning – but this applied to ordinary as much as to the political convicts.

A man's previous way of life was critical in determining the impact of the punishment. Men used to the living conditions and the food and work of labourers adapted easily to those aspects of the regime if not to captivity and penal discipline. Thomas Devaney (a labourer and Ribbonman recruited by Rossa for the Tradeston gasworks explosion), when released in 1896 on medical (largely mental) grounds, recalled that he was 'wild' at the thought of never seeing his family again. During his first three years he kicked against the discipline, and it went hard with him. His rations, which he thought were 'none too plentiful', were repeatedly reduced to the point, he claimed, where he almost became blind. He also remembered the intense cold of the refractory cells – 'I feel a shiver coming over me at the thought of them'. At last he came to the conclusion that his misbehaviour was exposing him to unnecessary suffering and he began to obey the rules, and to gain privileges. Unlike some of the other prisoners (Davitt in particular) Devaney made no complaint about the food, which he thought was good: 'We got 1lb of potatoes for dinner, 6oz of bread, and a fair look in at beef. Sometimes I have been unable to eat all the food.' He had worked as a carpenter and had also spent time in the blacksmith's shop: 'We had to work hard, but no harder than free men work.' And in general, 'I must say this much for Portland – if a man behaves himself and does his work he is well treated on the whole. The cells are comfortable, and in the winter time extra blankets are given out.' Once the decision had been made to release him he spent three weeks in the prison infirmary 'fattening

37 Clarke, *op. cit.*, p. 67.

up for my home-coming. They give you some fine nourishing food before you come out.'[38]

The Chatham Visitors' Report

Complaints about the treatment of John Daly, particularly the near-fatal administration of an overdose of belladonna, were ventilated in the press and Commons in the spring of 1890. It was then decided to ask the Visitors of Chatham prison to conduct an inquiry.[39] A pamphlet outlining Daly's supposed ill-treatment was published in Limerick in January 1890 by the Irish National League.[40] Large sections of the minutes of evidence published with the Chatham Visitors' Report deal with fairly trivial complaints, some barely significant in the context of convict prison life at the time, others petty annoyances and injustices no doubt, but again of the type that would be found in any residential institution under discipline. The manner of the inquiry itself was open, and no complaint or observation seems to have been suppressed.[41] The men were asked if they wished to submit complaints in writing, and if they did so the envelope was sealed, and opened in their presence by the Chairman of the inquiry, Judge Selfe. Egan

---

38 *Cork Examiner*, 20 August 1896, 5e–f, *passim*. He had spoken to some of his fellow offenders, but indicated that this was difficult to do: 'It's these snatched conversations that help to make one bear up. We think over in our cells every word which has been repeated, and treasure them up in our memory.' Devaney denied, however, that the Irish prisoners at Portland communicated with each other by tapping between the cells – 'it is chiefly the prigs [criminal prisoners] who resort to that. We kept ourselves as far apart from such characters as we could.'

39 PRO HO 144/925/A46664/31A; PRO HO 144/194/A46664C. Daly and his supporters attempted to link the overdose and other alleged ill-treatment to the refusal of the prisoners to assist the government in the *Times*–Parnell inquiry. Richard Pigott, forger of the Parnell letter, and Soames, representing *The Times*, were, however, each allowed access to the prisoners, as was Inspector Littlejohn of Scotland Yard.

40 *The Inhuman Treatment of John Daly and Other Political Prisoners in English Jails: Appeal to the People of Great Britain and Ireland*, Limerick, Irish National League, 1890. This publication received wide publicity in Irish newspapers, and prompted the Irish government to ask the Home Office for an inquiry (PRO HO 144/925/A46664/31).

41 This was not a specially constituted committee. Visitors were appointed by the Home Secretary to each convict prison, with the duty of visiting and inspecting and informing the Secretary of State of any concerns they might have. The Chatham Visitors were Judge W. L. Selfe (a county court judge) and Colonel Sir J. F. Lennard, together with two men of the respectable working class (appointed by the previous Liberal government) – C. J. Drummond and George Shipton. These men should have reported any irregularities in the running of the prison and it is a priori unlikely that they would in the course of their special inquiry discover them, since that would indicate a previous lack of vigilance or application. With some justice John O'Connor Power, MP, accused the Visitors of whitewashing the actions of the prison officials, and of being asked to sit in judgement on themselves (3 *Hansard*, CCCXLVIII, col. 873; 13 August 1890). The Visitors were assisted in the inquiry by an independent medical man, Sir James Risdon Bennett, former President of the Royal College of Physicians (PRO HO 144/925/A46664/42).

complained that members of staff were present when his submission was opened and he was to be questioned about it. It was pointed out that staff (and those who were in attendance were generally senior staff – junior staff being called only for specific reasons) could be excluded at his request. Daly asked that this should be done, and staff were requested to withdraw.[42] The manner of questioning occasionally betrays some impatience, but is almost always civil. As was customary at the time, prisoners had to stand while giving evidence, but then so also did the warders. What was not at all usual was to allow prisoners to remain in the room while staff were questioned. Daly was frequently allowed to interject, and to put questions to the witnesses.[43] This was particularly striking when Daly and Egan were allowed (or obliged) to confront a number of witnesses against whom they had made allegations of improper language or conduct, or of victimisation. Four full days of the seven-day inquiry were given over to such confrontations and face-to-face examinations of the complaints and allegations of Egan and Daly against fellow convicts and warders.[44]

For all the latitude extended to Daly and Egan, it could scarcely be doubted that the prisoners were at a disadvantage in pressing their case. Notwithstanding the political nature of their crimes, they were assumed, with their fellow convicts, to have lost their character. The weight of their word against that of staff was slight, and in the nature of the allegations there was rarely going to be much corroboration. The inquiry was not authorised to administer the oath (an omission which Daly deplored), and the advantages lay on the side of those who wished to cover up the unpleasant, rough and repulsive details of convict life. As with all other inquiries of this kind, it would have been in the witnesses' mind – staff and convicts alike – that they would remain in the prison, trying to make a life or a living, long after the inquiry was concluded. Nobody on either side of the counter was going to make enemies of colleagues with whom many years would have to be passed.

The psychology of the inquiry also weighed against complainers. What confidence could one have that the investigation was being conducted in good faith, and what value could be attached to the chairman's promise of indemnity? Pen and paper had been made available to help the prisoners prepare statements and make notes of the evidence they were to give, but this scarcely compensated for not having the advice of a lawyer or friend. Standing for hours while evidence was taken, wearing convict uniform, obliged to follow the etiquette of deference and submission, conscious of the inevitable return to a solitary cell and to prison life at the end of proceedings – all of this was daunting, taxing and inhibiting. Whatever one might make of the substance of the complaints of Daly and Egan,

---

42 *Chatham Visitors' Report*, Minutes of Evidence, qq. 2379–84, p. 73.

43 See, for example, ibid., qq. 2857–60, p. 85. This was an exchange on Gallagher's supposed insanity, and there were many other exchanges and interjections.

44 Ibid., qq. 2228–6215, pp. 68–173. This was unprecedented in the history of English prisons.

by far the most articulate and vociferous of the convicts to give evidence, they undoubtedly showed much self-possession and a deal of moral courage before the inquiry.

It is also fair to say that the convicts who wished to press complaints were scarcely doing so before an unbiased tribunal. The Visitors were likely to favour any official account of events for two reasons. First – and it is a tone that runs through all their questions – they had a strong reflexive middle-class English tendency to believe the authorities: this was Her Majesty's Prison, Chatham, and the presumption was that it would be run properly and that a mechanism of inspection, supervision and redress would correct breaches of duty by subordinate staff: axiomatically there would be no such failures by the superior grades, such as the governor, deputy governors, chaplain and medical officers. As in any human institution, mistakes and transgressions would occur, but they would be detected and remedied. Second, as noted, the Visitors were also conscious that it was their duty to detect irregularities, and any that now emerged and that they recognised as legitimate would fall on the debit side of the ledger of their effectiveness. Few bodies asked thus to judge themselves could be expected to return a true verdict.

The outcome of the inquiry (unlike that of the Devon Commission, for example) was never in doubt: with a few minor exceptions – failures of duty on the part of subordinate officers – complaints of ill-treatment were rejected. What cut across this fairly simple and predictable outcome, however, was the decision to take and publish verbatim minutes of evidence. Behind this lay several considerations. The 1867 Knox and Pollock Inquiry had failed to gain credibility because it was not seen as impartial and had not published the evidence on which it based its dismissive findings. The 1870 to 1871 Devon Commission had been necessary largely because of the lack of credibility of the earlier inquiry. It had gained authority and respect because of the standing, integrity and aristocratic independence of its chairman, and because it published in full the minutes of evidence. And although there were many embarrassing allegations and revelations about prison life in the evidence taken by the Chatham Visitors, and much that had the ring of truth about it, there was nothing other than the accidental poisoning of Daly that was truly damaging. Convict life was harsh: it was intended so to be. It was sometimes appallingly sordid and was conducted according to standards, etiquette and language not contemplated in the annual reports which dryly recorded its order, health and vigour – but all who lived in the grown-up world would have been surprised had it been otherwise found, or indeed if army and navy life had been free from the vulgar predilections and roughness in manner of working-class men under intense institutional pressure. These realities, encrusted with occasional examples of filthy language and unhygienic conditions, were no bar to publication.

Finally, there was the evidence of Daly and Egan, which was more likely to be received as doubtful than reliable, biased than unfair, and querulous and nit-picking than manly and substantive. For them to have made an effective case, it would have been necessary to accept with dignity the inevitable hardship of convict life and to limit their complaints to three or four major issues: a good lawyer would have advised this course. Muddling together issues of substance and principle and the long-spent tittle-tattle and inevitable inconveniences and petty unfairnesses of institutional life,[45] the men's evidence affirmed the general stance of the authorities: convict prisons were not comfortable places, but on the whole they were run fairly and complaints were improbable, inaccurate, poorly remembered or inappropriate. The publication of these minutes of evidence could only promote the official case, and, as a bonus, demonstrate forbearance in response to unreasonableness.

The Irish Parliamentary Party now focused on the issue of ill-treatment, and repeatedly raised it from 31 March 1890.[46] They were not mollified when the Chatham Visitors' Report was published and its attached verbatim minutes of evidence showed that the men had been encouraged to speak freely, and to lodge their complaints verbally or in writing. Some of the grievances – about food, for example – appeared to be relatively trivial, and contradicted by evidence of others of the Irish prisoners, who found their food satisfactory and even enjoyable.[47] The men were poor and many had relatives who lived far away, and so they could not receive visits: this was a frequent complaint. Others spoke of warders' petty injustices, and a number asserted their innocence and asked the Visitors for help in bringing their case before the Home Secretary. There were the complaints of warders' bad language, but one man (Thomas Callan) said that he had never heard it.[48] There were several mentions of visits from Scotland Yard to offer inducements in exchange for information during The Times–Parnell Commission. The egregious partiality of the authorities in the matter was also manifest in the Home Office's grant of permission for a representative of The Times and for Richard Pigott, the forger of the Parnell letter, to visit some of the men in prison, seeking their assistance.[49] John Daly's accidental poisoning with belladonna had nearly proved fatal, but the minutes show that during the inquiry he was given every opportunity to raise questions, remaining in the room while the medical officer, the compounder of medicine, and other witnesses, lay and medical, were examined.[50] The minutes

---

45 One of Daly's allegations, put to the instructor who was supposed to have said it, was 'How silly Daly looks when he says a thing'. Badinage rather than abuse by any criterion, surely (Chatham Visitors' Report, Minutes of Evidence, q. 3120, p. 93).

46 3 Hansard, CCCXLIII, col. 304; 31 March 1890. At this point the report was still being written.

47 Henry Dalton complained that his roast beef had been served to him cold, with bad potatoes – 'so cold that you could skim the fat off the liquor that was in the tin' (op. cit., Minutes of Evidence, q. 257, p. 9); James Gilbert took a very different view (ibid., qq. 540–2, p. 15).

48 Ibid., q. 708, p. 19. Callan also said that although he had been in a cold cell he was now 'very comfortable'; he got on reasonably well with the officers, the labour was not too hard, and he found the food variable (ibid., qq. 704; 707; 701 and 695, p. 19).

49 See the evidence of John Daly on this: ibid., qq. 1658–61, pp. 50–1; qq. 1681–9, pp. 51–2; see also Daly's post-release Daily Chronicle interview (12 September 1896, 3c).

50 See ibid., qq. 1–8, p. 1; qq. 751–8, p. 20; qq. 833–1313, pp. 22–36.

did, however, strongly suggest that some of the men were insane, or were feigning it rather well. This would prove to be a major focus for nationalist and Fenian condemnation.

Viewed overall, the Chatham Visitors' Report catalogued tittle-tattle about unfair treatment, but when closely examined some of this was seen to amount to little.[51] The unexceptional nature of most of the evidence was undoubtedly why the government decided to publish the minutes, dispelling rumours and reinforcing the credibility of the inquiry. But the nationalist MPs would not cooperate. In August 1890, John O'Connor Power,[52] a former secretary of the Supreme Council of the IRB, and who had himself been imprisoned in Ireland five times, pushed the issue forward in the Estimates' debates. The men had been and continued to be ill-treated. Traps were being laid for them; there was a system of bullying, petty persecution and annoyance, and they were severely punished for trivial or non-existent offences.[53] Warders used language 'so filthy that it could not be read to the Committee', and when the prisoners objected they were reported and punished.[54]

Pleading for clemency, O'Connor Power insisted that the men were political prisoners. Release was merited because of the indignities they had suffered, and their careless medical treatment. An ordinary prisoner poisoned by a double or treble dose of belladonna would long ago have been given his freedom. The dynamite scare was now completely over 'and the policy of dynamite had been abandoned as a futile and wicked policy'. The only reason the men were being kept in prison was revenge. England was alone in her 'implacable severity' towards political prisoners: even the exiled Communards had been allowed to return to their homes, and many were now active in French political life.[55]

---

51 The evidence of John Daly is particularly striking in this regard. He had good grounds for his complaint about belladonna poisoning, but many of his other complaints were unconvincing and diminished his credibility as a witness (op. cit., Minutes of Evidence (qq. 1314–519, pp. 37–44) provides a number of examples of his fairly petty complaints).

52 See above, p. 285, n. 34; pp. 307–8.

53 Power's allegations are drawn almost entirely from the evidence of John Daly. This included a dramatic incident on the third day of the inquiry when Daly presented the Commissioners with a piece of contraband newspaper which he had been given not long before being called in. The intention, he insisted, was to trap and discredit him (op. cit., qq. 1316–30, p. 37).

54 3 Hansard, CCCXLVIII, cols 858–93, passim; 13 August 1890 (summarised in The Times, 14 August 1890, 5c). Irish Members took particular exception to warders' use of filthy language. Thomas Sexton, the MP for Belfast West, referred to 'Language of the most obscene and filthy description' which he said was habitually used by the warders. Had government responded more vigorously the prisoners 'would have been saved from the indignity and torture of having such language continually applied to them'. Sexton asked that the men's term of imprisonment be shortened, and that in the meantime they be removed from Chatham (3 Hansard CCCXLVIII, cols 883–7; 13 August 1890).

55 The Times, 14 August 1890, 5e.

Home Secretary Henry Matthews denied all these charges and rejected all pleas. Prisoners were apt to make allegations about the hostility and ill-will which they imagined officials felt towards them, but why, among a thousand Chatham prisoners, should these men be singled out for ill-treatment? Although some of the warders might be brutal men, 'anything like systematic persecution was hardly possible when these subordinate warders were under the direct control of a staff of officers of the highest reputation and character'. A committee had investigated the allegations, and had fully exonerated the prison administration.[56]

The Irish Parliamentary Party remained in some difficulty in presenting the dynamitards' case. In an important Commons' speech towards the end of the turbulent session of 1891, John Redmond[57] moved an amendment to the Consolidated Fund Bill, calling for their amnesty. It could not be denied that the dynamite offences were 'of a senseless and cowardly character'. None of the offences, as far as he knew,[58] had resulted in 'actual loss of life', yet they were 'distinguished by such a recklessness of consequences' that it would not be unnatural for the Commons to view with impatience an appeal on behalf of men who had been convicted of such crimes.[59] All of the men, Redmond implicitly accepted, with the exception of Daly and Egan, had been justly convicted. He went on to argue that Daly and Egan's cases should be subject to a full review since doubt existed about their guilt, and that clemency should be extended to the other offenders.[60] Despite some back-bench Liberal support, the Irish members were unable to persuade the government either to order an inquiry or to grant clemency.

Amnesty deferred

By mid-1891 there remained in English convict prisons sixteen men convicted of treason-felony-related offences. These had been convicted in seven sets of trials

---

56 Ibid.

57 (1856–1918). Educated at Trinity College, Dublin; called to the English Bar, 1885, and the Irish Bar, 1887. He was, successively, nationalist MP for New Ross (1881–5), North Wexford (1885–91) and Waterford (1891–1918). After the split in the Irish Party and Parnell's death, Redmond led the Parnellite minority. Following reunification of the Irish Parliamentary Party in 1900, Redmond became leader, retaining that position until his death (and the demise of the Party) in 1918.

58 This was a fine point. A boy of 7 had been killed as a result of the January 1881 attack on Salford barracks. It was true, however, that none of the dynamitards had been charged with murder (see above, p. 342). It had been their intention, moreover, to act with disregard for life and it was only a mercy that no more had been lost.

59 3 *Hansard* CCCLVI, cols 1141–2; 3 August 1891. See the Home Office briefing papers for the debate at PRO HO 144/194/A46664C/19.

60 Daly always insisted that Egan did not know that he had buried explosives in his garden (see PRO HO 144/925/A46664/86: Daly to Dr Mark Ryan, 14 June 1892).

held between May 1883 and April 1885. With one exception all were serving life terms of penal servitude.[61] The dynamitards were to spend much longer in prison than the first wave of Fenians. They attracted much less sympathy and support from Irish opinion and liberal and radical English circles. The timing, as well as the nature of the dynamite campaign was a major factor in the lack of Irish sympathy. 'Advanced' national opinion, including the resources of Fenianism, had been harnessed to the Land War, and this dovetailed with the obstruction tactics of Parnell's militant parliamentary party. The dynamite campaign obscured and impeded these other struggles, which had attracted mass support, achieved some successes, and made nationalist opinion more cohesive than perhaps it had ever been. Terrorism in the cause of Irish independence enabled all nationalists to be portrayed as complicit in this type of violence – if not actually engaged in its promotion.[62]

Tens of thousands of Irishmen and women had migrated to the industrial conurbations of England and Scotland. Their presence emphasised the gap between the Fenians of 1865 to 1870 and the dynamitards. Romantic and militarily hopeless though they may have been, the Fenians could claim to have fought with honour: this was central to their notion of national regeneration. Appeals for leniency for both the Young Irelanders and the Fenians had conceded that they were foolish and misguided, and that they had without doubt broken the law and were therefore liable to its penalties. Yet it could always be said in their favour that they were men of honour – a point of some importance when the politicians were looking for acceptable ways to present an act of clemency to the public. How could one plead on behalf of men who left bombs in railway stations or blew up gasworks in densely populated neighbourhoods; and how could their amnesty be explained? The dynamitards had moved from the politics of national honour to a war of attrition fought with the tactics of terrorism, and they had to bear the consequences in terms of British public and political sentiment. Nor was Irish opinion reconciled to the dynamitards. The liberal-nationalist *Cork Examiner* had condemned the persecution of Irish immigrants in England during the bombing campaigns, but insisted that if the bombings had provoked ire in England, 'they have caused sorrow and yet profounder indignation in Ireland. Men differing widely on questions of national politics heartily agree

---

61 James Egan was serving twenty years. See *Return of the Names and Number of Persons now Suffering Sentences of Penal Servitude in Ireland and England as a Consequence of Conviction for Treason-Felony, Showing (a) Date of Conviction; (b) the Length of the Sentence; and (c) the Prison where the Convict is Imprisoned*, PP, 1890–91 [387], LXIV 725, 1. This return had been moved by Parnell.

62 As the 1887 use of forged letters by *The Times* to incriminate Parnell in the Phoenix Park murders showed. (There are many accounts of this affair, but see, for example, Robert Kee, *The Laurel and The Ivy*, Harmondsworth, Penguin Books, 1994, pp. 521–8.)

in reprobation of these hideous crimes.'[63] This condemnation extended across the whole nationalist spectrum.[64]

Unlike Young Irelanders or Fenians, moreover, the dynamitards were not Irishmen living in Ireland. This further weakened their standing since, whether forced exiles like Devoy or Rossa, or ordinary emigrants, or children born in America of Irish parents, they had ceased directly to share the fate of their compatriots. Certainly their right to conduct a campaign of terror in England, for which the Irish community might be expected to pay, rested upon their speculative and mystical notions about the unity of the 'Irish Race'. In the early years of their imprisonment, and particularly while the campaign continued, the dynamitards were an embarrassment to the Fenians and an obstacle to constitutional nationalists – both groups to which they might be expected to turn for assistance in obtaining better prison conditions and, eventually, an amnesty.[65]

For some years the nature of their crimes made it impossible to portray the dynamitards as martyrs of any kind. Had they taken extreme care to bomb only empty buildings or to take other precautions to prevent injury, it would still have been difficult to evoke sympathy for them or even to reduce hostility. But given that they had planted bombs in places where the public congregated, the fact that they had desired civilian loss, injuries and even deaths as a means of creating terror could not be argued away. All the rhetoric about the 'humanity' of dynamite and how it actually saved lives when compared to conventional warfare blew back in the faces of the dynamitards and their supporters as sophistry and

63 *Cork Examiner*, 23 March 1883, 2d. A few days later the newspaper returned to the theme, noting the worldwide feeling the bombing produced towards the Irish: 'The atrocities of which O'Donovan Rossa and men like him speak so calmly are no whit less detested amongst the native American population than they are amongst the English people' (ibid., 27 March 1883, 2d). And again 'A panic or gust of fury might deprive hundreds of thousands of Irish people in England of their homes and their bread. This would be glorious no doubt, for the gentlemen who, safely in New York, are living richly on contributions for dynamite' (ibid., 9 April 1883, 2c). Some English newspapers had not been unwilling to dwell upon the vulnerability of the Irish community. The Tory *Morning Advertiser* ran a piece fairly typical of the genre in March 1881, beginning, 'Englishmen are not inexhaustible in patient endurance . . .' and asking whether nothing could be done 'to stamp out the panic and peril in their midst' (Bodleian Library, Ms Harcourt dep. 348, f. 14).

64 In March 1885, James Stephens, the old Fenian chief, was one of several Irishmen expelled from safe haven in Paris, largely because of the dynamitards' activities. His health was poor and he was destitute. Stephens' wife told the *Freeman's Journal* that he was opposed to the dynamite campaign, that he had never sympathised with the dynamiters, and never ceased denouncing them. What he wanted was open war between England and Ireland, and he deprecated a resort to any methods but those of organised warfare. News of Stephens' difficulties led to the establishment of an aid fund in Ireland (14 March 1885, 7h; 19 March, 5g; 20 March, 5g–h, 6a).

65 Writing to Dr Mark Ryan from Chatham Prison, Daly (welcoming the first stages of the campaign for his amnesty) acknowledged that 'The people of Ireland . . . have never sympathized with the policy of dynamite'. He welcomed the amnesty campaign as a sign that the Irish people were beginning to think for themselves (Daly to Ryan, 14 June 1892: PRO HO 144/925/A46664/86).

cynicism. Their standing should also be viewed against the background of an Irish peasantry enjoying a fairness and security of tenure transformed over a thirty-year period, with further improvements in prospect. Nationalists in the towns gave firm allegiance to the parliamentary party, which represented their cause effectively and militantly and had not succumbed to the place-seeking of earlier times. The Roman Catholic clergy – especially at its lower levels – had become more openly nationalist, but theirs was a brand of nationalism essentially conservative and law-abiding, and (with a few individual exceptions) utterly anti-revolutionary. From Dublin Castle, in the charge of Conservative Chief Secretary Arthur Balfour, came repeated affirmations of a determination to repress Irish agitation. The pendulum had moved to the coercion side of the policy box once again.[66] Finally, there was manifest and common-sense justice in the retribution visited on the dynamitards. In the light of what they had set out to do, who could argue that they should not spend a very long time in prison?

These were the most impropitious circumstances for any reanimation of an amnesty campaign. For the mood to change it was necessary that nationalists be given reason to re-evaluate the dynamitards and to feel able to speak on their behalf without appearing to palliate terrorism. It was to be expected that the passage of years would soften memories of the dynamite campaign, while common humanity would channel some sympathy to the prisoners in the long and arduous duration of their confinement. But such a mood, were it based entirely on pity, would be insufficient to create the undertow of anger and urgency necessary for a clemency campaign to be politically effective. Signs of an underlying shift in mood came from the constitutional (occasionally semi-constitutional) nationalists who, as they had with the Young Irelanders and Fenians, began to draw electoral and political advantage from the cause of amnesty. This was sufficient for an alliance to be formed, and for a clemency campaign to become respectable.[67] The drivers of this movement would, as before, come from Fenianism, to whom, Lenin-like, a popular campaign had advantages for recruitment of the more advanced elements, as well as nurturing anti-British and pro-independence sentiments in the population at large. In 1890 the Amnesty Association was

---

66 Balfour (1848–1930) in March 1887 had been appointed by his uncle, Lord Salisbury, to be Irish Chief Secretary. He was strongly set against any Home Rule policy. He combined an enlightened policy on land questions with great firmness in response to extra-parliamentary agitation. In private conversation with Wilfrid Scawen Blunt (who controversially disclosed it) he allegedly said that he was intent on imposing severe sentences on the leaders of Irish agitation so that they should die miserably in their prisons. The misery of dynamitards – infinitely worse than agitators – by this reckoning could only be to state and public advantage (see *Freeman's Journal*, 16 January 1888, 5g; 17 January, 4e–f; see also Alex Egremont, *The Cousins: The Friendship, Opinions and Activities of Wilfrid Scawen Blunt and George Wyndham*, London, Collins, 1977, p. 132).

67 Irish agitation for amnesty seems to have begun first in the spring of 1889 in John Daly's home town, Limerick. A meeting later that year, chaired by the High Sheriff of Limerick, protested at Daly's 'inhuman treatment' at Chatham. This referred to the belladonna poisoning incident (PRO HO 144/925/A46664/27).

revived. Backed by a wide range of nationalist opinion, branches were subsequently established in Ireland's main towns and cities, and in several places of Irish settlement in Britain.[68]

In a November 1892 article on the dynamitards (probably written by Sir Robert Anderson) it was noted that the one subject which united Irish-American nationalists and Irish nationalists in general was amnesty. There had been much jostling on how far to extend the term. The Parnellites had at first restricted it to dynamitards, but the clerical (majority) wing of nationalism had extended it to all convicts in penal servitude for conspiracies to murder during the Land War, including those Invincibles who had escaped hanging. The Parnellite faction had then adopted this programme, 'clamouring for an indiscriminate amnesty to all vindicators of the unwritten law'. This, the article tartly noted, was naturally to be expected from the Liberal government which the Irish nationalists had placed and continued to uphold in office. And there would of course be financial advantages to the politicians should the amnesty campaign succeed – 'liberal thank-offerings from the Clan na Gael'.[69]

But whether viewed as a unifying cause in post-Parnell nationalism or a fairly cynical ploy for the self-advancement of Irish politicians, the moral character of the dynamitards needed to be transformed or – at the very least – there had to be a shift in how they were portrayed. The nature and fact of their deeds was incontrovertible: no one could say that these were innocent men;[70] no one could alter the appalling means they had adopted to further their cause. Some degree of moral equivalence could be wrung from accusations that they had been ill-treated. The more serious the cruelty, the more easily the men's terrorist identity could be diluted and obscured. Carelessness of human life could be transferred to the British government; the dynamitards could become victims of age-old oppression and vindictiveness. Thus afflicted, they would surely not be embarrassing objects for a clemency campaign.

The dynamitards had been based in and had operated from the United States of America, and it was there that the first steps were taken by Irish-American

---

68 The London branch was established in March 1892, on the initiative of the IRB. A national association, coordinating branch activity followed in August 1894 (Ryan, *op. cit.*, pp. 173–4).

69 *The Times*, 8 November 1892, 8a. The article pointed out that Rossa and Devoy, who had promoted the dynamite attacks, had been amnestied by Gladstone, as had five of the seven trustees of the 'Skirmishing Fund'. Losmasney and Melody had returned to England as dynamiters, while Condon (of the Manchester rescue) had become President of the Washington branch of Clan na Gael and was an active supporter of the dynamite policy. Daly (one of those for whom mercy was now solicited) had been indicted in 1868 for administering the Fenian oath, but not proceeded against (8c).

70 In one or two cases – particularly that of Daly's associate Egan – it was argued that there had been a wrongful conviction (see below, p. 386). The intensity with which this was argued and the eagerness with which it was taken up indicates – independently of the strength of Egan's case – the underlying unease with which the dynamitards' guilt was contemplated. Should Egan not be guilty, that in some way made the guilt of the others easier to bear.

politicians and others who sought the Irish vote. In April 1887, on the occasion of her jubilee, New York Governor David Hill, and both Houses of the State Legislature petitioned Queen Victoria for Gallagher's amnesty. The *New York Times* was scathing. The evidence against Gallagher was clear. Were it not, and if new information existed, then the newspaper would itself say a word on his behalf. Without such evidence it had to be asked whether pardoning such men was likely to encourage or discourage others like them. Besides the petitioners, were Americans prepared to concede that blowing up hotels and steamships were 'political offences'? Vote-gathering was one of the principal objectives of the petition.[71] Five years later, when the State Department announced that it had instructed the American Embassy in London to look into Gallagher's case – despite past Republican indifference to the matter – the newspaper denounced the initiative as an utterly transparent move in the light of the imminent election and observed that 'it must fill sensible Irishmen with disgust'.[72]

This was all true, of course, but vote-gathering is an inevitable feature of democratic politics. The application of American pressures (as distinct from pro-forma representations) on Gallagher's behalf was in any case unlikely for two reasons. Relations between the two countries were excellent, both politically and commercially, and the process of transforming Gallagher from a justly convicted terrorist into a victim of British penal cruelty had not yet progressed sufficiently. That would happen, but until it did, non-Irish-American opinion was unmoved.

Irish politicians now felt able to take up amnesty. Their motives varied, but the way had been opened by the Chatham Visitors' Report and a shift in the Irish public mood. The stand-off between the Irish party and the British government continued while Lord Salisbury remained in office. Amnesty momentum, while not as great as it had been for the Fenians, nevertheless began to gather pace. In January 1892, a petition was circulated in Dungannon, where Thomas Clarke's family had originated, and where he had lived as a boy. This was signed by clergy of all denominations, as well as professional men and gentry, and was presented to the Home Secretary without result.[73] To lesser offenders, however, some mercy had been shown, and the previous year the Irish-American

---

71 *New York Times*, 27 April 1887, 4c.

72 Ibid., 1 November 1892, 4a–b. A few months before, the Embassy had helped to arrange a visit to Gallagher by T. St John Gaffney, on behalf of Gallagher's family and friends (PRO HO 144/A46664C/108).

73 Le Roux, *op. cit.*, pp. 49–50. On 5 November 1895, Maud Gonne submitted an appeal on behalf of Clarke and the others. Testimonials for Clarke confirmed his good conduct before emigrating to America (PRO HO 144/195/A46664C/220). Because of the political use she made of a visiting privilege in an interview in the Paris *Figaro* on 22 May 1895, Maud Gonne was barred from Portland Prison by the Home Secretary (ibid., /219; PRO HO 144/194/A46664C/100). Her involvement in the amnesty campaign was unlikely to prove helpful.

Thomas Callan, convicted of conspiracy to cause explosions, had been released on serving five years of his fifteen-year sentence.[74]

In late May 1891, four of the political prisoners at Portland – John Curtin, Henry Dalton, John Daly and James Egan – retained John Redmond as their legal adviser.[75] As leader of the Parnellite nine-member minority of the Irish party, Redmond was well placed to raise the case of these prisoners in Parliament, and after the 1892 election had every inducement to do so. Sympathy for the men was growing (albeit slowly) and politicians who promoted their cause would be expected to benefit, at least within nationalist politics. Following the split and Parnell's death, Redmond's only way forward was to assume Parnell's reputation for militancy and an uncompromising stand on national issues. By becoming the men's legal adviser, Redmond was entitled to see them at regular intervals, and might also be able to persuade the authorities to allow access to certain official papers touching on their condition.

Gladstone had returned to power in August 1892, and his Home Secretary, Herbert Asquith, granted an application from the London Irish Political Prisoners Amnesty Association to visit the treason-felony prisoners.[76] Three months later, as the first parliamentary session of the new government got under way, Redmond appealed for amnesty through the columns of the *Fortnightly Review*, repeating his call for an inquiry into the supposedly unsafe convictions of Daly and Egan. He emphasised the distinction between ordinary and political prisoners. Law-breakers, no matter their motive, had to pay the penalty. But since the essence of all criminality is intention, a distinction could be drawn on grounds of motive. The man whose offence came 'not from any selfish sordid unworthy, or depraved motive, but . . . to advance the cause of popular freedom or national right, no matter how culpable, dangerous or stupid his methods may be, he is, and must be, a political offender as distinguished from an ordinary criminal'. Redmond did not argue that political prisoners should not be punished, but the amount of punishment had to depend on the culpability and danger of their conduct.[77]

74 PRO HO 144/209/A48131/21–2. There had been respectful representations from American friends (supported by the US Department of State), deteriorating health, some doubt as to the extent of culpability, and good conduct while in prison.
75 PRO HO 144/925/A46664/75. At around this time it appears that rules on visitors were relaxed, allowing Dr Mark Ryan and John Crowe (both known to the police as Fenians) to visit John Daly. This provoked an inquiry from the Irish government and an instruction from Henry Matthews, the Home Secretary, to tighten up again (PRO HO 144/925/A46664/84: 13 April 1892).
76 PRO HO 144/194/A46664C/49. The Association's previous applications had been refused by the Conservative government (ibid., /45).
77 J. E. Redmond, 'A Plea for Amnesty', *Fortnightly Review*, 52, 212 (1 December 1892), p. 722.

In the previous year (July 1891) and as one of his last Commons' actions, Parnell had moved for a return of the treason-felony prisoners then in custody.[78] This had shown that, with the exception of James Egan, who had been sentenced to penal servitude for twenty years, the men had all received life sentences. Redmond pointed out that, contrary to popular belief, not a single one of these prisoners had been convicted of dynamite offences. Despite the government having access to the Explosive Substances Act of 1883[79] (which provided heavy penalties for unlawfully or suspiciously possessing or using dynamite), all had been prosecuted under the Treason Felony Act of 1848. That prosecution decision, Redmond contended, must have been based on the weakness of the dynamite evidence alone. But having chosen to try the men for treason felony the government could not now logically deprive them of whatever advantage they could reap from being convicted of 'an essentially and admittedly political crime'.[80]

In the case of Daly and Egan, Redmond argued that the state of public feeling had been such that they were denied a fair and impartial trial. Daly had been undefended and the victim of a police plot. In support of the latter, Redmond quoted the claims of Chief Constable Farndale of Birmingham, who had stated that the man who handed Daly the parcels of dynamite just before his arrest was an RIC agent (and therefore, of course, an agent provocateur). This grave accusation had been taken up with Home Secretary Henry Matthews by Alderman Henry Manton,[81] on behalf of several members of the Birmingham Watch Committee.[82] What would have happened, Redmond asked, had Farndale been called at the men's trial and testified that the explosives had been planted on Daly: 'does any sane man believe it would have been possible to obtain a conviction?'

---

78 See *Return of the Names and Number of Persons now Suffering Sentences of Penal Servitude in Ireland and England as a Consequence of Conviction for Treason Felony, showing (a) the Date of Conviction; (b) the Length of the Sentence; and (c) The Prison Where the Convict is Imprisoned,* PP, 1890–1 [387], LXIV, 725. The return did not include those sentenced for explosives offences. Thus there was no mention of Michael Harkins, who had been serving a sentence of fifteen years and had been released in August 1891 on health grounds (tuberculosis) (PRO HO 144/209/A48131C/2).

79 46 Vict., c.3.

80 Redmond, *op. cit.*, p. 723.

81 (1809–1903). A wealthy jeweller prominent in Birmingham philanthropy, temperance and public service. Mayor, 1861, magistrate, 1865. Had a particular interest in children's welfare (he was a lifelong Sunday School teacher), reformatories, prisons and policing. An active Liberal who supported Gladstone after the Home Rule split. Manton wrote and published a pamphlet on the Daly–Egan case (Henry Manton, JP, *Turning the Last Stone: Printed for the Purpose of Supplying the Mayor, Alderman, and Councillors of the City of Birmingham with Information for their Private Use,* Birmingham, Robert Birbeck & Sons, 1895). He forwarded this to the Home Secretary in February 1896 (PRO HO 144/193/A46664B/58).

82 The allegations caused a sensation: see *The Times,* 24 September 1890, 4b–c.

The evidence against Egan was even weaker. Explosives had been found not on his person, but buried in his back garden. Daly was at least guilty of this offence (and therefore, it might be argued, of the treason felony of which he had been accused) since at the men's trial, both before and after sentence, he had insisted that he had buried the explosives, and that Egan had known nothing of them. Indeed, while on what he believed was his deathbed (overdosed with belladonna) Daly had pleaded to see Egan so that 'as a dying man' he might ask forgiveness for the wrong he had done him. The case against Egan, it had been conceded in Parliament both by the Liberal Home Secretary Harcourt and the Conservative Matthews, was deserving of an early review, yet the man was 'still wearing his life out in Portland'.[83]

Gladstone's government had come to office and remained there by virtue of the support of the Irish Parliamentary Party, but Redmond's amnesty received an immediate rebuff from the new Home Secretary Herbert Asquith.[84] Notwithstanding Egan's early release, there was little sign of movement. The first intimation of the new government's disinclination to grant a general amnesty came within days of the opening of Parliament when Asquith stated that it was not his intention to intervene in the case of John Daly, Egan's co-defendant. Daly would first be considered for release when he had served twenty years of his sentence (which would mean 1904).[85]

In the Queen's Speech debate John Redmond reviewed the history of Irish political prisoners back to John Mitchel and again questioned the convictions of Egan and Daly. The dynamite conspiracy was dead, and was it not time to amnesty the men and move on?[86] In a confident and devastating reply, which

---

83 Redmond, *op. cit.*, pp. 725–32, *passim*.

84 The US government, which had also tested the new administration on the question of amnesty for Gallagher and Curtin, was similarly rebuffed. See PRO HO 144/116AA/A/26493/78: Under-Secretary at Foreign Office to US Charge d'Affaires, 7 November 1892. The reply was formal and dismissive: 'the Sec[retary] of State regrets that he has failed to discover any grounds which would justify him in interfering either with the sentence of Gallagher or of Curtin.' For examples of the petitions submitted to Congress on the men's behalf in 1892 see National Archives, Washington, DC: Committee on Foreign Affairs, 52nd Congress 1891–6, HR52a. H.7.2. These resolutions represented Gallagher and his companions as innocent men, denied a fair trial in England. In one petition from Westchester Co., New York, for example, Gallagher's trip to England was said to be for the purpose of 'prosecuting his medical studies, and to obtain rest and recreation'. Another accused the British government of securing Gallagher's conviction through the use of 'bogus solicitors'. Yet another asserted that were the men to be given a fair trial they would be set at liberty.

85 4 *Hansard*, VIII, col. 675; 7 February 1893. See also col. 943 *et seq.*; 9 February 1893.

86 Ibid., cols 1707–9; 17 February 1893. Redmond published his speech as a pamphlet: John E. Redmond, MP, *The Case for Amnesty*, Dublin, William J. Ally & Co, 1893. Comparisons were also drawn between the case of Daly and Egan and the Walsall anarchists who in March 1892 had been found guilty of explosives offences. Three men had been sentenced to ten years' penal servitude (PRO HO 144/242/A53582/20; for commital details see *The Times*, 8 January 1892, 4f; 9 January 7f). These sentences were much more lenient than those passed on Egan and Daly, J. J. Clancy pointed out in a Commons question on 29 August 1893 (4 *Hansard*, LXVI, col. 1357 (Clancy was the nationalist Member for Dublin Co. North).

gave a flavour of his mastery of the Commons at the time, Asquith rehearsed the men's crimes. Of Daly's guilt he said that he had no doubt whatsoever. He had been arrested with three bombs in his possession, and had refused to give any account of how he had come by them. The police searched his room and found documents confirming that he was a member of the IRB, and in the back garden had found a canister containing more such documents, cartridges and a bottle of nitroglycerine. At his trial Daly had volunteered the information that he had placed these items in the garden without Egan's knowledge. Egan had now been released because there was nothing in the evidence to connect him with the dynamite conspiracy. Asquith did not doubt his connection with the IRB or that he had committed treason, but having served eight and a half years, he considered he had been punished enough – 'and it is upon that ground, and that alone, that Egan has been let out'.[87]

Asquith hammered home the nature of terrorism and gave an unequivocal pledge to see the dynamitards properly and fully punished. Short of murder itself he could not conceive any offence more heinous than those of which they had been convicted. They had plotted for months and made machines to destroy life and property 'without any regard whatever to the innocence or guilt, the responsibility, or the absence of responsibility, of those who would be the victims of their proceedings'. He nailed his colours firmly to the mast: 'So long as I hold the position I do, so long as I am responsible for the exercise of the prerogative of mercy, there is not one of them who shall receive any different treatment, or whose sentence shall be any sooner interfered with, than of any other criminal now lying in Her Majesty's gaols.'[88] There was such contempt in Asquith's declaration, and such a degree of clarity in the pledge, that any hope of mercy seemed to be extinguished during his tenure at the Home Office. The Liberal government had been the best hope for amnesty, and with Gladstone's Home Rule Bill polarising opinion within his own party and hardening the Conservatives in their Unionism, the dynamitards looked set to serve a minimum of twenty years of their life sentences – and very possibly more.

British politics entered the rapids. Gladstone brought forward his second Home Rule Bill. In his eighty-fourth year and with an anxious eye on his own party, he fought it through the Commons, to see it go down in the Lords. The now openly Conservative House of Lords blocked other important pieces of his legislation, challenging his mandate to govern. A major constitutional battle loomed, and Gladstone briefly considered leading a liberal and democratic crusade. The

---

87 4 *Hansard*, VIII, cols 952–3; 9 February 1893. And by releasing Egan, the only man whose guilt was in question, Asquith bolted the door more securely on the others. Sections of the Conservative press were nevertheless scandalised by the release (see PRO HO 144/193/A46664B (no piece number)). Asquith had taken the decision to release Egan on 18 January 1893, leaving the timing to be decided (ibid., /55). The announcement was made on 2 February (4 *Hansard*, VIII, col. 248).

88 4 *Hansard*, VIII, col. 954; 9 February 1893.

mood of the country now seemed firmly imperialist and Unionist, and he would almost certainly have lost – but in the event the confrontation was postponed for sixteen years. Isolated from his colleagues, crippled by cataracts, even the smoke of the volcano drifted away, and on 3 March 1894, ending an unparalleled and majestic political career of some sixty-one years, Gladstone took his *nunc dimittis*.[89] As a final twist in the unhappy relations between them, Victoria did not seek his advice on a successor, and chose to send for Rosebery rather than Spencer, whom Gladstone preferred. Gladstonian Liberalism was eclipsed. The Liberal Party rank and file wanted Sir William Harcourt rather than Rosebery, while the country could see no point in Gladstone's Cabinet without Gladstone. After some fifteen months of weak government Rosebery resigned office on 22 June 1895. In the general election Salisbury returned to power with an overwhelming majority of 152.[90] Ireland, in all this, was a sideshow, and the prisoners a sideshow within that. Paradoxically, the relative obscurity of the issue, the complexion of the government and the size of its majority enabled the new Home Secretary, Sir Matthew White Ridley, to begin the process of releasing the dynamitards without political uproar.[91]

Increasing public concern about the physical and mental health of the prisoners induced Ridley to institute a medical inquiry in December 1895. This was conducted by Dr Henry Maudsley and Dr David Nicholson.[92] On giving a pledge of confidentiality Redmond was invited to read the resultant report. This showed that the prisoners were suffering from a variety of physical ailments. The doctors, it would appear, were more willing to admit to these, which might be as much the result of normal ageing processes, or prior conditions, as of the rigours of imprisonment. Henry Dalton, John Daly, Patrick Flanagan and Terence McDermott were all considered to be in a good mental and physical condition; Henry Burton, Timothy Featherstone and Thomas Gallagher showed symptoms

89 See Richard Shannon, *Gladstone: Heroic Minister 1865–1898* (London, Allen Lane, 1999, pp. 557–64) for an appropriately distant and ironic description of Gladstone's last bleak weeks in office.

90 In the general election 340 Conservatives and seventy-one Liberal Unionists were returned, against 177 Liberals and eighty-two Irish Nationalists. The majority now became generally known as 'Unionists', although both Conservative and Liberal sections retained separate party machinery (R. C. K. Ensor, *England 1870–1914*, Oxford, Oxford University Press, 1964, p. 221).

91 Ridley (1842–1904) was educated at Balliol College, Oxford; Fellow of All Souls. Conservative MP North Northumberland, 1868–85; Blackpool, 1886–1900. Parliamentary Under-Secretary at Home Office, 1878–80; Financial Secretary, Treasury, 1885–6. Home Secretary, 1895–1900. Fifth Baronet and large landowner.

92 Henry Maudsley (1835–1918) was one of the leading mental health experts of the time, with extensive clinical and academic experience. Published a number of major texts on psychology and mental illness. David Nicolson (1844–1932) had worked in several convict prisons before transferring to Broadmoor Criminal Lunatic Asylum in 1876. At the time of his report he was Superintendent of that establishment. Served on numerous departmental committees; medical adviser to Home Secretary in criminal mental cases.

of minor physical ill-health. 'Wilson' (Thomas Clarke) had signs of valvular disease and persistent indigestion, but this caused him less discomfort at Portland than at Chatham. In mental health, Thomas Devaney was 'naturally' somewhat weak, and Albert George Whitehead (Murphy) while not mentally strong, was not considered insane. Indeed, the doctors observed (in Redmond's paraphrase): 'He seems to have enough cunning in his disposition to make him feign insanity as he is reputed to have done.' (Daly was also said to have complained 'in exaggerated fashion' of a variety of ailments.) The most controversial finding concerned Gallagher, whose physical health was good, despite having lost thirty-five pounds. Gallagher (a doctor himself) stated that he had no physical ailments. As for his mental health, Maudsley and Nicolson were unequivocal: Gallagher was not insane. They observed (again Redmond's paraphrase) that 'His answers were quiet and rational & his demeanour tho' dejected & somewhat sullen – natural and composed. In our opinion his mental condition exhibits nothing more than the natural effects of imprisonment upon a man of his education and temperament.'[93]

Thomas Clarke, Gallagher's prison companion, gave a very different account, according to which Gallagher and other men had been insane for several years. He insisted that Duff, McCabe, Flanagan and Casey (all Glasgow Ribbonmen released earlier on the expiration of their shorter sentences) had been insane.[94] Murphy kept the other prisoners awake with his night-time ravings and on one occasion was caught by Clarke eating crushed glass. He attempted to bring Murphy's condition to the attention of John Redmond, but his letter was suppressed. He also raised it with the Roman Catholic chaplain in the confessional. The priest agreed that Murphy was insane but said he could do nothing about it because of possible complaints to his bishop. Not long after, Redmond visited Clarke, who passed on the information. As a result of this another medical

---

93 Gallagher was then forty-five years of age. A précis of medical reports on the men, July 1893 to December 1895 is at PRO HO 144/195/A46664D/30. The original report (23 December 1895) is at /4; Redmond's notes (which are close and faithful) are at NLI: Redmond Papers: Ms. 15,222 (dated May 1895 by Redmond, but from internal evidence the notes seem to have been made on 30 March 1896, or shortly thereafter). There had been several reports on the men's health over the years. Five years before Redmond was allowed to look at the notes of Dr George Walker, the Chatham medical officer who had reported Gallagher to be in a poor physical state. Walker believed Gallagher to be feigning insanity (religious monomania) but the strain of so doing had reduced him mentally. Since Gallagher was deteriorating Walker asked for a second opinion which 'would relieve me of a great load of responsibility and anxiety'. The Convict Directorate rejected this request (PRO HO 144/116/A26493/66: Walker to Directorate, 4 February 1890; Gover to Directorate, 17 February 1890).

94 In October 1892, the assistant surgeon at Portland had found Duff to be insane or feigning insanity. He rejected reports which had appeared in the newspapers suggesting that McCann (aged 67) had completely broken down, that Dalton was suffering from rheumatism, and that J. G. Gilbert had received neither visit nor letter since his incarceration (PRO HO 144/194/A46664C/59).

commission examined the men, and the outcome on this occasion was their release on medical grounds.[95]

We have seen that the suspicion of malingering was endemic in the convict medical service, and the authorities were convinced that Gallagher (who seems to have been the first to become insane) was shamming. Being a medical man, one of the dynamitard leaders, and resourceful and determined, this may not have been an unreasonable suspicion.[96] There ensued what the authorities may have decided was a battle of wills, but which seems rather to have been the repeated punishment of the mentally ill. Certainly once a medical opinion had been given that the men were feigning insanity, their breaches of the rules would be taken as deliberate and part of an aggravated campaign of deception, and would be punished accordingly.

The account given by the medical commission which reported in 1890 was unequivocal. Gallagher commenced his campaign of pretended insanity in September 1887, and in the succeeding thirty months incurred sixteen punishments for refusing labour and improper language. For a four-month period over the autumn and winter of 1888 to 1889 he vomited his food. The commissioners considered this to be a deliberate attempt to damage his own health. He was taken into the infirmary and the vomiting stopped, but recommenced when he

---

95 Clarke, *op. cit.*, pp. 13–18. The March 1890 transcripts of the examinations of some of these men by the Chatham Visitors give several clear indications of insanity. Whitehead (alias Murphy) told the Visitors that 'mischievous beings' had made influential people on the outside exert their influence to prolong his confinement. He also complained that his brother was writing 'unlawful' and 'insolent' letters to the prison authorities under the direction of these enemies. As to prison itself, however, he made no complaint: 'They are treating me as well as the laws will allow them' (*Chatham Visitors' Report*, Minutes of Evidence, qq. 53–4, p. 3). Patrick Flannagan told the Visitors: 'I have power to show great signs and wonders by shutting the organs of my body, that is quite beyond your comprehension . . . I did it last time the dockyard clock was changed, at the hour of 8 o'clock; there were certain changes made in the dockyard clock through it' (ibid., qq. 179–82, p. 7). John Duff was convinced that there was a conspiracy among the prison staff to kill him, and that 108 different kinds of drugs including caustic acid and vitriol had been put in his food – 'In every article of food every day'. As a result, half of his stomach had been burnt away. He believed that all the prisoners had been drugged and that the system had been in operation for twenty-one years. These complaints caused the Chairman of the Visitors, Judge W. L. Selfe, to declare 'we are not here to have our time wasted with such preposterous nonsense as you are now talking' (ibid., qq. 611–75, pp. 17–18). The evidence of some of the Glasgow Ribbonmen (James McCullough, Peter Callaghan and James Gilbert, for example) suggests that besides being minimally educated, they may also have been slow-witted (ibid., pp. 10–17, *passim.*).

96 It is difficult to know whether the case of the Fenian leader Ricard Burke, who was diagnosed as insane while in prison and removed to Woking Invalid Prison, but who on his release claimed a successful imposture, was a factor in the judgement in Gallagher's case. Certainly there was malingering. John Daly told the Chatham Visitors that he had seen a man in the prison infirmary whom he thought was shamming insanity. A prison officer struck him violently on both sides of the face 'and this poor fellow in order to preserve the character of a lunatic not saying a word about it' (*op. cit.*, Minutes of Evidence, qq. 1557–9, p. 46).

was discharged. The prison medical officer, Dr Blandford, considered him to be 'a dangerous man, who will require very careful watching and management'.[97]

Release and transfiguration

With the Queen's Diamond Jubilee in the offing, amnesty was urged several times during the 1896 parliamentary session. The decision to release four men on grounds of their ill-health was made in the summer of 1896,[98] and was announced as a possibility in the Commons on 31 July, and as a definite decision on 13 August.[99] The Tories, hot against any such step while in opposition, found it advantageous in office. The men began to be freed from mid-August onwards. Thomas Devaney (sentenced in December 1883 for his part in the Tradeston gasworks explosion) was released on 18 August 1896, and immediately travelled to Glasgow where, as required, he reported to the police. Such had been the totality of his removal from the world that he expressed great surprise on being told of Parnell's death five years previously.[100]

In order to avoid sympathetic demonstrations, the four were released at irregular intervals, with the details being kept secret (even from relatives) until the last minute.[101] They were escorted to the train and, where necessary, were met by the police at rail junctions, and passed on. But with most of the prisoners now well known in nationalist circles because of amnesty appeals, it was unlikely that the releases would pass as quietly as the Home Office desired.

---

97 Cit. Clarke, op. cit., p. 20.

98 PRO HO 144/195/A46664D/10. Daly had first petitioned for release on grounds of ill-health, and medical mishandling of his case, in January 1892 (PRO HO 144/925/A46664/82). The petition was rejected. As noted, a number of men had by this time served their sentences and been released. This group comprised mainly the Ribbonmen recruited by Rossa, convicted as accessories in the Glasgow explosions and sentenced to seven years each. In 1893 James Francis Egan had been released in partial amnesty. He had been sentenced to twenty years' penal servitude, and even with maximum remission could not have expected to complete this sentence until 1900.

99 4 Hansard, XLIII, col. 1288; 31 July 1896; XLIV, col. 752; 13 August 1896. The announcement was worded to indicate that appeals for amnesty had not been a consideration. Because of the Portland medical officer's concern a medical panel had been appointed to review the treason-felony men. On receiving the panel's report, Sir Matthew Ridley told the Commons, 'I have felt it my duty, as I should in all similar cases, to advise the release on licence, on grounds of ill-health of four of the prisoners – viz. Daly, Devaney, Gallager and Whitehead.' Ridley had in fact been presented with the medical recommendations at a most opportune time, since on 31 July he had announced that he was granting first-class misdemeanant status to the Transvaal Raiders (a decision his officials considered ultra vires). This was received with Tory cheers, and provided the Irish with a springboard for renewed amnesty pleas for the dynamitards (4 Hansard, XLIII, col. 1269).

100 Cork Examiner, 19 August 1896, 5b. 'Parnell dead! Surely you are not in earnest' (ibid., 20 August 1896, 5e).

101 PRO HO 144/195/A46664D/10. The Home Secretary had directed 'it must be done gradually, and not too immediately'.

In July 1895, John Daly had been returned as MP for Limerick City (following the tactic successfully used in the 1869 Rossa election in Tipperary) even though his election was bound to be declared invalid.[102] Redmond had several times spoken in the Commons about Daly, distinguishing him from the other prisoners and insisting on the unfairness of his conviction. Because the case had been so well ventilated, the doubts which Redmond had attached to his conviction, and because he was free from the direct moral opprobrium of terrorism, Daly's was an obvious case for sympathetic attention. A Commons announcement had been made of his impending release on 13 August, but it took several days for arrangements to be made.[103] As on several past occasions in such cases, it was convenient that the parliamentary session ended the day after the announcement was made. Freed from Portland on the afternoon of 20 August 1896, Daly was taken away by his brother and J. P. Coughlan (of the London branch of the Amnesty Association). He remained strong in his political beliefs and had refused the suit of flannel underwear which the prison provided (his outer clothes were brought to the prison by his brother). On being handed his ticket of leave Daly was also given his discharge gratuity. He at first also refused this, since to accept would suggest that he acknowledged the justice of his sentence. But when told that continued refusal would mean suspension of his release, he gave way.[104]

Because his release was on a ticket of leave, and the authorities (it would seem) had warned him that his statements could affect the fate of imprisoned comrades, Daly at this point refused to discuss prison conditions with reporters, nor would he comment on the health of the others.[105] He apparently confirmed that Gallagher had become insane and was broken in health, the reporter covering this statement with the observation that this was a well-known fact.

102 Daly was returned on 13 July; the election was declared void in September 1895 (PRO HO 144/925/A45554/114–21).

103 The four men were informed on 1 August 1896 of their release on medical grounds, and were asked what arrangements they wished to make with their friends (Evelyn Ruggles-Brise to Troup, 7 August 1896: PRO HO 144/195/A46664D/11). See also 4 Hansard, XLIV, col. 752; 13 August 1896.

104 This was certainly a bluff on the part of the prison governor. The most detailed (but highly partisan) account of Daly's release was given by a special correspondent of the Cork Examiner (evidently a former acquaintance of Daly): 21 August 1896, 5f–g.

105 'I have left six men behind me in Portland Prison who have been comrades for close on 13 years. I must not forget them, and as I understand it is the intention of the government to advise Her Majesty to finish the sixtieth year of her reign by an act of clemency to the Irish political prisoners, I cannot say anything that would in any way tend to induce the Government to withdraw from that position' (ibid., 5g). This sounds implausibly formal, and was probably the reporter's summary of what Daly said. Daly later fully regained his political confidence and fire, and made a series of speeches which the Irish government considered to breach the conditions of his ticket of leave (which was to last for the rest of his life). The Home Office declined to act in the matter (PRO HO 144/925/A46664/146–50).

The moral transformation of the dynamitards through their suffering and supposed British brutality is evident in various of the phrases used in the account of Daly's release. He was described as 'much worn and haggard' and had been in the prison infirmary for some considerable time, but, the report continued, 'There is no sign that 13 years of British convict discipline has in any way daunted or broken the spirit of this victim of English misrule'. His hair was streaked with grey and he seemed 'prematurely enfeebled'; while his half-grown beard looked ill-kempt, but 'there is a fire in his eye and a spirit in his speech that might become the political enthusiast who has yet to learn what suffering is'.[106] This was a noble spirit re-entering the world from which he had been tyrannously and unjustly removed for so long: not a mention of dynamite and its uses, and brutality and callousness the sole property of the British government.

The releases of Albert Whitehead (alias John Murphy) and Thomas Gallagher, which also took place during the parliamentary recess, completed the dynamitards' moral transformation. Murphy had been convicted in May 1883, together with Thomas Clarke, and had served thirteen years. From the moment he was released, it was clear that he was in a state of complete mental collapse, barely able to talk and largely indifferent to his surroundings, except for a fear that he would be returned to prison. On the evening that he reached his mother's home, Murphy vanished and wandered at large for a fortnight before being recovered, still mentally bereft. Three weeks after his release from Portland he was dispatched to the United States of America in the custody of his brother, with a grant of $500 provided by the Cork Amnesty Association.[107]

Further concern and indignation was caused by Gallagher's condition, which was widely reported in the English and Irish newspapers. Having no immediate relatives in Ireland, he returned forthwith to the United States of America,

---

106 *Cork Examiner*, 21 August 1896, 5f and g, *passim*. In extreme nationalist circles there was possibly some lingering stigma attached to Egan and Daly: they had not descended completely into insanity like Murphy and Gallagher, but had merely broken down. Writing years after his release Tom Clarke apparently addressed this. 'I want no man's opinion of either Daly or Egan. The ordeal they went through under my eyes for years is a test of manhood as severe and searching as mortal man could be subject to, and I know in what spirit they met it and went through it' (Clarke, *op. cit.*, p. 6).

107 *Cork Examiner*, 8 September 1896, 6g. On the search for Murphy – a sensation which further stimulated indignation about his condition and ill-treatment – see *Cork Examiner*, 4 September 1896, 5c, and 5 September 1896, 5b; 8 September 1896, 4f. During the fortnight of Murphy's disappearance the newspaper carried a daily bulletin on the search for him. Murphy also took to wandering when he arrived in the United States of America, and was convinced that spies were poisoning his food (Pinkerton Agency Report, via British Consul, New York, 6 January 1897: PRO HO 144/195/A46664D/23A). Pinkerton's (instructed by the British Consulate) managed to interview Murphy at the Long Island Asylum, Amityville, on 5 January 1897. The report made it clear that he was unquestionably insane.

where his insanity was confirmed by a medical panel.[108] The Home Office was sufficiently uneasy about his condition as to fear suicide. It was decided to place him under the supervision of an attendant on release, notwithstanding the implication that would be drawn that his health had been destroyed.[109] Like Murphy, Gallagher suffered from delusions in connection with his imprison-ment, and for hours on end imagined himself to be in prison, and his friends to be warders. At first the doctors who examined him in America thought it possible Gallagher would recover, with the periods of delusion becoming less frequent and shorter in duration. In time, however, it became evident that no recovery was possible, and he was confined to a private insane asylum where he died twenty-nine years later.[110] The expenses were met from Clan and Amnesty Association funds, whose various organisations felt sympathy and obligation towards the released men, but also saw them as aids in internal as well as external struggles.[111]

The discharge of the four men in such a poor state immediately cast great doubt upon the value of the repeated assurances of the Convict Service and the Home Office; it also raised questions about the severity of penal servitude and the ill-treatment of Irish political offenders. A number of Unionist politicians were sceptical about the men's supposed ill-health and seemed to suggest that

108 Until the last the Portland medical officer gave an optimistic report on Gallagher, whom he considered to be 'quite sensible, and coherent . . . none of his old despondent symptoms present' (Report, 26 August 1896: PRO HO 144/195/A46664D/14). Outside doctors had a very different view. Dr Arthur Ferris pronounced Gallagher incurable. His condition was 'worse than death', and his companion, Whitehead (Murphy) was also demented. 'No one who sees Gallagher two or three times could for a moment doubt the reality of his insanity. To mistake his acts for shamming is inexplicable' (cit. Clarke, op. cit., pp. 20–1). The British Consulate in New York obtained sight of a medical report which confirmed that Gallagher was suffering from chronic mania manifest in outbursts of temper and violent assaults: 'He also shows extreme cunning. The form of insanity has a religious tendency, he impersonates a Priest, carrying a string of beads and a Bible. His case is considered hopeless' (Percy Sanderson to the Marquis of Salisbury, 21 January 1897, marked 'Confidential': PRO HO 144/195/A46664D/25).

109 Troup to Sir Matthew White Ridley, 21 August 1896: PRO HO 144/195/A46664D/10.

110 Dr Coomb's Sanatorium, Flushing, Long Island. For comments on the state of Gallagher on arrival in New York see Daily Chronicle, 7 September 1896, 4e and g. Eighteen months later William Redmond in a Commons speech confirmed the insanity of Gallagher and Whitehead (Murphy), and reported that one of them (he did not say which but it was prob-ably Whitehead) had broken out of the asylum and vanished (4 Hansard, LIII, cols 439–40; 11 February 1898).

111 NLI: Devoy Papers: Ms. 18,065 (13). Devoy agreed that Gallagher and Murphy were insane and could not be produced at meetings. Daly, though physically debilitated could address meetings. He was, wrote Devoy, 'a man whose gift of eloquence and personal popularity fit him to play a great part in the final settlement of the troubles which have for so many years divided Irish-Nationalists in America'. The Devoy faction was anxious to keep hold of Daly, and voted $5000 for the benefit of the prisoners. There was a deal of faction-fighting among the Fenian groups over the issue (ibid. (14), undated memorandum).

it was connected with some kind of arrangement between Redmond and the government. Redmond and his supporters lent some credence to this with the suggestion that they had secured the releases, when the more extreme nationalists had been unable to make any headway with their amnesty campaign.[112]

All speculation was swept aside, however, in a widespread press agreement that the men were not malingering, and in expressions of concern about the effect of lengthy terms of penal servitude. *The Times*, sceptical about the releases, demanded further information.[113] From most of the Irish newspapers there was forthright condemnation, the *Cork Examiner* speaking for many nationalists when it observed that 'The condition of those prisoners on their liberation is nothing short of a foul disgrace to the prison system and to the officials high and low by whose directions or with whose cognisance the destruction of mind and body was daily carried on.'[114] Drawing the lesson for convicts in general, the Liberal *Daily Chronicle* asked 'how many poor demented creatures are still in confinement' and complained that every time the newspaper had raised the matter of prison insanity it had been assured that the rate was no higher than in the general population. 'The condition of Dr Gallagher and his companions,' the *Chronicle* continued, 'is a sufficient comment on official assurances. It ought to rouse public opinion to demand the reform of an administration which spares the lives of offenders only to inflict on them this horrible and lingering penalty.'[115]

Radical and progressive circles in England also voiced their disquiet on a theme which had been on the reform agenda for some twenty years – the connections between Du Cane's iron-clad system of prison discipline and the incidence of insanity. The *Progressive Review* carried a well-argued essay from Bernard Molloy, MP, criticising Home Secretary Sir Matthew Ridley and (for his retrospective defence of prison discipline) Herbert Asquith. The latter remained emphatic in his views. Any suggestion that the Irish political offenders had been exposed to exceptionally rigorous treatment while in prison was utterly unfounded. Using blue books, Molloy showed that Portland Prison (from which Gallagher and Murphy had been released), with a slightly lower population than Dartmoor, had a rate of punishment some 50 per cent greater in 1894 and nearly two-fifths more in 1895: Portland's flogging, handcuffing and

---

112 *Cork Examiner*, 27 August 1896, 4f.
113 *The Times*, 7 September, 7f; 8 September, 7b–c. Of the men's insanity the newspaper observed 'It is surprising . . . that those conditions should be found to exist, to the satisfaction of the medical authorities, in the case of four of the dynamitards, precisely at the close of the last Session of Parliament' (7c).
114 5 September 1896, 5b.
115 *Daily Chronicle*, 7 September 1896, 4e. See also the extensive interview with Daly (then in Paris) published on 12 September under such headings as 'Portland A Living Tomb' and 'How Convict Life Kills' (3c–e).

manacling ran at twice Dartmoor's rate, as did dietary punishments in 1895.[116] The lunacy rates in the general population over fifteen years were twelve per 10,000, but in prisons it was 332 in 1896.[117] Although this comparison was open to many objections – not least that since 1878 when central government took over local prisons the magistrates had been wont to save on local expenditure by committing lunatics to the gaols – the disparity was of such magnitude as to suggest that prison discipline promoted insanity.[118] Molloy's essay, for all the questions that might be raised about its statistical analysis, nevertheless effectively presented some very troubling questions about the severity and ill-effects of prison discipline.

For the nationalist press the state of the four released men, Gallagher and Murphy in particular, lent great urgency to the plight of those who remained in prison. Any system which had reduced men to such a state, the *Cork Examiner* observed, was condemned before civilisation and humanity: 'It is a short but black and dismal record, reflecting foul disgrace on the men and the system responsible for such results.' The newspaper went on to hope that in the cases of the other prisoners 'the clemency of the Crown will not be withheld until they have been reduced to the same state as Murphy and Gallagher'.[119]

Little was said in those fulminations about John Daly, who may well have 'worked his ticket'.[120] Certainly his health returned with sufficient speed and to such a degree that within weeks he was able to undertake a lecture-tour in the United States of America under the auspices of the Clan-directed Irish Political Prisoners Fund Association.[121] A careful tone was struck. There were no grounds for triumphalism, and care was taken to avoid it. While there were no revolutionary threats such as the released Fenians had made, strong language was used on the issue of the remaining prisoners. At a meeting in Chicago in March 1898 the circumstances of Daly's conviction were rehearsed. It had been 'on evidence since admitted by a prominent English official to have

---

116 Bernard C. Molloy, MP, 'Insanity in Prisons', *Progressive Review*, 1, 2 (November 1896), p. 155. For the Home Office and Convict Service response see PRO HO 144/195/A46664D/21. Troup (Permanent-Under-Secretary) minuted 'The article is full of fallacies but may produce all the more effect on that account'.

117 Molloy, *op. cit.*, p. 160.

118 The connection was, however, overstated by penal reformers. See my *English Local Prisons 1860–1900*, London, Routledge, 1995, p. 644.

119 *Cork Examiner*, 27 August 1896, 4f. See also *Freeman's Journal*, 29 August 1896, 5i; 31 August, 4h ('Will the remaining prisoners be kept until they are hopelessly wrecked in constitution or mind?').

120 Since Daly had been an attendant in a Roman Catholic asylum at Burgess Hill, Sussex for two years prior to his arrest at Birkenhead he was familiar with the symptoms of physical and mental ill-health. He was undoubtedly a resourceful and cunning conspirator, well able to use this expertise.

121 An extensive file of press-cuttings of Daly's American lectures and interviews was compiled by the Home Office (PRO HO 144/195/A46664C/294A).

been an infamous fabrication'. Daly had undergone 'twelve and a half years of awful torture without flinching' and had been offered his freedom if he agreed to betray Parnell. His release had not been an act of clemency but a desire 'to relieve the government of the odium of having him die from the effects of ill-treatment'.[122] Again there was no mention of dynamite.

Dynamite again

Daly's and others like it were vigorous appeals for clemency, as well as a contribution to the dynamitards' book of amnesiac self-justification. These were not, however, attempts to confront the government. Indeed, through incapacity, discretion or fear for those who remained behind, the four who had been released, and their supporters and minders, had not sought to embarrass, beyond the expected calls for the completion of amnesty. The process of lobbying and pressurising was, however, brought to an abrupt stop with the discovery of yet another dynamite plot. This whole affair remains wrapped in layers of uncertainty and mystery, but appears to have been constructed in equal parts of adventurism on the part of particularly inept but generously funded Irish-American extremists, and penetration, inducement and the use of an agent provocateur by British intelligence.

The long-time enemy of Fenianism (and hardly less bitter opponent of Gladstone's Irish policy), Sir Robert Anderson, was probably involved in this last splutter of dynamitardism. In his 1906 memoirs Anderson insisted that the normal methods of law enforcement were inadequate to deal with terrorism and insurgency conspiracies. Legal procedures required everything to be done openly and above board. This was appropriate for crimes of the usual kind but not for Irish political offences: 'For a mine can be reached only by a counter-mine.'[123] This is close to an admission of entrapment or what was sometimes referred to in police language as 'allowing crime to mature'.

---

122 NLI: Devoy Papers: Ms. 18,065(i). John Daly continued to enjoy good health until 1911, when he became partially paralysed: this may have been a result of the syphilis from which he had suffered since 1878. He died in 1916. He had returned to his native Limerick, where with capital from the amnesty and aid funds he opened a bakery. Between 1899 and 1901 he was three-time elected Mayor of Limerick. Daly remained active in IRB affairs, though more as a senior figure than in day-to-day activities. Thomas Clarke married Daly's niece Kathleen, and his nephew Edward Daly was shot for his part in the 1916 Easter rising. A sympathetic chronicler of the Daly family, writing in times more innocent than our own (which have seen several miraculous recoveries follow releases on medical grounds) noted 'Released to die, he astonished the medical practitioners by seemingly regaining his normal health' (Dan Mulcahy, 'Life and Death of Commandant Edward Daly', The Kerryman, Limerick's Fighting Story, Tralee, The Kerryman, n.d. (?1947), p. 18).

123 Sir Robert Anderson, Sidelights on the Home Rule Movement, London, John Murray, 1906, p. 128.

In 1896 Anderson and his colleagues learned (possibly through an informer) that another dynamite expedition had been dispatched from New York.[124] Sensationally this group was led by Patrick J. Tynan, the 'No. 1' or leader of the Invincibles. Tynan had put together, instructed and funded the group which had slashed Burke and Cavendish to death in the Phoenix Park fourteen years before. He had subsequently escaped to the United States of America. Detectives followed the men from the moment they embarked in New York. It is uncertain to what extent Anderson's agent encouraged the party to proceed to Europe, whence one of the four, Edward Bell (alias Ivory), was further lured to Britain and arrest. Tynan and his confederates prudently remained in Belgium, The Netherlands and France, where they too were arrested. Bell was charged with Explosives' Act offences, and Anderson had to disclose to the Home Secretary the means by which he had been captured. Ridley did not think it proper to proceed with the prosecution. Anderson pressed the matter and the dispute was put to the Prime Minister, Lord Salisbury, who decided in Anderson's favour. The case went to the Old Bailey, but according to Anderson, the Law Officers had come to know that what he derided as 'the prize-ring rules' had been violated. On the second day of the trial the Solicitor-General announced that the prosecution would be withdrawn – to Anderson's great fury, since he had in the meantime negotiated a plea-bargain with Bell.[125] The other conspirators had been alerted to the fact of a traitor in their ranks and returned to the United States of America. Alarmed and vexed by allegations (doubtless inspired by Anderson) that the Irish dynamitards in France were acting in concert with

---

124 The *Nation* (Washington) had another explanation for the discovery but it was almost certainly incorrect. Tynan and his colleagues, the journal asserted, had been drinking heavily, and had explained their plans at each hotel at which they stopped 'when they were "full" – and they were generally "full", their expenditure on alcoholic drinks in one place being not less than $10 per day' (*Nation*, 24 September 1896, pp. 225–6).

125 Anderson, *op. cit.*, pp. 129–30. It is interesting to contrast Anderson's account with an equally vitriolic and solipsistic (but rather more breathless) version of events from Maud Gonne, then active in the Amnesty Association. She detected the hand of the British Secret Service immediately Bell was arrested and Tynan and the others were detained, and went to London where she raised funds and retained the distinguished lawyer Charles Russell (who had exposed the Pigott forgeries). The Irish barrister J. F. Taylor was briefed for Bell and asked for the notebook of one of the police witnesses, covering interviews he had conducted in Belgium: the judge so ordered. According to this account it was the Crown's reluctance to produce these notebooks that led to the withdrawal of the charge the following day (Maud Gonne MacBride, *A Servant of the Queen Reminiscences*, London, Gollancz, 1938, pp. 179–87). For more detail on the affair see William O'Brien and Desmond Ryan (eds), *Devoy's Post Bag, op. cit.*, Vol. 2, pp. 342–6). The *Pall Mall Gazette* which had initially trumpeted the success of the police was now indignant: 'The detection of crime . . . requires agents more effective than elderly officials who proceed by rule of thumb, and a staff recruited from the police force with every atom of initiative drilled out of it. Scotland Yard wants overhauling, and the collapse of the Bell case has given the Home Secretary an opportunity which he ought not to neglect' (21 January 1897, leader: 'Meddle and Muddle', 1a–b; see also 7c).

nihilists or anarchists to assassinate the Tsar, the French authorities took their own action. Two men were arrested in The Netherlands and Tynan was held in France. A fully equipped bomb-making laboratory was found at Antwerp.[126]

This was great cloak-and-dagger copy. Dynamite plots returned to the headlines at a most inopportune time for amnesty. A grand jury indictment had been preferred against Tynan in 1882 for his alleged part in the murder of Burke and Cavendish, and the British authorities sought his extradition to pursue this charge. This revived memories and emotions connected with one of the most brutal episodes in Irish revolutionary activities, and certainly hardened opinion towards the dynamitards – both those in prison and those who had been recently caught. The *Pall Mall Gazette* carried a two-column spread (including a sketch of Tynan) when it broke the news of the arrests.[127] The *Globe* in a leader headed 'Exchange no Robbery' mused on the curious coincidence that while 'strictly on medical grounds' Whitehead, Gallagher, Daly and Devaney had been released, 'four other gentleman of the same kidney' – Tynan, Kearney, Haines and Bell – had been arrested. The article gloated on the arrests and was quite confident that Kearney (who had been involved in the Tradeston gasworks explosion) and Haines would be extradited from The Netherlands ('however much our Dutch friends may differ from us in the matter of the Transvaal, their worst enemies would not suggest that they have any sympathy with dynamite outrage') and Tynan from France.[128] One might discount the knockabout tone of the *Globe's* leader, but there could be no doubt at all that it was correct in pointing to the achievement of the police and secret service in arranging, almost simultaneously, four arrests in three different countries. Any dynamite general receiving this news had to know that his organisation was totally and irremediably sold, bought and wrapped for delivery. This was the final foray of dynamite terrorism.

The *Daily Chronicle* sympathised with the Home Secretary's predicament in facing a new dynamite plot so close to his release of Daly, Gallagher, Whitehead (Murphy) and Devaney, and wondered if this were not the familiar reaction of the physical force party to any English concessions. But of the conspirators themselves it was dismissive. They were 'four farcically incompetent persons, provided with very large sums of money, bombs, incriminating correspondence, and every possibility of detection' and they had been 'snapped up by justice like a waterfly by a trout'.[129]

---

126 *The Times*, 15 September 1896, 7e–f; *Freeman's Journal*, 15 September 1896, 5b–h.
127 14 September 1896, 7a–b.
128 *Globe*, 15 September 1896, 4b. The newspaper also provided a round-up of the comments of the other leading dailies on the discovery of the plot. The *Daily Chronicle* devoted many columns to the plot, providing correspondents' reports from the several cities involved – New York, London, Glasgow, Rotterdam, Antwerp, Paris, Brussels and Boulogne. This was one of the newspaper sensations of the year (15 September 1896, 5g and 6a–d).
129 *Daily Chronicle*, 15 September 1896, 4d.

An alliance between anarchism, nihilism and Fenianism seemed unlikely, although the *Pall Mall Gazette* (now militantly Unionist) gave it some credence, as did some of the other dailies. The Tsar, who was about to undertake a state visit to France, would afterwards travel to England to visit the Queen. The most general reading of the plot was that Belgium had been chosen to manufacture the dynamite because of the difficulties of secretly obtaining the chemicals in Britain, or smuggling them from the United States of America. The Antwerp dynamite, it was surmised, would be used to attack the Tsar during his visit to England (or Scotland) as well as other targets, thus satisfying both the American backers of the scheme and the anarchists who had also supposedly given assistance.[130] Irish nationalist commentators, fully aware of Anderson's Unionist views, were inclined to see a connection between the arrests and the political needs of the Unionist Party.[131] This was too devious a connection, and the timing too difficult to manage, even for a man of Anderson's conspiratorial experience. Certainly government showed no inclination (even had it been able) to interfere with the discharge of Edward Bell's namesake, Joseph Bell, who was released on the day that the dynamite plot news broke, having served fourteen years of a twenty-year sentence for his 1882 dynamite offence.[132]

For the dynamitards remaining in prison, and the Amnesty Association which sought to free them, the Tynan-led expedition was a disaster. The Great Britain Amnesty Association spokesman put the best possible face on it. With the exception of Tynan he discounted any connection with any Irish political organisation: the Invincible accusations against the men were a result of the authorities' over-zealousness. Before the discovery of the plot they had hoped for the completion of the amnesty process within a few months, but he ruefully agreed that amnesty had now come to a halt.[133]

The lesser risk

Feelings about the prisoners nevertheless continued to be affected by the state of Gallagher and Murphy on their release, and the frequently repeated claims that the six remaining imprisoned dynamitards were ineluctably being reduced to the same mental and physical state by Du Cane's draconian convict system and superadded abuse. The various appeals for the men's release now uniformly represented them as victims. This transformation was of course easiest in the United States of America, remote from the bombings and all associated memories,

---

130 *Pall Mall Gazette*, 15 September 1896, 1a–b, 2a–b, 7a–b, 8a; 16 September, 8a–c; 17 September, 7a–c.
131 *Freeman's Journal*, 16 September 1896, 4e–f.
132 Joseph Bell was convicted in 1882 at Carlisle for damaging a building with explosives with intent to murder. He had earned maximum remission, and government would have found it difficult to prevent his release – though it might have delayed it for a time.
133 *The Daily Chronicle*, 15 September 1896, 6d.

and where popular politics required an unremitting canvass for Irish-American votes by politicians of many shades and all levels. Only three months after the Tynan expedition had been uncovered, a mass meeting was held in Boston, addressed by James Egan. There were twelve Irish political prisoners still in chains in English dungeons, four of whom were insane, Egan told his audience. The Amnesty Association expected to secure their release within six months, but in the meantime their families needed assistance, and when the men were released they would need support, since 'some are physical wrecks and others insane from prolonged prison life and its attendant severity and persecutions'. Egan urged subscriptions for 'these patriot sons of Ireland and their families, who represent the living, unselfish and self-sacrificing spirit of Ireland today'.[134]

Nor was windy rhetoric confined to former dynamitards. Two months later, John Redmond, showing a preference for a warmer style of oratory once the Atlantic had been crossed, claimed that English convict prisons held six Irish political offenders who had suffered for thirteen years 'all the horrors of the English penal servitude system as common malefactors'. Their crime was 'trying to save their country from that which was sucking out its life blood and destroying its people'. Over the previous five years he had visited the men every month or two. No one was left other than subordinates 'in the alleged conspiracy'. By way of illustrating how government had previously got it wrong, he recalled his interview with Asquith to plead for the release of Gallagher and Whitehead, whom Redmond knew to be insane: 'He [Asquith] laughed and said "I know better, they are shamming". Well after torturing these unfortunate fellow-creatures of ours for 4 or 5 years, at last they have admitted their insanity and released them.' From his personal knowledge two of the five men remaining in Portland (one man had been removed to an asylum) were insane, 'yet they are grinding out their poor lives within these prison walls'. Two more were broken in physical health and he daily expected that one or the other 'has dropped down dead in his prison cell'.[135]

A long resolution was then adopted, suitably encrusted with 'whereases' and 'resolveds' urging the United States of America to press for speedy releases. Britain should follow President Kruger's generous clemency towards the British subjects taken in arms against his government (a reference to the Transvaal Raiders) – even though their summary execution would have been sanctioned by international law. Finally, there was the often-cited example of the American

---

134 *Daily Item* (Boston), 17 December 1896: Irish-American Historical Society (New York), O'Callaghan Clippings, ff. 16–17.
135 NLI: Devoy Papers: Ms. 18,060 (unfoliated). The dynamitards, Redmond told his audience, were political offenders 'whose crime in the eyes of England is this – that by methods which probably most of us disapprove of they have endeavoured to free their country from the oppression that is sucking out the very lifeblood and ruining the happiness and prosperity of her people'. Redmond had visited Clarke and Dalton immediately before leaving for his American visit (PRO HO 144/195/A46664C/295).

Civil War: the British should follow the Union and treat the dynamitards as the defeated Confederates.[136]

With the medical releases settled, however, the British government showed little inclination to free the remaining prisoners, who, in the usual course of things, still had several years to serve before they would even become eligible for tickets of leave. Irish members continued to press and the Home Secretary to resist.[137] Amnesty pressures continued in Ireland, and the various pleas were linked to the Queen's Diamond Jubilee.[138] At the beginning of the 1898 session an amnesty motion was introduced into the Queen's Speech debate. William Redmond argued that the five men who remained in prison were not principals in the conspiracy.[139] In an unblushing volte-face on his brother's argument about John Daly, William Redmond implied that Daly was one of the ringleaders – and since he and others had been released, it was unjust to retain the remaining men. He objected to proceedings against the men having been brought under the Treason Felony Act, rather than the Explosive Substances Act, which had a lower maximum sentence. In a long and rambling speech he expressed his belief that the prisoners were absolutely innocent, and the victims of a panic which had gripped Britain in 1883. Their continued imprisonment was an old and open sore in Ireland. Within a few months they would have served fifteen years: it was time to release them.[140]

William Redmond's appeal for clemency attracted two curious supporters. William Abraham (MP for Cork, North East) thought it persuasive to state that he did not know if revolutionary methods would again be used in Ireland, 'but you will never find us using dynamite'. Instead, he told the House, 'we shall meet you openly on the field, as our forefathers did in 1798, and for that you cannot condemn us'. He concluded with a renewed plea for amnesty, so that 'in this year 1898 a message of peace will be given to Ireland'.[141] Lord Charles Beresford (MP for York) condemned the dynamitards in the strongest terms (he wanted to hang or shoot them) but insisted that those still in prison had been punished enough, and should be released to help foster a better spirit between the two countries.[142]

The Home Secretary was unmoved. He agreed with Gladstone and Asquith, who had declined to grant pardons. The men should be treated exactly as other long-termers, their cases individually reconsidered from time to time by the Home

---

136 Irish-American Historical Society, O'Callaghan Clippings, *op. cit.*, ff. 26–7: 'The Amnesty Movement; Great Meeting in New York', 23 February 1897.

137 4 *Hansard*, XLIX, cols 725–6; 18 May 1897.

138 Ibid., col. 1412; 27 May 1897.

139 Redmond was later corrected by the Home Secretary: there were six treason-felony prisoners remaining, not five (4 *Hansard*, LIII, col. 447; 11 February 1898).

140 Ibid., cols 434–41.

141 Ibid., col. 442.

142 Ibid., cols 443–5; 11 February 1898; see also PRO HO 144/195/A46664C/368.

Office. They had been found guilty of atrocious crimes – 'outrages calculated to bring loss of life to innocent people' – and their sentences were not excessive. The earlier releases – on grounds of health – did not affect the position of the remaining six prisoners. They would, during the course of the year, have served fifteen years and their cases would be reviewed. At that time they would each be considered individually, as others similarly situated – 'no better and no worse'.[143]

These Commons' exchanges were unlikely to shift government. Out of the public gaze, however, there were other representations. Michael Davitt was by now a well-established and respected MP. In connection with the 1898 Prisons Bill he was given permission to visit a number of prisons, including Portland. As a condition for this access he had promised not to make any undue use of the privilege to communicate with the dynamitard prisoners. He saw in their cells Clarke, Flannagan, Burton and Featherstone. McDermott, having a previous conviction, was not a Star-class prisoner, and was located on another landing. Wilson and Burton recognised Davitt, but did not speak on political topics. Davitt thought that Featherstone was tending towards feeble-mindedness – 'but both he & Flannigan were apparently never strong intellectually'. Clarke and Burton he found robust mentally, but showing the physical signs of their fourteen years' incarceration: 'Poor fellows how my heart bled for them . . . I did not speak, more than a minute to each & that was all about their health and labour.'[144] There is little doubt that in reporting to the Home Secretary, Sir Matthew White Ridley, Davitt mentioned the dynamitard prisoners. Counsel from such a source would not be set aside lightly, the more so since Davitt in the debates on the pending Prisons Bill had spoken moderately and with evident authority.

These influential and sympathetic voices coincided with a growing official and political sense that the men should be freed.[145] Time had caused passions to ebb, and another insanity or death would provoke an unhappy revival. Ireland was at peace, and the dynamitards in custody were an irritant and a risk: freed, they ceased to be an issue. The day was not very far off when, in the normal course, their sentences would expire and so a show of magnanimity involved no great loss of security or punishment. On 14 June Redmond was informed that it had been decided to treat Wilson (Clarke) as a twenty-year prisoner. With a

---

143 4 *Hansard*, LIII, cols 447–8; 11 February 1898. Michael Davitt and other Irish members spoke in the debate, repeating the familiar arguments for amnesty.

144 TCD: Davitt Papers: Ms. 9571 (unfoliated). The visits were conducted in the course of the Easter recess, 6–10 April 1898. During this time Davitt was able to visit Wormwood Scrubs, Bedford, Birmingham, Bristol, Dartmoor and Portland. At Dartmoor and Portland memories of his own imprisonment came flooding back, especially his release from Portland amidst the tragic news of the Phoenix Park murders: 'How little this place seemed changed? It looked as if I had only left it yesterday.'

145 See Troup to Sir Matthew White Ridley, 13 August 1898: PRO HO 144/195/A46664D/28.

remission of five years his sentence was now completed, and he would be released. A similar course would be taken with the other treason-felony prisoners.[146] Thus, with no great fanfare, the annual recitation of the wrongs of the dynamitards was brought to an end two months later when, with Parliament again safely in its long recess, the six were released at staggered intervals. Each had served some fifteen years of his life sentence.[147] Apart from the death penalty, these were the most severe sentences passed and carried out on Irish political offenders, reflecting the particular nature of the offences and the unwillingness of English politicians and administrations – Liberal and Tory – to palliate them.

146 PRO HO 144/195/A46664C/377.
147 PRO HO 144/195/A46664C/393. The men were brought to Pentonville Prison prior to their release. Clarke was freed on 29 September 1898. John Daly and James Egan travelled to London to meet him, and to fulfil a pledge that the three would share a bowl of punch on the day of their release (Le Roux, *op. cit.*, p. 53).

9

THE EASTER RISING

Prelude and preparations

By the early autumn of 1893 the future of Irish nationalism was again in the balance. In his eighty-fourth year Gladstone had presented his second Home Rule Bill, and in an unequalled parliamentary performance had seen it through eighty-two sittings. No other nineteenth-century measure took up more parliamentary time, and when it was given its third reading on 2 September 1893, Gladstone had amply discharged his promises and obligations to Ireland. Six days later, the Bill was crushed by the Lords, and Gladstone, looking to the narrow majority which he had won in the Commons, decided that he could not hope to win a general election on the issue.[1] Home Rule had further strained the loyalty of the Liberal Party, which it had earlier split. That it had been brought at all was a demonstration of Gladstone's extraordinary tenacity and unique authority.

The loss of the Bill, and Gladstone's retirement from office six months later, signalled more than a change of administration. Imperialism and Unionism continued their progress into the heart of British politics. Even when in the decade between 1905 and 1915 Liberalism flared again, it accommodated itself to a political discourse which Gladstone and his school of Liberalism would have rejected. It was to an imperialist consensus that the question of Ireland would again present itself.

The death of Parnell in October 1891 was for Ireland an event as significant as Gladstone's exit from politics. He died neither in tranquillity nor in triumph, but at bay among the ruins of a party which he had forged into an unequalled nationalist instrument. Like Gladstone, Parnell was far more than an accomplished political actor: he had catalytical properties. Even so, had he survived – and he was barely middle-aged when he died – he may have had to face

---

1 Of the many accounts of these events, Roy Jenkins' is one of the most recent. Coming from a veteran parliamentarian it vividly conveys the atmosphere surrounding the Bill, and, of course, Gladstone's extraordinary energy and talent (*Gladstone*, London, Macmillan, 1995, chs 34 and 35).

in Ireland the dwindling away of high political sentiment. In a partnership with Fenianism, Parnell had harnessed the enormous power of land-hunger and tenant grievances to the nationalist cause. English politicians of both parties had responded with a mixture of ameliorative and coercive measures. Even a mesmeric political figure might have found it difficult to drive forward a constituency which was rapidly achieving its ambition by becoming that most immovable and inward-looking of all groups: a proprietary peasantry. And that small-farmer class grappled fast to a conservative strain of Roman Catholicism, whose clergy and hierarchy were in a militant ultramontane phase, and whose laity were in triumphalist mood.[2] Land legislation struggles would continue, and government would blow hot and cold, repress and conciliate, but the war had been fought and won: the nationalists' successes and government's reforms were effective in changing the social structure of Ireland. In 1898 this found decisive expression in Gerald Balfour's Irish Local Government Act[3] – a measure aptly described as 'not far short of revolutionary'.[4]

As for the revolutionists, the Rossa–Clan na Gael dynamite campaign, which ground to a halt in the summer of 1887, demonstrated their impotence in face of the resources of the British state, and the indifference of the vast majority of the Irish in Ireland, England and the United States of America. Rossa had set himself to throw the fires of hell against England and had succeeded in blowing up a government office, along with several of his own agents. Through the rest of the 1880s and 1890s the IRB and Clan na Gael devoted their energies to organisational maintenance and a poorly supported campaign for the release of the dynamitards. Revolutionary dreams were still dreamt, but they were increasingly the consoling fantasies and reveries of ageing men caught up in the detail of political sectarianism. What could better attest the settled state of Ireland than the permitted return of the Young Irelander and Fenian John O'Leary, and even the old Head Centre himself, James Stephens?[5] Prosperous and settled at home, the majority of the Irish still looked for Home Rule, but appeared content that it should come through constitutional means, and, when it came, should leave intact the imperial connection.

The Boer War (October 1899 to May 1902) revived and radicalised certain advanced nationalist circles. Membership of the Gaelic League grew almost

2 R. F. Foster, *Modern Ireland 1600–1972*, Hammondsworth, Penguin, 1989, p. 433.

3 This measure came a decade after the highly successful Local Government Act which has transformed English county government (51 & 52 Vict., c.41).

4 '[I]t marked a decisive shift in power and influence . . . away from the landlord ascendancy class and towards "the democracy" of farmers, shopkeepers and publicans' (Francis Stewart Leland Lyons, *Ireland Since the Famine*, London, Fontana Press, 1985, p. 212).

5 Stephens returned to Dublin on 25 September 1891. Parnell had approached government on his behalf, and permission was given provided there were no public demonstrations. He lived quietly in a cottage, and died on 29 March 1901 (Desmond Ryan, *The Fenian Chief: A Biography of James Stephens*, Dublin, Gill & Son, 1967, p. 316; Mark F. Ryan, *Fenian Memories*, Dublin, M. H. Gill & Son, 1945, pp. 68–9).

fourfold. A number of the newly established county councils, controlled by nationalists, sent declarations of support to the Transvaal's President Kruger. Sinn Féin's beginnings can be traced to this period in Arthur Griffith's anti-war and autonomy-seeking Cumann na nGaedheal.[6] Opinion in Britain was to some extent divided about the war, with labour and radical politicians lending weight and authority to alliances of even more radical groupings. The same happened in Ireland, with the war bridging various strands of nationalist opinion. On 1 October 1899 a pro-Boer meeting was held in Dublin, with several nationalist MPs participating. Shortly thereafter Maud Gonne and Arthur Griffith formed the Irish Transvaal committee, one of its activities being a campaign against army recruiting. The Irish Party was strongly against the war and although MPs did not speak against recruitment in the House, some did so away from Westminister. This helped to ease relations between constitutional and more extreme nationalists. And, of course, there was a body of pro-Boer Irishmen in the Transvaal – the Irish Brigade of which John MacBride was the major.[7] All of this established a mood and connections which would have significant consequences over the ensuing decade and more.

In the United States of America the revolutionary chapbook was dusted down. Sympathy for the Boers was reflexive in Fenian circles. More importantly, the South African war coincided with a reuniting of the two principal wings of American Fenianism – the United Brotherhood and the United Irishmen. A secret circular issued to the merged United Organisation in September 1899 confirmed the union, and two months later it was determined that the Fenian condition that Britain should be engaged in a major war before a revolutionary action could be undertaken had now been met. The United Organisation did not have the numbers or resources to make adequate use of the opportunity, but it did have enough to allow it to make a beginning. The South African war had, it thought, rendered the British Army powerless to deal with similar problems elsewhere, and the Sudan would be yet another drain.[8] In the event, all this came to nothing: the South African war, after severe reversals, helped to make the British Army more effective, and that able Irish General, Horatio Kitchener, who decisively reconquered Sudan the previous year, did the same thorough job in South Africa. Having flared, however, the Fenian flame did not sink back to the levels of the previous thirty years. Sophisticated analysts in 1900 could already see the shape of a European war which would dwarf Britain's commitment to South Africa, and challenge the very existence of her Empire. But such insights were few, and largely unheeded: Ireland continued on her seemingly placid path.

6 Foster, *op. cit.*, pp. 456–7. Cumann na nGaedheal was founded in September 1900, drawing on the support which centred around the Transvaal committee.

7 Terence Denman, '"The Red Livery of Shame": The Campaign against Army Recruitment in Ireland, 1899–1914', *Irish Historical Studies*, 29, 114 (November 1994), 212–17, *passim*. MacBride would marry Maud Gonne in 1903, the marriage lasting for only a few years.

8 *The Times*, 20 January 1900, 4a; *Glasgow Herald*, 22 January 1900, 12a.

With revolutionary politics marginalised, and constitutional politics quiescent and diverted into local government, and the parliamentary party's distribution of spoils, the national impulse found expression in cultural regeneration. The achievement of literary figures such as Yeats, Synge, Hyde and O'Grady was to allow the Irishman and Irishwoman who lived highly Anglicised lives to recognise and take pride in a separate and ancient (if largely reconstructed) national identity. The preservation and revival of the Irish language was a potent part of this movement, as was enjoyment of Irish music. These national sensibilities extended to games (which had themselves been given a place of importance in English national life by the Victorians), and at the end of 1884 the Gaelic Athletic Association was formed under the significant patronage of Thomas Croke (Archbishop of Cashel), Michael Davitt and Charles Stewart Parnell.

The Gaelic League was founded in July 1893 to preserve and promote the Irish language, and by 1906 claimed 900 branches, with a total membership of 100,000.[9] Two of the three founders would play important parts in a new chapter of Irish nationalism: John (Eoin) MacNeill, an Ulster civil servant and later academic, in time became the Chief of Staff of the Irish Volunteers; Douglas Hyde became the first President of Ireland (under de Valera's 1937 Constitution). The third, Eugene O'Growney, was a priest, and Professor of Celtic Literature and Language at Maynooth College. Membership of the League was almost entirely confined to Roman Catholics, and the aims and spirit of the organisation were unreservedly nationalist and exclusionary.

The Irish cultural revival did not have to lead to revolutionary politics – it fed into constitutionalism, if anything with more ease. An Irish cultural identity was entirely compatible with Unionism, of the Southern variety at least. But – and it is a view that comes with hindsight as one looks back over the twentieth century's efflorescent nationalisms – the protective membrane between thought and deed can be breached by art's energising and sometimes transcendent properties. Myth, symbol, meaning and association can move from mental life to the psychological, and engender types of collective consciousness: thence it can be a few short steps to the social, political and military action.[10] When looked at from the other side, the equation becomes even more persuasive: vigorous nationalism, constitutional or violent, cannot exist without a cultural foundation, and this always proceeds from definition to degrees of exclusion and rejection.

The Irish cultural movement had more immediate consequences. It is a commonplace that English non-conformity imparted organisational skills and

9 Sydney Brooks, *The New Ireland*, Dublin, Maunsel & Co, 1907, p. 27. Brooks, a wholly naive English Home Ruler, saw the Gaelic League as being improbably immune from Ireland's several divisions: 'The whole essence of their attitude, towards Ireland was that it was Irish – not Catholic or Protestant, neither Separatists nor Unionist, but simply Irish.'

10 Colm Toibín writes persuasively about this, and the Irish setting of the 1890s to 1900s in 'Lady Gregory's Toothbrush', *New York Review of Books*, 48, 13 (August 2001), pp. 40–4.

confidence to its working-class laity in the course of its religious mission, and thus fed into English political life, deeply influencing Liberalism and Labour. So also the Irish cultural movement affected Irish political life. The many associations which carried forward literary, cultural and sporting activities taught organisation, bred leaders and demanded commitment. There were overlapping memberships. Men and women came together in nationally minded networks which were a form of nationalist mobilisation. A plethora of journals and debating venues allowed for the propagation, development and refinement of ideas and rubrics. The ensuing sectarianism and faction fights blunted energies, it is true, but also inspired the combativeness necessary for political development. The mass membership of these organisations, constantly honing their sense of nationality and sifting out the less committed, provided a steady if small flow of recruits for revolutionary nationalism.

This is not the place closely to map in detail the various paths which led to the steps of Dublin's Post Office on Easter Monday, 1916: the most general circumstance was the foundering of constitutional nationalism. This in turn had several causes. Depending on the Irish Party for its survival, Asquith's Liberal government promised a third Home Rule Bill, which it duly introduced in April 1912. Ulster Unionism had shown defiance, extending to military action from 1886, when Gladstone introduced his first Bill. The Lords had quashed Gladstone's second Bill and so Unionist insurrectionary determination had not been tested. By 1912, however, the position was much graver from the Unionist point of view, since the 1911 Parliament Act had asserted the legislative supremacy of the Commons. The Lords, with its overwhelming Unionist majority, could delay but no longer veto Home Rule, and the arithmetic of the Commons – 272 Unionists facing 272 Liberals supported by eighty-two Nationalists and forty-two Labour members – led to only one conclusion: some form of Home Rule was inevitable.

Ulster Unionism drew on a primarily nonconformist – largely Presbyterian – tradition that invoked many examples of righteous defiance of authority; it also had, in the Orange Order and kindred bodies, strong and effective sinews of popular organisation.[11] Ulster Unionists saw Home Rule as an attack on the British Constitution, and the political and religious components of that set of arrangements as its birthright. Unionists had few moral, political or religious scruples in taking direct action to preserve a structure considered to be beyond the powers and entitlement of Parliament (and especially the post-1911 Commons-dominated Parliament) to alter. The failure of Liberals to make Home Rule an explicit issue in the general election of January 1910 confirmed for Unionists that no mandate existed for such a monstrous change to the composition of the United Kingdom. This point was underlined by the equal representation in the

---

11 See Kevin Haddick-Flynn's lively *Orangeism: The Making of a Tradition*, Dublin, Wolfhound Press, 1999, chs 24–26.

Commons of the Conservatives and Liberals, and Liberal dependence on the Irish and Labour for its governing majority. Under the inspired leadership of Edward Carson a campaign of resistance was launched – part-intimidation and bluff – but sufficiently based on military organisation and popular support to cause any government to pause.[12] And its leaders were not stinting in their threats. In January 1912, F. E. Smith – a future Lord Chancellor of England – concluded a long and bitter speech against Home Rule with words that ran as close as was possible to the laws of sedition. Smith said he spoke for himself, but was confident that he spoke also for colleagues, when he said he would 'run any risk' – he chose his words carefully and advisedly – rather than allow the people to be 'defrauded by a Government which every election proved to have forfeited the confidence of the constituencies'.[13]

On 28 September 1912, ten days of meetings and processions culminated in an 'Ulster Day' of religious services, demonstrations and work stoppages. Summoning the most solemn memory and symbol of Presbyterianism, the National Covenant of 1638, an anti-Home Rule Ulster Covenant was initiated. The Covenant was signed by 218,000 men and a supporting document by 222,000 women. Four months later Carson's Ulster Unionist Council decided to raise a force of 100,000 men, to be called the Ulster Volunteer Force. Retired military men took over organisation and training, and high levels of efficiency were attained by many recruits. Negotiations between the government, nationalists and Unionists proceeded in various forms, but all inconclusively. The Curragh 'Mutiny' (though it was hardly that) of March 1914 showed that a section of the British Army in Ireland could prove unreliable in any attempt to enforce Home Rule in Ulster. The implications of this for a country on the brink of a major war were so appalling that by this one incident Ulster secured its exception from any Home Rule measure. On 24 April the point was decisively underscored when the Ulster Volunteer Force illegally and semi-publicly imported some 25,000 rifles of a modern pattern and three million cartridges through Larne, Bangor and Donaghadee, and Dublin Castle failed to act. This, *The Times* noted, 'establishes beyond all question that the passing of the Home Rule Bill must mean civil war'. Carson agreed arms and ammunition had been coming in

---

12 Harford Montgomery Hyde, *Carson: The Life of Sir Edward Carson, Lord Carson of Duncairn*, London, William Heinemann, 1953, ch. 9. Credible threats of forcible resistance went back as far as Gladstone's first Home Rule Bill in 1886, and Lord Randolph Churchill's playing of the 'Orange Card' (see R. F. Foster, *Lord Randolph Churchill: A Political Life*, Oxford, Clarendon, 1981, pp. 252–60). Carson (1854–1935) was born in Dublin. Educated there at Trinity College, he was called to the Irish Bar in 1889, and the English bar in 1892. Irish Solicitor General, 1892, English Solicitor General, 1900–6, Unionist MP for Trinity College, Dublin, 1892–1918. Leader of the Irish Unionist Party, 1910–21. Member of the War Cabinet. Appointed Lord Justice of Appeal, 1921.

13 *Liverpool Courier*, 23 January 1912, 8d (see cols a–e for the full speech). For F. E. Smith see p. 569, n. 56, below.

for some time. The last batch had been rushed because the crisis was close, but the policy had been unchanged for two-and-a-half years: 'if we were driven to it we should resist by force.'[14]

The Curragh incident showed Ulster Unionism's special relationship with the army, and destroyed any chance of finding a form of Home Rule acceptable to nationalists.[15] The Ulster gentry, together with those from other parts of Ireland, had made a disproportionate contribution to British military history and from before the time of Wellington had produced a caste whose peripatetic life was spent in the service of the Crown: from, but emphatically not of, Ireland. They were the self-conscious descendants of those who had conquered the country, and many insisted on the distinction between themselves and the defeated native Irish.[16] Asquith's government fully understood the background to the Curragh incident, and with a European war looming was paralysed by the fear of officer corps' dissatisfaction and the knowledge that many anti-Home Rule Irishmen occupied high positions in the army.[17] At the time of the Curragh incident, for example, Sir Henry Wilson was Director of Military Operations at the War Office (and indeed was destined to become Chief of the Imperial General Staff): already in close and sympathetic contact with militant Ulster Unionists, in retirement he became a Unionist MP (North Down) and military adviser to the first Northern Ireland government.[18]

14 The headline in *The Times* (27 April 1914, 10c) captured the moment exactly: 'Guns for Ulster', 'Castle Officials called from the Golf Links'. No evidence has come to light that the Ulster Volunteers were ever, or to any appreciable extent, the target of civil or military intelligence. Yet *The Times* was able to report that the majority of the 100,000 or so Ulster Volunteers had rifles, of which (following the April gun-running) 60,000 were 'thoroughly modern'.

15 This incident, which tested and broke the will of Asquith and his party on Ireland, is dealt with concisely and convincingly by Denis Gwynn in his *Life of John Redmond* (London, George C. Harrap, 1932, pp. 281–99). Sir Henry Wilson, who was treacherously a part of the plot, reveals much in his diaries (C. E. Callwell (ed.), *Field-Marshall Sir Henry Wilson, His Life and Diaries*, London, Cassell, 1927, Vol. 1, pp. 137–45). On Wilson's ingrained propensity for double-dealing see Sir Andrew Macphail, *Three Persons*, London, John Murray, 1929, pp. 3–99.

16 Wellington, born in Dublin, and periodically involved in Irish affairs (including a spell as Irish Chief Secretary and later a key role in Roman Catholic Emancipation) is reported to have observed of his Irish birth that being born in a stable does not make one a horse (see Elizabeth Longford, *Wellington: The Years of the Sword*, New York, Harper & Row, 1969, p. 129).

17 The gravity of the crisis was overshadowed by subsequent events – world war and the Easter rising among them – but there can be no doubt that it went to the heart of the constitutional relationship between Parliament and the army. Followed a month later by the Ulster gun-running, it seems to have shattered the nerve of Asquith and many of his colleagues (see *The Times*, 27 March 1914, 8a–e).

18 Sir Henry Wilson (1864–1922), born in Co. Longford, was a strong Unionist and Orange sympathiser, and a soldier politician of the greatest eminence. He made no secret of his sympathy for the Curragh officers, and during the Irish war of independence would repeatedly urge on the politicians (whom he more or less generally despised) a more vigorously repressive policy. He was assassinated by IRA men at the door of his house, just four months after entering the Commons. (For an account of Wilson's role in Irish affairs see his biography, drawn extensively

The Conservative Party, in its most Unionist and imperialistic phase, also teetered on the edge of unlawfulness. Bonar Law,[19] who had become leader in November 1911, firmly backed the stand of Carson and the other Ulster Unionists, and on 9 April 1912 took a leading part in a monster demonstration intended to warn the government of the consequences of the Home Rule Bill, which was to receive its first reading two days later. Standing alongside Carson and Craig, Law took the salute of some 100,000 Ulster Volunteers at Belfast's Balmoral Show Ground, and in an incendiary speech told the throng that in opposing Home Rule they were opposing tyranny. The Liberal government had sold themselves (to the Irish Party) 'and they thought they had sold you, but you were not theirs to sell'. Help would come in this crisis – and though he did not say what form it would take, he implied that it would be of a forcible kind.[20]

Events in Ulster, and their English echoes, challenged the Irish Parliamentary Party beyond its resources, energy and ability. Failing to understand or respect Ulster Protestantism, its leadership was unable to effect a direct compromise with the Unionists, to divide its opponents, find Ulster allies, or secure its position through negotiations and pressure on the British government. This was nationalism's perpetual blind spot. Since the time of the first Home Rule Bill, and long before, Irish nationalists, constitutional and revolutionary alike, had been unable to engage Ulster Unionism – perhaps because its Southern counterpart was more easily dealt with.[21] And, ironically for a party which had itself so successfully supported the Land League's direct action campaigns

from his journal: Callwell, *op. cit.* (2 vols).) Even after the December 1921 Treaty was signed, giving Southern Ireland Dominion status within the Commonwealth, Wilson remained unreconciled. His Unionism, indeed, was so strong that on 12 February 1922, in reaction to the post-Treaty disorder in Ireland, he told Winston Churchill and other ministers that the British government had only two courses open to it – to 'reconquer Ireland or lose the Empire' (ibid., Vol. 2, p. 326).

19 (1858–1923). Born in New Brunswick, educated in Canada and at Glasgow High School. Iron merchant in Glasgow. Secretary of State for Colonies and member of War Committee, May 1915 to December 1916. Chancellor of Exchequer and Leader of House in Lloyd George's War Cabinet, December 1916 to January 1919. Leader of Unionist Party in House, 1911–21; Prime Minister, October 1922 to May 1923.

20 *The Times*, 10 April 1912, 8c. Even more explicit and threatening was Law's remark later in July of the same year at a Unionist rally at Blenheim Palace: 'There are things stronger than Parliamentary majorities . . . I can imagine no length of resistance to which Ulster will go in which I shall not be ready to support them and in which they will not be supported by the overwhelming majority of the British people' (*The Times*, 29 July 1912, 8a). This was the voice of His Majesty's loyal opposition.

21 The analysis of Dorothy Macardle, historian of de Valera republicanism, is representative. The Ulster Unionists 'bore little resemblance to the Northern men who had been leaders of the national struggle in 1798. Their adherence to the Union was tenacious in the extreme, for to the Union and to their status of agents and garrison for Britain, they owed their position of power' (Dorothy Macardle, *The Irish Republic*, Dublin, The Irish Press, 1951, p. 76).

and Parnell's obstructionism (not to mention the lawlessness of the Land War), the nationalists had a self-deluding and certainly unrealistic belief in the British government's determination and ability to impose its will.

Other strands of nationalist opinion reacted more strongly to the formation and arming of the Ulster Volunteers. The possibility of a nationalist paramilitary movement was greatly stimulated by Unionism's step beyond the constitution. On the covert initiative of the IRB, the Irish Volunteers was formed in November 1913.[22] As events in Ulster and England unfolded its membership grew apace, and in six months had reached some 100,000.[23] Whatever effect this organisation had on the Ulster Unionists, its formation and ballooning membership alarmed the leaders of the Irish Party. A militia so strongly supported challenged an authority which, if sometimes fragmented, had, since the days of Parnell, been complete. And such a body, however strong the protestations that it was to be purely defensive and reactive, could not but raise fears in anyone versed in Irish history. In June 1914, John Redmond, the leader of the Irish Party, demanded and obtained the right to place a counterbalancing number of his own nominees on the Volunteers' national committee.

Two armed militias and a deteriorating political situation made disorder ever more likely. For many constitutional politicians, however, August 1914 provided an external enemy and a struggle which demanded the shelving of all sectional differences. Ulster Unionists and the Redmondite nationalists alike believed that their cause could be furthered by loyal support for the Empire. For Ulster this was certainly true, and on the outbreak of war many officers and men of the Ulster Volunteers went straight into the Ulster Division of the British Army. Redmond considered that nationalists could do no less. By carrying through the Home Rule Bill (which received the Royal Assent on 18 September 1914) Asquith had at least formally demonstrated his good faith. To keep his side of the bargain, Redmond urged members of the Irish Volunteers to enlist. The immediate cost of the several tens of thousands of enlistments, however, was a split in the Volunteers. The vast majority of men stayed with Redmond, while the dissidents seceded to a more militant and nationalistic body. The breakaway

22 The formation of the Volunteers was presented as a spontaneous response to events in Ulster, but it was actually initiated by the IRB – a fact which was withheld from many of the members of the founding committee (Piaras Béaslaí, *Michael Collins and the Making of New Ireland*, London, George Harrap, 1926, Vol. 1, p. 28). The Volunteer organisation was almost self-financing, with members paying weekly subscriptions and additional small regular payments towards the purchase of uniform and a rifle. The last was possible because of an earlier relaxation of the rules on the importation of arms into Ireland.

23 See 5 *Hansard*, LXIII, col. 764; 15 June 1914. Robert Kee, in *The Bold Fenian Men* (Harmondsworth, Penguin, 1989, p. 202, insists that the estimate of 80,000 given to the Commons by Augustine Birrell, the Irish Chief Secretary, was too low, and 100,000 was more accurate. He points out, however, that although their membership numbers were similar, the Irish Volunteers had few arms and had not achieved the levels of organisation and efficiency of the Ulster Volunteers.

group retained the title Irish Volunteers, while the Redmondite majority adopted the pointedly more conciliatory National Volunteers.[24] The cost of Redmond's stand as war-weariness mounted, and conscription loomed for Ireland, was the evaporation of his political capital and the sidelining of his party.

For more than twenty years Fenianism had been in the doldrums. The Land War had allowed it to guide a mass movement, and to recruit from its more militant adherents. The success of that struggle had dampened down the very fires which revolutionists had hoped would develop into a general conflagration. But given the abstract and theoretical concerns of conspiratorial societies, it was inevitable that the Irish cultural revival would cast some of the more zealous upon the shores of Fenianism. Men such as Patrick Pearse, Bulmer Hobson (a friend of Roger Casement), Michael Collins, Arthur Griffith and Seán MacDermott were sworn to the IRB and worked for the revolutionary cause in the various cultural and political organisations through which they had come.[25] The apostolic link with an earlier generation of Fenians was reinforced when the former dynamitard convicts Thomas Clarke and John Daly returned from exile.[26] These men reanimated the IRB, and made common cause with others such as Roger Casement, The O'Rahilly, Erskine Childers and Constance Markievicz, who were committed to various forms of militant and separatist nationalism. As the constitutional crisis heightened in Ireland and threats were exchanged between the militias and sections of their committees, nationalist fervour intensified and direct action became more acceptable to people who would a few years previously have peremptorily rejected it.

The Irish government's strategy was to ride the rapids. Fearful that intervention could incite the very forces which it hoped to suppress, Dublin Castle chose to

24 Kitchener, now Secretary for War, badly mishandled the induction of the National and Ulster Volunteers. The latter entered as intact units under their own officers into the Ulster Division. The National Volunteers were placed under Protestant officers. The argument, no doubt, was that the Ulster contingents had achieved high levels of efficiency and could therefore be taken into the army as operational units; the Irish Volunteers being less advanced in training needed different treatment. This was very likely true, but the unequal treatment may also have been prompted by a distrust of the Catholic Irish: who could tell where military training might lead them? There was about this an element of self-fulfilling prophecy, since the political consequences were highly damaging to Redmond: 'The Red Hand of Ulster was acknowledged; the Irish Harp was not. . . . Thanks to Kitchener, the surge of Irish loyalty was dissipated' (A. J. P. Taylor, *English History 1914–1945*, Oxford, Oxford University Press, 1976, p. 21; see also Frank Pakenham, *Peace by Ordeal*, London, Geoffrey Chapman, 1962, pp. 20–1).

25 Arthur Griffith was a member of the IRB at the time he founded Sinn Féin and although he left some years later, the IRB welcomed his open and non-revolutionary organisation as a means of spreading national thought. Michael Collins was sworn to the IRB in London in 1909 and was active in that organisation, the London Company of the Irish Volunteers, and Sinn Féin, until he returned to Ireland in January 1916 (Béaslaí, *op. cit.*, Vol. 1, pp. 18–19).

26 John Daly was thought by the police to be head of the IRB. His activities and associates were carefully watched. Thomas Clarke, however, was at the centre of IRB activities in Dublin, and was therefore the driving force of the IRB revival (see PRO HO 144/1454/1a).

dismiss as posturing much of what was going on in the more militant nationalist circles.[27] Reports from the Royal Irish Constabulary, moreover, were well informed and precise, and indicated that such a small and poorly armed body could scarcely mount a rising.[28] Optimism and insouciance so dominated that it was only in December 1913, in the face of rapidly heightening tensions, that the importation of arms into Ireland was prohibited. Since the Ulster Volunteers were already well armed, nationalists took this as further proof of the bias against them, and of Asquith's weakness in the face of Unionist bellicosity. A group of nationalists decided that the balance should be restored, explicitly taking the Ulster gun-running as their justification.[29] It was the gesture that counted, since neither purse nor opportunity could match Ulster's achievements. Two, who would later become more prominent in Irish revolutionary affairs (Erskine Childers and Darrell Figgis), travelled to Hamburg, where they purchased 1500 Mauser rifles and 45,000 cartridges. These weapons were successfully brought into Howth near Dublin and Kilcoole in Co. Wicklow.[30] All of this, it must be remembered, just nine days before the outbreak of the Great War.

Revolutionary possibilities were intensified by developments in Irish labour relations. A militant form of 'new unionism' – the organisation of semi-skilled and unskilled workers on non-craft lines – had been introduced into Ireland by James Larkin, a militant socialist.[31] Labour and social conditions in Dublin were

27 The chief authors of this policy were the heads of the Irish government: Augustine Birrell (1850–1933), Irish Chief Secretary, 1907–16; Matthew Nathan (1852–1937), Under-Secretary, 1914–16, archetypal Royal Engineer Imperial administrator. For their evidence to the Royal Commission on the Rebellion in Ireland, see Minutes of Evidence, pp. 2–27 (PP, 1916 [Cd. 8311], XI, 185). The *Report of the Royal Commission on the Rebellion in Ireland* (PP, 1916 [Cd. 8279], XI, 171, 13) placed the blame on both men for the British failure to anticipate and deal with the rising.

28 Béaslaí, *op. cit.*, Vol. 1, p. 82.

29 Significantly, most of the arms smugglers and funders were not members of the IRB, but were rather Anglo-Irish and upper-middle-class cultural nationalists. Roger Casement, Erskine Childers, Darrell Figgis, May Spring-Rice (a cousin of the British Ambassador to Washington) and Alice Stopford Green were the leading conspirators. For an account of the episode see Brian Inglis, *Roger Casement*, London, Hodder & Stoughton, 1973, pp. 241–66.

30 A thousand Volunteers had been mobilized to bring the Howth arms into Dublin on 26 July 1913. Almost by accident, soldiers who had been called, unavailingly, to the Howth landings opened fire on a jeering and menacing crowd which had followed them back to Dublin. Three people were killed and thirty-eight wounded in the centre of Dublin. A full account of the Howth landings was given in *The Times*, 27 and 28 July 1914, 9f and 10a–c. A further twist had been given to the screw which bore down on nationalist sentiments. The funerals of the three persons killed in the incident were organised by the Volunteers, and took an hour to pass. Bands played funeral music and a large firing party accompanied the procession (*The Times*, 30 July 1914, 10b–c).

31 (1876–1947). Born in Liverpool, became docker and then organiser. Founded Irish Transport and General Workers' Union in 1909. Led series of strikes and in 1913 confronted employers when a lockout was declared. This ended in victory for the employers. In late 1914 went to the United States of America, where he remained until 1923. Imprisoned in New York State for trade union activity. On the militant side of Irish labour and trade union activities until his death.

among the worst in the United Kingdom, and Larkin's evangelising, finding fertile ground, put him at the head of many bitter industrial actions. One of Larkin's principal assistants in the Irish Transport and General Workers' Union was James Connolly, a former soldier in the British Army, nationalist and revolutionary socialist.[32] In 1913 these two men led a strike against the lockout of William Martin Murphy, the Dublin tramways and newspaper owner, and other employers. In a confrontation on 31 August the police with some brutality suppressed a street riot. As a response to this and other clashes, and as part of a general programme for the advance of revolutionary socialism, in November 1913 Connolly established a workers' organisation which he called the Irish Citizen Army. Although never large in numbers, Connolly's relatively well-equipped and trained militia would play a central part in the events which were to follow.

Most of the pieces were now assembled for an armed outbreak in Ireland, but its form was by no means clear. On the outbreak of war Redmond had thrown his weight behind the British war effort.[33] In a Commons speech which was greeted with relief, enthusiasm and goodwill, Redmond spoke of the developments in Ireland which, over the previous generation had changed his country's attitude towards England and the Empire. The 'democracy of Ireland', he declared, would 'turn with the utmost anxiety and sympathy to this country in every trial and every danger that may overtake it'. In a bizarre flight of unreality he insisted that the government could deploy the army elsewhere, leaving Ireland's defence to the National Volunteers, in conjunction with the Ulster Volunteers.[34] Time would show this to have been the most fateful speech of Redmond's career. By giving full support without reserving a margin for bargaining and influence he displayed astonishing political naivety. Necessity, not generosity, is the driving force of politics – an axiom that had carried him to the top of his party, but which he now cast aside.

At the time it appeared that he had another card. Never a military power on the continental scale, the British Army was woefully short of manpower, and, at a time when conscription was scarcely thinkable, there was a need for volunteers. A crude and public bargain was politically impossible, but by holding back on Irish recruitment, Redmond gave Asquith another inducement to

---

32 (1868–1916). Born in Edinburgh, served in the British Army for some years until he deserted. Seven years in Dublin as socialist organiser, followed by seven years in the United States of America in similar activity. Returned to Ireland and became trade union and labour leader. For a concise (and entirely adulatory) account of Connolly's life and thoughts see P. Berresford Ellis (ed.), *James Connolly: Selected Writings*, Harmondsworth, Penguin, 1973, pp. 7–53.

33 The anti-recruitment campaign which had achieved some strength in the Boer War years and thereafter had by 1914 dwindled to sporadic acts of vandalism, occasional demonstrations and small poster campaigns. Notwithstanding its limited scale, however, anti-militarism was close to the heart of Irish nationalism, and was always apt to be revived. Redmond may not have been closely in touch with the extreme strains of nationalism, but should have sensed resistance to recruitment (see Denman, *op. cit.*, pp. 230–1).

34 5 *Hansard*, LXV, cols 1828–9; 3 August 1914.

proceed with Home Rule. Caught between Carson and Redmond, the government compromised by providing Home Rule, while at the same time bringing in a Suspensory Act which delayed implementation for twelve months or until the end of the war – whichever was the longer.[35] For all the disagreement and recriminations it had produced in the Irish Party, the Act evoked genuine enthusiasm in Ireland, and as he embarked upon a recruiting drive Redmond was confident that he and it would be carried forward on that flood of goodwill. In the haze of elation produced by the successful culmination of more than thirty years of parliamentary struggle, this view seemed unchallengeable: there had been a further and seemingly final consolidation and entrenchment of constitutional nationalism. By donning the recruiting sergeant's colours, however, Redmond took a final and fatal step down a short path which led to the immolation of his party and the negation of his own life's work.

From the standpoint of the IRB events had developed most favourably. Britain was engaged in a major war which dwarfed all others. Shortly after war was declared the IRB Supreme Council met and determined that a revolutionary opportunity existed and that it would accordingly strike for independence, whether or not military success was possible.[36] True to another of the Fenian beliefs the conspirators believed that national resurrection required the forces of republicanism openly to take the field: an insurrection required the moral authority of open warfare and the dignity of banners, uniforms, ranks and military etiquette: an Irish army would take the field on behalf of a Republic 'virtually established' since the foundation of Fenianism. The Empire was mobilising immense forces of men and technology, and modern communications allowed their rapid deployment. But even in the face of apparently insuperable odds Fenianism remained optimistic: immediate failure could lead to eventual success. One of the new leaders, Patrick Pearse, infused his politics with the Christian notion of redemption through sacrifice, insisting that the shedding of blood was essential for Irish rebirth.[37] His doctrine was comprehensively set out in a speech in Philadelphia

---

35 Government of Ireland Act, 1914: 4 & 5 Geo. V, c.90; Suspensory Act, 1914: 4 & 5 Geo. V, c.88.

36 Béaslaí, *op. cit.*, Vol. 1, p. 55.

37 Patrick Henry Pearse (1879–1916) was born of an English stone-carver father (who converted to Roman Catholicism) and an Irish working-class mother. Gifted with an exceptionally vivid imagination, he began to write at an early age. Educated at the Royal University, he was called to the Irish Bar, but did not practise. Sought the revival of the Irish language and founded St Enda's School for that purpose. Took a leading part in the Gaelic League. Founder-member of the Irish Volunteers (November 1913) and about the same time sworn to the IRB. Thereafter at the centre of revolutionary effort and conspiracy. For a discussion of Pearse's role in the events of 1916 (and before), particularly concentrating on his aspirations to sacrifice, see Seán Farrell Moran, *Patrick Pearse and the Politics of Redemption*, Washington, DC, The Catholic University of America Press, 1994. Ruth Dudley Edwards provides a warm but penetrating account of the man and the revolutionary in her *Patrick Pearse: The Triumph of Failure*, Victor Gollancz, 1977. Edwards raises but baulks at a thorough exploration of Pearse's sexuality, which seems to be close to the heart of his sacrificial politics.

in March 1914, in the course of which he emphasised the need to educate the young to national sacrifice and the continuity of the national struggle:

> If the men of '98 had not risen, if Emmet had not died, the men of '48 would not have risen, nor the men of '67. And if the men of '67 had not risen who in Ireland would be taking up the cause today. We have set our faces again towards the old paths, and we have taken up again the old work, and we hope to use the opportunities that the mercy of God has given.[38]

Completely insulated by poetic myopia and inexperience from the horrors of trench warfare, machine guns, high explosives and gas, and driven by what appears to be a psychosexual fascination with death, Pearse was able, sixteen months into the bloodiest war in human history, to describe those months as 'the most glorious in the history of Europe', and to write what may most charitably be described as nonsense: 'It is good for the world that such things should be done. The old heart of the earth needed to be warmed with the red wine of the battlefields.'[39] Connolly was scornful: 'We do not believe that war is glorious, inspiring or regenerating . . . Any person . . . who sings the praises of war is, in our opinion, a blithering idiot . . . We are sick of it, the world is sick of it.'[40] (Four months later, notwithstanding this scorn, Connolly would be drawn into knowing sacrifice, albeit his own, rather than the slaughtered masses which so aroused Pearse.) Connolly's debunking blast presumably represented majority opinion. But fixation on sacrifice as an end rather than a risk ensured that a conflict would take place: who can stop a suicide attack? The pragmatists in Dublin Castle made their judgements based on the probable actions of reckless but not suicidal men; Pearse and his close companions concluded that self-sacrifice and death was the most likely way to achieve their objectives. This logic also ensured that when the rising came it would not follow the lines of the 1865 to 1867 Fenian campaign – heavily penetrated plans, a cumbersome mustering of forces on conventional military lines, and eventually headlong and leaderless flight. There would, however, be a similar emphasis on national honour and display which

38 New York Public Library, Maloney Collection of Irish Historical Papers (NYPL, MCIHP), Box 5, 1HP87.
39 Patrick Pearse, *Political Writings and Speeches*, Dublin, The Talbot Press, 1952, p. 216. He went on to observe that war is terrible but not evil; many in Ireland dreaded it because they did not know it: 'Ireland has not known the exhilaration of war for over a hundred years. . . . When war comes to Ireland, she must welcome it as she would welcome the Angel of God.' Pearse dwelt on the forthcoming sacrifice in personal terms, writing poetry for his mother, in which he contemplated, *inter alia*, her pride and consolation in his sacrificial death: 'I do not grudge them: Lord, I do not grudge/My two strong sons that I have seen go out/To break their strength and die, they and a few/In bloody protest for a glorious thing/They shall be spoken of among their people/The generations shall remember them/And call them blessed' (Edwards, *op. cit.*, pp. 262–3).
40 *Workers' Republic*, 25 December 1915, 7c.

prevented Pearse and other leaders from embracing guerrilla or terrorist tactics. Theirs would be a stand-up fight, waged with the intent of quickening and rallying the Irish people through a display of bravery, self-sacrifice and honour: the creation of a myth for the times.[41]

The Easter rising

By 1915 Ireland was awash with militias. In addition to the principal bodies – Redmond's National Volunteers and Carson's Ulster Volunteers – there were the avowedly more extremist Irish Volunteers and the Irish Citizen Army, and there was also a small unit of riflemen of the American-affiliated Ancient Order of Hibernians. The latitude allowed to these organisations seems, at this remove of time, to have been quite extraordinary. Large bodies of armed men in various states of uniform, in formation and controlled by military commands, passed through the streets, and staged mock attacks on public buildings. When the IRB followed another of its recipes for heating public opinion, and repatriated and buried the remains of O'Donovan Rossa on 1 August 1915, armed and uniformed Volunteers accompanied the funeral procession, marshalled the crowds and fired the graveside salute.[42] Seven months before the Easter rising, Pearse led 1500

41 Pearse's acceptance of almost certain death for himself was eventually shared by Connolly, in whom one might have expected materialism and some sense of the world as it was to dilute the romantic ideal. As he left the headquarters of the Irish Transport and General Workers' Union to march his men the few hundred yards to the General Post Office to commence the rising, Connolly made it clear to William O'Brien, Secretary of the Dublin Trades' Council, that there was no chance of success: 'We are going out to be slaughtered' (Desmond Ryan (ed.), *Labour and Easter Week: A Selection from the Writings of James Connolly*, Dublin, At the Sign of the Three Candles, 1966, p. 21). It would appear that Thomas Clarke was of the same mind. Patrick Rankin, an IRB man from Newry, made his way to the GPO after the fighting started, arriving on the Wednesday. Clarke asked him what news he had of support from the North. Rankin replied that he knew of none. At this point it was surely evident to all the leaders that the rising's remote chance of success was extinguished, but Clarke was not downcast: 'He looked about 30 years younger and seemed so happy you would imagine you were talking to him in his old shop in Parnell Street.' (NLI: Patrick Rankin Papers: Ms. 22, 251, f. 8).

42 *Irish Independent*, 2 August 1915, 3h, 4a–b: 'Dead Fenian. . . . Enormous Crowds. . . . Impressive Pageant Through Dublin Streets . . . Ireland Represented' (photographs, p. 5). In his remarkable graveside oration Pearse looked forward as well as back when he declared: 'Life springs from death; and from the graves of patriot men and women spring living nations.' He was taken as referring to Rossa's grave, but was also looking forward to his own (*Political Writings and Speeches*, op. cit., pp. 133–7). John Devoy, the Clan na Gael leader, wrote to Sir Roger Casement about the funeral, which he described as 'a great demonstration, military as well as political, [which] had a splendid effect' (Devoy to Casement, 22 May 1915: NLI: Casement Papers: Ms. 13,073 (44/i)). The IRB put a huge amount of effort into the organisation of the funeral. The organising committee divided the work between thirteen subcommittees, membership of which was dominated by those involved in the leadership of the 1916 rising, including those who were subsequently executed. A souvenir booklet was published, consisting of an extended biography of Rossa and an account of the funeral: 'Diamuid O'Donnabháin Rossa 1831–1915'. A copy survives in the Labour History Archive and Study Centre, John Rylands University Library of Manchester (CP/CENT/PL).

Volunteers, about half of whom were armed, through the streets of Dublin and out to the Dublin mountains, where they practised military manoeuvres. Even more remarkably, the Irish Citizen Army a few weeks later was allowed to stage a mock attack on the seat of government itself: Dublin Castle.[43]

There were various strands in the Irish government's toleration of these displays, anabases and rehearsals. The Irish and National Volunteers were a response to the Ulster Volunteers. The difficulty for government was that while (for the duration of the war, at least) the loyalty of the Ulster Volunteers was not in question, and their suppression was not an issue, any move to dissolve the National or the Irish Volunteers would reek of bias, and would precipitate political and possibly military disorder. At the same time there was some sense in Dublin Castle that government was riding a tiger. There was also an element of collusive delusion. Redmond had claimed for the National Volunteers a role in the defence of the realm, and from its ranks men went in large numbers to the British Army. The Volunteers' agenda included, it is true, the possibility of countering any military action by the Ulster Volunteers in opposition to Home Rule; but that clash had been postponed for the duration of the war. Even the Irish Volunteers had apparently foresworn military action, reserving it only for an attempt to impose conscription, a repudiation of Home Rule, partition, or an attempt to disarm them: this list of eventualities also seemed to promise nothing worse than swagger and threat while the war lasted. As for Connolly's Citizen Army – it numbered not much more than 200, and, while bellicose, hardly posed a threat to the forces of the Crown.[44]

There were, in short, many reasons for inaction, and for high officials to keep their nerve, and bureaucracy abhors crisis. In so far as it vented feelings, sabre-rattling might be welcomed, and there were hardly any reasons why, in the midst of a war that was an unprecedented national haemorrhage and a voracious consumption of all kinds of resources, government would want to kick over the Irish wasps' nest. Only a major and protracted military and police operation backed by emergency powers could have disarmed and disbanded the militias. Besides the practical problems – Ireland was only lightly garrisoned – this would have produced an upsurge of bad feeling which could have destroyed morale among the Irish Catholics in the army and killed voluntary recruitment in the South; even-handedness would have seen as much in loyalist Ulster. The policy of conciliation which had been followed since 1868 would have been repudiated, its gains cast away, and at the height of Britain's danger and travail. The Chief Commissioner of Police urged suppression, but Dublin Castle preferred a longer

---

43 In the midst of the deluge of war news (much of it bad) these manoeuvres attracted little public and press attention. This well suited Clarke, Pearse and others of the inner core, since they were rehearsing for seizures which were actually made – and at Dublin Castle narrowly foiled – in the opening hours of the Easter rising.

44 See Sir Matthew Nathan's evidence to the Royal Commission on the Rebellion in Ireland (Minutes of Evidence, *op. cit.*, 2–4).

and supposedly more subtle and effective game. Augustine Birrell would later resign amidst nearly universal press and public execration in the wake of the Easter rising, yet it is scarcely conceivable that Asquith's government would have countenanced any policy other than that which he followed prior to April 1916: surveillance, prosecutions, imprisonment and deportations under the Defence of the Realm Act (DORA) and reliance on the ubiquitous paramilitary Royal Irish Constabulary.[45] Despite the restraint, moreover, Dublin Castle on the eve of the rising seemed to have some kind of round-up in preparation.

The IRB assessment of the situation is instructive. Writing to Roger Casement (who was in Germany on a Clan mission) John Devoy totted up the military balance sheet. British forces comprised some 94,000 – 'all Territorials, very poorly trained and officered, with very few competent non-commissioned officers and composed of the scum of England'. Volunteers numbered about 30,000, of whom the organisation was in direct and secure communication with 10,000. The Post Office (on Castle directions) refused to deliver Volunteer post, and all messengers were shadowed by the police. The Sinn Féin and Volunteer press had been suppressed and the national press was warned not to carry favourable news. 'No arrests have been made yet,' Devoy reported, 'but the footsteps of all our friends are dogged and they live in hourly expectation of going to gaol.' Nor had wartime precautions been neglected. Irish ports were closed and mined and much fortification was going on. Foreigners, including Americans, could enter the country only through Dublin: 'It is utterly impossible to get a cargo of arms in, and smuggling them would be very difficult and would bring severe punishment.' A Birmingham arms source had been closed off. The Irish Party was doing what it could to coerce the militants, and seeking to get them dismissed from their jobs. It was impossible to get American officers to undertake Volunteer training, since they would lose their US Army jobs. The new passport system had made contacts very difficult. With German help the Volunteers could win, 'if their hand is not forced so that they may be wiped out before they are ready'.[46]

Hemmed in though it was, the IRB grasped and fully exploited such constraints as there were on Dublin Castle, although it was far from sure when forbearance might break, with disastrous consequences for insurrection. There were, however, two pieces of information which Birrell and Nathan did not have and which surely would have dictated an immediate pre-emptive round-up: they did not understand

---

45 Macardle (op. cit., p. 144) notes that between November 1914 and 15 April 1916 there were almost 500 DORA prosecutions in Ireland. These resulted in deportations, exclusion orders and residence requirements. Ernest Blythe, a Volunteer organiser, was typical of those who ran up against the law during this period. A deportation order was made against him in May 1915, and when he refused to comply he was sent to Belfast Prison for three months. He was released conditionally and subsequently deported to England, where he was interned at the time of the rising (PRO HO 144/1454/1a and 3).

46 Devoy to Casement, 1 January 1915; NLI: Casement Papers: 13,073 (44/i: italics in original). Over the succeeding year Devoy, through Casement, and then directly, continued his efforts to extract arms and other assistance from Germany (See NYPL, MCIHP, Box 4, IHP74).

that Pearse was *intent* on a sacrifice, that his declarations should be taken literally, and that other key leaders would go along with him. Equally importantly they did not understand the IRB's clever knots within the Irish Volunteers. Pearse and his closest colleagues had tied another within the IRB itself; of the twenty members of the provisional committee which directed the Volunteers, only three or four knew of the secret plans before the first stages.[47] Operating in secrecy so complete that Dublin Castle got no hint of it, no more than their uninducted colleagues, Pearse and some IRB men worked through a secret directorate in the Irish Volunteers, that would, at the appropriate time, co-opt or bypass the open and formal leadership of Commander-in-Chief Eoin MacNeill, and which kept the rest of the IRB and all but a few of the most senior Clan na Gael men in ignorance of their plan. This device resolved the insurrectionists' conundrum which had utterly foxed the Fenians of the 1860s: how to carry forward and keep secret a conspiracy while conducting the necessary preparation to build and activate a mass organisation. And at the moment of action wavering and desertion were minimised. The Volunteers had been trained to military discipline. Many of those mobilised were in full or partial uniform, and in any event were in close formation. Disobedience in such circumstances was unlikely, moral and even the threat of physical force ensuring a near-automatic response.

It was by these means – with many subsidiary twists and turns – that just after midday on Easter Monday, 24 April 1916 Patrick Pearse, in full uniform, hat and sword, stood on the steps of Dublin's General Post Office. The building had a few minutes before been seized by a combined force of Irish Volunteers and Irish Citizen Army men, commanded by James Connolly. To a small crowd of passers-by Pearse proclaimed the Irish Republic, which the Fenians had long insisted was 'now virtually established'. Referring to the historical succession of insurrections and Ireland's 'old tradition of nationhood', he summoned Irishmen and Irish-women to fight for freedom. Religious, social and civil liberties were promised, God's blessing invoked and 'cowardice, inhumanity or rapine' abjured. The sentence which probably caused more antagonism in Britain and the Empire than any other referred to the support of the Central Powers – 'gallant allies in Europe'.[48]

---

47 Béaslaí, *op. cit.*, Vol. 1, p. 57. Devoy and the Clan were working to a more cautious and orthodox Fenian agenda. A German invasion and concurrent rising should not take place unless there were German victories, particularly at sea. Devoy was emphatic: 'No invasion of Ireland should take place unless England is also invaded: not less than 25,000 men and 50,000 rifles, with proportionate amount of artillery, should be sent to Ireland, if the seas are cleared' (NLI: Casement Papers: Ms. 13,073 (44/i), f. 11.

48 In the weeks and months which followed, this phrase allowed the rebellion to be portrayed as a German-funded stab in the back (see, for example, the initial assessment of the rebellion by *The Times*, 1 May 1916, 12c–d; editorial of 12 May 1916; 9a). The notion incensed popular feeling in Britain, and greatly enhanced the standing of the Ulster Unionists. The *New York Times* singled out the phrase as one which confirmed the treason of the rising: 'Even if revolt when the nation is at war be not treason, there can be no doubt about the quality of the act when alliance with the enemy is openly confessed' (4 May 1916, 10a).

The proclamation was signed by the seven members of the provisional government with the old Fenian Thomas Clarke heading the list.

The course of the rising is well known, and it is unnecessary here to review it in detail.[49] There had been hopes of German assistance in matériel and officers. Limited help was sent (captured Russian rifles) but there were last-minute changes in the arrangements for landing the cargo, and the vessel was intercepted by the British Navy – drawing successfully on both human and the still embryonic but effective electronic intelligence. MacNeill, the Volunteers' nominal leader, deceived by Pearse and his group for several months, now grasped the secret plan and unequivocally denounced it. As late as the Thursday prior to the Easter weekend (20 April), MacNeill learned that orders had been issued and that an insurrection was imminent.[50] Confronting Pearse, he was informed that the plans were so far advanced that nothing could stop them and, in particular, that German arms would be delivered within hours. MacNeill bowed to the fait accompli, only to revert to his original opposition the next day, when the full extent of the IRB deceit was revealed to him, together with the information that Roger Casement had been captured and the German arms' ship intercepted. The rising was now hopeless, and MacNeill sent orders to all units cancelling any special instructions they might have received; he also inserted a notice in the *Sunday Independent* cancelling all Volunteer manoeuvres and movements (which had been the IRB's cover for mobilisation). These actions destroyed almost all possibility of action outside Dublin, and hampered and confused action in the city.[51] Only a fraction

49 Of the many narratives the best undoubtedly remains Desmond Ryan's *The Rising* (Dublin, Golden Eagle Books, 1949), which was written while many of the participants were still alive and had vivid memories of the rising. Ryan's republicanism dominates the text, but the resultant flaws and disadvantages are more than compensated for by the access his partisanship gave him to the survivors. His *Remembering Sion: A Chronicle of Storm and Quiet* (London, Arthur Barker, 1934) – now out of print and comparatively rare – is an excellent introduction to the pre-rising milieu and atmosphere, as well as the events of Easter week. There were several contemporary or near-contemporary publications. The *Irish Times* published a type of compendium cum souvenir – *Sinn Féin Rebellion Handbook* (Dublin, Irish Times, 1917). This provided a chronology of events, the principal documents, names of the dead, and accounts of the courts martial, executions and deportations. A reproduction of the *Handbook*, with an introduction by Declan Kiberd, was published in 1998 (Boulder, Colorado, Roberts Rinehart/The Mourne River Press). Just under one-third of Tim Pat Coogan and George Morrison's excellent text and photographs of *The Irish Civil War* (London, Seven Dials/Orion, 1998) is devoted to the antecedents of the rising and the event itself.

50 F. X. Martin, 'Eoin MacNeill on the 1916 Rising', *Irish Historical Studies*, XII (March 1961), p. 248. This essay provides, with extensive comment and editorial support, two contemporaneous memoranda by Eoin MacNeill, one dated February 1916 and the other between June and October 1917.

51 There were clashes in Co. Dublin and Co. Meath, where barracks and RIC men were captured. The Wexford Volunteers did not act until the Wednesday following the rising and Galway units went into the hills, but did not engage Crown forces. Cork City Volunteers were effectively paralysed by the flurry of orders and counter-orders and indeed, on the urging of the lord mayor and bishop, surrendered their unused weapons to the military authorities. The Cork commandant was Thomas MacCurtain and his deputy Terence MacSwiney, both of whom would later die in the

of the Volunteer forces were mustered and deployed, and when Pearse stood on the GPO steps, it was in the certain knowledge that the rising was doomed, and that the sacrifice for which he had longed would shortly be consummated.

Since there were then no staff colleges for revolutionaries, the leaders had prepared themselves as best they could in military science, and, with the aid of those who had formerly been in the British Army, had achieved an elementary level of operational competence. But their tactics were flawed, an unhappy cross between guerrilla and conventional warfare. They divided up their forces in Dublin and seized and held a number of public buildings with the intention of forming a defensive ring against Crown forces, to buy time for a general rising of their own units and militant sections of the general population. As originally designed, the ring had included a route for reinforcement from the country-side.[52] The plan failed to address realities and contingencies, and assumed the availability of a far greater force than was actually deployed. The depleted ranks ensured little communication between the units and, with no mobility or ability to take the initiative, it was only a matter of time before superior British forces, fully armed and supplied and backed with machine guns and artillery, blasted and burned them out.[53] The guerrilla axioms of concentrating forces to overwhelm an enemy at a particular point, of tactical withdrawals and advantageous re-engagements and, fundamental to all this, constant mobility of units, were reversed by the IRB leadership, with utterly predictable results.[54] To Pearse

---

Anglo-Irish war. Limerick Volunteers, baffled by the confusing orders and without the expected German arms, decided not to act (see A. J. O'Halloran, 'The Irish Volunteers in Limerick City', in The Kerryman, *Limerick's Fighting Story*, Tralee, The Kerryman, n.d. (?1947), pp. 5–17). Inaction in Limerick and Cork removed from the rising its greatest potential support outside Dublin.

52 See William O'Brien's introduction to Ryan, *op. cit.*, p. 16.

53 The rebels' tactics helped them to do this. Spread out through several strongholds they did not have the manpower properly to secure danger points in the vicinity, or to safeguard escape and dispersal routes. Even within the commands, their inexperience showed. Three days into the siege of the GPO, the rebel commanders ordered the men to fill sacks of coal from the basement for window and door fortifications. No sooner had they done so than shells began to fall, fire started, and the coal had to be hauled away again (NLI: Patrick Rankin Papers: Ms. 22, 251, f. 9).

54 The leaders went about their military education in a curiously pedantic manner, drawing lessons from the Napoleonic and Franco-Prussian wars, for example. From the latter Connolly derived the notion that strongly fortified buildings were the basis for defending a town or village. These, he argued, were 'a principal object of the preparations of any defending force, whether regular army or insurrectionary' (see 'Street Fighting – Summary', *Workers' Republic*, 31 July 1915, 8b). Inferior and ill-equipped forces as the insurgents were bound to be should never have attempted defence, which simply concentrated and isolated them for mopping up. For a selection of Connolly's military writings see Berresford Ellis, *op. cit.*, pp. 199–231; for Béaslaí's benefit of hindsight criticisms see *op cit.*, Vol. 1, pp. 100–1. For contemporaneous (and sometimes factually inaccurate) comment see *The Times*, 1 May 1916, 12c; 2 May, 9e. It is probable, however, that full-blown guerrilla tactics could not have been used, since the IRB plan depended on a strong element of deception against their own forces as well as the British government. It was immeasurably easier to mobilise and control large units in fixed positions under these circumstances than to deploy groups of a dozen or less men, part-time soldiers at that.

and some of the other commanders this did not matter. On Friday, 28 April, a final communique was issued in which Pearse declared himself satisfied, even if they were to achieve no more – 'We have saved Ireland's honour'.[55] The following day, at about 3.30 p.m. Pearse, as Commander of the insurgent forces, surrendered his sword and issued an order for the outlying units to lay down their arms.[56]

The rebels fought bravely and, within the limits of their training, equipment and tactics, well. There was no rerun of the Fenian fiasco of March 1867. Hundreds had held their ground for five days in the face of a vastly superior enemy. Despite the fierce fighting, casualties were relatively low among the insurrectionists – fifty-six killed and an unknown but presumably proportionate number of wounded. Army and police casualties were much higher: 130 dead and many wounded. There was considerable destruction of private property, and loss of civilian life – 216 or more killed in Dublin and many more wounded.[57] For several weeks there was much confusion about the extent of the loss of life and property, and it is doubtful if an exact tally of either was possible. On 4 May the King sent a telegram of thanks to the Army and RIC for their wholehearted devotion to duty during the 'recent lamentable outbreak'.[58]

Retribution

Even had the Empire not been involved in the largest and most destructive war in its history, the rebels would have attracted severe punishment. As it was, here was a conspiracy which had resulted in a considerable and shocking loss of life and property, and which had diverted energy and resources at a time when great numbers of their countrymen were in peril and were dying at the front: here, to the most of the rest of the United Kingdom, was an act of base treachery and naked treason.

Thoughts about the nature and extent of punishment came after the need to re-establish order. By its failure to anticipate and prevent the rising, the civilian

---

55 Irish Times, *Sinn Féin Rebellion Handbook*, Dublin, Irish Times, 1917, p. 50. He continued, 'For my part, as to anything I have done in this, I am not afraid to face either the judgement of God, or the judgement of posterity.'

56 The *Manchester Guardian* (10 May 1916, 3b–e) published four historic photographs: Pearse negotiating his surrender; Constance Markievicz being taken into custody; the Plunkett brothers in custody; and John MacBride under escort. The surrender, en masse and under orders, would have a considerable effect on the organisation and experience of imprisonment, as we shall see.

57 See Macardle, *op. cit.*, p. 181. The *Irish Times* on 11 May estimated the dead to be 300, wounded 997, and nine missing (*Sinn Féin Rebellion Handbook*, *op. cit.*). *The Times* (13 May 1916, e–f) gave the civilian casualties ('so far as they are known') in Dublin as 694, including 180 deaths. Two hundred and sixteen civilians buried at Glasnevin Cemetery were certified to have died from gunshot or bullet wounds, but returns from other cemeteries were not yet in.

58 PRO WO/35/69/1.

administration at Dublin Castle was utterly discredited.[59] Chief Secretary Birrell was in England for the Easter holidays and returned on the evening of Tuesday 25 April; but his return was superfluous.[60] General Sir John Maxwell was dispatched from England, arriving on Friday, 28 April.[61] His mission was to restore order, for which task he was given plenipotentiary powers. By proclamation of the Lord Lieutenant the country had already been placed under martial law, with the concomitant suspension of the usual civil and criminal processes and protections.[62] Civil administration, with all its cautiousness, calculation and consultation, was swept aside: control took priority over conciliation.

Maxwell had no zest for his task, but he set about it in a methodical and professional manner, facilitated by the rebel's suicidal strategy of holding fixed positions. Rebel units were surrounded, larger cordons formed, house-to-house searches initiated and reinforcements deployed. Despite subsequent accounts sympathetic to the rebels, artillery was not widely used. Liberty Hall, Connolly's union headquarters, was bombarded, but the guns were otherwise used only when machine guns or rifles proved inadequate. The centre of the city was badly damaged, but outlying posts and their surrounding areas much less so. By noon on Saturday 29 April, Pearse, Clarke, Connolly and their GPO comrades had decided on capitulation, and sought terms. Not unexpectedly they were informed that only unconditional surrender would be accepted, although a broad hint was given that the rebel rank and file would receive clemency.[63] With the capitulation of the GPO and the Four Courts the rising was effectively brought under control. Orders were sent by Pearse and Connolly to the outlying commands, all of which laid down their arms the following day. London was informed, and on

59 English press comment ranged from the reproachful to the rabid. The latter, well exemplified in Horatio Bottomley's jingoistic John Bull, saw failure to anticipate and prevent the Dublin rising as further evidence of the ineptitude which had led to the then stalled state of the war (6 May 1916, 8b). The Royal Commission used more measured language, and distinguished between the various divisions of government and functionaries in apportioning blame. The police and the army were acquitted, as was the Lord Lieutenant. Augustine Birrell, the Chief Secretary, and Sir Matthew Nathan, the Under-Secretary, were blamed for policies and omissions which allowed the rising to occur (Royal Commission on the Rebellion in Ireland, op. cit., pp. 12–13).

60 See telegram, Asquith to Lord Lieutenant Wimborne, 25 April 1916, 4 p.m.: 'Your telegram of today, Chief Sec. Leaves for Dublin this evening. Take no action until he arrives' (Bodleian Library, Oxford: Ms Asquith, 41, f. 10).

61 Maxwell (1859–1929) was a highly experienced soldier. Served in Sudan, South Africa and Egypt. Retired, but recalled in 1914 on outbreak of war. Head of British Military Mission at French HQ before returning to Egypt. Had not wished to accept the Irish posting.

62 See the operational circulars and summaries of reports issued by GHQ, Home Forces, in connection with the rising (PRO WO/35/69/2). These documents include a veiled amnesty for the surrender by the Volunteers and Irish Citizen Army of arms, ammunition and explosives. Any member of these organisations found in possession of these items after 6 May would be severely dealt with. The implication was that surrender before that date would either be overlooked or treated leniently.

63 Sir George Arthur, General Sir John Maxwell, London, John Murray, 1932, pp. 249–50.

1 May it was announced that Dublin was now under control and safe. Although this was not entirely true (isolated sniping continued for another few days), legitimate authority had been restored.

The men marched out of the GPO and (the following day) the outlying strong-points, and eventually were brought under escort to Richmond Barracks. There detectives went among them, identifying the leaders, who were immediately removed. There appears to have been some friction between the military, who wished to have the men rapidly processed and moved out to England, and the police who wanted more time to make identifications.[64] Since the army was in control the identifications were curtailed – a move which saved several of the lesser-known leaders from more severe punishment.

On the Irish side the position was not as clear. The rising had no representative basis – if representation means the mandate of the ballot box. Indeed, writing of the prevalent mood, an Irish revolutionary concluded that there had never been a time 'when the conquest of Ireland by England now seemed complete'.[65] Pearse, Connolly and the other leaders were, of course, aware of the anomaly of their position: they were claiming to speak for the Irish nation, but had no tangible authority to do so, other than their own interpretation of nationhood and the apostolic succession of Fenianism. The IRB was the antithesis of a representative democratic organisation, and although more instinctively democratic, Connolly's brand of Irish Marxism allowed him to advance such serviceable rationalisations as false consciousness.[66] Yet it was undeniable that rebellion against the conqueror was a powerful theme in Irish history and national consciousness, and seemed to attract a retroactive form of legitimacy. Electorally unrepresentative, therefore, the rebels still needed to be handled with great care lest they acquire the standing acquired by the Young Irelanders and Fenians. The constitutional nationalists, who had been dealt the most severe blow by the rising, became aware of the aspiration to martyrdom by the rising's core of leaders, and of the consequences of their deaths: any substantial blood-letting would fulfil their principal objectives.

On the day that the last group of rebels surrendered in Dublin, Dillon, deputy leader of the Irish Parliamentary Party, wrote to Redmond in London counselling caution. Government should be advised of:

> [T]he *extreme* unwisdom of any wholesale shooting of prisoners. The wisest course is to execute *no-one* for the present. This is the *most urgent* matter for the moment. If there were shootings of prisoners on a large

---

64 NLI: Patrick Rankin Papers: Ms. 22, 251, ff. 13–14.

65 Béaslaí, *op. cit.*, Vol. I, p. 44: 'Men, women and children everywhere wore warlike badges in which the Union Jack was prominent. . . . All the political guides of the people predicted that winning the war for England was the only thing that mattered.'

66 For his version of the revolutionist's *vade mecum* see his reflections on O'Donovan Rossa's burial, 'Why the Citizen Army Honours Rossa', in Ryan (ed.), *op. cit.*, p. 70.

scale the effect on public opinion might be disastrous in the extreme. So *far* feeling of the population in Dublin is *against* the Sinn Feiners. But a reaction might very easily be created.[67]

And from Dublin Castle came much the same message from the outgoing and now discredited Chief Secretary: 'It is not an *Irish* rebellion,' he wrote to Asquith, 'It would be a pity if *ex post facto* it became one, and was added to the long and melancholy list of Irish rebellions.'[68]

It is a melancholy confirmation of the unwillingness or inability of politicians to learn from history, even when it matters most, that Birrell's advice was ignored and the rebellion was given a national character. Irish nationalism had repeatedly demonstrated that its more extreme and destabilising elements were energised by the creation of martyrs. An examination of the writings of some of the rebel leaders would have shown that they sought to apply the lever of martyrdom to a situation which they found unreceptive to physical force politics. And in their assessment of the effects of political executions they were correct. Looking back on the Easter rising from the vantage-point of the late 1920s, Churchill (who had a visceral hatred of the Irish rebels) took a line similar to Birrell's:

> The attempted German assistance, the mad revolt, the swift repression, the executions, few but corroding. Well it was said, 'The grass soon grows over a battlefield but never over a scaffold.' The position of the Irish Parliamentary Party was fatally undermined. The keys of Ireland passed into the keeping of those in whom hatred of England was the dominant and almost the only interest.[69]

At this defining moment in Anglo-Irish relations Asquith made a catastrophic error in casting the whole responsibility for Ireland on General Maxwell. Order has many elements, of which military security is certainly one of the most important. But fundamental though it is, military control does not stand alone – and certainly not in the medium and longer terms. Maxwell performed his tasks ably

---

67 Rolleston Denis Gwynn, *The Life of John Redmond*, London, George C. Harrap, 1932, p. 475. Dillon continued: 'I have no doubt that if any of the well-known leaders are taken alive they will be shot. But, except the leaders, there should be no court-martial executions.' (The rising had trapped Dillon and his family in Dublin, and Redmond in London.)

68 Leon Ó'Broin, *Dublin Castle and the 1916 Rising*, New York, New York University Press, 1971, p. 115. The Lord Lieutenant took a stronger line, writing to Birrell from the Vice Regal Lodge on Wednesday, 26 April, insisting 'with all the earnestness of which I am capable' that any doubt or hesitation in dealing with the rebellion would bring disaster to the government and would 'leave a stigma which afterwards would be felt to be most intolerable' (Bodleian Library, Oxford: Ms. Asquith, 41, f. 123).

69 Winston S. Churchill, *The World Crisis: The Aftermath*, London, Thornton Butterworth, 1929, p. 281.

and conscientiously within his professional understanding. It was inevitable that with Dublin Castle so discredited and Redmond damaged with it, advice would neither be sought nor needed from those quarters. But a number of critical judgements had to be made, and these were demonstrably beyond Maxwell's competence. The speed and manner with which courts martial and executions proceeded was not justified politically – nor, as it turned out, militarily. This was an unexpected rebellion by what seemed a shockingly large group, and cost much in life and property. But in the end the rebels were thinly spread, poorly prepared, led by amateurs, and, for all their bravery, no threat to a professional army: the loss of life amounted to no more than an hour or so of Western Front skirmishing. To hurry these aspirant martyrs to their graves, rather than subject them to the more deliberate and demystifying processes of law, was a major miscalculation for which Asquith must bear responsibility, as his rather belated intervention confirmed. In strictly retributive terms the leaders deserved death, and the philosophy of military justice would yield no other outcome. Any dispassionate calculation of state interests would surely have led to a different conclusion. But this balance was not attempted, and it was through the prism of the hasty and secret trials and executions that the lesser punishments, the internments, and many other things beside, would come to be viewed.

The executions

In the end, Maxwell executed fifteen men. Seniority in the conspiracy was the principal qualification, although reputation and ill-starred propinquity also operated. The Proclamation's seven signers were certainly destined for the firing squad.[70] In addition, all the commandants of the Dublin outposts were executed, except for de Valera who was saved by his possible American citizenship and probably also by being tried at a late date (8 May), when the Cabinet had concluded that aside from those cases already processed the executions should stop.[71] Two men who had not been in the leadership were shot. John MacBride had led the Irish Brigade in the Boer War, and this may have been taken by his court martial to be sufficient proof of high complicity in the rebellion – although despite his military experience MacBride had been excluded from the leadership,

---

70 The seven were Thomas Clarke, Seán MacDermott, Thomas MacDonagh, P. H. Pearse, Eamonn Ceannt (Kent), James Connolly and Joseph Plunkett. The last married his fiancée, Grace Gifford, sister-in-law of Thomas MacDonagh (who had been in the first group to be executed). The ceremony was conducted in the prison between 3 and 4 a.m. – shortly before Plunkett's execution (see 'Marriage Before Execution', *The Times*, 8 May 1916, 9f, 10a).

71 Two men were executed after de Valera's death sentence was commuted to life penal servitude – James Connolly and Seán McDermott – on 12 May 1916. Both had been at the heart of the conspiracy; both had signed the Proclamation, and both had been taken from the Post Office. On de Valera's own account of his citizenship, see below, p. 432, n. 85.

possibly because of his excessive drinking.[72] The other non-leader to be executed was Patrick Pearse's brother William, who played a wholly subordinate part and seems to have been sentenced because of his family connection.[73] A third man, Michael O'Hanrahan, was executed apparently because he had been second-in-command at the Jacob's Factory outpost, and had also been Quartermaster-General of the Volunteers. Only one man was executed from outside Dublin, and his was a singular case. Two days after the surrender, a rank-and-file Cork Volunteer, Thomas Kent, had killed a policeman while resisting arrest, and in consequence was sentenced to death and shot in Cork on 9 May.[74]

Asquith and the Cabinet were under intense privately expressed pressure to restrict the executions to the leadership. On 8 May four comparative unknowns were shot: Michael Mallin, Cornelius Colbert, Seán Heuston and Eamon Ceannt.[75] Later that day Asquith drafted a telegram to Maxwell: 'Four men shot this morning. Feel it my duty to represent grave danger of general and bitter resentment periodical [sic] vengeance on comparatively little known insurgents indefinitely prolonged. Reassuring statement needed without delay.'[76] This

72 At his court martial MacBride confirmed that he knew nothing of the insurrection and was never a Sinn Féiner. He had come to Dublin for a wedding, but 'finding a rebellion on I decided to join it as I always detested British rule'. MacBride thanked the court for a fair trial, concluding, 'I have looked down the muzzles of too many guns in the South African war to fear death, and now please carry out your sentence'. This speech was related to Tim Healy by the Crown Counsel in MacBride's case (Timothy Michael Healy, *Letters and Leaders of My Day*, London, Thornton Butterworth, 1928, Vol. 2, p. 563). According to Healy, General Blackadder who presided at the courts martial was much affected by the bearing of the insurgents and wished to save some of them, especially MacBride, 'but the accused wished to die'.

73 The balance may have been tipped in William's case by his having been drafted in by his brother on Good Friday to assist with the last-minute issuing of orders. For this purpose William signed himself 'Acting Chief of Staff' (See, for example NLI: O'Kelly Papers: Ms. 8469, Capt. William Pearse to Capt. Seán T. O'Kelly, 21 April 1916). Thomas MacDonagh's brother John also took part in the rising but was not shot or imprisoned. (He was interned – first at Knutsford Prison and them at Frongoch camp.)

74 The three Kent brothers had resisted attempts to arrest them, and the police and army had laid siege to their home. A head constable was killed, as was one of the brothers. Thomas Kent was sentenced to death, and his brother David to twenty years' penal servitude (see P. J. Power, 'The Kents and their Fight for Freedom', The Kerryman, *Rebel Cork's Fighting Story*, Tralee, The Kerryman, 1947, pp. 59–64).

75 Michael Mallin (1880–1916) had served in the British Army in India. Became Chief of Staff of Connolly's Irish Citizen Army and was Commandant at Stephen's Green. Cornelius Colbert (1896–1916) was bodyguard to Tom Clarke in the period before the rising, and saw action in Dublin. Seán Heuston (1891–1916) assisted Colbert in drill and musketry training at Pearse's St Enda's School. Commanded Mendicity Institute during rising (see Madge Daly, 'Seán Heuston's Life and Death for Ireland', The Kerryman, *Limerick's Fighting Story, op. cit.*, pp. 31–4). Eamonn Ceannt (1881–1916) helped plan the rising. Commanded South Dublin Union and Murrowbone Lane.

76 Bodleian Library, Oxford: Ms. Asquith 43, f. 9 (punctuation added). In Asquith's hand, and dated by archivist as either 4 or 8 May. Almost certainly the latter because of the obscurity of the men shot on that day. On 4 May Joseph Plunkett, Edward Daly, William Pearse and Michael O'Hanrahan were executed.

provoked a somewhat tetchy reply from Maxwell. He had confirmed no death sentences unless convinced by the evidence 'that the convict was either a leader of the movement or a commander of rebels', who were engaged in shooting down His Majesty's troops or subjects'. Connolly and MacDermott were to be tried that day (9 May) and 'If convicted they must suffer the extreme penalty.' These would be the last executions with the exception of any cases of proved murder of soldiers or police in the execution of their duty.[77] It would seem that at that point some form of political authority was sought for the remaining executions, since on 11 May Lord Kitchener, Secretary of State for War, telegraphed to Maxwell: 'Unless you hear anything to the contrary from Mr Asquith you may carry out tomorrow the extreme penalties upon MacDermott and Connolly.'[78] These (apart from Casement) were the last executions of the rising. On 20 May Maxwell assured Asquith that he would confirm no death sentence without reference to him.[79]

Courts martial proceedings in 1916 were brisk but did adhere to rough standards of elementary justice: clear charges were put, supporting evidence was called. The accused could cross-examine and call his (or her) own witnesses. The adjudicating panel took their duties and obligations seriously. The principal disadvantage a defendant suffered was the denial of legal advice during the critical stage of the taking of the Summary of Evidence. A great deal of discretion was given to the authorities with respect to procedure, and a distinction was drawn by them between a Field General Court Martial (the form for all the early trials) where legal representation was not allowed, and a General Court Martial, at which it was.[80] For a person not trained in the law, the difference between the actions and motives alleged against him or her, and the evidentiary requirements of the law, may have been far from clear. The defendant conceivably may not have had enough information to know how to plead to the charges or how to submit mitigation which was compatible with his own beliefs yet relevant to the charges. And there were other difficulties. The speed of the proceedings in disputed cases hardly allowed sufficient time to prepare a defence and locate witnesses and other evidence.[81] An appeal could be made only to the Competent Military Authority, and it was all but impossible to delay the execution of sentence pending appeal. Civil courts had very limited jurisdiction over military matters, and while the

---

77 Maxwell to Asquith, 9 May 1916: Bodleian Library, Oxford: Ms. Asquith 43, f. 11.

78 Kitchener to Maxwell, 11 May 1916: Bodleian Library, Oxford, Ms. Asquith 32, f. 18.

79 Maxwell to Bonham-Carter, 20 May 1916: Bodleian Library, Oxford, Ms. Asquith 42, f. 146.

80 PRO WO 35/68, Brigadier-General Sir Joseph Byrne (Inspector General, RIC) to GHQ, 23 May 1916. Colum Campbell provides a particularly useful description and analysis of courts martial procedure in *Emergency Law in Ireland, 1918–1925* (Oxford, Clarendon, 1994, pp. 54–101).

81 The very short time allowed between trial, review and (if approved) execution of sentence is in striking contrast with the pace of civil procedure. Some of the surviving documents of the prisoners – including emergency wills – emphasise the haste with which defendants went from the courtroom to the firing squad (see John MacDonagh's will (he was not executed) leaving all to his brother Thomas (who was executed), NLI: John MacDonagh Papers: Ms. 20648(5)).

1916 courts martial heard fairly straightforward cases, as the Anglo-Irish war developed and military jurisdiction expanded and cases became more complicated, it is extremely doubtful if justice could be said to have been done.

Still, in 1916, no innocent man was among the executed leaders, but in some cases there must be concerns regarding comparative guilt.[82] Writing in 1920 Timothy Healy noted that William Wylie had won the esteem of the Sinn Féiners because of the fairness with which he conducted the 1916 prosecutions.[83] At de Valera's[84] hearing, for example, his identity was established, and evidence was taken from the British officer to whom he had surrendered, to prove that he had commanded Boland's Bakery (the outpost at which he was taken). A British cadet who had been a prisoner at the Bakery gave similar evidence. The court questioned de Valera on his nationality – a point on which he himself made no claim except to insist that he had never regarded himself as a British subject.[85] The proceedings concluded, with findings and sentence to be announced at a later date. (As with all courts martial, proceedings and sentence were reviewed, and the latter was subject to confirmation.) De Valera left the court convinced

---

82 *The Times* criticised the decision to conduct the trials in camera: Asquith agreed (12 May 1916, 9a). A modern judgement has confirmed that courts martial meet Human Rights requirements: *R. V. Spear*, et al., [2002] UKHL31.

83 'He was one of the Officers' Training Corps during the War. British Army head-quarters required that he should, for the wage of a captain . . . prosecute Pearse and his companions' (Healy, *op. cit.*, Vol. 2, p. 627).

84 (1882–1975). Born New York of an Irish mother and Spanish father, raised by relatives in Co. Limerick. Educated in Dublin, graduate of University College. Joined Gaelic League in 1908. Commandant in 1916 rising. Condemned to death, reprieved and sentenced to life penal servitude. Released June 1917. His political career and devoted following made him a pervasive, frequently dominating, presence in Ireland until his death. See Tim Pat Coogan's definitive life, *De Valera*, London, Hutchinson, 1993.

85 De Valera's wife, however, had made representations to the Permanent-Under-Secretary at Dublin Castle, Sir Matthew Nathan (then in his last days of authority), pointing out that her husband had been born in New York of a Spanish father and Irish mother. She also contacted the US Consul in Dublin, and presented her husband's birth certificate (see John Brennan, 'Frongoch University – and After', The Kerryman, *Dublin's Fighting Story 1913–1921*, Tralee, The Kerryman, n.d. (?1948), p. 114). Doubt about citizenship contributed to the delay in de Valera's trial and the commutation of the death sentence. De Valera's citizenship remained a mystery to the British government, and at the request of the US State Department attempts were made to clear it up shortly before he was received at Dartmoor Prison. On 11 August 1916, Major E. Reade, the Dartmoor governor, reported that de Valera had given New York as his place of birth. He had asked his mother to find out whether his Spanish father had ever become an American citizen. If he had (and this was still undetermined) de Valera had told the governor he wished to claim American citizenship; if not he claimed Spanish citizenship. He had not become a British citizen, 'but he would have become an Irish citizen if that had been possible' (PRO HO 144/10309/50833/1). The British government, if not in 1916 then later, took the view that de Valera was not British and in October 1919, while he was an escaped prisoner and known to be at large in the United States of America, decided to exclude him from the United Kingdom: no visa would be issued, and he would be turned back at any port of entry (PRO HO 144/103009/50833/315944/15).

that he would shortly be shot.[86] Constance Markievicz underwent a similar process, conducting only minimal cross-examination and declining to call any witnesses of her own.[87]

Those who were condemned made no complaint: they had gone into the enterprise with open eyes. Tom Clarke was confident of eventual success: 'This insurrection, though it has failed, will have a wonderful effect on the country. . . . We will die, but it will be a different Ireland after us.' Seán MacDermott and James Connolly said much the same and in similar phrases.[88] Constance Markievicz's insouciance emerges from her account of events immediately after her surrender. As she and her comrades were marched away they discussed what seemed to be the only point in doubt – 'whether they would be shot or hung'.[89] With less bravado, Seán Heuston's last letter strikes a similar note of affirmative resignation: 'whatever I have done, I have as a Soldier of Ireland, in what I believe to be my country's best interest. I have, thank God, no vain regrets. After all, it is better to be a corpse than a coward.'[90]

Apart from core figures, the rebel's fate was determined as much by the automatic review which followed verdict and sentence as by the substantive court martial proceeding itself.[91] The sorting and sifting which went on after formal court proceedings closed could notionally make the difference between life and death – although apart from the principal figures there was a general policy of mercy. Maxwell appears to have been scrupulous in his reviews, and apart from William Pearse and John MacBride there were no obvious injustices. Indeed, in terms of culpability and intent, it seem obvious that many who were well qualified for execution escaped it. Of ninety sentences of death imposed by courts martial all bar fifteen were commuted – usually to penal servitude for life; many initial sentences of penal servitude for life were commuted to shorter terms. Ultimately, the length of one's sentence made little difference, since all

---

86 Earl of Longford and Thomas P. O'Neill, *Eamon De Valera*, Boston, Houghton Mifflin, 1971, pp. 48–9.

87 See the record of her Field General Court Martial, 4 May 1916: PRO HO 144/1580/316818/16. Most of the courts martial records (apart from a few such as Markievicz's which made their way into Home Office Records) are to be found in PRO WO/35/68; 71/344–9. See also Brian Barton's useful *From Behind a Closed Door*, Belfast, Blackstaff, 2002.

88 Béaslaí, *op. cit.*, Vol. 1, p. 122; Nora Connolly O'Brien, *Portrait of a Rebel Father*, London, Rich & Cowan, 1935, pp. 319 and 325–6.

89 NLI: Gore-Booth Papers: Ms. 21, 815: Eva Gore-Booth Memorandum, f. 9.

90 NLI: Sister Francesca MacDonagh Papers: Ms. 20, 647 (5) (unfoliated). Elsewhere in this letter (obviously written a very short time before his execution) Heuston asks for his outstanding salary to be paid to his mother, together with his superannuation: 'I take this opportunity for thanking you and all my railway friends for the kindness of the past years. I ask them all to forgive me any offence which I may have committed against them.'

91 The Law Officers had determined that the rebels' action amounted to 'intent to assist the enemy', under Defence of the Realm Regulation 50. Maxwell had ordered Field General Courts Martial, stipulating that sentences of death or penal servitude would be reserved for his confirmation (PRO WO/35/69/7).

remaining sentenced prisoners were freed in June 1917. The absolute difference between the capital penalty and any term of imprisonment made the caprice and chance of some of the sentences all the more pronounced. De Valera was a key figure in the rebellion – he was not a member of the core group, but one of those in the innermost circles, as well as an effective commander. His involvement and culpability thus was far greater than that of John MacBride or William Pearse, both of whom were executed. Nor did he exchange execution for a long and debilitating confinement, but within fourteen months was again at liberty. Comparatively minor figures were visited with death, major players with only a few months' imprisonment: the fortunes of war.

There is at least one record of the workings of chance at the reprieve stage of proceedings. As we have seen, MacNeill, repeatedly duped, had subsequently done all he could to thwart the IRB plan for the rising, short of betraying Pearse and the others to the British: he had sent out countermanding orders and advertised in national newspapers. As Commander-in-Chief of the Volunteers MacNeill was nevertheless arrested, brought before a court martial and sentenced to death. In Tom Jones' *Whitehall Diary* there is an account of his reprieve. Redmond went to Asquith and Lloyd George to plead for MacNeill's life, saying 'McNeill is our greatest Gaelic scholar.' Lloyd George then turned to Asquith and said 'Good God! We mustn't kill a Gaelic scholar.' And that, according to Redmond's recollection, 'settled it'.[92] Paradoxically, the British decision to proceed with the formalities of court martial, review by higher authority and confirmation or commutation of sentence probably conveyed a greater level of callousness and brutality than had the leaders been executed in a batch, in hot blood. The authorities were bound to follow procedure, but this meant that the executions were protracted, partly because competent legal staff were in short supply.

There was a coda to the executions, which received little, if any public notice. Under the Forfeiture of Property Act, 1870, the property of the executed rebels, and those sentenced to penal servitude was liable to be placed in administration.[93] On 15 May 1916, Major Price of Military Intelligence sought direction from General Maxwell on this matter. For the most part the rebels had been taken without money and had little property, but Price pointed out that £8-8-01/2d had been taken from Patrick Pearse and some money had been found on James Connolly: 'The countess Markievicz is said to rent or own two houses. James Connolly and the Citizen Army had a large holding at Croydon Park, Fairview, and they also held Liberty Hall, which stood on a valuable site.' Should the property be forfeited Maxwell would have to make the necessary declaration and

---

92 Thomas Jones, *Whitehall Diary*, London, Oxford University Press, 1969, Vol. 1, p. 13.

93 Forfeiture was abolished by this Act. The convict's property could be placed in administration, and the convict was liable for costs and compensation in his case (34 & 35 Vict., c.23, ss. 3, 4 and 9).

to arrange to take possession. Price suggested that the proceeds might be contributed to a compensation fund for the innocent victims of the rising.[94] Maxwell
and his advisers seem to have concluded that a forfeiture action was not generally
worth the trouble, though administrators were appointed for the property of
Countess Markievicz, W. P. Corrigan, F. Lawless and Dr Richard Hayes. When
these were released in June 1917, the question arose as to whether administration
should continue.[95] Since the convicts had been released on free pardon (as distinct from licence) their property was freed from restraint.[96] Rebels are generally
propertyless, but those few persons of property who took part in the rising were
able to retain it.

The long drawn-out series of trials, conducted *in camera*, and the daily terse
announcements of findings and sentence gave the civil population a sense of a
machine at work in their midst over which they had no control whatsoever.
Rumours abounded, and for the first month or more the combination of the
destruction and displacement caused by the rising, and military inexperience in
dealing with civil and political issues meant that the flow of information was
wholly inadequate. This affected many sectors of Irish – particularly Dublin –
life which had no connection whatsoever with the rising: administrative, public
service, legal and commercial information was critical for the restoration of
normal life, and often it was not provided or decisions were delayed.

The relatives and friends of those involved in the rising also sometimes
found it hard to obtain information. Eva Gore-Booth, Constance Markievicz's
sister, fell into this category. On the Sunday following the rising, as the last
of the rebels surrendered, there appeared a story in *Lloyds Weekly News* that
Constance's body had been found at Stephen's Green (where she had been
second-in-command). Eva was distraught, but recorded that in the 'terrible
days that followed' (as the trials got under way) she had almost wished the
soon-discredited story were true, 'so much worse does it seem to the human
mind to be executed coldly & deliberately at a certain hour by the clock, than
to be killed in the hurry and excitement of battle'.[97] There was a similar lack
of information in a letter from Knutsford Prison from John MacDonagh to his
sister. He had received no information on anything that had happened since
Easter Monday, outside of his own immediate affairs. He thought their brother
Thomas must be dead, since while in detention in Dublin he and the other
detainees had heard a rumour that all the signatories of the Proclamation would
be shot.[98]

---

94 Price to Maxwell, 15 May 1916: PRO WO/35/69/19.
95 PRO HO 144/1580/316818/64: Dublin Castle to Home Office, 27 June 1917.
96 The pardon signed by the King on 16 June 1917 remitted the balance of the convict's sentences
    (PRO HO 144/1453/311980/121 and 142).
97 NLI: Gore-Booth Papers: Ms. 21, 815: Eva Gore-Booth Memorandum, f. 4.
98 John MacDonagh to Sister Francesca MacDonagh, ? early May 1916: NLI: Sister Francesca
    MacDonagh Papers: Ms. 20, 647 (i) (unfoliated).

Reactions

Politicians and people

Having ventured so far down the road of total support for the war effort, if on no other ground, John Redmond was bound to condemn the rising. Formulation was everything, given that whatever he said was guaranteed a prominent place in the Irish political consciousness. Knowing the difficulties which his policy had already encountered in Ireland, speaking without first-hand information or (it would seem) more than cursory consultation with party colleagues, he was unequivocal in his denunciation. On behalf of the Irish Party and the 'overwhelming majority of the people of Ireland' he expressed his 'detestation and horror', joining with Carson in his desire that the rising would not be used as a political weapon against existing parties.[99] In an interview with an American news agency (apparently given on the day before the rebel surrender) Redmond rehearsed the reasons why it had been right for Home Rulers to back the British war effort, and did not stint in his condemnation of the rebels. They were the Party's implacable enemy and their rising was not half as much treason to the Allied cause as it was to Home Rule: 'I do not believe that this wicked and insane movement will achieve its ends. The German plot has failed.'[100] Those statements were surprisingly incautious, at the very least laying him open to the charge of again currying favour with the English, in a particularly unsavoury way because it was at the expense of his errant fellow countrymen, whose lives were now in the balance. The executions which Redmond must have known would follow the crushing of the rising cast a pall of horror over his remarks.

And the executions were not long in following. The first took place on 3 May (Patrick Pearse, MacDonagh and Clarke) and the last (Connolly and MacDermott) on 12 May. The secret proceedings, the terse public announcements of sentence and execution and, as the shootings continued, uncertainty about when they would stop, all had a galvanic effect.[101] Shaw, at best an ironic observer of Irish nationalism, condemned the executions both on the grounds that the men were prisoners of war and that the shootings would be counterproductive: all would take their place alongside Emmet and the Manchester

---

99 5 *Hansard*, LXXXI, col. 2512; 27 April 1916.

100 The interview was published as *The Voice of Ireland* (London, Thomas Nelson & Sons, 1916). The pamphlet contained some fifty or so messages of support for Redmond from Irish clubs and associations at home and throughout the world.

101 It was widely believed in nationalist circles that the public was excluded in order to hide injustice. Sir John Maxwell had directed that the hearings be closed to the public on security grounds. A subsequent appeal was refused, the Divisional Court taking the view that Maxwell had legitimately decided on closed proceedings because of safety and security concerns (*Rex v Governor of Lewes Prison*, The Times Law Report, 23 February 1917, 4a–b). Whatever the legalities, however, the decision to proceed in camera carried a high political cost, and long tarnished the reputation of British justice.

Martyrs as nationalist saints.[102] Dillon, who had been vehemently against the executions from the outset (and who was in the process of distancing himself from his leader), renewed his plea in the Commons on 11 May: 'It is not murderers who are being executed; it is insurgents who fought a clean fight, a brave fight, however misguided . . .' Asquith agreed that the great body of the rebels had conducted themselves 'with humanity', they had fought very bravely and 'did not resort to outrage'.[103] This generous and conciliatory statement was largely nullified by the subsequent executions of Connolly and MacDermott the following day.[104] And the forebodings of those who saw the executions as another episode in Ireland's potent martyrology were immediately fulfilled. Within a few years the 1916 courts martial were placed firmly in the category of procedural murder and the shootings in batches the driving home of a lesson that 'these men were entitled neither to open trial and proof of their guilt before execution, nor to the treatment of captured enemies'.[105]

It would have confirmed nationalist convictions that the courts martial were pro-forma justice had it become known that preparations for the disposal of the bodies were made before the hearings had been concluded. On Tuesday 2 May, as the first courts martial commenced, Brigadier-General J. R. Young, deputy Adjutant General at Maxwell's headquarters, issued detailed instructions for the executions and burials. In the event of sentences of death being imposed the condemned were to be segregated to the extent that circumstances permitted. They were to be asked whether they wanted to see chaplains, relatives or friends

102 *Daily News*, 10 May 1916, 4d. His claims for prisoner-of-war status were perhaps strengthened by the fact that – unlike the rebels who would follow them in the Anglo-Irish war – Pearse and all the leaders had fought openly, and they and as many of their followers who could afford it had been in uniform and made their own banners: their particular nationalist credo had made them scrupulous in this. The British view was that one could not opt out of citizenship and its obligations simply by donning a uniform: the high number of commuted death sentences, however, showed that the authorities knew that legal reasoning and logic was not their only guide. The question, being essentially political, was resolved by several standards and by these the executions were a capital error.

103 5 *Hansard* LXXXII, cols 951 and 956. Asquith favourably contrasted the behaviour of the Irish rebels with that of Britain's 'so-called civilised enemies'. Dillon's speech, together with the murder by a British officer of Francis Sheehy Skeffington (a well-known Dublin advocate of female suffrage and pacifism) and the internments, was considered by General Maxwell to have contributed to a deterioration in the Irish political situation. Since Dillon's claims were not refuted – 'The Sinn Féiners think that they were right, that the Government were to blame and that the executed rebels were "martyrs"' – Maxwell characterised Dillon's speech as 'unfortunate' and claimed that it had provoked 'a lot of racial feeling' (Bodleian Library, Oxford: Ms. Asquith 42, f. 146 and f. 150: Maxwell to Bonham-Carter, 20 May 1916). Dillon's speech was widely reported and attracted the attention of the Irish everywhere, including moderate Irish-Americans (see the *New York Times*, 12 May 1916, 1c and 3a).

104 *The Times* reported that opinion on executions was elusive, but (writing on the day Connolly and MacDermott were executed) the consensus was that the executions carried out to date should be sufficient (13 May 1916, 7e).

105 Robert Mitchell Henry, *The Evolution of Sinn Fein*, Dublin, Talbot Press, 1924, p. 221.

and these would be brought to Richmond Barracks by military vehicles, stationed there for that purpose. All visitors were to be taken back to their homes by 3.30 a.m. on Wednesday, 3 May, at which time the firing party would parade. The first condemned man would be brought out and face the firing party of twelve men and one officer, at ten paces. The rifles were to be loaded by men other than the firing party, so that one of the weapons had a cartridge but no ball. The firing party would be told of this arrangement, but none of them would know which rifle was loaded with a blank. There would be a different firing party for each of the men to be executed.[106]

After each man had been shot and certified dead by the medical officer, the body was to be placed in an ambulance, identified by a label on the breast. When the ambulance was full it was to go to Arbour Hill Detention Barracks where a working party would place the bodies close beside each other in the grave and cover them thickly with quicklime. (There was no mention of the bodies being stripped.) The grave was to be filled in – presumably only to the extent necessary to cover the bodies. An officer with the burial party was to keep a note of the position of each body, taking the name from the label, and a priest would conduct the funeral service.[107] Later on the day that General Young issued his instructions he was notified that Patrick Pearse, Thomas MacDonagh and Thomas Clarke had been sentenced to death and that General Maxwell had confirmed the sentences. The procedure was then set in motion by sending an officer to Kilmainham Prison and Richmond Barracks where the three men were variously held. The sentence and its confirmation was read to each man in his cell, and each was then kept in a separate room under observation until the sentence was carried out. These arrangements were generally followed, except for the preservation of the plan of the grave.[108]

General Maxwell was aware that the executed men would probably acquire an aura of martyrdom; with other officials and politicians he failed to anticipate how rapidly this would come, and the wide swathes of Irish opinion that would be affected. Urgent inquiries were made from London about the disposal of the bodies of the executed men – prompted no doubt by concerns about the disorder attendant on public funerals, and the likelihood of burial-places becoming places of pilgrimage. Maxwell assured Asquith that the proper steps had been taken:

106 Confidential memorandum, Brigadier-General J. R. Young, 2 May 1916: PRO WO/35/67/2. The executions were carried out at Kilmainham Prison.
107 Ibid. From these instructions it is clear that there was no truth in the rumour then circulating in Dublin (Macardle, op. cit., p. 185) that General Maxwell had ordered a grave to be dug for one hundred bodies.
108 At some point the procedure for recording the location of each body seems to have broken down or been lost. On 5 July 1932 de Valera's Irish Press reported that it had recently become possible to identify the remains. The Sergeant Major in charge of the preparation of the graves had, on his own initiative, placed a numbered brick at the head of each of the fourteen men interred in the mass grave, in order of burial (5 July 1932, 1f). The bodies remain in the grave, which was reconstituted in the 1950s and is now a national memorial.

'The Prime Minister should know that the bodies of all the executed martyrs are buried in quick lime, without coffins in the Arbour Hill Prison Grounds. This I understand is the ordinary prison procedure.'[109] In a Catholic country reverential and respectful treatment of the dead was a strong instinct, and the penal disgrace of the body of the condemned was viewed with particular horror and revulsion. 'A felon's grave' induced an immediate spasm in the nationalist psyche.

In his proclamation of the Irish Republic on Easter Monday, Pearse had abjured 'cowardice, inhumanity or rapine' in the conduct of the insurrection. Dillon had claimed and Asquith had agreed that the rebels had fought in a clean and humane way. There were no stories of brutality, looting, cowardice or – the old bugbear of Irish rebellion – drunkenness. The men had surrendered in order, in military formation, and under their commanders. The leaders had not attempted to escape, but in their defeat and captivity had accepted responsibility for the rising and had sought clemency for their followers; and they had died bravely, without recanting or seeking mercy. All this had an impact on the public mind as details of the rising and its aftermath became known.

Importantly for the reputation of the Volunteers, the men had behaved as good Catholics throughout the rising. Despite the total condemnation of the rebellion by their hierarchy, priests attended the men throughout the city – necessarily very dangerous missions. Priests of the Franciscan Capuchin Friary were particularly attentive.[110] On several occasions the rosary was recited in the GPO, and when transports of the rank and file were embarked for internment in England, they knelt together on the dirty planking of the cattle boats to pray.[111] This devoutness allowed several elements in the rising to combine into a potent mixture of nationalism, religion and self-sacrifice. When it became known that the rebel leaders had received the comforts of the Church before death their aspirations to popular marytrdom could not be thwarted.

Father Albert of the Capuchin Friary (who was particularly sympathetic to the republican cause) in December 1916 began to write about the continuing influence of the dead leaders in terms that hinted at the possibility of some form of supernatural intercession with its association of beatification. The deaths of MacDonagh and Pearse, brave and strong in their religion, had a great religious influence, he believed. Writing to MacDonagh's sister, Father Albert referred to the 'many interesting cases I have met recently . . . where men have received extra-ordinary graces through those dead friends whose life & death have brought

---

109 Maxwell to Bonham-Carter, 26 May 1916: Bodleian Library, Oxford, Ms. Asquith 43, ff. 140–1. Maxwell had been approached by Pearse's mother for the return of any papers or personal property found on him, or any prison writings. This matter had also been raised by Dillon. Maxwell asked for directions: 'I am sorry to raise such thing but with the Irish members on the war path I feel I ought to.'

110 NLI: Sister Francesca MacDonagh Papers: Ms. 20, 647(1) (unfoliated).

111 NLI: McGarrity Papers: Ms. 17, 512, Edward Martin, 'The Irish Rebellion of 1916. Personal Experiences. Reminiscences of English Convict Prisons'.

a religious as well as patriotic revival'.[112] In the Roman Catholic and Orthodox traditions, saints leave relics as tangible evidence of their earthly existence; to some believers these are possessed of beneficial or even miraculous powers. While the remnants of the rebels never attained full cult status, they developed intense political interest, tinged for some with distinct elements of piety. The collection of souvenirs and memorabilia attracted publishing and commercial interests in the months which followed the rising.[113]

When wed to romanticism this devotional patriotism became absurd. Constance Markievicz (who had kissed her revolver when she surrendered) sent a piece of the GPO flagpole to a friend. Her explanation well conveys the mix of patriotism, sentimentality and superstition which – although it might be derided by the unsympathetic – helped revive republican spirits. After the failure of the rising, the imprisonments and executions, she explained,

> [S]ome of the lads of the Fianna carried off the flagstaff on to which the flag that proclaimed the Republic was hoisted from the smoking ruins. This was cut into sections and one was given to me. I cut this little chip from it and am sending it to you as a tribute to your beautiful verses that are an inspiration to all lovers of freedom and justice.[114]

American opinion

Joseph McGarrity, a leading figure in extremist Irish-American circles, and a member of the Clan na Gael executive, denounced the British for violations of the laws of war. He promised punishment for those who had ordered the executions 'when the fortune of war' (by which he presumably meant German victory) 'places the power in Irish hands'. The executed men had gone to their deaths 'with the heroic courage of Robert Emmet and the Manchester Martyrs, proud that they were found worthy to die for Ireland and glorying in their martyrdom'.[115]

The mainstream American press was for the most part initially neutral about the rising. The *New York Times* carried full and lengthy reports of the fighting

---

112 Father Albert to Sister Francesca MacDonagh, 22 December 1916: NLI: Sister Francesca MacDonagh Papers: Ms. 20, 647(5) (unfoliated). Father Albert's political sympathies are made fairly clear elsewhere in this letter. Six years later he remained with the anti-Treaty forces throughout their occupation of the Four Courts, administering the sacraments to the dying and defying the order of the hierarchy to deny them to Republican (i.e. anti-Treaty) forces under arms (see Coogan and Morrison, *op. cit.*, p. 171, plate 200).

113 See, for example, the souvenir publication *Dublin and the Sinn Féin Rising* (Dublin, Wilson Hartnell & Co, 1916) which provided portraits, documents and pictures, together with descriptions of Volunteer relics, arms and accoutrements and the story of the rising.

114 NLI: Markievicz Papers: Ms. 24, 595. Constance Markievicz had founded the Fianna, a nationalist youth organisation of the scouting type, in 1909.

115 NYPL: Maloney Collection, Box 5, 1HP87.

and its aftermath, but was sparing in its editorial comment. In the midst of the series of executions it dismissed parallels between the Union's treatment of the Confederate leadership at the end of the Civil War and the British government's policy towards the leaders of the rising. The American War had ended before the questions of punishment and leniency came to be considered, but Britain was engaged in a terrible war the end of which was not yet in sight: 'It can hardly be doubted that in like circumstances any other Government would in like manner have enforced the law in its full rigour.' Some might doubt the wisdom of shooting Pearse, Clarke and the other leaders, taking the view that the rising was such madness that it would be more appropriate to treat them as fanatics rather than traitors, but 'war is a stern business and the subject who sets himself against his King or the citizen who rises against his Government when the nation is straining every resource to overcome enemies in the field, can hardly expect mercy'.[116]

The conservative Nation agreed on the character of the rising – 'murderous', 'a mad act' – and shared Redmond's characterisation that it was a thing of 'heartbreak and misery'. But it disagreed with the executions, even though the British government was well within the law, both civil and military. It is impossible for two nations to live intermingled with each other who were filled with desperate hate. Anything that intensified and perpetuated the hate is against the interests of the state. And – also referring to the American Civil War, but drawing the opposite conclusion to that of the New York Times – the British government should have taken a lesson from the United States of America in the way to deal with defeated rebels. The Irish rebellion appeared to be an affair of lunatic leaders and duped followers, and the soundest course was to imprison the guilty or put them in lunatic asylums 'and let time and second thought do their work'.[117]

But the fate of the Irish rebellion was always more likely to be affected by broad Irish-American sentiment than by the reflexively Anglophile WASP press. The rising brought mixed reactions – from bewilderment and caution to bitter rejoicing – but the executions were unlikely to produce anything but public condemnation among Irish-Americans of Roman Catholic stock. Some who felt uncertain about events in Ireland but worried about the shootings refrained from comment in the first days of the series of executions.[118] They were certainly

---

116 New York Times, 4 May 1916, 10a. For other reports on Ireland see 3 May, 1c, and 9 May, 8b–c.

117 Nation (Washington), 11 May 1916, 509c and 510a–b. Readers took opposite sides on the issue – dealing mercifully with the rebels as a wise act of state versus dealing ruthlessly with German-linked conspirators (ibid.,18 May 1916, 541a; 1 June 1916, 592a–b). On 10 August 1916, the Nation carried an article from London, 'A Defence of the Irish Executions', which comprehensively argued the justice of the sentences (ibid., 125c and 126a–b).

118 The New York Times found that the editors of local Irish newspapers agreed that the events had made a 'profound impression' but were otherwise unwilling to comment (4 May 1916, 2b).

right to be cautious, since the facts had reached the United States of America garbled to the point where it was reported that the executions had taken place in the Tower of London. The editor of *Ireland*, a Home Rule journal in New York, thought that the executions would have completely the wrong effect 'unless some very good reason were given for it'. Patrick Egan, a former US Ambassador to Chile and prominent Irish-American supporter of John Redmond, tried to turn the executions against Fenian circles in New York. If anyone should have been shot it was John Devoy who had received German funding and who was a 'destructive and dangerous agent'. Devoy with German money and Jim Larkin 'and his socialist-labour bunch' had persuaded a lot of good Irishmen into a hopeless cause. Devoy in New York and Larkin in Chicago had let other men spill their blood.[119]

Few Irish-Americans took this line, whatever they privately thought, and the way was cleared for denunciations. Justice Daniel F. Cohalan,[120] a prominent Democrat and Clan na Gael man, and close associate of John Devoy, party to the sending of Sir Roger Casement to Germany, and a prime mover in the American side of the rising, denounced the shootings in terms which showed his anger and indignation straining against the limitations of language.[121] Robert Ford, editor of the *Irish World*, was less extreme in tone, but condemned the executions on the grounds that Pearse and the others were prisoners of war and should not have been shot; reprisals would no doubt follow. John D. Moore, Secretary of the pro-German Friends of Irish Freedom called the executions 'murder', 'lynch law' and 'blood thirstiness' committed by a country that was doing its best to starve and destroy 'human beings of all ages, sexes and conditions in Germany, Austria and Hungary'.[122]

And with the denunciations of British action came execration of Redmond and the Irish Party. They had conspired to 'barter off Irish blood in England's interest', were 'pitiful whelps', pestilent traitors and ought to meditate on the fate of Judas.[123] Only Lawrence Ginnell had played the man's part in the Commons: Redmond was a 'shameless traitor'.[124] Details of the lives of the executed

---

119 Ibid., 4 May, 2b–c.
120 (1865–1946). Born Middletown, New York. Active in Irish-American politics in both the Democratic Party and the Tammany Society. Appointed to New York Supreme Court in 1912. A leading organiser of the American contribution to the Easter rising. In 1920 entered into a bitter dispute with Eamon de Valera over the leadership of Irish-Americans.
121 The executions were 'an atrocious crime and a colossal blunder', they were 'murder', an act of 'savage hate'. Badly beaten by the Central Powers, England had dragged the men to London 'to glut her savage hate upon them' (Cohalan thought the executions had been in the Tower). (*New York Times*, 4 May 1916, 2b).
122 Ibid., 2b.
123 *Irish World and American Industrial Liberator*, 6 May 1916, 4a–c.
124 Ibid., 13 May 1916, 4b.

dominated several issues of Ford's *Irish World* together with summaries of American reactions to the sentences, with particular attention to denunciations from normally pro-British newspapers and commentators.[125] For those Irish Americans with relatives among the dead, wounded and arrested, there were long lists of names and places of abode.[126] On 14 May a protest meeting was held at Carnegie Hall, with John Devoy and Judge Cohalan on the platform. The Hall itself was packed, as were the surrounding streets.[127] If anything, the pace and momentum of the campaign of protests accelerated. On 10 June 1916, some 10,000 to 15,000, it was claimed, assembled at Madison Square Garden to honour the rebel dead and to subscribe $26,500 for the relief of their families and those in prison. Women prisoners attracted special attention, as did Eamon de Valera as an American citizen and surviving leader. By August Nora Connolly had reached the United States, where she spoke about her father's captivity and stretcher-borne execution to great effect. This, coinciding with news of Casement's execution on 3 August, caused Sir Cecil Spring Rice, British Ambassador to the United States of America, to warn London to be prepared for a 'great explosion of anti-British sentiment'. Germans and the Irish would work together on the issue. There would be arson against British property and 'probably some hostile action in Congress'.[128]

The volatility of American opinion was well understood in London, where in late May Lloyd George and Balfour had met Grey, the Foreign Secretary, to discuss the situation. Grey and Lloyd George emphasised the negative effect that the rising had on Americans and argued that an agreement on Irish issues between the constitutional politicians would greatly assist in mending current perceptions. Balfour agreed, but pointed out the obvious – such agreement could not come soon, and in the meantime some other solutions must be sought. He proposed using a dispatch from Maxwell, to be formulated in 'direct and simple' military language to convey the truth to Americans. Uncertain as to whether Maxwell or anyone on his staff could write such a document, the dispatch could be addressed notionally to the War Office but Grey should have a hand in the final draft.[129] The notion that the assessment of a simple and honest soldier could shake American opinion was fanciful, however, and the proposal seems to have gone nowhere.

---

125 See, for example, ibid., 20 May 1916, 4c and 5; 3 June 1–2; 8 June, 2; 17 June, 1b–f, 7d–e; 8 July, 12a–b.

126 Ibid., 12 August, 1g.

127 The *New York Times* put the audience inside the hall at 3500, with another 4000 outside in the streets (15 May 1916, 1c and 2b).

128 Spring Rice to Foreign Office, 1 August 1916: Bodleian Library: Asquith Papers: Ms. 17, f. 30. During an American election year, he noted, the efforts of both parties were to make difficulties for Britain. All departments of government in Britain should show restraint.

129 Balfour to Grey, 29 May 1916: Bodleian Library, Asquith Papers: Ms. 30, ff. 105–6.

Home opinion

Of committed Irish republicans only a bitter reaction could be expected. The rising and the executions had immeasurably fortified their cause. But these effects were well beyond extremist circles, reaching those whose strong-rooted antipathy to all forms of republicanism was well founded. The speed with which Irish opinion shifted, and the nature and quality of the change, would be gauged across a range of organisations and individuals. Predictable but telling were the exchanges between General Maxwell and Dr Edward O'Dwyer, Roman Catholic Bishop of Limerick, over the matter of two pro-rebel priests in O'Dwyer's diocese whom Maxwell wanted removed from parochial work.[130] Replying to Maxwell's request, O'Dwyer declined to act against the priests, stating that he had no grounds on which to do so. But even had there been reason to act, it would have been impossible for him to take any part in proceedings he characterised as 'wantonly cruel and oppressive'. He contrasted the treatment of the Jameson Raiders with what had happened to the Irish rebels:

> You took care that no plea for mercy should interpose on behalf of the poor young fellows who surrendered to you in Dublin. The first information which we got of their fate was the announcement that they had been shot in cold blood. Personally I regard your action with horror, and I believe that it has outraged the conscience of the country.

Going on to denounce the deportations and internments, Bishop O'Dwyer condemned Maxwell's short period in charge as 'one of the worst and blackest chapters in the history of the misgovernment in this country'.[131] The bishop's bitter and unrestrained tone arose perhaps from the fact that the exchanges commenced on a fairly civil note on 6 May, in the midst of the executions, and finished five days after their full extent was known. The Roman Catholic Church in Ireland had a long and consistent history of denouncing political violence, and although he was something of a maverick, O'Dwyer's condemnation of the established authorities for their actions – placing them, at best, on a par with the rebels – was a blow to the moral basis of British government in Ireland. Nor was O'Dwyer on his own. A month after the executions, Tim Healy observed that he had never known such a transformation in opinion. The combination

---

130 (1842–1917). Edward Thomas O'Dwyer had a long record of pro-nationalist statements and actions, and had refused to join the other bishops' declaration against Parnell. He opposed Redmond in his support for the British war effort.

131 Cit. Béaslaí, op. cit., Vol. 1, p. 131. Maxwell forwarded his correspondence with Bishop O'Dwyer to Asquith, noting that O'Dwyer had without forewarning published it via the Cork Examiner. Although he was the only member of the Roman Catholic hierarchy to take this step, Maxwell feared that O'Dwyer's action had done harm and incited others to defy authority (Sir George Arthur, op. cit., p. 261).

of the executions and the 'ruffianism' of the army in the immediate aftermath of the rising had aroused a level of contempt and dislike such as he had never known.[132]

The Irish Parliamentary Party, fighting for its life, was in no position to turn the tide of feeling. Its most sensible strategy was to go with the current, attempt to get to its head and, when the time came, to redirect it. Asquith's six-day visit to Ireland on 12 May, and the concurrent cessation of executions,[133] did much to stabilise the Irish political mood, but it could no more stop the surge of sympathy for the rebels than had the statements of the nationalist leaders. Maxwell's political assessment on 20 May was astute. The Irish MPs, he wrote to Asquith, were taking advantage of the swing in the public mood to get the Sinn Féiners back into the nationalist fold, but he feared that the Irish Party had become discredited, and would be replaced at the next election by others 'less amenable to reason'. He noted how it had become increasingly difficult to draw a distinction between a nationalist and a Sinn Féiner, and that recruiting in Ireland had practically ceased. The shift in mood had found its way behind bars and barbed wire and showed itself in prisoners' correspondence. Whereas at first their letters were humble and apologetic, 'now the tone has become defiant, and it shows that they think themselves national heroes: though the Rebellion was condemned it is now being used as a lever to bring on Home Rule, or an Irish Republic.'[134]

The Irish newspapers, divided on party lines between the Unionist and moderate nationalist, were bewildered, then outraged by the rising. The staunchly Unionist *Irish Times* announced on 25 April that it had never been published in stranger circumstances, and went on to describe, on the basis of its limited information, the attempt that had been made to overthrow the government.[135] Days of confusion and combined editions followed, with the eventual announcement of the end of the rebellion.[136] The catalogue of destruction, loss of life and

---

132 Healy, *op. cit.*, Vol. 2, p. 568. The reaction of the Irish Parliamentary Party to the executions did it lasting damage. While it appears to be untrue that members of the party cheered the announcement that on 9 May the executions would continue, it damned the party in the eyes of many that only the maverick Larry Ginnell actually protested in the Chamber (see, for example, Béaslaí, *op. cit.*, Vol. 1, pp. 125–6). For the parliamentary record see *The Times*, 9 May 1916, 8a: this notes unspecified cheers and Ginnell's interjection of 'murder'.

133 Asquith arrived on the morning that Connolly and MacDermott had been executed, and was brought through the centre of Dublin *en route* to the Vice Regal Lodge in order to see the extent of the damage (*The Times*, 13 May 1916, 7e–f).

134 Maxwell to Asquith (undated, but possibly 20 May 1916; Bodleian Library: Ms. Asquith 42, ff. 151–5, *passim*). An autograph book kept by William O'Brien with entries from prisoners at Richmond Barracks, Dublin, Knutsford, Frongoch and Reading confirms Maxwell's observation. The inscriptions are patriotic and warlike, vow to return to the struggle and celebrate a German naval success (NLI: William O'Brien Papers: Ms. 15, f. 662).

135 *Irish Times*, 25 April 1916, 4c.

136 Ibid., 28 and 29 April, 1 May 1916 (combined edn), 2d.

trade, and misery inflicted by the rising concluded with a demand for 'A stern policy of suppression and punishment'. There was an attempt to bolster the position of the constitutional politicians, by publishing messages of support from Irish societies in Britain and overseas.[137] Birrell's resignation was described as a blessing, and the newspaper urged that a distinction be drawn between the leaders and their followers, and demanded a purge of the disloyal from the service of the state.[138] By 10 May, with the end of the executions in sight, the *Irish Times* rejected the demands that had been made for their cessation, which it considered premature; they likewise dismissed pleas for a return to civilian government. Martial law was a blessing, and for the first time in many months Dublin and parts of the provinces were enjoying real security of life and property: 'We have learned by bitter experience that the sword of the soldier is a far better guarantee of justice and liberty than the peace of the politicians.'[139] The newspaper was not over-sanguine, however, and when the last two executions were announced on 12 May it hoped that no others would be found necessary, with the exception of convicted murderers. At the same time it insisted that there should be no attempt to palliate the rebellion, and expressed bewilderment at Dillon's Commons speech and the Irish Party's half-hearted denunciation of the rebellion.[140]

In a combined edition covering seven days' missed publication, the *Irish Independent* declared that 'No terms of denunciation . . . would be too strong to apply to those responsible for the insane and criminal rising of last week. . . . It is as if foreign invaders . . . had brought their evil upon the erstwhile peaceful city of Dublin.' The leaders 'deserve little consideration or compassion . . . we care little about what is to become of the leaders who are morally responsible for this terrible mischief'. The newspaper, however, asked for 'special consideration' for the followers, many of whom were duped.[141] A week later, in the midst of growing pressure for mercy, the newspaper stuck by this line. The young followers who had been misled and tricked should be let off, the leaders 'dealt with as they deserve . . . weakness to such men at this stage may be fatal'.[142] By 13 May, however, with the executions of Connolly and MacDermott, and with the English liberal press pressing ever more strongly for clemency, the *Indpendent* felt able to call for a halt to executions, except for 'actual cool murder'.[143]

The *Freeman's Journal*, at this point the voice of the Irish Party, similarly failed to appear for several days, and when it did its line was cautious. The rebellion, the waste of property and destruction of life it condemned unreservedly ('stunning

137 Ibid., 2 May 1916, 3b.
138 Ibid., 5 May 1916, 8d–e; see also 3a–f for reporting on the aftermath.
139 Ibid., 10 May 1916, 4f.
140 Ibid., 13 May 1916, 4f.
141 *Irish Independent*, 26–29 April, 1–4 May 1916 (combined edn), 2a–b.
142 Ibid., 10 May 1916, 2c.
143 Ibid., 13 May 1916, 4c.

horror'), though it could not hold back from a party-political point: 'had Mr Redmond been Prime Minister of Ireland it would almost certainly have been averted'. It referred to Botha's crushing of the South African rebellion and his clemency thereafter, and urged the government to have careful regard for Irish feelings in the measures they would have to take.[144] With the last two executions the newspaper was more emphatic. Bitterness and disaffection were spreading. Secret trials, military sentences and executions would never before have been legal in Ireland. Robert Emmet and his companions were tried by judge and jury, as were William Smith O'Brien and the insurgents of 1867: 'We are not only under an uncontrolled despotism, but we have not even the protection that the people of Ireland had in 1798 and 1803.' The hurried trials and executions had been a 'fatal mistake' and far too much blood had been shed. 'Military Dictatorship' could not continue without disastrous consequences.[145]

But in the end it was English opinion which would decide how far to go in punishing the rebels, and ultimately, what severities might be justified in defence of British rule in Ireland. At this distance we have little evidence by which we might gauge popular sentiment. There was some jeering at the prisoners who were brought over from Ireland, and it seems that there was quite strong feeling against Roger Casement.[146] Occasional journal entries suggest puzzlement rather than anger, but journal keepers may be a special and more than usually reflective population.[147] The press certainly had a lot to say about the Irish revolt in reportage and editorial columns, but the tone and the values expressed faithfully followed party affiliations.

A common theme, irrespective of political colour, was the drawing of distinctions between the leaders and followers; there was also much comment on the German connection. The conservative *Liverpool Courier* picked up a widely expressed feeling when it welcomed the departure of Birrell, whose 'triflings', the newspaper insisted, had cost many gallant lives 'and forfeited others that were not so gallant'. The soldiers killed in suppressing the rebellion were dead and buried, the rebels 'who were tricked or bribed' into the rising were shot, yet Birrell retired gracefully with a bland apology for winking or blinking at the

---

144 *Freeman's Journal*, 26–29 April, 1–5 May 1916 (combined edn), 2c–e.

145 Ibid., 13 May 1916, 4c–e.

146 See below, p. 569, n. 58.

147 'The Rebellion in Ireland is quenched but there is still trouble because the rebels are being too severely punished . . . Ireland is our rebellious child and we don't a bit know how to handle her. If we would only try to understand her people better, instead of punishing them when they rebel, we should put an end to the trouble. Those rebels are made of good stuff' (Diary of Miss Viola Bantree, 15 May 1916: Imperial War Museum, Department of Documents). Kate Courtney (*Extracts from a Diary During the War*, London, Private Circulation, 1927) hoped that some good might come out of the conflict: 'Carson and Redmond join in condemning it, and I hope it may, at any rate, only be S. Africa over again, Redmond and his Nationalists being as Botha and his Boers' (30 April 1916). By the time it was over she was less sanguine: 'Too many executions. Unwise for future, if nothing worse' (5 May 1916).

event.[148] The *Courier* took a different line on the followers – 'wretched dupes'. These 'should be dealt with as leniently as circumstances and justice will permit'. There was a problem in disposing of such large numbers, but given the martial inclinations of these 'wild Irish lads' they could perhaps be employed in the French docks.[149]

The *Manchester Guardian* insisted that there were two things higher than the instinct of revenge – 'one is called justice and the other wisdom'. Writing on 10 May, the newspaper called for the suspension of the executions and the passing of cases from military to civil courts: 'Every life taken now, above all every life taken under martial law, is a new source of danger, and of permanent danger, to the relations between the British and Irish, and the word Irish means not only the people of Ireland, but the millions of Irish in America.'[150] The *Guardian* did, however, recognise that for military reasons some executions could not have been avoided. It also drew a clear distinction between leaders and followers. The following day, acknowledging that the mass of the Irish people had not supported the rebellion, the newspaper warned that the executions had 'stirred an old sentiment, have touched something that reverberates down long corridors of historic memory'.[151] Following this logic, on 12 May (too late by the time the newspaper appeared), the *Guardian* urged that Connolly and MacDermott should not be shot. It knew that Connolly was badly wounded and assumed that MacDermott was, and urged that the 'unwritten law' that the men be nursed back to health before being shot should not be followed, and the death sentence commuted to penal servitude. The terrible shooting of Francis Sheehy Skeffington without military authority and other incidents of a similar nature demanded atonement by some signal act of clemency.[152]

A month after the rising two polished and sagacious articles by the veteran journalist Henry Massingham (writing from Dublin) accurately diagnosed its cause. He described the volatile state of opinion in Dublin and looked to future developments. The authorities thought that military law had 'done rather well', but a Roman Catholic priest who had condemned the rising had told him that for every one sympathiser of Sinn Féin on Easter Monday, there were now ten.[153] Asquith's visit to Ireland had done good, in Massingham's view, but it came rather late. Political control should have been reasserted as soon as the last

---

148 *Liverpool Courier*, 4 May 1916, 4b. The editorial was headed 'Exeunt the Cap and Bells'.
149 Ibid., 4e.
150 10 May 1916, 4b: 'Every rebel who suffers the capital sentence is potentially a canonised hero. His blood may be the seed of sedition ages hence.'
151 Ibid., 11 May 1916, 4b.
152 Ibid., 12 May 1916, 4b. Skeffington (1878–1916) was a pacifist who disapproved of the rising. But while trying to stop looting he was arrested and subsequently shot on the orders of Captain J. C. Bowen-Colthurst, who was later found guilty of murder but found to be insane.
153 *Nation*, 20 May 1916, p. 208.

sniper was silenced or captured. Instead the military had been left in command, unable to deal with the special danger of extreme nationalism: 'Cast a thing like Sinn Féin adrift on the stormy Irish waters, after shooting or hanging its leaders and terrorising their followers, to what forces might you not deliver up Ireland? To John Devoy and the Clan na Gael?'[154]

154 Ibid., 27 May 1916, 247. It is said that popular opinion was initially so against the rebels that the crowds of rank and file were jeered as they marched under guard to the boats which would take them home to England. It is certainly true that the wives of British soldiers showed hostility to the men when they were moved from their place of temporary detention in the city centre to Arbour Hill barracks. But how quickly the hostility was displaced may be shown by John MacDonagh's account of his march to the Dublin docks in the course of which he removed his last tunic buttons to give as keepsakes to importunate sympathisers in the accompanying crowd (NLI: Sister Francesca MacDonagh Papers: Ms. 20, 647(1)).

10

INTERNMENT

A training camp in Wales

Still together

The character of the Irish prisoners, internees and sentenced must be understood. This was a group of rebels very different from any which had previously entered British custody. Most critically, the core, taken in arms, had surrendered as a disciplined body, and went into captivity as an army with its chain of command intact, or soon restored. Its leaders had not fled, but had chosen death or imprisonment in order to save the lives of their followers and preserve their organisation and what they saw as the integrity of the uprising. The core of activists was accompanied by a larger group, rounded up on suspicion. Some of these were justified detentions, others were merely sympathisers or innocents. Releases soon stripped away the less involved, and what remained was a disciplined body, under training, responsive to orders, and willing to exploit imprisonment as an opportunity for further struggle, as occasion offered. John Brennan, who fought in Dublin, compared his comrades with their forerunners thus:

> The Fenians, members of a militant organisation, but not an organised army, could be brutally punished individually as insubordinate convicts whenever they broke any of the prison regulations. It was extremely difficult, if not impossible, to deal similarly with the 1916 army, which, highly organised and disciplined, treated a gaol fight as a military operation and planned and carried it out accordingly.[1]

Failure to grasp this quality of the men in their charge placed the authorities, military and civil, headquarters and local, at a considerable disadvantage.

---

1 John Brennan, 'Frongoch University – and After', The Kerryman, *Dublin's Fighting Story 1913–1921*, Tralee, The Kerryman, n.d. (?1948), p. 115.

Legal issues

The surrender of the rebels and the several round-ups of suspects in Dublin and the provinces produced a large number of detainees. Manpower was not available to process them, and the best that could be done was to identify the leaders and other prominent activists,[2] and to put the followers where further investigations could be undertaken and, more importantly, where they could do no more damage. There was a parallel. In the 1865 to 1867 Fenian emergency habeas corpus had been suspended and several hundred men, Irish and Irish-American, were rounded up and detained on the Lord Lieutenant's warrant. These men had been held in Irish prisons – some for more than a year. The internments had been a significant drain on civil administration, and this could not be repeated in the midst of a major war. And, as the Fenians had demonstrated, there would be found among the guards – rank-and-file Irish soldiers, policemen and prison staff – some of whom could be seduced from their loyalty to the Crown: speedy removal from Ireland was imperative.

Detention, deportation and internment of untried persons raised several legal problems which had to be tackled immediately. Persons found guilty and sentenced by courts martial were in a clear enough position: a court martial sentence could be served in any part of the United Kingdom. Of the 183 persons dealt with by courts martial, 122 men and one woman were sentenced to penal servitude (some of these had been sentenced to death, commuted to life penal servitude); in addition, eighteen men were sentenced to various periods of imprisonment. The difficulty arose with those who had been detained but not processed by the courts. After the rising some 3200 persons were taken by the military and police. Of these, about 1200 were immediately or soon after released. Apart from the 183 dealt with by courts martial, 1863 were interned under the Defence of the Realm Act (DORA) Regulation 14b.[3] The total included hundreds who had been taken in arms, or who had surrendered under rebel colours, but the majority had been detained on suspicion of involvement in the rebellion, or connection with the revolutionary organisations.[4] It became clear from the number subsequently released that the net had been flung far too wide and a number had

---

2 Identifications were made by officers of the G Division of the Dublin Metropolitan Police, as the Dublin rebels were marshalled at Richmond barracks. The principal leaders were identified and sent for trial easily enough, but below that level there was some confusion and an element of hit and miss about the proceedings. Michael Collins, for example, an aide-de-camp to Joseph Plunkett in the Dublin GPO, escaped trial simply by leaving the group of suspects to which he had been assigned, and joining the rank-and-file detainees (Piaras Béaslaí, *Michael Collins and the Making of New Ireland*, London, George C. Harrap, 1926, Vol. 1, pp. 105–7. Tim Pat Coogan's biography of Collins also provides a graphic account of the initial sorting process (*Michael Collins*, London, Arrow Books, 1991, pp. 44–7).

3 5 *Hansard*, LXXXVI, col. 561; 18 October 1916.

4 A few, such as Ernest Blythe, had been deported prior to the rising, and were arrested in England and interned under Regulation 14b (PRO HO 144/1454).

been rounded up on mere tittle-tattle or malicious accusation[5]. Various problems would also arise from the fact that the cursory sorting and rapid removal of the suspects did not permit systematic and timely on-the-spot interrogation. Short-term security had been traded for intelligence and convictions.[6]

On 9 May 1916, General Maxwell urgently consulted the Irish law officers[7] on the legal predicament. It had proved impossible to bring any great proportion of the detainees to trial, since the nature of the fighting had left the authorities 'without sufficient evidence of identification to justify a court in convicting on a specific charge'. It would nevertheless be 'most prejudicial' to the safety of the realm to allow men who had been in open rebellion to remain at large while the war continued. Agreeing with Maxwell's assessment, the Irish law officers pointed to the limitations of DORA.[8] Its use would require information to be gathered in Ireland for production before tribunals in England. Equally unthinkable was the prospect of bringing the prisoners before Irish courts: 'Such proceedings would in most cases at least certainly prove abortive owing to the sympathy, apathy and cowardice of the jurors while they would keep alive in an aggravated form the burning embers of the recent conflagration.'[9] As long as internment continued in Ireland other constitutional difficulties lay in wait and could be activated by habeas corpus applications. DORA did not, in the law officers' opinion, provide any regulation which fully addressed the circumstances of the interned Irish rebels, and so they recommended an additional and retroactive regulation akin to Regulation 14b under the Act, which would specifically refer to the Irish rebellion. The whole problem should in any event be submitted to the English law officers.

English officials and lawyers were no less perplexed. The internees could not be brought to trial in England before civil courts, because their offences were committed in Ireland. Nor could they be tried by courts martial in England.

5 At least one member of Carson's Ulster Volunteers was arrested in error as he made his way to work in Dublin one morning. Despite his protests he was transported to Wakefield Prison, though released shortly after his arrival there (Eamon Martin, 'The Irish Rebellion of 1916. Personal Experiences. Reminiscences of English Convict Prisons'. NLI: McGarrity Papers: Ms. 17, 512).

6 Before and during the rising, and through much of the Anglo-Irish war of 1919 to 1921, British intelligence was far from adequate: it was divided between several agencies in Ireland and England, lacked strategic direction and coordination, and was poorly collated and disseminated. Eunan O'Halpin correctly notes the failure to collect intelligence about the internees ('British Intelligence in Ireland, 1914–21', in Christopher Maurice Andrew and David Dilks (eds), *The Missing Dimension: Governments and Intelligence Communities in the Twentieth Century*, London, Macmillan, 1984, pp. 54–77).

7 James Chambers (1863–1917), KC, Unionist MP for South Belfast, Solicitor General for Ireland, 1917; James O'Connor (1872–1931), PC, Solicitor General for Ireland, 1914–16, Attorney General for Ireland 1916–18, Lord Justice of Appeal, 1918–24.

8 Defence of the Realm Act, 1914 (4 & 5 Geo.V, c.29). Various amendments were made to this Act in the period 1914 to 1920.

9 PRO HO 144/1455/313106/1, annex.

Should a case be brought for an offence under DORA in England, internees would as British subjects be entitled to a jury trial.[10] The Home Office agreed with Maxwell that there were security problems involved in sending so many men back to Ireland for trial and, once there, the Cabinet was informed, it would be useless to bring them before juries, because in Ireland they 'cannot be relied upon to do justice'. Even if they were dealt with by courts martial in Ireland, the evidence in many cases would not be strong enough to ensure conviction, 'although there is no real doubt as to their connection with the rebellion'.[11]

A solution was proposed by English officials, however, that use might be made of DORA Regulation 14b. This allowed the Home Secretary, on the advice of 'a competent naval or military authority', and in order to secure public safety or the defence of the realm, to issue an order with regard to a place of residence, restriction of movement, reporting to the police or internment. Persons liable to such an order were (and the phrase would become notorious) those of 'hostile origin or associations'. There was a right of appeal to an advisory committee.

The Home Office was confident that the rebels' 'hostile associations' could be established by 'The known connection of the Sinn Féin movement with Germany, proved especially by the landing by Sir Roger Casement and the attempted landing of arms, and by the Rebels' proclamation which refers to the Irish Republic's "gallant allies in Europe"'.[12] There had been legal challenges to Regulation 14b, on the ground that it deprived British subjects of the right to trial, and authorised deprivation of liberty by fiat. This argument had been rejected by the High Court and by the Court of Appeal, but at the time of the Home Office memorandum it was possible that the case would go to the Lords (where it was rejected in May 1917[13]). In the event of a finding for the plaintiffs new legislation would be necessary, not only for the Irish rebels, but also for those thought to be subversive and who had been placed under various restrictions, as well as suspected spies and a range of detainees.[14]

---

10 Jury trial had by proclamation been suspended in Ireland but not in Great Britain. By virtue of Section 1(7) of the Defence of the Realm (Amendment) Act, 1915 (5 & 6 Geo. V, c.34) aliens had no right to jury trial under the Act, but this would not apply to the internees, all but a handful of whom were British subjects.

11 'Irish Rebels Interned in England', PRO HO 144/1455/313106/2, f. 1 (this document is dated 15 May 1916, and although signed by Home Secretary Herbert Samuel, it was prepared by the Home Office's legal adviser Sir Ernley Blackwell, in conjunction with the Permanent-Under-Secretary, Sir Edward Troup).

12 Ibid., f. 2.

13 R. V. Sir Frederick Loch Halliday, 32 Times Law Reports, 301; 33 Times Law Reports, 336.

14 'Irish Rebels Interned in England', op. cit. Another possibility mooted by the Home Secretary was to make a new regulation under the DORA, specifically applying the 14b procedure to rebellion. With the Irish internees, however, this would, the Home Secretary conceded, be open to 'the grave objection' of being retroactive legislation. (This latter point had in fact been raised by Asquith when he was consulted about the problem on 10 May: PRO HO 144/1455/313106/1.)

After some discussion Cabinet decided to follow the least complicated course: internments would be made under the 'hostile origin or associations' reading of Regulation 14b. There remained a further difficulty however. The advisory committee mandated by Regulation 14b did not meet the case of the Irish internees, since such committees were to be appointed 'for the purpose of advising the Secretary of State with respect to the internment and deportation of aliens'. The Irish were not aliens, and existing legislation did not permit special committees to be established for the purpose of dealing with them. In a move which concealed the difficulties, but which was of questionable legality, the existing structure was adapted to deal with the Irish internees by establishing a subcommittee. This consisted of Mr Justice Sankey[15] (who presided over existing 14b Committees), together with Mr Justice Ross[16] and Mr John Mooney, MP.[17] Mooney's attraction was that besides being an efficient member of existing Sankey committees, he was an Irish Nationalist MP.

The internment process would be initiated by recommendations under Regulation 14b.[18] These were to be made by General Maxwell as the 'competent military authority'. The Home Secretary in turn would issue the necessary internment orders. The men would be removed from the several prisons in which they had been lodged, and gathered together in an internment camp. Internees would then be given the opportunity to apply to the advisory committee for a review; there would at the same time be a review by the military authorities – a 'combing-out of the innocents'.[19]

The prisons

Transported from Ireland by cattle boat and then train, the internees were dispersed to six prisons in England, and two in Scotland, as shown in Table 10.1.

---

15 (1866–1948). Middle Temple, 1892; KC, 1909. King's Bench, 1914–28. Lord Justice of Appeal, 1928–9; Lord Chancellor, 1929–35. Knight, 1914; Viscount, 1932.
16 (1854–1935). Irish Bar, 1879; QC, 1891. Conservative MP, Londonderry City, 1892–5. High Court, Ireland (Chancery), 1896–1921. Lord Chancellor of Ireland, 1921–2.
17 (1874–1934). Barrister (Ireland and England). JP, Treasurer of the Irish Party. MP Dublin Co. South, 1900–6; Newry, 1906–18.
18 PRO HO 144/1455/313106/3.
19 Troup to Sir Robert Chalmers, Irish Under-Secretary, 23 May 1916: PRO HO 144/1455/313106/ 2 (Chalmers replaced Sir Matthew Nathan on 5 May 1916). On 19 May a notice was published setting out the procedure for wrongfully detained persons to obtain their release. Forms were available at the various places of detention which, when completed, would be compared with the information available to the military authorities (*The Times*, 19 May 1916, 9b). A large staff of clerks was employed at the Dublin barracks where a number of men were initially detained, and about twenty or more men were released each day (ibid., 24 May 1916, 5d). By the end of May some 800 detainees had been released (ibid., 1 June 1916, 5e). Feeling among the internees was against making an application to the advisory committee. Since the continued detention of persons obviously innocent of 'hostile associations' was likely to be politically embarrassing it was decided to review *all* internees (Béaslaí, *op.cit.*, Vol. 1, p. 111).

Table 10.1 Prisons used for internment (1916)[20]

Prison	Arrival date	Number
Knutsford	1 May	200
	3 May	308
	2 June	50
	7 June	41
	16 June	25
Stafford	1 May	289
	8 May	203
	13 May	58
Wakefield	6 May	376
	13 May	273
	2 June	100
Wandsworth	9 May	197
	13 May	54
	2 June	49
Glasgow/Perth	20 May	197
Woking	20 May	40
Lewes	20 May	59
TOTAL:		2519

For the most part, the internees spent only a few weeks in the various prisons before being released in the first groups of the obviously innocent, or being moved on to Frongoch internment camp.[21] Those considered leaders were put on a special list and were not sent to the camp (or were transferred from it). The experience of those retained in the prisons was very different from the Frongoch men.

Prison governors were given little initial guidance about how to treat the internees. There was consequently much confusion: they were neither convicted criminals nor on remand, nor were they civil prisoners. The official reflex in such uncertainty is to play it safe, and the first arrivals were accordingly subjected to the most restrictive regime, which confined them to separate cells for all but

20 Adapted from Sean O'Mahony, Frongoch: University of Revolution, Killiney, Co. Dublin, FDR Teoranta, 1987, p. 21. Knutsford and Stafford had been taken into military use for the duration of the war as military detention barracks, and contained a number of soldiers under punishment. The prison at Lewes was not the East Sussex county prison (then closed, but later reopened and used for the Irish political convicts). The internees were held in the former county prison, which had been taken over by the navy when East Sussex had acquired its new prison in the 1850s. Russians taken in the Crimean War had been held in this establishment. For a brief account of the men's journey to Lewes, Wandsworth and Barlinnie (Glasgow) prisons see NLI: Art O'Brien Papers: 8, 442 (unfoliated).

21 By mid-October, only 576 internees remained in custody (5 Hansard, LXXXVI, col. 561; 18 October 1916).

half an hour a day. Exercise consisted of walking a circle in silence, and the men were warned that any attempt to communicate would result in removal to punishment cells and restriction of diet to bread and water.[22] Deprived of money, possessions and the right to order food from outside, the internees were in a worse position than those remanded to face criminal charges.

Officials disagreed about how to proceed. On grounds of security, General John Maxwell had insisted that the internees should be prevented from communicating with each other.[23] Officials in England complied with Maxwell's instruction, but were aware that it could be represented that the Irish were being subjected to solitary confinement. After three weeks, Colonel Childs,[24] the War Office official who had been given responsibility for the Irish prisoners, pointed out that the conditions under which the Irish were being held 'practically amounted to solitary confinement' and asked whether the restrictions might be eased.[25] In response, Maxwell agreed that all but a small group of men (whom he named) might be placed on a more relaxed regime. The effect of this order was to confer the more favourable status and privileges that a civil prisoner could enjoy – rather more liberal in some ways than the conditions of confinement of a first-class misdemeanant.[26]

The first three weeks of confinement in England were an ordeal for most prisoners. They had, after all, been removed from their own country under great stress and in conditions of confusion, and had not been told their ultimate fate – how long they might expect to remain in prison, or how they could effect their release. Some had been greeted by crowds of hostile onlookers when they arrived in England or Scotland, and they were, of course, far from their families and friends, who did not know of their whereabouts. When these uncertainties and fears were dwelt upon in the nearly total solitude of cellular confinement, the effect on some men was drastic, and on all a strain.

There have survived several memoirs of these experiences. Patrick J. Maloney, a Tipperary man, spent a month in Barlinnie Prison, Glasgow, and kept a diary

---

22 Darrell Figgis, A Chronicle of Jails, Dublin, Talbot Press, 1917, pp. 74–5.
23 PRO HO 144/1455/313106/274. The order made sense if there was to be individual interrogation. This, however, proved impossible because the manpower was still not available to carry it through.
24 (1876–1946). Captain, then Major, Royal Irish Regiment. Assistant Adjutant General, 1916. Retired 1922, then Assistant Commissioner Metropolitan Police until 1928.
25 Wyndham Childs to Waller, 3 August 1916; PRO HO 144/1455/313106/274. In this letter Childs reviews the development of policy towards the internees.
26 First-class misdemeanants had to be designated as such by the sentencing court. Their condition was essentially that of a civil detainee. They were separated from criminal prisoners, and could receive meals and beer or wine from the outside, as well as books and newspapers. As far as practicable they could follow their trade or occupation in prison and keep their earnings. The immediate advantage to the internees was the privilege of mixing with their companions ('association' in prison parlance) for several hours each day.

of his experiences there.[27] Because he and his companions were transferred from Ireland at a relatively late date (20 May) they were not long under the solitary regime. Even so, their relief when it was announced to them that they would be treated as prisoners of war and allowed various privileges, including association, was considerable.[28] Darrell Figgis described the strain of solitary confinement at Stafford. A corporal of the guard ('a London Irishman') became friendly with him and Figgis asked what most of the men did during their long hours of solitary confinement. 'Most of them,' the corporal said, 'just sit on their stools and stare at the wall. It's horrible to see them. Lots of them are crying – some that you wouldn't think of. And a lot of them are praying, always praying. . . . It makes me feel bad to see them.'[29]

Stafford had been taken over by the military for the duration of the war, and the regime, designed for delinquent or recalcitrant soldiers, was both uncomfortable and a deterrent. Its most irksome aspect was the virtual solitary confinement. Even during exercise communication was forbidden, and although not compelled to work in their cells the men were initially denied all reading matter, paper and pens. Patrick Rankin recorded that on his second day at the prison his clothing was taken from him for fumigation (probably necessary, since the men generally had not had a clothing change since Easter Monday). In return he was given a set of thin dungarees, but no underclothing.[30] Food was on the scale given to criminal prisoners, and during the first weeks there was no supplementation.[31]

Once prisoner-of-war status had been granted (de facto) things improved enormously. Most importantly, the men were allowed out of their cells from 9 a.m. to 5 p.m. each day. The officer commanding the prison inspected at 11 a.m. and 2.30 p.m., and appears to have taken the men's complaints seriously. Rankin had been cheated of his watch and money by a staff sergeant under the pretence of official procedure, and on complaint these were returned to him: 'The O.C. was very just to us and acted like a gentleman.'[32]

---

27 This diary had a curious history. On Maloney's transfer from Barlinnie to Frongoch the document was confiscated, a grievance which Maloney took up with the advisory committee which reviewed his case. Despite an assurance from Mr Justice Sankey that the diary would be returned, Maloney was unable to recover it. The Home Office's legal adviser, Sir Ernley Blackwell, opposed the return of the dairy on the grounds that it could be treated as a relic of internment. He also argued that it was important that the Home Office should maintain its right to confiscate anything written in prison or in detention camps 'and it would be impossible to justify passing out stuff of this kind when we have the right to stop it' (PRO HO 144/1457/313643/4). As usual, Blackwell's views prevailed, and the diary was retained in the files – where it remains.

28 PRO HO 144/1457/313643, ff. 178 and 184.

29 Figgis, 1917, op. cit., p. 80.

30 NLI: Patrick Rankin Papers: Ms. 22, 251, ff. 14–16.

31 The allowance consisted of bread, potatoes and a little meat, which Rankin wrongly thought was horseflesh. Cocoa was served morning and evening.

32 Rankin, op. cit., f. 15.

Instead of walking silently around a concrete exercise ring seven paces apart, the men were now allowed to talk and even to sing. They sang Irish songs and marches, and were accompanied by mouth organs. Rankin mentions a staff sergeant who was particularly kind – perhaps because he was married to a Dublin woman. This sergeant had charge of the ground floor of the cell block, and from time to time asked the men to sing Irish songs 'which we did in great style'. The sergeant in charge of the top landing objected to the noise, but the kindly staff sergeant told them to sing on, whereupon the men on the top landing – unseen in their cells – joined in. As Rankin recorded, 'It was a great change from confinement.'

Soldiers under punishment were Stafford's main business and the Irish would often see them – Canadians, Australians and South Africans – marching up and down for hours in full kit. The contrast between the two groups of men was so great, noted Rankin, that 'we pitied them'. The internees' laundry was done each week by these military prisoners, and 'Despite orders to the contrary we put matches and cigarettes in our laundry, each week, for the unfortunate prisoners.'[33]

There was a certain amount of petty corruption at the prison (as at other military establishments). The top-landing sergeant brought in fruit at a 100 per cent mark-up. Early in July the men were entrained for transfer to Frongoch. Marshalled at the station, they gave a cheer for the commanding officer and each of the good sergeants. Last came the turn of the sergeant who had ill-treated them: 'Michael Collins gave the signal by a whistle and you should have heard the salvo from the former men, and the appropriate one for the latter, who was present: "Hell roast the Serg[ean]t". Of course all the Sergeants were aware of our intentions.'[34]

Conditions at Knutsford – also a military detention barracks – were harder. Diet was on the same scale as criminals during the first weeks, and they were allowed out of their cells only twice in the first week. (Rankin also complained of exercise being cancelled because of bad weather.) Bed-boards could not be let down until 8 p.m., which meant that the men had to sit on the floor or on backless stools. As at Stafford, NCOs were in charge of the various landings, while military prisoners guarded the internees and brought food. Two of the soldiers on the food party were armed (these may not have been military prisoners) and two unarmed soldiers served, while a sergeant supervised. Thomas Curran, in an account of his Knutsford confinement, claimed that he did not get a spoon until his second week.[35] Locked in their cells for twenty-three hours a day, monotony and isolation ground the men down. Only religious books were provided, which

---

33 Ibid., f. 16.
34 Ibid., f. 17.
35 Thomas Curran, 'A Brief Personal Narrative of the Six Days Defence of the Irish Republic', NLI: Joseph McGarrity Papers: Ms. 17, 510, f. 26.

limited amenity John MacDonagh (brother of the shot signatory Thomas) described as 'a God send'.[36]

During the initial weeks of their confinement, the men took their exercise in strict silence in groups of fifty, each man separated from his companion by a gap of some three yards. The prisoners were supervised by sergeants armed with revolvers, and soldiers armed with rifles and shotguns. Cut off entirely from the outside world, it was not until his second week at Knutsford that Thomas Curran learned from a sergeant of the shooting of Clarke, Pearse, MacDonagh, Plunkett and Ceannt. So closely were the men watched that it was a further three days before he could pass on this information.[37] Correspondence with the outside world was limited to two letters a week on purely personal matters.

Once more there was poor provision for personal hygiene. It was not until their third week at the prison that the men got a bath and a change of under-wear and, as Curran remembered, 'As most of us had not indulged in either since Easter Monday, four weeks previously, were greatly in need of both'.[38] On the Sunday of that week Alfred Byrne MP,[39] visited the prison and assured the internees that they would soon be released. No arrangements had been made for religious services, but on this Sunday, at Byrne's request, a Roman Catholic priest was sent for, and he conducted a short service (not Mass) in the prison chapel. Thereafter Mass would be said on Mondays and the prisoners attended Anglican Divine Service on Sundays.

There were several improvements during the fourth week. A Liverpool sympathiser (described as 'Mrs X' in Curran's account) visited the prison and asked that various Liverpool men whom she named be allowed to see her. She had brought food with her and, finding the men hungry, went out and bought more in town. She also gave news of developments in the outside world. At week's end there were many visitors, including Larry Ginnell MP, who obtained admission by giving his name in Irish, thus evading the prohibition order against him.[40] The men were paraded before the Knutsford commandant. There were a number of innocents among them, he said, together with men who had been forced into rebellion: an opportunity would therefore be given for the men to petition for release.[41]

---

36 John MacDonagh to Sister Francesca MacDonagh, undated, from Knutsford Prison: NLI: Sister Francesca MacDonagh Papers: Ms. 20, 647(i).

37 Curran, op. cit., f. 27. John MacDonagh, also in Knutsford, was probably informed at this time about the death of his brother Thomas. While in custody in Dublin the men had heard a rumour that the signatories of the Proclamation had been shot. Through oversight or callousness no one had confirmed this news (John MacDonagh to Sister Francesca MacDonagh, undated, from Knutsford Prison: NLI: Sister Francesca MacDonagh Papers: Ms. 20, 647 (i)).

38 Curran, op. cit., f. 28.

39 See below, p. 489, n. 164.

40 Ginnell was prosecuted for this. See p. 489.

41 Curran, op. cit., ff. 28–30.

Thereafter conditions were much better. In addition to the two letters out each week no limit was placed on inward correspondence. Mattresses and rugs were issued, together with books from the prison library. Parcels of food and comforts of various kinds arrived from relatives and friends, and were brought in by visitors. The military detainees were replaced as guards by detachments of the Manchester Home Defence Corps. Each corridor elected a captain who undertook all dealings with the prison authorities. Association was allowed in the yard for two hours each morning and afternoon, and abundant food arrived from outside.[42] The internees appointed their own orderlies. Detachments began to leave for Frongoch, and the cells they vacated were filled with new arrivals, mainly from Co. Galway.[43]

The first weeks at Wakefield were identical to those at Stafford and Knutsford – strict separation, silence and criminal discipline and diet. The last was so sparse that Eamon Martin remembered picking up a crumb of bread from the floor.[44] There was strong support from the Irish community once conditions were eased and visitors were allowed:

> Many priests and young ladies – mostly of Irish descent – came to see us when opportunity allowed. They brought us tobacco, cakes, and books. One fine young Kilkenny priest, stationed in England, telegraphed for some home made bread. He brought in a big parcel of it one day [and] shouted 'Come on boys, here's some rebel cake all the way from Kilkenny.'[45]

The men had been secluded for weeks, and now heard something of the out-side world. The naval engagement at Jutland on 31 May, though the outcome was inconclusive, was hailed as a British defeat. Kitchener's death six days later had a similar reception, with Eamon Martin recalling his record in India, Egypt and South Africa, and blaming him (as Commander-in-Chief) for the Dublin executions. That week the internees showed their delight by breaking all the rules: 'the warders were too stupefied and downhearted to attempt to quell our thinly veiled demonstration. We got a little of our own back during these few days.'[46]

---

42 John to Sister Francesca MacDonagh, 13 June 1916: NLI: Sister Francesca MacDonagh Papers: Ms. 20, 647 (i). He told her that he now had too much to eat because of visitors: 'I'm called out with every visitors' parade, most in account of being T[om]'s brother.'
43 Ibid., ff. 31–2.
44 NLI: McGarrity Papers: Ms. 17, 512: Eamon Martin, 'The Irish Rebellion of 1916. Personal Experiences. Reminiscences of English Convict Prisons', *passim*. See also Joseph M. Byrne, *Prisoners of War: Some Personal Recollections of an Irish Deportee*, Dublin, The Art Depot, 1917, pp. 16–22.
45 Ibid., f. 30.
46 Ibid., f. 35.

Relations between the internees and staff seem to have improved despite these incidents. According to Martin, this was due to the manly and orderly bearing of the men, who 'had such a frank and engaging appearance, that even their bitterest enemies found them almost irresistible'.[47] This may have been an over-rosy view of his comrades, but warders accustomed to dealing with Wakefield's usual criminal intake could scarcely have failed to note the contrast with the internees.

What probably cemented staff–inmate relations, however, was the influx of young female visitors whose respectability and respect for the internees could not be overlooked. These visitors asked the men for the names and addresses of their sweethearts, and promised to write to them; they also kept them busy signing their autograph books. When the transfer to Frongoch was announced some fifty young women came to see the men off – all, again according to Martin, in tears at the parting: 'They collected on the prison steps and gave us a royal send off, singing "Who Fears to Speak of 98", "Soldiers Are We" and "A Nation Once Again". One of them managed to smuggle in a large Republican Flag which she waved over us enthusiastically. The warders rushed then to quell the demonstration, but were absolutely powerless to prevent the ladies from giving enthusiastic expression to their pent up feelings.' Martin thought it would be worthwhile to endure similar hardships to experience again such a memorable farewell – 'and all it be remembered taking place in a prison in the very centre of England'.[48]

There survives but one brief account of imprisonment at Lewes Naval Prison under the separate regime. P. A. Sargeant of Dalkey, Co. Dublin, wrote to Hanna Sheehy Skeffington[49] on 6 June 1916, saying that the Lewes men expected shortly to be sent to a camp. Treatment had improved considerably, and they had been allowed newspapers and tobacco. Cell doors were left open between breakfast and dinner and they could walk in the prison corridors in addition to the two hours' exercise allowed in the barracks yard. They were locked up at 4 p.m. for the night. The evenings were long 'but with books and papers one manages to pass the time'.[50]

Hanna Sheehy Skeffington had herself heard the clang of the prison gate for unlawfully protesting at the exclusion of female suffrage from the Home Rule Bill. One of her many English suffrage contacts, Miss G. Allen, wrote to her about

---

47 Ibid., f. 37.
48 Ibid., ff. 36–7. 'We gave a wholehearted toast to these young ladies. They were the one bright feature that relieved the funereal monotony of one's existence in prison.'
49 (1877–1946). Widow of the murdered Francis with whom she had founded the Irish Women's Franchise League in 1908. Imprisoned for breaking windows in a suffrage protest in 1912. Took no part in the rising, but in its aftermath became a member of executive committee of Sinn Féin. Rejected the Treaty. Had extensive feminist and progressive contacts in England, and her correspondents at this time included Fenner Brockway, Sylvia Pankhurst, Sidney and Beatrice Webb, Philip Snowdon, the Pethick Lawrences, and many more.
50 P. A. Sargeant to Hanna Sheehy Skeffington, 6 June 1916: NLI: Sheehy Skeffington Papers: Ms. 22, 279 (ii).

the Lewes prisoners. The two women had obviously been in touch for some weeks, since Miss Allen had written to say that as the men were soon to be transferred to a central camp she would not need the funds that had hitherto covered her expenses.[51] Ten days later she had somehow heard of the move and had gone to the railway station just in time to see some internees entrained for Frongoch: 'The sergeant in charge gave me leave to speak to them, & afterwards a nice boy-officer came up & said as far as he was concerned I might come down to the platform to see them off.' Miss Allen bought oranges, bananas and newspapers for the men, who were also allowed to make purchases from the station buffet.[52] Another batch was sent to Frongoch two days later and Miss Allen performed the same kindness, as well as arranging for 2 lb of butter to be delivered to the prison every other day. The prison commandant, who had hitherto been very pleasant to Miss Allen, now told her that headquarters had warned him about sympathisers and others visiting the Irish rebels out of curiosity and coddling them: he would allow no coddling and no one should see a prisoner unless personally known to them. Miss Allen retorted that she did not think idle curiosity would motivate any suffragette – 'as we already knew a great deal about prisons'.[53]

Solitary confinement and its effects became one of the complaints in the campaign which nationalist MPs conducted during the summer and autumn of 1916. In an answer to Timothy Healy on 6 July, Home Secretary Herbert Samuel insisted that separate confinement had lasted for not more than a few days.[54] When the matter was pressed, however, the Home Office discovered that it had been misled by the War Office, and the 'few days' had been in some instances more than three weeks.[55] Protesters had alleged that solitary confinement was responsible for insanity, and an attempted suicide. Even an associated regime was said to have grave ill-effects on some. There had been two cases of insanity at Frongoch, one involving attempted suicide.[56] The relationship between imprisonment and insanity is notoriously difficult to determine.[57] It would have been surprising if the events of the rising had not had some severe after-effects

---

51 Miss G. Allen to Hanna Sheehy Skeffington, 12 June 1916, ibid.
52 Ibid., 23 June 1916.
53 Ibid.
54 5 *Hansard*, LXXXIII, col. 1640.
55 See PRO HO 144/1455/313106/274. One of the Frongoch internees who had been freed in the general releases of July wrote to Healy corroborating claims which had been made about solitary confinement, and alleging that at least one prisoner had become insane because of the experience. Healy passed the letter to the Home Office, and asked for an explanation. After an internal investigation had revealed that the Commons had in fact been misled on 6 July, a carefully worded reply was sent to Healy, evading the issue by standing on the old and rather sophistic Prison Commission distinction between solitary and separate confinement. The internees, the Home Office wrote, 'were not in solitary confinement in the strict sense of the term'. The letter also pointed out that at the time the original question had been asked, separate confinement had entirely ceased (PRO HO 144/1455/313106/274; Herbert Samuel to Timothy Healy, 12 August 1916).
56 Heygate Lambert to Waller, 8 August 1916; PRO HO 144/1455/313106/274.
57 See above, p. 396.

on those who had been jolted so traumatically out of civilian life, and if in some cases insanity had not resulted. It is certainly true that at best the internees received only the most cursory medical inspection on reception,[58] and any propensity to insanity is likely to have gone undetected and to have been greatly aggravated by the mental and emotional strain of solitary confinement.

The 'Special List'

Shortly after the removal of the internees to England, and their transfer from War Office to Home Office jurisdiction,[59] the Irish military authorities urged that the leaders should continue to be separated from the rank and file. Leaders were men identified by the Intelligence Department as 'rather of the agitator type . . . [who] would do a certain amount of harm with the other prisoners'.[60] This would necessarily be a small number, since those against whom there had been firm evidence had been brought to trial. What remained, therefore, was a group against whom there was some intelligence, generally speculative rather than firm.[61] Some of those on what came to be known as the 'Special List' were inadvertently moved into general custody, and on 20 June 1916 the War Office issued another list, which had been drawn up by MI5 rather than by the Irish Intelligence Department. These were 'specially dangerous' and were the only men that MI5 was anxious to keep separate. Although some subsequently vanished from the Irish military and political scene, the initial list did include several who

---

58 See diary of Patrick Maloney (PRO HO 144/1457/313643), f. 178; Figgis, 1917, *op. cit.*, p. 74. Apart from the wounded and obviously injured, medical examinations seem to have been conducted only after transfer to England, which in some instances would have been a matter of weeks after first receipt into custody.

59 As with most alien internees, the War Office provided camp accommodation and staffing, although ultimate responsibility rested with the Home Office. This dual responsibility was never completely or satisfactorily resolved. In practice, the Home Office took political responsibility for the camp and civil prisons at which the internees were lodged. Since staffing was entirely provided by the War Office, however, administrative oversight rested with that department. Especially in the early days, in consequence, some relatives and friends enquiring about internees were shuttlecocked between the War and Home Offices. See, for example, PRO HO 144/1455/313106/28. This file deals with an attempt by Mary MacSwiney to obtain information about her brother Terence. General Wyndham Childs sent her from the War Office to the Home Office, which was able to answer some of her queries, but which sent her back to the War Office for the rest. The file was annotated: 'General Childs ought not to have sent her here as HO is not concerned at present with the administration of Frongoch.'

60 PRO HO 144/1455/313106/57a (9 June 1916).

61 In some cases, however, there was firm intelligence. Ernest Blythe had been the subject of police surveillance for some time, and was issued with a DORA deportation order in May 1915. Blythe ('According to reliable information') had boasted that he had enrolled 5000 members of the IRB. On 24 March 1916, he was arrested and taken to Arbour Hill barracks. Deported on 8 April he was eventually interned in Brixton Prison under Regulation 14b. On 11 July he was sent to Reading, where the prisoners confirmed the MI5 assessment by electing him their leader (PRO HO 144/1454/3 and 11).

would prove dangerous opponents to British rule in Ireland.[62] In addition, several men who took leadership roles at Frongoch were transferred out in July.[63]

Acting on War Office advice, special accommodation was provided at Reading Prison, which at this time was designated as a place of internment for aliens.[64] The female wing was set aside for the Irish, and the men were transferred by the Army on 11 July 1916. The segregation of the leaders allowed all other internees to be removed to Frongoch.[65] In the event, it was decided to use all twenty-seven cells in the self-contained female block at Reading, and so fifteen men were drawn from the list provided by the Irish Intelligence Department, as well as the twelve identified by MI5. The process of identifying ringleaders and other dangerous men has a tendency to acquire a momentum of its own – driven by bureaucratic caution – and no sooner had the Reading wing been filled than the Frongoch commandant proposed several more men for segregation.[66]

In a smuggled letter a detainee (probably Seán T. O'Kelly)[67] at the end of October 1916 assured Art O'Brien of the Irish National Relief Fund that Reading

---

62 The list comprised only twelve names: P. T. Daly, Arthur Griffith, Thomas J. McSweeney (sic); Darrell Figgis, Pierce McCann, Herbert M. Pim, Dennis McCullough, Peter de Loughrey, John Milroy, Francis J. Healy, Dr T. Dundon, Joseph P. Connolly (see PRO HO 144/1455/313106/57a (20 June 1916)).

63 Thought was given to providing a special compound at Frongoch for the Special List men and emergent leaders. These included Seán T. O'Kelly, a future Irish President (PRO HO 144/1458). This had administrative attractions, but was dismissed for reasons of cost, since it was concluded that more land would have to be obtained and a small but separate camp constructed (PRO HO 144/1455/313106/168: Report on Frongoch Camp, 3 July 1916).

64 The male portion of the prison had three wings. One of these was set aside for 'Enemy Aliens', another for suspect 'Friendly Aliens' and the third for 'Criminal Aliens' (those with a criminal record or serving a sentence when war broke out, and segregated at Reading on the expiration of their sentences) ('A Brief Personal Narrative of the Six Days Defence of the Irish Republic. By a Captain of Head-Quarters Battalion of the Dublin Brigade of the Irish Republican Army', NLI: McGarrity Papers: Ms. 17, 510. This and other similar accounts appear to have been commissioned by McGarrity for publication in the United States of America).

65 PRO HO 144/1455/313106/140.

66 The effect of this was to raise these men's status among their comrades. On the evening that they were removed from Frongoch a farewell supper was laid on for them, concocted from various available supplies and with a cigar for each departing man. As they left the camp those remaining lined up to attention, giving the authorities no cause for intervention by refraining from saluting or cheering (Martin, op. cit., f. 48). William O'Brien, himself interned at Frongoch and then Reading, compiled a list of the Reading men. Seven were transferred from Frongoch on 24 July 1916 and seven were released from custody a week later: not a convincing demonstration of the intelligence services' ability to identify the most dangerous men among the internees (NLI: William O'Brien Papers: Ms. 13, 973).

67 The letter appears to be signed with the initials 'S.T.'. O'Kelly (1883–1966) had entered Republican politics through the Gaelic League, of which he became secretary. He was a founder member of Sinn Féin and the Irish Volunteers. After the Easter rising (in which he had been a staff captain) he was interned. He was a member of the first Dáil, and part of the delegation which unsuccessfully lobbied the Paris Peace Conference. Took anti-Treaty side in Civil War. His subsequent political career included several ministerial posts and (in 1945) the Presidency of Éire.

conditions were good. Concern had been expressed about the internees, and the correspondent wondered whether any of the Reading inmates had been sending letters of complaint to their friends and relatives. He would be surprised if this were so since there was no ground for serious complaint about the men's treatment at Reading: 'In fact it is often a matter of regret to many of us that conditions leave so little ground for complaint as we believe it would be better for us all from every point of view if the conditions were harsh and if we were obliged to keep up a fight for necessary alterations.'[68] Prison food was not too bad, and was supplemented by canteen purchases. One or two men sometimes complained to friends in London, 'but the general opinion here is that it is most difficult to satisfy these men and that they are only happy when grumbling'.

O'Kelly wanted supporters to concentrate on the condition of the convicted men and the internees at Frongoch. The latter should be sent home as soon as possible: 'I believe that to pass the winter under present conditions here would kill a number of them.' He went on to ask for visits to those of the Reading men who had not yet received one, and for a small sum of money and some writing materials for distribution among the men.[69]

This account is confirmed by a memoir of Thomas Curran.[70] Unlike Knutsford, Stafford and Lewes detention barracks, Reading was under civilian control and Curran described the governor (Captain Morgan) as 'a good natured and humane man'. Conditions were 'as little unpleasant as life in a jail could possibly be'. Cell doors were open from 7 a.m. until 10 p.m., and every rule was interpreted to the men's advantage. The diet was the best allowed by prison rules and was 'well cooked by German and Swiss chefs interned in the other wings'. The official allowance was supplemented by food sent in by friends. Classes were held in Gaelic, telegraphy and military training, and the internees conducted debates on a range of topics. A small manuscript journal *The Outpost* was produced and circulated.[71]

But for all its relaxed atmosphere, the authorities were well aware of the calibre of at least some of the Reading men, and they took care to intercept and copy their correspondence and to consult the intelligence service about contacts and visitors. All visitors to Terence MacSwiney and, one supposes, some or all of the others, were vetted in advance by Major Hall of MI5. MacSwiney's

---

68 NLI: Art O'Brien Papers: Ms. 8443 (unfoliated): 'S.T.' to O'Brien, 30 October 1916.

69 Ibid. When visited by a Dublin friend (J. O. Connor) on 27 October, the supervising warder noted that O'Kelly 'expressed himself highly satisfied with the treatment here, as far as the officials are concerned' (PRO HO 144/1458/9).

70 Curran had been a captain of the HQ Battalion of the Volunteers. He was deported to Knutsford and thence to Frongoch. Following an appearance before the Sankey Committee Curran was transferred to Reading.

71 'A Brief Personal Narrative of the Six Days Defence of the Irish Republic', *op. cit.*, ff. 39–41.

brother Peter, who travelled from New York to see him, was permitted a visit but a Mr D. O'Connor was deemed by Major Hall to be unacceptable.[72]

Frongoch Internment Camp

Given the connotations of imprisonment, it was politically advisable to move the internees to a camp. There were also very strong administrative reasons for this. For a variety of demographic, legal and administrative reasons the local prison population in England and Wales had fallen sharply on the outbreak of war. Many staff had enlisted in the armed forces, several large prisons had been taken out of service, while others held only a fraction of their maximum capacity. But the availability of accommodation depended on staffing as well as cells. The influx of some 2500 men between 1 May and 16 June would have increased the prison population by one-third and, even using reserve soldiers, would have been expensive and difficult to staff.[73] On 22 May, the Home Office insisted that 'the sooner we get [the internees] out of prisons into internment camps the better'.[74]

Physical conditions

Frongoch Camp in north Wales was located some three miles from Bala, not far from what was then the main road between Holyhead (which the mail-boat linked to Kingstown, near Dublin) and London: it was a few hundred yards from the railway station. The camp had a capacity of 1943 occupants.[75] The first Irish detainees arrived on 9 June, and the remaining previous occupants – German prisoners of war – were speedily removed.[76] The camp was even more makeshift than most wartime accommodation. It was, an inspector noted, divided into two sections and comprised 'a collection of regulation War Office huts, and . . . a

---

72 PRO HO 144/10308/9: memorandum of 5 November 1916. The Irish government wanted to deport Peter MacSwiney. The Home Office did not agree, but when in February 1917, Peter returned to New York an immigration order was issued prohibiting his re-entry (ibid., /14).

73 On prison numbers see *Report of the Commissioners of Prisons and the Directors of Convict Prisons* (hereinafter *RCP*), PP 1917–18 [Cd. 8764], XVIII, 109, 4.

74 PRO HO 144/1455/313106/3; War Office to Brigadier-General J. A. Byrne, Deputy Adjutant General, 22 May 1916.

75 PRO HO 144/313106/274; Lambert to Waller, 8 August 1916.

76 A few Germans who had been too unwell to move remained in the camp when the first Irish internees arrived, but were gone within a few days. Eamon Martin recalled only one German in the camp when he arrived – a man who was dying of consumption, and could not be moved (*op. cit.*, f. 38). The Irish prisoners befriended him, one of them being fluent in German. As a consequence, the prisoner was removed from the isolation hut in which he had been kept, and was taken away by ambulance (W. I. Brennan-Whitmore, *With the Irish in Frongoch*, Dublin, The Talbot Press, 1917, 20–1). Transfers from the various civil prisons took some time to complete. It was not until the end of June, for example, that Michael Collins was notified of his imminent transfer (Coogan, 1991, *op. cit.*, pp. 49–50).

disused distillery building'.[77] North Camp consisted of twenty-seven huts, each sixty feet long and sixteen feet wide. The pitched (and unceilinged) roofs rose to an apex of ten feet. There was sufficient accommodation to set aside one of the huts for religious purposes, another for activities such as painting, drawing and wood-carving, and a third as a YMCA recreational hall. The last was subdivided into various rooms, and had a piano and what was described as 'an American organ'. There were also the usual support services – a dining-hall and kitchen, wash-rooms and lavatories. The huts were poorly heated, having only plank floors, the whole construction being mounted on blocks. This lack of insulation meant that the huts were never properly heated, each being provided with only one slow-combustion stove.[78] The paths and areas between the huts were not paved, and in the midst of a spell of wet summer weather Michael Collins described conditions as cold and the surface of the compound as 'slippery, shifting mud'. A civilian canteen assistant in North Camp remembered 'Mud everywhere, deep liquid mud.'[79] When the weather was good the camp's fine surroundings became apparent – but when it rained all such impressions were blotted out by a sea of mud, wet feet and floors and general discomfort. Inspectors also noted that although the North Camp had a good dispensary, there was no covered accommodation for patients waiting to see the medical officers.

South Camp also had many deficiencies. It had been a whisky distillery, and before being taken over by the War Office had for some time been disused. The distillery equipment had been removed, and the various grain lofts and other parts of the building adapted to provide five large dormitories. Three of these were considered by inspectors to be unsuitable, being ill-lit and poorly ventilated. One was pronounced unsuitable for sleeping purposes, and a possible source of the colds and influenza prevalent in the camp. The others were 'more or less objectionable ... too depressing for use unless demanded by necessity'. In a smuggled letter, the inmate organisation went much further than the inspectors in condemning South Camp conditions. The lofts, they said, were unfit for human habitation – not simply unsuitable as the inspectors had indicated. Dormitories 1, 2 and 3 were infested with rats, while dormitory 1 had very poor ventilation. There were two lavatories *in* the dormitories and this, combined with the poor ventilation, meant that a stench was generated which persisted until midday: 'Men have fainted in the morning and one morning three men fainted.' Because

---

77 'Condition of Frongoch Camp', PRO HO 144/1456/313106/614. All details about the construction and condition of the camp are taken from this and subsequent reports, unless otherwise stated.

78 The incoming Irish were advised by the handful of departing Germans that the somewhat makeshift South Camp was to be preferred to the North, since even though dormitory conditions at the former were dreadful in the summer this was less of a hardship than 'the unbearable cold of North Camp in the winter' (O'Mahony, *op. cit.*, p. 24). As autumn drew in the inmates referred to North Camp as 'Siberia' (NLI: Seán O'Mahony Papers: Ms. 24, 450).

79 Michael Collins to Susan Killeen, undated (?28 June 1916), Coogan, *op. cit.*, pp. 50–1. This observation is confirmed by virtually all surviving correspondence and memoirs.

of this bad ventilation, it was claimed, men were losing their appetites and getting up in the morning feeling dazed and sleepy.[80] Eamon Martin's dormitory at one point held 200 in very overcrowded conditions. Men were so tightly packed in that they sometimes awoke in the morning and found themselves lying across their neighbour's bed. There was not enough space between the beds for men to stand while making them up.[81] By mid-October 1916 numbers at Frongoch had dropped well below 600, and there was sufficient space in North Camp for all to be transferred there. The internees had applied for this and wanted – not wholly unreasonably – to know why the transfer had not been made.

In addition to its inadequate dormitories, South Camp contained the camp hospital, as well as a dining-room, kitchen, doctor's surgery, barber's shop, some workshops and the usual wash-rooms and lavatories; it was also the location of the punishment cells. Overall it was described as being 'somewhat rough'. The one clear advantage that the South had over the North Camp was heating: instead of relying on slow-combustion stoves, heat came from a boiler house.

But to the internees North Camp was the preferred location, and removal to the South was seen as a punishment (which is why the commandant kept it in service). In October 1916, trouble erupted when the authorities attempted to identify and remove two men who through prior residence in England had become liable to conscription. The camp's remote style of discipline meant that although the two men appeared on the nominal roll, the camp staff could not match names to faces. The prisoners would not give up their comrades, all refusing to give names and numbers, or to answer roll-call. Those who were willing to identify themselves, the commandant decided, would be allowed to remain in the North Camp, and all refusers would go to the South Camp.[82] This was not a punishment, he insisted, but was necessary to separate the two groups because of supposed ill-feeling between them. This claim was undermined when men who later agreed to identify themselves were restored to the North Camp.

Most men had been bathed and given a change of clothing while they were in their various prisons, but many still arrived at Frongoch in such a filthy condition that the inmate administration feared an epidemic. Clean underclothing had been sent in by relatives and friends, but was somehow held up and not issued, while the camp authorities either did not have or would not provide a change for those who needed it: many had not had a change for more than a month.[83] The Inmate Council appointed a doctor from among their number

---

80 NLI: Seán O'Mahony Papers: Ms. 24, 450. Mimeographed compilation of inmate complaints prepared by Art O'Brien's Irish National Relief Association for circulation to press, MPs and neutral embassies.

81 Martin, op. cit., f. 39.

82 Some men gave their names voluntarily, others gave them by agreement with the refusers, with the intention of keeping open communications with the outside world via those not under punishment (Béaslaí, 1926, Vol. 1, p. 117).

83 Joseph Byrne, for example, went for six weeks without a change (op. cit., p. 56).

to organise the camp sanitary arrangements and to give lectures on hygiene, and this appeared to resolve the problem.[84]

In the seven months of Frongoch's operation, inmates bombarded the authorities with complaints about these and other deficiencies, a large proportion of which sympathetic MPs aired in the House. The inspectors' assessment was that, when taken for what it was, and with its various defects and limitations, the camp was adequately providing basic accommodation for large groups of men at a time of war and general scarcity. Frongoch

> is all that is necessary – as good in fact as is possessed by many battalions in training in England, or is provided for internment purposes in other parts of the country, and very much better than can be given to many thousands of loyal Irishmen who are bravely fighting against our enemies in foreign lands.[85]

No matter how convenient it was for nationalists and republicans to denounce it, the camp was spartan rather than inhumane. The rebels wanted prisoner-of-war status, and that was exactly what they got: Frongoch was a prisoner-of-war camp – not a concentration camp, and certainly not a prison.

'Buckshot Lambert'

Many of the difficulties which occurred at Frongoch were due to the heavy-handed management of Colonel Heygate Lambert, the commandant. Nothing survives in the files of any briefing he might have been given by the Home Office or War Office, but in any event this was unlikely to have been of a detailed kind, and certainly lacking in the necessary political directions.[86] The latter were absolutely essential since Lambert's political judgement was abysmal and his powers of leadership minimal. At Stafford, Wakefield and Reading the Irish prisoners had shown that they responded well to easy social relations – even when the regime was spartan. Common sense would have indicated that these were not men to bludgeon or browbeat – especially when the Frongoch population dwindled to the 500 or so activists and leaders. Lambert seems to have seen them in the character of enlisted men in the British Army and demanded from them the obedience, and deference, which class and rank expected and almost

---

84 Martin, *op. cit.*, f. 40. Martin recorded that for the few nights in his dormitory in South Camp rats and mice were active – all, presumably, eventually being killed or driven off by the men. Since the dormitories had been grain lofts a vermin infestation was to be expected – though not apparently by the camp authorities.

85 'Condition of Frongoch Camp', PRO HO 144/1456/313106/614. This document, ironically, was submitted the day after the camp was emptied by the Christmas releases of 1916.

86 All Frongoch records were transferred to London after the camp closed, and were subsequently destroyed.

invariably received. Had confrontation been intended, no better approach could have been adopted. Elsewhere, under de Valera's leadership, the convicts were determined on confrontation, and at a later stage in the Anglo-Irish war prisoners would generally attempt to provoke the authorities, but this was not the internees' attitude in the summer and autumn of 1916. Intent on appraising the rising, recovering from its traumas and attempting to see their way forward, they would have been content and relatively quiescent with a light hand on the reins.[87]

This was not what they got, and Thomas Curran (who had described the Reading governor as 'A good natured and humane man') recalled that the Frongoch men broke as many rules as they could and felt encouraged to do so because of Lambert: 'who did all he could to make things unpleasant for us and always interpreted rules and regulations to our detriment'.[88] His reception speech was of the 'you play ball with me, I'll play ball with you' variety. The prisoners could run the camp themselves, or he could – and his way was at the point of a bayonet. Anyone who tried to escape would be shot. All his sentries were armed with buckshot and '*you* all know how useful that is'. Since buckshot was mentioned to all newcomers, his nickname was inevitable.[89]

At Britain's lowest point every able and competent officer was engaged in the war effort – planning, intelligence, logistics or combat. It was inevitable that someone of Lambert's poor management abilities would be sent where he could apparently do little harm. But his combination of Colonel Blimp and Dad's Army more than once fanned the embers of rebellion at Frongoch. Worse than his confrontations, and his fairly frequent complaints to higher authority about his charges, was his embodiment of the qualities which the Irish rebels attributed to British governance – superiority, arrogance and bombast. He was a teaching-aid

---

87 The despondent mood of John MacDonagh was probably typical of many in the first months of their confinement: 'I hope the future will not be so black as sometimes it appears to me. All these things were to be & we've got to face them courageously. That was one of Tom's greatest points, his courage.' John MacDonagh was consoled by his religious beliefs and hoped that good days would come again (John to Sister Francesca MacDonagh, Knutsford Prison (undated): NLI: Sister Francesca MacDonagh Papers: Ms. 20, 647 (i)). Several weeks later at Frongoch the normally ebullient Michael Collins managed a less than spirited inscription for William O'Brien's autography book: 'Let us be judged by what we attempted rather than by what we achieved' (NLI: William O'Brien Papers: Ms. 15, 662).

88 A Personal Narrative of the Six Days Defence of the Irish Republic', *op. cit.*, f. 36.

89 Brennan-Whitmore, *op. cit.*, p. 13. The camp sergeant-major, who asked each new man if he had a jack-knife, was well liked, but known to the men and guards alike as 'jack-knives' (see also Byrne, *op. cit.*, p. 54). Lambert was no better at handling his own men. For small tips the guards were generally willing to post letters for the internees – thus bypassing the censor's department. This was discovered after a time and the guard changed. Lambert assembled and warned their replacements not to have dealings with the prisoners. Their predecessors had been sent away in disgrace and it was now up to them to uphold the honour of their regiment. As soon as they took up their duties, however, the new guards asked the prisoners whether they had letters to post home – Lambert having usefully advertised this source of petty revenue to his hard-up soldiers (NLI: Patrick Rankin Papers: *op. cit.*, ff. 18–19).

in the political education of revolutionaries rather than a counter-propagandist for fairness and restraint.[90]

What Lambert's superiors at the War Office wanted, and what Home Office officials and the politicians generally wanted, was for internment to be conducted quietly and without complicating further the deeply worrying Irish situation. Lambert lacked the wit or ability to deliver this and instead embarked upon a series of futile little battles. Only one conflict was not of his making – and it was an important one – the decision to seek out for forcible conscription those who through prior residence in Britain had become liable under the Military Service Act. He, however, made his basic position clear at an early point when he told the internees that they were not prisoners of war 'but were treated as such by the courtesy of government'.[91] He presumably located them somewhere between military delinquents and common criminals.

Within the first nine days of operation, dissatisfaction had soured both sides. Colonel Lambert indicated his displeasure in 'Notice No. 2', bearing his hand-written superscription 'Warning'. There was to be no unnecessary noise, running about and 'climbing inside and out'. Internees were not to speak to sentries or other staff, and were to keep a distance of at least five yards from any fixed post, and eight feet of the perimeter wire or other fences. Any man breaking this last rule was liable to be challenged and 'shot at sight'. Knives, apart from small penknives, were prohibited, as was any signalling or unauthorised communication outside the camp. He insisted that the internees should come to attention and salute his officers. A man who would not do this or say 'Sir' got twenty-four hours in the cells.[92] Another was sent to the cells for fourteen days for writing a 'false and impertinent letter'.[93]

Antagonism intensified when the men refused to do quarry work, and became yet worse when they refused to identify Hugh Thornton, who was wanted for military service. Despite the fact that Thornton gave himself up, a collective punishment was imposed.[94] The hut leaders complained to the Home Secretary about the punishments and Lambert's generally heavy hand. This elicited no

---

90 Brennan-Whitmore considered him conscientious and kindly but 'a type of Englishman who should never be placed in charge of Irishmen. Possessing an egregious idea of his own dignity and importance: utterly devoid of a sense of humour; he was totally incapable of treating us except as prisoners. That we might also be intelligent, reasoning and sentient human beings seemed altogether beyond his power of comprehension. In short, his nick-name was not altogether inappropriate' (*op. cit.*, p. 13).

91 NLI: Seán O'Mahony Papers: Ms. 24, 450 (unfoliated).

92 Eamon Martin, *op. cit.*, ff. 44–5.

93 NLI: Seán O'Mahony Papers: Ms. 24, 450 (unfoliated). The fourteen days were passed in alternate periods of three days on bread and water (the maximum allowed) followed by one day on a normal diet, then three more days on bread and water and so on. This was a severe punishment.

94 Thornton eventually identified himself and was tried and sentenced to imprisonment with hard labour for refusing conscription (Camp Committee (smuggled letter) to Timothy Healy, 4 October 1916: NLI: Irish National Aid Association Papers: Ms. 24, 324 (i)).

reply but Lambert insisted that the men now remove his soldiers' refuse as well as their own – perhaps his way of deriding complaints to higher authority. This was not a wise reaction, since there were several MPs who were more than willing to ventilate complaints. Indeed, John Dillon held his hand early in July only because he had been told that a 'very large' contingent would shortly be freed and he thought it better to direct his political effort to the removal of the remaining men from Frongoch to somewhere less remote.[95]

Lambert's inability to enforce his will in the face of the internees' obstinacy enraged him. The matter of identification rumbled on, and on 7 November he announced a new scheme, making hut leaders responsible for all in their huts and for their movements. The hut leaders refused to cooperate and all the internees were then paraded. Lambert turned out the guard, together with extra troops brought in from Chester – all fully armed. All internees were confined to their huts under threat of rifle and bayonet. The subsequent roll-call was a fiasco, with 342 men refusing to answer to their names. Fifteen hut leaders were charged with disobeying an order to line up their men to have them answer to name and number. The 342 were removed to South Camp, where they were punished with the loss of all privileges; the hut leaders were court-martialled. If the camp leaders could not run the camp in a proper and disciplined manner, Lambert insisted, he would do so at bayonet-point and 'if he had to have in it only dead bodies he would have discipline in it'.[96]

It was typical of Lambert's hamfistedness to cause a row over letters – another valuable carrot available to the wise administrator. Prisoners of war were entitled to post-paid letters. When they first arrived at Frongoch the Irish enjoyed this privilege.[97] On his own initiative Lambert directed that this should stop and the men should pay for stamps. This provoked a predictable response from the inmates, who (following a camp committee directive) continued to write and submit their letters unstamped, knowing that they would go into the camp censor's waste-paper basket. The inmate committee made an exception for married men and businessmen, and doubtless those prepared to tip one of the camp guards could get their letters posted.[98] The political impact was lost on Lambert: his charges became more dissatisfied and unified in their opposition to the camp administration, and had a further grievance to be hoisted by their supporters.

95 John Dillon to Irish National Aid Association, 6 July 1916: NLI: Irish National Aid Association Papers: Ms. 24, 366 (unfoliated).

96 Michael Staines (camp leader) to Alfred Byrne, MP, 8, November 1916 (smuggled letter), ibid.: 186 men identified themselves, many on the advice of the camp leaders, because of their age or state of health.

97 Several envelopes survive in the archives with postage-free 'Prisoner of War' overprints (see, for example, papers of Sister Francesca MacDonagh, NLI: Ms. 20, 647 (1)).

98 Martin, op. cit., f. 44. During this period, and later, batches of men were being released by the Sankey committee, and these also took out large bundles of letters.

Lambert failed to see where punishments could lead when imposed on such a determined body of men: he had little notion of costs and benefits. On 15 September he sentenced Patrick Daly to seven days in the cells on a bread-and-water diet for failing to come immediately when called for a route march. This was a minor offence and disproportionately severe punishment. Daly immediately went on hunger-strike and after three days, on the medical officer's directions, was removed to hospital. Lambert responded by charging Daly with failing to clean his punishment cell and refusing an order to eat his food. These offences were set down for hearing by court-martial, and the internees promptly retained Gavan Duffy to defend him, arguing that Lambert had acted *ultra vires*.[99]

Little reflection was required to realise that the republican movement could best be dealt with and even outmanoeuvred by giving fewest grounds for complaint.[100] Lambert thought he was engaged in a war of sorts with the internees' leaders: he was, but its outcome was decided by public relations and in this sphere he blundered along, handing them one victory after another. Executions, penal servitude, internment – and now a bullying martinet and helpless men – all made excellent copy for the republicans' increasingly able press and public relations machine. Staines, the camp leader, was certainly aware of this, and in reporting the various confrontations with Lambert asked that the information be typed up and sent to the neutral embassies, especially the Spanish. Copies were also to go to Dublin for circulation in Ireland.

And of course it got better. The courts-martial of the hut leaders also made a good story. Gavan Duffy was again retained to defend the men, and he made a very good job of it.[101] One was acquitted and the other fourteen were each sentenced to twenty-eight days' hard labour. These sentences were all confirmed

---

99 NLI: Irish National Aid Association: Ms. 24, 324 (1): Michael Staines (camp leader) to Timothy Healy, 7 October 1916.

100 Even the families of the internees were willing to give credit for decent treatment. Writing to her brother (then in Reading), Annie MacSwiney condemned Frongoch conditions – 'The whole business is a black scandal . . . wait until the war is over – then will come revelations.' But she went on: 'Miss Lynch said everyone was most kind at Reading and Dartmoor – there was courtesy and consideration on all sides – she said they couldn't have been nicer. That was what I found at Reading too. Why can't they be the same at Frongoch. Can they not see that they only make matters worse for themselves by such behaviour. The Commandant at Frongoch is doing his masters no good, and driving our men into lunatic asylums and consumption isn't the thing to help them. Storing up more bitterness in Ireland is poor work for themselves. Your Governor at Reading and the one in Dartmoor are doing England a good turn by introducing us to men who can do what their country demands of them without playing the brute and the bully' (Annie to Terence MacSwiney, 27 October 1916: PRO HO 144/10308/9: typescript of intercepted letter).

101 See NLI: Irish National Aid Association Papers: Ms. 24, 347 (unfoliated), 13 September 1916. Lambert even attempted to exclude the press from the camp's courts martial, but this was circumvented by the Judge Advocate, who moved the proceedings to a hut outside the perimeter wire and then admitted reporters from the *Manchester Guardian* (27 November 1916, 4g) and the *Irish Independent* (28 November 1916, 4h).

by the Commanding Officer of the Western Camp (under whose authority Lambert acted) except for Richard Mulcahy and T. D. Sinnott: these men were consequently discharged and returned to the North Camp.[102] Duffy called this outcome 'a very signal victory' – the sentences were very light and some had not been confirmed. The question remained about the 342 men in the South Camp under punishment: if Lambert did not release them, the Irish National Aid Association intended to take their case to the press. There would have been mileage in this also since as late as 19 December the Home Office had decided that the men under punishment in the South Camp would be denied Christmas post and parcels in line with Lambert's order.[103] The skids were already under his regime, however, and later that day Byrne telegraphed from the House of Commons that Christmas dinners and parcels would be allowed in the North and South camps: the politicians had seen where the advantage lay.[104] As it turned out, less that a week later the men – punished and unpunished, hard labour and acquitted – all sat down to Christmas dinner at their homes in Ireland.

Yet for all his defects Lambert was in a trying position. He had been given responsibility for some 1700 civilians, many fired with ardour of rebellion yet with only a smidgen of military discipline. And there remained after the summer releases a smaller number interned on the mistaken or malicious say-so of an RIC man or score-settling civilian who inevitably seethed with impatience and resentment. Many of his charges (as the photographs of the Dublin round-ups show) were very young men – scarcely out of their teens – and consequently likely to be immature, unruly and unamenable to discipline.[105] In addition, Lambert's threats of deadly force notwithstanding, these were men subject to the intense scrutiny and care of their compatriots, at home, in Britain and beyond the seas.

---

102 Gavan Duffy to Corrigan and Corrigan, 14 December 1916: NLI: Irish National Aid Association Papers: Ms. 24, 366. Richard Mulcahy (1886–1971) had been second-in-command to Thomas Ashe at Ashbourne during the rising. On release he became deputy, then chief of staff of the IRA. Supported the Treaty and became Minister of Defence as well as chief of staff of the army under the provisional government. Was a founder member of the Fine Gael and enjoyed an extensive ministerial career. After his release from internment T. D. Sinnott was one of the founders of the New Ireland Assurance Company.

103 The plight of the Frongoch men had been highlighted by collecting funds to send them Christmas parcels. Politically, it was a bonus that these could not be sent because the men were under punishment (NLI: Irish National Aid Association Papers: Ms. 24, 347 (unfoliated), reports of 16 and 18 December 1916).

104 Art O'Brien to Irish National Aid Association, 19 December 1916; Alfred Byrne to Irish National Aid Association, 19 December 1916: NLI: Irish National Aid Association Papers; Ms. 24, 366.

105 The various difficulties were recognised by at least some of the camp leaders. Noting that there were in the camp three young men aged 17 or under, and several under 20, a smuggled document commented: 'Camp life is anything but improving. They are (some of them) deteriorating and some effort should be made to get them out' (NLI: Seán O'Mahony Papers: Ms. 24, 450 (unfoliated)).

The official record of the 1916 internments ended with tributes to the staff, one of which must surely rank among the classics of damming praise. The Home Secretary, minuted Waller,[106] might wish to send letters of thanks to Captain Morgan (Governor of Reading) and Colonel Lambert (Commandant of Frongoch) –

> especially the latter, who, although he may not have been always tactful, has discharged an unpleasant and thankless task with great industry and business ability. He may have managed to set the men against him, but we created his worst difficulties for him by seeking out evaders of military service; and nothing has ever come to our knowledge to suggest that he was not perfectly fair and just to his prisoners, though admittedly strict.

Waller went on to note that it was only fair to say that every incident at Frongoch, however small, 'has been eagerly laid hold of, magnified, and exploited for political purposes'.[107] This last was indeed true, but it was either naive or disingenuous to imagine that one could lock up several hundred rebels, and not expect them and their friends to make politics from the incidents of that confinement. Colonel Lambert so aided them in this that he perhaps should have received from the IRB a letter to match his commendation from the Home Secretary.

Regime

Frongoch could serve any one of several purposes – basic training, transit, regrouping, or holding prisoners of war. For the latter purpose, the camp's geography had certain disciplinary implications. Unless it were subdivided and redivided into a number of secure compounds, the internees would have to be allowed to mix more or less freely. Since the purpose of the camp was containment, rather than punishment or reform, it followed that custody simply required a secure perimeter, and a sufficient guard to put down a concerted uprising or breakout.[108] The numbers involved, and their ambiguous legal standing, settled for the internees

---

106 Maurice Lyndham Waller (1875–1932). Family background artistic and architectural; educated at Rugby and Corpus Christi, Oxford. First served in the Admiralty, but after a year transferred to Home Office. Became a Prison Commissioner in 1910, Chairman in 1921, retired in 1928.
107 PRO HO 144/1456/313106/613.
108 The latter possibility had been greatly reduced by locating the camp in Wales rather than Ireland, since despite its proximity to the main London–Dublin road and rail links, escapers would have faced the difficulty of making their way through a probably hostile population to reach Liverpool or (more improbably) to cross the Irish Sea. It is curious nevertheless that no one completed an escape, especially since sympathisers in the Irish community on Merseyside could have hidden at least small numbers of men.

a question which had been in constant and bitter contention in the history of the imprisonment of Irish political offenders since Fenian times: the demand to be treated as political rather than criminal offenders. Without much fuss or bureaucratic debate it had been decided that all apart from those actually convicted would be treated as prisoners of war. (And, as we shall see in Chapter 11, even convicted prisoners were not to be treated as common criminals.)

From the outset, therefore, it was accepted that the men would be able to associate almost without restriction: not so much a concession as a necessity, in fact, since they had to organise much of their own lives. Commandants were elected for both camps, and each hut elected its own leader.[109] It followed that political and military as well as cultural and recreational pursuits would be observed, and that little could be done to regulate these. Eamon Martin, who complained about many of the camp's physical amenities, and who was Secretary of the General Council, was enthusiastic about the educational and cultural activities. Mass, breakfast and military drill were followed by afternoons of classes, as the internees drew on their own reservoir of talents. Instruction was offered in various languages, including Latin and French. There were three large Irish classes each evening; other subjects such as history, shorthand and book-keeping were also available. Covertly, a great deal of elementary military instruction was imparted.[110] Concerts were held twice a week and impromptu singsongs after the evening meal when there were no concerts: 'We had brilliant musicians, prize step-dancers and singers who were Feis Ceoil medalists, so that I can say without exaggeration that our socials were the acme of artistic finish and ability.'[111]

Martin mentioned frequent football matches, but Patrick Rankin remembered the ground being unsuitable for matches, because of the hilliness of the site.[112] The men seem to have adapted to this, however, and games and athletics let off a lot of steam. Given the connections between the Volunteers and the Gaelic Athletic Association, it was not surprising that there were among the internees three county captains who had not long before been in the All Ireland Championship, as well as other All Ireland hurlers and footballers.[113]

---

109 Béaslaí, op. cit., Vol. 1, p. 109.

110 On 20 September 1916, Michael J. Brennan (a prominent Volunteer, member of the Supreme Council of the IRB and of the military committee at Frongoch) smuggled a letter out to Art O'Brien, asking him to buy the British Army's basic training manual on signalling. He explained that the Frongoch signalling class had progressed so well that a book was now necessary: 'Needless to say such a book must come in surreptitiously, as it might be looked upon as endangering the cause of Small Nationalities, etc. etc.' O'Brien (ever methodical) noted that he had sent in one copy each of a manual on signalling and infantry training, together with two small signalling flags (NLI: Art O'Brien Papers: Ms. 8443).

111 NLI: McGarrity Papers: Ms. 17, 512: Eamon Martin, 'The Irish Rebellion of 1916. Personal Experiences. Reminiscences of English Convict Prisons', f. 40.

112 Patrick Rankin Papers: op. cit., f. 17. Rankin added 'but it was a very healthy place'.

113 Martin, op. cit., f. 41; Brennan, op. cit., p. 118.

Morale was sufficiently high for 'Frongoch Sports' in August and October. These included running, jumping and shot-putting. The vigour displayed in these activities was used to counter complaints about the quality and quantity of the food provided at the camp.[114]

Rules and regulations followed the usual War Office provision for prisoner-of-war camps for enlisted men,[115] and Colonel Lambert promulgated his version of this as soon as the internees arrived. The basic unit was to be a mess of between thirty and forty men. These were assigned to the same hut or dormitory, and would eat, work and have their recreation together.[116] The self-regulating messes each had an elected president; committees arranged activities: all this was notionally subject to Lambert's approval. The huts had to be cleaned to the required standard, and there were maintenance parties. There were also various special camp assignments such as kitchen work, and post, police and firemen. Importantly, at a time of near-universal cigarette- and pipe-smoking, internees were allowed tobacco. Carelessness in smoking, they were warned, would lead to the offending mess having its privileges curtailed; in particular, there was to be no smoking after lights out. A striking feature of the camp, as compared to a civil prison, was the limited role of the guard: only the officers, provost sergeants and censor went inside the wire; all others were posted outside.[117] These were precautions against trafficking and fraternisation, and to prevent soldiers' weapons from being seized.

Complaints

The first official camp inspection took place on 3 July 1916. Most arrangements were approved, but it was recognised that there had been problems with communications.[118] The camp authorities had not been informed that mail to and from Ireland was being censored in London. The only knowledge the commandant

---

114 5 *Hansard*, LXXXVI, col. 669; 18 October 1916. Internees insisted that the diet was indeed inadequate, and that they managed to keep up their strength through canteen spending, as well as parcels sent in by families, friends and supporters (Margery Forester, *Michael Collins: The Lost Leader*, London, Sphere Books, 1972, p. 57; Martin, *op. cit.*, f. 42 ('we were consequently somewhat independent of the ordinary camp rations')).

115 In the autumn of 1914 Chandler S. Anderson, a legal adviser to the US Department of State, inspected three British prisoner-of-war camps, two for other ranks and one for officers. His detailed report (forwarded by the US Ambassador in London to Sir Edward Grey, the Foreign Secretary) showed that Frongoch was run on similar lines and to a similar standard to the enlisted men's camps (PRO HO 45/10729/255193/(153) 'Internment and Treatment of Enemy Subjects').

116 These and following details are taken from 'Notice No. 1', issued by Colonel F. A. Heygate Lambert, Frongoch Camp Commandant, on 5 June 1916 (at PRO HO 144/1455/313106/8).

117 See 'Report on Frongoch Camp' (3 July 1916), PRO HO 144/1455/313106/168.

118 It had been claimed, however, that reasonably swift and efficient steps were taken to provide friends and relatives with information on the location of the detainees and means of contacting them and sending parcels (see official notice in *The Times*, 19 May 1916, 9b).

had of this was the censor's stamp on the envelopes. But there was also a camp censorship, and this was completely overwhelmed by the volume of mail. At the beginning of July there were still some 1500 men in the camp. About 1000 letters and 160 parcels arrived each day, and some 150 letters were officially posted out. The censors had been given several duties besides reading letters and examining parcels, and, as a result, a backlog of some 4000 letters had already accumulated.[119] The inspector considered that there was 'great irregularity' in the censor's department.

Nothing was said in the inspector's report on the subject of food, which became a major grievance. The internees received a steady flow of food parcels from Ireland and from local sympathisers. When they first arrived some of the men considered they were fed well enough. John MacDonagh, having money and access to the camp canteen, urged his family not to send any more food.[120] By mid-October, however, there were vociferous complaints on this subject. How much of this was political window-dressing for the campaign of complaints, and how far there was substance in the complaints is unclear. Given the state of the war and the nation's larder, and the degree of priority which would have been attached to an internment camp, it is likely that the complaints were not without foundation.

Both in quantity and quality the food was deficient, the prisoners insisted. The bread was of such poor quality during July that 160 men could not eat it at all. The potatoes were worse: 'It is practically impossible for an Irishman to imagine such potatoes – they are small, wet and soapy in appearance and texture.' On one occasion they were so bad that the camp doctor condemned them as unfit.[121] The meat ration was invariably New Zealand frozen and the 8 oz daily allowance included bone, fat and suet. Meat had three times been condemned as unfit for consumption – the last time having been offered to the soldiers of the guard, who had refused it. Friday fish was salt herring which was said to be so poorly cured that it also was unfit to eat: the men were paying for fish out of their own pockets.[122] Other complaints concerned margarine (not enough), tinned milk (unfit), vegetables (mainly preserved rather than fresh) and the regulation

---

119 Two men censored the mail. In addition to this they had to issue camp notices, arrange and supervise visits, attend the daily inspection as 'a kind of detective', act as bankers, be a means of communication between the prisoners and the commandant, attend the searches of new arrivals and make themselves 'au fait with all that goes on in the Camp'.

120 John to Sister Francesca MacDonagh, 27 June 1916: NLI: Sister Francesca MacDonagh Papers: Ms. 20, 647.

121 NLI: Seán O'Mahony Papers: Ms. 24, 450; mimeographed compilation of Frongoch and Aylesbury complaints. The details which follow, unless otherwise indicated, are all taken from this source.

122 The men had insisted on Friday fish to meet their religious obligation to abstain from meat on that day – despite the advice of their chaplain that this was not necessary. Cured herrings were supplied, but since they had not been gutted before being cured they were inedible (Brennan-Whitmore, *op. cit.*, pp. 50–1).

that all tinned foods sent in should be opened by the camp censor before being passed to the prisoners. These items then had to be eaten immediately or thrown into the pigswill.

Although an intelligence assessment was made of the internees' letters, the basic objective seems to have been to prevent political propaganda. The censor's comments on returned letters included 'Writer glories for having suffered in Ireland's cause'; 'Writer complains of lack of medical treatment in camp'; 'Complaints re Camp'; 'Refers to Casement's murder'; 'Refers to disturbances in Ireland'; 'I would rather rot in gaol than accept their privileges'; 'Refers to MacDavitt's escape'. The prisoners objected that rather than striking out the offending phrase and returning the letter to the writer for redrafting, the censors held it for a week or so before returning it. This meant that prisoners had a period of uncertainty as to whether or not their post had got through.[123] At the same time it was true that both individually and collectively the internees did make propaganda use of their letters, and gave directions to the Irish National Aid Association on this issue.[124]

For prisoners of any description visits from friends and relatives provide a vital bridge to the outside world, as well as distraction from the routine of prison life: visitors are light, colour and interest in a world reduced to grey routine; to internees indefinitely detained they provided hope of freedom and reunions. Almost universally, prison administrators have made visits part of the system of rewards and punishments: Lambert, failing to see the carrot, saw them only in a negative light: they had 'an unsettling effect on the prisoners'. Internees were supposedly entitled to one fifteen-minute visit a month. Visiting hours were limited to Tuesdays and Thursdays between 2 and 3 p.m.[125] Staffing and accommodation limitations meant that there could be only thirty-two visits in a week, which, with 1500 prisoners in the camp, made a nonsense of the monthly 'entitlement'. If every prisoner exercised his right to have a visit, his turn would come around only every forty-seventh week – an entitlement far inferior to the treatment of criminal prisoners in the most severe stage of discipline. This, together with the comparatively long distances that most visitors would have to travel,[126] constituted a legitimate grievance, which quickly inspired a protest campaign. Only the large releases of late July and August prevented a crisis, by reducing the volume of visits.

123 NLI: Seán O'Mahony Papers: Ms. 24, 450 (unfoliated).
124 NLI: Irish National Aid Association Papers: Ms. 24, 347 (unfoliated), letter from Frongoch subcommittee, 13 September 1916.
125 In addition, Lambert decreed that those not receiving visitors should be locked into their buildings during these hours (Martin, *op. cit.*, f. 44).
126 From London it was at least six hours to Frongoch by train (5 *Hansard*, LXXXIII, col. 1360; 4 July 1916). By boat from Dublin, with local travel on both sides, even longer hours and greater expenses were involved.

Colonel Lambert directed 'as soon as things become more settled' that the men should undertake route marches. This met with approval since it acknowledged the internees' military status and continued the kind of training they had frequently undertaken in the Volunteers. Indeed, whatever may have been their military deficiencies, they were reported to be 'extraordinarily well drilled', with many wearing 'the Sinn Féiner uniform and colours'.[127] Getting the men out into the splendid countryside of North Wales was a good move, if only to burn up energy and help dispel frustrations. The initiative was soured, however, when Lambert ruled that marches should be compulsory for all, and insisted that the old and unfit turn out alongside the fit young men. This then became another complaint winging its way to the outside world.[128]

Outside support

The Irish community

The recoil and realignment of Irish opinion was demonstrated by the rallying of sections of the Irish community to the support of the internees. Gratitude for this assistance runs through several accounts of internment. Some of the response was immediate and spontaneous, but as the weeks passed it became more organised under Art O'Brien's Irish National Relief Association, operating from London, with a sister organisation in Manchester. The Relief Association would eventually become an important arm of Irish revolutionary politics, but from the beginning it gathered and focused the energies and resources of sympathisers in the Irish community in England.[129] Because of the Military Service Act few young Irishmen liable to conscription remained in England, and so the internees were assisted by groups of women – mainly young it would seem – and a small number of sympathetic clergy. The internees' isolated and demoralised condition in their first weeks in the prisons has been described, as well as the boost given by visitors – and the food and comforts which they brought. For many men those demonstrations of support and respect resolved self-doubts and a wavering faith in the cause. The youth of the bulk of the internees and their female visitors doubtless blended nationalist fervour with romance.

Supporters in the Irish communities near the various places of detention managed visits and parcels after the first weeks of the men being moved to England, when the prison regimes were liberalised. Art O'Brien's organisation collected money from sympathisers and supporters throughout the country, and entered into correspondence – open and clandestine – with inmate leaders. These support mechanisms had not operated for either the Fenians or the

127 'Report on Frongoch Camp' (3 July 1916), *op. cit.*, p. 6.
128 NLI: Irish National Aid Association Papers: Ms. 24, 324 (i): Camp Committee to Timothy Healy, 4 October 1916, f. 10.
129 See below, pp. 483–8.

dynamitards – the former because the Irish community was not sufficiently well established in England and lacked the necessary self-confidence; the latter because their acts of terrorism were repugnant even in militant nationalist circles. By 1916, however, the Irish community was very much more established and secure, allowing some of its most respectable members to identify themselves as sympathisers; it was also more prosperous. Expressions of support were made easier by the scale of the Dublin rising, the numbers involved, and the Volunteers' generally respectable character, very ordinary backgrounds, and the fact that they were untried internees whose personal culpability for the death and destruction of the rising remained helpfully vague.

Of the men's gratitude for the support there can be no doubt. John MacDonagh wrote to his sister from Frongoch about 'These Irish people in Manchester, school teachers mostly [who] spent all their spare time & money on us. We shall not easily forget.'[130] It was a happy coincidence for the visitors and the internees that, the first few weeks apart, the school holidays allowed young female teachers the necessary time to organise and undertake visits. These also knew how to conduct themselves with the authorities, and were respectable, agreeable and no doubt attractive distractions for internees and soldiers alike, and therefore welcomed by all. The long-term effect of these visits and support activities was to reinforce the Irish revolutionary cause. The visitors were tangible proof to the men that their cause was widely supported, while each person who visited a camp or prison or was involved with those who did became a potential propagandist for Irish republicanism.

Relatives

Mary MacSwiney, one of the great termagants of Irish republicanism – a woman whose very name doubtless came to chill the blood of officials and politicians alike – served her apprenticeship in connection with Frongoch and Reading in 1916. It was Frongoch, however, that particularly stimulated her ire. Her brother Terence, who would become an icon of Irish independence, was arrested in Cork after the rising, and on 17 June 1916 transferred to Frongoch with the rank and file, but was then identified as a leader and put with the Special List men at Reading on 11 July. Mary, who was a committed Irish republican in her own right,[131] was a fierce defender of her brother and fastened herself on officialdom with terrier-like fierceness. She and Colonel Lambert were natural enemies.

---

130 John to Sister Francesca, 14 July 1916: NLI: Sister Francesca MacDonagh: Ms. 20, 647 (1). See also Eileen (?) Mallon to Sister Francesca, 24 July 1916: ibid. (5).

131 (1872–1942). Born London and educated at Queen's College, Cork. Taught in London and Dublin. Active in various republican organisations, including Sinn Féin. Strongly opposed Treaty and imprisoned for her activities during Irish Civil War. Her brand of republicanism denied the legitimacy of the new Irish State.

Following her first visit to Frongoch Mary complained at length to the Home Secretary. She catalogued the poor facilities, especially the overcrowded and poorly ventilated South Camp dormitories. In her brother's loft the men's sleep was affected by overcrowding and poor conditions including its one skylight which could not be opened when the weather was bad; they were also disturbed by the adjacent steam boiler and the camp dynamo: 'Want of sleep and impure air are infinitely worse than bad food, or insufficient food.' She taxed Samuel with denying these facts in his Commons statement.[132] With some justification, she objected to the very short visiting times (fifteen minutes) and asked to be allowed to see her brother again before she returned to Ireland, since it would be a long time before she could come back to Wales. Mary concluded by delivering a homily on British indebtedness to her brother, as well as British shortcomings.[133] The responsible Home Office official (Maurice Waller), anxious no doubt to avoid a second instalment of this sisterly encomium, granted the extra visit.

Mary's style of remonstration had other consequences. The day after the extra visit had been granted by Waller there arrived at the Home Office a strong letter of complaint from Lambert about her first visit to Frongoch. She was, he averred, 'a great mischief-maker', and at the camp had used language which 'had she been a man and not a woman, would have resulted in her being handed over to the Police under the DORA'. (This language was to become painfully familiar in Whitehall.) Because of her behaviour, Lambert had directed that she was not to be granted another visiting pass for some time; he also recommended that Terence MacSwiney be removed to Reading with the other leaders.[134] The Home Office (which may also at this time have received intelligence which gave a better idea of Terence MacSwiney's prominence in the Volunteers) acted immediately. Mary's visit was cancelled and a transfer order issued. Sir Edward Troup, the Home Office Permanent-Under-Secretary, telegraphed cancellation of the visiting order to Mary, but to her Cork address, rather than to the London address which she had given the Home Office. Unaware that her brother had been moved, Mary made the long journey to Frongoch. Lambert, in petty spite, would not tell her where her brother had been sent and refused to let her see any of the other internees. She made her way back to Ireland and learned through friends only on 15 July where her brother was being held. However disagreeable Mary MacSwiney had been to officials, this was a disgraceful runaround: a combination of carelessness on the part of some Home Office clerical officer and

132 Mary MacSwiney to Herbert Samuel (Home Secretary), 4 July 1916: PRO HO 144/10308, f. 2; 5 Hansard, LXXXIII, col. 13; 20 June 1916; col. 1005; 29 June 1916.
133 She reminded Samuel that Terence had not taken part in the rising, and that but for him and Thomas MacCurtain 'you would have had considerable trouble in the south of Ireland which *their* efforts kept peaceful. He had as much right to be an Irish Volunteer as Sir Edward Carson had to be an Ulster Volunteer and he maintained that right. You English talk a great deal about justice and Fair Play. If you had *practised* it a little more you would not have created the present situation in Ireland.'
134 Lambert to Waller, 8 July 1916: PRO HO 144/10308.

Lambert's bullying. Back in Cork, Mary dispatched another blast of complaint to Herbert Samuel. She again listed the camp's various deficiencies – physical, organisational and in regime – and demanded to know why these internees had been put on the same footing as the penal servitude men. She concluded with a characteristic thrust: 'If, as you said in the House of Commons, your sanitary inspector finds these conditions "perfectly satisfactory", I should suggest his testing his verdict by personal experience.'[135]

Mary MacSwiney was exceptional among the internees' relatives in her education, trenchant mode of expression and unfaltering self-confidence: she was not a woman that any sensible official would want to provoke. But she shared with many other relatives a determination to draw every grievance to the attention of the outside world, partly in affection and support for the imprisoned, but also out of her own desire to advance the republican cause by portraying internment as yet another manifestation of British cruelty and injustice. The realisation soon dawned on Mary MacSwiney and these other politically committed friends and relatives that the internees served the republican cause hardly less in captivity than at liberty. This was an unfortunate lesson for thoughtless or callous authority to drive home.

The Irish National Aid Association

As we have seen, at various phases in the development of physical force nationalism, movements for amnesty and assistance united a range of constitutional politicians with those on the extreme. This unity was by its nature fleeting, but it served the interest of both wings of the movement. Something similar happened after the 1916 rising, but such was the speed and direction of developments, and the cleavage between the Irish Parliamentary Party and the republicans, that the amnesty and assistance movement remained firmly under the control of the latter and became its useful instrument. Another distinctive feature of this new type of support organisation was that it provided the foundations for a semi-legal extension of the republican movement, involving networks of sympathisers willing to undertake a variety of tasks including clandestine communications, intelligence and public relations. The support and amnesty organisations in Ireland and Britain thus provided increasingly important tactical assistance in the prosecution of the armed struggle.

Possibly the first contact in the development of this relationship came on 29 June 1916, when the London-based Irish National Relief Fund sent £25 to the Irish National Relief Association in Dublin, stating that future funds would be sent equally to them and to the Irish Volunteers' Dependents' Fund.[136] In

---

135 Mary MacSwiney to Herbert Samuel, 19 July 1916: PRO HO 144/10308/5.
136 NLI: Irish National Relief Association Papers: Ms. 24, 324(1). Both the Dublin organisations had been set up in May, and amalgamated in August 1916. Committees had been set up in Manchester and Glasgow and these worked closely with Art O'Brien in London.

return, the Volunteers' Dependents' Fund asked the London organisation to arrange visits to the prisoners in England. This was agreed by Art O'Brien[137] (who ran the Relief Fund in London) and by 10 July the possibility was raised of renting a house at Bala and providing a woman worker to assist there with the Frongoch visits. Mary MacSwiney was asked to provide more information about this as she passed through Dublin on her way home from visiting her brother. From the outset, therefore, there was an emphasis on practical work as well as the public representation of the prisoners' cause. On 5 October 1916, the now amalgamated Dublin organisation (Irish National Aid Association) recognised the London Irish National Relief Fund as the collection and organising centre of the work in England.[138]

In Ireland and Britain the associations fielded an impressive array of sponsors on their letterhead – a mixture of Roman Catholic clergy and Irish worthies which betokened respectability and considerably widened the organisations' appeal.[139] As Irish opinion at home and abroad shifted in the weeks following the rising funds flowed in, reaching a total of £86,431 by February 1917. The largest donations came from Ireland (£32,833), the United States of America (£32,046), and Australia and New Zealand (£19,606).[140] The flow of contributions remained high throughout 1916, but with the Christmas general release from Frongoch dropped to what Art O'Brien some months later described as 'a lamentably low figure'.[141]

The relief and support work went well beyond the prisoners, though about half of the funds were expended in relief of the hardships caused by the round-up of some 2500 in the immediate aftermath of the rising. These arrests and internments it was claimed, together with numerous and widespread dismissals

137 See p. 487, n. 152.

138 NLI: Irish National Relief Association Papers: Ms. 24, 324 (1).

139 The Irish National Aid Association sponsors included clergy, various aldermen, John Dillon and Alfred Byrne, MPs, Dr Michael Davitt (Michael Davitt's son), Miss O'Rahilly (sister of the dead O'Rahilly) and the poet Dora Shorter (née Sigerson) whose husband Clement was editor of the *Illustrated London News*, as well as representatives of units of the National Volunteers and Dublin Trades Council. The ladies' committee was chaired by Miss Gavan Duffy and had branches throughout Dublin (NLI: Irish National Aid Association Papers: Ms. 24, 342).

140 NLI: Art O'Brien Papers: Ms. 8442 (unfoliated). England and Wales contributed only £1165 – but this may have been an accountancy distortion as these funds probably went to Art O'Brien's Irish National Relief Fund, and were directly expended on the prisoners in England. Several associations were involved in Australian fundraising, which seems to have been particularly responsive to the destruction and suffering arising from the insurrection. Funds were remitted from Sydney (Irish National Association of New South Wales), Petersburg, South Australia, Brisbane, Melbourne, Perth (United Irish League), Lismore, Bendigo and many other places. The Roman Catholic Church played a major role in these collections of sums which ranged from a few hundred to several thousand pounds. Large sums were sent to Dublin via the Revd Richard Bowden, the Administrator of the Pro-Cathedral (NLI: Irish National Aid Association Papers: Ms. 24, 322).

141 'Final Appeal' (August 1917), ibid.

from employment, had at one point affected the livelihoods of some 10,000 persons. More long-term obligations were assumed in meeting the needs of the families of the seventy-eight Volunteers who had been killed during the insurrection or had been executed. There were also the dependants of the 150 or so sentenced to imprisonment and penal servitude, the score who had been seriously wounded and the few who had become insane. As men were released from custody funds were disbursed to enable them to 'start life anew'. It was decided to invest the sum of £20,000 to make permanent provision for mothers, widows, orphans and other dependants.[142] At the other end of the range of activities, funds were used to provide comforts and supplies for internees, as well as assisting in the expenses of visits.[143]

As the months passed the funds undertook ever more obligations, and the work of collecting, distributing and accounting became more complex. Solicitors who had acted for Volunteers in Ireland and England were paid, though on a limited scale and sometimes rather tardily.[144] Claims were also considered from those who had not been Volunteers or dependants, but who had suffered as a result of the rising. Although this was an astute political move – in effect assuming the civil liability of government and thereby asserting a demand for loyalty – it necessitated considerable expenditure as well as much attention to distinguishing between genuine and bogus claims.[145]

The immediate dependants of the executed leaders received several forms of assistance. School fees were paid for a daughter of James Connolly until the end of 1918, and at that point his widow was given £1450 to invest in order to provide herself with an income. She was also given the funds necessary to place her son in an engineering apprenticeship. Thomas Clarke's widow, Kathleen, was similarly given £1500 in Dublin Corporation stock. The Pearse family (mother and sisters) was given various forms of financial and other aid, Grace Plunkett (née Gifford), who had married only an hour or two before her husband's execution, received a pension of £5 per month.[146] Michael Colbert, brother of

---

142 Ibid.

143 An appreciable sum was expended, for example, on providing tobacco for the Frongoch men (NLI: Irish National Relief Association: Ms. 24, 324(1)).

144 J. H. MacDonnell, the London solicitor who acted on behalf of republicans for the next several years, was paid only 3s. 4d. per head for representing internees before the Sankey Committee – half a dozen cases for £1. Gavan Duffy was paid 200 guineas for his courts martial work. Payment seemed to be determined by the funds available rather than the amount of work involved (NLI: Irish National Aid Association Papers: Ms. 24, 357(1) (unfoliated)).

145 For some personal claims of loss and hardship the applicant was asked to submit a letter of support from his or her parish priest.

146 The death-cell marriage attracted much attention because of its tragic and romantic circumstances. Grace subsequently found herself in very straitened circumstances, receiving little or no support from her own family or from the Plunketts. Working as an artist she had little money of her own, and was highly dependent on the small dole provided by the Aid Association. She became frantic when payments were delayed. Relations with the Association deteriorated,

Con (executed for his part in the rising), claimed that neither he nor his cousins could get employment and that his business (jockey and horse-trainer) had been destroyed because his clients would not do business with the relative of such a notorious rebel. The Association made a grant to assist him. Peter de Burca, whose education had been interrupted by the rising, was granted payment of his medical school fees, with assistance continuing until he was able to earn, in 1921.

Business claims included £50 to Mrs Bannister, owner of the Minerva Hotel (which would be used by Michael Collins during the Anglo-Irish war). Various firms applied for compensation for commandeered goods, including a motorbike, arms and ammunition. A woman whose son (and sole means of support) had been accidentally killed by a Volunteer received assistance, as did Jervis Street Hospital which submitted a claim for five patients treated for wounds received during Easter week.[147] Many of the grants for lost or damaged goods, destruction to premises and other losses due to the rising were quite substantial, with settlements going to £100 and more. Book-work and verification procedures in these transactions were meticulous, as surviving papers show. Great care was evidently taken that no grounds should be given for rumours of misuse or accusations of misappropriation.

The closure of Frongoch reduced the flow of donations and subscriptions, and caused some difficulties. Small sums had to be paid to assist immediate expenses and help the released men get on their feet. Some needed clothing and others needed assistance in finding employment or in being re-engaged in their old employment. A number of those whose names would become prominent during the Anglo-Irish war appear in the Association's correspondence at this time – Piaras Béaslaí and Michael Collins to name but two. (Collins became full-time secretary of the Association shortly after his release from Frongoch.) Commitments continued, in the form of the 139 convicted prisoners and their various dependants. And when the convicts were released they also needed assistance of many kinds, but nearly all boiling down to funds.[148] As the Anglo-Irish war developed there were a number of other calls upon the Association's funds, some

and in March 1919 she demanded to be put on the same footing as the other widows of the signatories of the Proclamation ('Please confine jurisdiction to this category as it is the one to which I belong'). Sinn Féin supporters in an American city had raised money for a memorial, taking the form of a group of statues depicting the death-cell wedding. Rather than have the monument built, Grace demanded the money to remove her from what she described as destitution. At various points she threatened to make her complaints public, and appears to have received a final payment in April 1919. The aid committee insisted that this was to be the last of the money allocated to her in November 1917; she demanded a written statement signed by Michael Collins, with the implied threat of publicity. It is not clear from the surviving papers how this conflict played out (NLI: Irish National Aid Association Papers: Ms. 24, 357(1)).

147 This claim was submitted on 20 March 1919, in response to a notice which the Association had published in the Irish press asking claimants to come forward (ibid.).

148 Constance Markievicz, for example, was given £50 on 30 July 1917 to meet her immediate expenses (NLI: Irish National Aid Association Papers: Ms. 24, 357 (1) (unfoliated)).

of which (such as the several thousand pounds spent on the funeral of Thomas Ashe) crossed the boundary between assistance and political campaigning.[149] A much stricter line was drawn between public and private expenses in the funeral of William Partridge (who had been at Lewes).[150]

The surviving papers show that while the objective had never been a purely philanthropic and humanitarian one, both the Dublin and London organisations became more directly involved with republican politics as time went on, and responded to the Sinn Féin and IRA agenda. They undertook such open tasks as the publication of the report on the ill-treatment of the Frongoch internees, the largely covert funding of the Ashe funeral, the building of multi-purpose contacts in Ireland, Britain, the US, and Australia and, as the Anglo-Irish war progressed, the payment of legal costs for those charged with IRA offences.[151] The two men at the heart of the organisation – Michael Collins in Dublin and Art O'Brien in London – were energetic and experienced administrators as able in the minutiae of finance as in dealing with solicitors or the press.[152] This legal face and its many resources would become invaluable to Sinn Féin and the IRA, and the needs of the prisoners and their dependants provided a *raison d'être* and the essential organisational underpinning. In a relatively short time the prison work of the Association became less important than its political functions.

An insight into the success of the Association in its public role, and the range of distinguished and respectable supporters it attracted, is given by the catalogue of the gift sale held at the Dublin Mansion House on 20 and 21 April 1917. The list included many impressive pieces – clothes, antiques, curios, jewellery, books and works of art. These gifts were donated by well-heeled and respectable Ireland and included several paintings by Augustus John as well as a blank canvas on which he would paint the portrait of the purchaser; John Lavery also offered a portrait. The bourgeois bidders could enjoy more than the

149 Ibid., 28 September 1917.
150 The Association paid for the public element in the funeral expenses of the Volunteer honour party, wreath and related payments. Partridge, a member of the Irish Transport and General Workers' Union, had been sent to assist with landing of the German arms in Kerry.
151 The Association collated and published the internees' various complaints about Frongoch which have been discussed in this chapter. This document lost some of its force, however, by being published at about the time the men were released and Frongoch ceased to be a live issue. See 'Official Report of the Ill-Treatment of the Irish Prisoners of War Interned at Frongoch Internment Camp', Cork, Irish National Aid and Volunteer Dependent's Fund Association, December 1916 (NLI: Art O'Brien Papers: Ms. 8442).
152 The two were in the very closest contact – by letter, telegram and courier. Only a few cypher messages have survived, but many others which more than hint at the volume and nature of the work are to be found in the archives. There is, for example, a three-letter exchange (12– 17 May 1921) concerning the release of Erskine Childers. There was information that this had provoked disagreements between the British civil and military authorities and O'Brien pressed for further details to assist his work in England (NLI: Kathleen MacKenna Napoli Papers: Ms. 22, 785).

normal *frisson* of the auction-room in the various items of somewhat gruesome revolutionary memorabilia on offer. These included Robert Emmet's wallet, as well as the block on which he was beheaded, the sword with which Lord Edward Fitzgerald had been wounded during his capture on 19 May 1798 and a piece of his outer coffin. And this being a very Irish auction, livestock was not overlooked: 'Three Irish Terrier Pups, two male and one female, all well-bred.'[153] Insurrection had already become worryingly domesticated.

Parliament

The most unrelenting parliamentary critic of internment and the treatment of the convicted was Lawrence Ginnell. He was elected for Westmeath in 1906, in the colours of the Parliamentary Party, sat virtually as an independent, was expelled from the Party and openly switched allegiance to Sinn Féin after the rising.[154] His career entered a new and more revolutionary phase when he greeted the first Commons announcement of the Dublin executions with the cry 'Murder'.[155] This was the start of a prolonged and bitter campaign. How many prisoners had been executed, and what were the capital offences of those who were neither signers of the proclamation nor leaders; what was the interval between capture and death; and what religious facilities were allowed to the condemned in their preparation for death? These were all issues about which public discontent was growing, and to which government – even as late as 10 May 1916 – had only vague and unsatisfactory answers.[156] Ginnell's probings included the Dublin executions and disposal of the bodies, the state of opinion in America, and a multitude of details concerning the prisoners.[157] As information was passed to him by militant republicans he moved from general and largely declamatory questions and charges to the more specific. By 26 June, for example, he had discovered the unsatisfactory state of postal deliveries at Frongoch,[158] and the following day it was political status for the convicts.[159] And on the day after there were other questions: a problem at Wakefield Prison; the property of

---

153 NLI: Art O'Brien Papers: Ms. 8442.
154 Ginnell (1854–1923) was a self-educated man who succeeded in being called to both the Irish and English Bars. After the East Clare and Kilkenny by-elections in the summer of 1917 he announced his abstention from Westminster. He was elected to the first Dáil Eireann, and imprisoned in May 1919. He took the republican side in the Irish Civil War. During his twelve or so years in the House of Commons he was removed from the Chamber on several occasions for breaches of procedure; he was also ejected from the Free State Dáil in 1922.
155 5 *Hansard*, LXXXII, col. 285; 8 May 1916. The expostulation followed an evasive answer to a multi-pronged question on the Dublin executions.
156 Ibid., cols 629–34; 10 May 1916.
157 Ibid., cols 2931–2; 1 June 1916; LXXXIII, col. 514; 26 June 1916.
158 Ibid., LXXXIII, cols 515–17.
159 Ibid., col. 702; 27 June 1916.

an executed prisoner, Dublin Castle Hospital and other matters.[160] And so on, almost on a daily basis: Ginnell became the IRB's parliamentary voice.[161]

A ban on his entry into any of the places of detention affected neither the flow of information to Ginnell nor his energy in using it, and his questions continued throughout July, resuming at full flow after the recess.[162] Because three – sometimes four – offices of state were involved in the internment of the Irish prisoners, there were opportunities to ask similar questions repeatedly – sometimes on the same day.[163] Until the internees were released, Ginnell bombarded government on Frongoch and the civil prisons, as well as the larger issue of release; the *Hansard* index testifies to his energy and persistence.

Ginnell had become the bitter, irreconcilable and (increasingly) abrasive voice of Irish republicanism in the Commons, but he was not alone in his campaign: senior members of the Irish Parliamentary Party, as well as the rank and file, played their part. John Dillon was much more active than his leader, John Redmond, in openly pursuing matters connected with the rising, martial law, executions and the prisoners. Indeed, in the roll of these questions, Redmond is almost entirely absent. Between May and December 1916, the principal voices were Dillon, Alfred Byrne,[164] Timothy Michael Healy[165] and Ginnell himself. The insurrection and its aftermath had badly wounded constitutional nationalism; the failure thereafter to conclude a Home Rule agreement dealt it a mortal blow. Redmond struggled to outflank the new Sinn Féin through confidential

160 Ibid., cols 855–8; 28 June 1916.
161 He was held in high regard by the internees (Brennan, *op. cit.*, p. 117).
162 See, for example, 5 *Hansard*, LXXXIII, cols 1356–7; 4 July 1916; cols 1505–6; 5 July 1916; cols 1638–47; 6 July 1916; LXXXIV, cols 318–19; 12 July 1916; cols 680–1; 17 July 1916; col. 1305; 24 July 1916; LXXXVI, col. 965; 24 October 1916. With Byrne, Ginnell was among the earliest visitors to the internees. The authorities considered them to be a bad and unsettling influence, and banned him. On 17 July Ginnell appeared at Bow Street on a DORA charge of attempting to evade the prohibition on his admission to any detention barracks. Knowing that he was banned Ginnell had signed his name in Irish (*The Times*, 17 July 1916, 5c). See also Thomas Curran's reference to Ginnell's illegal visit to Knutsford (Thomas Curran, 'A Brief Personal Narrative of the Six Days Defence of the Irish Republic', NLI: Joseph McGarrity Papers: Ms. 17, 510, ff. 29–30).
163 The three main departments were the Home Office, the War Office and the Irish Office. Sometimes the Foreign Office also became involved, usually in relation to American reactions to the events in Ireland. Ginnell was able to use this division of authority to multiply his opportunities in the Chamber, as, for example, on 26 October 1916, when he addressed two sets of questions to the Home Secretary, others to the Prime Minister, and yet another to the Under-Secretary at the Foreign Office (see 5 *Hansard*, LXXXVI, cols 1281–4 and 1353–4; 26 October 1916).
164 (1882–1956). Dublin Alderman. MP for Harbour Division of Dublin, 1915–18. Member of Dáil (Independent), Dublin City North, 1923–8, 1932–56. First Lord Mayor of Greater Dublin.
165 (1855–1931). Had been Parnell's secretary and later his colleague in the House of Commons. In 1883 he had been imprisoned in Ireland on treason charges, and played an important part in the land campaigns. After the split in the Irish Party, Healy led the anti-Parnellite Irish National Federation. Conservative and clericalist in his views, in 1922 Healy became the first Governor General of the Irish Free State.

negotiations, but there is in his private and political correspondence an ever more evident realisation of failure and a mood of bitterness and withdrawal.[166] He had no stomach for the complaints of prisoners and their supporters.

Members of the Irish Party covered much the same ground as Ginnell in their Commons questions, though generally they were less bitter in their tone, and less furious in delivery. Speaking only six weeks after the rising, Alfred Byrne, for example, presumed that it was the government's intention to win over Ireland. It could be done, he asserted, but only through kindness.[167] Arthur Lynch agreed. The government 'should rise to the great conception of a general amnesty . . . they should endeavour to release themselves from all smaller and petty considerations'.[168] Thomas Smyth took much the same line eight weeks later: 'None of us were in sympathy with the Irish Rebellion. We all deplored it, but we think that now a general amnesty should be given.'[169]

Too late Redmond fully grasped the situation. On 30 November 1916 he wrote to Asquith (whose premiership had only days to run), predicting exactly what would happen. After months of 'furious and angry agitation' the prisoners would be released. This would not mend things, but would rather be taken by extremists as a further proof that 'violent agitation is the only argument to which the British government will listen'. And he had no doubt about the impact of the organisation of the amnesty campaign. It provided a platform for the greatest enemies of the Irish Party, for 'inflammatory and bitter speeches'. Passions would be stirred, 'old race hatred lashed to fury' and there would be the gravest danger of bloody conflict between the people and the police and army.[170] The clarity and accuracy of his belated prediction could do nothing to change the outcome he feared. On 19 December, following Lloyd George's first Commons speech as Prime Minister, Redmond made an effective plea for the release of the internees and a week later they were freed.[171] They returned to Ireland and to popular acclaim, with, as he so bitterly predicted, little or no credit accruing to the Irish Party – and certainly no healing of political wounds.[172]

---

166 See, Denis Roleston Gwynn, *The Life of John Redmond*, London, George C. Harrap, 1932, chs 14 and 15.

167 5 *Hansard*, LXXXII, cols 2071–2; 1 June 1916.

168 Ibid., col. 2073.

169 5 *Hansard*, LXXXV, col. 255; 1 August 1916. Thomas Francis Smyth (1875–1939) was MP for South Leitrim from 1906 until his retirement in 1918.

170 Gwynn, 1932, *op. cit.*, p. 533. Gwynn notes that at this time 'in the morbid political atmosphere of London it was extremely difficult for Redmond to keep in touch with the trend of Irish opinion', but Redmond here has his finger on the Irish pulse.

171 5 *Hansard*, LXXXVIII, cols 1367–75; 19 December 1916. 'These men are dangerous so long as they are where they are. They cease to be dangerous – they become far less dangerous – the moment they are released' (ibid., col. 1371).

172 Feeling among the prisoners was particularly strong against the Irish Party (see Byrne, *op. cit.*, p. 56).

The tide against constitutional nationalism – more probably against the status quo in general – was by now flowing so fast that Redmond might well have concluded that it mattered little what he did. Even his closest colleagues were turning away: the nationalist cause, they believed, might be better advanced by creating difficulties for the British government than by perpetually seeking to show devotion to duty. The deputy leader of the Irish Party took a course which diverged from Redmond's by the day. As soon after the rising as he could, Dillon brought forward a resolution to check continuing executions, and to lift military rule. It was on this occasion that Dillon's own ambivalences burst the membrane of convention – to the indignation of a swathe of English opinion and the great benefit of his political reputation in Ireland and Irish America. Speaking to a bitter and noisily hostile House, Dillon attacked government policy before, during and after the rising. Tempers rose, especially when Dillon praised the courage of the rebels, even though they were misled. Heckled, Dillon was defiant: 'I say I am proud of their courage, and, if you were not so dense and so stupid, as some of you English people are, you could have had these men fighting for you, and they are men worth having.'[173] These and similar remarks caught a powerful Irish mood – even of some prison and police officers, it would seem.[174] But despite his stand then, and during the two years that followed, and the record of his long and honourable service in the cause of Irish nationalism, in December 1918 Dillon was evicted from a parliamentary seat held for thirty-three years. The majority against him was more than two

173 5 *Hansard*, LXXXII, col. 945; 11 May 1916. It was afterwards said by Lawrence Ginnell that at this point when the Easter executions were announced in the Commons, the Irish Party joined in the cheering. Tim Healy's brother and another anti-Redmond nationalist were in the House at the time, and denied that any cheering came from the Irish ranks. The story gained currency and persisted, however, much to the detriment of Redmond and his followers (Healy, *op. cit.*, Vol. 2, p. 564).

174 Darrell Figgis was arrested as part of the post-rising round-up of suspects. The acting governor of Castlebar Prison to which he was first taken kept up a rough front for the benefit of other staff and prisoners, but on entering Figgis' cell talked to him about the developing political situation: 'I remember him one morning bringing me the daily papers containing John Dillon's speech in the House of Commons denouncing the executions and imprisonments. He was glad, he said, that at least one man there had spoken out; and he insisted on reading to me those parts of the speech that pleased him most' (*Recollections of the Irish War*, London, Ernest Benn, 1927, p. 159). Figgis (1882–1925) had been a key figure in the Howth gun-running (see above, p. 415), and was active in the Irish Volunteers and Sinn Féin, in which organisations he was opposed to the growing control and eventual domination of the IRB. At the time of the rising Figgis was ostensibly living the life of a literary recluse on Achill Island, Co. Mayo. He was arrested and interned under DORA. On release Figgis returned to political activity, in 1917 becoming Secretary of Sinn Féin. The following year he was interned again following the 'German Plot'. He wrote books about his two imprisonments, as well as a memoir of his political activities. According to Ernie O'Malley, he was not popular with his comrades, who considered him vain and egotistical, with an unfortunate habit of making enemies (*On Another Man's Wound*, London, Rich & Cowan, 1936, p. 71). Besides his political and economic writings, Figgis produced a number of literary works.

to one, and the Sinn Féin victor was then in Lincoln Prison – Eamon de Valera. The change in the political currency had been under way since 1916.

When MPs spoke they addressed not only the House and their own constituents, but also the prisoners. And no one reviewing the tens and even hundreds of parliamentary questions in those months could fail to be aware that highly effective channels of communication flowed in both directions. Subject to the censorship of other publications, the internees found *Hansard* invaluable. By various means they conveyed outside the details of their grievances, and by raising them in similar terms the politicians assured the prisoners that the message had been received and that they had support in the outside world. Permission for the internees to have the daily *Hansard* was confirmed by the beginning of August.[175] Some months later Colonel Lambert protested to the Secretary of the Prison Commission, Maurice Waller (who had been seconded to the Home Office to take charge of the internment of enemy aliens and then the Irish rebels). *Hansard* was being sent to the camp on the Home Secretary's authority but he wondered whether the matter had been thoroughly considered:

> It means, of course, that the prisoners are being perpetually encouraged, both to discontent and disobedience, by the untrue and exaggerated statements of such people as Mr Byrne and Mr Ginnell, in their questions in the House. This of course does not render discipline any easier to enforce, nor do I think it is any advantage to the prisoners, who are encouraged to believe that they are suffering from ill-treatment which would never have entered into their heads, in many instances, if they had not seen these reports. Many a patient is made ill, they say, by his friends telling him that he looks so. Verbum sap.[176]

Lambert was probably right, but banning *Hansard* would only have heaped more coals on his head: *Hansard* had to be endured.

Revolutionary forcing-houses

From the late eighteenth century it has been an administrative axiom that free association between prisoners is a source of disorder and corruption. Writing of the unregulated gaols of the 1620s John Taylor, the Water Poet, described

---

175 5 *Hansard*, LXXXV, col. 225; 1 August 1916. The matter had been raised with the Home Secretary by Patrick White, Member for North Meath: 'Why does he refuse to allow the daily *Hansard* to be sent to the prisoners? Is there anything so vile in the statements and utterances made in this House that they are unfit to be read by prisoners?' The Home Secretary (Herbert Samuel) indicated that *Hansard* would be allowed.
176 Lambert to Waller, 18 November 1916: PRO HO 144/14561/313106/514.

them as 'An Universitie of Villany'.[177] For good reason classification and control of movement and association were priorities for prison reformers – whether reformatory or repressive. Treating the Irish internees as prisoners of war, government implicitly accepted that it would be able to exercise very little control over the men's life in captivity. The internees were to be put in the position of enemy prisoners of war, yet the parallels were far from exact. Captured belligerents of the Central Powers would on the cessation of hostilities return to their countries. No amount of national study and indoctrination in which they engaged while captive could be expected to harm British interests – and opportunities for further conventional military training behind the wire are limited. Indeed, in the history of prisoner-of-war camps, escape has been the chief risk.

The position of the civilian taken in arms or on suspicion was very different. Before captivity he was an occasional soldier in part-time or underground forces, now he is full time. All the influences which can be brought to bear by men with whom he must live in close proximity and comradeship are loosed upon him. The restraints and rewards of work, the duties and comforts of domestic life and wider social obligations, and the opportunities and absorptions of civil society are removed. The camp is a pressure-cooker. Those who cannot endure its lack of privacy, its loneliness, social strain and physical discomforts fall by the wayside. The militant, by contrast, is daily fortified in the cause. He relishes the authority which he and his comrades have constructed, and physical fitness, military instruction, and cultural and ideological indoctrination pass the time and justify and console him in his captivity. All the time the forces of law and established authority keep their distance, coming behind the wire mainly to inspect the men gathered in military formation, constantly confirming the authority of the insurgent organisation by communicating through its chain of command. Whereas for the captured soldiers of a regular military power, prison camp is a period of enforced waiting, inactivity, homesickness and frustration, for captive irregulars – pine though they may for freedom – it is an indoctrination and training camp. Some, perhaps even a majority, might drop out of the ranks on release: for these, captivity has been a shock and deterrent. This weeding out of the weak and uncommitted, however, strengthens rather than weakens the revolutionary organisation, since it completes with certainty a process of selection which in freedom might take years and consume much energy. And for those who remain active, the prison camp's experience is a second nativity and enduring badge of honour.

Faced with the influx of some 2500 internees, neither the Home Office nor the War Office had time to ponder too closely the sociology of prisoner-of-war camps; nor, had they done so, scope to propose an alternative course of action. The dispersal around eight prisons had merely been a stopgap. The average

177 *All the Workes of John Taylor The Water-Poet*, London, James Boler, 1630, p. 128 (facsimile: Menston, Yorkshire, The Scolar Press, 1973).

daily population of the fifty-six local prisons in England and Wales in 1913 to 1914 had been 14,352.[178] The war had had a significant impact on these numbers by absorbing much of the stage army of petty criminality and pugnacious masculinity, either by enlistment or by absorption into labour-hungry civil employment. At the same time, restrictions on alcohol consumption reduced offences of drunkenness and related criminal outbursts.[179] In addition, many warders had left the prison service to enlist.[180] Although the prison population in England and Wales had been dropping steadily since the turn of the century, there was a particularly sharp reduction once the war started.[181] This meant the closure of many prisons, the underpopulation of others and a considerable reduction in staff. Only by adding a military guard to the several civil prisons had it been possible to cope with the Irish rebels. By 1916 the army had become desperately short of men, and could provide prison guards only on a temporary basis: its own prison policy was to return men to the ranks as soon as possible. Quite apart from the diseconomies of dispersing the internees over several sites, there were considerable difficulties in running an internment regime in a prison designed for the separate confinement of criminals. By concentrating the internees in one place, and allowing them to run their own affairs within a secure perimeter, great savings could be made in army manpower and costs: with the ultimate threat of deadly force, the ratio of guards to inmates could be safely reduced to a level not possible in civil prisons. This, however, was to be a case of payment deferred. Michael Collins vaulted to leadership while in Frongoch. In an early letter from the camp he wrote: 'prating about home, friends and so on doesn't alter the fact that this is Frongoch, an internment camp. There is only one thing to do while the situation is as it is ... make what I can of it.'[182] Such an innocent undertaking – praiseworthy, even – easily passed the censor. Nationalist MPs, who condemned Frongoch as a revolutionary forcing ground, were entirely correct, even if they did not know the full extent of the training and regrouping that was going on.

The greatest challenge to the camp leadership was apathy. The British had no ideology capable of that assault on prisoners' minds which various forms of totalitarianism would bring to a high state of development later in the century. But there would very likely have been a decline into demoralisation and political detachment had the easy conditions of the first few months persisted. At that time, one of the internees recalled, 'we were as happy as prisoners could possibly

178 RCP, PP, 1914 [Cd. 7601], XLV, 361, 5.
179 Ibid., PP, 1916 [Cd. 8342], XX, 75, 5–6. Licensing restrictions were brought in under DORA regulations in order to control the excesses of civilian workers flush on war overtime earnings, and soldiers on leave.
180 Ibid., 20–1.
181 RCP, PP, 1917–18 [Cd. 8764], 109, 5. The prison population dropped by 68 per cent between 1913 and 1916.
182 Coogan, 1991, p. 50.

be'. Even complaints about food were to some extent diminished by the flow of parcels, while relations with the camp authorities were 'on the whole very good'. The prisoners' days 'passed in a round of concerts and games, tournaments and sports'.[183]

A number of conflicts promoted inmate solidarity and militancy. There was an attempt to renegotiate rates of pay for a voluntary work party which was completing essential construction work on the North Camp. The men had agreed to undertake heavy labour for the minuscule (even then) net hourly rate of $1\frac{1}{2}$d. The labour leader William O'Brien[184] persuaded them to strike and to renegotiate their pay. The prisoners' representative, M. W. O'Reilly, was asked to make the men's case to the camp administration. When he attempted to do so, the entire work party was placed under close confinement and given various punishments. Although O'Reilly was officially recognised as the prisoners' representative, with the title 'Principal Hut Leader', the commandant, acting on the military injunction against joint representations, found him guilty of insubordination and mutiny, and sentenced him to four days' bread and water and the confiscation of his Citizen Army uniform. When O'Reilly stated that the men had the right to renegotiate a contract into which they had freely entered, the camp commandant rather foolishly insisted that the prisoners had no rights, and had O'Reilly and O'Brien removed to Reading Prison.[185] This comment and the punishments did much to unite the men.

The internees removed ashes and refuse each day as part of their accepted housekeeping duties, but they did no work for the guard. Lambert now ordered them to remove ashes from the guards' huts, and the men refused. As punishment, sixteen were sentenced to isolation in the North Camp for seven days – no letters, parcels, visitors, books, tobacco or canteen purchases.[186] Their private property was removed (even devotional books) and until the intervention of the Roman Catholic priest they were forbidden to attend Mass. They were further punished by being locked up from 9 a.m. to 12 noon and 2 p.m. to 4 p.m. each day, and during this period were deprived of all furniture and domestic utensils and so had to sit on the floor. All recreation was prohibited. Since they showed

---

183 See Brennan-Whitmore, *op. cit.*, p. 51.

184 (1881–1968). Trade unionist and socialist. Founder member of the Irish Transport and General Workers' Union. Associate of Connolly and active anti-conscriptionist. Took no part in the rising but was interned because of his connections and militant reputation. Continued as a prominent trade unionist in Ireland until 1946.

185 NLI: William O'Brien Papers: Ms. 13, 973; O'Mahony, *op. cit.*, pp. 117–18; Brennan-Whitmore, *op. cit.*, pp. 65–7. O'Mahony states that O'Reilly received four days' bread and water; Brennan-Whitmore gives O'Reilly's punishment as seven days' bread and water. See also Béaslaí, 1926, Vol. 1, p. 113.

186 Food, tobacco and messages were sent to the men under punishment by a 'volunteer' work party organised by Michael Collins and others.

no signs of compliance, their punishment was extended to fourteen days and they were told it could become indefinite and be accompanied by a bread-and-water diet. Lambert also threatened a court-martial, penal servitude and return of the whole camp to Knutsford, Wandsworth and the other prisons, where they would be treated as criminals. As work party succeeded work party in refusal, the point was soon reached where over a hundred men were under punishment, and it was apparent that none would do the work and in consequence all would eventually be punished. Such an outcome would be politically unacceptable and so the Home Office withdrew support from the commandant.[187] By 4 October no men were under punishment.[188]

But the most bitter struggle concerned conscription, which was anathema to nationalists of all shades. Conscription did not extend to Ireland, but a number of the internees had become liable to military service because of prior residence in England.[189] It seems bizarre to think of men going from Frongoch to the British Army, but someone nevertheless decided forcibly to conscript the approximately sixty internees who through residence had become liable to service. There was a major obstacle to overcome, since, as has been noted, although staff knew the total number of internees they were holding and their names, they could not match names to faces.

Throughout the autumn of 1916 Lambert attempted to identify those to be conscripted, at one point penalising the entire camp because one man did not answer to his name at roll-call, and the others refused to identify him.[190] Various subterfuges were attempted, such as inviting certain men to draw clothing from the stores, or posting notices for supposedly unclaimed mail, parcels or messages from relatives.[191] The introduction of undercover agents was contemplated but

---

187 There was a feeble attempt at saving the commandant's face. In the letter announcing the decision not to persist with attempts to get the internees to remove the ashes, Maurice Waller, Secretary of the Prison Commission, concluded 'In announcing the decision to the prisoners the Secretary of State desires that you should make it clear that in his opinion you were right in requiring them to perform this duty and right in punishing those who refused, but the matter, being a trivial one, he does not desire to carry the punishment further' (PRO HO 144/ 1456/313106).

188 NLI: Irish National Aid Association Papers: Ms. 24, 324 (i). Camp Committee to Timothy Healy, 4 October 1916, f. 4.

189 Michael Collins and others had evaded liability by returning to Ireland shortly before the Act came into force. Irishmen remaining in Great Britain ('ordinarily resident') on 15 August 1915, aged between 18 and 41 and unmarried, became fully liable under s.1 (1) of the Military Service Act, 1916 (5 & 6 Geo.V, c.104). The Act, however, did not receive the Royal Assent until 27 January 1916.

190 O'Mahony, op. cit., p. 122. See the Manchester Guardian (27 November 1916, 4g) for an account of the court martial of fifteen internees for refusing to answer a roll-call. The fifteen had been chosen for trial because they were hut leaders and thus were deemed to be specially responsible in the matter (see also the Irish Independent, 28 November 1916, 4h and the Manchester Guardian, 1 December 1916, 4f–g).

191 Béaslaí, 1926, Vol. 1, pp. 115–16.

not pursued.[192] Despite the difficulties, however, the identification campaign was reasonably successful, and about fifty of the sixty-odd wanted men were brought before courts-martial and sentenced to various terms of imprisonment for refusing conscription.[193] There were several hunger-strikes, sometimes over individual and at other times general grievances. At one point some 200 men refused food for three days, ending their protest only when the authorities agreed not to press further a identification action they had initiated.[194] Individual prisoners went on hunger-strike over correspondence privileges, and usually seem to have been successful.[195] The authorities, with good political reason, feared hunger-strikes.

The two months before general release (November and December 1916) were, recalled Béaslaí, 'dreary and depressing'. The location of the camp, the severe winter, the punishments and loss of privileges all contributed to the hardship. When release came it was largely unexpected by the men.[196] Yet to some extent Frongoch was a successful venture for both sides. It worked as a place of detention, quickly and cheaply brought into action. And while it was a major source of grievances and endless parliamentary protests, there were no major disturbances, injuries or loss of life and – importantly for the battle of propaganda and morale – no prisoner successfully escaped.[197] The rebels could be equally satisfied with the experience. By living together under camp conditions strong bonds had been forged, much political and military knowledge acquired and reinforced, and men had been tested in struggles with the camp authorities. This last was important, and, given the past susceptibility of Irish conspiracies to spies and informers, honourable service as an internee at Frongoch was a touchstone of character. The daily ventilation of the specific and general grievances of the internees had done much to revive and spread the cause of republicanism, and to change the political atmosphere in Ireland. Once again, suffering – apparent or real – had transformed reputation and politics. On balance, the rebels had won the advantage.

192　As late as 16 December 1916 (and Frongoch was closed just over a week later) Lambert wrote to Maurice Waller urging the use of a detective planted in the camp to identify the agitators: 'If you could send me an intelligent Irish detective, who could be instructed to refuse to answer his name and number on the day after arrival, I could send him down on that plea to the South Camp, and the moment he had obtained the information required, all he would have to do would be to report to one of my staff (as others have done) that he was now willing to give his name and number, and he would be brought up before me. . . . Then . . . he could be released and return to you to report' (Lambert to Waller, 16 December 1916; PRO HO 144/1456/313106/571). This was an absurd proposal, since the antecedents of any man arriving at such a late date would have been questioned closely by the prisoners. Given the small size of the active Volunteer movement any imposter would have been quickly discovered and expelled or attacked. A much more practical ploy was to 'turn' one of the internees but there is no evidence that this was done.

193　O'Mahony, op. cit., pp. 122–5, passim; Béaslaí, 1926, Vol. 1, p. 115.

194　Brennan-Whitmore, op. cit., pp. 132–3.

195　O'Mahony, op. cit., p. 127.

196　Béaslaí, 1926, Vol. 1, p. 119.

197　One prisoner (apparently mentally ill) did escape and was at large for four days, but was recaptured a few miles away (O'Mahony, op. cit., p. 71).

The female internees

Of the 2500 or so internees, only five were women. This is hardly surprising, since with the conspicuous and remarkable exception of Countess Markievicz women had been assigned support roles in both the Irish Volunteers and Connolly's Citizen Army. Once the rising was under way, Pearse had made an appeal for support; men were wanted for fighting and women in support.[198] To this exclusion from the rebels' fighting ranks there was added the reluctance of the British authorities, striving to cope with large numbers of male suspects, to take into custody women who, on their own, were hardly seen as a danger.

Of the five women internees, the most remarkable was Winifred Carney,[199] who had been Connolly's confidential secretary, and who had set up her desk in the General Post Office alongside Connolly. She had been active as a female suffragist and was for some years an active and public figure in militant nationalism. Taken in the general surrender, she was regarded by Dublin Castle as 'one of J. Connolly's most devoted and trusted agents'. Despite her seniority, no charges were brought against her, and after she had been interned for six months it was proposed to release her on condition that she gave an undertaking and found two sureties of £25 each. Carney refused these conditions and was not freed until the general release of internees on Christmas Eve 1916.[200]

The other women internees were Helena Moloney, Maire Perolz, Brigid Foley and Ellen Ryan. All had taken support roles in the rising. Helena Moloney[201] had

---

198 Women of the Cumann na mBan acted as messengers during the rising, and smuggled arms from outlying dumps. Pearse (unlike Connolly) was firmly of the view that their role was support, not fighting. In a proclamation on the second day of the rising he stated, 'There is work for everyone; for the men in the fighting line, and for the women in the provision of food and first aid' (Macardle, *op. cit.*, p. 171). Despite Pearse's wishes, however, some thirty-four women and girls of the Cumann na mBan found their way into the General Post Office. They left the day before the general surrender, and most avoided arrest (Desmond Rynn, *The Rising*, Dublin, Standard House, 1949, p. 150).

199 (1887–1943). For four years before the rising Winnie Carney had been in charge of the women's section of the Irish Textile Workers' Union, an affiliate of the Irish Transport Workers' Union. It is almost certain that she was privy to the plans of the leaders. She admitted having acted as Connolly's 'typewriter' in the occupation of the General Post Office during the rising. This was disingenuously described by Lawrence Ginnell as 'precisely a continuation of the civil and legitimate work in which she had been previously engaged, and that under contract and trade union rules she had no option but to continue it' (5 *Hansard*, LXXXVI, col. 1554; 31 October 1916). In fact, while in the Dublin GPO with Connolly and the other leaders she held the rank of adjutant. Her seniority and active involvement was confirmed when she alone of the women was permitted to remain until the final evacuation of the building. In later life she remained strongly committed to radical social change and took the republican side in the Civil War (for which she spent several spells in custody). For further information on Carney see Helga Wogan's excellent note 'Silent Radical: Winnie Carney 1887–1943' (*Irish Labour History News*, 1 (summer 1986), pp. 3–4).

200 PRO HO 144/1457/314179/5.

201 (1883–1967). Had been an actress in the Abbey Theatre. During the 1913 lockout she was Countess Markievicz's assistant in running the Irish Transport and General Workers' Union

---

been with the Irish Citizen Army party which had assaulted Dublin Castle, and was arrested in the general surrender of rebel forces the following Saturday. Maire Perolz was a close associate of Constance Markievicz, whom she had assisted in Fianna activities. Foley and Ryan had also become involved in the rising through their trade union activities, and support for Connolly; Ryan was the sister-in-law of Seán T. O. Kelly, one of the leaders interned at Reading.[202]

Just over a month after the suppression of the rising the Home Secretary took the decision to continue the internment of the five women.[203] The Irish military authorities thought that they should be sent to Aylesbury, where Constance Markievicz had been consigned (though in the very different status of convicted felon), and where some twenty-four female non-Irish internees were held. This plan was not acceptable to the Home Office, Sir Edward Troup writing that 'it would be very undesirable to send the ladies . . . to Aylesbury and make them consort with German brothel keepers from Antwerp, but I have seen Sir Evelyn Ruggles-Brise and he promises to provide for them in a separate wing in one of his prisons, from which he will turn out the female prisoners'.[204] The mixing of Irish political prisoners with criminal prisoners – particularly those guilty of offences of moral depravity – provided a constant theme in nationalist protests.[205] The Home Office took no chances that the brothel-keepers of Antwerp would provoke further outbursts of sympathy. And all the senior officials were Victorians for whom the respectability of respectable women – rebels or not – was a matter of very great import.[206]

It took a fortnight or so to complete the arrangements to bring the women to England. Lewes Prison was chosen for their reception. (This was the then

soup-kitchens. Released in the general amnesty, Moloney immediately returned to organisation and agitation. She hoisted a banner on the roof of the ruined Library Hall, to signify the resumption of activities. Became a member of the executive committee of the reformed Sinn Féin, and took part in the formation of the Irish Women Workers' Union. On the republican side in the Civil War, she was imprisoned by the Free State government (for obituaries see *Irish Times*, 30 January 1967, 9c; *Irish Independent*, 30 January 1967, 2g–h).

202 On her release from internment in October 1916, she applied to visit O'Kelly at Reading before returning to Ireland. Since she had signed an undertaking to give no further trouble (which is why she was released), the Home Office issued a special permit for the visit (PRO HO 144/11458/8).

203 Brigadier-General J. A. Byrne (Deputy Adjutant General in Ireland) to Sir Edward Troup (Permanent-Under-Secretary, Home Office), 4 June 1916; PRO HO 144/1455/313106/6.

204 PRO HO 144/1455/31306/6. Troup, in 1880 the first clerk to enter the Home Office through the open examination, had occupied various posts before becoming Permanent-Under-Secretary in 1895. Evelyn Ruggles-Brise (1857–1935) joined the Home Office in 1881, and served as Private Secretary to five successive Home Secretaries, before being appointed by Asquith in 1895 to head the Prison Commission and Directorate of Convict Prisons.

205 See above, Chapters 2, 4 and 8.

206 This concern included the details of the female internees' transport to England. Their escort was to consist of wardresses and *plain clothes* policemen (PRO HO 144/1455/313106/6; letter of 4 June 1916).

mothballed county prison, not the military prison to which fifty-nine of the male internees had been consigned on 20 May.) The women arrived there on 21 June. Miss G. Allen, a veteran gaolbird in the cause of female suffrage, was in Lewes at the time and she promised Hanna Sheehy Skeffington to do what she could for them. The county prison, she wrote, 'is structurally far better than the Detention Barracks – but not as far as I know as good as 'D' Block Holloway'. She also had expert comment on the staff. If the prison had the same matron and head warder as previously, 'then the Irish prisoners will have two really good people to deal with. The doctor that used to attend Mrs Saunders when she was hunger-striking (she greatly liked him) is now alas at the Front & I am not sure who is doing the work.'[207]

Familiar with the needs of prisoners and the ways of prisons, Miss Allen offered to assist any of the prisoners' friends in Ireland who wished to send food by making arrangements with local tradesmen ('Most of them know me and are very obliging'). She gave a list of local prices for fruit, meat and butter; she also offered to book rooms. If the Irish internees were to stay at Lewes she recommended that some local arrangement should be made for a person to help them – 'as with the German prisoners'. She supposed that the women's MPs would ensure that they received as good treatment as the Germans.[208]

The women did not stay in Lewes, however, and in just over a week their number had fallen from five to three, since Brigid Foley and Maire Perolz were released by the Sankey Committee.[209] The remaining trio were then transferred to Aylesbury Prison, the hazards of Antwerp yielding to the realities of prison management.[210] By December only two female internees remained – Winifred Carney and Helena Moloney. Refusing to give the necessary undertaking to refrain from seditious activities and to provide sureties, these two remained in custody until the Christmas general release.

The Aylesbury prisoners fell into two groups: criminals and internees; some, however, were criminals who had been interned rather than convicted. Among these was an English prostitute whom the Irish women insisted had been interned because she numbered military men among her clients. The authorities' fear was

207 Miss G. Allen to Hanna Sheehy Skeffington, 23 June 1916: NLI: Sheehy Skeffington Papers: Ms. 22, 279 (ii).

208 Ibid.

209 J. H. MacDonnell, the republicans' preferred solicitor in England, represented the five women at the Sankey hearing. Reporting on 30 June 1916 to his Dublin counterparts, Corrigan and Corrigan, he observed 'I am rather surprised at the results of the ladies they only having let out 2 of the 5, in my opinion at least one of them was more dangerous than the three they kept in.' Understandably, but frustratingly, he did not indicate which of the two women was the dangerous one (NLI: Irish National Aid Association Papers: Ms. 24, 357 (1) (unfoliated)).

210 PRO HO 144/1455/313106/10. The cost of keeping the three at Lewes was prohibitive, since they had to be guarded on a twenty-four-hour cycle by a complement of female staff four or five strong. Aylesbury was a female prison where the marginal cost of another three prisoners – even if kept separate from the general population – was insignificant.

that she would pass on pillow-talk to her German husband, who was a waiter. The Irish internees were outraged that although she had come to Aylesbury suffering from venereal disease, she had not been segregated, and thus used the same sanitary facilities.[211]

Unlike Frongoch, it was possible at Aylesbury closely to supervise the internees – 'absolutely Russian', the women complained. No one apart from the Irish was allowed legal advice on her predicament, although solicitors could assist with private matters. Even then a wardress was always present 'so that the most delicate and private matters have to be discussed in the presence of a third party'.[212] Other communications with the outside were not easy. Visitors had to be approved and this was withheld or delayed when the applicants were sympathetic to the internees' cause.[213] In correspondence or visits no mention was allowed of prison conditions, other prisoners or the state of one's health. The internees sought to evade these restrictions by passing out uncensored letters. Detection could mean the loss of visits and correspondence for three months or more.[214]

The main complaint was the brawling that went on between prisoners in which 'the most filthy language [was] used'. Following one fight in which tongues and fists were used freely one of the combatants attempted suicide. Understandably, this atmosphere affected the other women on the internment wing. This can hardly have been helped by the cramped conditions. The cells were small, equipped only with a bed and table and the usual high prison window; lavatories were inadequate. Less substantially, the women complained that everyone had to do her own work, including cooking and washing up: it is hard to imagine how a residential institution of this kind could have been run otherwise. The food was good (though they implied this had not always been so) but the organisation of their wing was very bad, 'resulting in great dirt and discomfort'.[215]

The women were keenly aware of their own public relations potential – and in this they saw themselves as part of a larger group at Aylesbury, whose cases they believed the government was 'desperately anxious' to keep secret, since it could not grant releases without causing a scandal. They particularly mentioned two Belgian women – one whose husband was on active service, the other with

---

211 NLI: Sean O'Mahony Papers: Ms. 24, 450 (unfoliated). There were, the internees wrote, 'Hardly any true Germans' at Aylesbury. Two had been taken from neutral ships on their way to the United States of America. Nearly all were naturalised British subjects. Two Englishwomen had been interned because of their involvement in the Indian independence movement. A Swiss woman was also held under 14b because of alleged German sympathies. ('Absolutely false. . . . No German sympathies whatsoever.')

212 Ibid. It is noticeable that Carney, Moloney and the few other Irish female prisoners were, over the years, much more sympathetic to their criminal fellow prisoners than were their male comrades.

213 Mrs Darrell Figgis, Holford Knight (of the *Nation*), Art O'Brien and certain Irish priests fell into this category.

214 NLI: Sean O'Mahony Papers: Ms. 24, 450 (unfoliated).

215 Ibid.

a son in the Belgian Army. These women, it was claimed, were not allowed to send letters. The Irish prisoners suggested a number of English MPs and others who might be interested in Aylesbury, as well as the Irish Members, whom they hoped were about to go into opposition.[216]

Releases and amnesty

The Sankey Committee met in London and men were brought down from Frongoch in batches of between fifty and a hundred to appear before it. Each expedition took about three days: one day by train to and across London to be lodged either in Wandsworth prison or Wormwood Scrubs prison; the following day before the committee in what, perforce, were cursory hearings: five minutes seems to have been the average duration.[217] It is likely that the committee was guided by police and intelligence reports, but since the papers have apparently not survived it is impossible to know how extensive the briefings were.[218] After another night in their London prison the men re-entrained for Frongoch the following day.[219] The London prisons simply provided two nights' rather spartan accommodation, and few prisoners commented on them, though they had no great opinion of the Sankey Committee.[220]

The Irish National Aid Association provided basic legal assistance for the men appearing before the Committee in the form of a solicitor (J. H. MacDonnell) being on hand on the day. Having been refused release on 12 August, Seán T. O'Kelly asked to see a solicitor at Reading. A few weeks later Gavan Duffy asked for permission to visit his client under the conditions usually accorded to lawyers – the interview to be in the sight but not in the hearing of a prison officer. There was a division of opinion at the Home Office. Troup took the view that under

216 They named Charles Trevelyan (Liberal, Yorkshire Elland), Robert Outhwaite (Independent Liberal), Frederick Jowett (Labour, West Bradford), Sir William Byles (a radical Liberal, MP for North Salford: 'interested and keen on the Habeas Corpus aspect of it') as well as H. M. Hyndman (founder of the Social Democratic Federation) and Holford Knight of the *Nation*.

217 Byrne, *op. cit.*, p. 50.

218 The case of Ernest Blythe is indicative of prior intelligence briefings. He applied to the Sankey Committee shortly after internment, falsely denying he had any influence in the Volunteers. Were he released he promised not to take part 'in any political action whatever, either personally or by writing, until the end of the war'. Informed by MI5 that they considered Blythe a leader, the Committee turned him down (PRO HO 144/1454/6).

219 Although the Sankey Committee was also hearing conscription cases, it is hard to understand why they could not go to Frongoch, rather than bring some 1500 men to London in the midst of a war.

220 There was one telling encounter. At Wormwood Scrubs Eamon Martin fell into conversation with one of about eight conscientious objectors serving sentences of hard labour. He recalled: 'He was in prison for not fighting for his country while I was there for just the opposite reason. The majority of these fellows are frauds, but a few of them are genuine' (Martin, *op. cit.*, f. 52). Martin succeeded in convincing the Committee that he could be released, and was one of a party of about sixty freed on their return to camp.

present conditions the rule should be varied since 'we are dealing with persons concerned in a great conspiracy with the enemies of the country'. The Home Secretary, Herbert Samuel, overruled him and allowed Duffy's visit as a special concession, each subsequent application to be judged on its merits. He pointed out the incongruity of solicitors being able by right and with the usual confidentiality arrangements to visit convicted prisoners, while internees were denied these facilities.[221] This was an important decision, giving secure and private legal visits.

As Dillon had been promised, there was a particularly large release in July. On 12 July Troup wrote to Dublin Castle and to Lambert at Frongoch. He listed 460 internees whose release had been recommended by the Sankey committee. There was an evident determination to get the men back to Ireland as quickly as possible now that the decision had been taken. For this reason, individual notices of release would not be served, and Troup's list was Lambert's authority; it was passed to the Irish police so that the men would not be re-arrested.[222]

The military authorities in Ireland wished to avoid any demonstrations, so releases were staggered and the men sent by three different sea routes (Greenore, Rosslare and Kingstown); the Dublin North Wall route (which would bring them to the heart of the city) was not used. As an additional precaution against demonstrations, prisoners were not told of their impending release until the last moment. Each was informed that the Home Secretary had revoked internment under 14b and was given a railway warrant home and a day's rations or money in lieu. Lambert was directed that no man should be released in Sinn Féin uniform or wearing badges: if a man had no clothing other than the uniform, civilian clothes were to be supplied by the camp, and should this not be possible the Home Office was to be informed immediately by telegram.[223] These arrangements worked well, and this group of internees returned home without any notable demonstrations.[224]

Releases continued, but at a much slower pace. By August identification of the obviously innocent or wholly rank-and-file prisoners had been completed, and only a trickle now passed out of Frongoch. The camp population was whittled down to some 600; at its greatest number it had been 1775.[225] Dublin Castle now took a hand, requesting in September that the names of candidates for release should be referred to the Irish Police.[226] It says much of the poor organisation of intelligence that such a request should come after the bulk of the releases had been completed. There was some Home Office grumbling at this cumbersome

221 PRO HO 144/1458/5: minutes and correspondence 8, 13 and 26 September 1916.
222 Troup to Dublin Castle, 12 July 1916: NLI: Joseph Brennan Papers: Ms. 26, 196 (unfoliated).
223 Ibid.
224 For lists of the released internees and their routes home see NLI: Art O'Brien Papers: Ms. 8, 442 (unfoliated). This unorganised box also contains a number of letters smuggled from various prisons.
225 PRO HO 144/1455/313106/274; Lambert to Waller, 8 August 1916.
226 Either the Inspector General of the Royal Irish Constabulary or (where Dublin men were concerned) the Chief Commissioner of the Dublin Metropolitan Police (minute of 21 September 1916; PRO HO 144/1456/313106/370).

procedure, but in the end it was decided to comply with the wishes of the Irish administration.[227] A greater difficulty was to induce the internees to apply for release, and to formulate an undertaking which would not offend their reasonable scruples, but which would, at the same time, provide some security as to their behaviour. Having served several months in detention, hard-core Frongoch and Reading internees were likely to exert strong pressure on any waverers not to sign themselves out.[228] To pledge oneself out in this way, Herbert Samuel pointed out to Henry Duke, the new Irish Chief Secretary, would very likely be regarded as 'treason to the Sinn Fein cause'. Rather that post notices inviting men to apply for release, and thus invite rejection, he suggested, it might be better to work through the MPs and other persons of influence who had applied for the release of specific prisoners.[229]

The proposed wording of the undertaking, which was discussed by the Irish and Home Offices, also showed some difference in approach. The former wanted a relatively strong form of words committing the signer to abstain from any illegal act 'hereafter'. Home Secretary Herbert Samuel doubted whether 'many or indeed any' of the men could sign such a comprehensive undertaking. 'They might' he pointed out, 'ask whether such an undertaking would be given by an Ulster Unionist!' In place of the Irish Office proposal, therefore, Samuel suggested a pledge to abstain from sedition and any act likely to hinder the war effort for the duration of the war.[230]

The advantages of such releases were obvious. A man freed on an undertaking, should he honour it, was neutralised for the duration of the war; but should he break it he was morally discredited. And as men applied and were released, the residue could be portrayed as diehards, and a stronger case could be made for their continued detention: they were, in a sense, condemning themselves. Militants among the internees reasoned exactly to the contrary. A whittling away of the body of prisoners was demoralising for the residue, diminished the cause, broke faith with the dead, and damaged IRB hopes of resuming the struggle. A sizeable nucleus of resolute prisoners, on the other hand, provided a focus for an amnesty campaign and support organisation. Reasoning thus, the Frongoch Camp committee appointed William O'Brien and Michael Collins to go around the huts at night and instruct the men that any release application had to go for approval to the inmates' representatives before being passed to the authorities.[231]

---

227 PRO HO 144/1456/313106/381.

228 In the early stages the pressure seems to have arisen more from a sense of solidarity and *esprit de corps* than any threats (see Béaslaí, 1926, Vol. 1, pp. 111–12).

229 PRO HO 144/1456/313106/381: letter of 28 September 1916.

230 Ibid.

231 Edward MacLysaght (ed.), *Forth the Banners Go: Reminiscences of William O'Brien*, Dublin, At the Sign of the Three Candles, 1969, pp. 132–3. By 18 October 1916, nevertheless, the Irish Chief Secretary Henry Duke was able to tell the Commons that while in the past few applications for release had been made, they had become more frequent, and 'a considerable number' of releases had been agreed (5 *Hansard*, LXXXVI, col. 603).

The complaints of nationalist and avowedly republican Members of Parliament continued, concentrating on conditions and alleged injustices done to the internees. There were repeated demands that the remaining detainees – Helena Moloney and Winifred Carney at Aylesbury, and the several hundred men at Frongoch and Reading – should be released without signing an undertaking.[232] In a Commons debate on 18 October John Dillon insisted that among those remaining in custody, 'many are far more innocent than those who have been released' and that detention 'kept up a perpetual boiling of irritation in Ireland'. There would not be even 'the beginning of improvement' while men remained in prison.[233] Despite such powerful appeals from a party which long had close associations with his own, Asquith refused to countenance either a general release of prisoners or the suspension of martial law in Ireland.[234] When a substantial easing of discipline for the rising convicts was announced on 14 November 1916, there were renewed calls for the release of all prisoners, convicted and interned alike. The Home Secretary once more refused the request.[235]

Away from these scenes in the House, and the baiting of the more extreme Irish members, Redmond made a private appeal to Asquith. The prompt release of the internees, he wrote, was essential for the maintenance of the improved situation in Ireland, which was in the general interests of the Empire and the successful conduct of the war. There was a 'confident expectation' in Ireland that government would pursue a policy of conciliation involving the end of martial law, the release of the remaining internees and 'some mitigation in the treatment of the convicted prisoners'. Should these expectations not be met, particularly in relation to the internees, there would be 'a fresh outbreak of bitterness and exasperation' which might undo the good effected in recent months.[236]

Redmond's case was a powerful one, and carried the weight of the best friend the British government had in nationalist Ireland. The issue, however, was one which had to go to the Cabinet, and this would take some weeks. The Irish Members remained active, pressing details of camp and prison discipline and returning to the issue of amnesty.[237] In a supply debate on 19 December Redmond called for a general amnesty. Their release would be 'A Christmas gift to the Irish people'. Lloyd George procrastinated: he had been Prime Minister for a

---

232 Especially on 18 October, when there was a major debate on the government's Irish policy. See 5 *Hansard*, LXXXVI, cols 558–692 *passim*. By this date it was reported that there were 574 men and two women in internment (ibid., col. 561).
233 5 *Hansard*, LXXXVI, col. 679; 18 October 1916.
234 Ibid., cols 632–5.
235 Ibid., LXXXVII, cols 562–3 and 621, 14 November 1916. See also cols 953–6; 16 November 1916.
236 Redmond to Asquith, 30 November 1916: House of Lords Record Office, Lloyd George Papers: E/3/2/4.
237 See, for example, 5 *Hansard*, LXXXVIII, cols 832–3, 880–1; 14 December 1916; cols 1056–7; 15 December 1916; col. 1138; 18 December 1916; cols 1275–8; 19 December 1916.

few days only, and during that time he had been ill, and unable to consult with the Chief Secretary on the matter. He needed a few more days.[238]

Redmond's call was generally supported by George Wardle on behalf of the Labour Party, as well as various Irish members. The atmosphere was one of conciliation, but with some currents of bitterness.[239] The following day the usual tempo resumed, with Larry Ginnell launching a barrage, disclosing to the Speaker at one point that he had asked the same question thirteen times.[240] Referring to Ireland's contribution to the war effort, John Dillon urged conciliatory action.[241] On 7 December there had been a change of government. Lloyd George, the minister to whom six months before Asquith had given special responsibility for an Irish settlement, became Prime Minister, heading an all-party coalition. The leaders of the Irish Party felt his sympathy for them, and hopes rose that he would make a gesture via the internees and prisoners. After further enquiries and exchanges, Bonor Law, Chancellor of the Exchequer, on 21 December promised a statement before the House adjourned for the Christmas recess.[242]

The Irish Chief Secretary, Henry Duke, was not in his place to give this promise because he was attending a meeting of the War Cabinet. He wanted the internees released. Rebellion was now 'practically impossible'; there was more danger in keeping the internees than freeing them, since Irish sentiment sprang more from pity than agreement with the prisoners' views; and finally, release would assist rather than hinder the application of conscription to Ireland.[243] In a supporting memorandum, Duke analysed the character of the internees, now numbering about 530. Half were not seriously dangerous, 'though no doubt they will be troublesome'. Of the remainder perhaps one fifth were 'active people of ability' who would cause trouble 'by seditious conspiracy, by communication with the enemy, or, if they see any opening, by armed action'. Conscription would give this last group their opportunity. Despite police opposition, Duke thought the balance of advantage was for a general release of the internees. Any subsequent misbehaviour could be dealt with by DORA.[244]

Accepting Duke's proposal, the Cabinet made a number of broader points. Members were 'more especially influenced' by reliable information that continued

---

238 Ibid., cols 1371–3; 19 December 1916.

239 Timothy Healy castigated the previous Home Secretary, Herbert Samuel: 'I am delighted to think that he is out of office, and I hope he will never return to it, at any rate as far as anything connected with Ireland goes, because a more cruel and heartless administrator of the Acts he had to deal with never stood at that box.' Healy also attacked John Mooney, the nationalist member of the Sankey Committee (ibid., col. 1378). Herbert Samuel later intervened to describe Healy as someone who 'never, or rarely, strays from the realm of fancy into the realm of fact' (ibid., col. 1385).

240 Ibid., cols 1435–9; 20 December 1916.

241 Ibid., cols 1575–6; 20 December 1916.

242 Ibid., col. 1607; 21 December 1916.

243 Minutes of the Cabinet meeting, 21 December 1916: PRO CAB 37/162/4.

244 Ibid., Appendix: 'Untried Irish Prisoners: Frongoch and Reading'.

detention of the internees had contributed to the defeat of Australian conscription proposals. American opinion also had to be considered, and it was desirable to foster the view that the new coalition government was approaching Ireland 'in a generous but not timorous spirit'. Finally an impression had been allowed to grow in Parliament that there would be a favourable decision. Duke was authorised to announce the release with certain safeguards and to emphasise that it was 'an act of grace and conciliation'. Later that evening Duke rose to make the announcement for which Irish members had been waiting.[245] The statement was widely welcomed, with several expressions of hope of better feelings in Ireland. That there was unfinished business, however, was signalled by Ginnell the next day. Had the orders been sent to release the men from Frongoch, and the two ladies from Aylesbury? What of the convicts? And did the Under-Secretary for War have anything to say about the alleged illegality of the courts-martial which had followed the Dublin rising?[246]

The Home Office was determined to maximise the political benefits of the releases, and to get all internees back to Ireland for Christmas. It was decided to delay the release of the Reading men until after those at Frongoch had gone – the reasoning being that there would be less opportunity for the leaders to make a political splash if they reached Ireland after the mass of the rank and file.[247] A few anomalous cases were speedily cleared up or put to one side, showing how quickly officialdom could function when the fire of political advantage was lit under it.[248] At Frongoch the announcement was initially received by the internees with great reserve. Given Lambert's earlier manoeuvres it was taken as yet another trick to put names to faces. Eventually it was agreed that the hut leaders would compile the lists of names and addresses necessary for the release orders, and hand them to the camp adjutant.[249] A telegram from Holyhead on the morning of Christmas Eve announced that all the Frongoch men had embarked, and authority was then given to release the Reading prisoners, all of whom caught the last pre-Christmas transport home.[250]

On all sides Christmas cheer was evident. The Reading men thanked the governor warmly and, so the Home Office believed, 'appear to have parted from

245 5 *Hansard*, LXXXIII, cols 1763–4.

246 Ibid., cols 1813–14; 22 December 1916.

247 As late as 6.22 p.m. on 23 December Art O'Brien was reporting to the National Aid Committee in Dublin that the Reading governor had not received the expected Home Office instructions to release the Reading men. He added: 'Understand girls Aylesbury already left but have not seen them yet' (NLI: Irish National Aid Association Papers: Ms. 24, 378 (unfoliated)).

248 Some men had DORA exclusion orders against them; others were on parole. Three were in asylums and another three in civilian hospitals. All returned home when the hospital cases passed fit (PRO HO 144/1456/313106/613). Some, such as Ernest Blythe who had been under deportation orders in England prior to internment, were not allowed immediately to return to Ireland (PRO HO 144/1454/12).

249 Béaslaí, 1926, Vol. 1, pp. 119–20; Brennan-Whitmore, *op. cit.*, pp. 210–11.

250 PRO HO 144/1456/313106/613: 'Release of Irish Interned Prisoners', minutes.

him on the best of terms'. *The Times* reported that on arrival in Dublin some of the Frongoch men spoke of the kindness of the camp surgeon and of Adjutant Lieutenant Burns.[251] Maurice Waller recorded that the releases had been accompanied by 'no discordant note',[252] but the men reaching Dublin complained of conditions in the South Camp and of the tricks used to identify men liable for conscription. The kindness and support of the Irish community in England was extensively praised.[253]

Frongoch was to have its irritating afterlife for some three years. There was a correspondence about the books that the Reading men had left behind on their release. These had been purchased by the Irish National Aid Association, which demanded their return.[254] Then there was the winding up of the Frongoch canteen account. Because of their share in the profits on canteen sales and also the revenue arising from the sale of camp pigswill, the Irish internees were entitled to an official accounting and final settlement. (Significantly, the Home Office had no difficulty in accepting the Irish National Aid Association as the men's representative.) Art O'Brien was the tenacious instrument by which the amazingly voluminous correspondence was conducted between June 1917 and November 1919. At various times the Home Office, War Office, Irish National Relief Fund, Dublin and London solicitors, various MPs and assorted parliamentary questions were involved. Mere sanity requires that these files be skimmed rather than read in any detail. Behind them there are indications that the issue merely veiled a battle of attrition which had its well-understood part in the wider war. The final settlement confirmed this: £55 19s 8d. It is hard to know in what mood Michael Collins wrote to Art O'Brien 'We were under the impression that the amount should have been nearly double this, but no doubt War Office deductions account for the difference.'[255]

---

251 *The Times*, 26 December 1916, 3d.
252 PRO HO 144/1456/313106/613.
253 *Freeman's Journal*, 25 and 26 December 1916, 5f–g. The *Irish Times* carried a low-key account of the return, and paid it no editorial attention (26 December 1916, 6b).
254 NLI: Irish National Aid Association Papers: Ms. 24, 378 (unfoliated).
255 NLI: Art O'Brien Papers: Ms. 8, 442 (unfoliated). The War Office charged the fund for damage done to the camp by internees. For the Frongoch canteen account correspondence see Art O'Brien Papers: Ms. 8444 (iii).

11

IMPRISONMENT

War by other means

Under sentence

The courts martial which followed the rising sentenced ninety of the ringleaders and their associates to death. Of these only fifteen sentences were executed; the remainder had their sentences commuted to life or other long periods of penal servitude. Altogether, by original sentence or commutation, 122 men and one woman were sent to penal servitude and a further eighteen to ordinary imprisonment.[1] All were immediately removed to England: the convicts went to Dartmoor and Portland (Constance Markievicz to Aylesbury), and the eighteen hard-labour men to Wormwood Scrubs.[2] Since they had been sentenced by court martial there was no legal obstacle to these transfers.[3]

Political prisoners?

Since the mid-nineteenth century the convict prisons and (after 1865) the local prisons in England had been administered on the basis of a strict uniformity

---

1 Briefing document for Cabinet, August 1916; Lloyd George Papers, House of Lords Record Office, E/9/4/15. See also *RCP and Directors of Convict Prisons*, PP 1917–18 [Cd. 8764], XVII, 109, 11; 5 *Hansard*, LXXXVII, col. 562; 14 November 1916.
2 RCP, PP 1917–18 [Cd. 8764], XVII, 109, 11. Later, three of the convicts – de Valera, Richard Hayes and Desmond Fitzgerald – were sent to Maidstone 'for disciplinary reasons'. The convict distribution was then: Dartmoor, sixty-two; Portland, fifty-seven; Maidstone, three; Aylesbury, 1 (5 *Hansard*, LXXXVII, col. 562; 14 November 1916). Seventeen men had been sentenced each to one year's hard labour (imprisonment) and one to two years.
3 Section 133 of the Army Act, 1881 (44 & 45 Vict., c.58) allowed military prisoners (any person imprisoned by court martial) to be removed to any building in the United Kingdom designated by a Secretary of State to be a military prison (subject to the qualification set out in Section 63 (3)). See Opinion of Irish Law Officers, Ms Asquith, 43, ff. 47–8; Bodleian Library, Oxford. The legality of the courts-martial proceedings was challenged, chiefly on grounds of their in camera nature, eventually reaching a special Divisional Court on 23 February 1917. The case was dismissed, one judge (Mr Justice Darling) using such words as 'incongruous' and 'grotesque' and referring to 'the trivialities which had been submitted to the Court' (See *Times* Law Report, 23 February 1917: *The Times*, 4a–b. See also *The Times*, 31 January 1917, 3b and 13 February 1917, 4a–b).

which extended to the most minute points of discipline and procedure. The reception of the Irish convicts into the English system created a conflict of interest between the Prison Commissioners and the politicians. The former saw the Irish as a group for whom any special treatment or concessions would challenge the principle of strict uniformity, creating extra work for staff and envy and unrest among other prisoners. Nor, at this time, were the Irish the only political offenders in the Commissioners' custody, and the effect of the preferential treatment on the substantial group of conscientious objectors then serving sentences had to be considered. Politicians, however, had to cope with the evolving Irish situation. They needed to redirect the Irish sentiment which had swung so strongly to the rebels in the aftermath of the executions; they also had to placate American opinion. Ultimately, and despite initial statements to the contrary, there could be little realistic question of treating the Irish as ordinary criminals. A large section of their countrymen did not regard them as such, even though they disagreed with their politics and deplored their methods. To abide by the formalities of the law and penal regulations might aggravate the situation. This was a place where politicians, civil servants and prison administrators had been before, and while the individual office-holders had changed, the files told their story.

The Young Irelanders had in many ways been treated leniently and as special cases, although they were convicts. But by 1916 this precedent had been obscured by the passage of time and – more tellingly – the ending of transportation, and the recasting of penal servitude. Indulgences and privileges which might be allowed half a world away were not guides for life at Portland and Dartmoor convict prisons seventy years later. The precedents of the Fenians were closer in time, and were governed by the same framework of laws and regulations by which penal servitude operated in 1916.

The Fenians had also been treated exceptionally. Most importantly, there was the amnesty of 1869 to 1871 which had freed all bar the soldiers among them. Amendments to the prison regime had been few, but were important. By informal decision, not referred to in Home Office files, their exemption from flogging for extreme indiscipline was an implicit acknowledgement of their special status, even though only one prisoner (O'Donovan Rossa) placed himself at risk of such punishment. They were, additionally, and frequently through political intervention, given more special visits and letters than ordinary convicts, and they were worked in separate parties. These were hardly major indulgences and were within the ordinary discretion of the Directors of Convict Prisons, on grounds of either compassion or security.[4] In all essentials – accommodation,

---

4 Throughout this and following chapters the titles 'Directors of Convict Prisons' and and 'Commissioners of Prisons' should be taken as interchangeable. After the Prison Act of 1898 (61 & 62 Vict., c.41) the two bodies were effectively united. Choice of style and title in the official correspondence and files thereafter largely related to responsibilities within the Prison Commission, and is sometimes confusingly arbitrary.

regime, labour and uniform – the Fenians were treated as ordinary convicts. There was even less question of the dynamitards receiving special treatment. None of this, of course, altered the fact that these were not individual, outcast and shame-wracked miscreants: the Fenians and even the dynamitards were held within a halo of political scrutiny which in itself and if only for self-interested reasons caused administrators to treat them with particular care.

Special consideration had been shown in three cases of relatively recent date – Mrs Georgina Weldon, W. T. Stead and the Transvaal Raiders. Georgina Weldon was convicted of criminal libel in March 1885 and sentenced to six months' imprisonment without hard labour. Stead, the campaigning editor of the then Liberal *Pall Mall Gazette*, in the course of an investigation into the immoral traffic in young girls had, in November 1885, been sentenced to three months' imprisonment without hard labour. In both these cases there was a sharp public reaction. Georgina Weldon, although convicted, had actually proved the truth of her libel. Stead had committed a purely technical and innocent breach of the law and was undisputably a public benefactor.[5] Despite official opposition to creating precedents the Home Secretaries of the day (Harcourt and Cross) intervened and had the prisoners removed to the First Division – decisions of questionable legality.

The case to which the Irish politicians particularly drew attention, however, was that of the Transvaal Raiders, who had in July 1896 received various sentences of up to fifteen months for offences under the Foreign Enlistment Act, 1870 (33 & 34 Vict., c.90). The country was turning to imperialism and these sentences, particularly the fifteen months passed on the Raid's leader Dr Jameson, were widely condemned. A Conservative Home Secretary (Sir Matthew Ridley) made a somewhat shifty use of the Royal Prerogative, pardoning Jameson and his followers on condition that they agreed to serve their sentences in the First Division. They agreed and were immediately transferred: Jameson was released even from this gentle custody on medical grounds after he had served only four months.[6] These cases proved, to the full satisfaction of the Irish members at least, that in prison administration where there was a political will a way would be found. They were correct, of course, as the subsequent treatment of the Irish prisoners would show. But political will is based on advantage and necessity, and in the summer of 1916 these still had to become clear in the government's Irish policy.

5 I provide an account of these cases in my *English Local Prisons 1860–1900*, London, Routledge, 1995, pp. 373–5.
6 Ibid., pp. 375–7. For a judicious account of the Transvaal Raid see Elizabeth Packenham's *Jameson's Raid*, London, Weidenfeld & Nicolson, 1960. This was one of the first high-profile cases which would make Edward Carson's name (he was Junior Counsel for the defence) and is discussed in Edward Majoribanks, *The Life of Lord Carson*, London, Victor Gollancz, 1932, Vol. 1, ch. 17.

Except for eighteen men sentenced to hard labour, those serving time for offences connected with the rising were convicts; that is to say, subject to the punishment of penal servitude. The precedents allowed a great deal of latitude as to how ordinary prisoners could be treated were their offences political in nature or (to a lesser extent) motivation. This had been given a legislative basis as a result of the cases described above. Section 6 of the 1898 Prisons Act allowed the courts to send offenders to any one of three divisions of imprisonment – the First Division gave most privileges, and amounted to little more than having to stay in prison, but otherwise living as normal a life as confinement would allow. The Second Division had been established expressly for prisoners of respectable backgrounds, not convicted of offences of violence, personal gain or moral turpitude. Second Division prisoners were kept apart from the truly criminal and had privileged arrangements for letters and visits.

The eighteen whom the courts martial had sentenced to ordinary imprisonment had been more leniently treated because of their youth, or their lesser involvement in the rising.[7] All had been sentenced to hard labour, and therefore were not eligible for placement in the First or Second Division. They could only move into these more privileged regimes by a conditional pardon, or if the hard labour element in their sentence was remitted. In the latter case they would then become eligible for recategorisation as First or Second Division prisoners. There was a further complication in this, however: as a guard against political interference recategorisation was reserved for the Visiting Committee, not the Home Secretary.[8]

Attempts to secure political or prisoner-of-war status for the rebel convicts nevertheless began almost immediately, but on 22 June, 16 August and 22 August 1916, Herbert Samuel was emphatic that the convicts were being treated as ordinary cases under the penal servitude rules.[9] This was true, but only just. There were three matters in which special consideration had been given. Several extra visits had been granted on the instructions of the Home Secretary and these had been conducted in a special room. Two ex post-facto justifications were given for these: any convict could receive a special visit where circumstances justified it; and the special room which was provided was not intended as a privilege, but as a means of ensuring closer supervision. A similar type of evasive explanation was given for the practice of working the Irish political convicts in

---

7 Ten of the Wormwood Scrubs men were under the age of 20 (PRO HO 144/1453/311980).
8 Criminal Justice Administration Act, 1914 (4 & 5 Geo. V, c.58, s.16(2)).
9 See 5 *Hansard*, LXXXIII, col. 337; 22 June 1916: 'I can find nothing in the past treatment of Irish prisoners that would be a precedent for exceptional measures in this respect.' Ibid., LXXXV, col. 1855; 16 August 1916: 'they are not entitled to any special treatment on the ground that their offences were of a political character'. Ibid., col. 2472; 22 August 1916: 'they must be subject to the same rules as other prisoners, and they cannot be allowed to receive newspapers or presents'. On 16 and 22 August Samuel contradictorily added that the Irish prisoners had been given an extra allowance of books.

separate parties at Dartmoor and Portland. Since all the men belonged to the 'Star Class' (essentially first offenders of previous good character) and there were no other Star Class prisoners at Portland or Dartmoor, they had to be separated from convicts of other classifications.[10] Finally, certain of the Irish convicts had been allowed to receive technical and educational books, including material in Irish. This privilege was allowed under the ordinary convict rules.[11] All of this was contrived to allow the Home Secretary to insist that no special concessions had been made. In fact, although in truly exceptional circumstances some of these privileges might be extended to the odd convict here and there, they were being granted to the convict rebels with an exceptional and telling degree of liberality. Any decision on further privileges, however, could not hide behind small print and quibbles.

In addition to the argument of substance that the Irish convicts had been convicted of political and politically inspired crimes, and should be treated as such, or as prisoners of war, another, more subtle case was made at the time – possibly emanating from the lawyers in the Irish Parliamentary Party.[12] The reason the English law did not distinguish between political and ordinary criminal offences, the argument went, was because in the institution of the jury, the English courts provided a substantial degree of protection from the arbitrary acts of the executive branch of government. But since the Irish rebels had been tried by courts martial they had been denied this protection, and therefore deserved to receive political status. Two grounds were given for rejecting this view. The first not so much addressed, but rather stepped around it. The courts martial were established under statute, and in dealing with the rebels were exercising their authority under the Defence of the Realm Act (DORA). It followed that they were regularly constituted courts of law. The second response was that the rebels were not the only court martial prisoners in civil prisons. Military offenders sentenced to penal servitude under Section 58 of the Army Act, 1881 (44 & 45 Vict., c.58) served their sentences in civil prisons, as ordinary convicts – and indeed penal servitude (unlike ordinary imprisonment) had no mechanism to deal with different categories of offenders.[13]

Administrative perturbation

These somewhat abstract considerations failed to soothe either the Home Office or the Commissioners, both of whom wished the rebels elsewhere. They fretted about the practicalities, and to an extent used them to revisit the basic allocation

---

10 For a description of the convict divisions see *New Rules Proposed to be Made by the Secretary of State for the Home Department for the Government of Prisons*, [HCP199], PP 1904, LXXX, 435, 1.

11 Memorandum of 17 October 1916: PRO HO 144/1453/311980/31.

12 The Home Office document which was intended to brief ministers against this case does not make it clear where or from whom it originated (see PRO HO 144/1453/311980/31, f. 6).

13 Ibid., f. 7.

of responsibilities. There were various preliminary inquiries during the latter part of May, while arrangements for the transfers to England were being made. Many prisoners had arrived in rebel uniform and had asked that this clothing should be sent to their friends – as the standing orders provided it might.[14] What was to be done with this clothing and equipment? Should prisoners' letters be submitted to the military authorities before they were dispatched? How should visits be conducted, and should reference be made to the censor's department of the Irish police before visits were authorised? The men were being kept apart from other convicts, an arrangement that amounted to placing them in the Star Class. Since Star Class was reserved for offenders of good character not previously imprisoned, could their employment history and previous mode of life be ascertained and this information passed on to the Commissioners? As for those sentenced to ordinary imprisonment, their numbers hardly justified segregation. Would there be any objection to their being placed with ordinary criminal prisoners?[15]

The prospect of receiving Countess Markievicz was regarded with particular misgivings. The Chairman of the Prison Commission hoped that she might be kept in the Irish Female Convict Prison.[16] Were she to be sent to Aylesbury she would have to be placed in a small group of Star Class prisoners, 'which contains the German and Swedish convicts, Wertheim and Bournonville'.[17] And in a display of concern not shown towards the male convicts, Ruggles-Brise worried about the Countess' visiting arrangements because of the distance of Aylesbury from Ireland. This was a feeble objection, since Portland and Dartmoor were far less accessible than Aylesbury. But the truth of the matter was that the Commissioners did not want the lady: 'Unless there are urgent reasons for this

---

14 Eoin MacNeill was one of a party of twelve convicts transferred to Dartmoor at the end of May. Several of the men, it was reported, wore Volunteer uniforms (*The Times*, 1 June 1916, 5e).

15 Sir Evelyn Ruggles-Brise (Chairman of the Prison Commission) to Home Office, 15 May 1916; PRO HO 144/1453/311980/4.

16 He may have read her post-rising profile in *The Times* which described her as 'one of Dublin's stormy petrels'. At times of popular excitement the Countess was to be seen 'rushing about' haranguing individuals and crowds with 'a curious swift shrill rush of words, and giving the impression of a well-meaning but ill-balanced and hysterical personality' (1 May 1916, 12b). The prospect of complaints from and about such a prisoner was not enticing.

17 Mrs Lizzie Wertheim was a demi-mondaine who had acquired British citizenship by marriage. Teamed with a male companion (Breeckow) she attempted to gather naval intelligence by making herself agreeable to officers. Arrested, tried and found guilty at the Old Bailey on 20 September 1915. Breeckow was sentenced to death (executed 26 October at the Tower) and Wertheim, thought to be acting under his influence (though this almost certainly was not so), to ten years' penal servitude. Mlle Eva de Bournonville was a Swede of French extraction who was detected early in her brief spying career, and whose subsequent offer to work as a British double-agent was turned down. Tried at the Old Bailey on 12 January 1916, she was sentenced to death, later commuted to life penal servitude (see Sidney Theodore Felstead, *German Spies at Bay*, London, Hutchinson & Co, 1920, pp. 113–18 and 187–95).

transfer, the Directors would for this and other reasons deprecate it.'[18] This last sentiment was dutifully echoed the next day in a letter to the military command in Ireland. 'It would,' Troup (Permanent-Under-Secretary) wrote, 'be extremely inconvenient to receive the one female convict in Aylesbury Convict Prison, where she would have to associate chiefly with two German spies under sentence of penal servitude; and Mr Herbert Samuel [Home Secretary] hopes that it may be possible to arrange for her to be kept in Female Convict Prison in Ireland.'[19] But the Countess, the military authorities decided, was too dangerous an influence to remain in Ireland, and so she went to Aylesbury, where, as we shall see, she enjoyed the stimulating company of spies, a bank robber and a clutch of domestic murderers.

It was in fact the male convicts who posed most problems. On 22 June the independent nationalist (now de facto Sinn Féin) MP Alfred Byrne asked the Home Secretary for special privileges to be granted to the Irish prisoners, to allow MPs to visit them once a month, observing that 'the treatment of Irish political prisoners in the past makes these visits essential'.[20] On the matter being referred to the Prison Commission, Sir Evelyn Ruggles-Brise reflexively objected to any 'differential treatment'. Visits should be governed only by the stage system on which 'the whole discipline of a Convict Prison depends'. Privileges had to be earned, and it would be a great mistake to interfere with this provision. There was, moreover, the question of who merited indulgence. Sentences covered everything from the mere possession of arms to 'cold-blooded murder of British soldiery'. Surely, Ruggles-Brise argued, 'the facts of each case should be ascertained before any general order for indulgence is given'. In any event, if the Irish as a class were deemed improper associates for the ordinary felon population, 'it would be better that they should be removed to a separate place of confinement under military authority'.[21] The Commissioners, in other words, were no more keen to receive the male prisoners than they were the Countess Markievicz.

Ruggles-Brise's line was accepted by Sir Edward Troup, and drafted into a Commons reply which Home Secretary Herbert Samuel duly delivered. He recited the increasing visiting privileges which could be earned under the progressive stage system. Byrne had referred to the past treatment of Irish prisoners, but Samuel insisted that he could find 'nothing in the past treatment of Irish prisoners that would be a precedent for exceptional measures in this respect'.[22] Troup had noted that 'certain relaxations' had been allowed to the treason-felony prisoners, 'but it must be remembered that the conditions of p[enal] s[ervitude] were much more severe then than now. Moreover the Fenian troubles

18 Ruggles-Brise to Home Office, 15 May 1916, op. cit.
19 Letter of 16 May 1916; PRO HO 144/1453/311980/4.
20 5 Hansard, LXXXIII, col. 337; 22 June 1916.
21 PRO HO 144/1453/311980/12.
22 5 Hansard, LXXXIII, col. 337; 22 June 1916.

of those days did little harm compared with the present rebellion.'[23] The latter was a debatable point, and raised the previously unexplored notion of applying the doctrine of retribution to offenders whose offence was agreed to be conscionable. On the same day that Byrne asked his question about visiting privileges, the directors referred to the Home Office petitions which they had received from Eamon de Valera and Robert Brennan.[24] The two had applied for pens, ink and paper – de Valera to further his study of mathematics, Brennan for literary work. The directors did not object to de Valera's mathematical work, but saw problems with Brennan's request. If materials were supplied for novel-writing, other prisoners could claim facilities to carry on their trade, and the prison would be put to the trouble of examining what Brennan produced. The larger question, however, was whether 'having regard to the peculiar circumstances of their convictions' these men were to receive privileges not granted to ordinary convicts. If they were, then they should be removed from convict prisons and placed under military authority.[25] The Home Office accepted the reasoning. De Valera was told that he was not yet eligible for the privilege he sought, and Brennan was simply turned down. There was, an official noted, 'no intention of treating them as prisoners of war'.[26]

Within a few weeks of this declaration, however, the Home Office was dealing with a War Office minute setting out suggestions as to how the two departments might deal with petitions from 'Irish Prisoners of War'.[27] The Home Office kept a closer hold on its terminology, and found 'Irish Prisoners' or 'Sinn Féin Prisoners' or 'Irish Rebels' acceptable alternatives to 'Prisoners of War'. But despite the linguistic discipline it was not easy to sustain the line that these were no more than ordinary convicts. Frederick Dryhurst,[28] one of the Prison Commissioners, minuted his colleagues about a visit he had paid to Portland in early July, during which he spoke to twenty-four of the fifty-seven Sinn Féin prisoners. They were, he recorded, 'a distinctly prepossessing set of men – well spoken, of more than average education'. They made no complaints 'but on the contrary, when they said anything more than that they had no application or

---

23 PRO HO 144/1453/311980/12. No reference was made to the dynamitards.

24 (1881–1964). Member of the IRB and the Irish Volunteers, had not been able to join the rising in Dublin, but was subsequently arrested. He took the anti-Treaty side in the Civil War, and was a lifelong associate of de Valera.

25 Ruggles-Brise to Troup, 22 June 1916; PRO HO 144/1453/311980/65.

26 Minute of 29 June 1916; PRO HO 144/1453/311980/65.

27 PRO HO 144/1453/311980/17. Thomas Ashe also petitioned for writing materials. Prior to his imprisonment, he explained, he had written a great deal as an essayist and story-teller, and had also attempted dramas: 'I am nearly certain that at some future date I will have to resort to writing in order to gain a livelihood. I could very well fit myself for such work during my study time in prison if allowed to write' (Dartmoor, 20 June 1916. The request was refused on 23 November 1916: PRO HO 144/1459). On Ashe see pp. 610–14, below.

28 Dryhurst transferred to the Home Office from the Post Office in 1899. Private Secretary to Asquith, then Senior and Principal Clerk; Prison Commissioner, 1903. Retired 1917.

complaint to make, it was to the effect that they were well-treated, that the system was fair, and that the Officers were kindly and considerate.'[29] This last was particularly well received and served to enhance the men's credibility with officials.

The prisoners whom Dryhurst interviewed ranged in their occupations from labourers to a member of Dublin Corporation and a solicitor. Dryhurst quizzed them about the causes of the rebellion, and received a variety of replies including the abiding national spirit, fear of conscription and resentment at being robbed of Home Rule. 'If one could forget the terrible things that were done during the Rebellion,' Dryhurst wrote, 'it would be hard to believe that such men as these could be capable – I will not say of committing, but even of looking on at or assenting to such acts.' While there must be a great variation in degrees of guilt among men, Dryhurst evidently believed several who declared that they had been deceived as to the purpose of the Easter Monday mobilisation: 'One man, a teacher at a Roman Catholic School or College whom I found reading Tacitus, said that he had never been in favour of violence, that he had protested against the use of violence a month before, and that he had nearly cried when he saw Sackville Street when he was brought away from Dublin.' Another man said that they had been told that the Easter Monday parade was a rehearsal for a bigger parade which was to take place on Whit-Monday and that he was in uniform 'and would have been shot if he had not obeyed orders'. Had this man been in plain clothes he would have got away, as he had 'arranged to take his wife and the children to the pictures on Easter Monday night'.

But with few exceptions, the prisoners had expressed no regrets for the rising or the loss of life and property it had wrought; nor had they done so in letters to friends. They were perhaps fortified by their belief that their imprisonment would not be prolonged. One of them, a former journalist, said that while he did not like prison 'he had got to stick it out'. Another, speaking of the political outlook, thought that things would improve 'but it would be a long time before he would see them. However, God is good.'[30] Reading Dryhurst's memorandum it is hard to believe that this group would easily blend into the general population of prisons, or could readily be deprived of its political certainties and solidarity by the enforcement of convict discipline.

Out of a spirit of natural rebelliousness, or as part of a strategy to continue the struggle in prison, de Valera and other leaders proved troublesome more or less from the outset. As noted above, de Valera had almost immediately asked for writing materials to carry on his mathematical studies and, as an exceptional case, this had eventually been granted.[31] A special visit was allowed in August 1916 to enable a family friend, Father Thomas Roche of Castletownroche, to

29 PRO HO 144/1453/311980/18.
30 Ibid.
31 De Valera petition, PRO HO 144/10309/50833/315944.

discuss personal business with him.[32] These were small concessions, but ordinary convicts were unlikely to receive them, as de Valera and his companions would have known. Far from inducing a more compliant mood, however, they seem to have suggested that the authorities could be pressed further. On 11 August, responding to an enquiry from the US State Department, de Valera gave a mettlesome reply to an enquiry about his citizenship. If he were not an American he was (through his father) a Spaniard. He had never become a British citizen, but would have become an Irish citizen had this been possible.[33]

De Valera's leadership of the Dartmoor men was unquestioned, and almost by default he began to develop a simple but effective means of battling with the prison authorities and engaging his followers. The response of the governor and his staff showed that they were lumbering along behind rather cluelessly while de Valera set the agenda. The technique was carefully to pick an issue, take an action which broke the rules, be punished and respond to the punishment with further and more widespread breaches of the rules. Supporting this was a campaign of constant complaining.[34] Essential to all of this was a good channel of communication with the outside, and a range of supporters who would gain publicity and press the matter in the Commons.

The first incident may serve to illustrate many which followed. In mid-October 1916, de Valera was put on a charge for throwing an 8 oz loaf of bread to John McArdle, another prisoner: strictly against the rules but not easy to justify any punishment to the outside world. He admitted the offence: it was not the first loaf he had thrown to a fellow prisoner and it certainly would not be the last.[35] The charge was adjudicated and on being 'punished in the ordinary way' with two days' close confinement and two days on bread and water, de Valera refused to eat or work. He argued that he had been right to give the prisoner bread because the man was hungry, and the reason for that was an insufficient diet.

The authorities had been foolish to allow themselves to be provoked in the first place – they inevitably looked mean and spiteful and de Valera's defence invited questions about the convict diet. Now under his further punishment de Valera told the prison medical officers that he would refuse food and that if

---

32 De Valera's conversation was reported. He had told Father Roche that the food seemed insufficient for the first six weeks, but that he had got more by asking. At first he had been afraid he would go mad, but he now had plenty of books: 'Tell the boys we are all well and to keep the old flag up' (ibid., /50833/8).

33 Ibid., /6 and /1.

34 Between 14 August and 14 October a section of the sixty-five Irish convicts at Dartmoor complained persistently. Thirty-two men made sixty-three applications, as compared to thirty-two of the 403 ordinary convicts, who made fifty applications during the period. The Irish convicts at Portland, by contrast, had not lodged a single complaint: de Valera seems to have made the difference (PRO HO 144/10309/50833/12).

35 Major E. Reade to Prison Commissioners, 18 October 1916: ibid., /11.

an attempt were made to feed him forcibly he would refuse food 'until he was killed'. He accompanied this by a flow of anti-British and pro-German sentiments. Because he was on hunger-strike he was removed to the prison hospital, and in support the other Irish convicts intimated that they would also go on hunger-strike. Rather late in the day Major E. Reade, the Dartmoor governor, realised that events were slipping away from him, and wrote to the Prison Commission. De Valera, he emphasised, was a 'Personality' and 'A real firebrand and fanatic to whom the others looked up, together with his lieutenants Richard Hayes and F. Fitzgerald'.[36] Major Reade believed that if de Valera were transferred to Maidstone Prison, Hayes and Fitzgerald and the other men could be managed. The Prison Commission on this occasion read the danger signals. All three men would be transferred immediately and (anticipating a parliamentary question) Major Reade was to supply information on the supply of food at Dartmoor. No further punishment was to be inflicted without the authority of the Directors.[37]

De Valera's health and mental state were now a cause for concern, and while the deputy medical officer was able to give some reassurance, it was a mixed message. The prisoner had been receiving extra diet since his reception at Dartmoor, and his weight had increased from 163 to 171 lb. At the time of writing (20 October) de Valera was in the prison hospital 'recuperating from the effects of 48 hours voluntary starvation; otherwise general health is good. . . . Mentally he is sane.' He had been pleasant and civil while in the hospital,

> but he maintains the attitude of (1) A father to his children with reference to the other Irish prisoners, e.g. says it hurts him to hear the others ordered about by the Warders, etc. etc. . . . (2) Insisting that he is a prisoner of war like the Belgians, & should be treated in exactly the same way that the Belgians have been treated by the Germans all thro' this war – *his own words*.

De Valera subsequently condemned hunger-striking, and it is interesting to note that at this point he had been on hunger-strike and threatened to renew it if punished again:

> Forcible feeding he will consider as causing an injury to his health, and that will be sufficient grounds for him to refuse all food in future,

---

36 PRO HO 144/110309/50833/11. Richard Hayes (1878–1958) was a boyhood friend of de Valera, and in the rising had taken part in the Asbourne engagement under Thomas Ashe, for which he received a sentence of twenty years' penal servitude. Supported the Treaty and enjoyed a career as politician and man of letters. F. Fitzgerald was actually Desmond Fitzgerald (1888–1947) who had fought at the GPO and received a long-term sentence of penal servitude. After release became the Dáil's Director of Propaganda during the Anglo-Irish war. Took the Treaty side in the Civil War and subsequently followed political, literary and journalistic career.

37 Correspondence, 19–21 October 1916: PRO HO 144/10309/50833/11–13.

whether under punishment in his cell, or in hospital – 'It would be war to the bitter end'. I consider Prisoner to be of a determined and fanatical temperament, & I fully believe he will carry out his threats re. hunger-striking, at any rate for a long period. He is at present quite fit to be forcibly fed. Prisoner looks upon every thing from the political point of view, and he believes apparently that every man and child of English origin is imbued with hatred for Ireland, and is constantly endeavouring to injure her.[38]

On 27 October the Prison Commission ordered the immediate transfer of de Valera, Hayes and Fitzgerald to Maidstone Prison, which was chosen because its medical staff were experienced in dealing with hunger-strikers. To emphasise the penal nature of their removal the men were moved by train, in convict uniform, in restraints and escorted by uninformed officers.[39] The escorting staff reported that when he was put in shackles for the transfer de Valera had said to them, 'you'll see John Bull shackled up like this before long'.[40] Within two weeks of his arrival at Maidstone de Valera had lodged a petition objecting to the method by which he had been transferred and the public scrutiny to which he had been subjected en route. He also protested that he was being obliged to labour with and therefore associate with other convicts.[41] He continued to press the issue in the following days, and was supported in this in the Commons by questions from Byrne, O'Shaughessy and Ginnell.[42] A great deal of effective

---

38 Dr E. Battiscombe to Major E. Reade, 20 October 1916: PRO HO 144/10309/50833/12. Dr Battiscombe added that when he visited him in the separate cells, de Valera accused the medical staff of ill-treating all the Irish, 'but would give no particulars'.

39 PRO HO 144/10309/50833/315944/4. De Valera subsequently complained of the indignity of being transferred in chains. During the twelve-hour journey the three men were chained 'so that when one of us had to perform the natural functions he had to drag his two companions with him and violate every law of common decency. The provision of a sufficient escort would have made the chaining quite unnecessary'. There was much meat here for sympathetic MPs – as the Home Office well realised.

40 Ibid., /11: Reade to Dryhurst, 30 October 1916. De Valera had rather oddly added that had he been a director he would have dealt with his transfer in the same way.

41 De Valera petition, 9 November 1916: PRO HO 144/10309/315944/4. He objected to the degradation of being associated with criminals, and to the opportunities it gave to such prisoners on discharge to approach and attempt to dupe their families. He probably lodged his protest on arrival at Maidstone, but would have had to await a hearing by the governor and the governor's response before being allowed to lodge a petition.

42 See questions by Byrne and O'Shaughessy, 5 Hansard, LXXXVII, cols 561–3; 14 November 1916; cols 1634–5; 23 November 1916. The Prison Commission appeared to be unmoved by the brouhaha and proposed that the three transferees should not be allowed the privilege of talking at their new prison 'until they shall have proved themselves fit for it by a long period of good conduct'. This provocative proposal was peremptorily overruled by the Home Office (R. J. Wall to Home Office, 14 November 1916; Reply 28 November 1916: PRO HO 144/10309/50833/315944/3).

publicity had flowed from the throwing of the 8 oz loaf; a battle of attrition was being waged against the most immediately available representative of British authority; the morale, solidarity and standing of the convicts had all been substantially strengthened: a rebel success.

The Commissioners' dissatisfaction grew in succeeding weeks. Ruggles-Brise and his colleagues doubted whether they would have adequate political backing. Statements by Samuel in August did not reassure them.[43] When Parliament reassembled Alfred Byrne and others again called for the Irish convicts to be given privileges, especially extra letters and visits. Fighting for his political life amidst the rapidly shifting tides of Irish politics Dillon described the convicts as not so much enemies of Britain as of the Irish Party. Anxious to prevent any further progress to martyrdom he urged better treatment, insisting that 'No modern civilised State treats political prisoners as common convicts. England occupies an unenviable pre-eminence in this matter.'[44] Asked to comment on these and many similar interventions from the Irish benches, the Commissioners reiterated their objections to differential treatment: if such privileges were to be allowed, the men should be put under military control. The rebels had come into the civil prisons only because there were no penal servitude prisons under War Office control. Until recent times it had been accepted that military prisoners, both convict and local, should be confined under civil jurisdiction, but since the War Office had now taken control of the short-sentence military prisoner, there seemed to be no reason why it should not do the same for long termers. Under War Office administration, the rules for the Irish convicts' treatment need not be as rigid as those for civil convicts, but as long as they remained in the civil system they must be subject to its code.[45]

It had been suggested that the Irish should be segregated in a special prison, under the Commissioners' administration. This was also rejected by Ruggles-Brise since it 'would be to accept the demand for special treatment of grave political offences; would require a special set of rules to be laid before Parliament, and would, I am afraid, be creating much difficulty and danger for the future, when worse crimes than these might be perpetrated from so-called political motives'.[46] Ruggles-Brise did not see a major inconsistency in this position. He was willing to agree to a relaxed regime for Irish political offenders – but only

---

43 On 16 August Samuel reaffirmed that the men had been criminally convicted and were not entitled to special treatment because of the political nature of their offence. He added, however, that a liberal allowance of books had been given, and that they would be allowed technical and educational books, as well as books in Irish (5 *Hansard*, LXXXV, col. 1855; 16 August 1916). The decision to allow extra books was seen by the Commissioners as an ominous departure from the rules. Samuel reiterated his position on privileges a week later (ibid., col. 2471; 22 August 1916).
44 5 *Hansard*, LXXXVI, cols 677–8; 18 October 1916.
45 Minute by Evelyn Ruggles-Brise, 6 November 1916; PRO HO 144/1453/311980/30.
46 Ibid.

under the army's jurisdiction. The dangers, evidently, only arose when the Commissioners themselves were asked to take charge.

Even on something as ostensibly trivial as allowing notebooks for literary use, the Commissioners could be unyielding. Responding to political pressures, the Home Secretary directed a limited rule change to allow prisoners 'accustomed to literary work' to have notebooks on condition that they were not used to write about prison or political matters. Ruggles-Brise reluctantly submitted an extremely restrictive draft rule. This was rejected and a less rigid reformulation was requested. Submitting the further draft, Ruggles-Brise entered a formal protest. There would be nothing in future to stop a convict writing about non-political matters, and selling the product 'with the attractive advertisement of having been composed in prison'. This would be a deplorable development:

> I cannot but regard this privilege as contrary to the public interest, and I do not think that at my interview with the Secretary of State this morning I sufficiently dwelt on this point. Such a privilege would, moreover, be tantamount to conferring on a man sentenced to penal servitude the most valuable of the privileges allowed to prisoners of the First Division. If the Secretary of State desires this to be done, of course it will be, but I hope it will not be done without serious consideration.[47]

Troup provided additional wording to tighten the rule while preserving its essence, but this can hardly have satisfied Ruggles-Brise. To the Commissioners this confirmed that the Irish convicts were a transforming presence in the penal system and the sooner they were ejected from it, the better.

Concentration at Lewes

The Commissioner's objections notwithstanding, the politicians decided in November and December 1916 to match the conciliatory release of the internees with concessions to the convicted prisoners. They had been given writing materials 'for literary work'; visits and letters were increased to one-monthly intervals and – most importantly – they were allowed to associate and talk together during certain hours 'so long as good order was maintained'. Since these privileges placed them in a category far superior to that of their criminal (and conscientious objector) colleagues, it was decided to collect them all together at Lewes – previously used as a local prison, but specially designated a convict prison for the purpose.[48]

---

47 Ruggles-Brise to Troup, 31 October 1916; PRO HO 144/1453/311980/29.
48 This designation was necessary for legal purposes (RCP, PP 1917–18 [Cd. 8764], XVII, 109, 11–12).

Apart from the Commissioners, there were various legal and bureaucratic obstacles to be addressed. Some prison rules were embodied in legislation, and changes were not easily brought within ministerial discretion. There were two possible solutions. Since most of the prisoners had been convicted under DORA, a new regulation could have been brought to give the Home Secretary the necessary discretion in the administration of their punishment. This, however, was thought to be undesirable 'especially because it would raise the claim on the part of other persons sentenced to imprisonment under DORA to be allowed preferential treatment'.[49] The other possibility was to change the Convict Prison Rules to allow for special treatment for those sentenced under DORA. The difficulty here was that any draft had to be laid before the House for thirty sitting days. This could lead to some political opportunism on the part of Irish Members, but even more problematical was the delay which would be involved. A draft change laid before Parliament in November would not be effective until late February or March of the following year – assuming there were no political difficulties.

Given ministers' strongly expressed wishes for progress, Troup recommended that preferential treatment might best be given under existing rules 'without straining them unduly'. Showing what a senior civil servant could do when given the political spur, he creatively analysed the rules, seizing every ambiguity and loose phrase to show how the regime might be made more lenient. Visits, he argued, might be permitted more frequently than once a month.[50] And, although association and communication between prisoners were severely restricted, a phrase in the relevant Convict Rule (no. 70) could be used to grant this privilege 'in such manner as the governor may direct'. The men could be allowed to talk during exercise and, since they were to eat together, at mealtimes. Books and writing materials were already allowed greatly in excess of the usual allowance, and could be given even more freely if the Irish were kept apart from other convicts. For security reasons, however, Troup considered it inadvisable to allow friends to supply the writing materials.

There was now flexibility even on food and dress. The Convict Rules did not prohibit prisoners' friends from supplying them with *additional* food or clothing. The only difficulty was Rule 23 which directed that prisoners should be compelled to wear prison clothing. But, argued Troup, 'strictly speaking' the rule would not prevent any *extra* clothing from being provided by prisoners' friends, but this would have to be worn in addition to the uniform. This last, Troup minuted, was not likely to be taken up if the Home Secretary wished to make concessions on food and clothing, 'but, from the point of view of prison discipline and administration it seems undesirable to give way on this point'.[51]

---

49 Memorandum by Sir Charles Troup, 'Treatment of Irish (Sinn Fein) Convicts, 13 November 1916'; PRO HO 144/1453/311980/34. The 'other persons' were the conscientious objectors.
50 Ibid., f. 3.
51 Ibid., ff. 4–5.

All these ingeniously wrought concessions should, Troup argued, be conditional on good behaviour. He proposed that the three convicts who had been transferred from Dartmoor to Maidstone for misbehaviour and 'bad influence' (a reference to de Valera) should not be allowed to rejoin their comrades in the enjoyment of the various privileges of the relaxed regime. This was a token rearguard action, however, and knowing the certain reaction of the Irish convicts to a continued exclusion of de Valera and the others, the Home Secretary vetoed Troup's suggestion, and directed that the three men should rejoin their companions 'so long as they behave well'.[52] The authorities had to weigh up the advantages of concentrating the men at Lewes, against the possibility that this would increase the chances of collective indiscipline. Informing the prisoners of their transfer and of the easing of their conditions, it was emphasised that these advantages were dependent on good conduct. The Commissioners hoped that the men would be placed under an obligation of honour to abide by the rules. They got a foretaste of their new regime when they were transferred in plain rather than convict clothes, with no chains or handcuffs (which were standard convict requirements). In return they were asked to give their parole not to communicate with anyone *en route*, and to obey their warder's instructions.[53]

This optimism was soon dashed when at Lewes there began acts of defiance which in the case of ordinary prisoners would have resulted in severe punishment. As the rising's senior surviving commandant, de Valera had asserted his leadership in Dartmoor, and this was confirmed at Lewes.[54] The men had no doubt that their military structure had survived and retained its entitlement to their oathbound loyalty. Whereas the authorities hoped that they would respond in a conciliatory way to their improved conditions, the prisoners saw removal to Lewes as an opportunity to continue their struggle against the British by whatever means they could command. In a letter smuggled out of the prison at Easter 1917, de Valera emphasised their continuing identification with the cause of militant nationalism:

52 Ibid., f. 5, marginal minute by Herbert Samuel.
53 Before transfer the privileges they would enjoy at Lewes were read out to them. The most important, of course, was bringing them together in one prison. This, being obvious, was not referred to, but the monthly visits and letters, writing materials and talking together during exercise were emphasised (PRO HO 144/1453/311980/186: letter from Commissioners to governors of Dartmoor, Maidstone, Portland and Wormwood Scrubs, 5 December 1916).
54 When Eoin MacNeill was received at Dartmoor, de Valera took advantage of the men being mustered for exercise to step forward, call them to attention, salute MacNeill and order 'Eyes Left' as a demonstration of respect to the former Commander-in-Chief of the Irish Volunteers (Dorothy Macardle, *The Irish Republic*, Dublin, Irish Press, 1951, pp. 201–2). At Lewes some of the prisoners had wished to elect a commanding officer, but in order to avoid friction it was decided to ask de Valera, as the rising's senior surviving officer, to accept the position. Thomas Ashe and Thomas Hunter, next in seniority, agreed to act as deputy commanding officers (Piaras Béaslaí, *Michael Collins and the Making of a New Ireland*, London, George G. Harrap, 1926, Vol. 1, pp. 149–50).

We regard ourselves at present as, in a very special way, identified with the cause the ideals and aspirations for which our common comrades died last Easter. We feel that any important action of ours will too have a reflex effect on last Easter's sacrifice and on any advantages which have been secured by that sacrifice.[55]

Developments fully justified Ruggles-Brise's forebodings. The government's decision was announced to the Commons on 14 November 1916 by Herbert Samuel. The Irish prisoners would be brought together to be given the privileges of the later stages of penal servitude. In addition, they were to be allowed notebooks for literary purposes, and monthly letters and visits; association would be allowed at certain fixed times, 'with permission to talk together so long as quiet and good order is maintained'.[56] It took some weeks to complete the transfers, but by December 1916 all were collected at Lewes. These included de Valera and his two Maidstone companions, and the Wormwood Scrubs men, who were serving sentences of hard labour.[57]

The last of the relaxations – permission to talk together – was announced in somewhat ambiguous terms. It was not clear whether the men were granted permission to talk only when they were brought together for association, or whether they had general permission to talk, provided they did so without disorder. Naturally it was the latter which the men insisted upon: this view was also taken by the governor and his staff, to whom no more detailed instructions were given. The lack of clarity was compounded by staff shortages, resulting in lax supervision when the men first arrived. There appears subsequently to have been a drift in the discipline, and a warning was issued that there was too much

---

55 University College, Dublin (UCD): De Valera Papers: P150/529: De Valera to Simon Donnelly, Easter 1917.

56 5 *Hansard*, LXXXVII, cols 562–3; there had been strong representations from the Irish nationalists the previous month about prison conditions. These protests came from the leaders of constitutional nationalist opinion as much as from members who had taken up the Sinn Féin cause. John Dillon, while continuing to condemn the rebellion, in the cause of conciliation demanded political status for the convicts. 'No modern state,' he insisted, 'treats political prisoners as common criminals.' By continuing to deal with the convicts as though they were merely criminals, 'you are maintaining the bitterest spirit in Ireland'. In France or Italy or any other continental country they would not be treated in that way. To grant political status would 'in no conceivable way interfere with the maintenance of law and order' (5 *Hansard*, LXXXVI, col. 678; 18 October 1916). The privileges announced on 14 November were in fact extended, and within a few months the Irish National Aid Association was sending magazines in to the men. On 10 March 1917, R. A. Marriott, the Lewes governor, agreed to Michael Collins' request that the men receive shamrocks to be worn in the prison on St Patrick's Day (NLI: Irish National Aid Association Papers: Ms. 24, 387). These privileges went far beyond even Troup's imaginative reading of the convict rules.

57 5 *Hansard*, LXXXVIII, col. 466; 30 November 1916; ibid., cols 807–8, 12 December 1916. Those who were serving sentences of imprisonment were held in the prison's 'F' (formerly female) wing, separated from their penal servitude comrades in the main body of the prison.

talk and not enough labour. Following this, labour discipline improved and talking was reduced, but it was still fairly free. One of the directors, on a routine inspection, noting the amount of talking, ordered that it was to cease entirely at labour. When a prisoner was subsequently punished for breaking the rule, the entire body staged a work-strike. The governor (Major Marriott) withdrew the punishment, and all returned to work.[58]

At this point de Valera sent a long statement of protest to the Commissioners; it ran to three-and-a-half closely written foolscap pages and took up two petition forms. The transfer to Lewes, he argued, had been interpreted by the prisoners and their friends as removal 'from the jurisdiction of the criminal department of the Home Office'. But they were still being treated as criminals. He objected to the silence rule in itself ('the refinement of cruelty') and to the rigour with which it was being applied to the Irish. The men were not unwilling to work: 'Labour *as labour* we rather welcome for its own sake and as an employment, be it digging, carting manure, carrying sacks of coke on our backs or scrubbing our halls.' Given their previous training, some could not hope to be efficient at it. But they would not 'take very kindly' to penal labour 'monotonous and soul killing', and while at Dartmoor he had himself refused to pick coir because the task was 'degrading'. He denied that the men had abused their privileges at Lewes. The morning exercise period was too short, considering the limited number of WCs on the parade grounds. The machines for hair-cutting and shaving were instruments of torture. There were delays in forwarding letters, so great that it almost nullified the privilege they had been granted of more fre-quent letter-writing. The prisoners had been told that the governor had to punish them for indiscipline: 'The governor,' he commented, 'is to be a mock judge, the trial a farce, the predetermined sentence being already in the judge's coat-tail pocket.'[59]

This list was the stuff of many disputes and strikes to come. Ruggles-Brise immediately wrote to the Home Secretary on barely restrained 'I told you so' lines. Were these ordinary circumstances, the directors would have reacted strongly to the governor's surrender of his authority to the convicts, 'but the Convict Prison at Lewes is not being governed under ordinary circumstances'. At the time when the concessions had been announced 'by the late Secretary of State',[60] it was anticipated that there would be difficulty in maintaining order and discipline, and 'It is not too much to say that the maintenance of a proper standard of prison discipline is incompatible with the liberty which these men enjoy, to converse without restraint at their daily exercise'. Strongly disapproving of the governor's action, the directors did not propose to blame him officially.

58 These details are taken from the report of Inspector J. R. Farewell to the directors, 24 March 1917; PRO HO 144/1458/311980/86.
59 PRO HO 144/11458/311980/315944/5: de Valera to Commissioners, 2 March 1916.
60 Sir George Cave had replaced Sir Herbert Samuel as Home Secretary on 10 December 1916 in Lloyd George's coalition.

Vigorous measures had to be taken to prevent the repetition of such 'acts of gross insubordination', or if the acts could not be prevented, their adequate punishment. An inspector (effectively an assistant Commissioner) was immediately to be sent to Lewes to warn the convicts, who would be specifically assembled to hear him. Any future act of insubordination, the prisoners would be warned, 'either singly or in combination,' would lead to punishment and the withdrawal of all the privileges which had been granted. If these warnings were not heeded and punishments were met by a hunger-strike, the prisoners would be distributed in small groups throughout all the prisons in England and Wales. Anticipating that this strong line might lead to trouble, the directors proposed to reinforce the staff at Lewes, with officers made available by the closing of Dartmoor.

Having expressed his disapproval at the policy adopted by the previous Home Secretary, which had ended in the predicted tears, Ruggles-Brise could not resist a flourish. The present state of affairs could not be allowed to continue. Kindness and consideration had been made an excuse for further demands: 'The Directors would not be discharging their public duty if they tolerated the insubordination which has already arisen, and is likely to be repeated under present conditions, and they would be glad to learn that the Secretary of State concurs with the action they propose to take.'[61]

The Inspector chosen to give the formal warning was J. R. Farewell, who went down to Lewes without delay. Obviously the proclamation of a formal warning to an assembly of men already excited and disaffected could have had a disastrous outcome, and Farewell made careful preparations. He arrived at the prison a week before the day on which he intended to issue the warning, taking particular guidance from the Roman Catholic chaplain, Dr Andrew O'Loughlin,[62] who had been with the Irish at Portland, and was now their pastor. O'Loughlin cautioned that any address should be deferred until after St Patrick's Day (17 March). The men, he said, thought that they were not being treated as leniently as had been promised, and while they might take a warning quietly, they might be 'explosive'.

Delaying his address, Farewell made a number of visits of observation. He found the men orderly in all respects, except that they talked at labour. Apart from their unwillingness to obey the silence rule, Farewell saw 'no tendency among the men to misconduct', and in all other respects they were quiet, orderly and well behaved. Dr O'Loughlin reported that the majority of them

---

61 Ruggles-Brise to Troup, 7 March 1917; PRO HO 144/1458/311980/78. A test case had been brought on behalf of two of the Lewes men, Gerald Doyle and Cornelius O'Donovan, challenging the validity of the procedures by which they had been convicted. This was first heard on 12 February before the Lord Chief Justice and two others, and then before a seven-judge special Divisional Court on 23 February. The habeas corpus application was rejected (*The Times*, 13 February 1917, 4a–b; 23 February, 6e; 24 February, 4a–b).

62 (1867–1928). Born in Middlesex. Educated at English College, Rome; DD, Ph.D. Had been transferred from his post at Portland to assist in managing the Irish convicts. Returned to Portland when the men were released in June 1917.

were devout Roman Catholics, and that they were beginning to settle down and to follow his exhortations to industry so that they might prevent the moral deterioration produced by long confinement and slackness of work.[63]

Reporting to the Commissioners, Farewell dwelt upon the special nature of the prisoners. They had been brought together in one prison, recognised as a class apart: 'they are bound together by the common tie of their race and ideals, their cause, and their suffering, and they are permitted to study Gaelic which alone feeds their enthusiasm for their cause.'[64] Farewell noted that they had elected a committee composed of de Valera, MacNeill and Eamon Duggan,[65] of whom the dominant, most influential and reputedly most uncompromising member was de Valera.

The Commissioners had prepared Farewell's statement to the prisoners, and having divided the men into three groups he addressed them in succession. He took the precaution of keeping a reserve of warders concealed in an adjoining room lest there should be a disturbance; each of the three parties was in addition accompanied by their usual warders. Farewell read the statement 'slowly and deliberately'. This was an encounter without precedent in English prison history. In so far as they collectively refused to obey certain orders, and would respond unconditionally only to the orders of their appointed leaders, the men were mutineers, subject under the Convict Rules to the most severe of prison punishments: flogging. Having listened attentively to the Commissioners' message, the men returned quietly to their cells for lunch. When in the afternoon they were mustered for labour, they refused to commence work until Farewell had seen their three-man committee.

Negotiation with a prisoners' committee was also unprecedented in English prison history. The Commissioners had not authorised this meeting, but having received instructions to deal with the trouble at Lewes, and faced with the prisoners' solidarity, Farewell had little choice in the matter. Because of Dr O'Loughlin's view that de Valera was the committee's most obstinate member, Farewell decided to see him alone. De Valera, somewhat incoherent and agitated at times, nevertheless delivered a clear message. Government intended to treat the Irish more harshly than other convicts, and the men would act accordingly. Farewell denied harsh treatment. On the contrary, they were subject to the normal prison discipline, with certain special ameliorations. The two swiftly reached a deadlock. The conversation with MacNeill and Duggan (professor

---

63 Farewell to Commissioners, 24 March 1917; PRO HO 144/1458/311980/86. The following details of Farewell's visit to Lewes are taken from this file.

64 Ibid. He added, in parenthesis, 'There is reason too to believe that this learning of Gaelic is at the bottom of much of their talking.'

65 (1874–1936). One of the older prisoners, a solicitor. He fought in the Dublin GPO, and became IRA Director of Intelligence on his release from prison. Elected to the first Dáil, he was one of the plenipotentiaries who negotiated and signed the Treaty in December 1921. Ministerial career in the Free State government.

and solicitor) lasted longer, but had the same outcome. MacNeill claimed that the undertaking they were given when they were moved from Dartmoor had been broken, and that from what they had seen at Portland, Dartmoor and Maidstone, the rule of silence which was to be imposed on them was more rigorous than that imposed on ordinary criminals, who spoke surreptitiously and to whom a certain latitude was extended. Apart from the silence rule, MacNeill complained that they had been given work not suitable for long-sentence men. They were '"required to make bags", "ply a needle all day long", "old women's work, and yet be silent as old women never were".' Most of them were 'lusty young men prepared and able to do a day's work' but to enforce a rule of silence on them was cruel. In an additional breach of faith, extra warders had been sent to the prison. They had no complaint against the officials, and their protest was directed at the harsh form of discipline which it was proposed to introduce.

Farewell could only repeat the official line. They should abandon their protest and petition the Home Secretary. This failed to convince, and the three leaders indicated that they could not get the prisoners to return to work. Though disappointed, Farewell was impressed by their demeanour: 'very calm very much in earnest, and feeling the responsibility of the attitude they were taking'. Given little leeway by the Commissioners, Farewell nevertheless felt able to rescind the order that the men should be broken into separate working parties. Labour was resumed, but so also was talking: 'It is restrained, and there is very much less than there was a week or ten days ago and is more or less negligible in degree from a disciplinary point of view, but with the all-important exception that it is in defiance of the order.' He and the governor decided not to press the point since the men had threatened another work strike. Never had Farewell experienced a more difficult position, 'or felt more conscious of failure', but 'to a man' the prisoners would follow each other; they had 'a grim determination to risk everything to resist the rule'. The only solution, Farewell concluded, was to transfer them in small groups to other prisons, but this he cautioned against. It would cause a political outcry at a very critical time, 'and may lead to a serious fracas with a very determined body of men which would require [a] much larger force than is available at the prison'.

Farewell took a conciliatory position. There was some validity in the men's case that the talking rule had intentionally been relaxed; they were, apart from this one issue, orderly and obedient. This was not to be given the same significance as disobedience in ordinary criminals. Talking at labour would not interfere with control, nor would it encourage idleness. There was no question of it leading to moral contamination (in these circumstances), nor was talking likely to provoke bickering and quarrels, since this could be punished by the authorities and would, in any case, 'bring them under the reprobation of their comrades'. As for the one ground which remained, that talking would facilitate combinations and plots, this they could do in any case while talking at exercise.

No action should be taken which would allow them to be represented as martyrs. They would make the most of any tightening of discipline to induce supporters and friends to believe that government had betrayed them: 'they revolt in order to get questions asked in Parliament and inflame Irish sentiment.' They conducted themselves well as a matter of policy, so that when they got hold of what they considered a legitimate grievance they could make the most of it. To concede to the men 'seems like a counsel of despair, and a weakening of authority'. But the combination had not been brought about by any sinister plotting. Rather the men had been officially recognised as a separate class 'afforded every opportunity, indeed almost encouraged to combine'. In justice and in common humanity was it right to expect these men 'bound together as they are by the closest ties of common ideals (however misguided), comrades, some of them blood relations' to maintain silence except when at exercise?

Ruggles-Brise and his colleagues pondered this unwelcome report for almost a month. If, as Farewell thought likely, any attempt to enforce the silence rule either in the prison or by shipping the men out could provoke violent resistance, what thanks would government give when the news became public in Ireland, America and Australia? Though in a convict prison, the men were not isolated, and because of the well-organised system of visits the news would quickly become public.[66] Farewell's report would almost certainly be seen by the Home Secretary, which would leave the Commissioners in the difficult position of justifying a major confrontation and its consequences over a rule that permitted talking during exercise but not at labour: proportion and sense were lacking. The climbdown was total, with whatever face-saving was possible. On 19 April the Home Secretary wrote to Major Marriott at Lewes Prison, ostensibly responding to a petition which the prisoners' committee had lodged on 22 March. He was to summon Duggan, de Valera and MacNeill and tell them that while the government was satisfied that the privileges announced on 14 November had been granted as promised, Sir George Cave (the new Home Secretary) recognised that there had been 'some misunderstanding' as to the privilege of talking during labour. It had been intended that this should be confined to the hours of exercise, but the Home Secretary was now prepared to allow it during labour, so long as it was not abused 'in such a way as to interfere with the work or lead to noise or disturbance'. Talking would be prohibited if work or discipline were adversely affected.[67]

66 The Irish National Aid Association gave financial assistance for visits and also organised visits from sympathisers for those whose friends and relatives could not come. Michael Collins gathered and collated information gained during these visits (see correspondence in NLI: Irish National Aid Association Papers: Ms. 24, 387).

67 PRO HO 144/1458/331980/86. Only one hard labour (imprisonment) man now remained at Lewes. This was James Wilson, who was serving two years, the maximum sentence of imprisonment then allowed. Art O'Brien protested that with his comrades gone from the wing of the prison set aside for them, Wilson was in virtual solitary confinement. The Home Office decided that Wilson could work and associate with the convicts. This was a clear breach of the rules, but no one was going to argue about it (NLI: Irish National Aid Association Papers: Ms. 24, 324(2): O'Brien to Troup, 21 March 1917; H. B. Simpson to O'Brien, 20 March 1917).

Rebellion

The respectable and orderly demeanour of the Irish convicts belied a determination to continue their struggle against the government *whatever* concessions
were granted. Bolstered by their Lewes victory, in late May de Valera, MacNeill
and Duggan determined on a further campaign. They may have been prompted
to act by broad and favourable political changes. The United States of America
had entered the war on 6 April 1917, and the pressure which the Americans
had exerted on Lloyd George (it was an election year in the USA) was reinforced
as coming from an invaluable ally. On 21 May Lloyd George, taking up a
proposal by John Redmond, announced the convening of an Irish Convention.
The prisoners' leaders probably calculated that this was the moment to press
forward their own campaign.

On Whit Monday (28 May) 1917, when the Lewes convicts were being
mustered for labour, de Valera stepped out of the ranks and handed a note to
the principal warder in charge: 'The Irish people demand that we be made
prisoners of war. Until the Government declares our status as such we refuse to
do any labour, except those services directly necessary for ourselves, namely –
cooking, laundry etc.' The note was signed 'E. de Valera, acting for the body
of prisoners'. The men on parade then gave three cheers. The governor was
summoned, but was unable to persuade the prisoners to work, and so they were
returned to their cells and the governor telephoned the Commissioners.[68]

On receipt of the Lewes news the Commissioners – still smarting from their
earlier climbdown – decided on a hard line. The strike was to be dealt with
as a breach of discipline, and there would be a collective loss of privileges.
All letters and visits were suspended, as was associated exercise. Apart from the
men who had agreed to continue cooking, laundry and other maintenance
tasks, all prisoners were confined to their cells, being unlocked only for exercise
and to use the lavatories. Any men causing trouble at exercise (which was to
be of the very restricted kind normally afforded to criminal prisoners) would be
locked up until further orders. The response of the prisoners to this was to refuse
all exercise.[69]

Not so very helpfully, the Commissioners reminded the Home Secretary that
on 27 March they had informed him that if political considerations made it
necessary to suspend the normal convict rules for the Irish prisoners they would
comply, waiving the authority vested in them for maintaining law and order in
the prisons 'and ask for definite instructions from the Government as to how
these men are to be dealt with'. If it was now decided not to enforce discipline
in the normal way, by bringing the prisoners before the Board of Visitors, or
before one of the Commissioners in their statutory capacity as Directors of
Convict Prisons, and, by inflicting the usual punishments and loss of privileges,

---

68 Evelyn Ruggles-Brise to Troup, 29 May 1917; PRO HO 144/1453/311980/112.
69 Ibid., f. 2.

the government would have to decide on its course of action. In the Commissioners' opinion there were two possibilities. The prisoners could remain locked up until they decided to end their protest, and accept work and exercise on the same terms as criminal prisoners. Having accepted normal penal discipline it might be decided at some future time to restore the privileges they had forfeited by their work-strike. The alternative course of action was to concede the demand that they be treated as prisoners of war. On this the Commissioners offered no opinion, but reminded the Home Secretary that they had previously suggested to him ('on more than one occasion') that the army should take charge, 'and they are not aware of any legal difficulty of handing over Lewes prison to the War Office for this purpose'.[70]

The Commissioners had one other caution. Should the Home Secretary wish the prisoners to be tried by a Commissioner sitting as Director, then it would be necessary that the warning conveyed by the Inspector during his March visit be carried into effect, and that the men be distributed in groups of not more than thirty to Parkhurst, Portland and Maidstone prisons (some remaining at Lewes) where they would be deprived of all privileges and subject to the normal discipline of penal servitude. If these punishments were met with a hunger-strike, 'which is not improbable', then the men would be split up into even smaller parties of not more than a dozen and sent to prisons throughout the country where they could be fed forcibly.[71]

The warning of the way in which events could develop must have had a chilling effect on any political desire to force a conclusion through normal disciplinary means, since it might ultimately have led to men dying throughout the country, and over a period of several weeks. Hopes for the revival of constitutional nationalism which Lloyd George and John Redmond had vested in the Irish Convention would have been hopelessly crushed.[72] At the same time action had to be taken, and on Friday, 1 June 1917, the Home Secretary agreed that each man should face adjudication by a director, who would punish according to the earlier warning, and distribute the men in batches of thirty around the various convict prisons.[73]

---

70 Ibid., f. 4. And since a number of civil prisons had been taken over by the military for the duration of the war, there was no practical obstacle to this course.

71 Ibid., f. 3.

72 The hunger-strike would be used to considerable effect at a later point, but, as noted, de Valera opposed its use at Lewes – although the Commissioners did not know this. In late March, anticipating that he would be moved from Lewes, he issued orders to the men as to what they should do in the event of the government deciding to disperse them. The orders included the following: 'You may be tempted to hunger-strike. As a body do not attempt it whilst the war lasts unless you were assured from outside that the death of two or three of you would help the cause – as soldiers I know you would not shrink from the sacrifice – but remember how precious a human life is. Nothing but the highest motives can justify taking it away.' (UCD: De Valera Papers: P150/529: 23 March 1917).

73 Evelyn Ruggles-Brise to Troup, 4 June 1917; PRO HO 144/1453/311980/112.

At Lewes, de Valera issued his own orders on Whit Monday, 28 May. A copy of these was found and passed to the Commissioners – perhaps planted as a warning of what was to come. No understanding or parole of any kind was to be given to the authorities. If on Sunday the men were released for chapel no man was to return to his cell: 'The idea is to compel them to bring in the military if we can.' There were to be no personal quarrels with officers 'on any account', since this would ruin their case. If they were not released for chapel, and were not given exercise on Monday morning, then a campaign of destruction would begin by breaking the upper panes of cell windows: 'Reason, to get more air. The cells are the Black Hole of Calcutta.' Prisoners were also ordered to attempt sabotage if they were released for Sunday chapel: 'try to stop the locks with buttons etc. or strain the hinges so that they cannot easily be locked again. Perfect order – no rows with officers.'[74]

Deeply worried about what might transpire, Major Marriott sought an undertaking from each man that if released from his cell he would go to and from chapel in an orderly way. Some fifty men gave the undertaking, but the majority would not, despite the urgings of the Roman Catholic chaplain. It was then decided that there would be no chapel, and all staff would be kept on duty. De Valera's general order was then found and confirmed the wisdom of the governor's decision.[75] On the Sunday evening (3 June) de Valera gave the chief warder a note for the governor:

> Sir, I wish to inform you that if on tomorrow evening we are still confined in this manner we shall be compelled to take steps of our own to secure a proper supply of fresh air. The doctor is already aware what confinement in the atmosphere of these cells means for the men who are suffering from swollen glands, etc.[76]

74 UCD: De Valera Papers: P150/529; see also Earl of Longford and Thomas P. O'Neill, *Eamonn de Valera*, Boston, Houghton Mifflin Company, 1971, p. 56.

75 The missing of Mass on Sunday was a serious matter for devout Roman Catholics, and the episode was used to blacken de Valera as an atheist (see R. Brennan, *Allegiance*, Dublin, Browne and Nolan, 1950, pp. 131–3; see also for this incident Béaslaí, 1926, Vol. 1, pp. 155–6). The allegation was instigated by Dr O'Loughlin, who suggested to the Inspector (not Farewell this time, but Colonel J. Winn) sent down to oversee the removal of the men from Lewes that if the story were made known in Ireland 'it would alienate all sympathy on the part of the really religious Catholics (the basis of the Sinn Fein movement)'. O'Loughlin hoped that the Home Secretary would make use of this point in any Commons statement. He took the view that the men were 'subordinating their religion to their purposes of revolt'. The chaplain's nose may have at this time been somewhat out of joint, since he told the Inspector that his influence over the men was nil, and they were completely out of hand as far as he was concerned (Colonel J. Winn to Commissioners, 6 June 1917; PRO HO 144/1453/311980/121). At the same time Dr O'Loughlin cultivated good relations with the men's supporters and sympathisers. On 5 May 1917, he wrote to Michael Collins (now at the Irish National Aid Association) giving assurances about the Lewes diet and thanking Collins for 'your kind help in so many ways' (NLI: Irish National Aid Association Papers: Ms. 24, 387 (unfoliated)).

76 Enclosure at PRO HO 144/1453/311980/112.

There was alarm in Whitehall about these developments. Sir Ernly Blackwell, the Home Office Legal Adviser, showed the Commissioners' letter to the Irish Chief Secretary, Henry Duke, who said he would inform the Prime Minister, 'as this incident might affect the Cabinet's decision as to the release of these convicts'.[77] The Commissioners insisted that 'The situation at Lewes is very grave' and that 'the contumacy has reached a very acute stage.' The men could not be moved from Lewes except by force since it was probable that they would refuse to leave their cells and would have to be carried. And it would not end there: 'if they went by train there would probably be scenes of disorder in public places and . . . when they arrived at their destination they would probably adopt the same tactics. . . . The whole difficulty would therefore began again in another Convict Prison.' They sought approval to remove the men either singly or in small parties of two or three, commencing with de Valera and the other leaders. All, by their disobedience, had forfeited privileges, and so would be removed in convict dress and in restraints. With their leaders gone the Commissioners hoped that 'a considerable section' would abandon their rebellious attitude. If they did not, however, the policy of decanting them to other prisons would continue.[78] Anxious to be rid of the troublesome Irish to the army it is possible that the Commissioners were drawing the blackest possible picture, but considerable disruption was more than likely.

Since the authorities had not granted prisoner-of-war status and were evidently preparing to neutralise the work-strike, de Valera's destruction campaign proceeded. It began with the breaking of cell windows. This was followed by attacks on cell doors and the smashing of the gaslight covers. Colonel Winn (who besides being an inspector was Secretary of the Prison Commission) reported that it was 'quite a new experience in prison life to have howling going on, punctuated by crashing of bed boards against the doors, and window smashing. When they commenced on the gas box glass, there was a tremendous hullabaloo with cheers etc.'[79] Two men broke the bricks that separated their cells and began to dismantle the whole wall, before they were stopped. One of these (McNestry) was removed to the punishment cells, but managed to shout out as he was being moved, which provoked a barrage of door-pounding. This last was a danger, since the Lewes cell doors were not iron-lined and could therefore have been smashed by persistent ramming with cell furniture. It was therefore decided to remove all bed-boards, stools and other items that could be used to batter or lever, unless the men gave undertakings not misuse them.

Dr O'Loughlin advised that the point of all the destruction was to compel the introduction of the military, 'so that these men can boast that by their efforts they have forced the Government to place them under Military control as Prisoners

77 Minute of 31 May 1917; ibid.
78 Ruggles-Brise to Troup, 4 June 1917; ibid.
79 Winn to Commissioners, 6 June 1917; PRO HO 144/1453/311980/121.

of War, and thus hope to gain kudos with the so-called Military Volunteers in Ireland'.[80] Little did de Valera or his comrades then know that the Commissioners also devoutly hoped that the army would take control of Lewes, removing the whole tiresome and messy problem from their otherwise orderly convict system.[81]

In accordance with the plan, the leaders were the first to be moved, and the rank and file followed over the succeeding days in parties which never exceeded seven men. Even as this got under way, however, destruction mounted. Some parties went by train, others, whom the authorities did not think they could trust to behave in public, went by car. One party from whom trouble was expected behaved well, Colonel Winn reported, 'But . . . one can never tell what may happen, as these . . . are such men of mood.'[82]

Within four days the men were more or less equally distributed between four prisons: thirty each at Parkhurst and Portland; twenty-eight at Maidstone; and thirty-one retained at Lewes. Dr O'Loughlin had contributed his knowledge of the men's character and antecedents, which altogether 'was most valuable in deciding on the destination and method of deportation of each man'.[83] He had also disclosed what one of the men had told him about their future course of action. They would do nothing that ordinary convicts do, and would not work; they would not exercise with ordinary convicts, nor would they allow their hair to be clipped with clippers used on other convicts, 'so that they should not contract venereal disease'. They would insist also on attending Sunday Mass. Various forms of protest were evidently contemplated in furtherance of these demands, but not a hunger-strike, Colonel Winn reported, 'as they did not wish to be considered as copying "Suffragettes"'.[84]

This, Ruggles-Brise decided, was the moment to do away with all political privileges and subject the men to the full rigours and controls of convict discipline. In his memorandum of 5 June 1917, reporting to the Home Secretary of the actions at Lewes, Ruggles-Brise could not prevent a tone of triumph and satisfaction from seeping through – and indeed more than a little vindication. Maidstone, Parkhurst and Portland governors were to be told that the Irish had forfeited all privileges by their bad behaviour. All outstanding letters and visits were to be cancelled and the ordinary convict allowance would be calculated on the basis of time served and good behaviour. A reception letter would be allowed on arrival at the men's new prison, and this and any future letters and visits

---

80 Ibid., memorandum, 7 June 1917.
81 The Commissioners' published account of the Lewes events – transfer thither, privileges, refusal of prisoner-of-war status, outbreak of indiscipline and destruction, transfer out and, finally, pardon and release, was a model of non-committal civil-service prose (see RCP, PP 1917–18 [Cd. 8764], XVIII, 109, 11–12).
82 Winn to Commissioners, 7 June 1917, PRO HO 144/1453/311980/121. The following day he reported that some of the men sang a little in the train, 'but not to attract attention very specially'.
83 Ibid., Report of 8 June 1917.
84 Ibid.

which they might earn would be referred to the Commissioners for censorship and approval. But since all were now subject to the ordinary convict rules they would remain in the Star Class – enjoying its very limited privileges, chief of which was segregation from non-Star prisoners.[85]

As the central mover in the Lewes troubles, de Valera received special treatment, and was removed on his own under Winn's supervision. De Valera's transfer in convict dress and in restraints was intended to emphasise his reinstated penal status. He was to be told that misconduct would be dealt with under the ordinary procedure of the Convict Rules; that is, depending on the gravity of the offence, there would be a hearing before the governor, or the Board of Visitors, to be followed by the usual punishment.

Since his incarceration de Valera had several times openly committed one of the most serious of prison offences – mutiny – for which flogging was prescribed. The threat of submission to the usual course of prison justice should have been salutary. But as with Rossa, and the other Fenians imprisoned in the late 1860s, such a punishment was effective only as a deterrent if there was a realistic prospect that it would be carried out, and no one believed that it would be politically acceptable to flog de Valera and his comrades. In such circumstances, the most severe punishments which could be imposed were confinement to a stripped-down punishment cell, with restricted diet, loss of remission or loss of privileges. These had the political consequence of increasing the likelihood that in Ireland the prisoners would be viewed as martyrs, rather than refractory convicts. Dietary punishment and cellular confinement had the further drawbacks, moreover, that in repeated doses a prisoner's health would be affected or even that the prisoner would seize the initiative and go on hunger-strike.[86] The transfers had already been reported in Irish newspapers with some exaggeration, as had the events at Lewes: Irish public opinion was ripe to be outraged, and de Valera and his followers were primed for sacrifice. Government failed to recognise that every opportunity would be seized to engage it in struggle, or that the majority of the prisoners regarded themselves as still being on active service. The normal rules of punishment and penal discipline could, in these circumstances, fan rather than smother disorder.

85 Evelyn Ruggles-Brise to Home Office, 5 June 1917: PRO HO 144/311980/121. He had no inkling that the men would be released within eleven days, and had he known, his feelings may have been mixed. Shot of the problem, but no punishment visited on those whom he evidently thought deserved it.

86 Curiously enough, no political capital had been made of two cases of insanity among the convicts (Tierney and Halpin). Both had been removed to asylums, where the Irish National Relief Fund arranged visits and other support (NLI: Irish National Aid Association Papers: Ms. 24, 324(2), letters of 28 February and 16 March 1917). One man, J. T. Cullen, had been freed under the rule which allowed for release on compassionate health grounds – essentially to die. With the assistance of the Aid Association Cullen was transferred to a sanatorium in Ireland, where he died almost immediately from what Michael Collins claimed was 'illness contracted in prison' (ibid). Despite this comment, Cullen's case was not taken up politically.

The behaviour of the convicts at their new prisons showed an unabated determination. On his arrival at Maidstone, for example, de Valera immediately started to break up his cell. Interviewed by the governor, he refused to stand or to button his prison dress. When moved to another cell he immediately started to damage it. He took the view, his biographers report, that 'There were fewer punishments than there were ways of breaking prison discipline'.[87]

Constance Markievicz

Constance Markievicz was the only woman among the rebel leaders, and probably the only woman known to have fired a gun that week.[88] For her part in the rising (she was second-in-command at the St Stephen's Green outpost) she was sentenced to death, as was her commanding officer, Michael Mallin. He was executed; she, 'solely & only on account of her sex', was reprieved and her sentence commuted to penal servitude for life.[89] Her biographer, Anne Marreco, reports that mercy came as an anti-climax, Constance exclaiming to her sister at Mountjoy prison, 'Why don't they let me die with my friends?'[90] Constance's guilt was certainly as great as that of some of the men who were executed but Maxwell had enough sense not to add to the obloquy of martyr creation by shooting a woman.[91]

87 Longford and O'Neill, op. cit., p. 59; Béaslaí, 1926, Vol. 1, p. 156.

88 Later she was to say that the Citizen Army was the only place she knew where command was given according to merit and that she had been appointed second-in-command the day after she joined, with instructions to take over entirely if anything happened to Connolly (PRO HO 144/1580/316818/16).

89 Schedule, Field General Court Martial, Constance Georgina Markievicz, 4 May 1916: PRO HO 144/1580/316818/16. Constance had been the object of much speculation and rumour, with many seeing her actions as being particularly shocking and against the grain of her sex. An Australian doctor, who had been staying at the Shelbourne Hotel, close to her command, cast her as a piratical termagant. He had seen her 'dressed as a man, with two revolvers stuck in her belt, at the head of a band of rebels. I was informed by an Irish doctor that she had shot six of them for hanging back when the soldiers appeared on the scene' (Dr Cecil D. McAdam reported in the New York Times, 15 May 1916, 2d–e). The story of her shooting her own men was without foundation, but the rumour is indicative of her reputation in respectable circles at this time.

90 For a time after the rising it appeared that Constance would have welcomed death; she certainly expected it (NLI: Gore-Booth Papers: Ms. 21, 815: Eva Gore-Booth Memoir, f. 9). See also Anne Marreco, The Rebel Countess: The Life and Times of Constance Markievicz, London, Weidenfeld & Nicolson, 1967, p. 212. The same author reports that Maura Perolz, also imprisoned for her part in the rising, found Constance in a state of exultation in the two days between the passing of the death sentence and the reprieve. Once the death sentence was respited she was removed from Kilmainham to Mountjoy Prison.

91 In his report to the King on 6 May 1916, Asquith gave an account of the Cabinet meeting that day. At Asquith's request General Maxwell gave a report on the situation in Dublin and the rest of Ireland. Maxwell had commuted the Markievicz death sentence, Asquith reported, and 'He was instructed not to allow the death sentence to be carried out in the case of any woman' (the Germans had eight months before committed what the British considered to be a war crime when Nurse Edith Cavell was executed at dawn on 12 October 1915, for assisting Allied officers) (PRO CAB/41/37/19: Asquith to George V, 6 May 1916).

The weeks after the rising were particularly gruelling. Not only did she know that many of her friends had been shot, but in solitary confinement in her Kilmainham cell awaiting her own court martial she heard the volleys that took Clarke, Pearse and MacDonagh on 3 May and William Pearse, Daly, Plunkett and O'Hanrahan the following day. Since General Maxwell did not confirm her sentence of penal servitude for life until 6 May, she must also have heard the execution of John MacBride on 5 May. She was transferred to Mountjoy on 7 May 1916. Her sister Eva, who visited a few days later, wondered whether she should tell her of the executions at Kilmainham that day of Ceannt and Connolly but Constance had already been told of these.[92] To anyone these would have been harrowing and indelible experiences, and to someone of Constance's sensitivities and loyalties an appalling nightmare. Not only were there the repeated execution volleys, but in some cases following shots as the *coup de grâce* was administered.[93]

Constance and her supporters claimed that for several months after the executions this awful experience was given an extra dimension because she was cut off 'from ordinary human companionship'.[94] If this phrase means that her only or principal companionship came from visitors, prison officials and other prisoners, it is true, but it raises the question of who would have qualified to provide this companionship – presumably only family, friends, and sympathisers – and that is not the nature of imprisonment for anyone. It is true that the ordinary convict regime at Mountjoy and Aylesbury meant long periods of confinement in one's cell. Supper was served at 4.30 p.m. and lock-up for the night was 5.30 p.m.; at weekends the periods of solitude were even longer. But Constance had been worldly-wise enough to seek employment on the one work party that was guaranteed more out-of-cell time than any other: the prison kitchen.

The hardship of which Constance most complained was the long daily period of cellular confinement. It was not simply solitude to which she objected, but solitude peculiarly combined with lack of privacy. Each cell had a spyhole concavely recessed into the door, which Constance described as being carved and painted to resemble an eye, with eyelashes, eyebrow and pupil – the last fitted with a shutter which the warders could operate in order to look into the

---

92 NLI: Gore-Booth Papers: Ms. 21, 816: Eva Gore-Booth Memoir, ff. 6–7. It is possible that this visit was on 8 May, but since Eva refers to the execution of Connolly and Ceannt on the same day, it seems safer to take the later date, 12 May (Ceannt was executed on 8 May). Constance was greatly concerned about other friends and during one of her sister's visits passed her a note (written on toilet paper) listing these, and giving addresses and other details. Eva was instructed not to write but to reply 'first chance by hand & tell me *Christian names* next visit' (NLI: Eva Gore-Booth Papers: Ms. 21, 816: undated but probably Eva's first visit).
93 See plea on behalf of Markievicz, c. January 1917: PRO HO 144/1580/316818/11.
94 Ibid.

cell. The eye – possibly painted by an imaginative sadist, or given form by Constance's fancies – had a depressing effect.[95]

It hardly seemed likely that Constance Markievicz posed the kind of security and control problems that necessitated the transfer to England of convicted and interned men, but she had established and was using effective channels of communication with the outside world. This had the potential of making propaganda and embarrassing the government, and there was always a residual danger that her escape could be engineered.[96] After she had been at Mountjoy Prison for two months, therefore, General Maxwell wrote to the Home Office, requesting her removal to England. The prison was not secure from leakages of information. Lady visitors were thought to be one source of the information which was getting out, and the visiting justices the other. Noting that there were sixteen visiting justices at the prison, Maxwell pointed out that eight of these were appointed by Dublin Corporation, 'which it is well known, has strong Sinn Féin sympathies. . . . It is obvious that the Dublin Corporation members would be most likely to attend and inspect the prison.'[97] The Home Office, as we shall see, had been somewhat reluctant to accept the female internees who had been sent to England the month before, and certainly there was no question of holding them in ordinary prison accommodation. A female wing had been specially cleared for them. Constance Markievicz was in a different category again, and while she could be accommodated in England, she could not be allowed to mix with the five women internees at Lewes. She would have to take her chances, rather, with the Aylesbury criminal convicts.[98]

On 4 August authority was given to transfer Constance from Mountjoy to Aylesbury Convict Prison. She travelled via London and Holloway Prison, arriving at Aylesbury on 8 August.[99] As with the male convicts during the first six months of their incarceration, Constance was treated as an ordinary criminal, and as a first-timer of good character was placed in the Star Class. This meant little by way of privileges, but involved separation from women thought to be more steeped in crime. After some time, a small but important concession was granted, and as with de Valera and certain others among the men, she was allowed to have writing materials, or rather, drawing materials. She had the

95 Marreco, op. cit., pp. 220–1; May Churchill Sharpe (Chicago May: Her Story, London, Sampson Low & Co, 1929, p. 186) refers to the 'eye' thus: 'Poor Countess Markievicz told me her "eye" pretty nearly drove her mad. For the first week she was there . . . she said she had to walk the floor every night, trying to exorcize the devilish thing. Punishment was bound to follow if you defaced it or were caught covering it.'

96 On 19 July 1916, General Maxwell complained to Herbert Samuel about Constance's communications, almost certainly through the visiting justices.

97 PRO HO 144/1455/313106/6; PRO HO 144/1580/316818/10.

98 Edward Troup to Brigadier-General J. A. Byrne (Deputy Adjutant General, Ireland), 6 June 1916: PRO HO 144/1455/313106/6.

99 PRO HO 144/1580/316818/7.

regular convict diet and was obliged to work. At first she was assigned to the sewing-room and then, by her own request for more energetic work, was put in the kitchen. Because of her social connections, and also presumably because of her curiosity value, quite a number of people wished to visit, and these requests were liberally granted.[100] These visitors brought light, colour and variety into a daily round which otherwise was the epitome of monotony and monochrome.

Constance was cast into the company of her criminal comrades very much more than were her male counterparts. Of the twenty Star Class women whom Constance joined at Aylesbury twelve had been convicted of wilful murder, one of attempted murder, three of manslaughter and one of wounding. These, of course, were offences to which Constance has aspired in her military actions on Stephen's Green, although she operated at a wholesale rather than a retail level, and was motivated more by national loves and hates than the pitiful domestic miseries of her prison companions.[101] There were some refined and educated women among her companions, but others were 'the lowest of the low'. The worst penalty that could be inflicted on 'patriot rebels', she wrote, was to associate them with 'low class criminals'.[102] She strongly objected to some of the immoral conversations – 'The "gay life" and how to "put away" a baby without being caught were always being discussed; disgusting jokes were passed around.' This conversation, which was conducted surreptitiously in violation of the supposed silence rule was, Constance insisted, 'a torment to some of the ordinary prisoners, and a gradual training in vice to others'. She saw her own experience as part of a general strategy of the British government to destroy the moral character of the Irish prisoners – 'to try and break them mentally, morally and physically by herding them with the worst criminals, depriving them of books, writing materials and decent companionship and confining them in unsanitary and disued prisons'.[103]

As women in other parts of the prison had been involved in prostitution, or had led sexually immoral lives, there was, Constance wrote, 'one horror always hanging over our heads, and that was the fear of catching loathsome diseases'. The kitchen in which she worked served the Borstal section of the prison, which she said contained up to 150 young women.[104] The food-trays on which

---

100 Dryhurst (Prison Commissioner) to Troup (Under-Secretary, Home Office), 27 March 1917: PRO HO 144/1580/316818/33A.

101 None of the Star Class women with whom Constance was accommodated had been convicted of prostitution, though eight had illegitimate children. Seven had been convicted of the murder of these children (presumably babies). It is probable that the other murders had a domestic background (see letter of Dr S. F. Fox (governor) to Prison Commission, 21 December 1916: PRO HO 144/1580/316818/10).

102 *San Francisco Examiner*, 7 December 1919, 6f. This retrospective article was written as the Anglo-Irish war was entering its most violent phase, and Constance expected re-arrest.

103 Ibid., 16f–g.

104 This was no exaggeration on Constance's part. The average daily population of Borstal girls at Aylesbury in 1916–17 was 165 (RCP, PP, 1917–18 [Cd. 8764], XVIII, 109, Appendix no. 1).

these prisoners were served were often returned to the kitchen 'in a state too disgusting to be described'. It was not possible to keep them clean. This problem became more acute when the Medical Office began to examine the Borstal girls for venereal disease. Those who proved positive had their mess-tins marked with a 'D' and instructions were given to keep these separate from the others. No adequate provision was made for this, however, and as the Medical Officer diagnosed more cases, the 'D' trays became hopelessly mixed up with the others.[105]

The 'extreme dirt' seems to have been the characteristic which Constance found most striking 'after you have got used to being amazed at the [silliness] . . . of it all'. As was said of the armed services at the time, the prison's public surfaces were scrubbed and polished, but behind the scenes there was a great deal of sordidness. The prisoners' baths were so dirty that Constance and others refused to use them until they were cleaned – 'Vermin was constantly crawling over one.' The porridge ladle which was used to dole out the evening meal was left for the night, Constance claimed, 'in a dirty pail with the brush which was used to sweep out the lavatory'.[106]

Constance's partisanship sometimes outran the accuracy of her memory. In September 1916, she complained about the prison food. Since she had lost eight pounds in weight during her first month at the prison she was asked to go into the infirmary where she could be put on a special diet. She turned this offer down, preferring to stay with the kitchen work party. She had complained that the state of her teeth made it hard for her to eat the prison meat. Orders were given for it to be minced for her, and she was referred to the dentist who fitted her with a denture. Her weight thereafter increased to its original level. She continued to complain to her visitors about the food, but at no time returned any of it. In February 1917, she told two visitors (Miss Esther Roper and Lady Clare Annesley) that she could not eat the fish because it was the 'large variety which fed on human beings', and therefore had only the rice that accompanied it. She also told them that she lived on only bread. This was untrue, since she ate a range of prison foods.[107]

Three years later in Hearst's *San Francisco Examiner* the Countess stuck to her story of very poor food and drastic loss of weight: 'The black bread did not agree with me and they put me into hospital when my weight dropped to about 98 pounds. It had been 136 pounds when I left Mountjoy gaol, and even that was a good deal below my normal weight.[108] Because of her unique position of leadership in the rising, and her subsequent rebel career, Markievicz's Home

Office file, with its many prison entries, has survived in a full state. It may be said with some confidence therefore that she was never in hospital at Aylesbury prison and that her weight dropped to 120 pounds, rising to 129 pounds at some of her monthly weighings.[109]

Like her male comrades, Constance Markievicz was undoubtedly shocked by convict conditions in England, and there were certainly many aspects of the convict's life which were sordid, and which left a sense of both physical and moral contamination. She had, for example, been given (and retained throughout her time at Aylesbury) a mattress 'so dirty that I cannot describe it'. The notion that she was sleeping on such an object must have preyed on her mind – as it would on any person with decent sensibilities and background. Contamination also came from her convict clothing, passed on from another woman who had been released: 'The shoes were full of holes which let in wet and snow.'[110] But these were the normal conditions of penal servitude, not part of a British plot to break the spirit of the Irish political prisoners. And nowhere in her accounts of imprisonment does Constance draw attention to her privileges over and above the lot of the common convict – a generous allowance of extended visits and correspondence, books and writing materials.

Constance continued her war against the Crown through the prison authorities. Her exaggerations and complaints were battles in this conflict, but she also acted more directly and at times defiantly. On her first morning in the Aylesbury sewing workshop she refused to stand when the governor made her rounds of inspection: 'Firmly, but politely, I refused to show respect to any British official.' After Dr Fox had passed through the warders coaxed and threatened Constance. She remained obdurate, and the next morning the warder announced that in future the governor did not wish the women to stand, since it interrupted their work: 'So the first morning I won a victory for the unfortunate people.'[111]

To become a medical doctor and a governor of a prison required outstanding qualities in a woman at this time. To dress in men's clothes and lead a socialistic militia in rebellion against the British Empire betokened an equally remarkable personality. As might be expected, Dr Fox and the rebel Countess did not peacefully co-exist at Aylesbury. Dr Fox apparently did not leave a memoir of her career, and her official correspondence dealing with Constance is carefully neutral, if cool. Constance was subject to no such restraint: 'A more unsuitable person to control a gaol it has never been my misfortune or experience to come across, though I have had some experiences.' She described Dr Fox as 'a woman with neither heart nor imagination'. The condemnation continued with revealing hauteur: Dr Fox did not even possess 'The instinct of an ordinary coachman

---

109 PRO HO 144/1580/31618/18: Attachment.
110 *San Francisco Examiner*, 7 December 1919, 16d.
111 Ibid., 16c. Constance was not above a little self-congratulation: 'This episode put me on good terms with my fellow convicts in the workroom.'

which makes him pride himself of the good condition of the animals under his charge'.[112]

Constance continued to over-egg the pudding in her conversation with visitors. On a visit in January 1917, she told Esther Roper and Lady Clare Annesley that her court martial had been unfair and that a sentry had been placed on the door to prevent the entry of witnesses in her favour. She asked them to pass this information on to Gavan Duffy. None of the others whose accounts of their court martial have survived made this complaint, and the consensus was that as far as procedure went, the courts martial were fair. Her court-martial papers show clearly that she was second-in-command at Stephen's Green and that she was armed and fired shots. She did not deny this, and evidently expected the death penalty that was passed on her. The court-martial record shows that she asked questions of one witness, declined to question another and did not wish to call witnesses on her own behalf. She told the court 'I went out to fight for Ireland's freedom and it doesn't matter what happens to me. I did what I thought was right and I stand by it.'[113] There was no truth whatsoever in her claim that she had been unfairly treated.

From prison she did what she could to harass officialdom. Misrepresentation of her treatment was one way to do this, pestering another. Esther Roper told her that supporters and sympathisers were constantly approaching the Home Office trying to get concessions for her, including daily visits. Constance then asked her 'to send as many people as she could each day to worry the officials, as that was the only way to get anything out of the government'. Constance also said that all those who wished to see her should apply to the Home Office for visits, and if she were asked she would say that she knew them 'even if she had never heard of them'.[114]

Appalled and moved by the condition of the Dublin poor, Constance could not wholly stifle her sympathies for some of her fellow inmates at Aylesbury – repulsive though she found their moral standards. While she was at the prison there were a number of suicide attempts among the Borstal girls. One tried to cut her throat, another set fire to her cell, several attempted hanging, and others swallowed buttons and huge needles: 'Poor girls! It seemed so wicked and futile to drive them to this.'[115] One of the women, a 'gangster's moll', had been

112 Ibid., 16b. Constance objected to Dr Fox's lectures on the progress of the war, which were given in the prison chapel: 'and to ensure my receiving a kindly welcome from the convicts she had given a lecture on "Easter Week Rebellion" mentioning me shortly before my arrival. Later on the convicts explained to me that this was the reason they had not been over-friendly on my arrival.' That there was hostility to the Irish at Aylesbury – both staff and prisoners – was confirmed by 'Chicago May' (see May Churchill Sharpe, *op. cit.*, p. 84).
113 PRO HO 144/1580/316818/16.
114 Ibid., Principal Matron's note of visit by Miss Esther Roper and Lady Clare Annesley, 26 January 1917.
115 *San Francisco Examiner*, 7 December 1919, 6f.

involved in a shooting incident between her rival lovers. This lady, who went by the sobriquet 'Chicago May', seems to have become a close companion, drawn to Constance by adversity and nationality. The two women met by chance some years later and renewed their acquaintance.[116]

Constance passed the hours of her cellular solitude in a number of ways. She had been allowed a notebook in which to do literary work, conditional only on her not writing about politics or prison life. In March 1917 she asked Frederick Dryhurst, a Commissioner who was visiting the prison, if she could have a notebook with plain rather than lined paper, since she had made various pen-and-ink drawings to accompany her poems. Dryhurst immediately agreed to this.[117] She received an allowance of incoming letters so generous that it included postcards.[118] (No convict on a monthly allowance of one letter in and one out would have accepted postcards.)

Certainly these privileges would have taken some of the edge off solitude, but did not remove its impact. Hanna Sheehy Skeffington, who knew Constance well, supposed that she felt the pains of imprisonment keenly: 'Madam, who loved the fresh air, sunlight and freedom, must have suffered a lot from prison. It must have shortened her life by many years.'[119] Some indication of her introspection and spirit at this time was given in a 1926 letter to Esther Roper (written after Constance's sister Eva had died). She expressed her sense of loss, but also some of her sense of Eva's presence, and recalled that when she was in Aylesbury the two had agreed to try to get in touch for a few minutes each day:

> I used to sit at about 6 o.c. & think of her & concentrate & try & leave my mind blank, a sort of dark still pool, & I got to her & could tell her how she sat in the window & I seemed to know what she was thinking. It was a great comfort to me. When I got out, I lost this in the bustle and hurry of life; but now just in the last few days I seem to get in touch again.[120]

---

116 'Chicago May' (May Churchill Sharpe) was born near Dublin in 1876, and ran away from home at the age of 13, living in New York and London. For her involvement in the Guerin shooting she received a sentence of fifteen years' penal servitude and was deported to the United States of America after some ten years. She claimed that relatives and friends took the Volunteer side in the 1916 rising (see Sharpe, op. cit., ch. 22; Marreco, op. cit., pp. 228–9; Esther Roper (ed.), Prison Letters of Countess Markievicz, London, Longman & Co, 1934, pp. 147–76).

117 Dryhurst to Troup, 27 March 1917: PRO HO 144/1580/316818/33a.

118 Three of these postcards survive: two sent on St Patrick's Day 1917, and one at Easter that year (NLI: Frederick J. Allen Papers: Ms. 26, 765).

119 NLI: Sheehy Skeffington Papers: Ms. 24, 189: Memoir of Countess Markievicz by Hanna Sheehy Skeffington, f. 3.

120 Constance Markievicz to Esther Roper, undated (? summer, 1926): NLI: Eva Gore-Booth Papers: Ms. 21, 816 (unfoliated).

The privileges for the male convicts announced by Herbert Samuel on 14 November, particularly the concession of talking together, highlighted Constance's isolation. The fact that there were other Irish rebels at Aylesbury with whom she was allowed no contact must have been particularly tantalising for her. The men had been brought together at Lewes so that they could enjoy an enhanced regime, whereas she continued to have the limited and at times highly undesirable company of Chicago May and other criminals. Peremptorily Ruggles-Brise had determined that it would be extremely difficult to allow privileges to Constance as she was on her own at Aylesbury. He therefore proposed that no action be taken.[121] Nothing in the files or in her own accounts or the memoirs of friends indicates that she found the company of the German spies Wertheim and Bournonville any more acceptable than the murderers and infanticides among whom she lived.

Once the male convicts had been brought together at Lewes, and the issue of their de facto political status had apparently been settled, more weight was put behind the campaign to improve Constance's position. Several people took a hand in this, including such usual suspects as Alfred Byrne, who forwarded a statement about Constance that had more than likely been put together by Art O'Brien.[122] This emphasised that alone of the Irish convicts Constance was unable to enjoy the privileges of association and conversation, 'not because of any faulty conduct on her part, but because she is a woman'. The company to which Constance had been restricted since her arrest, the statement argued, was that of 'the dregs of the population'. She had no one to speak to apart from prostitutes who had been convicted for murder or violence, 'and the atmosphere and conversation in which she has lived all this time has been "the atmosphere and conversation of a brothel"'.[123] This statement recognised implicitly the practical difficulty arising from Constance being the only female convict among the rebels, but claimed that this could be resolved by 'a little commonsense adjustment on the part of the authorities': the nature of this adjustment was not specified.[124]

The 'commonsense adjustment' boiled down to two possibilities: the opening of a female wing at Lewes or sending Constance to Holloway Prison in London,

121 Memorandum, Evelyn Ruggles-Brise to Home Office, 10 November 1916: PRO HO 144/1453/311980/34.
122 See above, pp. 483–8.
123 Dr Fox, governor of Aylesbury Prison, objected to this characterisation of her charges. Among the Star Class women (Constance's group) there was no direct evidence that any had been a prostitute, though eight (of the twenty) had illegitimate children. Many of the Star Class 'cannot by any means be classed as "the dregs of the population". Several have had no charge of murder or violence at all and are quite decent well-behaved women.' She also said that the assertion that the atmosphere and conversation was that of a brothel was 'a gross exaggeration' (Dr S. F. Fox to Prison Commission, 21 December 1916: PRO HO 144/316818/10).
124 PRO HO 144/1580/316818/10.

where there would be greater ease of access for her friends and she would be allowed visits of perhaps an hour a day, to compensate for the lack of suitable association and conversation. Neither of these suggestions found favour with the Prison Commission. Frederick Dryhurst (who had special responsibility for women prisoners) argued that the Lewes proposition was impossible, and that the female wing there was being used for those Irish convicts sentenced to imprisonment. He passed on Dr Fox's information about the Aylesbury women with whom Constance was classed and observed that it was impossible to prevent female prisoners from talking, and that in any event they got the privilege of 'conversational' exercise earlier in their sentences than did men. After four months at Aylesbury conversation was allowed on Sunday afternoons between women in adjoining cells, who sat outside their cells for this purpose. Sensing perhaps that he was missing the point of the case that had been made on Constance's behalf, Dryhurst noted that if she had objected to conversing with her neighbour, she could have gone without it.[125]

There were further attempts to persuade the Commissioners to take the Lewes option. Captain J. H. White, DSO, had approached Henry Duke, then the Irish Chief Secretary, and had pressed the case. 'Countess Markievicz,' he wrote, 'is one of my very greatest friends and in many ways one of the finest women that ever breathed. It's horrible to think of her in the surroundings she now is when but for her sex she would immediately have the privilege of associating with decent and sympathetic people granted to the men.' White suggested her transfer to Lewes to be with the other Irish convicts. She did not want the privilege of freer association in Aylesbury.[126] Duke was sufficiently taken with this plea to forward it to the Home Office, which replied that it was impossible to do as suggested, outlining the privileges she was receiving at Aylesbury and denying that she was living in the atmosphere and conversation of a brothel.[127]

When the internees were freed, the IRB through its front organisations began to campaign for the release of the convicts, and Constance, because of her name, character and circumstances was particularly useful in dramatising the issues. On 27 December 1916, John O'Dowd, MP for Sligo (the county in which Constance had been born and raised), pressed her case and was told that she had received

125 Ibid., Minute of 22 December 1916. He added that since she was unable to associate with the male Irish convicts he had extended her monthly visits to three-quarters of an hour.
126 White to Duke, 21 December 1916: PRO HO 144/1580/316818/11. White urged Duke to help: 'I am sure that Ireland would appreciate her being treated chivalrously.'
127 Ibid., Minute of 3 January 1917. The Home Office did not explain fully why it was impossible to remove Constance to Lewes. The principal objection was not that the female wing had been allocated to those serving sentences of imprisonment. Lewes had been brought into use solely for the Irish and had abundant accommodation in several wings. Staffing was probably the main obstacle – assuming that the notion of Constance associating with the men was acceptable to all. She would have required three or even four wardresses to look after her, and the cost of this would have been prohibitive.

all the privileges extended to the men, except association – and that because she was the only female convict among the Irish rebels.[128] Early in 1917 Art O'Brien, through the Irish National Relief Fund, protested that the government had not kept the pledge which Samuel had given on 14 November. The male convicts had been collected together at Lewes and given the promised concessions. The Home Office had refused to make similar arrangements for Constance because of 'puritanism and officialism'.[129] This appeal was renewed on 17 and 23 February 1917. Miss Louie Bennett, a prominent Irish female suffragist and labour activist, wrote on behalf of the Irishwomen's International League.[130] She rehearsed the complaints about Constance and referred to the moral character of her Aylesbury companions ('lowest type of criminals . . . close association with prostitutes of infamous character'), but somewhat to her credit did not leave it there. She added that the circumstances had shown 'the serious need for a reform of the system which exposes moral women prisoners to the dangers of contact with professional prostitutes'.[131] Art O'Brien followed in the same tack, insisting that the directors of convict prisons were making no real effort in the matter, that government had given a clear pledge and that the impasse was 'a callous breach of faith'.[132]

Spurred by the various representations, C. P. Scott of the *Manchester Guardian*, on 25 February 1917, raised Constance's case privately with Lloyd George. Did he propose to do anything about the differential treatment she was receiving? She had to choose between 'solitary confinement and association with the lowest female criminals and prostitutes', while the male leaders had been allowed to associate with each other. Lloyd George was unimpressed. He was not willing to do anything to improve her conditions and remarked that 'a little solitary confinement would do her no harm'.[133]

It was an altogether different story in the United States of America. In the critical weeks when that country was considering whether or not to join the Allied cause, the British Embassy cabled that the story was circulating that Countess Markievicz was being ill-treated in Aylesbury. This prompted Lord Hardinge at the Foreign Office to write to Troup. Since he was sure that the stories of ill-treatment were without foundation he did not see how the Embassy could be instructed to say that the Countess was to receive better treatment. He asked instead for some facts which could be used to avert the agitation on Constance's behalf: 'It is most important just now that there should be no fly in

128 O'Dowd to Home Secretary, 27 December 1916: PRO HO 144/316818/12.
129 NLI: Art O'Brien Papers: Ms. 8, 442 (unfoliated).
130 Bennett (1870–1956) was an associate of Winifred Carney in the Irish Women Workers' Union. She went on to a career in the Irish trade union movement and Labour Party.
131 Louie Bennett to Home Secretary, 17 February 1917: PRO HO 144/1580/316818/20.
132 Art O'Brien to Home Secretary, 23 February 1916: PRO HO 144/1580/316818/21.
133 Trevor Wilson (ed.), *The Political Diaries of C. P. Scott 1911–1928*, London, Collins, 1970, p. 264.

the ointment.'[134] Troup emphasised the supposed benefits of the Star Class, the extra privileges accorded to her and her facilities for literary composition. He even injected an idyllic note: 'She . . . writes poetry and makes drawings.'[135]

Art O'Brien's Irish National Relief Fund had proposed a compromise on the question of Constance's association: she should be brought to Holloway and allowed a visit of one hour's duration a day.[136] This proposal stood no chance of success. Constance had been removed from Dublin in large part because of the stream of visitors she was receiving and the information and views which she was able to pass out. To place her in a prison close to the centre of London, where access would have been infinitely easier for a range of friends, supporters and sympathetic politicians and journalists, and where she could hold court for an hour a day, was surely an attractive option for her. And the complaints about the nature of her associates would have remained: Holloway functioned as a local prison and a major portion of its intake consisted of drunks, prostitutes, petty thieves and public brawlers. This stage army had, if anything, even more potential to be represented by republican sympathisers as the dregs of society. Given no encouragement, the Holloway option was not vigorously pursued.

A confidential offer had come from another source, and the failure of the Home Office to take it up justifies at least some of the complaints of inflexibility against it. By December 1916 only Carney and Moloney remained at Ayles-bury[137] and Carney approached the authorities to allow her to have contact with Markievicz. On 1 December she petitioned the Home Secretary, drawing attention to the privileges that had recently been granted to the male convicts, especially that of association. Countess Markievicz was the only female convict among the Irish rebels, 'and is therefore debarred from enjoying the greatest of these privileges, which is association with friends. From experience I know that the other concessions will make comparatively little difference to her comfort if she is cut off from companionship.' Carney offered herself for the same convict treatment as the Countess if the two were allowed association: 'I will freely and gladly agree to live in the prison and conform to the rules with regard to food, work, hours of exercise and clothes if necessary . . . I pledge my word of honour not to make either now nor at any future date, political capital out of this

---

134 Lord Hardinge of Penshurst to Sir Edward Troup, 26 March 1917: PRO HO 144/1580/316818/33a.
135 Troup to Hardinge, 27 March 1917: ibid.
136 NIL: Art O'Brien Papers: Ms. 8442 (unfoliated).
137 Ellen Ryan signed the required undertaking and was released. There was no question of Carney and Maloney being released, stated Home Secretary Herbert Samuel, 'even if they were willing to give the prescribed undertaking' (5 *Hansard*, LXXXVI, cols 175–6; 12 October 1916). This remained the position at the end of October (5 *Hansard*, LXXXVI, col. 1554; 31 October 1916). Shortly afterwards, however, Samuel was prepared to release one of the two (Winifred Carney) provided she found sureties and gave an undertaking (5 *Hansard*, LXXXVII, col. 233; 8 November 1916; see also ibid., col. 379; 9 November 1916). Carney did not avail herself of this offer.

arrangement.'[138] The concession, had it been granted, would have been short-lived, since within three weeks Carney, with the other internees, was to be set free – but it was a kind and compassionate gesture. Prisoners, Oscar Wilde had insisted, were the 'only really humanizing influence in prison'.[139] This may have been fanciful exaggeration, and they certainly could not be allowed to arrange the terms of their confinement, and so the reply was inevitable. Miss Carney was informed that the Secretary of State had considered her petition 'but is unable to accede hereto'.[140] Constance continued to be cast among her criminal crew.

Whatever the intentions of the government, the Countess was in a position which compared unfavourably with that of her male co-convicts. With the departure of Winifred Carney and Helena Moloney in the Christmas release of internees, any prospect of association with other political offenders was lost. Early in March Robert Lynd, a Belfast-born and sympathetic journalist, raised her plight in the pages of the Nation. The male convicts were permitted to meet each other for an hour each day. This privilege was an acknowledgement that the Irish political prisoners belonged to a special class. The Countess Markievicz was allowed a visitor once a fortnight. By way of compensation for her situation as the sole female political convict, surely she should be allowed a daily visit of one hour. The letter appeared on St Patrick's Day, 1917, but evoked no response from the Home Office.[141]

Amnesty for the convicts

Two days after the internees returned to Ireland (Christmas Eve, 1916), Dillon announced that his party would campaign for the convicts, asking that their cases be reopened and sentences revised. The Freeman's Journal went further, however, and asked for a general amnesty: a week later Dublin Corporation endorsed this appeal.[142] It was one thing to release unconvicted internees, some of whom were possibly wholly innocent of any involvement in rebellion or

---

138 Petition of Winifred Carney, 1 December 1916; PRO HO 144/1457/314179/8.
139 Daily Chronicle, 28 May 1897, 10d: 'Their cheerfulness under terrible circumstances, their sympathy for each other, their humility, their gentleness, their smiles of greeting when they meet each other . . . are all quite wonderful and I myself learned many sound lessons from them.'
140 Reply to Carney Petition, 11 December 1916; PRO HO 144/1457/314179/8.
141 Nation, 17 March 1917, p. 803.
142 The Times, 27 December 1916, 4c; 9 January 1917, 7f; Freeman's Journal, 25 December 1916, 4d. The Irish National Aid Association seems to have been laggardly in this campaign, since as late as 28 March 1917 Art O'Brien wrote to urge it to begin agitating for amnesty and expressing surprise that it had not done so before. This was a particularly opportune time, he wrote, since the Russian provisional government had been universally congratulated for its leniency towards political offenders. If the Association had insufficient resources to lead a campaign it should make its position clear and ask some other body to take the lead (O'Brien to Irish National Aid Association, 28 March 1917: NLI: Irish National Aid Association Papers: Ms. 24, 324(2)).

subversion, and none of whom had faced a court; it was quite another to release men who had been sentenced to lengthy terms of penal servitude and imprisonment by a court – albeit a military one. The release of the internees had, moreover, been a means of testing Irish opinion, and also the behaviour of those released. The last was reassuring, at least in the early months of 1917. The rising's trauma and confusion had been succeeded by a period of calm, which was reinforced by martial law. According to William O'Brien, the released internees, as well as the Volunteers who had not been interned, for their various reasons kept 'quiet and out of the way. Nobody advocated any particular course to be followed.'[143]

As in the aftermath of Young Ireland, and the Fenians, there was a regrouping around the issues of relief for the families of those who had been executed, the convicts and the internees. But beneath the relatively calm surface a great deal of hatred and bitterness seethed, and daily intensified. The IRB had survived, had taken in new blood at Frongoch, and now awaited a chance to resume its military activities; the Irish Volunteers were in the process of reorganisation. A by-election in North Roscommon provided a chance for the more militant nationalists to strike a blow against the Irish Parliamentary Party, and the father of the executed Joseph Plunkett was put forward as a candidate and sturdily supported by the militants. His victory – by 3022 votes to 1708 – in what had been a safe Irish Party seat was a sensation, but may have lulled the British government into believing that militancy was willing to take the parliamentary path – even though after election Plunkett followed the Sinn Féin line of refusing to take his Westminster seat.

The North Roscommon defeat was viewed by Redmond and the other parliamentary leaders as a disaster, a view which was confirmed by further Sinn Féin victories in by-elections in May, July and August. The Irish convicts provided the basis for business as usual in the Commons. Militant nationalists continued to ask the type of question that they had put before the freeing of the internees, scarcely needing to change the wording.[144] To the bafflement of the Irish Party, government seemed set on keeping the Irish pot boiling, with a series of DORA arrests and re-arrests and removals from Ireland. This seemed to John Dillon to be a reversal of a policy of conciliation which had 'haltingly no doubt and slowly' been developed by government the previous autumn. 'Our task,' he told the government, 'has been for a long while difficult, and you are making it impossible.'[145]

---

143 Edward MacLysaght (ed.), *Forth the Banners Go: Reminiscences of William O'Brien*, Dublin, At the Sign of the Three Candles, 1969, p. 137.

144 Byrne and Ginnell were vociferous and untiring. See, for example, 5 *Hansard*, XC, col. 446; 13 February 1917; ibid., col. 1342; 21 February 1917; ibid., XC, col. 20; 5 March 1917; ibid., XC, cols 1439–41; 16 March 1917. Even Frongoch made a reappearance, with Larry Ginnell demanding to know by what statutory authority books had been withheld from internees, and where did blame lie for a case of insanity among them? (ibid., XCI, cols 1937–8; 21 March 1917).

145 5 *Hansard*, XC, col. 1787; 26 February 1917.

A number of factors were coming together which would make it impossible for government further to resist amnesty for the convicts. One was the declining fortunes of the Irish Party, and the urgent need to give it a boost. This in itself was far from sufficient to produce a change in policy, however. On 6 April 1917 the geometry of Irish politics shifted significantly, with the entry into the war of the United States of America. Irish-American opinion was raised in significance and influence, and regard had to be paid to President Wilson's pronouncements on the right to self-determination of small nations. Still government clung to the line that disciplinary concessions had been made to the convicts and it was neither legal nor expedient to go further.[146] Irish members responded with questions about prison conditions, the legality of courts-martial convictions, and – repeatedly – demands for amnesty. The frequency of the questions and their repetition exactly replicated the campaign which had been waged over Frongoch, except that the flow of information from the prisoners was not so good, and the questions and comments had, perforce, to be more general.[147]

In an attempt to set a new course, on 21 May 1917, Lloyd George announced the establishment of an Irish Convention, at which Nationalists and Unionists and other representatives would attempt to iron out their differences.[148] The principal parties welcomed the announcement, but the cross-over Sinn Féin Member, Larry Ginnell, sounded an uncomfortable note of reality when he reminded the House that the 'men at Lewes' had to have a place at the Convention, if it was not to be a 'fraud and deception'.[149] In a seething hour-long rant against his former colleagues in the Irish Party ('hired tools against their own country' and 'degraded and unnatural followers of their philandering leaders'), Ginnell insisted that they could not negotiate for Ireland.[150] Henry Duke responded to amnesty demands with an ambiguous statement that 'The time had not yet come to reopen the cases.'[151] The issue was pressed the following day and two days after that, with the same outcome.[152] On 25 May T. P. O'Connor, one of the Redmondite nationalists condemned by Ginnell and others for selling out to the British, intervened in the Whitsun adjournment debate to plead for the convicts' release. There was no act the government could do, O'Connor insisted, 'which would do so much to help to appease the very troubled feelings

---

146 5 *Hansard*, XCII, col. 1291; 4 April 1917; ibid., col. 1317; ibid., col. 1504; 17 April 1917; ibid., col. 1841; 19 April 1917; ibid., col. 2194; 24 April 1917.

147 Ibid., col. 2611; 26 April 1917; ibid., XCIII, cols 616–17; 4 May 1917; ibid., col. 896; 8 May 1917; ibid., cols 1065–6; 9 May 1917; ibid., col. 1331, 14 May 1917; ibid., col. 1481; 15 May 1917; ibid., cols 1600–1; 16 May 1917.

148 Ibid., XCIII, cols 1995–2000; 21 May 1917. On behalf of the Irish Party John Redmond fulsomely welcomed the announcement.

149 Ibid., XCIII, col. 2029; 21 May 1917.

150 Ibid., cols 2027–38; 21 May 1917.

151 Ibid., col. 1953; 21 May 1917.

152 Ibid., cols 2121–2; 22 May 1917; cols 2509–10; 24 May 1917.

in Ireland today.'[153] This heartfelt plea from constitutional nationalism found no response, and so the dreary exchanges resumed after the recess, questions alternating between Alfie Byrne and Larry Ginnell, with sniping at the Convention supplementing their usual prison fare.[154] The disciplinary removal of the convicts from Lewes stimulated further heated questions and interventions.[155] While putting up a stern front, however, the coalition government was moving to a decision, and on 15 June, the Unionist, Andrew Bonar Law, Chancellor of the Exchequer, rose to announce an amnesty 'without reservation, of the prisoners now in confinement in connection with the rebellion of 1916'.[156] On behalf of the Irish Party John Devlin was sufficiently carried away to imagine that the prisoners returning to Ireland would 'lend a hand in the softening of racial acerbities and the creation of that better feeling which will bring peace and blessings to Ireland'.[157] A chapter in Irish history may have closed, but Devlin was indulging himself in another, of pure fantasy. The reality was found in the enthusiastic reception of the released convicts on their return to Ireland.[158] In portentous synchrony, reports of the homecoming appeared side by side with letters of condolence, accounts of obsequies and obituaries of John Redmond's younger brother Willie, killed while leading his men over the top in a Flanders' infantry charge.[159]

Constance Markievicz was the last to return home. Her sister and four friends (Esther Roper, Helena Moloney, Marie Perolz and Dr Kathleen Lynn) had travelled to Aylesbury with her summer clothes, and brought her back to London. That afternoon Constance and Eva had tea on the House of Commons

153 Ibid., col. 2082; 25 May 1917.
154 Ibid., XCIV, cols 24–6; 5 June 1917; cols 489–90; 7 June 1917.
155 Ibid., cols 307–9; 7 June 1917; cols 500–1; 8 June 1917; cols 595–7; 11 June 1917; cols 775–6; 12 June 1917; cols 1158–9; 14 June 1917; cols 1299–300; 15 June 1917.
156 Ibid., cols 1384–5; 15 June 1917. The pardon was signed by the King on 16 June, and remitted the balance of their sentences; the prisoners were not placed on licence (PRO HO 144/1453/311980/121 and 142).
157 Ibid., col. 1387; 15 June 1917.
158 The men had first been marshalled at Pentonville and thence travelled back to Ireland via Holyhead. Although their movements were kept secret almost to the last, thousands of sympathisers had waited through the night to greet them at the Kingstown Ferry terminal and at Westland Row Station, with (as *The Times* put it) 'frantic enthusiasm'. Dublin detainees, including Count Plunkett and Cathal Brugha, were released at the same time (ibid., 19 June 1917, 3b). The Irish National Aid Association had bought outfits of clothes for the released men, Irish goods being bought as far as possible (NLI: Irish National Aid Association Papers: Ms. 24, 324(2)). Such was the speed of their release that much of the men's property remained at Lewes, from where Michael Collins retrieved it, with the assistance of Dr O'Loughlin (ibid., Ms. 24, 387 (unfoliated)).
159 Major William Redmond, MP was killed on 7 June, and the Irish newspapers devoted many column inches to his death, while at the same time covering the imminent release and then the return of the Irish convicts (see, for example, *Freeman's Journal*, 19 June 1917, 4f–g, 5a–c and 3c–e; *Irish Independent*, 19 June 1917, 3f–g, 4a–b).

terrace with Alfred Byrne and Captain Jimmy White.[160] The journey home next day culminated in scenes of enthusiasm as great or surpassing those which had greeted the men.[161] Constance, in her womanhood and particular presence, in her character of rebel leader, befriender of Dublin's poor, and, above all in her imprisonment, had been transformed and, with the released men, became a powerful force in the currents then shaping Irish political life.

The designation of events as turning points in a nation's history can easily be overdone. No one who has studied the photographs or newsreels of the crowds which turned out to greet the returned convicts can, however, doubt that powerful feelings had flowed to the surface and crystallised around the event. The size of the demonstration, the evident intensity of feeling, the respectable dress of so many of the participants and – here and there – unmistakable signs of a guiding and organising hand, all indicate that Irish republicanism had been transformed in its public reception.[162] Here it was now, in the open, full of confidence, bearing forward the convicts amidst the flags, emblems, uniforms and roars of public approval. Thirteen months had passed since the first drafts of prisoners had left for England, leaving behind a foolish and wholly defeated rebellion, a gutted political movement, vast destruction of life and property and a resentful and bewildered populace. The vigour and speed of the resurgence could then scarcely have been imagined by the most enthusiastic rebel, still less the part which executions, camps and prisons would play in these events.

160 Marreco, *op. cit.*, p. 233; *Freeman's Journal*, 19 June, 6d; 20 June, 5b, *Irish Independent*, 20 June, 4a. The *Independent* had completed its volte-face on the punishment of the rising's leaders, and covered their homecoming with enthusiasm.
161 For Constance's own account of her homecoming see NLI: Eva Gore-Booth Papers: Ms. 21, 816: Constance to Eva, n.d. but *c*. 20 June 1917. She reassured her sister, 'You will be thankful to hear that people in command are not in favour of a fight now & do not want to shed useless blood (this of course is private)'.
162 Tim Pat Coogan and George Morrison reproduce an excellent photograph in their *Irish Civil War* (London, Seven Dials, 1998, p. 99). For newspaper accounts see the *Freeman's Journal* and *Irish Independent*, 19 and 20 June 1917. These newspapers also carried photographs.

12

ROGER CASEMENT

A question of honour

The not so secret agent

It is frequently asserted that Roger Casement was the last of the Easter rising leaders to be executed. This is untrue – Casement never was part of the leadership, was not privy to its plans, and left Germany in a submarine determined to do what he could to prevent the rising. What is true is that the British government regarded him as one of its most dangerous enemies in Ireland, a prime mover, and a vital link in the German–Clan na Gael conspiracy. It put a price on his head and tried to kidnap him in neutral Norway. In the course of time Casement's marginality to the 1916 rising became clear, but in what follows here it is important to bear in mind the information which was available to the British government in April 1916. Casement arrived in Ireland on a German submarine, accompanied by an arms freighter. He had negotiated with Berlin, and had secured a widely publicised statement of policy on Ireland in the event of a victory by the Central Powers – and in 1916 that victory did not seem improbable. British intelligence had Casement under observation since 1913, knew of his role in the Howth gun-running, his association with John Devoy and the Clan, his mass meetings in America, his contacts with the German Embassy in Washington, and his activities during eighteen months in Germany. Casement had indeed sought the limelight, using his literary skills and familiarity with international relations to campaign in the United States of America against the Allied cause.[1] Within weeks of his death he would be described by a leading British propagandist as 'the chief leader of these [1916] rebels'.[2]

The capture of such a man would be greeted as a major triumph, all the more so when his arrival in Ireland coincided with the most serious rebellion against British authority in over a hundred years. Casement the fumbling conspirator, the man of inaction, the dreamer paralysed by his scruples, the troubled

1 Casement's American articles were gathered together by Joseph McGarrity and issued as a booklet (*The Crime Against Europe: A Possible Outcome of the War of 1914*, Philadelphia, Celtic Press, 1915). This was widely circulated, with German-American, and probably German, support.
2 NLI: McGarrity Papers: Ms. 17, 601 (10).

manic-depressive, would emerge in interrogation and trial, but this diminished view of the man was unacceptable – unthinkable – to his captors, if for no other reason than its measure of their triumph. In seizing Casement, they assured themselves, they had brought to his long overdue reckoning one of the most malign and repugnant enemies of the British Empire.

One other preamble may throw light on what follows. No one who has studied Casement's voluminous papers – letters, memoranda, poems, articles, journals, jottings and mere scraps – could fail to be aware of the man's unusually fraught emotional makeup. It spills off the pages, in affection, condemnation, declaration, insecurity, self-centredness and (usually) pessimistic introspection. In dealing with others extravagance in emotion is never far away, and this not infrequently led to an abandonment of critical faculty, abundant sentimentality, lack of proportion and episodes of paranoia. All of this was heightened and kept constantly in motion by the lack of a settled abode and way of life, and an acute need to find personal groundings in the Irish national movement. As it happened, Joseph Conrad had met Casement in the Congo, and on two brief occasions thereafter. Allowance must be made for Conrad's detestation of German imperialism in the strength of his observations, made a week or so after the allegations against Casement had first been outlined in committal proceedings. But even so discounted, the novelist's eye seems true enough. Here was a man, thought Conrad, 'properly speaking, of no mind at all. I don't mean stupid. I mean that he is all emotion. By emotional force (Congo Report, Putumayo, etc.) he made his way, and sheer emotionalism has undone him. A creature of sheer temperament – a truly tragic personality: all but the greatness of which he had not a trace. Only vanity. But in the Congo it was not visible yet.'[3] Lest all this seem too harsh, it is in no way incompatible with the view of many, who affirmed Casement to be sympathetic, kindly and generous, abstemious and to an unusual degree modest in personal contacts.

A fatal mission

Roger Casement's story is widely known, at least in outline. At one level it is straightforward enough. During a distinguished career in the British consular service, in the course of which he won national honour and international acclaim for exposés of atrocities in the Belgian Congo and Brazil, Casement was knighted in June 1911. He retired with a pension in June 1913, expressing his 'very keen regret at severing my connection with a Service I have so long been associated with'. The following year he went to the United States of America, arriving three weeks before Britain declared war on Germany. Four months after

---

3 Joseph Conrad to John Quinn, 24 May 1916: NLI: McGarrity Papers: Ms. 17, 601 (2). For other observations on Casement see G. Jean Aubry (ed.), *Joseph Conrad, Life and Letters*, London, William Heinemann, 1927, Vol. 1, pp. 324–6.

that, Casement's pension was withdrawn because of what the Foreign Office deemed to be his pro-German activities.[4]

Had he confined himself to Clan na Gael's fundraising, and sabre-rattling to Irish-American audiences, Casement would have suffered none but financial losses. Coinciding with his arrival in the United States of America, however, a group associated with the Irish Volunteers succeeded in landing 1500 rifles in Ireland, and as a leading plotter, Casement was propelled along by a wave of Irish-American enthusiasm.[5] For all his previous hard-headed consular work, Casement lived in a ferment of anguish and indecision, while the constancy of his anti-English feelings grew daily more virulent. Caught up in the excitement of meetings, and given a shrewdly warm reception by veteran Fenians, he was tumbled into a revolutionary conspiracy for which he possessed neither aptitude nor stamina.[6] He stepped into a world run by rules of which he had little knowledge, invested with purpose, energy and ruthlessness he could not hope to match.

Unlike Devoy and others of Clan na Gael, Casement had achieved an eminent position in conventional society, and his consular background naturally led to the proposal that he should represent the Clan in discussions with the German Foreign Office in Berlin.[7] This was the more easily undertaken because after three

---

4 The Foreign Office had been aware of Casement's growing attachment to unconstitutional nationalism for some time (see PRO CO 904/195 which reports on his movements in 1913–14). Unfortunately a good portion of this file is in undeciphered telegrams – but that in itself shows with what seriousness Casement was watched. The offence that precipitated the breach was a letter to the *Irish Independent* (5 October 1914, 3e) urging Irishmen not to become supporters of the British war effort. Ireland could not afford to export her young men. Germany had never wronged Ireland 'and we owe her more than one debt of gratitude'. It was not until 8 December 1914, when Casement had been formally received by the German government, that his pension was stopped 'until further notice'. At his trial it was shown that Casement continued to draw his pension until 7 October 1914. Each quarter payees were required to sign and encash a voucher, so there was no question of the pension continuing by default. Casement's continued drawings for two months after the outbreak of war, and up until the last possible payment before he sailed for Germany, embellished his prosecutors' case (see George H. Knott (ed.), *Trial of Sir Roger Casement*, Edinburgh and London, William Hodge & Co, 1917, p. 16; *The Times*, 27 June 1916, 3b). Casement's view (which he put in his trial statement) was that he had earned his pension, and it was assigned by law.

5 'The Irish here would make me into a Demi-God, if I let them. In Philadelphia they have christened me, a deputation told me "Robert Emmet". They are mad for a Protestant leader' (Casement to Mrs Alice Stopford Green, 26 July 1914: NYPL: MCIHP, Box 1, IHP9). It is a measure of Casement's mercurial temperament that five weeks later he wrote to his cousin, Gertrude Bannister: 'I don't like the U.S.A. The more I see of it the less I like it. The people are ignorant and unthinking and easily led by anything they read in their rotten papers. The press is the worst in the world' (1 September 1914: NLI: Casement Papers: Ms. 13, 074 (9/ii)).

6 And it was easy to be misled by enthusiastic meetings. Patrick Rankin recalled such a rally addressed by Casement in Philadelphia in September 1914. Several hundred young men attended, in uniform but not armed. Casement's call for volunteers to go to Ireland was met by loud cheers. The following week, however, not a single recruit turned up (NLI: Patrick Rankin Papers: Ms. 22,251, f. 3).

7 A number of Casement's notes and articles on the German–Irish alliance are to be found in the MCIHP, *op. cit.*, Box 2, IHP34.

months, revolutionary life in America had lost some of its lustre for Casement, while, at the same time, his presence was beginning to irk Devoy and other Clan leaders.[8] The decision to go, however, was Casement's alone, and when his sister subsequently criticised the Clan leaders, Devoy replied that she was utterly mistaken 'that either I or anyone else in America urged or asked him to go'.[9] On 15 October 1914, Casement sailed from New York to Christiania (now Oslo) on board the Norwegian ship *Oskar II*.[10] From Christiania he went to Germany, where he was to spend some eighteen months, until his fatal return to Ireland.

Beginning with the highest of hopes, Casement's mission dwindled into inactivity, frustration and ill-health. From extravagant pro-German sentiments, he swung to equally inflated denunciations: 'they are swine and cads of the first water – not one of them with the soul of a rat or the mind of a cur'.[11] In German eyes, Casement rapidly declined from the status of veteran diplomat to whining neurasthenic; from the fully accredited representative of a potential ally, he became an obstacle to German–Clan cooperation. In latter days, indeed, both sides communicated around rather than through him. The mission's high point came shortly after Casement's arrival in Berlin, when he negotiated the Imperial government's statement on Ireland which was promulgated in a formal

---

8 Devoy's frustration with Casement is reflected in a comment made after the latter's capture and imprisonment: 'We knew he would meddle in his honest, but visionary way to such an extent as to spoil things, but we did not dream that he would ruin everything as he has done. He took no notice whatever of decisions or instructions, but without quarrelling, pursued his own dreams. . . . He was obsessed with the idea that he was a wonderful leader and that nothing could be done without him' (Devoy to Laurence de Lacey (intercepted letter), 20 July 1916: PRO HO 144/1636/311643/53). This retrospective assessment must be read as part of Devoy's careful post-rising distancing of himself from Casement (see p. 565 below). It is true, however, that Devoy's doubts about Casement were such that he advised him not to go to Germany. Once there, he advised him to stay (NLI: Devoy Papers, Ms. 18, 139 (unfoliated)).

9 Devoy to Agnes (Nina) Newman, 15 August 1915: NLI: Devoy Papers: ibid.

10 British intelligence attempted to intercept him, but a naval boarding party failed to make an identification. The British Embassy in Christiania tried to enlist Casement's disreputable servant, Adler Christensen, in a kidnap. Christensen alerted Casement from the outset, and the plot failed. Over the following months this episode absorbed a wholly disproportionate amount of Casement's energy, generating a considerable correspondence with the United States of America and a formal complaint by Casement to the British Foreign Secretary, Sir Edward Grey (see NLI: Casement Papers: Ms. 13, 081 (2/iii); 13, 084 (1–5) and (9)); Charles Emerson Curry (ed.), *Sir Roger Casement's Diaries* (Munich, Arche Publishing Co, 1922) are also devoted to this incident). It is telling of Casement's character that he should go to war and be astonished when the enemy sought to harm him. In his death cell he fretted that the full and true story be told, and some of his last instructions concerned certain papers on the matter which he wished his cousin to locate (ibid., Ms. 14, 100: Casement to Gertrude Bannister, 20 July 1916).

11 Casement memorandum, April 1916: NYPL: MCIHP, Box 1, IHP26. He continued his fulmination: 'They certainly deserve to be thoroughly well taught in the first rudiments of humanity and kindliness – for as they are, they are lower than the Congo Savages in most things that constitute gentleness of mind, heart or action.'

declaration on 20 November 1914.[12] Adhering as always to the Fenian doctrine on England's adversity, the German proclamation was hailed by the Clan as a great success, and, through the German Embassy, Devoy on 1 January 1915 sent a congratulatory message.[13] The declaration doubtless cheered Irish-American revolutionists, but it seems unlikely that the German government served its greater purpose of demoralising Irish soldiers fighting in the British Army, or Irish civilian opinion.

The Clan had given Casement three tasks, one of which – winning German political and public opinion – was accomplished in the November declaration. The other two were beyond his capabilities. He was to obtain German military assistance for an Irish rising and, related to that, to recruit a military unit from Irish prisoners of war in German hands. In the end, Casement was so unsuccessful and paralysed by bitterness in his relations with his hosts that German military assistance was negotiated directly between Devoy and the German government, with Casement being informed of the outcome via his own deputy in Germany, Robert Monteith.[14] Within a year of arriving Casement was enraged with his hosts and at odds with those who had sent him, vexing and draining the time and energy of both.[15]

The unit which Casement attempted to form was modelled on the Boer War's Irish Brigade.[16] The concept drew on an Irish exile military tradition going back to the seventeenth century. Of all of Casement's anti-British acts, his recruiting missions among the 2500 or so Irish prisoners whom the Germans had specially assembled at Limburg Camp raised most doubt among his friends and most disgust and anger among his opponents. The combination – intentional or not

---

12 PRO HO 144/111637/311, 643/184. Attached to this file are letters to Eoin MacNeill and Mrs Alice Green. There is also an English version of the November Declaration, and a German version from the *Norddeutscher Allegemeine Zeitung* of 20 November 1914. These materials had been sent in a covering envelope via the neutral Netherlands, and (of course) intercepted by the British Postal Censor. Sir Basil Thomson later forwarded the items to the Home Office so that he could tell Mrs Green that they were no longer in police hands.

13 NLI: Casement Papers: Ms. 13, 073 (44/i): 'I must congratulate you on the splendid way in which you have done your work.... The Declaration was all that could be expected in the present military and naval situation.'

14 Robert Monteith, who had strong labour sympathies, was an early member and organiser of the Volunteers. At the request of the IRB he travelled to Germany, via the United States of America, in early September 1915. From there he travelled covertly to Germany, via Norway and Denmark. His memoir (*Casement's Last Adventure*, Dublin, Michael F. Moynihan, 1953) is a detailed account of his time with the Irish Brigade, his arrival in Kerry with Casement, and his subsequent activities.

15 The Casement–Devoy correspondence is too extensive for review here, but at one point it became so bitter that both men resolved to break contact (Devoy to Casement, 21 November 1915: NLI: Casement Papers: Ms. 13, 073 (vii)). Casement's hostile attitude towards the Germans is splattered through the correspondence from about the beginning of 1915.

16 Casement confirmed that he had taken the idea from John MacBride's South African unit (NLI: A. S. Green Papers: Ms. 10, 464 (16): Brixton memorandum).

– of financial and other material inducements, and an element of menace was indefensible. In the end Casement himself came to see this episode as morally flawed and sordid. The parade of wounded and exchanged soldiers who gave evidence at Casement's trial proved devastating, and allowed exaggerated or untrue evidence to be given voice.[17] Nor were his efforts effectual. Addressing the prisoners en masse Casement received a sometimes brutally hostile reception, being jeered and heckled, and on at least one occasion jostled and struck.[18] He was then reduced to the indignity of having a German escort to guard him from his fellow countrymen.[19] Persistence produced not a brigade, but a group not much over fifty, some of whom were genuinely attracted to Casement's ideas, a few who hoped to escape military custody, and others of whom were rogues or fools. Casement's first comment to the German authorities served to characterise the entire enterprise: 'They are mercenaries pure and simple and even had I the means to bribe them I should not attempt to do so.'[20]

By the spring of 1915 Casement was in despair.[21] The year that followed – forced inactivity, German evasions, what he saw as bureaucratic snubs, and the humiliating realisation that the Irish Brigade was a total liability – wore down Casement's mental and physical health. He lashed out in all directions. To

---

17 It was said, for example, that soldiers who refused to join the Irish Brigade had their bread ration reduced from 750 to 300 grammes per day, and turnips substituted for potatoes. Casement's counsel, Sullivan, elicited the fact that the bread ration was reduced *before* Casement appeared and that other dietary changes were common to all British prisoners (*The Times*, 27 June 1916, 3c). This correction of the facts, however, had little impact on the overall impression created in the public mind of bullying helpless prisoners. Casement denounced as a 'horrible insinuation' and 'an abominable falsehood' the suggestion that 'I got my own people's rations reduced to starvation point because they did not join the Irish Brigade.' Rations had been reduced throughout Germany because of the Allies' blockade (*The Times*, 29 June 1916, 3b). The draft agreement establishing the Brigade is in the Devoy Papers (NLI: Ms. 18, 081 (xi)).

18 For British accounts of these visits see PRO WO/141/5.

19 For this evidence see Knott, *op. cit.*, pp. 16–43, *passim*; *The Times*, 27 June 1916, 3c. An account of Casement's recruiting rebuff was given by John Redmond on 15 May 1915 (press-cutting, John Devoy to Joseph McGarrity, 18 May 1915: NYPL: MCIHP, Box 4, IHP73). As a conventional military formation a brigade normally consists of two or three battalions commanded by a brigadier general. Casement's unit rose to little more than an infantry company in numbers.

20 René Maria MacColl, *Roger Casement: A New Judgment*, London, Hamish Hamilton, 1956, p. 166. On 4 April 1915, the British received 'definite evidence' – possibly from an exchanged prisoner – that Casement was recruiting for an Irish brigade (Sir Basil Thomson, *The Scene Changes*, London, Collins, 1939, pp. 241–2). Casement's first two recruits were Sergeant MacMurrough and Corporal Timothy Quinlisk, whom he thought 'looked like rogues'. About the latter he was completely right. In November 1919 Quinlisk tried to decoy Michael Collins to capture in Dublin. When he tried again a trap was set for him and, his guilt proved, he was shot by the IRA (Piaras Béaslaí, *Michael Collins and the Making of a New Ireland*, London, George C. Harrap, 1926, Vol. 1, pp. 392–402).

21 Though he still had enough energy and motivation to contribute to the German propaganda organ, the *Continental Times*, according to Joseph McGarrity, who identified two and possibly three pieces as being of Casement's authorship (NYPL: MCIHP, Box 5, IHP90).

Joseph P. McGarrity,[22] his New York friend, he denounced the same Irish Americans who months before had thrilled him as 'contemptible', his bitterness leaping off the page: 'They have talked – floods of talk – but they have not even subscribed money, much less attempted any overt act for Ireland. They have killed England with their mouth a thousand times – but when it came to a job of work they were "all of a tremble"'. He affirmed his own willingness to die, but if he did so alone, it would be for 'a lost and dishonoured cause'. Unless American supporters paid for the maintenance of the Brigade (still not formed) and Casement's own living expenses, he intended to abandon his mission and to let the British government have 'what satisfaction it can get from trying me for high treason'.[23]

At this point Casement was still sometimes willing to give the Germans the benefit of the doubt. They were offering 'great help' and promising more than any other government had given. Were the Irish not willing to grasp the opportunity and help themselves 'then in God's name let us have done with the lie'. He pondered his justification for forming the Brigade and exposing soldiers to the penalties he inevitably faced, especially when he was uncertain about how far the Clan would support them and honour its agreement.[24] A fortnight later he returned to the theme. The Germans wanted action ('cooperation in arms') before they would do anything. He had tried to persuade them to take the first

---

22 (1874–1940). Born in Co. Tyrone and emigrated to the USA in 1892, settling in Philadelphia. Became a tavern-owner and liquor-merchant. Joined Clan na Gael in 1893 and in 1912 was elected to its executive. During Casement's stay in the USA McGarrity formed a high opinion of him, and was one of the last of the Irish leaders to see him before his departure for Germany. Casement wrote frequently from Germany to McGarrity, and in December 1915 asked him to look after his sister – an obligation which McGarrity accepted and discharged over several difficult years. After the Treaty, McGarrity took the republican side and remained an irreconcilable until his death. He was expelled from the Irish Free State in 1939.

23 Casement to McGarrity, 29 April 1915: NYPL: MCIHP, Box 1, IHP21. Casement's romanticism and detachment is underlined by a bizarre and rather repulsive war eulogy: 'If today when all of Europe is dying for national ends, whole peoples marching down with songs of joy to the valley of eternal night, we alone stand by idle or moved only to words, then we are in truth the most contemptible of all the peoples of Europe. Germany if she won a thousand times over could not bring freedom to such a people as this.' Despite having told McGarrity to show the letter wherever he thought it might help, Casement had second thoughts and marked in pencil 'better burn this' (the war eulogy was very likely derived from Pearse's death paen (see p. 418, above)).

24 Casement to McGarrity, 5 May 1915: NYPL: MCIHP, Box 1, IHP22. Without consulting Devoy, Casement had undertaken the considerable financial burden of funding the Irish Brigade. On learning of this, Devoy was emphatic that the Germans should pay. The Clan's limited funds were better used in Ireland, the Brigade's upkeep was beyond its resources, and if they were to fund it, the US government would be able to seize Clan assets. Between departure from Germany and May 1915, Casement received $6500 from Devoy. From all the surviving documents it appears that he was treated fairly by the Clan. Despite his money worries, moreover, Casement refused German financial assistance when it was offered (see Devoy to Casement, 22 August 1915: NLI: Casement Papers: Ms. 13, 073 (44/vi)).

step by providing arms, to create an Irish momentum. They had demanded proof of seriousness: 'They said, in effect "get them yourselves – you have millions of your people in the USA and they should do that".'[25] Casement saw the weight of the German argument, and the validity of its test, but this simply stoked his anger and added to his frustration.

By the end of the year Casement concluded that his mission was utterly hopeless – 'delays, delays, delays – always delays. They break my heart.' Elsewhere he wrote: 'It is all so black and dead . . . I am worse than useless and only a burden and in a clog.' He thanked McGarrity for his support and kindness and asked him to look after his sister, since he could do nothing for her. He and the others were worthy of a far better agent than Casement had been – 'poor broken me'. Some good might have come out of his mission, but he could do no more then or in the future 'for the seat of power within me is giving way'.[26]

Two days before writing his letter Casement had been invited to meet a German liaison officer. Rather than take this as a positive sign he (annotating the invitation) fumed about the delay: 'This is a typical example of German "thoroughness". After four or five months since the question was raised – and my wishes expressed and a year (tomorrow) after the Agreement was submitted . . . I get this letter and it takes two days to reach me.' So weak was Casement's sense of proportion and grasp of the times that a one-day postal delay triggered a tirade. He would go to Berlin to meet the liaison officer but should the outcome be unsatisfactory he was ready to depart: 'I am quite sick to heart of this Government and everything and person connected with it.'[27] By early April 1916, Casement had concluded that the Germans had repudiated their agreement, and had decided to treat the men of the Brigade as deserters or prisoners of war.[28]

That his difficulties were personal as well as (or rather more than) political was shown by his reaction to the forced departure of St John Gaffney, the US

---

25 Ibid., 20 June 1915.
26 Ibid., 24 December 1915. Casement urged McGarrity not to let his breakdown be known to his sister or to the British. From this and many other indications it seems clear that his manic-depressive temperament at some point (or points) gave way, and he cracked up almost completely. That he could be up as well as down was demonstrated in his cogent and well-argued article against Irish conscription, completed two months before – 'Ireland and the World War' (NLI: McGarrity Papers: Ms. 17, 590 (3)).
27 Casement note, Tosson, 22 December 1915: NYPL: MCIHP, Box 1, IHP5. Two months later Casement asked that one of the solders of the Irish Brigade be discharged and sent to the USA on his behalf. This letter is annotated 'no answer was given to this request – the customary form of official courtesy in this country' (ibid., 24 February 1916). Information on Casement's condition and the progress of his work got back to Devoy and the Clan, who clearly believed in cutting their losses. On 8 March 1916, Devoy referred to the Irish Brigade (which then numbered sixty-nine) which needed funds. He would not permit fund-raising – 'we have better work to do and must not be interfered with' (ibid., IHP75, Box 4).
28 Ibid., Casement note, 11 April 1916.

Consul in Munich. The Irish-born Gaffney, a lifelong supporter of the nationalist cause, had held a dinner for Casement at which various anti-British sentiments were expressed (thus violating US neutrality laws).[29] Casement sent a long and somewhat rambling letter of consolation, ending with a passage of obvious sincerity: 'For your friendship to me, a lonely man, far from friends and with so many doubts, anxieties and perplexities to make my way dark I thank you from the bottom of my heart and I am sure every Irishman worthy of the name will thank you too.'[30]

In his final letter to his sister Agnes ('Nina') Casement gives a bleak account of this period when he 'often and often' prayed for death. Months before he embarked for Ireland, which he knew would be a fatal mission, he was begging for death: 'I was so lonely, and I could do nothing and go nowhere.' Six times in 1915 he had tried to leave Germany, and in July had obtained a passport and set out 'but had to return to stand by those poor chaps [the Irish Brigade] and help them'. There was another attempt to leave, early in 1916.[31]

During this period of Casement's despair IRB plans developed without his knowledge or assistance. On Devoy's urging the Germans agreed to send to Ireland 20,000 rifles and ammunition, but none of the other *matériel* and staff support which had been requested.[32] Casement and Robert Monteith were summoned to the General Staff to be told of the plans. Although he considered the German aid to be 'most inadequate' and likely to lead only to a failure, Casement kept silent. He insisted that he should go with the expedition, and this was agreed: at this point he was convinced of the Germans' 'entire insincerity'. They wanted to do as little as possible, at least cost to themselves, and regardless of the final outcome – to do enough to be able to say they did what they could. 'They are wholly selfish,' he recorded, 'wholly untrustworthy and to sum it all up – not gentlemen.'[33]

29 The US government may also have heard that in August 1915 Gaffney had asked the German government to obtain passage to America for Casement by a ship of a neutral country – 'the fact of his presence there could not fail to secure wider and fuller support for the German cause' (NLI: McGarrity Papers: Ms. 17, 590 (2)).

30 Casement to Gaffney, 1 November 1915: NYPL: MCIHP, Box 1, IHP4. Devoy commented bitterly: 'Every note he struck was one of despair. And he told everything to every fellow who called on him' (Devoy to Laurence de Lacey, 20 July 1916 (intercepted letter): PRO HO 144/ 1636/311643/53). This letter was found in a raid on de Lacey's premises by the US authorities and handed over to the British).

31 Casement to Nina, 25 July 1916: NLI: Casement Papers: Ms. 13, 600 (unfoliated).

32 See letter of John Devoy, 3 January 1916, confirming that the Germans had improved on their offer of assistance but would not provide 'the main thing' (probably German officers). Devoy was about to send this information to Ireland by courier (NYPL: MCIHP, Box 4, IHP73).

33 Casement memorandum, 16 March 1916, Berlin, NYPL: MCIHP, Box 1, IHP26. Devoy did not consider the Germans to be unreliable: 'they did everything we asked but they were weary of his impracticable dreams and told us to deal directly with them here.' Casement had no more to do with the shipload of arms 'than the man in the moon'. Dublin had made the request, Devoy had

At another point he confided to his diary that the General Staff 'are all cads, scoundrels or cowards – and invariable liars'.[34]

In view of later claims that Casement had gone to Ireland to try to stop the rising, and an emphatic prosecution insistence to the contrary, Casement's correspondence at the time is important. On 30 March 1916 – almost a fortnight before embarkation for Ireland – Casement wrote about his position to Count Georg von Wedel, head of the English Department at the German Foreign Office (and a man whom Casement respected). Within a few days it was likely that he would be gone from Germany, embarked upon the mission planned by the General Staff: 'I am thus a passive agent, powerless to act according to my judgement, and with a course of action forced upon me that I wholly deprecate.' He had gone to the General Staff, expecting to hear a plan to land arms, but instead 'I found myself confronted with a proposal for a "rebellion" in Ireland I believed to be wholly futile at the best and at the worst something I dreaded to think of. I had *always* been greatly opposed to any attempted revolt in Ireland unless backed with strong foreign military help.' According to Casement he had been told that unless he agreed to their plan the General Staff would cancel all aid and inform Devoy that it was because of Casement that they did so. Thus, he argued, he was trapped: the plan was doomed, but, should he not go along with it, relations between Germany and the Clan might be ruptured. Even at this point, however, Casement wholly failed to understand his own subordinate place in developments. He complained that Devoy and 'Irishmen at home' had without consulting him and in opposition to his known views 'decided to attempt some form of revolution in Ireland'. He now hoped for little but disaster.[35]

transmitted it, and the Germans had replied within nine days (Devoy to Laurence de Lacey, 20 July 1916: PRO HO 144/1636/311643/53).

34 Ibid., Box 2, IHP39, Casement Diary, p. 53. This outburst was apparently prompted by the discovery that the Germans had not told him that they could send cypher messages to their Washington Embassy.

35 Casement to von Wedel, 30 March 1916, NYPL: MCIHP, Box 1, IHP31; there is a contemporary copy of this letter in the MacNeill Papers (NLI: Ms. 10880). Casement worried about the men in the Irish Brigade (which, in the event, was not sent), who had been promised they would be sent only with an ample German force. For himself, he had obtained poison against the eventuality of capture. After the war letters were discovered in Germany and passed to the Home Office via the military and intelligence authorities. These, noted Lt. Col. J. Hall of the intelligence service, 'bear out the attitude which he took when interrogated in London after his arrest' (PRO HO 144/1637/311643/194a). The intelligence services had, at the time, emphatically denied Casement's version of events, including his claim that he had gone to Ireland to try to stop the rising, and that he had been forced into a corner by the German General Staff. These papers, which were not officially registered until 1960, confirmed Casement's claims beyond a doubt. They did not affect the substance of his treason, but they surely were substantial mitigation, and might have saved his life had the Cabinet known about them.

Casement did not believe that Irish insurrectionary forces could prevail – and for all that he had been out of Ireland since August 1914 he had a good idea of the resources available and the likely reaction of the general population to a rising. He could not see beyond the failure, however, to what might follow, and all his reasoning suffered from his compulsion to put himself at the centre of the picture. Ruminations in his diary make it seem as though the rising was his personal trouble and trap. If he persisted in criticisms – 'its stupendous idiocy, its fundamental falsity, its foredoomed failure' – he would be held up 'to all ages in Irish history' as a traitor, someone who failed his country's cause and prevented the German empire from assisting revolutionary Ireland: 'My God! Was ever a sane man in such a position.' He concluded that the landing of arms should go ahead, since that did not necessarily involve bloodshed, and was the wish of the organisation in Ireland and America. He hoped to get ashore before the arms and that he could then stop the rising and simply arrange for the delivery of the rifles.[36]

At least some of his determination to go was fired by his own depressed and despairing mental state. Germany had become hateful to him, and life there a horror. His euphoria on landing in Ireland, even in such circumstances, indicates his condition. He was, he told his sister,

> [f]or one brief spell happy and smiling once more. I cannot tell you what I felt. The sandhills were full of skylarks, rising in the dawn. The first I had heard for years . . . and all round were primroses and wild violets and the singing of the skylarks in the air, and I was back in Ireland again.'[37]

The euphoria was dissolved soon enough by painful reality. As noted, the insurrection was originally planned to commence on Easter Sunday, 23 April, and on 12 April Casement embarked by submarine from Emden. For security reasons the *matériel* had been dispatched to arrive not earlier than 20 April. Knowing his negative views of the plans, the General Staff probably did not want Casement to arrive too far in advance of the guns. By accident or design the submarine broke down, and returned to port. In consequence Casement did not arrive in Ireland until the small hours of Friday, 21 April. The local Volunteer unit had not been properly forewarned, and he landed in circumstances and in a physical and nervous condition that made detection and capture almost inevitable.[38] Luck was not on his side, and by that afternoon he was in

---

36 NYPL: MCIHP, Box 2, IHP39; NLI: Casement Diary (typescript), p. 22.

37 Casement to Nina, 25 July 1916: NLI: Casement Papers: Ms. 13, 600.

38 René MacColl, whose book on Casement was published in 1956, was able to interview a number of survivors who were in Tralee at the time of Casement's capture, and provides interesting details (*op. cit.*, pp. 200–13).

the custody of Tralee RIC.[39] Although he succeeded in passing a message to the IRB leaders, they were set on their self-sacrificing path, and the rising – countermanded, agreed and then again countermanded – commenced on Easter Monday.[40]

In view of the position which Devoy and others took on Casement's negative approach to the rising, and the efforts they made to distance themselves from his judgements, it should be noted that in January 1915 the leadership of the Clan (including Devoy) was equally cautious. Devoy emphasised that German success in the war – particularly at sea – was the essential prerequisite for a successful rising in Ireland. He told Casement (who was expected to adhere to this approach in negotiations with the German General Staff) that 'No invasion of Ireland should take place unless England is also invaded: not less than 25,000 men and 50,000 rifles, with proportionate amount of artillery, should be sent to Ireland, if the seas are cleared. With that force they [the Clan leadership] are satisfied they could answer for Ireland.'[41] In attempting to stop the rising, therefore, Casement was doing no more than following the Clan line: 20,000 rifles nowhere nearly met Devoy's list of conditions of sixteen months before. It was not only Casement's neurotic defeatism that lay behind his last mission to Ireland. What he did not know was that the IRB leadership had determined on a sacrificial rising and were moving to a very different drum.

39 The British intercepted and deciphered German diplomatic radio messages out of Washington, as well as naval radio traffic; they were also handed material seized by the US authorities on 19 April in a raid on the offices of Wolf von Igel, a German espionage agent. This included a message from the Dublin leaders, transmitted via Devoy, requesting that the arms be landed *between* Good Friday and Sunday, 23 April. This suggests confusion in the transmission dates, and it may be that contradictory messages reached the Germans (see MacColl, *op. cit.*, pp. 191–2; Monteith, *op. cit.*, chs 11 and 12). Precise information on the intelligence operation against Casement is still not available, but it is likely that the Admiralty informed the government that he was on his way to Ireland. The fact that the submarine which took Casement to Ireland had no radio, and the sequence of accidents which resulted in his capture, suggest that the authorities had good but not precise knowledge of where he would be landed. See PRO HO 144/1636/311643/53; see also the foreword by Sir Basil Thomson to Hugh Cleland Hoy's *40 O.B. or How the War Was Won* (London, Hutchinson & Co, 1932), p. 8: 'For weeks the Germans had been telling the Admiralty Intelligence about the movements of Sir Roger Casement without dreaming that their messages were being intercepted and their code deciphered.' See also PRO WO 904/94 for other documents on Casement's capture and detention.

40 The message was passed on the day of his capture via Father F. M. Ryan and by Robert Monteith (PRO HO 144/1636/311643/51 and /53). Two Volunteers, Cornelius Collins and the Kerry Commandant Austin Stack, were subsequently charged under the Defence of the Realm Act (DORA) with aiding and abetting Casement to land German weapons in Ireland. Tried by court martial they received long sentences of penal servitude, but were released in the general amnesty of June 1917 (PRO WO 35/68).

41 NLI: Casement Papers, Ms. 13, 073 (44/i): Devoy to Casement, 1 January 1915.

Trial

Casement was already under interrogation when London got news of the Dublin rising. His passage thither had been swift, and on his arrival on Easter Sunday he was immediately escorted to Scotland Yard. Taken in flagrante delicto, Casement made little attempt to withhold information from his questioners – Sir Basil Thomson,[42] head of the CID, and Captain Reginald Hall,[43] head of Naval Intelligence. The Dublin news inflamed opinion even further against Casement, and led to a Commons question from the jingoistic Pemberton Billing.[44] Could the Irish Chief Secretary confirm that Casement had been brought to London, and could he give the nation and the House an assurance that 'this traitor' would be shot forthwith? Cheers indicated what a good many MPs thought.

The rising created much initial confusion, and what might have been a straightforward, if sensational progress through committal and trial procedures was halted while government pondered whether to proceed against Casement via the civil courts or, as they had against the other leaders in Ireland, by court martial. Certainly there was no doubt that had Casement's mission (which was seen as the landing of arms) succeeded, events in Dublin might have taken a different turn.[45] Having briefly been confined at Brixton Prison, Casement was handed over to military custody and held squalidly incommunicado in the Tower. Under twenty-four-hour surveillance by three soldiers, his cell was lit night and day. No papers or writing material were allowed, and neither was he given a change of clothes; by systematic intent or bungling (probably a mixture of both) he was denied contact with his friends.[46] Gavan Duffy, his solicitor,[47] finally saw

---

42 (1861–1939). Eton, New College and Bar. Colonial Service, then governor of convict and local prisons in England. Head of CID and Assistant Commissioner, Metropolitan Police, 1913–19; Director of Intelligence, 1919–21. Prolific author.

43 (1870–1943). Naval career including Director of Intelligence, Admiralty War Staff, 1914–18. Rear Admiral, 1917; retired 1919. Unionist MP West Derby Division of Liverpool, 1919–23, Eastbourne, 1925–9. Principal Agent of Unionist Party, 1923–4. In a curious twist, Hall succeeded to the seat of F. E. Smith, Casement's prosecutor. Smith had held the West Derby division for the Conservatives until his elevation to the Woolsack as Lord Birkenhead.

44 (1880–1948). Served in Boer War and (1914–16) Royal Naval Air Service. Broke wartime truce between parties and was elected as an Independent for East Hertfordshire, 1916–21, campaigning for a strong air policy. For his Casement question see 5 Hansard, LXXXI, col. 2462; 25 April 1916. Billing's question followed shortly after Augustine Birrell (Chief Secretary for Ireland) gave the first news of the Dublin Rising to the Commons (ibid., cols 2460–1).

45 General Sir John Maxwell to Asquith, 24 May 1916: Sir George Arthur, *General Sir John Maxwell*, London, John Murray, 1932, p. 260.

46 Gertrude Parry (née Bannister) left a memoir of her cousin describing the difficulties placed in the way of herself and Alice Green in trying to contact Casement and provide assistance for him (NLI: Casement Papers: Ms. 13, 079, ff. 10–11).

47 George Gavan Duffy (1882–1951). Son of Young Irelander Sir Charles Gavan Duffy (see p. 44, n. 129 above). Educated in France and at Stonyhurst. Practised as a solicitor in London. Joined Sinn Féin and was elected for South Dublin in 1918 general election. Represented Sinn Féin at Versailles Peace Conference, and was one of the plenipotentiaries in the Anglo-Irish Treaty

him on 9 May, and found him disoriented, filthy, covered in flea-bites, and still wearing the clothes in which he had landed in Kerry. Casement's condition was explained to his old friend Alice Green,[48] who, despite utter disagreement with the course he had taken, and her disapproval of the rising, joined with his cousin Gertrude Bannister in doing all she could to help him. Green's complaint to Asquith about the manner in which Casement was being held contained a scarcely veiled threat to pass the information to the American newspapers.[49] At this point (with the Dublin executions completed) it was decided to proceed against Casement in the civil courts, and on 15 May he appeared at Bow Street Magistrates' Court on a charge of High Treason.[50] Committal proceedings were conducted before Sir John Dickinson, the stipendiary magistrate, and Casement was remanded to Brixton Prison. Here he remained throughout committal and trial proceedings, being removed to Pentonville (a 'hanging prison') after conviction and sentence.

Although Casement had talked freely to his captors and did not dispute the facts against him, he entered a plea of 'not guilty' to the charge of high treason. This plea was based not on the facts but on intent: he insisted that he acted as a patriotic Irishman rather than a traitor to the Crown.[51] Casement's leading counsel Serjeant Sullivan[52] refused to mount a political defence, as urged by

negotiations; Minister of Foreign Affairs in Provisional Government. Defended civil liberties in first years of Irish Free State; President of Irish Supreme Court, 1946. By taking up Casement's defence he closed the door on the large legal practice he had built up in London; his firm insisted that the partnership be dissolved. Duffy had to wait for nine days before he was permitted access to Casement. This exceptional delay was neither explained nor excused. He was able to get messages to Devoy in New York, letting him know what Casement had told him and the authorities (PRO HO 144/1636/311643/53).

48 (1847–1929). Born in Kells, Co. Meath. Historian and hostess of London salon for writers, scholars and politicians. Involved with the Howth gun-running. Supported Treaty and became a member of the first Irish Senate.

49 PRO HO 144/1636/311643/12. Casement had still not been charged.

50 A consideration in departing from the original decision to try Casement before a court martial was the desire to bring a treason charge, which, it was thought, would create a greater impression in neutral countries – the USA in particular (see Major-General Sir Wyndham Childs, *Episodes and Reflections*, London, Cassell & Co, 1930, p. 112. Childs, interestingly, condemned the circulation of the diaries and considered Casement to be 'an idealist and a very brave man').

51 Casement wrote to Alice Green and others asking them to provide examples of speeches praising those such as the Poles and Czechs who had rebelled or repudiated their allegiances. He wished to make the point that 'the very thing I did has been done again & again by *far* greater men . . . men whom the English nation are asked to honour and praise for ever'. The British Constitution itself was based on an act of betrayal, '*calling in a foreign prince & foreign army* to overturn the Throne'. He asked for the names of the leaders of the Whig Revolution of 1689 (Letter, undated, to Alice Green and others, NYPL: MCIHP, Box 1, IHP10).

52 (1871–59). Duffy's brother-in-law. Son of Alexander Martin Sullivan (Young Irelander, and later constitutional nationalist). Born in New York, began career there as a journalist. Moved to Dublin, Irish Bar, 1892, English Bar, 1899. Sullivan hardly distinguished himself in the conduct of Casement's defence. His cross-examination was weak and his arguments tended to ramble,

Bernard Shaw, and as Casement himself desired, and chose instead a technical defence based on an improbable reading of the law of treason.[53] But the 'not guilty' plea ensured that there would be a full trial. Indeed, even the committal hearing lasted for three days. In the event, a defended trial suited the government interests. Already there were signs that the courts martial and executions in Dublin had backfired. Far better, therefore, to give Casement due process of civil law, and to spell out against him a case of squalid and ignominious betrayal and German sympathies, rather than high patriotic principles. Starting on 26 June, the trial lasted four days.[54] He was duly found guilty and sentenced

even if one accepted his legalistic (rather than political) strategy. Emotionally and intellectually he seems to have been completely out of his depth, and the transcript suggests that he was intimidated by the venue, the high office of the judges and his trial opponent. He may also have been unnerved by his knowledge that Casement was a homosexual who gloried in his condition, and who wished this fact to be put to the jury (see MacColl, *op. cit.*, p. 228; *Irish Times*, 16 April 1956, 5f). Sullivan's dislike of Casement (certainly in 1956) was obvious: 'He took up the attitude that we pigmies could not understand the conduct of great men, and had no right to pass judgement on it. . . . Everyone seems to forget, as I have sometimes done myself, that Casement was a megalomaniac' (ibid.). On the trial's penultimate day Sullivan broke down, and failed to appear at all on the last day. His junior, Artemus Jones, had to close the defence case. An American lawyer, Michael Francis Doyle (who had acted for Casement in a libel matter against the *New York World*) had come over apparently with the approval of the British Ambassador, Spring Rice, to assist in the trial. According to Tim Healy, Doyle was received by the Foreign Secretary and described the impact of the Easter executions on American opinion. His exact role in the preparation of Casement's defence is not clear, but he was probably a contact of McGarrity, which makes Spring Rice's endorsement puzzling (see Inglis, *op. cit.*, pp. 334–5; Timothy Michael Healy, *Letters and Leaders of My Day*, London, Thornton Butterworth, 1928, Vol. 2, p. 570; Harford Montgomery Hyde (ed.), *Famous Trials: Roger Casement*, Harmondsworth, Penguin, 1963, p. 26; William O'Brien and Desmond Ryan (eds), *Devoy's Post Bag, 1871–1928*, Dublin, C. J. Fallon, 1948–53, Vol. 2, p. 497). The final member of the defence team was an old acquaintance of Casement's, Professor John Hartman Morgan, who assisted with the constitutional elements in the brief.

53 Shaw's early reaction had been different. Nine days after Casement's capture in Tralee, Shaw wrote to Massingham (editor of the *Nation*), taking the view that the rising was 'rather ghastly'. With the Dublin executions still going on, Shaw urged a different course with Casement: 'If they send Casement to Broadmoor, no great harm will be done. If they shoot him, he will be canonized with Emmet & Lord Edward, and do mischief for years to come. It is supremely important that he should be made ridiculous' (Shaw to Massingham, 30 April 1916: Dan H. Lawrence (ed.), *Bernard Shaw: Collected Letters 1911–1925*, London, Max Rinhardt, 1985, p. 398). Shaw's proposed defence was privately printed by Clement Shorter (*A Discarded Defence of Roger Casement, Suggested by Bernard Shaw. With an Appendix of Comments by Roger Casement, and an Introduction by Clement Shorter*, London, February 1922). Only twenty-five copies were printed, one of which is held at the British Library. There is a typed abstract in the MCIHP (Box 2, IHP42).

54 For an account of the trial see *The Times*, 26 May 1916, 3a–b (grand jury indictment); 27 June, 3a–c; 28 June, 3a–c; 29 June, 3a–d (trial), 30 June, 6a–c (conclusion and sentence) (original trial materials are to be found at the Public Record Office: J17/662; J93/3; KB12/217–18, and in the Casement Papers, NLI: Ms. 13, 088). The charges of high treason against Casement and Julian Daniel Bailey (the soldier) were the first for which a bill of indictment had been drawn under

to death by the Lord Chief Justice. The appeal was heard on 17 July, and, as Casement had expected, was summarily dismissed.[55] Leave to appeal to the House of Lords had to be obtained from Casement's chief prosecutor, the Attorney General – Sir Frederick (F. E.) Smith,[56] who had himself more than flirted with treason in Ulster just a few years previously, and who remained a diehard Unionist. Scrupulousness about his own record might have obliged Smith to allow even an uncertain weak case to go to the Lords, but Smith experienced no such difficulty.[57] Casement's execution was set for 3 August.[58]

the Indictments Act, 1915 (5 & 6 Geo.V, c.90). The intention of this statute was to modernise the language used in the drafting of bills of indictment. In his charge to the Middlesex Grand Jury the Lord Chief Justice explained the nature of the offence of high treason and emphasised the necessity to prove overt actions. These were the various acts of incitement at Limburg Camp, the seduction from their allegiance of several soldiers, and Casement's trip to Ireland by submarine and the simultaneous attempt to land arms and ammunition. At the conclusion of Casement's trial no evidence was offered against Bailey on the charge of high treason. The soldier had simply been a prop in the drama.

55 See Knott, *op. cit.*, pp. 207–87. On the eve of his appeal Casement wrote to Father Edward Murnane, from whom he was receiving religious instruction: 'Tomorrow I go to the Appeal Court to hear my Counsel against the indictment – & I shall return here. That is the one thing I am sure of. However interesting from the point of view of "the history of treason law in this country" I anticipate no other interest than that of listening to the arguments for and against, and coming back to the place I started from in the morning' (Casement to Murnane, 16 July 1916: NLI: Casement Papers: Ms. 14, 100). He had, however, taken some interest in the reprieve campaign, giving instructions for a letter to the press to Gertrude Bannister in the course of a visit on 24 July. Both he and Miss Bannister were warned that the use of visits for this purpose were prohibited, and that a recurrence would result in visits being stopped (PRO HO P. Com. 9/2330).

56 (1872–1930). Academic lawyer, 1894–1903; KC and Bencher of Gray's Inn, 1908; Unionist MP, Walton Division of Liverpool, 1906–19. Solicitor General, 1915; Attorney General, 1915–19; Lord Chancellor, 1919–22. Active service in France, 1914. Baron, 1919, Viscount, 1921, Earl, 1922. Director of ICI and of Tate and Lyle, 1928.

57 Smith (later Lord Birkenhead) appeared to shift somewhat in his attitude towards Casement, but his fundamental objective was clear enough – the man's destruction. He was willing to allow Casement's defence team to use the diaries as an indication of insanity, and thus to save Casement's life. The price of this, of course, was Casement's acceptance of the diaries as genuine, and the consequence would have been his confinement as a perverted lunatic and the besmirching of his cause. If this could not be achieved, then the second best outcome for Smith was Casement dead. Speaking in New York sixteen months after the event, Smith said 'Nothing gave me greater pleasure than the execution of Casement' (*Boston Post*, 14 January 1918: NYPL: MCIHP, Box 12, IHP 174). Such language (if correctly attributed) was utterly inappropriate for a law officer, and one who within two years would be Lord Chancellor of England.

58 The case was, of course, a national sensation, and in the popular newspapers there was a deal of satisfaction about the outcome. The headline (and half-page report) of the *News of the World* was typical (2 July 1916, 3a–c). Northcliffe's *Daily Mail* (which then had the country's largest circulation) was unrelenting: 'A Paltry Traitor Meets his Just Fate'. Sub-headings included 'Sentence Received with a Cynical Smile' and 'The Diaries of a Degenerate' (30 June 1916, 1).

Prison

At Brixton, Casement was treated as a remand prisoner, with the allowance of letters and visits provided by prison regulations.[59] Conditions, according to his cousin, were 'infinitely better' than at the Tower. He was allowed to receive civilian clothes (and changes) as well as books and newspapers, and there were daily visits.[60] For the most part he was treated as any other prisoner under potential sentence of death. On the Home Secretary's instructions, special suicide precautions were taken. He was held in the prison hospital, and warders were with him constantly: one during daytime hours and two at night.[61] The embers of the Dublin rising were barely cold, the war continued, and the authorities wished to ensure that Casement passed out no message that would have either political or military repercussions. Thus, when Alice Green visited on the morning of 19 May, the governor (C. Haynes) himself supervised, to ensure that their conversation was confined to personal matters, and Casement's legal defence.[62] Usually correspondence would have been censored and noted in the prison, but all Casement's correspondence, in and out, went to the Prison Commissioners.[63]

Duffy and Casement's friends attempted to ease his conditions. He was a heavy smoker suffering from the denial of tobacco. In what appears to have been a prearranged sequence of letters, on 20 May Gavan Duffy wrote to Colonel J. Winn, Secretary of the Prison Commission, asking that Casement be allowed to smoke. The rules for remand prisoners did not permit this, Duffy knew, but he argued that as the case was an exceptional one (though surely only in terms of notoriety) 'I trust you may be able to relax the ordinary prison rule

---

59 The regulations were strictly applied (PRO P. Com. 9/2321/50454/26).
60 NLI: Casement Papers: Ms. 13, 079, f. 11. During one of these visits there was a bitter confrontation between Casement and Richard Morten, one of his oldest friends. Hyde claimed that this was about Casement's homosexuality (1963, *op. cit.*, p. 80). Casement's letter of reconciliation shows deep distress, but does not refer directly to the cause of the row (NLI: Casement Papers: Ms. 13, 600: Casement to Morten, 11 June 1916).
61 Extra staff were assigned to Brixton for the special watch (PRO P. Com. 9/2322).
62 PRO P. Com. 9/2316. The precaution was not wholly effective, since among the Casement Papers there is a plan of the fort on Banna Strand in which Casement was captured. This shows the location of certain rabbit holes in which, presumably, Casement had hidden documents or other items. Whether these were ever retrieved (or whether the RIC or the IRB searched the area) is unclear (NLI: Casement Papers: Ms. 13, 088(2)). Casement also managed to smuggle out a last message to Ireland, dated 2 August 1916. Eighteen months later Gertrude Parry handed this to de Valera. (ibid., Ms. 14, 100 (unfoliated)).
63 PRO P. Com. 9/2317. The packages were accompanied by a form which was used in the case of aliens, underlining the security reasons behind the censorship. A number of Casement's letters were suppressed on Sir Ernley Blackwell's instructions. On 29 July – six days before the execution – Blackwell directed 'the four letters to him are trivial and are not to be given to him'. A plea from Casement to his friend Alice Green, asking her to see that he was buried in Ireland, was also suppressed. The Permanent-Under-Secretary, Sir Charles Troup, minuted: 'the publication of this letter would open out an unpleasant controversy in an unpleasant way – and to have to reply to it would be unfortunate however clear the answer' (PRO HO 144/1637/311643/108).

and I have little doubt that the medical officer at the prison would recommend this course'. The medical officer was not consulted at all, and at the Prison Commissioner Frederick Dryhurst simply minuted 'Please reply that on the medical officer's recommendation the prisoner is being allowed to smoke.'[64]

Encouraged by Duffy's success with tobacco, Casement's cousin Gertrude Bannister wrote to the Home Office on 5 June to enquire whether she might have fruit sent in. Here too the response was reasonably flexible. Casement, the Prison Commissioners noted, was already receiving a hospital diet, and if the medical officer thought that fruit was needed it would be better that he should purchase it. There was no objection therefore to Miss Bannister sending in money to be expended at the medical officer's discretion.[65]

In his last weeks Casement determined to convert to Roman Catholicism as the religion of the majority of his countrymen – a curious decision given his earlier insistence on the importance of the Protestant contribution to Irish nationalism.[66] On 5 June Gavan Duffy wrote to the Prison Commission asking that Casement should be allowed visits from a priest, and that the visits should be permitted as freely and under the same conditions as visits from the regular prison chaplain – that is, on as many occasions as both should desire and out of sight and hearing of prison officials. This raised difficulties, since the rules did not permit a prisoner to change the religion which he declared on reception. If there were additional security concerns (Casement had, after all, used a Tralee priest to pass a message to the leaders of the rising) they do not appear in the

---

64 PRO P. Com. 9/2318. Duffy's initial allusion to the medical officer suggests prior consultation, since this was a well-tried device when the authorities wished to bend the rules but required a point of authority which avoided accusations of favouritism and the creation of open precedents.

65 PRO P. Com. 9/2320: memorandum of 6 June 1916. Initial approval for the fruit came from Sir Ernley Blackwell.

66 Casement acknowledged his own uncertainties in the matter of conversion, and from the condemned cell wrote movingly to the priest from whom he was receiving instruction in Roman Catholic doctrine (Father Edward Murnane): 'There are times when I feel my doubts are settled and then they revive, and I cannot say what motive actuates me. It is very hard to be sure of one's convictions – to be certain always one is convinced. I thought I was – and today and yesterday I am not sure: and questions came to me from myself that I find no answer to. The trouble is – am I *convinced*? Or do I only think I am? Am I moved by love or fear? I can only accept, in my soul, from love – never from fear; and part of the appeal *seems*, at times, to be to my fear. The more I read the more confused I get, and it is not reading I want, but companionship. . . . And then I don't want to jump or rush or do anything hastily just because time is short' (NLI: Casement Papers: Ms. 14, 100: Casement to Murnane, 16 July 1916). The Roman Catholic hierarchy raised difficulties about Casement's conversion, but Father Thomas Carey, Pentonville's Catholic chaplain, discovered that as a child Casement's mother had had him baptised in that faith (this was confirmed by Gertrude Parry: NLI: Casement Papers: Ms. 13, 079, f. 1). In his last letter to his sister Nina Casement gave the date of his baptism as 5 August 1868 at Rhyl (ibid., Ms. 13, 600 (unfoliated)). Formal conversion was therefore unnecessary, and there only remained ministry to the dying. Carey wrote about Casement's last hours and moments: 'He died with all the faith and piety of an Irish peasant woman. . . . It was an edifying Catholic death . . . I have no doubt that he has gone to heaven' (NLI: Casement Papers: Ms. 13, 078 (7)).

official correspondence.[67] No obstacle was placed in the path of conversion. On 12 July 1916, the Revd Thomas Carey, the Pentonville Roman Catholic chaplain, asked permission for Casement to make his confession and for a Bishop to come to the prison to confirm him. These requests were granted.[68]

Upon removal from Brixton, Casement wrote to the governor, C. Haynes, thanking him for his kind treatment. A version of this letter appeared in the *Irish Independent* some sixteen years later.[69] The tone and style of the body of the text have the ring of Casement's courtliness about them, as well as his obsession with national traits:

> Before I had the misfortune, as I will term it in truth, to be taken out of your custody on my journeys to and from this prison to Bow Street, I want to thank you very warmly and sincerely for your unfailing courtesy, manliness and kindness to me.
>
> From the time you took me into custody at Euston on Easter Sunday and again took me to the Tower on Easter Tuesday, you showed me the best side of an Englishman's character – his native good heart. Robert Louis Stevenson once said 'an Irishman's hatred of England is natural, right and sincere. It is against a rule and a government, and is not based on any personal end. It is impersonal and may be most unselfish.' I hope my feeling is something of that kind.

At Pentonville he was subject to the normal regime for a prisoner under sentence of death. This included the wearing of convict clothes, an indignity which he resented (or so the *Daily Express* reported with some relish.)[70] He would don civilian clothes for his appeal and for his execution.[71]

Campaign for reprieve

Next only to his decision to go to Germany, Casement's fate was shaped by the fall on 17 May 1916 of England's last Liberal government, and its replacement

---

67 The Home Office response to Duffy's request referred only to the prison rules: 'It does not appear that the Rev. E. Murnane is visiting Casement in his spiritual capacity, but merely an ordinary visitor. In that case it seems most desirable that his visits should take place within sight and hearing' (PRO P. Com. 9/2319). Father Murnane was attached to the Dockhead Church, Bermondsey.

68 The chaplain asked that a priest other than himself should hear the confession ('one who is more of a stranger to him than I now am') and suggested the Revd T. J. Ring of Saints Mary and Michael's Church, Commercial Road (PRO P. Com. 9/2329).

69 *Irish Independent*, 16 September 1932, 1d.

70 It is difficult to know whether Casement was bothered by his convict uniform. His cousin, Gertrude Bannister, was distressed to find him so dressed. The *Express* clearly had a channel to the intelligence services, and may simply have been relaying a report intended to diminish Casement's status (1 July 1916, 1d).

71 Hyde, 1963, *op. cit.*, p. 157.

by a Liberal–Unionist coalition. Whatever indulgence Asquith as head of a Liberal government could have extended to Casement (and Asquith's tendency to reinforce reconciliation with leniency would have been joined to the expediency of placating Irish opinion in the aftermath of the rising executions) the wishes of his coalition partners were central to Asquith's own survival.[72] The coalition government included such champions of Ulster Unionism as Carson and F. E. Smith, as well as Bonar Law and Arthur Balfour. The narrow and partisan claims of these new colleagues had, moreover, acquired great moral force on the Somme, when on 1 July thirteen British divisions attacked a still-intact German defensive line on a twenty-mile front. On that first day the British Army suffered the greatest losses in its history: 19,000 dead and 57,000 casualties.[73] Of this number, one division, the 36th Ulster Division, suffered a loss of seventy-nine officers and 1777 men and (in a significant departure from the normal ratio of killed to wounded) 102 officers and 2626 men wounded. Ulster Unionism's claim for consideration had been sealed in blood, bravery and loyalty.[74] The contrast with Dublin's Easter rising could not have been greater, and hardly needed emphasis by Unionists. It was in these sombre and unpromising circumstances that reprieve appeals were launched.

At this point there was Cabinet disagreement on Casement's fate. Early in July Asquith informed the King that several ministers, including Sir Edward Grey (Foreign Secretary) and Lord Lansdowne (a determined anti-Home Ruler), took the view that it would be better were Casement kept in confinement as a criminal lunatic 'than he should be executed without any smirch on his character, and then canonised as a martyr both in Ireland and America'.[75] No immediate decision was necessary, however, as Casement's appeal was still pending. The option of confinement as a criminal lunatic had to a large extent been pre-empted, since the defence had refused the Attorney General's offer – though it was perhaps possible that the Royal Prerogative could have been exercised conditionally. But before sentence had been pronounced, Casement's friends in Ireland, England and the United States of America had been moving.

---

72 And necessity alone determined outcomes, as Churchill had observed rather sourly to his wife a few months previously when he himself was out of office: 'It is *need* alone that counts. Nothing else is considered' (Martin Gilbert, *Winston S. Churchill*, London, Heinemann, 1971, Vol. III, p. 680).

73 A. J. P. Taylor points out that these losses were the heaviest suffered in such circumstances by any army in the 1914–18 war (*English History 1914–1945*, Oxford University Press, 1976, p. 60).

74 The *Official History of the War: France and Belgium 1916* (p. 404) drew attention to the fact that 1 July (old style) was the anniversary of the Battle of the Boyne and contended that the remembrance of that day 'filled every Ulsterman's heart with certainty of victory'. The officer commanding the Ulster Division, General Oliver Nugent, emphasised a similar point in a letter to Carson: 'The losses were formidable before we ever reached the first line; but the men never faltered and finally rushed the first line, cheering and shouting "Boyne" and "No Surrender" . . . I can hardly bring myself to think or write about it. It was magnificent beyond description' (Ian Colvin, *The Life of Lord Carson*, London, Victor Gollancz, 1936, Vol. III, p. 184).

75 Asquith to George V, PRO CAB41/37/25.

There were a number of individual offers of help, but the most concerted efforts centred around petitions.[76] In England Sir Arthur Conan Doyle launched a petition in conjunction with Clement Shorter of the *Sphere*.[77] Doyle considered Casement's crime to be very bad indeed, aggravated enormously by Casement's having taken government money all his life. He thought that he was mentally unhinged 'and that his honourable nature would in a normal condition have revolted from such an action'. He did not, however, urge mental condition as the basis of a petition. The line he favoured was absolutely to acknowledge Casement's guilt and the justice of the sentence while at the same time urging the political wisdom of magnanimity. The petition should be signed by men 'who have shown no possible sympathy for Germany or pacific leanings'.[78] Shorter agreed, and the petition followed Doyle's wording almost exactly, and no one subsequently approached was a person whose motives could be misconstrued.

The petition circulated for the following three weeks, Shorter and Doyle seeking to get the maximum number of influential signatures, but conscious of the fatal timetable and of the need to allow government to deliberate. Given the general opinion of Casement's crime and the temper of the times, quite a remarkable and impressive group of thirty-eight signatures was obtained. Literary figures included (besides Doyle himself) John Masefield, Arnold Bennett, G. K.

---

76 Josiah Wedgewood wrote to Redmond on 9 May 1916. If there was still time he was willing to do what he could to help obtain a commutation of sentence: 'We ought not to have his blood on our heads, when the cause for which we are fighting is as near as we believe it to be the cause of God. We both know that he is mad – mad with that glorious madness that sees only the heavens and cares nothing for this earth. There is nothing mean and self-seeking about that form of lunacy, and for it one can only have the deepest pity and charity' (Cicely Veronica Wedgewood, *The Last of the Radicals: Josiah Wedgewood, MP*, London, Jonathan Cape, 1951, p. 115).

77 Doyle (1859–1930) was at the height of his considerable fame. He had known and admired Casement for some years and had been involved with E. D. Morel and others in the Congo Reform Association. His Irish parents, Roman Catholic upbringing (though he was no longer a believer) and support for Home Rule no doubt added to his interest in Casement's plight (for correspondence see NLI: Casement Papers: Ms. 13, 073 (28/ii)). Clement Shorter (1857–1926), editor of *The Sphere*, 1900–26. Civil servant, then journalist, editor and biographer (particularly the Brontës). Married (1896) Dora Sigerson, Irish poet and writer (daughter of Dr George Sigerson, nationalist and man of letters).

78 Doyle to Shorter, 2 July 1916: Casement Petition Papers: BM Add. Mss. 63596, ff. 4–6. The petition, addressed to Asquith, admitted Casement's guilt and the justice of the sentence but argued that he should not be executed. It drew attention to what it called 'the violent change' in Casement's attitude towards Britain, as shown, for example, by the wording of his acceptance of his knighthood, and continued: 'Without going so far as to urge complete mental irresponsibility, we should desire to point out that the prisoner had for many years been exposed to severe strain during his honourable career of public service, that he had endured several tropical fevers, and that he had experienced the worry of two investigations which were of a peculiarly nerve-trying character. For these reasons it appears to us that some allowance may be made in his case for an abnormal physical and mental state.' The document also pointed out that Casement's execution would harden opinion among some of the Irish, and would be used against Britain in the United States of America (PRO HO 144/1637/311643/79).

Chesterton, John Drinkwater, John Galsworthy and Jerome K. Jerome. Academics and professionals were represented by Sir Clifford Allbutt, Regius Professor of Physics at Cambridge, and Sir Thomas Barlow, President of the Royal College of Physicians, as well as both Beatrice and Sydney Webb. The President of the Baptist Union signed, as did the Bishop of Winchester. Several journalists – generally of Liberal or left-of-centre journals – gave their support: H. W. Massingham (then of the *Nation*), C. P. Scott, the distinguished editor of the *Manchester Guardian*, A. G. Gardiner of the *Daily News*, G. P. Gooch of the *Contemporary Review*, and of course Shorter himself as editor of the *Sphere*. Sir Sydney Olivier,[79] Permanent Secretary of the Board of Agriculture and Fisheries, raised some official eyebrows by giving his support.

The responses of those who refused to sign were usually courteous. Rudyard Kipling, Nobel Laureate, and then at the height of his fame as 'The Poet of Empire', would have been a hugely influential signatory, but he declined in a one-sentence letter: 'I find myself unable to sign the petition you sent me re. Roger Casement, and I return it accordingly.' Kipling's only son had served with the Irish Guards and had been killed in September 1915, and a more bitter rejection might have been expected.[80] Sidney Colan was in favour of amnestying the Sinn Féin rank and file, 'a politic as well as a merciful course to take'. But Casement, a traitor, should be hanged – 'without regard to the consequences, unless indeed he could be confirmed as a lunatic'. He doubted whether there were proofs of insanity.[81] John Burns (who had resigned from government on the outbreak of war) refused to sign because he thought that the petition campaign would do no good, and might do harm. In any event, he did not believe that the sentence would be carried out.[82] Burns' namesake James Crichton Burns was emphatic in his refusal. He recognised the humane spirit behind the petition but could not accept that Casement was mentally unbalanced. On the contrary,

> He appears to me to be astute and clear headed, a peculiarly mean and contemptible traitor – a liar and a sneak, who richly deserves the punishment to which he has been sentenced. Magnanimity is all very well, but it would be sheer poltroonery to allow any deference to the views of the United States or of the Neutral countries that have never seen fit to protest against German atrocities.

79 Olivier (1859–1943) may have been drawn to the petition because of his Colonial Service background; he had also, for some four years, been a secretary of the Fabian Society.

80 Ibid., 9 July 1916, f. 138. It was Kipling's tragedy, of course, that he had exerted his influence to have his 17-year-old poorly sighted son admitted to the army (see Rudyard Kipling, *The Irish Guards in the Great War*, Staplehurst, Spellmount, 1997, pp. 9–10).

81 Ibid., 11 July 1916, f. 114.

82 Burns had been a labour leader, street agitator, prisoner, MP and Liberal minister. He had taken a significant interest in penal reform in the 1890s. Whether his signature would have been influential is doubtful, but it would hardly have been harmful.

He also refused to accept that there was any similarity between Casement's case and the amnesty granted by the Union in the American Civil War.[83] Another correspondent was more abrupt and indignant: 'I am strongly in favour of the immediate execution of the traitor Roger Casement and I entirely disagree with this petition.' Alice Green attempted to collect signatures from a small group of prominent figures, to go privately to Herbert Samuel, the Home Secretary. 'So far,' she informed William Cadbury, 'all for different reasons have refused to sign.'[84]

The Doyle–Shorter petition was sent to Asquith on 24 July, who two days later (and significantly, without comment) passed it on to the Home Office.[85] With just over a week until the day fixed for Casement's execution a response had to be agreed quickly. Sir Ernley Blackwell, who took the leading official role in Casement's case, immediately drafted a two-and-a-half page memorandum refuting the petition clause by clause.[86] Casement had not undergone a violent change in opinion which could be taken as an indication of mental instability. The petitioners had drawn attention to Casement's obsequious letter to the King at the time of his knighthood as an example of his drastic shift. This, Blackwell pointed out, was described by Casement as 'a piece of official politeness'. Indeed, Casement had argued that he was obliged to accept the knighthood, and Blackwell quoted from his journal for the day (15 June 1911) on which he received notification of the honour: 'Letter from Sir E. Grey telling me of knighthood! Alack. To Uxbridge. Lovely boy scout and Chaney's baker lad. Putumayo telegram 1/7½d. Cigarettes 10d. Papers 7½d. Stamps 2/=.'[87] The entry showed not only how unmoved Casement had been by the award, but also that he was *genuinely* unmoved, since the entry contained homosexual observations

---

83 Ibid., 13 July 1916, ff. 106–9.

84 NLI: Casement Papers: Ms. 8358 (3): July 1916: 'The upper classes are intensely hostile, the lower classes uninformed & silent. The clergy outdoing the laymen in "imperialism".' There was nevertheless some discreet lobbying. Haldane (once a powerful Liberal eminence, but now immobilised by spurious allegations of pro-Germanism) did what he could, but on 31 July informed Alice Green that he thought the Cabinet would not alter its decision: 'The horrors of war are terrible' (ibid., Ms. 13, 000 (unfoliated)).

85 By this time most members of the Cabinet had seen the medical report on Casement, based on an examination of his diaries. Doctors Smith and Craig had on 10 July concluded that the evidence was too meagre to certify insanity (see below, p. 586, n. 123). On 14 July Asquith informed the King that the report found Casement to be abnormal but not certifiably insane (PRO CAB41/37/26). Five days later the Cabinet again considered the matter, and, Asquith informed the King, unanimously decided that Casement should hang (PRO CAB41/37/27).

86 In drafting his memorandum Blackwell was assisted by Basil Thomson, who provided information on Casement's political and private activities (Sir Basil Thomson, 1939, *op. cit.*, p. 302). Ernley Robertson Hay Blackwell (1868–1941) came from a well-known St Andrews family. Bar (Inner Temple), 1892. Appointed to Home Office in 1906 as a result of the Adolph Beck case. Handled petitions from prisoners, and advised on the exercise of the Royal Prerogative in capital cases. First-class golfer, captain of the Royal and Ancient (1933). Married in his sixty-ninth year.

87 Ernley Blackwell Memorandum, 26 July 1916: PRO HO 144/1637/311364/79.

that Casement would never have contemplated showing to anyone else, and therefore there could be no question of assuming a false insouciance.[88]

The quotation also served, and was intended to draw attention to, Casement's perverted and immoral proclivities, and thus supported another of Blackwell's refutations of the petition's claim that Casement had 'an honourable career of public service'. His diaries and ledgers of 1910 to 1911 showed evidence that Casement's private life was 'of the filthiest description', and that 'whether he was in South America, England or Belfast his leisure was entirely taken up in finding accomplices or victims and there are several instances where he succeeded in corrupting youths and one of attempting to corrupt a child of 11 years of age'. Had this evidence come to light, 'It is quite certain that his honourable career in the public service, would have come to a sudden termination'. While Casement's mental and physical state might be abnormal, it did not appear that this had affected his crime.

Blackwell brushed aside the argument that Casement's execution would have a bad effect on Irish-American opinion: he doubted whether it would affect any opinion which was not already hostile. Opinion at home and in the Empire, and of the Allies ('and the French in particular') would see reprieve merely as an act of weakness. In the midst of a war Britain could not act as had the Union at the end of the American Civil War. Casement was not merely a misguided Sinn Féiner, but someone whose primary object was to help Germany and so to enable Ireland to regain her freedom: 'The time has certainly not come when we should be willing to extend an amnesty to British subjects who may for one reason or another adhere to Germany.'

Neither the Permanent Secretary (Troup) nor the Home Secretary (Herbert Samuel)[89] disagreed. The former did note that the petition was 'a very moderate statement of the reasons for reprieve'. The Home Secretary was of similar mind, and minimised, the influence which the petitioners were likely to wield in Britain. He observed, however, that the signatories were not entirely without weight, and directed that Conan Doyle's offer to refrain from publication should be accepted: 'the names of many of them carry so much weight with the American public that the effect might be serious there.'[90] Seeking to avoid embarrassment

---

88 Ironically, Casement's explanation that his apparently warm acceptance of the knighthood was merely formal politeness was at his trial strenuously challenged by the prosecution.

89 (1870–1963). Previously President of Local Government Board, Postmaster General and Chancellor of the Duchy of Lancaster. Declined to join Lloyd George's government in December 1916. Leader of Liberal Party, 1931–5.

90 PRO HO 144/1637/311643/79. Samuel wrote to Doyle the day after the petition had been formally acknowledged, stating that government preferred that it not be published. He dangled an empty hint of favourable consideration: 'All the circumstances relating to the case of Casement are receiving the earnest consideration of the Government' (Samuel to Doyle, 27 July 1916: Casement Petition Papers: *op. cit.*, f. 9). Doyle passed the message to Shorter: 'I suppose in the face of this request we may not publish.'

to the government, and to preserve whatever influence the petitioners might hope to have, Doyle and Shorter probably miscalculated in keeping the petition confidential. Most of the signatories came from what could have been portrayed as more sentimentally inclined walks of life, but many were figures of national and international renown, and some, by any criterion, were persons of sober authority. When the petition had been passed from Downing Street to the Home Office an anxious accompanying note about publication showed Asquith's uncertainty as to the political repercussions. Had it become known that a well-backed plea for clemency had been made, it is possible that others might have spoken for reprieve. This in turn might have strengthened Cabinet sympathisers. Binding their loyalty with an offer of public silence, Doyle and Shorter probably discarded the only trump in their weak hand.

And the Doyle–Shorter petition was the only one likely to have had an effect. With so many Unionists in the Cabinet, petitions from Irish nationalists were valueless scrip, and even the pleas of unquestionably respectable and manifestly non-political personages counted for little. This despite the state of feeling in Ireland. In a matter of three or four days Alice Green alone received the signatures of thirteen bishops, 128 parish priests, 118 justices of the peace, 310 councillors, mayors and other local government officials, and 1276 private persons. A greater number of pledges were sent to Colonel Maurice Moore's Committee.[91] In addition to the organised petitions a number of individuals wrote privately or publicly urging mercy, though in the nature of things some of these were hardly likely to be productive. W. B. Yeats wrote to Asquith from Calvados. The handwriting was not his, though the covering letter and the signature on the petition certainly were. Blackwell noted: 'Madam Maud Gonne McBride is also staying at the above address at present!' (Indeed it seems that either she or her daughter had copied out the petition for Yeats: certainly her association with the document in no way enhanced its influence.)[92]

In a letter to the *Manchester Guardian* Bernard Shaw argued the case that he had urged on Casement as his defence.[93] The trial had been fair, but certain issues had not been addressed – the unprosecuted treason of the Ulster Unionists, and those in Britain whose actions had helped convince Germany that an attack on France would fail to find a British response. Because Ireland was part

---

91 NLI: Casement Papers: Ms. 13, 088 (9). All the petitions were sent immediately to Asquith (for correspondence on the petition organised by Colonel Maurice Moore and Agnes O'Farrelly see NLI: Maurice Moore Papers: Ms. 10, 564 (1–6)). Blackwell, on 2 August 1916, responded by regretting that the Home Secretary could find no grounds to interfere with 'the due course of law'.

92 PRO HO 144/1636/311643/45. Yeats had crossed to France to renew his by now ritual proposal of marriage. This was rejected, and Yeats then seriously contemplated marriage to Maud's 20-year-old adopted daughter (he was 51) (see Margaret Ward, *Maud Gonne: A Life*, London, Pandora, 1990, pp. 112–13. As Ward observed, 'The situation verged on the ludicrous'). No matter how high Yeat's reputation subsequently rose, at this time he appeared to the Home Office as a semi-Bohemian poet with a Fenian reputation and some very unsavoury associations.

93 *Manchester Guardian*, 22 July 1916, 4b. The letter ran to almost twenty column inches.

of the United Kingdom it could not be argued that his action in pursuing his country's independence established Casement's guilt, any more than five centuries of Turkish rule had extinguished a Serbian's right to fight for independence. Most telling of all, there was the fact that if Casement were executed he would become a national hero in Ireland, and 'Ireland has enough heroes and martyrs already, and if England has not by this time had enough of manufacturing them in fits of temper, experience is thrown away on her'.

The Archbishop of Canterbury had been approached, and supported reprieve, but, considering that it would be inappropriate for the head of the Established Church to intervene publicly in such a politically fraught matter, he privately consulted the Lord Chancellor (Lord Buckmaster) and also Herbert Samuel. The latter had been a parliamentary ally of Casement during the Congo investigations, and had then spoken in glowing terms of Casement,[94] and the Archbishop (as he doubtless intended) evoked memories when he wrote of his own high regard for the man during those years.[95] Others also wrote privately, drawing on whatever credit or standing they had.[96] Alice Green renewed a fleeting acquaintance with General Louis Botha (the Boer leader and then Premier of South Africa) to seek his intervention. She outlined Casement's career, the difficulties of his current situation and drew various political parallels with Masarayk and others – and, by implication, Botha himself.[97]

The Irish Party had lost most by the rising (and would eventually lose all), but from motives both political and self-interested, as well as humane fellow feeling, a substantial minority sought mercy for Casement.[98] John Dillon, Redmond's deputy, made a personal appeal to Asquith, but Redmond himself refused to intervene.[99] In a memoir undated but possibly written not long after Casement's death, Joseph McGarrity, the Clan na Gael leader and friend of

---

94 4 *Hansard*, CXXXV, col. 1262; 9 June 1904. In a debate on the Congo atrocities Samuel (then in opposition) had described Casement as 'a gentleman of the highest standing and reliability, and whose good faith even the Congo Free State had not ventured to challenge'.

95 MacColl, *op. cit.*, pp. 216–18.

96 NLI: Casement Papers: Ms. 13, 078 (1).

97 Alice Stopford Green to General Louis Botha, 16 June 1916: O'Brien and D. Ryan, *op. cit.*, Vol. 2, pp. 499–502.

98 In the general election of December 1910 the Irish Party had obtained eighty-four seats. A deputation which waited on Asquith on 26 July 1916 handed in a petition signed by thirty-nine of these (*News of the World*, 30 July 1916, 7e). The deputation was led by Arthur Lynch, who had been (with John MacBride) a co-founder of the Irish Brigade in the South African War. In January 1903 he had been found guilty of treason and sentenced to death, which sentence was commuted to penal servitude. He was elected MP for Clare, pardoned in 1907, served in the British Army during the war and assisted in recruitment in Ireland. Lynch was a very apt leader of the delegation (see p. 618, n. 44, below).

99 Redmond may have been influenced by the extracts from Casement's diaries, which he had of course been shown. Denis Gwynn, the sympathetic biographer of both Redmond and Casement, following the 1936 publication of William J. Maloney's *The Forged Casement Diaries*, strongly intimated that Redmond considered the diaries to be genuine. Redmond had left a note in his

Casement, noted, 'Redmond says no man has injured Ireland as much as Casement. He promised that he would tell the Government not to execute Casement if it asked his opinion before doing so but he would make no petition for his pardon of any kind.'[100]

On 17 July, Eva Gore-Booth wrote to Sir Edward Grey offering evidence that Casement had in fact gone to Ireland to try to stop the rising. This consisted of a statement from Father F. M. Ryan, the priest to whom Casement had spoken while in custody in Tralee on 21 April (the day he was captured). Ryan stated that Casement had told him he had come to Ireland in order to stop the rising and asked him to spread the news.[101] Eva claimed that while under interrogation at Scotland Yard on Easter Sunday Casement wished to send a message to the Irish leadership, but had not been allowed to do so. She argued that another execution would aggravate the situation in Ireland. Casement was a national hero, and clemency would do much to conciliate ordinary Irish people.[102] This letter was circulated by Herbert Samuel on 21 July, but Blackwell, worried that the waverers in the Cabinet would find it persuasive, had circulated with it his own memorandum countering the claim of a peace mission. He also attached a portion of the transcript of Casement's interrogation by Hall and Thomson at Scotland Yard.[103] The waverers were stiffened.

In that desperate summer of 1916, with the war in the balance, Britain could not afford to be indifferent to American political opinion, and sections of that, in turn, were sensitive to the Irish-American electorate. Attempts were made to

papers describing what he had been shown. In a letter to Bulmer Hobson, Casement's protegé and friend, Gwynn confessed that he had deliberately omitted Redmond's statement from his *Life of Redmond* 'because I thought that most people would regard his evidence as conclusive' (30 October 1936: NLI: McGarrity Papers: Ms. 17, 604 (5)). When Henry Nevinson went to the Commons on 31 July 1916 to solicit support for Casement's reprieve he was well received by a number of Irish and Liberal MPs, but when he mentioned Casement's name to Redmond he 'turned rudely away . . . merely saying, "Please don't," and no more' (Henry Woodd Nevinson, *Last Changes Last Chances*, London, Nisbet & Co, 1928, p. 117).

100 NYPL: MCIHP, Box 5, IHP87. McGarrity made a number of other interesting comments on the reprieve campaign. Dillon worked for reprieve and T. P. O'Connor did not believe the government would execute Casement. McGarrity also claimed that the Attorney General (F. E. Smith) 'sent word that if Sir R. pleaded insanity he would get off'. He noted that Shaw thought that Casement should have no counsel but Doyle (an American lawyer who advised the defence). And, as we have seen, Shaw had written a speech for Casement which he wanted him to read before the jury retired. Two of the jurymen, according to McGarrity, said that 'if they had read his speech they would not have convicted him'.

101 NLI: Casement Papers: Ms. 13, 078 (7): Father F. M. Ryan to Gavan Duffy, 12 July 1916.

102 Eva Gore Booth to Sir Edward Grey, 17 July 1916: PRO HO 144/1636/311643/53. This letter must also have been shown to the press. The *Weekly Despatch* reported that the letter was being hawked around and dismissed it. For its readers' interest, it revealed that the cell in which Casement was being held had been previously occupied by Seddon, 'the murderer of Miss Barrow' (30 July 1916, 2f).

103 Ibid. See also Thomson, 1939, *op. cit.*, p. 302.

turn this chain of sensitivities to Casement's account. Some thought that the timing was propitious, since both US Presidential and Congressional elections were but four months away. In a dispatch to Sir Edward Grey on 16 June the British Ambassador in Washington warned that Irish-Americans were ready to mount an anti-British campaign: 'Pamphlets are in readiness to be published the moment that Casement is executed and the funds are already at hand for their distribution.' Should Casement not be executed, however, this would also be taken as a grievance, since (unlike the leaders of the Easter rising) he was a Protestant. But in any event American public opinion would condemn his execution: 'There is a great unanimity among the friends of England here that Casement's execution would be, from the point of view of pure expediency, at any rate a very great mistake.'[104]

American politicians were initially not unwilling to take up Casement's cause, despite his German associations. On 22 July Senator Martine of New Jersey moved a resolution requesting the President to ask for a stay of Casement's execution to allow new facts to be introduced. The resolution was flawed, however, in that it referred to Casement's 'hasty (so-called) trial'. This wording offended a sufficient number of Senators for the resolution to be referred to the foreign relations committee, which after several days produced a majority for a resolution omitting all reference to Casement and instead asking the President to transmit the Senate's hope that the British government would 'exercise clemency in the treatment of Irish political prisoners'.[105] The resolution, even watered down, was carried by only a majority vote – forty-six to nineteen.[106]

Such a weakly worded resolution was unlikely to influence the British government (now agreed that Casement should die) which, after all, had periodically to endure Congressional expressions of sympathy with extreme Irish nationalism. To have an impact such resolutions needed Presidential endorsement, and at this Woodrow Wilson baulked. The electoral consideration was irrelevant, since

---

104 Spring Rice to Grey, 16 June 1916: House of Lords Record Office, Lloyd George Papers: E/9/4/14, p. 2.

105 The resolution was prepared by Senator Stone and proposed by Senator Pitman (see NLI: Casement Papers: Ms. 13, 088 (10)). Casement's sister, Mrs Agnes (Nina) Newman, sat through several of the Senate debates on the resolution (*Irish World*, 5 August 1916, 1b–f). She had received no encouragement from American officialdom. Within days of Casement's arrest the State Department had turned down her request for an interview with the President to plead on her brother's behalf (*Liverpool Courier*, 2 May 1916, 5d).

106 The *Manchester Guardian*, sympathetic to Casement's cause though it was, noted the resolution's weakness, observing that its adoption 'followed an unfavourable report by a majority of the Foreign Relations Committee on a resolution requesting clemency for Roger Casement' (31 July 1916, 4g). Casement's supporters must have wondered if their cause would not have been better served by silence from the Senate rather than such a pointedly weak and general resolution. The militant Irish-American press were as pleased to greet another martyr as they would have been had clemency been shown – perhaps even more so. Ford's *Irish World* gave Casement's life story under the page-wide banner headline 'England Executes Another Champion of Humanity' (12 August 1916, 3a–g).

the Irish were embedded in the Democratic Party to such an extent that a switch of allegiance would have been impossible. Nor were Wilson's sympathies likely to lie naturally with the Irish: he had won his 1912 nomination against a Tammany Hall interest, and, as Spring Rice, the British Ambassador, noted some time after Casement's execution, Wilson was 'by descent an Orangeman and by education a Presbyterian'.[107] There is also some suggestion that Wilson could accommodate his disinclination to intervene on Casement's behalf with his electoral interest by allowing the rumour to gain currency that he had privately intervened on Casement's behalf.[108]

The diaries

The aspect of Casement's trial and execution which produced most bitterness in Irish opinion, and which particularly set his case apart from that of the other rebel leaders, was the use made of his diaries. At a distance of eighty-six years it hardly seems conceivable that senior officials and ministers should connive at the circulation of the private diaries of a prisoner under sentence of death, for whom the legal process was not exhausted – but that, to put the most charitable gloss upon it, was what ministers allowed themselves to be backed into. Over the intervening decades the contempt of Casement's friend, the liberal journalist Henry Nevinson, rings out:

> anyone who may have attempted by such means to blacken the character of, and prejudice our feelings towards, a man who stands in acute danger of a degrading and hideous death, is, in my opinion, guilty of a far meaner and more loathsome crime than the worst that could possibly be unearthed in the career of the criminal himself.[109]

For a man with a triple life – retired consul, insurrectionary conspirator and cruising homosexual with a penchant for boys and very young men – Casement

---

107 Stephen Gwynn (ed.), *The Letters and Friendships of Sir Cecil Spring-Rice: A Record*, London, Constable & Co, 1929, Vol. 2, p. 393. He added, however, that as leader of the Democratic Party, in which the Irish played a prominent part, 'he is bound in every way to give consideration to their demands'.

108 'Great pressure has been brought to bear on the President to interfere with a personal request, and had he done so he would have placed the Irish supporters of the Democratic party under great obligation to himself personally. It was no doubt with some such object that the rumour of his intervention was put about' (Spring Rice to Grey, 4 August 1916: PRO HO 144/ 1637/311643/181).

109 *Manchester Guardian*, 25 July 1916, 10d. Henry Woodd Nevinson (who had known Casement since 1906) argued comprehensively for reprieve – Casement's attempt to stop the rebellion, his humanitarian services, the pragmatic case for not adding another martyr to the Irish list and the case for treating insurgents as prisoners of war. His account of Casement is full of interest: *op. cit.*, ch. 4.

was remarkably nonchalant. In keeping with his itinerant bachelor lifestyle, he deposited his property in various places, including in the scattered items a chronology of his sexual fancies, lusts and encounters. He did nothing to retrieve or destroy this material before embarking for Germany. The most superficial reflection should have convinced him that domicile in Berlin entailed certain notoriety, execration and investigation in Britain. Indeed, the apprehension of his blunder in leaving behind such dangerous goods and the outcome – however dimly perceived – came to him before the British government admitted it had laid hands on his property. Two letters to John Devoy, sent shortly after his arrival in Germany show that the possibilities had begun seriously to worry him. He requested Devoy to remove his belongings to a place of safety, but it is not clear to which papers he referred.[110] It may be that Casement feared that his revolutionary comrades might read the journals and ledgers.[111] Rarely has someone so clearly foreseen his own destruction, and done so little to avoid it.

In a long letter, dated 11 November 1914, and dealing mainly with war developments, and details of his own mission, there occurs the following passage: 'My chief concern is for my sister in Ireland and for my papers with Bigger[112] and at the Agents in London. How foolish of me not to have got them over to the USA! Now the Enemy will get them I fear. They are in a state of mind that sticks at nothing – as you will realize – and so angry and frightened too.'[113] Only ten days later Casement revealed his anxieties even more clearly, and began, perhaps, to prepare the ground for an explanation: 'The way they tried to destroy Parnell by a divorce scandal when they failed to down him with the Pigott forgeries and how they tried to murder so many earlier Irishmen. Well they are just the same today.'[114] There is no record of Devoy having acted.

---

110 See Devoy to Casement, 1 January 1915: NLI: Casement Papers: Ms. 13, 073 (44/i). This twenty-five-page letter, sent through the German Embassy in Washington, was Devoy's first to Casement after Casement's arrival in Germany. Devoy confirmed a prior wireless message that he had put Casement's papers in a safe place, but from all the other news in the letter this was most unlikely to include material in England or Ireland. William Joseph Maloney (*The Forged Casement Diaries*, Dublin, The Talbot Press, 1936) suggests that Casement was concerned about his political papers. While that is possible, there was unlikely to be anything of a conspiratorial nature in Casement's papers before the summer of 1914. His political and cultural views had been well published. Far more likely was Casement's concern about personal material.

111 Devoy gave some indication of his own likely reaction when he mentioned in a letter to Casement a man named Brogan who had trouble with his wife – 'not for an ordinary transgression in the way of infidelity, but because of a charge of a baser and more disgraceful kind, which made it desirable that he should get out of her reach and the jurisdiction of the courts here' (28 May 1915: NLI: Casement Papers: Ms. 13, 073 (44/v).

112 Francis Joseph Bigger (1863–1926), a Belfast solicitor, antiquarian and Irish cultural enthusiast. He and Casement had met at a Féis which Bigger had organised in 1904.

113 Casement to Devoy, 11 November 1914: NYPL: MCIHP, Box 1, IHP20.

114 Casement to Devoy, 21 November 1914: ibid. Casement had been indelibly marked by Parnell's fall (see his poems in NLI: Casement Papers: Ms. 12, 114, which include three odes to Parnell, written when Casement was 27).

He may have discounted Casement's anxieties as being all of a piece with his other exaggerated moods, or he may not have had the means to do anything about papers in England, which could well have been under police observation.[115]

At some point – whether before or after his arrest is unclear – Casement's fears were realised, and some at least of his diaries and other papers were seized in his former lodgings at 45 or 50 Ebury Street.[116] These are curious documents, consisting of daily records of visits, activities and daily expenditure. Interspersed with domestic trivia and routines there were, from time to time, sexual observations. These consisted of notes of boys and men whom Casement found pleasing and attractive, many speculations about their sexual organs, and accounts of his sexual importuning and acts. These entries are not in formal narrative and continuous prose, but are rather like private shorthand – intended to remind the writer of intimate observations and feelings.[117]

Although arguments raged for many years after Casement's death, there can now be no doubt that the diaries and ledgers are genuine.[118] And while one

---

115 See Devoy to Casement, 1 January 1915: NLI: Casement Papers: 13, 073 (44/i). In a later letter to Casement (28 March 1915) Devoy reported that British agents in the United States of America were making every effort to gather information about him. (ibid. (44/iii)).

116 In one of his memoirs Thomson stated that the trunks containing the diaries were seized when the authorities had first received evidence of his treachery some months previously. Elsewhere, however, it is clear that Casement's views were known shortly after the outbreak of war – that is, some twenty months prior to his capture and interrogation. This seems the most likely timing (*Queer People*, London, Hodder & Stoughton, 1922, pp. 75–6, 90). A number of accounts were offered by Thomson over the years of the finding of the diaries – which must strengthen the suspicion that they were located and prepared for use some time before Casement's capture (see William J. Maloney, *op. cit.*, ch. 15).

117 Hyde, whose *Famous Trials: Roger Casement* is the best of the books dealing with Casement's trial and a great deal of the background, provides a short selection of extracts (appendix 4).

118 Casement's counsel, Serjeant Sullivan, stated that at no point did Casement deny that the diaries were his 'and he never authorised anybody else to do so' (*Irish Times*, 11 April 1956, 5f.). Saving only the possibility that forensic tests on the writing, paper and inks should demonstrate otherwise, their authenticity seems beyond doubt. There are, for example, a number of facts in the diaries that subsequently were verified, and which could not have been known to a forger (see, for example, PRO HO 144/1637/311643/139). Certainly the question of authenticity continues to generate discussion. Roger Sawyer and Angus Mitchell were commissioned to edit the diaries of Casement's Putumayo expeditions in 1910–11, and soon found themselves in disagreement as to whether the recently declassified documents were genuine (*Guardian*, 28 February 1998, p. 6). The result has been two sharply differing books: Roger Sawyer (ed.), *Roger Casement's Diaries, 1910. The Black and the White*, London, Pimlico, 1997; Angus Mitchell (ed.), *The Amazon Journal of Roger Casement*, London, Anaconda, 1997. A more recent report based on modern examination techniques asserts that the diaries are genuine (Goldsmiths College, 'The Giles Document Laboratory Report on the So-called Black Diaries (PRO HO 161/1–5) Associated with Sir Roger Casement', London, Goldsmiths College, 2002); see also W. J. McCormack, *Roger Casement in Death*, Dublin, University College Dublin Press, 2002. While I believe that the diaries are genuine, their authenticity or otherwise does not affect the central issues of this chapter: should a government blacken the name of a man in peril of his life, and should it use private information and documents for post-mortem character assassination?

cannot be certain that he performed all or even most of the sexual acts he records (since the diaries evidently played a part in Casement's psychosexual life), it seems probable that a number of the encounters he describes actually took place.[119] In certain towns which he visited in South America he discovered and frequented homosexual meeting places, where gratis or otherwise he obtained sexual gratification. On occasion, Casement recorded several acts of sexual congress in one day or evening. It was his preference to adopt the passive role in these encounters and to seek a number of partners: reading the entries one is struck by the similarities to the life of the bath-houses of pre-AIDS San Francisco.[120] Casement's post-mortem examination showed that he had undergone the physical changes of someone who habitually engaged in anal intercourse.[121]

Whatever reaction the diaries would produce today (and in truth they amount to little more than easily available pornographic accounts of penetrative sex), in 1916 they undoubtedly cast Casement in an utterly scandalous and pathological light. In a document he prepared for the Cabinet ostensibly to address the question of whether Casement could benefit from an exercise of the Royal Prerogative, Blackwell outlined Casement's sexual proclivities and activities in terms which made no attempt to hide disgust and revulsion. The diaries and ledgers, he wrote, show that Casement for years had been 'addicted to the grossest sodomitical practices'. Blackwell offered his own interpretation of Casement's psychopathology:

---

119 An affidavit by Dr Herbert Spencer Dicky, who for some days travelled on the Amazon with Casement, was used to try to exculpate Casement from the charges of depravity, but rather seems to confirm that he collected pornographic material in the form of notes of imaginings or recollections. On receiving a bundle of correspondence Casement told Dicky that Arthur Conan Doyle (who did write to him about the Amazon, seeking material for what would become his fantasy novel *The Lost World*) had asked him for examples of sexual depravity among the Indians. Having worked among them, Dicky began to tell of instances of which he had seen or heard. Casement wanted details and went off and got a notebook in which he recorded what he was told. Dicky and others inferred that this notebook may have been the notorious diary (which was in fact several journals) but it was much more likely to have been used by Casement for his own erotic purposes (Affidavit of Dr Herbert Spencer Dicky, 16 May 1938: NLI: McGarrity Papers: Ms. 17601 (3)).

120 For a modern (and not unsympathetic) account of this milieu see Randy Shilts, *And the Band Played On: Politics, People and the AIDS Epidemic*, New York, St Martin's Press, 1987. There is an indication that Casement continued his sexual activities in Germany, and was on one occasion arrested by the German police and then released (see *Daily Mail*, 26 April 1916, 5c; n. 127, below). This may have been black propaganda on the part of the British, but it would not have been out of keeping with a man as lonely and sexually driven as Casement evidently was – at least from time to time. For its part, the *Mail* thought the report was a ruse to cover Casement's gun-running movements.

121 See letter of 3 August 1916 from Dr Percy R. Mander, surgeon at Pentonville Prison, to Sir Herbert Smalley, Medical Commission of Prisons; 'I made the examination, which was the subject of our conversation at the Home Office on Tuesday, after the conclusion of the inquest today, and found unmistakable evidence of the practices to which it was alleged, the prisoner in question had been addicted.' With a certain amount of dissecting-room humour Dr Mander went on to detail the physical changes which he had noted (PRO HO 144/1637/311643/141).

Of late years he seems to have completed the full circle of sexual degeneracy, and from a pervert has become an invert – a 'woman' or pathic who derives his satisfaction from attracting men and inducing them to use him. The point is worth noting for the Attorney General [F. E. Smith] had given Sir E. Grey [Foreign Secretary] the impression that Casement's own account of the frequency of his performances was incredible and of itself suggested that he was labouring under hallucination in this respect.[122]

Under English law the diaries offered no prima facie grounds for sparing Casement the death penalty on grounds of insanity, although the eminent doctors who examined them emphasised that on their own the documents were insufficient to decide whether Casement was certifiable.[123] Blackwell, who did not disclose this important reservation to the Cabinet, was prepared to concede

---

122 House of Lords Record Office: Lloyd George Papers, E/9/4/11, p. 3. The point about Casement's frequency of sexual performance is interesting in another regard. It is usually assumed by those who write on the topic that the Attorney General, F. E. Smith, having been Casement's political opponent, would be unrelenting in Casement's prosecution. Here, however, by suggesting that Casement's diaries were in some part sexual fantasy he was taking a charitable view with regard to character, and opening the possibility of the diaries displaying a mental state apt for pardon on grounds of insanity. And as noted, Joseph McGarrity recorded that the Attorney General had 'sent word that if Sir R. pleaded insanity he would get off' (NYPL: MCIHP, Box 5, IHP87). George Bernard Shaw later argued that by suggesting this line of defence Smith had proved 'his complete sincerity . . . by characteristically disregarding his obligations as Crown Counsel and advising the defence to plead insanity and use the documents to prove their plea' (*Irish Press*, 11 February 1937, 9c). Shaw by this time took the view that the diaries were simply material that Casement had collected for his Putumayo campaign. (This was an untenable theory since some of the sexual passages relate to Irish and English incidents, observations and fantasies. Having withheld the diaries from critical inspection, the Home Office was unable to refute the theory.) Even at the time the material was being shown around, however, Shaw (who never saw the diaries) assumed that the allegation against Casement was not that he indulged in the practices he described but that he had amused himself by writing such 'an imaginary autobiography or diary' (ibid., 15 March 1937). A number of theories about provenance and authenticity were collected by Casement's defenders and are now in the McGarrity Papers (NLI: Ms. 17, 601 (1–13)).
123 The diaries and ledgers were assessed by Dr R. Percy Smith, and Dr Maurice Craig who confirmed that the documents contained 'definite evidence of sexual perversion of a very advanced type'. The facts before them were too meagre to certify insanity, but the writer's absorption in his subject and at times his conduct 'suggest much more mental disorder than is usually met with in a person who is suffering only from a perverted instinct' (Report, 10 July 1916: PRO HO 144/1636/311643/40). Smith (1853–1941) was one of the leading mental health physicians of the day and a writer on insanity and the law. Craig (1866–1935) was equally prominent in the field, and at the time was a mental health consultant at Guy's and adviser to the RAMC on shell-shock and mental illness in soldiers. It is significant that the reservations of these two eminent doctors as to Casement's sanity were not further explored by means of the personal examination that they clearly indicated would be necessary to come to a more conclusive judgement.

that the diaries offered evidence of 'abnormality and disordered judgement' and often in cases of murder – particularly murder of a sexual character – it was possible to trace an indirect connection between that type of crime and an obsession such as Casement displayed. But here there was no such connection:

> No one who had read Casement's report to the Foreign Office on the Putumayo atrocities (at a time when his sexual offences were of daily occurrence), his speech from the dock in arrest of judgment, his private letters to his friends, and the long, closely reasoned and able comment upon the trial and the Lord Chief Justice's charge to the jury (prepared with a view to his appeal) could doubt for a moment that intellectually at any rate, Casement is very far removed from anything that could properly be described as insanity.[124]

For those who wished to see him destroyed, the diaries had the considerable advantage of dishonouring Casement's name and casting a pall over his public service, while at the same time disarming those who got up petitions. And while the diaries were of such a gross and disgusting nature that they opened a gap for those who were willing to see Casement reprieved on grounds of insanity, Blackwell effectively preluded this both by argument and authority.[125]

The circulation of the diaries had to be handled with great care, lest ministers or senior civil servants were seen to be directly involved in an action which at the very least was unethical, sordid and undignified. The exact sequence of events is now impossible to discover, but it is unlikely that the Home Secretary, Herbert Samuel, was asked for or gave his approval. This was a notoriously divided Cabinet – soon to disintegrate completely – and there remains no record of ministerial expressions of concern that confidential material had at the very least been leaked or, as must have been evident to all but the wilfully ignorant, that a campaign against Casement was being orchestrated by officials. It is certainly to Samuel's discredit that as Home Secretary he made no enquiries about the matter and took no steps to stop what by any standards was a morally and legally questionable action against a man whose life was in the balance.

Neither is Blackwell's precise role in the affair clear. His determination to block mercy for Casement is evident in his memoranda. There is no record, however, of his having shown the Casement diaries to journalists, and indeed his 15 July memorandum challenged the Foreign Office view that because of Irish-American opinion Casement could not safely be hanged unless the nature

---

124 House of Lords Record Office: Lloyd George Papers, E/9/4/11, p. 3.
125 There survives a letter of 14 May 1916 from Sir Cecil Spring Rice, the British Ambassador, to an American correspondent. Casement, he wrote, had for some years been sexually abnormal, but that did not prove insanity. Should there be other evidence of mental abnormality, however, he was willing to forward it to London (NLI: McGarrity Papers: Ms. 17, 601 (13)).

of his private life were first made public. This consideration of American opinion struck Blackwell as humiliating, but he also raised the more central issue: 'There are obviously grave objections to any sort of official or even inspired publication of such facts while the man is waiting trial or appeal, or even awaiting execution.' What might happen later, however, Blackwell saw as quite another matter. There was not 'the slightest objection to hanging Casement, and *afterwards* giving as much publicity to the contents of his diary as decency permits, so that at any rate the public in America and elsewhere may know what sort of man they are inclined to make a martyr of'.[126]

Remarks about the legal proprieties were all very fine, but Blackwell knew well enough that they were quite redundant since material from the diaries was already in circulation – a fact which he acknowledged later in the memorandum when he dismissed the view that to execute Casement would be counterproductive: 'Casement's value as a martyr is already a good deal discounted. His private character is by this time pretty generally known in London. The "Daily Express" on three occasions has openly stated that he is a moral degenerate, addicted to unmentionable offences, and has cited his "diaries" in proof.'[127] The juxtaposition of these remarks with the earlier observation that there were 'grave objections' to any official or officially inspired circulation of his material is certainly curious. Blackwell and his colleagues showed no concern that the Casement diaries were being shown around London, and that an official whom they all knew (Captain Hall) was briefing on them. This was no haphazard leak by an indiscreet or indignant official, but is instantly recognisable as a well-organised campaign of

---

126 Memorandum for Cabinet, 15 July 1916: House of Lords Record Office: Lloyd George Papers: E/9/4/11.

127 Ibid. See the *Daily Express*, 30 June 1916, 1c: 'It is common knowledge that Sir Roger Casement is a man of no sense of honour or of decency. His written diaries are the monuments of a foul private life. He is a moral degenerate.' On 1 July the *Daily Express* (1d) again referred to the dairies 'which reveal him in the light of a moral degenerate, abandoned to the most sordid vices. They are unprintable, and their character cannot even be hinted at.' The *Express* returned to the diaries on 13 July, suggesting that those who were petitioning on Casement's behalf should be permitted to look at the diaries. Were this done 'no man of Mr Nevinson's high character, and certainly no minister of religion would ever mention Casement's name again without loathing and contempt' (1g). Rumours (and possibly material) were in circulation *before* Casement's landing in Ireland. The *Daily Mail* obliquely alleged that Casement had been arrested for homosexuality under Germany's criminal code (26 April 5c). This report, which it described as 'curious' and 'mysterious', circulated in London on 15 April, simultaneously with a Danish newspaper report carried by the Reuter's wire (though the Danish report was of swindling). All this indicates a high state of knowledge and preparedness on the part of British intelligence and counter-espionage. As for Casement's reported arrest on a vice charge in Germany, Blackwell annotated the press-cutting in the file: 'I think the incident may have occurred. It is not improbable that C[asement] sh[oul]d be arrested on such a charge during his stay in Germany having regard to his habits. No doubt he w[oul]d be released as soon as his identity was discovered' (PRO HO 144/1636/311643/38). This episode is discussed in some detail, but necessarily speculatively, in Maloney's *The Forged Casement Diaries*, *op. cit.*, ch. 6.

black propaganda. If Blackwell and his colleagues thought it improper to deal with Casement in such a way while his life was in the balance, why did they not stop the campaign? The answer, of course, is that they had given at least tacit approval for the briefing of journalists, diplomats and others, and that they wanted to strike poses of judicial fairness at the same time.

On 23 July there was a more direct call for the rejection of the petitions, and for Casement to hang. This took the form of a short article in the *Weekly Despatch* signed by 'An MP', which official records indicate to be George Terrell.[128] One can now only speculate on the relationship between Hall and the intelligence services and Terrell. It may well be that Terrell was moved by his own anger to write the piece, but it is also possible that Hall had prompted it. Terrell set out the case for not hanging Casement, and dismissed it: not a single valid argument could be advanced 'to show why he should live a day longer than the law allows'. Under the subheading 'His Depravity' Terrell went on to refer to the diaries: 'His life, as outlined by himself, has been one continuous immersion in the depths of depravity.' This document 'should destroy the last flimsy foundation of the sentimental plan that a rebel dead is a greater danger than a rebel alive.' Those busy with his reprieve should acquaint themselves with the contents of the diary, Terrell suggested, 'and I am satisfied they will desist'.[129]

The man who undertook the actual business of showing the diaries around was well used to the role of cut-out or deniable middleman, and was well connected with useful journalists. He was the country's leading counter-espionage agent, Captain Reginald Hall. Since November 1914 Hall had been involved in the whole range of his country's intelligence struggle against the Central Powers including the developing insurgency in Ireland and anti-British German–Irish cooperation in the United States of America. He worked in close cooperation with Scotland Yard and, through the Navy's interception of German wireless traffic and breaking of German codes, had been aware of Casement's activities almost from the earliest days in Germany. Hall was behind an attempt to flush out Irish revolutionary cooperation with Germany (including the possible landing of Casement) by running the decoy yacht *Sayonnara* up and down the west coast of Ireland.[130] It was to Reginald Hall and Basil Thomson of Scotland Yard that Casement was brought on his arrival in London. As noted, the surviving papers and memoirs of officials are curiously imprecise as to when the Casement

128 (1882–1952). Manufacturer and Unionist MP for Chippenham, 1910–22. President, National Union of Manufacturers, 1916–32; Treasurer, National League for Freedom.

129 *Weekly Despatch*, 23 July 1916, 5e. Terrell's article was trailed in the *Daily Mail* on the previous Friday. The *Sunday Herald* (also on 23 July 1916) carried too short paragraphs also referring to 'his now notorious diary [which] puts him absolutely beyond any claim on sympathy' (see PRO HO 144/1636/311643/38).

130 For this and any other episodes in Hall's murky and distinguished wartime career (including his role in black propaganda) see Admiral Sir William James, *The Eyes of the Navy: A Biographical Study of Admiral Sir Reginald Hall*, London, Methuen, 1955.

diaries were found. There is no reason to suppose that Thomson withheld investigation until Casement was captured. He was a notorious traitor, and it is hardly to be imagined that all his London connections would not have been thoroughly checked. It is entirely possible, likely, indeed, that both Hall and Thomson knew of the diaries, and may even have read them when they interrogated Casement. At some point – exactly when is unclear – Thomson had typescripts prepared, as well as photographs of certain pages of the journals. Hall then undertook the task of circulation.

Hall's part in the circulation of the diaries was disclosed in 1937 when William Maloney's book was serialized in the *Irish Times*.[131] Hall had shown diary extracts to Ben Allen, an Associated Press correspondent in London, telling him that his agency could have exclusive publication rights. In accordance with AP's procedures, however, Allen had insisted that he verify the extracts by showing them to Casement. This was not agreed, but Hall and Allen met on several occasions, and further typewritten extracts were shown.[132] When Maloney named Hall in his *Irish Press* article Hall made no attempt to deny his part in the affair, or to contradict Allen's account of events (which was eventually deposited in the National Library of Ireland).[133]

London's ruling circles were relatively homogeneous and discrete. The extracts were shown around the clubs and to Members of Parliament. The King, a possible avenue for those seeking mercy, was also shown the material, and he in turn passed it to Bishop Hensley Henson, then Dean of Durham.[134] Extracts were also shown to Walter Page, the American Ambassador, who even before he had seen them had heard the rumours that information 'of an unspeakable filthy character' had been withheld from Casement's trial. If these facts were to

131 *Irish Times*, 1 March 1937, 6d–f; *Irish Press*, 3 March 1937, 6 February 1937, 17c; 18 February, 15c–d.

132 Statement by Ben Allen, Ms. 13, 542. This document is in the form of a statutory declaration made by Allen on 2 August 1960.

133 Sir William James, Hall's biographer, in an exchange of correspondence with Denis Gwynn, Casement's biographer, confirmed that in Hall's papers he had found a copy of Maloney's articles on Casement. These categorically stated that Hall had shown typewritten extracts to Ben Allen of Associated Press, and that these extracts had been prepared for circulation: 'Knowing Hall as well as I did I never doubted for a moment that if these articles were untrue Hall would have at once challenged them . . . I have no doubt that Thomson had given Hall the photographs of the diary which he had taken' (NLI: Denis Gywnn Papers: Ms. 21, 814 (unfoliated)).

134 Hensley Henson (1863–1947) when a canon of Westminster Abbey had in 1912 preached a sermon against the Peruvian Amazon Company's activities on the Putumayo as part of an upsurge in public and political opinion based on Casement's report. He resisted legal threats from the company, and preached further sermons on the subject in the course of a visit to the United States of America in the summer of 1912. Henson, who had headed Oxford House in Bethnal Green in 1887–8, had an interest in social and educational questions. He had a distinguished academic and Church career, becoming Bishop of Hereford in 1918 and of Durham in 1920.

become public, he wrote, 'it will be well that our Government had nothing to do with him or his case, even indirectly!'[135]

Casement's reputation was based on his humanitarian campaigns against the abuse by Europeans of native peoples, and appeals on his behalf were likely from fellow campaigners. John H. Harris, a former Congo missionary, was, at the time of Casement's trial, secretary of the Native Races Protection Committee. He had known Casement for several years, and with sufficient trust, admiration and respect to nominate him in 1910 for the Commission of Inquiry on the Upper Amazon – the Putumayo which was to be the final phase of Casement's illustrious career in human rights. When he first heard of the diaries Harris had been convinced that a 'serious mistake' had been made, since Casement's character had previously been 'a perpetual and vigorous protest against the prevailing morality'. There had been no sign of vice in the Congo or South America, and Casement's enemies would certainly have used it against him had there been any. If, therefore, the diaries were in Casement's own hand, then it was surely proof that he was mentally unhinged.[136]

Harris wrote to the Archbishop of Canterbury, who in turn contacted the Home Secretary. In consequence Harris was invited by Blackwell to visit the Home Office, where he inspected the diaries. Deeply shocked, Harris wrote again to the Archbishop (with a copy to Blackwell). As a result of what Blackwell had shown him:

I must admit with the most painful reluctance that the Roger Casement revealed in this evidence is a very different man from the one up to whom I have looked as an ideal character for over fifteen years. My distress of mind at this terrible revelation will I am sure be fully appreciated by your Grace. The only consolation is that there appears to be no certain evidence that these abominable things were practised in the Congo – it may be that our presence checked them.

135 On the evening of Tuesday, 1 August Page dined with Asquith, who told him that the Cabinet would not stay Casement's execution. Asquith asked if Page had heard about the diary, and when Page said that he had been given photographs of parts of it Asquith said, 'Excellent, and you need not be particular about keeping it to yourself' (Thomson, 1939, *op. cit.*, p. 305). The previous day Asquith had made an angry statement to the House of Commons (in response to a question from Carson) confirming that the Germans had murdered Captain Charles Fryatt of the merchant marine. Asquith promised retribution for this crime against the law of nations and the usages of war (*The Times*, 1 August 1916, 10a). On 23 June 1916, Fryatt had been captured on board his ship *Brussels*. The previous year he had successfully fought off a submarine by attempting to ram it. For this offence he was shot at Bruges on 27 July 1916. The British government regarded the court martial and sentence as murder. This incident outraged British public opinion and extinguished any hopes Casement's supporters may have had: Casement was now seen, above all, as a German agent (see *News of the World*, 30 July 1916, 7e, which juxtaposes news of the failure of Casement's appeal with Captain Fryatt's execution).
136 PRO HO 144/1636/311643/53. Harris (1874–1940) was an active Liberal, briefly an MP (Hackney, 1923–4), and was knighted in 1933.

Harris had obtained a few signatures to a 'limited appeal' he had made on Casement's behalf and he told the Archbishop that he felt it 'only due to these gentlemen that I should write and ask them whether they still wish their signatures to be appended – this I am doing at once'.[137] It was not long before information which had been laid by gentlemen before gentlemen began to seep down to less refined social strata: the scatological value of the diaries was too high, the gossip too hot, the *schadenfreude* too intense.

The charges of homosexual degeneracy fitted well with national stereotypes, smouldering at all times, and easily fanned in wartime. Just as the French were associated with licentiousness and heterosexual immorality, sections of the German ruling classes were supposed to indulge in perverted sex – 'Hunnish practices'.[138] This reputation would of course bloom after the war, and still evokes the nightlife of the Weimar Republic. In the still cautious and coy language with which sexual matters were discussed during the First World War, room was made to denounce German sexual perversion as yet another manifestation of the wickedness of the enemy. So damaging was this charge that it was given an explicit airing in John Buchan's best-selling *Greenmantle* (published in 1916).[139] Had Casement's immorality taken the form of promiscuous sex with women it is doubtful that his character could have been damaged much by the publication of his diaries. A record of sexual fantasies and acts with men and boys was by far the most damaging and politically apt weapon which Casement could have presented to his enemies.[140]

Propaganda, information and disinformation have since biblical times had their places in the armaments and habits of governments: and patriotic lies, defamation and scandal-mongering are essential ordnance in modern warfare. The

---

137 Ibid. The implication was that despite the revelations he himself would petition on Casement's behalf (see also NLI: McGarrity Papers: Ms. 17, 604 (5)). Colonel Maurice Moore, then organising a mercy petition in Ireland, referred to stories being 'secretly disseminated from official sources'. Casement was a man of unblemished character, he insisted, and the rumours should be scorned as the Pigott forgeries before them (*Freeman's Journal*, 31 July 1916, 4b).

138 In January 1918 Pemberton Billing, the demagogue MP, would, in his journal *Vigilante* allege that the British ruling classes were also permeated with perverted practices, and that the German government had a Black Book in which were listed some 47,000 British perverts. See also *John Bull*, 8 July 1916, 9a; 22 July, 1a; 12 August, 1a.

139 This book, as with the two others in the Richard Hannay trilogy, was a fiercely anti-German tract, delivered as an adventure story, reprinted seven times during the Great War. In one scene Hannay confronts the chief villain Colonel Von Stamm in his drawing-room: 'the room of a man who had a passion for frippery . . . a perverted taste for soft delicate things'.

140 Writing from Washington on the day after Casement's execution, Sir Cecil Spring Rice indicated that on the whole American opinion had not reacted as sharply as had been expected: 'The agitation in Congress is rather checked by the dread that some publication will be made expressing the private character of Casement, which makes statesmen somewhat wary of making impassioned encomiums which may afterwards be made to assume a somewhat ridiculous aspect' (Rice to Grey, 4 August 1916: PRO HO 144/1637/311643/181). Herbert Samuel wanted Rice's letter to go to the Cabinet.

High Victorian morality of statesmen who saw (or appeared to see) falsehood and dirty dealing as demeaning to the state was probably little more than a passing affectation of those totally secure in their power. In the extremity of the second and uncertain year of the Great War, fairness and impartiality to Casement had perhaps to give way to the necessities of state.[141] Certainly both the Allies and the Central Powers had by then long disregarded truth and chivalry in the conduct of warfare. Survivors of the Somme, and the relatives and friends of the thousands of dead and horribly maimed, might question the value of fairness to Casement's reputation as a concern of the state for which they had suffered. One is left with the bones of a debate which may have become threadbare but has hardly been settled: to what extent may we use morally questionable, undemocratic and unconstitutional methods against those whom we consider to be acting immorally, undemocratically and unconstitutionally?

Admiral Sir William James, Reginald Hall's biographer, was well acquainted with his subject and his circle. He regarded Hall as 'a great man [who] did more to win the war than most of the other leading figures'.[142] At the same time James had come to believe that Hall's action was discreditable, mitigated somewhat by Basil Thomson's role in the affair. A man in the Thomson–Hall circle had also concluded that the men's campaign with Casement's diary was to their discredit but 'it should be remembered that the war was at a critical stage, that the possibility of defeat and surrender to the enemy was a real one and that in those anxious and tense days many things were done which would not be done in times of less strain'.[143]

Yet this was no maverick operation – the seniority of those involved was guarantee enough of that. A number of ministers were well aware of what was going on, and those who were not may have been wilfully ignorant. One (F. E. Smith, the Attorney General) actually showed extracts to friends. The nature of ministerial rank is responsibility, and this applies with particular weight in a case such as Casement's. This episode, therefore, must be accounted to the shame of British government. Here was a man caught firmly in the toils of his own folly and fractured character and brought fairly to book by the law. In criminal justice, above all, government is obliged to act with fairness and restraint. The contending forces are unbalanced – the power and authority of the state versus an individual whose reputation is damaged and resources strained even before a guilty finding. In the Casement trial there was to be no question as to guilt, but

141 Captain Reginald Hall's counter-espionage work included the dissemination of false information – an activity which was seized upon by those who believed that the Casement diaries were forged (NLI: Denis Gwynn Papers: Ms. 21, 814 (unfoliated)).

142 Ibid.

143 Ibid. One of Hall's close colleagues drew attention to what he considered the ingratitude of the Admiralty in allowing him to retire without honour or recognition. The explanation offered was that there were several men in prominent positions 'who had sworn vengeance against Hall for his part in disclosing the contents of the Casement diary'.

the use of the diaries (and the denial of leave to appeal to the Lords) were an unacceptable application of power – the central evil which the Allies had pledged themselves to destroy.

An aggravated death penalty?

Aggravated forms of the death penalty had been largely abandoned in England in the eighteenth century. The last hanging, drawing and beheading took place in 1817; the last burning to death in 1789.[144] Aggravation in the form of dishonour to the corpse after death persisted longer, with mandatory dissection and/or gibbeting of the bodies of murderers not being abolished until 1834.[145] And when the public execution of murderers ceased, the requirement that the body of the culprit be buried within the prison grounds was both a precaution against necromancy, and further punishment and degradation.[146] In strict terms Casement was not subjected to an aggravated death penalty, but he was dealt with in a way which undoubtedly increased the weight of the most extreme penalty.

Stripping of honours

Despite his denial of all British identity and eschewment of all the advantages which his service to the Crown had brought him – a knighthood and pension – Casement was slow to repudiate these tokens of his allegiance. He would certainly have strengthened his moral stance had he renounced title, income and allegiance publicly or privately before departing for Germany. The requirements of conspiracy were pleaded, but it is also likely that both income and title were useful at a time of critical change. [147]

---

144 Leon Radzinowicz, *A History of Criminal Law and its Administration from 1750*, London, Stevens & Sons, 1948, Vol. 1, pp. 226–7 and ch. 7 generally.

145 Albert Hartshorne, *Hanging in Chains*, London, T. F. Unwin, 1891, p. 110; 4 & 5 Will. IV, c.26: Abolition of Hanging in Chains Act, 1834.

146 Capital Punishment Amendment Act, 1868 (31 & 32 Vict., c.24, s.6).

147 Casement claimed that he had made his standard application for a pension in September 1914 because Clan na Gael colleagues had advised him to do so, in order that he should not draw attention to himself at a critical time, and to convince British agents that he remained in the United States of America. Casement handed the pension payment to McGarrity 'begging him to give it to some charity or to the Irish cause' (NLI: Dr Charles Curry Papers: Ms. 17, 021: Casement Memorandum, Munich, 26 March 1916; A. S. Green Papers: Ms. 10, 464 (1b)). This explanation addresses the implied accusation of venality and hypocrisy levelled against him, but the broader question must remain whether it had been right, for some time prior to this, to continue to draw a Crown pension. Nor does this Clan na Gael advice account for Casement's drawing of a pension at all. He had left Foreign Office service with protestations of 'very keen regret', and had applied for a premature pension on health grounds (NLI: Casement Papers: Ms. 13073 (43)).

Fortified with the honours of his distinguished public service, Casement the defendant was vulnerable to the disgrace of being stripped of them. In 1905 he had been awarded the CMG in recognition of his Congo work. He had not, he told a friend, been consulted about the honour, it was a source of embarrassment to him, but he did not take the decisive step of declining it.[148] Six years later, in June 1911, without warning or consultation, Casement was awarded a knighthood for his services on the Putumayo, and accepted the honour in a letter which he at the time described as 'cold and formal enough', but which produced a very different impression when read at his trial.[149]

While in Germany Casement had written to Sir Edward Grey complaining of the plot against him by the British Consul in Christiania, Mansfelt Findlay, and returning the insignia of the CMG, the George V Coronation Medal 'and any other medal, honour or distinction conferred upon me by His Majesty's government, of which it is possible to divest myself'.[150] The problem was that by the time Great Britain and Germany had been at war for six months Casement had been in Germany for three of those months, and had already begun his recruiting missions among the Irish prisoners of war, advertising himself as Sir Roger Casement.[151] He thus exposed himself to the distasteful charge that he was using his title to gull unsophisticated soldiers, prisoners in a foreign land who were without the guidance of their officers. With the King's consent it was decided to deprive Casement of his knighthood and CMG immediately following conviction and sentence, and the necessary letters patent and order were issued. The ordinance executing this decision was served on him in his cell.[152]

148 See NLI: A. S. Green Papers: Ms. 10, 464 (1b); Casement Papers: Ms. 13, 079, f. 3. Casement evaded formal investiture and the insignia of the Order were discovered after his death, still unopened in the Foreign Office package.

149 Casement was correct in claiming that the words were 'cold and formal' even if they did not appear to be so to the layman. The language of the envoy and the courtier overlapped, and persisted (as did their equivalents in commerce and law, for example) because they were useful templates. The letter of acceptance of the knighthood only slightly departed from the usual submission of 'humble duty' and declaration of being 'very deeply sensible' of the honour which 'His Majesty . . . has been so graciously pleased to confer on me'. The opening paragraph was, ironically enough, a frank statement of Casement's difficulty: 'I find it very hard to choose the words, in which to make acknowledgment of the honour done to me by the King' (Geoffrey Vincent de Clifton Parmiter, *Roger Casement*, London, Arthur Barker, 1936, p. 85. See also NLI: A. S. Green Papers: Ms. 10, 464 (1b); Casement Papers: Ms. 13, 079, f. 6).

150 Casement to Sir Edward Grey, 1 February 1915 (NLI: Casement Papers: Ms. 13, 081 (2/iii); see also Curry, *op. cit.*, p. 191).

151 Knott, *op. cit.*, pp. 17, 30, 33.

152 PRO HO144/1636/311643/38. Only three precedents for degradation had been identified – the last in 1621. The term 'degradation' was technical in this context, but by juxtaposing the official announcement of the stripping of honours with renewed references to Casement's diary, the *Daily Express* (1 July 1916, 1d) with some relish gave the term its everyday meaning.

Character assassination

Little more needs to be said about this. Although they were used primarily to counter pleas for reprieve, the diaries were also deployed, as Blackwell stated to the Cabinet, to destroy Casement's character and reputation after his death. To the extent that 'decency permits', the diaries could be publicised so that in America and elsewhere people 'may know what sort of man they are inclined to make a martyr of'.[153] This 'decency' limitation was not the convention of decent behaviour by government – but rather the extent to which lewd and obscene passages could be published. It is impossible to imagine such a step being contemplated in the case of a common murderer in many of whose belongings the authorities had over the years found evidence of a bizarre or disgusting private life. Blackwell would have argued that Clarke, Pearse, Connolly and the others recently executed had already become Irish republican icons, and that Casement should not rise to a similar rank. Pragmatically he had a case, but in taking this course he weakened Irish constitutionalism and narrowed the moral gap between legality and insurrectionism.

The transient nature of Blackwell's gains was exemplified in the journey of Alfred Noyes, a poet and Murray Professor of English literature at Princeton, who played a part in presenting the British war policy to the United States of America. On 31 August 1916, he wrote of Casement in the *Philadelphia Public Ledger*, describing him as the chief leader of the rebels: 'I cannot print his own written confessions about himself, for they are filthy beyond all description. But I have seen and read them and they touch the lowest depths of human degradation ever reached. Page after page of his diary would be an insult to a pig's trough to let the foul record touch it.'[154] When in 1936 William Maloney published his book *The Forged Casement Diaries*, Noyes' remarks about Casement were reprised in the *Irish Press*. Within weeks Noyes had reappraised his judgement and called for an independent inquiry into the authenticity of the documents. This was imperative for justice to be done. He added that he regarded the report on which he had based his original remarks (presumably Hall's typescript and photographs) as 'utterly unreliable'.[155] Noyes went on to write his own book (*The Accusing Ghost*),[156] completing his passage from British propagandist to

---

153 Lloyd George Papers: *op. cit.*, E/9/4/11, p. 4.

154 NYPL: MCIHP, Box 12, IHP174; NLI: McGarrity Papers: Ms. 17, 601 (10).

155 Ibid., Scrapbook; *Irish Press*, 2 February 1937, 6d–g; 3 March 1937, 8f; see also 6c–d. Noyes (who had worked in the Foreign Office News Department in 1916) had been shown a copy of the diary for a few minutes, but never had the original or a copy in his own possession (*Two Worlds for Memory*, London, Sheed and Ward, 1953, p. 133).

156 Alfred Noyes, *The Accusing Ghost or Justice for Casement* (London, Victor Gollancz, 1957, p. 12). 'For some years now the ghost of Roger Casement has been beating at my door.' The reference is to W. B. Yeats' poem, 'The Ghost of Roger Casement'. For an account of Noyes' retraction (and the consequent rewording of Yeats' poem) see Richard J. Finneran (ed.), *The Poems of W. B. Yeats*, New York, Macmillan, 1983, pp. 306–7 and 671–2.

Casement partisan. Hall, Thomson, Blackwell, Troup and their ministerial superiors had forced Noyes and others into denunciations of British integrity – ironically on the basis of a wrongful belief that the diaries were forged and that Casement was an innocent.

Mode of execution

In considering hanging as a method of execution it is impossible not to accept that terror and degradation are intrinsic to the punishment. Historically, it has been regarded as a mercy to permit an alternative mode of death, such as shooting or beheading. In his last days Casement seems to have been calm and reconciled to his fate.[157] He remained troubled about the mode of execution, however, which he had long considered undignified and degrading.[158] Five days before his death he wrote to Alice Green referring to past executions for high treason, which had been by beheading. He also expressed a preference to be shot – 'but I suppose that cannot be'. In the absence of either alternative to hanging in the prison, Casement expressed a desire to be executed in public: 'I believe there is a reason good in law for it, just as in humanity for it.' It was his hope that a public execution would allow him by bearing and demeanour to obtain some dignity for the proceedings and for himself – something a hurried fumble in the execution shed would not do. He insisted that his offence was 'a public one, the most public one, an offence against the Realm – so the punishment must be in public'.[159]

157 Fenner Brockway, a leading anti-conscription activist (and later MP) was released from Pentonville three days before Casement's execution. On the evening of 26 July he had seen Casement taken out for exercise: 'His face was wonderfully calm, though his complexion was sallow. He came out apparently seeing nothing but the sky and the sun, and for a moment or two stood with his hands behind his back looking into it.' Warders beckoned Casement into the exercise yard, but when he returned to the prison building an hour later he looked again at the sky and the now setting sun: 'These two glimpses have left a very moving and vivid impression on my mind' (Brockway to Hanna Sheehy Skeffington, 31 July 1916: NLI: Sheehy Skeffington Papers: Ms. 22, 279(ii)). This account is also in the Casement Papers (Ms. 13, 088 (11)), with a description by Canon Carey of his last meeting with Casement, and his peace and tranquility on that occasion. See also Brockway's *Inside the Left*, London, George Allen & Unwin, 1942, pp. 73–5.

158 In his final letter to von Wedel before leaving Germany, Casement dwelt on his fate should he fall into British hands. He had provided himself with poison in order 'to avoid the indignities and infamies reserved for me should I fall into the hands of the government I have dared (so unwisely) to defy' (30 March 1916: NYPL: MCIHP, Box 1, IHP31.).

159 Casement to Alice Green, 29 July 1916: typescript copy at PRO HO 144/1637/311643/108. As noted this letter was suppressed on the recommendation of Blackwell, with the concurrence of Troup. The latter thought that Casement was mistaken in law 'but the publication of this letter would open out an unpleasant controversy in an unpleasant way – and to have to reply to it w[oul]d be unfortunate however clear the answer' (ibid.).

As for the law, he contended that the 1868 Capital Punishment Act had provided only for the private execution of murderers, and it therefore remained possible for a person guilty of treason to be executed in public.[160] It is possible that he had got the idea from press speculation, relayed to him via Gavan Duffy, since the first mention of the possibility of a public execution was in *The Times* on 15 May, six weeks before Casement's trial.[161]

These suggestions were taken seriously at the Home Office, where a review of precedents and statutes supported the view that a traitor's execution could still be conducted in public, though there was no obligation on government so to do. Troup pointed out that the Forfeiture for Felony Act, 1870 (33 & 34 Vict., c.23, s.31) repealed sections of the Treason Act, 1814 (54 Geo. III, c.146) referring to drawing the condemned to the place of execution on a hurdle, severing the head from the body, and quartering. These changes left only the requirement that the condemned 'shall be taken to the place of execution and be there hanged by the neck until he be dead'. Should the government have wished it, therefore, Casement could have been executed in public – but such a ceremony, evoking Robert Emmet and the Manchester Martyrs, was precisely what it did not want.[162]

Disposal of remains

From the funeral of the Young Irelander Terence Bellew MacManus which breathed life into the Fenian movement in 1861, to the 1915 funeral of O'Donovan Rossa, so skilfully exploited by Pearse and the IRB, the dead had taken their place in Irish revolutionary ranks. The bodies of the 1916 leaders had in consequence not been released to their families and friends, and the Home Office was determined that Casement would also be buried anonymously within the walls of Pentonville Prison.

The prospect of a Pentonville burial caused Casement particularly great distress, and five days before his execution he wrote to Alice Green (the letter was suppressed) asking her to do what she could to ensure that his body was handed over to friends and relatives for Christian burial in Ireland. The letter, written on 29 July 1916 under conditions of great distress and strain, and without legal assistance, was based on a misreading of the law of treason. Casement argued that 'all the precedents of history' were on the side of his wish to have his body handed over to friends and family. In the case of Robert Emmet, his friends

---

160 Capital Punishment Admendment Act, 1868 (31 & 32 Vict., c.24). The Act (see s.2) referred only to murderers.
161 *The Times* (3a) took the view that in cases of high treason execution had to be in public. It reviewed law and practice, including the sentence passed on William Smith O'Brien.
162 See the discussion between Samuel, who was prepared to contemplate execution by shooting, should Casement request it, and Troup and Blackwell, who did not wish to extend this honourable option to him (PRO HO 144/1636/311643/52).

were given the body for secret interment. 'I do not think,' Casement confidently stated, 'there is a single precedent for treating a person convicted of High Treason with ignominy *after death*.'[163] Here he was completely wrong. In the past the penalty had been aggravated by the mangling and display of the corpse (and, indeed, disembowelment while still alive) – precisely because the crime was regarded as the worst of all possible crimes. Any omission of those aggravations was by Crown clemency. Indeed, having found the Young Irelanders guilty of treason, the government of the day had to obtain parliamentary sanction for not inflicting what by 1848 had come to be seen as a barbarous penalty.[164] Blackwell was right when he minuted Casement's letter as 'bad law and worse history'. But he failed to remind the Cabinet that the 1868 Capital Punishment Act, which required burial within the prison precincts, applied only to those executed for murder, and that discretion could have been exercised in Casement's case. Perhaps with that in mind, and lest Casement's plea should catch the popular imagination, it was suppressed.[165] Gertrude Bannister did attempt to obtain Casement's remains, and Professor J. H. Morgan wrote strongly in her support.[166] Despite her pledge of private burial, however, her plea stood no chance of succeeding.

After execution the body was stripped; the clothes in which Casement had gone to his execution were searched (as a guard against a last message to be smuggled beyond the walls).[167] Following post-mortem and inquest the body, naked or in underclothing – the papers are not clear on the point – was put into a prison grave, without a coffin, and drenched with quicklime.[168] There it lay, a continuing irritant in Anglo-Irish relations for almost fifty years until, in very

163 PRO HO 144/1637/311643/108.

164 See above, pp. 43–4.

165 PRO HO 144/1637/311643/108. At least one prominent politician was in favour of public executions. Twenty years before, Winston Churchill had recommended that moderate numbers of those who wished should witness executions: 'Justice in every form should not shrink from publicity. The last expiation which she extracts from man should not be hidden from the eyes of his fellow creatures.' These were sentiments directly in line with Casement's. Churchill, however, was no longer in government, having resigned as Chancellor of the Duchy of Lancaster in November 1915. He favoured capital punishment throughout his life, but thought that a murderer or traitor should be allowed to address the crowd (Randolph Spencer Churchill, *Youth: Winston S. Churchill, 1874–1900*, London, Minerva, 1991, p. 338).

166 Morgan to Samuel, 4 August 1916: NLI: Casement Papers: Ms. 13, 078 (7).

167 Casement had given no indication that he would attempt to resist, but it was decided to employ an assistant executioner (Robert Baxter) as well as hangman John Ellis. The medical officer reported that the execution had taken place without difficulty, and that Casement had died from a fracture of the vertebrae (i.e. not strangulation) (PRO P. Com. 9/2331).

168 This mode of burial of the executed was followed until 1926 (P. Com. 9/2340). Over the years permission was given to members of Casement's family to visit Pentonville, and pray by his grave. Instructions were given to ensure that these visits were completely private (see P. Com. 9/2332). From the papers it seems that the families of other executed persons were allowed such visits.

different political times, the British government handed it over to the government of the Irish Republic for which Casement had worked apparently with so little success.[169] On 23 February 1965, Casement's remains were returned to Ireland, to lie in state and process through crowded Dublin streets. On Monday 1 March, Casement was laid among the figures of the Easter rising, the Anglo-Irish war and Fenians of earlier generations.[170] The last surviving leader of the rising, Eamon de Valera, again President of the Republic of Ireland, in his eighty-third year and ailing, gave the graveside oration.[171] This was the final formal honour, but vindication had come more than four decades previously, with the formation of the Irish state.

With the body, so with the property. There were obvious political possibilities in Casement's papers, and so most of those in government possession (including, tantalisingly, a prison diary) were destroyed. Eleven days after the execution, Duffy applied for Casement's papers, expressing a willingness that the political items should wait until the end of the war for release. To settle the issue Blackwell recommended that all remaining papers be destroyed and Samuel agreed.[172]

169 The London-based Roger Casement Committee had in 1935 been told by John Dulanty, the Irish High Commissioner in London, that it would be unwise to raise Irish hopes of repatriation of the body, since this was 'now a physical impossibility' (NLI: Casement Papers: Ms. 13, 078 (8)). No authority was quoted for this statement, which presumably was based on the assumption that after nineteen years in a quicklimed grave the remains had completely dissolved. The 1965 repatriation proved this to be untrue (NLI: Sheehy Skeffington Papers: Ms. 24,122; Casement Papers: Ms. 13, 600 (unfoliated)).

170 See PRO P. Com. 9/2340. At Casement's inquest (conducted immediately after the execution) Gavan Duffy asked the coroner to release the body to him. This was refused, and the burial order was issued to the Pentonville governor (Irish Times, 4 August 1916, 4h). The Daily Express (4 August, 1e) reported Duffy's request, and his condemnation of the refusal to release the body, as 'a monstrous act of indecency'. The newspaper disagreed: 'Only the flabby sentimentalists will agree with this view.' On returning from South Africa, Captain Tom Casement approached the authorities, drawing to their attention his own honourable war service. He asked permission to take his brother's remains to Ireland for burial. With the Anglo-Irish war at its height of mutual slaughter and atrocity there could have been no question of such an emotive funeral and the request was peremptorily refused (PRO HO 144/1637/311643/194–5).

171 During an official visit to London in September 1953 de Valera had at a luncheon asked Churchill to authorise the return of Casement's remains to his family in Northern Ireland. Churchill said he would look into the matter and wrote privately to de Valera saying that for legal reasons the request would have to be refused; he was wary of introducing new legislation and of opening old disputes. De Valera wrote back disputing the legal argument and pointing out that it was the retention of Casement's remains that was keeping the dispute alive (PRO P. Com. 9/2334). The following year the Casement Committee renewed the request on the occasion of Churchill's eightieth birthday, pointing out (inaccurately) that Churchill was the last surviving member of the 1916 Cabinet which had dealt with Casement's case. No reply was made to this letter (PRO P. Com. 9/2335).

172 PRO HO 144/1637/311643/176: these materials were destroyed on 16 August 1916, possibly by Blackwell himself (see also PRO P. Com. 9/2327 for the first decision to withhold Casement's papers). The destroyed papers included Casement's last letter to his brother Tom (ibid., /194).

Apart from the papers there were the small items of property which Casement had been allowed to retain in his cell. In the hours before his execution, on a scrap of paper he listed the friends to whom he wanted the items to go as keepsakes. All would pass to Alice Green, who would dispose of it as requested. But while the property was eventually handed over via Duffy, his executor, the scrap of paper was not, for Casement had strayed into the political. At the bottom of his tiny bequests he had written – and they were surely the last words he wrote: 'And for the rest – my good will to all men: to those who have taken my life equally to those who have tried to save it – all are my brethren now. Roger Casement, 2 August, 1916 11:00 p.m.'[173]

Aftermath

The strong shifts in nationalist opinion following the earlier executions should have been warning enough. Some reasoned that there would be a return to constitutional paths – such had been the experience after the Fenian campaign (which included the Clerkenwell rescue and Manchester executions), and even more so during the dynamitard episodes. On paper, Redmond's Irish Party in 1916 still dominated Irish Catholic opinion and commanded its loyalty. He was 'safe hands', loyal, and in thrall to Home Rule and government's good faith. Casement's execution had been unavoidable, was evidence of the strong purpose and hand of government, and cleared the way for conciliation and constitutional advance after the war. All of this seemed sound sense to those operating in London in the midst of the Empire's greatest war.

Reaction was swift. Sir Cecil Spring Rice cabled from Washington five days after the execution that

> the extreme Irish organisation is much strengthened and embittered and has received unexpected additions from moderates. . . . This means violent action in Congress and elsewhere, pressure [on] Government and crimes here and in Canada. . . . We are using [Casement's] journal not for publication but to warn politicians, press and church against running Casement as a patriotic martyr.

---

173 PRO HO 144/1637/311643/169. Cabinet had that day devoted the greater part of its proceedings to what Asquith described as 'a further and final discussion of the Casement case'. This further discussion was prompted by new materials (most likely the claim that Casement had gone to Ireland to try to stop the rising) and the appeals 'from authoritative and friendly quarters in the United States'. Agreeing that there were no grounds for reprieve, Sir Edward Grey was asked to draw up a statement of reasons for the refusal to spare Casement, primarily, it would seem, for use in the United States of America. (PRO CAB 41/37/29: Asquith to George V).

Spring Rice reported that the respectable press had dropped the topic but that extremist agitation was going on and could be expected to break out 'in a more violent form'.[174]

On the day of Casement's execution the Cork Board of Guardians had adjourned its meeting 'to mark our sense of horror and detestation at the murder of Sir Roger Casement'.[175] This was but the first of many protests. The *Irish Times* denounced all such views a disgrace and libel. Casement had been fairly treated and his guilt clearly established. It was permissible to argue that a reprieve might have been granted on grounds of clemency or policy, but it was 'sheer treason' to say that Casement's punishment was not just and lawful.[176] The *Freeman's Journal*, organ of the Irish Party, fully reported the execution, but was conspicuous in its editorial silence.[177] In England the Conservative press had no doubts about Casement's fate. He had been treated more than fairly, insisted the *Liverpool Courier*, and it would have been perfectly proper had he been court-martialled and shot within hours of his arrest. But perhaps he wished that this had happened since he had been condemned to the 'more ignoble death by hanging'.[178] The *Daily Express* was unrelenting: 'Casement Pays the Penalty; Crowds Cheer The Hanging of a Traitor.'[179] By contrast, the *Manchester Guardian* considered the execution to be 'a ghastly blunder' which would lie in the way of an Irish settlement and would prejudice British interests abroad; it deplored the creation of a martyr from a man otherwise discredited before the world. The politicians, in refusing clemency, 'have had eyes and ears for nothing but the

---

174 Spring Rice to Foreign Office, 8 August 1916: PRO HO 144/1637/311643/170. Such was the volatility of opinion that a few days before Spring Rice had been more sanguine. Ford's *Irish World* had reacted predictably. Had the British government kept faith with Home Rule there would have been no Casement affair. The execution of Casement was on a par with Germany's execution of Edith Cavell. But the *New York Times* had remained editorially silent (though the news was given a full column on the front page and two and a half columns and a large portrait inside) and the *New York Tribune* had 'to general surprise' run a 'frank and courageous article supporting the British government's action'. Some of the Hearst newspapers (generally anti-British) had appeared in mourning, but on the whole the effect of Casement's execution was not as great as some had thought it might be. Congressional agitation had been checked by the diaries – 'the dread that some publication will be made exposing the private character of Casement' (ibid., /181: Spring Rice letter to Foreign Office, 4 August 1916).

175 *The Irish Times*, 4 August 1916, 4h. The Board pointed out that neither Jameson nor de Wet had paid for their rebellious crimes as had Casement. This sympathy alarmed the Castle. A circular was issued on 29 August, directing the RIC to report all local bodies which expressed similar views. The police should name the body, the nature of the resolution and the numbers voting for and against (PRO CO 904/195). On the legal and political issues arising out of the Jameson Raid, see my *English Local Prisons 1860–1900*, London, Routledge, 1995, pp. 375–7.

176 *Irish Times*, 4 August 1916, 4e.

177 *Freeman's Journal*, 4 August 1916, 5g.

178 *Liverpool Courier*, 30 June 1916, 4b.

179 4 August 1916, 1e.

hot resentment of the present, that clamour for blood which rises so vehemently in times of excitement from normally placable and kindly men'.[180]

The Times took the conventional view of Casement's guilt and sentence. He had a fair trial – which he acknowledged – and his crime was the most heinous of all offences. His guilt was compounded by the mass of crime and misery caused by the rebellion of which he was an accomplice. As for his execution – 'No one even questions the justice of his fate.' The question of clemency turned entirely on the issue of expediency, and of that government was the best judge. But the newspaper protested against the use of the diaries: 'attempts which have been made to use the Press for the purpose of raising issues which are utterly damaging to Casement's character, but have no connexion whatever with the charges on which he was tried.' These matters should have been raised in a public and straightforward manner or else left 'severely alone'. It would have been better had Casement been shot on his arrival in Kerry, but he was not, and whatever virtue there was in the pomp and circumstance of a great state trial 'it can only be weakened by inspired innuendoes which, whatever their substance, are now irrelevant, improper, and un-English'.[181]

In Catholic and nationalist Ireland the reaction to the circulation of Casement's diaries and journals was very different from what Blackwell expected, and the *Daily Express* had predicted.[182] Far from preventing Casement's martyrdom by blackening his character, the diaries were widely denounced as infamous forgeries which showed with what unrestrained ruthlessness government dealt with its Irish enemies. 'No one,' wrote Gertrude Parry, 'ever believes a word that comes from England about an Irishman. The loathsome beasts thought they would ruin his name. Never.'[183] A controversy raged for several decades, which every time it flared up, lacerated and re-embittered Irish opinion, both at home and in the United States of America.[184] Casement's supporters adamantly refused

---

180 29 July 1916, 6b; 31 July 1916, 4c and 4g; 3 August 1916, 4c.

181 *The Times*, 30 June 1916; 4 August 1916, 3a and 7b. There is a lofty indifference to Irish nationalist opinion in the sentence 'No one even questions the justice of his fate'. The Moore–O'Farrelly petition correspondence shows that men of eminence and position from many walks of public and religious life were deeply concerned with Casement's fate. Moore told Asquith that he and his colleagues had confined their petition approaches to such substantial personages so as not to stir up the country, but that 'Hundreds of thousands of signatures could be obtained with the greatest ease' (NLI: Maurice Moore Papers: Ms. 10, 546 (5)).

182 Denouncing Casement as a 'moral degenerate' the day after he was sentenced, the *Daily Express* had insisted: 'There is no danger whatever that Ireland will ever look upon Casement as a martyr. The Irish people know all about him and his character . . . Ireland does not make martyrs of such people' (*Daily Express*, 1 July 1916, 1d).

183 NLI: Casement Papers: Ms. 14, 100: Gertrude Parry (née Bannister) to Nina (Mrs Agnes Newman), 4 May (?) 1917.

184 It also provided republican and nationalist newspapers with a perpetual issue for the denunciation of British injustice, and a potboiler for its newspapers and journals (see, for example, John Devoy's *Gaelic American*, 11 October 1924, p. 2: 'Irish martyr sent to his doom on foul and

to believe that there could be a dark side to the character of a man of such nobility and bravery.[185] Firmly lodged in the canon of Irish martyrs, every attempt to foist the diaries on him evoked bitter memories. Recognising this, however belatedly, the British government retreated into silence, and it was not until 1959 that permission was given for historians and other persons of standing to inspect the diaries. Even then, it continued to be asserted that they had been forged.[186]

There are strong indications that at least some of the Irish leaders accepted the authenticity of the diaries, but were understandably embarrassed and coped through silence or evasion. Two of the plenipotentiary delegates to the Anglo-Irish negotiations, the solicitor Edward Duggan and Michael Collins, were enabled by Lord Birkenhead to view the documents. Collins was familiar with Casement's handwriting and believed the diaries to be genuine. After discussions with Collins and Birkenhead, Duggan also took this view.[187] In 1936, William Maloney, author of *The Forged Casement Diaries*, asked de Valera (then head of the Free State government) to contribute a Foreword to the book. This invitation was declined in a letter the careful wording of which is suggestive, and which for all its evasiveness appeared to leave de Valera personally non-committal on the question of authenticity.[188] On 17 February 1937, de Valera in the Dáil refused to back a proposal for an Anglo-Irish committee of inquiry, making the ambiguous comment that 'Roger Casement's reputation is safe in the affections of the Irish people, the only people whose opinions mattered to him.'[189] Republican pride and politics, and the prudishness of Ireland's ultramontane Roman Catholic state, required that the truth about Roger Casement and his diaries be restricted to a very small group indeed: silence for the cognoscente, faith and denial for the generality.

---

loathsome testimony; was convicted before he was tried.' The story (and language) was continued the following week).

185 Two types of explanation were offered – outright forgery and the confusion (deliberate or accidental) of exhibits from his Congo or Putumayo trips with Casement's own journals. His protegé Bulmer Hobson, for example, insisted that when Casement had come back from the Putumayo he had shown him photographs of the tortured and maimed victims of the rubber collectors, and the shockingly indecent diary kept by one Armando Normand which he had secured, and which was part of the evidence he was sending into the Foreign Office (NLI: John MacDonagh Correspondence, Ms. 20648 (9): Bulmer Hobson, 'Memories of Roger Casement', f. 4). It was Hobson's view that the Foreign Office knowingly circulated Normand's disgusting diary as Casement's (f. 6). This was also Gertrude Parry's line. (See her various letters to Nina, Casement's sister, in NLI: Casement Papers: Ms. 14, 100 (unfoliated)).
186 See Inglis, *op. cit.*, pp. 373–88 for an even-handed account of the forgery debates.
187 NLI: McGarrity Papers: Ms. 17, 601 (6): Edward Duggan Memorandum, n.d. (c. 1933). Duggan's advice (probably to Maloney, who was at that time writing *The Forged Casement Diaries*) was not to open the matter again.
188 Ibid., Ms. 17, 604 (5).
189 *Dáil Eireann Debates*, LXV, 331; 17 February 1937.

The 1916 circulation of the diaries justly earned opprobrium for the British government. This was added to abiding anger at Casement's execution, and contempt for the supposed forgery. These were potent ingredients in a national mood that drew easily on a bank of grievances and from time to time erupted into Anglophobia. The return of Casement's remains to Ireland in 1965 began the process of healing this particular sore in Anglo-Irish relations. The evolution of social and sexual opinions over the past four decades perhaps completed it.[190] Even Catholic and nationalist opinion (or most of it) could, however reluctantly, come to accept Casement's sexuality alongside his position in Irish history, reality and myth. It is certain, however, that whatever short-term advantage the British government derived from the circulation of the diaries – and it was never much – the long-term damage to its reputation in Ireland far exceeded that inflicted on Casement.

190 The change was some time in coming. Casement's biographer Denis Gwynn in 1955 supplied the National Library of Ireland with information suggesting that the diaries were genuine. Acknowledging his letter, the Library's distinguished head, R. J. Hayes, said he would file it, adding, 'but I think it would be better not to make it available for a number of years' (Hayes to Gwynn, 13 December 1955: NLI: Denis Gwynn Papers: Ms. 21814; see also Gwynn's letter to Bulmer Hobson, 30 October 1936: McGarrity Papers: Ms. 17, 604 (5)).

13

SINN FÉIN, 1917–19

Nationalism's crisis

The Easter rebellion, and the manner of its suppression, devastated constitutional nationalism. While the Irish Republican Brotherhood (IRB) regrouped and re-established itself, fed by a reflexive sympathy for the defeated insurrectionary forces, Redmondism began to disintegrate. A Home Rule measure which divided the nation, which so imperfectly met national aspirations, and which was in any event suspended for the duration of the war, was ever more widely taken as evidence of England's perfidy, and Redmond's impotence and gullibility. Ulster Unionism rode high in Asquith's coalition, certainly able to veto nationalist aspirations. Protestant Ulster contributed so mightily to the war effort – and at all levels – that it neutralised Redmond's credit for enlisting southern Catholics. The upheaval through which they had come, and the uncertain direction of their country's development, fed Irish uncertainty and restlessness as 1916 wore on. By the end of July, an astute observer of the Irish scene noted, 'Redmond had not only become unpopular, but hateful to the populace'.[1] The implications were devastating, but to Asquith, and then Lloyd George and their colleagues, Ireland was a sideshow in a mighty struggle for national and imperial survival, in which unity was paramount and loyalty the cardinal virtue.

Two months after the Easter rising the High Tory Lord Hugh Cecil painted a pessimistic but prescient view of Ireland's prospects. The Irish public opinion on which Redmond relied for his support was, Cecil thought, opposed to republicans, but was 'still more opposed to any vigorous measures for repressing them'. This had been the keynote of Dillon's memorable speech to the Commons, and was reflected in early and urgent calls for amnesty. Sinn Féin would reorganise, using the old methods of boycotting, intimidation and outrage. The Germans would give secret assistance and if the war lasted long enough there would be a second rebellion. Redmond could restrain republicanism only by supporting the firm enforcement of the law, 'and this he neither can nor will do'. Conciliation was

---

1 Timothy Michael Healy, *Letters and Leaders of My Day*, London, Thornton Butterworth, 1928, Vol. 2, p. 573.

largely pointless since government of Ireland by Redmond alone would be even weaker than under Birrell, with Redmond advising him. In the circumstances, the best course, for the duration of the war, was to suspend all constitutional discussion while enforcing 'the just supremacy of law'.[2]

This solution, however, was no more likely to be effective than others then being canvassed. Ireland, north and south, was in a ferment which no ukase could still. Unionist and Nationalist forces pressed unappeasably forward, the demands and chances of war energising rather than tranquillising. For its part, imperial government was locked into the fine balances and imperatives of coalition, a number of which went to the heart of Irish affairs. Irish antagonisms, which for their resolution needed energy, imagination and decisive political manoeuvre in open ground, were instead left to gather force.

There was a period of deceptive tranquillity. The Christmas return of the internees was an act of conciliation, and it appeared to have the desired effect, since most chose to keep to themselves in the spring of 1917, though a small group in Dublin was already buying arms.[3] That underlying changes had taken place in the mood of the country would be amply demonstrated in a series of by-elections, the first being North Roscommon in February 1917. George Plunkett (a papal count), father of Joseph Mary Plunkett (executed for his part in the rising) and of two convict sons, stood against Redmond's man for a seat which for decades had been in the Irish Party's possession. Supported by IRB organisation and manpower, Plunkett won overwhelmingly and promptly announced that he would not take his seat: 'I recognise no Parliament in existence has a right over the people of Ireland.'[4] This was the first in a string of Redmond defeats in

2 *The Times*, 30 June 1916, 5a.

3 John Brennan, 'Frongoch University – and After', The Kerryman, *Dublin's Fighting Story 1913–1921*, Tralee, The Kerryman, n.d. (?1948), p. 120. Purchases were made from Irish soldiers stationed in Dublin. The authorities remained understandably jumpy and, on 22 February 1917, rounded up a number of suspects under Defence of the Realm Act (DORA) regulations. Those detained included J. J. O'Kelly, Darrell Figgis and John T. O'Kelly (*The Times*, 23 February 1917, 6e).

4 *Freeman's Journal*, 6 February 1917, 5g. The newspaper (at that time the voice of the Irish Party) described the result as 'a very heavy blow' (4b). There was a bitter exchange between the War Office and the Home Office in the wake of Plunkett's election victory. In June 1916 Plunkett had been excluded from Ireland under DORA Regulation 14b, on the authority of the General Officer Commanding-in-Chief in Ireland. When the internees were released from Reading and Frongoch in December 1916, Plunkett applied for permission to return to Ireland. The Home Office consulted the Irish Office, which agreed to the request. Plunkett's electoral victory raised a storm within officialdom. The Army Council asked by whose authority the deportation order had been revoked, and on discovering that the Home Office and Dublin Castle had agreed it between them, protested at the exclusion of the military authorities from the decision. Such consultation was a matter for the Irish government, the Home Office rather tartly replied. Despite the failure to consult on this occasion, it had been decided that the interned rebels should be released and returned to Ireland, and 'it would have been difficult in the circumstances then existing to defend the retention in England of a person whom it had not been thought necessary to intern' (Letters of 20 and 29 March 1917: PRO, HO 144/1458/315663/18). In 1918 Plunkett would be interned in Birmingham Prison as part of the 'German Plot' round-up (see ibid., /31; see also PRO HO 144/1496/362269/2).

May, July and August 1917. At South Longford, despite all the efforts of John Dillon, who personally directed his party's campaign, an IRA convict then in Lewes, Joseph MacGuinness, won a narrow victory on the inspired slogan 'Put him in to get him out'.[5] On the day he was released under general amnesty, Eamon de Valera (presumably won over by MacGuinness' victory) announced his candidacy in the East Clare by-election. Plunkett's platform had been obscure, and he had stood as an independent, donning Sinn Féin colours only after election. De Valera was, by contrast, completely forthright: he was a Sinn Féiner who wanted independence for Ireland. He was rewarded by a landslide 3000 majority in an electorate of only 8000.[6] At Kilkenny a month later William Cosgrave won again for Sinn Féin on a similar scale. After his election de Valera was described by Dr Fogarty, Roman Catholic Bishop of Killaloe, as 'the brave and honourable representative of East Clare . . . who stood for the honest policy of Irish independence, which should have behind it, and, please God, would soon have behind it, the whole manhood of Ireland, both North and South'.[7]

With Redmond's party in the deepest trouble, Lloyd George turned to smoke and mirrors, and initiated essentially futile talks about a way forward. An Irish settlement of some kind moved up the agenda when, on 6 April 1917, the United States of America entered the war. Redmond had been offered immediate, but very limited, twenty-six-county Home Rule (Carson had been given a different deal), and when he refused this Lloyd George took up his suggestion that there should be an Irish convention. Whatever 'substantial agreement' such a meeting might reach, Lloyd George promised to abide by its terms. It was, as Robert Kee notes, a Lloyd George formula which combined 'surface plausibility with apparent concession while throwing the onus of success on to other shoulders than his own'.[8] Redmond's desperation and ultimate lack of understanding of Ulster Unionism lent a false credibility to this initiative.

The Irish Convention, as it was called, was a doomed venture. While nationalists and southern Unionists might make common cause against partition, the northern Unionists had secretly been given an absolute guarantee by Lloyd George, and had no reason whatever to negotiate – indeed would have been foolish to do so. On the other side, Irish labour and, more importantly, Sinn Féin, boycotted the proceedings. The Convention puttered along from July

---

5 MacGuinness was a Longford man, whose brother was influential in the constituency. Advised by de Valera and others in Lewes Prison he had declined the nomination, but the Sinn Féin leadership went ahead regardless (Piaras Béaslaí, *Michael Collins and the Making of a New Ireland*, London, George C. Harrap, 1926, Vol. 1, pp. 151–4).

6 *Freeman's Journal*, 12 July 1917, 3d. The seat had seen Daniel O'Connell's historic victories in 1828 and 1829, which added symbolic significance to de Valera's victory. He referred to the historic nature of the result in his victory speech, which he made in Volunteer uniform. *Freeman's* bitterly observed that 'East Clare has declared for revolution by an overwhelming majority' (2b).

7 *The Times*, 3 October 1917, 3b.

8 Robert Kee, *Ourselves Alone*, Harmondsworth, Penguin, 1989, p. 25.

1917 until April 1918 utterly inconsequentially, daily emphasising the impotence and growing irrelevance of constitutional nationalism.

Sinn Féin regroups

Some clarification is necessary on names. The Easter rising arose from a triple-sealed IRB conspiracy. It was worked through the Volunteers and enlisted the cooperation of Connolly's Citizen Army. By a process of association and mis-understanding, however, the rising became known as the Sinn Féin rebellion, and those who were 'out' as Sinn Féiners. The convicts and internees were described as Sinn Féiners in government files and official correspondence, and political statements, and the connection was fixed firmly in the public mind. In due course the misperception adjusted organisational facts, but at the time of the rising and thereafter the Sinn Féin label was completely misapplied. The Sinn Féin movement, which was totally peaceful, had nothing whatever to do with the rebellion.[9]

In the period after the release of the internees and convicts the reorganised IRB needed a political outlet, as did other militant nationalists. The Volunteers retained a military structure which could not be adapted to political purposes, and was, in any event, proscribed. Sinn Féin was seen – never mind mistakenly so – as the vehicle of militant nationalism, and by-election victories against the constitutional nationalists were being achieved in its name. Logic and conveni-ence dictated that militants should unite under the Sinn Féin banner. Once this strategy was accepted the movement entered a period of rapid growth. In April 1917 there were no more than 166 Sinn Féin branches numbering perhaps 11,000 members. Six months later there were 1200 branches ('clubs') and perhaps a quarter of a million members.[10] Such an expansion, with the return from Britain of the internees and convicts, transformed the movement. This change was recognised at the Sinn Féin convention (Ard-Fheis) on 25 October 1917, when republicans and traditional Sinn Féiners adopted a vague but com-mon platform. The compromise in words extended to organisation, and Arthur Griffith and Count Plunkett withdrew in favour of Eamon de Valera, who was then unanimously elected Sinn Féin president.

9 Sinn Féin developed between 1905 and 1908 out of the ideas and organisational work of Arthur Griffith and Bulmer Hobson. Taking the Austro-Hungarian dual monarchy as a model, Griffith argued for legislative independence in Ireland, such as was said to have operated during Grattan's Parliament of 1782 to 1800. The economic doctrines of the movement included protectionism and a degree of self-sufficiency; the political programme envisaged a separate Irish civil administration. Of particular importance was the notion of seeking election but refusing, if successful, to attend Westminster. The movement attracted little support before 1914, but its anti-conscription policy tapped an important spring of popular feeling.

10 F. S. L. Lyons, *Ireland Since the Famine*, London, Fontana, 1985, p. 390.

Shadowing this unification of the open political movement, the reorganisation of the IRB and the Volunteers proceeded rapidly, under the direction of Michael Collins and other militants. The Volunteers elected de Valera as their president, thus symbolically uniting the political and military wings of militant nationalism. As Hugh Cecil had predicted, IRB men, and others, cooperated in Volunteer training, reorganisation and re-equipping. Arms raids began on private houses. Drilling took place on such a scale it could not be concealed, and in rural areas sporadic and apparently popular land redistribution took place. These moves could not be ignored by government, and there were a number of DORA arrests and deportations. The goodwill and sanguine expectations which had accompanied the release of the 1916 internees and convicts evaporated.

The unravelling of authority

Two events drove forward the forces of renewed rebellion. The first was the treatment of newly imprisoned Sinn Féiners, particularly (as a result of forcible feeding) the death of the hunger-striker Thomas Ashe on 30 September 1917. The second event had more widespread repercussions. Since the outbreak of war there had hung over Ireland the threat of conscription. The measure had been introduced elsewhere in the United Kingdom, and the Allies' acute manpower shortage in the spring of 1916 led the War Cabinet to provide the legal framework for its extension to Ireland. As though by calculation the newly aligned forces of nationalism were cemented in resistance, creating a tide of militancy throughout the country.

Thomas Ashe

So many junctures of Anglo-Irish history have been described as being 'decisive' that there must be some reluctance in adding another to the list. The death of Thomas Ashe, however, was a powerful element in the organisational revival of physical force nationalism, and in its renewed appeal for popular support. The struggle for moral dominance involved many battles and skirmishes whose outcome often allowed one side to emerge with credit or to throw moral opprobrium on the other. Sometimes honours – or dishonours – were evenly drawn, but from the death of Thomas Ashe onwards the political balance swung against British policy, while the best that constitutional nationalism could hope for was a neutral outcome – a position that in the longer term must prove disastrous.

The British government and its Irish administration had a difficult position to defend: the failure to grant Home Rule, the success of Ulster Unionism, and – looming always – the possibility of Irish conscription. Government's natural advantage was an appeal to all who held property, position and responsibility: who, other than government, could uphold law and keep disorder at bay? Nationalists other than republicans sought to use the law and political processes to advance their cause, and while they might occasionally venture into extra-legal protest such as demonstrations, did so reluctantly, knowing that such tactics could spiral out of control. Constitutionalists believed that the law and the political process remained outside party politics, that they were mechanisms which, if not entirely impartial, might be won by the Irish cause. Both the British government and the Irish Party, therefore, were especially vulnerable to anything which challenged and damaged the basis of law and the integrity of its enforcement. The death of Thomas Ashe was a disaster for the status quo, and a triumphant advance for republicanism.

It was of little account that the death of Thomas Ashe was an accident, or that Ashe had chosen to put himself in the way of death. The public was not to know, moreover, that in his case a perceived duty to the dead was reinforced by his recent election to the presidency of the IRB Supreme Council. His public persona was that of a decent and upright young Irishman. Even those nationalists who condemned his politics acknowledged his bravery and the strength of his patriotism – however misguided.

Like many of those who found their way into the IRB and Volunteer leadership, Ashe came from the lower-middle class, and on the outbreak of war was a national schoolteacher.[11] In the Easter rising he commanded at Ashbourne, Co. Dublin, one of the few operationally successful Volunteer operations, capturing four Royal Irish Constabulary barracks, together with quantities of arms and ammunition. Two sergeants and four constables were killed in the course of these engagements. After the general surrender Ashe was sentenced to death, commuted to penal servitude for life. (And he was certainly more deserving of the death penalty than William Pearse or John MacBride.) With the other convicts he was released in June 1917, and immediately resumed political activities, being part of the secret regrouping of the IRB and campaigning openly in East Clare on behalf of Eamon de Valera. Some weeks later he was again arrested, charged with delivering a seditious speech, which the prosecution (not unfairly) said could be taken as a threat to renew Irish insurrection should the war go against the British.[12] A district court martial on 11 September imposed a sentence of two years' imprisonment with hard labour: this was the longest sentence of imprisonment (as distinct from penal servitude) that could then be passed. On review, one year of this sentence was remitted, and Ashe began to serve his time in Dublin's Mountjoy Prison.

Imprisonment with hard labour meant the regime of an ordinary criminal, and in protest against this Ashe and some forty comrades began a hunger-strike.[13] The Irish government, disillusioned by the militants' response to successive displays of leniency, determined that it would not grant political status, and commenced forcible feeding. The strikers' demands (described as 'extravagant' by The

11 Trained as a teacher at De La Salle College, Waterford. Active both in Irish Volunteers and Gaelic League. In 1914 collected funds for both organisations in USA.
12 The Times, 4 September 1917, 8c; Anon., The Death of Thomas Ashe, Dublin, J. M. Butler, 1917, p. ix.
13 The Times, 21 September 1917, 3b.

Times[14]) were for optional work (instead of obligatory hard labour), unrestricted conversation and smoking, and separation from ordinary prisoners. Granted, this would have been civil detention rather than punishment.

Despite its extensive infliction on suffragettes, forcible feeding was a crude and risky procedure, in which medical staff remained inexperienced. A tube was fed down the throat via the mouth or, if the prisoner resisted, the nose; liquid nutrients were then pumped into the stomach. Ashe was 33 years old and said to be of 'fine physique', but after a session of forced feeding on the evening of 25 September he became very ill, was released to a local hospital, and died there a few hours later. The inquest was told that in the week before his death Ashe, who disobeyed the regulations and destroyed prison property, had been subjected to a number of punishments. The Dublin Lord Mayor, Lawrence O'Neill, had found him without bed, bedding, books, and even boots.[15] Sleeping badly on the cell floor, forcible feeding had found him in a weak state after a hunger-strike lasting four or five days.[16]

In condemning forcible feeding as 'inhuman and dangerous', and recommending its discontinuance, the coroner's jury found that the inexperienced assistant medical officer had performed the procedure unskilfully. The Castle was censured for not acting more promptly, especially when the condition of Ashe and other prisoners had been reported by the Lord Mayor, and Sir John Irwin.[17] The jury condemned Mountjoy's deputy governor for violating prison rules, and inflicting punishment beyond his authority. But, they continued, 'we infer he was acting under instructions from the Prisons Board at the Castle'. For their part, the authorities at all levels, from prison to Dublin Castle, pleaded that to treat Ashe in any other way was beyond their power: they exuded weakness and hypocrisy, and seemed to lack humanity and reasonableness.[18]

This death was a disaster for the Irish government, and an immeasurable boon to Sinn Féin.[19] The death of any prisoner under circumstances which suggested prolonged and officially sanctioned ill-treatment would be a cause for public

14 Ibid., 27 September 1917, 3b.
15 *Freeman's Journal*, 28 September 1917, 5e. The authorities justified the removal of furniture, cell equipment and other items on the grounds that they were being destroyed or used as tools to inflict damage on the prison or to make noise. Anon., 1917, pp. 15, 68.
16 Anon. 1917, pp. 83–4 and *passim*.
17 Irwin was Chairman of the Visiting Justices Committee, Dublin prisons, 1900–19. Paper manufacturer, active in public life and good works.
18 *Freeman's Journal*, 2 November 1917, 5d; Anon., 1917, p. 84. The jury – mainly tradesmen and shopkeepers – was eminently respectable, precisely the group whose support was critical to the Irish administration and constitutional nationalists.
19 Sir Basil Thomson (Director of Intelligence in the London Metropolitan Police) was at this time visited by Major Price of Military Intelligence in Dublin who told him that things were very bad in Ireland: 'Sinn Féin has been losing ground and wants to have a martyr. Now they have Thomas Ashe, the hunger-striker who died in hospital after being forcibly fed . . . clear the Government made a blunder' (*The Scene Changes*, London, Collins, 1939, pp. 354–5).

concern and anger, and the repulsive details of forcible feeding and mean-minded bullying punishments were all too easily grasped. The difficulty of controlling a group of healthy young men set on a campaign of destruction and disobedience was overlooked or ignored: there had been such an apparent imbalance in power that the state forfeited any right to a fair hearing. Appearing for the next-of-kin, Timothy Healy, KC, the Nationalist MP, was vengeful, sarcastic, histrionic and disbelieving in his examinations: a sympathetic coroner gave him all the necessary leeway. Opinion, which had been shifting on uncertain moorings, swung violently: *The Times*, with some understatement, described the death as 'unfortunate'.[20] Healy's overstatement was closer to the mark: Ashe's death, he insisted, had moved Ireland more than the 1916 executions or more than anything since the hanging of Allan, Larkin and O'Brien in 1867.[21] The IRB, supreme impresario of martyrs' funerals, carried off Ashe's with the usual brio and impact. Ashe had been among the very top leadership of the IRB, was young, a dutiful Catholic, and demonstrably brave: his was an easy case for canonisation. At his inquest Dublin's Lord Mayor had (possibly creatively) recalled Ashe's last words to him: 'I die in a good cause', and had commented, 'It is for his country to decide whether it is in a good cause or not'.[22] Sinn Féin determined to provide an answer.[23]

The Irish government was in a state of unconcealable confusion – irrational severity, followed by undisguised weakness. Sinn Féin grew proportionately more confident. In total defiance of public order regulations, Ashe's vast funeral procession was accompanied by armed and uniformed Volunteers; a salute was fired at the graveside. Michael Collins, in the uniform of Vice-Commandant of Volunteers gave the oration: the volley just fired, he proclaimed, was 'the only speech which it is proper to make above the grave of a dead Fenian'.[24] Only a few months amnestied from Aylesbury convict prison, Countess Markievicz appeared in the Citizen Army uniform which she had worn during the rising. Every means was employed to underline the continuity of intent and organisation, and the resurgence of rebel spirit.[25]

---

20 *The Times*, 27 September 1917, 3b.
21 Healy, *op. cit.*, Vol. 2, p. 586.
22 *The Times*, 28 September 1917, 5b.
23 Ashe's example and sacrifice fortified the more active of the Volunteers. Seán Treacy, who had been on hunger-strike with Ashe, subsequently recalled the man: 'It was an honour to be walking in the prison ring beside Thomas Ashe' (Desmond Ryan, *Sean Treacy and the 3rd Tipperary Brigade*, London, Alliance Press, 1946, p. 39).
24 Béaslaí, 1926, Vol. 1, p. 166.
25 *The Times* reporter wrote that Ashe's funeral on 30 September 1917 was 'the largest, and in some ways the most impressive, demonstration which I have ever seen in Dublin'. The cortège stretched for at least three miles and included a 'vast number' of representatives of civic, political and cultural organisations, as well as women's groups and nationalist boy and girl scouts; there was a 'tremendous' display of Sinn Féin banners and emblems. But surely a matter for greater government concern than any of these, there was in the procession a contingent of at least a hundred Roman Catholic clergy, led by the Archbishop of Dublin (*Freeman's Journal*, 1 October 1917, 4a–b, including photograph of firing party).

Some weeks later Henry Duke, the Irish Chief Secretary, explained to the War Cabinet how Sinn Féin had been allowed to proceed with the Ashe funeral on such a large scale. Ashe's lying in state was at the City Hall and, visited by thousands, indicated the measure of popular opinion. Duke then consulted the General Officer Commanding and the Commissioner of Police, who told him that it would be impossible to interfere with the funeral 'without provoking the bitterest antagonism and social disorder'. Duke told the Cabinet that about 15,000 people followed the funeral (newspaper reports put the numbers much higher) 'in an impressive and orderly manner'. There had been two criticisms of government's role – allowing Volunteers to parade in uniform and the firing of a volley over the grave.[26] Duke offered no explanation for the former, assuming perhaps that the public order difficulties were obvious. As to the use of arms, the number had been 'extremely small'. They had been smuggled into the cemetery, he thought in the hearse, and despite the vigilance of the police (likely no doubt to be discreetly exercised in the midst of a large and emotional crowd) the organisers had succeeded in smuggling them away.[27] All in all, it was hardly an explanation of events that would have convinced the Cabinet that the Irish government had a grasp on events, as distinct from responding as best it could.

To *The Times* the situation was 'very delicate': Ashe's death had given an impetus to Sinn Féin, which had previously begun to lose ground because of its lack of intelligible policy. The day before the funeral the Irish Privy Council in an emergency meeting had completed the necessary formalities to allow the General Prisons Board to bring in special rules for the treatment of DORA prisoners. These new rules met the Sinn Féin prisoners' demand for political status, and the hunger-strike was called off.[28] Two particularly ill prisoners were

---

26 The two more prominent critics of government's apparently weak stance were Dr John Mahaffy (Provost of Trinity College, Dublin) and Lord Midleton (leader of the southern Unionists).

27 PRO CAB 23/4: War Cabinet, 15 October 1917.

28 The rules, approved on 29 September, were thereafter known as the 'September Rules' (PRO HO 144/1453/311980/138). The modified regime was as follows: separation from other prisoners; no reception bath; to be searched by a special officer; special cells for all and to be allowed to rent more comfortably equipped cell if so desired, and to use own furniture, etc.; on payment, a prisoner would housekeep for them; outside food at own expense, likewise books, and newspapers (subject to approval); no prison work; generous allowance of visits and letters and special visiting room. These ameliorations were substantially the same as those authorised by Churchill in 1910 for the treatment of those whose offences 'however reprehensible, do not involve personal dishonour' (5 *Hansard*, 15 March 1910, cols 178–9). Churchill (then Home Secretary) had been prompted to act by the unease caused by the prison treatment of the suffragettes. The ameliorations, which could be granted at the discretion of the Prison Commissioners in suitable cases, were incorporated into the Prison Rules for England as Rule 243A (*RCP and the Directors of Convict Prisons, 1909– 10*, PP, 1910 [Cd. 5360], XLV, 277, 19. There was an Irish as well as a suffragette connection, since the need for rule changes to accommodate political offenders had first been urged on Churchill as the incoming Home Secretary by Wilfred Scawen Blunt, who had himself been imprisoned for two months in 1887 for political offences committed in the course of the Land War (see Wilfred Scawen Blunt, *My Diaries*, London, Martin Secker, 1920, Vol. 2, p. 307; PRO HO 144/1107/ 200655. I am grateful to my student Alan Baxendale, who pointed out these connections).

immediately liberated under the 'Cat and Mouse Act', lest there should be further prison fatalities.[29] The concessions were further evidence of ineptitude. 'Had they been justifiable,' *The Times* admonished, 'they should have been made before Ashe's death. If they were not justifiable they should not have been made at all.' Nor was impuissance manifest only in relation to prisoners:

> For weeks past men have been tried and sentenced by court-martial for the wearing of green uniforms and the carrying of hurley sticks but during the last two days these uniforms have been worn and these sticks carried freely in the streets of Dublin. The continued absence of firm and logical policy at Dublin Castle must have the worst possible results.[30]

The Irish government's loss of credibility was also signalled in other ways. The Sinn Féin prisoners were to be removed altogether from Mountjoy, pending which the Irish Chief Secretary accepted an offer from the Lord Mayor to provide food to those who were suffering from the effects of their hunger-strike.[31] Intended as conciliation, acceptance of the food simply confirmed the authorities' culpability and faltering legitimacy. The Lord Mayor had also moved the adjournment of the Dublin Corporation's monthly meeting, 'as a mark of respect to the memory of Thomas Ashe'. Ominously for British authority and the Irish Parliamentary Party, the Roman Catholic clergy continued their realignment.

In London there was deep consternation. Through Arthur Henderson (Secretary of the Labour Party) and George Barnes (Labour Member of the War Cabinet) John Dillon asked the Cabinet to consider the critical nature of the situation in Dublin. Should any more prisoners die there would be 'desperate feeling'. Dillon urged that all political prisoners should be immediately placed under special rules. Henry Duke (who was then in Dublin) was asked to make a report to the next Cabinet meeting.[32]

Duke's assessment was hardly reassuring. Hunger-strikes for political status and treatment were continuing, and forcible feeding had been condemned at the Ashe inquest by 'medical witnesses of great credit'. If the prisoners could not be fed forcibly there were five possible courses of action. The hunger-strike could

---

29 This Act, introduced in 1913 to deal with suffragette hunger-strikes, allowed the Home Secretary (in Ireland the Lord Lieutenant) to authorise the temporary discharge of a prisoner whose health had deteriorated 'due in whole or in part to the prisoner's own conduct in prison'. On the restoration of health the prisoner could be returned to custody, the period at liberty not being counted against the sentence being served (Prisoners (Temporary Discharge for Ill-Health) Act, 1913 (3 Geo. V, c.4, s.1)). The new rules, which, *inter alia*, allowed for the supply of food other than prison diet, were based on the 1910 Churchill Rules.
30 *The Times*, 22 November 1917, 3b.
31 Ibid., 3 October 3b; *Freeman's Journal*, 2 October 1917, 3e.
32 PRO CAB 23/4: War Cabinet 242 (1 October 1917).

be allowed to proceed, and the prisoners could be released one by one as their condition became dangerous. The men could be fed forcibly, incurring the medical risks. Ringleaders could be removed to another prison 'perhaps in England', making it easier to deal with the remainder. The demands could be conceded, placing the prisoners in a condition that went no further than mere detention. Finally, Duke suggested, the hunger-strikers would be discharged from prison, but using DORA regulations deported from Ireland.[33]

The Home Secretary (Sir George Cave) was far from willing to accept transfers to the English prisons. All forty or so prisoners on hunger-strike had been committed for political offences, such as wearing uniforms and drilling. In English law there was no such thing as a political prisoner. Apart from Stead and the Jameson Raiders only two political cases had been treated as first-class misdemeanants, and Rule 243A provided the most lenient form of discipline possible in the English system. Cave (and even more the officials behind him) did not want to have to cope with a group of political internees. After a lengthy discussion a compromise was agreed. Only certain of the leaders among the prisoners would be transferred to England, and all Sinn Féin prisoners, both in Ireland and England, would be given the benefit of Rule 243A.[34]

Mountjoy's striking prisoners had been released, but fifteen others from provincial centres were transferred to the refitted Dundalk Prison (which had been used previously for wounded soldiers). These were given privileges, which amounted to internment conditions, including unlimited association, daily visits and superior food. In England, the Home Office fretted lest conscientious objectors, also imprisoned under DORA, should begin to demand similar privileges.[35] The Castle's cup of humiliation was not yet drained, however, and on the day of their transfer to Dundalk the prisoners began a new hunger-strike, because they contended their food was for criminals rather than for the civil detainees they had now become. In under a week Duke decided to release all the men, who were greeted at the prison gate by a large crowd, which cheered them away.[36] At Cork Prison a hunger-strike was immediately declared by the Sinn Féin prisoners, and they too were released on 21 November. Although the government claimed the face-saver of the Cat and Mouse Act, hunger-striking had again proved to be a politically devastating weapon.[37] There was little the prison authorities could do to counter it. Excessive force could kill a determined or delicate prisoner, and the procedure was not only brutal but accident-prone. A subsequent Home

---

33 Ibid., War Cabinet 244 (3 October 1917). If the existing DORA regulations did not allow deportation a new one could be brought in, Duke noted.

34 Ibid.

35 PRO HO 144/453/311980/138. Sir Edward Troup would have none of it, however: 'Irish prisons have not . . . been regarded in the past as models to be followed in English Prison Administration.'

36 The Times, 4 October 1917, 9b; 19 November 1917, 5a; Irish Independent, 4 October 1917, 2g; 19 November 1917, 3g.

37 Freeman's Journal, 22 November 1917, 6f; Cork Examiner, 22 November 1917, 4f.

Office circular issued on 8 December to all prison governors did not seek to circumvent the strikes, but rather to shift responsibility for forced feeding and other potentially embarrassing decisions from the lay to the medical spheres. Medical officers were given responsibility in each case, and instructed to ensure that correct procedures were followed and recorded.[38]

Sinn Féin's sweeping electoral victory was more than a year away. Few, looking at the massive dominance of Redmond's party in the Irish parliamentary representation, could have imagined its utter destruction. Constitutional politicians could nevertheless feel tremors in the ground they had hitherto so confidently trodden, and were anxious not to cede patriotic fervour to Sinn Féin. A few MPs had already changed their colours and would push the Sinn Féin line notwithstanding. Politicking at Westminster was in any case propelled by popular feeling about Ashe. The result was a relentless and repeated returning to the question, once Parliament resumed on 16 October. Alfred Byrne,[39] vocal in the Sinn Féin cause since the Easter rising, asked whether the Irish Secretary was aware of Irish indignation about Ashe's death, whether forcible feeding had been stopped after Ashe's 'murder', and whether the meeting of the Irish Privy Council to change the prison rules had anything to do with the foreign notice that had been taken of Ashe's death.[40] He returned to the issue after the inquest, fortified by expert evidence that the feeding procedure had been dangerous 'even in the most skilled hands'. Would the government now abolish this method of punishing prisoners?[41] Would there be an inquiry into the matter in the light of the inquest verdict and rider? Would there by criminal indictments?[42]

Even among Irish Members Byrne took a hard and intemperate line, and his interventions were to some extent discounted. The veteran nationalist politician William O'Brien, who had gone against the grain of many of his natural supporters to speak on recruiting platforms in 1914 and 1915, and whose central idea in Irish politics was national conciliation, could not be dismissed as a

---

38 PRO HO 144/172/233014/118: 8 December 1917. Forced feeding was also used on conscientious objectors (who were also undergoing imprisonment at this time). Despite these instructions, (or because of the unintended signal they gave) for the duration of the Anglo-Irish war forcible feeding was never again attempted against Irish hunger-strikers. It would seem that no medical officer was willing to risk a fatality and the inevitable outcry and lifelong stigmatisation. In modern times this has remained a controversial issue with difficult ethical, legal and administrative dimensions, and periodically tested by difficult cases (see John Williams, 'Hunger-Strikes: A Prisoner's Right or a "Wicked Folly"?', *The Howard Journal of Criminal Justice*, 40, 3 (August 2001), pp. 285–96).

39 See p. 489, n. 164, above.

40 5 *Hansard*, XCVIII, col. 24; 16 October 1917; cols 660–1; 23 October 1917. The Speaker rebuked Byrne for using the word 'murder' (see also col. 1015; 25 October 1917; cols 1603–4; 1 November 1917).

41 Ibid., cols 2317–18; 8 November 1917.

42 Ibid., cols 2331–2; 8 November 1917; XCIX, col. 392; 14 November 1917.

firebrand.[43] In the great debate on Irish government on 23 October 1917, his criticisms of the executive were detailed, rational and given from the perspective of one who wished to see the cause of peaceable and orderly Home Rule advanced. He was excoriating on the handling of Ashe and similar offenders. Ashe's offence had been comparatively trivial, certainly not meriting such a heavy sentence. But if imprisoning Ashe and his companions was folly, then to subject them to a criminal prison regime was 'little short of madness' unless government really wanted another outbreak. When, against its wishes, Ashe's coroner allowed probing of the facts about how the Mountjoy men were being treated, government instructed officials to refuse to give evidence. But enough was elicited for O'Brien to say that the details of forcible feeding and other types of brutal treatment were 'barbarities so revolting that if ever the facts get out they will horrify all civilised men as they have horrified Irishmen'.

Other Irish members followed in similar tones, as a few examples will show. Arthur Lynch,[44] who at different points in his remarkable career had been sentenced to death for treason, served a term of imprisonment and was pardoned, described Ashe's death as having 'sent a shock throughout the whole of Ireland'. The situation was one of the gravest of the past 100 years with 'a sense of some impending great event' which he hoped would not be a tragedy. This revulsion in Irish sentiment could have been averted had government from the first day treated Ashe and the others as political prisoners. The refusal to do this, Lynch believed, arose from government's wish 'to pander to a sentiment of revenge'.[45]

William Anderson[46] was one of several members who reminded the House that the direct action of Ashe and his like had been learned from events in Ulster, where without any legal sanction seditious speeches had been made, similar to the one for which Ashe had been imprisoned. By its treatment of Ashe, who was punished in all sorts of pettifogging ways for asserting his claim to be a political

---

43 O'Brien (1852–1928) had himself been imprisoned in Ireland several times during the Plan of Campaign. He later believed in discussion and conciliation between all parties in Ireland, Nationalist and Unionist, landlord and tenant. He owned and edited several newspapers over the years in the promotion of his views.

44 (1864–1934). Born Australia, Irish father and Scottish mother. Settled in London. Drawn into Irish nationalism via Gaelic League and Amnesty Association; associate of Maud Gonne. Co-founded (with John MacBride) the Irish Brigade in South Africa, and was Colonel of its Second Brigade. Elected MP for Galway in 1901; on his return to the UK to take his seat was sentenced to death, commuted to imprisonment; pardoned in 1907. Lost much support when in 1918 he took part in a recruitment drive. Forfeited his seat (Clare) in 1918 election. Thereafter practised medicine in London. At the time of this speech a moderate, if slightly eccentric, nationalist. Accused by anonymous Clan na Gael correspondent of desertion and looting in South Africa (NLI: Devoy Papers: Ms. 18, 138).

45 5 Hansard, XCVIII, col. 758; 23 October 1917.

46 (1877–1919). Chairman of Independent Labour Party, 1911–13, Labour Party, 1914–15. Member for Attercliffe Division of Sheffield, 1914–18. Died in influenza epidemic.

prisoner, and by his death, government was feeding revolutionary forces in Ireland 'for that man received a funeral such as no man has received since Parnell died'. These events were looming over and impeding the Irish Convention, and if it failed there was not the least doubt that there would in the coming few years be 'very dreadful history in Ireland'.[47]

The left was generally sympathetic to the Irish cause, and among the few English MPs who spoke against the government on Ashe's death there were some who had a direct experience of imprisonment. Philip Snowdon[48] was unable to win from the Home Secretary any softening in English prison punishments on the back of the Ashe inquest. He wanted forcible feeding stopped, together with dietary punishments ('mean and dangerous to health') and the punitive removal of cell furniture and equipment. Sir George Cave peremptorily refused these requests, insisting that forcible feeding was only ever used in the last resort 'as a medical measure to preserve . . . life'. This prompted Arthur Lynch's derisory interjection 'to save life you destroy it'.[49] That, of course, was the problem: had Ashe only lived. . . .

Transfer to English prisons

The Cabinet decision to transfer to England leaders among the Sinn Féin prisoners was made on 3 October.[50] Some ten weeks elapsed before Duke, the Irish Chief Secretary, sought to make use of it. On 14 December 1917, he wrote to the Home Secretary, Sir George Cave, reminding him of what had been decided. He had not so far found it necessary to use the facility, but expected soon to send three men over.[51] The Home Office, in the person of Troup, the Permanent-Under-Secretary, immediately began to wriggle. The Cabinet decision cited by Duke referred to the conditions at the time it was made (i.e. the Mountjoy hunger-strike) and extended only to 'Certain ringleaders among the Sinn Féin prisoners'. Circumstances had changed and the whole matter ought to be reconsidered: 'it would be a pity to enter upon a course which would have to be abandoned afterwards.'[52]

It was incumbent on the English administration to accept the Irish prisoners 'however great the trouble they may cause' if their transfer would help to resolve the difficulties in Ireland. But would transfers solve the Irish government's problems? Troup thought not. If transferred to England the men would go on

---

47 5 *Hansard* XCVIII, cols 769–70; 23 October 1917.

48 (1864–1937). Labour leader. Would be Chancellor of Exchequer in MacDonald governments of 1924 and 1929.

49 5 *Hansard*, XCIX, cols 561–2; 15 November 1917.

50 PRO CAB 23/4: War Cabinet 244.

51 PRO HO 144/22523. The October crisis had, of course, been settled by releases.

52 Ibid., /3: Troup memorandum, 18 December 1917. The paragraphs which immediately follow are from this document.

hunger-strike, as in Ireland. They were under the misapprehension that mutinous conduct had wrought the release of both the Frongoch and Lewes men; they knew that hunger-striking had worked in Ireland, and the one man who had died had become a martyr whose death had 'materially promoted the Sinn Féin cause'. If faced with a hunger-strike, government had three possibilities: it could release the prisoners; feed them forcibly; or warn them they would be allowed to starve themselves to death, and then see the confrontation through.

If the first of these options were adopted, and the men released, what was the point of transferring them to England? If, alternatively, they were to be force-fed other difficulties presented themselves. The prisons would cope if only a small number were involved, but this type of feeding could not, in any event, be kept up indefinitely. There was also the possibility that someone would die, which would provoke the same reaction as had Ashe. This would inflict polit-ical damage, and was also unfair to the medical officers who were laid open to allegations of incapacity or even murder. As for the last option – warning of the consequences of hunger-striking and seeing it through to the end – some prisoners might heed the warning and abandon their hunger-strike. But some might persist, and in that event would government be prepared to let a number of them die – 'one by one in prison by self-inflicted starvation'? There would be enormous pressure for releases. If the fact that a hunger-strike was under way were concealed (to avert political pressure) then government would be open to the charge of having allowed the prisoners to die when they might have been saved.

Troup also pointed to a legal difficulty arising from the leading case of *Leigh v. Gladstone*, in which it was held that it was the duty of the medical officer to preserve the life of a prisoner by any means available, including forcible feed-ing. If this case could be applied, then (as the Lord Chief Justice had hinted) a medical officer who allowed his prisoner to die when he might have saved him by forcible feeding could be liable to a manslaughter charge.[53] The difficulty might be resolved by legislation which absolved the prison authorities from responsibility in cases where prisoners chose to starve themselves. But even here there were complications: not all prisoners could be allowed to choose to die – 'a murderer cannot be permitted to escape the gallows or penal servitude by suicide'. Legislation, in any event, would be difficult or impossible to bring in, yet without it Troup could not see any advantage in transferring the men to England.

There were also, in Troup's view, some positive drawbacks in transferring the Sinn Féin prisoners to England, even if the difficulties which he had outlined

---

53 *Leigh v. Gladstone*: 26 *Times Law Reports*, 139. This was a case brought by Mrs Marie Leigh (a suffragette) against the Home Secretary and others, claiming damages for assault by forcible feeding. The defence was that minimum force was used and the feeding was necessary to save her life. The case report (140b) contains a graphic account of forced feeding.

were somehow resolved. The transfer would itself be exploited as a new grievance. In Ireland the Sinn Féin prisoners were enjoying the benefits of Rule 243A. If these privileges were discontinued on their transfer to England there would be a new set of protests. If, however, they were allowed to bring the privileges with them, confusion would be created in the English prisons. Finally, bringing the Irish detainees to English prisons could stir up the conscientious objectors, who for some time had been threatening to go on hunger-strike. Should the Irish successfully go on hunger-strike, winning their release, the conscientious objectors would follow them. This might produce a hunger-strike on such a large scale that immediate release would be the only course.

Some of Troup's talk was little more than speculative scaremongering – a probing of the politicians' resolution – but the Home Secretary was convinced, or found it convenient to appear so. Two days after receiving Troup's memorandum he wrote to Duke. He had been rather alarmed by the request that three Irish prisoners be placed in English convict prisons and 'various others' later on. The 30 October Cabinet decision had referred to one or two ringleaders, and Cave had understood those to be serving only short sentences. He endorsed Troup's argument against receiving a number of Irish prisoners and noted (undoubtedly at Troup's suggestion) that convicts received from Ireland (i.e. persons serving sentences of penal servitude, as distinct from ordinary imprisonment) could not be given the privileges of Rule 243A. Cave felt bound to comply with the original Cabinet decision regarding the three ringleaders, 'but I hope you will not ask to go further'.[54]

Conscription

Thomas Ashe's death, and its inevitable and far-reaching aftermath, was a wound self-inflicted by Dublin Castle. In the spring of 1918, however, a far greater blow against peace and stability in Ireland was inflicted by the Imperial government. Irish nationalist opinion was united against conscription – constitutionalists because it would wash away their support in the country; republicans because it violated their claims to national self-determination. Opposition was vociferous, and warnings from the government's sympathisers were many and sombre.[55]

54 Sir George Cave to Henry Duke, 20 December 1917: PRO HO 144/22523.
55 With the exception of the Ulster Unionists. Carson from the beginning had pressed for conscription to be universal throughout the United Kingdom (see Harford Montgomery Hyde, *Carson: The Life of Sir Edward Carson, Lord Carson of Duncairn*, London, William Heinemann, 1953, pp. 400, 406 and 432). Voluntary enlistment, in Carson's view, was reducing the loyalist manhood of Ireland, to the advantage of the nationalists; he also held, as a Unionist, that as a matter of principle Ireland should have the same status and obligations as other parts of the United Kingdom (see also Ian Colvin, *The Life of Lord Carson*, London, Victor Gollancz, 1936, Vol. 3, pp. 131–5).

By the autumn of 1917, British manpower requirements were critical.[56] In Britain, changes in conscription regulations and a vigorous 'combing out' of reserved positions in industry had maximised the intake of men, but still attrition exceeded supply. Throughout the winter of 1917 to 1918 Germany had been preparing a major offensive on the Western front, aided greatly by the removal of Russia from the war, and the virtual collapse of Italy. Where the Germans would strike was not known, but that they would was not in doubt. On 23 March 1918, Sir Henry Wilson, the newly appointed Chief of the Imperial General Staff, discussed with Lloyd George the initial allied defeats of what would be a prolonged German advance. He again urged conscription to take in all men up to the age of 50 and 'of course' Ireland.[57] By late April the Germans came to within forty miles of Paris and military pressure to conscript Ireland was intense. The Americans were now contributing to the war effort, and promised to increase their monthly transports, but President Wilson asked that conscription not be enforced in Ireland, 'as his task would be rendered very difficult'.[58] Lloyd George vacillated. On 16 April 1918, a Bill to extend conscription to Ireland passed the Commons and in August Lloyd George agreed to bring in the necessary executive Order in Council as soon as Parliament reassembled. By this time, however, the tides of war were flowing strongly the other way. Germany faced collapse and the Cabinet split on the issue of conscripting Ireland, with a majority opposing it.[59] Up until the end of the war, even with the Central Powers manifestly defeated, the military continued to press for Irish conscription, being supported in this by the Ulster Unionists and by important sections of the Conservative Party.

From its inception conscription troubled and to a some extent divided English political circles, but it galvanised Ireland – the constitutional nationalists, Sinn Féin and the Roman Catholic hierarchy on the one side, Ulster Unionists on the other. Five months before the Easter rising John Devoy wrote to Roger Casement in Germany, explaining the revolutionary advantages as he saw them: 'The *threat* of resistance has staved off Conscription for a while, given us time and, what is better, it has given us the "flesh and blood" appeal which is the only means of getting money here. We are getting it at last and because of that appeal only.'[60] In Ireland Volunteers were directed to 'resist to the death' any attempt to conscript

---

56 Since the start of the Somme (1 July 1916) the British had lost 1.5 million men. By mid-autumn 1917, 780,000 had been sent out to replace them. There was a total reserve of 90,000. This was a very narrow margin, and few men were coming into the army (Thomson, 1939, *op. cit.*, p. 358).

57 Major-General Sir C. E. Callwell, *Field-Marshall Sir Henry Wilson: His Life and Diaries*, London, Cassell, 1927, Vol. 2, p. 74 (see also pp. 76 and 81).

58 Ibid., p. 82.

59 Ibid., pp. 135–6.

60 Devoy to Casement, 21 November 1915: NLI: Casement Papers: Ms. 13, 073 (44/vii).

them.[61] As the measure passed the Commons, Dillon (who on Redmond's death the month before had become leader of the Irish Parliamentary Party) warned Lloyd George that 'All Ireland will rise against you', and led his colleagues out of Westminster.[62] The Irish Chief Secretary contended that conscription in Ireland would be tantamount to recruiting Germans, and that additional troops would have to be sent to enforce it.[63] The Roman Catholic Primate, Cardinal Michael Logue[64] (an entrenched conservative, who had helped to cripple Parnell and who condemned the de Valera version of Sinn Féin) led the standing committee of Irish Bishops in a public statement which denounced Irish conscription as 'an oppressive and inhuman law, which the Irish people have a right to resist by all means that are consonant with the laws of God'.[65]

Two days after the passage of the Military Service Bill the Lord Mayor convened a representative conference at Dublin's Mansion House. This meeting did much to unify Irish nationalist opinion on the issue, and bestowed even more credibility on Sinn Féin. An anti-conscription pledge (drafted by de Valera) was agreed, and the following Sunday was administered at church doors throughout the country. Sinn Féin and the Parliamentary Party agreed a temporary electoral pact; a National Defence Fund was launched; a one-day general strike was held on 23 April; and it was decided that the Irish anti-conscription case should be presented to the President and Congress of the United States of America.[66] This, A. J. P. Taylor suggested, 'was the decisive moment at which Ireland seceded from the Union'.[67]

The 'German Plot'

The British response to the upsurge in Ireland was both precautionary and repressive. On 1 May the moderate Conservative Henry Duke was replaced as Irish Chief Secretary by Edward Shortt, a Lloyd George Liberal, who was charged with putting down 'the Irish-German conspiracy' with a stern hand.[68] In addition,

---

61 [U]se every weapon . . . be it knife, pitchfork, rifle or bomb . . . make . . . death or capture dearly purchased by the lives of enemies.' The Volunteer who was taken should never consent to wear a British uniform, nor obey orders 'in prison or out of prison' (An tÓglach, 14 September 1918, 1, 2, 1b).

62 Irish Independent, 17 April 1918, 3f; 5 Hansard, CIV, cols 1475–1592, 10 April 1918; cols 1738–1816, 11 April 1918; cols 1832–1998, 12 April 1918; cols 2013–93, 13 April 1918.

63 Lyons, 1985, op. cit., p. 393.

64 (1839–1924). Condemned the Land League's Plan of Campaign, and after the O'Shea divorce opposed Parnell's continuance as leader of the Irish Parliamentary Party. Patron of the Gaelic League, temperance campaigner and promoter of rural works and reafforestation.

65 Irish Independent, 19 April 1918, 3g.

66 Ibid., 20 April 1918, 3d–e.

67 A. J. P. Taylor, op. cit., p. 104.

68 Thomas Jones, Whitehall Diary, London, Oxford University Press, 1971, Vol. III, pp. 8–9. Duke (1855–1939) was a Conservative MP, 1900–6, 1910–18, and Irish Chief Secretary, 1916–18. He was subsequently appointed as a judge. Shortt was a Liberal MP, 1910–22. Barrister; Irish Chief Secretary, 1918; Home Secretary, 1919–22.

Field Marshal Lord French[69] was appointed Lord Lieutenant on 11 May, replacing Lord Wimborne.[70] The decision to replace a civilian with a soldier indicated a determination to enforce conscription, and to suppress any consequent disorders; it also, at least informally, shortened the lines of communication between the military and civil administrations in Ireland. On tabling the Home Rule Bill, Lloyd George declared his intention of issuing the Order in Council for conscription, and privately advised the new Lord Lieutenant 'to put the onus for first shooting on the rebels'.[71] The difficulty with this crude carrot-and-stick routine was that the time had long passed when the version of Home Rule on offer was attractive or even acceptable to a significant section of the population, who in consequence saw only the waving of the British stick. On its side, the War Cabinet united in believing that for either Home Rule or conscription to succeed in Ireland, the rule of law had to be re-established: stern measures were necessary.[72]

These were not long in coming. Less than a week after his arrival in Dublin, Lord French announced the discovery of a 'German Plot'.[73] A strong proclamation was followed by the arrest of most of the Sinn Féin leadership, including Eamon de Valera and Arthur Griffith. There had been plenty of warning of what was pending. The capture of an Irishman on a mission from Germany was announced on 17 April.[74] A week later certain amendments were announced in DORA regulations regarding powers of deportation.[75] On 8 May, Sir Edward

---

69 Field-Marshal Sir John French (1852–1925), Chief of Imperial General Staff, 1911–14; Commander-in-Chief UK Forces, 1916–18; Lord Lieutenant, 1918–21. Only Irish Lord Lieutenant to sit in Cabinet. Viscount, 1916; Earl of Ypres, 1922.

70 (1873–1939). First Viscount Wimborne; Lord Lieutenant, 1915–18. Conservative, then Liberal, politician.

71 Callwell, op. cit., Vol. II, p. 98.

72 Jones, op. cit., Vol. 3, p. 9; Charles Townshend, The British Campaign in Ireland 1919–1921, Oxford University Press, 1975, pp. 8–9.

73 Both Piaras Béaslaí (1926, Vol. I, ch. IX) and Dorothy Macardle (The Irish Republic, Dublin, Irish Press, 1951, p. 253) are emphatic that there was no plot, but this is not necessarily conclusive.

74 Irish Independent, 18 April 1918, 3c. This was Joseph Dowling, whose identity was not disclosed at the time. Dowling kept his counsel, and Marcardle stated that he had been sent by the Germans on their own initiative. This seems implausible since they had well-established channels through Devoy and Clan na Gael. In later years both the Irish and British governments had good reasons for reticence. British officials would later claim that fear that the Germans would learn the extent to which the Admiralty had broken their naval codes prevented the publication of the strongest evidence of the plot (Thomson, 1939, op. cit., pp. 371–3; see also (though it is largely culled from Thomson's book) Admiral Sir William James, The Eyes of the Navy, London, Methuen, 1955, pp. 168–9). An element of mystery remains. Hugh Cleland Hoy (40 O.B. or How the War Was Won, London, Hutchinson, 1932, pp. 142–8) suggests that the mission was a genuine attempt by the Germans to discover the state of affairs in Ireland, but this fails to convince. It is possible, of course, that British intelligence engineered the incident. See below, p. 767.

75 Irish Independent, 25 April 1918, 2d.

Carson addressed the Irish situation in *The Times*. The government, he insisted, 'have the clearest evidence in their possession that the Sinn Féin organization is, and has been, in alliance with Germany'.[76] This letter in itself was a major pressure for action.

Through his detective double-agent Ned Broy, Michael Collins had advance notice of the intended round-up which he passed on without revealing his source. De Valera was warned not to return to his home, but rejected the advice.[77] All but a few of the Sinn Féin leadership decided not to resist arrest or to evade it, but to allow the action to act as a warning to the country: the sentences and internments of 1916 to 1917 had been so clearly counterproductive. Replacements were available to carry on the work, and 'by the fact of being in jail we would have a unifying effect . . . by placing the whole nation behind us as a matter of national honour'.[78] Altogether, seventy-three men and women were gathered up on 17 May 1918, of whom sixty-one men and two women were sent to England.[79] Significantly (and fatefully), Michael Collins who by mere accident had escaped the arrest, and now the driving force in the IRB, had decided to 'go on his keeping'. Cathal Brugha also avoided arrest: both men were active in military preparations. Failure to take these men and their immediate followers would prove to be expensive for British policy. While Sinn Féin's political leaders sat in English prisons, Collins and Brugha tightened their grip on militant forces in Ireland.[80]

The 1918 to 1919 internments

The first weeks

As planned, detainees remained in Dublin for only a few hours before embarking from Kingstown, having been presented with DORA internment orders marked

---

76 *The Times*, 8 May 1918, 7c. This was also the day that the Irish Office wrote to the Home Office about accommodation for those who might be interned or banished from Ireland. The Home Office was not anxious to become involved again, and on 13 May replied, pointing out that those detained or deported under DORA Regulation 14b would be the responsibility of the military authorities. The Isle of Man would be an unsuitable location for an internment camp, because of its proximity to Ireland. Frongoch could again be made available. This exchange confirms that a deal of planning and preparation went into the 'German Plot' (PRO HO 144/ 1496/362269: Home Office to Irish Office, 13 May 1918).

77 Béaslaí, 1926, Vol. 1, pp. 189–90.

78 Darrell Figgis, *A Second Chronicle of Jails*, Dublin, Talbot Press, 1919, pp. 16 and 9–19, *passim*. What Figgis and the others did not know was the length of time of their confinement. Would their decision have been the same had they realised that they would be interned for ten months?

79 RCP, PP, 1918 [374], XXVII, 759, 22.

80 The arrests, recalled John Brennan, put those still at liberty under a 'crushing burden' (*op. cit.*, p. 121). This may have increased cohesiveness and efficiency.

for Frongoch.[81] Once in Wales, however, the men were held at a military transit camp at Holyhead, where they were informed that they were not to go to Frongoch, but were to be broken into two parties – one of which would go to Gloucester Prison, the other to Usk. On their onward journey two days later, the internees encountered civilian hostility, but were treated decently by their military escorts.[82] Within a few days the sixty-one men and two women would be distributed among eight prisons.[83]

Military involvement was not as great as it had been in 1916, largely because of acute manpower shortages, and a lesser sense of crisis about Irish developments. The prisons were also running with a much depleted staff, since there had been a dramatic reduction in the population of ordinary prisoners, and many warders had gone into the armed services.[84] There was concern that in their reduced state the prisons would not be able to cope, and governors were told that should they have doubts about the adequacy of their staff they should apply immediately to the District General Officer in Command for a military guard.[85]

The decision not to re-open Frongoch caused friction between the War and Home Offices. The Prison Commissioners complained that they had been presented with the problem as a result of a military decision, yet were not being given any extra resources. In time of war military needs are paramount, and on 23 May the War Office simply informed the Home Office that the Army Council could offer no assistance. The Council did, however, promise military escorts should it prove necessary to move the internees. Ruggles-Brise, the Prison Commission Chairman, protested that this decision might have 'untoward results'. All was now quiet (in early June 1918) but with the prolongation of their detention the men's restlessness and discontent would increase. A few soldiers – even if over age – would assist. The initial military assistance had been withdrawn from two

81 All the internment orders (except for the two women) specified Frongoch, but the Home Office was unable to persuade the War Office to reopen the camp (PRO HO 144/1496/362269). On 22 May the Home Office accordingly informed Dublin Castle of the seven prisons around which the internees had been distributed. Two considerations probably weighed against Frongoch: numbers were too small to justify the expense of reopening the camp; and, as has been seen, army experience of the Irish in the relatively relaxed surroundings of a prison camp was decidedly unhappy (see PRO HO 144/1496/362269/2, 22 May 1916).

82 Figgis, 1919, pp. 32-3.

83 PRO HO 144/1496/362269/2. A list, dated 22 May 1918, gave the location of all the internees. After the main wave of arrests Mrs Kathleen Clarke (widow of the executed Tom Clarke) was also arrested. Removing this woman from her five children, when her husband and her brother (Edward Daly) had been executed two years before, smacked of heartlessness (Healy, *op. cit.*, Vol. 2, pp. 599–600).

84 Memorandum of Sir Edward Troup, 10 June 1918, PRO HO 144/1496/366265. By the spring of 1917 the population of English prisons had been reduced from 16,727 (31 March 1914) to 9299 – a fall of just under half. In consequence seventeen prisons were closed, and staff transferred to make up the shortfall caused by enlistments for military service (5 *Hansard*, XCII, col. 1317; 4 April 1917).

85 Memorandum of H. B. Simpson, 20 May 1918; PRO HO 144/1496/366265/1a.

prisons, as it inevitably would from the remainder. Responsibility for any mishap would lie with the War Office, and not the Commissioners.[86]

The Home Office shared Ruggles-Brise's concerns, and on 10 June 1918, Sir Edward Troup wrote to the War Office. The internees were demanding Frongoch conditions, and these were impossible to grant in prison. When the men were informed that their regime had been made 'as liberal as the circumstances will allow' it was possible that prison staff would be unable to cope with any consequent disorder. In this eventuality it was essential that military assistance should be available. Soldiers still at the prisons should be left there, and where removed they should be replaced. Repeating Ruggles-Brise's warning, Troup took a tone unusual in correspondence between one department of state and another: 'These prisoners, though accommodated in civil prisons, are detained at the instance of the military authorities and for military reasons, and very serious consequences may ensue if the Governors cannot rely upon the co-operation of the military authorities in maintaining discipline among them.'[87] A copy of this letter was sent to Edward Shortt, the Irish Chief Secretary, soliciting his intervention with the War Office. From the records it would seem that Shortt, having got rid of the internees, cared little about the subsequent interdepartmental dispute, and declined to intervene.

To the prison governors the position looked rather desperate. Knowledgeable and confident prisoners presented petitions demanding Frongoch conditions, and threatened violence. In 1916 to 1917 the Irish had shown what they could do, and the Usk governor insisted that their threats could not be regarded as 'mere bunkum'. Some of the younger Usk men, indeed, might welcome a chance to create a disturbance just to relieve the monotony, and were that to happen all the internees would join in, he had no doubt. He was fearful as to the outcome:

> [W]ith their unlimited opportunities to conspire, and . . . their physical standard as compared with that of my staff, they would not be easy to overpower if a disturbance occurred while they were out of their cells. Only three of the 20 internees are over 40 years of age, whereas only three members of the Prison Staff are under 40 and those are nearing that age. The whole of the internees, too, are drilled men.

Usk had a military guard, but this was little consolation. The soldiers, who were members of the Royal Defence Corps, were 'not of the robust type of many of the internees, and in order to avoid the risk of their being overpowered and

---

86 Memorandum of Sir Evelyn Ruggles-Brise, 7 June 1918, ibid.

87 Troup to War Office, 10 June 1918; PRO HO 144/1496/366265/1a. In a covering personal note to General Macready (then Adjutant General) Troup added: 'The prisoners were sent for internment in England at Lord French's request – and a successful mutiny by them in an English prison would cause great excitement in Ireland which is quiet for the moment and might have very mischievous consequences on the situation there.'

losing their weapons, the use of firearms might conceivably have to be resorted to'. Apart from the danger of a mutiny there were matters of simple security. The prison walls were 'far from unscalable' and in consequence had constantly to be guarded. There was, moreover, no military depot nearby, and the guards had had to be sent from a considerable distance.[88]

The peril of the Commissioners' position was kept from the internees, who, had they rioted, could seriously have embarrassed the government. Since they had been neither charged nor convicted, the Gloucester governor immediately put himself in the wrong by insisting that they should be treated as ordinary prisoners. The men responded with demands to be treated as prisoners of war. Thinking that the internees would be held at Frongoch, the Home Office had not provided advance guidance on this critical issue. When threatened with trouble, the governor immediately backed down: no official would be thanked for a riot, and evasion and temporising could well pass on the problem. The prisoners, moreover, included many who had previously been in prison under DORA, and who spoke confidently about the schedule to the Act and its interpretation by Prison Commission standing orders.

The internees' basic demand was for free daytime association: cell doors opened at 7 a.m. and kept unlocked until 9 p.m. Their other requirements in effect reestablished the Frongoch and Reading regimes. All their property was to remain in their possession. They wanted to subscribe to Irish and English newspapers – and also to be permitted to buy, receive and retain books. Parcels of food, clothing and literature were to be allowed, together with three letters out each week. There were to be monthly visits from relatives and friends, and unlimited inward correspondence. If the prison could not set up a shop the governor should grant facilities for outside purchasing of food, clothes and literature. Perplexing though all of this was for the unprepared governor, he was particularly surprised to be told that the prisoners would do no work – or at least do only that which they wished. Even more astonishing was the demand that they should smoke as they wished: 'Smoking in a prison', he exclaimed.[89]

The upshot of the prisoners' statement was a procrastinating request from the governor that the men draw up for submission to the Home Office a schedule of their proposed regime. This was agreed, but in the meantime the internees insisted on their full rights. The governor was uncertain about how to proceed, but was willing, pending further instructions, to concede to the prisoners' demands, provided Figgis (their spokesman) 'as an Irishman' gave his word of honour that they were the conditions allowed at Reading two years before.

Two days after the prisoners handed in their schedule, the Home Office sent its reply. The conditions were for the most part agreed, and there was certainly

88 Usk Governor (W. Young) to Prison Commissioners, 6 June 1918; PRO HO 144/1496/366265/1a.
89 Figgis, 1919, op. cit., pp. 38–9.

no dispute but that they had been allowed at Reading in 1916. As a result of its previous negative experience the Home Office wished to impose some constraints on daytime association, and also, possibly, to get the men used to being periodically locked in their cells.[90] This enhanced control, and was one of the Home Office conditions that Figgis asserted 'was afterwards to take on a sinister twist'. In particular, the Home Office wished the men to be locked in their cells for two out of their three meals. The governor justified this to them by pointing out the extent to which his staff had been depleted since 1916. The prisoners responded that since their arrival they had given no trouble, and at the next mealtime ignored staff intimations that they should return to their cells (no direct orders were issued, and so a confrontation was avoided). The Home Office insisted, however, that the prisoners should receive ordinary prison fare, and not the special diet allowed in 1916.[91]

The oddest and most far-reaching of the amendments to the 'Reading Rules' was an initial prohibition on all correspondence, in or out. Within a few days of the arrests, Edward Shortt 'very decidedly' gave instructions that the detainees should not be allowed to reveal their location. No justification was offered to the prisoners for this embargo, and the Home Office pointed out that it meant that the prisoners could not telegraph or write in any way which indicated where they were: 'To allow them to write letters which obviously conceal the place of internment would give rise to very unfavourable comment.'[92] An additional consideration was that for some days, the men's friends and relatives thought they had been taken to Frongoch.[93] Under existing law and regulations the embargo was unenforceable. The men were entitled to receive parcels, which meant that friends and relatives had to know where these should be sent. The governor had to agree, which meant that a postcard was sent to every prisoner's home, so that all knew at least where their relatives were being held.

The blanket embargo on letters could not be maintained, and on 1 June the internees were informed that they would be allowed to receive and send three letters weekly.[94] All the men immediately telegraphed to relatives and

90 It was impossible to meet the men's wish that they should be treated exactly as they had been at Frongoch, since camp conditions could not be replicated in prison (PRO HO 144/1496/366265/1a: memorandum of 8 June 1918).

91 Figgis, 1919, op. cit., pp. 44–5.

92 The Home Office insisted that it would be 'quite impossible' to maintain the embargo for more than a few days (PRO HO 144/1496/362269/6: memorandum of 24 May 1918; see also memorandum of H. B. Simpson, 20 May 1918, PRO HO 144/1496/366265/1a).

93 It was not until 22 May that Arthur Griffith's wife learned that her husband was at Gloucester Prison, and that because a form had been sent to her from the governor, asking for his clothes (Maud Griffith to Home Office, 28 May 1918: PRO HO 144/1458/316093/8).

94 The Usk internees had warned that they would take direct action were the ban on letters not lifted, and the governor, William Young, later reported that 'It was not an easy matter to hold them in check during the suspension of their letters . . . suggestions of "trouble" and "commotion" were far from rare' (PRO HO 144/1496/366265/1a: letter of 6 June 1918).

friends. Because of censorship delays, however, ordinary mail was delayed for between a fortnight and a month. News of these delays got into the Irish press, whereupon an unrealistic pledge was given that in future they would be no greater than twenty-four hours. In fact, the difficulties continued to the end of internment.[95]

With ordinary criminals separation was a security and control mechanism, an intensification of punishment, and a device to prevent or at least limit contamination. There was no difficulty whatsoever in imposing the regime. When the Irish convicts had been allowed full association at Lewes in 1917 they had resisted the authorities, and had brought the prison to the verge of a riot.[96] Then, as some eighteen months later, it was politically undesirable to use military force. Since association could not reasonably be denied the internees, security could best be enhanced by breaking them into smaller groups, spread around several prisons. On past performance there was a good chance of violent resistance should the prisoners anticipate this move; subterfuge was necessary. According to Figgis, the Gloucester governor tricked them into having one meal in their cells (pleading a weekend staff shortage), giving his word that he had no ulterior motive. De Valera, Griffith and Figgis were all suspicious, fearing double-dealing. They decided, nevertheless, that if the authorities were determined to break them up they should not resist. Within a short time of returning to their cells they were brought out under close escort, and in several parties most were dispersed to other prisons. The stay at Gloucester had been rather

95 See complaint for Mrs Maud Griffith, 4 June 1918: PRO HO 144/1458/316093/8. From Home Office records it is evident that the normal inefficiencies of a bureaucracy in wartime were to blame for the postal delays. In addition, almost all the governors appear to have misread the Commissioners' directive of 31 May 1918. Governors had been instructed to send in 'all letters written by and all letters received for the prisoners, including postcards, telegrams, books and newspapers and any messages contained in parcels'. This would in itself delay correspondence, but all the governors (except at Reading) took it upon themselves additionally to read the correspondence, and to inform the Commissioners of anything interesting that was found (see PRO HO 144/1496/362269/159). Ironically enough, after several months' experience, relatively few instances of suspect mail had been penetrated by the postal censors – 393 cases of suspicious mail in the eight months up to 15 March 1919. This was out of a total of more than 25,000 letters, 745 telegrams and 1585 newspapers and other publications examined in the period between 14 July 1918 and 15 March 1919 (Ninth and Final Report of Directorate of Military Intelligence on the Correspondence of the Irish Internees; PRO HO 144/1496/362269). The War Office contended that postal censorship was useless because numerous unauthorised letters were variously passed out of the prisons (PRO HO 144/1496/362269: Report of Directorate of Military Intelligence, 21 March 1919). The Home Office disagreed, believing that even if it was not quite watertight, censorship did serve a useful purpose (presumably the gathering of general intelligence). In response to War Office criticisms it proposed a closer search of internees who were released, and taking their parole that they were not carrying out messages (ibid., /167; Minute of 25 February 1919).

96 See above, pp. 533-5. By 1919 the Prison Commissioners were describing the Lewes disturbances as 'The Lewes Prison mutiny of 1916'. RCP, PP, 1919 [374], XXVII, 759, 22. The leader of the Lewes mutiny was, of course, de Valera.

less than a week.[97] The internees were now distributed between Usk, Reading, Birmingham, Hull, Lincoln and Durham prisons: eleven remained at Gloucester; the two women were at Holloway.[98] Care had been taken to keep to small groups those who were thought to pose particular problems of potential disruption: leaders were separated from followers. On arrival the men were informed of new, stricter conditions.

The female internees

These were the ostensibly most notorious of the Sinn Féin women. Kathleen Clarke, the widow of Thomas Clarke, was the niece of the dynamitard John Daly, sometime member of the Supreme Council of the IRB and a convict for some twelve years. Her brother Edward had commanded the Four Courts Volunteers, and had been executed on 4 May 1916. Constance Markievicz was the most prominent woman to have taken part in the Easter rising, and continued to be seen in the active and leading circles of Sinn Féin. Maud Gonne MacBride was a Sinn Féin supporter, but not a member of that or any other organisation. The decision to arrest her seems to have been based more on the prominence she acquired as the widow of John MacBride. The couple were estranged for many years, and she had not been in Ireland at the time of the rising, though she subsequently returned there from France despite a prohibition order.[99] She reached Ireland late in 1917 or in the first days of the New Year.[100] When she was arrested in Dublin on 15 May 1918, therefore, she was in some senses a fugitive, though one which authority had not energetically sought out. Indeed, apart from her name and violation of a travel order it would have been hard to justify her arrest.

97 The men arrived at the West Camp, Holyhead, on 18 May, were lodged in Gloucester on 20 May and transferred out on 25 May 1918 (NLI: Seán O'Mahony Papers, Ms. 24, 456 (unfoliated)).

98 RCP, PP, 1919 [374], XXVII, 759, 22–3; PRO HO 144/1496/362269/2. Thus de Valera was in a group of only six at Lincoln, Figgis one of five at Durham, and Cosgrave, Hurley and Hayes were in a similar-sized group at Reading; Griffith had ten companions at Gloucester. The two largest groups were Birmingham (thirteen including Count Plunkett) and Usk (twenty). The two women – Countess Markievicz and Maud Gonne – were at Holloway; they were joined later by the widowed Kathleen Clarke. Aylesbury had ceased to be used for female convicts, accommodation at Liverpool being made available instead. Holloway offered more suitable facilities for the few female internees.

99 PRO HO 144/1465/321387/1. On her return to England from France on 17 September 1917, Maud Gonne was accompanied by her son John (aged 13), her adopted French daughter Germaine, known as Iseult (23) and her French cook. Her long-time suitor W. B. Yeats accompanied the party (Yeats had been able to get a passport to travel to France on the grounds that he was engaged in propaganda work: PRO HO 144/1465/312387/1a). On arrival Maud was served with a notice under DORA Regulation 14e, forbidding her onward journey to Ireland.

100 PRO HO 144/1465/321387/6.

Maud Gonne's position as an exile of many years and a widow with a young son cast doubt over her confinement from the beginning. This was surely a case of defective intelligence on the one side and inflated notoriety or reputation on the other. Six months into her confinement even Lloyd George took the view that her long absence abroad had undermined her political influence in Ireland.[101] Interest was taken in her case by the Liberal MP, Joseph King,[102] who sought in the first instance to secure a visit to Holloway for her son John (also called Seaghan, later Sean) and adopted daughter Iseult. An undertaking was secured from William Brace, the Home Office minister (to the annoyance of the Irish Office, which was against the visit).[103] As usual, the Home Office showed more political sense in the matter than the Irish Office, since it would have been hard to justify denying a mother (a widow at that) access to her young son to discuss his schooling and other domestic matters. In the event the visit (monitored by the Holloway governor) passed off uneventfully.

Writing to the Lord Mayor of Dublin three weeks into her confinement, Maud protested bitterly about conditions. She was being kept in secret, not charged, not even told why she was locked up, allowed no visits and not allowed to consult a solicitor. She was in a tiny cell, about seven by thirteen feet, for eighteen hours a day. Only during the time that the cells were being cleaned and in the exercise yard was she able to speak to Constance Markievicz and Kathleen Clarke. They were allowed only three small scraps of writing paper ('such as this is written on') each week and when they had finished writing pen and ink were removed. No Irish or Labour newspapers were allowed, but from the little information she could gather ('in such rags as the *Daily Mail*') she judged things to be going on well in Ireland. The more she and the others were ill-treated, the worse for England's reputation abroad. She therefore felt more useful in prison, where she did little but care for her son's education and nurse her rheumatism.[104]

In a letter the following day to her housekeeper (or friend) she repeated these complaints, adding only that they were allowed to go into each other's cells for about an hour each afternoon. She asked for a work by St Thomas Aquinas, 'for one needs sound doctrine if one does much meditation to prevent imagination going wild'. Having made various domestic arrangements she asked for prayers

---

101 See below, pp. 634–5.
102 (1860–1943). Educated at Trinity College, Oxford; Barrister, Liberal Member for North Somerset, 1910–18. Later stood (unsuccessfully) as Labour candidate.
103 5 *Hansard*, CVII, col. 168; 18 June 1918; PRO HO 144/1465/321387/14. The Irish Chief Secretary, Edward Shortt, did not want her son to visit, on the somewhat fantastical grounds that 'a woman like Mrs MacBride might have taught her son a sort of code that could be used in ordinary conversation' (ibid., memorandum of 18 June 1918). Shortt was also anxious that the boy should not return to Ireland, though his being under 16 years old may have made this hard to enforce.
104 Maud Gonne MacBride to Lord Mayor of Dublin, 8 June 1918: PRO HO 144/1465/321387/23. This letter was one of several stopped by the postal censor and returned to Holloway.

for her son, who was terribly alone on his own in London, and about whom she could get no news. Apart from this she was content, doing more good in prison than at liberty: 'The secrecy in which we are kept shows England's uneasy conscience about her bogus plot.'[105]

To her adopted daughter she made identical complaints, asking her to consult Irish friends and get a recommendation for a solicitor: 'He must be sympathetic to the Irish movement.' Food was adequate and she and the others were not hungry. (With a housewife's practicality she urged Iseult (who had been sending food in) not to send butter or sugar – 'They are claiming our rations here.' Her arrest 'was too absurd if it were not so wicked'. She was in full agreement with Sinn Féin principles, but was not a member, and her poor health prevented her from taking part in any activity.[106]

There seems to have been a great deal of heavy-handedness in stopping these and other letters, since the reasons given included that the letter exceeded twenty lines, or that Maud mentioned the conditions of her imprisonment, or that she had claimed that she was not allowed to see a solicitor. When the letters were returned so also was a cheque for £5, which she had sent out for her son's maintenance. Some of Maud's letters were angry and provocative ('I was kidnapped in the streets of Dublin on 19 May by 5 suspicious looking ruffians who had no warrant for my arrest') but repeatedly sending them back to her for different reasons was little more than Kafkaesque tyranny.[107] She was an anxious, intemperate and querulous woman, but no threat to state security: her treatment was inappropriate and disproportionate.

Maud eventually got a solicitor, but it was a marked and worrying deterioration in her health, rather than legal advice, that secured her release. There was concern about the political consequences of her breakdown in prison, though at first this possibility was treated with scepticism. M. L. Waller, now very well attuned to the political dimension of internment, first sounded a note of caution on 12 September 1918, and asked for an up-to-date medical report.[108] This coincided with a letter from Maud's son Seaghan which claimed that his mother was in a poor state of health, specifically that her left lung was afflicted, that she had lost nearly two stone (28 lb) since being imprisoned, and that she was suffering from episodes of delirium. Because of her poor medical treatment and

---

105 Maud Gonne MacBride to Miss Barry O'Delaney, 9 June 1918: ibid. This and the following letter were stopped by the postal censor.

106 Maud to Iseult Gonne, undated (c.8 July 1918): ibid.

107 Maud Gonne to Edward Shortt, 26 June 1918: PRO HO 144/321397/23.

108 George W. Russell (the poet AE) wrote to Shortt at Dublin Castle on 7 September. He had received letters from Maud Gonne complaining of her poor health and loss of weight. The Holloway medical officer had not been inclined to view her condition as serious, and specifically concluded that her previously affected lung was healthy. Russell contradicted this: 'I can say as one who has known Madame Gonne since I was a boy that her sister and herself are both inclined to be tubercular and have been treated for tuberculosis' (PRO HO 144/1465/321387/30).

continued detention without charge she was threatening hunger-strike. Seagan also asked for more frequent visits, since he had seen her only twice since her arrest.[109] The letter was hardly the composition of a 14-year-old, but publication of its claims and sentiments would have been devastating. A flurry of medical reports followed, with examinations by the Holloway medical staff and an outside consultant. These at first equivocated, but within a few days the deputy medical officer confirmed a weight loss of 16 lb and a deterioration in her condition ('to some extent') since her arrival at Holloway.

Stephen Gwynn[110] and W. B. Yeats managed to see Edward Shortt in Dublin to express their concern. They proposed that she be released on condition that she went to France, and Shortt was willing to accept this solution. French consent would be necessary, but since she had already worked for a considerable time for the French Red Cross and was no political danger to the French government, Shortt saw no difficulty in making arrangements. He wrote to Sir George Cave, enclosing a lengthy sealed letter from Yeats to Maud urging her to take the French solution, adding, 'Personally I should be extremely glad if it could be arranged'. Her health was not good, and although there did not appear to be any immediate danger 'her family history makes it extremely probable that she will suffer more from imprisonment than ordinary persons'.[111] Cave was in complete agreement; her health had recently been unsatisfactory and were it to become worse 'as is not unlikely' she would probably have to be released unconditionally. Yeats' letter had been delivered to her and if she agreed to go, Cave would leave it to Shortt to approach the French government.[112]

Maud pondered Yeats' letter for several days, then asked him for further advice. Meanwhile medical opinion became more negative, with the suspicion being voiced for the first time that tubercular activity might have resumed. Seagan now applied to have his mother examined by a doctor of his choice. This was agreed, and on 22 October Dr F. W. Tunnicliffe (Harley Street and King's College Hospital) submitted his report. There had been a reactivation of her former pulmonary tuberculosis. His recommendation was unambiguous: 'If the disease is to be arrested she required active medical and open air treatment in a suitable climate without delay.'[113] On 24 October Lloyd George intervened. He had been told of her health problems and that it would be fatal for her to

109 Seaghan Gonne MacBride to Home Office, 11 September 1918: ibid., /32. Seaghan (who later became an IRA leader and then constitutional political and international jurist) also applied a certain amount of pressure by writing a general letter of protest about the internment to the *Manchester Guardian* (7 October 1918, 8c). This (possibly overseen by Art O'Brien) may have been his first publication.

110 (1864–1950). Man of letters and nationalist politician. MP for Galway city, 1906–18; served with Connaught Rangers during Great War. Attended Irish Convention.

111 Shortt to Cave ('Secret and Confidential'), 9 October 1918: PRO HO 144/1465/321387/36).

112 Cave to Shortt ('Confidential'), 10 October 1919: ibid.

113 Ibid., /38.

remain in Holloway. She had been detained because of her Sinn Féin activities, 'but it is urged that her long absence abroad has detracted from her political influence in Ireland, and that her release would not be dangerous, whereas if she died in prison an impetus would be given to Sinn Féin'.[114]

Action followed fairly swiftly, and on 29 October 1918, Maud was released temporarily to go into a nursing home under the charge of Dr Tunnicliffe. Once out she petitioned to move to a private address, again enlisting the support of Joseph King, MP. When no immediate decision was forthcoming she moved anyway, and since all the arrangements for her release had been made verbally officials were unable to do much, though even had they had evidence that she had violated a written undertaking, it is doubtful that they would have found it expedient to re-arrest her. Through her son Maud now asked permission to return to Ireland, to be treated at a sanatorium run by her Dublin physician. Letters pleading on her behalf continued to come in, with Reginald Roper[115] urging Lloyd George to release her in the interests of promoting cooperation with the Irish, and Ezra Pound (then editor of the *Little Review*) warning the Home Secretary that her death or the permanent injury to her health 'will certainly do no good to anyone, nor to the situation in Ireland'.[116]

By the time of Maud's release Holloway conditions seem to have improved. The women had a landing and bathroom to themselves (prison numbers continued to fall on the female as well as the male side, so there was no want of accommodation), and to a large extent appear to have been allowed to organise their own routine. Hanna Sheehy Skeffington remembered that they 'sewed, embroidered, wrote or painted all day'. But for the first month or two, and probably more from neglect or inertia than policy, they had rather more restrictions on outside contacts than the men – as Maud Gonne's difficulties with letters and visits indicate. And for all the apparent harmony and productive feminine activities they contrived to work into their regime, Holloway was not a pleasant place to be: 'Madam [Markievicz] who loved the fresh air, sunlight and freedom, must have suffered a lot from prison. It must have shortened her life by many years.'[117]

As with the men, time hung heavily, and when (after Maud Gonne's release) Constance and Kathleen saw a cell being prepared for a newcomer they speculated with some excitement who it might be. Constance hoped that it might be Hanna Sheehy Skeffington, 'for she'll tell us all about America'. It was: Hanna (who had been on a Sinn Féin tour of the United States of America) was interned under DORA for returning to Ireland without a permit.[118] Arrested at

114 Frances Stevenson to S. W. Harris, 24 October 1918: ibid., /40.

115 (1860–1943). Liberal Member for North Somerset, 1910–18. Subsequently contested Ilford and York for the Labour Party. Barrister; published on political topics and on education and the arts.

116 Pound had been urged to write by Lady Cunard: PRO HO 144/1465/321387/41.

117 Memoir of Constance Markievicz by Hanna Sheehy Skeffington: NLI: Sheehy Skeffington Papers: Ms. 24, 189, f. 3.

118 On Hanna Sheehy Skeffington see p. 461, n. 49, above.

her sister's house in Dublin, she was immediately removed to England, reaching Holloway on the morning of 10 August 1918. Hanna had been down this course before as a suffragette, and had decided on her tactics. From the moment of arrest she took no food, and on arrival at the prison announced her intention to hunger-strike and – a disabling stroke – refused to be examined by the medical officer. Since that gentleman would take the responsibility for any mishap, he announced that it would be dangerous in the circumstances to force-feed her. This led to an immediate capitulation by the authorities, and her internment order was changed to a deportation order and obligatory residence in England, Shortt (then the Irish Chief Secretary) noting: 'In any case having regard to the tragic story of her husband it is impossible to let her die. I am endeavouring to see her sister Mrs Kettle this afternoon.'[119]

So keen was Dublin Castle to be rid of Hanna that, exceptionally, she was released on Sunday, 11 August. She was warned not to attempt to go back to Ireland, to which she replied that she did not like the order but would do nothing without first informing Scotland Yard. Hanna or her friends contacted the *Manchester Guardian* which in a leader condemned the way she had been treated, and the deportation order under which she was now obliged to remain in England: 'She is a deeply wronged and suffering woman. Would it not, on the plane of pure expediency, let alone justice or sentiment, be wiser to let her do and say what she likes in her own land rather than subject her to [what] to Irish minds has every evidence of persecution?'[120] Following this, and other representations, Shortt backed down altogether, and withdrew even the deportation order. On 16 August, a week after her arrest, she was told that she could return to Ireland.

This well-publicised fiasco undoubtedly harmed the authorities; it also confirmed the hunger-strike as a powerful weapon. Following Ashe, it would seem, no medical offer was willing to take the risk of forcible feeding. Had the male internees at this point embarked on a determined hunger-strike they may well have won their release. The weapon would be used to great effect by internees in 1920, as we shall see, and with tragic results by convicted prisoners.

Hanna's release was all the more striking because she was not the innocent that some then implied. She was certainly a wronged woman, but the murder of her husband and aftermath to the Easter rising had caused her to identify with the Sinn Féin cause. She had been prohibited from leaving Ireland, but in 1916 had clandestinely made her way to the United States of America, where she embarked on a lecture-tour to promote Sinn Féin, to condemn the British for

---

119 PRO HO 144/1584/16. Hanna's brother-in-law, Lieutenant T. M. Kettle, had been a moderate nationalist politician. Following Redmond's line he had enlisted, and was killed on the Western Front (see J. B. Lyons, *The Enigma of Tom Kettle: Irish Patriot, Essayist, Poet, British Soldier*, Dublin, The Glendale Press, 1983).

120 *Manchester Guardian*, 13 August 1918, 4c. The same issue (4f) reported a resolution from Dublin Corporation condemning the manner of her arrest at her sister's home and demanding that she be charged and tried, or released.

the manner in which the rising had been put down, and, of course, to speak of the murder of her husband. On her return in 1918 she was accompanied by Nora Connolly (James Connolly's daughter) and Margaret Skinidder who (according to Special Branch) had at one time been Constance Markievicz's secretary: these were highly suggestive friendships.

On her return to England from America Hanna was shadowed by Special Branch, which reported her (in conversation with her sister) as saying, inter alia, 'I think that the rebellion failed through the Sinn Féiners having a fit of nerves, otherwise it might have won. Sinn Féin is weakening and I am going to reach Ireland to rouse it up as I have always had a good following in Dublin.'[121] While in Liverpool (where she landed) and Glasgow she was seen to meet several prominent Sinn Féiners, and in Liverpool on 14 July she addressed the Roger Casement Sinn Féin Club. During her various encounters she was supposedly overheard to say 'A distressed widow story goes well.'[122] Whether or not she said it, it was certainly true. Unless she crossed the line from sedition to direct incitement or (improbably) action, Hanna was doubtless immune from arrest and certainly from detention.

At Holloway the three detainees never did get to hear Hanna's account of her American trip. The weeks, and then the months of confinement and uncertainty took their toll. The women worried and fretted. Writing to her daughter, Maud expressed concern for Kathleen Clarke: 'she eats so little, she has never been well since her husband's & brother's deaths & she cannot sleep in the prison beds. She is fretting for her children & is getting very weak.'[123] And having left the prison, amidst all the joy at seeing her children again, Maud continued to worry about her companions, and wrote to Hanna Sheehy Skeffington about her 'heartbreak' at leaving them: 'They are so brave and uncomplaining & so willing to suffer for Ireland.'[124]

Kathleen Clarke was released on 12 February 1919, having been interned for nine months.[125] Constance Markievicz was again on her own (as when a convict at Aylesbury, three years before). The Home Office was sensitive to charges that it was imposing solitary confinement (against which there were various prohibitions and safeguards in the prison regulations). Accordingly, when her sister Eva applied for special visiting privileges in February 1919, she was assured of a sympathetic response. Eva asked to visit fortnightly without the 'humiliating conditions' that had led other Sinn Féin relatives to forgo visits. These conditions

---

121 PRO HO 144/1584/12. The words and phrasing have a whiff of the police notebook, but the sentiments were probably authentic.

122 Ibid., /12.

123 Maud to Iseult Gonne MacBride, undated (c. 8 July 1918): PRO HO 144/1465/321387/23.

124 1 November 1918: NLI: Sheehy Skeffington Papers, Ms. 24, 106 (unfoliated).

125 Irish Independent, 14 February 1919, 3d. She was reported to be very weak and ill, and stayed at the London flat of Eva Gore-Booth until she was fit to return to Ireland, where a public reception was planned.

included the presence of a wardress in the room, a pledge not to talk politics (or speak in a foreign language), and not to publish any details of the conversation. Troup was inclined to grant the request, explaining to the Irish Office that Constance was now 'practically in solitary confinement', and that fortnightly visits had been granted under similar circumstances at Aylesbury. If no concessions were made on the 'humiliating conditions' it seemed unlikely that Constance would receive any visits, and this was thought to be a special hardship since she had no fellow prisoners for company. Dublin Castle agreed, and fortnightly visits were granted in the sight but not the hearing of a prison officer. Eva was required to give an undertaking not to discuss political topics, but this seems not to have been a problem.[126]

The stricter regime

With the male internees distributed across the country, the initial *laissez-faire* was discontinued. The new regulations, Figgis recalled, 'were bad'. It is difficult to agree with him, since in essence the men were treated as civil detainees, but as being consigned to a prison rather than to a camp. They were kept apart from other inmates as far as possible, civil and criminal, tried and untried. Unlike criminal prisoners they were not obliged to take a reception bath (a point of honour rather than hygiene) and they were allowed to retain their civilian clothing, which could be augmented by purchase or gift. Although lodged in separate cells, the internees, provided they behaved well, could associate at work and during exercise and recreation, 'and at such other times as may be convenient'.[127] They could retain their private property, documents and books. After the first few weeks, books, magazines and newspapers could be purchased, provided these were not considered to be objectionable. In addition, they could have two prison library books each week. Cells had to be cleaned and tidied each day and beds made up, but should the internees object to these tasks, they could employ a prisoner to do them. There were two exercise periods a day, and they were also to be allowed 'such open air recreation in association as the weather and staff exigencies permit'. They could attend chapel, if they wished, and the chaplain could make cell visits. Whoever wished to work would be paid prison rates.[128] The diet – a generous interpretation of the allowance for civil prisoners – could be supplemented with outside purchases; tobacco could also be bought.

---

126 PRO HO 144/1580/316818/75.

127 All following details of the regime are taken from the relevant memorandum, 'Regulations as to the Treatment of Persons other than Aliens Ordered to be Interned in H.M. Prisons under the Defence of the Realm Act'. A copy of this document is at PRO HO 144/1496/362269/163a. These regulations were made under DORA Regulation 14b, para. 3, and were approved by the Home Secretary on 24 May 1918 (see PRO HO 144/1496/362269/8: Troup to Cave, 23 May 1918).

128 There is no record of any of the internees having done such work, the rates of payment for which were pitiful.

Internees were allowed three letters weekly out and in, the outgoing letters being restricted to one sheet of notepaper not exceeding twenty lines. On special application, however, extra letters or longer letters might be permitted. A limit of thirty lines was stipulated for incoming letters and all correspondence was to be confined to personal or business matters: political or military subjects, complaints about detention or 'exaggerated complaints of their health' were prohibited.[129] Parcels containing books and newspapers were allowed, but examined; surplus books could not be sent home in case they contained coded messages. Food and clothing would also be checked by the censor, and any food that was rationed in England would be deducted in equal measure from the prisoners' rations.

The internees' chief morale problems were undoubtedly the indeterminacy of their confinement, and (in the absence of visitors) their isolation. There were also the strains of close custody: Figgis complained particularly of this at Durham. Other internees moved fairly freely between cells, the wing, the association room and (at Reading) the exercise yard. At Durham the five internees either had to be in their cells or in the association room, and could move only under escort; this meant that wherever they went soldiers went also, and took up sentry positions. And since there were insufficient soldiers for individual escorts, the prisoners were compelled to keep together: 'We moved, literally, by majority vote in all our acts – a kind of democracy in nightmare, that taxed, not always successfully, our resources of patience.'[130]

This account of Durham conditions was, to some extent, confirmed by the governor. Writing to 'The English Secretary for Ireland' on 31 October 1918, Figgis' wife Millie had protested at the close confinement of the twelve internees at Durham and the lack of exercise and poor diet. This went to the Home Office, and was passed to Durham for comment. The governor stated that the prisoners got 'close' on an hour's exercise in the morning – 'but most of them are too lazy to turn out for it FIGGIS IN PARTICULAR'. The prisoners also played modified versions of Rounders and Fives and were in good health and spirits. He agreed that the prisoners' association room was too small, but no other was available: 'the heat and stuffiness in that room is to me often unbearable, but of course an Irishman can stand more of this sort of living than an Englishman in fact he does not care for too [much] fresh air etc. etc.'[131]

---

129 The internees used codes, allusions and nicknames to evade the censors. The censors allowed this to continue in order to collect intelligence. The Fourth Report of the Directorate of Military Intelligence included an extensive annex of code words and nicknames (PRO HO 144/1496/362269).

130 Figgis, 1919, p. 67.

131 PRO HO 144/4481: Governor to Home Office, 5 November 1918. The capitals are in the original. There was, from other comments in the report, little love lost between the governor and Figgis, whom he asserted (also in capitals) no longer to be the head of the prisoners and not popular with his companions.

The prisoners and their supporters continued to press for visits, and outside pressures on the matter had also continued.[132] On 11 August, three months into their confinement, permission was given for quarterly half-hour visits. Only near relatives would be allowed – a maximum of two at a time – and these had to give a written pledge to keep conversation to private matters. Names had to be submitted and prior agreement obtained from the governor.[133] The solicitors' rather than the ordinary visits' room was used, and a 'discreet and sensible officer' supervised, making notes of what passed. Political matters would be reported, and any attempt at secret or coded conversation or use of a foreign language (such as Gaelic) terminated the visit.[134] The Irish argued that these conditions were more severe than those imposed on criminals and on other internees. Criminals received visits once every three months, but they were not restricted to visitors who were 'near relations', nor did their visitors have to give such pledges. An additional consideration was that neither members of Sinn Féin nor their 'near relations' would give promises to the British government.

The determination to exclude all but near relations, and the stringent conditions imposed even on them meant, the Home Office noted, that very few visits had been made to the internees. But this, it was argued, 'does not seem to be a sufficient reason for now extending the privilege to friends as well as relatives'.[135] Requests from friends to visit were accordingly firmly rebuffed. This curtailment of access to the outside world inevitably affected morale. At the same time clandestine communications were established so effectively that the Directorate of Military Intelligence had to admit that censorship (as distinct from intelligence gathering) had been 'practically valueless' because the internees at all prisons had devised means to evade it.[136] The Home Office wished to continue

---

132 This had continued unabatedly from the earliest days of confinement, Mrs Griffith (among many others) demanding immediate communication with her husband on domestic matters and also information about parcels, letters and visits (PRO HO 144/1458/316093/8). On 12 June 1918, Mrs de Valera had submitted what amounted to a questionnaire on her husband's conditions of confinement – all the more effective, perhaps, because of its tone of wifely concern and domestic priorities (PRO HO 144/10309/50833/27). Several related Commons interventions were made in the adjournment debate on Ireland on 25 June 1918 (5 Hansard, CVII, cols 905–1014, passim).

133 'Visits to Irish Interned Prisoners', cit. Figgis, 1919, p. 87. Although Figgis stated that the new ruling on visitors was introduced on 11 August, formal authority (which necessitated part revocation of the rules of 24 May 1918) was not signed by the Home Secretary until 5 September 1918 (PRO HO 144/1496/362269/8).

134 Possibly in response to this condition, on 5 August Figgis submitted a petition to the Home Secretary in Irish. Waller, a Home Office official, replied that petitions must be in English. Figgis pressed the matter and Blackwell, the Home Office legal adviser, marked the file 'This is simply an impertinence' (PRO HO 144/4481).

135 Minute, 15 January 1919: PRO HO 144/1458/316093/18. This reaffirmed decision arose from an application by Thomas Martin, a London-based architect, to visit Arthur Griffith and W. L. Cole at Gloucester.

136 'Letters and articles which did not pass through Censorship constantly appeared in the Irish Independent, St. Enda's Magazine, Irish Fun and The Leader' (PRO HO 144/1496/362269).

the censorship and considered either searching the internees released on parole, or requiring from them a pledge not to carry messages. On consideration neither course was adopted.[137]

The tedium of confinement, aggravated by its indeterminacy, bore down heavily. The end of the war raised prisoners' hopes. The recollection that the 1916 internees had been home for Christmas was especially tantalising, and hope did not die until Christmas Day itself.[138] Then, much to the chagrin of the detainees, rumours recommenced in the New Year. It was hard enough to endure prolonged imprisonment, Figgis recalled, but it was even harder to do so 'while we were the prey of papers from home that told us, with varying shades of confidence, that we were surely to be released the following day, or the day after at most'.[139] Disappointment that there had not been a Christmas release was evident in a bitter letter from Mrs Griffith to the Home Secretary on 13 January 1919. Having recapitulated a number of complaints about her husband's arrest she demanded 'what on earth do you mean to do with my only relative?'[140]

The internees organised themselves to pass the time as best they could. At Lincoln there was a short-lived manuscript journal in circulation. Called *The Insect*, this ran through four issues from 1 September to 20 October 1918, its contents ranging from the humorous (including drawings and cartoons) through poetry to political comment and analysis. Some of the political pieces were tedious, and there was much routine abuse of England. Analysis of war news favoured the Central Powers, and included a poem which rejoiced at an air-raid on London. More cut off than the general population (which was itself subject to a fairly well-manipulated press), the prisoners fed on hopes of a German victory, which could mean both their own release and victory for their cause. Four weeks before the German capitulation *The Insect* dismissed 'the fancied importance of Allied victories'. The Germans had merely retired to their winter lines where 'they ought to hold the Allies for practically an indefinite period'. Indeed, there could be a sudden German attack: 'The situation remains full of hope and great possibilities.'[141] The journal's next issue (which

---

137 Ibid., /167.
138 There was one notable release just after Christmas (the timing was significant). Count Plunkett was released on medical grounds on 30 December. The Birmingham Prison medical officer considered his condition to be such that had he caught influenza he would probably have died (PRO HO 144/1458/315663/30).
139 Figgis, 1919, p. 98. See also the reports of censored mail from the Directorate of Military Intelligence, particularly in the period 16–31 January 1919 (PRO HO 144/1496/362269).
140 Maud Griffith to Edward Shortt, 13 January 1919: PRO HO 144/1458/316093/17. The Home Office was unmoved: 'The letter has been ack[nowledged], & I think hardly requires a further reply.'
141 NLI: Seán O'Mahony Papers, Ms. 24, 458. The manuscript, on exercise book pages, comprises some 228ff. The tone of the journal is forced, and the tedium of the men's experience shows

did not appear) would have had to account for the Armistice. It is apparent from this material what a devastating blow the Allied victory must have been to the internees, even though they may have hoped for some act of clemency to mark the war's end.[142]

The febrile mood of the prisoners at this time, and the Home Office's desire to contain it, was shown by an incident at Gloucester Prison, to which several prisoners had been transferred from Usk. The transferees refused to surrender their money, which at Usk they had been allowed to keep. The commissioner with special responsibility for the Irish internees, M. L. Waller, wrote to the Irish Office. There was a genuine security concern, since cash could assist escape, and the rules forbade its possession. Of the two evils – a possible outbreak were the money confiscated, and the risk of having it in circulation – Waller concluded, 'the best plan is to avoid an outbreak in this prison which has hitherto been quiet. I do not like it . . . but every other kind of precaution is now being taken against escapes, so perhaps we had better risk it for the sake of quiet. What do you think?' Since there had been escapes from Usk, and the even more sensational escape of de Valera and his companions from Lincoln had taken place little more than a week previously, the exchange was a demonstration of bureaucratic prudence, and a desire to lay off some risk. Power at the Irish Office may have been something of a betting man, however, and by return of post he agreed that the transferees could retain their cash.[143]

The Durham internees contrived some easement of their confinement when, on giving their parole, permission was given to attend a Christmas Day service at a nearby Roman Catholic church. The privilege was extended to a New Year's Day service, but a subsequent application to attend the church every Sunday was refused on security grounds.[144] The Gloucester men had also asked to attend an outside church on Christmas Day. They would not give individual paroles,

through. The few humorous items are all on the lame side. The competition for 'My Best Girl' included an entry from de Valera in praise of mathematics (he was referred to as the 'Great White Chief'). An election address supposedly by a member of Cumann na mBan contesting the North Galway constituency includes a proposal to change parliamentary rules to allow no more than four women to speak at once. At Gloucester the internees' journal was edited by Arthur Griffith. Unfortunately no copies appear to have survived (PRO HO 144/1469/362269: Second Report of the Directorate of Military Intelligence, f. 1).

142 Military Intelligence reported that some of the internees took some consolation for Germany's defeat in the emergence of the Soviet Union. The censors quoted Constance Markievicz: 'Freedom has dawned in the East; the light that was lit by the Russian democracy has illuminated central Europe, is flowing Westward. Nations are being reborn, peoples are coming into their own and Ireland's day is coming' (Second Report, Directorate of Military Intelligence, f. 15: PRO HO 144/1496/362269).

143 Waller (Home Office) to Power (Irish Office), 15 February 1919: PRO HO 144/1496/362269/162.

144 'If it became a regular thing naturally friends would waylay them, letters be passed etc. etc.' (Minute, 6 January 1919: PRO HO 144/1496/362269/148).

insisting that Arthur Griffith's parole should cover the whole group. This was unacceptable to the Home Office and the request was refused.

Escapes

Four men escaped from Usk prison on 23 January 1919, forcibly demonstrating the difficulties of allowing internment conditions in prisons intended to be run on penal lines.[145] This basic problem was aggravated by staff shortages. Usk's evening lock-up was at 8 p.m., but on the internees promising to behave as though staff were present, it was put back to 9.45 p.m. Indeed, since the men gave no trouble, the governor on occasion gave permission to keep cell doors open all night. There was no apparent abuse of this privilege, and the influenza epidemic then raging, and the needs of the sick, made a necessity out of an exception. Much weight was placed on the fact that the men had given their parole not to abuse the privilege, and this had been underwritten by the Roman Catholic priest. An analysis of modern escape (by Provisional IRA men from Whitemoor Prison on 9 September 1994) refers to this creation of trust and other expectations among staff as 'conditioning'. The Sinn Féin prisoners of 1919 may not have used the term, but they knew and used the concept.[146] The internees were located in the old female block, which under the liberal lock-up arrangements they had entirely to themselves from early evening until morning. During this time it was relatively simple to force one of the windows. Because of their seclusion, and the lack of a night patrol, the escape was not noticed until the following day, by which time the four men were well away. Special Branch put its ferry-watchers on alert, and increased surveillance of certain addresses in London, but all too late.[147] Sir Edward Troup concluded that the men having given their word of honour not to misbehave, the Usk governor was not to blame: 'We have up till now found that the Sinn Féiners kept to their word of honour. Apparently they are deteriorating.'[148]

While the Usk men were planning their escape, de Valera and two companions were doing the same at Lincoln, aided by Michael Collins' increasingly

---

145 The four were Herbert ('Barney') Mellowes, Frank Shouldice, Joseph McGrath, MP, and George Geraghty (see *Irish Independent*, 24 January 1919, 3c; *Freeman's Journal*, 24 January 1919, 3e). McGrath (1888–1966) later rose to prominence as a Sinn Féin politician and minister under the First and Second Dáils, the provisional government and the first Free State government. He retired from politics and became a successful businessman and a major figure in bloodstock and racing.

146 Sir John Woodcock, *The Escape from Whitemoor Prison on Friday 9th September, 1994* [Cm. 274], London, HMSO, 1994, pp. 71–2; see also General Sir John Learmont, *Review of Prison Service Security in England and Wales and the Escape from Parkhurst Prison on Tuesday 3rd January, 1995* [Cm. 3020], London, HMSO, 1995, pp. 121–3.

147 The addresses included the Irish National Relief Committee at Holborn and Fintan Murphy at Brixton (PRO HO 144/1496/362269/157).

148 PRO HO 144/1496/362269/157.

effective apparatus. Coded messages in Irish and Latin and elliptical English were passed out.[149] A wax impression was taken of a key, the result sent out, and a key duly made and smuggled in – in a cake, of course. After some problems in getting an exact fit, de Valera made his escape on the night of 3 February 1919, accompanied by Seán McGarry and Seán Milroy.[150] The great tradition of prison escapes was honoured throughout, and although a torn bedsheet was not required, the night of de Valera's escape was the last opportunity for a fortnight, until the return of a waning moon. Michael Collins and Harry Boland crossed from Ireland to assist, and despite some mishaps the three escapers were successfully got away. De Valera hid in Manchester for two weeks, returning to Dublin on 20 February. All the internees were released not long after, but this escape received wide publicity in America as well as Ireland and Britain, and did much to promote the Sinn Féin cause.[151] Military intelligence (which was monitoring the internees' post) reported that the escape had raised morale and reduced the internees' 'impatience for release'.[152] Behind the scenes, the escape was the occasion for repeated Prison Commission sniping at the War Office for failing to provide military assistance.[153]

149 There had already been a clear indication of the efficacy of de Valera's lines of communication. On 17 November 1918, the intelligence service reported that he had smuggled out of the prison a letter which was read at a Sinn Féin general election meeting. This corresponded word for word with a letter seized by MI9 and addressed to 6 Harcourt Street, Dublin (Sinn Féin headquarters). The prison investigated, and concluded that the duplicate letter had been smuggled out by a paroled prisoner (PRO HO 144/10309/50833/9). It was thought that de Valera used other prisoners to conduct his coded correspondence, since his own was 'harmless'. He corresponded en clair about family matters, however, and the exchanges with his mother in Rochester (New York) were 'harmless though intensely hostile in tone' (Second Report of the Directorate of Military Intelligence, Lincoln, f. 1: PRO HO 144/1496/362269). Privacy was hard to defend in prison, and de Valera must have felt the intrusion.

150 Milroy (1877–1946) had been Sinn Féin Director in the general election of 1918. After his escape he was elected (1921) to the legislatures of both Northern Ireland and the Free State, and later to the Irish Senate. Just over a month after his escape, de Valera's other companion, Seán McGarry, made a dramatic appearance at a Sinn Féin concert in Dublin's Mansion House, where he delivered a speech, before making his getaway. It was feared at the time (5 March 1919) that this incident would be seen as a provocation by the authorities and would impede releases of the internees. The decision to end internment had already been taken by the War Cabinet, however, and the first releases were under way (The Times, 6 March 1919, 7c; PRO HO 144/1496/362269/179).

151 For an account of the escape see The Earl of Longford and Thomas P. O'Neill, Eamon de Valera, Boston, Houghton Mifflin, 1971, ch. 7. The government's inquiry into the escape, and official and ministerial reaction to it are given in PRO HO 144/1496/362269/163a. The official inquiry failed to spot how de Valera had obtained the impression of the key used to exit the door in the prison wall. Evelyn Ruggles-Brise in his report to the Home Secretary suggested that an impression had been taken from an inner door of the same pattern. De Valera's Home Office file (which is an amalgamation of Home Office and Prison Commission papers) is unaccountably devoid of material on his Lincoln internment.

152 PRO HO 144/1496/362269/135, f. 11.

153 Ruggles-Brise to Home Secretary, 11 February 1919: PRO HO 144/1496/36229/163a, f. 4.

After the Usk and Lincoln escapes, the Home Office reviewed its politics. The Lincoln escape, Troup noted, 'clearly arose from the comparative freedom allowed to these interned men within the prison'. Since they were interned rather than imprisoned, however, Troup did not think that regulations could be made more severe. Prisoners of war were liable to be searched, but Troup doubted whether it was worth while to start this, and searching would probably not have prevented the escape; they could, however, supervise the internees more closely. The Commissioners increased the deployment of warders, and Troup, reviving a continuing grievance, thought that the War Office should be called on to match this with a military guard.[154]

For their part, the Commissioners drew much the same lessons. Although in prison, the internees were on no account to be associated with ordinary prisoners. Their regime was intended to minimise constraints, consistent only with safe custody. The internees were also experienced in the ways of imprisonment. De Valera had previously given much trouble, and anticipating difficulties a senior governor had been assigned to Lincoln to deal with him and the others; a precautionary military guard had also been provided. But soon after the internees' arrival, the Lincoln governor had reported that they were behaving well and (somewhat naively) had ventured 'I feel that they and I understand each other.' He thought that the military might be removed. This was not done, but the soldiers were directed to intervene only in case of serious trouble, such as a riot. The Commissioners observed (rather unnecessarily) that the Lincoln governor had been deceived, and this had contributed to the lapses which had allowed de Valera's escape.[155] There had been overconfidence: 'The lessons of Usk and Lincoln show that these men cannot be trusted, and if escape is to be prevented,

154 Memorandum by Troup, 11 February 1919: PRO HO 144/1496/362269/163A. The Home Office was unable to obtain more soldiers. In 1918, the Army Council had pleaded the demands of war in refusing the Home Office's plea for assistance; in mid-February 1919, three months after the Armistice, the excuse was demobilisation. Soldiers would be available only to assist the police or in the case of disorder in a prison (War Office to Home Office, 17 February 1919). Ruggles-Brise minuted that 'it seems useless to press the War Office further in this matter, and we must endeavour to make the necessary provision for safe custody with our own officers. Luckily the numbers of warders now returning from the War give us a small margin' (Minute, 22 February 1919: PRO HO 144/1496/362269/164).

155 Another echo of 'conditioning': the Commissioners meant that the internees had created a set of false expectations intending to lull the governor and his staff. The inquiry into the Lincoln escape got two important details wrong. The Commissioners correctly believed that de Valera's outside contacts had helped to make the critical key. They were wrong about his means of communication with them. It was not through a released internee that instructions were sent in and out, but by coded correspondence, including (in a cartoon Christmas card) an actual drawing of the key. The Commissioners also wrongly concluded that he had obtained the key pattern from the lock of a disused lavatory. In fact, de Valera had taken advantage of his position as altar-server to obtain an impression of the chaplain's keys on wax left over from the chapel candles (The Earl of Longford and Thomas P. O'Neill, Eamon de Valera, op. cit., pp. 81-6; Commissioners to Troup, 11 February 1919: PRO HO 144/1496/362269/179).

military assistance, both inside and outside the walls is essential.' A sufficiently strong force of warders would be deployed inside to keep the internees under observation 'like ordinary prisoners'. The remaining Lincoln internees would be removed to Birmingham and Lewes prisons.[156]

Parole

In the early months of 1919 the internees were becoming increasingly restive and difficult to contain: the Usk and Lincoln escapes unsettled them further. Throughout the winter there had been some releases, fourteen absolute and un-conditional, others paroles of a few weeks. As noted, Hanna Sheehy Skeffington was freed in August within hours of her detention. Maud Gonne MacBride was released at the end of October 1918, and Kathleen Clarke in mid-February 1919 (the former because of her hunger-strike, and the latter two on medical grounds).[157] One man was discharged on the recommendation of the DORA Advisory Committee, and another because of continued family illness; yet another was handed over for criminal proceedings. Most, however, were freed on medical grounds. Of those granted conditional paroles, serious family illness or the death of a relative secured release for between one and three weeks.[158] 'Family' was interpreted widely, and leave was given to attend a niece's funeral or because a nephew was ill.[159] Successive waves of illnesses and death arising from the influenza pandemic encouraged a fairly liberal view of requests for compassion-ate parole. Darrell Figgis had several irritating and unnecessary exchanges with the authorities. He was considered to be a major Sinn Féin figure, and con-sequently had two parole applications turned down. He had claimed that his wife was dangerously ill, but failed to provide supporting medical evidence. Even he obtained parole, however, when in addition to his wife's illness there was a fire at his flat.[160]

---

156 After the escape there were fourteen prisoners at Lincoln; ten were to be transferred to Birmingham and four to Gloucester (Commissioners to Troup, 11 February 1919: PRO HO 144/1496/362269/163a). The transfers were overtaken by influenza at Birmingham and Gloucester prisons and by the releases of the following month (see PRO HO 144/1496/362269/ 179; ibid., Troup minute of 25 February 1919).

157 PRO HO 144/1496/362269/17.

158 The process was far from automatic. In late November Count Plunkett had applied for parole to attend his father's funeral, and to attend to family business. He was turned down because the funeral had already taken place (PRO HO 144/1458/315663/29).

159 PRO HO 144/1496/362269/172, schedule of releases.

160 He had applied twice in November and been refused, but in late February, after damage to his flat as the result of a neighbourhood fire, was given ten days' parole. Shortly after arriving back in Dublin he was informed that because of influenza at Durham prison, he would not be required to return to custody (PRO HO 144/4481). Figgis' temper and lack of a sense of proportion may be seen in a petition which he lodged a month before his release, complaining that the locum medical officer at Durham had addressed him 'as a menial'.

Although some of the internees were young and relatively fit men, several were much older and more unfit; the 1918 internees were far less youthful than those of 1916. One of the least fit was Lawrence Ginnell, MP, who had so emphatically assumed Sinn Féin colours that he had been interned.[161] His Reading companions noted a degree of mental unstability.[162] In January 1919, Ginnell (who was described by the governor (F. G. C. M. Morgan) as 'always excitable and objectionable') ordered the prison medical officer out of his cell, shouting 'you treat me as a criminal. Your predecessor treated one of us as a malingerer and shammer – we will not stand insolence.' At the same time Ginnell threw a tin of rice over the doctor.[163] At about this time Ginnell wrote to President Wilson, protesting at the internments and asking for his intervention. This letter was suppressed by the censor. Early in March 1919, Ginnell was examined by the Reading medical officer, who discovered clear signs of arteriosclerosis 'of a degree that is unusual even at his age . . . he is tremulous, very excitable and even at times violent. In my opinion he is [a] man "old for his years" and his mental condition is very unstable.' Three days later Ginnell was released.[164]

Older people are also more likely to have complicated business and personal affairs than the young. The welfare of the clients of his newly established

161 Between 1916 and June 1918 Ginnell had several brushes with the law. On 27 July 1916, he was expelled from the Commons for defying the Speaker. The following day he was fined £100 (or six weeks' imprisonment) for using a false name to enter Knutsford detention barracks. Although this was reduced on appeal he still refused to pay and served three weeks in the first division at Pentonville. There were other clashes with the Speaker (in December 1916, and July 1917) and on 26 March 1918 he was up before a Dublin court for inciting cattle-driving, for which he was ordered to enter into six months' bail for the sum of £500 and provide two sureties of £1000 each, or to serve six months (The Times, 27 March 1918, 3b).

162 According to censored post. On 28 January 1919, George Nicholls wrote from Birmingham Prison that a recent transferee had reported on 'poor Ginnell', who had become 'most peevish and irritable'. His companions had concluded that 'the mental strain is too much for him' (Report of Directorate of Military Intelligence, 25 February 1919: PRO HO 144/1496/366269/155). The censors themselves reported that owing to ill-health or other causes Ginnell did not appear to be 'in a normal state of mind'.

163 This was a grave offence, for which an ordinary prisoner might have been seriously punished. On the incident being reported, M. L. Waller at the Commission noted that were Ginnell punished 'the other men would all be up in arms'. He asked the medical officer to treat the assault as 'the act of a man who was not quite responsible'. This was done (Memorandum by Waller, 24 January 1919: PRO HO 144/1496/366265/155).

164 PRO HO 144/2137: medical officer's report, 4 March 1919. Three months after his release Lawrence Ginnell was sentenced to four months' imprisonment for inciting people to boycott the police. He was released on health grounds after three months (Freeman's Journal, 9 June 1919, 4b; 5 September 1919, 3b). In 1923 Ginnell travelled to Washington, DC to stage a protest occupation of the representative offices of the Irish Free State. He died of natural causes in a hotel. He was remembered by The Times as the inventor of cattle-drives (18 April 1923, 8d).

insurance business was the ground given by William T. Cosgrave in seeking parole.[165] This was not granted, although he was allowed a special visit from his Dublin lawyers, Corrigan and Corrigan. His health was not so poor as to require medication, but the Reading medical officer put him on a hospital diet, for which he was grateful. In September 1918, Lawrence Ginnell (his fellow internee at Reading) petitioned for Cosgrave's release on humanitarian grounds, but this failed when the medical officer reported Cosgrave to be in good health. The following month, Alfred Byrne, MP (now in the Sinn Féin interest) applied for a special visit. Since Cosgrave was not one of those who had recently mis-behaved themselves at Reading (threats had been made following a meeting of the internees) this was granted with the usual stipulations – conversation was to be restricted to personal and family matters, and was to be in the sight and hearing of a prison officer. Byrne was indignant: 'I could not under any circum-stances accept the visit under such insulting conditions.'[166] In early February 1919, Cosgrave was provisionally granted parole for seven days because of the dangerous illness of an uncle: this was to be activated only if the illness became more dangerous, which it apparently did not.[167] A month later, however, Cosgrave was released.

Relatively liberal in releasing individuals on specific grounds, the War Cabinet refused to countenance any general release, despite the Lord Lieutenant's urgings.[168] Pressures continued to mount as the prisoners festered; there must also have been a debilitating sense of unfairness as the individual discharges and paroles continued, and a futile comparison of cases.[169] Reading's governor, C. M. Morgan, gave a sombre warning on 2 February 1919. The men's mood and the shortage of staff meant that things could not continue as they were: 'discipline must be restored or the men released.' Morgan had several times complained about the indiscipline of the Irish, but had been told not to punish them, and to keep matters peaceful. He reported that the internees had declared that they intended to go on making demands and to use a refusal for further disobedience. This would result in punishments and a general campaign of resistance. The Home Office replied that the Secretary of State recognised

---

165 (1880–1965). Sentenced to death, commuted to five years' penal servitude for his part in 1916 rising, during which he fought at the GPO. Became Treasurer of Sinn Féin and member of first Dáil. Supported Treaty and succeeded Michael Collins as Chairman of provisional govern-ment. First President of the Executive Council of the Free State. Founded the pro-Treaty party Cumann na nGaedheal in 1923.

166 Byrne to Home Office, 21 October 1918: PRO HO 144/1582/13.

167 Ibid., /14.

168 The Times, 8 February 1919, 3e; PRO HO 144/362269/172.

169 For the first few months the internees seem to have maintained their morale. Writing to Sister Francesca MacDonagh from Reading on 28 August 1918, Dr Richard Hayes was cheerful about her brother Joseph, who was with him in Reading. The tone of the letter was more than conventional reassurance (NLI: Sister Francesca MacDonagh Papers: Ms. 20, 647 (5) (unfoliated)).

the difficulties, and would render support if there should be an outbreak. As demobilisation proceeded, Troup noted, and warders became available, it was desirable that they should be assigned to Reading, 'to deal at once and effect-ively with any attempt at mutiny'.[170] Despite these assurances, however, the Prison Commissioners were sufficiently disturbed by Morgan's report to ask that it be put before the Home Secretary, and that the Irish Chief Secretary should be warned that discipline should be enforced or the internees released.[171]

Despite the number who had honoured their parole when released on com-passionate grounds, the prisoners' collective word of honour could not be taken: this was the lesson of the Usk escapees. Nor, at a lesser level, could the fact that they were confined in relaxed conditions, and accorded a variety of privileges, be taken to constitute an implied understanding that the prisoners would 'play fair'. These were 'difficult and crafty men' whose 'fixed practice' was 'to beguile the Prison Authorities with an assumed good behaviour and quietness of demeanour'. Quite simply, 'these men cannot be trusted'. And if they could not be trusted, it followed that there could be no repetition of the basic error of permitting an internment-camp regime in a civilian prison. In future, they would have to be subjected to the same regime of security and control as criminal prisoners, namely, 'continuous observation, and the right to search persons, cells and property'.[172]

General release

Release, when it came, owed more to expediency and the forces of nature than political clemency. It is true that the 'German Plot' internments had probably been more to the disadvantage than the advantage of government, but, as we shall see, the Irish situation as it developed in the early months of 1919 could

---

170 Troup to M. L. Waller, 8 February 1919: PRO HO 144/1496/362269/172. The warning was prompted by a meeting at which the internees, voicing various complaints, informed the governor of a unanimously agreed resolution: 'The Irish interned prisoners demand collectively and individually release or immediate trial, otherwise there would be trouble' (PRO HO 144/1496/366265/155). Morgan attached to his letter of warning statements from two warders about the men's indiscipline. They were doing all they could to be difficult, would not work and broke up chairs for firewood: they were 'most unreasonable and selfish and do all that is possible to give trouble' (ibid., /172).

171 With the Home Secretary's agreement Troup wrote to Macpherson (Irish Chief Secretary) enclosing the Reading reports. The internees were seeking an excuse for an outbreak and in order to avoid this the governor and his staff were exercising an extraordinary amount of patience and forbearance: 'No notice is taken of an Irish flag which is kept hanging from a cell window: and when Mr Ginnell amused himself by throwing his plate of rice pudding over the head of the medical officer, nothing was said!' Unless there was a general release there would be a smash-up or hunger-strike. Things were at their worst at Reading, but governors and staff elsewhere were feeling the strain (Troup to Macpherson, 4 February 1919: PRO HO 144/1496/362269/172).

172 All quotations from Commissioners' letter to Permanent-Under-Secretary Troup, 11 February 1919: PRO HO 144/1496/362269/163a.

easily have persuaded the authorities that law and order were best served by a continuation of internment. In the meantime government was faced with a breakdown in inmate discipline, demoralisation of governors and their staff, and the certainty that there would soon be a confrontation. Balancing the difficulties of restoring discipline and the disadvantages of releasing the internees, it was recognised that the former would most likely involve serious disturbances, hunger-strikes and political damage. Release seemed a reasonable and calculated risk. In the meantime, nature increased the pressure for a decision, and provided political cover. The influenza pandemic which swept the world in three waves of mounting severity, starting in the summer of 1918, could be represented as a *force majeure*. And there was the reality that Irish reactions to deaths in custody were a significant consideration for government. The first of these was Richard Coleman, who died at Usk on 9 December 1918.[173]

The fatality was widely reported in Ireland, and led to comment, even from constitutionalists, on the doubtful wisdom of continuing internment when faced with influenza. After seven months in prison, the *Irish Independent* observed, no man would be in a condition to resist the disease: 'If what happened at Usk is typical the wonder is that there have not been more deaths. It is nothing short of tyranny to keep these men in prison any longer.'[174] The inquest on Coleman provided yet more ammunition for critics, since the coroner refused to hear from the dead man's comrades. This inflamed suspicions that the authorities had something to conceal.[175]

Coleman had the customary Sinn Féin funeral. Stage-management and political exploitation were not, however, sufficient explanations for the large crowds which turned out in bad weather to line the streets and to follow the cortège – some 15,000 people, according to the *Irish Independent*. The funeral was led by sixty Volunteers and fifty priests, followed by the flower-covered hearse and firing party. The procession included numerous private carriages, the Sinn Féin executive, the Lord Mayor in his official carriage, a band, and units of Dublin Volunteers. The last, in military formation, marching under command, numbered between 300 and 400. Volleys of blanks were fired at the graveside, and the Last Post was sounded. Prominent female republicans such as Mrs Pearse, Mrs Eamonn Kent, Countess Plunkett and the widow Mrs Joseph Mary Plunkett were in close attendance. Even the weather contributed to the mood: 'Rain fell heavily.'[176] Such was the temper of the times that this event – however bathetic to the detached modern observer – powerfully boosted the Sinn Féin cause.

---

173 In 1916 Coleman had received a sentence of three years for his part in the Easter rising, and he was freed in the general amnesty of June 1917. He was subsequently sentenced under DORA, but was one of those released from Dundalk Prison after their short hunger-strike. He had been an obvious target in the 'German Plot' round-up.
174 *Irish Independent*, 12 December 1918, 2e; see also 10 December, 3e.
175 Ibid., 3a–c.
176 Ibid., 16 December 1918, 3d–e, *passim*.

Repetitions, with consequent ratchetings of hatred and fervour, were awful for government to contemplate, yet were distinctly possible – as was a two- or three-coffin *fête des morts*.

There had been a notable death at Gloucester (Pierce McCann, MP) where several prisoners were so ill as to require nursing outside the prison. McCann's funeral party was received in Ireland by a large crowd, including 500 Volunteers and leaders such as Michael Collins and Richard Mulcahy.[177] When the epidemic further gathered pace, it was decided that it would be prudent – both on political and public health grounds – to grant a general release.[178] This started on 5 March 1919 and was completed within four days.[179] Some prisoners were too ill to travel, and were detained until they were sufficiently recovered.[180] Another lesson was well remembered from 1916 to 1917, and, to avoid demonstrations in Ireland, releases were staggered by the Home Office, with priorities being dictated in part by medical reports.[181] The fact that a general release was under way was also obscured by granting compassionate paroles until the last days. Robert Brennan was freed from Gloucester on 14 March 1919, ostensibly because of his father's illness. The Irish Office asked that his release be arranged discreetly. He was not to be required to give any undertaking and no date was to be fixed for his return. This was an unconditional release, but without saying so.[182]

Apart from those whose health did not allow immediate release, there was only one other rather curious hitch. On 8 March 1919, when governors were notified that all the remaining internees were to be released, an exception was made for Edward Bulfin, who was held at Durham. He was detained because he was an Argentine citizen with a deportation order against him. His file, for some reason, was not readily available to the Home Office, and it was decided

---

177 *Freeman's Journal*, 10 March 1919, 5d. Pierce McCann was at the time of the Easter rising the County Commandant of the Tipperary Volunteers and was subsequently elected to the Commons, taking his seat in the Dáil. He died on 6 March, the day after releases had started. His remains were accompanied back to Ireland by his parents and several newly freed internees, including Dr Richard Hayes, John O'Mahony and Frank McGuinness – all MPs elected in December 1918, who were now members of the Dáil (NLI: Sean O'Mahony Papers: Ms. 24, 452 (unfoliated)).

178 PRO HO/144/1496/362269/179; RCP, PP, 1919 [374], XXVII, 759, 22.

179 The operation went smoothly but three Birmingham prisoners, notified of their release on 6 March, refused to go unless their comrades were released as well. This proved to be the smallest kind of obstacle, however, since all were released the following day. The one woman remaining in custody at this time, Constance Markievicz, was released on 7 March ('to be sent out quietly this evening'). (PRO HO 144/1496/362269/179). Her reception in Dublin on 15 March, however, was far from quiet, and again thousands paraded through the streets in her honour (*Freeman's Journal*, 17 March 1919, 7c–d).

180 RCP, PP, 1919 [374], XXVII, 759, 22.

181 PRO HO 144/1496/362269/185.

182 PRO HO 144/11681/3. In May 1930, Brennan's play *Bystander* was produced at the Abbey Theatre. He asked the Home Office for a photograph of himself in convict dress – a request that did not amuse officials.

to hold his brother Frank Bulfin, also detained at Durham, since Edward's file contained adverse reports on Frank. The Bulfin brothers, kept company by Arthur O'Connor, remained in custody for a further two weeks. Edward Bulfin's deportation was still under consideration and the other two men elected to wait in prison until a decision was reached. The governor sought the Commissioners' advice on whether censorship and visiting rules applied to the two voluntary 'detainees'. Waller questioned whether Frank Bulfin and Arthur O'Connor should be allowed to remain in prison 'at the expense of the state'. Censorship was no problem, since that had effectively been abandoned. While the two volunteers remained, it was decided they should be subject to the rules for internees.[183] The situation was resolved on 22 March when Edward was removed to Liverpool Prison to await deportation, and his brother and Arthur O'Connor were discharged.[184]

Within officialdom, the releases were marked by a sad little set of minutes. On 26 April 1919, the Irish Chief Secretary, Ian Macpherson, wrote to Home Secretary Shortt (who, as it happened, had been Macpherson's immediate predecessor in the Irish Office) on behalf of the Irish government, expressing thanks for the 'great services' of Home Office officials in connection with the Irish internments. 'In particular,' Macpherson wrote, 'we would ask that you might convey to the warders our deep appreciation of great tact and patience displayed by them . . . often under the most difficult and provocative circumstance.' The prisoners, 'though chafing under restraint without trial' found little to complain of and some prisoners had spoken 'in not unsympathetic terms of the treatment they have received'. A generous tribute, never conveyed to the prison staff because of the Commissioners' fear that it might prompt an application for a money reward.[185]

183 Minute by M. L. Waller: PRO HO 144/1496/362269/183.
184 Waller to Power, 24 March 1919; ibid.
185 Waller to Power, 24 March 1919; ibid., /183; Chief Secretary's Office to Waller, 15 April 1919; ibid., /184.

14

'FRIGHTFULNESS'

Ireland, 1919–22

Through the looking glass

Shortly before 6 p.m. on 8 July 1921, Major-General Sir Nevil Macready, General Officer-in-Chief Commanding British Forces in Ireland, paid a visit which he could not have possibly anticipated when he took up his post fifteen months before. Nor could he have imagined the conditions under which he would make it. Eamon de Valera, President of the Irish Republic and de jure fugitive, had made the Dublin Mansion House his headquarters. Passing through cheering crowds, Macready was effusively greeted by Larry O'Neill, Dublin's irrepressible Lord Mayor.[1] The purpose of the visit was to conclude truce terms with the IRA's representatives.[2] The men with whom he sat down – Robert Barton and Eamon Duggan – had been specially released from custody a few days previously. Agreement was reached the following afternoon, and on 11 July 1921, a cease-fire and stand-off commenced: the Anglo-Irish war came to a stop.[3] No one was certain how long the Truce would last, but peace hopes were high, and many recognised that in this agreement between Irish rebels and the British government a wholly new stage had been reached in relations between the two countries.

Ireland had been in an ever-intensifying state of war since the beginning of 1919. Many hundreds of lives had been lost, vast quantities of public and private property destroyed, and tracts of the country reduced to lawlessness, terror and paralysis. Civil authority had broken down in many places and ways, and a new state had been established in six of the counties of Ulster. Government was faced with the necessity of sending in a large army of occupation and, with an

---

1 *Irish Times*, 9 July 1921, 5d–e; 11 July, 3d–e; *Freeman's Journal*, 9 July 1921, 5a–e (including photograph).
2 The Irish Republican Army (IRA) had gradually replaced Irish Volunteers as the name of the armed movement. This occurred in popular usage during 1918, though Constance Markievicz was signing her affiliation thus in late 1916 (NLI: Eva Gore-Booth Papers: Ms. 21, 816, clandestine letter). Throughout much of the Anglo-Irish war, however, the two names remained interchangeable.
3 For the Truce terms see *Arrangements Governing the Cessation of Active Operations in Ireland*, London, HMSO, 1921 [Cmd. 1534]; also at PRO HO 45/20094.

uncertain outcome, taking measures which would possibly bring on it the odium of nations. The IRA, ill-equipped, depleted in manpower and under immense pressure, had no reserves on which to draw. Burnings, bombings, killings and atrocious actions had been carried out by both sides. Was Ireland on the verge of a form of nationhood acceptable to a majority of its people, or was more terrible devastation to sweep the country? Had militant Irish nationalism now reached its culmination, or was this merely another stage in a history of rebellion and repression?

It is neither possible nor necessary for the purposes of this volume to give a detailed account of the political, legal and military developments in the two and a half years between the outbreak of the Anglo-Irish war, and its effective ending with the Truce. So much was compressed into these months, and the shifts and complexities were so many, that only a full-length study could hope to do justice to them. The overall sense, however, may be conveyed in a word which became an unavoidable adjunct to Irish reports and commentary: 'frightfulness'. These months certainly commenced with a high level of political tension and a sense of impending conflict, yet nothing which had previously occurred – except perhaps the revolt of 1798 – could have prepared the population for what was to come. There developed in Ireland an irregular war of considerable intensity into which ever more sections of the community were drawn, and it was not only property which was immolated, but also decency and compassion.

The newspapers of the day convey the sequence and pace of crisis, conflict, bloodshed, brutality and destruction in a way that no modern analyst could hope to achieve. In what follows I have made extensive use of these sources, but know that no selection can capture fully what it was to live in such a disintegration of economic, civil and political life. The deterioration was dramatic. On 22 January 1919, the day on which the Irish newspapers reported an ambush and killings at Soloheadbeg, Co. Tipperary, the main stories were the first meeting of the Dáil and items of foreign news. There was little comment on terrorism that day or the next, other than Tipperary being declared a military area. Bolshevism and Europe's turmoil provided the day's quota of worries for the thinking person.

Jump to 9 July 1921 and all is changed. The *Irish Times*, organ of southern Unionism, reported the bombing of a train and the murder of a tramways inspector; attacks on auxiliaries; arson at an army depot; the kidnapping and killing of an ex-soldier and the dumping of his placarded body; the killing of a process server; the kidnapping of a juror; raids on the mails; bombing of the police; robbery at a post office; discovery of an IRA dugout, arms and ammunition; and the kidnapping of litigants in a civil case.[4] A flick back and forth in the newspaper files shows that this day was relatively uneventful – there were many, many which were worse.

---

4 *Irish Times*, 9 July 1921, 5e–f. The nationalist *Freeman's Journal* carries much the same range of stories, concentrating on the killing of Catholics at Newry; the inquiry into the Mallow shootings; shooting at soldiers; the possession of arms and a challenge to a death sentence (5g–h; 6c–h).

A bad day, selected at random, might have been 21 March 1921, when over one weekend fifty-two people were victims of the fighting, twenty-five of whom were killed. The English *Daily News* called this 'the bloodiest weekend for many weeks in Ireland'.[5] And the killings did not abate. Two days later the same news-paper reported twenty-three people killed in twenty-four hours; the day following that another twenty-three were dead.[6] And there was the supporting chorus of burnings and bombings, retaliation and counter-retaliation, robbery by both sides, kidnappings, public whippings, beatings, cutting the hair of young women, torture, mutilation, intimidation, insecurity and fear – truly frightfulness writ large.

The political basis for terror

Political and military struggle had intensified during the period of the 'German Plot' internments. The December 1918 wipe-out of the Irish Parliamentary Party was the mirror image of Sinn Féin's triumph. With many of its leaders and candidates in prison, and subject to a range of handicaps and hindrances, the fledgling party achieved outstanding results, soaring from seven to seventy-three seats.[7] Sharpened political focus, the abstention of Labour and a growing climate of intimidation meant a virtual elimination of independents, and a Unionist increase from eighteen to twenty-six seats: there seemed to be no middle ground, and politics was given over to intensity and fierceness. A year previously, in the autumn of 1917, Sinn Féiners had lost three by-elections in a row and the party was in the doldrums; in March and April 1918 the Irish Party had won two seats in a contest with Sinn Féin. And while before the 'German Plot' round-up Sinn Féin continued to make inroads into constitutional nationalism, few anticipated the rout to come. The threat of conscription, above all, but also deportations and internments and (in July 1918) the proscription of Sinn Féin and the Gaelic League, all recharged the cause of physical-force nationalism. Now all barriers were swept away: Redmond was dead (on 6 March 1918), his party crushed, the Irish Convention had trickled to an ignominious close, and lawful nationalism could point no way forward.

Much suffering, and loss of life and property would be inflicted by guerrilla war and military and police counter-insurgency in the two and a half years between the 1918 general election and the Truce. These might be seen as obviously arising from the character and declared mission of Sinn Féin, and its popular endorsement. This was not at all apparent in December 1918, when votes were cast. Piaras Béaslaí, a militant republican, insisted that the outcome of the election was 'not to be taken as indicating a sudden and complete conversion

---

5 *Daily News*, 21 March 1921, 1d.

6 Ibid., 23 March 1921, 1g; 24 March, 1a–b.

7 Dorothy Macardle, *The Irish Republic* (Dublin, Irish Press, 1951 pp. 262 and 919–22) gives a republican analysis. For the Irish Party view see *Freeman's Journal*, 14 December 1918, 4c–d.

of the Irish people to Republicanism. . . . The vote . . . was largely an anti-Irish Party vote, and also a gesture of protest against the English Government's actions in Ireland'.[8] Sinn Féin itself remained a coalition, with a substantial faction still adhering to notions of boycott, civil resistance, abstention from Westminster and an ultimate settlement with the British not far removed from Redmond's Home Rule; some would still have accepted a dual monarchy. Other Sinn Féiners were wholly committed to a republic, and nothing but; and even here there were degrees of certitude. The party's general election manifesto was vague, even as such documents go, and had been so mutilated by the Dublin Castle censor that a key clause promising to make use of 'any and every means available to render impotent the power of England and to hold Ireland in subjugation by military force or otherwise' had been excised.[9] Read and pondered, this might have caused some who were inclined to cast their vote for Sinn Féin to think again. But the possibility that an uncensored manifesto might frighten off as many or more voters than it encouraged was too subtle for Dublin Castle. And even of those who thought that support for Sinn Féin could lead to some form of armed conflict, how many conceived the debasing cruelty, bitterness and destruction of that struggle?[10]

By suppressing and censoring the authorities drained Ireland of genuine political engagement, boosted nationalist unity and forced a greater pace of struggle. The 'German Plot' had left the field clear for figures such as Michael Collins, Cathal Brugha[11] (Volunteers' Chief of Staff), his deputy Richard James Mulcahy,[12] and Rory O'Connor.[13] In the summer and autumn of 1918 this group began to put together the basis of what would become an effective fighting machine, structurally and operationally much closer to modern urban guerrilla and terrorist groups than to 1916's gallant, romantic and very correct insurrectionism in the Fenian tradition. And Catholic Ireland – or at least parts of it

---

8 Piaras Béaslaí, *Michael Collins and the Making of a New Ireland*, London, George C. Harrap, 1926, Vol. 1, pp. 250–1.

9 Macardle (*op. cit.*, pp. 919–22) provides both the original and censored versions of Sinn Féin's electoral address.

10 Several of the German Plot internees were cautious about Sinn Féin's electoral success. One, writing from Durham Prison, expressed the view that the result was due to a wave of enthusiasm and not based on any real understanding of Sinn Féin's aims and objects. He urged that Sinn Féin should bridge this gap in understanding by undertaking a propaganda campaign (PRO HO 144/1496/362269: Directorate of Military Intelligence, Seventh Report on the Correspondence of the Irish Internees).

11 (Charles Burgess) (1874–1922). Born Dublin, mother from Yorkshire, father Irish. Second-in-command to Eamonn Ceannt in the rising (during which he was wounded). Killed by Free State forces in civil war.

12 (1896–1971). Second-in-command to Thomas Ashe at the 1916 Ashbourne attack on the RIC. On release from Frongoch became Deputy Chief of Staff of the Volunteers, subsequently Chief of Staff of the IRA. Supported Treaty and became Chief of Staff of Free State Army. Later a leading Fine Gael politician and minister.

13 Macardle, *op. cit.*, pp. 262 and 919–22. For O'Connor see n. 64, below.

– was ripe for some kind of political violence. There was widespread anger at being cheated over Home Rule and a sense that drastic change was in the making. In a society so rural and with such a strong instinct for place, this discontent spontaneously led to organisation and action. No direction or exhortation from a conspiratorial centre was necessary to stimulate land distribution, cattle-driving and arms' raids on private houses: these sprang directly from the tradition of Irish agrarian unrest. Local groups, themselves part of a culture of secret societies, easily transformed into units of Volunteers. Much was accomplished quite independently of Dublin.[14] By the time of the German Plot arrests there had grown up in the south-west of Ireland 'a lawlessness reminiscent of the old days of the Land League or even the Defenders'.[15] Preventive police measures were taken, including the 'proclaiming' of the most disaffected counties under powers derived from the Criminal Law and Procedure Act, 1887. Fairs, festivals and other meetings were prohibited in certain districts which were designated 'Special Military Areas'.[16]

Against this background of disorder the threat of conscription united all shades of nationalist and Roman Catholic opinion in a way that British ministers seemingly could not grasp. Vows of resistance translated easily enough into promises of action against the British government, in whatever circumstances. Men whose place was reserved in the Western Front killing machine had little to lose in embracing the Sinn Féin alternative. Writing in An tÓglach (the Volunteer journal) Ernest Blythe from internment called for bloody war against conscription: 'We must recognise that anyone, civilian or soldier, who assists directly or by connivance in this crime against us, merits no more consideration than a wild beast, and should be killed without mercy or hesitation as opportunity offers.' Anyone who assisted in conscription, even if only by applying for exemption, 'must be shot or otherwise destroyed with the least possible delay. In short, we must show that it is not healthy to be against us, and then those who are not going to be against us must be with us.'[17] Many who previously would

---

14 See, for example, Dan Breen, My Fight for Irish Freedom, Dublin, Talbot Press, 1924, pp. 6–10; Robert Kee, Ourselves Alone, Harmondsworth, Penguin, 1989, pp. 38–9. Note the very strong sense of locality in Tom Barry's Guerilla Days in Ireland, Dublin, Anvil Books, 1962.

15 Kee, op. cit., p. 39.

16 The Criminal Law and Procedure (Ireland) Act, 1887 (50 and 51 Vict., c.20) authorised certain inquisitorial proceedings, special juries and transfer of venue to a court outside a proclaimed area (for a discussion of these powers see Colm Campbell, Emergency Law in Ireland, 1918–1925, Oxford, Clarendon Press, 1994, pp. 16–18 and 54–8).

17 An tÓglach, I, 4 (14 October 1918), 1b and 2a. Piaras Béaslaí, then editing An tÓglach, had been handed the article by Michael Collins, to whom it had been smuggled by Blythe. This was therefore no private outburst, but a statement of intent, endorsed at the highest level (see Béaslaí, 1926, Vol. 1, p. 211). Blythe (1889–1975), a member of the Sinn Féin executive, and Irish Volunteers' organiser for Munster and South Connaught, was several times imprisoned under DORA. He took the Free State side in the civil war, served in various ministerial capacities and became a director of the Abbey Theatre.

have dismissed this as dangerous ranting now countenanced or supported it: rhetoric teetered towards reality.

Political channels petered out. There were the highest expectations of the Versailles Peace Conference, which opened on 20 January 1919, and which amidst the terrible destruction of the Great War was intended, *inter alia*, to give a hearing to the claims of smaller nationalities. The belief that this body would interfere in the domestic affairs of one of the victorious allies was, even for the times, absurdly naive. Sean T. O'Kelly[18] was dispatched to Paris, where his energetic lobbying was so much ploughing of the sands; the victors' prestige was at its highest: as former friends of the Central Powers (some still thought them clients) Sinn Féin had neither political nor moral currency. President Wilson refused to receive O'Kelly, or any other Sinn Féin representative.[19] Some small consolation was given to republicans by the dispatch to Ireland of a three-man commission of inquiry, which arrived in Dublin on 3 May.

While these attempts to enlist international support faltered, the ground was being cleared for the next stage of conflict. Pursuing Sinn Féin's basic doctrine (an assembly in Ireland of those elected to Westminster, and a boycott of the latter) the Dáil was convened on 21 January 1919. All Irish MPs had been invited to attend. Not surprisingly, none but Sinn Féin responded; and of the seventy-three Sinn Féin members who had been elected, thirty-six (including de Valera and Arthur Griffith) were in English prisons. Representing the overwhelming majority of those returned in the November 1918 election, the Dáil was acutely conscious that it was the first such assembly to meet in Ireland since the 1800 Act of Union. A provisional ministry was appointed which, over the succeeding months, set up a parallel and semi-covert civil administration. Backed by popular sentiment, moral coercion and armed force, this body gnawed at the foundations of British governance. In promulgating a Declaration of Independence (which emphasised its continuity with the Republic declared on Easter Monday, 1916), the Dáil made a plea for international recognition. In the 1916 Republic diehards had their emblem and touchstone. 'We have declared for an

18 (1883–1966). Former General Secretary of the Gaelic League; a founder member of Sinn Féin. Staff Captain in the Dublin GPO during the rising, and subsequently interned. Took the anti-Treaty side in the Irish Civil War. Long political career in de Valera's Fianna Fail. President of Éire, 1945–9; first President of the Irish Republic, 1949–59.

19 In the immediate post-war period, Wilson was preoccupied with a settlement which would not *extend* the territories of the victorious allies, and also with the establishment of the League of Nations. In both of these complex fields of negotiation Ireland was a sideshow and possible trap (see Louis Auchincloss, *Woodrow Wilson*, New York, Lipper/Viking, 2000, p. 92). For electoral reasons, however, Wilson could not afford to appear wholly indifferent to Irish nationalism. On 1 April 1918, agreeing to a monthly draft of 120,000 American soldiers, he had warned of US repercussions should conscription be enforced in Ireland. By 27 February 1919, he was nevertheless reported by Reuter's as telling a member of the Congressional Foreign Affairs Committee that the Irish question was a matter for Ireland and England (this statement was subsequently denied). See Macardle, *op. cit.*, pp. 248, 278, n.10, and (on developments in Paris) pp. 281–2.

Irish Republic and will not live under any other law' declared Liam Lynch in 1917,[20] thus stating the position of uncompromising republicanism, which has survived through and beyond the twentieth century.

The renewed declaration of the Republic had more to do with keeping faith with those who had died in 1916 than with practical politics: it was a powerful symbolic commitment which found widespread approval in a movement that affected to be repelled by the intrigues of conventional politics and politicians. Its electoral mandate (though almost certainly this did not extend to war) allowed the Dáil to claim a moral justification for the use of violence. This helped to bridge a gap between the more 'advanced' elements of direct-force nationalism and the general population, and allowed Sinn Féin and its armed (if largely autonomous) wing, the Irish Republican Army, to avoid or to minimise the charges of secrecy, lack of authority and criminality which the Roman Catholic hierarchy had levelled against Fenianism. From the convening of the first Dáil, Fenianism entered the mainstream of Irish politics.

The Anglo-Irish war

The collapse of the Central Powers was a bitter defeat for Irish republicanism. Both in the United States of America and in Ireland the old Fenian doctrine of England's adversity had nourished dreams of a settlement forced on the defeated British Empire which would include Irish independence. As we have seen, within weeks of the rout of the German armies the interned leaders at Lincoln Prison (including de Valera) were persuading themselves that retreats were simply withdrawals to winter quarters, and that victory – or at least victories – would come in the spring.[21] With the Armistice all illusion evaporated: the IRB had placed all its chips on a losing number. Worse, the principle of my enemy's enemy had led it to oppose Irish republicanism's two oldest allies: France and America. Ulster Unionism, by contrast, had made its sacrifice and was entitled to its reward. The vast contribution of southern Catholics to the British war effort had been nullified in the destruction of the Irish Party.

It is not surprising that in these circumstances there was much confusion. The electoral victories were hard to read, but they were not a mandate for war. British imperialism appeared stronger than ever. Fenianism was emphatic – there was no chance of a military victory unless the British oppressor was engaged in a major war. Collins and the other military leaders tinkered with the

---

20 Florence O'Donoghue, *No Other Law*, Dublin, Irish Press, 1954, p. 18. Lynch (1890–1923) was one of the major figures of Republicanism. Member of the IRB, Commander No. 2, Cork Brigade, IRA. Led various attacks on British forces; captured General Lucas. Took anti-Treaty side in Civil War. Became IRA Chief of Staff on 26 March 1922 and (after split) again on 30 June 1922. Cornered and shot by Free State troops on 10 April 1923.

21 See above, pp. 641–2.

reorganisation of the Volunteers on conventional lines, but knew that there was no point in a rerun of the 1916 rising. How, then, to go forward? There was no strategy, but in some localities groups of young men cried out for *any* action. Terrorism and guerrilla war were discovered, rather than contemplated: strategy emerged from the haze of action, tactics were makeshift and exploratory; the war grew in a haphazard fashion.

The parallel state

Between January 1919 and the spring of 1920, there were numerous small-scale terrorist incidents, the pattern of which – a growing and loosely coordinated challenge to the state – only slowly became discernible. Despite window-dressing, government faced the unquestionable collapse of conventional policing. Official pronouncements still insisted that the problem was merely murder gangs, yet a full-scale campaign of counter-terror was put in hand. As civilians were drawn from conviction or intimidation, if only passively, into the struggle, government lost the inducement (and restraint) of appealing to moderate nationalist opinion: indeed, there now existed no constitutional party with the necessary mandate. And though Sinn Féin remained a coalition, elements of which might have provided negotiating partners, the prolonged absence of Eamon de Valera, at first in Lincoln Prison, and then in the United States of America, meant that the pace would be set by the military rather than the political wing of the movement.

And the soldier was hardly subject to political control. True, in August 1919, by taking oaths to the Republic and the Dáil, the IRA notionally became the de jure armed force of the Dáil.[22] It remained operationally and in most other ways responsible to its own elected executive, which in turn was under IRB rather than Dáil control. In any event, the organisation was more locally than centrally driven, and took military rather than political initiatives. Without a political process and negotiations, terrorism and counter-terrorism spiralled in a rapid succession of hundreds of incidents. This marked the second phase of the war,

---

22 The relationship between the Dáil and the Volunteers (which in the Dáil Declaration of Independence on 21 January 1919 had been described as the IRA) remained ambiguous. Although many IRA units took an oath of allegiance to the Dáil, many did not, and subsequent events showed that loyalty to the IRA itself was far stronger than the Dáil oath. This was reinforced by the IRA's mode of organisation, which combined the election of officers with the discipline of command. The leaders of the rising based their authority on an interpretation of Irish destiny, as did the IRA. The Dáil claimed through its electoral mandate to represent Irish national aspirations. These were two very different sources of authority – one based on revelation, the other on the ballot box: conflict between them was inevitable. Dorothy Macardle, writing within the de Valera canon, treats the relationship between Dáil and army with some coyness and opacity – as well she might – given de Valera's subsequent difficulties with both (*op. cit.*, pp. 290–2 and 304–5). More than he intended, Ernie O'Malley, in his telling of the soldier's tale, reveals much ambivalence and many reservations about the oath and Dáil–IRA relations (*On Another Man's Wound*, London, Rich & Cowan, 1936, ch. 9, *passim*).

and lasted until the end of 1920. During the final six months or so, until the Truce of 11 July 1921, government effectively lost even daytime control of large swathes of territory; there was combat between the flying columns of both sides, with civilians repeatedly, certainly uncomfortably, frequently frighteningly and sometimes fatally pinched between two masters.

Ten years after England and Wales, Ireland, in a period of political tranquillity and optimism, was given local government reform in the Local Government (Ireland) Act, 1898. This abolished the previous, essentially oligarchical, forms of rural local government and provided county and borough councils, regularly subject to election on a ratepayers' franchise.[23] Financed by local taxes, substantially grant-aided and (apparently not always effectually) supervised by the Irish Local Government Board, these new councils were of great importance to local political and economic life: they were also major dispensers of patronage. Throughout the Catholic parts of Ireland local councils were dominated by Redmond's Irish Party; Unionism controlled the Protestant areas. With the Irish Party wiped out, it was inevitable that control of local government in Catholic urban and rural areas would also pass to Sinn Féin.[24] This duly happened in January 1920, when the bulk of local administration fell to Sinn Féin candidates.[25]

As we have seen, town and city councils and corporations had adopted resolutions in favour of clemency for the Fenians and even the dynamitards.[26] Now in Sinn Féin hands or substantially under its influence, local government in itself and in relation to the Dáil became the sinews of the administrative struggle – alongside the embryonic Sinn Féin departments, courts and police.[27] The Dáil's other shadow departments – finance and agriculture – also began to function, generally more in symbolic than substantive ways. Military encounters could be assessed by deaths and casualties, weapons seized, barracks held or destroyed, territory controlled: although the pattern of victory and defeat swayed and changed, there was a great deal of certainty about these individual outcomes. Civil administration was a less tangible but scarcely less important arena.

---

23 Local Government (Ireland) Act, 1898 (61 & 62 Vict., c.37). (English local government had been reformed by the Local Government Act, 1888 (51 & 52 Vict., c.41).) In addition to county and borough councils, subordinate rural district and urban district councils were provided for medium and small towns and townlands.

24 For an instructive account of the significance of Irish local government in the 1920–2 period see Tom Garvin's 1922: The Birth of Irish Democracy, Dublin, Gill & Macmillan, 1996, pp. 63–91.

25 Sinn Féin captured eleven of Ireland's twelve cities and boroughs, and 172 of the 206 councils (Macardle, op. cit., pp. 326–7). See also Irish Times, 19 January 1920, 5c–e; Evening Telegraph [Dublin], 19 January 1920, 1a–c.

26 See pp. 218–21, 235, 381–3, above.

27 The British authorities were aware that local government was being used as the mechanism through which Sinn Féin took control. Hence the later attacks by the Black and Tans and auxiliaries on local officials, such as mayors (see Jeudwine memorandum, 22 April 1921; PRO CO 904/232).

To whom should rates be paid, and how disbursed; which local government board – Dublin Castle's or the Dáil's – should command obedience? Nor was this a matter of purely organisational conflict – everyday citizen choices were made regarding local government, police and courts.

Political and military struggle permeated every nook and cranny. Tax-collectors were shot at; Sinn Féin courts deliberated and handed down decisions which were willingly or fearfully obeyed. Assassination and attacks drove the RIC from normal policing duties, leaving the way clear for Sinn Féin police, who arrested criminals and brought them before its courts. Sinn Féin did not have prisons[28] but could and did pass sentences of banishment from Ireland, backed by threats of injury or death.

On the IRA side there was an increasing ruthlessness and an ever less con-strained embrace of terrorism. This was more brutal and uninhibited than the 1880s dynamitard campaign, and on an incomparably larger scale. Face-to-face killing of the unarmed or helpless by members of the community in which they live has a particular quality of horror about it, whether the victim be a trouble-some magistrate, a policeman, an off-duty soldier, a government official or a suspect civilian. On a lesser scale, shaving the heads of young women who kept company with soldiers or police, burning a home, and issuing a banishment order were all brutal acts intended to strike terror across a community well beyond the immediate victim. This was the level of personal violence contem-plated by Richard Mulcahy when in Frongoch Camp he demanded that scruples be set aside:

> To have a real revolution, you must have bloody-minded fierce men, who do not care a scrap for death or bloodshed. A revolution is not a job for children, or for saints or scholars. In the course of revolution, any man, woman or child who is not with you is against you. Shoot them and be damned to them.[29]

Terror tactics

On 21 January 1919 (the day the first Dáil convened) the ability to divest oneself of scruple and pity was demonstrated when local IRA men shot dead two RIC constables who were escorting a load of explosives to a quarry at

---

28 Although there is at least one account of a 'prison': *Freeman's Journal*, 9 June 1920, 3e. Three men had been brought before a Sinn Féin court charged with illegally demolishing a wall. Two of the three refused to make reparation and were sentenced to be marooned on an island for three weeks. The two stoned and drove off an RIC rescue party, saying it had no authority to release them.

29 *Cit.* Tomás Ó Maoileón, in Uinseann MacEoin (ed.), *Survivors*, Dublin, Argenta Publications, 1980, pp. 82–3.

Soloheadbeg, Co. Tipperary.[30] This sordid incident was to be seen as the beginning of the Irish War of Independence.[31] The killing of Constables McDonnell and O'Connell was wholly intentional and was as important as the seizure of the explosives themselves. Dan Breen, the leader of the ambush party, had planned the action to raise Volunteer morale (which had plummeted with the ending of the Great War and the evaporation of the threat of conscription). The police escort at Soloheadbeg apparently would not have been allowed to surrender and save their lives: 'Our only regret was that the escort had consisted of only two Peelers instead of six. If there had to be dead Peelers at all, six would have created a better impression than a mere two.'[32] And, although Treacy's comrades subsequently disputed its meaning and intent, Treacy is on record as having said several weeks before the ambush, apropos of poor discipline in his IRA unit: 'If this is the state of affairs, we'll have to kill someone, and make the bloody enemy organise us.'[33]

Soloheadbeg provided a telling foretaste of how things would develop. The authorities immediately proclaimed South Tipperary a 'Military Area' and prohibited fairs, markets and meetings. Reinforcements were brought in and garrisons were established in villages which previously had rarely seen a policeman. An initial reward of £1000 (subsequently raised to £10,000) was offered for the ambushers. All of this (at least in retrospect) was welcomed by Breen and his

---

30 *Freeman's Journal*, 22 January 1919, 3d; 23 January, 3d. After a peremptory challenge the two constables, James McDonnell and Patrick O'Connell, were shot dead in an ambush which included three local IRA men who would establish fearsome reputations. These were Dan Breen, Séamus Robinson and Seán Treacy, all friends since childhood. Breen (1884–1969), who had been sworn to the IRB by Treacy, backed the anti-Treaty side in the Irish Civil War, but in 1927 became the first republican to take the Oath of Allegiance. Treacy (1895–1920) took part in a number of actions during the twenty-one months after Soloheadbeg, and was killed in a spectacular gun battle with police in Dublin in October 1920. Séamus Robinson was born in Ballagh, Co. Tipperary. After Soloheadbeg he operated in Dublin, taking part in two attacks on the Lord Lieutenant; active in flying column attacks. Constable James McDonnell, a widower with seven children, was close to retirement. Since he had lived in that rural area for thirty years, it is highly probable that Breen and Treacy were at least on nodding terms with him.

31 Piaras Béaslaí disputed Breen's claim that this was the first armed action since 1916 in which police were killed. There had been, he insisted, several armed encounters between the police and IRA in 1918, wounds inflicted and policemen killed (Béaslaí, 1926, Vol. 1, pp. 271–2; Breen, *op. cit.*, p. 39).

32 Breen, *op. cit.*, p. 44. There is disingenuousness in Breen's attempt to soften this brutal statement with a sentimental tribute to his two victims: 'They were Irishmen, too, and would die rather than surrender . . . we would have preferred to avoid bloodshed; but they were inflexible.' Breen claimed that the ambushers had twice called on the constables to surrender, but this hardly accords with his plans for an outrageous incident which would grip the country. It is hard to believe that the five-day wait of the ambushers could have had any other acceptable outcome for Breen and his comrades. Seán Treacy, on being asked about Constable McDonnell's death, is reported to have described it as regrettable but 'unavoidable' (Desmond Ryan, *Sean Treacy and the 3rd Tipperary Brigade*, London, Alliance Press, 1946, p. 41).

33 Ibid., pp. 55–6. See ch. 5 for an exculpatory account of the ambush.

comrades: 'Our little band had unmasked the British. They had to come into the open and let the world see that they held Ireland by naked force.'[34] Less welcome was the reaction of the local community. The two constables had been popular figures, and both were cast in the mould of the rural and easy-going policeman. Former friends – even within the IRA – shunned the band. Breen bitterly recalled that he and his companions were refused shelter even in cattle byres 'on nights so inclement that one would not put out a dog'. And this in the midst of a very cold winter. The local priest denounced the killers, declaring that they would bear the mark of Cain to their graves. (Not all clergy took this view, and it was a priest who eventually provided food and shelter.) Even the IRA leadership seemed appalled by the brutality of the incident (though such squeamishness soon passed). Arrangements were made to smuggle the men to the United States of America, assistance which they indignantly refused.[35]

These reactions were a benchmark. As shootings, bombings, killings, assaults and burnings multiplied in the following months and years, the degree of brutality necessary to attract particular notice, much less condemnation, necessarily rose. Shortly after Soloheadbeg Michael Collins, addressing a somewhat apprehensive Sinn Féin executive meeting, extolled the benefits of disorder and, Shiva-like, demanded creative devastation. Darrell Figgis recalled the remarks which were delivered with the contemptuous air of a fighting man to civilians: 'He spoke with much vehemence and emphasis, saying that the sooner fighting was forced and a general state of disorder created throughout the country . . . the better it would be for the country. Ireland was likely to get more out of the state of general disorder than from a continuance of the situation as it then stood.'[36] This epitomised the doctrine of terrorism, just as Soloheadbeg had been the deed: Collins and his comrades had their strategy.[37]

The strategy did not require central control, and was all the stronger for this. Even to get cooperation between these bands was difficult, and some months were to pass before the 'Flying Column' emerged.[38] This highly mobile formation, usually not more than thirty strong, drew men from several units, lived off the country and gave a concentration of firepower in engagements with police and

---

34 Breen, op. cit., p. 50.

35 Ibid., pp. 52–9, passim; Ryan, 1946, pp. 88–9. According to the military censor, internees who referred to Soloheadbeg in their correspondence condemned the incident 'and deplored it as injurious to the cause by alienating public sympathy' (PRO HO 144/1496/3162269: Seventh Report on Correspondence of Internees, Directorate of Military Intelligence).

36 Darrell Figgis, Recollections of the Irish War, London, Ernest Benn, 1927, p. 243.

37 Tim Pat Coogan notes that it was not until June 1919 that the Sinn Féin executive authorised a killing (Detective Inspector Hunt) but that guerrilla warfare developed from Soloheadbeg onwards (Ireland Since the Rising, London, Pall Mall Press, 1966, p. 25).

38 The columns, according to Coogan, were the invention of Dick McKee, Commander of the IRA's Dublin Brigade (ibid., p. 27).

military: it could then melt back into the population.[39] Such actions were still undertaken on a local footing, albeit within an expanded area, and it was not until the war's closing stages that attempts were made to organise at what was called divisional level, pooling the resources and men of up to eight brigades and several hundred men. But this level of operation remained untested, and the full implications of the deployment of what was approaching conventional military formations were undigested. Poor communications and even worse logistics combined with uneven training, uncertain discipline and a high degree of localism would probably have made large formations more advantageous to the British than to the IRA. Leading IRA figures such as the divisional commanders Liam Lynch and Earnie O'Malley were conscious of their own lack of training and experience at this and much lower command levels, and seemed to learn from crisis to crisis and from an unsystematic if urgent study of military manuals.[40]

And so the war developed on the basis of local initiatives, the centre responding to circumstances for the most part, rather than directing them, successful because of its adaptive pragmatism rather than any military doctrine. Strategy was still sometimes articulated as the old Fenian one of a general uprising. This meant little since it was displaced by the consequences of carrying out the preparatory work: the arms raids and the counter-raids; the killing of Crown officials and suspected informants; police and military crimes and excesses, and IRA reprisals; counter-reprisals and so on, in what would essentially reach an equilibrium of terror.[41] To fight this war, Volunteers were told, 'forget the Company of the regular army'. The IRA did not aspire to become a standing regular force and if it attempted to do so it would fail. Rather, 'Our object is to bring into existence, train and equip as riflemen scouts a body of men . . . capable of acting as a self-contained unit, supplied with all the services that would ordinarily be required in the event of martial action *in this country*.'[42] Preparation for an old-style national and territorial general uprising gave way to the realisation that – certainly in the southern part of the country – the war of attrition already under way had become a form of general rising. And until the very last stages of the Anglo-Irish war local units were more like loosely affiliated franchises than branches of their parent organisation.

The war thus unfolded pell-mell and reactively. Republican propaganda certainly did not give the impression that the Dáil underwrote systematic terrorism, but rather sought to portray the daily attacks as a series of spontaneous

---

39 Béaslaí, 1926, Vol. 2, p. 96.

40 See, for example, O'Malley, 1936, chs 19–21, *passim*.

41 Ibid., p. 111: 'We had thought in terms of a general, simultaneous rebellion throughout the country; now Headquarters endeavoured to teach us to train, arm and equip and to carry out minor operations, for the seizure of arms' (this referred to the spring of 1919). See also pp. 118–19 for a description of the IRA's organisational structure.

42 *An tÓglach*, 1, 2 (14 September 1918), 1b–2a.

and local reactions to British restrictions, reprisals and atrocities.[43] The war was entering its final stages before the Fenian doctrine of a general rising was explicitly set aside. Commitment to general insurrection could be a considerable convenience for localities which wished to organise and secretly parade rather than act. In any event, the British, no more than local IRA commanders, were unwilling passively to await the general uprising. Attrition to both sides mounted, and terror and counter-terror ever more obviously sustained Sinn Féin's parallel civil administration, and alienated the civil population from the Crown.

Although the IRA remained pitifully weak in organisation, and certainly in resources,[44] the essence of its development was its relationship with the broad mass of nationalists who had deserted the Irish Parliamentary Party, and who remained uncertain of the way ahead. As time went on and the struggle intensified, with cruelties and atrocities on both sides, this broad and hesitant mass, in a paradoxical way, became more rather than less committed. If it required a great mental, emotional and moral effort to support an IRA which killed men in the street, outside their church, on their doorsteps, in their beds and in front of their families, then once that commitment was made it was easier to go forward than back. And the general sympathy was a war resource. It provided the information which is the essence of any war, and guerrilla war in particular. The Irish Civil Service, Post Office, railways and public administration were generally riddled with IRA informants – including a number of well-placed police and prison officers.[45] Material help was also forthcoming – money, food, shelter, labour. All of this created a momentum in which it became easier to sympathise than not, and harder to withhold assistance, requested or not. In turn, British forces came to much the same view as the revolutionists – that the Irish people (or at least the Roman Catholic majority), unless they gave evidence to the contrary, were to some degree in the service of the enemy.

43 In the autumn of 1919 Dublin IRA men were told by Richard Mulcahy, their Chief of Staff, that the Dáil was anxious that no armed action should be traced to the IRA, and if it were it might be necessary to repudiate the men involved (Desmond Ryan, 1946, p. 177). As late as February 1921, Ernie O'Malley was urging the Editor of the *Irish Bulletin* to acknowledge the full role of the IRA (O'Malley, *op. cit.*, p. 279).

44 It had the great advantage of being grossly overestimated by the British who in the spring of 1920 gave a strength of between 100,000 and 200,000. At this time Collins considered the IRA's effective strength to be no more than 3000 fighting men (Richard Bennett, *The Black and Tans*, London, Edward Hulton, 1959, p. 29). Another account has Collins saying that in all of Ireland there were not more than 1000 fighting men: it is reasonable to suppose that he had no precise knowledge of numbers that must constantly have fluctuated. The Dublin Brigade of the IRA in the closing stages of the war had a nominal strength of 3500, of whom not more than 1000 were armed. Of these only about 15 per cent were free to take part in an action because of their employment (Charles Dalton, *With the Dublin Brigade 1917–1921*, London, Peter Davies, 1929).

45 Michael Collins' network of informers extended to the London Post Office, where his agent, Sam Maguire, continued to work throughout the Anglo-Irish war. Béaslaí claimed that Collins had been able to intercept and decode almost all civil service, army and police messages (*op. cit.*, Vol. 1, pp. 220–1; Vol. 2, p. 180).

Heroes and bandits

Wars need heroes, bravery and tales of derring-do. Personalities always matter in a predominantly peasant and local society, and legends generate energy. Eamon de Valera was of course known and respected throughout the country, as were Michael Collins and the other leaders whose names emerged as the war went on. But fighting men such as Breen, Barry, Treacy and O'Malley captured the popular imagination in a particularly raw and atavistic way, with daring raids, escapes and repeated acts of audacity and bravery.[46] When Breen and Treacy escaped from 'Fernside' (a sympathiser's house in north Dublin) on 12 October 1920, shooting their way through a large raiding party, and Breen made his way, badly wounded, to the safe haven of an ordinary and randomly selected Dublin home, the two men confirmed their place in republican mythology, and created the image of the tough, daring and resourceful rebel. And the British Army, maladroit as ever in the field of propaganda, confirmed Breen's moral ascendancy by shooting his unresisting host – Professor John O'Carolan: pimpernel bravery contrasting with the cowardly shooting of an unarmed prisoner.[47] A final twist came two days later when Treacy was shot to death on a Dublin street, but not before killing two of his opponents.[48]

A legend of a different kind was created six weeks later, when on 28 November 1920, Tom Barry's West Cork flying column ambushed a lorry convoy of auxiliaries at Kilmichael, near Macroom. After fierce fighting, including an alleged false surrender by some of the auxiliaries, the entire detachment was wiped out, their arms, equipment and notebooks seized and the lorries in which they had been travelling set alight. Some of the column were so shocked by the close-quarters fighting and carnage that Barry drilled them on the spot, marching and countermarching for five minutes by the light of the burning tenders.[49] Two

---

46 The rescue from custody of Sean Hogan (one of the Soloheadbeg ambushers) by Breen, Treacy and others on 13 May 1919 resulted in a gunfight and the killing of two RIC men. This incident, in its recklessness and loss of life, was a national sensation and established the fame and notoriety of the raiders (*Irish Independent*, 14 May 1920, 5c; 15 May, 5d–e; *Freeman's Journal*, 14 May 1920, 5d; 15 May, 3d).

47 Desmond Ryan, 'Fight at Fernside', The Kerryman, *Dublin's Fighting Story 1913–1921*, Tralee, The Kerryman, n.d. (?1948), pp. 133–41; Breen, *op. cit.*, ch. 12; Ryan, 1946, ch. 10; Professor Carolan made a deathbed statement, testifying that the raiding party had made him face the wall before shooting him in the head (*Irish Independent*, 13 October 1920, 5a–b; 22 October, 6f). The army account had Carolan being shot by the two fugitives (*The Times*, 13 October 1920, 10e).

48 *Irish Independent*, 15 October 1920, 5a–b.

49 Barry, 1962, p. 46; Stephen O'Neill, 'Auxiliaries Annihilated at Kilmichael', The Kerryman, *Rebel Cork's Fighting Story 1916–21*, Tralee, The Kerryman, 1947, pp. 83–5. In a later account ('Auxiliaries Wiped Out at Kilmichael in their First Clash with the IRA', The Kerryman, *With the IRA in the Fight for Freedom: 1919 to the Truce*, Tralee, The Kerryman, 1953, 120–8) Tom Barry provides the significant information that before the ambush the local parish priest heard the IRA men's confessions, and blessed them.

IRA men were killed in the encounter, but the rest successfully evaded converging army and police forces.

The republican bond with the general population was strengthened by Crown reprisals. Following the Kilmichael ambush, for example, neighbourhood houses, farms and commercial premises were burnt, and the Macroom auxiliary unit posted a notice threatening to shoot on sight any male appearing in public with hands in his pockets. Martial law was declared in the counties of Cork, Tipperary and Limerick; all businesses and shops in Cork city were forcibly closed between 11 a.m. and 2 p.m. on 2 December 1920 to show respect for those Auxiliaries killed in the Kilmichael ambush.[50] Rebellion and reaction gripped fiercely with the inevitable ratcheting-up of nationalist feeling, the squeezing out of neutrals and elevation of the status of the IRA.

Between 1 January 1919 and the commencement of the Truce on 11 July 1921, it has been calculated that there were just under 9000 'outrages', including 2564 raids for mail, 3218 for arms, twenty-five occupied barracks destroyed, and 405 police and 150 soldiers killed (and 196 civilians).[51] It is no wonder that Breen, Barry, O'Malley and others would hear their names and exploits sung in homes where they sheltered and gatherings where they relaxed. It is, however, remarkable that it was not until three weeks before the Truce was signed that a member of the English cabinet – the diehard F. E. ('Galloper') Smith, now Lord Chancellor Birkenhead, no less – was prepared to admit that 'a small war' was under way in Ireland, adding that the situation would be dealt with at 'whatever degree of sacrifice' was necessary.[52]

Despite the singing and celebration, however, there were many parts of Ireland where action was infrequent or trivial, and where IRA units were torpid, ill-trained, largely bereft of arms, and quite unresponsive to HQ urgings. Ernie O'Malley, who cycled large tracts of the country as an IRA organisation officer, was forced to conclude of several districts that the popular atmosphere was so unreceptive, or that the local officers were creating such obstacles, that action was impossible or unlikely. The shoot-outs, raids, ambushes and burning barracks were always, for some areas, somewhere else.[53] But it was the fiery images and the audacity which stirred feelings, and the increasing brutal and uncaring police and military activity which provided the fixative.

---

50 *Cork Examiner*, 30 November, 1920, 5a; 2 December, 5c; 3 December, 5a.

51 Charles Townshend, *The British Campaign in Ireland 1919–1921*, Oxford, Oxford University Press, 1975, pp. 160–1.

52 5 *Hansard*, XLV (Lords), col. 690; 21 June 1921. The admission came in a debate on a motion (Earl of Donoughmore) urging the government to open negotiations with the republicans. Birkenhead conceded that the history of the previous three months was one of 'the failure of our military measures to keep pace with, and to overcome, the military measures which have been taken by our opponents'. He promised that this would be put right.

53 Richard Bennett (*op. cit.*, pp. 134–5) points out that in November 1920 there had been no trouble reported in thirteen of the twenty-six counties, and that the IRA's efforts remained concentrated in Dublin and the south and west.

Iron in the soul

The police and army mutation from forces of community and state to one of repressive occupation was both unavoidable and inexcusable. The *raison d'être* of Crown forces was the law, and when they broke it they did double damage, slashing at a quickly rotting fabric. The insurgents suffered no such hindrance, however, even when they committed acts of great callousness and cruelty. Their sympathisers seem quickly to have looked away on these occasions, and certainly the killing of disarmed or off-duty soldiers found no place in songs of celebration. Ernie O'Malley, in a well-known narrative, described the shooting of three British officers captured near Fethard, Co. Tipperary. He told the three that they were to be shot as a deterrent to the British of the district, who were shooting their prisoners. There was no trial, but to formalise the killing, to turn it from murder into an execution, a procedure was observed. The three were told they would be shot at dawn the following morning. The condemned were offered a clergyman, or a sympathetic civilian, to sit with them. They were given writing materials for a last letter, and O'Malley promised to return their personal possessions to relatives. In the morning there was a walk to the place chosen for execution, blindfolds, the condemned asked if they were ready, the shots of the firing-squad and the *coup de grâce* for each twitching body. 'None of us wants to do it', O'Malley had said to them, 'but I must think of our men.' In his narrative he had added, 'I could not see the ultimate implications of our proposed action'.[54] This incident, an act of deterrence and retaliation, showed how far the conflict was removed from Collins' later claim in the *New York American* that although individuals were being marked down for IRA killing, only the British armed forces and their 'spies and criminal agents' were attacked: 'Prisoners of war were treated honourably and considerately, and were released after they had been disarmed.'[55] There was no way an organisation as locally based as the IRA could guarantee standards in the treatment of prisoners.[56]

And there were those for whom there were no final formalities, shot in the streets, or in their beds. On Bloody Sunday (21 November 1920) when Michael Collins' men killed fourteen British officers (as far as can now be said all but one serving in intelligence) nine were in their pyjamas as they died (a Sunday morning had been chosen) and a number were killed in the presence of wives or

---

54 O'Malley, 1936, pp. 331–2. 'I was putting myself in the place [of the condemned]. My turn might come, too, and soon' (ibid., p. 330). Charles Dalton, a Dublin Volunteer, recorded a similar reaction to the killing of four British officers lined up against the wall in the hallway of their hotel: 'Knowing their fate I felt great pity for them. It was plain they knew it too. As I crossed the threshold the volley was fired . . . the sights and sounds of that morning were to be with me for many days and nights' (*op. cit.*, pp. 106–8).

55 Béaslaí, 1926, Vol. 1, p. 335. Those interviews were given in 1922.

56 Tim Pat Coogan (1966, p. 30) describes both Black and Tan and IRA atrocities, noting that some of the Volunteers 'were just as degenerate'.

girlfriends, one of whom at least had to be prised away before her man could be shot.[57] There was also the case of Alan Bell, a retired magistrate, employed at Dublin Castle in tracking down the bank deposits that constituted Sinn Féin's National Loan. Collins had Bell taken off the morning tram in which he travelled each day and shot on the pavement amidst the crowds on their way to work.[58]

The campaign in England

The IRA's English campaign of 1920 to 1921 was overshadowed by the daily catalogue of atrocities coming out of Ireland, then by Irish independence, and by the civil war which followed. Accounts of the times have largely neglected or underplayed this episode, which, though brief, was many times more destructive than the dynamitard expeditions of the 1880s or the Fenian actions of 1865 to 1867. No comprehensive or satisfactory account of the English campaign exists.[59] Rory O'Connor, who might have been able to give an overview, was executed extra-judicially by the Free State government in December 1922. Other participants were low in seniority and access to general plans. Art O'Brien, who very likely played some part in directing the campaign, was not in a position in the wake of the Treaty to own to it. What follows, therefore, is a partial account, pieced together from newspaper reports and such other material that is available. The intention was to bring home to the electorate in Great Britain the nature of the 'frightfulness' in Ireland. This would not be served by an atrocity, and some care was taken to avoid bloodshed (except in pursuit of Black and Tans). Shots were fired and injuries inflicted, but few lives were lost,

57 There are several accounts of Bloody Sunday, James Mackay's partisan *Michael Collins: A Life* (Edinburgh and London, Mainstream, 1996) being one of the most recent (see ch. 11). Béaslaí (1926, Vol. 2, ch. 4) gives the contemporary republican version of the incident. Part of the justification for this extraordinarily brutal action went beyond the men's role as intelligence officers. Collins and his associates had for some time claimed that small groups of British officers were operating as death squads (ibid., Vol. 1, ch. 23). In a later account of the killings Béaslaí insisted that the IRA GHQ had 'unmistakable evidence that there was a conspiracy to murder Irish citizens, planned, engineered and carried out by the Intelligence Department of the English forces in Ireland, with the sanction and approval of their General Headquarters Staff'. This was the justification for Bloody Sunday. These claims cannot now be checked ('Fourteen British Officers and Agents Executed in Dublin on "Bloody Sunday"', The Kerryman, *With the IRA in the Fight for Freedom: 1919 to the Truce*, pp. 114–19).

58 *Irish Times*, 27 March 1920, 7d–e. According to Dorothy Macardle, Bell was a resident magistrate 'noted for his services to British Intelligence Departments in Ireland' (*op. cit.*, p. 332). In addition to his investigations of banks he was known to be enquiring into the attack on the Lord Lieutenant and a murder. It is significant that Bell's killers were able to leave the scene and disperse without hindrance.

59 Thus that diligent, if partisan, chronicler Piaras Béaslaí only briefly discussed IRA and IRB support in England and Scotland in his survey, 'The Anglo-Irish War' (The Kerryman, *With the IRA in the Fight for Freedom: 1919 to the Truce*, pp. 5–13; see p. 10).

although the cost of damage to property up to November 1922 was estimated at £1,188,000.[60]

The English campaign originated in the summer of 1920 when the IRA convened a meeting of its officers. Among the issues discussed was the increasing number of military and police reprisals, including the destruction of the houses of supposed IRA sympathisers and also the burning of district creameries. Particularly militant IRA leaders such as Liam Lynch[61] and Terence MacSwiney[62] pressed for action in England to bring home to English public opinion the damage then being wrought in Ireland by Crown forces.[63] Rory O'Connor, the IRA Director of Engineering, was given command of this campaign.[64]

There were several large Irish communities in England and Scotland, from which IRA recruits and auxiliaries were drawn. These were people with good local knowledge, some second or third generation immigrants, or so long settled that they could pass as English. Events in Ireland, and the polarisation of opinion on the national question, swept up people who previously had little connection with republicanism. Their involvement often began with cultural or general political interests in Irish nationalism: the various front organisations were important reservoirs of manpower. One such recruit, Edward Brady, was probably typical. Aged 19, Brady was drawn into Liverpool republican circles through his sympathy for Irish political internees. After short service in various non-military republican organisations (such as the Irish Self-Determination League and the Irish Trading Club) he was 'spotted' and invited to join the Birkenhead IRA.[65] As was usual, he broke off contact with overt organisations, and began to train in smallarms, bomb-making and other black arts of the urban guerrilla. Because Brady had lived in England since childhood, his Irish identity was well concealed:

---

60 PRO HO 144/4645/132. This figure applied to England and Scotland, though the bulk of damage was English. On Sunday, 27 November, in the midst of various arson attacks, an IRA party being chased by police fired shots, and an innocent bystander was killed (*Daily Telegraph*, 29 November 1920, 13d; 30 November, 11f). Another innocent man was killed on 16 May 1921 by an IRA assassination gang seeking a former policeman who had served in Ireland. The victim died some days later (*Morning Post*, 23 May 1921, 8f).

61 See above, p. 659, n. 20.

62 (1879–1920). Interned following Easter rising. Active in Volunteers and Sinn Féin on release; member of First Dáil (mid-Cork); Commandant, First Cork Brigade, IRA. Succeeded Thomas MacCurtain as Lord Mayor of Cork. Re-arrested and sentenced by a military court under DORA and died after a seventy-four-day hunger-strike in Brixton Prison.

63 O'Malley, 1936, p. 168.

64 Rory (Roderick) O'Connor (1893–1922) graduated in arts and engineering from University College, Dublin. Worked in Canada as a railway engineer. Returned to Ireland and was wounded and interned in 1916. Close colleague of Collins, but opposed Treaty. Executed on 8 December 1922, without trial, by the Free State government – one of its first actions – as a reprisal for assassination of Seán Hales, a pro-Treaty member of the Dáil.

65 The story of Brady's involvement with the IRA is taken from his rather breathless memoir ('Some of the most dramatic and thrilling episodes of my life'): Edward Mark Brady, *Ireland's Secret Service in England*, Dublin, Talbot Press, 1928.

he was simply a respectable young clerk. Activists appear to have been thin on the ground, and were periodically further reduced by police action. Energetic, well educated and competent, within weeks Brady became second-in-command of the whole of Merseyside, filling the place of a man deported to Ireland and interned under the Restoration of Order (Ireland) Act (ROIA).[66] A few months later, in consequence of the arrest of his superior, Brady took control of all IRA operations on Merseyside – most of Lancashire (including Liverpool), Cheshire and part of Yorkshire.

In addition to men such as Brady, swept into the movement for a few months, there were other more serious revolutionaries at work. These were sent over from Ireland to induct, train and oversee new recruits, and to plan and carry out actions themselves.[67] In overseeing the English campaign Rory O'Connor sought retaliation for Crown actions in Ireland; he also hoped to divert and drain military and police resources, while bringing home to the electorate the nature and consequences of British policy in Ireland. Subsidiary goals included the procurement of *matériel* for use in Ireland, and the militarisation of nationally minded young men in Britain's Irish communities.

Early in November 1920, O'Connor crossed to England and addressed 150 Merseyside IRA men about the campaign.[68] The details, worked out in succeeding days, included a plan to burn twenty of Liverpool's large cotton and other warehouses and timber yards. On Saturday, 27 November 1920, large quantities of petrol, paraffin and bolt-cutters were purchased, and fifteen large and destructive fires were set.[69] This was a serious and politically damaging act against one of the Empire's principal ports, and police reaction was immediate and intense.[70] Besides the investigation of particular crimes, there seems to have been a policy of harassing front organisations through raids and conspicuous surveillance.[71] The headquarters of the Irish Self-Determination League at Shaftesbury Avenue, London, and the Gaelic League in the same building were raided, as were Art O'Brien's offices in Adam Street, Adelphi, and those of Sean MacCraith and Fintan Murphy. Correspondence and files were removed from all these premises;

66 10 & 11 Geo. V, c. 31: see below, p. 682.
67 These experienced activists had been promised by the IRA commanders at the July 1920 meeting at which the English campaign had been agreed (O'Malley, 1936, p. 168).
68 Brady, *op. cit.*, pp. 26–7. O'Connor probably addressed similar meetings elsewhere in England at this time. It is noteworthy that even with such numbers of men, and their untried nature, police intelligence was very limited.
69 *The Times*, 29 November 1920, 14a.
70 Among the precautions, instructions were issued to post offices to notify the police of suspicious telegrams – either of content, or handed in by suspicious (i.e. Irish) people. Likely locations such as Liverpool, Glasgow and Manchester were particularly targeted, under the general authority of the Home Secretary (PRO HO 144/4645/5 and 6).
71 Thus on 16 December 1920 there were raids in Bayswater, London, during which a number of documents of the Irish Self-Determination League were seized (*Morning Post*, 17 December 1920, 7b).

there were similar actions in Liverpool.[72] The intention, no doubt, was to create an impression of vigilance and to put pressure on known Sinn Féin figures. Patrols were increased in vulnerable areas and various precautions were taken. The residence of the governor of Brixton Prison was placed under guard, because of possible retaliation for the death of Terence MacSwiney six weeks before.[73] There was extra security at the Houses of Parliament, where the public galleries were closed. Other Whitehall buildings were restricted, and Downing Street was barricaded and policed.[74]

This activity had little effect on the campaign, which had the great advantage of being able to use people unknown to the police. On 13 December there was an unsuccessful attempt to blow up Braidhurst Viaduct near Motherwell, which carried one of the main railway lines between England and Scotland. Two days later a Manchester rubber-works was the target.[75] On 12 February 1921 (Saturday was the night favoured for fire-setting) there were attacks on various premises in the Manchester area – rubber, chemical and oil plants.[76] During arson attempts in Manchester on 19 February, shots were fired by the raiders and some £30,000 worth of damage was done.[77]

An attempt to fire an oil-works at Wandsworth on 15 January 1921 was interrupted by police. Even though the arsonists fired at the unarmed beat-constables, one was arrested and (since the homes of those arrested were invariably searched) press-cuttings and correspondence were found which established his Sinn Féin connections. Three more (out of the party of twelve) were subsequently arrested and committed for trial.[78]

Found guilty of a variety of arson offences and of possessing firearms (but not of firing at the constables) two men were each sentenced to eight years' penal servitude and a third to four years. The fourth, granted bail and tried separately, was not convicted.[79] At sentencing, Thomas O'Sullivan told the court he had set the fire because of what was happening in Ireland: protest meetings had been held in England, but the public took no notice. James Moran said much the same, adding that many friends had been burnt out in Ireland. The judge was

---

72 *Daily Herald*, 2 December 1920, 1b.

73 Ibid.

74 *Daily Telegraph*, 29 November 1920, 13f; *The Times*, 30 November 1920, 14b.

75 *Daily Chronicle*, 14 December 1920, 1c (one of the piers of the viaduct was slightly damaged).

76 The attacks were at Rochdale, Sailsworth, Rayton and Oldham; the damage was reported to be slight (*Manchester Guardian*, 14 February 1921, 5a–b).

77 Ibid., 21 February 1921, 5a–c.

78 *The Times*, 22 January 1921, 4f. Their occupations were interesting: two clerks, a schoolteacher and a cable operator. All lived close to the oil works. The incident showed their amateurism, and certainly none was possessed of even the basic skills of conspiracy, the police task being made considerably easier because of documents found in their possession and at their homes (see also *The Times*, 17 January 1921, 7b; 29 January, 7b; 8 February, 4b; 18 February, 7b).

79 *The Times*, 19 February 1921, 7f. It is possible that this man cooperated with the police in return for leniency.

clearly taken by the men's youth (they were aged 19 and 20), their courtroom demeanour and their education, and did not pass the heaviest sentences available to him.

Another trial, concluded at about the same time, resulted in the conviction of three much older men for conspiracy to murder and arson. These charges arose out of the Liverpool fire-setting on the night of 27 November 1920. Unlike the young Wandsworth men, these were labourers. Sentences of ten years' penal servitude and two years' imprisonment were passed.[80] One of the men (Neill Kerr) appealed and found a niche in legal history when his conviction for conspiracy to murder was overturned by a majority verdict of the Court of Criminal Appeal – the first time this had occurred in the history of that court.[81]

Various arrests were made in Scotland, arising from similar events. Seven men stood trial in Glasgow in February on rioting, attempted wounding and wounding charges. Four were found guilty and received sentences of eight and ten years' penal servitude.[82] A month later there was a trial of sixteen men at Edinburgh on conspiracy to endanger life and property and arms and explosives charges. The police gave evidence of finding a 241-foot live fuse, together with detonators, gelignite cartridges (more than 900 in one bag) and the explosives samsonite and stomonal; arms and ammunition had also been found.[83]

Judging by the proportion of acquittals and 'not proven' verdicts, these trials seem to have been conducted fairly, throwing out cases in which evidence was weak. Feelings were mounting, however, even in judicial circles. Passing sentence in the Glasgow case of rioting and attempted murder, the judge was reported as remarking:

> It is no good winking at the fact that there had congregated in parts of Scotland an alien populace who had not a drop of Scottish blood in their veins, and were indifferent to the great historical associations of that country, and for whose national feelings they cared nothing at all. They were cosmopolitan adventurers.[84]

---

80 Neill Kerr aged 57 and his companion James McCaughey were convicted of both charges; Matthew Fowler was found guilty on the lesser one (*The Times*, 15 February 1921, 7d).

81 There was abundant evidence of Kerr's connections with Sinn Féin including a letter from de Valera in New York, conveying his greetings as President of the Irish Republic. Kerr also had military training material. There was, however, no direct evidence connecting him to a conspiracy to murder, and the Court of Criminal Appeal (Darling and Avory, J J; Salter, J, dissenting) found that the trial judge should have directed that the charge should not go to the jury (*The Times*, 23 March 1921, 4d).

82 *Morning Post*, 10 February 1921, 9f.

83 Nine were found guilty and seven acquitted; sentences of between one and five years were imposed (*Morning Post*, 21 March 1921, 8c).

84 *Morning Post*, 10 February 1921, 9f.

Young men continued to come forward, however. Fire-setters struck Merseyside farms on 9 March 1921 – three on the Cheshire side and half a dozen or so on the Lancashire side. In these raids six men (two of whom carried revolvers) were captured, and a fireman was killed when his engine overturned while attending a fire.[85] Fires had been set in the Kent and Surrey outskirts of London the previous month.[86] Extensive damage was caused in London as a result of a window-smashing campaign, reminiscent of the suffragettes.[87] At the end of March more than £50,000 worth of damage was caused in farm-fires between the Tyne and Tees.[88] On the night of 22 May 1921 there was widespread and coordinated fire-raising in fourteen districts on Tyneside and Teeside, including North Shields, Wallsend, Chester-le-Street, Jarrow, Stockton and Newcastle. These were more varied than the Merseyside targets (probably because of the police watch on the more obvious premises). Water and gas mains were blown up, and a number of businesses and public services were fired – railway stations, a cinema, a garage, haystacks, a timber yard and a shipyard and drapery stores. Three men were arrested (two of whom were armed), but the scale of the attacks indicated a substantial IRA capacity, as well as a paucity of police intelligence.[89]

This was confirmed when, despite the arrests arising from the earlier campaign, there was a new wave of attacks on Merseyside in the more difficult circumstances of long days and light evenings. Telephone and telegraph wires were cut whole-sale, and on such a scale that it took two to three days to restore the network.[90] A few days after that there was an attempt to blow up Liverpool petrol storage on the premises of the London and North Western Railway.[91] Police arrested five men in connection with the cutting of the telephone and telegraph wires, but this failed to stop wire-cutting in Leeds, Bristol, London, Kent, East Sussex and South Wales on the night of 7 June.[92] More serious offences were averted by luck. A shot (which missed) was fired through the window of a Board of Trade building in South Kensington, in an attempt to kill a former Black and Tan.[93] At Middlesborough a man was arrested in possession of 70 lb of high explosives – a quantity that could have done very serious damage indeed.[94]

---

85 *Daily Chronicle*, 11 March 1921, 3e; *Pall Mall and Globe*, 11 March 1921, 3c; *Morning Post*, 10 March 1921, 8b.
86 *The Times*, 8 February 1921, 7c.
87 *Daily News*, 21 April 1921, 1d; 22 April, 1d. Because plate-glass windows were targeted, costs were very high. The attacks continued throughout April.
88 *Manchester Guardian*, 28 March 1921, 5a–b.
89 *Daily Chronicle*, 23 May 1921, 1f.
90 *Morning Post*, 4 June 1921, 3d.
91 Ibid., 6 June, 7f.
92 *Daily Telegraph*, 9 June 1921, 11d. Some of the wire-cutters were armed and used cars to travel between various sites.
93 *Daily Chronicle*, 27 Mary 1921, 1d.
94 *Morning Post*, 4 June 1921, 3d.

And there were attacks other than destruction of property. Through the seizure of mails in Ireland and its Post Office contacts, the IRA was able to pinpoint the identities, addresses and sometimes the movements of individual Black and Tan and Auxiliary officers, and to order that they be killed at home, or their homes burned down. On Merseyside fourteen homes were identified and eight actually burned down; in London a number of fire-raids were carried out and several people were injured. These attacks might have become dangerously successful had not the Truce intervened.[95]

English units of the IRA – particularly on Merseyside – were also used to enforce Sinn Féin's anti-emigration policy. Parties of US-bound emigrants were detected and 'persuaded' to return to Ireland. Passports and transatlantic tickets were confiscated, and when replaced by the authorities, the emigrants' money was also taken. These raids were called off after a short time, but the fact that parties of IRA men could raid hotels and interrogate and terrorise guests showed the extent of republican support and organisation in Irish communities in England, and the boldness of the activists.[96]

Only a week before the Truce came into operation sixteen men were convicted in Manchester (and two acquitted) of treason felony and variously sentenced to between three and thirteen years' penal servitude. The sentences reflected what an official file described as their 'relative prominence in a very grave conspiracy'. Fires were set in Manchester on 2 April 1921, and police received information that the Erskine Street Irish Club in Manchester was involved. The club was raided and arrests were made. Twenty-one men were variously charged with treason, felony, conspiracy, fire-setting and attempting to set fires, and possessing firearms and explosives with intent. Five were charged with attempted murder of police constables. An arsenal of arms, ammunition and explosives had been seized on the premises.[97] The Club was described as 'probably the worst of the Sinn Féin conspiracies'.[98]

Despite setbacks, the IRA was prepared to extend its English campaign. In April 1921, Richard Mulcahy, the IRA Chief of Staff, narrowly escaped capture in Dublin but left papers behind as he fled. These revealed plans for the destruction of shipping in Liverpool, as well as further fire-setting and an attack on Manchester's electricity plant. Some of these schemes were within days of being put into effect.[99]

Altogether there were fifty-five convictions for crimes committed in England and Wales before the Truce. The offences ranged widely from the burning of haystacks of little value to destruction in the region of £200,000. Some men

95 Brady, *op. cit.*, pp. 65–8.
96 Ibid., pp. 44–55.
97 On 12 May 1921, the men's desperado status was heightened by an attempt to escape from Manchester Prison (PRO HO 144/4645/82).
98 PRO P. Com. 7/260; *Manchester Guardian*, 16 July 1921, 9g.
99 Béaslaí, 1926, Vol. 2, p. 214.

were charged with shooting at the police (usually in connection with a fire or explosives attack) and others with the acquisition and possession of explosives, arms and ammunition. Convictions were also obtained for the cutting of telegraph wires, purchasing arms, inciting soldiers to steal arms and ammunition, and attempts to commit the range of substantive offences.[100] Operations did not cease with the Truce, although the pace did decline and switched from attacks to building up the IRA's *matériel* – stealing gelignite and other explosives in fairly large quantities, and stealing or purchasing arms. A letter found on one offender stated: 'The truce does not in any way affect us as regards getting the stuff away.'[101] Eighteen offenders were tried for post-Truce, pre-Treaty offences and, in the nature of revolutionary conspiracies (including the split in the IRA), a certain number of offences which were committed in the months and years that followed.[102]

Early in 1922 there was an attempt to break the back-up of the Sinn Féin organisation in Merseyside by using the deportation and internment powers of the Restoration of Order in Ireland Act. Major-General Sir Wyndham Childs, who moved from the War Office to take charge of Special Branch in December 1921, took the lead in this. In conjunction with the Chief Constable of Liverpool he arranged a round-up of more than a 100 'Irish undesirables'. Trains were laid on to take the deportees to Liverpool where, with the Merseyside contingent, a destroyer took them to Dublin. The scheme did not have a happy ending, however, since a writ of habeas corpus was granted and the deportations were held to be illegal. Then, according to Childs, 'I had the mortification of seeing the whole crowd released and awarded damages by way of Compensation for their wrongful arrest'.[103]

The security authorities were aware that further attacks were contemplated, and on 10 June 1921 a conference of senior officials was convened at the Home Office, consisting of heads of intelligence, police and the Home Office.[104] It was

100 See list at PRO HO 144/4645/412340/102. This document, which includes a limited description and commentary on the offences, was compiled at the time when a general amnesty was being considered.

101 Ibid., f. 4.

102 The last offences in the Home Office list concerned a conspiracy to steal arms from Chatham barracks. The three offenders (James Creena, Henry Collins and H. J. Friday) came to trial at Kent Assizes on 15 February 1922, and received sentences of between nine and eighteen months' hard labour. Kate Evans, the only woman in this group, was convicted with her husband of stealing explosives and passing them to the IRA organiser J. P. Connolly; she was given seven years' penal servitude.

103 Major-General Sir Wyndham Childs, *Episodes and Reflections*, London, Cassell & Co, 1930, pp. 205–7, *passim*.

104 The meeting (which was opened by the Home Secretary) included the Permanent-Under-Secretary (Sir Edward Troup), Sir John Baid, General Sir W. T. F. Horwood (Commissioner of the Metropolitan Police), Sir Basil Thomson (Director of Intelligence), J. W. Olive (Assistant Commissioner, Metropolitan Police) and the home counties' chief constables (Buckinghamshire, Surrey, Berkshire, Hertfordshire, Essex and Kent) (PRO HO 144/4645/68a).

feared that there would be an IRA push before the Truce came into effect and various measures were agreed to protect London. The chief of these was the establishment of barriers on important roads on the periphery of the Metropolitan Police area. These would be manned by five or six armed policemen and would control motor traffic leaving London after 9 p.m., and in both directions after 10.30 p.m. Cars would be stopped and documents examined. The location of the barriers would be varied and where the local force had insufficient manpower the special constabulary would be called out. Sir Basil Thomson agreed to issue to the chief constables a special summary of intelligence, 'on the condition that each Chief Constable personally burns his copy as soon as read'.[105] Such a major operation, involving a great deal of public attention and some inconvenience, and great expense, indicated that the IRA's English campaign had bitten deeply, and that the organisation was thought to have the resources and energy for further attacks. But the minds of the IRA leaders had now turned back to Ireland, and the momentous circumstance of the Truce. The 'Ring of Steel' was not needed.

The British response

Between Irish nationalists and republicans and an acceptable form of self-government there were two major obstacles. One was Ulster. That this was such a barrier was partly of the nationalists' own making. A central plank of all nationalist platforms was the political unity of the island of Ireland and the concomitant assertion that Ulster Unionists were deceived or self-deceived about their national identity. The short period in the 1790s when some Ulster nonconformists and Roman Catholics made common cause in the United Irishmen was endlessly reprised. At some point Ulster Protestants would supposedly return to the national fold. Any separate arrangement for them was unthinkable. Unable to bow to geopolitical facts, nationalists were weakened in their principal and morally most justifiable demand – national self-determination for the overwhelming majority who wished it in the remaining twenty-six counties. This myopia would follow Irish envoys into the final negotiations (and beyond). The other obstacle to Irish self-rule is often mentioned, but the mere words 'fear of the break up of the Empire' do not today convey the strength of the political charge they carried.

A sense of the end of things, of civilisation in upheaval was ubiquitous. Hopes of a return to 'normality' evaporated – frighteningly for some, exhilaratingly for others. The still-falling debris of empires with all the attendant disturbances dominated international news. Part of the penalty imposed on the defeated Central Powers – German, Austro-Hungarian and Ottoman – was dismemberment and loss of empire. But that any territorial loss should be suffered by one of the

105 Ibid.

victorious allies was unthinkable, and that a section of the United Kingdom itself should secede would, the reasoning went, shake the Empire when stability and assurance were most needed. The 1916 rising had sent shock-waves far afield. In Moscow it was seen by British diplomat Bruce Lockhart and his colleagues as 'a severe blow to British prestige', ranking with Gallipoli and the surrender at Kut.[106] In the following decades the rising and the Anglo-Irish war were analysed and pondered in India, Burma, Palestine, Cyprus and more distant colonies.[107] The safety of the Empire, the rule of a few over the multitudes, rested on several factors, but one of them was established beyond all doubt in the sepoy mutiny of 1859: the notion of imperial invincibility. When that was ruptured, rebellion flourished, conflagration took hold, and authority had to be speedily and sometimes bloodily re-established. There were important differences, of course, in the degree and type of firmness that could be shown in some distant colonial possession, and to one's errant fellow citizens a few hundred miles from Fleet Street. But imperial government needed to be seen to act with confidence and firmness, and totally to rule out any question of the break-up of the United Kingdom. It is easy now, some eighty years after the event, and in a supposedly postcolonial world, to miss the fears and determination behind this doctrine. And providing the emotional underpinning to postwar imperialism was the question that any generation of survivors must face – does this or that act keep faith with those who died or were maimed in the Great War?

The second prong in the imperial case was an immediately practical one. How could a seaborne empire be safe with the possibility that at its heart there existed an independent island, lying athwart its seaways, which could be denied as a base or for harbours of refuge? Indeed, was it even remotely acceptable that these might fall into the hands of a hostile France or Germany? Before the full advent of airpower this strategic argument seemed unanswerable: Britain would be in mortal danger were Ireland to be let go. She could not become a corrosive and dangerous example to the outside world, another curfew-bell for empire, nor could she be given the possibility of the kind of strategic alliance her rebels had several times sought in the past – with Spain, with France and, latterly, with Germany. And in those immediate postwar years dissolution did not seem so remote: Bolshevism had survived and now frantically promoted revolution wherever and however it could.

106 R. H. Bruce Lockhart, Memoirs of a British Agent, London, Putnam, 1941, pp. 151–2.
107 See Andrew Selth, 'Ireland and Insurgency: The Lessons of History', in Small Wars and Insurgencies, 2, 2 (August 1991), pp. 302–5. Selth and Tony Geraghty (among others) point out that the IRA campaign also had a marked and ironic influence on British military doctrine, convincing an influential group of officers that a formation resembling the flying column could be a successful addition to conventional military forces. With Churchill's support this led to the formation and use of the Special Operations Executive (SOE) in 1940–5 and eventually to the establishment of the Special Air Service (SAS) (Tony Geraghty, The Irish War, London, HarperCollins, 2000, pp. 346–7).

The Irish administration

Standing on the imperatives of imperial doctrine, and conscious of the tides sweeping Europe, Lloyd George and his Cabinet determined to prosecute the war in Ireland to its conclusion. This meant an overhaul of the Irish government. On 12 April 1920, a new Chief Secretary, Sir Hamar Greenwood,[108] was appointed, together with a team of senior civil servants. Sir Nevil Macready took over as General Officer Commanding (GOC) British forces in Ireland, his combined experience of leadership in the military and the police commending him particularly for the post.[109] Greenwood, however, inherited an Irish administration which was markedly inferior to the Whitehall machine, and which a committee of inquiry in May 1920 found to be 'quite obsolete' as an executive body and non-existent as a means of informing and advising the Irish government on policy.[110] As a result of this report, one of the greatest of British civil servants, Sir John Anderson, was drafted in to head and reform the Castle as a department of state.[111]

As the principal advisers to government and monitors of the implementation of policy it was important that the Irish administration should have had good working relations with the army (whose line of reporting was to the War Office) and the police. The latter, notionally, came under the direct control of Dublin Castle, but as the months passed, this control became increasingly difficult to assert. The civil inability to control the police, and the growth of indiscipline in the force in turn became key elements in the breakdown of order in Ireland, the destruction of British authority, and the loss of much public support in Britain.

As noted, Macready assumed his position at about the same time that Anderson and his assistants were drafted in to take over the civil administration.[112] At the outset, Macready refused the joint appointment as head of the army and the police – even though Lloyd George, when announcing his appointment, had referred to his 'distinguished military career [and] experience as head of the

---

108 (1870–1948). A Canadian-born lawyer who became a Liberal MP in 1906. Would be a member of the British team which negotiated the Treaty. Like many coalition Liberals, subsequently switched to the Conservatives and was an MP for that party, 1924–9, and its Treasurer, 1933–8. Created Viscount, 1937.

109 (1862–1945). After successful military career became Commissioner of the London Metropolitan Police in 1918. Had commanded both police and troops during South Wales coal strikes (1910) and dealt successfully with London police strike in 1919. Persuaded by the Lord Lieutenant (Lord French, his former Commanding Officer) to accept the Irish post.

110 Report of Sir Warren Fisher (Head of the Civil Service), 12 May 1920. House of Lords: Lloyd George Papers: F/31/1/32.

111 Anderson (1882–1958) had a brilliant civil service and political career, becoming an independent MP in 1938, then Home Secretary (1939–40) and Chancellor of the Exchequer (1943–5) in the wartime government. Created Viscount Waverley, 1952.

112 Macready's appointment was announced to the Commons by Lloyd George on 29 March 1920, and he took up his post shortly afterwards (5 *Hansard*, CXXVII, col. 870). Anderson arrived in Dublin six weeks later, on 22 May.

largest police force in the world'. Macready, who had strong Liberal beliefs and, initially at least, great admiration for Lloyd George, had been troubled by the unconstitutional actions and threats of the Ulster Unionists. He was a firm supporter of Home Rule and seems to have had a distaste for police work and (certainly towards the end of his time in Ireland) politicians alike.[113] In declining to head the police as well as the army, he argued, not unreasonably, that the task of overhauling the Irish police was in itself likely to require a full-time appointment. In the light of later developments refusal of joint command was a tragic miscalculation. The demoralisation and incapacity of the Irish police, and ill-considered measures to rectify these, led to an undermining of the army's own morale and ability to do its job.

The man chosen to head the police – and the last part of the senior management of control – was not Macready's first choice. Instead of Lieutenant General Sir Edward Bulfin, Major-General Hugh Tudor[114] took the post. Despite the title (Police Adviser), which did not suggest executive authority, Tudor had complete control and responsibility. His position in the hierarchy of authority was uncertain but, backed by Lloyd George and Churchill, he soon won for himself considerable freedom of action, despite having no previous police experience and little feeling for politics. Tudor was unwilling to do what Macready most wished of him – to bring the police under the same discipline as the army. Instead, he allowed a slackness in organisational control and responsibility to develop. Ultimately disastrous, this was at first useful to Lloyd George and other Cabinet hard-liners when the police, during the summer of 1920, began to develop tactics of unofficial reprisals against the civilian population.[115]

Coercion and conciliation

British policy was to resist republicanism and as the struggle developed the doctrine emerged that this was to be done by intensified coercion, intended to procure a dominance which would allow conciliation: this was the path well trodden in the previous seventy years of policy-making. Dictated by events, however, the form, intensity and scope of coercion now left little and then no room for conciliation. The operation was envisaged and presented to domestic and international opinion as a police drive against criminal gangs, and politicians promoted this public fiction long past the time when they, together with much of the British press and public, had ceased to believe it. The military were

---

113 The evolution of his views on politicians may be gleaned from his memoir, *Annals of an Active Life*, London, Hutchinson & Co, 1924, Vol. II, *passim*.

114 (1871–1965). Wounded in both the Boer War and the Great War. Admired by the Secretary of State for War, Winston Churchill.

115 Uncertainty in lines of responsibility suited Lloyd George and Churchill who approved of the reprisal and retaliation policy of the Black and Tans and auxiliaries, and whose strongest suits were ambiguity, uncertainty and evasiveness (See Townshend, *op. cit.*, pp. 81–2, 100, 163).

reluctant to accept a policing role, drawing them into politics, and inevitably corroding morale and discipline. Presentation and operational logic, therefore, required the police to be the leading element. The RIC was reorganised and an attempt was made to reconstruct the intelligence service, which had been greatly damaged by penetration and assassination. At the same time, the Restoration of Order in Ireland Bill was introduced to provide the necessary legal powers for an attack on rebellion. Receiving the Royal Assent on 9 August 1920, this measure greatly strengthened the hand of the GOC.[116]

The British response was immediate but narrow, and failed to grasp the dynamic and expanding nature of Irish disaffection. Asquith's Liberal administration had fed a furnace of Unionist ire, especially in 1910 to 1911, and Unionist members of the coalition government wanted to rewrite history. Lloyd George, imbued with a sense of impending political extinction, was their captive. Edward Shortt had been replaced by Ian Macpherson as Irish Chief Secretary on 13 January 1919.[117] As with other coalition Liberals, Macpherson was still a reflexive Home Ruler, but this merely hardened a determination to restore law and order to Ireland: further constitutional progress depended on this.[118] Macpherson had no inducements to woo moderate or would-be moderate opinion: Ulster Unionists were firm in their unwillingness to contemplate any but the most restrictive form of Home Rule, allowing very little more than local government powers.

By the the end of 1919 a cabinet committee on Ireland, chaired by the Unionist Walter Long, and including Lord Lieutenant French as well as Macpherson, produced a new and emasculated version of Home Rule. This proposed two parliaments – one in Dublin and the other in Belfast – with a Council of Ireland consisting of members of both bodies, to assist in coordination and possibly to provide the basis for future unity. The measure[119] gave little more than local

---

116 Restoration of Order in Ireland Act, 1920 (10 & 11 Geo. V, c.31). The Act allowed the Irish government to issue regulations for the prevention of disorder, to try civilians before courts martial and to allow courts martial to take over from civil courts the conduct of business ranging from summary jurisdiction to capital cases, including coroners' proceedings and county and High Court matters. Regulations permitted trial in civil proceedings without a jury, transfer of prisoners to other parts of the UK and the retention of local authority finance where local authorities failed to discharge their obligations. Where a defendant could be subject to the death penalty a court-martial panel had to include a legally qualified member. In the discretion it conferred on the executive the Act was an open-ended and hardly constitutional statute – in spirit, if not in letter. It would not have been tolerated in peacetime Britain. Section 1(i) provided that regulations should be laid before the House 'As soon as may be after they are made'. The safeguard was an address to the King, from either House, which in practical terms meant nothing, since government (and specially the coalition) controlled both Houses. Given the life, death and property powers involved, the safeguards were disgracefully weak.

117 (1880–1937). Liberal MP Ross and Cromarty, 1911–31 (National Liberal, 1931–5). Under-Secretary for War, 1916; Irish Chief Secretary, January 1919 to April 1920; Minister of Pensions, 1920–2; Recorder of Scotland, 1931–7.

118 5 *Hansard*, CXIV, col. 1544; 3 April 1919.

119 Government of Ireland Act, 1920 (10 & 11 Geo. V, c.67).

government powers and satisfied few in Ireland. It was clearly unacceptable to nationalists, republican and constitutional, north and south. It left southern Unionists isolated – a politically unviable entity in a Catholic and nationalist state. Ulster Unionists, who had not sought their new state, were protected from all-Ireland Home Rule, but at the cost of incorporating a substantial and stubbornly irredentist minority, and the possession of a permeable and troublesome frontier. Nor were British interests protected: Sinn Féin was bound to capture the southern parliament, and would use it as before – to constitute a separatist legislature and government. Except for the desire to preserve the coalition by introducing Irish partition, it is impossible to see why this scheme became the basis of constitutional policy in Ireland.[120]

Militarisation

As the impracticality of separating the mass of southern nationalists from Sinn Féin became apparent, a primarily military policy was embraced: the restoration of order by applying sufficient force. Only the army had the necessary manpower, firepower and mobility. But militarisation had problems. Labour unrest in Britain, from the 1919 police strike to the various industrial confrontations, and behind much of this the perceived threat of Bolshevism, necessitated an adequate home garrison. A variety of pressing imperial commitments within Europe and beyond also had to be met. Nor can the psychology of the postwar army be overlooked. The country had suffered more than the largest loss of manpower in its military history: the imperial edifice, coming close to destruction, had been cracked from top to bottom. The end of the war and demobilisation had stripped the army of much of its experienced manpower, and what was available to send to Ireland was often inexperienced, or – what could be worse – brutalised by several years of trench warfare.[121] But even well-seasoned soldiers to be fully effective would have required extensive training and orientation to Irish conditions. Throughout 1920 and up to the Truce in July 1921, therefore, the British Army in Ireland was operating at or beyond its limits of doctrine, manpower and skills. This was acknowledged by General Macready in a gloomy memorandum for cabinet in May 1921. It was agreed that the army would be reinforced by at least sixteen

---

120 Béaslaí's comment is of course strongly partisan, but was shared across a surprising political spectrum in the parliamentary debate on the measure – from High Tories and Gladstonian Liberals to well-intentioned Labour: 'probably no Act of the British Parliament was treated with such universal contempt, or made so ludicrously futile, as the so-called Home Rule Act ... but it fulfilled its real purpose – the creation of Partition' (1926, Vol. 2, p. 226).

121 Following the June 1920 mutiny of 350 men of the Connaught Rangers at Jullindur, Punjab, there must have been grave doubts about the use of Irish Catholics in the Crown forces in Ireland. The mutiny had been caused by the news from Ireland, which led the men to refuse to 'soldier for England'. One mutineer was shot and sixty-one others sentenced to between two and twenty years' penal servitude. These prisoners were released after 1922 (see below, pp. 766–7).

battalions. This was to be matched by the introduction of far-reaching and draconian powers – martial law throughout nationalist Ireland, a blockade of Irish ports, mass internments, press censorship and all the apparatus of an army of occupation.[122]

Facing a population some of whom were plain-clothes, part-time soldiers, with a larger number prepared to give active aid and comfort, and a majority of apprehensive onlookers, at best neutral, and working (for the most part) within the law and under the constant scrutiny their own press and international journalism, the British could scarcely apply their advantage of strength. Intelligence was hopelessly organised – divided jealously or incompetently between police and army, Dublin and London, and none working it effectively.[123] Indeed, once a certain point in the transfer in allegiances had taken place, and numbers of the clerical classes and minor public functionaries had crossed to the other side, the IRA had won the intelligence war. Among the consequences of this victory was the effective destruction of British intelligence officers and agents.[124] Many in the ranks of public employment passed on vital information while presenting every appearance of loyalty: and how were the loyal and disloyal to be distinguished?[125]

Without adequate intelligence, moves to counter the IRA could only be blunt, frequently indiscriminate and therefore politically counterproductive. With their intelligence superiority, by contrast, the republicans were able to direct their energies and resources and nullify many moves against them. Local knowledge and connections provided the IRA with a large degree of protection against infiltration, while a campaign of assassination deterred those who might be 'turned' or who, opportunistically or from conviction, offered information to the authorities.[126] Once confidence in the ability of the Crown to protect its

---

122 Townshend, *op. cit.*, pp. 181–4; see also CAB 24/123: Wilson to Cabinet, 24 May 1921.

123 Charles Townshend's meticulous analysis of the collapse of British rule in Ireland provides several discussions of the failures to collect, collate and use intelligence (*op. cit.*, pp. 90–2, 125–8).

124 Most notably on 21 November 1920 ('Bloody Sunday'). There is a considerable literature on this, but see esp. T. Bowden, 'Bloody Sunday – A Reappraisal', *European Studies Review*, 2, 1 (1972), pp. 25–42.

125 For an account of IRA intelligence activities see Townshend (*op. cit.*, pp. 125–31 and *passim*). Michael Collins' recent biographer, James Mackay, who also brings together much information on this topic, points out that Nancy O'Brien, Collins' cousin, was selected by the Irish Permanent-Under-Secretary, Sir James MacMahon, to be his confidential clerk. Miss O'Brien, needless to say, took full advantage of her opportunities (*op. cit.*, p. 125 and ch. 8, *passim*). Nor was this the only such incident: Piaras Béaslaí's cousin Lily worked for the head of Military Intelligence (Colonel Hill Dillon) as his confidential typist – with similar results (p. 147).

126 Michael Collins was the principal figure in the campaign against informers and British agents, and authorised various of the killings. These incidents are catalogued by a number of authors (see, for example, Robert Kee, *Ourselves Alone*, Harmondsworth, Penguin, 1989, chs 7 and 8; Mackay, *op. cit.*, chs 8–11). But Collins' authority was not necessary for those killings, as is made clear in the memoirs of Tom Barry, Dan Breen, Ernie O'Malley and others. The IRA's

sources, agents and officials was lost, there was a further downward spiral in the collection of intelligence.[127] In April 1920 Lord Robert Cecil emphasised the futility of the coalition's policy: 'Let us be perfectly certain of this, that we are drifting through anarchy and humiliation to an Irish Republic.'[128]

Because it pits a force inferior in numbers and equipment against a superior enemy, guerrilla warfare must be hit and run – concentration, ambushes, raids and killings, and then dispersal, concealment and escape. To prevail, conventional forces must be well trained, with a high degree of motivation, and they must be given mobility and be supported by an operationally efficient intelligence apparatus (collection, collation, interpretation; swift, appropriate and secure dissemination). In all of these the British scarcely made the grade. Roads were not good, and in many areas were particularly apt for ambushing, necessarily slow-moving convoys. The railway system was progressively denied to Crown forces through a Sinn Féin orchestrated boycott of military supplies and troop transports (with the bonus of provoking army retaliation, thus denying the railways to irate civilians); similar actions affected shipping.[129] This was the worst possible situation for the army and police. Obliged to defend fixed points – towns, barracks, military bases, public buildings, bridges, communications centres and the like – and to patrol somewhat haphazardly over difficult terrain, it was inevitable that whole areas would be denied to them, and that even the simplest of journeys would be conducted as military expeditions. In the middle of 1921 Colonel Hugh Elles, a tank commander, submitted a dire report. The army, he reported, was bogged down – 'besieged'. He described a trip from Dublin to Cork:

> [O]ne may fly, one may go by [destroyer] and be met by escort at the docks, or one may go – very slowly – by armed train. . . . On the other hand, the population moves when, where and by whatever route it wishes. This is a curious situation for a force whose *raison d'être* in the country is to maintain order.[130]

---

success in 'sealing up' the civilian population is shown in statistics given in the Commons in April 1920. In connection with 1089 IRA attacks committed between 1 January 1919 and 29 March 1920, 210 arrests had been made. These had produced eighty-one convictions with another sixty-two awaiting trial.

127 By the autumn of 1920 the army recognised the IRA success in using the population as an intelligence source, warning that every move of the army and police 'are carefully watched at all times'. The slightest weakness would be observed and would lead to attack (GHQ confidential manual, October 1920: PRO WO. 32 *Sinn Féin and the Irish* 4308/79/Irish/708).

128 5 *Hansard*, CXXVIII, col. 966; 26 April 1920. Cecil was one of the most effective of the critics of the Government of Ireland Bill, which he repeatedly argued was a waste of time and would never be implemented in the south. He made a number of devastating attacks on government policy, and the lawlessness of both sides.

129 Townshend, *op. cit.*, pp. 69–70, 109.

130 Colonel Hugh Elles to Field Marshall Sir Henry Wilson, Chief of the Imperial General Staff, 24 June 1921: circulated to Cabinet (PRO CAB 24/124, Cabinet Paper 3075). It was not

Counter-terrorism

In the summer of 1920 the army was reinforced by eight battalions, and available motor transport was doubled. But this policy of rushing about and showing the flag barely addressed critical military and political developments. Operating entirely in guerrilla and terrorist mode, the IRA was not to be threatened, never mind eliminated, by convoy patrolling, roadblocks and searches. It certainly made some of their operations difficult and hindered the transportation of arms and explosives, as well as communication, and there was always a chance arrest or unlucky identification in a block search or street stop. But British operations were in large part a blundering around. The civil population, to whom the military display of authority was directed, was hardly likely to be impressed by troops passing through – whether or not they conducted searches and raids. Military law had been proclaimed in the south-west on 10 January 1920, and extended on 4 January 1921. In many ways this simplified operations, by giving responsibility and authority unambiguously to the military, but its enforcement required a generous deployment of soldiers. A curfew had been imposed on Dublin in February 1920, and on Cork in July, and the extra troops and their increased mobility were certainly useful in curfew patrols, and also for defending police stations and barracks. But, in the first months of Macready's command, there was little sense of carrying the fight to the IRA, or of adapting organisation, training and tactics to a counter-guerrilla campaign. General Jeudwine wrote of the gradual reassertion of government authority after the introduction of fresh powers to extend courts martial under the Restoration of Order in Ireland Act.[131] This was a considerable misunderstanding of the vulnerability of authority in these circumstances: the fires of disorder could not be extinguished one by one.

Crown forces were goaded by the seeming impunity conferred on the IRA by the constraints of legality, and from time to time this frustration murderously vented itself. Thomas MacCurtain was commandant of the Cork Brigade of

---

until the spring of 1921 that the army began to counter IRA flying columns with its own highly mobile units moving on foot across country, bivouacking and concealing themselves as necessary. This method achieved some success, but was not taken up by the high command, and was far too late in the campaign (Townshend, *op. cit.*, p. 177). O'Malley (1936, pp. 332–3) describes the British columns as 'wearing civilian clothes and equipped somewhat like our columns, or in full war kit with helios for signalling and blood hounds for tracking. . . . They slept during the day, usually, and tramped into the night.' Some of these columns would try and pass themselves off as out-of-district IRA men in order to obtain intelligence from the local population.

131 Memorandum, Major-General Sir Hugh Jeudwine, 22 April 1921: PRO CO 904/232. Jeudwine (1862–1942), of Huguenot descent, had an extensive and successful army career before being posted to Ireland to command the Fifth Division in 1919. He remained on active service until the Treaty.

the IRA; he was also Lord Mayor of Cork. Since he was an avowed Sinn Féiner, his secret life was no secret, and he received many threats and warnings. When, on 19 March 1920, an RIC man was shot near Cork, local police and army units decided to kill MacCurtain. The area around his house was cordoned off by soldiers, plain-clothes and uniformed police. In the early hours of 20 March a group of men broke into his home and shot him. MacCurtain died of his wounds shortly thereafter, and at the subsequent inquest the jury returned a verdict of murder 'organized and carried out by the Royal Irish Constabulary, officially directed by the British Government'. Lloyd George, the Lord Lieutenant, the Irish Chief Secretary and three members of the RIC were named as murderers.[132] The murder and the inquest caused a sensation throughout Ireland.

In June 1920 the extent to which some of the senior RIC staff were prepared to countenance and encourage unofficial and illegal reprisals was revealed in a widely reported speech by newly appointed Munster Divisional Commissioner, Colonel G. B. F. Smyth. Police at Listowel, Co. Kerry, had mutinied when ordered to vacate for the army their comparatively safe barracks and take up what they saw as more dangerous forward posts in out-stations. Smyth, in what was supposed to be a placatory and morale-building speech, on 18 June explained why the army had to be quartered in towns. He went on to urge retaliation against the civil population. Should a barracks be burned down then the best house in the locality was to be commandeered, 'the occupants thrown out in the gutter – the more the merrier'. Should the commands of army and police patrols not be obeyed immediately they should shoot 'and shoot with effect'. Persons approaching with their hands in their pockets or who were 'in any way suspicious' were to be shot down. Although they would occasionally shoot innocent persons, Smyth assured his audience that they were sometimes bound to get the right people: 'The more you shoot, the better I will like you, and I assure you no policeman will get into trouble for shooting any man.' He went on to hint at secret killings already carried out. A constable objected to these extraordinary instructions, and submitted his immediate resignation. Smyth ordered the man's arrest, but this was prevented by his colleagues, and indeed

---

132 *Cork Examiner*, 19 April 1920, 6f. Transcript of Coroner's Inquest, PRO CO 904/472. In an interview with the *Daily Express*, Lord French, the Lord Lieutenant, absurdly insisted that MacCurtain had been murdered by his own side for not being active enough: this story was believed by nobody and simply brought government into further disrepute (see 5 *Hansard*, CXXVIII, cols 188–9; 19 April 1920; cols 534–5, 22 April 1920). It was widely believed that District Inspector Swanzy had led the raiding party, and as a protective measure he was transferred to Lisburn, Co. Antrim. Michael Collins ordered Swanzy's death and on 22 August he was shot. His death triggered anti-Catholic riots in Lisburn and nearby towns.

another five constables also immediately resigned in protest.[133] The 'Listowel Mutiny' inevitably achieved widespread national and international publicity.[134]

On 26 June 1920, there was another instance of the breakdown of law and order. In retaliation for the IRA capture of a high-ranking officer (General Lucas, commanding the 16th Brigade), Fermoy soldiers left barracks and caused damage of £18,000 in the town.[135] Two points were worrying about this: reprisals by the military on the property of innocent civilians devastated any hope of winning over or neutralising the population at large; and politicians and others in authority grew nervous whenever soldiers ran out of control. Because of problems with army morale, the need to control any form of reprisal and – above all – the lack of results from the measures hitherto adopted, country-wide martial law increasingly found its way into official discussions.[136]

The Black and Tans

Assassinations, political uncertainty and threats to families produced a dramatic increase in police resignations: by the end of May 1920 these were running at 200 per month, as compared to some twenty-five per month before the war.[137] By the spring of 1920, a British military analysis concluded, the RIC were 'practically confined to barracks in the more remote districts and were in imminent

---

133 The account of this meeting must be treated with some caution since it was first carried in the *Irish Bulletin* (Sinn Féin's propaganda sheet) on 9 July 1920; one of the constables at the meeting handed his note of what had transpired to Arthur Griffith (Macardle, *op. cit.*, pp. 360–2). On the other hand, the substance of what was alleged to have been said was never convincingly put in doubt. Smyth certainly denied the remarks attributed to him, but fourteen constables insisted the report was correct (5 *Hansard*, CXXXI, cols 2386–91; 14 July 1920). A few weeks after the speech Colonel Smyth was shot at the County Club in Cork, supposedly with the words 'Were not your orders to shoot at sight? Well, you are in sight now, so prepare.' Bennett (*op. cit.*, p. 64) regards this speech as 'improbable', but so notorious had Smyth's Listowel address become that it is entirely possible he was shot with these words. Dan Breen had previously tried to kill Smyth, but shot someone else in his place. Three months later Breen killed Smyth's brother, Major G. O. S. Smyth, at the Fernside shoot-out (see above, p. 667) and in his memoirs described the two men as members of 'a bloodthirsty, ill-starred family' (Breen, *op. cit.*, p. 148).
134 For a republican account see 'Lee-Sider', 'Caused Mutiny in Listowel; Shot in Cork', The Kerryman, *Rebel Cork's Fighting Story 1916–21*, pp. 75–82.
135 On this incident see George Power, 'The Capture of General Lucas', ibid., pp. 43–5.
136 The political implications of nationwide martial law were formidable since it would amount to an acceptance that a form of war (rather than a police action) was being conducted (see the review of the previous several months by Major-General Sir Hugh Jeudwine: PRO CO 904/232, memorandum of 22 April 1921).
137 T. Jones, *Whitehall Diary*, ed. K. Middlemas, Oxford, Oxford University Press, 1971, Vol. 3, p. 17. The resignation rate was hardly surprising in the light of the casualties being sustained. In the province of Munster 241 policemen and soldiers were killed between 1 January 1919 and 31 March 1921. In the other three provinces 127 men were lost in the same period (memorandum, Major-General Jeudwine, 22 April 1921: PRO CO 904/232).

danger of collapse'.[138] Policing in the previous civil sense was now impossible, but policing of some sort had to be restored. The pool of willing suitable Irishmen to fill police vacancies was so small that it was necessary in the spring of 1920 to recruit non-Irish ex-servicemen. Insufficient police uniforms were available for these new men (which in itself is indicative of the level of planning and the pace of things), and so they were kitted out in a mixture of khaki and police clothing: the Black and Tans had arrived. Despite the makeshift nature of their uniforms, however, they were equipped with good motorised transport and modern weapons.

To integrate such drafts into a well-disciplined police force in times of stability and peace would hardly have been easy, but to bring them into the much-weakened RIC, and to deploy them on police duties among an ever more hostile population was to abandon normal civilian policing in favour of a paramilitary gendarmerie. This was a body which needed the tightest discipline and control, and would not get it, which needed training and would not get it, and which needed, at the very least, time to adjust to police life, but which was immediately deployed. The Black and Tans would give the screw of violence and counter-violence a further turn, and would so embitter the Irish population that the very name continues to carry a considerable political and emotional charge.

In the summer of 1920 necessity carried the government even further. At the end of July a new body was established, at first known as temporary cadets, and then special constables, and eventually the name that it would bear until its dissolution – the Auxiliary Division of the RIC. Brigadier-General Frank Crozier, an Ulster Unionist, commanded.[139] By September 1920, the division had an operational strength of about 500, in five companies. Three months later it was 1000-strong with twelve companies.[140] Recruits – all former army officers – elected their own commanders, and, outside Dublin, operated in virtually independent companies. Mobile and well armed, they were dispatched to the most disturbed parts of the country: their service background apart, this was a band of mercenaries, recruited and allowed to conduct themselves as soldiers of fortune. They had considerable military experience, and could operate with brio and

138 Ibid.
139 (1879–1937). Born in Co. Leitrim. Served in the Boer War and retired on half pay in 1908. Had been active in militant Ulster Unionism, and in 1914 had established the West Belfast Regiment of the Ulster Volunteer Force. Served throughout the Great War. A much-decorated, professional soldier, he came to Ireland fresh from anti-Bolshevik missions in Poland, Latvia and Estonia. He saw Sinn Féin as a subspecies of Bolshevism. See his article 'The RIC and the Auxiliaries' (*Manchester Guardian*, 28 March 1921, 7a–c), in which he discussed the raising of the Division and argued that it should be subject to military rather than police law and discipline.
140 Townshend, *op. cit.*, Appendix II, p. 210. Auxiliaries were paid £1 per day and were guaranteed a year's engagement (see *The Times*, 27 September 1920, 10f and 3b: 'The life is an open air one, and will doubtless appeal to many ex-officers').

initiative; they also had a number of irremediable drawbacks. The division had been raised too quickly and was trained only in the sense that it came 'pre-trained'. That being so, conventional infantry experience hardly fitted it for guerrilla warfare in Ireland, and – even had the British Army had the capacity to do so – no further training was given. Finally, although it had a considerable degree of mobility it had no clear mission and little or no intelligence capacity. All dressed up with nowhere to go, it is hard to see this force as little more than a counter-terror body in the most specific sense of that term: it is impossible to see it as part of any developing strategy; it was precedent to strategy. This narrowly conceived instrument was to strike in various rebellious districts of the country with the intention of convincing the population that the Crown's capacity for terror and the infliction of pain was as great as that of the IRA.

By the autumn of 1920 the newly strengthened RIC and Auxiliaries (and to a lesser extent the army) were regularly engaging in reprisals and had committed a number of atrocities against the civilian population.[141] In part this was a response to the IRA deployment of flying columns and an increased pace of ambushes and killings, and in part simply reflected indiscipline and lack of control.

All of this would have taxed but might have been mastered by a determined dictatorship, operating without moral or legal restraint. But unbridled counter-terror of the kind that totalitarian governments of various hues would establish and refine throughout the twentieth century was not available to British politicians and soldiers, even had they been willing to countenance it. The framework of the British ideology (if it could be called such) was conservative, constitutional and Christian, and those in authority were obliged to work within the law and to respect the property and personal rights of their Irish fellow citizens. The war pushed these religious and political beliefs beyond their limits, and both the Irish executive and the Cabinet each contained men who daily (if not hourly) shifted between the defeatist and the draconian. Thus General Macready reported that 'where [official] reprisals have taken place, the whole atmosphere of the surrounding district has changed from one of hostility to one of cringing submission'.[142] Yet four months before Macready had urged a bold gesture of generosity to begin to win over the Irish.[143] Others were less divided in themselves, with Walter Long sententiously revealing that 'the Irishman is easily dealt with if you stand up to him, but he is the worst man in the world from whom to run away'.[144] Churchill, one of the leading hawks, veered between a scarcely disguised

---

141 Professor Lee's comment is astute: 'The new recruits were too few to impose a real reign of terror, but numerous enough to commit sufficient atrocities to provoke nationalist opinion in Ireland and America, and to outrage British liberal opinion' (J. J. Lee, *Ireland 1912–1985: Politics and Society*, Cambridge, Cambridge University Press, 1989, p. 43).

142 Macready to Wilson, n.d., after 27 September 1920: Anderson Papers: PRO CO 904 188(1), f. 398.

143 Macready to Frances Stevenson, 25 May 1920: House of Lords: Lloyd George Papers: F/36/2/14.

144 Long to Lloyd George, 18 June 1920: House of Lords: Lloyd George Papers: F/33/2/27.

selective murder policy and (in the end) a curious personal sentimentality towards the Sinn Féin leaders.[145] Absorbed by postwar negotiations and settlements, and a complex political situation at home, Lloyd George did not give Ireland his full attention until mid-1920, when in public he became bellicose and dismissive of Irish national claims. In a speech (presumably intentionally) patronising and dismissive at Carnarvon on 9 October 1920 he reflected on the 'uncertainty' of the Irish temper and (referring to the form which acceptable Home Rule might take) insisted that dangerous weapons such as armies and navies were better under the control of the Imperial Parliament. After three years of restraint in the face of murder the patience of the police and army had given way 'and there has been some severe hitting back'. Appearing to justify all that was being done in the name of the Crown in Ireland, he observed that the police felt the time had come to defend themselves 'and that is what is called reprisals in Ireland'. He promised to 'restore order over there, by methods very stern'.[146] Elsewhere he denounced Irish national claims as 'a sham and a fraud'.[147] These remarks provoked predictable reactions in Ireland, but feeling in England was far from easy. Sir Edward Grey (former Foreign Secretary) and Lord Robert Cecil ob-served that Lloyd George had given a very incomplete account of the form that reprisals were taking. On 'apparently overwhelming evidence' these included the burning and destruction of buildings and other property, firing rifles and throwing bombs at random, killing and wounding civilians. Crown forces had also 'driven women and children of all ages and in all conditions of health in terror to the fields and mountains'. These acts had been revenge for 'horrible outrages' in the districts concerned, but had not been confined to the perpetra-tors. It was alleged that these acts had been sanctioned by ministers, including the Prime Minister: 'These are grave charges, and require full, open and imme-diate investigation by a constitutional tribunal.'[148]

The chances of such an inquiry were nil. Reprisals were government's blind-eye policy and had reached such a pitch, *The Times* warned, that they were creating permanent bitterness and undermining what respect remained for law and order in Ireland. As long as these illegal actions by the police continued,

145 On Churchill's enthusiasm for counter-terrorism see Townshend, *op. cit.*, p. 100; Greenwood (before he went to Ireland) wanted to shoot Sinn Féiners 'at sight and without evidence, and frightfulness generally'. Wilson wanted to proclaim certain Sinn Féiners as hostages and shoot five for every policeman murdered (Stephen Roskill, *Hankey, Man of Secrets*, London, Collins, 1970–4 (3 vols), Vol. 2, p. 153).

146 Note of speech, Under-Secretary to Lord Chancellor, 19 October 1920: Anderson Papers: PRO CO 904 188(1), ff. 519–20; *The Times*, 11 October 1920, 16a–d, *passim*.

147 D. G. Boyce, 'How to Settle the Irish Question: Lloyd George and Ireland 1916–21', in A. J. P. Taylor (ed.), *Lloyd George: Twelve Essays*, London, Hamish Hamilton, 1971, p. 15.

148 *The Times*, 14 October 1920, 10a; see also Asquith's unequivocal condemnation of outrages 'committed in the name of, or at any rate by the officers of the law in the uniforms of soldiers and policemen – not in hot blood, but calculated, planned and organised, and of which the victims had been innocent, inoffensive civilians' (ibid., 30 October 1920, 12c).

the public would assume either that government regarded them with 'a certain lenience' or that it could not stop them.[149] These fears were confirmed when, in response to the killing of the popular District Inspector Burke (who had been celebrating his promotion at a local pub) on 20 September and the wounding of his brother, an RIC sergeant, Black and Tans attacked the town of Balbriggan, Co. Dublin. Twenty-five houses were set on fire, together with shops and a hosiery factory; firearms were discharged and hand grenades thrown. Two young men were bayoneted to death.[150] Two days later there was a similar incident in Co. Clare, when, following an ambush in which five of their comrades were killed, the RIC (regulars and Black and Tans) set fire to buildings in Ennistymon, Lahinch and Miltown Malbay and killed three people.[151]

These and many other outbreaks and reprisals by the RIC, Black and Tans, auxiliaries and army caused alarm and indignation in England.[152] The *Manchester Guardian* spoke for many when it condemned the burning of the town of Mallow by Black and Tans as the 'largest act of incendiarism yet performed by any of these mutineers' and compared it to the German atrocity at Louvain.[153] And among those who should have been the Crown's most loyal supporters in Ireland indignation sometimes boiled over. Opening the Ennis Quarter Sessions Judge Bodkin condemned the outrages on both sides. The IRA's actions 'shamed their

149 *The Times*, 20 September 1920, 12e.
150 *Freeman's Journal*, 22 September 1920, 3a–b and 5a–b. A deputation led by the local clergy went to Dublin Castle to plead for protection.
151 *Freeman's Journal*, 24 September 1920, 5a–b; *Irish Independent*, 23 September 1920, 5d. It was alleged that dum-dum bullets had been used in the ambush, creating 'a gruesome and bloody sight'. In none of the IRA war memoirs is the use of dum-dum ammunition mentioned (though it hardly would be). This type of bullet which expanded and broke caused horrific wounds, and was prohibited by articles 22 and 23 of the 1907 Hague Convention. Bennett, describing this incident in his history of the Black and Tans, and drawing on repeated statements in the Commons by Greenwood, asserts that dum-dums were used at Ennistymon and Lahinch (*op. cit.*, p. 94). Tim Pat Coogan and George Morrison point out that the Irish Volunteers in 1914 inadvertently brought outdated ammunition of the type prohibited by the Hague Convention. (*op. cit.*, p. 85). Certainly given their soldiering background, the sights of dum-dum injuries would have particularly provoked the Black and Tans and auxiliaries. For a republican account of the ambush at Rineen and the reprisals at Lahinch and Ennistymon, see Ernie O'Malley, *Raids and Rallies*, Dublin, Anvil Books, 1982, ch. 4.
152 Because of the press restrictions and penalties under the Restoration of Order (Ireland) Act (ROIA) Britain-based journalists were freer to report than their Irish colleagues. Consideration was given to a prosecution of Hanna Sheehy Skeffington under the Act because of an interview she gave to the *Daily Herald* (14 December 1920, 2a) claiming that Crown forces were ill-treating women. The case went to the Director of Public Prosecutions, who concluded that it would not be wise to proceed: 'this woman is quite capable of instancing with names and dates certain of the incidents mentioned'. If she pleaded justification there would have to be adjournments and investigations. But, the DPP concluded, 'Knowing the record of the lady I feel pretty sure that she will give us the opportunity [to prosecute] before very long' (PRO HO 144/1584/20).
153 30 September 1920, 6b.

common humanity', while the 'reprisals by Crown forces should be known by their legal names . . . arson and murder'.[154]

There can be no doubt, however, that some ministers and senior officials were satisfied with these developments. General Tudor, the police commander, told Sir Henry Wilson that the police, Black and Tans and intelligence officers were all carrying out reprisal killings on those they identified as Sinn Féin and IRA. In his diary for 23 September 1920, Wilson recorded that 'Winston saw very little harm in this, but it horrifies me.'[155] Reviewing the documents and memoirs a distinct impression emerges that Lloyd George and the hawks fully realised what was going on in Ireland, and saw it as a form of morally justified or at least politically necessary repression. It would eventually have to be reined in, but in the meantime, and until it worked, whatever had to be done would be done to mislead, placate and keep the lid on English opinion. The Irish administration was bare-faced and brass-necked in explaining away or denying reprisals. Sometimes the magnitude of the incident passed beyond the skills of evasion. The sack of Balbriggan was raised in the Commons a month after the event (Parliament had been in recess) and occasioned a remarkable observation from Greenwood. He conceded that the incident had taken place. Up to 150 Black and Tans had gone to the town determined to revenge their comrade. He had been unable to discover which of the men had killed or who had set fire to the town. To this admission of conspiracy and cover-up he added the remarkable statement, which achieved instant notoriety: 'I have yet to find one authenticated case of a member of this auxiliary division being accused of anything but the highest conduct characteristic of them.'[156]

Besides waiting for the hard medicine to work, there was a feeling that one had to pull back on the reins with great care. Ireland was in a state of undeclared but undoubted war, the Crown forces contained many violent and war-hardened men, there had been a police strike in England the year before, and the notion of having to deploy the army to contain or disarm a police mutiny was a nightmare. Hamar Greenwood, the Irish Chief Secretary, reported to Cabinet on 27 September 1920 that police discipline needed 'very delicate and sympathetic handling in view of the provocation which the Police have received and the extreme tension of feeling which now prevails among all ranks'.[157]

154 *The Times*, 14 October 1920, 10a.
155 *Cit.* Townshend, *op. cit.*, p. 116, n. 76. Churchill's attitude to reprisals and retaliation in Ireland was well known. During the debate on Labour's censure motion (20 October 1920) Lord Robert Cecil observed: 'I know the Secretary of State for War [Churchill] has no respect for law or justice.' Despite protests he refused to withdraw this statement (5 *Hansard*, CXXXIII, col. 975).
156 5 *Hansard*, CXXXIII, cols 938 and 947; 20 October 1920.
157 Chief Secretary for Ireland (CSI) Weekly Surveys, 20 September 1920: PRO CAB 27 108/185.

The final months

Ambushes and killings by the IRA continued at an undiminished pace, including Bloody Sunday and the Macroom ambush. Between 1 August and 1 November 1920, sixty-five policemen and twenty-three soldiers were killed.[158] Retaliation was now scarcely restrained or disguised, and consisted of burning and looting homes and commercial premises, shootings (including innocent bystanders), beatings, public floggings and other instances of torture. On the night of Saturday, 11 December 1920, Crown forces set extensive fires in the principal streets of Cork, causing millions of pounds' worth of damage and severely disrupting the city's economy: there was also a great deal of looting and brutality.[159] This was a reprisal for an IRA ambush in which an Auxiliary was killed at Dillon's Cross, near the city.[160] Official explanations included Greenwood's absurd claim that the inhabitants had fired their own town. An army inquiry was duly instituted, but its report was not published. On 29 December the British Labour Party published its own inquiry into events in Ireland, strongly condemning actions by Crown forces (which it meticulously documented), and calling for negotiations between the government and Sinn Féin.[161] Earlier in the autumn Asquith had made clear the objections of the independent Liberals to the coalition's Irish policy, arguing that its logic was a reconquest of the island and its forcible subjugation. Though perhaps not beyond British powers, this course, he asserted, 'will never be sanctioned by the will or the conscience of the British people'.[162] Lloyd George and his Cabinet were seemingly impervious to these and other criticisms and proposals, and were evidently determined to ride them out. On 10 December, when he told the Commons that he was prepared to hold discussions with certain members of the Dáil as individuals, Lloyd George made it clear that the government's position was unchanged. He also announced a stepping-up of the anti-IRA campaign – an expansion of

158 5 *Hansard*, CXXXIV, col. 1380; 11 November 1920.
159 For a republican account of this episode see F. O'Donoghue, 'The Sacking of Cork', The Kerryman, *Rebel Cork's Fighting Story 1916–21*, pp. 47–58.
160 *Irish Independent*, 13 December 1920, 5a–c; 14 December, 3 (photographs), 5a–d; *Cork Examiner*, 13 December 1920, 5a–g. Dillon's Cross itself was the subject of an extended arson attack. Fire reprisals on a smaller scale had been going on in Cork and surrounding areas for some weeks.
161 On 11 November 1920, speaking in the Commons on behalf of the Labour Party, W. Adamson (leader of the Parliamentary Labour Party) anticipated its findings. What had being going on in Ireland had done almost irreparable damage to Britain's international standing: 'Day after day, as we open our newspapers, and read the terrible accounts of the things that are occurring in Ireland, we are absolutely ashamed of our methods of governing that country' (5 *Hansard*, CXXXIV, col. 1414). Adamson (1863–1936) was Secretary for Scotland, January to November 1924 and again 1929–31.
162 *The Times*, 5 October 1920, 11f.

the martial law zone and new offences which would be liable to the death penalty.[163]

But the tide of unease in Britain was rising and could not be ignored. Unable or unwilling to stop unofficial reprisals, or to escape the suspicion that it was encouraging them, government decided to take them over and make them official. The first of what would eventually be 150 official reprisals was taken on 1 January 1921 at Midleton, Co. Cork. Seven houses were destroyed because the residents had failed to give information about a nearby ambush in which three policemen had been killed. One hour's notice was given; permission was given to remove valuables, but not furniture.[164] Whatever the political sympathies of those who lost their homes, the authorities must have realised the deadly danger in which residents would have placed themselves had they given information about an impending IRA operation. One view of this was that government, which notionally was supposed to be protecting them, was unable to do so, and was punishing them for its own incapacity: in effect exposing them to a double peril. But minding one's own business was not to be permitted, and on 1 January 1921, the military governor of Cork (Major-General Strickland) issued a proclamation to that effect. The civil population was directed to refuse aid and comfort to the IRA and to report persons suspected of being in possession of arms. Neutrality was deemed to be inconsistent with loyalty and would incur heavy sanctions.[165] In response to attacks on military vehicles in Dublin and elsewhere, leading nationalists and republicans were carried on board army lorries, tied or chained in a prominent position. This was not permitted under martial or civil law, but nothing seems to have been done to stop it.[166]

Fighting had extended into the towns. Attacks on the military and police in Dublin were incessant, as was arson and other means of destroying supplies and property. 'The roar of bombs, and the report of guns,' recalled Béaslaí, 'were familiar sounds to the ears of all, by day and by night, and the most peaceful and unmilitary citizen learned to distinguish between the sound of a revolver, a rifle, a machine gun and a bomb.'[167] Plain-clothes police, armed and moving around the city in squads, were brought in to help counter these attacks; Sinn Féin alleged that these squads were authorised to kill, and to conduct other extra-judicial

---

163 5 *Hansard*, CXXXV, cols 2601–11; 10 December 1920. The non-negotiable points (announced on 16 August) were: no secession from the United Kingdom of Ireland or any part of Ireland; the six counties to be a separate issue; and protection for the security of the United Kingdom (5 *Hansard*, CXXXIII, col. 694).

164 *Irish Independent*, 3 January 1921, 5a.

165 *The Westminster Gazette*, 3 January 1921, 1d.

166 Béaslaí, 1926, Vol. 2, p. 15.

167 Ibid., Vol. 2, pp. 154 and 158. Contemporary newspapers, both in layout and content, support Béaslaí's recollection entirely.

operations against suspects. Some of the government's statements seemed to go out of the way to encourage this view.[168] The army and police conducted block searches, closing off sections of towns with trucks and barbed wire, 'combing out' persons and property. These measures generally seem to have allowed escapes and were in any event announced by the arrival of several hundred troops. Without reasonably precise intelligence blanket sweeps were not a useful deployment of resources. Far more successful were the foot patrols introduced in the spring of 1921. These moved through the city streets stopping and searching pedestrians. This was the most effective tactic yet adopted in the anti-IRA campaign. These patrols were more difficult to anticipate and avoid than the round-ups by noisily heralded lorry-borne troops, and mingling with pedestrians and having available all the natural cover of the streets was much more difficult to attack.[169] A resident of Dublin in those months recalled: 'It was an atmosphere of war, but of war conducted amid all the outward trappings of peace. Men and women went about their daily affairs to the accompaniment of grenade explosions and small arms fire.'[170]

By this time the whole southern part of Ireland was under martial law.[171] By the end of February 1921, over 2000 men were being held in Irish internment camps.[172] On 1 February executions began for offences under martial law regulations (as distinct from civil law). Found guilty by court martial of possessing arms and ammunition, Cornelius Murphy was shot at Cork.[173] After legal wrangling, six more men were shot at Victoria Barracks, Cork, for the same offence at the

---

168 To select but one of many, distinguished only by its provocative cynicism James O'Neill and Patrick Blake were brought before a Dublin court martial charged with murder. They were acquitted on 19 November 1920 and on returning home to Limerick the following day were killed, allegedly by Crown forces. Hamar Greenwood acknowledged the murders and commented that 'The police have been unable to obtain any information as to the perpetrators of this crime, but are still making investigations' (5 *Hansard*, CXXXV, col. 649; 25 November 1920). Such a statement shows that he had passed caring about credibility.

169 Béaslaí, 1926, Vol. 2, p. 234.

170 Donal O'Kelly, 'The Dublin Scene: War Amid the Outward Trappings of Peace', The Kerryman, *With the IRA in the Fight for Freedom: 1919 to the Truce*, Tralee, The Kerryman, 1953, pp. 25–30, p. 27.

171 This left little room to make the government's case. The tone of its public relations may be discerned from the draft preamble to the declaration of martial law: 'Irishmen! Understand this: Great Britain has no quarrel with Irishmen; her sole quarrel is with crime, outrage and disorder; her sole object in declaring MARTIAL LAW is to restore peace to a distracted and unhappy country; her sole enemies are those who have countenanced, inspired and participated in rebellion, murder and outrage' (PRO CO 904/232).

172 5 *Hansard*, CXXXVIII, col. 2023; 3 March 1921.

173 *Freeman's Journal*, 2 February 1921, 3d. The following day, however, Joseph Murphy (no relation) had his death sentence (for murder) commuted to life penal servitude (ibid., 3 February 1921, 5a–b). For a description of procedure in such courts and of military tribunals in martial law areas see Campbell, *op. cit.*, pp. 69–101.

end of the month.[174] Later that day the IRA shot six British soldiers in retaliation. More executions followed, however, and on 14 March 1921 six men were hanged in Dublin – four for treason and two for being involved in the killing of British officers on Bloody Sunday.[175] Far from deterring republican sympathy and activities, the March executions occasioned a day of mourning in Dublin, with some 20,000 people assembling outside Mountjoy Prison as the executions were conducted, two at a time, at hourly intervals.[176] In a country with such a strong sense of family, the popular imagination focused on the bereaved mother and father. Each time the bells tolled for an execution the crowd fell to its knees and began to pray. Dorothy Macardle is to be believed (and is supported by news photographs) when she writes of the crowd: 'emotions of grief and anger were overpowering. An impression remained which nothing could efface.'[177]

Between 1 November 1920 and 7 June 1921, when Patrick Maher became the last man to be executed in the Anglo-Irish war, twenty-four men were executed. Little or nothing was accomplished militarily, while from first to last anti-British and pro-republican sentiment consolidated. The first execution in the series – the 18-year-old medical student Kevin Barry – set the pattern. Barry

174 The six (who were shot in pairs at fifteen-minute intervals) were Thomas O'Brien, Daniel O'Callaghan, John Lyons, Timothy McCarthy, Patrick O'Mahony and John Allen (*Irish Independent*, 1 March 1921, 5a–c). The Very Revd Canon O'Sullivan, who had acted as chaplain during the executions, told the press that 'They died like brave men. They were like schoolboys going on a holiday, and they marched firmly to their doom.' The impact of such words, and such an image, can be imagined. The Roman Catholic clergy and hierarchy were now in the majority firmly behind the republican cause. John Allen had appealed to the civil courts, but the Irish King's Bench had ruled that a state of war existed and that therefore Sir Nevil Macready was entitled to exercise life-and-death powers in the martial law area. For the duration of the state of war, the High Court declared, it could not 'control the military authorities, or question any sentence imposed in the exercise of martial law' (*King v. Murphy*, *Irish Report*, 1921, II, 190–201; *King v. Allen*, *Irish Report*, 1921, II, 272). See also 271: 'The proceedings of a military Court derive their sole justification and authority from the existence of actual rebellion, and the duty of doing whatever may be necessary to quell it, and to restore peace and order.' In *Rex v. Murphy* the High Court held that notwithstanding an erroneous decision by the court martial on a point of law, the death sentence on Murphy should stand (*Irish Report*, 1921, II). In this instance however, General Macready commuted Murphy's sentence to penal servitude for life.

175 A third man, Frank Teeling, had also been sentenced for his part in the Bloody Sunday killings but had escaped with Ernie O'Malley in January. Patrick Moran (one of those hanged) had been offered, but refused, the opportunity to escape (O'Malley, 1936, *op. cit.*, pp. 264–75).

176 *Irish Independent*, 15 March 1921, 5a–c; *Freeman's Journal*, 15 March 1921, 5a–c. The six were Thomas Whelan, Patrick Doyle, Patrick Moran, Frank Flood, Thomas Bryan and Bernard Ryan. The men were executed in pairs at 6, 7 and 8 a.m. Religion and politics intermingled in last statements – dangerously so for British authority. Whelan the night before had said 'I feel a taste of Heaven already' and Moran 'I would not be here but for God's will' (ibid., 5c).

177 *Op. cit.*, p. 425. Around this time Eileen MacGrane, in whose possession various of Collins' papers had been found, became the first woman since 1916 to be sentenced by court martial (Béaslaí, 1926, Vol. 2, p. 153).

had been sentenced to death for his part in an ambush on a military ration party in Dublin.[178] One of the soldiers was killed in the resulting firefight, and Barry was taken at the scene with a loaded pistol. Before his execution Barry signed an affidavit claiming that he had been tortured during interrogation in order to extract the names of his companions. There was no doubt that he was guilty as charged, however, or that he was liable for the sentence imposed upon him. Private Patrick Washington, the soldier who had been killed (not six soldiers, as Dorothy Macardle states), was the same age as himself.[179] The anger of the military authorities is understandable, but it would have been more politic to reprieve Barry on grounds of his age. The great difficulty, no doubt, was police and army morale – already very mercurial. But then again, that was the point: politics had given way to military imperatives, and the army was trained and equipped for one thing only – the destruction of opposition by the application of superior force. The psychopolitical dimensions of armed conflict were greatly simplified or ignored altogether. A crowd of some 2000, praying and deeply moved, gathered at the prison on the morning of Barry's execution, and his entry into the pantheon of Irish nationalism was immediate.[180]

The effect of the Barry execution was doubtless intensified when, six weeks later, a parish priest and a young man of the district, Timothy Crowley, were murdered by a party of Auxiliaries at Dunmanway in Co. Cork. The 73-year-old Canon Magner had received a threatening order to toll the bell of his church on Armistice Day. His murder was presumably the penalty for failing to comply with instructions; the young man was killed simply because he was there. The whole incident was witnessed by a magistrate, who insisted on an official inquiry. In a reprise of the Skeffington killing five years before, the Auxiliary who had fired the shots was found guilty but insane. No other members of the party were charged. The effect of the murder and farcical trial can be imagined: even the Cabinet was disturbed.[181]

The British government had allowed a momentum to develop in Ireland, seeing this fierceness and energy as a military instrument which could be bent to its purpose. The spirit of indiscipline which affected the RIC, Black and Tans, Auxiliaries and even army units at times looked more like counter-revolution than mere counter-terror. General Crozier, who had commanded the Auxiliaries, resigned on 19 February 1921 when he discovered that subordinates whom he

---

178 For an account of the raid on 20 September, see the *Freeman's Journal*, 21 September 1920, 6f–g; *Irish Independent*, 21 September, 5a–b.

179 *The Times*, 2 November 1920, 12a; *Irish Independent*, 2 November 1920, 5a–b; 5 *Hansard*, CXXXIV, cols 705–10; 4 November 1920.

180 On leaving the prison the chaplain all but confirmed Barry as a holy martyr, declaring 'I never met a braver man. He died with prayers on his lips for every one – his enemies and all' (*The Times*, 2 November 1920, 12a).

181 Macardle, *op. cit.*, pp. 418–19; Timothy Michael Healy, *Letters and Leaders of My Day*, London, Thornton Butterworth, 1928, Vol. 2, pp. 620–1.

had removed for indiscipline and crimes had been covertly reinstated. He argued that the dismissed Auxiliaries had, in effect, blackmailed the British government, and their reinstatement was a precaution against public disclosures in England about what had been going on in Ireland.[182] His account of events is full of plots and double-dealing by politicians. But even discounting the temper and tempo of his narrative, parts of Ireland had come close to being free-fire zones and places of private enrichment for many Black and Tans and auxiliaries. This criminal behaviour appalled the British officer corps – it brought shame and discredit upon the army, and caused problems when soldiers were rotated out of Ireland to other duties. The shameless and cynical denials and evasions of Greenwood, Lloyd George and other ministers confirmed military contempt for 'the frocks'.

If the army was a pillar of the Establishment, the Church was little less. On 22 February 1921, the Archbishop of Canterbury, Dr Randall T. Davidson, in a Lords speech, denounced the government's Irish policy in unstinting terms, prefacing his remarks by an unequivocal condemnation of the 'insane wickedness' of the murderous gangs with which Crown forces had to contend. Dr Davidson quoted Judge Bodkin, the Irish County Court judge who had spoken out on the events at Lahinch on 22 September 1920. It was true that the Sinn Féin outrages were worse than those of the Black and Tans: 'We not only condemn them, but we exhaust every epithet in denouncing them.' But he drew a distinction between the wrongdoing of irresponsible individuals and those holding 'official and authorised positions', asserting 'you cannot justifiably punish wrongdoing by lawlessly doing the like'. There was a growing uneasiness in the country, and 'unutterable mischief' was being done overseas.[183]

A fortnight after the Archbishop's speech Crown forces obligingly supplied an example of the official lawlessness in question. Since Sinn Féin had made a sweep of local government as well as parliamentary seats it followed that most local officials were Sinn Féin or IRA activists. From their intelligence the army and police knew of these men's secret affiliations, but without evidence were powerless to act through the legal processes. This frustration engendered some atrocious acts, such as the MacCurtain murder a year previously. The intense national and international reactions to this killing were not sufficient barriers when on 7 March 1921, George Clancy, Mayor of Limerick, Michael O'Callaghan,

---

182 Frank Percy Crozier, *Ireland for Ever*, London, Jonathan Cape, 1932, pp. 129–33; *Impressions and Recollections*, London, T. Werner Laurie, 1920, pp. 255–62. Although Crozier's account of events was later discredited to some extent as the result of a civil suit, his denunciation of the indiscipline and crimes of Crown forces had an understandable impact on opinion in Ireland, Britain and abroad.

183 5 *Hansard*, XLIV [Lords], cols 79–91, *passim*; 22 February 1921. Timothy Healy also drew a distinction between the crimes of Sinn Féin, and those of Crown forces: 'The sins of ignorant youths without experience or training are to be judged differently from those of an organised administration preaching law and order in the King's name. . . . The Sinns at least don't pretend to rob or kill victims for their good' (*op. cit.*, Vol. 2, p. 643).

a former mayor, and an IRA man, James O'Donoghue, were all murdered in their homes – Clancy and O'Callaghan in front of their wives.[184] There was a pro-forma and inconclusive military inquiry and in the Commons Lloyd George stoked further Irish fury when he employed the shop-worn lie that Clancy and O'Callaghan had been murdered by their own people.[185]

Endgame

There had to be a change in Ireland, and Lloyd George had to choose. The fiction that this was simply a policing operation had become untenable and was threatening to become disastrous. One possibility was to talk to the Irish leaders, and Lloyd George signalled, with varying degrees of conviction, his willingness so to do throughout the autumn of 1920. The difficulty, of course, was to find a basis for negotiation, and this meant within the government as well as with the other side: altogether this path was strewn with many difficulties. The alternative – and it must daily have become clear it was the only one – was to treat the Irish insurrection as a full-blown war, put the army in control, and take all necessary measures. Although he headed a sometimes shaky coalition Cabinet, Lloyd George faced a Commons of which he was undoubted master.[186] Provided he got ministerial support, in other words, he could carry through whatever measures he wished. But the way forward was far from clear, and rather late in the day Lloyd George sought to keep his options open. Even while indicating a willingness to talk, in December 1920 he had steered Cabinet agreement for a four-county introduction of martial law.[187] Although General Macready was not allowed to go as far as he wished, particularly in the use of the firing squad, a severe regime was imposed, including street and district searches, curfew, the use by patrols of prisoners as hostages, reprisals and other measures of intensification of control which searched, sifted, controlled and intimidated – and of course antagonised – the civilian population.

184 *The Times*, 8 March 1921, 12a; *Irish Independent*, 8 March 1921, 5a–c. Clancy (1879–1921) seems to have been active on the political and cultural side of republicanism, rather than the IRA. He was well known as a promoter of the Irish language, and had taken a leading part in de Valera's East Clare election. Elected Mayor of Limerick in January 1921. Michael O'Callaghan (1880–1921) had preceded Clancy as Mayor and had for many years been a municipal councillor. He had, during his term of office, repeatedly been threatened with death and rarely slept at home.

185 5 *Hansard*, CXXXIX, cols 256–7; 8 March 1921; CXL, col. 422; 7 April 1921. The Irish Attorney General had stated that 'The motive for these abominable crimes is very obscure'. Lloyd George was unequivocal in attributing blame to the IRA.

186 In the 1918 general election independent Liberals (as distinct from those who supported Lloyd George) were all but eliminated (twenty-six independents against 134 coalition Liberals). The Labour Party had risen from thirty-nine to fifty-nine, but this was insignificant in the face of a combined Unionist–Liberal block of 473. Irish nationalist non-Sinn Féin representation had dwindled to a handful.

187 Townshend, *op. cit.*, pp. 134–5; see also Thomas Jones, *Whitehall Diary: Ireland 1918–1925*, London, Oxford University Press, 1971, pp. 41–4.

By mid-1921 it was plain that counter-insurgency measures had not worked. Elections under the partitioning Government of Ireland Act were to be held on 25 May. With the six north-eastern counties removed, Sinn Féin would sweep the remainder of Ireland: there was no possibility that the Dublin Parliament would assemble on the scheduled date, 28 June. The Act, it is true, had provided (under Section 72) a fall-back position in the form of direct rule as a Crown Colony should less than half the new members agree to take the oath. The war would continue indefinitely. In that event further military measures could be taken, some of which had proved efficacious in the Boer War. Troop levels were to be more than doubled, and used to run blockades across the country, to intern tens of thousands of suspects; to intensify, in other words, the searching, sifting and control of movement. All of this would be backed by country-wide martial law and severe punishments, including the death penalty. Press censorship would throw a veil over the workings of this repressive machinery.[188] This might have worked, and certainly after 1922 the Free State was to proceed some way along that path in its suppression of the anti-Treaty forces. But the Free State government was Irish and had the support of the overwhelming majority of the Irish population, whereas a British military government might prevail, but could never succeed.

Having attempted to start talks with various pre-conditions – the surrender of IRA arms, the exclusion of Ulster (and of Michael Collins), the denial of independence and a republic[189] – on 24 June the British government invited Eamon de Valera as 'the chosen leader of the great majority in Southern Ireland', together with Sir James Craig (now Premier of Northern Ireland) to a conference in London: no pre-conditions were set. Two events had preceded this historic move: the total victory outside Ulster of Sinn Féin in the May general elections; and the King's speech on opening the new Northern Ireland Parliament on 22 June. The first was a clear enough victory, but it is worth noting that in the twenty-six counties Sinn Féin candidates were almost entirely unopposed, and this may be read in different ways considering the fraught nature of the times. In the six counties a pact between Sinn Féin and the Nationalists (now the last electoral remnant of Redmond's party) ensured that twelve of their candidates won seats. Outside Ulster the only opposition to Sinn Féin

---

188 See Townshend, *op. cit.*, pp. 134, 147–8 and 195–6. A document which came into Collins' hands in the weeks after the Truce suggested that some at least in British military circles were thinking along counter-insurgency lines which US forces would use in Vietnam some fifty years later: versions of 'strategic-villages' into which the non-combatant civil population would be gathered; and 'free-fire' zones allowing all those outside these protected settlements to be deemed hostile elements (Béaslaí, 1926, Vol. 2, pp. 268–9). One of those concerned in this scheme, which was to be implemented should the Truce break down, was Andy Cope, Assistant Under-Secretary at Dublin Castle, and the Dublin go-between for the British and Irish sides.

189 Emissaries of varying degrees of authority and secrecy operated throughout the spring of 1921, and the two sides also staked out their positions in newspaper statements and interviews and (in Lloyd George's case) parliamentary statements (see Macardle, *op. cit.*, ch. 45).

came from four members returned for Trinity College, Dublin and two Dublin Co. senators. Labour, which could have expected to pick up a reasonable number of seats, abstained in favour of Sinn Féin representing the national interest. Sinn Féin could credibly claim to have been endorsed as the government of Ireland, and its armed wing as Ireland's army.[190]

A decisive move towards a negotiated settlement came with the King's speech on the opening of the new Northern Ireland Parliament. This arose from the King's deep unease and from outside advice. There had been conversations between Tom Casement (brother of Roger Casement) and General Jan Smuts. The latter was attending the Imperial Conference in London, and with the consent of de Valera, Tom Casement raised with him (and other delegates) the Irish imbroglio. Knowing that his speech to the Northern Ireland Parliament would be closely scrutinised for signs of political movement, the King consulted Smuts, who helped prepare a speech which was more to the King's satisfaction than the original government draft. This was delivered on 22 June and two days later a letter was sent to de Valera, inviting him to London to discuss terms for peace.[191] De Valera insisted that before talks could begin there should be a truce, and after the intervention of Lord Midleton, leader of the southern Unionists, this was agreed. On the afternoon of 9 July the terms of that truce were agreed between Macready and IRA representatives. Advantageous to the IRA, it had the effect of freezing the military situation in Ireland (though behind the scenes both sides prepared for renewed war).[192] The Truce confirmed that the British had been fought to a standstill – certainly within the existing state of law and military deployment. The republican cause was immensely strengthened, with the veteran parliamentarian Timothy Healy conceding that Sinn Féin 'had won in three years what we did not win in forty'.[193] De Valera had taken up

---

190 Lord Salisbury quoted Old Ireland (which he described as a leading Sinn Féin journal): 'The George-Greenwood story about a "murder gang" presupposed that the IRA acted independently of Dáil Eireann. Ireland, in fact, stands by the gunman' (5 Hansard, XLV (Lords), cols 662–3; 21 June 1921).

191 The decisive strategic factor was the establishment of an Ulster Parliament and through it the resolution of the Ulster issue. Politically, Chamberlain (as leader of the Unionist portion of the coalition) and Birkenhead were probably decisive in urging Lloyd George to take advantage of the King's speech (Frank Pakenham, Peace by Ordeal, London, Geoffrey Chapman, 1962, pp. 76–9).

192 Townshend (op. cit., pp. 198–9) points out that the IRA continued to drill, train, recruit and procure arms. Up to 10 September there were 128 breaches of the Truce in the Martial Law Area, a pace which increased thereafter. As various trials in Britain would show, IRA arms procurement continued at full pace, and by all means. Macready protested that the Truce had allowed the IRA to transform itself from a 'disorganized rabble' into 'a well-disciplined, well-organized and well-armed force'. He was of course closing his eyes to the army's preparations for a resumption of hostilities on a considerably greater scale.

193 As for the methods, Healy, a senior member of the Bar, fell back on the usual clichés: 'You cannot "make revolutions with rose water", or "omelettes without breaking eggs"' (op. cit., Vol. 2, p. 640).

open quarters at Dublin's Mansion House, and a number of key republican figures who were prisoners or internees were released to assist him. Thirty-four members of the Dáil remained in custody, however, and there was no provision for a general release.[194]

Five months elapsed between the Truce and the signing of the Treaty which secured Irish independence. Civilian rejoicing throughout the country was not universally shared by IRA militants, some of whom did not understand why a truce had been agreed and who (with good reason) feared a fatal loss of momentum were it prolonged.[195] As is well known, the Irish side was bitterly divided on the terms of the Treaty, which was signed in London in the early hours of 6 December 1921. De Valera and other important figures rejected the Treaty and in the Dáil debates argued for its repudiation. In a close-run vote on 7 January 1922, the Dáil nevertheless accepted the Treaty by a majority of sixty-four to fifty-seven. On 14 January 1922, sixty pro-Treaty members of the Dáil, elected to the Dublin Parliament in the May 1921 elections, and four members from Trinity College convened and elected the provisional government which was to see through the execution of the Treaty from the Irish side, to draw up a constitution and prepare for elections, and in general prepare for the establishment of the Irish Free State. Two days later the Lord Lieutenant received Michael Collins and his colleagues at Dublin Castle and authority passed from the British to the provisional government. The withdrawal of British forces began at once; the several hundred internees had been released from their camps in Ireland and on 12 January an amnesty had freed almost 400 persons convicted of political offences before the Truce, including a number under sentence of death. Those convicted in Britain or convicted of offences since the signing of the Truce continued, for the time being, to be detained.

Within months a state of civil war would engulf the new state. Authority had decayed rapidly in the period between the Truce and the Treaty. The IRA was not subject to the military controls of living in barracks, and it had lost much of the enforced discipline of war. To return these men to the regularities and routine of civilian life would have taxed a strong and wealthy government, and the Irish Free State was neither of these. Authority was re-established, but at a cost that still marks Irish national life. The prisons would fill up again and the executioner be put to his trade. A great stream of political aspiration had taken a new course, but its smaller tributaries would continue to deposit republicans in

---

194 In June 1921 there were forty-two IRA men under sentence of death. Michael Comyn, KC (described by Macardle as Senior Counsel to the IRA) applied for a Writ of Prohibition to stop courts martial from proceeding, arguing that they were illegal tribunals. The application was rejected by the Irish courts and was appealed to the Lords. While that appeal was pending the army suspended executions and the King also requested that executions should cease in Ireland (Macardle, *op. cit.*, p. 465, n. 8).

195 See O'Malley, 1936, p. 336; *The Singing Flame*, Dublin, Anvil Books, 1978, chs 1 and 2; Breen, *op. cit.*, pp. 166–7.

Irish and English prisons until and beyond the new millennium. With the establishment of an independent Irish state the politics of imprisonment were drastically redefined, but certain dynamics remained. From time to time prisons in Ireland and Britain would become cockpits for bitterly fought political, moral and psychological contests. Prisoners and their sympathisers would ever appeal to the broader community with the strength and certitude of the vanquished. Ireland, which had refined and elaborated this form of struggle, would have to find a way of establishing and maintaining democratic authority against the mandate of dead and living martyrs and of those for whom intention transmuted crime from the base to the noble, and guilt to axiomatic innocence.

15

BANG AND WHIMPER, 1919–22

Problem and opportunity

As public administration – particularly criminal justice – began to crack in Ireland, the Irish government looked to Britain for immediate practical support. For all the reasons discussed above, the Irish prisons were encumbered with particular difficulties. Staff could be suborned or intimidated, or were sympathetic to the republican cause. Visiting committees included a proportion of local politicians or their nominees, frequently of uncertain loyalty. Political and security problems also arose from the easy assembly of large crowds outside the prisons at times of crisis, and from the comparative ease with which contraband and correspondence could be smuggled. While no general transfer of internees, convicts and those sentenced to imprisonment was contemplated, the Irish government sought relief through selective removals. The English prison system, accustomed to ordinary criminal prisoners of a tractable disposition, generally posing few security risks, was physically and managerially unprepared for the new tasks, and undertook no systematic review of the problems it might face in the light of the developing situation in Ireland. In the resulting sequence of confrontations and crises the political, official and administrative components of the English system frequently lacked coordination, and at times were at odds with each other. It was understood that the political prisoners and detainees would continue to promote their cause, and to make trouble where they could. What was not appreciated was how quickly this could be done, and on what scale; neither was there an understanding of how intensified conflict in Ireland would fuel troubles in English prisons. For their part, the prisoners and detainees drew on past experience and developed new tactics as they went along; they were supported by a strong and ever more sophisticated aid association, fronting for Sinn Féin and the IRA.

Internees and deportees

Pass the parcel

By mid-1919 the Home Office and the Prison Commission had three years' experience of recent Irish political offenders – most of it bad. From the respectable rather than the criminal classes, these prisoners were far more difficult to handle than ordinary criminals. Refusing to submit to penal discipline, they had no sense of shame for their deeds, displayed no remorse, and could not be subjected to certain disciplinary punishments. Curtailment of letters and packages was possible, but the more drastic measures – solitary cells, dietary and corporal punishment – were politically inflammatory. Dietary punishment had in fact been turned back on itself, and after the death of Ashe government strongly wished to avoid any more Irish deaths in custody. The republican movement was not fully aware of government's vulnerability on this issue, but once it grasped the leverage, internment became virtually impossible, and even the custody of convicted prisoners uncertain.

Bolstered by outside support – sometimes literally outside the prison – republican prisoners misbehaved in Irish prisons, causing severe disruption to the system as a whole. The history of staff collusion (sympathetic or coerced), the ready availability of outside help, and the ease with which fugitives could find shelter and support meant that escape, even from conditions of maximum security, was a daily possibility. The loss of a well-known rebel would damage British authority, and discomfit ministers and officials to a point where resignations might be necessary, ripples of humiliation and incompetence travelling well beyond the precipitating incident.

Against this background, on 30 May 1919, Dublin Castle asked the Home Office to provide accommodation for Pierce Beasley, MP and Daniel P. Walsh.[1] Both had been convicted by courts martial under the Defence of the Realm Act (DORA) and sentenced to two years' imprisonment (in Walsh's case with hard labour). As noted, court-martial prisoners could be imprisoned anywhere in the United Kingdom, and so there was no legal impediment to their transfer to England were the Home Office to agree. In making the request, Dublin Castle did not mention Béaslaí's recent escape and recapture, but disclosed that the men's continued detention at Mountjoy Prison was difficult because of their great influence over the other Sinn Féin prisoners and the likelihood of their causing trouble.[2]

The Home Office dragged its feet, and the Irish authorities had to send a reminder on 17 June. A week later the Home Secretary agreed to the transfer, commenting that 'the removal of Irishmen convicted in Ireland to a prison in this country is open to serious objection' but he was prepared to assist in view of

---

1 Beasley (Gaelicised Piaras Béaslaí – his preferred form) was born in Liverpool of Irish parents in 1881. Edited An tÓglach and worked closely with Michael Collins. Elected MP for East Kerry, 1918. Imprisoned in Mountjoy, March 1919; escaped, but recaptured several weeks later. Took Free State side in civil war, but resigned from politics in 1923. Michael Collins' biographer. Published extensively in Irish and English. Daniel Patrick Walsh was a dispatch handler in Collins' Intelligence Section. Involved in operations to protect Breen and Treacy after the Fernside incident (see above, p. 667).
2 PRO HO 144/1734/2.

the 'special circumstances' in this case. The men were sent over on 2 July 1919 (Walsh to Leeds and Béaslaí to Birmingham). Only at this point did the Irish authorities admit how very difficult Béaslaí had been.[3] Because of already well-established precedents of Irish political offenders demanding and eventually winning special treatment, both the Leeds and Birmingham governors requested advance directions from the Prison Commission. Waller, the Commissioner who had taken special responsibility for Irish political offenders since 1916, in turn wrote to the Home Office. On 17 July 1919, Sir Ernley Blackwell directed that both Walsh and Béaslaí were to be treated as political offenders (notwithstanding Walsh's hard labour sentence). Sir Evelyn Ruggles-Brise, Chairman of the Prison Commission, received the Home Office directive with foreboding. Whatever privileges the two men were given they might go on hunger-strike. Should that happen, they might have to be temporarily discharged (under the Cat and Mouse Act)[4] with the additional complication that they would then have to be prevented from returning to Ireland. Reiterating his basic argument on Irish politicals, Ruggles-Brise urged that if they were to be given a special ameliorative regime, they should be returned to Ireland. He did not conceal his disappointment and unhappiness about the Home Secretary's decision to accept new transfers from Ireland.[5]

Ruggles-Brise had not spelled it out, but the two men were in themselves only part of the problem. His deeper concern was that they had opened a door through which a swarm of Irish prisoners – particularly difficult prisoners, at that – would be propelled. These misgivings were realised on 18 September 1919, when Dublin Castle requested places for another six men. This group had so misbehaved at Maryborough Prison that they had all but halted normal administration. They had torn off their clothes and sang and shouted so loudly as to be heard throughout the building. Even ordinary prisoners, the letter intimated, wanted rid of them. Once again Ruggles-Brise vainly protested. The case had not been made out for the transfer of the six men, he insisted, nor was it clear why they could not be kept at Maryborough if a military guard were provided. And why, he demanded, if these transfers had to be carried out, could not some be sent to Scotland? The time had surely come when the Scots might reasonably be asked to take a small share of the burden.[6]

---

3 C. Munro, governor of Mountjoy Prison, wrote to E. Goldie-Taubman (his counterpart at Birmingham Prison) informing him that Béaslaí had escaped on 2 March 1919 using a rope-ladder thrown over the prison wall by confederates. While awaiting trial a file and a thin coil of rope had been found in loaves of bread sent in for him (these escape bids were arranged by Michael Collins). After sentence by court martial Béaslaí refused to work and therefore earned no remission.

4 Prisoners (Temporary Discharge for Ill-health) Act, 1913 (3 Geo. V, c.4).

5 PRO HO 144/1734/2.

6 Ruggles-Brise to Troup, 24 September 1919: PRO HO 144/1734/3. Ruggles-Brise drew on Waller's experience of the Irish prisons to suggest how the men might be handled at Maryborough, but the Home Office declined to forward these suggestions on the grounds that it should not be seen telling another department of government how to do its work.

This issue was not, however, pressed on the Scottish Office, and when a year later it was, the Scottish Secretary successfully fielded it. With the Anglo-Irish war entering its final phases, and law and order in crisis throughout Southern Ireland, both Dublin Castle and the Home Office asked the Scottish Office for help with Irish prisoners. Robert Munro,[7] Secretary of State for Scotland, responded that it would be 'inadvisable' to accept them unless there was a real shortage of accommodation in Irish and English prisons. (This was a safe proviso for the Scots since there was so much spare accommodation in England that entire prisons, such as Chelmsford, had been mothballed.)[8] Munro's reasons for withholding help boiled down to the strength of Sinn Féin support in Glasgow and Lanarkshire. This was 'a somewhat dangerous position' which would probably be made worse were political prisoners to be brought over. In addition, Munro noted, certain agrarian troubles in Scotland looked like spreading. Anticipating the Home Office response that England also had several large concentrations of Irish immigrants, in addition to a threatening wave of industrial unrest, Munro urged that it was better to concentrate the Irish prisoners since 'the means at the disposal of the Government for dealing with civil disorder are so weak'.[9] Whatever was felt in the Home and Irish Offices about Munro's position, his refusal to cooperate could be overcome only if the matter were referred to Cabinet, whose decision was far from certain. It was decided to let the matter lie, and so Scotland escaped the fractious Irish transfers.

The Scots' resistance was indicative of how much trouble was expected. Given the strong opposition at official level, political intervention was necessary. On 29 September 1919, Home Secretary Edward Shortt (who had been Irish Chief Secretary until the previous January) met the Irish Lord Lieutenant, Lord French, in London. Despite previous disagreements over policy and friction in their working relationship, French persuaded Shortt that broader imperial interests

7 (1868–1955). Liberal MP, Roxburgh and Selkirk, 1918–22. Edinburgh University, Scottish Bar, 1893; KC, 1910. Secretary of State for Scotland, December 1916 to October 1922.

8 Because of a rapidly falling prison population many prisons had been closed. During 1920–1 receptions into prisons in England and Wales for those convicted on indictment had dropped by 38 per cent and for those convicted summarily by 74 per cent in comparison to average receptions in the five years ending 1913–14: these figures include the transfers from Ireland. This steadily falling trend meant that a significant amount of spare accommodation was available, since the daily average population in local prisons had halved in comparison to 1908–9. There was, however, a shortage of the prison staff necessary to use this spare capacity and it would have been expensive to reactivate closed prisons (see RCP, 1920–1, PP 1921 [Cmd. 1523], XVI, 423, 4, 6, 16 and 25.

9 Munro to Shortt, 5 October 1920: PRO HO 144/1734/157. Munro could also have pointed out that the average daily population in Scottish prisons had not fallen in the post-war period to anything like the extent that it had in England. In 1920 it was 1874 compared to 2603 in 1914. The volume of Scots offending seems to have consisted of petty offences and average sentences were consequently shorter than in England (see *Annual Report of the Prison Commissioners for Scotland, 1920*, PP, 1921 [Cmd. 1255], XVI, 501, 5 and 17).

required the removal from Ireland of the six difficult prisoners.[10] A more extensive programme of transfers was also mooted, and Shortt agreed to French's suggestion that Chelmsford Prison be reactivated for this purpose.[11] This met some of Ruggles-Brise's concerns about the handling of political offenders alongside ordinary criminals, but the setting aside of a whole prison was a much worse outcome to the political consultations than the English officials had imagined: small groups of difficult men were bad enough, but the Shortt–French agreement suggested that a pipeline had indeed been opened through which the Irish government would pump its most difficult characters.

The Prison Commissioners made their dissatisfaction known, and in a memo of 6 November 1919 set out conditions for receiving the Irish, while pointing out that their safe custody could not be guaranteed unless they were held in separate confinement. This was to remain a contentious issue for the following two years. Given proposed numbers, it was decided that a special set of rules would apply at Chelmsford. By 8 December this document had been agreed and signed by both Shortt and French – an extraordinary and unprecedented step in Home Office relations with Dublin Castle. Equally remarkable, and a confession that normal criminal justice principles had gone by the board, was the decision that the new rules would apply equally to convicted prisoners and internees.

The Shortt–French agreement had arisen out of a series of minutes from English officials, and was intended to provide a political safeguard of sorts for the Home Office in the event of protest campaigns by or on behalf of the prisoners. This may have been the idea, but no official agreement or set of rules would deflect the ire of prisoners and protesters away from those who actually exercised custody: concessions cleared the way for new demands. A Home Office explanation that it was simply acting as an agent for the Irish government was irrelevant. Troup noted that the Shortt–French rules had no legal authority. Had this become generally known, it would have provided the republicans with a stick of some weight.[12] And haunting the whole enterprise was the spectre of hunger-strike, of which Ruggles-Brise had warned some months previously. This was taken up by H. B. Simpson, Assistant Secretary at the Home Office, who saw it as the most critical question for the politicians: the Prison Commissioners were entitled to

---

10 On the sometimes difficult working relationship between French and Shortt during the latter's period as Irish Chief Secretary (April 1918 to January 1919) see Eunan O'Halpin's *The Decline of the Union: British Government in Ireland 1892–1920*, Dublin, Gill & Macmillan, 1987, ch. 6.

11 Troup to Dublin Castle, 6 October 1919: PRO HO 144/1734/3.

12 French's position in Ireland was very different from that of previous Lords Lieutenant. The difficulties endemic in the Chief Secretary–Lord Lieutenant relationship had been resolved in favour of the latter. In Ireland, French exercised a firm control over civil authority, and, because he was a soldier, a great deal of informal authority over the military. This pro-consular status finds a distinct echo in the agreement – and indeed the very concept of an agreement – that French signed with Shortt (for the reorganisation of Irish government at this time see O'Halpin, 1987, pp. 158–69).

know how far the politicians' resolve went. Since steadfastness would involve deaths, policy had to be decided by Cabinet, and until then it seemed pointless to take up lesser matters of penal discipline with the Irish government.[13] Troup agreed, and asked for a memorandum to be prepared, setting out the issues.

This duly went to Cabinet and led to the Shortt–French agreement. Thus underwritten, the go-ahead was given to the transfer of a few of the most difficult from the ranks of both the convicted prisoners and internees. Because of the Prison Commissioners' strong concerns a military guard would be provided. For reasons that are not now clear, Chelmsford Prison was not brought back into use, and instead the men went to Wormwood Scrubs.[14] The issue of hunger-striking was side-stepped. It was initially decided to greet the prisoners with a declaration that hunger-striking would not procure release, and to display such a notice in all cells. Simpson argued that this was more likely than not to be taken as a provocation, and so on 16 December it was decided that notices and declarations would be withheld until a strike threat was actually made.

The Manchester escape

While these discussions were going on, those hard-case prisoners who had already been received were showing their mettle. The Prison Commission had decided to concentrate some of these. The inevitable happened, and on Saturday, 25 October 1919, Austin Stack and four others made a spectacular escape from Manchester Prison.[15] The poor state of security and control was highlighted by the daring simplicity of the escape. A long ladder was made to order in the locality. This was openly wheeled through the streets, and propped against the prison wall when Stack and his companions were exercising. They overcame the guard and shinned over the wall. Outside, bicycles were waiting and the men made their various ways through the darkening streets to safety and concealment.[16] Since it was Saturday afternoon only a small number of warders were on duty. Stack had been so confident of success that he had left a note in his cell explaining to the governor that the men had been *obliged* to escape because of the violation of pledges given respectively by Chief Secretaries Duke

---

13 H. B. Simpson, Minute, 8 November 1919: PRO HO 144/1734/4.

14 Wormwood Scrubs, being laid out in 'halls' (cell houses), lent itself to a convenient separation between the Irish politicals and criminal prisoners. It was operating at a fraction of its capacity, and could be brought into use immediately and economically. It did, however, have the disadvantage (as will be seen below) of being located in London.

15 *Manchester Guardian*, 27 October 1919, 7a; *Daily Telegraph*, 27 October 1919, 11d.

16 Stack (1880–1929) was the Kerry Commandant of Volunteers who failed to rescue Roger Casement, and was himself arrested when he went to the local police station to make enquiries as to the stranger on Banna Strand. He was a leading figure in the campaign for political status for those convicted of offences connected with the Easter rising. A member of the anti-Collins faction of the IRA, Stack was later imprisoned by the Free State government.

and Shortt not to deport Irish political offenders to England, and to place them in an internment camp rather than a prison. The note was topped and tailed with some flair, prefatory sentences declaring that 'It is hardly necessary to say that we deny the right of the British Government to imprison Irishmen. That is well-understood nowadays throughout the world.' Stack apologised for his deception (what exactly this was is not clear), and confirmed that the men had no complaint against the governor.[17]

Had the full story become known, it is probable that there would have been damning press and parliamentary comment.[18] Béaslaí was an escaper; Walsh, his co-deportee, a trouble-maker: Stack was a senior and experienced IRA officer. Any sensible evaluation pointed to maximum security, and this at the very least meant separate cellular confinement and a consequently restricted regime. Instead, all the benefits of fairly free association and easy communications with the outside world were allowed. The episode has also to be seen as part of operations within a low general prison population[19] and few expectations of disciplinary or security difficulties: indeed, at that time an escape assisted from outside was so rare as to be unthinkable. But these were no ordinary criminal prisoners, shuffling through their sentences, down in spirits, submitting to their lot, devoid of resources, known to the local police, with nowhere to go but well-known haunts and associates.

Some letters from Austin Stack to Sister Francesca MacDonagh (the sister of Thomas, shot in 1916) should have given an indication of the high spirits and easy connections which the Manchester prisoners enjoyed. In early June he informed Sister Francesca that ten men had been transferred from Belfast Prison 'for a change of air'. Prior to this they had not left their cells for fourteen weeks and all were in consequence in poor health. The Manchester regime gave them several hours' open-air exercise each day. With that, and all the food and tobacco sent in by friends in Manchester and Ireland ('there is no luxury that we are not getting'), and the generous allowance of visitors and letters, 'we are again in fine form – like gamecocks'.[20] Towards the end of August 1919, Stack again praised

---

17 PRO HO 144/1734/8. The escapers were John Boland (30); Piaras Béaslaí (36) (his second over-the-wall escape); Cornelius Connolly (30); Daniel P. Walsh (37); Patrick McCarthy (22); and Austin Stack (39). (For Béaslaí and Walsh, see above, p. 667, n.1). Cornelius Connolly was commandant of Skibbereen Battalion, West Cork Brigade, IRA. Later member of Tom Barry's Flying Column. All in all, an experienced and formidable group of IRA men.

18 Only one enquiry was made in the Commons, and this was evaded by the Home Secretary (5 *Hansard*, CXX, cols 712–3; 29 October 1919). There were no follow-up questions.

19 See n. 8, above. The docility of the prison population, convict and local, was shown by the dramatic fall in prison punishment rates – in local prisons the lowest ever recorded (RCP, 1920–1, *op. cit.*, 14).

20 Austin Stack to Sister Francesca MacDonagh, 8 June 1919: NLI: Sister Francesca MacDonagh Papers: Ms. 20, 647(4) (unfoliated). It may not be too fanciful in the circumstances to note the considerable fighting abilities of the gamecock. These letters were either not subject to censorship, or it was done very quickly, since they were postmarked only a day after the date of writing. Prisoners used an extensive lexicon of code words and allusions.

the Manchester committee of Art O'Brien's Irish National Relief Association, and the other supporters who had done so much to help them. The men's health was fine: 'we are having a good time – that's the long and short of it.'[21] These letters did not point to an escape attempt, but they indicated high morale, good health and an abundance of local contacts with whom the men were in fairly free communication. A few warning lights ought to have come on.

But since details did not seep out, the Home Office and Prison Commission quickly closed the book. Ruggles-Brise submitted an account to the Home Secretary, but provided no information on the means by which the outside help had been orchestrated. He ritually renewed his plea that his prisons be spared these men. Troup, in his review for the Home Secretary, implicitly agreed with Ruggles-Brise since he concluded that the men could not have escaped had they been confined under normal disciplinary conditions, or had there been an effective military guard. Ruggles-Brise had recommended no more than a 'severe caution' to the governor and subordinate officers. With Troup's endorsement this finding was accepted by the Home Secretary on 2 December 1919. [22] None of the issues thrown up by the escape had been addressed and English prisons continued to operate as before, with governors and their staff working within their usual and now inappropriate expectations.

Confrontation and control

This failure to upgrade boundary security and to modify the central elements in the regime is all the more remarkable when viewed alongside Dublin Castle's plans. In late November and early December 1919, a master coup against republicans was in the making. This was intended to decapitate by rounding up and deporting, as internees, the top layers of leaders. Orders were signed on 2 December under DORA Regulation 14b for the arrest of a carefully selected group – a police wish-list – including Cathal Burgess, MP, Michael Collins, MP, Alderman Thomas Kelly, MP, and the Countess Markievicz, MP.[23] The orders were to be executed on 8 or 9 December, the men to go to Wormwood Scrubs and Markievicz to Holloway. By this time Collins had penetrated Dublin Castle and the police. Only immediate and secret army action would have offered a chance of closing the net. Humiliatingly for the Castle no arrests were made and news of this failure became public. But even had this group been gathered

---

21 Ibid., Austin Stack to Sister Francesca MacDonagh, 20 August 1919. Stack particularly praised Miss Gertie O'Connell (a schoolteacher) who had sacrificed virtually all her holidays on their account.

22 PRO HO 144/1734/9

23 PRO HO 144/1734/10A. For Michael Collins, see p. 451, n. 2, above; Constance Markievicz, pp. 537–49. Thomas Kelly was an Alderman of Dublin Corporation; Acting Joint Secretary, Sinn Féin during absence of executive members after 'German Plot', April 1919; arrested December 1919. Elected Lord Mayor of Dublin while in prison, January 1920.

together in an English prison under internment conditions it is doubtful whether security and control could have coped.

The intended round-up had major consequences for the English prison system since the prospectus of the *coup de main* had been used to extract an agreement from the Home Office (in the teeth of Prison Commission objections) to receive at Wormwood Scrubs a further and unspecified number of Irish political offenders and internees. French and his security advisers took immediate and full advantage of the agreement. Four men were delivered on 12 December 1919; by mid-February 1920 this had risen to seventy, with an anticipated maximum of 200 to 300.[24]

The chemistry of confrontation was now assembled and was ignited by a number of challenges of growing intensity. Fearful of protest across a spectrum of opinion in Ireland, in Britain and abroad, the authorities repeatedly backed down to the point where normal imprisonment became impossible. There was an early taste of what was to come. On 17 February 1920, Major A. V. Briscoe, Governor of Wormwood Scrubs, informed the Prison Commission that the internees objected to fortnightly searches, as required by the regulations. Joseph McGrath, the men's leader, insisted that these were harassing and unnecessary, since the prisoners received no outside goods. Whether or not the men received outside items through legitimate channels was beside the point: searches were undertaken to discover contraband, which included everything from harmless but unauthorised comforts to weapons and the means of escape. Ignoring this basic security and control requirement, however, the Home Office consented to stop the searches.[25]

Against all common sense, the Commissioners decided that their Wormwood Scrubs difficulties were due largely to the arrival of Joseph McGrath and his leadership of the internees.[26] In a memorandum to Shortt, Ruggles-Brise painted a cosy picture of life before McGrath (and one quite at odds with his earlier accounts of the Irish prisoners). The internees 'who are on the whole a responsible body of men, were apparently content to live quietly under the regulations which were approved with much care and thought.' With McGrath, however, there began 'a recurrence of the trouble with which we became so familiar when the Irish convicts under de Valera were at Lewes'. Now organised behind the leadership of one man, the Wormwood Scrubs men would obey him 'whatever their own feelings and inclinations might be'. With a prospect of internee numbers increasing to 200 or 300, the position was grave. Having laid so much of

---

24 Ruggles-Brise to Shortt, 19 February 1920: PRO HO 144/1734/16; see also A. V. Briscoe to Prison Commissioners, ibid.

25 PRO HO 144/1734/12.

26 McGrath (1888–1966) had participated in the Easter rising and was subsequently imprisoned. Elected MP for Dublin in the 1918 general election and again imprisoned in 1920. Supported Treaty and became a minister in the provisional government. Retired from politics and enjoyed successful career in business, bloodstock and horse-racing.

the blame for unrest on McGrath, however, Ruggles-Brise identified the 'root cause' of the defiant and rebellious attitude of the men at Wormwood Scrubs and elsewhere as the fact that '*they are interned in a Prison and are made subject to Prison regulations* in many respects identical with those in force for convicted prisoners'.[27]

This was not a statement of sympathy with the internees, but another attempt to be rid of them to the army. The request of the Lewes convicts in 1916, Ruggles-Brise pointed out, had been for recognition of their status as belligerents and confinement in a military camp. This had been refused and 'grave difficulties' had been avoided only by general amnesty. From the beginning, he had argued for army responsibility – 'the safest and best and wisest method of custody for these Irishmen'. The previous few years had amply demonstrated the mischief and trouble which might occur 'if by continued contumacy prisoners force themselves into a situation where close cellular confinement is the only remedy against their insubordination'. This experience arose not only from the Irish, but from the conscientious objectors, who had to be kept in cellular confinement for periods of up to several weeks because they would not give undertakings to abstain from disorder. Such close custody required constant medical care: many had to be released. Besides this, they disturbed the order and discipline of their prisons and 'caused public scandal by shouting and yelling from their windows to the annoyance of people living in the neighbourhood'.[28] Ruggles-Brise went on to forecast (remarkably accurately, as it turned out) that these difficulties would have a reprise at Wormwood Scrubs, and there would, in addition, be medical difficulties and releases on grounds of ill-health.

A change of course would defeat the intention of the Irish government, which was to keep the men out of Ireland and in safe custody in England. Ruggles-Brise had been to see Shortt's successor as Irish Chief Secretary, Ian Macpherson,[29] and inferred that Macpherson did not see much of a problem in the recognition of belligerent status that would be implied by placing the men in an army camp. This being the case, he concluded that the only objection to military internment was removed and recommended transfer as soon as possible. Anxious for a done deal, he went to the War Office and enquired about a suitable camp. The best seemed to be the former alien internment camp at Oswestrey, in the process of being dismantled but still sufficiently intact to accommodate several thousand men; it was also close to a concentration of troops.[30] Soft-soaping a minister, finding a camp and getting army agreement were all very different

27 Ruggles-Brise to Shortt, 19 February 1920: PRO HO 144/1734/12.
28 Ibid.
29 Sir James Ian Macpherson (1880–1937). Educated at Edinburgh University; Bar, 1906, KC, 1919. Liberal MP, Ross and Cromarty, 1911–36 (National Liberal after 1931). Deputy Secretary of State for War, 1918; Chief Secretary for Ireland, January 1919 to April 1920; Minister of Pensions, April 1920 to October 1922.
30 Ruggles-Brise to Shortt, 19 February 1920, *op. cit.*

things, as Ruggles-Brise found out when he tried to put his plan into operation. An army bureaucracy unable to baffle civilians in such matters would have been a pitiful thing indeed.

The Wormwood Scrubs governor, Major A. V. Briscoe, had supplied the list of woes which Ruggles-Brise had relayed to the Home Secretary.[31] Things had gone well, he insisted, until McGrath had arrived. Demands then began for small concessions which, on their being granted, stimulated the appetite for more.[32] He gave an illustration of the state of things. Briscoe had discovered that Gubbins, one of the internees, had a cheque-book. This was regarded as being in the same category as cash, which prisoners were not allowed to have, lest they suborn staff or breach security. Asked to surrender his cheque-book, Gubbins refused to do so without McGrath's authority. Briscoe then approached McGrath who, 'in a most defiant and insolent way', threatened that if the cheque-book were taken by force there would be very serious trouble indeed for Briscoe and his staff. His position was now difficult, Briscoe complained. The regulations gave little or no power to punish the internees – he could deprive them of association, of exercise or magazines – 'and these powers are futile', since acting under McGrath, the men would probably evade the punishment. 'Numberless' demands were being made for razors, knives, food, extra letters and visits and longer periods of association, and if these were not granted there would be grave consequences along Lewes lines. If a man were punished by cellular confinement for insolence or disobedience his cell door would be broken open, and in any case virtually all the men would follow McGrath and be punished. There would be a general breaking up of the prison, and staff would be unable to handle the men when they were allowed out of their cells, as they must be, for exercise.

This Cassandran recital ended on a self-pitying note. As a faithful public servant Briscoe was prepared to do his best to preserve safe custody, but he and his staff considered prison to be unsuitable for internment: an army camp was the right place. Failing that, he did not see how he could continue the government of the prison without greatly enhanced powers of punishment. The atmosphere and the constraints under which they had to work were having the greatest effect on staff 'seeing as they do, day by day the Governor browbeaten and insulted by defiant men asking for privileges which cannot be granted'.[33]

---

31 Briscoe to Prison Commissioners, 19 February 1920, ibid. It is possible, even probable, that Ruggles-Brise encouraged Briscoe to complain: he may even have indicated the line to be followed.

32 There was close contact with Art O'Brien's still flourishing Irish National Relief Association. A revealing exchange between O'Brien and the Prison Commissioners at this time gives a glimpse of the prison's liberal regime. The prisoners had asked O'Brien to send in two sets of war pipes, two practice chanters and one side drum with sticks and belt. O'Brien asked for permission, but was told that there was no lack of such instruments in the prison (NLI: Art O'Brien Papers: Ms. 8444(i) (unfoliated), c. March 1920).

33 Briscoe to Prison Commissioners, 19 February 1920, op. cit.

The memoranda of Ruggles-Brise and Briscoe were submitted on the same day to Cabinet by Shortt (who had a propensity to deal with problems by drawing others in). His covering note confirmed Briscoe to be an experienced and competent governor, in whose judgement he had full confidence. The matter was urgent and Shortt sought Cabinet authority for the transfer of custody from the Home Office to the War Office. Whether Lloyd George allowed a full discussion on the matter is not clear, but Shortt could not carry his proposal and was obliged to retain responsibility for the Irish internees.

Unable to shed the internees, Ruggles-Brise decided to shift McGrath. By prior arrangement Briscoe called at the Prison Commissioners' office and formally repeated his assessment that McGrath was a fountainhead of danger and unrest, and would cause trouble at the evening lock-up on that day (Saturday, 21 February 1920) unless his demand for the extension of association were granted. Shortt was out of town for the weekend, but with Troup's agreement it was decided that Ruggles-Brise, accompanied by the Under-Secretary of State, Major John Baird, MP, and Major Briscoe, would forthwith lay their difficulties before Ian Macpherson, the Irish Chief Secretary. Macpherson saw them immediately and Ruggles-Brise outlined the steps which in the view of the Prison Commission required urgent action to stabilise the situation at Wormwood Scrubs.[34] The removal of McGrath was item number one. Macpherson agreed, and signed an order under DORA Regulation 14b, transferring McGrath to Brixton. The plan of action required the removal of any leader who took McGrath's place, and the revocation of Regulation 14b, as the instrument governing the confinement of the Wormwood Scrubs internees. It was to be replaced by the ordinary prison powers of punishment. In the event, both of these changes were dead letters. McGrath was succeeded by the aptly named Lawless, who even more effectively engineered several acts of collective disobedience without retaliatory transfer. Almost immediately, moreover, Troup overruled the decision to revoke detention under Regulation 14b, which would have undoubtedly multiplied troubles, both in the prison and among sympathisers and supporters at large.

Ruggles-Brise's plan also called for the removal of persons under punishment to other parts of Wormwood Scrubs. This was never apparently followed through, since it would probably have meant moving internees from the Wormwood Scrubs building assigned to internees to another in which ordinary inmates were held. This would have certainly provoked protests, and would have been represented as bad faith in the conduct of internment and an attempt to degrade the prisoners. Following his 1916 experience Ruggles-Brise also wanted, in the event of collective action, to break the internees into smaller groups to be distributed around the country. The Home Office did not consent to this, taking

34 Ibid. Untitled eight-point memorandum, annotated by Troup, dated 21 February 1920. The details immediately following are taken from this document.

the view that dispatching small groups of internees to prisons around the country would multiply rather than reduce difficulties, since at each institution they would be entitled to and would assert their right to internment conditions. The effect of these transfers on ordinary Irish criminals held in the same prisons had also to be considered. As the number of internees continued to increase it was far from certain that sufficient self-contained accommodation was available in prisons outside London to hold them all in small detachments. Staffing had also presented difficulties, and was addressed by Ruggles-Brise's plan. All Wormwood Scrubs warders were to be notified that they might be called in at all hours of the day and night, whatever their regular hours of duty. For these services, and any danger to which they might be exposed, they would receive a bounty.[35]

Anticipating that some of these decisions would be taken as provocations by the internees, it was decided to call on the pre-emptive and deterrent assistance of the army. (This also had the advantage of involving the army in the whole exercise, perhaps inserting a wedge which would ultimately shift responsibility.) In the midst of all this, Briscoe's frustration and anger at the way he had been treated was not lost to sight ('brow-beaten and insulted by defiant men'): it was resolved 'To use force, at an opportune time, to obtain the cheque-book from Gubbins'. The last (and it is not clear if it was ever attempted) would in all probability have exposed poor Major Briscoe to yet further derision; Gubbins, well forewarned, would not have had the cheque-book, and the prison-wide search, accompanied by the confinement to cells of all internees, which would have been necessary to recover it (if indeed it could be found) would have been the almost certain occasion of violent resistance and protest, and would have been difficult to justify to the outside world.[36]

Hunger-strike

Wormwood Scrubs: first phase

The actual removal of Joseph McGrath to Brixton Prison presented no difficulties, and was effected on the afternoon of Saturday, 21 February 1920. An immediate problem which neither Ruggles-Brise nor Troup seem to have anticipated was that at Brixton McGrath, strictly segregated from the criminal prisoners, was virtually in solitary confinement. This was taken by the internees and their

---

35 The suggestion of a bounty may have reflected continuing unease about the loyalty of Wormwood Scrubs warders, who had gone on strike in August 1919. A number had then been dismissed, but reverberations continued (see 5 Hansard, CXXV, cols 740–1; 17 February 1920).

36 To contemporaries Briscoe's disproportionate interest in Gubbins' cheque-book may have had a comical element owing to the emergence and frequent use of 'gubbins' as a slang word during the First World War – a term denoting anything that one might be too lazy or forgetful to name (see Eric Partridge, A Dictionary of Slang and Unconventional English, London, Routledge & Kegan Paul, 1984).

supporters and sympathisers as a severe punishment of a man who had never been charged or convicted before a court, nor indeed before a prison tribunal.

The intention to transfer any man who stepped into McGrath's position of leadership at Wormwood Scrubs was impractical, as the Commissioners fairly quickly realised. Followed through, it might simply have led to a decanting from Wormwood Scrubs to Brixton – where, presumably, the process would simply have continued: taken to absurdity, a perpetual circular traffic. What was certain was that McGrath had a strong following among the internees, and that their protests would not be long delayed once the details got back to Wormwood Scrubs. And so it proved to be. On 15 March James Lawless protested at McGrath's Brixton conditions. The authorities had asked for three volunteers to go with McGrath to be company for him. This assumed a level of cooperation which Briscoe must have known did not exist. Lawless demanded McGrath's return to Wormwood Scrubs by 18 March, or the transfer of half the men to Brixton. Should this ultimatum not be met, there would be a hunger-strike. Two days later Lawless was told by Major Briscoe that Brixton had been designated as a place of internment and that therefore there should be an inflow of prisoners transferred from Ireland, which would end McGrath's isolation. Lawless then wrote to McGrath seeking confirmation. The letter was not forwarded, but assurances were given that McGrath was well and comfortable. This failed to satisfy, and on the morning of Friday, 19 March the men commenced a hunger-strike.[37]

The reaction of the authorities showed that they had not the slightest intention of standing firm to the point of death. Food was placed in the cells, and was removed and replaced by fresh meals at the appointed time. (The records describe the food as 'enticing', but give no other details.) Lawless was willing to stop the hunger-strike if McGrath himself assured them that he was being treated properly. Joined to this was a demand for improved food at Wormwood Scrubs (specified in some detail) and for the dispatch of three men to Brixton to be McGrath's companions. By Sunday, 21 March, the medical officer was expressing deep concern about one of the prisoners (W. Ryan) who had a rheumatic heart condition; the strain of the hunger-strike meant that he might have heart failure at any time. A death in custody – even of a previously ill person – would have spelled disaster and Troup directed that Lawless be taken to Brixton to see McGrath, noting for the file that it seemed right 'to do what is possible to prevent Ryan's dying today'.[38] Returning to Wormwood Scrubs, Lawless consented to call off the hunger-strike if the men got the same hospital diet as McGrath's at Brixton, and if three companions were provided for him.

37 PRO HO 144/1734/22; 101 of the 104 internees at Wormwood Scrubs joined the strike.
38 PRO HO 144/1734/22. He also recorded the deputy governor's belief that McGrath had been looking for an excuse to go on hunger-strike, and that the men's true intention was to force their release.

Edward Shortt, the Home Secretary, was again out of town and so Troup, under the pressure of Ryan's imminent death, agreed to Lawless's demands: Shortt subsequently gave retroactive approval to Troup's action.[39] By 8 p.m. that evening the prisoners were taking food again, rejoicing in their victory.

William O'Brien remained on hunger-strike, but both sides seemed to agree that his was not part of the main struggle. O'Brien, who was not a member of Sinn Féin, the Volunteers or the Citizen Army, had been interned in 1916, largely because of his association (via the Irish Transport and General Workers' Union) with James Connolly.[40] On release he had confined himself to the reorganisation of his union, and the work of the Irish Labour Party, of which he was General Secretary. Although government would later claim that O'Brien was suspected of being involved 'in a murderous conspiracy that has resulted in the deaths of so many loyal servants of the Crown in Ireland',[41] there was no evidence against him, and the charge had no basis, other than O'Brien's general and open stance against British government. There had been a number of protests against his detention, and a request that he be released to campaign in a by-election at Stockport, in which he had been nominated for Labour.[42] O'Brien continued to refuse food, or to be removed to hospital. On 25 March the Home Office insisted that he had been warned of the consequence of his hunger-strike, but on the following day seemed willing to consider his removal to a nursing-home, which was then agreed.[43] After several weeks of nursing and on parole O'Brien was unconditionally released, Bonar Law being unable to justify the original arrest and serious accusations.[44]

This episode was simply one of a misconceived arrest, and delay in government backing down. There was at this stage no question of releasing any other detainee, and another attempt to force the issue was inevitable, and expectations that hunger-striking would be used again were fulfilled in little over a fortnight. In protest against the refusal of four applications for temporary parole, Lawless called a new hunger-strike on 9 April. The action would last until the outstanding cases were dealt with and a guarantee given that requests for compassionate

39 Ibid. Troup minuted Shortt: 'I have no doubt that they will think they have secured a success and sooner or later will make further demands – but I do not think we could have defended refusing these small points when the result w[oul]d be Ryan's death, and within a day or two either release of the others or their death.'

40 O'Brien (1881–1968) had been active in the trades union movement from an early age, and was a founder member of the Irish Transport and General Workers' Union. Prominent in the anti-conscription movement, and an associate of Connolly (though not in armed struggle) he was an obvious target in any round-up of troublemakers. Twice briefly returned for Labour to the Dáil (1922–3 and 1927), he concentrated on Labour and trade union activities for the remainder of his career.

41 Bonar Law statement to House of Commons, 26 March 1920 (5 Hansard, CXXXVII, col. 767).

42 Ibid., col. 49; 22 March 1920.

43 Ibid., col. 724; 25 March 1920; col. 769; 26 March 1920.

44 Ibid., CXXIX, cols 621–2; 13 May 1920.

parole would be dealt with within twenty-four hours of receipt of the telegram informing of the illness or death of a family member.[45] Troup urged Shortt immediately to take the matter to Cabinet, since, were any of the hunger-strikers to die, 'his death will be made an excuse for attempted murder of Ministers in this country'. In the event, the Irish government stood firm, and the hunger-strike was called off on the evening of 10 April, having lasted a day and a half. Reporting to the Home Office, deputy governor H. M. A. Hales claimed that the strike had been half-hearted and unpopular, that some men did not abide by it, and that facing defections, Lawless was looking for an excuse to call it off: 'The whole affair was a piece of "bluff", conceived [on the assumption] that the Irish Government would concede everything by return of post.'[46]

The 'bluff' had been much encouraged by events at Dublin's Mountjoy Prison, where a hunger-strike had commenced on Monday, 5 April 1920. On 31 March the Mountjoy leaders, Frank Gallagher and Thomas Hunter,[47] had demanded that DORA internees should be treated as prisoners of war. In the face of official silence, thirty-six men refused food on 5 April, joined by twenty-nine more the following day; by 9 April ninety men were on strike. The medical officer indicated that a number (presumably because of prior health conditions) were in a grave condition.[48] On 11 April he informed Dublin Castle that fatal collapses were imminent. The following day the Roman Catholic chaplains reported that the men were in a very weak condition and urged their release or the immediate grant of regime concessions: the Mountjoy prisoners were being treated worse than the internees in England. In the Commons, the Irish Party Member T. P. O'Connor reminded government of the devastating impact on constitutional nationalism of the death of Thomas Ashe, 'the reason we have seven representatives here today instead of 77'.[49] Three days later Dublin Castle decided to grant 'ameliorative' treatment to DORA detainees. This offer was rejected. Rumours in the London newspapers that the protesters were about to be released were denied, but that evening the news from Mountjoy was that there had been two collapses from heart failure, and although one man had rallied, both were in a very grave condition.

---

45 The four requests for parole had been made on compassionate grounds – two cases of a child's illness, one of a mother's illness and one an application to consult the prisoner's own doctor (PRO HO 144/1734/24).

46 Ibid.

47 Gallagher (1893–1962) would endure several hunger-strikes, including one lasting forty-one days. An author and journalist, he sided with the anti-Treaty side and was imprisoned by the Free State government in 1931. His subsequent career included broadcasting and several years on the staff of the National Library of Ireland. Thomas Hunter had participated in the 1916 rising; adjutant to Eamon de Valera at Lewes Prison.

48 Almost certainly he was wrong about this, as later and much more prolonged hunger-strikes would show. Prisoners had also learned to fake symptoms (Ernie O'Malley, 'In British Jails', The Kerryman, *Dublin's Fighting Story 1913–1921*, Tralee, The Kerryman, n.d. (?1948), pp. 193–8).

49 5 *Hansard* CXXVII, col. 1542; 13 April 1920.

Dublin Castle attempted to hold its line: convicted prisoners would be treated as such, the untried would get the benefits due to them and DORA internees would receive an enhanced regime. On 13 April ameliorations were extended to about forty men. This conferred privileges according to the rule promulgated on 29 September 1917.[50] Thereafter the momentum of the hunger-strike took over. On the afternoon of 14 April the medical officer certified sixty-six men to be in 'immediate danger', and they were released on parole for periods he specified. Dublin Castle gave as a precedent the release in England of William O'Brien, who had now been allowed to go in to a nursing-home. This, however, was a fig-leaf. O'Brien (not even a Sinn Féiner) had been an internee. Thirty-one sentenced men (as distinct from internees) were among those released from Mountjoy, and this Bonar Law told the Commons the following day had been a mistake. Sentenced men were 'in no case entitled to be released on parole'.[51] Enquiries showed that careless wording in the Lord Lieutenant's order had caused the convicted men to be released.[52] The doctor's conviction that death was imminent in these cases is curious since (excepting those with prior health conditions of a grave character) later that year Terence MacSwiney showed that men could survive on hunger-strike for seventy-five days or more.[53] Nor was this exceptional. Subsequent experiences have shown that healthy men can survive without food for comparable periods.[54] It is likely that the recommendation to release so many prisoners after such a short period on hunger-strike was based, in fairly equal parts, on inexperience, faked symptoms, bureaucratic caution and a degree of sympathy (or fear) on the part of the prison officials.

But whether due to an error in transmission or interpretation, the release of so many prisoners from Mountjoy inevitably had an effect in England. Since the

---

50 See *Manchester Guardian*, 22 April 1920, 16c, which reprints these rules.

51 5 *Hansard* CXXVII, cols 1810–11; 15 April 1920. Of the thirty-one men sentenced, twenty-one had been convicted under DORA and ten under ordinary law (Minute of 5 May 1920; PRO HO 144/1734/27A).

52 Lord French's order had been rushed to the prison by Lawrence O'Neill, the Lord Mayor of Dublin – an indication of the atmosphere of panic and political pressure. The document had directed that any of those prisoners whom the medical officer certified to be in immediate danger of death were to be released, with no mention of distinction between convicted and unconvicted. On 6 May, in response to C. F. Palmer (MP for The Wreckin), Denis Henry, the Irish Attorney General, admitted that the Lord Lieutenant had not explicitly excluded sentenced men, and the Mountjoy governor 'unfortunately applied the directions to all prisoners, and as a result a number of convicted men were erroneously discharged' (5 *Hansard*, CXXVII, cols 2212–13). The incident had been a panicky shambles.

53 MacSwiney, in fact, was not in particularly good health when he commenced his hunger-strike (see below, pp. 737–8).

54 See, for example, Chris Ryder's account of the Maze hunger-strikes of 1981 which led to several deaths (*Inside the Maze*, London, Methuen, 2000, chs 10 and 11). Kieran McEvoy (*Parliamentary Imprisonment in Northern Ireland*, Oxford, Oxford University Press, 2001, ch. 4) relates the modern hunger-strike to republican tradition and the broader objectives of its recent campaign in Northern Ireland.

Irish government's newly promulgated rules for an ameliorative regime were bound to be taken as a benchmark by Irish prisoners, Ruggles-Brise and Troup agreed to examine their possible effect on the English prisons.[55] They correctly anticipated further actions and, sure enough, on 21 April 1920, a new hunger-strike started at Wormwood Scrubs. Four days later 108 men were refusing food, and the medical officer reported that he did not expect the strike to collapse as the previous one had: 'last time the strike was ordered against the desires of a considerable minority, whereas now each man is acting on his own initiative.'[56] The Dublin releases had boosted the Scrubs' men's hopes and stiffened resolve.

This strike was much more ambitious than the previous one. In a letter setting out their case, the men reminded Briscoe that they had been at Wormwood Scrubs, uncharged and untried for over three months: 'This is contrary to the laws of humanity, and we demand unconditional release.'[57] Troup pointed out that the new Wormwood Scrubs strike significantly differed from Mountjoy's, in that its goal was unconditional release rather than ameliorations. Government needed to agree its response. Should the men be released because life was in danger, 'it will of course be impossible to hold any more prisoners under internment orders'. If it was decided they would not be released, then whatever their condition, they should be warned, 'though of course they will, after what has happened [in Dublin] pay no attention'. And if the men were to be released because their health was deteriorating it was difficult to know what to do with them: 'We can hardly keep them all in nursing homes at twelve guineas a week!'[58]

Wormwood Scrubs: in earnest

After the previous false starts and the prisoners' rather uncertain leadership there were hopes that this latest hunger-strike would fizzle out. This time, however, Sinn Féin took a more direct interest, and, greatly encouraged by the Mountjoy events, determined to turn Wormwood Scrubs into a major propaganda exercise. One of the principal reasons for deporting the men to England was to deprive them of the stimulus of immediate public support. London Sinn Féin decided to address this by mounting protests outside the prison. On Sunday, 25 April Art O'Brien, Sinn Féin's most senior representative in England, and Chairman of the Irish Self-Determination League, organised a large demonstration outside the prison. Estimates of numbers varied between 2000 (Metropolitan Police)

---

55 PRO HO 144/1734/27.
56 Medical officer to governor, 25 April 1920: PRO HO 144/1734/64.
57 *Daily Mail*, 24 April 1920, 6a.
58 Troup to Shortt, 22 April 1920: PRO HO 144/1734/25A. Two days later Dr Treadwell, Medical Inspector of Prisons, reported that he had been unable to find suitable military or civil hospital accommodation in London.

and 7000 (*Daily News*).[59] Eighteen League branches were represented, and the crowd was led by bands and pipers in the singing of Irish patriotic songs. Father Thomas Roche of Holy Trinity, Dockhead Parish, Bermondsey, recited the rosary in Irish.[60] O'Brien issued a statement claiming that the majority of the 150 internees had been on hunger-strike since the previous Wednesday morning (21 April) and that many were rapidly reaching a state of collapse. All the hunger-strikers were determined, as had been their comrades at Mountjoy, to secure their liberty or to succumb to the effects of the hunger-strike.[61] The crowd had been large and exuberant, but the police gave a crumb of comfort to the Home Office by reporting that only about 1000, including many women, appeared to be in sympathy with the strikers. The prison governor went further and estimated sympathisers to be only a few hundred, with the rest made up of sightseers.[62]

The prisoners had greeted the first demonstration by setting fire to their bedclothes and throwing them out of cell windows, shouting their determination to continue the strike. The following evening they took more vigorous action, and by 7.15 p.m. had smashed almost all cell doors, coordinating this destruction with the demonstration. As the crowd assembled, the prisoners yelled that the doors were off their hinges. Upper portions of cell windows were also smashed and a number of prisoners pressed themselves through, waving republican flags and cheering. Art O'Brien and Father Roche were in attendance, the latter leading prayers. The size of the crowd was estimated at between 10,000 and 20,000.[63] The hunger-strike had become a national sensation. In the Commons, the Home Secretary refused to give an undertaking to bring the men to trial: they had been arrested on suspicion and could apply to bring their cases before a judicial tribunal.[64] Lord Robert Cecil initiated an adjournment debate, memorably and presciently arguing that Ireland was drifting through anarchy and humiliation to a republic.[65]

---

59 PRO HO 144/1734/64. See also *Daily Herald*, 26 April 1920, 1d–e; *Morning Post*, 26 April 1920, 8e; *Daily Chronicle*, 26 April 1920, 1d; *Manchester Guardian*, 26 April 1920, 7f and g. Announcements were sent out by the Irish Self-Determination League, and advertisements placed in the press (see, for example, *Daily Herald*, 1 May 1920, 2a–b. The advertisement contained an appeal to protect the 'Irish Priests and Irishwomen' who had been attacked during the demonstrations).
60 Father Roche appears to have been a visiting priest at Holy Trinity, and the *Catholic Directory* for 1921 shows that he had by then departed.
61 *Morning Post*, 26 April 1920, 8e.
62 PRO HO 144/1734/64. This was whistling in the wind.
63 *Morning Post*, 27 April 1920, 7g; *Daily Telegraph*, 27 April 1920, 9d; *Manchester Guardian*, 27 April 1920, 9c; *Daily Herald*, 27 April 1920, 1d–e. All the national newspapers carried the story.
64 5 *Hansard*, CXXVIII, cols 833–5; 26 April 1920. Unlike the earlier batches of detainees, there was no mechanism for automatic review, and it was extremely unlikely that individuals would apply for a hearing. Unwillingness to submit their cases to a tribunal could be taken, the Home Office doubtless reasoned, as a tacit admission of guilt.
65 5 *Hansard*, CXXVIII, col. 966; 26 April 1920.

The hunger-strikers had been tightly organised. The smashing of cell doors had commenced at 7 p.m. at the sound of a whistle. Half an hour later the whistle was blown again and the men rushed to the top landing. Because of the previous night's experience this had been cleared and secured with barbed wire. Pushing the warders aside, the prisoners climbed over the barbed wire, broke cell window frames and began to shout and wave flags at the crowd. Deputy governor Hales asked them to leave the windows, and when they refused summoned the military guard (1st Battalion Coldstream Guards) who marched into the prison. The men then moved away from the windows and were locked in undamaged cells. By 9.45 p.m. the prison was quiet and the prisoners were offered hot soup.[66]

The hunger-strike now swept up all but a few internees. Confined to their cells, the men were unable to greet the following night's demonstration, which Special Branch reported to be several thousand strong – including many sightseers.[67] A section of the crowd was hostile and scuffles broke out, causing Art O'Brien to protest to the Home Office that the demonstrators were not receiving the police protection to which they were entitled.[68] In the Commons the Home Secretary, referring to the disorder, had remarked that the Sinn Féin demonstrators had got the worst of it.[69] O'Brien protested that this was an inappropriate remark. His own deep involvement in all aspects of Sinn Féin's activities, and his knowledge that the Home Office knew of his role, lent a monumental quality of chutzpah to O'Brien's complaint, and it received short shrift from Troup, on behalf of Shortt. The police, Troup informed O'Brien, would protect peaceful persons from violence, but could not prevent counter-demonstrators. The Secretary of State did not accept O'Brien's claims that his demonstrators were making orderly and legitimate protests. The object was to encourage prisoners who were acting illegally and who had committed serious offences in the prison. The demonstrations had been conducted provocatively and many who were taking part carried blackthorns and other weapons. O'Brien should discontinue his protests.[70]

---

66 Hales to Home Office, 27 April 1920: PRO HO 144/1734/64. There was abundant spare accommodation at the prison. It had 1418 cells and a daily average population of only 237 (RCP, 1920–1, *op. cit.*, appendix 1, p. 28).

67 Special Branch to Home Office, 27 April 1920: PRO HO 144/1734/64. The principal Sinn Féin figures at the demonstration were J. J. McGrath, Art O'Brien and Mrs Eady.

68 O'Brien to Home Office, 29 April 1920: PRO HO 144/1734/64. Many of the demonstrators had been injured, O'Brien reported, including two girls who had had their heads cut open by stones, and five men, one of whom was so badly injured he might lose an eye.

69 Press reports had greatly exaggerated what had happened, he claimed, and there had been practically no disorder. The counter-demonstration on the night of 27 April, Shortt insisted, 'did not amount to very much disturbance and, so far as I am led to understand the Sinn Féin processionists got the worst of it' (5 *Hansard*, CXXVIII, col. 1366; 28 April 1920). The *Manchester Guardian's* report (28 April 1920, 9b) agreed that there had not been much of a disturbance, but also indicated that the demonstrators' marshalls had controlled the crowd.

70 Troup to O'Brien, 1 May 1920: PRO HO 144/1734/37 (see also ibid., /62).

Far from moderating, the protests became more intense, attracted stronger street opposition and spread to other cities. Despite Shortt's assurances to the Commons, the 27 April counter-demonstration had been larger and more pugnacious than ever before. The Irish Self-Determination League had also been active in other cities. There was a baton charge in Glasgow, and for some days the threat of a dock-strike in Liverpool.[71] Art O'Brien and the ubiquitous J. H. MacDonnell had been excluded from Wormwood Scrubs while the hunger-strike was going on, the authorities taking the view that they would simply encourage the strikers. Visiting the Home Office to challenge this decision, O'Brien argued that his ability to give information about the condition of the prisoners helped to keep the demonstrators orderly. If he could not visit the prisoners generally could he at least have access to Lawless and other leaders? The Home Office thought not. A day or so later, however, Troup had second thoughts, and directed that information was to be given on the condition of each prisoner whom O'Brien would name on a daily list. Besides meeting his complaint about the lack of information for the demonstrators, this decision allowed O'Brien to respond to the many telegrams he had been receiving from the prisoners' relatives in Ireland. The governor of Wormwood Scrubs made the necessary arrangements. Access to the prison itself was still denied.

Outside the prison violence intensified. On Wednesday, 28 April, as darkness fell, the demonstrators were attacked by hostile crowds. On a wet evening clods of mud and stones were thrown, and small groups of demonstrators were split off

---

71 A dock-strike in Liverpool, had it succeeded, would have been a major problem for the government, and besides the immediate difficulty with military supplies for Ireland might even have spread beyond Liverpool. (Certainly there was a mood for this, since on 10 May London dockers refused to load the *Jolly George* with munitions for Poland which were to be used against the Bolsheviks.) Sinn Féin, however, seems to have overplayed its hand, and by lack of funds and consultation brought itself into opposition with the Labour leadership. The announcement that a strike would be organised was made without preparing the ground, and provoked a warning from James Sexton, MP, Secretary of the National Union of Dock Labourers, that his union would not be used for political purposes (*Manchester Guardian*, 29 April 1920, 11a; 5 *Hansard*, CXXVIII, col. 1343; 28 April 1920). Attempts to call the dockers out were resisted, with union officials insisting that only they had this authority (*Manchester Guardian*, 29 April 1920, 9e). At noon on Thursday, 29 April, nevertheless, between 1500 and 4000 Irish dockers at Liverpool commenced a strike. From the outset this action was doomed. It flew in the face of an increasingly hostile attitude from the Union of Dock Labourers, reinforced by the leadership of other unions and the Labour Party, all fearful of sectarian division. In any event, a strike by a few thousand out of a workforce of about 37,000 (15,000 of whom were Roman Catholics) could at best be marginal. Twenty-four hours into the strike, the Liverpool Chief Constable reported the numbers to be about 1000 and that the work of the docks was hardly affected; indeed 'at South Dock 600 were turned away this morning because there was no work for them'. A demonstration of about 2500 had taken place: 'mostly women and Jews took part; there was no disorder at all' (PRO HO 144/1734/64). The *Manchester Guardian*, on the contrary, pronouncing the demonstration a success, described the dock-strike as 'to all intents and purposes a failure'. James Sexton again denounced the attempt to manipulate the Dockers' Union for political ends (*Manchester Guardian*, 1 May 1920, 11e; photograph 9b–c).

from the main body and assaulted. Two men took refuge from their pursuers in houses, and had to be rescued by police. Six more were reported injured and police drew batons to prevent further disorder.[72] Sinn Féin brought out more supporters the following evening, and this was matched by even more counter-demonstrators. Mounted police were deployed to clear away what the *Daily Chronicle* described as 'one of the biggest demonstrations London has ever witnessed'.[73] Even allowing for journalistic hyperbole, events were spinning out of control. Sinn Féin now showed its determination to meet violence with violence by providing a strong body of stewards. These, armed with hurley sticks, were positioned on the sides of the column. Estimates of numbers differed wildly. The *Daily Telegraph* reported 5000 on the heath outside the prison, of whom only 1000 were Sinn Féin supporters. The *Morning Post* put the crowd size at 30,000 with fresh relays of counter-demonstrators coming in during the evening, and a core of only 300 Sinn Féiners.[74] The following night (Friday, 30 April) demonstrators came prepared, with a 'flying column' of stewards in steel helmets, and a casualty clearing station.[75] There was no demonstration on 1 May, but Ireland and the hunger-strike was a bitter issue at Labour meetings throughout the country.[76]

The noise, fury and attention had greatly bolstered the hunger-strikers, and on Friday, 30 April the prison reported that all but four of its 221 internees were on hunger-strike.[77] Although prisoners had been without food for only nine days (and latecomers to the strike for less than that) there was already deep concern. Thirteen were removed to the Metropolitan Hospital, where they immediately began to take food and behaved well: 'like lambs', according to the matron. The hospital secretary reported that the improvement in the men's condition was so rapid that they would be ready for removal on the following Monday, 2 May.[78] St James' Infirmary, Wandsworth, agreed to accept forty-four cases. Dr W. R. K. Watson, the prison medical officer, informed the Home Office that in the event of an internee suddenly becoming unwell he would use all his resources to keep him alive until authority was given to remove him to hospital. It is unclear from this whether Dr Watson intended to force-feed, but in any event the Home Office agreed with his decision, which usefully shifted responsibility from politicians and officials to the doctors. The authorities' lack

---

72 *Daily Mail*, 29 April 1920, 5c; *Daily News*, 29 April 1920, 1a.

73 *Daily Chronicle*, 30 April 1920, 1e.

74 *Daily Telegraph*, 30 April 1920, 7e; *Morning Post*, 30 April 1920, 7g–h. The *Morning Post's* reports savoured the attacks upon the demonstrators: 'Lively Scenes at Wormwood Scrubs' and 'London Sinn Feiners' New Experience'.

75 *Daily Chronicle*, 1 May 1920, 1e; *Daily News*, 1 May 1920, 5f; *Daily Mail*, 1 May 1920, 5e.

76 *Manchester Guardian*, 3 May 1920, 7–8, *passim*; *Morning Post*, 3 May 1920, 4c–d.

77 PRO HO 144/1734/64. This figure, much larger than that being reported by the newspapers, is obviously more reliable than the various outside estimates.

78 Ibid.

of experience of the effects of hunger-strike was evident in Dr Watson's report of 2 May. Five prisoners were taking food 'in the ordinary way' and another six were on a special diet. But such was the condition of the remainder that Dr Watson insisted that they must be taking some nourishment.

Over the succeeding ten days the authorities lost their nerve and effectively gave Watson the power to decide who should be transferred to outside hospitals, and at what point. By 3 May fifty-three men were in bed in their cells. Lawless warned that the strike would continue to the bitter end, and were the men not freed 'it will be a question of the great release'. Privately officials were agreed that the men were determined to continue.[79] The following day Dr Watson reported A. Stack, J. McGuill and M. Quinn to be 'dangerously weak', and protested that they and others were being allowed to wander about the prison even though they were now in a condition which made it unsafe to use the stairs. If, however, they were kept in their cells, and allowed out only to use the adjacent lavatories, they could continue for some time without appreciable risk. But, he cautioned, 'as things are there is always the danger of syncope'.[80] Troup, with Shortt's approval, directed that Dr Watson (rather than the governor) should decide whether a prisoner was confined to his cell or held in the prison hospital.

A few days before, reports of the men's rapid recovery in the outside hospitals had begun to come in, and so a decision was necessary as to what would happen when they were completely recovered. 'This,' Troup minuted 'is the next difficulty.' Indeed it was, and on 6 May Dr O. F. N. Treadwell, the Medical Commissioner of Prisons, addressed it. Hospitals could not with propriety detain recovered men (and in any event, no guard had been provided at any of the hospitals). Two difficulties arose should the men be brought back to prison. If they were removed forcibly from within their precincts, the hospitals would be placed in such an awkward position that they might refuse to accept any future cases. And even if there was a successful return to custody, the men could start another hunger-strike and might then decide to continue it if returned to outside hospitals.

With these issues unresolved, the internees continued to be transferred to hospitals and nursing-homes. The 192 hunger-strikers at Wormwood Scrubs on 1 May had dropped to 180 by the morning of 6 May.[81] Large batches were removed on Friday and Saturday, 7 and 8 May: forty-seven, split between St James' Infirmary and Highgate Infirmary on the Friday, and a further thirty on the Saturday. Two days later another twenty-eight men were sent out when it was announced that Aiden Redmond, one of the Mountjoy hunger-strikers,

---

79 PRO HO 144/1734/64.
80 Dr W. R. K. Watson to Prison Commission, 4 May 1920: PRO HO/144/1734/64. 'Syncope' meant swooning, fainting, collapse, with possibly serious consequences.
81 Shortt replying to T. P. O'Connor: 5 Hansard, CXXVIII, col. 2218; 6 May 1920.

had died.[82] By 11 May there remained only forty-four men at Wormwood Scrubs, of whom eleven were accepting food. Dr Watson thought that two of the hunger-strikers – Lawless and Maloney – were clandestinely taking nourishment, but the thirty-one undoubtedly on strike were showing considerable weakness. Troup ordered that these be transferred to hospital. Two days later – whether they had belatedly joined the strike or whether Dr Watson had been wrong in his guess about secret feeding is not certain – Lawless and Maloney were also thought to be in a weak state. Their transfer to hospital, ordered that day, cleared all hunger-strikers from the prison.

No attempt was made to return the men to Wormwood Scrubs once hospitals reported their recovery. The Home Office seemed to hope that the problem foreseen by Troup would go away. It did, but not in the way that Shortt and his officials had hoped. On Sunday, 16 May twenty-three of the twenty-four internees recovering at the Metropolitan Hospital, Dalston, simply walked out. Later that day all thirty internees at Marylebone Hospital also departed. This concerted action had been decided by Art O'Brien, who had made the necessary preparations for supporters to receive and secrete the fifty-three absconders. Special Branch was immediately alerted, but the following morning astonishingly reported that it had been unable to trace the men's movements.[83] Five days after the walkouts Sir Basil Thomson, Director of Intelligence and head of CID, informed the Home Office that Joseph MacDonagh and several others had reached Dublin. The majority remained in London, mainly in the Dalston area, but 'It is very difficult to ascertain what they are doing.'

Not all the internees left their hospital – possibly because of the limited accommodation that O'Brien had at his disposal. Sixty-one remained at Highgate on 18 May, and when they were given passes to go out all but four returned. At the hospital they received crowds of visitors daily. Two days previously, however, all the internees at Marylebone had walked out in a (presumably humorous) protest against the shortage of food. The Daily Mail reported that because of the unexpected admission of several patients and the illness of the hospital steward there was a shortfall in lunch servings. Despite being offered special rations of pressed beef and boiled egg in lieu, the internees 'rose in a body and . . . walked out of the institution with a number of sympathisers who were visiting them'.[84]

By this time the internees were sufficiently confident of the government's pusillanimity to demand railway passes to allow them to return to Ireland.[85]

---

82 Daily Herald, 10 May 1920, 1d. Redmond had been released from Mountjoy three weeks previously and had in the meantime had an operation for appendicitis. The Herald's headline, 'Mountjoy Man Dead', and the short report which followed, implied however that Redmond's death was related to his hunger-strike.
83 PRO HO 144/1734/71A.
84 Daily Mail, 17 May 1920, 7e. The newspaper also reported that some of the nurses had been reduced to tears by the behaviour of the internees.
85 The first request had been made on 5 May by J. H. MacDonnell, acting on behalf of five released internees (PRO HO 144/1734/49).

The Irish government and the Home Office continued to dither. The latter took the view that having provided prison space in England when requested, it had done its duty: disposal of the walkout strikers was an Irish problem. On 10 May a decision was sought from Dublin Castle. The men transferred from Wormwood Scrubs to the Metropolitan Hospital had fully recovered and the hospital secretary refused to accommodate them for more than another twenty-four hours. Action was therefore imperative, and the Irish officials were cautioned that should the men refuse to return to prison there was no legal basis for re-arrest on the authority of the deportation orders which had transferred them to England.[86]

Still the Irish government vacillated, despite renewed Home Office protestations of urgency. Most of the internees were now at large, with a few in hospital and half a dozen or so non-strikers remaining in Wormwood Scrubs. J. H. MacDonnell demanded a decision incessantly, as did the Irish press.[87] The Home Office could not answer these enquiries and demands, and from 20 May referred them to the Irish Office. It was understood that Hamar Greenwood (Irish Chief Secretary) was inclined to revoke the internment orders but that he wanted the backing of a Cabinet decision: 'It is of course for the Chief Secretary and not for the Home Secretary to obtain this decision' insisted Troup.[88]

Sensing government paralysis, and frustrated by the uncertainty of their own legal status, and the pressures of work and family, internees vociferously demanded the return of their personal property and for rail passes to be issued. These requests were accompanied by threats of legal action. Deliberations proceeded in Dublin and on 25 May Power at the Irish Office was informed by the Under-Secretary at Dublin Castle that the Irish government's legal advisers were clear that the internees who had been removed to hospital from prison were thereby rendered free and immune from further confinement or re-arrest in England without the preparation of fresh deportation orders in Ireland. In these circumstances there was no authority to withhold the men's personal effects.

This bald statement of the legal position hardly helped the Home Office, and the following day Troup rather acidly pressed for further instructions. Most of the men remaining in hospitals were fit for discharge and the hospitals wanted them to go. Were they to be released, and if so, did the Irish government wish them to be given railway warrants? On the same day Hamar Greenwood

---

86 Draft telegram, Home Office to Dublin Castle, 10 May 1920: PRO HO 144/1734/49.

87 See, for example, the *Freeman's Journal* (11 May 1920, 3c and 4e; 12 May, 7e; 13 May, 5b; 14 May, 3e–f) for the concluding days of the strike and releases. Demand for the men's return to Ireland appeared with increasing emphasis from 22 May onwards (5g); 26 May (4e) ('the shiftiness of officialdom'); 29 May 1920 (4e).

88 Troup to Power (Irish Office), 19 May 1920: PRO HO 144/1734/49.

asked the Home Office to treat the men as if they had been unconditionally released, to return their personal property and to issue railway warrants. Troup was uncertain that this had the necessary authority, and asked for urgent confirmation from the Home Secretary. Shortt would not accept responsibility, and on 28 May telegraphed to Greenwood: 'Bonar Law has arranged a conference with the P[rime] Minister and myself on Ireland & the internees to-morrow. Would it be possible for you to come over.'[89] In the event, Cabinet again postponed a decision.

In the meantime the Home Office continued to be harassed by the hospitals. On 25 May one wanted to know if the men could be given their letters without censorship, and on the same day the Islington Poor Law Guardians, conscious no doubt of potential demands on their ratepayers, wrote supporting the men's application for their property and for warrants home. Two days later much the same message came from the law firm of Charles Russell & Co on behalf of several of the men. Sir Charles Russell drew attention to the expenses that fell on them during their enforced stay in England. Some left for Ireland daily, yet the governor of Wormwood Scrubs refused to hand over personal property – 'a vexatious and unnecessary proceeding which can only increase existing irritation without producing any good result'. Even Russell's admonition failed to elicit a full and honest response. Knowing that legally the men were free and unencumbered, the Home Office on 3 June still wrote that while the governor of Wormwood Scrubs had been instructed to hand over personal property, the men were not at liberty to return to Ireland, and if they did they would be liable to re-internment: 'Railway warrants therefore would not be issued.'[90] At this point, as far as the official records go, the exchanges ceased, and it must be presumed that whether at liberty to do so or not, all or most of the released Wormwood Scrubs men returned to their homes in Ireland.

After this dwindling away there remained a handful of prisoners whose cases had not been decided – either because they were not at Wormwood Scrubs or because they had not gone on hunger-strike. The three men who had been transferred to Brixton Prison as McGrath's companions, encouraged by the freedom forced by their comrades, went on hunger-strike on 10 June. One of these (J. Gibbons) demanded trial or release; the other two (T. Byrne and P. Dunne) sought unconditional release. Dr G. B. Griffiths, Brixton's medical officer, reported Dunne as saying that 'it was a rotten thing to be kept in prison for months without a trial and then to have to resort to this sort of thing to get free'.[91] The official records do not disclose the fate of these three men, but it seems that they were released under the general tidying up which followed the Wormwood Scrubs débâcle.

89 Shortt to Greenwood, 28 May 1920: PRO HO 144/1734/49.
90 PRO HO 144/1734/49.
91 PRO HO 144/1734/91.

Remand and convicted prisoners

The transfer to England of internees was authorised under the Defence of the Realm Regulations (DORR), but the status of persons convicted or remanded by civil courts in Ireland was quite different. This position had been confirmed from time to time, and as late as July 1920 Sir Edward Troup reminded Dublin Castle that there existed no power to detain in England prisoners who had been sentenced by civil courts in Ireland.[92] Within a month this deficiency was remedied with the enactment of the far-reaching Restoration of Order (Ireland) Act, 1920 (ROIA). Thereafter convicted prisoners could be transferred from Ireland to any other part of the United Kingdom, the power extending to those convicted before, as well as after, the passage of the Act. The Irish government would therefore make transfers as of right, rather than by special warrant or as a concession by the Home Office.[93] And, as before, those sentenced by district courts martial could be transferred to any part of the United Kingdom. Given the Scots' opt-out, this meant England and Wales.

The offences which these prisoners had committed were all unquestionably political in motivation, yet a distinction was drawn between those detained under DORA (referred to as 'politicals'), and those convicted by courts martial, who were held to be criminal cases. In the summer and autumn of 1920 most of these convicted prisoners were held at Liverpool and Manchester prisons (one was at Wormwood Scrubs). Care was taken to keep them as far apart from each other as possible, as at this point numbers were low enough to permit this. The intention was to prevent combinations hunger-striking or undertaking other forms of disobedience. This seemed to work, and although a few refused food as part of a campaign for political status and privileges, they soon gave up. Since these men were considered to be fully fledged criminal prisoners, sentenced by the courts, they would not be allowed to win release through hunger-strike. If they did refuse food, only the prison medical officer could decide on forcible feeding. Troup asked the Irish government to keep down the number of convicted transferees to a level at which medical staff might cope. He also requested confirmation of the no-release decision. And if indeed this was not firm, he wanted to know what would be done with any hunger-striker who was released, since after the Wormwood Scrubs experience it was unlikely that any hospital would accept them as patients.[94]

The Irish government continued to dither, its eyes no doubt on the pressures and balance of advantages in Ireland. This uncertainty cut across the basic principles of prison administration, as the Home Office and Prison Commissioners would intermittently expostulate. But when a prisoner tested the resolve of the

92 Troup to Anderson, 19 July 1920: PRO HO 144/1734/105.
93 Restoration of Order (Ireland) Act, 1920 (10 & 11 Geo. V, c.31, s1(3)(e)). The Act received the Royal Assent on 9 August 1920.
94 PRO HO 144/7134/103 and 105.

731

authorities, and the Home Office held the reins, the response was firm. Thus in July 1920 John Crowley, on hunger-strike at Manchester prison, was forcibly fed for three days, at which point he half promised to give up if he were allowed to wear his own clothes. Relating this to the Irish authorities, Troup emphasised that the Prison Commissioners were much against making the concession: 'They think that Irish prisoners (other than "politicals") if sent to English prisons must conform to English prison rules. If we give way in this case others will strike for the same privilege: then there will be other demands: and so it will go on.'[95] As it happened, the issue was not forced since Crowley gave up. Troup and the Commissioners were right: it was hard for most men to starve themselves without the solidarity and moral support of companions.

This firmness and success in avoiding more hunger-strikes was noted in Dublin and almost immediately brought further requests for assistance. John Anderson, now Under-Secretary at Dublin Castle, thanked the Home Office for its assistance and apologised for giving 'a great deal of trouble which events have proved to be unnecessary'. The policy of the Irish government on offences 'arising out of the present disturbed state of the country' was to detain only those whom it was intended to bring to trial as soon as possible. Any such person who was convicted would not be allowed to force his release by hunger-striking. To enforce this policy it had been agreed 'by your kindness' that any convicted prisoner who threatened to hunger-strike 'or otherwise to become refractory' would be transferred to England. Up until 11 August 1920, twenty-four prisoners had been transferred and none had persisted in their hunger-strike. On that day another twenty-two hunger-strikers had been transferred to England. As far as Anderson knew all had taken food prior to departure and had continued to do so on arrival.[96]

Of remand prisoners presently held in Ireland, Anderson reported, all but three or four remained on hunger-strike. It had been decided to winnow out this group, and those charged with lesser offences would be released. The medical officer thought that if any of the remainder were transferred to England they would take food. On this basis the Home Secretary had agreed to accept them, with the express proviso that no man was to be sent unless he ate before departure. This, Anderson felt sure, would mean that the men would continue to eat on arrival in England. The Admiralty had promised a ship, but this had not come, and because of the delay and therefore the increased debility of some of the men it had not been possible to send all who had been chosen. The men had all been charged with grave offences – involvement in attacks on the army and police and the possession of arms, ammunition, military manuals and equipment.[97]

Despite its experience of Dublin Castle promises, the Home Office took Anderson's assurances at face value – perhaps because of his high standing in

95 Ibid., /106.
96 Anderson to Shortt, 12 August 1920: PRO HO 144/1734/114.
97 Ibid. and /117.

Whitehall. There was chagrin, therefore, when some of the transferred remand prisoners continued to hunger-strike in England. The Home Office, feeling that undertakings had been broken, prepared for releases under the Cat and Mouse Act and informed Dublin Castle accordingly. Two men, who had been refusing food for nine days, were extremely weak, Troup telegraphed on 3 September 1920, and would therefore be released the following day: 'Secretary of State protests strongly against sending prisoners to England in this condition and must request that it may not be done again.'[98] This was an awkward development for the Irish government, which was faced with a determined hunger-strike at Cork prison; this would be greatly strengthened were the two men released in England. It was 'most important' that these men were not freed, Anderson telegraphed back. The Cork hunger-strikers had been charged with similar offences and had been on hunger-strike for much longer. The Irish Chief Secretary would be in London the following day and Anderson trusted that he and the Home Secretary could speak. As for the protest about sending debilitated hunger-strikers to England, clear instructions had been given that none were to go who did not take food before embarking, and enquiries would be made.[99]

Besides problems with the unconvicted there were difficulties with convicted prisoners. This had led to several disagreements between the Home Office and Dublin Castle. Some issues had been resolved, but the political needs of the Irish Office continued to generate requests which irritated and perplexed the English administrators. On 19 April 1920, the Irish government set out its intentions regarding political status. The general principle was that those arrested and imprisoned for political offences should be entitled to be 'differently treated' both with regard to the place of confinement and regime. This was not as straightforward as it sounded, however, since several types of offences were excluded from the political category, even though they could be committed only by persons with political motivation. Exclusions fell into three groups. Group A consisted of homicide, assaults or similar offences against the person. Group B included burglary, housebreaking, larceny, malicious damage, cattle-driving and the like – property offences. Group C was undoubtedly political and comprised offences that the Irish government particularly wished to deter. These were riot, firearms offences, unlawful assembly and 'speaking or writing words inciting or encouraging persons to commit any of the offences set out at A, B, or C'.[100] Since offences in any of the three groups could be politically motivated, political

---

98 Troup to Anderson (telegram), 3 September 1920: PRO HO 144/1734/132. The two men were John Joseph McCarthy and Daniel O'Brien, being held at Winchester Prison.

99 Anderson to Troup, 4 September 1920: PRO HO 144/1734/132-3. The Winchester problem resolved itself. The governor had instructions that the men were not to be force-fed, but these were countermanded by the prison Commissioners. The prison doctor then persuaded McCarthy and O'Brien to accept food.

100 PRO HO 144/1734/27. The details immediately following are taken from this document, which was also printed in the *Manchester Guardian* on 22 April 1922, 16c.

status was to be very limited, and largely meaningless in the light of what was happening in Ireland.

The document addressed procedures. A 'political' would go to a designated non-criminal prison, with a special regime. Those tried and convicted for a political offence before any court would, unless they had been sentenced to penal servitude, be entitled to the same treatment as untried political offenders except that they would not be permitted freedom of movement within the prison, or association or conversation other than at permitted times. They would also be limited weekly to one visit from one person and a letter in and out.

Against this framework a number of more detailed stipulations were laid down. Most importantly, political privileges were dependent on 'an orderly submission' to the rules and regulations: misbehaviour would deny access to the special regime, and possible removal to another prison. A person committed as a political prisoner and subsequently convicted of a non-political offence would be treated as an ordinary criminal prisoner. Claims for political treatment which the Irish law officers considered unfounded would be referred to a committee comprising two members of the prison's Visiting Committee (one to be nominated by the prisoner) and chaired by a judge.

The rules for the political regime were set out in two parts. The first (Schedule A) was to be available as soon as the prisoner was received into custody and the second (Schedule B) came into operation at the special prison. The rules were an amalgam of the various privileges available to the untried, civil prisoners and first-class misdemeanants. Schedule A provided for separation from ordinary prisoners, exemption from a reception bath and uniform (both of which political prisoners found degrading), search only by a specially designated officer, and excusal from work, hair-cutting and shaving. Smoking, own clothing, outside food (or the unconvicted diet) and a moderate amount of alcohol, books and newspapers were all available at the prisoner's expense. Relatives and friends could be corresponded with daily, and the Visiting Committee could enlarge this allowance for special reasons. Special cell furniture and equipment were to be provided, and at the prisoner's own cost the governor could provide a person to undertake 'any unaccustomed tasks or offices' (essentially cell cleaning). Schedule B gave freedom of movement and conversation between 9 a.m. and 6 p.m., 'subject to orderly behaviour'. Two weekly visits were allowed, one person on each occasion.

Compared to the restrictions and deprivations imposed on criminal prisoners with the intention of promoting security, emphasising the punitive nature of the regime and enforcing a degree of degradation, this was a substantial amelioration of confinement. To avoid administrative confusion and friction between those who did and those who did not have these privileges, however, the greatest possible separation of political from non-political prisoners was necessary. A completely separate prison was ideal, though the regime could probably have been operated in a self-contained wing.

The new rules were intended to apply to political prisoners in Ireland, but immediately the document was received at the Home Office Troup noted the problems for England. They went some way beyond the ameliorations given to the internees at Wormwood Scrubs (who of course were neither charged nor convicted). If Wormwood Scrubs were to continue to hold internees, Troup observed – and he was writing on 24 April 1920, when the first hunger-strikes had yet to run their course – the internees would surely sooner or later claim equality of treatment.[101] Troup sent the Irish document to the Prison Commissioners for analysis and comment. On closer examination it appeared that the rules under which men were held at Wormwood Scrubs either met the requirements of the new rules or (as often happened in the prisons when there was a will to do so) could be fudged to do so. Only on three points were the English rules or practices less generous. The provision of a weekly letter in and out was well out of line with the Irish daily allowance, and at Wormwood Scrubs the prisoners were not permitted freedom of movement around the prison. The same hours of association were given, though at slightly different times. There was also a marked difference in the number of visits: one a month at Wormwood Scrubs against two a week under the Irish rules. To raise the level of privileges to this level would, Ruggles-Brise contended, place a great strain on his staff, especially since visits were no longer to be confined to near relatives. Many priests and others would apply, and this would undoubtedly lead to a large increase in traffic. No mention was made of the extra work in censoring a daily allowance of letters in and out, but Ruggles-Brise observed that freedom of movement around the prison would be 'very undesirable'.[102]

On receiving these comments Troup noted that persons arrested and detained under DORA without any charge being laid were treated as 'political' under the Irish rules, and this applied equally when they were sent to England without any charges being laid. The use of the term 'political' was unfortunate 'in those cases where the real crime is complicity with murder'. As for the immediate implications for the Wormwood Scrubs internees, Troup observed that they had nearly all forfeited all privileges through their misconduct (in the hunger-strikes) and therefore (since good behaviour was a necessary qualifier for privileges) 'nothing further need be done just now'.[103] But within four months, government would face a prison challenge of an entirely different magnitude.

Terence MacSwiney's hunger-strike

Digging in

No single prison event during the Anglo-Irish war had a greater impact on its outcome than the hunger-strike of Terence MacSwiney, Lord Mayor of Cork and Commandant of the Cork IRA. Arrested with ten others while presiding over

---

101 Troup Minute, 24 April 1920: PRO HO 144/1734/27.
102 Ruggles-Brise Minute, 27 April 1920: PRO HO 144/1734/27.
103 Troup Minute, 20 April 1920: ibid.

an IRA meeting in the Cork City Hall (which the raiding party thought was an illegal Sinn Féin court), MacSwiney was brought before a District Court Martial at Victoria Barracks, Cork, on 16 August 1920 on four charges.[104] He refused to recognise the validity of the proceedings ('Illegal court, not assembled by the Irish Republic'). Invited to address the presiding officers before sentence, he made a remarkable commitment: 'I have decided that I shall be free alive or dead in a month as I will take no food for the period of my sentence.'[105] Sentenced to two years' hard labour, MacSwiney was immediately shipped to England, arriving at Brixton prison at 4.30 a.m. on the morning of 18 August 1920. He died there at 5.30 a.m. on 25 October, after a hunger-strike lasting seventy-four days.

From the beginning there seems to have been an awareness on the part of the officials that this might prove to be a difficult case. It was certainly in a different category from the Wormwood Scrubs hunger-strikers, who had drifted back to Ireland ten weeks previously. That had been an embarrassment, and although it made DORA look ridiculous, it hardly dealt a body-blow to the state. This was different. MacSwiney was a convicted man, and notorious besides: his forced release would be devastating. Ten days into the hunger-strike Lloyd George emphasised his government's duty to preserve law and order: 'If the Lord Mayor were released every hunger-striker, whatever his offence, would have to be let off. A law which is a respecter of persons is no law.' Were government to give way there would be a wholesale breakdown in the machinery of law.[106] As the days and weeks passed government had these observations brought home to it with ever greater force. Both sides knew that the play was for the very highest stakes.

---

104 The charges were: unlawful possession of a cipher issued to the RIC; unlawful control of a cipher (an alternative charge); unlawful possession of a document recognising the authority of Dáil Eireann; unlawful possession of a seditious document. He disputed and was acquitted on the charge of unlawful possession (PRO HO 144/10308/16A and /41). The cipher, ironically enough, concerned the transport to England of hunger-strikers and other prisoners: 'Admiral can do nothing till he knows number of prisoners, whether hunger-strikers, number of escort, date and place of embarkation.' The telegram, from the Inspector General of the RIC to the County Inspector, had come from one of the IRA's many agents and sympathisers in the Post Office. The court martial was conducted fairly with an abundance of evidence given by several witnesses. Proceedings were open to the public, but names and addresses were required, and those attending were subject to search.

105 *Cork Examiner*, 13 August 1920, 6a. The *Examiner* gave a slightly different and more disdainful version of MacSwiney's words: 'I simply say that I have decided on the term of my detention whatever your Government may do. I shall be free, alive or dead, within a month.' (This speech is also given in C. Harrington, 'Arrest and Martyrdom of Terence MacSwiney', The Kerryman, *Rebel Cork's Fighting Story 1916–21*, Tralee, The Kerryman, 1947, pp. 31–3.)

106 *Morning Post*, 26 August 1920, 5g. He insisted that the Mountjoy releases some weeks previously had been followed by 'an outbreak of cruel murder and outrage', including the shooting of a defenceless man within sight of the altar of his church. There had been no expression of regret, even in that case, from the political organisation to which MacSwiney belonged.

MacSwiney had equally little room for manoeuvre. He had given an unambiguous pledge, which had received wide publicity. He was a senior IRA figure, and some sixty of his comrades had commenced a hunger-strike in Cork Prison days before. The loss of face to himself and his organisation had he given up would have been devastating. There were two matters in his past which reinforced his determination. Together with his commanding officer, Thomas MacCurtain, MacSwiney had an uncertain record during the Easter rising, when he had failed to steer his way through the MacNeill–Pearse orders and countermands. On Easter Sunday morning MacCurtain and MacSwiney had dispersed their forces and, with assistance from local clergy, subsequently handed in weapons: the final message from Pearse had come too late. Although he was not alone in failing to act under the circumstances MacSwiney always felt tainted by the Cork failure. Even his fearsomely republican sister Mary reminded the Home Secretary in 1916 that had it not been for the efforts of her brother and MacCurtain 'you would have had considerable trouble in the South of Ireland'.[107] Mary wrote later that Terence knew no appeasement of the grief of those Easter days of failure until he was dying in Brixton Prison.[108]

Responsibility to the dead, the tug of the grave – a core element in republican political ethics and ideology – also welded MacSwiney to his death or freedom pledge. He had succeeded Thomas MacCurtain in the office of Lord Mayor of Cork, as well as Commandant of the Cork IRA. As noted above, five months previously a mixed force of police and soldiers had isolated and surrounded MacCurtain's home, entered and shot him dead.[109] Such a death of such a man, and the knowledge that he now trod in MacCurtain's shoes, could not but deeply impress MacSwiney, and lend him a mortal determination.[110]

Despite its recent experience with the Wormwood Scrubs hunger-strikers, the prison medical service had still not developed a good understanding of prolonged refusal of food: until the Cork hunger-strike no one would test themselves to the death.[111] MacSwiney's medical examination on arrival at Brixton gave the doctor concern about his ability to withstand the strains of progressive starvation. His physique was not good. In youth he had suffered from pleurisy, and twice

---

107 Mary MacSwiney to Home Office, 4 July 1916: PRO HO 144/10308/2.

108 Dorothy MacArdle, *The Irish Republic*, Dublin Irish Press, 1951, p. 178.

109 See above, pp. 686–7.

110 At his court martial MacSwiney stated that he realised that he might meet MacCurtain's fate (PRO HO 144/10308/16a). MacSwiney's fierce commitment was undoubtedly bound up with his ties of friendship and sense of loss for his dead comrade.

111 The Cork strike, which started with some sixty participants, soon faded, and by 16 September only eleven men persisted. A month later the first striker died on the fifty-eighth day. He was Michael Fitzgerald, Commandant of the First Battalion, Second Cork Brigade, IRA. A second striker, James Murphy, died on the same day (25 October 1920) as MacSwiney (*Cork Examiner*, 20 October 1920, 5b; 26 October, 6g).

had seen a doctor for heart problems. He had not eaten, he declared, since his evening meal on Thursday, 12 August.[112]

Three days after his arrival at Brixton MacSwiney (who had immediately been placed in the prison hospital) dictated a defiant note to the hospital warder and schoolmaster clerk who were in attendance: 'My undertaking on the day of my alleged Court Martial that I would be free, alive or dead, within a month, will be fulfilled.' (Like the medical officer MacSwiney had no idea that the human frame – even one as imperfect as his – could survive for two and a half months without food.) He projected himself on to the broader Anglo-Irish struggle: 'Knowing the revolution of opinion that will be thereby caused throughout the civilised world and the consequent accession of support to Ireland in her hour of trial, I am reconciled to a premature grave. I am prepared to die.'[113]

This form of struggle had a particular appeal to MacSwiney's temperament, and his belief that endurance is a cardinal virtue. One of his convictions was for the possession of a seditious document – his own speech to Cork City Council some weeks before, upon his election as Lord Mayor, in which he outlined his beliefs about the Anglo-Irish war. It was not from his perspective a contest of vengeance, but of endurance – 'it is not they who can inflict most but they who can suffer most can conquer. . . . Those whose faith is strong will endure to the end and triumph.'[114]

The Home Office and the Prison Commissioners were deeply worried by this case. Dublin Castle, which in the light of Ashe's death might have been expected to be equally careful, was altogether more gung-ho. On the day after MacSwiney's arrival at Brixton Geoffrey Whiskard telegraphed the Home Office: 'This man is not to be released. It is intended to forcibly feed him. You are aware that he is entitled to be treated as a political prisoner. Please wire daily about him.' The tone of the message did not please Home Office officials, who considered themselves to be helping the other department for reasons of state, but did not like to be taken for granted in an affair which already reeked of disaster and endless trouble. The reply was fairly curt: 'It is not intended to feed MacSwiney. Medical Officer says that his state of health is such that artificial feeding would

---

112 PRO HO 144/10308. Calculation of the length of his hunger-strike is based on the date he gave for his last meal.

113 PRO HO 144/10308/1. The original of this document is at /24. This was more than bravado, as the long hunger-strike would show. But at the time the message was dictated MacSwiney must have anticipated an early death. By 24 August the headlines in the *Freeman's Journal* pointed to imminent death: 'Dying for Ireland; Terrible Tragedy Drawing to Its Close in Brixton Prison; Condition Grows Worse; Lord Mayor Asks for No Mercy; Will do His Duty Until Death.' All this was grouped under an eight-column banner 'Defiant Message From Cork's Dying Lord Mayor' (3a–h).

114 Notes for the speech at PRO HO 144/10308/16a. This passage is well known, having been given wide circulation by republicans. Less familiar are his concluding words denouncing British rule in Ireland as 'a thing of evil incarnate' with which there would be no parley: 'We ask for no mercy and we will make no compromise.'

be unsafe.'[115] But in view of the Irish government's determination not to give way to a hunger-strike in this case, a solemn warning was issued to the prisoner by Dr Treadwell, the Medical Commissioner, that he (MacSwiney) alone would be responsible for the consequences of refusing food. He was asked if he wanted to see a priest.[116]

The decision not to force-feed was not unqualified. Dr W. D. Higson, the Brixton medical officer (who conscientiously considered the medical ethics of treatment throughout), told his patient in the presence of his priest that after his physical ability to resist taking food broke down, he would make every effort to introduce nutriments into his system 'for the purpose of prolonging, if not saving, his life'.[117] The following day Higson reported to the Home Office that he had done everything with the exception of physical force to induce his patient to take food and had also repeatedly spoken to his wife, sister and spiritual advisers in the hope that they would help him overcome 'the prisoner's almost fanatical determination not to take food while he is under detention here'.[118]

The question of MacSwiney's determination arose when Dr Higson was summoned to the Home Office for a strategy meeting with Home Secretary Edward Shortt, Home Office Legal Adviser Sir Ernly Blackwell and Dr Treadwell. Higson questioned whether MacSwiney was an apt case on which to test government's resolute position on hunger-striking. He was, Higson argued, 'a very different type of man from the ordinary Sinn Féin prisoner and from the point of view of gaining public support it would be much easier if the first case in which it was decided to let a prisoner die were a case of a prisoner convicted of some criminal offence involving stronger moral reprobation'. Shortt disagreed. It was preferable for the test case to be 'a well-known man and a leader rather than the case of some unknown and ignorant dupe'. Dr Higson took a different tack. MacSwiney had tubercular trouble. In an ordinary case this might lead to a medical officer recommending release should such a patient become dangerously ill. Did this offer a way out? The Home Secretary was scornful: 'Such a policy would mean that any scoundrel with a weak heart would have to be released quickly because he could not be forcibly fed.' He did, however, agree with Higson's decision that when MacSwiney became too weak to resist he would have to consider feeding him.[119]

It was a great convenience to agree that this was a medical rather than an administrative or political problem – though transparently it was a problem which might be resolved by political means. Two days later Shortt summoned

115 Ibid., /21. On Whiskard see n. 180, below.
116 The instruction to issue a formal warning came from Sir Ernly Blackwell (ibid., /22).
117 By this time MacSwiney had been without food for ten days (ibid., /34).
118 Higson to Home Office, 24 August 1920: ibid., /37.
119 Ibid., /49a. This document consists of a note of the meeting signed by Blackwell and Treadwell – an unusual proceeding (certainly the confirmatory signatures) – which indicates that Shortt wished to have something to show the Cabinet in the event of political fallout.

another meeting, this time involving external medical consultants (Drs. Craig and Beddard), as well as Doctors Treadwell and Higson. It soon became clear that Shortt was fishing for medical sanction to force-feed. Were that done the political problem might well be solved. The medical side, by contrast, was cautious and anxious not to be used as a political convenience. Shortt suggested that Higson had always had it in mind that it would be necessary to force-feed MacSwiney at some point. This was denied. What had been contemplated was not forcible feeding, but Higson's intervention at the latter stages, when MacSwiney's will-power declined to the point where he could no longer refuse to take food in liquid form. And it was also possible that in such circumstances MacSwiney might revive to the point where forcible feeding would have to stop.[120]

There was much fencing around these issues with Shortt constantly prob-ing for decisive medical intervention which could solve the problem, and the doctors pointing to the various complications. Shortt wanted to know whether MacSwiney had now reached the point where the shock and effort of attempt-ing to resist taking food were lesser dangers than his continued self-starvation. The medical men were evasive, though Craig pointed out that had MacSwiney been a patient in a mental hospital he would have been fed by now. What would happen, Shortt wanted to know, if nothing were done? The outside consultants did not think his lung problem would kill him, but warned that circulation might slow to the point of clotting – and that would kill him. By the end of the discussion it was agreed that it was better not to force-feed. Troup summed it up: 'balancing chance against chance there seemed to be more to be gained by taking the chance of refraining from feeding'. MacSwiney's will and powers of endurance would be tested, but not his power physically to resist or to bear the shock of force-feeding.

While these discussions were going on MacSwiney was in slow and steady decline, and protests and expressions of concern mounted. The first and most voluble of the protests came from Mary MacSwiney, who followed her brother to London and on 20 August presented herself at the Home Office, accompanied by Art O'Brien, and demanded an interview with Shortt. This was not granted, but Blackwell saw her and confirmed that the government was determined not to release her brother. This provoked a warning letter to Shortt which, had he had a mind to do so, might have provided the basis for a criminal charge against Mary herself. She impressed on Shortt the seriousness of what he proposed to do: 'If you let my brother or any of his comrades die in prison, we shall hold you personally responsible for murder. We are not accustomed to bluff – what we say we mean, so if you imagine that any of these men are bluffing and will take

---

120 Ibid., /64. At Shortt's request the outside doctors confirmed this agreement, and a note to that effect was submitted (on Dr Beddard's Harley Street notepaper). All Higson could do was to continue to try and persuade MacSwiney to eat, to deal with his discomforts and pains as they arose and to give what further treatment he would permit.

food at the end, you are mistaken.' She emphasised that none of the mothers or sisters or wives would intervene to bring about an end of the hunger-strike and concluded: 'I warn you to beware how you cause the death of a second Lord Mayor of Cork.'[121]

Mary remained in constant attendance during her brother's hunger-strike, which she blamed entirely on the British government. Her formula was simple: if her brother was released the problem would be resolved. Until then she protested at his confinement, continued to demand his release and was unwavering in her support for the hunger-strike. When Dr Higson told her that he would have to consider feeding her brother when he became too weak to resist, it produced 'an hysterical outburst as she regarded it merely as a way of prolonging the agony'.[122] Sir Norman Moore (President of the Royal College of Physicians) was brought in as a medical consultant by the MacSwiney family and supporters. He explained to Mrs Muriel MacSwiney (wife) and the two sisters, Mary and Annie, the danger in which Terence had placed himself, and later told Dr Higson that he had found them quite obdurate in their determination not to influence MacSwiney to take food. He reported that 'they seemed even more determined if possible than he was'.[123] These women remained adamant to the end – whatever their private thoughts and feelings may have been.

Interventions

There were expressions of concern and protests from what might be termed the usual circles. On 23 August, the pro-republican Roman Catholic Archbishop of Melbourne, Dr Daniel Mannix (who two weeks previously had been refused entry to Ireland and removed to England on board a destroyer) accompanied by the Bishops of Killaloe and Ballarat, had visited MacSwiney at Brixton. They had previously given undertakings to do nothing to encourage MacSwiney in his hunger-strike, but their presence was in itself a considerable boost for MacSwiney and his supporters.[124] There had been an attempt to bring the Lord Mayor's chaplain to Brixton, but as the request (made by Cork's Deputy Lord

---

121 Mary MacSwiney to Shortt, 20 August 1920: PRO HO 144/10308/23. She received a bland reply the next day, reiterating the government's position and confirming that owing to the state of his health her brother could not be fed forcibly. Mary continued to issue warnings particularly to Lloyd George ('we shall hold him responsible for my brother's murder'). Since the decision not to release him had been a Cabinet decision 'then each member of that Cabinet who does not publicly resign as a protest, will be held, by the Irish Nation, to account for that murder' (Labour History Archive and Study Centre, John Rylands University Library of Manchester: Labour Party Archives, CA/MAC/7.i: Mary MacSwiney to Council of Action, 4 September 1920).

122 Ibid., /49a.

123 PRO HO 144/10308: 25 September 1920.

124 Ibid., /26.

Mayor) inexplicably demanded that the British government should provide the transport and it refused to do so, this clerical visitation failed to come off.[125]

The hunger-strike was lead news in the Irish newspapers, over the weeks occupying thousands of column inches and hundreds of banner headlines. It is hard to convey the fever of sensation, pity and increasing bitterness. The un-expectedly protracted length of MacSwiney's agony daily consolidated support for him and his cause. In England the case was of lesser but still considerable import. Predictably, various liberal and humanitarian bodies became involved. The Central Office of the Society of Friends in a letter to the Home Secretary argued that 'the death of the Lord Mayor of Cork in prison will create such passionate feeling in Ireland as will very greatly decrease the possibility of reconciliation'.[126] Similar statements were submitted by bodies such as the Irish Peace Conference, the Fellowship of Reconciliation, the National Health Insurance Committee, the County of Cork and the High Sheriff of Cork (an appeal to the King). Govern-ment appeared unmoved, and on 24 August issued a statement which nailed its colours to the mast as firmly as MacSwiney had his. The decision not to release MacSwiney had been made by the Cabinet and the government would stand firm; the Irish government had concluded that release would be disastrous. In the light of these facts, interviews with the Home Secretary to urge MacSwiney's case could serve no useful purpose.[127] This stance was confirmed by a statement issued by Lloyd George (then in Lucerne) to Reuters on 25 August.[128]

But it was not only republican fellow travellers, liberals and pacifists who were drawn into the drama. The Times, long a staunch exponent of the benefits of British rule in Ireland, had under its editor Henry Wickham Steed become a bitter and telling critic of Lloyd George's Irish policy.[129] On 23 August it ran a trenchant editorial. Had MacSwiney been sentenced for complicity in murder or serious outrage government would be justified in allowing him to suffer the

---

125 Thomas MacCurtain had appointed the Franciscan Father Dominic as chaplain to the Cork Brigade of the IRA. Arrested in January 1921 and sentenced to five years' penal servitude Father Dominic was released in January 1922. During the civil war he sympathised with the Republicans, though ministering to both sides. Certainly this was no neutral, unworldly or cloistered priest (see Florence O'Donoghue, 'A Patriot Priest of Cork City', The Kerryman, *Rebel Cork's Fighting Story 1916–21*, Tralee, The Kerryman, 1947, pp. 65–7).

126 Letter of 23 August 1920: ibid., /36.

127 Ibid., /44.

128 See *Morning Post*, 26 August 1920, 5g. In correspondence with petitioners ministers confirmed this statement as government's final position. Writing to the Labour Party on 5 September Bonar Law stated 'There is little to add.' While recognising the part that sentiment plays in human affairs, the government could not take a step (MacSwiney's release) which 'would inevitably lead to a complete breakdown of the whole machinery of law and Government' (Bonar Law to J. S. Middleton (Assistant Secretary, Labour Party), 5 September 1920, Labour Party Archives, CA/MAC/II, i–iii: Labour History Archive and Study Centre, John Rylands University Library of Manchester).

129 Steed (1871–1956) had worked for The Times since 1896, mainly as a foreign correspondent. Foreign editor, 1914–19, editor, February 1919 to November 1922.

consequences of hunger-striking, 'But his offences are not of this character; and in the eyes of his fellow countrymen, bear no moral stigma. If he dies the majority of the Irish people will conscientiously regard him as a martyr, and the government as his murderers.' The editorial recalled the death of Thomas Ashe and its aftermath: did ministers desire a similar outcome? And if their calculation was different – 'the eventual surrender of their prisoner' – the game was still risky since he could persist to the end, and by his death 'stir the angriest depths of Irish feeling': the situation could well be irretrievable.[130] Government, by this reasoning, was boxed into a corner: it lost if MacSwiney starved himself to death, and it lost if it allowed itself to submit to the release of a convicted prisoner. *The Times* thought the latter would inflict the lesser damage.

It is extraordinary that ministers could not follow this simple logic. Having refused food for a number of weeks MacSwiney's health would by any criteria be sufficiently damaged for government to contrive release under the provisions of the Cat and Mouse Act without losing too much face. Yet nowhere in the MacSwiney papers is there any discussion of temporary release. Instead, there were ever more public statements by ministers to limit rather than increase options, even while advice from those who saw MacSwiney every day confirmed that he was utterly determined. Part of government's stubbornness came from the Unionist domination of the coalition. On 23 August Arthur Balfour telegraphed his support for the no surrender policy. The same day Bonar Law wrote to the Home Office asking if 'vitamans' (*sic*) could not be surreptitiously introduced into MacSwiney's water to 'help keep him going'.[131] Anything, in other words, even trickery scarcely compatible with the dignity of a department of state, rather than any kind of release, however conditional and short term.[132]

The King's duty

As the hunger-strike progressed national and international attention focused on Brixton Prison.[133] The Irish Self-Determination League followed much the same

---

130 *The Times*, 23 August 1920, 11b–c.

131 PRO HO 144/10308/34. Dr Treadwell (to whom this scheme was put) thought it 'injudicious'. A substance tasteless in water would make little difference. If MacSwiney became suspicious he would refuse water as well as food, with the inevitable result of a more rapid deterioration: 'Mr Bonar Law should be informed that the prisoner is constantly supplied with appetising soup jelly and custard. He would not be in the least likely to take water which he *knew* had been doctored.'

132 There is no explicit reference in the official papers, but the Wormwood Scrubs débâcle may have been a factor in refusing to contemplate the release of MacSwiney under the Cat and Mouse Act. What, if released, he could not be taken when restored to health? He certainly had the resources to go into hiding.

133 Even the most pro-republican newspapers were, however, forced to cut back their coverage by the length of the hunger-strike, an exhaustion of prose, and the spiralling violence in Ireland (See *Freeman's Journal*, 2 October 1922, which gave only six column inches to MacSwiney (5e)).

programme of demonstrations that had gathered large numbers at Wormwood Scrubs earlier in the year, although momentum could not be sustained during the ten weeks of the strike.[134] The issuing of statements of government's determination not to give in – including Lloyd George's Lucerne telegrams – all built up a sense of deepening public crisis. Behind the scenes an important section of the establishment was becoming deeply disturbed. Sir John Scott, High Sheriff of Cork, a southern Unionist and undoubted loyalist, asked the King to intervene to have MacSwiney moved from Brixton to an outside hospital.[135] At about the same time Redmond Howard (a Home Ruler) also telegraphed the King. Exceptionally, the King's reply, which cannot have been read with any satisfaction by government, was made public: 'I am commanded to express His Majesty's appreciation of your assurances that, in spite of the very grave condition of affairs in Ireland, the work of reconciliation between the two races may yet be accomplished.'[136] The emphasis on reconciliation rather than standing firm, and the fact that permission appeared to have been given to publish the reply were strong hints of the King's unease.

An important section of southern Unionism had approached the King confidentially through the former Commander-in-Chief of Ireland, General Sir Bryan Mahon, an Irish Privy Councillor.[137] The political position of southern Unionists, he wrote, had latterly shifted considerably, and the majority now favoured 'Dominion Home Rule'. Mahon could see government's difficulty over MacSwiney, but believed that his death in prison would cause 'hatred and bitterness against England which will take generations to eradicate and will also stir up religious strife'. Any hope of settlement would be ended for a generation. Exercise of the Royal Prerogative would be appreciated by all classes in Ireland and would assist a settlement.

Lord Stamfordham, the King's Private Secretary, replied to Mahon's letter, which had immediately been forwarded to the Home Secretary. Mahon had probably seen the correspondence in the press about the exercise of the Royal Prerogative:

> The King heartily deplores the present terrible condition of things in Ireland and the increasing spirit of retaliation and revenge resulting in the deplorable loss of life among both parties in the strife. What you say of the affection of the Irish people for His Majesty is gratifying to the King, who has always reciprocated this feeling, and therefore

---

134 See the *Morning Post*, 25 August 1920, 5g; 28 August, 5f. Numbers dwindled by 31 August.
135 PRO HO 144/10308: 26 August 1920. Scott was Chairman of Cork Unionist Association, prominent in public affairs and commerce, a senior Alderman and past mayor; he was also a member of the Synod of the Church of Ireland.
136 *Morning Post*, 26 August 1920, 5g.
137 (1862–1930). Born in Galway. Military career included India, Egypt, Sudan and South Africa. General Officer Commanding Irish Division, 1914; Commander-in-Chief, Ireland, 1916–18.

he sorrows all the more for that misery which at the present time casts a shadow over the daily life of the Irish people.[138]

That this was not an empty and formal statement was shown by exchanges between King and government, which had they become public would have had a devastating effect on public opinion. The King could not with any propriety have allowed more than a hint of his views to emerge, and so they remained deeply buried in government files. There would no doubt have been incredulity on the part of Sinn Féin members had they known that the King, the ultimate symbol of Empire and British rule in Ireland, had entered into a strongly worded conflict with his government over MacSwiney. But George V acted on what he saw as his duty of welfare and protection towards his Irish subjects.[139]

From Balmoral Stamfordham telegraphed on 25 August 1920 that His Majesty was sure that government was 'seriously considering' the case of the Lord Mayor of Cork: 'Were he allowed to die in prison results would be deplorable from every point of view. His Majesty would be prepared to exercise clemency if you so advise and believes that this would be wise course. Lord Mayor should not return to Ireland but be accommodated in private house under precautionary rule.' Whether this would have been a practical arrangement or even acceptable to MacSwiney is not clear, but it was a reasonable proposal and, since it came from the head of state, worthy of at least cursory investigation – if only for form's sake. Inexplicably this telegram produced no answer – not even an acknowledgement. The following day the King telegraphed again, using the first person to emphasise his concern and sense of urgency: 'I had hoped to receive answer to yesterday's telegram. Meanwhile I am receiving appeals from many quarters including editor of Manchester Guardian to exercise my prerogative. The Government know my view and while appreciating difficulty of their position I still advocate clemency. George R.I.'[140]

Late in August virtually all ministers were out of London, leaving Shortt in charge. Never one to grasp responsibility, Shortt summoned Balfour and Churchill back to town (Lloyd George was still abroad) to consider MacSwiney's case in the light of the King's views. Lloyd George's reply to Mary MacSwiney's plea on behalf of her brother had appeared in the press that morning, and this apparently left no room for compromise or fudge. A telegram to the King was agreed: 'Mr Shortt deeply regrets that the decision of the Cabinet must stand.

---

138 PRO HO 144/10308/204.

139 Seven years previously, when the Cat and Mouse Act Prisoners (Temporary Discharge for Ill-Health Act, 1913 (3 Geo. V, c.4)) was being considered, the King had confidentially expressed his distaste ('something shocking, if not almost cruel') at the forcible feeding of the suffragettes. He hoped that with the passage of the Act it might be possible to cease the practice (Harold Nicolson, *King George V: His Life and Reign*, London, Constable, 1952, p. 212). The King's views failed to sway government on the issue.

140 PRO HO 144/10308/63A. This file had been marked 'Very Confidential'.

The Irish Chief Secretary informed Mr Sec. Shortt that the release of the Lord Mayor of Cork would have disastrous results in Ireland and would probably lead to mutiny of both military and police in South of Ireland.'[141] There was not the slightest evidence to support the last statement (and certainly there is no mention of it elsewhere in these and related papers), but army and police mutiny was as grave a prospect as could be imagined. Coming in the forum of official advice to the monarch from the government it was a blunt warning to keep out of the affair.

Thus warned off the King could go no further without provoking a serious constitutional confrontation. He signalled that he would continue to watch developments, of which the government had been remiss in not keeping him abreast. With the exception of Shortt's replies to his two enquiries, he telegraphed, 'King has not had any official information about the Lord Mayor of Cork and has to rely on newspaper reports.'[142] Concern and displeasure were thus made clear, but the only outcome was to force the government to arrange that copies of the regular reports received from Brixton should be sent to the King.

Body-snatching

By early September the outcome was no longer in doubt, and the issue for government narrowed – how to deal with MacSwiney's body: everyone knew what Sinn Féin could do with such a funeral. The Irish government was emphatic that it would be undesirable to give MacSwiney's body to his relatives in London. The result would probably be 'a great procession in London [and] also one in Dublin'. The body might then be taken by road to Cork 'with a demonstration at every town on the way'. If possible, Dublin Castle wanted the body taken by the navy to Cork, and there handed over.[143] Troup sought legal advice and on 9 September Sir A. H. Dennis, the Treasury Solicitor, outlined the law. Were a *felo de se* verdict returned, it was open to the coroner to issue directions as to the disposal of the body, which would probably be interment in a cemetery serving Brixton.[144] Three days later the Metropolitan Police (which was concerned about public order problems should MacSwiney's body be processed through London) asked whether a decision had yet been made on the matter: would the relatives get the body? At this point Dennis added to his earlier explanation of the law. Should there not be a *felo de se* verdict MacSwiney's next of kin could claim the body, but in the event of a *felo de se* finding the coroner was bound to

---

141 Shortt to King, 26 August 1920: ibid.
142 King to Balfour, n.d. (?26 or 27 August) 1920: ibid.
143 Troup Memorandum of conversation with Whiskard, 7 September 1920: PRO HO 144/10308/ 206a.
144 Sir A. H. Dennis to Sir Edward Troup, 10 September 1920: ibid., /206a. The coroner held these powers under the Interments (*Felo de Se*) Act, 1882 (45 & 46 Vict., c.19, s.2).

order burial in England. The Home Office had no power in the matter, but had an obligation to see the coroner's directions enforced by issuing the necessary warrant to his officers and to the police.[145]

Setting out the issues Troup argued that there were public interest considerations 'which might negate the claim of the Executors to immediate possession of the body'. He asked Dennis if prison authorities could send the body to Cork to be handed over to MacSwiney's executors:

> The matter may prove in the course of a day or two one of great political importance, and I think the Government would not be willing to assent to the view that they are under compulsion to hand over the body to the relatives at Brixton except on the highest legal authority, i.e. where the result would be a dangerous demonstration in London and probably a still more dangerous one in Dublin.

Troup asked Dennis to obtain the Opinion of the Attorney General (then in Scotland).[146]

At this point MacSwiney's condition was fairly stable although his decline was inexorable. Appeals from religious and other groups continued to come in, with the Bishop of Southwark and various establishment figures variously expressing concern and seeking some form of clemency. Muriel MacSwiney continued to refuse to persuade her husband to eat, as did Mary, who was said to be very bitter and anti-British in her conversation. Because of the prolonged fast – of which there was little experience – there was some suspicion that one or the other (or both) of these women might be smuggling in food. This seemed to be confirmed on 11 September when a small piece of an unidentified substance was found in MacSwiney's cell. Hoping for evidence of fraud, this was immediately sent for analysis – and proved to be soap. A week later the prisoner's faeces were analysed in another attempt to show fraud: this also gave no indication that food was being taken.[147]

---

145 PRO HO 144/10308/206a. Dennis pointed out that the Home Office had no power to impose conditions on MacSwiney's executors.

146 Ibid., /206a. This letter was marked 'Secret'. In thinking that government would force the MacSwiney executors to obtain a High Court order before handing over the body, Troup had in mind the case of *Fox* (which concerned a gaoler who withheld the body of a prisoner until his relatives settled an outstanding prison bill). On this occasion the court had ruled that the body could not be withheld, and had granted a writ of mandamus. *Fox* was given more general form by Mr Justice Kay in the case of *Williams*. Troup's hope was that a public interest argument would prevail notwithstanding this case law.

147 Ibid., /253a and /256a. Official experience was based on the suffragette hunger-strikes. These had rarely lasted for more than a week or two before the risks and ill-effects of forcible feeding had compelled the women's release (see Emmeline Pankhurst, *My Own Story*, London, Eveleigh Nash, 1914, chs 4 and 5; E. Sylvia Pankhurst, *The Suffragette Movement: An Intimate Account of Persons and Ideals*, London, Longmans, Green, 1931, pp. 312–19, 438–54).

MacSwiney's endurance was an object of speculation well beyond the Home Office. Dr Angus MacPherson, Assistant Medical Secretary of the British Medical Association, in early October had joined in press speculation that perhaps nutrition was being administered in the form of medicine.[148] Art O'Brien responded on behalf of the family and supporters and invited Dr MacPherson to consult Sir Norman Moore, President of the Royal College of Physicians, who had been attending MacSwiney on behalf of his family. Moore, O'Brien wrote, would assure his medical colleagues that 'no nourishment, whatever, either in liquid or solid, has entered the system of the Lord Mayor of Cork, either by internal or external application, since the time of his arrest.'[149] As much as it was in the government's interest to find evidence of fraud, it was in Sinn Féin's to ensure that no food was introduced (perhaps as a means of sabotaging or as a dirty trick by government, at whatever level) and that the strike should appear to the world as unquestionably and unimpeachably genuine. Around this time, and for a few weeks previously, one senses in the exchanges a growing wish on the part of the family that MacSwiney should die sooner rather than later, and claim his victory. Release as an invalid to a private nursing-home would by now have hardly been worth such agony. Such was MacSwiney's impact in Ireland and beyond that militant republicans preferred death to release.[150]

By 21 October there were intimations that the end was near. The previous day MacSwiney had been able to refuse food and to reason and argue with the doctor, but during the night he had entered a delirium and had begun to scream. The medical officer administered morphia and also made the decision, in view of the patient's mental state, to give small quantities of milk and dextrose. The following morning his condition was considered to be very grave. Dr G. B. Griffiths, the senior medical officer (who had taken over from Dr Higson in early September) reported a change in the attitude of MacSwiney's family and friends 'who

---

148 See, for example, *Pall Mall Gazette*, 2 October 1920, 5a. This reported a French case of survival for sixty-three days without food. On 24 September the MacSwiney family issued an emphatic denial that they had ever supplied food, in any form, to Terence (ibid., 5d).

149 O'Brien to MacPherson, 11 October 1920: NLI: Art O'Brien Papers: Ms. 8444(i) (unfoliated). O'Brien made a rather extraordinary offer to MacPherson on behalf of the family. Little was known about the effects of depriving the body of nutriment and apparently the London medical profession was not interested in the topic – 'even though they have in their midst a most outstanding case on the subject'. MacSwiney's relatives would not give information to the press, but he thought they would be willing to pass it (through him) to the medical profession. On 14 October, MacPherson replied. He agreed that the case of the Lord Mayor would interest the medical profession but did not see how the facts could be collated since there could be no direct access. His concluding observation was perhaps unexpected: 'Personally I have the greatest respect for anyone who is making a sacrifice for a cause or principle of the justice of which he or she is convinced.'

150 'The result was inevitable; we hoped he would not be released when his body was almost used up. . . . He had become a symbol of part of a new nation; disciplined, hard, clear, unsentimental, uncompromising, a conscious using of vigour to build up strength' (Ernie O'Malley, *On Another Man's Wound*, London, Rich & Cowan, 1936, p. 203).

are always about here and beg me to "let him die in peace" and tell me that "I am only prolonging the torture"'. In feeding his patient Griffiths considered he was doing no more than what six weeks previously he had told MacSwiney and his wife he should do if MacSwiney became unconscious or unable to resist: they had then agreed this to be a reasonable thing for a doctor to do. Griffiths now found the demands to let his patient die 'quite distressing'.[151]

Light feeding continued and MacSwiney, who had become unable to control his functions and whose naked and emaciated body needed constant turning, was given intensive nursing care.[152] Relatives were excluded from time to time, which led them to allege that he was being fed when they were not present. Dr Griffiths reported on 23 October that he did not, apart from the condition of his patient's heart, expect 'an immediate termination'. MacSwiney's hold on life was now very weak indeed, however, and Griffiths wanted to keep him as quiet as possible. This was not assisted by Mary MacSwiney who, volatile at the best of times, and now under immense mental, emotional and physical strain, allowed her detestation of the prison functionaries and all they represented to erupt into unacceptable behaviour. Dr Griffiths had to contend with much of this abuse, and on the evening of 22 October Mary came to see him in his surgery to protest about his continued feeding of her brother. He reported that she had 'behaved in an extremely unpleasant and disorderly manner', the upshot of which was that she was banned from the prison.[153] Other members of the family were not excluded. Mrs Muriel MacSwiney sat in a passage outside the ward and could see her husband at any time, day or night, except when the nurses were with him. His brothers had been allocated a room in the prison hospital, and had the same access. By mistake Mary and Annie were admitted to a waiting-room adjacent to the prison gatehouse. Once in, they refused to leave. After some time the Home Office was consulted, and Shortt himself directed that they be ejected, by force if necessary. The police were then called and persuaded the sisters to leave.[154]

---

151 Griffiths memorandum, 21 October 1920: PRO HO 144/110308/261a.

152 Shortt was insistent that the course of MacSwiney's treatment was entirely and exclusively a medical matter: 'If the doctors think lime-juice would ease him, help him to live, and give him another chance of seeing sense, they will be perfectly justified in trying to persuade him to take it, and, indeed, if necessary, forcing it upon him' (5 *Hansard*, CXXXIII, cols 1041–2; 20 October 1920). The last words were too strong by far, and evoked the image of a terminally ill man being manhandled. The next day he backtracked: 'In this case forcible feeding consists merely in holding a cup to his lips, and the swallowing has been voluntary. In any case, forcible feeding is not only legal, but many times a duty' (ibid., col. 1053; 21 October 1920).

153 Griffiths memorandum, 23 October 1920: PRO HO 144/10308/261a. He found the other sister, Annie, 'not quite so troublesome' but thought nevertheless that she was behind the difficulties that were being made over feeding. In the Commons the Home Secretary made no reference to the sisters' behaviour in justifying the decision to exclude them: 'The directions were all given purely on medical grounds . . . because of the extremely bad effects they had upon the condition of their brother' (5 *Hansard*, CXXXIII, cols 1334–5; 25 October 1920).

154 PRO HO 144/10308/261a.

The previous day Mary MacSwiney had directed a characteristically intemperate letter to Shortt, who was even less likely than normal to tolerate her
outbreaks. She protested that in a Commons statement in order to discredit him
Shortt had suggested that her brother had voluntarily taken food. Neither she nor
any other relative had given him food, she insisted: 'Of all the infamies possible
to an individual, or a government, that of lying about an unconscious victim,
who for the time being is in their power, is the most vile.'[155]

Outside interest intensified. This protracted and agonising death attracted
national and international attention. His name and his cause had achieved
worldwide recognition, almost all of it sympathetic on grounds of general humanity. Careful arguments about the rule of law were lost in the drama and pity of
MacSwiney's plight. Only a fraction of those persons or individuals who are disturbed by government action, or who disagree with it, write in. By 25 October,
nevertheless, government had received 189 telegrams and 159 letters on
MacSwiney's behalf, with a significant representation from Labour Party branches,
trades unions, various Irish organisations and some local authorities (mainly in
Ireland).[156] The Liberal Party, now almost entirely Lloyd George's fiefdom, was
not represented at all, though a number of individual Liberals doubtless were.
But on any reckoning MacSwiney's action was a major boost to his cause, and a
blow against the government. He had seen his arrest and imprisonment as an
opportunity, which his endurance enabled him to seize.

That endurance and Dr Griffiths' medical and nursing resources were finally
exhausted at 5.30 a.m. on Monday, 25 October.[157] All relatives (including Mary
and Annie) were immediately admitted to see the body. The inquest was set
for 27 October, and both sides prepared to struggle for the body. The Home
Office, the Irish government and the Metropolitan Police all hoped for a
felo de se verdict, and a favourable direction from the coroner. The relatives
were backed by Art O'Brien and the significant resources he could command,

---

155 Mary MacSwiney to Shortt, 22 October 1922: ibid., /261. The letter continued in the same
   vein. The previous day Shortt had in fact quashed a suggestion by the MP for Hackney,
   Horatio Bottomley, that food had been smuggled to MacSwiney (5 *Hansard*, CXXXIII,
   col. 1053; 21 October 1920). The statement which had incensed Mary was a one-liner (also in
   answer to Bottomley) on 19 October. In view of his great suffering and as a gesture to Ireland,
   Bottomley had urged clemency for MacSwiney, then in his sixty-eighth day without food, and
   inter alia, had asked whether there had been any feeding whatsoever. 'Not on the part of the
   prison authorities,' Shortt replied (5 *Hansard*, CXXXIII, col. 769; 19 October 1920).
156 PRO HO 144/10308/263a and 263b. It is uncertain who at the Home Office ordered the
   tabulation.
157 The nationalist Irish newspapers broke out their banner headlines, long-prepared feature articles,
   and photographic portraits, poems and tributes from all sections of nationalist and Catholic
   society. His death coincided with that of Joseph Murphy, the second man to die in Cork
   Prison, and whose hunger-strike had lasted for seventy-six days. Murphy's passing, completely
   overshadowed by MacSwiney's, received only four column inches in the *Freeman's Journal*
   (26 October 1920, 5c).

including good legal advice and a purse long enough to make an immediate High Court application.

Hamar Greenwood, the Irish Chief Secretary, was prepared to ignore legal requirements. On the day after MacSwiney's death, he wrote to Shortt saying that it would be very dangerous to Dublin to allow the body to be brought there *en route* to Cork. The body should be transported by the government directly to Cork; this was the 'only course'. Adding further pressure he concluded: 'I know that the Prime Minister and Bonar Law do not want any legal technicalities to alter this plan.' At this point Troup and the Home Office planned to take the body to a convenient port and then by the navy to Cork, where it would be handed over to the relatives.[158]

This was what eventually happened, but not quite in the way that government had hoped. On the morning of the inquest a meeting of the principal ministers was held at Downing Street. It was agreed (despite Greenwood's earlier thoughts that the law might simply be side-stepped) that in the event of a 'natural causes' verdict, the body would be handed over to the relatives. No notes of what transpired at this meeting have survived, so it is impossible to be sure exactly what produced the decision, but it may well be that, on balance, it was thought that MacSwiney's executors would succeed in a mandamus application. There may also have been some appreciation that the sequence of events so far had been a political disaster, which it would be unwise to cap by body-snatching. Greenwood, immediately the decision was made, telegraphed Dublin to ensure that steps were taken to prevent public disorder on the arrival of the body, and between Dublin and Cork as it was progressed homewards.[159]

The inquest did return a 'natural causes' verdict.[160] J. H. MacDonnell, on behalf of the family, informed the coroner that the body was to be buried in Cork. The coroner then refused to give his certificate, saying that this was out of his jurisdiction. Seeing disaster, MacDonnell attempted to withdraw his information, but the coroner would not cooperate. There ensued impasse, and MacSwiney's body remained in the hands of the Prison Commissioners at Brixton Prison. Troup saw an opportunity to bargain with the relatives, to get them to transport the body directly to Cork. He left a rueful memorandum of the outcome:

But when Mrs MacSwiney, Mr Art O'Brien and Mr MacDonnell came to the H[ome] O[ffice] and saw the S[ecretary] of S[tate] it was perfectly plain no such bargain was possible. They had made all arrangements for the funeral in London and simply demanded the body sh[oul]d be given them. As there was now no question that they

---

158 PRO HO 144/10308/265a.
159 Ibid., cipher telegram.
160 *Freeman's Journal*, 28 October 1920, 6a–b.

were entitled to it, the S. of S. (after communicating formally with the Coroner who said he was quit of the case and did not care what we did) decided that the body must be given up: and Sir E. Blackwell instructed the Pr[ison] Comm[issione]rs to this effect and informed Mr MacDonnell.[161]

MacSwiney's obsequies were protracted, each stage meticulously organised, faultlessly combining dignified mourning with republican tribute and display. In accordance with Irish Catholic practice the remains were removed from Brixton Prison to St George's Cathedral at Southwark (then centre of a significant Irish presence in London). The chief mourners were admitted to the prison chapel and an honour party of eighteen of MacSwiney's fellow prisoners bore the coffin to a hearse in the prison yard. At the Cathedral an overflowing congregation (mainly but not exclusively Irish) heard a requiem mass conducted by Dr Daniel Mannix, Archbishop of Melbourne, and the Bishops of Southwark and Portsmouth. On its way to Euston Station the mile-and-a-half-long funeral procession took over thirty minutes to pass, and was watched by a silent, bareheaded and respectful crowd of many thousands. There were none of the clashes between republicans and their opponents which had been a feature of the Wormwood Scrubs and Brixton demonstrations, and the respectful attitude of the spectators (which included many non-Irish) was received very well in Ireland. The cortège was led by uniformed Volunteers and pipers. There then came several hundred priests together with Dr Mannix, the Bishop of Portsmouth and many Irish dignitaries. Art O'Brien's touch was sure, and the balance between politics and taste seems to have been sufficiently maintained, even though twenty-seven branches of the Self-Determination League were represented in the procession.[162] To match the solemnity of the London scenes, Sinn Féin, with the support of the Irish Labour Party, had organised a day of mourning in Ireland – restricted public transport and the closure of licensed premises and restaurants. This seems to have been widely supported for a mixture of reasons – sympathy, support and coercion in unknowable ratios.[163]

The London demonstrations would have been magnified many times over had Sinn Féin plans to land the body in Dublin gone ahead. When the funeral party arrived at Holyhead it encountered a concentration of police – local, Metropolitan and armed Auxiliaries. The steamer *Rathmore* had been provided by government to ship the body directly to Cork. Sir Hamar Greenwood had directed that twenty relatives and friends could travel with the coffin,

161 PRO HO 144/10308/271.
162 *The Times*, 29 October 1920, 9a. *Freeman's Journal*, 29 October 1920, 6a–d; photographs, 30 October, 3. The Irish MPs T. P. O'Connor and Joseph Devlin had attended the Southwark service, but apparently did not join the procession.
163 Ibid., 28 October 1920, 5a–c.

but this offer was refused. After an undignified tussle in the funeral van of the mail-train, the coffin was transferred to the *Rathmore* and left for Cork. The funeral party (without Muriel MacSwiney, who had been taken ill) continued to Dublin by the mail-boat.[164]

Despite this seizure a vast congregation spilled out of the Dublin Pro-Cathedral into surrounding streets for the celebration of a requiem mass, and there were similar religious services and secular demonstrations throughout the country.[165] Arriving at Cork, the coffin was landed in the harbour tug *Mary Tavy*. There followed a stand-off during which the local officials refused to accept it without instructions from the relatives from whom it had been seized. Eventually (and once the point had been made) the coffin was removed to Cork City Hall, to lie in state. The army laid down conditions for the funeral – the procession was not to be more than a quarter of a mile in length, and was not to include any military formations; only one republican flag was allowed (to be placed on the coffin). In return for observance of these rules soldiers and police would not interfere, or make their presence provocatively pro-minent. Whether the funeral organisers complied strictly with the army's rules is uncertain, but both photographs and reports indicate a vast funeral throng. This and what must have been very heightened feelings did not lead to violence or disturbance.[166]

Aftermath

In the latter days of MacSwiney's hunger-strike every newspaper in Ireland, most in Britain and many throughout the world had carried reports. Had MacSwiney been killed in a shoot-out with the army or police his death would have been a passing thing. For many days after the funeral a number of Irish newspapers continued to appear in mourning columns, and countless articles appeared alongside messages and declarations of sympathy from political and cultural organisations, public bodies (now mainly Sinn Féin dominated) and numerous individuals. The topic dominated the nationalist and pro-republican press, and the *Cork Examiner* continued to publish tributes a week after the funeral and beyond. The generally Anglophile *New York Times* had made the story its front-page lead on 26 October. Its editorial ('Irrepressible Ireland') had reached a reluctant judgement. Whatever mistaken judgement had led MacSwiney to starve himself to death, and however impossible it had been for the government to surrender to him, 'the world will at present consider only the outstanding result. It sees an Irishman willing and glad to die if only the cry of

---

164 Ibid., 29 October 1920, 5a–b; 30 October, 9d; 5 *Hansard*, CXXXIV, cols 347–50; 3 November 1920.

165 *Freeman's Journal*, 30 October 1920, 3 (photographs) and 9a–c.

166 *Cork Examiner*, 1 November 1920, 5d–h; *Freeman's Journal*, 1 November 1920, 5c–e.

his nation can the better make itself heard.'[167] No matter that the editorial went on to urge nationalists to accept as inevitable the fact of partition and the offer of Home Rule, MacSwiney's death had achieved its 'outstanding results'.

In Ireland, Lord French and Sir Hamar Greenwood continued to place all their government's chips on suppression and coercion, despite the message conveyed by MacSwiney's death. By this stage they appeared to have no option, given government's basic position. On the day after the MacSwiney funeral 18-year-old Kevin Barry was executed for his part in an armed raid in Dublin. This was the first postwar execution, and while it signalled a determination on the part of the government, the failure to use political judgement was more a sign of weakness than strength. There had been appeals for a reprieve from all over the world, and these and the national mood might more advantageously have been addressed by a tactical rather than judicial or doctrinaire response. The young medical student, fortified by the sacraments and declared sympathy of his church, joined MacSwiney in Sinn Féin's formidable college of martyrs. The fact that the soldier killed in the raid had been the same age as himself was lost in the torrents of emotion the hanging unleashed.[168] Feelings in Ireland had been raised to the highest pitch, as though by a deliberate act of government.

There had been a hunger-strike in Cork Prison from the day before MacSwiney's arrest, and this now posed a tricky problem for Sinn Féin, which from the outset had put MacSwiney at the centre of its campaign. The Cork hunger-strike lacked the stature and drama of the Lord Mayor's lone struggle. More than sixty men had started, but by 16 September numbers had dwindled to eleven, and despite the Cork Examiner's boasting ('In the history of hunger-strikes this is probably a record!') the story, because of the drop-outs, lacked a heroic dimension.[169] Not even the death of Michael Fitzgerald on 17 October, the fifty-eighth day of his strike, put the Cork hunger-strike on an equal footing with MacSwiney. Fitzgerald had commanded the first battalion of the IRA's Second Cork Brigade, and was given a large funeral, and many tributes.[170] A second hunger-striker, Joseph Murphy, died on 25 October, and this death was completely overshadowed by MacSwiney's on the same day.[171]

After Joseph Murphy's death an uneasy tone creeps into reports from Cork. On 2 November nine men were still on strike and reported to be weak. A week later the Examiner's report was a mere one-and-a-half column inches, and two

---

167 New York Times, 26 October 1920, 1a–b; portrait 7a–f; editorial 16b. In the days before MacSwiney's death the newspaper had carried on its front page the bulletins on his condition issued by the Irish Self-Determination League – an indication of Sinn Féin's close attention to public relations.

168 See Freeman's Journal, 2 November 1920, 5a–b; photographs 3; Cork Examiner, 2 November 1920, 5a. Ernie O'Malley (op. cit., pp. 203–4) vividly describes the prostration of popular grief.

169 Cork Examiner, 16 September 1920, 5e.

170 Ibid., 20 October, 5b.

171 Ibid., 26 October, 6g.

days later this had dwindled to half an inch.[172] On 12 November the Bishop of Cork appealed for an end to the hunger-strike, and an *Examiner* editorial agreed, pointing out that the men were now in their ninety-fourth day.[173] MacSwiney, with exceptional fortitude and strength (and artificial feeding in his last days) had shown that a man could survive on hunger-strike for seventy-four days. While little was known about the effects of prolonged starvation, by the ninety-fourth day it must have been apparent to anyone who looked at the matter with a cold eye that the remaining nine strikers were receiving some kind of nutriment. Although weak, they were not in the prostrate state that the other deaths had shown would set in after a certain stage. To continue the strike any longer would have incurred charges of fraud and bathed the whole thing in farce. The Bishop's plea was a boon (as may have been intended) and was followed immediately by a letter from Arthur Griffith to the men. This ended what could have become an embarrassing and potentially damaging episode.[174]

'Politicals' and politicals

The MacSwiney hunger-strike was unquestionably a major event in the Anglo-Irish war, and a republican victory. Had it been followed by a mass of other strikes, determinedly carried through, it is possible that an Anglo-Irish settlement might have arrived earlier. But MacSwiney's doctrine of triumph through endurance, while finding many admirers, attracted few followers. Government had shown its determination, and few doubted its extreme unwillingness to back down. Only rare men or women could contemplate going through MacSwiney's agony, and a campaign which collapsed would have hampered the republican cause. In the nine remaining months of the Anglo-Irish conflict the possibility of hunger-striking remained an issue for prison administration, but it did not again reach the crisis level of Wormwood Scrubs or MacSwiney.[175] Prison battles were fought instead over the comparatively narrow ground of privileges.

Uncertainty and lack of a clear decision-making structure aggravated the difficulties of applying Irish rules in English prisons, especially as the Irish government continued to send over small batches of men – always for special reasons – some of whom they chose to designate as 'political'. There were repeated complaints about this macedonian mix from the Prison Commissioners and in

172 Ibid., 9 October, 4f; 11 October, 5e.
173 Ibid., 12 November 4d and g.
174 Ibid., 5f. In the 1981 hunger-strikes at Northern Ireland's Maze Prison, forty-six days was the shortest period of survival and seventy-three days the longest; the average was sixty-two days. These were all young men, apparently in good health, and their deaths make utterly improbable claims of a ninety-four-day hunger-strike. See n. 54 above.
175 See, for example, 5 *Hansard*, CXL, col. 2047; 21 April 1921.

late November Shortt asked for a statement of these problems. On 30 November 1920, M. L. Waller responded.[176]

At the time of writing there were six politicals at Brixton Prison. These, who had been there for some months, constituted a manageable group. There had been no political transferees for some time, but on 27 November Wormwood Scrubs had received fourteen men from Ireland, sent without notice, of whom five had been deemed political. Simultaneously, Dublin Castle had telegraphed the dispatch of another twenty men, including thirteen politicals: this brought the total in this category to twenty-four.

The Commissioners' chief bugbear was the privilege of association. Long experience had shown that this was used for planning escapes, as at Usk and Lincoln, mutinies, as at Lewes, or hunger-strikes, as at Wormwood Scrubs. The more prisoners there were with political privileges, the greater the danger. Another difficulty was that there were ordinary Irish criminal prisoners in almost every prison in England, and the mixture of the two types inevitably caused friction. If the twenty-four politicals were concentrated in Brixton certain security problems would arise because of the layout of the prison. Placing the group near the boundary wall, as would be necessary, would increase the risk of escape 'with or without rescue'.

A further issue was that some politicals had been given express permission to wear their own clothes, while others had not. Understandably, this created irritation and jealousy. The previous August such an own-clothes man had to be sent to Preston Prison (where he remained alone) in order to avoid placing him with other Irish prisoners. Of a recently received batch from Ireland, seven had been designated on an unsigned list as not being entitled to ameliorations, while the remainder had been marked as 'entitled'. No other instructions or information were provided about the men's offences (which under the Irish rules qualified or disqualified political privileges), and so the Commissioners had decided to allow all to continue to wear their own clothes. There were continuing general difficulties with documentation. Status information was sometimes sent after the men had arrived and no offence detail was provided: lists and instructions were unsigned, or initialled indecipherably or written in lead pencil or altered. All of these defects raised questions of reliability, authority and accountability.

The Commissioners drew attention to the original July 1920 agreement with the Irish government. No limit had been fixed to the number of politicals to be sent over, but it had been understood that they would be as few as possible. There were no problems with prisoners who were not entitled to political privileges. They were split up into small groups and distributed among prisons all over the country and were easily absorbed. But when the ordinary rules

---

176 PRO HO 144/1734/17: Waller to Shortt, 30 November 1920. The details which follow are taken from this memorandum.

of imprisonment were not applied and special privileges were given 'it may be taken as certain that trouble is not far off'. The Irish government was requested not to send any more prisoners entitled to wear their own clothes, and, if feasible, to withdraw that privilege from the men just arrived. If at all possible political status itself should be denied to these men, and if that were not acceptable then the Irish government should not send any more in this class.

Political status was the principal issue. Those not granted such privileges would be subject to the ordinary rules, with a few extra security modifications. Hunger-strikers would be dealt with under the regular standing order, with the addition that daily reports on the men's condition were to go to the Irish Office (for transmission to Dublin) as well as to the Commissioners.[177] Prisoners without political status would wear prison uniform. They were not to be placed in any of the special classifications (for example, juvenile adults, second division misdemeaneant or Star) and were to be located and worked at the governor's discretion on the understanding that they were to be kept as far apart from each other as circumstances and facilities would allow. Their location was 'occasionally and unobtrusively' to be changed, especially after friends had begun to pay visits.

Part of the normalisation of the Irish prisoners' treatment was the reception photograph. This was to be treated ostensibly as a matter of ordinary procedure, 'so that the Irish prisoners will not think they are being treated differently from any other prisoners'. But should they resist, and if it looked as though force would have to be used, no further action was to be taken until nearer their discharge. No mention was made of fingerprinting.[178] The Irish Office was to be given photographs and full and systematic descriptions, was to be involved in censoring letters and to have lists of visitors (other than near relatives), who had to receive its prior approval. By this time J. H. MacDonnell had been given general authority to visit all the Irish prisoners as their legal adviser.

Governors were warned that they should 'regard it as certain that these men and their friends are considering the possibilities of effecting an escape, and that should there be a weak spot . . . advantage will be taken of it sooner or later'. They were therefore to pay 'minute personal attention' to all prison arrangements. Assistance was to be sought from the local police, who, if possible, were requested to assign a plain-clothes officer to watch boundary walls. Attempts to assist escape had previously been made at the back or rear of the prison, and these areas should receive particular attention. Bachelor warders

177 This and the detail immediately following were taken from the confidential 'Memorandum to Governors of Prisons Containing Sinn Féin Prisoners', dated 26 October 1920 (at PRO HO 144/1734/206).
178 This was raised the following year, when on 23 August 1921 Scotland Yard asked for the fingerprinting of those convicted of a scheduled (penal servitude) offence. Negotiations between Sinn Féin and the British government were by this time under way, however, and it was decided not to press the matter.

sleeping in the prison were to constitute an emergency reserve. Since there had been escapes through visitors overpowering staff at the prison gate, and in the visiting boxes, the number allowed in the sallyport (the space between the outer and inner gates) was to be limited and indeed not too many visitors were to be allowed into the prison at once. Both the gatekeeper and the visits officer should have means to call for assistance. Suspicious visitors were to be searched for weapons and other contraband, and if they objected the visit would be cancelled.

Dublin Castle, for all the Commissioners' repeated representations and admonitions, seemed unable to resist the inclination to send specially privileged prisoners. On 2 December 1920, with the Anglo-Irish war entering its final and most intensive months and strain showing on all sides, Shortt again protested, this time to Hamar Greenwood (Irish Chief Secretary since 12 April 1920). Shortt urged a radical solution: no privileges for any convicted prisoner transferred to England.[179] This proposal appeared to have little effect, since a month later Geoffrey Whiskard, Assistant Under-Secretary at Dublin Castle,[180] asked for four Brixton prisoners to have political status. Shortt's letter to Greenwood had not been overlooked, Whiskard insisted, and the Irish government was attempting to persuade the army to make arrangements (presumably in Ireland) 'which will relieve you of these political prisoners altogether'. He rather gave the game away, however, by referring to his approach to the army as having engendered 'some controversy'.[181]

At about the same time Waller, on behalf of the Prison Commission, was again complaining to the Home Office. There were now at Brixton some twenty Irish prisoners receiving 'political amelioration'. The Commissioners did not wish to have more than twenty-five, since Brixton was the only place at which they could be held. Indeed they did not want many more Irish prisoners, whether privileged or not. There were about 400 in all, plus the convicts transferred from Maryborough, and if many more were sent, some would have to go to Scotland to avoid having large groups at any one English prison. A strong representation should be made to the Irish government that no more politically privileged prisoners should be transferred to England: 'The difficulties, which are real enough in any case, are so much increased by the presence of ordinary Irish prisoners in nearly all the prisons.'[182]

In addition to the complexities of handling a mixture of privileged and non-privileged prisoners in one prison, governors were worried about the likelihood of escapes and attacks. Some had already asked for police assistance. In August

179 Shortt to Greenwood, 2 December 1920: PRO HO 144/1734/196.
180 Geoffrey Granville Whiskard (1886–1957); educated at St Paul's, Wadham College, Oxford (double first); Home Office, 1911; Assistant Secretary, Dublin Castle, 1920–2; Colonial Office (Irish Section), 1922–5. Distinguished civil service career thereafter; KCB, 1943.
181 Whiskard to Troup, 3 January 1921: PRO HO 144/1734/196.
182 Waller to Home Office, 5 January 1921: ibid.

1920, the Chief Constable of Birmingham agreed to put three of his officers inside the prison, and to increase the watch at night to four, all armed with revolvers. The Home Office approved, provided that they were trained in handling revolvers and understood that their weapons were to be used only for self-defence or as a last resort in the event of an attack.[183] A month later police informed the governor of Durham that an armed attack on his prison was 'not improbable'. This prompted him to borrow a machine gun and rifles from the army and to post two experienced former machine gunners to sleep in at night. A plain-clothes policeman patrolled outside between 5 and 7 p.m. The Governor (H. M. A. Hales – formerly at Wormwood Scrubs) was confident that should there be a raid during daylight hours, when a full complement of staff was available, he could deal with it. He was, however, unhappy about the siting of the prison since the land beyond the boundary walls was 'either unfrequented or crowded with low-class hovels. A large party could collect either on the fields or these habitations without attracting notice.' Hales was cautioned by headquarters in the same terms as the Chief Constable of Birmingham. Firearms were an ultimate measure to repel a violent attack on the prison. The machine gun and its possibilities alarmed the Commissioners more than a little, and they insisted that Hales must be present to control his men (though how he was expected to do this around the clock was not explained).[184]

Despite administrators' tensions, the Irish National Relief Association's assessment of conditions was fairly relaxed. Of Durham the Association observed: 'Prison warders considerate; treatment fair; food rather short, certain complaints as to quantity but not quality; none on hunger-strike; all wearing prison clothes; general health good except William O'Brien . . . Governor Hales same as in Wormwood Scrubs during last hunger-strike.' Leicester received a similar report. All men were being treated as criminals, and were in prison clothes; none on hunger-strike, although the leader (Robert O'Moore) had applied to the Home Office for political treatment. The warders and governor were considered 'fairly decent', and all the men were in good health.[185] As these reports were intended purely for internal Sinn Féin consumption, their low-key assessments seem to indicate that the various governors who expected external armed attacks may simply have had the jitters.

---

183 Chief Constable, Birmingham, to Home Office, 28 August 1920: PRO HO 144/1734/126.

184 Correspondence, Hales and A. J. Wall (Secretary of the Prison Commission), 28 September and 8 October 1920: PRO HO 144/1734/156.

185 NLI: Art O'Brien Papers: Ms. 8444(i) (unfoliated), report compiled around November 1920. These assessments, no doubt intended for the use of both the Association and Sinn Féin, survive only as fragments of what appears to have been a fairly comprehensive exercise. They are notable for their seeming objectivity and a complete absence of rhetoric. The Association's solicitor (J. H. MacDonnell) compiled what appear to be complete lists of Irish political prisoners in England in November to December 1920. These were tabulated by prison, with personal and some legal details (ibid., Ms. 8443 (unfoliated)).

With the troubles in Ireland at their most intense in the weeks before the Truce, there was a scare at Manchester Prison, where prisoners claimed to have overheard remarks suggesting that there might be an attack. At this time several men were awaiting trial on arms and conspiracy charges in connection with the Erskine Street Club affair,[186] and Troup thought an attack 'very likely'. Ruggles-Brise wanted to put two or three armed night-watchmen into the prison, and this was approved by the Home Secretary. The police were asked to take extra precautions when the men were brought up for trial.[187]

After his 1916 excursion to Lewes with de Valera and the other Easter rising convicts, Dr A. J. O'Loughlin returned to his post as Roman Catholic chaplain at Portland, whence in July 1921, a few days before the Truce, he sent an encouraging prospectus to Sister Francesca MacDonagh, whose cousin George was at the prison. He represented Portland as a cross between a monastic retreat and a resort:

> The place is so airy that all employment is practically out of doors. Yes we have services . . . Sunday is a day of rest, spent between chapel and recreation. I am glad to say we have a good choir & the services are very hearty. They all made a novena for the feast of Our Lady of Perpetual Succour. So you can see that their religion suffers no decline.

Ever the conscientious representative of the Prison Commissioners, O'Loughlin reported that the Irish prisoners were 'going along quietly'. As far as he knew they were not planning demonstrations or protests: 'I am glad of that, because nothing can be gained in that way. I have seen so much of it in all these years here. It . . . only entails loss of letters & other privileges.' The start of negotiations, and the visits to London by de Valera and Craig (which O'Loughlin had announced in chapel), had encouraged the men, who felt that if a settlement were reached they would soon be home. He ended on a kindly note. Cousin George would be writing home soon, and after a while his letters would become more frequent (as he earned more privileges) – 'but I trust they will not be here long enough to gain this enlargement'.[188]

The final phase

The Truce was signed on 9 July 1921, and two days later there was military disengagement in Ireland. But even as negotiations got under way between Sinn Féin and the British government, the Irish prisoners continued to cause problems for the English prison system. On 16 July 1921, Irish political convicts mutinied

---

186 See above, p. 676.
187 Correspondence, 20 June 1921: PRO HO 144/1734/196.
188 Dr A. J. O'Loughlin to Sister Francesca MacDonagh, 4 July 1921: NLI: Sister Francesca MacDonagh Papers: Ms. 20, 647 (5) (unfoliated).

at Dartmoor.[189] This was judged by M. L. Waller to have been 'an awkward affair which came near to success'. Like the Manchester escape of October 1919, the Dartmoor outbreak had been carefully timed for a Saturday, when fewer than half the warders were on duty. IRA prisoners had been allowed to exercise together, and through their leader (McCarvill) had given an undertaking not to make trouble; eighty or so nevertheless refused to fall in after exercise and began shouting and singing and throwing their clothes on to the ground. All off-duty staff living near the prison (about eighty in all) were summoned, most bringing their staves. The prisoners were forced back to their cells, with six of their number and four staff suffering injuries.[190] The governor may have been lulled by the political negotiations then under way, but it is clear that not only had he violated the instructions in Waller's circular of 26 October 1920 on the handling of these prisoners, but also basic precepts of prison-keeping. To allow eighty men, young, fit, prepared and willing to obey the commands of their leaders, to assemble together in a half-staffed prison was simply negligent. The governor's argument would no doubt have been that it was better to purchase the cooperation of the Irish prisoners through what appeared to be an acceptable risk than incur the inconveniences of their unrest.

The mutiny had several postscripts. There was the automatic attempt to pass the parcel to the army which, as usual, failed. A military guard was immediately deployed at the prison, but in the straitened conditions of the times the Army Council indicated that it had insufficient manpower to stay beyond early October. That extra staffing was needed was shown by another incident, in September. Sixteen Irish prisoners, convicted in England of political offences, refused to obey orders and threatened that unless they were allowed to join the main body of the Irish political prisoners (convicted in Ireland) there would be a general disturbance in the prison by all the Irish (now 200-strong).[191] Staffing deficiencies at the prison were once more thrown into sharp relief. The Home

---

189 Initially the Prison Commissioners had given a qualified welcome to the transfer of political *convicts* (as distinct from internees and those sentenced to imprisonment) and had made special arrangements for their reception at Dartmoor, including the appointment of a Roman Catholic chaplain. The Irish convicts were administratively useful, since the normal convict population in England had dropped to such a low level that there were problems in running the prisons (PRO P. Com. 7/260/1802/55).

190 PRO HO 144/1734/225.

191 These sixteen had been convicted in the Erskine Street Club conspiracy, and all sentenced to penal servitude (see PRO HO 144/1749/2). On 29 August 1921, Patrick O'Donoghue (who had been sentenced to fifteen years' penal servitude and sent to Dartmoor) petitioned to be transferred to D wing, which contained the IRA prisoners convicted in Ireland. O'Donoghue pointed out that (as stated in his speech from the dock) his offence had been committed as an IRA officer. He also repeated his protest against 'the humiliation of associating with any of the criminal classes'. The petition was refused. (O'Donoghue was Collins's principal contact in Manchester. Played major part in Manchester Prison escape of November 1919. Participated in de Valera's escape from Lincoln Prison.)

Office asked the Army Council to delay the removal of the military guard. A bizarrely belated review discovered the prison to be sixty short in its complement of warders. This serious shortfall could not be remedied easily since it would take time to get Treasury approval for recruitment. An alternative was to reduce the Irish contingent by 120, dispersing these around local prisons. Following this course, Dartmoor could manage with only thirty-five extra staff. It was decided to adopt this plan and to ask for interim army coverage. The War Office was approached on 30 September 1921. Should the negotiations then going on between the British government and Sinn Féin break down, the Home Office acknowledged, it might become necessary to withdraw the military from Dartmoor. But should the army now be unable to help it might become impossible to receive any more prisoners from Ireland. In turn this could mean the deployment to Ireland (for prison guard duty there) of 'a larger number of soldiers than the relatively small number now stationed in Dartmoor'.[192]

In the meantime, the Home Secretary had second thoughts about removing a section of the Irish from Dartmoor, since there was a danger of Sinn Féin representing this as an attempt during the Truce to alter the condition of the Irish prisoners for the worse (the men would also have posed major problems in security for the local prisons). The Prison Commissioners were to make the best arrangements they could to keep the men at Dartmoor in one group, but Shortt agreed that should any of them mutiny or threaten disorder he would be prepared to authorise removals — 'at any rate of the leaders'.[193]

Echoes of the Dartmoor mutiny continued even after the Treaty had been signed. On his release under the general amnesty Lyang, one of the rioters of 16 July 1921, claimed in the *Freeman's Journal* that when the prisoners were driven inside he had been forced to run the gauntlet of warders, and had subsequently been thrown down some stairs. He had been so badly injured, in fact, that he had spent seventeen days in hospital. The Home Office admitted that there had been a riot at Dartmoor, but insisted that it had been suppressed with no more than necessary force. Lyang had received a scalp wound in the course of these events, but he had not been ill-treated as he claimed.[194]

Threats of disorder and hunger-striking continued. On 14 October Michael Collins, in London for the negotiations, had gone to Pentonville Prison. He explained the Truce terms to the thirty-six political prisoners who were being held there. This was little more than a morale-building exercise, but it raised expectations of a substantial improvement in conditions. Against the rules, they

---

192 Home Office to War Office, 30 September 1921: PRO HO 144/1734/208.
193 PRO HO 144/1734/208.
194 *Freeman's Journal*, 18 January 1922, 4c; 5 *Hansard*, CL, col. 804; 14 February 1922. Lyang pointed out in his *Freeman's* interview that the deputy governor of Dartmoor was Major French, son of the Irish Lord Lieutenant Lord French. His claim (which has an undoubted ring of truth) is that the worst assaults took place after the men had been returned to their cells, when the leaders were removed to the punishment block.

began to talk during exercise. This resulted in cautions and, when the offence was repeated, in punishments. In a now-familiar escalation of confrontations and punishments, eleven prisoners went on a hunger-strike, while others started to destroy their cells. The latter were placed in restraining-jackets for twenty-four hours by the governor, Major Blake, ostensibly as a precaution, but more likely as further punishment. The prisoners refused to don the jackets, and declined to work, saying that they were political, not criminal prisoners. Reporting this to the Prison Commission, Blake lamented that the Roman Catholic chaplain unfortunately had no influence over them.

The Pentonville men demanded talking, exercise, separation from criminal prisoners and permission to smoke. Sensing that things were getting out of hand, Blake equivocated. He could not allow talking during exercise – it was against the rules – but the men could go to the reception block each day and talk to him about their home lives and other matters.[195] All the men, he reported, took the view that since the peace talks were under way they should be released as soon as possible. Blake blamed the delays on de Valera, claiming in his report to the Commissioners that 'This has caused a distinct fall in de Valera's stock and has made him quite unpopular'. In exchange for a promise of good conduct Blake departed from the Commissioners' instructions of 26 October 1920 and housed the men together, apart from the criminal prisoners. He could not possibly allow smoking. Diet was really a medical question, he explained, and this meant that where necessary the prison doctor would arrange some extra food: 'This satisfied them.'[196]

Justifying his actions, Blake emphasised that his priority was quietness and good order. Thirty-six Irish political offenders continually shouting and smashing up would affect the morale of the remaining 900: 'I would not allow my prisoners to dictate terms to me. But these men are rather different and it is Diplomatic to humour them a little.' He was evidently rather taken with them, and indeed they must have contrasted favourably with the petty and often habitual criminals who were Pentonville's more usual population. 'They are really very decent fellows,' he wrote, 'merely suffering from the characteristics of their Race – Obstinacy, Pugnacity and an imaginary sense of injustice.' (Beside this insight an anonymous Home Office hand noted 'Major Blake is himself Irish'.)

Blake had avoided a major disturbance, but the Home Office was not wholly pleased. To Troup, the basic lesson of the previous five years was that when the Irish were allowed to associate they would conspire and act together. He

---

195 Ironically enough, the Prison Commissioners (now under a new chairman and with a new outlook) the following year greatly loosened the no-talking rule for all prisoners (RCP, 1921–2, PP, 1922 (Session 2) [Cmd. 1761], II, 1015, 72, Appendix 10).

196 PRO HO 144/1734/217. Blake was intent on representing himself in the best possible light to the Commissioners, so it is difficult to judge the accuracy of his report. It seems unlikely that an explanation of the respective competencies of the governor and medical officer would have satisfied the prisoners, and persuaded them to drop their protests.

lamented to the Commissioners that bringing the Irish together might allow Blake to manage his thirty-six prisoners at Pentonville, but it set a precedent which would cause problems for other prisons. It would be easy for Irish prisoners at Dartmoor, and elsewhere where they were in large numbers, to act together, over-power warders and smash up the prison. He confirmed that the Home Secretary had 'definitely decided against separating Sinn Féin from ordinary prisoners and giving them political treatment'. The Home Office would not reverse Blake's decision on separation since this 'would no doubt lead to a big row, and so long as he can manage them I don't know that it matters much. It does not imply any political privileges.'[197]

Amnesty

Troup was right that it did not matter much what Blake did. Political events now accelerated.[198] The Treaty was signed by the Irish plenipotentiary delega-tion on 6 December. Within twenty-four hours Downing Street issued an order releasing all those detained under ROIA, Regulation 14b.[199] The fate of the convicted prisoners was not so swiftly resolved (though five convicted women, three of whom were serving life, were at this point released in Dublin). For a month it was uncertain if the Treaty, which had split the republican move-ment, would be accepted, or the war resumed. But after acrimonious debate the document was narrowly ratified by the Dáil on Saturday, 7 January 1922. Five days later Geoffrey Whiskard (now acting under the authority of the pro-visional government) telegraphed to Troup requesting that, in conformity with the amnesty which had been announced, Irish prisoners convicted of offences of a political nature should be released as soon as possible. Working on a list of prisoners in English prisons for politically motivated offences committed in the twenty-six counties which would form the Irish Free State, the Home Office that same day (12 January 1922) authorised all the releases. The exodus comprised 534 prisoners who had certainly been committed for political offences in Ireland and Britain, and a further three whose status was uncertain.[200] (The three were later declared by Dublin Castle not to be Sinn Féin prisoners.) Excluded from the releases were persons convicted of offences in the six counties of Northern

---

197 Ibid. Troup's memorandum went to Shortt, who simply confirmed it.
198 Largely leaving penal matters behind. Yet only two days before the Treaty was signed, Dublin Castle announced that it had deported to an English prison eight men who had attempted to escape from Mountjoy (*Manchester Guardian*, 6 December 1921, 8c).
199 *Manchester Guardian*, 8 December 1921, 7a. There were scenes of great rejoicing in Ireland as 220 men were released from Kilmainham, and 1700 from Ballykinlar Camp and 50 from Rath. This surely contributed to the pro-Treaty majority which emerged in the population at large (photograph of Kilmainham releases, *Manchester Guardian*, 10 December 1921, 7b–e).
200 Those convicted in England were released under a separate Royal Warrant: PRO P. Com. 7/260/412340/106.

Ireland, persons convicted of ordinary crimes, police and soldiers. The prisoners
– both those sentenced to ordinary imprisonment and those sentenced to penal
servitude – were distributed throughout the country, with a large concentration
at Dartmoor.[201] By 23 January all had been released, except for one man, too
unwell to discharge, and another whose Sinn Féin status was uncertain.[202]

Problems of definition, place and time meant that after the bulk of the
cases had been dealt with a number of anomalies and politically sensitive decisions lingered. Less complicated matters were dispatched first. Ordinary criminal
prisoners held in English prisons who had been sentenced for offences committed
in the twenty-six counties were transferred to Irish prisons. On 27 January 1922,
the provisional government asked that any offender who at the time of conviction
had been a member of the armed forces or the police should not be repatriated
to Ireland. This was agreed, and twelve ex-members of the Royal Irish Constabulary were retained in England to complete their sentences. The Irish escort
which arrived to take back to Ireland the criminal prisoners brought with them
a former soldier and a former policeman, each serving court-martial-imposed
sentences of penal servitude. This brought to twenty-four (out of an agreed total
of thirty) prisoners returned to England from the twenty-six counties. A separate
arrangement was made with the government of Northern Ireland for the repatriation of its criminal prisoners.[203]

Other groups remained. One comprised those who had been convicted of
offences committed in England – especially during the IRA arson and destruction campaign. These divided again into those guilty of offences committed
pre- and post-Truce. On 11 February 1922, fifty-five persons sentenced between
24 January 1921 and 18 July 1921 were granted remission of sentence by Royal
Warrant. The distinction between pardon and remission of sentence may seem,

201 The distribution was as follows: Imprisonment: Bedford 7; Birmingham 6; Bristol 3; Brixton 8;
   Canterbury 9; Cardiff 6; Carlisle 2; Carmarthen 2; Carnarvon 2; Dorchester 10; Durham 6;
   Exeter 4; Gloucester 8; Hull 16; Ipswich 10; Leicester 8; Lincoln 10; Liverpool 5; Maidstone
   (local) 6; Newcastle 5; Northampton 5; Nottingham 5; Pentonville 36; Portsmouth 1; Preston
   14; Shepton Mallet 5; Shrewsbury 6; Swansea 2; Usk 2; Wandsworth 34; Winchester 11;
   Worcester 3; Wormwood Scrubs 26. Penal Servitude: Dartmoor 190; Maidstone (convict) 1;
   Parkhurst 29. This list totals 503 and not the figure of 534 on which Troup worked. It is
   possible that the missing twenty-nine were undercounts at some of the prisons (and Portland
   seems to have been missed out). There may also have been some releases which Troup's list
   had not taken into account (See PRO HO 144/1734/221). A further confusion is that the
   Prison Commissioners reported a total Irish political population of 700 for the greater part
   of the year – 400 in local and 300 in convict prisons. Since the Commissioners' reporting
   year ended on 31 March 1922, one can only assume that some of these 700 (particularly in the
   local prisons) were released in the normal way, or their sentences expired (see RCP, 1921–2,
   PP, 1922 (Sess. 2) [Cmd. 1761], II, 1015, 4).
202 There was a certain amount of outrage in Conservative circles in England at the release of a
   number of notorious and serious offenders who had served such a small portion of their sentence (5 Hansard, CLV, cols 2300–1; 29 June 1922).
203 PRO HO 144/1734/224.

in the circumstances, to be of little practical importance, but had any of these offenders subsequently been re-convicted in the United Kingdom (a distinct possibility, given the civil war then being waged in Ireland) it would have been possible to withdraw their remission for the earlier conviction.[204] The offences of the prisoners released as a result of this remission included shooting with intent to murder and do grievous bodily harm, conspiracy (arson and murder), possession of arms, ammunition and explosives with intent, inciting soldiers, cutting telegraph wires and treason felony. As a reciprocal measure, and in the same spirit, on 11 February 1922, Michael Collins, head of the provisional government, proclaimed an amnesty for all members of the British armed forces, police and civil service for acts committed over the previous six years.[205] After some internal debate government determined to close the books, and on 1 April 1922 a further fourteen prisoners were freed on Royal remission of sentence. These had been convicted between 5 November 1921 and 15 February 1922 of a variety of offences, all committed post-Truce.[206]

As with the Fenians fifty years previously, there was particular sensitivity about soldiers who had violated their oath of loyalty and aided the republicans in various ways. The Connaught Rangers' mutineers fell clearly into this category. On 28 June 1920, 350 men of the 1st Battalion, stationed at Jullundur in the Punjab, had protested at the news from Ireland by laying down their arms. Sixty-two were brought before courts martial for mutiny and associated offences. One man (James Daly) was sentenced to death and executed; the others received sentences of between two years' imprisonment and twenty years' penal servitude.

At the conclusion of the Anglo-Irish war a number of ex-officers of the British Army began a campaign to free these mutineers.[207] Their loyalty had been tested to destruction by the deployment of Black and Tans in Ireland and the atrocities arising from the reprisal policy. Hard things had been done on both sides, and justice and reconciliation would be served by amnesty. In

---

204 PRO HO 144/4645/106; PRO P. Com. 7/260/412340/116. These offences had been committed before 11 July 1921, 'and attributed to motives connected with the political movement in Ireland'. See also Churchill's Commons statement (5 *Hansard*, CL, col. 592; 13 February 1922). There was at least one case (and probably more) of forfeiture of a government pension. Patrick O'Donoghue, convicted and sentenced to fifteen years' penal servitude for his part in the Erskine Street Club conspiracy, under the Felony Forfeiture Act, 1870, also forfeited an annual pension of £37 12s. 7d. Six weeks after his release he applied for a restoration of this pension, which request seems to have been refused (PRO HO 144/1749/3).

205 5 *Hansard*, CL, col. 592; 13 February 1922. This reflected sentiment in Britain (ibid., cols 639–40).

206 PRO P. Com. 7/260/412340/116; HO 144/4645/116. Only a week before these releases Shortt had told the Commons that the amnesty agreement did not apply to offences committed in Great Britain subsequent to the Truce (5 *Hansard*, CLII, col. 256; 21 March 1921).

207 Those who campaigned included Sir Bryan Mahon, Colonel Maurice Moore and Captain Stephen Gwynn, and a number of other former officers (Macardle, *op. cit.*, p. 364).

December 1922, William Cosgrave, the Irish Prime Minister, held discussions with the War Office about the soldiers. Release of the thirty-nine remaining mutineers was ordered on 3 January 1923, the Free State government arguing that this act of clemency would assist the passage of its own Amnesty Bill through the Free State legislature.[208]

There remained another soldier in custody. Joseph Dowling had been a prisoner of war in Germany, and was captured on 12 April 1918 as he came ashore on an island off the Galway coast on a secret mission. Dowling, who had been a member of Casement's Irish Brigade, was regarded as being in a different and worse category than the Connaught Rangers since he had been convicted of 'voluntarily serving and aiding the enemy and persuading British soldiers to do the same'.[209] The British government thought that Dowling's release would create an undesirable precedent for several others (presumably not Irish) serving sentences for similar offences. The Free State maintained its interest, and periodically pressed Dowling's case, finally securing his release.

During the Anglo-Irish war the republican side carried out numerous armed robberies to finance its activities. One such was carried out by Coleman, Ruddy and Dempsey, who held up a car at West Calder and stole £2000. Was this an act of free enterprise criminality, excluded from amnesty, or was it a political act? In the latter case what was the explanation for an act committed during the period of the Truce, when both sides had pledged to refrain from aggressive measures? General Richard Mulcahy, revolutionary transformed into Minister of Defence and Chief of Staff under the provisional and the Free State governments, made enquiries of his old comrades. Two stories emerged. The robbery 'was beyond any doubt the outcome of erroneous orders conveyed to them [Coleman, Ruddy and Dempsey] by Irish political leaders in Scotland'. The Free State government sought the men's release as an act of grace by the British government and undertook to repay the stolen £2000. It also intimated that men high up in the IRA command structure (including Liam Mellows, the IRA Director of Purchases and later bitter opponent of the Treaty) had issued orders for the robbery in an attempt to wreck the peace treaty. With these explanations and assurances the three men were released.

Other cases which caused difficulty included the widow Mrs Elizabeth Eadie, the sister of James Connolly, and described by the police as one of the most prominent of the extreme republicans in the country. She had been convicted at the Old Bailey on 21 July 1922 of possessing explosives with intent, and

---

208 The Free State Amnesty Bill applied to soldiers, police and other Crown servants guilty of offences during the Anglo-Irish war, and was an essential measure in the construction of normal relations between the two countries (PRO HO 144/3724/1, 3 and 5). The Connaught Rangers were released from Maidstone, Parkhurst, Shrewsbury, Winchester and Bedford prisons.

209 Ibid., /6. Dowling's landing had been the occasion for the launch of the German Plot round-ups.

sentenced to two years' imprisonment. She was a determined opponent of the Treaty and the provisional government. Herbert Wrigley had been convicted of possession of a revolver and IRA documents and according to Special Branch was a 'dangerous fanatic who might commit acts of violence to further [the] Irish Republican cause in this country'. The Irish government indicated that it would accept the British decision in these two cases.[210]

There were several men serving sentences in Northern Ireland prisons for offences committed after the signing of the Treaty. These men had been caught up in the disorder which had attended the establishment of the Northern Ireland state, and the Free State government sought their release as part of the policy of closing the books, and because clemency would be politically advantageous to it. Two men in particular were named: John McCurtain, whose brother had been a commandant in the National Army, killed by republicans in Tipperary, and John Flood, whose brother had been shot by the British in March 1921.[211]

The British government in the years immediately following undertook to act as intermediaries with the Northern Ireland government to review the cases of prisoners who had been sentenced because of their part in the 'invasion' of Northern Ireland in 1922 to 1923. The Northern Ireland Prime Minister, Sir James Craig, agreed to allow the British government to review these cases and to accept the resultant recommendations.[212] Thirty-three men were released on 25 January 1926. With these releases[213] the British penal system ended the part it had played in the Anglo-Irish war and its immediate aftermath, though not, of course, its involvement with Irish revolutionary politics. New cohorts had already entered the system, and would have a presence there for most of the twentieth century.

210 Ibid., /3. Other cases discussed at this time included Bernard Mara, a sailor who while on leave in Co. Carlow asked soldiers to sell their rifles (four years' penal servitude) and McKinstry (ten years), Lavery and Kearny (five years each), for possessing arms and ammunition.

211 Ibid., /5.

212 PRO HO 144/6065.

213 The last man to be released for offences committed in the twenty-six counties was probably Arthur Casey. At the suggestion of the IRA Casey had joined the RIC and had stolen arms. At a General Court Martial in Dublin on 12 April 1922, he had been sentenced to life penal servitude (commuted to ten years) for this offence, and for aiding an ambush. Casey (who admitted stealing arms but denied assisting the ambush) petitioned several times under the terms of the amnesty, but was refused because his offences were considered to be acts of treachery. After two and a half years he repudiated Sinn Féin (which had shown no interest in his case). He was released on 11 January 1926, when, with remission, he had served the equivalent of five years' penal servitude (PRO HO 144/17627).

BIBLIOGRAPHY

ORDER OF BIBLIOGRAPHY

Archives
Other unpublished material
Cases, statutes, parliamentary papers and official publications

- Cases
- Statutes
- Annual reports
- Reports of Royal Commissions, Select Committees and Departmental Committees
- Returns
- Miscellaneous
- Official and related publications

Books, essays and journal articles
Journals, newspapers and works of reference
Libraries

Archives

Abercorn Papers: Northern Ireland Public Record Office
Frederick J. Allen Papers: National Library of Ireland
Sir Robert Anderson Papers: Public Record Office
Asquith Papers: Bodleian Library, Oxford
Joseph Brennan Papers: National Library of Ireland
Buckingham Papers: British Library
Carlingford Papers: Somerset County Record Office
Casement Papers: National Library of Ireland
Casement Petition Papers: British Library
Clarendon Papers: Bodleian Library, Oxford
Communist Party Archive: Labour History Archive and Study Centre, John Rylands University Library of Manchester
Cranbrook Papers: British Library
Dr Charles Curry Papers: National Library of Ireland
Davitt Papers: Trinity College, Dublin

Derby Papers: Knowsley Hall, Lancashire
De Valera Papers: University College, Dublin
Devoy Papers: National Library of Ireland
Dillon Papers: Trinity College, Dublin
Fenian Brotherhood Papers: Catholic University of America, Washington, DC
Lloyd George Papers: House of Lords Record Office
Gladstone Papers: National Library of Ireland
W. E. Gladstone Papers: British Library
Gore-Booth Papers: National Library of Ireland
A. S. Green Papers: National Library of Ireland
General Sir Charles Grey Papers: University of Durham
Denis Gwynn Papers: National Library of Ireland
Harcourt (Lewis) Papers: Bodleian Library, Oxford
Harcourt (Sir William Vernon) Papers: Bodleian Library, Oxford
Irish American Historical Society (New York)
Irish National Aid Association Papers: National Library of Ireland
Irish National Relief Association Papers: National Library of Ireland
Labour Party Archive: Labour History Archive and Study Centre, John Rylands University
    Library of Manchester
Larcom Papers: National Library of Ireland
John Martin Papers: Northern Ireland Public Record Office
Mitchell Library, Sydney
Sister Francesca MacDonagh Papers: National Library of Ireland
John MacDonagh Papers: National Library of Ireland
Joseph McGarrity Papers: National Library of Ireland
Maloney Collection of Irish Historical Papers: New York Public Library
John Martin Papers: Northern Ireland Public Record Office
Mayo Papers: National Library of Ireland
Maurice Moore Papers: National Library of Ireland
Murgatroyd Papers: Manchester Central Library
Kathleen MacKenna Napoli Papers: National Library of Ireland
National Archives, Washington, DC
National Archives of Ireland
National Library of South Africa, Capetown
O'Brien Papers: Trinity College, Dublin
Art O'Brien Papers: National Library of Ireland
William O'Brien Papers: National Library of Ireland
William Smith O'Brien Papers: National Library of Ireland
O'Donohoe Papers: National Library of Ireland
O'Donovan Rossa Papers: National Library of Ireland
O'Hagan Papers: National Library of Ireland
Father Michael O'Hickey Papers: National Library of Ireland
O'Kelly Papers: National Library of Ireland
Sean O'Mahony Papers: National Library of Ireland
Public Record Office, London
    • Cabinet
    • Colonial Office

- Courts
- Foreign Office
- Home Office
- Prison Commission
- War Office

Patrick Rankin Papers: National Library of Ireland
Redmond Papers: National Library of Ireland
Rose Papers: British Library
Royal Archives, Windsor
Sheehy Skeffington Papers: National Library of Ireland
James Stephens Papers: National Library of Ireland
Archives Office of Tasmania
State Records Office of Western Australia

Other unpublished material

Bantree, Miss Viola. 'Diary', Imperial War Museum, London
Curran, Thomas. 'A Brief Personal Narrative of the Six Days Defence of the Irish Republic', National Library of Ireland: Joseph McGarrity Papers: Ms. 17, 510
Goldsmiths College, 'The Giles Document Laboratory Report on the So-called Black Diaries (PRO HO 161/1–5) Associated with Sir Roger Casement', London, Goldsmiths College, 2002
McManamin, Francis G. 'The American Years of John Boyle O'Reilly: 1870–1890', Ph.D. dissertation, The Catholic University of America, 1959
Maloney, Patrick J. 'Prison Diary', Public Record Office: HO 144/1457/313643
Martin, Eamon. 'The Irish Rebellion of 1916. Personal Experiences. Reminiscences of English Convict Prisons', National Library of Ireland: Joseph McGarrity Papers: Ms. 17, 512
Robinson, President Mary. Address to Reform Club, London, 15 May 1997: 'Tribute to Daniel O'Connell'
Takagami, Shin-Ichi. 'The Dublin Fenians, 1858–79', Ph.D. dissertation, Trinity College, Dublin, 1990

Cases, statutes, parliamentary papers and official publications

Cases

Leigh v. Gladstone and Others (1909) (26 *Times Law Reports*, 139)
Regina v. Spear, v. Boyd, v. Williams, etc, (2002 *HL* 31)
Rex v. Governor of Lewes Prison (*The Times Law Report*, 13 February 1917, 4a–b; 23 February, 6e; 24 February, 4a–b)
Rex v. Sir Frederick Loch Halliday (32 *Times Law Reports*, 301; 33 *Times Law Reports*, 336)
Rex v. Murphy (1921), *Irish Report*, II, 190
Rex v. Allen (1921), *Irish Report*, II, 241

Statutes

Treason Act, 1351: 25 Ed. III, c.2
Abolition of Punishment of Death Act, 1832: 2 & 3 Will. IV. c.62
Abolition of Hanging in Chains Act, 1834: 4 & 5 Will. IV, c.26
Transported Convicts Amendment Act, 1843: 6 & 7 Vict., c.26
Prevention of Crime and Outrage (Ireland) Act, 1847: 11 & 12 Vict., c.2
Treason-Felony Act, 1848: 11 & 12 Vict., c.12
Suspension of Habeas Corpus (Ireland) Act, 1848: 11 & 12 Vict., c.35
Transportation for Treason (Ireland) Act, 1849: 12 & 13 Vict., c.27
Penal Servitude Act, 1853: 16 & 17 Vict., c.99
Peace Preservation Act, 1856: 19 & 20 Vict., c.36
Penal Servitude Act, 1857: 20 & 21 Vict., c.3
Prison Act, 1865: 28 & 29 Vict., c.126
Suspension of Habeas Corpus (Ireland) Act, 1866: 29 & 30 Vict., c.1
Suspension of Habeas Corpus (Ireland) Continuance Act, 1867: 30 & 31 Vict., c.1
Suspension of Habeas Corpus (Ireland) Continuance Act, 1868: 31 & 32 Vict., c.7
Capital Punishment Amendment Act, 1868: 31 & 32 Vict., c.24
Irish Church Act, 1869: 32 & 33 Vict., c.42
Nitro-glycerine Act, 1869: 32 & 33 Vict., c.113
Forfeiture of Property Act, 1870: 33 & 34 Vict., c.23
Irish Land Act, 1870: 33 & 34 Vict., c.46
Ballot Act, 1872: 35 & 36 Vict., c.33
Prison Act, 1877: 40 & 41 Vict., c.21
Army Act, 1881: 44 & 45 Vict., c.58
Interments (*Felo de Se*) Act, 1882: 45 & 46 Vict., c.19
Criminal Law and Procedure (Ireland) Act, 1887: 50 & 51 Vict., c.20
Local Government Act, 1888: 51 & 52 Vict., c.41
Local Government (Ireland) Act, 1898: 61 & 62 Vict., c.37
Prison Act, 1898: 61 & 62 Vict., c.41
Prisoners (Temporary Discharge for Ill-health) Act, 1913: 3 Geo. V, c.4
Defence of the Realm Act, 1914: 4 & 5 Geo. V, c.29
Criminal Justice Administration Act, 1914: 4 & 5 Geo. V, c.58
Suspensory Act, 1914: 4 & 5 Geo. V, c.88
Government of Ireland Act, 1914: 4 & 5 Geo. V, c.90
Defence of the Realm (Amendment) Act, 1915: 5 & 6 Geo. V, c.34
Military Service Act, 1916: 5 & 6 Geo. V, c.104
Restoration of Order in Ireland Act, 1920: 10 & 11 Geo. V, c.31
Government of Ireland Act, 1920: 10 & 11 Geo. V, c.67

Annual reports

Twelfth Annual Report of the Directors of Convict Prisons in Ireland, PP, 1866 [3745], XXXVIII, 465
Thirteenth Annual Report of the Directors of Convict Prisons in Ireland, PP, 1867 [3805], XXXVI, 273
Report of the Commissioners of Prisons and the Directors of Convict Prisons 1909–10, PP, 1910 [Cd. 5360], XLV, 277, 1

Report of the Commissioners of Prisons and the Directors of Convict Prisons, PP, 1917–18 [Cd. 8764], XVIII, 109

Report of the Commissioners of Prisons and the Directors of Convict Prisons, PP, 1919 [Cd. 374], XXVII, 759, 1

Annual Report of the Prison Commissioners for Scotland, 1920, PP, 1921 [Cmd. 1255], XVI, 501, 1

Report of the Commissioners of Prisons and the Directors of Convict Prisons 1920–21, PP, 1921 [Cmd. 1523], XVI, 423, 1

Report of the Commissioners of Prisons and the Directors of Convict Prisons 1921–22, PP, 1922 (Session 2) [Cmd. 1761], II, 1015, 1

Reports of Royal Commissions, Select Committees and Departmental Committees

Royal Commission on Transportation and Penal Servitude, PP, 1863 [3190], XXI, 1

Report of the Commissioners on Treatment of the Treason-Felony Convicts in the English Convict Prisons, PP, 1867 [3880], XXXV, 673, 1

Commission of Inquiry Into the Treatment of Treason-Felony Convicts (Devon Commission), PP, 1871 [C.310], XXXII, 1

Inquiry As to the Alleged Ill-treatment of the Convict Charles McCarthy in Chatham Convict Prison, PP, 1878 [C.1978], LXIII, 769, 1

Report of the Commissioners Appointed to Inquire into the Working of the Penal Servitude Acts (Kimberley Commission), PP, 1878–9 [C.2368], XXXVII, 1

Report of the Visitors of Her Majesty's Convict Prison at Chatham as to the Treatment of Certain Prisoners Convicted of Treason Felony, PP, 1890 [C.6016], XXXVII, 629

Royal Commission on the Rebellion in Ireland, PP, 1916 [Cd. 8279], XI, 171

Evidence Taken Before the Royal Commission on the Rebellion in Ireland, Appendix of Documents, PP, 1916 [Cd. 8311], XI, 185

The Escape from Whitemoor Prison on Friday 9th September 1994 [Cm. 2741], London, HMSO, 1994

Review of Prison Service Security in England and Wales and the Escape from Parkhurst Prison on Tuesday 3rd January, 1995 [Cm. 3020], London, HMSO, 1995

Returns

A Return for Each Gaol and House of Correction in the United Kingdom, Stating (1) The Name and Designation of Every Person Confined for Charges of Printing and Publishing Seditious and Blasphemous Libel, or for Uttering Seditious Words, or for Attending Any Seditious Meetings, or for Conspiring to Cause Such Meetings to be held, or for Any Offence of a Political Nature, from the 1st day of January 1839 to the 1st day of June 1840. . . . The Treatment before and after Conviction or Sentence of that Class of Prisoners, as to Dietary, Clothing, Bedding, Hours of Locking Up and Opening of Cells; Use of Candles, Firing, Pens, Ink and Paper, Correspondence with Friends, Visiting of Friends, Use of their Own Money to better their Dietary or Comforts; Place and Hours Allowed for Exercise; Confinement, whether Solitary or not; whether Employed or not in Menial Offices, or other Particulars, in such Prisons as those Prisoners are Confined, PP, 1840 [600], XXXVIII, 691, 1

Return of All Persons Committed to or Detained in Prison in Ireland by Warrants of the Lord Lieutenant or Chief Secretary for High Treason or Treasonable Practices, or Suspicion Thereof, PP, 1849 [13], XLIX, 381, 1

Return of the Correspondence Relative to the Change in the Medical Management of the Mountjoy Convict Prison, whereby Dr. McDonnell was Deprived of Office of Medical Superintendent without Compensation, PP, 1867–8 [502], LVII, 519, 1

Return of the Names and Sentences of the Fenian Convicts Now Proposed to be Released Stating What Portion of Their Sentences is Unexpired and Distinguishing Between Those Confined in Australia and Those in Great Britain and Ireland, PP, 1868–9 [72], LI, 531

Return of the Fenian Convicts Recently Released, Showing in Each Case the Offence; the Date of Conviction; the Sentence; the Term of Sentence Unexpired; the Cost of Passage Money Provided; and the Total Expenses Incurred in Connection with the Release, PP, 1871 [144], LVIII, 461

Return of the Names, the Dates of Conviction, and the Sentences of the Irish Convicts Still Remaining Under Punishment in English Gaols, or in the Penal Settlements, for Complicity in One or Other of the Offences Known as the Manchester Rescue and the Clerkenwell Outrage, Both Committed in the Latter Part of the year 1867, PP, 1871 [430], LVIII, 463

Copy of All Affidavits Used in the Court of Queen's Bench, Either in Obtaining or Showing Cause Against a Conditional Order for a Criminal Information Made in Last Hilary Term, on the Application of Daniel Reddin Against Dr. Burns, the Medical Officer of Chatham Convict Prison, PP, 1873 [366], LIV, 287, 1

Return of the Names of Any Persons Now Suffering Imprisonment on Account of Their Conviction, Either as Principals or Accessories, of the Murder of Serjeant Brett at Manchester, 1867; Of the Names of Any Persons Now Suffering Imprisonment under Convictions for Treason-Felony Under the Crown and Government Security Act of 1848; And, of the Names of Any Persons Suffering Imprisonment Under Sentences of Courts Martial in Ireland for Offences Against the Articles of War, Appearing to be Connected with their Complicity with the Fenian Conspiracy; Specifying in Each Case the Date and Nature of the Sentence, the Court before Which They Were Convicted, the Nature of the Charge, and the Mode in which the Sentence is Carried Out, PP, 1874 [119], LIV, 493

Return to an Order of the Honourable The House of Commons, dated 16 February 1875 for Copy 'of Certificate by the Clerk of the Crown for the County of Dublin of the Conviction and of the Judgment in the Case of the Queen against John Mitchell tried at a Court of Oyer and Terminer and Gaol Delivery, held at Dublin on the 26th Day of May 1848:' 'Extract from the Government Gazette published, by authority, at Hobart Town on 14th June 1853 containing an Official Notification of the Escape of John Mitchell, and offering a Reward for his Apprehension:' And, 'Copies of any Despatches from the Lieutenant Governor of Van Diemen's Land relative to the Ticket of Leave granted to the said John Mitchell, and to his Escape from the Colony', PP, 1875 [50], LXII, 155, 1

Return of the Conditional Pardons Granted to Persons Convicted of Treason-Felony and Other Offences of a Political Character since and Including the year 1865, PP, 1881 [208], LXXVI, 381

Return of the Names and Numbers of Persons now Suffering Sentences of Penal Servitude in Ireland and England as a Consequence of Conviction for Treason-Felony, Showing (a) Date of Conviction; (b) the Length of the Sentence; and (c) the Prison Where the Convict is Imprisoned, PP, 1890–1 [387], LXIV, 725

Miscellaneous

The Reception of Convicts at the Cape of Good Hope, PP, 1850 [1139], XXXVIII, 223, 1

Correspondence on the Subject of Convict Discipline and Transportation, PP, 1852–3 [1601], LXXXII, 1, 105

Correspondence Reporting the Publication in the United States of Incitements to Outrages in England, PP, 1882 [C.3194], LXXX, 53, 1–3

New Rules Proposed to be Made by the Secretary of State for the Home Department for the Government of Prisons, PP, 1904 [HCP 199], LXXX, 435

Arrangements Governing the Cessation of Active Operations in Ireland [Cmd. 1534], London, HMSO, 1921

Official and related publications

Convictism: Report of the Proceedings of a Public Meeting Held in the Court House at Grahams Town on Wednesday, 4 July, 1849 on the Subject of the Order in Council Constituting the Cape of Good Hope a Penal Settlement, Graham's Town, Godlonton & White, 1849

Residents of Stellenbosch, *Letter to the Governor*, Stellenbosch, 1849 (National Library of South Africa)

Rules and Regulations for the Government of the Convict Prisons, London, George E. Eyre & William Spottiswoode, 1858

Standing Orders (Convict Prisons) London, George E. Eyre & William Spottiswoode, 1865

Rules to be Observed in Mountjoy Male Prison, Dublin, Alexander Thom, 1867

Rules and Regulations for the Government of Convict Prisons, London, HMSO, 1886

Books, essays and journal articles

American Historical Society, *Annual Report*, Washington, DC, 1942

Amos, Keith, *The Fenians in Australia*, Kensington, NSW, New South Wales University Press, 1988

Anderson, Sir Robert, *Sidelights on the Home Rule Movement*, London, John Murray, 1906

Anon., 'An American Opinion of Fenianism', *Dublin University Magazine*, LXVIII (November 1871)

Anon., 'Our Dead Comrades', *The Celtic Magazine*, XI (February 1884), pp. 91–7

Anon., *The Death of Thomas Ashe: Full Report of the Inquest*, Dublin, J. M. Butler, 1917

Anon., *Dublin and the Sinn Féin Rising*, Dublin, Wilson Hartnell & Co, 1916

Anon. (? Robert Anderson or Howard Vincent), 'The Dynamite Party: A Word in Season for British Electors', London, The British Protestant, c.1886 (British Library Pamphlet 8145 ss. 17; reprinted from *The Times*)

Anon. (P.L.), 'The Fenian Brotherhood', *Blackwoods Magazine*, CXC, 1151 (September 1911), pp. 378–93

Anon., 'The Fenian Conspiracy in America and in Ireland', *Dublin University Magazine*, LXVIII (April 1866), pp. 465–7

Arthur, Sir George, *General Sir John Maxwell*, London, John Murray, 1932

Athearn, Robert Greenleaf, *Thomas Francis Meagher: An Irish Revolutionary in America*, Boulder, University of Colorado Press, 1949

Aubry, G. Jean (ed.), *Joseph Conrad, Life and Letters*, London, William Heinemann, 1927

Auchincloss, Louis, *Woodrow Wilson*, New York, Lipper/Viking, 2000

Barton, Brian, *From Behind a Closed Door: Secret Court Martial Records of the 1916 Easter Rising*, Belfast, Blackstaff Press, 2002.

Barry, Tom, 'Auxiliaries Wiped Out at Kilmichael in their First Clash with the IRA', The Kerryman, *With the IRA in the Fight for Freedom: 1919 to the Truce*, Tralee, The Kerryman, 1953, 120–8

——, *Guerilla Days in Ireland*, Dublin, Anvil Books, 1962

Bateman, Robert J., 'Captain Timothy Deasy, Fenian', *Irish Sword*, 8 (1967–8), pp. 130–7

Béaslaí, Piaras, 'The Anglo-Irish War', The Kerryman, *With the IRA in the Fight for Freedom: 1919 to the Truce*, Tralee, The Kerryman, 1953, pp. 5–113

——, 'Fourteen British Officers and Agents Executed in Dublin on "Bloody Sunday"', The Kerryman, *With the IRA in the Fight for Freedom: 1919 to the Truce*, Tralee, The Kerryman, 1953, pp. 114–19

——, *Michael Collins and the Making of New Ireland*, London, George G. Harrap, 1926 (2 vols)

Bell, J. Bowyer, *The Secret Army*, London, Anthony Blond, 1970

Bennett, Richard, *The Black and Tans*, London, Edward Hulton, 1959

Berlin, Isaiah, *The Roots of Romanticism*, London, Chatto & Windus, 1999

Bernstein, Samuel, *Auguste Blanqui and the Art of Insurrection*, London, Lawrence & Wishart, 1971

Blunt, Wilfrid Scawen, *My Diaries: Being A Personal Narrative of Events, 1888–1914*, London, Martin Secker, 1920 (2 vols)

Bowden, T., 'Bloody Sunday – A Reappraisal', *European Studies Review*, 2, 1 (1972), pp. 25–42

Boyce, D. G., 'How to Settle the Irish Question', in A. J. P. Taylor (ed.), *Lloyd George: Twelve Essays*, London, Hamish Hamilton, 1971, pp. 137–64

Brady, Edward Mark, *Ireland's Secret Service in England*, Dublin, Talbot Press, 1928

Breen, Dan, *My Fight for Irish Freedom*, Dublin, Talbot Press, 1924; Anvil Books, 1981

Brennan, John 'Frongoch University – and After', The Kerryman, *Dublin's Fighting Story 1913–1921*, Tralee, The Kerryman, n.d. (?1948)

Brennan, R., *Allegiance*, Dublin, Browne & Nolan, 1950

Brennan-Whitmore, W. J., *With the Irish in Frongoch*, Dublin, Talbot Press, 1917

Brockway, A. Fenner, *Inside the Left: Thirty Years of Platform, Press, Prison and Parliament*, London, George Allen & Unwin, 1942

Brodrick, Hon. George Charles, *Memories and Impressions: 1831–1900*, London, James Nisbet & Co, 1900

Brooks, Sydney, *The New Ireland*, Dublin, Mannsel & Co, 1907

Buckle, George Earle (ed.), *The Letters of Queen Victoria*, London, John Murray, 1926 (3 vols)

Buckley, Cliona McDonald, 'Robert McDonnell (1828–1899)', *Journal of the Irish College of Physicians and Surgeons*, 3 (1973), pp. 66–9

Burchell, R. A., *The San Francisco Irish: 1848–1880*, Manchester, Manchester University Press, 1979

Butt, Isaac, *Ireland's Appeal for Amnesty*, Glasgow and London, Cameron & Ferguson, 1870

Byrne, Joseph, M., *Prisoners of War: Some Recollections of an Irish Deportee*, Dublin, The Art Depot, 1917

Callwell, Major-General Sir C. E., *Field-Marshal Sir Henry Wilson, His Life and Diaries*, London, Cassell, 1927 (2 vols)

Campbell, Colm, *Emergency Law in Ireland, 1918–1925*, Oxford, Clarendon Press, 1994

Campbell, John, *Thirty Years' Experience of a Medical Officer in the English Convict Service*, London, T. Nelson & Sons, 1884

Canning, Paul, *British Policy Towards Ireland 1921–1941*, Oxford, Clarendon Press, 1985

Carlyle, Thomas, *The Works of Thomas Carlyle*, ed. H. D. Traill, London, Chapman and Hall, 1896–1901 (vol. 10)

Casement, Roger, *The Crime Against Europe: A Possible Outcome of the War of 1914*, Philadelphia, PA, Celtic Press, 1915

Casey, John Sarsfield, *Journal of a Voyage from Portland to Fremantle on Board the Convict Ship 'Hougoumont', Cap. Cozens, Commander October 12th, 1867*, ed. Martin Kevin Cusack, Paget, Bermuda; Bryn Mawr, PA, Dorrace & Co, 1988 (on deposit in the British Library; National Library of Ireland)

Childe-Pemberton, William Shakespear, *Life of Lord Norton (Right Hon. Sir Charles Adderley, KCMG, MP) 1814–1905: Statesman & Philanthropist*, London, John Murray, 1909

Childs, Sir Borlase Edward Wyndham, *Episodes and Reflections; Being Some Episodes from the Life of Sir Wyndham Childs*, London, Cassell & Co, 1930

Choille, Breandán MacGiolla, 'Fenian Documents in the State Paper Office', *Irish Historical Studies*, 16 (1968–9), pp. 258–85

Churchill, Randolph Spencer, *Youth: Winston S. Churchill, 1874–1900*, London, Minerva, 1991

Churchill, Winston Spencer, *The World Crisis: The Aftermath*, London, Thornton Butterworth, 1929

Clarke, Thomas J., *Glimpses of an Irish Felon's Prison Life*, Dublin and London, Mannsell & Roberts, 1922

Cluseret, General Gustave Paul, 'My Connections with Fenianism', *Frazer's Magazine*, 6, 31 (NS) (July 1892), pp. 31–46

Cohn, Stan and Taylor, Laurie, *Psychological Survival: The Experience of Long Term Imprisonment*, Harmondsworth, Penguin, 1972

Colvin, Ian, *The Life of Lord Carson*, London, Victor Gollancz, 1936 (3 vols)

Conquest, Robert, *The Great Terror: A Reassessment*, London, Pimlico, 1992

Convict of Clonmel (?Richard Pigott), *Things Not Generally Known Concerning England's Treatment of Political Prisoners*, Dublin, The Irishman, 1869

Coogan, Timothy Patrick, *Ireland Since the Rising*, London, Pall Mall Press, 1966

——, *Michael Collins*, London, Arrow Books, 1991

——, *De Valera: Long Fellow, Long Shadow*, London, Hutchinson, 1993

—— and Morrison, George, *The Irish Civil War*, London, Seven Dials/Orion, 1998

Costello, Francis, J., *Enduring the Most: The Life and Death of Terence MacSwiney*, Dingle, Brandon Book Publishers, 1995

Courtney, Kate, *Extracts from a Diary During the War*, London, Private Circulation, December 1927

Croker, T. Crofton (ed.), *Memoirs of Joseph Holt, General of the Irish Rebels, in 1798: Edited from his Original Manuscript, in the Possession of Sir William Betham*, London, Henry Colburn, 1838 (2 vols)

Cronin, Sean (ed.), *The McGarrity Papers*, Tralee, Anvil Books, 1972

Cross, Richard Assheton, *A Political History*, London, privately printed, 1903

Crozier, Frank Percy, *Impressions and Recollections*, London, T. Werner Laurie, 1920

——, *Ireland for Ever*, London, Jonathan Cape, 1932

Currant, Charles, 'The Spy Behind the Speaker's Chair', *History Today*, 18 (1968), pp. 745–54

Curry, Charles Emerson (ed.), *Sir Roger Casement's Diaries. His Mission to Germany and the Findlay Affair*, Munich, Arche Publishing, 1922

Cussen, John, 'William Smith O'Brien in Van Diemen's Land, 1849–54', *Old Limerick Journal*, 23 (1988), pp. 77–81

Dalton, Charles, *With the Dublin Brigade 1917–1921*, London, Peter Davies, 1929

Daly, Madge, 'Seán Heuston's Life and Death for Ireland', The Kerryman, *Limerick's Fighting Story*, Tralee, The Kerryman, n.d. (?1947)

Davis, Richard, 'Patrick O'Donohoe: Outcast of the Exiles', in Bob Reece (ed.), *Exiles from Erin: Convict Lives in Ireland and Australia*, London, Macmillan, 1991

——, 'The Reluctant Rebel: William Smith O'Brien', *Tipperary Historical Journal* (1998), pp. 46–55

——, 'Unpublicised Young Ireland Prisoners in Van Diemen's Land', *Tasmanian Historical Research Association Papers and Proceedings*, 38 (3 and 4), December 1991

——, *William Smith O'Brien: Ireland – 1848 – Tasmania*, Dublin, Geography Publications, 1989

——, *The Young Ireland Movement*, Dublin, Gill & Macmillan, 1987

—— and Davis, Marianna (eds), *The Rebel in His Family: Selected Papers of William Smith O'Brien*, Cork, Cork University Press, 1998

Davitt, Michael, *Leaves from a Prison Diary: Or Lectures to a 'Solitary Audience'*, London, Chapman and Hall, 1885 (2 vols)

——, *Life and Progress in Australasia*, London, Methuen, 1898

Denieffe, Joseph, *A Personal Narrative of the Irish Revolutionary Brotherhood*, New York, Gael Publishing Co, 1906; republished Dublin, Irish University Press, 1969

Denison, Sir William, *Varieties of Vice-Regal Life*, London, Longmans, Green, 1870 (2 vols)

Denman, Terence, 'The Red Livery of Shame: The Campaign Against Army Recruitment in Ireland, 1899–1914', *Irish Historical Studies*, 29, 114 (November 1994), pp. 212–17

Dillon, William, *Life of John Mitchel*, London, Kegan Paul, Trench & Co, 1888 (2 vols)

Doan, Van Toai and Chanoff, David, *The Vietnamese Gulag*, New York, Simon & Schuster, 1986

Dohney, Michael, *The Felon's Track or History of the Attempted Outbreak in Ireland Embracing the Leading Events in the Irish Struggle from the Year 1843 to the Close of 1848*, New York, W. H. Holbrooke, 1849; Dublin, M. H. Gill & Son, 1914

Downling, Patrick J., *California: The Irish Dream*, San Francisco, CA, Golden Gate Publishers, 1988

Du Cane, Sir Edmund Frederick, *The Punishment and Prevention of Crime*, London, Macmillan, 1885

Duffy, Sir Charles Gavan, *Four Years of Irish History 1845–1849*, London, Cassell, Petter, Galpin & Co, 1883

——, *Young Ireland: A Fragment of Irish History 1840–1850*, London Cassell, Petter, Galpin & Co, 1880; also T. Fisher Unwin, 1896 (2 vols)

Edwards, Ruth Dudley, *Patrick Pearse: The Triumph of Failure*, London, Victor Gollancz, 1977

——, *The Faithful Tribe*, London, HarperCollins, 1999

Egremont, Max, *The Cousins: The Friendship, Opinions and Activities of Wilfred Scawen Blunt and George Wyndham*, London, Collins, 1977

Ellis, P. Berresford, *James Connolly: Selected Writings*, Harmondsworth, Penguin, 1973

Ellman, Richard, *Oscar Wilde*, London, Hamish Hamilton, 1987

Ensor, Robert Charles Kirkwood, *England 1870–1914*, Oxford, Oxford University Press, 1936

Evans, A. G., *Fanatic Heart: A Life of John Boyle O'Reilly 1844–1890*, Nedlands, University of Western Australia, 1997

Felstead, Sidney Theodore, *German Spies at Bay: Being an Actual Record of the German Espionage in Great Britain During the Years 1914–1918*, London, Hutchinson & Co, 1920

Feuchtwanger, E. J., *Gladstone*, London, Allen Lane, 1975

Figgis, Darrell, *A Chronicle of Jails*, Dublin, Talbot Press, 1917

——, *A Second Chronicle of Jails*, Dublin, Talbot Press, 1919

——, *Recollections of the Irish War*, London, Ernest Benn, 1927

Finneran, Richard J. (ed.), *The Poems of W. B. Yeats: A New Edition*, New York, Macmillan, 1983

Fitzgerald, Revd Philip, *A Narrative of the Proceedings of the Confederates in '48 from the Suspension of the Habeas Corpus Act to their Final Dispersion at Ballingary*, Dublin, James Duffy, 1868

——, *Personal Recollections of the Insurrection at Ballingary*, Dublin, John F. Fowler, 1861 (rare: See NLI, Larcom Papers, 7698)

Fitzpatrick, David, *Oceans of Consolation: Personal Accounts of Irish Migration to Australia*, Ithaca, NY, and London, Cornell University Press, 1994

Forester, Margery, *Michael Collins: The Lost Leader*, London, Sphere Books, 1972

Foster, Roy F., *Lord Randolph Churchill: A Political Life*, Oxford, Clarendon Press, 1981

——, *Modern Ireland 1600–1972*, Harmondsworth, Penguin, 1989

Garvin, Tom, *1922: The Birth of Irish Democracy*, Dublin, Gill & Macmillan, 1996

Gathorne-Hardy, Alfred (ed.), *Gathorne Hardy, First Earl of Cranbrook: A Memoir, with Extracts from his Diary and Correspondence*, London, Longmans & Co, 1910 (2 vols)

Geraghty, Tony, *The Irish War: The Military History of a Domestic Conflict*, London, HarperCollins, 2000

Gilbert, Martin, *Winston S. Churchill*, London, Heinemann, 1966–88

Gladstone, William Ewart, *Two Letters to the Earl of Aberdeen on the State Prosecutions of the Neapolitan Government*, London, John Murray, 1851

'Glencree', *Scientific Warfare or the Resources of Civilisation*, (?) New York, Private Circulation, 1888

Graham, Merrilyn and Bamford, David, 'Chartists and Young Irelanders: Towards a Reassessment of Political Prisoners in Van Diemen's Land', *Tasmanian Historical Research Association Papers and Proceedings*, 32 (June 1985), pp. 68–74

Gray, Tony, *The Lost Years: The Emergency in Ireland 1939–45*, London, Warner, 1998

Green, E. R. R., 'The Fenians', *History Today*, 8 (1958), pp. 698–705

——, 'The Fenians Abroad', in T. Desmond Williams (ed.), *Secret Societies in Ireland*, Dublin, Gill & Macmillan, 1973

Griffith, Arthur (ed.), *Meagher of the Sword: Speeches of T. F. Meagher in Ireland, 1846–1848: His Narrative of Events in Ireland in July, 1848; Personal Reminiscences of Waterford, Galway and His Schooldays*, Dublin, M. H. Gill & Son, 1916

779

Gwynn, Denis Rolleston (ed.), *Reminiscences of a Maynooth Professor, Walter McDonald, D. D.*, London, Jonathan Cape, 1925

——, *The Life of John Redmond*, London, George C. Harrap, 1932

——, *Young Ireland and 1848*, Cork, Cork University Press, 1949

Gwynn, Stephen Lucius, *Collected Poems*, London, Brickwood & Sons, 1923

—— (ed.), *The Letters and Friendships of Sir Cecil Spring Rice: A Record*, London, Constable, 1929 (2 vols)

Haddick-Flynn, Kevin, *Orangeism: The Making of a Tradition*, Dublin, Wolfhound Press, 1999

Hammond, John Lawrence Le Breton, *Gladstone and the Irish Nation*, London, Longmans, Green, 1938

Harrington, C., 'Arrest and Martyrdom of Terence MacSwiney', *The Kerryman, Rebel Cork's Fighting Story 1916–21*, Tralee, The Kerryman, 1949, pp. 31–3

Harrisson, Tom, *Living Through the Blitz*, London, Collins, 1976

Hartshorne, Albert, *Hanging in Chains*, London, T. F. Unwin, 1891

Hattersley, Alan Frederick, *The Convict Crisis and the Growth of Unity*, Pietmaritzburg, University of Natal Press, 1965

Healy, Timothy, *Letters and Leaders of My Day*, London, Thornton Butterworth, 1928 (2 vols)

Henry, Robert Mitchell, *The Evolution of Sinn Féin*, Dublin, Talbot Press, 1920

Hobhouse, Stephen, *An English Prison From Within*, London, George Allen & Unwin, 1919

Hodges, John George, *Report of the Trial of William Smith O'Brien for High Treason at the Special Commission for the Co. Tipperary. Held at Clonmel, September and October, 1848: with the Judgement of the Court of Queen's Bench, Ireland, and of the House of Lords, on the Writs of Error*, Dublin, Alexander Thom, 1849

Hoy, Hugh Cleland, *40 O.B. or How the War Was Won*, London, Hutchinson, 1932

Hughes, Robert, *The Fatal Shore: A History of the Transportation of Convicts to Australia*, London, Collins Harvill, 1987

Hyde, Harford Montgomery, *Carson: The Life of Sir Edward Carson, Lord Carson of Duncairn*, London, William Heinemann, 1953

——, *Famous Trials: Roger Casement*, Harmondsworth, Penguin, 1963

Inglis, Brian, *Roger Casement*, London, Hodder & Stoughton, 1973

Ingraham, Barton L., *Political Crime in Europe: A Comparative Study of France, Germany, and England*, Berkeley, University of California Press, 1979

Irish Times, *Sinn Féin Rebellion Handbook*, Dublin, Irish Times, 1917; republished Boulder, CO, Roberts Rinehart/The Mourne River Press, 1998

James, Admiral Sir William, *The Eyes of the Navy: A Biographical Study of Admiral Sir Reginald Hall*, London, Methuen, 1955

Jebb, Major Joshua, R. E., *Modern Prisons: Their Construction and Ventilation*, London, privately printed, 1844

Jellinck, Frank, *The Paris Commune of 1871*, London, Victor Gollancz, 1937

Jenkins, Roy, *Gladstone*, London, Macmillan, 1995

Johnson, Nancy E. (ed.), *The Diary of Gathorne Hardy, Later Lord Cranbrook, 1866–1892: Political Selections*, Oxford, Clarendon Press, 1981

Jones, Thomas, *Whitehall Diary*, ed. K. Middlemas, London, Oxford University Press, 1969–71 (3 vols)

Kee, Robert, *Ourselves Alone*, Harmondsworth, Penguin, 1989

——, *The Bold Fenian Men*, Harmondsworth, Penguin, 1989

——, *The Laurel and the Ivy: The Story of Charles Stewart Parnell and Irish Nationalism*, Harmondsworth, Penguin, 1994

——, *The Most Distressful Country*, London, Penguin Books, 1989

Keneally, Arabella, *Memoirs of Edward Vaughan Keneally, LLD*, London, John Long, 1908

Keneally, Thomas, *The Great Shame: A Story of the Irish in the Old World and the New*, London, Chatto & Windus, 1998

Kerryman, The, *Dublin's Fighting Story (1913–1921): Told by the Man Who Made It*, Tralee, The Kerryman, n.d. (?1948)

——, *Limerick's Fighting Story: Told by the Man Who Made It*, Tralee, The Kerryman, n.d. (?1947)

——, *Rebel Cork's Fighting Story 1916–1921*, Tralee, The Kerryman, 1947

——, *With the IRA in the Fight for Freedom: 1919 to the Truce*, Tralee, The Kerryman, 1953

Kickham, Charles, *Knocknagow: or the Homes of Tipperary*, Dublin, Gill & Macmillan, 1978

Kiernan, T. John, *The Irish Exiles in Australia*, Dublin, Clonmore & Reynolds, 1954

Kinealy, Christine, *This Great Calamity: The Irish Famine 1845–52*, Dublin, Gill & Macmillan, 1994

Kipling, Rudyard, *The Irish Guards in the Great War*, Staplehurst, Spellmount, 1997

Kircheimer, Otto, *Political Justice: The Use of Legal Procedures for Political Ends*, Princeton, NJ, Princeton University Press, 1961

Knott, George H. (ed.), *Trial of Sir Roger Casement*, Edinburgh and London, William Hodge & Co, 1917

Lalor, James Fintan, *Collected Writings*, Dublin and London, Mannsel & Co, 1918

Lawrence, Dan, H. (ed.), *Bernard Shaw: Collected Letters 1911–1925*, London, Max Rinhardt, 1985

Le Caron, Major Henri (pseudonym Thomas Miller Beach), *Twenty-five Years in the Secret Service*, London, William Heinemann, 1892

Lee, J. J., *Ireland 1912–1985: Politics and Society*, Cambridge, Cambridge University Press, 1989

Le Roux, Louis N., *Tom Clarke and the Irish Freedom Movement*, Dublin, Talbot Press, 1936

'Le Sagart', 'The Coming Convention. Its Policy', The Society of United Irishmen, *Preamble and Constitution*, Philadelphia, PA, United Irishmen, 1880

Lockhart, R. H. Bruce, *Memoirs of a British Agent: Being an Account of the Author's Early Life in Many Lands and of his Official Mission to Moscow in 1918*, London, Putnam, 1941

Longford, Earl of and O'Neill, Thomas P., *Eamon De Valera*, Boston, MA, Houghton Mifflin, 1971

Longford, Elizabeth, *Wellington: The Years of the Sword*, New York, Harper & Row, 1969

Lyons, Francis Steward Leland, *Charles Stewart Parnell*, London, Fontana, 1977

——, *Ireland Since the Famine*, London, Fontana, 1985

Lyons, J. B., *The Enigma of Tom Kettle: Irish Patriot, Essayist, Poet, British Soldier*, Dublin, The Glendale Press, 1983

Macardle, Dorothy, *The Irish Republic*, Dublin, Irish Press, 1951 (4th edn)

MacBride, Maud Gonne, *A Servant of the Queen Reminiscences*, London, Gollancz, 1938

MacColl, René María, *Roger Casement: A New Judgement*, London, Hamish Hamilton, 1956

McConville, Seán, A History of English Prison Administration 1750–1877, London, Routledge & Kegan Paul, 1981

——, English Local Prisons 1860–1900: Next Only to Death, London, Routledge, 1995

——, 'The Victorian Prison: England 1865–1965', in Norval Morris and David J. Rothman (eds), The Oxford History of the Prison, New York, Oxford University Press, 1995, pp. 131–67

McCord, Norman, 'The Fenians and Public Opinion in Great Britain', in Maurice Harmon (ed.), Fenians and Fenianism, Dublin, Sceptre Books, 1968, pp. 35–48

McCormack, W. J., Roger Casement in Death or Haunting the Free State, Dublin, University College Dublin Press, 2002

MacDonagh, Oliver, The Emancipist: Daniel O'Connell 1830–47, London, Weidenfeld & Nicolson, 1989

McDonald, Walter, Reminiscences of a Maynooth Professor, ed. D. R. Gwynn, London, Jonathan Cape, 1925

MacEoin, Uinseann (ed.), Survivors, Dublin, Argenta Publications, 1980

McEvoy, Kieran, Paramilitary Imprisonment in Northern Ireland, Oxford, Oxford University Press, 2001

McGrath, William, 'The Fenian Rising in Cork', Irish Sword, 8, 33 (1968), pp. 322–5

Mackay, James, Michael Collins: A Life, Edinburgh and London, Mainstream Publishing, 1996

MacLysaght, Edward (ed.), Forth The Banners Go: Reminiscences of William O'Brien, Dublin, At the Sign of the Three Candles, 1969

Macphail, Sir Andrew, Three Persons, London, John Murray, 1929

McPherson, James M., Battle Cry of Freedom: The Civil War Era, New York, Oxford University Press, 1988

Macready, Sir Cecil Frederick Nevil, Annals of an Active Life, London, Hutchinson & Co, 1924 (2 vols)

MacSuibhne, Peadar, Paul Cullen and His Contemporaries: With Their Letters from 1820–1902, Naas, Leinster Leader, 1961

Majoribanks, Edward, The Life of Lord Carson, London, Victor Gollancz, 1932 (2 vols)

Maloney, William Joseph Marie Alois, The Forged Casement Diaries, Dublin and Cork, Talbot Press, 1936

Manjendie, Vivian Dering, 'Nitro-glycerine and Dynamite', The Fortnightly Review, 33 (January to June 1883), p. 643

Manton, Henry J. P., Turning the Last Stone: Printed for the Purpose of Supplying the Mayor, Alderman, and Councillors of the City of Birmingham with Information for their Private Use, Birmingham, Robert Birkbeck & Sons, 1895

Marreco, Anne, The Rebel Countess: The Life and Times of Constance Markievicz, London, Weidenfeld & Nicolson, 1967

Martin, F. X., 'Eoin O'Neill on the 1916 Rising', Irish Historical Studies, 12 (March 1961), pp. 226–71

Marx, Karl and Engels, Frederick, Collected Works, London, Lawrence & Wishart, 1985

——, Ireland and the Irish Question, Moscow, Progress Publishers, 1971

Matthew, H. G. C., Gladstone 1809–1874, Oxford, Clarendon Press, 1991

——, The Gladstone Diaries, Oxford, Clarendon Press, 1995

Maume, Patrick, 'Parnell and the IRB Oath', Irish Historical Studies, 29, 115 (May 1995), pp. 363–70

——, The Long Gestation: Irish Nationalist Life 1891–1918, Dublin, Gill & Macmillan, 1999

Mezzeroff, Professor, *Dyanamite Against Gladstone's Resources of Civilization or the Best Way to Make Ireland Free and Independent*, New York, c.1882

Mitchel, John, *Jail Journal; or Five Years in British Prisons*, London, R. & T. Washbourne, n.d. (original edn New York, 1854)

——, *The Crusade of the Period and Last Conquest of Ireland (Perhaps)*, New York, Lynch, Cole & Meehan, 1873

——, *The History of Ireland from the Treaty of Limerick to the Present Time: Being a Continuation of the History of the Abbé Macgeoghegan*, Glasgow, Cameron & Ferguson, 1869 (New York, Sadleirs, 1867)

Mitchell, Angus (ed.), *The Amazon Journal of Roger Casement*, London, Anaconda, 1997

Molloy, Bernard C., MP, 'Insanity in Prisons', *The Progressive Review*, 1, 2 (November 1896), pp. 155–62

Monaghan, Jay, *Australians and the Gold Rush: California and Downunder*, Berkeley, University of California Press, 1966

Monteith, Captain Robert, *Casement's Last Adventure*, Dublin, Michael F. Moynihan, 1953

Moody, Theodore William, *Davitt and Irish Revolution 1846–82*, Oxford, Clarendon Press, 1982

Moran, Seán Farrell, *Patrick Pearse and the Politics of Redemption*, Washington, DC, The Catholic University of America, 1994

Morash, Chris and Hayes, Richard (eds), *Fearful Realities: New Perspectives on the Famine*, Dublin, Irish Academic Press, 1996

Morgan, Kenneth Owen, *Consensus and Disunity: The Lloyd George Coalition Government 1918–22*, Oxford, Clarendon Press, 1979

Morley, John, *The Life of William Ewart Gladstone*, London, Macmillan, 1903 (3 vols)

Mulcahy, Don, 'Life and Death of Commandant Edward Daly', The Kerryman, *Limerick's Fighting Story, 1916–21*, Tralee, The Kerryman, n.d. (?1947), pp. 18–23

Mullen, Richard and Munson, James, *Victoria: Portrait of a Queen*, London, BBC Books, 1987

Nevinson, Henry Woodd, *Last Changes, Last Chances*, London, Nisbet & Co, 1928

Newsinger, John, *Fenianism in Mid-Victorian Britain*, London, Pluto Press, 1994

——, 'Old Chartists, Fenians and New Socialists', *Éire-Ireland*, 17, 2 (summer 1982), pp. 19–45

Nicolson, Harold, *King George V: His Life and Reign*, London, Constable, 1952

Nolan, Peter, 'Fariola, Massey and the Fenian Rising', *Journal of the Cork Historical and Archaeological Society*, LXXV, 75, 221 (January to June 1970), pp. 1–11

Norman, E. R., *The Catholic Church and Ireland in the Age of Rebellion: 1859–1873*, London, Longmans, 1965

Noyes, Alfred, *The Accusing Ghost, or, Justice for Casement*, London, Victor Gollancz, 1957

——, *Two Worlds for Memory*, London, Sheed & Ward, 1953

O'Brien, Nora Connolly, *Portrait of a Rebel Father*, Lonon, Rich & Cowan, 1935

O'Brien, William, 'Was Fenianism Ever Formidable?', *Contemporary Review*, 81 (January to June 1891), pp. 680–93

O'Brien, William and Ryan, Desmond (eds), *Devoy's Postbag 1871–1928*, Dublin, C. J. Fallon, 1948 and 1953 (2 vols)

O'Broin, Leon, *Dublin Castle and the 1916 Rising*, New York, New York University Press, 1971

——, *Fenian Fever: An Anglo-American Dilemma*, London, Chatto & Windus, 1971

O'Callaghan, Sean, *The Informer*, London, Bantam Press, 1998

O'Cathaoir, Brendan, *John Blake Dillon, Young Irelander*, Dublin, Irish Academic Press, 1990

——, 'Terence Bellew McManus: Fenian Precursor', *Irish Sword*, 16, 63 (1985), pp. 105–9

O'Donnell, Peadar, *The Gates Flew Open*, London, Jonathan Cape, 1932

O'Donoghue, Florence, 'A Patriot Priest of Cork City', The Kerryman, *Rebel Cork's Fighting Story, 1916–21*, Tralee, The Kerryman, 1947, pp. 65–7

——, *No Other Law*, Dublin, Irish Press, 1954

O'Farrell, Patrick, *The Irish in Australia*, Kensington (NSW), New South Wales University Press, 1987

O'Fiaich, Cardinal Tomás, 'The North and Young Ireland', *Tipperary Historical Journal* (1998), pp. 19–31

O'Halpin, Eunan, 'British Intelligence in Ireland, 1914–21', in Christopher Maurice Andrew and David Dilks (eds), *The Missing Dimension: Government and Intelligence Communities in the Twentieth Century*, London, Macmillan, 1984, pp. 54–77

——, *The Decline of the Union: British Government in Ireland 1892–1920*, Dublin, Gill & Macmillan, 1987

O'Hegarty, Patrick Sarsfield, *The Victory of Sinn Féin: How It Won It, and How It Used It*, Dublin, Talbot Press, 1924

O'Leary, John, *Recollections of Fenians and Fenianism*, London, Downey & Co, 1896; republished Shannon, Irish University Press, 1969 (2 vols)

O'Lochlainn, Colm (ed.), *More Irish Street Ballads*, Dublin, The Three Candles, 1968 (2nd edn)

O'Mahony, Sean, *Frongoch: University of Revolution*, Killiney, Co. Dublin, FDR Teoranta, 1987

O'Malley, Ernie, 'In British Jails', The Kerryman, *Dublin's Fighting Story 1913–1921*, Tralee, The Kerryman, n.d. (?1948), pp. 193–8

——, *On Another Man's Wound*, London, Rich & Cowan, 1936

——, *Raids and Rallies*, Dublin, Anvil Books, 1982

——, *The Singing Flame*, Dublin, Anvil Books, 1978

O'Neill, Stephen, 'Auxiliaries Annihilated at Kilmichael', The Kerryman, *Rebel Cork's Fighting Story 1916–21*, Tralee, The Kerryman, 1947, pp. 83–5

O'Reilly, John Boyle, *Moondyne: A Story from the Underworld*, London, G. Routledge & Sons, 1889

O'Toole, Fintan, 'O'Schindler', *The New Republic*, 11 October 1999, pp. 48–52

Owens, Garry, 'Patrick O'Donohoe's Narrative of the 1848 Rising', *Tipperary Historical Journal* (1998), pp. 32–45

Packenham, Elizabeth, *Jameson's Raid*, London, Weidenfeld & Nicolson, 1960

Packenham, Frank (Francis Angier Packenham, 7th Earl of Longford), *Peace by Ordeal: An Account, from First-hand Sources of the Negotiation and Signature of the Anglo-Irish Treaty 1921*, London, Geoffrey Chapman, 1962 (first published 1935)

Packenham, Thomas, *The Year of Liberty: The History of the Great Irish Rebellion of 1798*, London, Hodder & Stoughton, 1969

Pankhurst, Emmeline, *My Own Story*, London, Eveleigh Nash, 1914. Facsimile in Marie Mulrey Roberts and Tamar Mizuta (eds), *The Suffragettes: Towards Emancipation*, London, Routledge/Thoemmes Press, 1993

Pankhurst, Sylvia, *The Suffragette Movement: An Intimate Account of Persons and Ideals*, London, Longmans, Green, 1931

Parmiter, Geoffrey Vincent de Clifton, *Roger Casement*, London, Arthur Barker, 1936

Pearse, Patrick, *Political Writings and Speeches*, Dublin, Talbot Press, 1952

Pease, Z. N., *The Catalpa Expedition*, New Bedford, MA., George S. Anthony, 1897

Pelling, Henry and Reid, Alastair, J., *A Short History of the Labour Party*, London, Macmillan, 1996

Quigley, Dr, *The Irish Race in California and the Pacific Coast*, San Francisco, CA, A. Roman & Co, 1878

Quinliven, Patrick and Rose, Paul, *The Fenians in England 1865–1872: A Sense of Insecurity*, London, John Calder, 1982

Radzinowicz, Sir Leon, *Adventures in Criminology*, London and New York, Routledge, 1999

——, *A History of Criminal Law and Its Administration from 1750*, London, Stevens & Sons, 1948–86 (5 vols)

—— and Hood, Roger, 'The Status of Political Prisoners in England: The Struggle for Recognition', *Virginia Law Review*, 65, 8 (1979), pp. 1421–81

Redmond, John E., 'A Plea for Amnesty', *The Fortnightly Review*, 52, 212 (December 1892), pp. 722–32

——, MP, *The Case for Amnesty*, Dublin, William J. Ally & Co, 1893

——, *The Voice of Ireland*, London, Thomas Nelson & Sons, 1916

Reece, Bob (ed.), *Exiles from Erin: Convict Lives in Ireland and Australia*, London, Macmillan, 1991

——, *The Origins of Irish Convict Transportation to New South Wales*, Basingstoke, Palgrave, 2001

Roche, Mrs John Boyle (ed.), *Life of John Boyle O'Reilly, by James Jeffrey Roche, Together with his Complete Poems and Speeches*, New York, The Mershen Company, 1891

Roper, Esther (ed.), *Prison Letters of Countess Markievicz: Also Poems and Articles Relating to Easter Week by Eva Gore-Booth and a Biographical Sketch by Esther Roper*, London, Longmans, Green, 1934

Roskill, Stephen, *Hankey, Man of Secrets*, London, Collins, 1970–4 (3 vols)

Rossa, Jeremiah O'Donovan, *My Years in English Jails*, New York, American News Co, 1874; condensed and revised edn (ed. Seán Ua Cearnaigh), Tralee, Anvil Books, 1967

Rossa, Margaret O'Donovan, *My Father and Mother were Irish*, New York, Devin-Adair, 1939

Rudé, George, *Protest and Punishment: The Story of Social and Political Protesters Transported to Australia 1788–1868*, Oxford, Clarendon Press, 1978

Ruo-Wang, J. P. Bao and Chelminski, R., *Prisoner of Mao*, Harmondsworth, Penguin, 1976

Rutherford, William, *'67 Retrospection: A Concise History of the Fenian Rising at Ballyhurst Fort, Tipperary*, Dublin, O'Loughlin, Shields & Boland, 1903

Ryan, Desmond, 'Fight at Fernside', The Kerryman, *Dublin's Fighting Story 1913–1921*, Tralee, The Kerryman, n.d. (?1948), pp. 133–41

—— (ed.), *Labour and Easter Week: A Selection from the Writtings of James Connolly*, Dublin, At the Sign of the Three Candles, 1966

——, *Remembering Sion: A Chronicle of Storm and Quiet*, London, Arthur Barker, 1934

——, *Seán Treacy and the 3rd Tipperary Brigade*, London, Alliance Press, 1946

——, *The Fenian Chief: A Biography of James Stephens*, Dublin, Gill & Son, 1967

——, *The Rising: The Complete Story of Easter Week*, Dublin, Golden Eagle Books, 1949

Ryan, Dr Mark Francis, *Fenian Memories*, Dublin, M. H. Gill & Son, 1945

Ryder, Chris, *Inside the Maze*, London, Methuen, 2000

Rynne, Stephen, *John Devoy*, Kildare, The John Devoy Memorial Committee, n.d.

Sachs, Albie, *The Jail Diary of Albie Sachs*, London, Harvill Press, 1966

Saville, John, *1848: The British State and the Chartist Movement*, Cambridge, Cambridge University Press, 1987

Sawyer, Roger (ed.), *Roger Casement's Diaries, 1910: The Black and the White*, London, Pimlico, 1997

Selth, Andrew, 'Ireland and Insurgency: The Lessons of History', *Small Wars and Insurgencies*, 2, 2 (August 1991), pp. 299–322

Shannon, Richard, *Gladstone: Heroic Minister 1865–1898*, London, Allen Lane, 1999

Sharpe, May Churchill, *Chicago May: Her Story*, London, Sampson Low and Co, 1929

Shaw, Alan George Lewers, *Convicts and the Colonies*, London, Faber & Faber, 1966

Sheelye, Julius H., 'Dynamite as a Factor in Civilization', *North American Review*, 320 (July 1883), pp. 1–7

Shilts, Randy, *And the Band Played On: Politics, People and the AIDS Epidemic*, New York, St Martin's Press, 1987

Short, K. R. M., *The Dynamite War: Irish-American Bombers in Victorian Britain*, Dublin, Gill & Macmillan, 1979

Shorter, Clement King, *A Discarded Defence of Roger Casement, Suggested by Bernard Shaw. With an Appendix of Comments by Roger Casement, and an Introduction by Clement Shorter*, London, privately printed by Clement Shorter, 1922

Sigerson, George, *Political Prisoners at Home and Abroad*, London, Kegan Paul, Trench Trübner & Co, 1890

Sillard, P. A., *The Life and Letters of John Martin. With Sketches of Thomas Devin Reilly, Father John Kenyon, and Other 'Young Irelanders'*, Dublin, James Duffy & Co 1901 (2nd edn)

——, *The Life of John Mitchel with an Historical Sketch of the '48 Movement in Ireland*, Dublin, James Duffy & Co, 1901 (2nd edn)

Skeffington, Francis Sheehy, *Michael Davitt: Revolutionary Agitatory and Labour Leader*, London, MacGibbon & Kee, 1967

Smith, A. H., 'The Cranbrook Papers: Stray Letters from a Politician's Archive', *British Library Journal*, 12 (1986), pp. 172–5

Smith, Beverly A., 'Irish Prison Doctors: Men in the Middle, 1865–90', *Medical History*, 26 (1982), pp. 373–7

Stephen, Sir James Fitzjames, *A History of the Criminal Law of England*, London, Macmillan, 1883 (3 vols)

Takagami, Shin-Ichi, 'The Fenian Rising in Dublin, March 1867', *Irish Historical Studies*, 29, 115 (May 1995), pp. 340–62

Taylor, A. J. P., *English History 1914–45*, Oxford, Oxford University Press, 1976

Taylor, John, *All the Workes of John Taylor The Water-Poet*, London, James Boler, 1630; facsimile, Menston, Yorkshire, The Scolar Press, 1973

Thomas, James Edward and Stewart, Alex, *Imprisonment in Western Australia: Evolution, Theory and Practice*, Nedlands, University of Western Australia Press, 1978

Thomson, Basil, *Queer People*, London, Hodder & Stoughton, 1922

Thomson, Sir Basil, *The Scene Changes*, London, Collins, 1939

——, *The Story of Scotland Yard*, London, Grayson & Grayson, 1935

Thornley, David, *Isaac Butt and Home Rule*, London, MacGibbon & Key, 1964

Thorpe, Andrew, *A History of the British Labour Party*, London, Macmillan, 1997

Toíbín, Colm, 'Lady Gregory's Toothbrush', *New York Review of Books*, 48, 13 (August 2001), pp. 40–4

——, *The Irish Famine*, London, Profile Books, 1999

Touhill, Blanche M., *William Smith O'Brien and his Irish Revolutionary Companions in Penal Exile*, Columbia and London, University of Missouri Press, 1981

Townshend, Charles, *The British Campaign in Ireland 1919–1921*, Oxford, Oxford University Press, 1975

Tracey, Herbert, *The British Labour Party: Its History, Growth, Policy and Leaders*, London, Caxton Publishing Co, 1948 (3 vols)

Trant, Thomas, *Reply to Father Fitzgerald's Pamphlet Entitled His 'Personal Recollections of the Insurrection at Ballingarry in July, 1848.' With Remarks on Irish Constabulary, and Hints to All Officials*, Dublin, McGlashan & Gill, 1862 (rare: see NLI: Larcom Papers, Ms. 7698)

Troup, Sir Edward, *The Home Office*, London and New York, C. P. Putnam's Sons, 1925

An Ulsterman (pseudonym George Sigerson), *Modern Ireland: Its Vital Questions, Secret Societies and Government*, London, Longmans, Green, Reader & Dyer, 1868

Ward, Alan Joseph, *Ireland and Anglo-American Relations, 1899–1921*, London, London School of Economics and Political Science; Weidenfeld & Nicolson, 1969

Ward, Margaret, *Maud Gonne: A Life*, London, Pandora, 1990

Wedgwood, Cicely Veronica, *The Last of the Radicals, Josiah Wedgwood, M.P.*, London, Jonathan Cape, 1951

White, Terence de Vere, *Kevin O'Higgins*, Dublin, Anvil Books, 1986

——, *The Road of Excess*, Dublin, Brown & Nolan, 1946

Williams, John, 'Hunger-strikes: A Prisoner's Right or a "Wicked Folly"?', *Howard Journal of Criminal Justice*, 40, 3 (August 2001), pp. 285–96

Wilson, Trevor (ed.), *The Political Diaries of C. P. Scott 1911–1928*, London, Collins, 1970

Wogan, Helga, 'Silent Radical: Winnie Carney 1887–1943', *Irish Labour History News*, 1 (summer 1986), pp. 3–4

Woodham-Smith, Cecil, *The Great Hunger: Ireland 1845–9*, London, Hamish Hamilton, 1962

Woodward, Sir Llewellyn, *The Age of Reform 1815–1870*, Oxford, Oxford University Press, 1962 (2nd edn)

Yeats, William Butler, *Tribute to Thomas Davis* [Meeting held in Dublin on 20 November 1914], Cork, Cork University Press, 1947

Journals, newspapers and works of reference

Argus (Melbourne)

Australian Dictionary of Biography

Birmingham Daily Mail

Birmingham Daily Post

Boston Daily Advertiser

Britannia and Trades Advocate (Hobart)

British Medical Journal

Catholic Directory
Celtic Magazine
Clare's Weekly (Perth)
Colonial Times (Hobart)
Cork Examiner
Cornwall Chronicle (Tasmania)
Dáil Eireann Debates
Daily Alta California
Daily Chronicle
Daily Express
Daily Herald
Daily Item (Boston)
Daily Mail
Daily News
Daily Telegraph
Dictionary of Irish History 1800–1980, D. J. Hickey and J. E. Doherty, Dublin, Gill and MacMillan, 1980
Dictionary of National Biography
Dictionary of Slang and Unconventional English, Eric Partridge, London, Routledge & Kegan Paul, 1984
Dublin Evening Mail
Dublin Evening Post
Encyclopaedia Britannica (11th edn)
Evening Star
Evening Telegraph (Dublin)
Flag of Ireland (Dublin)
Fortnightly Review
Forward (Glasgow)
Fraser's Magazine
Freeman's Journal
Gaelic American (New York)
An Gaodhal
Glasgow Herald
Glasgow Weekly Citizen
Globe
Hansard
Herald (Perth)
Hobart Mercury
Hobart Town Advertiser
Hobart Town Daily Courier
Hobarton Guardian
Illustrated Sydney News
Inquirer and Commercial News (Perth)
Irish-American (New York)
Irish Exile (Hobart)
Irish Felon
Irish Independent
Irish News (New York)

Irish Press
Irish Republic
Irish Times
Irish Tribune
Irish World and American Industrial Liberator (New York)
Irishman
John Bull
Labour World
Launceston Examiner (Tasmania)
Leeds Mercury
Liverpool Courier
Liverpool Mercury
Lloyds Weekly
Manchester Guardian
Medical Directory
Mercury (Hobart)
Morning Advertiser
Morning Post
Nation (Dublin)
Nation (London)
Nation (Washington, DC)
Nevada Journal
News of the World
New York Daily Times
New York Herald
New York Times
New York Tribune
Northern Whig (Belfast)
An tÓglach
Oxford Companion to Irish History, ed. J. S. Connolly, Oxford University Press, 1998
Pall Mall Gazette
Pall Mall and Globe
Perth Gazette
An Phoblact
Punch
Salford Weekly News
San Francisco Examiner
Saturday Review
South African Commercial Advertiser
Spectator
Standard
Sunday Herald
Sydney Morning Herald
The Times
United Irishman (John Mitchel's newspaper 12 February to 27 May 1848)
United Irishman (New York, ed. O'Donovan Rossa)
Vigilante
Washington National Republican

Washington Sunday Herald
Weekly Despatch
Western Australia Police Gazette
Western Australia Times
Westminster Gazette
Who Was Who
Who's Who
Who's Who of British Members of Parliament, ed. Michael Stenton and Stephen Lees, Hassocks, Harvester Press, 1976–81
Workers' Republic (Dublin)

Libraries

J. S. Battye Library, Perth
Birkbeck College Library
Bishopsgate Institute Library
Bodleian Library, University of Oxford
British Library (Euston and Colindale)
British Library of Social and Political Science
Cambridge University Library
Catholic University of America, Library
Cooper Union for the Advancement of Science and Art (New York)
Dublin Local Studies Collection (Gilbert Library)
Foreign Office Library
Home Office Library
Institute of Historical Research, University of London
Irish American Historical Association
John Rylands University Library of Manchester
King's College, London, Library
Lambeth Palace Library
Library of Congress
Manchester Central Library
Marx Memorial Library
National Library of Ireland
National Library of South Africa
Mitchell Library, Sydney
New York Public Library
Prison Service Library
Queen Mary, University of London, Library
Radzinowicz Library, University of Cambridge
Reform Club Library
San Francisco Public Library
Squire Law Library, University of Cambridge
State Library of Tasmania
Trinity College Dublin Library
University of London Library, Senate House

INDEX

Note: Numbers in bold type indicate a section devoted to a subject; *bis* and *ter* denote the appearance of an item on a page twice and thrice, respectively. A number of subjects Gaelicised their names, though both forms sometimes continued to be used: preferred versions have been followed, except where direct quotation or immediate context indicated otherwise. The same approach has been followed with 'Mc' and 'Mac'. With few exceptions unsigned newspaper articles and editorials are not indexed.

Land League: suppression of 322; its tactics 24; mentioned 343

Lansdowne, Lord: favours lunacy confinement for Casement 573

Lapham, Capt. Samuel (Superintendent of Convicts): biographical note 89 n 174; dismissed convict service 89 ter; and O'Brien 81, 87

Larcom, Thomas (Irish Under-Secretary): biographical note 145 n 19; and Dartmoor prison 156 n 69; mentioned 120 n 24, 158 238

Larkin, James: biographical note 415 n 31; and Dublin lockout 416; mentioned 442

Larkin, Michael: executed at Manchester 132–3

Law, Bonar (Chancellor of the Exchequer): announces amnesty 552; and anti-Home Rule campaign 412; and Mountjoy hunger-strike 721; and release of internees 506; mentioned 573

Lawless, F.: administrator appointed for 435

Lawless, James: at Wormwood Scrubs prison 719–20, 728

Lawson, James (MP) 115 n 12

Lavery, John: and Aid Association sale 487

Le Caron, Henri (alias Beach, Thomas Billis): on Fenian influence 143 n 12; penetrates Clan na Gael 119 n 22; mentioned 342 n 48, 348 n 78

Leeds prison 707

Lefroy, A. O'Grady (Acting Colonial Secretary, W. Australia) 210 n 306

Leicester prison: and 1922 amnesty 765 n 201; mentioned 759

Lennard, Col. Sir J. F.: and Chatham inquiry 373 n 41

Lewes county prison: acts of defiance at 524–30; ban on talking at **526–30**; designated a convict prison 522; destruction at 534–5; and female internees 499–500; further campaign at **531–7**; magazines allowed at 525 n 56; proposed for Markievicz 546 bis; shamrocks allowed at 525 n 56; mentioned 756

Lewes naval prison: internment at 455 bis; regime at 461

Liberal party 750

Liddell, Sir Adolphus (Home Office Permanent-Under-Secretary): bars American lawyer 362; criticises Earl of Devon 198 n 249

Lilly, Dr G. Herbert (Assistant Surgeon, Portland prison): examines Davitt 323

Lincoln prison: escape from 643–4; and 1922 amnesty 765 n 201; and prisoners' journal 641–2; mentioned 631 bis, 756, 761 n 191

Listowel mutiny 687–8

Liverpool prison: and 1922 amnesty 765 n 201; mentioned 631 n 98, 652, 731

Lochee, Francis: biographical note 204 n 275; and Fenian convicts 204–5

Lockhurst, Bruce: on Easter rising 679

Logue, Cardinal Michael: opposes Irish conscription 623 bis

Lomasney, William Francis (Fenian and dynamitard): biographical note 228 n 56; blows himself up 353; costs dynamite campaign 348; denounces Rossa's activities 345 bis; and 1869 amnesty 228–9; and London attacks 350 n 86; reconnoitres for dynamite campaign 337; mentioned 382 n 69

London: as Fenian target 332; wartime bombing of 326; mentioned 328

Lowe, Robert (Home Secretary): biographical note 253 n 151; on Davitt 278 bis; and Melody amnesty 253–4

Luby, Letitia: and relief fund 215 n 2, 218 n 13

Luby, Thomas Clarke: arrested 123; becomes National Fund trustee 333; biographical note 116 n 15; denounces Skirmishing Fund 332; and dynamite campaign 340; and origins of Fenianism 116; punished in prison 170; sentenced and removed 154; mentioned 120 n 24, 275, 360

Lucas, Brig.-Gen.: captured by IRA 688

Lushington, Godfrey (Home Office Permanent-Under-Secretary): on Daly conviction 351 n 89; on Davitt's re-arrest 313–14

Lynch, Arthur (MP): biographical note 618 n 44; and Casement reprieve petition 579 n 98; and death of Ashe 618–19

Lynch, John: remembered by Rossa 163 n 102

Lynch, Liam 671

Lynd, Robert (journalist): his plea for Markievicz 549

Lynn, Dr Kathleen: and Markievicz 552

Lyons, John: executed 697 n 174

Lyons, Dr Robert: biographical note 197 n 244; condemns Rossa's punishment 180 n 176; member Devon Commission 197; seeks expatriation waiver 249 n 134

McAdam, Dr Cecil D.: on Markievicz 537 n 89

Macardle, Dorothy: on Bell shooting 670 n 58; on Dáil–IRA relationship 660 n 22; mentioned 698

McArdle, John: and de Valera protest 518

McBride, John: and Irish Brigade 407; trial and execution 430 bis, 538; mentioned 425 n 56, 433–4, 618 n 44